Short Story
Criticism

Guide to Thomson Gale Literary Criticism Series

For criticism on	Consult these Thomson Gale series
Authors now living or who died after December 31, 1999	*CONTEMPORARY LITERARY CRITICISM (CLC)*
Authors who died between 1900 and 1999	*TWENTIETH-CENTURY LITERARY CRITICISM (TCLC)*
Authors who died between 1800 and 1899	*NINETEENTH-CENTURY LITERATURE CRITICISM (NCLC)*
Authors who died between 1400 and 1799	*LITERATURE CRITICISM FROM 1400 TO 1800 (LC)* *SHAKESPEAREAN CRITICISM (SC)*
Authors who died before 1400	*CLASSICAL AND MEDIEVAL LITERATURE CRITICISM (CMLC)*
Authors of books for children and young adults	*CHILDREN'S LITERATURE REVIEW (CLR)*
Dramatists	*DRAMA CRITICISM (DC)*
Poets	*POETRY CRITICISM (PC)*
Short story writers	*SHORT STORY CRITICISM (SSC)*
Literary topics and movements	*HARLEM RENAISSANCE: A GALE CRITICAL COMPANION (HR)* *THE BEAT GENERATION: A GALE CRITICAL COMPANION (BG)* *FEMINISM IN LITERATURE: A GALE CRITICAL COMPANION (FL)* *GOTHIC LITERATURE: A GALE CRITICAL COMPANION (GL)*
Asian American writers of the last two hundred years	*ASIAN AMERICAN LITERATURE (AAL)*
Black writers of the past two hundred years	*BLACK LITERATURE CRITICISM (BLC)* *BLACK LITERATURE CRITICISM SUPPLEMENT (BLCS)*
Hispanic writers of the late nineteenth and twentieth centuries	*HISPANIC LITERATURE CRITICISM (HLC)* *HISPANIC LITERATURE CRITICISM SUPPLEMENT (HLCS)*
Native North American writers and orators of the eighteenth, nineteenth, and twentieth centuries	*NATIVE NORTH AMERICAN LITERATURE (NNAL)*
Major authors from the Renaissance to the present	*WORLD LITERATURE CRITICISM, 1500 TO THE PRESENT (WLC)* *WORLD LITERATURE CRITICISM SUPPLEMENT (WLCS)*

ISSN 0895-9439

Volume 93

Short Story Criticism

Criticism of the
Works of Short Fiction Writers

Jelena Krstovíc
Project Editor

THOMSON
━━━━━✴━━━━━™
GALE

Detroit • New York • San Francisco • New Haven, Conn. • Waterville, Maine • London

THOMSON

★

GALE

™

Short Story Criticism, Vol. 93

Project Editor
Jelena Krstović

Editorial
Kathy D. Darrow, Jeffrey W. Hunter, Michelle Lee, Thomas J. Schoenberg, Noah Schusterbauer, Lawrence J. Trudeau, Russel Whitaker

Data Capture
Frances Monroe, Gwen Tucker

Indexing Services
Laurie Andriot

Rights and Acquisitions
Margaret Abendroth, Margaret Chamberlain-Gaston, Edna Hedblad

Imaging and Multimedia
Dean Dauphinais, Leitha Etheridge-Sims, Lezlie Light, Mike Logusz, Dan Newell, Christine O'Bryan, Kelly A. Quin, Denay Wilding, Robyn Young

Composition and Electronic Capture
Gary Oudersluys

Manufacturing
Rhonda Dover

Associate Product Manager
Marc Cormier

LIBRARY OF CONGRESS CATALOG CARD NUMBER 88-641014

ISBN 978-0-7876-8890-5

ISBN 0-7876-8890-8
ISSN 0895-9439

Printed in the United States of America
10 9 8 7 6 5 4 3 2 1

Contents

Preface

Short Story Criticism (*SSC*) presents significant criticism of the world's greatest short-story writers and provides supplementary biographical and bibliographical materials to guide the interested reader to a greater understanding of the authors of short fiction. This series was developed in response to suggestions from librarians serving high school, college, and public library patrons, who had noted a considerable number of requests for critical material on short-story writers. Although major short-story writers are covered in such Thomson Gale series as *Contemporary Literary Criticism* (*CLC*), *Twentieth-Century Literary Criticism* (*TCLC*), *Nineteenth-Century Literature Criticism* (*NCLC*), and *Literature Criticism from 1400 to 1800* (*LC*), librarians perceived the need for a series devoted solely to writers of the short-story genre.

Scope of the Series

SSC is designed to serve as an introduction to major short-story writers of all eras and nationalities. Since these authors have inspired a great deal of relevant critical material, *SSC* is necessarily selective, and the editors have chosen the most important published criticism to aid readers and students in their research.

Approximately three to six authors, works, or topics are included in each volume, and each entry presents a historical survey of the critical response to the work. The length of an entry is intended to reflect the amount of critical attention the author has received from critics writing in English and from foreign critics in translation. Every attempt has been made to identify and include the most significant essays on each author's work. In order to provide these important critical pieces, the editors sometimes reprint essays that have appeared elsewhere in Thomson Gale's Literary Criticism Series. Such duplication, however, never exceeds twenty percent of an *SSC* volume.

Organization of the Book

An *SSC* entry consists of the following elements:

- The **Author Heading** cites the name under which the author most commonly wrote, followed by birth and death dates. Also located here are any name variations under which an author wrote, including transliterated forms for authors whose native languages use nonroman alphabets. If the author wrote consistently under a pseudonym, the pseudonym will be listed in the author heading and the author's actual name given in parentheses on the first line of the biographical and critical introduction. Uncertain birth or death dates are indicated by question marks. Single-work entries are preceded by the title of the work and its date of publication.

- The **Introduction** contains background information that introduces the reader to the author and the critical debates surrounding his or her work.

- The list of **Principal Works** is ordered chronologically by date of first publication and lists the most important works by the author. The first section comprises short-story collections, novellas, and novella collections. The second section gives information on other major works by the author. For foreign authors, the editors have provided original foreign-language publication information and have selected what are considered the best and most complete English-language editions of their works.

- Reprinted **Criticism** is arranged chronologically in each entry to provide a useful perspective on changes in critical evaluation over time. All short-story, novella, and collection titles by the author featured in the entry are printed in boldface type. The critic's name and the date of composition or publication of the critical work are given at the beginning of each piece of criticism. Unsigned criticism is preceded by the title of the source in which it appeared. Footnotes are reprinted at the end of each essay or excerpt. In the case of excerpted criticism, only those footnotes that pertain to the excerpted texts are included.

- Critical essays are prefaced by brief **Annotations** explicating each piece.

- A complete **Bibliographical Citation** of the original essay or book precedes each piece of criticism. Source citations in the Literary Criticism Series follow University of Chicago Press style, as outlined in *The Chicago Manual of Style,* 15th ed. (Chicago: The University of Chicago Press, 2006).

- An annotated bibliography of **Further Reading** appears at the end of each entry and suggests resources for additional study. In some cases, significant essays for which the editors could not obtain reprint rights are included here. Boxed material following the further reading list provides references to other biographical and critical sources on the author in series published by Thomson Gale.

Indexes

A **Cumulative Author Index** lists all of the authors that appear in a wide variety of reference sources published by Thomson Gale, including *SSC*. A complete list of these sources is found facing the first page of the Author Index. The index also includes birth and death dates and cross references between pseudonyms and actual names.

A **Cumulative Nationality Index** lists all authors featured in *SSC* by nationality, followed by the number of the *SSC* volume in which their entry appears.

An alphabetical **Title Index** lists all short-story, novella, and collection titles contained in the *SSC* series. Titles of short-story collections, separately published novellas, and novella collections are printed in italics, while titles of individual short stories are printed in roman type with quotation marks. Each title is followed by the author's last name and corresponding volume and page numbers where commentary on the work is located. English-language translations of original foreign-language titles are cross-referenced to the foreign titles so that all references to discussion of a work are combined in one listing.

In response to numerous suggestions from librarians, Thomson Gale also produces an annual paperbound edition of the SSC cumulative title index. This annual cumulation, which alphabetically lists all titles reviewed in the series, is available to all customers. Additional copies of this index are available upon request. Librarians and patrons will welcome this separate index; it saves shelf space, is easy to use, and is recyclable upon receipt of the next edition.

Citing *Short Story Criticism*

When citing criticism reprinted in the Literary Criticism Series, students should provide complete bibliographic information so that the cited essay can be located in the original print or electronic source. Students who quote directly from reprinted criticism may use any accepted bibliographic format, such as University of Chicago Press style or Modern Language Association (MLA) style. Both the MLA and the University of Chicago formats are acceptable and recognized as being the current standards for citations. It is important, however, to choose one format for all citations; do not mix the two formats within a list of citations.

The examples below follow recommendations for preparing a bibliography set forth in *The Chicago Manual of Style,* 15th ed. (Chicago: The University of Chicago Press, 2006); the first example pertains to material drawn from periodicals, the second to material reprinted from books:

Morrison, Jago. "Narration and Unease in Ian McEwan's Later Fiction." *Critique* 42, no. 3 (spring 2001): 253-68. Reprinted in *Short Story Criticism.* Vol. 57, edited by Jelena Krstovic, 212-20. Detroit: Gale, 2003.

Brossard, Nicole. "Poetic Politics." In *The Politics of Poetic Form: Poetry and Public Policy,* edited by Charles Bernstein, 73-82. New York: Roof Books, 1990. Reprinted in *Short Story Criticism.* Vol. 57, edited by Jelena Krstovic, 3-8. Detroit: Gale, 2003.

The examples below follow recommendations for preparing a works cited list set forth in the *MLA Handbook for Writers of Research Papers,* 6th ed. (New York: The Modern Language Association of America, 2003); the first example pertains to material drawn from periodicals, the second to material reprinted from books:

Morrison, Jago. "Narration and Unease in Ian McEwan's Later Fiction." *Critique* 42.3 (spring 2001): 253-68. Reprinted in *Short Story Criticism.* Ed. Jelena Krstovic. Vol. 57. Detroit: Gale, 2003. 212-20.

Brossard, Nicole. "Poetic Politics." *The Politics of Poetic Form: Poetry and Public Policy.* Ed. Charles Bernstein. New York: Roof Books, 1990. 73-82. Reprinted in *Short Story Criticism.* Ed. Jelena Krstovic. Vol. 57. Detroit: Gale, 2003. 3-8.

Suggestions are Welcome

Readers who wish to suggest new features, topics, or authors to appear in future volumes, or who have other suggestions or comments are cordially invited to call, write, or fax the Associate Product Manager:

Associate Product Manager, Literary Criticism Series
Thomson Gale
27500 Drake Road
Farmington Hills, MI 48331-3535
1-800-347-4253 (GALE)
Fax: 248-699-8054

Acknowledgments

The editors wish to thank the copyright holders of the excerpted criticism included in this volume and the permissions managers of many book and magazine publishing companies for assisting us in securing reproduction rights. Following is a list of the copyright holders who have granted us permission to reproduce material in this volume of *SSC*. Every effort has been made to trace copyright, but if omissions have been made, please let us know.

COPYRIGHTED MATERIAL IN *SSC*, VOLUME 93, WAS REPRODUCED FROM THE FOLLOWING PERIODICALS:

Australian Literary Studies, v. 20, May, 2002. Reproduced by permission.—*Baker Street Journal,* v. 49, March, 1999. Copyright © 1999 by The Baker Street Irregulars. All rights reserved. Reproduced by permission.—*Commonweal,* vol. 69, November 21, 1958. Copyright © 1958, renewed 1986 Commonweal Publishing Co., Inc. Reproduced by permission of Commonweal Foundation.—*Dalhousie French Studies,* v. 44, fall, 1998 for "Finding a Room of One's Own in Colette's *La Vagabonde*" by Hope Christiansen. Reproduced by permission of the publisher and author./ v. 67, summer, 2004 for "A Delicate Balance: Becoming a Woman and a Writer in Colette's *Claudine &lsdquo;a l'école'* and *La Maison de Claudine*" by Stephanie Schechner. Both reproduced by permission of the publisher and the respective authors.—*Durham University Journal,* v. 85, January, 1993; v. 87, January, 1995. Reproduced by permission.—*English Language Notes,* v. 41, June, 2004. Copyright © 2004, Regents of the University of Colorado. Reproduced by permission.—*The Explicator,* v. 59, summer, 2001; v. 61, fall, 2002. Copyright © 2001, 2002 by Helen Dwight Reid Educational Foundation. Both reproduced with permission of the Helen Dwight Reid Educational Foundation, published by Heldref Publications, 1319 18th Street, NW, Washington, DC 20036-1802.—*Extrapolation,* v. 37, spring, 1996. Copyright © 1996 by The Kent State University Press. Reproduced by permission.—*Folklore,* v. 108, 1997 for "'The Rules of Folklore' in the Ghost Stories of M. R. James" by Jacqueline Simpson. Copyright © 1997 The Folklore Society. Reproduced by permission of Taylor & Francis, Ltd., http//:www.tandf.co.uk/journals, and the author.—*The French Review,* v. 58, February, 1985. Copyright © 1985 by the American Association of Teachers of French. Reproduced by permission.—*Meanjin,* v. 46, December, 1987 for "The Economics of Realism: John Morrison" by Ivor Indyk. Reproduced by permission of the author.—*Modern Fiction Studies,* v. 46, fall, 2000. Copyright © 2000 by Purdue Research Foundation, West Lafayette, IN 47907. All rights reserved. Reproduced by permission of The Johns Hopkins University.—*New Republic,* v. 139, December 8, 1958. Copyright © 1958 by Harrison-Blaine, Inc. Renewed 1986 by The New Republic, Inc. Reproduced by permission of *The New Republic.*—Nottingham French Studies, v. 43, summer, 2004. Copyright © The University of Nottingham 2004. Reproduced by permission.—*Overland,* v. 58, winter, 1974. Reproduced by permission.—*Papers on Language and Literature,* v. 40, fall, 2004. Copyright © 2004 by The Board of Trustees, Southern Illinois University at Edwardsville. Reproduced by permission.—*Prairie Schooner,* v.34, spring, 1960. Copyright © 1960 by University of Nebraska Press. Copyright © Renewed 1988 by the University of Nebraska Press. Reproduced from *Prairie Schooner* by permission of the University of Nebraska Press.—*Romance Quarterly,* v. 36, May, 1989. Copyright © 1989 by The University Press of Kentucky. Reproduced with permission of the Helen Dwight Reid Educational Foundation, published by Heldref Publications, 1319 18th Street, NW, Washington, DC 20036-1802.—*Studies in English Literature 1500-1900,* v. 41, autumn, 2001. Copyright © 2001 The Johns Hopkins University Press. Reproduced by permission.—*Studies in Short Fiction,* v. 19, summer, 1982; v. 29, fall, 1992. Copyright © 1982, 1992 by *Studies in Short Fiction.* Both reproduced by permission.—*Studies in Twentieth Century Literature,* v. 20, summer, 1996. Copyright © 1996 by *Studies in Twentieth Century Literature.* Reproduced by permission.—*Unisa English Studies,* v. 11, March, 1973. Reproduced by permission.—*University of Mississippi Studies in English,* v. 11-12, 1993-95. Copyright © 1995 The University of Mississippi. Reproduced by permission.—*Victorian Newsletter,* fall, 1998 for "'A Warning to the Curious': Victorian Science and the Awful Unconscious in M. R. James's *Ghost Stories*" by Brian Cowlishaw. Reproduced by permission of *The Victorian Newsletter* and the author.

COPYRIGHTED MATERIAL IN *SSC*, VOLUME 93, WAS REPRODUCED FROM THE FOLLOWING BOOKS:

Andrew, Ray Vernon. From *Wilkie Collins: A Critical Survey of His Prose Fiction with a Bibliography.* Garland Publishing, Inc., 1979. Reproduced by permission of Routledge/Taylor & Francis Group LLC., and the author.—Campbell, Ramsey. From *Meddling with Ghosts: Stories in the Tradition of M. R. James.* The British Library, 2001. Reproduced by permission of The British Library.—Clark, Leslie. From "Brunch on Moon River," in *The Modern American Novel and the*

Thomson Gale Literature Product Advisory Board

The members of the Thomson Gale Literature Product Advisory Board—reference librarians from public and academic library systems—represent a cross-section of our customer base and offer a variety of informed perspectives on both the presentation and content of our literature products. Advisory board members assess and define such quality issues as the relevance, currency, and usefulness of the author coverage, critical content, and literary topics included in our series; evaluate the layout, presentation, and general quality of our printed volumes; provide feedback on the criteria used for selecting authors and topics covered in our series; provide suggestions for potential enhancements to our series; identify any gaps in our coverage of authors or literary topics, recommending authors or topics for inclusion; analyze the appropriateness of our content and presentation for various user audiences, such as high school students, undergraduates, graduate students, librarians, and educators; and offer feedback on any proposed changes/enhancements to our series. We wish to thank the following advisors for their advice throughout the year.

Breakfast at Tiffany's

Truman Capote

The following entry presents criticism of Truman Capote's *Breakfast at Tiffany's*. For general discussion of Capote's short fiction, see *Short Story Criticism,* Volumes 2 and 47.

INTRODUCTION

Breakfast at Tiffany's is Truman Capote's lighthearted novella about the irresistible Holly Golightly, a nineteen-year-old prostitute and self-proclaimed "traveler" whose purpose in life is to have fun. The unnamed narrator of the work, an aspiring writer, recounts the events of his first year in New York, from 1943 to 1944, when he lived in the same apartment building as Holly. Holly entertains a series of lovers and is eventually arrested for her unwitting involvement in the drug trade. Published in 1958, Capote's 26,000-word story both looks back to a more innocent time and reflects the concerns of postwar America, including the emerging sexual revolution and the New York Mafia. Like Capote himself, the novel's narrator is gay, and there are frequent references in the novel to homosexuality and to unconventional morality. The novella also showcases the author's fascination with wealth, parties, and the Manhattan elite, showing the discrepancy between its perceived glamour and its reality. Other important themes include freedom, security, narcissism, and the outsider. *Breakfast at Tiffany's* was adapted for the screen by Blake Edwards in 1961 and the film version, starring Audrey Hepburn, has become even better known than Capote's short novel; Hepburn's portrayal in the film made Holly Golightly an iconic figure. Despite being one of Capote's most admired works, *Breakfast at Tiffany's* has generated surprisingly little critical commentary. This is partly because interest in the film has eclipsed notice of the novella, although, as critics are quick to point out, the two differ vastly. Many view the film as missing some of the most important elements of the book, noting that it turns the work into a conventional love story with unconventional characters neatly packaged in Hollywood style. Scholars who have written about the novella have focused on the work as a character study of Holly, who is seen both as a study of innocence and the prototype of today's liberated female.

PLOT AND MAJOR CHARACTERS

The story of *Breakfast at Tiffany's* is told by an unnamed narrator, a writer who has returned to the neighborhood in New York where he had come to seek success in 1943. It is now fifteen years later and he is back in the old neighborhood after receiving a call from Joe Bell, a bartender who gives him news of a mutual friend—Holly Golightly. Joe has photographs, taken by I. Y. Yunioshi, of an African sculpture that he believes is modeled after Holly. The narrator learns that the woman who is the subject of the sculpture was traveling with two men in Africa and that she stayed briefly with tribesmen before disappearing. After seeing Joe Bell, the narrator walks back to the old brownstone where he had his first New York apartment. It takes the narrator back to his first year in the city and his friendship with Holly.

At first Holly, who lives in the apartment below the narrator's, pays the narrator little attention, only "using" him when she loses her key. She had previously "used" her upstairs neighbor, Mr. Yunioshi, as her "doorbell convenience." One night in September, 1943, Holly climbs the fire escape to the narrator's room to flee an unwanted male guest. They quickly become friends. Holly calls the narrator "Fred" because he reminds her of her brother, who is in the army. She reads his work and tells him of her weekly visits to Sally Tomato in Sing Sing—he pays her $100 just to visit him. She asks the narrator if she can sleep in his bed, and when she thinks he is asleep she starts talking about Fred and crying. When the narrator asks her why she is crying she says she "hates snoops" and climbs back down to her room.

The next day, Holly apologizes and invites "Fred" to her apartment for a drink, which turns out to be a party. Holly is always giving or going to parties; she is devoted to having fun. She is careful not to form attachments, or to have a real home. She explains that she does not even name her cat, because it does not really belong to her. At the party the narrator meets numerous socialites, including O. J. Berman, a Hollywood agent who tells him that Holly is a "phony, but a real phony." The narrator also encounters "Rusty" Trawler, a millionaire, and Mag Wildwood, a fashion model. Mag is Holly's sometimes roommate, and Holly has her eye on Trawler, a known homosexual, because of his immense wealth. Mag is engaged to a Brazilian diplomat, José Ybarra-Jaegar.

One day in October the narrator and Holly spend a day together. They tell each other about their childhoods. Holly says she left home at fourteen, and then confesses that everything she has told him has been a lie. Later, the narrator discovers that Holly is making plans to move to Brazil.

At Christmas Holly asks the narrator to help her trim her Christmas tree, and she gives him an expensive, antique bird cage; he gives her a St. Christopher's medal from the famous jewelry store Tiffany & Co. Holly had told him that she loves Tiffany's because it calms her down and helps her when she is depressed. She goes to Tiffany's when she gets the "mean reds"—a state of angst and fear. When she goes to Tiffany's, she says, she feels that nothing really bad could happen.

In February, Holly, Rusty, Mag, and José take a trip. Holly recounts the details of the trip to the narrator. In Key West, Mag got badly sunburned, and Rusty was injured in a fight. Both were hospitalized, so José and Holly traveled to Havana. Mag had become suspicious that José and Holly are lovers, so Holly told Mag she is a lesbian. Holly also informs the narrator that she has given a copy of his story, without his consent, to O. J. Berman. They argue, and Holly throws the narrator out of her apartment.

After the fight, the narrator leaves the birdcage by Holly's apartment door. Later he finds it outside with the garbage, and retrieves it. Holly and the narrator do not speak for some months. The following spring, the narrator notices a man lurking around the brownstone. It is Doc Golightly, a horse doctor. He assumes the man is Holly's father, but finds out he is her husband, and that Holly's real name is Lulamae Barnes. Doc tells the narrator how he found Lulamae and Fred stealing food from him in Tulip, Texas. Their parents had died and he took them in. He married Lulamae when she was fourteen; she later ran off even though she had seemed happy. Doc pleads with the narrator to reunite him with Holly. When Holly sees Doc she is calm and happy, for she cares deeply for Doc; he saved her and gave her confidence, but he loved a "wild thing" and made a mistake when he thought he could tame her. Doc Golightly returns to Texas.

While riding the subway one day, the narrator learns that Rusty Trawler has married Mag. When he gets back to the apartment building, he hears noises from Holly's apartment. José arrives with a doctor and finds the apartment in disarray and Holly in a terrible state.

Fred has been killed in the war. After this, Holly no longer calls the narrator "Fred." José moves in with Holly. She begins cooking and learning Portuguese. She is pregnant, and she says she wants to have nine children with José. She insists she is in love with him and wants to move to Rio.

On the morning of September 30th, 1944, Holly invites the narrator to go horseback riding in Central Park to say farewell to her favorite horse. Holly intends to move to Brazil with José. A group of boys jump from behind the bushes and spook their horses while they are riding, and the narrator falls off. While Holly is taking care of him back at his apartment, two detectives burst in to arrest Holly for her connection with Sally Tomato's drug ring. The narrator and Joe Bell try to get Holly released from jail. Mag and Rusty Trawler will not help, but O. J. Berman does, so long as his name is not connected with the incident.

The narrator goes to feed Holly's cat and finds José's cousin packing his things. He gives the narrator a letter for Holly. The narrator takes José's letter to Holly, who is in the hospital, having lost her baby in a scuffle with the police. Holly hardens when she realizes that José has abandoned her. After she gets out of the hospital, Holly leaves for Rio. The narrator gathers her things, including her cat, and brings them to her at Joe Bell's bar. On the way to the airport, Holly tosses the cat out of the limousine. She then realizes that she and the cat do belong to one another, jumps out, and looks for him. When she can't find him, the narrator promises her he will. Holly tells the narrator she is scared. She heads to the airport and Brazil. That was the last time the narrator saw Holly.

The narrator notices that Holly is mentioned less and less in the news and finds himself longing to be with her once again. He reads in the headlines of a newspaper about Sally Tomato's death and how Holly is believed to be in Rio. A man named Quaintance Smith moves into her old apartment. Little is heard about Holly until the narrator receives a postcard in the spring. She has met someone new and is looking for somewhere to live. He wishes he had an address to write Holly and tell her that he has found her cat.

MAJOR THEMES

The central theme in *Breakfast at Tiffany's* is the tension between human beings' need for security and their desire for freedom. Holly embodies this theme, as she moves through her life seeking somewhere to call home while resisting being pinned down to any place. The narrator, like Holly, has come to New York to find freedom. But unlike Holly, by the end of the book he finds himself free yet secure, settled in, and connected to

New York. Holly has escaped from Texas and Doc Golightly, whom she loves but cannot stay with because she cannot compromise her independence and individuality. Although she desires security, she hates cages of any kind; she is a "wild thing" who refuses to be confined to any role not of her own making. She tries out a number of personas—Hollywood starlet and New York lady of the evening—but always refuses to give up her identity to be something she is not. She is, as O. J. Berman says, a "phony," but a *real* phony. There is a streak of narcissism in her (she does not really relate to anyone or anything except as an extension of her own desires), but she is also self-aware and honest about who she is and what she is trying to be. She wants love, wealth, and stability, but she also knows that she values her autonomy too much to let it be taken away, so she lives her life half in fantasy to avoid the responsibilities that might threaten her freedom.

Both main characters, the narrator and Holly, are outsiders who want to belong. Both are strangers to New York and long to be part of it. Yet Holly cannot belong if it means being something she is not—at least not on her own terms. The card on Holly's door reads "Miss Holiday Golightly, Traveling," and her apartment is full of packing crates. She is completely nonjudgmental about people's sexuality (she says that "a person ought to be able to marry men or women"), and she does not do what is expected of her. She is a romantic who wants love but does not believe she must have it on society's terms. The narrator is an outsider not only because he is a stranger in New York and uneasy among the glamorous people he meets, but also because of his unconventional sexual orientation. The characters' outsider status and sense of identity are emphasized by the way they are named and not named in the novella. The narrator is unnamed to highlight the sense that he does not belong, just as Holly does not name her cat because it does not belong to her. Holly changes her name from Lulamae Barnes to Holly Golightly to try to fit into city life so people will not know who she really is. Yet she *is* Holly Golightly; she has assumed that identity and become that person, and is true to that identity even to the end of the novella when she is wandering the world, looking for a permanent home.

CRITICAL RECEPTION

When *Breakfast at Tiffany's* first appeared in 1958 in a collection with three other short stories, it received mixed reviews. Some regarded it as among Capote's best work, while others viewed it as "slight" and a little too slick—style without substance. However, reviewers and readers were almost universally charmed by the work's central character, Holly Golightly, and she was quickly seen as Capote's most important creation. When

the movie adaptation of the novella appeared in 1961, it was an instant hit, and the name *Breakfast at Tiffany's* has since been more closely associated with Edwards's film than Capote's original. Capote was reportedly dissatisfied with the film, in particular with the choice of Audrey Hepburn as Holly; he had picked Marilyn Monroe to play the role. He was also upset with the changes made to the story, in particular to the ending.

Since the novella first appeared, there has been little detailed critical analysis of the work. The most thorough critical examination of the work has been by Ihab Hassan, who has focused on the character of Holly Golightly. Hassan argues that with Holly Capote fashions a new heroine and also gives shape to the theme of narcissism that runs through his work. William Nance also offers an analysis of the novella, one that again focuses on Holly and also views the novella as a sign of Capote moving from inward-looking stories to one that faces the real world. Other commentators have written about the thematic concerns in the novella, including its ideas about freedom, security, traveling versus belonging, the outsider, social conformity, sexuality, innocence, and integrity. Important symbols in the novel, it has been noted, are the wooden sculpture of Holly, the birdcage, Holly's cat, and Tiffany's jewelry store. Several critics have commented on the differences between Capote's novella and Blake's film adaptation, pointing out that the Hollywood version of the film in many regards bears little resemblance to Capote's work, with its wholesome feel and characters that are stripped of their complexity. While *Breakfast at Tiffany's* has not generated much critical commentary, the novella continues to be widely read, and it remains Capote's best known work of fiction.

PRINCIPAL WORKS

Short Fiction

A Tree of Night and Other Stories 1949
Breakfast at Tiffany's (novella and short stories) 1958
Selected Writings 1963
A Christmas Memory (novella) 1966
The Thanksgiving Visitor (novella) 1967
Music for Chameleons: New Writing (semi-fictional stories) 1980

Other Major Works

Other Voices, Other Rooms (novel) 1948
Local Color (nonfiction sketches, travel essays) 1950
The Grass Harp (novel) 1951

The Grass Harp (play) 1952
Beat the Devil [adaptor, with John Huston, of a novel by Thomas Helvick] (screenplay) 1954
The Muses Are Heard (nonfiction) 1956
In Cold Blood: A True Account of a Multiple Murder and Its Consequences (nonfiction novel) 1965
House of Flowers (play) 1968
The Dogs Bark: Public People and Private Places (essays) 1973
Answered Prayers (unfinished novel) 1986

CRITICISM

Alice Ellen Mayhew (review date 21 November 1958)

SOURCE: Mayhew, Alice Ellen. "Familiar Phantoms in the Country of Capote." *Commonweal* 69, no. 8 (21 November 1958): 236-37.

[*In the following early review of* Breakfast at Tiffany's, *Mayhew praises Capote's prose but finds the work a little too slick in parts and its ending not entirely satisfactory.*]

In the title story, and longest piece, of his new collection, Truman Capote changes his set from the decaying mansions of the Southern back country to Manhattan's East Side. His main character (her Cartier card reads: *Miss Holiday Golightly, Traveling*) expresses herself in an odd mixture of tough talk, cosmopolite chatter and French salutations. But the veneer is thin. The familiar Capote phantoms try to haunt the stage—love, absent and somber—and Mr. Capote re-examines those rare, childlike moments of promise in lives that seem otherwise destined for loneliness.

Because his lovers are, most often, children and older people who really are still children, and because the objects of their love are sometimes unrealistic, Mr. Capote appears, at first, whimsical. But his accusations are not capricious. His disparate matings point up the allegory of love's freakish status in the world. Though we have accepted its conventional modes, we have never learned that it must be free, various and all-encompassing. The old judge, in his earlier book, *The Grass Harp,* says, "We are speaking of love. A leaf, a handful of seed— begin with these, learn a little what it is to love. First, a leaf, a fall of rain, then someone to receive what a leaf has taught you, what a fall of rain has ripened. No easy process, understand; it could take a lifetime, it has mine, and still I've never mastered it—I only know how true it is: that love is a chain of love, as nature is a chain of

life." And there are, in Mr. Capote's pieces, those who seem to have a queer potentiality for love; they are eccentric or under-age. Miss Dolly Talbo, one of his elderly "children," answers, "Then I've been in love all my life," as she recounts the mementos of her affection: the color pink, a dried honeycomb, an empty hornet's nest, a jaybird's egg, her Negro friend, a little boy. Miss Golightly's collection is more sophisticated bits and ends: horses, a dumb-but-tender brother, a narcotics king, a Brazilian diplomat, a nameless cat, and the quiet dignity of Tiffany Jewelers. But Miss Dolly Talbo comments on the isolation. For these characters to divulge the habit of love (and they invariably do, being congenitally blabby) is foolishness because, "It's best not to show such things, it burdens people and makes them, I don't know why, unhappy."

Truman Capote's spare and beautiful prose, as well as his theme, recalls, somewhat, the work of Carson McCullers, who also writes with deceptive simplicity and underlying intensity of odd-assorted lovers. Often, Mrs. McCullers' heroes outgrow their strange predilections or destroy them. Their affairs flourish briefly in spite of their eccentricity as presentiments or symbols of that power. Mr. Capote's lovers, those whom the world has not corrupted, hold the outside permanently in abeyance with the single-minded assurance of the simple. They are bound to each other because they can hear the silent explosions of love. They are the world's waifs. Not unexpectedly, they are almost all orphans.

This, by way of comparing Truman Capote's most recent orphan, because he is a writer of enormous talent and sensitivity; yet, there is, unquestionably, a quality of slickness about *Breakfast At Tiffany's.* The flavor has changed from bittersweet to acid. Now we are asked to accept a child-woman, a bad-little-good-girl (I would have preferred it the other way round) who, even in the context of very broad comedy, strains our credulity and patience; who declares her love with, "I'd stop smoking if he asked me to," assures us that she'd rather have cancer than a dishonest heart, and refers to death as the fat woman. To be sure, this is Miss Golightly at her worst moments, and she has some genuinely affecting and humorous ones. Of course, it all comes out in the end that Miss Golightly, alias Lulamae Barnes, was a child-wife from Tulip, Texas, long before we met her picking her way Twenty-One and El Morocco, by way of Hollywood, and with a means of support all too visible. But, unlike *Other Voices, Other Rooms* with its sinister cravings of desire, or the poignant, tentative loves in *The Grass Harp,* Mr. Capote has to *tell* us that Miss Golightly is a genuine personality and not just a very clever stage device. This necessitates embarassing little speeches which do not proceed naturally from the core of the writing: ". . . it's better to look at the sky than live there. Such an empty place; so vague. Just a country where thunder goes and things disappear," she says.

The end of the story devolves into a razzle-dazzle of vaudeville. The police pursue Miss Golightly because of an innocent involvement in a dope ring, her Brazilian lover, sensitive to scandal, hastily departs, and she jumps bail to disappear from our sight forever, with only a tearful regret for her abandoned cat. Later on, there is a card from South America, enigmatic and deliberately high-spirited and, still later, an African mask turns up that bears a striking resemblance to Holly Golightly. We are left with our madcap memories and a pious desire that she has arrived where she belongs but we are unaffected by such tricks upon the sentiments. Mr. Capote, himself, has spoiled us for them.

The other three stories are little more than vignettes, distinguishable only because of Mr. Capote's easy way with the language. **"House of Flowers,"** the same title and locale as his Broadway musical, is a sort of slice-of-folk-life plus moral. **"A Diamond Guitar,"** the relationship of two prisoners who attempt an escape, is primarily a story of unrequited love, inchoate and diffuse. Only **"A Christmas Memory"** is reminiscent of Capote's earlier work, but it seems more as if the author were imitating himself in this story of the old woman and the small boy, each other's best friend, and their last Christmas together. It is written in tender colloquial style and fairly brimming over with Poignance!

Gordon Merrick (review date 8 December 1958)

SOURCE: Merrick, Gordon. "How to Write Lying Down." *New Republic* 139 (8 December 1958): 23-4.

[*In the following early review of* Breakfast at Tiffany's, *Merrick notes that the novella is a character study reminiscent of* The Great Gatsby, *but asserts that while F. Scott Fitzgerald was constantly scratching the surface of his main character, for Capote the surface is everything.*]

It has been ten years since Truman Capote was introduced to the public, reclining on a sofa, hilarious in tattersall vest and blond bangs. Today, if we may judge from the jacket illustration of his new book, *Breakfast at Tiffany's,* the bangs are almost gone but he is still lying down. Is he enacting an allegory? His production has been slight. At a time when one gets the impression that literary merit is evaluated by the pound, Capote and his publishers have had the hardihood to bring out a book that couldn't weigh more than a few ounces. Flying in the face of yet another current trend, he treats the English language as if it were here to stay and writes a prose of the utmost clarity and precision. These facts should be enough to predispose us in his favor.

Let us hope so, for on the basis of the current offering, Capote might easily be underestimated by the very people who oversold him when he first appeared. *Breakfast at Tiffany's,* according to the publisher, consists of "a short novel and three stories." There is nothing here for anybody in search of a "major" novelist but at his best, Capote is very, very good, as is illustrated by the fragment called **"A Christmas Memory"** which appears at the end of this collection. It is just that—a memory of a Christmas season when the author was seven and living with an endearing, childlike old female relative. It is full of kitchen smells and tastes, of outdoor excursions to gather nuts and holly, of the world of things and of childlike human warmth. One is tempted to quote, but it is contrived of so many small touches that one would be obliged to quote it all to convey its whole flavor. It is nostalgic but the observation never blurs or softens, it is affectionate but never sentimental. It is also very funny. One would like it to go on and on but it soon stops. The public image of the author, wan and recumbent, comes to mind and one is grateful that he has found the energy to write this much.

On the other hand, there is the "short novel" which gives this book its title. I think it is fair to assume that it is intended as a study of character, one Holly Golightly, a young lady of nineteen with some fairly free and easy attitudes towards the world. Her past is mysterious, her life at the time we are introduced to her is tumultuous with the animal cravings of the shady gents with whom she surrounds herself and on whom she preys. Eventually, she gets involved inadvertently in a dope ring, is arrested, has a miscarriage of a baby which would otherwise have been born illegitimate, breaks bail provided by a loyal friend, and skips the country. All this is plotted with dazzling skill.

We have met Miss Golightly before. Christopher Isherwood has written of her, or someone so like her that it makes no difference. She has a streaky blond head like a boy's, she has a body like a boy's, she talks like a boy. She is spoiled, inconsiderate, anti-social and, in spite of her casual way with a man, basically frigid. She is the romantic adolescent's projection of the ideal woman who will make no demands on anybody's manhood. Having divested herself of desirability for the fastidious by her declared promiscuity, she can remain just a good chum as she strolls across the room stark naked. Capote writes of her with rapt admiration.

The point of Miss Golightly is that she believes in love. As one of the characters says of her, "She's a *real* phony." In the words of the young lady herself, "A person ought to be able to marry men or women or—listen, if you came to me and said you wanted to hitch up with Man o' War, I'd respect your feelings." She's obviously a comfortable girl to have around, if you're inclined to get a crush on a horse or some other eccentric love object.

In structure and plan, this story is curiously reminiscent of Scott Fitzgerald's *The Great Gatsby*. Aside from the effect achieved by the prose, which is at once stylish, detached and colloquial, aside from the unabashed use of theatrical device, a startling parallel may be drawn between the two central characters. Both have cloaked their pasts in elaborate fantasies. Having done many things for which they might be called to account, both are tripped up ironically by something they *didn't* do. Both are betrayed by love. The great difference is that Fitzgerald was constantly scratching away at the surface, revealing the horror and emptiness below; for Capote, the surface is everything. There is only an occasional hint of an awareness that all is not for the best in Holly Golightly's world. As a consequence, his story is never more than clever entertainment, as entertaining, say, as something tossed off by Somerset Maugham, though he lacks too, perhaps, that foxy grandpa's popular touch.

The other two items in the collection may be disposed of briefly. One is called **"House of Flowers"** and all that need be said of it is that it served as the inspiration for a Broadway musical comedy of considerable charm. The other, **"A Diamond Guitar,"** concerns one of those mute, doomed loves that occur, we learn in books, between men in lowly circumstances, in this case between two inmates of a prison farm. This is Tennessee Williams country and Capote would be well advised not to stray into it again.

"Childlike," but not "childish," is the essential word in any discussion of Capote's work. His naïve enthusiasm for Holly Golightly is the child's enthusiasm for the mysterious adult world. "Brats and niggers," as he has one of his characters say of his work, are his special material, at least the former. On the basis of his performance to date, it would be as foolish to expect of him a full-bodied work of mature fiction as it would be to expect him to hold himself erect while sitting for his portrait.

It is tempting to explore the reasons for what is apparently a case of arrested development but it would entail touching on personality and therefore go beyond the bounds of strict literary criticism. If Capote is lying down the better to suck his thumb, it need not concern us once the basic distinctions have been made.

We have a tendency in this country to praise violently and, the aftermath to any excess, to hate ourselves for it the next morning. Every season must have its quota of masterpieces but God help the poor writer who turns out later to be something less than a genius. This is, of course, wasteful of talent, both great and small. We would be wiser and would better serve the national culture of which we hear so much if we learned to count our blessings with greater measure and discrimination.

Truman Capote is no genius, despite the manner of his presentation ten years ago, but his music, when in tune, is clear and lovely and I hope that it will still be heard long after Holly Golightly has been forgotten.

Ihab H. Hassan (essay date 1960)

SOURCE: Hassan, Ihab H. "Birth of a Heroine." In *The Critical Response to Truman Capote,* edited by Joseph J. Waldmeir and John C. Waldmeir, pp. 109-14. Greenwood, Conn.: Greenwood Press, 1999.

[*In the following essay, originally published in* Prairie Schooner *in 1960, Hassan contends that in Holly Golightly Capote introduced a heroine who embodies the new ideal of the misfit hero.*]

For ten or fifteen years now some critics of the novel have been going around, like Diogenes, with a lamp in their hand looking for a good novelist in the broad light of day, and some, like John the Baptist, have been crying aloud in the wilderness. This is well: death and taxes take their toll, the Cold War is still on, critics quarrel with themselves, and who does not yet know that ours is an age of organized conformity? But there is a "new" type of hero born to American fiction, and whether we call him saint or criminal, rebel or victim, rogue or picaro, his heart, though not entirely pure, is in its place. The moment, it seems, has found the character to embody its absurdities and crazy yearnings.

All of which brings us to Holly Golightly, the heroine of Capote's latest novella, ***Breakfast at Tiffany's*** Holly may remind some people of Salinger's Holden Caulfield, Bellow's Augie March, or even Kerouac's ragged collection of holy bums. But we had better let Holly remind us of Joel Knox, the protagonist of Capote's first novel, ***Other Voices, Other Rooms,*** or of no one at all. For in a real sense the story of Capote—and, incidentally, of a good part of contemporary fiction—can be told by following the transformation of one type of personage into the other. It is a story, of course, that requires a preamble.

Capote has two styles, two moods, which he uses within the ambit of romance, that form so ably defined by Richard Chase as possessing "a formal abstractness," veering more freely towards "the mythic, allegorical, and symbolistic" modes, and rather prone to "ignore the spectacle of man in society." Of the two styles one may be called "nocturnal," the other "daylight." The nocturnal style makes the greater use of dream imagery, uncanny trappings, supernatural motifs; it is shot through with the sense of underlying dreadfulness, and reveals to characters the disintegration of their psyche in "the instant of petrified violence." In **"Miriam," "Shut a**

Final Door," "A Tree of Night," "The Headless Hawk," and *Other Voices, Other Rooms* what the characters seek, like a dark Narcissus, is the most secret knowledge of their *identity*. But if the supernatural defines the nocturnal mode of Capote, humor defines his daylight style. The style, evident in **"My Side of the Matter," "Jug of Silver," "Children on Their Birthdays,"** and *The Grass Harp*, assumes the chatty, first-person informality of anecdotes. It specifies character and admits the busy-ness of social relations more than its darker counterpart. And the scene which it lights upon is usually the small Southern town, not the big city which witnesses in abstract horror the so-called alienation of man from his environment. In the daylight mood, the characters break through the circle of autism and introspection in a broad gesture of *love*—compare Joel's moment of hallucinatory self-revelation at the Cloud Hotel with Collin's humorous, nostalgic, and loving recognition as he remembers Sister Ida and her thirteen children cavorting in a sunny stream. Capote's latest creation, however, goes still farther than the retrospective Collin, who confesses that his life seems more like "a series of closed circles, rings that do not evolve with the freedom of the spiral. . . ."

With *Breakfast at Tiffany's,* the closed rings begin to evolve into a spiral, some open and continuous motion of the heroine's spirit, Miss Holiday Golightly, Traveling, as her Tiffany cards insist. But whether the driving motion of a spiral, so endless and implacable, possesses more freedom than a circle affords is a conundrum only Euclid may solve.

Holly, like Capote's other protagonists, is not yet out of her teens: "It was a face beyond childhood, yet this side of belonging to a woman." But her initiation began long ago, before she becomes the child-bride, at fourteen, of Doc Golightly, a horse doctor in Tulip, Texas; begun, probably, when she lost father and mother and was dumped with her brother Fred, half starved, on "various mean people." The process of that initiation remains secret—there are intimations of outrage and misery beyond a child's endurance—for Holly behaves as if past and future were no more substantial than the air she breathes; but its results are none the less permanent: a wild and homeless love of freedom. When we see her during the war years in that New York brownstone of the East Seventies, she is fully nineteen, and she strikes us as an improbable combination of the *picaro*, the courtesan, and the *poète maudit*.

Improbability is indeed the quality she uses to criticize a dreary and truthless round of existence, and artifice—she is an inspired liar—to transform it. "I'll never get used to anything. Anybody who does, they might as well be dead," she cries at one point, and we realize that her rebellion against the *given* in life, the useful and prudential, is one of the sources of her vitality. It is

as her dwarfish friend and Hollywood agent puts it, the "kid" is a "*real* phony," and her specialty is presenting "horseshit on a platter." Screwball, phony, or saint—some will find it more convenient simply to say "sick, sick, sick"—it does not take us very long to recognize Holly's hold on experience. Her "philosophy" is quite elementary—and hopelessly at odds with the times. "I don't mean I'd mind being rich and famous," she tells the narrator. "That's very much on my schedule, and some day I'll try to get around to it; but if it happens, I'd like to have my ego tagging along. I want to still be me when I wake up one fine morning and have breakfast at Tiffany's." When Holly's dream comes true—the vision symbolized by the "*ordre, luxe, et volupté*" of Tiffany's which she employs to cure her spells of "the mean reds"—she wants to be no other than herself. Implied here is no revulsion against one's identity, no holy surrender or unattachment. Holly is in fact very much attached to this world, and therefore to herself. In this respect, she seems the opposite of Salinger's Holden Caulfied with whom she shares the quixotic gift of truth, and shares the ability to gamble everything on a wayward love for, say, Man O'War—Holden's ducks in Central Park—or her brother Fred—Holden's sister, Phoebe. But also unlike Holden, whose stringent idealism limits the scope of his *joy,* Holly's truth refers to no self-transcending ideal. As she candidly admits:

> Good? Honest is more what I mean. Not law-type honest—I'd rob a grave, I'd steal two-bits off a dead man's eyes if I thought it would contribute to the days enjoyment—but unto-thyself-type honest. Be anything but a coward, a pretender, an emotional crook, a whore: I'd rather have cancer than a dishonest heart.

Her loyalty to others—the inmate Sally Tomato, for instance—is a loyalty to her own feelings for which she is willing to risk all.

Morality, we see, is defined in the privacy of the passing moment. But as the phantasmal vision of young Knox was followed, in Capote's novels, by the elegiac insight of a more mature Fenwick, so does the latter give way to Holly's sustaining faith in the honesty of the heart. The last allows Capote's heroine to implicate herself in a wider range of experience than her predecessors could encompass; it permits her to check her code against the play of reality in a manner Knox and Fenwick would have been powerless to command. But the crazy valor of Holly does not prevent her from carrying the customary burden of pain; the price of unorthodoxy, the intensity of her involvement with life, is fully paid. In this she is not unlike the hipster whose badge, the dark glasses, she constantly wears. Holly has no possessions other than the moment requires—she is "camping out" in New York. Like the ugly tomcat she picks up by the river one day, her existence is thoroughly improvised: "I don't want to own anything until I know I've found the place where me and things belong together." And like a wild thing she lives in the open sky; but she knows, too, that "it's better to look at the sky than live there. Such an empty place; so vague. Just a country where the thunder goes and things disappear." When her beloved brother, Fred, dies in the war—her brave soul goes berserk, the jaunty dark glasses are shattered, and her true piteous human nakedness is revealed—when her Brazilian lover abandons her pregnant, when she becomes involved in a narcotics scandal and the friends who fed on her emotional bounty desert her, when she jumps bail and takes off for Latin America, and thence to darkest Africa, the defiant spiral of her life, swirling into the unknown, leaves us breathless and afraid that so much light can diffuse itself into darkness, that such brave exuberance could be the product of greater desperation. And indeed Holly herself becomes afraid. On her way to the airport she stops in Spanish Harlem to let "her" cat off, admonishing it in a scene frankly sentimental to find a proper home for itself. Then she breaks down: "I'm very scared, Buster. Yes, at last. Because it could go on forever. Not knowing what's yours until you've thrown it away."

Holly Golightly may be what we should all like to become if we could put away comfort and respectability in an insured bank account; and her breezy excesses of fancy as of intuition may be, again, just what our stuffy age most requires. In her case the misfit hero certainly shows a fitting genius for *living*—rebellion here is secondary, spontaneous. But Capote himself is not entirely taken in by Holly's verve and piercing glitter. His tale, though lovingly told, has wit and sharp precision. As Holly sweeps through her zany adventures, one becomes conscious of a groundswell of gentle criticism. Mildred Grossman, the grind whom the narrator recalls from his schooldays, may be a "top-heavy realist," but Holly by the same token must be considered a "lop-sided romantic"; and antithetical as the two girls seem, both "walk through life and out of it with the same determined step that took small notice of those cliffs at the left." Even Holly's incorrigible tomcat finds at last a home with potted palms and lace curtains, a home and a name; but for Holly the narrator can only pray that she may be granted, sometime, somewhere, the grace of knowledge and repose. Narcissus found both in a reflected image; Holly, whimsical child of old Faust, looks for them beyond a vanishing horizon. For Holly—sooner or later we must say it—is a child too. She is premature in ways both delightful and regressive. (The latest avatar of Capote's Wizard Man is the "fat woman" who haunts Holly's "red nightmares," threatening to inflict punishment, withhold love, or destroy everything high and rare). But does not childhood itself, to which adults wend back in such tortuous ways, present a criticism of maturity for which we seldom have a ready answer?

Criticism, the interplay of views, is sustained by right form. The form of *Breakfast at Tiffany's* approaches perfection. It has pace, narrative excitement, a firm and subtle hold on the sequence of events from the first backward glance to the final salutation. A novelette in scope, it still manages to treat a subject usually accorded the fuller scope of the picaresque novel with marvelous selectivity. The point of view, the tone, the style herald no technical discoveries in the field of fiction: they simply blend to make the subject spring to life. Capote allows the story to be told in the first person by a struggling young writer whose vantage of perception, now in the shadow, now in the light, captures the elusive figure of Holly with the aid of such minor figures as Joe Bell and O. J. Berman. The device is both revealing and discreet, for there is, no doubt, something about Holly's complexion that cannot bear too sharp a light. By establishing the right relation between his narrator and subject, Capote also strikes the right tone. For though the whole story is unfolded backwards in one sweeping flashback, the tone is not, like *The Grass Harp*'s elegiac. Elegy, where so much hope is called to question, is out of place. The tone comes closer to that of an invocation, a blessing: hail, Holly, and farewell. Criticism, as we have noted, is implied, patronage never. What keeps the tone from becoming patronizing—look at that wonderful spoiled child!—is the style. The style matches the exotic quality of the subject with its clear-headedness, matches whimsy with wit, though here and there, as in the description of the cat, Capote indulges himself in a superfluous flourish of imagery. Holly's lack of self-criticism is balanced by the searching temper of the narrator. Tension and control are maintained. This is evident in the most casual bit of description. Here is one of Holly:

> She was still on the stairs, now she reached the landing, and the ragbag colors of her boy's hair, tawny streaks, strands of albinoblond and yellow, caught the hall light. It was a warm evening, nearly summer, and she wore a slim cool black dress, black sandals, a pearl choker. For all her chic thinness, she had an almost breakfast-cereal air of health, a soap and lemon cleanness, a rough pink darkening in the cheeks. Her mouth was large, her nose upturned. A pair of dark glasses blotted out her eyes.

Holly Golightly will remind a good many readers of Isherwood's Sally Bowles, and remind the greater community of movie-goers of Julie Harris's fine rendition of that role. But it is not chauvinism, we hope, that compels us to recognize her peculiarly American quality: her quixotic ideas of hope, sincerity, truth. (Sally may or may not have stood up for the gangster Tomato, while Holly could not have done otherwise.) Though Holly's life is completely open-ended, and her "initiation," once again, brings with it no confirmation or knowledge—neither does it bring nostalgia—it is a life, like Verena's, that leaves behind it a trail of love and affection. Secret doors, which might have remained forever closed, are unlocked where she passes, and even savages commemorate her presence in carved images. She is in this, we see, like other heroes of contemporary fiction, scapegoats and liberators all, and if we refuse to emulate them or accept their painful destiny, noting in our wisdom their shortcomings, we cannot in good conscience ignore the truth their proud fate so urgently implies.

Breakfast at Tiffany's happens also to include three short stories earlier published in magazines. The best one can say of them is that they have great charm and that they represent a livelier awareness of interpersonal relations, a more open concern with people, than some of Capote's earlier, and perhaps better, stories showed. Some will feel that **"A Diamond Guitar"** owes much to Carson McCullers—the tense style and the doctrine of love are hers—and others that **"House of Flowers,"** which sustained the frills and trills of a Broadway musical, discovers no new aspect of Capote's imagination, an imagination that the fairly autobiographical sketch, **"A Christmas Memory,"** helps us understand.

It is the novelette itself that gives new shape to the emergent pattern of Capote's work, a pattern, as we said, that reflects the central concerns of contemporary fiction. For as Joel, Collin, and Holly stand for knowledge through dream, love, and free action, they also represent typical attitudes struck in the post-war novel. Joel embodies the current feeling that our world is now discovered, our life organized, our vision confined to some lost room of childhood. The only freedom we still possess is the freedom to dream, and as reality becomes more intractable our dreams become compulsive. Collin Fenwick, in his nostalgic and backward glance, expresses the need to redeem the present, to redeem reality through love, a need to which the contemporary novel is intensely dedicated. As for Holly, she approaches the ideal of the new picaresque, the free-wheeling hero who insists on the freedom to experience and to denounce precisely because that freedom is no longer tolerated by society. In all cases, the American hero, equally so much more innocent *and* experienced than of yore, remains an outsider, a fugitive from the dominant concerns of American life, hiding in secret rooms or up a chinaberry tree, or still "lighting out for the territory ahead," which is now situated in Africa.

William L. Nance (essay date 1970)

SOURCE: Nance, William L. "*Breakfast at Tiffany's*." In *The Worlds of Truman Capote*, pp. 107-24. New York: Stein and Day, 1970.

[*In the following excerpt, Nance presents a detailed study of Holly Golightly, comparing her to Capote's other characters and discussing her relationship with the narrator.*]

Breakfast at Tiffany's almost completes the movement in Truman Capote's fiction from the submerged world of childhood to the real world of people and events. It employs the same New York setting as **"The Headless Hawk"** and **"Shut a Final Door,"** but there the resemblance ends. Between those stories and this one, Capote the writer has grown up. The early stories were inward-turning, conscious of the outside world only as a symbolic extension of inner fears. *Breakfast at Tiffany's* on the other hand, is as topical as Winchell's column, as cool and sophisticated as the tough, eccentric society it talks about. Its unnamed narrator, an aspiring writer who might well be Capote himself during his first months in New York, is an older Collin Fenwick who has set his own affairs in order and begun to look around him at the world. He observes it more objectively than before, but once again his attention is focused on a dreamer-heroine whose prototype is the elderly friend of **"A Christmas Memory."** This story, too, is a memory.

> I am always drawn back to places where I have lived, the houses and their neighborhoods. For instance, there is a brownstone in the East Seventies where, during the early years of the war, I had my first New York apartment . . . a place of my own, the first, and my books were there, and jars of pencils to sharpen, everything I needed, so I felt, to become the writer I wanted to be.

(*S* [*The Selected Writings of Truman Capote*] 162)[1]

The tone suggests that nothing is to be taken too seriously, and nothing is.

The narrator explains that he would probably never have thought of writing about Holly Golightly except for a conversation with Joe Bell, a bartender and mutual friend, that "set the whole memory of her in motion again" (*S* 163). In a now familiar pattern, the frame is set up to enclose a dreamlike past experience that still leaves its glow. Holly had been a tenant on the floor below, and this was "a long time ago." But it was just the previous Tuesday that Joe Bell called, "a croak of excitement in his froggy voice," and asked him to hurry over.

Bell has just had a visit from a photographer who also once lived in the brownstone and who, according to Winchell's column, has just spent two years in Africa. He has left some photographs of a Negro man proudly displaying a wood carving of "a head, a girl's, her hair sleek and short as a young man's, her smooth wood eyes too large and tilted in the tapering face, her mouth wide, overdrawn, not unlike clown-lips" (*S* 164). It is simultaneously a typical primitive carving and "the spit-image of Holly Golightly" (*S* 165), and the story is that the girl passed through the village with two white men, both sick with fever, and for a time "shared the woodcarver's mat" (*S* 166).

Holly's two former friends make what they can of this clue, so slight and so long-awaited. Bell admits that he was in love with her, though he never wanted "to touch her. . . . You can love somebody without it being like that. You keep them a stranger, a stranger who's a friend" (*S* 167). The narrator leaves and, let down and lonely, wanders by the brownstone and looks at the mailboxes where he first saw her card: "*Miss Holiday Golightly*; and, underneath, in the corner, *Traveling*" (*S* 168).

The narrator catches his first sight of Holly by leaning over the bannister, "just enough to see without being seen" (*S* 169). Her custom is to ring other tenants' bells, since she keeps losing her own keys, and it is the dismayed protesting of the photographer on the top floor that attracts the new resident's attention. From his point of vantage he notices first the "ragbag colors" of Holly's "boy's hair," then observes that in spite of her black evening dress and chic thinness she has "an almost breakfast-cereal air of health" (*S* 169). Dark glasses hide her eyes, giving latitude to his speculation about her age: "It was a face beyond childhood, yet this side of belonging to a woman. I thought her anywhere between sixteen and thirty; as it turned out, she was shy two months of her nineteenth birthday" (*S* 169). Though the setting could hardly be more different, here is a young observer peering down, like Collin from the attic, at a childlike heroine who has much more in common with Dolly Talbo than the sound of her name. Holly is, at the moment, giving the brush-off to an oily, thick-lipped man, punctuating his angry dash down the stairs with the advice, "The next time a girl wants a little powder-room change, take my advice, darling: *don't* give her twenty cents!" (*S* 170).

During the next few days, Holly begins calling on her new neighbor for door-opening chores. He wonders whether she is a model or a young actress but decides that she hasn't time for either. He sees her at a wide variety of places with an equally wide variety of men, and carries on further research by examining the contents of her trash can. In this manner he learns that her reading is confined to tabloids, travel folders, and astrological charts, and that she receives V-mail letters "by the bale" (*S* 171). He observes that she has a cat, and that she plays the guitar and occasionally sings, "in the hoarse, breaking tones of a boy's adolescent voice" (*S* 171). Her usual repertoire of Broadway show tunes is occasionally varied with others that "smacked of piney-woods and prairie." The one that seems to be her favorite goes: "*Don't wanna sleep, Don't wanna die, Just wanna go a-travelin' through the pastures of the sky*" (*S* 172).

The narrator's relationship with Holly Golightly moves along in this private-eye fashion until, one night in September, she turns the tables by appearing on the fire es-

cape and tapping at his window as he lies reading in bed. Wearing only a bathrobe, she explains that she is escaping a drunken "beast." She says she particularly loathes "men who bite," and loosens the robe from her shoulder to show him the mark. She apologizes for intruding but explains that he looked "so cozy. Like my brother Fred. We used to sleep four in a bed, and he was the only one that ever let me hug him on a cold night. By the way, do you mind if I call you Fred?" (*S* 173). After a moment she adds, "I suppose you think I'm very brazen. Or *tres fou*. Or something." When he denies it she seems disappointed: "Yes, you do. Everybody does. I don't mind. It's useful" (*S* 173). She tells him that except for his size he looks like Fred, who was six-feet-two. "My other brothers were more your size, runts. It was the peanut butter that made Fred so tall. Everybody thought it was dotty, the way he gorged himself on peanut butter; he didn't care about anything in this world except horses and peanut butter" (*S* 174). She insists he "wasn't dotty, just sweet and vague and terribly slow; he'd been in the eighth grade three years when I ran away" (*S* 174). Fred's defining characteristic seems to be that he is odd, that people call him crazy. Holly accepts him without reserve, just as she accepts the oddities in herself and even takes pride in them. Joel Knox and Miss Bobbit achieved their strength and freedom by the same kind of acceptance.

The narrator tells Holly he is a writer, and she asks him to tell her "the story part" of something he's written. When he explains that they're "not the kind of stories you can tell" (*S* 174), she asks him to read her one. He nervously reads one he has just finished, about two women who live together, one of whom prevents the marriage of the other by anonymously spreading scandal. His listener's apparent boredom chills him, and at the end she asks, "if it's not about a couple of old bull-dykes, what the hell *is* it about?" (*S* 175). By now he is "in no mood to compound the mistake of having read the story with the further embarrassment of explaining it" (*S* 175). Holly goes on to assure him she has nothing against Lesbians, and even to ask if he knows a nice one she might get as a roommate. She had one in Hollywood, she explains, and found her an excellent homemaker. "Of course people couldn't help but think I must be a bit of a dyke myself. And of course I am. Everyone is: a bit. So what? That never discouraged a man yet, in fact it seems to goad them on" (*S* 176).

Holly talks on, half-revealing another strange facet of her life. Reminded that it is Thursday, she mentions that she pays weekly visits to a man in Sing Sing, a notorious criminal named Sally Tomato who used to frequent Joe Bell's bar. One day she was contacted by a "lawyer" who asked if she wanted to "cheer up a lonely old man" and make a hundred dollars a week, and she found the offer too "romantic" to turn down. Pretending to be his niece, she takes messages from the lawyer such as,

"It's snowing in Palermo," or "There's a hurricane in Cuba." She describes visiting days at the prison in terms reminiscent of **"Children on Their Birthdays"**: the occasions are "sweet as hell," the wives dressed in their finery and the children shining as if they were going to get ice cream. It's like "a party," and because there is no grille, "all you have to do to kiss somebody is lean across" (*S* 177). When the narrator expresses concern at all this, she says, "Don't worry, darling. I've taken care of myself a long time" (*S* 179).

She pulls the covers up to his chin and lies down beside him, looking "like a transparent child" (*S* 179). He pretends to sleep, and after a long time feels her delicate touch on his arm, feels her tears against his shoulder, and hears her whisper, "Where are you, Fred? Because it's cold. There's snow in the wind" (*S* 179). He asks why she is crying and she jumps up, says she hates "snoops," and climbs back out the window.

Holly's closest relative among the Capote heroines is Miss Bobbit; all her asserted exploits notwithstanding, she is just as child-wise and sexless as that little girl. She has, however, been pursuing her dream much longer than Miss Bobbit has and knows much more about sadness. Her companion's warning about the Tomato affair seems to have made her feel the chilliness of her isolation, the vulnerability beneath her hard shell. The narrator himself feels lonelier than usual during the next few weeks, but finally he receives a note inviting him for drinks. He is admitted that evening by a gnomelike man who informs him that Holly is in the shower. The room is bare except for suitcases and unpacked crates, one of which serves as a table for martini mixings, another for a lamp and phone. He warms to the room immediately, liking its "fly-by-night look" (*S* 181). The little man, speaking in "a jerky metallic rhythm, like a teletype," abruptly demands of the newcomer:

"So what do you think: is she or ain't she?"

"Ain't she what?"

"A phony."

"I wouldn't have thought so."

"You're wrong. She is a phony. But on the other hand you're right. She isn't a phony because she's a *real* phony. She believes all this crap she believes. You can't talk her out of it. . . . Benny Polan, respected everywhere, Benny Polan tried. Benny had it on his mind to marry her, she don't go for it, Benny spent maybe thousands sending her to headshrinkers. Even the famous one, the one can only speak German, boy, did he throw in the towel. . . . She's strictly a girl you'll read where she ends up at the bottom of a bottle of Seconals. I've seen it happen more times than you've got toes: and those kids, they weren't even nuts. She's nuts."

(*S* 181-182)

Holly Golightly, a remote descendant of the heroine of **"Master Misery,"** has not let the psychiatrists steal her dreams. She belongs to a later generation of Capote heroines who have learned to preserve their integrity by safeguarding their uniqueness. Society helplessly admires her and considers her crazy at the same time, but Capote and his narrator have only admiration for her.

The little man identifies himself as O. J. Berman, a Hollywood actor's agent. He discovered Holly living with a jockey at Santa Anita at the age of fifteen and arranged a minor part in a movie, only to have her turn it down at the last moment. He describes her as a "goddamn liar," but his disapproval is only superficial, as his presence on this occasion suggests. Within a half hour the apartment is crowded with prosperous looking middle-aged men, each apparently surprised not to be the only guest. Holly floats among them carrying her cat.

Eventually she joins the narrator, and stays long enough to give him a considerable new insight into her thinking. She explains that she didn't want to be a movie star because it requires the sacrifice of one's ego, and "I want to still be me when I wake up one fine morning and have breakfast at Tiffany's" (*S* 187). Holly's life of traveling is really a search for a home, a place "where me and things belong together" (*S* 187). She hasn't found the place yet, but she knows it will make her feel like Tiffany's does, with the sense of security, the "quietness and proud look of it" (*S* 188).

She asks the narrator if he knows what the "mean reds" are, and distinguishes them from the blues, which only make you sad. "But the mean reds are horrible. You're afraid and you sweat like hell, but you don't know what you're afraid of. Except something bad is going to happen, only you don't know what it is" (*S* 188). He confesses that he knows the feeling and says some people call it *angst*. He suggests that a drink can help, but Holly says she's already tried that, and also aspirin and marijuana. What does her the most good is going to Tiffany's: "It calms me down right away; . . . nothing very bad could happen to you there, not with those kind men in their nice suits, and that lovely smell of silver and alligator wallets" (*S* 188). Unable to make a home of the near-at-hand paradise, she dreams of settling down with Fred after the war in a more distant one. "I went to Mexico once. It's wonderful country for raising horses. I saw one place near the sea. Fred's good with horses" (*S* 188).

The character of Holly Golightly was, Capote says, inspired by a real girl who told him many of the things Holly tells the narrator in the story.[2] If the above reflections were among these, this anonymous young lady may deserve considerable credit for helping to shape his literary career. Whether or not this is the case, her technique for handling the "mean reds" seems to be Capote's own. His early stories were all about the "mean reds," and the antidote he found was the dream. Joel Knox made the transition by finding his "proper place," but had to retire from the real world to do it. His later counterparts, because they try to live in the world, must consequently be travelers. Holly, realizing as Miss Bobbit did that "the next best thing is very often the best," makes do for the time being with the artificial peace of Tiffany's.

Holly's immediate plan is to finance the next leg of her journey by marrying a wealthy "middle-aged child" (*S* 185) named Rusty Trawler. Meanwhile she acquires a roommate, a grotesquely tall, horsey fashion model named Mag Wildwood, and, learning that Mag is engaged to a Brazilian with presidential aspirations, begins laying plans to snare him for herself. The narrator has encountered this man, named José, in the apartment and is "charmed" by his physical perfection and bashful manner.

Not long after the party in Holly's apartment, the narrator has his first story accepted by a small university review. Elated, he pounds on Holly's door and shows her the letter. At first she objects to his not being paid, but then, realizing that he wants congratulations rather than advice, she offers to take him to lunch. He waits in her bedroom, which has the same "camping-out atmosphere" as her parlor except that it houses an extravagant double bed. Finally dressed, she cups her hand under his chin and says, "Listen, I'm glad about the story. Really I am" (*S* 197).

It is a Monday in October, 1943, and a beautiful day. They have a drink at Joe Bell's and watch a parade on Fifth Avenue. "Afterwards, avoiding the zoo (Holly said she couldn't bear to see anything in a cage), we giggled, ran, sang along the paths toward the old wooden boathouse, now gone" (*S* 198). Holly puzzles him by describing, in vague, impressionistic terms, a childhood which seems "happy in a way that she was not, and never, certainly, the background of a child who had run away" (*S* 198). When he finally gets her to admit that she has been on her own since she was fourteen, and that the pretty recollection isn't true, she explains, "But really, darling, you made such a tragedy out of your childhood I didn't feel I should compete" (*S* 198).

He spends a number of "hither and yonning days" with Holly, but after a time he gets a nine-to-five job which makes their meetings rare. Now and then he sees her, usually with Rusty, Mag, and the Brazilian. Late in the winter, Holly gives him an account of a trip to South America. Leaving Mag and Rusty along the way, she had gone to Havana with José and had a wonderful time. To convince Mag that she hadn't "spent the whole time sleeping with José," she claimed to be a dyke.

"Leave it to me: I'm always top banana in the shock department. Be a darling, darling, rub some oil on my back" (*S* 203).

While he does so she tells him she has shown his story, now published, to Berman and that he is impressed. Berman agrees, however, that he's on the wrong track: "Brats and niggers. Trembling leaves. *Description.* It doesn't *mean* anything" (*S* 203). Tempted to bring his hand down hard on her bare buttocks, he asks her to give an example of "something that means something." When she mentions *Wuthering Heights,* he objects that she's referring to "a work of genius"; then, learning that she knows only the movie, he annoys her with his disdain.

> "Everybody has to feel superior to somebody," she said. "But it's customary to present a little proof before you take the privilege."
>
> "I don't compare myself to you. Or Berman. Therefore I can't feel superior. We want different things."
>
> "Don't you want to make money?"
>
> "I haven't planned that far."
>
> "That's how your stories sound. As though you'd written them without knowing the end."
>
> (*S* 204)

In this scene especially, Capote teases the reader with the suspicion that the narrator of *Breakfast at Tiffany's* is himself. There is no doubt about the resemblance, or about the role of this story in Capote's gradual transition from fiction to non-fiction. The rather surprising insertion of Holly's critique on obviously early-Capote writing may be a tribute to the real-life girl who seems to have had more influence on his literary career than all the professional critics put together. For he has followed Holly's advice to the letter. *Breakfast at Tiffany's* itself fills the prescription that he abandon brats and trembling leaves, and *In Cold Blood* has solved the financial problem. Of course, what Capote really found in the Ur-Holly, as in the other women who inspired his heroines, was a new avatar of his constantly unfolding self.

This bizarre literary discussion brings the narrator's friendship with Holly to a temporary close. Spring comes, and one day he sees a man studying Holly's name card and looking up at her window. Later he notices the man following him and whistling Holly's plaintive tune about the *pastures of the sky.* Apparently in his early fifties, he has "a hard, weathered face, gray forlorn eyes" (*S* 205). He joins the narrator at the counter of Hamburg Heaven, explaining, "Son, I need a friend" (*S* 206), and shows him a worn photograph of seven people on the sagging porch of a wooden house—five children and himself with his arm around a plump blond girl. He says the blond girl is "her," and identifies a tow-headed beanpole as "her brother, Fred."

The narrator looks again at "her" and sees the resemblance. "You're Holly's *father*."

The man blinks, frowns. "Her name's not Holly. She was a Lulamae Barnes. Was," he says, "till she married me. I'm her husband" (*S* 207). He is Doc Golightly, a horse doctor and farmer from Texas, who married Lulamae at the age of fourteen after his first wife's death. She and Fred had appeared one day, having escaped from the "mean, no-count" family that had kept them since their parents died of TB. Doc was kind to his young wife, but after a time she began taking walks. "Every day she'd walk a little further: a mile, and come home. Two miles, and come home. One day she just kept on" (*S* 209).

When the narrator springs the name "Lulamae" on her, Holly thinks Fred has come and runs down the stairs looking for him. She is disappointed at finding Doc but treats him kindly and, as she admits to the narrator the next day in Joe Bell's bar, lets him take her to bed. Apparently feeling guilty (for the first time in their acquaintance), she explains, "Anyone who ever gave you confidence, you owe them a lot" (*S* 211). She says they spent the latter part of the night in a bus station, Doc all the while thinking that she was really coming home with him, even though she told him she was not fourteen any more, and that she was not Lulamae. "But the terrible part is (and I realized it while we were standing there) I am" (*S* 211).

Joe Bell brings them another drink and she says to him, "Never love a wild thing, Mr. Bell . . . the more you do, the stronger they get. Until they're strong enough to run into the woods. Or fly into a tree. Then a taller tree. Then the sky" (*S* 212). Holly's words, which would be an appropriate text for **"A Diamond Guitar,"** are spoken in a voice slightly blurred with drinking. She offers a toast to the absent Doc: "Good luck: and believe me, dearest Doc—it's better to look at the sky than live there. Such an empty place; so vague. Just a country where the thunder goes and things disappear" (*S* 212).

For various reasons, the narrator doesn't see Holly again for some time. Fired from his job and threatened by the draft, he has his own case of the mean reds. When he sees headlines proclaiming Rusty Trawler's fourth marriage, he assumes that he has married Holly and gets even more depressed. "For I *was* in love with her. Just as I'd once been in love with my mother's elderly colored cook and a postman who let me follow him on his rounds and a whole family named McKendrick" (*S* 213). A while later he buys a paper, finishes the article, and learns that Rusty has married not Holly but Mag Wildwood. Arriving home, he hears a terrible racket in Holly's room but, strangely, no quarreling voices. At his knock the noise stops, but the door remains locked. He is trying to break it down when a frightened José

rushes up the stairs accompanied by a doctor and enters the room with his key.

Almost everything in the apartment is broken. Holly is on the bed, staring blindly and "whimpering like an exhausted, fretful child" (*S* 214). The doctor tells her she must sleep, and she says, "He's the only one would ever let me. Let me hug him on cold nights. I saw a place in Mexico. With horses. By the sea" (*S* 214). The doctor gives her an injection and José shows the narrator a telegram from Doc telling Holly that Fred has been killed in action.

Holly does not talk about Fred any more and stops calling her friend by that name. Through the summer she lives in relative isolation. Far from becoming bitter, however, she seems happier than the narrator has ever seen her. She is trying to learn Portuguese and begins most of her sentences with "After we're married—" though José has never mentioned marriage. This is notwithstanding the fact, she informs her friend, that José knows she is six weeks pregnant. She says she is delighted at the fact and even wishes she had been a virgin for José. This leads to a brief survey of her sex life. She denies that she has "warmed the multitudes" that some people suspect; she has, to be precise, had eleven lovers. This is "not counting anything that happened before I was thirteen because, after all, that just *doesn't* count. Eleven. Does that make me a whore?" (*S* 217). She explains that she doesn't have anything *against* whores. "Except this: Some of them may have an honest tongue but they all have dishonest hearts. I mean, you can't bang the guy and cash his checks and at least not *try* to believe you love him. I never have. . . . I sort of hypnotized myself into thinking their sheer rattiness had a certain allure" (*S* 218). She concludes that, in fact, Doc and José have been her only "non-rat" romances.

Earlier, in a conversation with Mag Wildwood overheard by the narrator, Holly had said that she liked a man who sees the humor of sex rather than being like "most of them, . . . all pant and puff" (*S* 195). Insisting she would rather be "natural" than "normal," she emphasized the visual approach and suggested leaving the lights on while making love: "Men are beautiful, a lot of them are, José is, and if you don't even want to look at him, well, I'd say he's getting a pretty cold plate of macaroni" (*S* 195).

Holly's response to José is not, in fact, very different from the narrator's own appreciation of his handsomeness. What we really come to know of Holly in **Breakfast at Tiffany's** makes the account of her sexual exploits seem as fictional as Tico Feo's admittedly were in **"A Diamond Guitar"**—a fact of considerable interest in view of the strong similarity between the two characters in other respects. As in Capote's other stories, sexuality is more convincingly negated than affirmed. On the other hand, Holly's efforts to avoid the dishonesty of whores by "making herself love" practically anybody seem never quite successful—even in the case of José, as she goes on to show. Acknowledging that he's not really her idea of "the absolute finito," she lists some of his questionable traits such as worrying about what people think, taking "about fifty baths a day," turning his back to get undressed, making too much noise when he eats, and having "something funny-looking about him when he runs" (*S* 218).

If, she goes on, she were free to pick anyone in the world, she would more readily select Nehru, Wendell Willkie, or even Garbo. "Why not? A person ought to be able to marry men or women or—listen, if you came to me and said you wanted to hitch up with Man o' War, I'd respect your feeling" (*S* 218). Holly says she's completely in favor of love, that it "should be allowed." And, she says, she does love José, for he has helped her escape at least to some extent from the mean reds. She has even thrown away her horoscope, having decided the only answer is that good things happen to you only if you're honest.

> Not law-type honest—I'd rob a grave, I'd steal two bits off a dead man's eyes if I thought it would contribute to the day's enjoyment—but unto-thyself-type honest. Be anything but a coward, a pretender, an emotional crook, a whore: I'd rather have cancer than a dishonest heart. Which isn't being pious. Just practical. Cancer *may* cool you, but the other's sure to.
>
> (*S* 218-219)

Holly's ideal of love is simply not a sexual one, nor is it likely to be satisfied by any real human being she will meet. The ideal relationship she aspires to is approximated by the narrator's own relationship with her: tender but distant, and consisting largely of admiration for her brilliance and strength. That Holly makes honesty to self her guiding principle is not surprising when we remember that on the deepest level she is the Capote-narrator's alter ego, representing for him—as Miss Bobbit did for Billy Bob—the strange, unconventional side of himself. In admiring Holly he is being true to himself, making that act of acceptance that has been the dominant impulse in most of Capote's writing.

The end of summer passes in a blur of pleasantness, for their friendship has reached "that sweet depth where two people communicate more often in silence than in words" (*S* 219). But as the time for parting draws near, the narrator feels increasingly jealous of José and of Holly's future in general, "infuriatingly left out—a tugboat in drydock while she, glittery voyager of secure destination, steamed down the harbor with whistles whistling and confetti in the air" (*S* 219). Like Collin at the end of *The Grass Harp*, he feels threatened by the end of one section of his life.

The thirtieth of September, his birthday, is "unlike any other I've lived" (*S* 219). Holly invites him to go horseback riding in Central Park. Slapping her flat stomach, she says, "Don't think I'm out to lose the heir. But there's a horse, my darling old Mabel Minerva—I can't go without saying goodbye to Mabel Minerva" (*S* 220). She tells him that she and José will be flying to Brazil in a few days. He follows her down the street in a trance, protesting that she can't just "run off and leave everybody." At the stable he helps hoist him onto an old mare she declares is "safer than a cradle," then mounts her own silvery horse and takes the lead.

The fun lasts only a few minutes, for all at once a gang of Negro boys jump at them from the bushes, throwing rocks, cursing, and whipping the horses. His horse bolts, and Holly chases him through the park and down several blocks of noon-day Fifth Avenue traffic before she and a mounted policeman manage to bring him to a stop between them. She puts him into a taxi, expressing serious concern for his welfare. Touched and embarrassed, he mumbles, "honestly. I don't feel anything. Except ashamed. . . . And thank you. For saving my life. You're wonderful. Unique. I love you" (*S* 222). Holly is a blurred vision: he sees three of her, then four, then faints.

The evening papers are filled with Holly, not as the catcher of a runaway horse but as a "DOPE-SMUGGLING ACTRESS," accused of complicity in Tomato's narcotics racket because of the "innocent" message-bearing which she has, in fact, recently stopped. Under the subheading, "ADMITS OWN DRUG ADDICTION," Holly is quoted as admitting that she has "had a little go at marijuana" and commenting that it is less destructive than brandy, though unfortunately she prefers the latter.

Once again the innocent dreamer becomes a prisoner; as always, she is at odds with a literalistic, moralistic society. One fact not mentioned in the articles is that Holly was arrested in the narrator's bathroom. He was soaking in Epsom salts while she sat on the edge of the tub, "waiting to rub me with Sloan's liniment and tuck me in bed" (*S* 225). The situation has its similarities to the confrontation between tree-dwellers and town in *The Grass Harp*. When a burly woman detective barges in and puts her hand on Holly's shoulder, she coolly tells her, "Get them cotton-pickin' hands off of me, you dreary, driveling old bull-dyke," and is slapped so hard "her head twisted on her neck" (*S* 225).

Holly's wealthy "friends" disappear. The narrator visits her in the hospital and learns that she has "lost the heir" and, in fact, come close to death.

> Christ, I nearly cooled. No fooling, the fat woman almost had me. She was yakking up a storm. I guess I couldn't have told you about the fat woman. Since I

didn't know about her myself until my brother died. Right away I was wondering where he'd gone, what it meant, Fred's dying; and then I saw her, she was there in the room with me, and she had Fred cradled in her arms, a fat mean red bitch rocking in a rocking chair with Fred on her lap and laughing like a brass band. The mockery of it! But it's all that's ahead for us, my friend: this comedienne waiting to give you the old razz. Now do you see why I went crazy and broke everything?

(*S* 228-229)

The "mean reds," expanding into the "fat mean red bitch," resemble the mad laughing Santa Claus that frightened Sylvia in **"Master Misery."** Death, which presided over Capote's early stories, is present all through his later ones, though held at bay by friendship and the pursuit of life-sustaining dreams.

Holly is at present facing several preliminary deaths, and her fast-approaching departure will be a sort of death for the narrator. She asks him about José and he hands her a letter in which that individual, frightened by the drug scandal, courteously bows out of her life. She knows in advance what it will say and asks for her purse, explaining, "A girl doesn't read this sort of thing without her lipstick." Finally, "armored" with cosmetics, she scans the letter "while her stony small smile grew smaller and harder" (*S* 229).

Holly's plan is to use her ticket for Brazil to escape from the country. The narrator tries to dissuade her, arguing that even if she does make it she can never come back. Both of them have visions of "iron rooms, steel corridors of gradually closing doors" (*S* 231). Finally her departure day arrives, dark with rain. "Sharks might have swum through the air, though it seemed improbable a plane could penetrate it" (*S* 233). The narrator, eluding police surveillance, cleans out Holly's apartment, and they rendezvous at Joe Bell's bar. Bell has hired a Carey Cadillac to take her to the airport, but gruffly refuses to drink to her "foolishness" and only thrusts some flowers at her before locking himself in the men's room.

Holly shocks the narrator by abandoning her cat in Spanish Harlem. She has never named it, intending to wait until they found a home; now she explains, "Independents, both of us. We never made each other any promises. We never—" (*S* 236). At a traffic light she jumps out of the car and runs back down the street, looking for the cat. Unable to find him, she finally allows herself to be led back to the car, shuddering. "Jesus God. We did belong to each other. He was mine" (*S* 236). The narrator promises to find the cat and take care of him, but she whispers, "But what about me? I'm very scared, Buster. Yes, at last. Because it could go on forever. Not knowing what's yours until you've thrown it away. The mean reds, they're nothing. The fat woman, she's nothing. This, though: my mouth's so dry, if my life depended on it I couldn't spit" (*S* 236).

Holly escapes to Rio and her name gradually disappears from the gossip columns. In the spring a postcard comes: "*Brazil was beastly but Buenos Aires the best. Not Tiffany's, but almost. Am joined at the hip with du-hvine $enor. Love? Think so. Anyhow am looking for somewhere to live ($enor has wife, 7 brats) and will let you know address when I know myself. Mille Tendresse*" (*S* 237). The address never comes, and eventually he moves out of the brownstone because it is "haunted." He wishes he could tell her about the cat. After weeks of searching, he had found him. "Flanked by potted plants and framed by clean lace curtains, he was seated in the window of a warm-looking room: I wondered what his name was, for I was certain he had one now, certain he'd arrived somewhere he belonged. African hut or whatever, I hope Holly has, too" (*S* 237).

Breakfast at Tiffany's is a showcase for Holly Golightly. O. J. Berman introduced her as a "*real* phony" who honestly "believes all this crap she believes," and the remainder of the story is a gradual exposition of the content of this belief. We learn that her idea of love is a non-sexual focusing of esthetically oriented feeling, just as it was for Randolph, Judge Cool, and Dolly Talbo. Honesty to oneself, or acceptance of one's identity, is as important to her as it came to be for Joel Knox. All her life she has known deprivation and death and fought a desperate battle against fear. It is, finally, the awareness of death that keeps her from feeling at home anywhere and impels her on a constant search for something better. Here at the end of *Breakfast at Tiffany's*—which is, except for the genial **"Among the Paths to Eden,"** Capote's last fictional "word" on life up to the time of *In Cold Blood*—we learn what seems to be Holly's deepest motivating force. Her regret at losing her nameless, battered "slob" of a cat, far from being a sentimental excess on her part (and the narrator's), is an intensely serious expression of a profound fear of relinquishment. Just as the dominant willed movement in Capote's fiction is acceptance—of things, persons, life—so its deepest fear seems to be of the inner principle of rejection that leads one to throw away those few and tenuous possessions life does permit. The fight against death must be carried on even in the innermost recesses of the self.

Holly's values are those of the Capote-narrator: she is a part of himself set free like a broken-stringed kite to wander toward an ambiguous land of dreams and death. Her brief presence is his own breakfast at Tiffany's, his taste of the idyll which always vanishes, leaving pain. Shortly before her departure he achieves a loving acceptance of this fact by an inner movement that parallels that of Collin in the tree house when he felt himself simultaneously receding from Dolly, the Judge, and Verena and embracing them all in a common sympathy. While he and Holly are riding in the park, just before his horse bolts, he feels an unexpected change of mood:

"Suddenly, watching the tangled colors of Holly's hair flash in the red-yellow leaf light, I loved her enough to forget myself, my self-pitying despairs, and be content that something she thought happy was going to happen" (*S* 221). This attitude of blended acceptance and relinquishment sustains him from that time on, through the vaguely sexual but deliberately unheroic climax of the horseback chase and the crisis over Holly's arrest. At the end, like Mr. Belli in **"Among the Paths to Eden,"** he thanks his heroine for the memory and wishes her well.

When ***Breakfast at Tiffany's*** was published in 1958, Capote was well on his way toward the nonfiction novel. He had gradually shifted himself from the center of his fiction to the edge—from the role of protagonist to that of a highly detached narrator. He had moved from a private dream world to one that was identifiable, topical, even journalistic. He had come increasingly to build his stories around real people he had met, most of them women who resembled the elderly lady who was his first close friend. Outside of the fiction, a long series of developments had been leading him in the same direction. . . .

Notes

1. *The Selected Writings of Truman Capote* (New York: Random House, 1963), p. 162. Quotations from this volume are identified in the text by *S* and the page number.

2. Truman Capote, recorded interview with William L. Nance, November 10, 1966.

Leslie Clark (essay date 1978)

SOURCE: Clark, Leslie. "Brunch on Moon River." In *The Modern American Novel and the Movies,* edited by Gerald Peary and Roger Shatzkin, pp. 236-46. New York: Frederick Ungar Publishing Co., 1978.

[*In the following essay, Clark compares Blake Edwards's 1961 film adaptation of* Breakfast at Tiffany's *with Capote's text.*]

In the midst of Holly Golightly's cocktail party in Truman Capote's ***Breakfast at Tiffany's*** a Hollywood producer named O. J. Berman offers the unnamed young writer-narrator a curious description of their outlandish hostess. "She isn't a phoney because she's a *real* phoney," Berman asserts, pleased to think he understands her.

The more we know of Holly the more Berman's self-contradictory observation comes to make deep sense. Holly lives conspicuously in a world of amoral, high-priced hustling, and she looks and acts like a girl on the make. But she never pretends to be much else. She may practice phoniness (her role as a society playgirl is a euphemism for a kind of informal prostitution), yet she *is* genuine. Her refusal to serve as a state's witness against someone she thinks has been good to her ("Testify against a friend I will not.") demonstrates her integrity even as this act precipitates her downfall. She may be, as she says, rotten to the core, but at the core she has a sense of honor.

O. J. Berman makes the identical pronouncement about Holly in the Blake Edwards film version of ***Breakfast at Tiffany's*** (1961); she is a "*real* phoney." And this time also we can take his meaning to stand as the thematic centerpiece of the work. However, Edwards is not in the least interested in Holly's convictions about decency and fair play. She qualifies as a *real* phoney because she believes wholeheartedly that glamor can fulfill dreams, just as she is susceptible to fairy tales and making wishes on a star.

Edwards gallantly rewards Holly's fantasizing with a happy fairy-tale ending, even though love and matrimony-ever-after are assuredly not what Capote's Holly had in mind.

New York Times film critic A. H. Weiler aptly described Capote's 1958 novella as a "wistful memoir." Set in New York during the wartime 1940s, it is a bittersweet, ironic study of how a nineteen-year-old girl is forced into womanhood before her time. She wants to play the society game like a gambler after high stakes, not for the money but for a chance at getting what she never had, which is, paradoxically, what only money can buy. Capote's writer-narrator calls her a "glittery voyager," committed to her makeshift headful of dreams. The difference between Holly and virtually everyone else we encounter is that, in O. J.'s words, "she believes all this crap she believes." Who beside Holly would seek after an elusive vision of peace in New York City and would latch on to the tolerant benevolence of Tiffany's, because "nothing very bad can happen to you there"?

Despite her romantic idealism, Capote's Holly is resilient, self-aware, and knows how to take care of herself; her beliefs give her the tenacity to survive. Most of the episodes missing from the film are those in the novella in which Holly displays her own strength and ability to manage (or manipulate) a situation. She nurses Mag Wildwood back to health after the famous cocktail party and moves Mag into her apartment; then she has no qualms about seducing her friend's rich South American "prospect" José. She saves the writer-narrator's life after a runaway horse nearly kills him; as a consequence, her illegitimate child miscarries (a development not in the film). Most of all, she *does* take the plane to Brazil, "travelling light," looking for whatever it is in the world that feels as nice as Tiffany's.

For Blake Edwards the fantasy of Tiffany's as a sanctuary from the pain of reality is the kind of dreaming that renders Holly fragile and soon despoiled. His Holly is deemed appealing precisely because she *cannot* take care of herself. She is just so vulnerable, so waiflike. Instead of the boyish elegance of Capote's heroine, her particular attraction is the fragility of Audrey Hepburn's acting. Accordingly, there is considerably more discretion about exactly how she collects her nightly fifty-dollar "powder room" tips in posh restaurants. (Edwards sugarcoats it for us, more, I suspect, from personal design than from concession to the moral standards of Hollywood, 1962.) For Blake Edwards, Holly is hooked, just as she started hooking, for the sake of dreaming and her own romantic impulses. And it is her dreaming which has sold her down (Moon) river.

It is a long distance from the Libertyphones and V-letters of the novella's world to the affluent, glossy, magazine-cover ambience of the film, and from Capote's admiring study of a character with spunk to a situation piece close to a gently sudsy, rather than soap, opera. The effect has been to lighten the substance. There are no pink panthers in the lush afterglow of a New York summer in the film version of *Breakfast at Tiffany's,* but it is a place as clean and sparkling as a brimming champagne glass, and just as giddy with promise. Well, almost.

Beneath the high-class swank of plush brownstone addresses, of fashion models and designer dresses, of handsome "kept" young authors, it is all just a big fake. From beginning to end, Holly Golightly leads a confetti existence, at best a charming but precarious masquerade. And no scene demonstrates this as does the cocktail party, the film's showcase for imposture. Blake Edwards looks on with the eye of a person long practiced at the art of appearances, and his camera takes a witty, malicious pleasure at betraying it. But what the removal of "masks," comic and otherwise, reveals is a sad, rather frightened humanity.

As it happens, even while his caustic attitude exposes the whole "scene" as sham, Edwards makes its enticements strong and compelling. Full of visual gags, wisecracks, bandbox color, slapstick, corny stunts, and a bouncing Henry Mancini score, the party is also the movie's one fully *auteurist* sequence, nicely anticipating Edwards's 1968 film with Peter Sellers called *The Party:* that whole movie is the party and almost nothing else. As for *Breakfast at Tiffany's,* Blake Edwards has explained:

> The thing I do take credit for was the party. . . . It was indicated in the screenplay; there were certain things written down such as a couple of speeches. But the general party was only indicated and I had to improvise it on the set. . . .[1]

In *Breakfast,* the party is how deception "looks." The scene begins with a tracking shot of O. J. Berman trying to talk to a stuffed green parrot in a cage, the bird looking larger than life (ironically, it is a movie producer who walks the border between the real and the phoney). Berman's next move is to a curvaceous blonde who says her name is "Irving." And so it goes; a succession of masks. It looks glib and silly, but the editing imposes a cutting edge that gives this strange roomful of dissemblances an unexpected, rather startling poignancy.

We see Holly in conversation with a young man wearing a picturesque black eye patch; later the camera cuts back to him having an argument so heated that he slides off the patch and exposes a perfectly normal eye beneath. A tipsy woman is laughing to herself in a large mirror; the camera pans away to watch the party, then pans back to her, now sobbing at her wretched reflection, black mascara running down her face. Two women are exchanging small talk; one glances away briefly, while the other suddenly elevates out of the frame, seated on the shoulders of a man who then stands nonchalantly sipping a drink. The other woman looks back, and we are left with her bewildered reaction. The trouble with subterfuge, with putting others on or "faking them out," Edwards seems to indicate, is how isolated people can become behind their exteriors, and how treacherously those exteriors can fail them.

Even Holly herself, with her preposterously long cigarette holder, is transparently acting the golddigger. But it is Mag Wildwood, a walking punchline from Arkansas, who passes out on the zebra-skin rug and puts the exclamation point to Edwards's proceedings. The party shows itself for what it is: a dizzy and more than somewhat devastating debacle. Mag typifies the vacuity around her, part of the big swindle Edwards sees foisted like angelfood cake on people who are hungry. (It is not all so self-righteous, of course, but it is intended to create something of a moral hangover.)

The party Capote describes is also the big scene of the novella, although it does not compare with Edwards's elaborately staged production, so disproportionate in length to the rest of the film. Capote's fête, more or less a stag affair, is memorably described: "It was as if the hostess had distributed her invitations while zigzagging through various bars; which was probably the case." As for Mag, Capote is more amused than disheartened by the charade of a Southern Cracker in the guise of a New York fashion sophisticate. In all, Mag Wildwood is a fuller presence in the novella. Her "career" and temperament—the materialism, the big city bitchery—contrast with Holly's throughout. The movie Mag is a caricature, a wild side show who never reappears after the party.

But the masks and facades *do* reappear in other guises in Edwards's film. Paul Varjak's wealthy mistress is introduced as his "interior decorator," and she calls him "Lucille" on the telephone when her husband unexpectedly walks into her end of the conversation. Holly's former husband, Doc Barnes, is mistaken for a detective, and he in turn offers the startling revelation of Holly's hidden married past. But perhaps the most facetious example of imposture is the Japanese photographer played by Mickey Rooney. And fraudulence directly affects the growing liaison between Holly and Paul (the film's version of Capote's unnamed writer-narrator).

Paul pretends that his being expensively "supported" will give him a chance to write. Holly pretends that her hustling will some day fulfill her dream of owning a horse ranch in Mexico with her brother Fred. To facilitate her goal, Holly keeps a mirror, lipstick, and perfume in the mailbox so that she can put on her "face" before confronting the world of her late-night escorts. The only way for Holly to evade facades is by way of the apartment fire escape. There she takes refuge from too-adamant callers, and there she asks Paul to help her take Doc to the bus depot, because she "can't play the scene alone." (Holly's immersion in a world of deception is reaffirmed by Edwards's mise-en-scene in the sequence where Doc meets Paul in Central Park to talk about Holly. Their discussion takes place in front of a deserted band shell—a correlative to Holly's "empty performance" of which these two people are privileged spectators.)

Basically, what Truman Capote admires as a style, an éclat, which Holly and her entourage fully recognize for its artifice, Edwards regards more severely as he commiserates with Holly's misguided spirit. Capote has respect for Holly and a sense of camaraderie with her. But Edwards demands that Holly come to terms on screen with the deceit of her fantasies. When she receives news of the death of her adored brother, Fred, Holly finds her dream of a home for the two of them shattered like glass. Edwards's camera cuts to a high, omniscient overhead shot and holds on Holly lying on her bed. She is a broken carnival doll amidst the wrecked junk of her bedroom. It is only after this expression of grief, the acknowledgment of dreams destroyed, that Edwards allows his own brand of happy ending for his heroine: the Right Man comes along. The conclusion hinges on perhaps the most essential change in the movie, the transformation of Paul Varjak, Capote's nameless narrator, into a respectable, and most importantly, *heterosexual* hero. In translation: Audrey Hepburn wins George Peppard.

The attachment between Holly and Capote's narrator is possibly of the heart but not of the body. Despite the feelings of kinship (they are both Southerners living in the same New York building) and the deep sympathy between them, there are never any moments of boy-girl interest. When he describes her physically, he praises only her qualities which are the most ambiguously feminine: he likes the tawny streaks of color in her "boy's hair," her slim and straight-hipped figure, and the "hoarse, breaking tones of a boy's adolescent voice" when she plays her guitar and sings. But usually his concern is platonic, surrogate brotherly. He is a spectator and a confidante. And when he does admit jealousy about Holly's other men, it is a carefully qualified declaration: "For I *was* in love with her. Just as I'd once been in love with my mother's elderly colored cook and a postman who let me follow him in his rounds and a whole family named McKendrick. That category of love generates jealousy too."

The movie adaptation, by Edwards and screenwriter George Axelrod, eliminates the many innuendos and implications of homosexuality in the novella. The changeover to a "straight" character is essential to analyzing the contours of the film and helps to interpret the new ending, a possibly irksome one for viewers demanding a "faithful" screen version. A. H. Weiler in the *New York Times* (Oct. 6, 1961), for one, expressed his dissatisfaction about Blake Edwards's remade male protagonist:

> In transforming him from a dispassionate admirer, as amoral as Holly, into a gent being subsidized for purely romantic purposes, by a rich, comely woman, the character loses conviction. . . . *Breakfast at Tiffany's* loses momentum as it heads toward that happy ending. . . .

In conceiving his film, Blake Edwards knew exactly how forbidden the intimations of Capote's original might be. He later recalled:

> Today, you could do it a lot closer. In those days, it frightened many people. It was too cynical; you touched on subjects that I believe people would be afraid to dramatize—the homosexual influence of the leading man, the sexual relationships of Holly that were so amoral—she lived with lesbians because they're good housekeepers—and things like that that have a great wonderful sardonic humor to them. You couldn't say things like that on the screen. . . .[2]

However, what Edwards *was* able to "say" in the film lies within the realm of possibilities which the story's lack of explicitness makes available. More to the point, the suppression of homosexuality in the writer-narrator is more consonant with Edwards's heterosexual romanticism: in the fairy-tale setting, Paul Varjak belongs as a lover not a friend. Simply, Edwards does give the story an ending, while Capote leaves it unresolved. Interestingly, Holly complains to Capote's hero, after listening to him read some of his stories, that they sounded as though he had "written them without knowing the ending." The novella's Holly disappears in the African bush, apparently, and Capote begins his story as a recollection of the time a few years ago when the narrator had known her.

Capote's Holly has as tough a spirit as she has imagination; she would rather wander, a vagabond, than disown her soul: "Be anything but a coward, a pretender, an emotional crook, a whore: I'd rather have cancer than a dishonest heart." Holly's noncomformity is her most vivid trait; her destination is unknown, but somehow, her fate is secure: she is not lost, she has just gone looking.

For Blake Edwards, Holly reaches her Moon River (it virtually pours down on her in the rainstorm at the film's end) when she quits yearning after gold-plated counterfeits of happiness and accepts the limitations of her own human self. It is a relinquishment of sorts, having her use her common sense and forget all that phoney nonsense in her head, but it is such a comfortable solution. Thus the fancy-free, arrogant, gutsy child-woman Capote's writer knew succumbs to tears and a tender embrace in Edwards's film and never even comes close to an airport. The rain-drenched kiss in the alleyway, creating a family tableau of Holly, Paul, and her no-name cat, in effect persuades by its very insubstantiality; the undeniable delight of the scene comes out of its unbelievable magic, especially in contrast to a garbagestrewn alley (psychologically an astute location since it undercuts sentimentality).

Holly and Paul hire a yellow cab to carry them off to their happy ending. The connection between going and coming in cabs is, thinking back, a special one. Even before the title credits rolled, in a long shot of an early summer's morning at sunrise, a yellow taxi glides rapidly down Fifth Avenue and pulls up in front of Tiffany's. Holly gets out. Nothing else happens, except the sound of the lyrics of "Moon River" on the sound track, but the materialization and movement of the cab down the empty street suggests such a consummate sense of a wondrous and privileged excursion out of the everyday, that it is exactly reminiscent of coming down the yellow brick road with another country girl named Dorothy. The absolute quiet of the street, the "breakfast" of the solitary Holly indulging in private make-believe, sets up a dreamy unreality that is always latent in the rest of the film. The completion, not of the dreams but of the dreaminess, comes in the other cab ride at the end of the film, where, after she refuses to listen to Paul's pleading with her not to run away any more, Holly "learns" about how people belong to each other and, presumably, finds another place like Tiffany's right there in Paul's arms. She can settle down at last, and cat will have a name.

Holly and Paul are thus transformed into the prototype of the ideal American couple of their era; their stroll around New York during the day they spend together has a well-fed, suburban satisfaction to it. Their tribulations are exotic, but the success they seem promised to achieve is an affluent, middle-class ever-after. The pasts are risqué but forgivable, and their social acceptability is never at stake. And such upbeat people, glad and hopeful of an upbeat fate, bear faint resemblance to the idiosyncratic, exceptional, and offbeat characters of Truman Capote's novella.

But the conformist ending does not do much to conceal Blake Edwards's deep streak of cynicism, inextricable from an even more deeply felt romanticism. Robert Haller, in writing on Edwards's famous private eye, Peter Gunn, noticed the same quality of disenchantment: "Through most of Edwards's films, the comedies, mysteries, and dramas, there runs an undercurrent of bitterness. . . . This bitterness transforms comedy into an anagram for anguish. . . ."[3] It is more of a prose than a poetic sensibility, and it shows little comprehension of the subtler idea of romance Truman Capote described, but neither can Edwards's sensibility be understood completely by such an explicit comparison to that of the novella; he is, in the film, true to the spirit of what he sees.

It is as someone with a sour stomach for reality, and a temperament for romantic, highly-colored love stories, that Blake Edwards imagined *Breakfast at Tiffany's.* He is, in fact, quite similar in style and approach to the character of Joe Bell, the dyspeptic bartender in Capote's novel (and not in the film), who customarily arranges fresh cut flowers in his bar, who sucks Tums to placate his indigestion, and who, from a great distance—say, as far as Moon River is wide—loves Holly Golightly very much.

Notes

1. Interview in *Cahiers du Cinema in English,* No. 3, 1966.

2. *Cahiers du Cinéma in English,* No. 3, 1966.

3. *Film Heritage,* Summer, 1968.

Helen S. Garson (essay date 1980)

SOURCE: Garson, Helen S. "Never Love a Wild Thing: *Breakfast at Tiffany's.*" In *Truman Capote,* pp. 79-89. New York: Frederick Ungar Publishing Co., 1980.

[*In the following excerpt, Garson examines the character of Holly Golightly and discusses the novella's plot and major concerns.*]

Like other Capote works, *Breakfast at Tiffany's,* written in 1958, received mixed notices. The same critic who said the novel was "among the best things he has written" later changed his mind and called it "slight." Another stated that the earlier fiction of Capote was "much better, truer." Yet another found something of Capote's to praise, and most readers regarded *Breakfast at Tiffany's* as the culminative effort of his daylight stories. Whatever their opinions of the merits of the work, reviewers noted certain resemblances to several Capote fictions, pointing out the kinship of Holly Golightly, the heroine, not only (as previously noted) to Miss Bobbit of **"Children on Their Birthdays"** but also to Joel of *Other Voices, Other Rooms* and Collin of *The Grass Harp.*[1]

Undeniably, Holly is similar in various ways to both the male and female figures of the most admired of Capote's stories: she is young and childlike, slight but attractive, friendly yet remote, her personality a touching mixture of innocence and sophistication. Like Miss Bobbit, Holly has made herself into a presence. She has deliberately created a personality to get her what she wants, and she is memorable for her own unique qualities. Furthermore, like Joel and Collin, Holly is a type of traveler. But where Joel and Collin are searching to find love and identity, Holly is seeking experience also. She has a great hunger to explore, to live each moment completely, to do and see everything.

Orphaned early, Holly and her younger brother Fred led a harsh existence in foster homes in Texas. When they ran away, they were taken in by a kindly horse doctor, who was widowed and the father of children older than Holly. Doc Golightly soon fell in love with the fourteen-year-old girl and married her. However, the marriage didn't last long. The child, then known as Lulamae Barnes, ran off again. She assumed the name and identity of Holly Golightly, big city girl, partygoer, traveler, and lady of the evening.

All of these events took place before the beginning of the story, which is told by a writer who, like Holly, had come to New York to seek success during the early years of World War II.

When the story opens, the unnamed narrator has returned to the neighborhood in which he had his first apartment and where he had met Holly in 1943, more than fifteen years before. At that time both are tenants in an old brownstone walk-up building, where a fire escape takes the place of an elevator; the area is the East Seventies near Lexington Avenue. Holly lives in the apartment below the narrator's, and for a while she uses him only as a "doorbell convenience," a substitute for her lost key. One night, however, when Holly climbs the fire escape to the narrator's room to get away from an unpleasant man in her apartment, she and the narrator become friends.

In spite of the great differences in the way they live, the narrator soon is Holly's confidant, but their friendship is brief. At the end of a year, Holly flees the United States to avoid testifying against a criminal she likes, a drug dealer named "Sally Tomato." Because Holly has found Sally "an okay shooter," she makes her decision against the "badgers," applying her own code of ethics: "My yardstick," says Holly, "is how someone treats me." After instructing the narrator to find her the names of the fifty richest men in Brazil, Holly leaves the country with his help. A single postcard, without a return address, arrives from Brazil soon afterward. He never hears from her again.

Years later, the narrator comes back to his old neighborhood because he receives an excited call from Joe Bell, the bartender, who, like several other men, was devoted to Holly. Joe has been given some photographs of an African wood sculpture, which is a carved head modeled after Holly Golightly. An African tribesman was the sculptor. Little more is known of the background of the episode except that the subject of the artwork was traveling with two men in Africa, where she shared for a brief time the tribesman's hut before riding off once more. Joe Bell's call, the photographs, and the view of the brownstone in which he and Holly had lived take the narrator back in memory to his first year in New York and to reminiscences of Holly.

The story of Holly's life in New York, which has just been summarized, is now told by the narrator. He recalls Holly with tenderness, a feeling shared by Joe Bell, who speaks of his special kind of love for her. Joe's is not an erotic passion; neither is the narrator's. Both men are kind and generous to Holly, for she provokes deep affection and loyalty in them; yet, they never join the ranks of her many lovers. Her seeming helplessness, her irresponsibility, and her childlike unselfconsciousness attract them as much as these qualities draw the men who provide for her financially.

In many ways Holly leads the fantasy existence children dream about. She appears to be at a continual birthday social, not only because she constantly gives or goes to parties, but also because her style of living is devoted to having fun. "I'd rob a grave. I'd steal two-bits off a dead man's eyes if I thought it would contribute to a day's enjoyment," says Holly. She does whatever is necessary to maintain her way of life. Her rules are her own, derived from a desire for independence and the need to survive in a world she has known to be cruel or indifferent to those who are unprotected.

A girl of some beauty but little talent—she plays the guitar well—Holly utilizes her looks and charm to pay her expenses. Although she once had an opportunity to become a movie actress, she walked away from the chance. In Hollywood she had been taken in hand by an agent, O. J. Berman, who saw to it that Holly was made over into starlet material. Berman wanted to get Holly into the movies, but Holly had no such intention. She stayed around long enough to improve her English, learn some French, and glamorize her appearance. "I was just vamping for time to make a few self-improvements," she tells the narrator, letting it be understood that she has not deceived herself into thinking she has talent.

Self-deception is not one of Holly's failings, although she is an extraordinary liar. It doesn't trouble her to beguile others when it suits her purpose. She constructs a world around her to make things as pleasant as she can, inventing stories when the truth is too painful to discuss. Berman, who calls Holly "a phony," modifies it to "a *real* phony," because, he claims, "she believes all this crap she believes." The narrator doesn't think of Holly that way. To him she is a "lopsided romantic," someone "gluttonous" for life, rather than a pretender.

Since her moral code differs from that of society, Holly has no qualms about lying. To protect herself or to keep people from getting too close, or from knowing too much about her, she fabricates. She fictionalizes when reality is grim and threatens to bring on the "mean blues" (sadness), or the "mean reds" (fear). Unwilling to share her memories of her early life, Holly invents a beautiful fantasy childhood for herself when the narrator tells her of his own unhappy boyhood. Holly also lies when a situation is not to her liking. At a party, when an acquaintance, Mag Wildwood, barges in and draws the attention of all the men, Holly retaliates by insinuating that Mag has a terrible social disease. Another time, to keep Mag from learning that she has slept with Mag's lover, José, Holly breezily pretends she is a lesbian, partly to deceive Mag and partly for the humor of the deception.

José is no loss to Mag, though, for she gets what she really wants, marriage to Holly's millionaire playboy lover, Rusty Trawler, an unattractive, middle-aged homosexual, an American fascist. He disgusts most of Holly's friends, particularly the narrator, who insists that Holly tell him how she feels about Rusty. Holly's answer is very revealing, for it encompasses an important element of her philosophy. She informs the narrator, "You can make yourself love anybody."

The idea of love keeps Holly from thinking of herself as a prostitute. She claims that she cared about all the men who paid for her favors. "I mean," she says, "you can't bang the guy and cash his checks and at least not *try* to believe you love him. I never have." Making yourself "love" anybody is what helps Holly to hold on to the way of life she has chosen. Yet, unpleasant as the idea may be, it shows Holly as existing in the same manner as Mag Wildwood, whom she detests and whom the narrator scorns. It is ironic that Mag marries Trawler, thus securing her future, but Holly is not able to follow a similar course.

Deciding to marry José, Holly chooses to ignore her relationship with Doc Golightly, claiming that the marriage could not be legal because of her age when they were wed. Because she becomes pregnant, Holly plans to go with José to Brazil, where she expects to marry him. She tells the narrator that, aside from Doc, José is her "first non-rat romance," and that she loves José. He makes her feel fine, taking away her sadness and her need for escape. The narrator notes that Holly's romance with José seems to change her. Not only does she appear content and happy, but her way of life is different also. She no longer sleeps all day and goes out all night, but instead behaves like a wife, shopping, cooking, taking José's clothes to the cleaner. Holly talks merrily of the future with José as her husband and of having many, many children.

That future never comes for Holly. José abandons Holly when her name appears in the paper as a playgirl linked with the drug ring headed by Sally Tomato. The narrator takes José's letter to Holly, who is in the hospital, having lost her baby in a scuffle with the police. When Holly sees the letter, a visible change comes over her. She seems to age and harden. She asks the narrator for her cosmetics, because "A girl doesn't read this sort of thing without her lipstick." Holly applies lipstick and rouge, eyeliner and eyeshadow, puts on pearls and dark glasses, sprays herself with perfume and lights a cigarette, readying her protective coating for what she expects to see in the letter.

The covering doesn't help. Briefly, Holly is devastated. She labels José "a rat" like all the others, although she finally agrees bitterly with the narrator that José's reasons for giving her up—his religion and his career—are valid for the kind of man he is. Holly then decides to flee the country, using the ticket for Brazil that José had bought her. Her reason for flight is not only that she wants to avoid helping the state's case against Sally; she says she'd rather the "fat woman"—that is, death—took her. Holly, with a practicality and cynicism learned early in life, knows that the publicity she has had will be harmful to her "particular talents," and she doesn't relish trading the high life for a marginal existence. Even though the narrator tries to dissuade her, Holly does not listen. He argues with her, telling her she will never be able to return to the United States, because she is under criminal indictment and will be jumping bail. A toughened Holly responds: "Home is where you feel at home. I'm still looking."

For a time it seemed that Holly had found her dream, her "place where me and things belong together." Her relationship with José might have been like her vision of Tiffany's, with "quietness and the proud look of it; nothing very bad could happen to you there." Before she met José, she had hoped that she and her brother Fred might one day make a home together, perhaps in

Mexico, near the sea. But Fred is killed in the war. After her bout of grief, Holly turns to José, ready to give up her independence for the security of belonging to someone.

Holly, however, seems fated to continue doing what her calling card says: traveling. She has always thought of herself, somewhat regretfully, as being like a wild creature and feels pity for those who are attracted to the untamed. Because she is fond of Doc Golightly, whom she left, she cautions Joe Bell, advising him never to give his heart to a wild thing: "the more you do, the stronger they get. Until they're strong enough to run into the woods. Or fly into a tree. Then a taller tree. Then the sky. That's how you'll end up. . . . If you let yourself love a wild thing. You'll end up looking at the sky." Nevertheless, Holly knows and asserts to her friends that looking at the sky is preferable to living there, for it is "such an empty place; so vague."

Living in the sky is the opposite of breakfasting at Tiffany's, Holly's symbol of the good life. But there is a dichotomy in this. Holly recognizes that she must find shelter, that she cannot run all her life; yet she also wants freedom. When she buys the narrator an elegant birdcage he has admired, she makes him promise that he will "never put a living thing in it." She has an abhorrence of cages of any kind. Still Holly longs for a quiet place, somewhere to settle and make a home.

Symbolic of Holly's divided beliefs is the relationship she has with her cat, a street tom that Holly found one day near the river. Although she has looked after him lovingly for some time, as she prepares for flight to Brazil she disposes of the cat in Harlem. Both her action and her defense of it unwittingly parallel José's treatment of Holly. Her explanation to the narrator of her behavior is that she and the cat were independent, that they had no ties to one another. Having said that, Holly changes her mind and searches frantically for the cat, but she cannot find him. Filled with regret, she tells the narrator of her feelings for the cat. When the narrator promises he will find the cat and take care of him, Holly confesses her most private, deep-seated fear of what her life will always be: "Not knowing what's yours until you've thrown it away."

If Holly had found her Tiffany's, she would have given the cat a name, an indication of having roots at last; but Holly never achieves that. When they first meet, the narrator has hopes for Holly's future. Because the narrator is young and inexperienced, the older, worldly O. J. Berman disagrees with his optimism about Holly, saying, "She's strictly a girl you'll read where she ends up at the bottom of a bottle of Seconals." Years later, when Joe Bell displays the African pictures of the sculptured piece, it is apparent that Holly has never found her place, her Tiffany's, and that she is still traveling.

One wonders whether she still sings the country song of years before: "Don't wanna sleep, Don't wanna die, Just wanna go a-travelin' through the pastures of the sky." The sky, however, is that lonely, empty place which both attracted and repelled Holly.

Capote once said in an interview that he had modeled Holly after a girl he had known in the early forties, and that in what he had written, "everything about her personality and her approach to life" was "literally true." Also, the prototype Holly did go to Africa. After the war, someone traveling in the Belgian Congo actually saw a wooden sculpture of her head. That, said Capote, is "all of the evidence of her existence that remains."[2]

Nevertheless, at the end of the fictional story, the narrator concludes on a more hopeful note. He tells of having seen Holly's cat one cold winter day, sitting in the window of a comfortable-looking room. Convinced that the cat has a name in that setting and a home where he now belongs, the narrator muses about Holly, the other wild thing; his words are almost an invocation as he hopes she might also have found a place for herself at last.

Much of *Breakfast at Tiffany's* is muted in tone. Although there is a great deal of humor in a number of episodes, in the dialogue, and in some of the Damon Runyonesque characters, the liveliness exists inside a frame of memory. That remembrance has, like many of Capote's stories, an autumnal sound.

Although Holly and the narrator meet in the summer, the friendship really begins in the fall, one night when "the first ripple-chills of autumn" are in the air. Over a period of a year the two become close, much as sister and brother, not as lovers. Holly even calls the narrator by her actual brother's name, Fred. Affection and understanding grow between them as "Fred" struggles to become a successful writer and Holly's romance with José flourishes. The next autumn, though, brings Holly's departure and the separation that will never be altered.

On a stormy October day, the narrator, who describes himself as "wind-blown and winded and wet to the bone," gathers Holly's belongings together. Carrying her rain-soaked possessions, he meets her at Joe Bell's bar, where Joe refuses to drink to Holly's departure. He cares too much for her and cannot bear to see her go. As she leaves, Joe thrusts a bunch of flowers at Holly, but, emblematically, they fall to the floor. The wind whips through the streets as the narrator and Holly go towards the airport. And Holly is gone.

Years later, when the narrator, now a famous writer, returns to the old neighborhood, it is once again October, a season of haziness and memory. He comes back in a downpour of rain, an afternoon which reminds one of the day of Holly's departure. It suggests the end of a cycle, the days of the past, which "blow about in memory, lazy, autumnal, all alike as leaves"; and now there is the waning day, the fallen leaves yellowed, covering the pavement, wet and slippery from the rain. The mist in the air touches everything, creating a sense of loneliness.

Breakfast at Tiffany's goes full circle. The beginning, which is actually the ending, has a gentle feeling of nostalgia. One hears in the background the echo of "gone" and "was," from *Other Voices, Other Rooms,* as the narrator walks towards the old brownstone apartment house, which stands "next to a church where a blue tower-clock tells the hours." This use of the past, memory, and sweet sadness is an identifying element of Capote's style. It is what some critics object to, labeling it style without substance. But this seems unfair caviling. For it is just that characteristic which sets off the story, encloses it, as if it were a narrative scene inside a crystal paperweight.[3] At the same time that it pleases and delights, it suggests something else, a pleasurable melancholy for the days that are no more.[4]

Notes

1. Alfred Kazin has the two different views, first in *The Open Form: Essays for Our Time* (New York: Harcourt, Brace, and World, 1961), p. 213; then in *Bright Book of Life* (New York: Delta, 1974), p. 209. Irving Malin prefers the earlier work; see *New American Gothic* (Carbondale: Southern Illinois University Press, 1962), p. 159. And Mark Schorer praises the mood, in *The World We Imagine: Selected Essays* (New York: Farrar, Straus, 1968), p. 294. For other comments on the novel, see also: Walter Allen, *The Modern American Novel in Britain and the United States* (New York: E. P. Dutton, 1964); Alfred Kazin, *Contemporaries* (Boston: Little, Brown, 1962); and Ihab Hassan, *Radical Innocence: The Contemporary American Novel* (Princeton, N.J.: Princeton University Press, 1961).

2. *Playboy,* March 1968, p. 62.

3. Capote's love of paperweights dates back to a visit he paid Colette in Paris in 1947. She called them "snowflakes," which he interpreted to mean "dazzling patterns frozen forever." "The White Rose" appeared first in the *Ladies Home Journal,* July 1971, but is reprinted in the collection *The Dogs Bark* (New York: Random House, 1973).

4. Sadness and melancholy, as in Tennyson's "Tears, Idle Tears," when the poet is looking back "on the happy autumn fields / And thinking of the days that are no more."

Helen S. Garson (essay date 1992)

SOURCE: Garson, Helen S. "Those Were the Lovely Years." In *Truman Capote: A Study of the Short Fiction,* pp. 28-41. New York: Twayne Publishers, 1992.

[*In the following excerpt, Garson compares Holly Golightly with the character Lily Jane Bobbit in Capote's story "Children on Their Birthdays."*]

From the day of its publication in 1958 *Breakfast at Tiffany's* has been a much-loved book. More than 30 years after its appearance, book reviewers continue to compare female characters to Holly Golightly, Capote's unforgettable heroine.

Numerous conflicting stories have been told about the model for Capote's portrait. An actual person sparked the fictional creation, but who that person was remains a topic of debate. Typically, Capote embroidered and embellished the truth, telling different versions of the origin of Holly Golightly to interviewers over the years, and also to his biographer. All of these statements are at odds with novelist James Michener's recollections of the original "starlet-singer-actress-raconteur" he knew to be Holly.[1]

Although an actual person may have provided the mold for the heroine, Holly is yet another fantasy creature, a beautiful, captivating, elusive, lovable, and haunting young woman, a mixture of the romantic and the tragic. Generally regarded by critics as an expanded, older version of the adolescent Lily Jane Bobbit of **"Children on Their Birthdays,"** Holly has many of the same personality traits: wisdom beyond her chronological age, brashness, courage, a longing for something that proves unattainable, and a separateness which makes her different from earthbound human beings. We respond affectionately to both Lily Jane and Holly, laughing at and with them, and mourning their loss. However, because *Breakfast at Tiffany's* is the longer, more complex fiction in which the major character is more fully drawn, the minor characters funnier, and the setting more completely realized, it is the more memorable work.

Mr. C., the narrator of **"Children"** [**"Children on Their Birthdays"**], has an expanded role in the novella. Though he has no name except the one Holly gives him briefly, he is obviously meant to be the young Capote, starting out as a writer in New York; even the birthdays are the same, September 30.[2] In *Breakfast at Tiffany's,* however, the Capote figure is more than an observer. He is an involved participant who falls in love with Holly and helps her whenever she has problems. He is friend, listener, defender, brother, and ultimately biographer of this captivating creature.

This story, resembling other Capote pieces in its mixture of tenderness, melancholy, and humor, is enclosed and protected in a frame of memory, inviolable, like figures carved on an urn, caught in a moment of time past. As in many of Capote's stories, time is the silent yet relentless figure in the background. In reality, autumn and winter must eventually succeed spring and summer; the church clock must toll the hours, signifying the passage of time and time-bound life. But memory, misted over with all its happy and unhappy moments, remains. The narrator's recollections are stirred by a phone call and a visit to a barman named Joe Bell. Returning to a neighborhood he knew well 15 years earlier, he learns that Joe has obtained a recent photo of a sculpted African head and that this head bears an uncanny resemblance to a much-loved person out of the past, Holly Golightly. After the bartender relates what little information he has concerning the background of the photo, the narrator walks through the neighborhood streets, back to the brownstone where he first met Holly.

It was wartime when the hopeful young writer met Holly, who lived in the same building as he. Holly, not quite 19, was a young woman who lived on "powder room money," a girl who looked like a breakfast cereal ad, but lived solely for fun and excitement. The larky atmosphere, the casual encounters, the easy money, the nightclubs, the dancing in the streets and partying with service officers—all speak of a wartime philosophy. The whole world seems young. Champagne bubbles up in glasses, in spite of or because of the war, but the war is very far away, even for Holly, whose beloved brother is at the front. When he is killed, however, her one tie with the past and normal life is destroyed.

Holly's card vaguely identifies her occupation as "traveling." The word is apt for the way she lives. Holly never stays anywhere for very long. She is a person searching for love, for a home, for a happy and safe life—all symbolized in her mind by Tiffany's. Orphaned early, the then Lulamae Barnes married Doc Golightly when she was only a child. Although she loves him—he was like a kind old father to her—she ran away. From that moment she has had a series of fantasy lives. In Hollywood, where for a time she concentrated on improving herself, Lulamae became Holly; she lost her hillbilly accent, learned a little French, became a starlet, and gained enough sophistication to realize she could not become a star. She then headed for New York to try for another kind of fame and fortune as a New York socialite. The elusive Holly is depicted as someone balanced between childhood and womanhood. In spite of her numerous lovers, she appears untouched by sordidness, and is surprisingly naive in many ways. Having had no childhood, she creates a child's world where she makes up the rules. Her girlish enthusiasm is contagious, so that all men feel more alive in her company.

In New York, although fortune eludes her, she does find fame, that is, notoriety, when she unwittingly becomes a courier for a mobster named Sally Tomato. This experience ends her only "non-rat" romance, when her skittish lover abandons her. The publicity also causes her to flee the country to avoid the courts and keep from betraying Sally, for she is an advocate of the honest heart in all circumstances. The streetwise side of Holly recognizes that her "career" in New York has been blemished and part of her life is over. Because of this mishap, once again Holly becomes a traveler. After sending a single postcard to the narrator, she fades into the soft haze of the past, a past revisited briefly when Joe Bell sends for the narrator.

All of Holly's fantasizing has a melancholy side, however, for it is really only a dream. Beneath the surface of gaiety lies the knowledge that nothing lasts. There is loneliness at the core of the dreamer. Though always surrounded by people, Holly gives the impression of being alone, still the little girl, Lulamae Barnes, still running, still searching for a home never to be hers. She knows she is one of those wild creatures who live in the sky, always an empty place; her favorite song tells plaintively of traveling "through the pastures of the sky." At times Holly confesses to the narrator her awareness of transiency, and in a sorrowful moment of revelation tells him we do not even recognize the wonder of lovely days until they are gone. Then it is too late to bring them back. For the narrator, however, they can be recalled, though only in memory.

Holly may seem like Miss Bobbit in her unchanging hope for something better, something more, but there is a far greater strain of melancholy in Holly. Holly, unlike Miss Bobbit, seems to know, at least at a subliminal level, that life will never give what it seems to promise children. Miss Bobbit dies before knowledge dims her radiance. Holly, however, even as a child, never had the kind of innocence Lily Jane has. There is a depth of sadness in her unknown to the younger girl. In spite of Holly's determination to be happy and have everything possible, she has been battered by existence and has endured poverty, hunger, loss, and abandonment.

An authority on abandonment, Holly has learned to face the world with style, even if it is veneer. When the narrator tries to tell her gently about the defection of her lover, Jose, Holly first puts on her makeup, her perfume, her earrings, and her dark glasses before she reads Jose's letter, in which he informs her that he will not marry her. A young woman who has built her personality partly on dissemblance and make-believe, partly playful, partly defensive, Holly has her own kind of armor to protect her from the harsh world. This is what leads her former Hollywood agent, O. J. Berman, to call her "a phony," but also to note that "She isn't a phony because she is a *real* phony. She believes all this crap she believes."[3]

Berman also predicts that Holly one day will finish "at the bottom of a bottle of Seconals." Although Holly battles frequently with fear and depression, in the tenderness of the narrator's memory, however, she is always young and unchanged. Still, the images associated with Holly lend themselves to both visions, Berman's and the narrator's: a birdcage she presents to the young writer, given with the admonition that he must never put anything in it; the cast-off cat she takes in, refuses to name, and then abandons when she flees New York; the yellow roses she loves (reminding the reader of the death of Miss Bobbit in **"Children on Their Birthdays"**); the flowers Joe Bell attempts to give her when she is leaving, flowers that fall to the floor (again reminiscent of the flowers Miss Bobbit never gets in the last scene in the short story). The downpour of rain as Holly flees New York carries with it the wind of desolation, an ache not obviated when the narrator discovers the cat at a later time ensconced in a lace-curtained window in Harlem. He hopes then that Holly too will find a place where she belongs, but that hope, the reader recognizes, may be as ephemeral as her promise to keep in touch.

Although both the short story and the novella end with a sense of loss in their images of mist and rain, a much more powerful minor key runs through the conclusion of the later work, for summer is still in the air in **"Children on Their Birthdays."** The rainbow that crosses the sky preserves the feeling of childlike hope, but in *Breakfast at Tiffany's* the autumnal season of heavy rain and yellowed leaves suggests only the winter to come.

However, *Breakfast at Tiffany's,* like **"Children on Their Birthdays,"** is also lighthearted in many ways. Once again, Capote's humor is found in characters, dialogue, and events. He plays with names: Joe Bell takes phone messages; Rusty Trawler is a much-married man who has been involved in sex scandals.[4] Runyonesque characters from New York and Hollywood fill the novella. There is a chase scene with horses. And the star of the story herself provides slapstick and bawdy humor. *Breakfast at Tiffany's* shows Capote at his best, in total control as humorist, stylist, symbolist, imagist, and tone painter, characteristics that marked his fiction and nonfiction prose of the fifties and sixties.

Notes

1. See Michener's "Forewrd" in Lawrence Grobel's *Conversations with Capote* (New York: New American Library, 1985).

2. Capote also makes an oblique reference to another autobiographical detail, when he speaks of being fired for "an amusing misdemeanor." He is prob-

ably referring to the Robert Frost episode at the *New Yorker*. See Helen S. Garson's *Truman Capote* (New York: Ungar, 1980) and Gerald Clarke's *Capote: A Biography* (New York: Simon & Schuster, 1988).

3. *Breakfast at Tiffany's,* in *A Capote Reader* (New York: Random House, 1987), 241-242; hereafter cited in text as *Breakfast.*

4. The names Lily Jane in "Children on Their Birthdays" and Lulamae in *Breakfast at Tiffany's* appear to have a relationship to the author's mother, whose name was Lillie Mae before she changed it to Nina.

Chantal Cornut-Gentille D'Arcy (essay date 1996)

SOURCE: Cornut-Gentille D'Arcy, Chantal. "Who's Afraid of the Femme Fatale in *Breakfast at Tiffany's?*: Exposure and Implications of a Myth." In *Gender, I-Deology: Essays on Theory, Fiction, and Film,* edited by Chantal Cornut-Gentille D'Arcy and José Angel García Landa, pp. 371-83. Amsterdam: Rodopi, 1996.

[*In the following essay, Cornut-Gentille D'Arcy analyzes the character of Holly Golightly to expose how the film adaptation of Capote's novella incarnates the traditional western religious conception of woman as a potential "femme fatale."*]

Even in its present rather hacked state, the wording of the title for this paper, especially in its interrogative opening, echoes Edward Albee's famous play *Who's Afraid of Virginia Woolf.* The allusion to Albee's play is by no means accidental. On the contrary, it is meant to signal three directions in the analysis of the film *Breakfast at Tiffany's.* In the first place, the reference to the femme fatale, instead of the missing and reverberating "Virginia Woolf," anticipates how this essay will centre on the character of Holly Golightly as someone desperately struggling to secure a "room of her own"—no matter how one chooses to understand the term "room." Secondly, as might be recalled, it was not its dramatic *form* that gave Albee's creation its renown. The cosy living room setting of the play pointed rather to it traditional lay out. It is, therefore, on the level of its allegorical dimension that the play challenged the audience to find meanings and to make relevant connections. The same could be said to apply to Blake Edwards' *Breakfast at Tiffany's,* a film based on Truman Capote's novel of the same title for, under the cover of a straightforward fairy tale-like story, utterly conventional in its cinematic realism, the film can be seen as actually engaging the audience with long-standing and immediate social issues. By way of introducing the third point, it might be as well to recall the major theme of *Who's*

Afraid of Virginia Woolf. The play starts off with an amiable get-together at a professor's house. As the dinner party proceeds, an atmosphere of emotional strain builds up, spiralling around an inexplicable void. In this hollow centre lies a private myth sustained by the characters' dread of reality. The disclosure of the secret—the fact that the son of George and Martha is imaginary—finally opens the way to harrowing reconciliation. Bearing in mind that myths "serve to explain and/or to express some important reality of life and nature" (Ruth 1990: 161), and that they are "recurrently present, both in and out of history, both past and present" (Irons 1992: 91-2), the characters' self-deception concerning their inexistent son could be taken as a paradigm of people's blurred view of themselves and others in everyday life. If this insight is given a feminist slant and applied to *Breakfast at Tiffany's,* then the mild and romantic surface meaning of the story, for all its apparent recognition of the woman's perspective, suddenly emerges as downright fraudulent.[1]

The aim of this essay is therefore to expose how the Creation story, as a powerful myth, uncovers a hidden message in the film about male attitudes towards women. In order to do this, I will examine the character of Holly Golightly, and show how she, against all odds, incarnates the traditional Western religious conception of woman as a potential "femme fatale." Once this more cryptic ideological stance is revealed, the psychological implications in the story become much wider; consequently, the film can no longer be viewed as a conventional fairy-tale. Finally, given the unprecedented ability of cinema to direct and even institutionalize behaviour patterns, the political function of *Breakfast at Tiffany's* in manipulating both male and female viewpoints, at a time of economic readjustment, should not be underestimated.[2]

We meet Holly Golightly as she alights from a taxi in the small hours of the morning—a stunning but faceless, solitary figure in a deserted avenue. With sunglasses and a long black evening dress shielding her from any attempt to identify her, she emerges as a princess of darkness to impersonate the mythological figure of Lilith, a sinister deity of the night who attacked, seduced and devoured solitary men. In the twelfth century, this ancient Mesopotamian legend was appropriated and inserted into the Judaeo-Christian heritage with Lilith now referred to as the first woman who escaped from Adam to give full rein to her own sexual fantasies with demons (Bornay 1990: 25). When Eve was created as a replacement, Lilith continued to live outside the Garden of Eden as a diabolic and extremely erotic night spirit who invaded the bodies and the senses of unwary men (Phillips 1988: 71-2). Just like this mythical figure, Holly, insinuatingly attired in black—with all the connotations this colour brings to mind—is a creature of the night. As a prostitute, she also incar-

nates the rebellious and self-affirmative Lilith in being a disturber of the (supposedly) right order of things.

During the Middle Ages, the story of Lilith slowly merged into the biblical account of Eve. The witch is Lilith who torments men at night, but the witch now is also Eve who lost Paradise (Ochshorn 1981: 119-20). If the block of flats where Holly lives is looked upon as a microcosm of established order, it is plain that her return home invariably takes on the dimension of a disruptive onslaught on the community in the form of some kind of debauchery or other—her total disregard in ringing her neighbour's bell at all hours of the day and night, her promise to Mr Yunioshi to allow him to take "those photographs we mentioned" (erotic photographs?), men friends clinging to her or embracing her on the way up the stairs, disappointed lovers banging at her door and shouting words of abuse, huge noisy parties ending in police raids, or simply herself, trying to reach her door in a drunken fit, either on her own or over a man's shoulder.

These pictures comply perfectly well with the view traditionally enforced by patriarchal religion that female initiative and will are evil. Eve caused the fall by asserting her will against the command of God. She was tricked by the serpent because, as a "weak creature not endued with like strength and constancy of mind" (Stone 1977: 198), she had less potential for self-control and moral strength than Adam (Timothy I, 2:14). It was her lack of moral force or reasoning power combined with her supposedly greater potential for sensuality which eventually led to a sexual interpretation of the fall. According to this interpretation, the act of eating the forbidden fruit is an euphemism for a sexual relationship between Eve and the snake or, the eating of the fruit gives Eve a sexual awareness which leads her to seduce her husband (Phillips 1988: 79-81). The idea of Eve's weakness was, in this way, linked to the idea that Eve was diabolical. Thus, Eve becomes the vehicle for the intrusion of lechery as well as sin in the created order, and hence the concept of women's evil potential to seduce men. Being in close league with the devil, the femme fatale is endowed with special powers over men which they are incapable of resisting. One of these devilish attributes, as in the pagan story of Pandora[3] that runs parallel to the myth of the Creation, is Beauty. Admittedly, this point would appear to be much more incisive if the role of Holly was played by Lana Turner or by Barbara Stanwyck, for the femme fatale in *Breakfast at Tiffany's* is not portrayed as a dangerous virago. On the contrary, she is presented as a charming manipulator of men and a naïve victim all in one. The contrast between the heroine in this film and the devastating vamps of classical Hollywood cinema reflects an essential difference in the historical conceptualization of woman. In her analysis of Max Ophuls' film *La signora di tutti,* Mary Ann Doane asserts that the cinematographic construction of the femme fatale as a kind of holocaust derives, in a sense, from a systematic repression of history (1991: 127-131).[4] With this idea in mind, it becomes possible to view the basic characteristics attributed to the femmes fatales in classical film narratives—their ominous beauty, voluptuous voices and rapacious glances (invariably omens of catastrophe)—as direct transpositions of the myth of Lilith, irrespective of historical developments. Thus, the characters on screen (especially in silent movies) are usually overcoded abstractions representing an *idea* of woman rather than any woman in particular.

Breakfast at Tiffany's, however, seems to depart from this determinism through the film's apparent attention to the concreteness and specificity of the socio-historical moment. The casting of Audrey Hepburn as Holly Golightly is of great significance in the film for, while her appearance can be said to expose something of the reality of women and women's situation in the sixties, it also reflects the inarticulate, and yet persistent, prejudice of inherited religious axioms. As mentioned above, according to patriarchal Western tradition, woman's progenitor was Eve, mother of evil and precipitator of the Fall. But the specific implications of the myth came to be that, since Eve resides in each and every woman, women's bodies are evil, seductive, damning and dirty. If every woman is a potential femme fatale—that is, literally fatal to man, either by causing his death, or because of her power to castrate him (as Cleopatra with Antony)[5]—then a religious straightjacket somehow had to be imposed on such dangerous creatures, and it appeared in the form of a new female model: Mary, perfect in her submission and sexual purity. The major appeal of Hepburn's beauty derives from the combination of her flawless features and a vicarious identification with this new religious ethic of the sexless woman. She embodies a notion of femininity as "Half kitten, half fairy-Queen" (Bornay 1990: 145) which was less aggressive since the vision that her physique inspires is not one of a dangerous and castrating witch, but rather that of a virginmartyr who is also an enchantress.[6] Hence, the choice of Audrey Hepburn to act the part of Holly Golightly seems to have been determined by misogynistic religious assumptions since it is her infantile looks and meagre constitution that serve to highlight the new twist in the Eve myth by veering the focus of attention from the (still present) evil, insatiable nature of woman to this new image of woman as enfeebled, weak and in need of manly guidance.[7] Audrey Hepburn's looks therefore adequately reflect the way a woman is supposed to function in a God-ordained world: as a dependent child needing manly guidance and correction—a point that is highly magnified in the scene when Doc Golightly tells Paul about Lulamae Barnes, the child wife he had picked up "like a wild thing." However, if attention is focussed on the wom-

an's *actions* rather than her looks then the message that emerges is totally different for the trajectory of the narrative will then seem to trace, on the contrary, the heroine's efforts to wriggle out of this patriarchal "cage" of protectionism: she tries to use men rather than be kept by them. As stated before, Holly Golightly is presented as someone who assumes a freedom of choice that is not often in evidence in real life and whose life is totally given up to sex. She thus personifies the impudence and brazenness inherent to Nietzsche's view of woman as a castrating figure (Doane 1991: 61). Several details subtly underline the femme fatale vein in the character. For instance, the presence of the cat could be understood as a constant reminder of the sphinx as emblem of the devouring woman. Likewise, the extravagantly long cigaretteholder Holly uses during her party can be viewed as a potent phallic symbol displaying her affirmative power and dominant position over her male guests. Admittedly, as Paul Varjack befriends Holly, the more lethal aspect of her character as a femme fatale seems to recede and give place to a more humane and tender trait: that of a woman suffering from the pangs of instability, indecisiveness and loneliness. However, the femme fatale streak could be said to persist in the hypnotic effect Holly exerts on the male protagonist throughout the story. Moreover, it clearly slips into the discourse again when she coldly discards him, in the public library, as "yet another rat" leaving him, to all effects, "unmanned."

There is a further point to be made concerning the actress's physique. According to Richard Dyer, Audrey Hepburn's beauty was "exquisite, an ideal," and yet, he remarks, she was "ridiculously, nearly gawkily—thin" (1993: 59). Dieting and thinness only began to be female preoccupations when women became active in public life and the labour market. This is when, in Naomi Wolf's words, thinness became "a social expedient that would make women's bodies into the prisons that their homes no longer were" (Wolf 1992: 184). Hence, the role of Audrey Hepburn as exponent of this standard of beauty, points in two directions. On the one hand, it could be interpreted as reassuring the establishment with the suggestion of a continuing and inherent female weakness and controlled sexuality. In other words, the vision of a barely formed girlish figure sustained male ego by inspiring men's protective instincts while calming their deep subconscious fears concerning the hot topics of the moment (1961), namely, women's emancipation and sexual freedom. On the other hand, Audrey Hepburn's adolescent body could also be understood as accentuating the part of Holly in that dream world that lies between childhood and maturity, for *Breakfast at Tiffany's* is undeniably informed by a sort of Oedipal perception.

Except for the opening scenes, the spectator is cued to identify with the perspective of the male character. In this way, the focus is kept mainly on what the chief *male* consciousness experiences. Consequently, a psychological ruse can be said to steer the growing awareness of viewers as they accompany the two main characters on their trip from childhood experience to adult assimilation.

The spectator's initial view of Holly cannot, in any way, be censorious since it soon turns out that Paul Varjack, the audience's chief eyewitness, is himself a gigolo. This probably accounts for the misleading objectivity or seemingly liberal approach in the presentation of Holly. She is depicted as radically different from the standard, conventional woman. She is stunningly beautiful, especially as she emerges on her way to Sing Sing jail to visit Sally Tomato, displaying more good taste in her clothes than in her choice of men-friends. She is amusing in her manner, above all in her affected gaiety and her overuse of French and chic *argot;* bemusing in her total lack of propriety—when she directly asks the new neighbour, who has requested to use her telephone, to look for her brown shoe while she gets dressed or when she calls at his window and pleads to spend the night in his apartment; she is entirely uncultured, shockingly materialistic and totally amoral—but always attractive. Much more so than Paul's confident and domineering protector (Patricia Neal), fittingly dressed in a shapeless cape or in twin-suits accentuating her middle-age curves—details that both play off Hepburn's girlish appearance and highlight the motif of the mother figure. In a discernible Freudian pre-oedipal paradise, Paul, the over-grown male child, is attached to his "mother," both as the caring love-object and as his object of desire. As he happily basks in the material security provided for him, he is at leisure to observe the comings and goings of the imp of a woman living downstairs. His growing fascination with Holly activates the process of oedipalisation and before long, he comes to reject the protection of the mother figure as being a claustorphobic pressure that robs him of his real autonomy: "The thing is, I can help her (Holly) and it's a nice feeling for a change," he tells his protector when informing her of his decision.

Lacan singles out the "mirror-stage" as a fundamental and climactic event within this elating period. Half awake and half asleep, Paul Varjack identifies his own image or situation with a statue, grotesquely attired with the dog mask, seemingly about to enfold the cat face in its arms. The dog and cat masks add a Dickensian touch as carnivalesque mirrors—more authentic than reality itself in their caricaturing of real beings. A deconstruction of the scene could therefore render the following reading: as an antique, the statue symbolizes the long standing, immutable "establishment." The in-disputably male dog mask in place of the head exemplifies how it is *man's* duty to guard and protect the established order while it is his potential for selfless love and faithfulness that will ultimately tame the wild, independent and loveable Cat. Paul Varjack internalizes an illusion of wholeness and, at the same time, the reflection provokes in him a feeling of alienation since the image is also perceived as Other. This scene in the film could therefore be understood as marking the splitting of the subject. The separation of the now unified being from the mother is made patent by the middle-aged woman's innocent but nauseating attempt at impersonating the cat. From then on, Paul Varjack embodies the father figure or Lacan's "paternal metaphor" and will strive to structure and give form to Holly's chaotic drives through the law of paternal authority.

For all her naïve abandon and her exhausted, played-out gaiety, Holly is also portrayed as floating somewhere between the real world and fantasy land. As a prostitute, she makes sexual fantasies proliferate all around her while deluding herself that she is actually using her lovers. This misconception is underlined by the animal imagery in the film. As mentioned before, the cat mask typifies Holly as a specimen of the feline species. By a law of nature, cats hunt rodents for food. Likewise, Holly pursues "rats" for, as a prostitute and femme fatale, she thrives on this worthless type of man. That is, her supposed autonomy or liberty depends entirely on men and the virility of men.

Holly's quest for the Other—be he father, brother, seducer or mirror image—initially involves her in wild gropings towards some dim and vague fulfilment: she speaks of Mexico as some limbo-land where she and her brother can live a dream life and she ineffectively struggles to amass enough money to make that dream a reality. The "room of her own" she is searching for is therefore not a concrete space in the sense Virginia Woolf described it. Holly already possesses what could be a cosy living-place. However, her most prominent articles of furniture are a pile of suitcases and empty shelves, indicating how escape is always pending. Nor is the "room of her own" related, in any way, to independence, autonomy and the flourishing of female qualities. It might be added too that this instability of Holly's, together with her determination not to "belong to anyone," and her nostalgic "I'm just not Lulamae any more, I'm not," when reminded that she was once Lulamae Barnes, are all character traits that go to confirm Lacan's famous view of woman as inexistent in the symbolic order, and his suggestion that since it is impossible to delimit or define the feminine, it can never be captured or pinned down (Duchen 1988: 79). Such a perspective could fuel a feminist construction of Holly's "fatalistic" attitude and actions as attempts to disrupt the Symbolic or "dislodge" the Masculine in her refusal to be named, caged or subjugated by patriarchal authority. However, there is no denying that the story relentlessly brings the audience to the climactic closing scene with Paul's pompous and dogmatic sermon provoking in Holly an unmistakable "bombshell" of self-knowledge.

> You know what's wrong with you, Miss, whoever you are? You've got no guts, you're afraid to stick out your chin and say OK life's a fact . . . you call yourself a free spirit, a wild thing and you're terrified someone will stick you in a cage. You're already in that cage. You've built it yourself . . .

This abrupt vision of love, loneliness and mutability plainly marks the end of any autonomous femininity in Holly. The perfidiousness of the film stems from the *illusion* that Holly has changed from being a transgressor as well as a passive object in man's trafficking into an active subject able to reap the benefits of her own decisions. In other words, the story cannot be said to move from male domination to female control. On the contrary, the reverse would probably be closer to the truth for, as a femme fatale, Holly at least had the potential, if not the power, to threaten and even disrupt the male establishment. The last scene showing the "wild thing" and her animal counterpart melting in the male embrace is therefore actually depicting the capitulation of the femme fatale. Hence, although *Breakfast at Tiffany's* may at first seem anomalous in the evident focus of the film on the female and feminine sensibility, in its repressive, secretive mode it in fact does not represent any type of departure from more openly patriarchal films.

However, I would also argue that the real villain in this surreptitious portrayal of the femme fatale is not Patriarchy as such, or Christianity, but Capitalism. The rise of a capitalist economy, Engels argued in *The Origin of the Family, State and Private Property,* is what deprived women of many of their traditional powers and areas of authority. By stressing the commercial aspect of ownership and making estate management a male-dominated enterprise, women were denied a real role in public life. Engels' solution to the problem was to urge women to enter more fully into the work force as a means of abandoning their confinement to private, domestic labour. It is interesting to note how, in times of crisis, as during the Second World War, it was women's productive contribution in defence industries that permitted America to enter the Second World War (Zinn 1986: 398). However, even though millions of women had responded to the intense wartime appeals and joined the traditionally male workforce, in the post-war period of adjustment to peace-time economy, they were encouraged—and even forced—to turn their jobs over to the returning veterans and resume their full-time commitment to home and family (Chafe 1991: 83). *Breakfast at Tiffany's* appeared in 1961, at the end of a decade marked by a veritable cult of feminine domesticity. The underlying theme in the film could therefore be interpreted as serving a double political function at a time when the economic situation in America required renegotiating female positions in society. First of all, behind Holly's autonomy and independence (fatal to the establishment) lies a story of disappointment and frustration: her delinquent methods of acquiring money, her failure to catch a husband, be it Rusty Trawler or José, and her subsequent loneliness all point to a marketing technique employed to warn both male and female viewers of the dangers inherent in female emancipation. On the other hand, the scenes in the film that reflect her gross incompetence in purely domestic activities, such as knitting or cooking, seem to indicate that no job was more exacting, more necessary or more rewarding than that of a housewife, that housework is a matter of knowledge and skill, rather than of dull and unremitting effort. A dominant theme in *Breakfast at Tiffany's* could therefore be this covert idealization of the housewife, both as a means of exhorting women to look upon the home as their "rightful" place and as a male defensive buildup in preparation for what was already in the air as female liberation in its early phases, foreshadowing Betty Friedan's *The Feminine Mystique* (1963).

Another arresting feature in the film is the centrality given to Tiffany's—a sanctuary of investment and consumption—as a haven of peace and security. It is interesting to note how, in one of the first scenes, the camera is placed indoors, showing only a reflection of Holly standing in front of the shop window. This picture could be understood as shrewdly underlining the way in which Holly is viewed by the "establishment" as an "outsider." The imposing jewellery shop is, however, the place Holly turns to for consolation and reassurance when afflicted with "the mean Reds" and where she and Paul have their friendship sealed by their cheap premium ring. The young couple's conversation with the assistant reveals how, for all his unshakable *savoir-faire* and kind disposition, he (the attendant) is totally disconnected from the world outside: he learns, for example, that gift tokens in packets of crisps still exist. This detail enhances the picture of Tiffany's as a symbol of the "dream era" when the economic upsurge was slowly blotting out the deprivations and sacrifices of the war period (Tindall 1988: 1275). The major catalyst in promoting economic expansion after the war had been the unleashing of consumer demand as a means of adapting American factories to peace-time necessities. The efforts of marketing specialists to engineer a revolution of rising expectations and self-gratification were directed more particularly at women.

In *Woman's Consciousness, Man's World,* Sheila Rowbotham showed how the social concept of the home as a refuge from the world of work masks the fact that domestic activity itself helps reproduce capitalist society

(1973: 81-84). The potential to *spend* of housewives was therefore the target of marketers and, as denounced by Betty Friedan: "their lack of identity . . . their lack of purpose was translated into dollars" (quoted in Wolf 1991: 64).[8] Here again, the choice of Audrey Hepburn for the part of Holly Golightly has important repercussions since, at a time when the economy of the country depended on spiralling consumption, a new definition of perfection emerged to make sure that the growing number of women who combined their jobs with the home would keep consuming at the levels they had been accustomed to when they had little else of interest to occupy them. This is when a modern form of beauty myth was devised, with modern advertisers selling diet products, specialized cosmetics and anti-aging creams over and above household goods. Audrey Hepburn's physique could therefore be translated as indirectly assuring busy and tired working women, and bored and dispirited housewives that "achievement" was within their scope if only they relied on the expertise of the cosmetics industries and the fashion dictates of clothes manufacturers. A look at what this "achievement" really entailed brings us right back to square one: women's sexual appeal or the female propensity, inherited from Eve, to ensnare men. Thus, it seems that *Breakfast at Tiffany's* does not simply depict an atypical femme fatale, it also glamourizes the political economy of the time.

As an overall conclusion, I would therefore state that, as in *Who's Afraid of Virginia Woolf,* an enigmatic void is created and sustained throughout the film *Breakfast at Tiffany's* by the fact that the character of Holly Golightly, a prostitute and thus a person popularly considered to be a disturber of a (supposedly) right order of things, is played by Audrey Hepburn, renowned for her cherubic beauty and sophisticated demeanour.

The choice of Audrey Hepburn for the part of Holly is therefore an important marker of the ideological stance behind the tale. First, the character she brings to life exhibits the Christian reflection of Eve as a femme fatale who, like Lilith or Pandora before her, was endowed with diabolical beauty and sensuality to cause disruption and evil. The actress's angelical face and girlish slenderness reflect, on the other hand, an additional myth imposed on women. The cult of the Virgin Mary killed off the threatening eroticism of the female by elevating female weakness and dependency above vulgar sex. Thus, *Breakfast at Tiffany's,* in presenting Audrey Hepburn as a delightful anachronism, is really about the myth of female emancipation—an attempt to anaesthetize women's growing political consciousness. Holly's independence is a mere illusion for she is, in actual fact, the real victim of the "rats" she tries to ensnare. Hence, while Paul Varjack's oedipalization entails giving up his life as a gigolo to assume the role of "father figure," Holly's acceptance of his manly embrace marks her real capitulation as a potential threat to patriarchal society. Consequently, the film cannot be described as feminist in its valuations since it ultimately sanctions male domination at a time when feminism was becoming a public presence in America. Besides, the message that transpires from *Breakfast at Tiffany's,* together with the appeal and elegance of the female protagonist, could also be interpreted as reinforcing an economic conception of woman's place in society while promoting women's potential as consumers as the country was moving from one stage of capitalism to another. Hence, translated into economic terms, *Breakfast at Tiffany's* seems, on the contrary, to tacitly reinforce the myth of the femme fatale by convincing women that Audrey Hepburn's glamour was both erotic and exotic and totally within their reach, if only with a little artificial help from cosmetic and fashion industries.

Notes

1. The fundamental plot in *Breakfast at Tiffany's* conforms perfectly with the general guidelines offered by publishers to potential authors of Harlequin novels: "Harlequins are well-plotted, strong romances with a happy ending. They are told from the heroine's point of view and in the third person. There may be elements of mystery or adventure but these must be subordinate to the romance. The books are contemporary and settings can be anywhere in the world as long as they are authentic" (Modleski 1992: 21). According to Anne Cranny-Francis (1990), the Harlequin novel, just like romance in general, is structured by two central ideas or aims: the characterization of a strong, male figure, the hero, and the romance and marriage between him and the heroine. So, although romance may at times *seem* to be concerned with female subjectivity and female problems, its ultimate aim is more likely to keep women in their place by upholding the dominant masculine ideology.

2. This was the dominant view in Althusserian-based film theory in the 1970s. See, for classic formulations, Jean-Louis Baudry's "Ideological Effects of the Basic Cinematographical Apparatus" (1974/ 75) and "The Apparatus" (1976); Christian Metz's "The Imaginary Signifier" (1975) and Stephen Heath's *Questions of Cinema* (1981). In feminist film theory, Laura Mulvey's seminal "Visual Pleasure in the Narrative Cinema" (1975) also takes this general view. For a good summary of these and other ideology-based theories, see Robert Laspsley and Michael Westlake's *Film Theory: An Introduction* (1988), esp. pp. 1-31 and 67-104. For a thorough attack on Marxist-based film theory, see Noël Carroll, *Mystifying Movies: Fads and Fallacies in Contemporary Film Theory* (1988).

3. Zeus, taking his revenge on mankind, fashioned out of clay the most beautiful creature ever created and sent her to Epimetheus as a present. Disobeying orders, the beautiful Pandora promptly opened a jar in which Prometheus had confined all the Calamities that might plague mankind (Graves 1966: 1.143-5). This story therefore reflects a genuine myth which runs parallel to the story of the Creation: Pandora and Eve are calamities who, because of their feminine characteristics of curiosity, craftiness, impetuosity *and* fatal beauty, eventually destroy mankind's happiness.

4. In her book *Femmes Fatales*, Mary Ann Doane dedicates three chapters to the analysis of three different films centring on the figure of the femme fatale: Charles Vidor's *Gilda* (1946), Max Ophuls's *La signora di tutti* (1934) and G. W. Pabst's *Pandora's Box* (1929).

5. One of the most famous characterizations of the beautiful woman, the vamp who captivates a man so that he becomes so obsessed by her that he gives everything up for love, is probably Shakespeare's portrayal of Cleopatra who "unmans" Antony by seducing him away from his former manly life of war. Hollywood has adapted the story twice: *Cleopatra* (Cecil B. de Mille, 1934), with Claudette Colbert in the title role and *Cleopatra* (Joseph L. Mankiewicz, 1963), with Elizabeth Taylor.

6. With this point in mind, a tenuous feminist argument emerges if Audrey Hepburn's loveliness is seen as reflecting, not a woman as such, but an *idea* of woman—a substance upon which male desires might be executed. In this sense, she would not be a femme fatale, nor would she be a prostitute, but rather the object on which men prostitute *themselves* (See Greene and Kahn 1985). This is also the general view taken by Krutnik (1991), esp. pp. 75-91.

7. The cult of the Virgin Mary dates from before the Reformation and is therefore Catholic. The Marian ideal sustained by Catholicism derives in great part from a divinely-ordained family Structure: The Sacred Family. According to this divine plan, the Virgin Mary is free from sexuality but wholly dedicated to domestic life. Anglican doctrine and Protestant doctrine on this matter stem from different theological presuppositions, although the results for women are roughly the same. For Luther and Calvin the Fall meant that Eve had lost her power and independence. She was therefore to be imprisoned in her husband's home as a punishment. In other words, a wife must be subject to her husband for a good reason: "That she

who first drew man into sin should now be subject to him, lest by the like womanish weakness she fall again" (Stone 1977:197).

8. Mary Ann Doane analyses the incidence of this phenomenon in the 40s in her study of women's films (1987), although her approach is an interesting mixture of sociology and psychoanalysis, centred around the cultural/psychological concepts of female narcissism. See esp. pp. 22-38.

Tison Pugh (essay date fall 2002)

SOURCE: Pugh, Tison. "Capote's *Breakfast at Tiffany's*." *The Explicator* 61, no. 1 (fall 2002): 51-3.

[*In the following essay, Pugh notes the importance of homosexual elements and allusions in* Breakfast at Tiffany's.]

The predominant heterosexuality of Holly Golightly's lifestyle has eclipsed the queer thematics of Truman Capote's **Breakfast at Tiffany's,** and thus the subtle homosexual presence in the novella has gone unnoticed by many scholars. To overlook the queer aspects of Holly Golightly's world is to miss key moments of the text that provide a better understanding of the novella's sexual dynamics.

Foremost, Capote describes Holly's two closest friends—the narrator and Joe Bell—as homosexuals, though he does so with such a delicate touch that many critics have failed to recognize these characters as gay. The first clue to the narrator's homosexuality lies in Holly's formulation of how to determine if a man is gay: "If a man doesn't like baseball, then he must like horses, and if he doesn't like either of them, well, I'm in trouble anyway: he don't like girls" (38). These words resonate in the reader's mind when the narrator reports the contents of Holly's bookshelves ("of the books there, more than half were about horses, the rest baseball") and then feigns interest in horses: "Pretending an interest in *Horseflesh and How to Tell It* gave me sufficiently private opportunity for sizing Holly's friends" (35). If this passage fails to convince us that the narrator holds no interest in horses and, therefore, no interest in heterosexuality, the episode when Holly takes him horseback riding, to disastrous effect, also figures him as a homosexual under her horse/baseball rubric.

Second, when Holly tells the narrator that she will not testify against Sally Tomato, she calls the narrator a name laden with queer meaning: "Well, I may be rotten to the core, Maude, *but:* testify against a friend I will not" (102-03). In homosexual slang, "maude" signifies a male prostitute or a male homosexual (*Dictionary of*

Slang and Unconventional English). Third, the narrator himself makes a veiled reference to his homosexuality when he compares his rain-soaked trip from Holly's apartment to Joe Bell's bar to another difficult journey he had made years ago: "Never mind why, but once I walked from New Orleans to Nancy's Landing, Mississippi, just under five hundred miles. It was a light-hearted lark compared to the journey to Joe Bell's bar" (105). Nancy's Landing is Capote's creation; it does not exist geographically. According to *A Dictionary of the Underworld,* "Nancy" refers either to the posterior or to "an effeminate man, especially a passive homosexual." "Nancy's Landing," then serves as Capote's code phrase for a gay resort, a make-believe, southern Fire Island or Provincetown. Thus, the narrator's coy rejoinder that the reader should "[n]ever mind why" he made the trip appears as a subtle move to direct attention away from his self-confession.

We perceive a hint of Joe Bell's homosexuality in the list of his passions; he enjoys, in addition to hockey players and Weimaraner dogs, "Our Gal Sunday (a soap serial he had listened to for fifteen years), and Gilbert and Sullivan," both of which indicate less stereotypically masculine aspects to his character. Capote develops the reference to Gilbert and Sullivan further, noting that "[Bell] claims to be related to one or the other, I can't remember which" (4). Since Sullivan is rumored to have been a homosexual because of the many coded references to sexual partners in his diaries, the passage slyly hints that the bartender is part of Sullivan's "family," a fellow gay man to his beloved composer. One could, of course, argue that, because Capote does not specifically state to which composer Joe Bell is related, he could be "related" to the heterosexual Gilbert. Such an interpretation, however, would have to ignore a final touch of Capote's characterization of Joe Bell that emphasizes the bartender's feminine qualities: he "arranges with matronly care" the flowers at the bar (5).

Descriptions of Joe Bell's bar also subtly hint that it is a gay bar: its anonymity suggests that it is hidden from general view; the narrator remarks that it has no neon sign to attract attention to itself (5). Gay bars did not advertise themselves as such in the 1950s, and patrons had to learn about their locations through word of mouth. Furthermore, the narrator mentions that the windows of the bar are mirrors (5). Mirror windows allow patrons to see outside but do not allow passersby to look in; to this day many gay bars have such mirror windows to protect the privacy of their patrons. Though we see very few customers inside the bar besides Holly and the narrator, two men enter together when the narrator prepares to leave after conversing with Joe Bell (10).

Critics have long recognized that Holly's friendships with the narrator and Joe Bell are asexual, but it is imperative to note the queer reasons for the platonic na-

ture of these relationships. Thus, we can see that Holly's friendships with gay men are one sign of her progressive sexual politics. Indeed, Holly's words to the narrator about gay marriage remain topical today: "A person ought to be able to marry men or women or—listen, if you came to me and said you wanted to hitch up with Man o' War, I'd respect your feeling. No, I'm serious. Love should be allowed" (83). (A possible irony: under Holly's rubric of sexuality, in which love of horses indicates heterosexuality, would the narrator be straight if he loved Man o' War?)

Holly Golightly's queer world marks her as a participant in the sexual struggle against conformity and conservatism, rather than as merely a lovely young innocent who inspires protective and paternal love. And Capote makes it clear that she leaves a queer legacy behind her when Quaintance Smith, who "entertained as many gentleman callers of a noisy nature as Holly ever had" (110), moves into her old apartment. The name "Quaintance" is an allusion to George Quaintance, a painter of the 1940s and 1950s, whose art bordered on soft-core gay pornography. Holly Golightly's queer world lives on even after she flees the constraints of New York City for her own freedom.

Works Cited

Capote, Truman. *Breakfast at Tiffany's and Three Stories.* 1958. New York: Vintage, 1993.

Partridge, Eric. *A Dictionary of the Underworld.* New York: Macmillan, 1950.

———. *A Dictionary of Slang and Unconventional English.* 8th ed. New York: Macmillan, 1984.

FURTHER READING

Criticism

Capote, Truman, with Eric Norden. "*Playboy* Interview: Truman Capote." In *Truman Capote: Conversations,* edited by M. Thomas Inge, pp. 110-63. Jackson: University Press of Mississippi, 1987.

Capote and Norden discuss the "new morality" and Holly Golightly as the prototype of today's liberated female.

Krämer, Peter. "The Many Faces of Holly Golightly: Truman Capote, *Breakfast at Tiffany's,* and Hollywood." *Film Studies* 5 (winter 2004): 58-64.

Explores the treatment of Capote's Holly in Blake Edwards's film adaptation of the novella.

Morris, Alice, Eleanor Perényi, Clay Felker, Doris Lilly, John Malcom Brinnin, and Joan Axelrod. "In Which TC's *Breakfast at Tiffany's* Upsets Mr. Deems." In *Truman Capote: In Which Various Friends, Enemies, Acquaintances, and Detractors Recall His Turbulent Career,* edited by George Plimpton, pp. 161-65. New York: Doubleday, 1997.

Conversation among several of Capote's associates about the circumstances surrounding the publication of *Breakfast at Tiffany's.*

Reed, Kenneth T. "Three Novel-Romances." In *Truman Capote,* pp. 71-93. Boston: Twayne Publishers, 1981.

Suggests that *Breakfast at Tiffany's* is a celebration of innocence and an affront to middle-class respectability.

Smiley, John. "Breakfast of Champions." In *The Power of Myth in Literature and Film,* pp. 24-34. Tallahassee: University Presses of Florida, 1980.

Examines *Breakfast at Tiffany's* as an example of how myths are appropriated in literature, pointing out Capote's use of archetypal characters and situations.

Additional coverage of Capote's life and career is contained in the following sources published by Thomson Gale: *American Writers Supplement,* **Vol. 3;** *Authors and Artists for Young Adults,* **Vol. 61;** *Beacham's Encyclopedia of Popular Fiction: Biography and Resources,* **Vol. 1;** *Concise Dictionary of American Literary Biography,* **Vol. 1941-1968;** *Contemporary Authors,* **Vol. 5-8R;** *Contemporary Authors New Revision Series,* **Vols. 18 and 62;** *Contemporary Authors—Obituary,* **Vol. 113;** *Contemporary Literary Criticism,* **Vols. 1, 3, 8, 13, 19, 34, 38, and 58;** *Contemporary Novelists,* **Eds. 1, 2, and 3;** *Contemporary Popular Writers;* *Dictionary of Literary Biography,* **Vols. 2, 185, and 227;** *Dictionary of Literary Biography Yearbook,* **Eds. 1980 and 1984;** *DISCovering Authors; DISCovering Authors 3.0; DISCovering Authors: British; DISCovering Authors: Canadian Edition; DISCovering Authors Modules,* **Eds. MST, NOV, POP;** *Encyclopedia of World Literature in the 20th Century,* **Ed. 3;** *Exploring Short Stories; Gay and Lesbian Literature,* **Ed. 1;** *Literature and Its Times,* **Vol. 3;** *Literature Resource Center; Major 20th-Century Writers,* **Eds. 1 and 2;** *Major 21st-Century Writers,* **Ed. 2005;** *Modern American Literature,* **Ed. 5;** *Nonfiction Classics for Students,* **Vol. 2;** *Reference Guide to American Literature,* **Ed. 4;** *Reference Guide to Short Fiction,* **Ed. 2;** *Short Stories for Students,* **Vol. 2;** *Short Story Criticism,* **Vols. 2 and 47;** *Something about the Author,* **Vol. 91;** *Twayne's United States Authors; Twentieth-Century Literary Criticism,* **Vol. 164; and** *World Literature Criticism,* **Vol. 1.**

Colette
1873-1954

(Full name Sidonie-Gabrielle Colette; also wrote under the pseudonyms Colette Willy and Willy.) French short story writer, novelist, and journalist. For additional information on Colette's short fiction, see *Short Story Criticism,* Volume 10.

INTRODUCTION

One of the best-known French writers of short fiction in the twentieth-century, Colette is lauded for her insightful observations on love, sensual prose style, and realistic characterizations of women. Her protagonists are said to offer the first genuine instances of feminine perspective in French fiction. Although many of Colette's writings were originally published as novels, critics regard them as novellas and observe that much of her fiction defies generic categorization. Colette's best-known work is the novella *Gigi* (1944), about an adolescent girl in training to be a *cocette,* the highest class of courtesan in French society. It was made into a motion picture in 1958. Drawing upon autobiographical influences, Colette's stories often focus on the personal and domestic aspects of life and explore such subjects as marriage and women's freedom. Colette's work has generated a great deal of criticism, much of which discusses the autobiographical quality of her fiction, her study of female sexuality, her innovative use of language and narrative voice, her explorations of female space, her theme of femininity as a form of disguise, and the presence of the mother figure in her work.

BIOGRAPHICAL INFORMATION

Colette was born in 1873 in the village of Saint-Sauveur-en Puisaye, in Burgundy, France. She was the daughter of a retired army captain, Jules-Joseph Colette, a taxcollector with local political aspirations, and his wife, Adele Eugenie Sidonie Landoy. Colette's mother, known as "Sidonie" or "Sido," was a quietly unconventional woman. Colette enjoyed a happy childhood and she credited her own success later in life to her mother's wisdom and naturalness. When she was twenty, Colette married the journalist Henri Gauthier-Villars, who by most accounts was a fraud who used Colette's talents for his own ends. Colette wrote four novels under his pen name, Monsieur Willy. The novels, about a young girl named Claudine, were a huge

success. In 1906 Colette divorced her husband and became a music-hall mime, touring the circuits with moderate success for six years.

In 1912 Colette married Henri de Jouvenel des Ursins, the editor-in-chief of *Le Matin,* for which she was the literary correspondent. They had a daughter, Colette de Jouvenel. During the 1920s Colette wrote prolifically and became well known in French literary circles. By 1927 she was acclaimed as France's greatest woman writer, and in the 1930s was made a member of the Belgian Royal Academy. She married again in 1935, this time to Maurice Goudaket, a Jewish businessman-turned-journalist with whom she was to have her longest and happiest union. In 1945 Colette was elected to the Académie Goncourt, over which she presided beginning in 1949, and in 1952 to the Légion d'Honneur. Over the last two decades years of her life she became progressively more immobile because of a debilitating form of arthritis, but she continued to write. Colette died on August 3, 1954 in Paris.

MAJOR WORKS OF SHORT FICTION

Colette began writing under the direction of Gauthier-Villars, producing a series of novels that brought them both national celebrity. In 1904 she attempted to establish herself as a writer independent of her husband by publishing *Dialogues de Bêtes* (1904; *Animal Dialogues*), a series of poetic conversations between a cat and a dog who make observations about the sexes and the wonders of nature. For the next thirty-five years, Colette produced mostly short fiction, including story collections and more than a dozen novellas.

Most of Colette's short fiction explores the intricate patterns and nuances of love relationships. This is seen early on in her reflective pieces in *Les Vrilles de la Vigne* (1908; *The Tendrils of the Vine*) as well as the short novel *La Vagabonde* (1910; *The Vagabond*), about a strong-willed woman who refuses to relinquish her freedom for the sake of love. Her 1913 short story collection *L'Envers du Music-Hall* (*Music-Hall Sidelights*), inspired by her experiences as a music-hall dancer and mime, looks at the emotional lives of the performers and their relationships. Colette's most famous work, the novella *Gigi,* is a lighthearted love story about a teenage girl from a family of high-class courtesans who is wooed by a handsome playboy millionaire. Despite its fairytale quality, the work explores questions of female sexuality, power, and freedom.

Married life is the subject of numerous novellas and short stories by Colette, including the collection *La Femme cachée* (1924; *The Other Woman*), which portrays men and women who feel confined within their marriages. In "The Hand," a newlywed woman, while lying next to her sleeping husband, is disturbed by conflicting feelings of attraction and revulsion as she contemplates her husband's hand. Older women are often characterized especially sensitively in Colette's work, as in the novella *Chéri* (1920) and its sequel *La Fin de Chéri* (1926; *The Last of Chéri*), which depict the love affair between an aging courtesan and a beautiful young man she nicknames Chéri. A relationship between an older woman and a younger man is also the subject of the short novel *La Naissance du Jour* (1928; *Break of Day*). Many critics have suggested that Colette's mother provided the model for the positive qualities Colette admired in older women. Colette revered her mother throughout her life, portraying her as an idealized, almost mythic figure in *Sido* (1929) and *La Maison de Claudine* (1922; *My Mother's House*). In both of these works, Sidonie is depicted as independent and generous, possessing an instinctive understanding of nature, and loved by her children, spouse, neighbors, and animals.

Several of Colette's short works portray characters whose nostalgia for their lost childhood prevents them from fully participating in their present lives. For example, *The Last of Chéri* and *La Chatte* (1933; *Saha the Cat*) focus on young men who resist the responsibilities of adulthood and marriage by retreating into fantasy and their idealized memories of the past. Women's freedom is a frequent theme, seen for example in *Julie de Carneilhan* (1941), in which the heroine's newfound independence is undermined by feelings of weakness, disillusionment, and loss when she agrees to visit her former husband who has fallen ill. Colette had numerous female lovers, and her bisexuality was the basis for the novella *Ces Plaisirs* (1932; *The Pure and the Impure*), which emphasizes the juxtaposition of masculine and feminine characteristics in all individuals, blurring conventional notions of gender, sexuality, and morality.

CRITICAL RECEPTION

Criticism of Colette's fiction concentrates on her stories and novellas; after the early Claudine novels, she wrote mostly shorter fictional works. Her short fiction earned her the highest literary honors that could be bestowed on a woman in France. When she died in 1954, Colette was her country's most famous female writer, and the first woman to be accorded a state funeral. Her champions admired the fluidity and intensity of her style, as she blurred the boundaries between fiction and autobiography. They lauded her evocative prose and sensual descriptions and her strong, resilient, and unconventional female characters. But despite her ostensible success, many early commentators dismissed Colette as an undisciplined writer whose subjects were trivial and who focused too heavily on women's emotional lives. They viewed her writing as deficient in structure, too overtly feminine, overly reliant on spontaneous outpourings of emotion, and lacking in political purpose.

For the first few decades after her death, critics focused on the autobiographical aspects of Colette's writing, pointing out where her life and fiction converged. Commentators paid attention too to the relationship between her narrators and the world and her characters and the objects surrounding them. Beginning in the 1970s, feminist scholars began to look at the themes of female space, sexuality, and male dominance in Colette's writing, noting the social critiques embedded in her work. Some argued that her focus on the joy and pain of individual existence and on domestic space served to highlight the question of the nature of the female self. Further, many suggested that the unconventional structure of the stories and novellas sought to draw attention to the different type of space—physical and emotional—in which women live. Since then, critics have shown keen interest in the unusual narrative strategies employed in Colette's writing and the fact that her fiction defies categorization. Her stories, novellas, and even novels lack intricate plotting; the focus is on patterns of relationships rather than patterns of ideas or events. It has been suggested that the reason Colette's fiction is unusual in its narrative design is because it represents women differently—not within the confines traditionally imposed on them. Colette's stories, fusing fiction and autobiography, interior life and exterior space, systematically deconstruct gender stereotypes by refusing to fix women's images and movements in the area surrounding them. In the twenty-first century, interest in Colette's writing continues, with critics paying particular attention to the author's views on gender differences, her narrative techniques, and her portrayal of the conflicted female self.

PRINCIPAL WORKS

Short Fiction

Dialogues de Bêtes [*Animal Dialogues*] [as Colette Willy] (short stories) 1904; enlarged and published as *Douze Dialogues de bêtes* 1930

Les Vrilles de la Vigne [*The Tendrils of the Vine*] [as Colette Willy] (short stories) 1908

La Vagabonde [*The Vagabond*] [as Colette Willy] (novella) 1910; republished as *Renée la Vagabonde* 1931

L'Envers du Music-Hall [*Music-Hall Sidelights*] (short stories) [as Colette Willy] 1913

Mitsou; ou, Comment l'Esprit vient aux Filles [*Mitsou; or, How Girls Grow Wise*] (novella) 1919

Chéri (novella) 1920

La Maison de Claudine [*My Mother's House*] (novella) 1922

Le Blé en Herbe [*The Ripening; Ripening Seed*] (novella) 1923

La Femme cachée [*The Other Woman*] (short stories) 1924

La Fin de Chéri [*The Last of Chéri*] (novella) 1926

La Naissance du Jour [*Break of Day; A Lesson in Love; Morning Glory*] (novellas) 1928

La Seconde [*The Other One; Fanny and Jane*] (novella) 1929

Sido ou les Points cardinaux (novella) 1929; revised 1930

Ces Plaisirs [*The Pure and the Impure*] (novellas) 1932; republished as *Le Pur et l'Impur* 1941

La Chatte [*Saha the Cat*] (novella) 1933

Duo (novella) 1934

Bella-Vista (novella) 1937

Le Toutounier (novella) 1939

Chambre d'Hôtel [*Chance Acquaintances; Hotel Room*] (short stories) 1940

Julie de Carneilhan (novella) 1941

Le Képi 1943

Gigi et autres Nouvelles (novellas) 1944

Trois . . . Six . . . Neuf [*Three . . . Six . . . Nine*] (short stories) 1944

The Stories of Colette 1958; republished as *The Tender Shoot and Other Stories* 1959

The Collected Stories of Colette 1983

Other Major Works

Claudine à l'École [*Claudine at School*] [as Willy] (novel) 1900

Claudine à Paris [*Claudine in Paris*] [as Willy] (novel) 1901

Claudine en Ménage [*The Indulgent Husband*] [as Willy] (novel) 1902

Claudine s'en Va: Journal d'Annie [*The Innocent Wife*] [as Willy] (novel) 1903

Journal à Rebours [*Looking Backwards*] (memoirs) 1941

L'Etoile Vesper [*The Evening Star*] (meditations, memoirs) 1946

Le Fanal bleu [*The Blue Lantern*] (diaries) 1949

Oèuvres complètes. 15 vols. (fiction, nonfiction, and drama) 1949-50

Oeuvres complètes de Colette. 16 vols. (fiction, nonfiction, and drama) 1973

Earthly Paradise: An Autobiography Drawn from Her Lifelong Writings (autobiographical writings) 1975

CRITICISM

Elaine Marks (essay date 1960)

SOURCE: Marks, Elaine. "Anecdote and Meditation: Daily Adventures." In *Colette*, pp. 174-85. New Brunswick, N.J.: Rutgers University Press, 1960.

[*In the following excerpt from her full-length study of Colette's works, Marks examines the author's first-person writings and observes that they express her relationship to the world.*]

> To choose, to note the conspicuous, to preserve the unusual, to eliminate the banal, is not my concern, since, almost always, it is the ordinary that excites and animates me.[1]

Thirty-three of the fifty-seven titles included in the *Oeuvres complètes* are works written in the first person. Both in quantity and in quality these works, originally written as newspaper chronicles or as short stories and articles for different anthologies or as advertisements or as single books, dominate Colette's literary production. Although they treat a wide variety of subjects—animals, plants, music halls, Sido, childhood, fashion, Willy, travels, old age, love in all possible forms, Parisian events, famous writers and murderers, Colette's daughter, Bel-Gazou, France—and although the manner of presentation may be an anecdote, a dialogue, a description, a short or long meditation, Colette's first-person writings are of interest essentially as the expression of a relation between the narrator, "Colette," and the world.

These first-person writings are neither diaries nor intimate journals. With the exception of *Mes Apprentissages,* they tell nothing, or very little, of Colette's private affairs. They reveal, not a life, but a style of living and a style of writing. The reader's intimacy with Colette is both real and illusory. In the aesthetic distance that separates Colette from "Colette," the real woman is transformed into a fictional character who, drawing on the memories and the experiences of the original model, becomes the distinctive voice that rules a charmed but very real domain.

This voice is first heard in *Les Vrilles de la Vigne.* Published in 1908,[2] *Les Vrilles de la Vigne* contains the same major themes as those that were elaborated in the *Claudine* novels: childhood, nature, love and solitude.

But the treatment of these themes takes a new form, and the atmosphere in which they are developed changes. Colette has put aside the fictional universe she created in her first novels in favor of brief chapters sustained and unified by a single voice.

Thus, at the beginning of her independent literary career, when Colette took off the mask and wrote in her own name, she did not choose the novel as her vehicle of expression. The *Dialogues de Bêtes,* the last pages of *La Retraite sentimentale* and *Les Vrilles de la Vigne* clearly show that Colette, left to herself, tended toward poetic revery and anecdote rather than toward fiction. This change from fiction to revery, from Claudine to "Colette," is accompanied by a movement away from the adult human world to the world of memory and the world of animals. The importance accorded to memory and animals in these early independent works, the need to communicate in relative solitude both with the past and with elemental, primitive forces, is indicative of Colette's withdrawal from the human world as she had transposed it in the *Claudine* series and experienced it in the years spent with Monsieur Willy.

Many of Colette's first-person writings follow this same pattern of withdrawal. In her novels, Colette creates characters involved in situations which reflect certain of her own experiences, temptations and premonitions. In her first-person writings, she creates a character who, free from the conventions of plot and action, reveals, as it were, the fruits of these involvements, in a commentary on life as seen by one who has temporarily withdrawn from it. The freedom, both in content and expression, to be found in such works as *Les Vrilles de la Vigne,* counterbalances the controlled rigidity of many of the novels and short stories and serves to illuminate the characters and situations created in these more conventional works.

Both in matter and in manner *Les Vrilles de la Vigne* anticipates the entire range of Colette's first-person writings. It stands in much the same relation to these writings as do the *Claudines* to the later novels. *Les Vrilles de la Vigne* establishes a general pattern, a pattern on which, in her first-person works, she elaborates but from which she never deviates.

The book thus marks a point of arrival and a point of departure. It takes its title from the lyrical opening pages, among the most beautiful that Colette ever wrote. In **"Les Vrilles de la Vigne,"** she describes a nightingale who is caught while sleeping one night by the tendrils of the vine and who thereafter sings in order to keep awake, eventually becoming enchanted with its own voice. Through the image of the nightingale, Colette symbolically portrays her childhood, her first marriage and the liberation that came with the discovery of her talent. Writing, Colette implies, has become for her,

as singing for the nightingale, a mode of life, the necessary element for survival.

Colette reveals the quality of her voice to herself and to the reader in these opening pages, and she introduces a first-person narrator, "Colette," whose desire it is to write "Everything that I know, everything that I think, everything that I divine, everything that enchants me and wounds me and astonishes me,"[3] and who thereby heralds the advent of all that part of Colette's work which falls under the heading of meditations and reminiscences: *La Naissance du Jour, Mes Apprentissages, Le Pur et l'Impur, De ma Fenêtre, Trois . . . Six . . . Neuf . . . , Belles Saisons, L'Etoile Vesper* and *Le Fanal bleu.*

As is the case with *Les Vrilles de la Vigne,* the titles of these meditations and reminiscences are all symbolic and mark different stages of Colette's life and development. *La Naissance du Jour* symbolizes the birth of a new attitude toward life, a new renunciation and a new acceptance. *Mes Apprentissages* evokes the years of apprenticeship, both as a writer and as a woman, which Colette spent with Monsieur Willy. *Le Pure et l'Impur* indicates her refusal to accept conventional morality. *De ma Fenêtre* portrays her immobility, her arthritis, which, forcing her to stay in bed, permits her to see and to live in only that part of the world which is visible from her window. *Trois . . . Six . . . Neuf . . .*[4] refers to Colette's unwelcome, yet ever-increasing changes of residence. *Belles Saisons* calls up the eternal beauty of the natural world for one who is forced to live mostly in memory. *L'Etoile Vesper* symbolizes Colette's decline. *Le Fanal bleu* describes the narrowing of her world to those objects which are illuminated by an electric light bulb, shaded by a piece of blue paper. The light of the *fanal bleu* in Colette's window announces to the world that she is, despite her illness and her great age, still alive.

As Colette grows older, the autobiographical elements in these meditations and reminiscences increase. "Novels, short stories, embellished episodes, skilful arrangements of fiction and truth, I managed to do all this. But now the difficulty of walking and the years put me in a situation where I no longer sin by lying and banish from me all occasions for flights of fancy."[5] The Colette who can be known most fully, therefore, is the ailing, arthritic Colette of *L'Etoile Vesper* and *Le Fanal bleu.* A series of masks and models have been discarded, until finally, just before death, the character and the woman meet.

These works vary in quality but not in kind. A flower, an evening wind, people reading in the park, one of Sido's letters and Colette starts off on a path that leads from the present to the past and back again to the present, recalling the voices of friends, the color of the sea, a summer in Provence, an incident from her childhood, combining these with the hardships of war, the pains of arthritis, an unexpected visit, a short conversation with her faithful companion.

A rambling promenade of this sort, even in the company of Colette, may become tedious, but this tedium is the ransom required to redeem from captivity, the captivity of laziness and habit, one's own attentiveness to detail, one's own often dormant senses. Colette compels her readers to look, to smell, to taste, to touch, to hear. She forces them into a new and intimate relation with living things and with objects. And as there is no sudden illumination in Colette's world, tedium is the prerequisite of wisdom. Colette the moralist is ever present in Colette the sensualist, drawing from the smallest detail a lesson, and always the same lesson, that lucidity is more precious than happiness and that lucidity demands constant vigilance.

"Nuit Blanche," "Jour Gris" and **"Le Dernier Feu,"** the three lyrical monologues in *Les Vrilles de la Vigne,* are short poems in prose, rhapsodic evocations of mood and landscape. In **"Nuit Blanche,"** the narrator, beginning with a description of "our bed," proceeds to tell of a night of insomnia during which the memory of a garden is linked with the memory of love and of pleasure. "You gave me flowers without thorns. . . ."[6] At the end of a rather audacious evocation of Sapphic caresses, there is a concluding sentence which foreshadows and perhaps explains the origin of the relationship between Léa and Chéri: "You will give me pleasure, bent over me, your eyes full of maternal anxiety, you, who are seeking in your passionate friend the child you never had."[7]

In **"Jour Gris"** and **"Le Dernier Feu,"** the narrator speaks to her anonymous though clearly feminine lover, contrasting the maritime country in which they are with the country of her childhood. Perhaps the most striking note in these monologues is that of melancholy, a melancholy which is always associated, in Colette's world, with love. Here the melancholy is a result both of physical love and of the loss of the narrator's "true" love, her childhood. The juxtaposition of childhood and homosexuality is not fortuitous. As shall be seen later, in a discussion of Colette's "masterpieces," the link lies in the word "pure."

The three chapters in *Les Vrilles de la Vigne* which compose the "Valentine" cycle are forerunners of Colette's longer first-person short stories: **"Bella-Vista"** in *Bella-Vista,* **"Chambre d'hôtel"** and **"La lune de pluie"** in *Chambre d'Hôtel,* **"Le Képi"** and **"Le Tendron"** in *Le Képi* and **"La Dame du Photographe"** in *Gigi.*

> It is insane to think that the periods without love are "empty spaces" in a woman's existence. On the contrary. . . . These "empty spaces" which took it upon themselves to furnish me with anecdotes, with troubled, lost, incomprehensible or simple characters who tugged at my sleeve, used me as witness, then let me go, I did not know then that they were more romantic interludes than my own personal dramas.[8]

Colette spent these "periods without love" in Paris or in French provincial hotels. The "romantic interludes" are transformed into short stories in which Colette appears as narrator, observer and character. Ostensibly these are "real" stories, based on real anecdotes, about people whom Colette meets in her travels; sometimes, as in the **"Valentine"** stories, **"Le Képi"** and **"Le Tendron,"** real friends supposedly tell Colette their past or present experiences. The air of authenticity is reinforced by the presence of other real people: Willy, Georges Wague, Annie de Pène, Paul Masson.

The atmosphere in these stories is always mysterious. What is Valentine's "disguised sorrow"? What is the connection between Monsieur Daste and the dead birds? What is Madame Ruby? Why does Monsieur Haume never stop looking at his watch? What is the strange relation between Colette's past and the two sisters who live in her old apartment? Why does the photographer's wife attempt to kill herself? Why does Albin Chaveriat, at the age of seventy, refuse the invitation of a friend whose household abounds in young girls?

Colette would have one believe that the people whose stories she narrates are all ordinary people, each possessed of a particular secret, living a particular drama, a drama that would have passed unnoticed were it not for the writer who, observing the tics and the habits of her habitual or chance acquaintances, divines, intuits, imagines and creates. If one were to protest that a person such as Madame Ruby, supposedly a Lesbian but really a man, or the series of coincidences that bring together the characters in **"Chambre d'hôtel"** hardly seem ordinary, Colette would undoubtedly answer that the protest reveals inability to see, that everyone does have a secret, that everyone, at some time, is caught in a web of coincidences. Colette never fails to use such phrases as "the lover of young girls," or "the betrayed lover," or "the spinster," thereby implying that her characters belong to, and behave in a manner appropriate to, a general class of humanity.

That "Colette" attracts confidences and confessions, there can be no doubt. Her name is known even to chance acquaintances, and as she is a willing card player and a good listener, it is not very difficult to engage her socially. What is most revealing about "Colette" is that she is quite obviously unable to bear the solitude for which she pretends to yearn. Her arrival at a hotel is followed by a period of uneasiness caused by the strangeness of her room, the difference in the air and the necessity of speaking to unknown people. Her one desire is to return immediately to Paris. And yet, although she frequently reiterates that her acquaintances and their problems bore or annoy her, that she prefers the company of her dog or her cat to human contacts, once the initial presentations have been made, "Colette" quite willingly plays the role of detective or accomplice and soon finds that her room is livable, the air refreshing and the people interesting.

Her fear of solitude, a strong curiosity and a very real affection for human beings, an affection which "Colette" is often reluctant to admit, invariably propel her toward others. But it is not merely by chance that the secrets she discovers, the dramas in which she becomes entangled, reflect her own secrets, her own private dramas, that the "real" first-person short stories should bear so strong a resemblance to the invented third-person short stories. The "real" world of her experiences and her created world are very much the same. The only important difference between the two is that in the "real" world the revelation is double. A mystery is resolved, and "Colette" is partially unmasked. The moral of the story, and there is always a moral, supports the double revelation and becomes an apology for the drama, its actors and its narrator.

> Whenever I think of her, I always see her firmly entrenched behind scruples that she modestly called annoyances and sustained by outbursts of feminine grandeur, humble and everyday, a grandeur which she misjudged by inflicting on it the name of "a very small life."[9]

The women, of which "my friend Valentine" is the first, are the unsuspecting heroines of Colette's first-person short stories. They are always courageous and always unaware of their courage, which, were it not for Colette, would have passed unnoticed. Colette lifts these women from oblivion, demonstrating once more that drama and heroism, far from being exceptions, are integral parts of many a "very small life."

The narrator, "Colette," also shares in this "feminine grandeur, humble and everyday." Her own daily life, her own "scruples," which she, too, modestly calls "annoyances," constitute in fact the second, complementary drama in these stories, a drama which she pretends to ignore. This lonely woman, so ready to apply the adjective "courageous" to others—is she not, by implication, the most courageous of all and her stories the proof of this courage that grapples with the daily adventure, attempting to give it a meaning and a value?

Aside from the very specific nature of the subject matter, **"Music-Halls"** in *Les Vrilles de la Vigne* and Colette's later music-hall anecdotes, *L'Envers du Music-Hall* and **"Gribiche"** in *Bella-Vista,* belong with the first-person short stories. In the music hall as in her chance acquaintanceships, "Colette" is both an outsider

and a participant, more conscious of the task of illuminating the life of her companions than of the fact that she is revealing her own. Colette's music-hall stories are documents on a world that no longer exists, sentimental tales in which the moral twist often seems excessive. One begins to wonder whether poverty and hard work are always attributes of heroism and dignity, whether intellectual mediocrity always implies moral superiority and whether Colette is not relying a little too much on her own facility to move from the particular to the general.

It is in the light of Colette's pre-music-hall existence, her life with Monsieur Willy, that this emphasis on pride, dignity and morality is brought into proper focus. If it weakens the anecdotes, it nevertheless strengthened Colette. The music-hall stories, for all their local color, are essentially studies in the development of the character "Colette."

The diversity of such chapters in *Les Vrilles de la Vigne* as **"La Dame qui chante," "Le Miroir," "En Baie de somme"** and **"Partie de pêche"** is characteristic of the varied chronicles and often unrelated anecdotes that fill the pages of such works as *Dans la Foule, Les Heures longues, La Chambre éclairée, Le Voyage égoïste, Aventures quotidiennes, Journal à rebours, Mes Cahiers, Trait pour Trait, Journal intermittent, La Fleur de l'Age, En Pays connu, A Portée de la main* and *Mélanges.*

Colette could and indeed did write about anything and everything that came within the range of her own daily adventures. There is not one of her voyages, not one of the well-known people she met, not one of the sections of Paris in which she lived, hardly a succulent meal eaten, a change in women's styles, a child encountered, that is not carefully and faithfully transcribed. Colette achieved a major triumph in bringing into the body of literature a very unusual record of the peoples, places and things observed, in a long lifetime, by one woman. But the subject that dominates *Les Vrilles de la Vigne,* the subject to which Colette devoted many pages in the works cited above, not to mention one novel, *La Chatte,* and six short books, *Dialogues de Bêtes, La Paix chez les Bêtes, Autres Bêtes, Prisons et Paradis, Flore et Pomone* and *Pour un Herbier,* the subject which, along with love and childhood, obviously stands highest in her favor, is that of the animal and vegetable kingdoms. Even more perhaps than her relations with human beings and human events, Colette's contacts with flora and fauna reveal the limits and the depths of her anecdotes and meditations.

Notes

1. *Le Fanal bleu,* 8.

2. In subsequent editions of *Les Vrilles de la Vigne,* new chapters were added and original ones omit-

ted. This discussion deals only with those chapters which appeared in the 1908 edition.

3. "Les Vrilles de la Vigne," *Les Vrilles de la Vigne,* 207. This quotation may be compared to a similar one in *La Naissance du Jour,* 56.

4. *Trois . . . Six . . . Neuf . . .* is the title of a play written by Michel Duran and reviewed by Colette on February 9, 1936, *La Jumelle noire,* 313. Colette speaks in her review of "valises opened as soon as they are closed," and this perhaps accounts for the similarity in the titles.

5. *L'Etoile Vesper,* 303.

6. "Nuit Blanche," *Les Vrilles de la Vigne,* 218.

7. *Ibid.,* 220.

8. *Bella-Vista,* 133.

9. "La Dame du Photographe," *Gigi,* 129.

Bibliography

For a complete bibliography of Colette's published writings see the *Oeuvres complètes de Colette* and Elaine Marks, "Colette: A Critical Study" (doctoral thesis, New York University, 1957).

Oeuvres complètes de Colette. Paris, Flammarion, 1948-1950. This definitive edition of Colette's works is being translated and published in England by Secker and Warburg and distributed in the United States by Farrar, Straus and Cudahy.

Volume VIII: *La Naissance du Jour, La Seconde, Prisons et Paradis, Nudité.*

Volume IX: *Le Pur et l'Impur, La Chatte, Duo, Le Toutounier, Belles Saisons.*

Volume X: *La Jumelle noire.*

Volume XII: *Journal à rebours, Le Képi, De ma Fenêtre, Trois . . . Six . . . Neuf . . .*

Volume XIII: *Gigi, L'Etoile Vesper, Mes Cahiers, Discours de réception.*

Volume XIV: *Le Fanal bleu, Pour un Herbier, Trait pour Trait, Journal intermittent, La Fleur de l'Age, En Pays connu, A Portée de la main.*

Les Vrilles de la Vigne. Paris, Editions de la Vie Parisienne, 1908.

La Naissance du Jour. Paris, Flammarion, 1928. (*A Lesson in Love.* Translated by Rosemary Benêt. New York, Farrar and Rinehart, 1932.)

Bella-Vista. Paris, J. Ferenczi et fils, 1937. (See: "Bella-Vista," "Gribiche," "The Rendezvous" and "The Patriarch" in *The Tender Shoot and Other Stories.* Translated by Antonia White. New York, Farrar, Straus and Cudahy, 1959.)

Trois . . . Six . . . Neuf . . . Paris, Corrêa, 1944.

L'Etoile Vesper. Genève, Editions du Milieu du Monde, 1946.

Le Fanal bleu. Paris, J. Ferenczi et fils, 1949.

I. T. Olken (essay date January 1963)

SOURCE: Olken, I. T. "Imagery in *Chéri* and *La Fin de Chéri.*" *Studies in Philology* 60, no. 1 (January 1963): 96-115.

[*In the following essay, Olken discusses sensory imagery in the novellas* Chéri *and* La Fin de Chéri, *arguing that it sets the tone for the works and helps the reader to better understand relations between characters and objects in the novellas.*]

An understanding of the basic components of Colette's mature use of sensory imagery is vital in any discussion of her writing, particularly in **Chéri** and **La Fin de Chéri,** her most important novels. Throughout these two books there is an immediate stress placed upon the definition of the characters as they move through a physical world. Immediate perception is constantly in the foreground, transposed into image and symbol, which act as devices basic to the location of the various characters, singly and in their interrelationships.

I. Sound Imagery

The thing heard, in much the same way as the thing seen, has a direct sensory effect. But there is one fundamental difference between the literary presentation of sound and visual image.[1] If an author tells us that something is red, green or yellow, we can be fairly certain that each reader will be thinking of much the same color, with variants within the range of red, green and yellow as spectral divisions. With sound, however, this is not always the case. Since there are no adjectives subdividing the sound spectrum as there are for the color spectrum, a more devious stylistic device is required to evoke a specific sound than is required to evoke a specific color. For literary purposes, sound may be elicited in two ways: onomatopoeia may be employed, in which case the desired sound is specifically imitated and placed before the reader as a model; or the sound may be represented through a complex of comparisons, to a certain onomatopoeic, but to a greater extent synthetic, i.e., explained verbally, element by element, through metaphor and simile. The consequences of this difference determine the extent of the use of sound as image in **Chéri** and **La Fin de Chéri.** First, sound is not employed as extensively for the purposes of emphasis and foregrounding of characters as is color. It needs too much explanation, too much verbal expansion, and one of the outstanding qualities of both these novels is their terseness and tightness of detail. Secondly, where sound is used, the development of the image is rather slow and diversified in effect. And since the concentrated form of both novels gives them their impact and pace, sound descriptions would slow them down, dissipating the desired effect.

This ambiguous quality serves well, however, in the one case where sound acts as a foregrounding element, a crucial indicator of personality, and this is in our introduction to Charlotte Peloux, Chéri's mother. During the course of this introduction one is struck primarily by the sharp quality of the tones: "En marchant sous l'ombre des acacias, entre des massifs embrasés de rhododendrons, et des arceaux de roses, Léa écoutait un murmure de voix, percé par la trompette nasillarde de Mme Peloux et l'éclat de rire sec de Chéri" (24).[2] We think that this, perhaps, is merely a single occurrence of a vivid image until we find it repeated on the very next page: "Il rit mal cet enfant, songea-t-elle. Elle s'arrêta un instant, pour mieux entendre un timbre féminin nouveau, faible, aimable, vite couvert par la trompette redoutable" (25). In both passages we have not only the voice of Charlotte Peloux, but that of others as well: Chéri with his dry laugh, and Edmée with her hesitant, timid tones, pleasing but too weak to make any impression. The contrast is further intensified by the fact that it is Léa in both cases who hears and mentally records these voices, as though another witness were at our side, to confirm our own impressions. Léa's acuity of perception is thus stressed at the same time that the other voices receive initial definition. The "rire" of Chéri, mentioned in both passages, will be discussed later.

It is only several paragraphs beyond this point that we are given the final touches so that we can be sure of the author's intention: "—Il faut la marier, il faut la marier! continua Mme Peloux qui ne répétait jamais moins de deux fois une vérité première. Nous irons tous à la noce! Elle battit l'air de ses petits bras et la jeune fille la regarda avec une frayeur ingénue" (26). Colette announces her inventions; she tells the reader that whenever Charlotte speaks, he will hear her words twice. And this holds true, with rare exceptions, throughout the first novel. It is the second statement, though, which sharpens the sound image and makes it more precise. "Elle battit l'air de ses petits bras," and the image begins to take form with the comparison of Charlotte to some kind of bird. Several pages later, the bird itself appears when Charlotte, near hysterics, "se frappa les seins en poussant des appeals de paonne" (32). The sound of the pea hen, the shrill, raucous cry, accompanied by the batting of useless wings that doubles the intensity and insipidity—this is Charlotte Peloux. "Elle trompettait fort et faux" (28), and her voice is the one constant reminder of her inevitable presence: "Léa mit

une main sur son oreille et Chéri déclara, sentencieux:—Ça serait trop beau, un après-midi comme ça, s'il n'y avait pas la voix de ma mère" (28). The image is fixed and this portrait in sound is repeated often in the first novel: "Elle [Léa] imita la trompette de Mme Peloux en battant des avant-bras:—'L'ombre d'elle-même! l'ombre d'elle-même!'" (53); "La trompette de ma mère vénérée ne lui a pas fait bouger un cil" (56); "Mme Peloux battait l'air et minauda" (63); "Ah! les voilà, trompettait Mme Peloux. Et la forte voix basse de la baronne scandait:—Le p'tit ménage! Le p'tit ménage" (63); "—Je pensais aussi aux Briquettes comprimées, heureusement, flûta la trompette étouffée" (125).

There is in these examples a mélange of parts. It is not the actual sound of "trompeter" alone which carries the image. This verb is commonly used when referring to the scream of the eagle and other large birds. But it is certainly not the eagle to which Charlotte Peloux is being compared. Rather, the sound image that recalls the bird must be reinforced by the movement of wings, in this case of "avant-bras," and also by the repetitious quality of Charlotte's speech, the bird-like monotony of repeated cry and tone.

Another element is admixed, that of metallic, tinny music, a grotesque wind ensemble of trumpet, clarinet, flute and fife, as in the fourth example of the above group, in which the baroness seans as Charlotte carries the melody. We have later excerpts from this same recital: "Elle se mit à nasiller comme une clarinette" (209); "C'est vrai, c'est vrai, approuva en petit fifre Charlotte Peloux" (246); "Les cristaux vibraient au son de sa voix perçante" (250). Charlotte rarely "says" anything. The quality about her that is the most notable is not the content of her remarks, but her manner of expression. She "s'élança en criant" (25), "haleta" (28), "glapit" (28), "soupira" (34), "clama" (62), "minauda . . . gémit . . . s'esclaffa" (74), "rectifia de tous ses poumons" (65), "piaulait" (68), "aboya" (250).

Earlier, Léa had called her the "Harpie nationale" (15), presenting this aspect of Charlotte by way of introduction and setting in motion the sharp sound picture we are to have of her. Later, it is strengthened by Chéri's comment: "Mame Peloux . . . préparait en haut ses poisons du lendemain" (81). Verbal poisons of this type precipitate the following scene, one of the few occasions on which we find Charlotte temporarily silenced: "Un soir, Charlotte lança à trois reprises et comme à l'étourdie, par-dessus les chrysanthèmes du surtout, le nom de Léa au lieu de celui d'Edmée. Chéri baissa ses sourcils sataniques:—Madame Peloux, je crois que vous avez des troubles de mémoire. Une cure d'isolement vous paraît-elle nécessaire? Charlotte Peloux se tut pendant une semaine" (80).

The chaotic potpourri of sounds, as given voice by Charlotte, serves its purpose. As mixed as the total simile may be, it gives clear definition to Charlotte. Sound is her element as surely as color is Léa's. Colette can give in this way all the intrusive, discordant characteristics of Charlotte, at the same time setting her apart from Léa and Chéri. With the interpolation of the bird motif, we have the added bit of vanity, studied self-consciousness and hollow, preening femininity that not only describe Charlotte but distinguish between her stridency and the calm beauty and quiet grace of Léa. Compare Charlotte and Léa in sound, the latter immediately described with a voice "douce et basse" (13), "féminine" (14). Léa is characterized by soft tones and whispers: "Elle murmura, comme on calme une bête" (15); ". . . souffla Léa avec un jet de fumée" (28); "Elle parla sans élever la voix" (51); or even by silence: Chéri is "habitué aux demi-silences de sa sage amie" (58). He spends "certains après-midi de plaisir long et parfaitement silencieux chez Léa" (108). Charlotte at her best can only mimic the silence of others: Mme Peloux intimidée imita son silence" (74).

The images conveyed through these sound descriptions have two different evocative levels, that of immediate auditory effect and that of meaning within the system of symbols of the language. "Murmurer," "soupirer," "gémir," "souffler" are vivid in that they are onomatopoeic representations. "Trompeter" serves almost equally in both functions. It can evoke in the reader the idea of harsh and metallic sound as produced by the instrument, or it can convey the more musical and lyric melody of the same instrument. This evocative power is limited to the one or the other depending upon the intention of the author. The aspect of sound referred to as musicality is, of course, the basis for most sensorial harmony and concord in literature of any genre.[3] It will have a greater importance in poetry, but will also play a major rôle in prose works written by authors who have a strong feeling for rhythm and melody. Colette herself once remarked that she should have been a composer; she claimed that there existed in music a purity, a completeness of expression that could never be achieved in writing.[4] Nevertheless, her prose always strives toward this quality of unity. The reproduction of the natural and immediate flow of speech, the recapturing of even subliminal perception, both effectively transmuted into descriptive language—these seem to be the principal tasks Colette set for herself. It would be convenient here to use the term "organic form" in specifying the ingenuous unity that is the object of her reverence, with especial reference to her use of sensory imagery. But this term has recently been pushed too far to the side of biological analogy. The distinction between art and living being is thereby almost eliminated, rather than heightened.[5]

Whatever the vocabulary we choose, the point to be stressed here is the underlying primitive function of sound, which Colette presents in the two novels through the reproduction of animal-like utterance, combined with musical intonation. The animal motif recurs in the use of sound to portray other characters apart from Charlotte Peloux. Chéri himself is often described in this way: ". . . tandis qu'il murmurait des paroles, des plaintes, tout un chant animal et amoureux" (39); "Elle écoutait, mêlés au clapotis du tremble et aux grillons qui ne s'éteignent ni nuit ni jour, les grands soupirs de chien de chasse" (41); "Il rit, on jurcrait un lévrier qui va mordre" (43). Actual animal cries are reserved exclusively for Charlotte's cronies: "Baronne, vouz ne coupez pas à mon quatre-vingt-dix, chevrota Mme Aldonza" (62); "—Un homme au couvent! hennit en basse profonde Mme de la Berche" (67); "—Oui, oui! dites tout; jappèrent les trois vieilles" (68).

Charlotte fares well in comparison with these three. "Au moins Charlotte a une apparence humaine, elle" (62), remarks Léa as she quietly watches the scene. And her remark sets up one of the bases for a hierarchy Colette is to establish within this society of courtesans, old and young. It is a hierarchy of sound, with the three cronies at the bottom, a little below Charlotte, who rules this lower roost. At the top are Chéri and Léa. The higher the position held by anyone on this scale, the greater his awareness and sensitivity. With regard to sound perception, we see this markedly in the case of Léa. Sounds literally permeate her:

> Il disait ces choses basses, d'une voix assoupie, dont Léa écoutait le son plein et doux et recevait le souffle tiède sur son oreille.
>
> (36)

> Chéri feignait le sommeil, la langueur, pour pouvoir mieux serrer les dents et fermer les yeux, en proie à une fureur de mutisme. Mais elle l'écoutait quand même, couchée contre lui, elle écoutait avec délices la vibration légère, le tumulte lointain et comme captif dont résonne un corps qui nie son angoisse, sa gratitude et son amour.
>
> (48)

> Puis elle entr'ouvrit une fenêtre, tendit l'oreille pour écouter elle ne savait quoi. Un vent humide et plus doux avait amené des nuages, et le Bois tout proche encore feuillu, murmurait par bouffées.
>
> (70)

> Un petit éclat de rire étranglé, qu'elle ne put retenir, avertit Léa qu'elle était bien près de s'abandonner à la plus terrible joie de sa vie.
>
> (137)

In all these examples except the last, the sounds themselves are buttressed with other sensory images, or synaesthesia is employed to bring forth the full impact of the sounds. But sound itself remains the focal point, and one is left with the impression that Léa literally bends under the weight of the vibrations of the air around her. The primitive aspect of sound is well illustrated by the "rire étranglé" of the last example. Produced within herself, this sound warns Léa of the danger of the situation.[6]

Chéri, too, reacts in the realm of sound. He has retained a "sauvage délicatesse de l'ouïe" with its accompanying "plaisirs compliqués" and "sagaces terreurs" (163). His reactions to sound are as strong, though perhaps not as fine, as Léa's. His "délicatesse" is a nervous reaction; he prefers, for example, to move noiselessly: "Le long d'un corridor à demi éclairé de bleu, il avançait sans bruit, pareil à une figure flottante dans l'air, car il avait exigé, du haut en bas de sa maison, d'épais tapis. Il aimait le silence" (171). This is a trait which he may have acquired partially through Léa, in reaction to the almost incessant din in Peloux's Palace. He is almost as sensitive as Léa to nuances and minor tones, to the total implications of the sounds he hears: "Chéri se mit à fredonner en marchant, mais il s'aperçut au son de sa voix qu'il ne fredonnait jamais, et il se tut" (92); "Il . . . leva la tête vers le jour doré, le jardin mouillé d'arrosage, les merles qui brodaient une arabesque vocale sur le cri sec et multiplié des passereaux" (241). In effect, what Chéri lacks in total definition, in body, is almost compensated for by his perception of sound, which defines him as well as the object perceived. Colette gives us here an almost perfect guide to Chéri's mental state, further reinforcing the value of the sound image. This is precisely why his laugh has an unnatural quality about it. Léa remarks on this, as does Edmée: "Tu ne ris que par méchanceté, ou par moquerie. Ça te rend laid" (15); "Il rit, de son rire maladroit et contraint" (84); "Il riait tout bas et ne semblait pas gai quand il riait" (167).

Just as other forms of sensory imagery define and establish settings and milieu, sound is an indicator of time. Chéri's sensitivity further serves in that it is generally he who notes the passing of time, the hour of the day, the bell that rings on the hour. After his marriage to Edmée, he develops an almost morbid feeling for time in its movement, as it is signaled by various clocks and natural phenomena: "Le timbre d'un cartel anglais, au mur, sonna huit heures.—Oh! flûte, grommela Chéri. Desmond, fais-moi une commission au téléphone" (94); "Quand il frissona de froid et qu'il entendait les merles annoncer l'aurore, il se leva" (105); "La pendule d'émail sonna. Chéri se dressa brusquement et s'assit" (142); "Janson-de-Sailly sonna l'heure et Chéri, la tête levée, recueillit au vol les tintements de cloche comme des gouttes de pluie" (162).

For pure musical effect, we must return to Léa. It is the sound of her voice alone that produces melody and song. The soft and full tones of her laughter are a vital part of Chéri's mental picture of her, and serve a like function for the reader. Our perception of Léa is strongly colored by the sounds she utters. There is also the implicit contrast between the sound of her laughter and Chéri's: "Mais un grand rire innocent, sur une gamme grave et descendante, résonna, étouffé derrière une tenture et précipita l'intrus dans une tourmente de souvenirs" (211); "Le grand rire innocent résonna de nouveau, et Chéri chercha la source de ce rire, là, ici, ailleurs, partout ailleurs que dans la gorge de la femme au poil gris" (211); "Elle rit d'un rire incomparable, qui commençait haut, et descendait par bonds égaux jusqu'à une grave région musicale réservée aux sanglots et à la plainte amoureuse. Chéri leva la main inconsciemment pour une supplication" (225).

It is particularly in **La Fin de Chéri** that such extended descriptions of Léa's voice are given. Earlier, the physical proximity of Léa. Chéri's life with her which he took as a matter of course, rendered him less susceptible to any single isolated aspect of her personality. But in this last meeting of the two, Chéri finds himself in an intolerable world, a tantalizing world, peopled with voices and sounds so familiar to him that for a moment he can almost believe that nothing has changed. His acuteness becomes a curse, and he raises his hand as though to ward off some power inherent in this familiar laughter, a sound which has become the symbol of everything that Léa had once been. All that remains is a cadenza, and then the swan song. Confronted with this enormous stranger, "coiffée en vieux violoncelliste," he finally closes his eyes in desparation: "Il retenait un terrible élan de rancune et de supplication, le besoin de crier: 'Cesse! Reparais! Jette cette mascarade! Tu es bien quelque part là-dessous, puisque je t'entends parler . . .'" (217). He opens his eyes again only to be faced with the "placide désastre installé devant lui" (218). Léa's burst of laughter constantly recalls the past: "Chéri goûta, au son grave et rond de ce rire, un plaisir qu'il n'eût supporté longtemps" (218). It is almost with relief, however unpleasant, that he notices the unfamiliar locution in Léa's speech: "Il n'aimait pas ce 'hein' nouveau et saccadé, qui ponctuait les phrases de Léa" (218). The stranger in front of him is then transformed for one final moment: "[Elle] rendit encore une fois un son féminin, tinta tout entier d'une harmonie intelligente. Mais le revenant, rendu à sa susceptibilité de fantôme, exigeait, malgré lui, de se dissoudre" (228). Even the "revenant" is but an illusion. Chéri crosses from one unreality to another. When he arrives in the street, it is an unfamiliar and strange one. His head swims with the color, the jewels, the sounds of a memory that hangs in front of him like a scrim, blocking out all possibility of clear perception in the world on the other side. And it is the auditory impression that is stressed here, making us painfully aware of Chéri's state of mind: "Il y eut encore entre eux, pendant la retraite de Chéri, quelques paroles, le bruit d'un meuble heurté . . . un rire de Léa, qui s'arrêta à mi-chemin de sa gamme habituelle, ainsi qu'un jet d'eau coupé dont la crime, privée soudain de sa tige, retombe en perles espacées . . . L'escalier passa sous les pieds de Chéri ainsi que le pont qui soude deux songes, et il retrouva la rue Raynouard qu'il ne connaissait pas" (229). The preceding scene of substantial clarification, of possible reasonable solution of a dilemma is only an anticlimax for Chéri. His perception is distorted; he can no longer synthesize its components, nor reintegrate them into any meaningful whole.

Edmée, as we should suspect, remains outside this sphere of sound definition. Only twice in the course of the two novels do we find her vitally aware of sounds. In the first novel, still hesitatingly jealous, yet irresistibly drawn to the Pandora's box of Chéri's past, she goes through his belongings, looking for letters from Léa: "Qu'est-ce que tu fais là? Bien qu'il l'eût interpellée presque bas, le son de la voix de Chéri atteignit Edmée au point qu'elle plia en avant comme s'il l'eût poussée" (83). In *La Fin de Chéri*, Edmée reacts to another voice with so completely opposite a movement that the contrast is inevitable. This time it is the voice of Dr. Arnaud: "D'en bas monta, par la fenêtre entr'ouverte sur le jardin, la voix de baryton du docteur Arnaud, qui chanta . . . Edmée fit vers cette voix un mouvement de tout son corps, mais se contraignit à ne pas tourner la tête du côté du jardin" (185). Otherwise, Edmée herself is described in only the most perfunctory manner, and places little or no visible interest in the voices or sounds around her. She changes and her voice quality reflects this change, but she never succeeds in thrusting herself solidly into any scene. She is pointedly oblivious to the comings and goings of Chéri in the second novel, or at least she chooses to exclude him from her awareness as though he were an unnoticed shadow: "Il entra sans frapper, à sa manière, dans le boudoir de sa femme. Mais Edmée ne tressaillit pas, et n'interrompit pas sa conversation téléphonique, que Chéri écouta" (165); "Elle tourna le dos à Chéri, et ne l'entendit pas venir . . . Au moment même, Edmée perçut son mari, ne cria point de suprise et se retourna sans hésiter" (184).

This lack of sensitivity to Chéri's and Léa's world associated with Edmée is part of the same artistic pattern which places her outside the area of any vivid sensory definition. She neither reacts to the intensities which surround her, nor does she receive definition through them. Here, she perceives movement, voice and tone only outside the scope of Léa and Chéri. Theirs is a realm of susceptibility to vocal shadings, pitch and timbre that she can never enter, even after having lived at its periphery for more than seven years. She moves, rather, toward the level of Charlotte Peloux, coming to resemble her strikingly in *La Fin de Chéri*, in attitude, expression, and even voice quality: "Ça fait fatal.— Comme tu aimes les expressions de ma mère, dit-il [Chéri] pensivement" (162).

II. Tactile Imagery

The visual image is certainly the most familiar form of sensory image in literature. Colette relies heavily upon it, but she also make extensive use of touch. The transfer of this sense from the level of physical perception to that of artistic description involves the same kind of general structuring. The tactile image, like the visual image, is a sensation or act of perceiving, but it can also stand for or refer to abstract qualities. It serves as both "presentation and representation . . . [existing] as 'description' or as 'metaphor.'"[7] There is, in Colette's writing, a further dichotomy in the use of this sense as image, distinguishing between indications of space and time. In *Chéri* and *La Fin de Chéri*, both of these functions are important, alternating as any given scene demands.[8]

The definition of minor characters is most often achieved through description rendered in terms of touch. And it is generally through Léa's or Chéri's immediate and intense tactile perception of them that they receive any sharp definition at all. "Les trois femmes regardèrent le jeune homme . . . Léa ne se trompa point à l'expression effarée, vaincue, des yeux de la jeune fille. Elle se donna le plaisir de la faire tresaillir en lui touchant le bras. Edmée frémit tout entière, retira son bras et dit farouchement tout bas:—Quoi? . . .—Rien, répondit Léa. C'est mon gant qui était tombé" (27). In this passage we have a good indication of the unity of impression that Colette is to maintain constantly in her description of Edmée. Rarely does the "jeune fille muette et docile" emerge as an imposing personality. The reader's ideas about her are set in this description, to be reinforced whenever she appears in the first novel. At the same time, Léa's gesture represents, in no uncertain terms, her own personal reaction to and distance from Edmée. Léa recognizes instinctively that she is facing a rival; she taunts the young girl who is mesmerized by Chéri's strange beauty as he stands motionless against the wall. Edmée reacts to any simultaneous stimulus as would someone sipping a delicate and aromatic wine, were his nostrils to receive suddenly the impact of a strong, unpleasant odor from another source.

Edmée changes from the unimposing nineteen-year old girl, "qui a vécu si enfermée, si seule," to the busy young matron, the serious "ange gradé," who enthusiastically supervises the running of her hospital. When Chéri visits the hospital, he makes the rounds of the wards with Edmée: "Elle traversa une salle et posa sa main en passant sur l'épaule de Chéri, mais il sut qu'elle voulut par ce geste de tendresse et de possession délicate, faire rougir d'envie et d'irritation une jeune infirmière brune qui contemplait Chéri avec une candeur de cannibale" (187). Edmée's gesture is a sure indication of her remoteness from Chéri and states unequivocally her own feelings. Were she still in love with her husband, she would touch him impulsively, spontaneously; the gesture would have meaning as an unpremeditated reaching out toward a human being she needed and loved. This is not the significance of the movement. There is no feeling, no affection in her touch, only possession manifested gently to the subaltern. Chéri is quite aware of what is happening; he interprets the scene for the reader, and his own acceptance of the situation explains its meaning most eloquently.

Other minor characters are mentioned relatively early in the novel in terms of touch:

> Les paumes à bourrelets de Lili, les moignons déformés de mère Aldonza, les doigts durs de Charlotte Peloux avaient saisi ses mains, ses manches, son sac de mailles d'or. Elle s'arracha à toutes ces pattes et réussit à rire encore. . . .
>
> Et elle s'élança dans le vestibule, mais la porte s'ouvrit devant elle et un ancêtre desséche, une sorte de momie badine la prit dans ses bras:—Léa, ma belle, embrasse ton petit Berthellemy ou tu ne passeras pas!
>
> Elle cria de peur et d'impatience, souffleta les os gantés qui la tenaient, et s'enfuit.
>
> (68)

This scene has a double function. Berthellemy, "ancien amant de Léa," imposes his aged, withering presence at a crucial moment. For Léa, who has always prided herself on her choice of handsome young men, is now faced dramatically with the intrusive fact of her own aging and her prospective loneliness. Berthellemy touches her just after she has escaped the grasping, clutching fingers of Lili, Madame Aldonza, and Charlotte Peloux. The shattering physical moment of contact with the "pattes" of the shriveled, hard old women is strengthened and doubled in intensity and magnitude by the psychological shock of contact with the "os gantés" of Berthellemy. And Chéri's emotional presence remains tantalizingly in the background, by way of contrast, even though he is no longer on the scene.

Desmond, too, is defined by touch. He is one of the few characters in the two novels whose development and change are progressive, rather than regressive. His whole story is told in the one gesture of the hand-shake: "Il [Desmond] serra la main de Chéri dans une main qui avait changé. D'étroite et fondante, elle s'était faite large, exigeante, camouflée en main probe et un peu dure. 'La guerre . . .' persifla Chéri en lui-même (183). Colette uses an unexpected verb, "camouflée," to indicate immediately to the reader that this is a description rendered from the point of view of Chéri. It is he who makes a qualitative judgment of Desmond, denigrating the changes which have everywhere occurred following the war of 1914. He tries to deny his own weakness through a negative estimate of Desmond, who all too

solidly represents the post-war world of reality. *Ecce homo,* the crass, materialistic man of commerce; this is what Chéri wants to believe. To him, the business world, the world of engagement in practical affairs, and hence Desmond, represent movement toward superficiality, away from feeling and meaning, which was the past. "Je voudrais que les gens ne soient pas des salauds, je veux dire uniquement des salauds . . . Ou bien je voudrais simplement ne pas m'en apercevoir" (206). He does not want to notice, but the physical immediacy of Desmond's hand precludes the possibility of ignoring the changes that have come about.

The baroness de la Berche appears in the foreground only once. With the heat of July weighing oppressively over Paris, Chéri offers to take her for a ride in the country. After stopping for refreshment at an inn on the way back to the city, the baroness suggests that they remain overnight and return early the next morning. Chéri refuses and the baroness "lui envoya une forte claque sur l'épaule.—Oui, oui. Tu vas circuler dans la journée mais tu rentres à la cagna tous les soirs. Ah! tu es bien tenu! Il la regarda froidement" (192). Once on the road, Chéri becomes very nervous as he dwells on the baroness' remark, the untruth of which he dares not contradict for fear of further sarcasm on her part. He comes within inches of colliding with a cart without lights which is moving on the road in front of him. "C'est à cet instant qu'une grosse main se posa légèrement sur son avant-bras.—Fais attention, petit. Il n'attendait, certes, ni le geste ni la douceur de l'accent. Mais rien ne justifia l'émotion qui les suivit, et ce noeud, ce fruit dur dans sa gorge. 'Je suis idiot, je suis idiot,' se répétait-il. Il avança moins vite et il s'amusa des rayons brisés, des zigzags d'or et des plumes de paon qui pendant quelques instants dansèrent autour des lanternes, dans les larmes qui emplissaient ses yeux" (193). The masculine baroness whom Chéri has known since childhood, whom he has made fun of and laughed at, suddenly becomes a part of his world because she lays her hand on his arm in a moment of sincere feeling and sympathy. In spite of her grotesque appearance and unpleasant manner, her warmth and momentary softness provoke him to tears, the first and last he sheds in all the time since he has left Léa.

One other character is introduced through the sense of touch, la Copine: "Une nuit ils [Chéri and Desmond] retrouvèrent la blonde Loupiote, chez son amie dont on oubliait toujours le nom terne: 'Chose . . . vous savez bien . . . la copine de la Loupiote . . .'" (100). She makes so little impression that one cannot even remember her name. But Chéri, sitting quietly on the mat that first evening, looks at her often, "avec une fixité pénible et interrogatrice." He is fascinated by the pearls she wears around her neck and the color of her hair: "Un moment Chéri tendit la main, caressa du bout des doigts les grosses perles creuses et légères, puis il retira sa main avec le frémissement nerveux de quelqu'un qui s'est accroché les ongles à une soie éraillée. Peu après, il se leva et partit" (100-101). "La Parque asservie" has no symbolic name in the first novel; she is only "la Copine"; but she represents as vividly here, as she will later, the destruction of a dream past. Chéri always seeks around him, in people, in objects, some reminder of Léa. He thinks he has found it in the red hair and pearls of la Copine, but when he reaches out to touch his reality, it vanishes before him, leaving only tinted hair and artificial beads. The sensation even causes a nervous reaction in him and he must either back away or deny the validity of his past. So he retreats and leaves the apartment soon afterward.

Thus, even through the definition of minor characters, Léa and Chéri are reaffirmed in their central position. It is one of the characteristics of these two novels that the sensory images, wherever they occur and whatever form they take, are decisive in maintaining the original focus projected by the author. At no point is there any radical break in the direction or tempo which has been established; nor do sensory images, when used to portray emotion or feeling, in any way detract from their intensity. Touch serves to locate the minor characters, but only in relation and with relevance to the major personages. The success of the presentation of these minor characters is due in large part to Colette's ability to sort out the many facets of their personalities, always choosing the most germane, those which define character in its essence.

The description of tactile sensation serves on the one hand as a common denominator of perception; on the other, as a highly selective force at work in specifying action and feeling which has already been outlined in broad strokes. As a common denominator, it gives the idea of immediate physical contact, acting in this way as a base line for reader perspective. That is, throughout a narrative, and in **Chéri** and **La Fin de Chéri** solely in the narrative, images based on touch set the tone of physical immediacy or remoteness. This relative proximity will be the prime indicator throughout of the psychological states of the characters. This is manifest, beginning with Léa's relationship to Chéri which is in effect a continuum of maternal affection and concern, broken for a period of time by their liaison (the maternal aspects of which never really disappear and, in fact, are reinforced by the amorous relationship). This maternal attitude is so basic that Léa often thinks of Chéri and refers to him as a "nourrisson méchant." Their physical intimacy is thus one of constant shifting from the warmth of parental concern to the passion of lovers:

> Léa sourit de le voir tel qu'elle l'aimait, révolté puis soumis, mal enchaîné, incapable d'être libre, elle posa une main sur la jeune tête qui secoua impatiemment le joug. Elle murmura, comme on calme une bête:— Là . . . là . . . Qu'est-ce que c'est . . . qu'est-ce que c'est done. . . .

> Il s'abbatit sur la belle épaule large, poussant du front, du nez, creusant sa place familière, fermant déjà les yeux et cherchant son somme protégé des longs matins. . . .

(15)

> Il disait ces choses basses d'une voix assoupie, dont Léa écoutait le son plein et doux et recevait le souffle tiède sur son oreille. Il avait saisi le long collier de Léa et roulait les grosses perles entre ses doigts. Elle passa son bras sous la tête de Chéri et le rapprocha d'elle, sans arrière-pensée, confiante dans l'habitude qu'elle avait de cet enfant, et elle le berça.

(36)

The second passage occurs shortly before the liaison has begun, the first, during the last year of their time together. But the tone is unmistakably similar.

The pervasiveness of Léa's physical presence and gestures is so strong that Chéri regards them almost as a magical cure to all indispositions. What problem cannot be solved, what unhappiness not dissipated, what ill not remedied by the touch and gesticulation of Léa! And so he attempts to use this magic on his young wife when she is upset: "Que de larmes sur cette jeune femme qui se débat devant lui! Que fait-on pour tant le larmes? Il ne savait pas. Tout de même, il étendit le bras, et comme Edmée reculait . . . il lui posa sur la tête sa belle main dounce . . . en essayant d'imiter une voix et des mots dont il connut le pouvoir: Là . . . là . . . Qu'est-ce que c'est . . . Qu'est-ce que c'est donc . . . là . . ." (86). But the magic does not have the usual effect. Edmée bursts into further tears, while Chéri "avait dépassé le moment cuisant de sa propre émotion, et s'ennuyait" (87). His annoyance turns to anger at Edmée's incessant complaint, and finally, "il lui toucha l'épaule d'un index dur, elle en souffrit comme d'une meurtrissure grave" (88). The harsh words exchanged between the couple seem only the cement used in an edifice, the building blocks of which are these moments of intense physical and psychological contact. Their entire relationship has already been defined a few pages earlier, in a comparison which left nothing to the imagination: "Il retira son bras avec brusquerie et la jeune femme glissa au creux du lit comme une écharpe détachée" (77).

The physical and psychic metamorphoses of Léa are the object of some of the most concentrated attention and artistry that Colette ever devoted to a character in her novels. The sense of touch, used alone as a descriptive or psychological device, could not account for the integrity of effect achieved in Chéri's last encounter with Léa. In this final meeting all the senses are brought into the field, the sense of touch allying itself immediately with that of vision. But if sight presents reality in all its incredible form and vestment, touch poignantly reaffirms the psychological and physical barrier between Chéri and Léa: "Eh! mon Dieu, petit, c'est toi? Il avança comme en songe, baisa une main.—Monsieur Frédéric Peloux, la princesse Cheniaguine. Chéri baisa un autre main, s'assit" (211). No distinction is made between the two hands; they are both strange. Léa herself is not even described in human terms, let alone familiar ones: "Sa main claqua sur sa cuisse comme une croupe de cavale" (217). When Léa touches Chéri, her hand no longer caresses his skin, nor is there any of the delicateness of perfume. Instead it is a hand heavy with rings, artificial and disguised, with no further possibility of meaning for him: "Léa lui frappa l'épaule, y laissa sa main à grosses bagues. et comme il inclinait un peu la tête, sa joue perçut la chaleur de cette lourde main" (220). The hand touches him again, "une grande main, bossuée de bagues qui se leva à la hauteur des lèvres de Chéri" (229): the grotesque, preposterous, unfeeling hand of an old woman. The distance between these two human beings is complete and irrevocable. The tactile description gives a smoothness and fluency to the scene, adding to the dream-like quality of this reality vehemently denied out of existence.

As a selective device, touch indicates motion and feeling of a different, more specific nature. In some of its effects, it closely resembles the type of presentation employed in *pointillisme,* with one important difference. When Colette uses the sense of touch to specify the choice of a particular aspect of an object or person in *Chéri* and *La Fin de Chéri,* there is little of the terse, jagged quality in her images or descriptions that is often associated with pointillist technique *à la* Goncourt. As with their use of inversion, the Goncourts were concerned with achieving certain impressionistic effects when they employed pointillist phrasing.[9] Colette's purpose is more precise: "Elle [Léa] lui brossa les orcilles, rectifia la raie, fine et bleuâtre, qui divisait les cheveux noirs de Chéri, lui toucha les tempes d'un doigt mouillé de parfum et baisa rapidement, parce qu'elle ne put s'en défendre, la bouche tentante qui respirait si près d'elle" (20). Léa chooses the individual components of Chéri's beauty, the objects of her admiration, and sets them in a mental row, to be admired by the reader as well. This is no single occurrence. Colette frequently uses this method of introducing tactile images, of pointing out to the reader the sources of Chéri's beauty and Léa's fascination: "Mais elle . . . tapotait de la main le jeune corps qui lui devait sa vigueur renaissante, n'importe où, sur la joue, sur la jambe, sur la fesse, avec un plaisir irrévérencieux de nourrice" (46); "Elle toucha de l'index, comme pour désigner et choisir ce qu'il y avait de plus rare dans tant de beauté, les sourcils, les paupières, les coins de la bouche" (52).

This same device is applied to the description of other characters. Edmée, in the second novel, is efficient, self-composed, business-like. She attempts to reach Chéri through touch, but only rarely, and with no real concern: "Aussi laissa-t-il glisser la douce main posée

sur sa manche" (252). However, there are tactile images in which Edmée appears, with the emphasis strongly placed on her hardness and competence. These are pointed descriptions of her: "Edmée posa sur son bras une main qui frémissait déjà d'irritation mais qui se faisait légère" (167); "Elle délaissa toute invite voluptueuse, s'assit, posa une main sur le front de Chéri:—Malade?" (241); "Elle jeta sur le corps étendu une couverture . . . et elle tendit soigneusement l'étoffe sur une main pendante, avec un peu de pieux dégoût, comme si elle eût caché une arme qui a peut-être servi" (242). Only once is Edmée's gesture a purely feminine reaction: "Edmée sourit sans répondre, pencha la tête et remonta, en la pinçant entre deux doigts, la dentelle qui bornait le décolletage de sa robe" (195). But her provocative gesture is almost vulgar and her "impudence" has already prompted Chéri to remark on the shocking aspect of her appearance: "Attentive à ne choquer personne, elle choquait pourtant à la manière d'une parure trop neuve, ou d'un coursier de second ordre" (247). Her efficiency is not sufficient to compensate for this lack of grace: "Les domestiques et Chéri redoutaient ce qu'en Edmée ils pressentaient plus bas qu'eux" (247). Edmée touches the lace on her dress and all these elements are incorporated into the gesture that Chéri sees. Earlier, Chéri had mentally pictured a scene at the hospital: ". . . et il [Dr. Arnaud] tiendra dans sa grosse main au coaltar ta petite patte au phénosalyl" (239). But this tone of light sarcasm is rendered blunt a few pages later: "D'ailleurs, l'hôpital avait enseigné à Edmée des gestes professionnels, non point doux mais assurés, qui atteignent un point visé sans avertir ni effleurer la sone environnante" (242). The aseptic mood is continued here in the description of Edmée's hands and touch. The imagery of the hospital, the barren, unfruitful tainting of everything that comes in contact with Edmée epitomizes the "bonne entente monstrueuse" between Chéri and Edmée. Chéri is nothing more to her than one of the patients in her hospital. She tends to his superficial comforts, but remains impassive at the sight of his agonies.

A third and final use of the sense of touch is in the immediate recognition of object or person, in what might be called factual recognition as opposed to psychological perception. The pictorial aspect of detail is the sharpest in this type of imagery. Inanimate objects are artfully presented; Léa's bed is a "chef-d'oeuvre considérable, indestructible, de cuivre, d'neier forgé, dur à l'oeil et cruel aux tibias" (18). Chéri sitting nervously in Desmond's apartment, "gratta la nappe comme à l'examen" (178). The same scrutiny applies to people as to objects; of Deamond, "Il noua ses mains l'une à l'autre, et la flerté commerciale eraqua dans ses phalanges" (178). Or, a gesture familiar to everyone, "Il [Chéri] étendit ses jambes, les baigna dans une région fraîche des draps" (280). Chéri, in the dark trenches, recognizes any object given to him: "Noirs de terre et de crasse humaine, ses doigts de soldat avaient su palper, à coup sûr des elligies de médailles et de monnaies, reconnaître la tige de la feuille des plantes dont il ignorait les noms . . . 'Hé Pêloux, dis vouâr é-c'est qué j'tiens là?' Chéri revit le gars roux qui lui glissait sous les doigts, dans l'obscurité, une taupe morte, un petit serpent, une rainette, un fruit ouvert ou quelque ordure, et qui s'écriait: 'Ah! qu'i d'vine bien!'" (163). This quality of Chéri's sensitivity, this feeling for the distinctive form and texture of objects, issues in a series of tactile descriptions, partially emphasizing Chéri's acuity, partially by way of introducing pure graphic detail: "L'alcool . . . effaçait sous ses doigts l'âpreté des surfaces non polies et des étoffes" (235). One image implies touch without actually expressing it: "Il désignait le sac noir du bout de l'index, avançant le doigt et reculant le corps comme si le sac eût été vivant" (236). The handbag might as well have been a living thing; it was one that had belonged to Léa. One has the impression that were Chéri actually to touch it, the shock would provoke physical pain.

The weight of sensory perception drags Chéri down, like a chronic affliction, almost to the level of immobility. One moving detail is all that is needed to make this idea precise: "Il entra chez son coiffeur, tendit ses mains à la manucure et glissa, pendant que des paumes expertes substituaient leur volonté à la sienne, dans un moment d'inestimable repos" (282). But the key to la Copine's apartment is an enormous physical presence, cumbersome in his pocket. When he arrives there, "sa maladresse à tâtonner autour de la serrure, le grincement de la clef, accélérèrent un moment son coeur" (282). He moves through the flat as though in a dream, and when his automatic decision is finally reached, the suicide scene is phrased completely in terms of the tactile sensations involved in his meticulous and fastidious preparations for death:

> Sans se lever, il chercha une attitude favorable, finit par s'étendre sur son bras droit replié qui tenait l'arme, colla son oreille sur le canon enfoncé dans les coussins. Son bras commença tout de suite à s'engourdir et il sut que s'il ne se hâtait pas ses doigts fourmillants lui refuseraient l'obéissance. Il se hâta donc, poussa quelques plaintes étouffées de geindre à l'ouvrage, parce que son avant—bras droit, écrasé sous son corps, le gênait, et il ne connut plus rien de la vie au delà d'un effort de l'index sur une petite saillie d'acier fileté.
>
> (285)

Throughout this paragraph we are given a vivid account of Chéri's slightest gesture. We follow each of his movements, we hear him complain, we can almost feel the arm that bears the weight of the body, the fingers, tingling and nearly uncontrollable. The childish determination prevents the scene becoming one of melodrama, since all is put in terms of the sensations involved. We assume that these sensations are all that is

in Chéri's mind at the moment. But then we reach the final words of the paragraph, of the novel, and there is a strange feeling of something missing, something omitted, some vital remark or comment as adjunct to the physical gestures that occupy Chéri and ourselves. For during this instant, the extreme simplicity of the narrative, its purely graphic quality, is misleading. In the final line comes the mordant reality of this inescapable denouement which we have really been expecting all along. The impact of the scene is heightened through description which takes the form of a series of natural and direct images. The irony is implicit, for Chéri's death *is* only physical; his spiritual demise goes back in time to the moment of his irrevocable break with Léa.

Sound and tactility are crucial in setting the tone, first for reader perspective, second, in the placement of characters and objects, one in relation to the other. Physical and psychological detail operates at both levels. The element in Colette's writing which one critic calls "questo stupendo accordo di elementi contrari" is often the fusion of object and perception of object through physical sensation.[10] Style, as Proust once pointed out, is never an ornament, but rather, a reality of vision, the revelation of a particular universe. Colette presents her particular universe through the senses. She offers no explicit formula by way of resolution to the specific problem she states in *Chéri* and *La Fin de Chéri*. But her own attitude and answer are implicit in her preference for an idiom that externalizes and materializes thought and feeling.

Notes

1. For a discussion of visual imagery in Colette, see I. T. Olken, "Aspects of Imagery in Colette: Color and Light," *PMLA* LXXVII (1962), 140-148.

2. All page references to *Chéri* and *La Fin de Chéri* are to the text in Vol. VI of *Œuvres complètes de Colette* (Paris: Flammarion, 1949).

3. "Le côté le plus important de ce sens [l'ouïe], c'est la musicalité qui ne s'exprime pas seulement directement dans les fréquentes comparaisons tirées du domaine de la musique, mais aussi, ce qui est plus important au point de vue stylistique, indirectement dans ce sens des moyens sonores du langage qui se manifeste dans le désir constant de faire harmoniser les sons des mots avec ceux perçus par les sens, tout en renforçant les sensations auditives, qu'il s'agit de décrire." Irene Frisch Fuglsang, "Le Style de Colette," *Orbis Litterarum,* 3 (1945) p. 10.

4. Jean Larnac, *Colette, sa vie, son œuvre.* Paris: Simon Kra, 1927, p. 203.

5. René Wellek, "Concepts of Form and Structure in Twentieth Century Criticism," *Neophilologus,* 79 (1958) p. 8.

6. The primitive function of sensory imagery is treated more fully elsewhere; cf. I. T. Olken, "Imagery in *Chéri* and *La Fin de Chéri:* Taste and Smell," *French Studies,* 16 (1962), 245-262.

7. René Wellek and Austin Warren, *Theory of Literature* (New York: Harcourt, Brace, and Co., 1942), p. 177.

8. This stands in contrast to the writing of Proust, in which the sense of touch serves almost exclusively to evoke a temporal flight into the past, as in the combined sensation of taste and touch in the *madeleine* episode. The element of time as it relates to perception has been treated in a study by Hans Meyerhoff, *Time in Literature* (Los Angeles: University of California Press, 1955).

9. Stephen Ullmann, *Style in the French Novel* (Cambridge: Cambridge University Press, 1957), pp. 167-173.

10. Carlo Bo, *Della Lettura e altri saggi* (Firenze: Vallechi, 1953), p. 229.

Donna Norell (essay date 1981)

SOURCE: Norell, Donna. "The Relationship between Meaning and Structure in Colette's *Rain-Moon.*" In *Colette: The Woman, the Writer,* edited by Erica Mendelson Eisenger and Mari Ward McCarty, pp. 54-65. University Park: The Pennsylvania State University Press, 1981.

[*In the following essay, Norell examines Colette's interest in the occult, as demonstrated in* La lune de pluie, *in which the supernatural is a major theme.*]

It has been generally accepted that Colette's famous imperative "Look . . . look . . ." is a call to readers to look more objectively at the world about them, to shed their prejudices and their preconceived ideas in an effort to see that world as it really is. Colette's own considerable descriptive powers were so firmly rooted in long-standing habits of observation that Thierry Maulnier wrote: "Colette never supposes, she sees, she hears and she notices, implacably."[1] His is a judgment almost universally shared by critics, who agree that she was, in fact, a writer who took no detail for granted.

Many of Colette's readers discover with surprise, therefore, that she dabbled in the occult. Her fascination with the material world and her insistence on the importance of the senses in evaluating terrestrial phenomena might seem to preclude the idea that she could be seriously interested in such activity. That is not the case. Colette gives the senses the chief role to play in interpreting the world only because most of the time she is dealing with material phenomena, which must be sensually perceived. But her basic canon of objectivity holds true for every kind of experience. In the twenty or so volumes of fiction, essays, and correspondence that she left to posterity, references to the occult reveal that Colette had direct contact with certain occult practices and that, although she was far from being credulous, she at no time dismissed occult phenomena as nonsense.

Her ventures into this domain were, however, both haphazard and intermittent. Her first important encounter with it took place early in the century, when she accompanied a friend to visit a Russian psychic "Saphira." The friend, a lesbian, was told that she would soon run off with a young man. This event, which none but the psychic foresaw, proved to be true. Over the years, Colette visited other psychics, of various kinds. Two women, "the sleeping woman of Caulaincourt Street" and Elise, "the woman with the candle," demonstrated, she says, a "not very believable (but verified) infallibility" (*L'Etoile Vesper,* XIII: 271)[2] to read the past and the future of their clients; while a third, whom she calls simply "Mme B . . ." and who "saw" the spirits of Colette's father and brother (*Sido,* VII: 216-219), gave her pause to reflect by mentioning certain facts known only to Colette herself. These visits were few in number, but Colette mentions them time and again in her essays.[3] She finds them fascinating, because they are incomprehensible. Looking back, some thirty years later, on her initial experiences, she writes:

> Who will give me the key to Saphira? How does one distinguish, among all that hodge-podge of tinsel, banality, Slavic origins, kabbalistic names, make-up, huge rings and fitted frock coats, the extent to which he possessed real lucidity and powers of sorcery, to use the word that satisfies me the most?
>
> (*L'Etoile Vesper,* XIII: 269-270)

That showmanship, and even quackery, often play a role in such practices, she readily admits, but her observations left her persuaded that there is sometimes an authentic gift involved. An essay of 1922 sets out her position on the whole subject:

> Do I believe, then, in this candle that burns and drips tears of stearin, in the images of the future and the past its disagreeable-smelling fumes form and dissipate? Not exactly. Yes and no . . . Let's get this clear. Pierre Faget and his colleagues in magic . . . they only make me shrug my shoulders. Reading coffee grounds is childish. Playing with yarrow sticks is gross superstition. But the woman with the candle . . .
>
> (*Prisons et paradis,* VII: 396)[4]

Colette's view remained unchanged until her death. She held that, although one must not be blindly superstitious, anything may be possible in this world: personal experience is the only real test.

This is precisely the position taken by the narrator of *La Lune de pluie* when confronted with the enigma of Délia Essendier, sister of Rosita Barberet. In this *nouvelle,* published in 1940 and the only one of Colette's fictional works in which the occult is a major theme, the narrator is presented with a whole series of riddles. Why is Rosita so secretive about Délia? Why has she been crying? How can "thinking" make Délia so tired? What does Délia do with the scissors? Though the narrator is reluctant to abandon her original idea that Délia is pining for her estranged husband, these and other considerations lead her to say: "Since I had come to know Délia Essendier, it . . . seemed to me that more than ever I needed to know [things] by myself, and without consulting anybody else" (p. 385). None of the explanations she can think of seems to stand. Yet she is completely unprepared for Rosita's disclosure that Délia is practicing black magic, that the young woman is attempting to "convoke" Eugène Essendier and thereby weaken and destroy him.

To believe or not to believe in black magic? That is the question posed to the reader of *La Lune de pluie.* It is never openly presented as such. Colette has long had the reputation of a writer who weds prose style to matter. In *La Lune de pluie* she goes farther than that. The entire work is built upon a network of structural elements—narrative movement, digressions, symbols and leitmctifs, symmetrical characterization and relationship of characters—so carefully arranged that all serve to decoy the reader into a position where he is obliged to pose this ultimate question to himself, and even to answer it in a certain way.

The tale (for such it may be called) gives the impression of being constructed upon very informal lines. The narrative seems rambling. Passages on what is ostensibly the subject—"the Barberet story" (p. 374)—are interrupted by reminiscences and discussions of apparently irrelevant topics. Close examination reveals, however, that there is not one narrative movement but two, and that the digressions have important functions of their own.

The narrator begins by relating how, on her first visit to her new typist Rosita Barberet, she discovered that Rosita was living in an apartment in which she herself had once spent many unhappy hours brooding on the unfaithfulness of her (now ex-)husband. As she recognizes one familiar object after another—the window catch, a panel of old wallpaper, the ceiling rosette, the floor plan, the sound of a door, the slope of the front steps—she is left in no doubt but that the house was previously her own. What renders the situation even more strange is that it is because of a man from B . . . , whose accent recalls that of her former husband, "that other man from B . . ." (p. 367), that she has visited the house once more. At her next visit, she learns that

the apartment is shared by Rosita's sister Délia, who, estranged from her husband, spends most of her time in the room the narrator calls "*my* room." The coincidence becomes too much to resist. She penetrates into the room, sees the young woman on the divan, and believes she has found in her what she later calls "my young self that I would never be again, that I never stopped disowning yet regretting" (p. 378). Thus is born the narrator's fascination for Délia Essendier.

The double narrative movement arises out of the narrator's decision to keep secret her discovery of the "coincidence." Colette establishes the duality in the opening scene. There, she presents, in carefully alternated passages, the banal conversation and gestures of Rosita and the narrator, as well as the secret small discoveries that the latter is simultaneously making. For example:

> I lifted the muslin curtain with my forehead and placed my hand on the window catch. Immediately, I experienced the slight, rather pleasant giddiness that accompanies dreams of falling and flying . . . For I was holding in my hand that singular window catch, that little cast-iron mermaid whose form my palm had not forgotten, after so many years. [. . .]
>
> Not having put her glasses on, Mlle Barberet noticed nothing . . . [. . .] a few square inches of wallpaper remained bare: I could distinguish its roses whose color had nearly vanished, its purple convulvus fading to grey and . . . I could see again all that I had once left behind. [. . .]
>
> "This view is pretty . . ."
>
> "Most of all, it's bright for an upstairs storey. Let me arrange your papers, Madame [. . .]."
>
> (p. 361)

And during all the rest of the *nouvelle* the narrator continues, through an alternating inner-outer movement of past description and monologue, to relate what is, in effect, two separate series of events: one, external, centering on the activities of Délia and Rosita; another, internal, centering on the narrator's own reactions and thoughts. Each furnishes the reader with a series of mysteries, strange events, and questions, which are one by one cleared up or answered in the course of the story, but only as they give way in turn to new mysteries, events, and questions.

Actually, the story has begun with an emphasis on strangeness, for the narrator's interest in Délia has been engendered by her discovery of the coincidence of the lodging. It is nourished, however, by concerns that are narcissistic (and not altruistic, as her readiness to accede to Rosita's request that she "talk to" Délia, might suggest). This explains why she is so slow to understand that there is something sinister about Délia's behavior. She is given a whole series of clues, dating even from before the discovery that she has once lived in the apartment. Rosita seems to lie about the length of time she has lived there (p. 360); she does not want to discuss her sister at all (p. 368); she is vague about the nature of Délia's "sickness" (p. 371); she says that Délia has an *idée fixe* (p. 377). As for Délia herself, she claims that her "work" is extremely fatiguing, though she seems to do nothing but lie about all day; she says also that it is good for her to touch pointed objects (p. 392); "I'm looking after him," she says, ironically, of her "boyfriend" standing in the street (p. 394). But so caught up is the narrator by the coincidence of the lodging, that for a long time she fails to realize that the picture she has painted of Délia's psychology has its counterpart only in her own memory.

The reader soon ceases to marvel at the "coincidence." Instead, one's attention is drawn first to the clues, that is, to the many small mysteries in the behavior of the two sisters, and secondly to the narrator's changing attitudes. More than once the latter is tempted to wash her hands of the sisters, but each time something occurs to change her mind. Early in the story, she experiences a moment of aversion on learning that Délia is unhappily married, for, she says, she does not care for "other people's conjugal difficulties" (p. 372); then, her first sight of the "rain-moon"—a halo of refracted light on the wall—and the news that Délia is actually living in her old room reawaken her interest (pp. 372-373). A similar movement takes place when she first suspects Rosita of jealousy, because, she admits, she does not like jealousy either; but again the movement is checked, this time by another mystery—when, reluctantly, she knocks once more at the sister's door, Délia's prostrate form bars her way (pp. 380-382).

It is only after this visit, about halfway through the story, that the narrator herself analyzes the situation. Her awareness of her own emotional attachment to Délia, an attachment in which, however, affection plays no part, now becomes equal to the reader's understanding of it. She says: "Yet I did not like Délia Essendier, and the cherished companion whom I sought, was it not my former self, its pathetic form stuck between the walls of this wretched lodging like a petal between two pages?" (p. 388). She understands that she has *wanted* the coincidence to be significant. Now she sees, as well, that the sisters present a mystery far more challenging than the strangeness of the original event. And so, as has always been her habit, she seeks enlightenment in her own experience. But no amount of reflection sheds light on the enigma of Délia's behavior. Nor, indeed, does further investigation, for Délia's bizarre replies to her questions furnish more mystery than explanation, and the only conclusion supplied by her observations is that the resemblance she has believed to exist between Delia's situation and her own former one has no basis in fact:

"It's fatigue." But what kind of fatigue? That caused by an unhealthy life? No unhealthier than mine, and just as healthy as that of other women and girls of Paris. A few days earlier, Délia had touched her forehead and clutched at her temples, saying: "That's what makes me tired . . . And that . . ." The fixed idea, yes, the absent, the unfaithful Essendier . . . In vain I contemplated that perfect beauty—and, studied feature by feature, Délia's face was flawless—in vain I sought there signs of suffering, signs, that is, of suffering from love.

(p. 394)

The narrator has finally joined the reader in remarking the oddity of the two sisters' conduct. But the reader's interest in her psychology will continue, for her reaction to Rosita's revelations will be every bit as intriguing as was her reaction to the coincidence of the lodging.

With Rosita's disclosure, the narrator comes into possession of all the facts. The disclosure takes place in two stages—the initial one at the sisters' apartment, and its continuation the next evening at the home of the narrator. The latter remarks that Rosita herself has changed. "In less than two weeks," she says, "my 'old young girl' had become a real old maid" (p. 397). And, even though for her visit to the narrator's she has redonned her usual correct costume, Rosita "seemed to have repudiated forever the two little ringlets on her shoulder. The brim of her hat came down over the mournful snail-shaped bun, symbol of all renouncements" (p. 406). This change is significant: Rosita has given up the struggle to save Eugène, believing him doomed.

The tale is remarkable for the abruptness with which it ends. The day after Rosita's visit, the narrator renounces the two sisters, even though she is still enough attracted to Délia to arrange to meet her "by chance" three more times. Then, one final time, she happens to see Délia from afar. Délia is wearing widow's weeds. All the events preceding this last one are reported with commentary, but the last incident is described briefly, cryptically. The abruptness of the ending strikes the reader, for it is extremely effective dramatically. In the course of the narrative, mystery after mystery has been dispelled or cleared up, but not the final mystery of Eugène's death. And, at intervals during her rambling recital, the narrator has informed the reader of her views on a good many subjects, but on the last and most important subject she is silent. The result is that the reader finishes the story with two questions uppermost in his mind. Has Délia's magic actually been successful? And what is the narrator's opinion on the matter?

On the surface, it appears that the reader is free to judge of these questions for himself. But there is evidence that Colette actually wishes to influence the reader, that she wishes, in fact, to oblige him to abandon a good part of any skepticism to which he may be prone.

The first corroboration of this idea can be found in the inner narrative movement, which suggests that the narrator is secretly willing to admit of the efficacy of Délia's activities. Very early in the story, she has shown herself to be secretive, by concealing from the sisters—for no very clear reason—her discovery of the "coincidence." Later, she conceals something else from them, something more important: a familiarity with the occult. Immediately after her first visit, long before she suspects that any untoward activities are taking place in her former abode, she reminisces on her own visits to psychics. "Among fortune-tellers," she says, "those to whom a fleeting gift of second sight is given on our behalf, are rare" (p. 366). It is a statement of faith. Further passages mention similar experiences (pp. 374, 402-403). And, indeed, the narrator confesses that even on the subject of black magic she is not uninformed. "Certainly," she says, "on the subject of simple and popular magic, I was not so unknowledgeable as I had wished to appear in Mlle Barberet's eyes" (p. 403). The inner narrative and the digressive passages are thus useful. They serve, in part, as a portrait of the narrator, leading the reader into her mind so that he may be influenced by her attitude whether he wants to be or not. And they also show that she is not the complete skeptic she pretends to be in front of Rosita Barberet.

They do more. They reveal that, despite the impression she gives the reader of confiding everything about herself, it is completely within the narrator's character to withhold important information. And if she does that with Rosita, why not with the reader as well?

The reader at whom this particular deceit is aimed is, of course, the die-hard skeptic, whose attitude is such that he has decided *a priori* that any so-called experience of the occult is so much nonsense. Ordinarily, such a reader might be expected to dismiss the story from his mind once he gets to the end of it, even assuming that he does get to the end. But the narrator has laid down a special trap for him. Throughout the story, she has continually emphasized the fact that all her judgments are based on observation of empirical data; she has given numerous examples of this type of reasoning.[5] She therefore appeals to the skeptical reader on his own ground of rationality, so that if he accepts the idea that the data she presents on "the Barberet story" is accurate, then he must also accept the conclusion implied. But why does she not state what that conclusion is? Because the conclusion to which the narrator is obliged to come is one at which the rational mind balks. The skeptical reader who identifies with the rational viewpoint repeatedly expressed by the narrator becomes, then, at the end of the story, a skeptic at bay.

Other influences are at work on the more pliable reader. The subject matter of the digressive passages themselves is significant here, for they fall into two main groups. One group deals with what the narrator's past can conjure up of strangeness, that is, with coincidences and contacts with the occult. More than once, in these passages, she concludes that nowhere has she encountered anything quite like the two sisters. For instance:

> Thus, I reckoned up everything inexplicable that had more or less become part of my experience thanks to dull-witted intermediaries, vacant creatures whose emptiness reflects fragments of destinies, modest liars and vehement visionaries. None had done me harm, none had frightened me. But those two dissimilar sisters . . .
>
> (p. 404)

The second group deals with her current activities—writing, bicycling, dining out, going to the flea market, and entertaining her mother, whose presence, she says, "recalled my life to dignity and to kindness" (p. 396). These two types of passages seem to have little in common; but, in fact, the harmlessness of the *voyantes* and the eminent sanity of the narrator's own activities serve to set the present situation in relief and to point up the reason for her uneasiness: "the Barberet story" is singular because it is of evil.

What disturbs the narrator, then, is not Délia's practice of the occult, but her evil intent. After the renouncement, the latter's attraction lingers on, but the narrator is prudent. Recalling the three "chance" meetings, she says of Délia: "Something unnamable, deep within me, stirred and spoke in her favor. But I did not respond" (p. 415). The truth is that Rosita's disclosure has pushed her to the limits of her credulity, for Rosita has insisted that the practice of black magic is far from rare. "She [Délia] isn't the only one who does it. It's quite common," she says (p. 401). "In our neighborhood there are lots who repeat the name. [. . .] It's well known" (p. 412). The narrator muses on this idea: "Whispers, an ignorant faith, even the habits of a whole neighborhood, were *those* the forces, the magic philters that procure love, decide questions of life and death, and move that haughty mountain: an indifferent heart?" (p. 412). She offers no answer, and the reader is left with the question still open three pages later, when the narrative ends.

The double narrative movement and the digressive passages both support, therefore, the idea that, however much the narrator may *wish* not to take the idea of black magic seriously, her rational mind is tempted to accept it, because even in her own broad experience the case is exceptional. Rosita has believed in it all along, and, since events suggest finally that the latter's opinion on this one case has been well-founded, the implication is that perhaps her remarks on society as a whole repose on something more solid than superstition as well. The idea that, under the apparently humdrum stream of everyday life, there flows a darker, persistent current which many people cannot or do not choose to recognize is suggested many times by Rosita. "And the confectioner from downstairs, what has she done, then, with her husband?" she asks. "And the dairy-man from number 57, it's a bit strange that he's a widower for the second time, isn't it?" (p. 408). "It's very well-known" (p. 412). Rosita reproaches the narrator for her ignorance: "A person as well-educated as you . . ." (p. 407). And, indeed, in the lives of the two sisters themselves the narrator has seen evidence that people, and events, are not always what they seem.

This idea is central to the deeper significance of **La Lune de pluie**: the notion that individuals and society as a whole have often a hidden side which we are sometimes reluctant even to know. Certainly, Délia Essendier is not what she seems when the narrator first meets her; nor, according to Rosita, is the little society of the *quartier,* which the narrator had always considered so innocent and picturesque. And Délia and her fellow-practitioners of magic are not even exceptional in this way. Colette suggests, by her portrayal of the other two major characters, that the situation may be universal. The narrator has shown herself to be garrulous or secretive according to the moment. And in Rosita's eyes, her image is that of a "woman alone" (p. 395), that is, of the separated or divorced woman obliged to live, in that first decade of the century, outside respectable society; yet we know, through what the narrator says about herself, that her conduct gives rise to no scandal and that her activities are, in fact, thoroughly wholesome.

As for Rosita, she is, oddly enough, the key personage of the three. Colette has distributed the weight of the narrative interest more or less equally on the three women. The plot, or dramatic interest, weighs most heavily on Délia, since both the narrator and Rosita are interested primarily in her. The psychological interest is, of course, borne by the narrator, in her reactions to events both inner and outer. But the import of the tale is concentrated in Rosita. She is quite unlike Délia. As she says, "First of all, there is a certain difference of age between us, and she is dark. Besides, as far as our characters are concerned, we're not at all alike" (p. 373). She is also different from the narrator, in that she is considered respectable where the narrator is not, and in that she harbors ideas completely at variance with those sanctioned by the respectable society of which she is a part, while the narrator displays no such leanings. And, whereas Délia and the narrator have "hidden" sides, Rosita reveals considerable paradox within herself. This "old young girl," whose correctness of dress and manner is the first thing one notices about her, invites the narrator to watch her step, saying "My sister is lying on the floor" as if she were saying "My sister has gone to the post-office" (p. 382). Even her beliefs are unsoundable. "And what about the devil, Rosita?" asks the narrator, attempting to comprehend the other's ideas. And Rosita replies, surprised: "But,

Madame, what do you mean? The devil is for imbeciles. The devil, just imagine . . ." (p. 413). In a flash of intuition, the narrator guesses that "it's in Rosita, so colorless and prim, that one must seek the solution to this little puzzle" (p. 395). And, indeed, it is Rosita's character which most accurately reflects the central meaning of the tale: that paradox and strangeness are but the obverse of the commonplace.

The characteral significance is supported, in part, by symbolic names. Actually, the narrator herself is never named. To all appearances, she is one of the many Madame Colettes whose lives resemble their creator's own. But Rosita calls her simply "Madame," so that that assumption is never completely valid and the ambiguity of her identity merely adds to the general atmosphere of secrecy surrounding her. On the other hand, "Rosita" signifies "little rose," and is coupled here with the surname Barberet, a play on the French word *barbare* (Latin *barbarus;* Greek *barbaros*), meaning, in its first sense, an outsider, a foreigner, a stranger, and in its second sense, an uncivilized person. Together the two names are perfectly descriptive of Rosita, who in many respects is an innocent young girl but who places faith in practices banned by the civilization to which she presumably belongs.

Her enigmatic sister is "this Délia who did not want to be called Adèle" (p. 415). Adèle is a saint's name,[6] but Délia is an epithet of the goddess Artemis, derived from the name of her birthplace, Delos. The adoption of the name Délia is therefore symbolic of her intention. Less innocent than Rosita, she has abandoned altogether the Christian religion into which she has been born, in order to participate in rites that seek their origin in pagan antiquity. The name Délia is well chosen, for Artemis is goddess of the hunt and of the moon. It is therefore apt that she should assign to herself that identity while she "hunts" Eugène Essendier under the auspices of the "rain-moon."

These names form part of a network of minor symbolic elements designed to support the main idea and to add to the accumulated impression of strangeness. The central symbol is the one designated by the title, the "rain-moon." In the story, the term refers to a halo of refracted light, by which the sunlight separates into its component colors as it passes through thick glass and is projected on the wall. It seems at first to be merely one more of the many things the narrator recognizes as she confirms the fact that the apartment was once her own. But, unlike the other objects, it is mentioned again and again, and takes on additional importance with every repetition. Although the narrator has once considered it to be a symbol of hope, Rosita says that her sister is afraid of it, that Délia calls it "an omen" (p. 372). Later, the narrator asks: "A blind alley haunted by evil plans, was that what had become of the little apartment where

once I had suffered so innocently, under the guardian-
ship of my rain-moon?" (pp. 403-404). In folklore, the
term used in its original sense signifies something else:
a moon with a diffused halo around it, and the belief is
that the "rain-moon" betokens rain for the morrow.[7] So
Délia is right. Just such an announcement, just such an
"omen" it turns out to be, not of love requited but of
death.

A system of number and color symbolism is related to
the central symbol and to the central meaning of the
tale. The number three, which has mystical overtones
because of its association with the Trinity as well as
with various unholy mythical trios, recurs often. There
are three women, of whom now one and now another
becomes prominent, depending upon which aspect of
the tale is being considered. Three segments of society
are also presented: the wholesome one in which the
narrator moves, the strange but harmless milieu to
which the *voyantes* belong, and the sinister world of the
two sisters. Three times the narrator speaks of her experiences of the occult and three times she arranges to
meet a weakened Délia in the street. Symbolically, three
represents the synthesis of duality and unity, so that its
use here evokes the idea that room must be made in our
concept of reality for the hidden side, for the incomprehensible, because it, too, is part of the whole.

Seven is equally important. "The three is after the
seven," observes Rosita, as she rearranges the narrator's
pages (p. 362). She offers to retype the last page, since
"it will only take seven minutes" (p. 362). As she arrives to confide in the narrator for the last time, the
clock strikes seven, and her revelations are delayed
only long enough for her to drink "a glass of Lunel
wine" (p. 406), which is, she says, "a magic drink" (p.
406). In the language of the occult, the number seven
signifies completion, termination, and so in despair
Rosita tells the narrator that Eugène is doomed, that
"six moons have already passed, the seventh is here, it
is the fatal moon, the poor man knows that he has been
summoned" (p. 407).[8]

Significantly, the number of colors in the spectrum and
so of the "rain-moon" itself is seven, with the seventh
color being violet. Mention of this color runs like a refrain throughout the tale, as Rosita asks what color of
typed copies she should make: "In violet or in black?"
(p. 362). But at the last visit she does not ask. "Like a
stranger, Rosita listened and said, 'Very well . . . Fine
. . . In black and in violet . . . It will be finished
Wednesday'" (p. 398). And events do prove finally that
the two colors signify the same thing, for when the seventh and fatal moon is past Délia wears "a dress whose
black turns to violet in the sunlight" (p. 415). The seventh color, like the seventh moon, is death.[9]

La Lune de pluie is not a particularly profound work,
although Colette is a far more profound writer than she

is currently given credit for. But in any case, this tale
certainly provides ample evidence that she is a superb
craftsman. What seems to be a rambling but simple narrative is actually a tightly constructed maze of significant detail, ordered in such a way as to lead the reader
down one or more paths of the author's choosing. Even
in her use of digression Colette achieves considerable
economy, for she ensures that at one and the same time
these apparently superfluous passages dramatize the exterior action, offer the reader insight into the narrator's
psychology, and provide the skeptic with food for
thought.

Many of these passages also add to the immense accumulation of suggestive matter that Colette amasses to
back up the main idea. References to coincidences,
mysteries, presentiments, experiences with the occult,
symbolic names, numbers and colors, and, of course,
the ever-recurring "rain-moon": the sheer weight of
these is impressive. Events, we are shown, are not necessarily what they seem, nor are people. Every phenomenon has two aspects, the seen and the unseen, and, in
that, it resembles the room wherein Délia weaves her
spell, "dark on one side, bright on the other" (p. 363).
What we consider to be true depends, like the color of
Délia's dress, on our perspective.

So suggests Colette in *La Lune de pluie,* where the
narrator consciously chooses to rely on her rational
mind, on her experience, on *herself,* but in the end can
only suspect.

Is Colette, finally, asking the readers of *La Lune de
pluie* to believe in the occult? Not necessarily, for her
intention is always to tell a good tale. But many times
in her works, she expresses the thought that man is
afraid of anything which upsets his serenity, his sense
of being in control. Any occult phenomenon will disturb him in that way. Of her own contacts with the occult, Colette wrote: "I believe that during my lifetime I
have not consulted more than four or five persons gifted
with second sight. But it gives me pleasure to recognize
that their various gifts had the potential to upset our human view of events" (*L'Etoile vesper,* XIII: 268). The
structure of *La Lune de pluie* is designed to do the
same thing.

Notes

1. *Introduction à Colette* (Paris: La Palme, 1954), p.
   58.

2. Unless otherwise stated, all references to Colette's
   works are to the fifteen-volume *Oeuvres complètes*
   (Paris: Flammarion, 1948-1950). References to
   works other than *La Lune de pluie,* which is in
   Volume XI, will give both volume and page numbers. Translations are mine.

3. The most important passages dealing with the occult are, in addition to *La Lune de pluie,* the following: *Aventures quotidiennes,* VI: 428-431; *Sido,*

VII: 216-219; *Prisons et paradis,* VIII: 394-396; *L'Etoile vesper,* XIII: 264-273; *Journal intermittent,* XIV: 260-261.

4. Pierre Faget was a country sorcerer whose arrest and trial caused a minor sensation in France during the winter of 1921-22.

5. See, for example, p. 359, where the narrator discusses the differences in the wear of cuffs and sleeves between scribes and typists; and pp. 384-385, where she remarks on how the movements of certain animals betray their species, and how certain gestures and tics reveal the innermost thoughts of people.

6. The Benedictine abbess, Saint Adela, daughter of Dagobert II, c.675-c.734.

7. In a letter to Lucie Saglio, tentatively dated by researchers as mid-September 1940, Colette wrote: "You know, it's the moon that has a rainbow halo around it and that announces bad weather" (*Lettres à ses pairs* [Paris: Flammarion, 1973], p. 135).

8. According to J. E. Cirlot's *A Dictionary of Symbols* (trans. Jack Sage [New York: Philosophical Library, 1962], p. 223), seven is "symbolic of perfect order, a complete period or cycle." *The Encyclopedia Americana* (Canadian ed., 1950, Vol. 24) gives this explanation: "Various reasons have been given for the peculiar regard had for this number, such as that seven is a symbol of completeness, being compounded of three and four, perfect numbers, they being representable in space by the triangle and the square."

9. Color symbolism is more variable than number symbolism. However, Cirlot says that a superficial classification will have the "cold, 'retreating' colors" ("blue, indigo, violet and, by extension, black") corresponding to "processes of dissimulation, passivity and debilitation" (p. 50). The novel suggests a movement from violet to black in the progressive debilitation of Eugène that will end in his death. This idea is consistent with the more obvious symbolism of violet in the tale, for violet derives most of its symbolism from its relationship to the number seven, being the seventh and last color of the spectrum. Beyond it lies (in non-scientific terms) the void (i.e., blackness). As an echo of seven, therefore, violet acquires the meaning of something ended or completed, and in *La Lune de pluie* that something is Eugène's life. In this way, black—a universal symbol of death—is but the extension of violet, or, in other terms, Eugène's potential death realized.

Robert D. Cottrell (essay date 1982)

SOURCE: Cottrell, Robert D. "Colette's Literary Reputation." In *Women, the Arts, and the 1920s in Paris and New York,* edited by Kenneth W. Wheeler and Virginia Lee Lussier, pp. 8-13. New Brunswick, N.J.: Transaction Books, 1982.

[*In the following essay, Cottrell contends that Colette's reputation in the 1920s was as a "feminine" writer, which may explain why she exerted so little influence on writers in the 1930s and 1940s.*]

In 1920, at the age of forty-seven, Sidonie Gabrielle Colette published *Chéri,* the novel that has often been considered quintessential Colette and that firmly established her reputation in France as a popular novelist. With the publication of this novel, Colette's fame, both as a writer and as a "personality," began to equal that of the two other women writers whose literary reputations, although sadly tarnished today, shone brightly in the twenties. Colette soon became as famous as the mercurial Countess Anna de Noailles, whom Janet Flanner in 1933 called "the greatest poetess France has ever possessed,"[1] and the prolific novelist Radchilde, who in 1889 had published her first and most notorious novel, *Monsieur Venus,* which prompted the debauch-prone Verlaine to exclaim: "Oh, my dear child! If you could invent a new vice, you would be the benefactress of mankind."[2]

A closer look at the nature of Colette's literary reputation in the twenties (as distinct from her fame as a "personality"—actress, dancer at the Moulin Rouge, journalist, model for the New Woman in the postwar years) reveals that she was invariably praised as a "feminine" writer. In the review of *Chéri* that appeared in 1920 in the *Nouvelle Revue Française,* the most prestigious literary journal of the day, noted critic and novelist Benjamin Cremieux praised Colette's prose as being the best "feminine prose" in French literature.[3] Cremieux declared that French women writers of earlier generations—Marguerite de Navarre, Madame de Staël, and George Sand among others—"wrote no differently from men," whereas Colette was an exquisite manipulator of "feminine prose."

If French critics of the twenties—male critics, for no woman commented in print on Colette's work until 1928—extolled Colette's literary style, they tended either to ignore or disparage the subject matter of her novels. She was, they all agreed, a supreme stylist, with an infallible sense of rhythms of the French language. Perhaps compelled by a sense of gallantry, they avoided serious consideration of the values implied in her fiction, populated by resilient women and feckless men. Virginia Woolf expressed the problem clearly when she observed late in the twenties that "both in life and in art the values of a woman are not the values of a man." Since the "established values" of society are essentially those of man, the male critic "will see [in a novel written by a woman] not merely a difference of view, but a view that is weak, or trivial, or sentimental, because it differs from his own."[4]

The concept of feminine prose, so often mentioned in the twenties in connection with Colette's work, must be seen in the context of French literature of the first couple of decades of this century. These years were marked by an avalanche of books by dozens of women writers, nearly all of whom have by now sunk below the horizon of critical attention. Readers (or critics) in the twenties saw in Colette's novels not innovation, but an exemplary expression of certain themes that reappeared with obsessive frequency for some twenty years in the mass of books by women authors, themes that help define what was meant in France in the twenties by "feminine" literature.

There appears over and over in those books a particular kind of lyrical celebration of nature. Anna de Noailles, whose rapturous rhetoric is much less appreciated today than it was by an earlier generation, vibrated tinglingly as she felt herself in tune with all of nature. "I was star, foliage, wing, scent, cloud."[5] Although Colette eschewed Anna de Noailles' grandiloquence and ornateness, in the twenties her fame rested in part, as it does today, on her ability to evoke flowers, plants, and the various moods of nature with a lucidity, tough-mindedness, and tender anthropomorphism unique in French literature. For Colette, as for most women writers of the time, nature was a garden, an enclosure that approximated a room of her own. It was a refuge from the murky world of society, often Parisian society, from the hypocrisy of men.

If nature figures prominently in the feminine literature of the first twenty years of this century, so does the human body. Reacting against the nineteenth-century tendency to study "sentiment" as if it were an entity isolated from the body, French women writers at the beginning of our century sang caressingly and sensuously of their bodies, which they perceived as being in communion with nature. There is a reflection of this fusion of the female body and nature in the *art nouveau* of the period, for here too the flowing lines of the hair and limbs often merge with plants to become part of the general configuration of voluptuous, curvilinear forms.

A character in Colette's fiction, who more than likely possesses no mind to speak of, is above all a corporeal presence. Her female characters are often shown peering into a mirror, scrutinizing their face, neck, shoulders, and arms for signs of fatigue or aging. They examine each others' bodies lucidly and harshly, as if they were examining fruit or vegetables at the market. With even greater care, they examine the male body, or rather the body of a male adolescent with long eyelashes, graceful limbs, and just barely defined pectorals.

In *The Last of Chéri* two aging cocottes discuss the strong and weak points of a man they both know:

> "Oh, my dear, what a disappointment! Tall, yes, that goes without saying . . . in point of fact, rather too tall. I'm still waiting to be shown one, just one who is well put together. Eyes, yes, eyes, I've got nothing to say against his eyes. But—from here to there, don't you see (she was pointing to her own face), from here to there, something about the cheeks which is too rounded, too soft, and the ears set too low . . . oh, a very great disappointment. And holding himself as stiff as a poker."
>
> "You're exaggerating," said Lea. "The cheeks—well what about cheeks? they aren't so very important. And, from here to there, well really it's beautiful, it's noble; the eyelashes, the bridge of the nose, the eyes, the whole thing is really too beautiful! I'll grant you the chin: that will quickly run to flesh. And the feet are too small, which is ridiculous in a boy of that height."
>
> "No, there I don't agree with you. But I certainly noticed that the thigh was far too long in proportion to the leg, from here to there."
>
> They went on to thrash out the question, weighing up, with a wealth of detail and point by point, every portion of the fore and hind quarters of this expensive animal.[6]

An unsettling scene bordering on the indecent? Probably, at least from a male reader's point of view, but couched, as is always the case in Colette, in language of the kind she found in *Lady Chatterly's Lover*. In 1932 she wrote to Lady Troubridge, who had sent her a copy of D. H. Lawrence's novel: "What do you think of this poor childish excited person, the author of Lady-What's-Her Name's Lover? It's terribly adolescent and immature. . . . What a narrow province obscenity is, suffocating and boring."[7] Colette's own fiction depicts a milieu of loose morals, seductive and unscrupulous courtesans, aging roués, baby-faced gigolos, painted denizens of Sodom and Gomorrah. Yet her characters, at least her female protagonists, have an inflexible sense of propriety and morality, which has little to do with an official code of morals.

Many French women writers of the first two decades of this century, evoking their bodies in a kind of pantheistic rapture, found men intolerably crude, insensitive, pretentious. Hence another feature of this literature: an astonishing proliferation of books that deal, discreetly and lyrically, with lesbianism or, to use the word preferred by the writers themselves, sapphism. As portrayed in this literature, lesbianism is the impulse of a tender, often bruised feminine spirit that finds comfort by seeing itself reflected in a kindred spirit. Emerging from their whalebone corsets and multiple petticoats like a butterfly from its chrysalis, French women writers often introduced sapphism in their work as a means of expressing a sensuality no longer brutalized, lacerated, or denied. This sapphic melody, bittersweet and verging on the elegiac, is a narcissistic celebration of self. Sapphism in this literature is, like nature, a refuge, an asylum, a sanctuary. Criticizing Proust for having misrepresented lesbianism in *Remembrance of Things Past*, Colette wrote that "two women enlaced will never be for a man anything but a depraved couple, and not the melancholic and touching image of two weak beings who have perhaps taken refuge in each other's arms, there to sleep and weep, to flee from man who is often cruel, and to taste, better than any pleasure, the bitter happiness of feeling that they are alike, small, forgotten."[8]

This view of lesbianism may seem quaint and outmoded today, too bittersweet to be in fashion. Colette's depiction of sapphism is representative of the way it was treated by French women writers in the early years of this century. Celebration of nature, preoccupation with the body, and interest in lesbianism are subsumed in the larger and more general theme of love. Perhaps at no period in French literature has love been analyzed more deftly, more variously than in the books published by the now forgotten women writers of the first two decades of the twentieth century. Of these authors, many of whom offered subtle insights into the nature of love, only Colette is read today.

On those rare occasions when critics in the twenties alluded to the values expressed in Colette's fiction, in Colette's view they were hostile. The remarks of Colette's second husband, the aristocratic Henri de Jouvenel, newspaper editor and politician, are typical. She reports that he said to her: "Can't you write a book that is not about love or adultery or a semi-incestuous relationship or a parting? Isn't there anything else in life?"[9] Jean-Paul Sartre, writing much later but in the same vein, observed that "a woman's book is one that refuses to take into account what men do. Many men have never written anything but feminine books."[10] Sartre was not speaking specifically about Colette when he made this comment, but Simone de Beauvoir was when she said disapprovingly that Colette "was after all very much engrossed in little stories about love, housekeeping, and animals."[11]

These remarks by Sartre and Simone de Beauvoir suggest why Colette exerted so little influence on the writers who emerged as the dominant and most powerful figures of the thirties and forties in France. Like most women writers of her generation, she did not "take into account what men were doing." In the fifties, novelist and journalist Claudine Chonez commented bitterly that women writers of Colette's generation "missed out on surrealism, missed out on the broad movement toward the social novel before 1914, missed out on the postwar anxieties."[12] Many male writers did too. But the generation of writers born in the first years of this century,

who in the twenties were writing or publishing their first books, were determined not to miss out. Most of these younger writers, such as Simone de Beauvoir and Simone Weil, had not only been university-trained but trained specifically in philosophy. Literature to them meant something very different from what it meant to Colette, whose formal education had ceased at the equivalent of junior high school. Political events in Europe during the thirties, especially the Spanish Civil War and the ever-increasing threat of World War II, made Colette's work, with its faint fin-de siècle aroma, almost as remote as the century of Louis XVI.

During the thirties and forties Colette continued to write, producing the serene, majestic, and exquisitely mannered books of her old age, on which her reputation may ultimately rest. That her voice remained perfectly pitched was, all the younger writers agreed, astonishing. But she was thought of as being outside the mainstream. When Germaine Bree and Margaret Guiton published their influential *An Age of Fiction: The French Novel from Gide to Camus* in 1957, they did not discuss Colette. In their preface they observed that Colette "remained aloof from the principal currents of the time." After her death in 1954, Colette was not forgotten in France, but her books were set aside. So were they in this country. In the early thirties, an American reader could have bought an English translation of most of Colette's novels. In 1973, only four were in print in the United States. Since then, almost all her novels have been reissued in this country.

Notes

1. Janet Flanner, *Paris Was Yesterday, 1925-1939*, ed. Irving Drutman (New York: Viking, 1972), p. 93.

2. Quoted by André David, *Radchilde* (Paris: Editions La Nouvelle Revue Critique, 1924), p. 22. Unless indicated otherwise, all translations in this article are my own.

3. Benjamin Cremieux, *La Nouvelle Revue Française* 15 (1920): 938-40.

4. Virginia Woolf, *Granite and Rainbow: Essays* (New York: Harcourt, Brace, 1958), p. 81.

5. Quoted by Evelyn Sullerot, *Histoire et mythologie de l'amour: huit siècles d'écrits feminins* (Paris: Hachette, 1974), p. 230. This is probably the best survey of French women writers from the Middle Ages to the present.

6. Sidonie Gabrielle Colette, *Chéri* and *The Last of Chéri,* trans. Roger Senhouse (New York: Farrar, Straus, & Young, 1951), p. 218. In the past few years, several critical works have been published that study the significance of the body in Colette's

fiction: Marcelle Biolley-Godino, *L'Homme objet chez Colette* (Paris: Klincksieck, 1972); Elaine Harris, *L'Approfondissement de la sensualité dans l'oeuvre romanesque de Colette* (Paris: Nizet, 1973); Yannich Rech, *Corps feminin, corps sensuel: essais sur le personnage feminin dans l'oeuvre de Colette* (Paris: Klincksieck, 1973).

7. Quoted by Yvonne Mitchell, *Colette: Taste for Life* (London: Weidenfeld & Nicolson, 1975), p. 91.

8. Sidonie Gabrielle Colette, *La Vagabonde,* vol. 4 of the Fleuron edition of *Oeuvres complètes* (1948-50), p. 191. In the English-language translation, *The Vagabond* (New York: Farrar, Straus, & Young, 1955), this passage is on p. 188.

9. Sidonie Gabrielle Colette, *La Naissance du jour,* vol. 8 of the Fleuron edition, pp. 18-19. In the English-language translation, *Break of Day* (New York: Farrar, Straus, & Cudahy, 1960), this passage is on pp. 18-19.

10. Jean-Paul Sartre, *Situations IX* (Paris: Gallimard, 1972), pp. 18-19.

11. Quoted by Biolley-Godino, *L'Homme objet,* p. 140.

12. Claudine Chonez, "Hier, aujourd'hui, demain," *La Table Ronde* 99 (March 1956): 63.

Marianna Forde (essay date February 1985)

SOURCE: Forde, Marianna. "Spatial Structures in *La Chatte*." *The French Review* 58, no. 3 (February 1985): 360-67.

[*In the following essay, Forde argues that the dominant theme in the novella* La Chatte *is the search for and defense of a space, which informs the action, provides a complex organizing element, and aids interpretation of the work.*]

The characters in Colette's novels are intimately linked with the spaces which they occupy, remember, or search for. This study of **La Chatte** intends to show that in addition to extending and illuminating characterization, the spatial structures in this novel inform the action, provide a complex organizing element, and are an essential factor in the interpretation of the story.

First published in 1933, **La Chatte** is a product of Colette's maturity and one of her most popular novels. It has been the subject of several studies, focusing on character, point of view, theme, and genesis.[1] There has not been any study of space in this novel. Three recent dissertations on Colette, one of them entirely and the other two partially concerned with the question of space, exclude **La Chatte** from their discussion of that subject.[2]

The method chosen here for analysis of spatial structures in **La Chatte** is the system of binary oppositions developed in separate ground-breaking studies by Jean Weisgerber and Michael Issacharoff.[3] While recognizing the monumental and enduring importance of the work of Gaston Bachelard, Joseph Frank, Georges Poulet,[4] and others who have written about literary space, Weisgerber and Issacharoff prefer an approach by binary oppositions as part of a way to distinguish between verbal space in the narrative and psychological space or concrete space in the real world. Bachelard, for example, with his concept of "topo-analyse" or "l'étude psychologique systématique des sites de notre vie intime" (p. 27) does not make this distinction. For Issacharoff, "un décor verbal est avant tout un *système* fait de signes spatiaux, ceux-ci étant constitués par une série d'oppositions" (p. 119). In this signifying structure formed by binary oppositions, the various possible pairs (up/down, open/closed, static/dynamic, etc.) will not have *a priori* meaning but will acquire meaning by virtue of their function in each individual system. Objects, clothes, gestures, and larger motions will be part of the space.

La Chatte is a story of marital failure. A dominant theme shaping the plot is the search for and the defense of a space. When he marries Camille, Alain leaves his family's old-fashioned home and beautiful garden in Neuilly to go with her to live temporarily in a borrowed modern apartment in a triangular building called the Quart-de-Brie. Scorning certain antiquated details of Alain's house, Camille initially prefers the modernity of the apartment, but as she settles into married life and entertains the idea of a family, she develops a preference for the lodgings being constructed for the young couple adjacent to the Neuilly home. Explaining this reversal to Alain she says, "Mais tout de même . . . Et puis c'est ta maison, ici, ta vraie maison . . . Notre maison . . ." (p. 68).[5] Alain mentally replies, "Pas ici, pas ici—pas encore" (p. 69), and in a turnabout of his own he now prefers to stay in the modern apartment to keep Camille from invading the home and garden where Saha the cat was his constant companion. As the marital incompatibility increases, the story consists of Alain's frequent physical and psychological flights from the apartment back to his home, the space of his bachelor solitude. His primary preoccupation is this: "Comment empêcher Camille d'habiter MA maison?" (p. 99). Camille's attempt to kill Saha gives Alain justification for his final flight. Camille has not been allowed to enter his space, nor have they been able to make a new space together.

This article will focus primarily on the dominant spatial polarity in *La Chatte,* the down/up pair, and on imagery and some secondary pairs closely related to it. Three other pairs which are initially more apparent to the reader may be mentioned here first in passing: old/modern, noble/common, animate/inanimate. Many of the details describing Alain's home, servants, family business, garden, clothing, and cat fall into the old, noble, and animate categories, whereas Camille's clothing, gestures, family occupation, and the borrowed apartment which she initially prefers may be classified under the opposite term of each polarity. In a longer study each one of these pairs could be examined in detail, revealing further the complexity of the spatial structures in this novel. What is relevant for my present purpose is that these three more obvious polarities seem at first to magnify Alain's character at Camille's expense. Critics have tended to take sides rather vigorously in the marital dispute, and those who favor Alain cite, in addition to Camille's attempt on Saha's life, her brash modernity, her lack of refinement, and a hard, brittle, even inhuman quality in her character which harmonizes with the mineral substance of the walls and furnishings in the Quart-de-Brie apartment.

One critic, after brushing a condemnatory portrait of Camille, proposes the garden as an antidote to all the evils of contemporary society, thereby making Camille seem representative of that society: "But *La Chatte* is a parable and a warning and should be interpreted as such. As the powerless witness of the systematic degredation of humans through the 'rat race,' its abusive demands, the abuses of power and the violence and crimes they lead to, Colette feels the need to return to the primal innocence, the unrepressed world of Nature."[6] Nature, represented by his garden, is one of Alain's spaces, and this quotation identifies Colette with Alain through that space. The animate/inanimate pair creates an extended opposition in some readers' minds, lining up Alain, the garden, and Colette herself against the Quart-de-Brie and Camille, thus suggesting authorial favoritism and approval. How can Alain be at fault when Colette has endowed him with her well-known love of nature?

But the down/up pair, the most penetrating and complex of the spatial structures in *La Chatte,* adds density to this deceptively simple story and sheds a new light on the representation of nature. In the most obvious example of this opposition, the height of the Quart-de-Brie is constantly contrasted with the level of the garden lawn, and in Alain's perception this is a contrast between the unnatural and the natural. Camille is fearless in the apartment's elevation, but Alain is beset by a definite uneasiness expressed by recurring marine imagery. "Tout cet horizon chez soi, dans son lit . . . Et les jours de tempête? Abandonnés au sommet d'un phare, parmi les albatros" (p. 50). In this space Alain has "le

mal des airs" (p. 99). In contrast, his beloved *pelouse* represents *terra firma,* security. To many, a high-rise may well symbolize the undesirable aspects of modern society while a tranquil lawn suggests sanity, but in *La Chatte* this particular contrast is presented through the emotional screen of Alain's fears. This fact and the following image give a peculiar twist to the idea of what is natural. In his fatigue Alain expresses this wish: "Dormir là, sur l'herbe, entre le rosier jaune et la chatte" (p. 63). The recumbent position, characteristic of Alain and a sign of his inertia, here coincides with and intensifies the relatively lower position of the lawn as a symbol of his need for security.

It is indicative of the structural importance of the downward signs that the novel begins and ends with one. The first example, on page one, is the first glimpse of Alain: "Elle en appelait du regard à son fiancé, vaincu au fond d'un fauteuil." The significance of this first sign of inertia and withdrawal—sunk down in the chair, Alain is separate from and unresponsive to Camille—is magnified by the focus of narration. Generally in *La Chatte* the focus of narration resides in Alain; Camille is seen from the outside. In this sentence, however, although Camille is still perceived from the exterior as she appeals to Alain by a glance, he too is seen by her as well as by what Mieke Bal calls the *narrateur-focalisateur*[7] and by the reader, both of whom also see her see him. Since Camille's glance is seen strictly from the outside, she does not become a true *focalisateur* here in this sentence, although she very nearly does. Bal defines this as a seeing with: the *narrateur-focalisateur* sees with the character (p. 41). In the context of this study of space Camille's glance serves to direct the reader's gaze toward Alain's position. The significance of this technique is confirmed by the presence of an almost identical situation in the final paragraph of *La Chatte* which recalls and clarifies the earlier scene. At the end of the story "Alain à demi couché jouait, d'une paume adroite et creusée en patte, avec les premiers marrons d'août" (p. 183). This return to the downward position in a more extreme form is underlined by an identical *focalisation*. Camille, on her feet and leaving, turns to look at Alain, and again the *narrateur-focalisateur* and the reader see her see him. Here she gives not a glance intended as communication but a direct look at a totally unaware Alain, psychologically incapable of any communication. She directs the reader's eyes toward Alain playing with chestnuts in an animal-like posture. He has regressed so far into his solitude by the end of the story that the adverb *humainement* relating to Saha's manner of watching Camille's departure places Alain at least a step below the cat on the scale of life. This more obvious final message refers back to and heightens the meaning of the reader's initial vision of Alain.

Between these two framing figures there are numerous other downward signs shaping Alain's space, some of them again created by his physical position. One of the scenes in which a recumbent Alain observes Camille moving about on her feet occurs the morning after the wedding night. Alain lies in bed and reacts with disapproval while Camille parades in the nude. This scene reproduces the anecdote which Colette recounts in **"Nudité"** and which figures among the sources for **La Chatte**—the confidences of a young neighbor shocked by his new wife's too abrupt loss of modesty[8]—and shows an important coincidence of genesis and sign. In two other scenes Alain stands in the garden looking up at his mother in a higher position. Their conversation in the second of these scenes, where his mother stands above him on the *perron,* leads her to exlaim, "Mon Dieu! quel enfant!" (p. 169). His lower position and her exclamation emphasize his emotional immaturity.

Alain's oneiric space is also part of the downward direction of the down/up structure. The dream is a descent by stages, complicated by swirling motion and shadow. Alain consciously cultivates his dreams as an escape into his own private world. One of his psychological returns to the dream occurs at the crucial moment when Alain and Camille are watching fireworks from the Quart-de-Brie balcony and Alain begins to realize that Camille is responsible for Saha's fall. Some of the brilliant constellations recall shapes from his dreams, and Alain makes mental note of them for subsequent use. "J'ai trop négligé mes rêves . . ." (p. 145). Margaret Davies interprets the music and fireworks accompanying this scene as "a sort of recall to his dreams, an announcement of the triumph of the fantasy world."[9] Since, in addition to the constellation forms, the fireworks also contain specific pendent and falling shapes, the spatial structure here confirms and enlarges upon Davies's observation, visually reinforcing the link between the recall of the fireworks and the self-centered world of the dreams.

Alain's garden, already five steps lower than the house, displays various pendent shapes and botanical symbols coinciding with them. The elms bring hanging shapes together with suggestions of age and claustrality: "De très grands arbres, d'où pleuvait la noire brindille calcinée qui choit de l'orme en son vieil âge, [. . .] défendaient [la maison] du voisin et du passant" (p. 12). More curiously, a dead tree standing upright in the center of the lawn and mentioned four different times makes a devastating statement about the garden space, carrying the first term of the old/modern polarity to its ultimate conclusion. Two vines extend this symbolism. The *chèvrefeuille* draping the tree in the first scene suggests the idea of the loving couple by association with Tristan and Iseut.[10] In **La Chatte** the *chèvrefeuille* offers "le miel de ses premières fleurs" as Camille serves "les sirops de dix heures" to Alain (p. 8), associating the

honeysuckle with Camille. Alain seated passively in his armchair is then the dead tree. On the second appearance of the tree, the polygonum vine, which has a hermaphroditic flower, specifically hangs down from its arm-like branch, joining a cluster of suggestions to this pendent shape: self-sufficiency, self-love, and death. The idea of death is again evoked by the branch of poisonous laburnum hanging directly in front of Alain's window. In one scene the laburnum actually points to the cat sitting under it on the window sill. The garden is poisonous and so is Alain's feeling for Saha, because they stunt his emotional growth, keeping him attached to the past and to himself. An unchanging heart shaped bed of red sage which delights Alain on his final return to the garden clearly represents his own heart, protected and ensnared in this private space.

All of the above botanical symbols, coinciding with examples of downwardness, are also highlighted by framing and focalizing techniques. Either they are seen through windows, or Alain's eyes are specifically directed toward them. Significantly, the *focalisation* in these instances is minimal, a seeing with limited knowing. It is a device to draw attention to the signs; but the diminished knowing, clearly indicated by the author, is also important in itself: "Il leva les yeux sur son domaine d'enfant privilégié, qu'il chérissait et *croyait* connaître" (p. 32, emphasis mine). Alain sees the beauty of the garden, but he does not understand its limitations and dangers as a space for his life.

Three more binary pairs extend the effect of the down/up group. In the first scene of the novel, Alain's repeated lethargic escapes toward the garden—his glance in that direction, his going down into the garden, his later flight further into its shadows—establish a slow rhythm against which is set contrapuntally a contrasting series of action verbs describing Camille's energetic movements, a continual staccato in the *passé simple*. This contrast produces the static/dynamic pair. Camille is a study in perpetual motion. She is constantly defining her own space by her gestures. Her clothing, hair, and make-up display a dynamic color scheme, black and white with touches of red, whereas the greens and blues associated with Alain's space are quietly adjacent on the color scale. A character trait related to Camille's dynamic spatial structure is her sexual aggressiveness.

A past/future contrast also takes shape in the first pages of **La Chatte.** Camille shuffles cards and sets them out cabalistically to play at predicting the future. Here and throughout the novel when information and scenes outside the present are evoked, the future is generally expressed in Camille's words, through her plans and prophesies; the past is more often recounted in Alain's memories. This polarity belongs to the aspect of time, but the visual component of these anachronisms relates them to space also. Alain's downward space seems accentuated by his passiveness and by the past orientation of his thoughts. Camille's upward space is enriched by both the dynamic element and the visual content of the future evocations.

A final binary group has already been suggested by the sheltering trees in the garden: Alain's space is claustral. It may be contrary to expectation that in the closed/open pair an outdoor space appears closed and a small city apartment is open. The Quart-de-Brie apartment is open because of its height and the many windows which provide a view of the entire city. By contrast, the windows in Alain's house open only onto his garden, from one private space to another, and each window frames a symbol of death.

In the threatening openness of the Quart-de-Brie, Alain has to find claustral spaces to shelter his solitude. He acquires the habit of escaping from the marriage bed to finish the night alone on a narrow couch in the small *salle d'attente,* first closing all the curtains. "Il fermait de part et d'autre les rideaux opaques d'étoffe cirée [. . .]. Il respirait sur son corps l'arôme même de la solitude, l'âpre parfum félin de la bugrane et du buis fleuri" (p. 122). The botanical references transport the atmosphere of the garden to this sheltering nook and also make yet another symbolic statement. The *bugrane,* also called *arrête-boeuf,* rest-harrow in English, is known as a troublesome weed whose long roots impede the progress of the plow. This anti-progress symbol relates to Alain's side of the past/future and old/modern polarities. Sometimes Alain's flight takes him to the balcony of the apartment, where an infuriated Camille finds him awaiting the dawn, huddled in a tight little group with Saha. Basking together in their nostalgia for the garden, they shut Camille out from the private emotional world which encloses them.

Must we then totally condemn Alain on the basis of his downward, static, past-oriented, claustral, poisonous, and moribund space, and for his inertia, withdrawal, egotism, and immaturity? The text expresses hope through his mother's attitude as she listens to him talk of divorce: "Elle écoutait son fils avec douceur, sachant que certaines causes fructifient en effets imprévus, et que l'homme est obligé, au long de sa vie, de naître plusieurs fois sans autre secours que le hasard, les contusions, les erreurs" (p. 171). There will be hope for Alain if he can be reborn at some future time and finally free himself from the womb of the garden. Often in Colette's work the native village and the garden are places of rest and renewal, offering necessary asylum for convalescence after the artificial life of the city and the bruising experience of sentimental disillusionment. But the text of *La Chatte* suggests that if asylum is more than temporary it becomes destructive. Colette must sympathize with Alain because of his love of na-

ture and his love for a cat, but the difference between the two is the author's ludicity: nostalgia for the garden has finally to be overcome. Jean-Pierre Richard observes that Colette portrays her own mother's garden as a potentially claustral space, but that there are necessary avenues of escape from this maternal paradise, the low walls, for example, which are in reality "ouvertures déguisées":

> La question est alors de savoir, non pas pour le personnage maternel lui-même bien sûr, mais pour ceux qui dépendent de lui, la jeune Colette et ses deux frères, comment s'affranchir d'un lieu si parfaitement fait à leur mesure: comment en sortir pour être individuellement eux-mêmes, comment, en somme, y venir, ou plutôt peut-être aller au monde. [. . .] Le jardin c'est aussi le lieu dont il faut savoir s'extraire si l'on veut arriver, vraiment, à l'existence. Faute de quoi on s'y étouffera, étiolera, désespérera peut-être.[11]

In separating Alain from complete identification with and justification by Colette, I am in agreement with the conclusion reached by Mieke Bal through an entirely different route, her study of *focalisation.* According to Bal, readers have been falsely led into assuming the identification because Alain is vested with the focus of narration more often and on more levels than Camille: "Alain, en tant que personnage et en tant qu'instance, est avantagé" (*Narratologie,* p. 53). This advantage, the initially less flattering view of Camille, and the tendency to identify Alain with Colette through the garden conceal Camille's qualities at first.

Once Alain is separated from the shelter of authorial favoritism, a fairer picture of Camille can emerge. Are not some of Camille's negative qualities—her lack of refinement, her habit of taking initiative—reprehensible only when measured against a certain ideal of passive femininity? They do not justify the extreme condemnations of some critics.[12] On the symbolic level they show a realism concerning progress, which is sometimes accompanied by an offensive disregard for the refinements of the past. On the positive side, Camille's space is open, upward, dynamic, modern, and future oriented. As a rootless outsider, Camille is unencumbered by tradition. The text shows her often creating her own space. She is a healthy, energetic young woman whose hard edges soften somewhat as she evolves toward the desire to create a home and start a family. The suggestion of new life emanating from Camille contrasts curiously with the repeatedly mentioned dead tree in the middle of Alain's garden, that "fût desséché" (p. 63).

Many readers cannot forgive Camille for trying to kill Saha, and she does seem heartless, relentlessly stalking the cat on the balcony. But who is Saha? On one level she is a character with serious claims on Alain's affections. If this makes a triangle in the character structure, the basic spatial structure is nevertheless binary. Except for her jumping and other motions, Saha does not have her own space but shares all of Alain's spaces. Because of this, Saha seems also to be an aspect of Alain's space, as well as being almost an aspect of his self, through the qualities which he thinks they have in common. Far from being a mere plaything, Saha has the uniqueness of a *grand amour,* and this love is an intensely integral part of Alain's innermost being, "son secret, qui était un secret de pureté" (p. 150). In **La Chatte,** "pureté" designates the untouchable fantasy world as opposed to the brashness of the real world.

In spite of Alain's protestations that Saha is not a rival for her, "Tu ne peux avoir de rivales que dans l'impur" (p. 55), Camille is correct in not believing him: "Il y a rivale et rivale, dit Camille sarcastiquement" (p. 150). Saha is the most tangible barrier between the young woman and Alain's private self. Camille's attempt on Saha's life is a desperate attempt to reach Alain. But Camille has forgotten that one does not easily kill a cat, nor another person's self-centeredness. Camille is guilty of violence, and a quotation cited above seems to identify Camille and her space with violence, crimes, and abuses of power. But actually one can say that the spatial structures of **La Chatte** put power—in the form of the past, tradition, and elitism—on Alain's side, the power of the passive status quo, which must take some of the responsibility for the frustrated counter-violence it inspires. Certainly the author's sympathies go out at least as much to Camille as to Alain; there is a delicate and intriguing equilibrium at work in the conception of these two contrasting protagonists.

Notes

1. Mieke Bal, *Complexité d'un roman populaire: ambiguïté dans "La Chatte,"* (Paris: La Pensée Universelle, 1974); M. Bal, "Narration et focalisation," in *Narratologie: essais sur la signification narrative dans quatre romans modernes* (Paris: Editions Klincksieck, 1977), pp. 21-58; Beverly Bourgoyne, "*La Chatte* par Colette: 'un pas de trois',' *Proceedings, Pacific Northwest Conference on Foreign Languages, Twenty-first Annual Meeting,* 21 (3-4 Apr. 1970), 24-26, ed. Ralph W. Baldner (Victoria, B.C.: U. of Victoria); Claire Quilliot, "Colette, *La Chatte* et le métier d'écrivain," *Revue des Sciences Humaines,* 33, No. 129 (Janvier-Mars, 1968), 59-77; J. Carrascal Sanchez, "Les Personnages et l'élément comparatif dans une œuvre de Colette: *La Chatte,*" *Revue du Pacifique: Etudes de la Littérature Française* 2 (1976), 50-60.

2. Ann Leone Philbrick, "Space as Metaphor and Theater: The Individual's Search for Place in Selected Works of Colette," *DAI* 40: 5889A; Simone Robaire-Lavoie, "Les Structures dans l'œuvre romanesque de Colette," *DAI* 39: 2261A-62A; Rose-

mary Smith Virk, "The Poetic Imagination of Colette," *DAI* 35: 4568A.

3. Weisgerber, *L'Espace romanesque* (Lausanne: Editions l'Age d'Homme, 1978); Issacharoff, "Qu'est-ce que l'espace littéraire?", *L'Information Littéraire,* 30 (1978), 117-22.

4. Bachelard, *La Poétique de l'espace* (Paris: Presses Universitaires de France, 1974); Frank, "Spatial Form in Modern Literature," *Sewanee Review,* 53, Nos. 2-3, and *The Widening Gyre* (New Brunswick: Rutgers U. Press, 1963); Poulet, *Les Métamorphoses du cercle* (Paris: Plon, 1961) and *L'Espace proustien* (Paris: Gallimard, 1963), to name just a few works by these authors.

5. For page references to *La Chatte,* Le Livre de Poche edition (Paris: Hachette, 1960) was chosen because of its availability.

6. Anne Duhamel Ketchum, "Colette and the Enterprise of Writing: A Reappraisal," in *Colette: The Woman, The Writer,* ed. Eisinger and McCarty (University Park: The Pennsylvania State U. Press, 1981), p. 28.

7. Mieke Bal, *Narratologie,* p. 40, formulated this term to indicate the solidarity of the two *instances, narrateur* and *focalisateur,* when they operate on the same level in relation to their objects. Bal created the word *focalisateur* to indicate the performer of *focalisation,* this latter notion having been formulated by Gérard Genette (*Figures III,* Paris: Seuil, 1972, p. 206), who was the first to separate *focalisation* from *narration* in literary theory. Genette uses *personnage focal* for the performer of *focalisation,* but Bal's *focalisateur* is both more versatile and more precise. Bal's very interesting study proposes important modifications of Genette's analysis.

8. In *Belles Saisons* (Paris: Flammarion, 1955).

9. Davies, *Colette* (New York: Grove Press, 1961), p. 89.

10. Marie de France, *Lais* (Oxford: Basil Blackwell, 1947), p. 125.

11. Richard, "L'Ail et la grenouille," *La Nouvelle Revue Française,* 308 (1978), p. 101.

12. Elaine Marks, *Colette* (New Brunswick: Rutgers U. Press, 1960), describes Camille as less human than the cat; for another critic Camille is an example of the negative subtype of the young adolescent woman in Colette's writing; Sylvie Romanowski, "A Typology of Woman in Colette's Novels," in *Colette: The Woman, the Writer;* Anne D. Ketchum calls Camille "cette femme égoïste et basse" in *Colette, ou la naissance du jour* (Paris: Lettres Modernes, Minard, 1968).

Bethany Ladimer (essay date May 1989)

SOURCE: Ladimer, Bethany. "Moving beyond Sido's Garden: Ambiguity in Three Novels by Colette." *Romance Quarterly* 36, no. 2 (May 1989): 153-67.

[*In the following essay, Ladimer argues that the common subject of the three novellas* La Chatte, La Fin de Chéri, *and* Le Blé en Herbe *is the constitution of the female self.*]

Many of Colette's novels retrace at least a portion of a characteristic itinerary: the heroine, or female protagonist, leaves the sanctuary of her mother's home while still quite young to embark upon amorous adventures, almost invariably disappointing, and then returns, often with advancing age, to a serene acceptance of the wisdom of Colette's mother, Sido. This pattern of return to the place of origin is of course not exclusive to Colette's heroines; indeed, it applies equally well to male protagonists in the works of other novelists, and one might even say that in this respect Colette's heroines follow an essentially male model. The constitution of the female self emerges each time as the major theme, and most critics would probably agree that the self arrives at its full potential and expression of identity only with reference to the mother. Yet the development of this theme is tied to an aesthetic of ambiguity, which largely results from the simultaneous portrayal of conflicting parts of the self. In the novels written after 1920, the narrative often involves a triangle with one man and two women, and in *Le Blé en Herbe* (1923), *La Fin de Chéri* (1926), and *La Chatte* (1933) the principal character is male. These three novels share many other characteristics, including a particular type of ambiguity connected to the mother or mother figure. This article argues that the constitution of the female self is also the subject of these three novels in which the protagonist is a young man.

In terms of the narrative, Alain, Chéri, and Phil find themselves in a similar situation. They are poised at a decisive moment early in life between two women who represent the mother figure and a young wife or lover. In Alain's case, the maternal role is shared by the cat and Mme Amparat, Alain's mother; the cat stands between Alain and Camille. In Chéri's case, the memory of Léa prevents Chéri from joining Edmée in a new postwar life. Phil's attachment to Mme Dalleray interferes with his feelings for Vinca. The young man's dilemma represents not only a rite of passage, as critics have seen in the case of Phil and Chéri, but also a less banal moment of decision for the self between two modes of existence.

In *La Chatte, La Fin de Chéri,* and *Le Blé en Herbe* the reader is invited, primarily by means of "focalizing" techniques, to share in the thoughts and feelings of the three male characters.[1] Nevertheless, the reader experiences ambivalence toward them because their point of view often conflicts with the textual realities of the young man and woman as described by the symbolic system, i.e., the set of descriptive elements within the text considered in their relationship to each other. Although the male characters have an excellent opportunity to argue their cases, they do not ultimately serve as a model of conduct within Colette's literary universe, as I shall demonstrate. The women, on the other hand, display certain compelling, positive characteristics, even in the portraits sketched by the male focalizers.

Thus, in *La Chatte,* Alain does his best to persuade the reader that Camille is insensitive, even cruel, and because everything is seen from Alain's point of view, the reader is made to share Alain's longing for the garden in which he grew up, as well as his admiration for his cat. Yet the symbolic system descriptive of Alain and Camille hints that Camille's "negative" qualities are "reprehensible only when measured against a certain ideal of passive femininity."[2] The reader is ambivalent about the breakup of the marriage and Alain's return to his mother's house and the company of his cat. In *La Fin de Chéri,*[3] Chéri and Edmée create a similar puzzle, in that Chéri's nostalgia for Léa is understandable to anyone who has read *Chéri.* The subjectivity of the narrative, heightened by the lyricism of the painful scene between Chéri and the now aged Léa, creates much sympathy for him. In contrast to his own sensitivity and idealism his wife Edmée appears to Chéri brash and opportunistic. But occasional shifts of focalization as well as the symbolic system provide glimpses of Edmée that seem to justify her conduct when she turns away from Chéri (e.g., pp. 121-25).

There is less ambiguity in *Le Blé en Herbe,* because Phil regards Vinca with affection in the early chapters, although as the narrative develops he becomes increasingly fearful and estranged. There is also less ambiguity because Phil's point of view is more often qualified by ironic interventions by the narrator-focalizor. Phil's nostalgia for his untroubled childhood love with Vinca is nevertheless made accessible to the reader, even if she/he is left wishing at the end of the novel that Phil could commit himself more wholeheartedly to the new relationship with Vinca, and that her victory were not so heavily qualified.

A close examination of the characters reveals that the entire symbolic system which describes them is composed of a set of binary pairs. Camille, Edmée, and Vinca are each described by one term, while the men are each characterized by the opposite term. The three basic categories of binary pairs are active vs. passive, future vs. past, and exposure vs. self-protection. Each category contains several subordinate pairs, which are also actualized to define the space with which the character identifies. The masculine spaces provide a key to the interpretation of the ambiguity in these novels.

Camille as Alain sees her has been described in Marianna Forde's insightful analysis of spatial relations in *La Chatte*. Forde has stressed that Camille is active, energetic, and healthy (Forde, pp. 365-76). Her coloring is vivid, and Alain associates it with vigor, noting "sa vigoureuse odeur de brune" on the morning after their wedding (p. 47). She is a creature of appetites, for food and for sex, and of robust health. She gains weight, in "the most attractive way" (p. 111).[4] Camille channels and projects her energy into activity in the present and plans for the future. When Alain abandons her, she makes vacation plans for herself; she is not immobilized by this traumatic event.

Camille's loud voice and manner of speaking draw the attention of the old servant Emile, who resents her assertiveness and the fact that she makes herself understood (p. 67). As elsewhere in Colette's works, a character's use of language, or failure to speak, is a distinguishing feature; here, "la parole de Camille la situe socialement; par sa volonté de s'affranchir, Camille souligne ses origines bourgeoises. . . ."[5] Alain regards Camille as lacking in refinement. She is a modern girl, liberated from certain conventions and representative of the values of the twentieth century, who sometimes offends Alain's older, aristocratic sensibility.

Alain's household is also disturbed by Camille's voice, which carries beyond the garden, exposing her to the world outside. In a more general way, Alain dislikes Camille's openness, her willingness to reveal her feelings, to expose herself, through words and gestures.

Edmée, like Camille, seems always to be busy and in motion. In the aftermath of World War I, she works in a hospital for the wounded, and she projects herself into her work with pleasure and a sense of accomplishment. Together with Chéri's mother, she is thoroughly involved in making money. To his friend Desmond, Chéri confesses that this disgusts him (p. 52). More simply, Edmée's engagement with practical reality disconcerts Chéri: when she informs him that she has taken care of household repairs and that she has made a profitable sale of stock that afternoon, his response is "Bien . . . et moi, dans tout ça?" (pp. 38-39). Chéri tells Desmond that "ma fortune, eh bien, la petite, ma femme, s'en occupe.—Oh! blâma Desmond, choqué" (p. 50). The implication is that a man ought not to let his wife usurp his masculine role as Edmée has done.

Perhaps Edmée's most striking aspect for Chéri as well as for the reader is the extent to which she has evolved with respect to her image in *Chéri.* Like Léa, she has adapted to changed circumstances and the passage of time, and, like Léa, Edmée has freed herself from potentially painful involvement with Chéri. Edmée also resembles Camille in that she has a survivor's response to her realization that Chéri has moved out of her reach: she turns toward the doctor with whom she works (p. 125). Chéri is displeased with the changes that have occurred in Edmée, making her more assertive, and after a quip from Edmée, he reacts: "La réplique de sa femme lui déplut. Il la voulait distinguée, et muette, sinon insensible, dans ses bras" (p. 37).

It is interesting to compare the following portrait of Edmée to the image of Camille as she appears to Alain and his servants: "Quelque chose d'outrageant rayonnait à travers son suave contour. Une indiscrète lueur décelait celle qui veut parvenir et qui n'a connu encore que le succès . . . Edmée ne se réclamait que par un seul signe: L'impudence. Attentive à ne choquer personne, elle choquait pourtant à la manière d'une parure trop neuve, ou d'un coursier de second ordre, les êtres que leur nature ou leur absence d'éducation rapprochait de la subtilité originelle. Les domestiques et Chéri redoutaient ce qu'en Edmée ils pressentaient de plus bas qu'eux" (p. 129). Chéri here makes essentially the same distinction that Alain made between an *arriviste* with modern, upwardly mobile values and a member of an older, established order. By implication, Chéri is describing Edmée's adaptation to the present and her orientation towards the future.

Vinca has often been misunderstood by critics as a "positive subtype" among Colette's fictional women, while Camille has been seen as "negative subtype."[6] I would argue that Vinca and Camille, or Vinca and Edmée, resemble each other more than they differ, and that their textual reality reveals these resemblances as well as the similarity in each novel of their characterization vis-à-vis the male protagonist.

By virtue of her extreme youth, Vinca is by far the most androgynous of Colette's women. She is often seen by Phil this way: "Ses quinze ans fiers et gauches, entraînés à la course, sales, durcis, maigres et solides, la rendaient souvent pareille à une houssine cinglante et cassante, mais ses yeux d'un bleu incomparable, sa bouche simple et saine étaient des œuvres achevées de la grâce féminine" (p. 45). The two parts of this description, one strong, athletic, and suggestive of virility, the other insistent upon the feminine beauty of her blue eyes, recur throughout the novel. Vinca is literally named for the periwinkle color of her eyes. They are a metonym for her femininity, but they are also the locus of her strength. They reveal by means of their color Vinca's dominance over Phil: "Elle l'éblouit, en lui jetant au visage le rayon bleu de ses grands yeux ouverts, dans un brusque et ferme regard" (p. 156). At other moments, her eyes join forces with her other vivid colors (the yellow of her hair, the white of her teeth, her terra cotta skin), all indicative of energy and strength, to subjugate Phil: "Le bleu rare de ses yeux, ses joues assombries par le fard chaud qu'on voit aux brugnons d'espalier, la double lame courbe de ses dents, brillèrent un moment avec une force de couleurs inexprimable dont Philippe se sentit comme blessé" (p. 69).

It is hardly surprising that Phil sometimes sees Vinca as frightening. His fear develops after he has begun his relationship with Mme Dalleray: ". . . il contemplait la force évidente d'un corps chaque jour féminisé, les durs genoux ciselés finement, les longs muscles des cuisses et des reins fiers. 'Comme elle est solide!' pensa-t-il, avec une sorte de crainte" (p. 110). As the novel progresses, Vinca becomes increasingly active, expressive, and articulate, and Phil's reaction is increasingly ambivalent. He is offended by what he considers to be the "brutality" of her jealousy (p. 156), but Vinca continues to voice her jealous anger in an articulate stream of words which recall Phil to reality, distracting him from his reverie of Mme Dalleray. "Toutes ses paroles sont aussi surprenantes que cette force que je lui ai vue souvent, quand elle nage, quand elle saute, quand elle lance des cailloux. . . ." (p. 160). Her words and her voice are also a source of her strength. Like her eyes, they reveal her to others and are highly expressive. Phil is literally charmed and seduced by her whispered speech at the end of the novel, despite his fears: "Elle parlait d'une voix insaisissable et pourtant Philippe ne perdait pas une de ses paroles. L'absence de timbre lui causait un plaisir infini. Ce n'était plus la voix de Vinca, ce n'était la voix d'aucune femme" (p. 177).

Vinca also resembles Camille and Edmée in that she is almost always busy and in motion. Phil observes the pleasure she takes in her food (p. 69). He is also struck by her joyous acceptance of her sexual initiation (p. 187). She has no regrets at leaving their childhood love behind and she faces the future serenely. Destined to become Phil's wife, she nonetheless displays a propensity for business, and her father regrets that she had to abandon a small commercial arrangement with a local merchant (p. 73).

Although the focus of narration usually resides within the man, the reader is also given the opportunity to evaluate him on the basis of his appearance. Consistent with Colette's technique of representing moral and psychological traits by means of physical characteristics, the man is occasionally seen in each novel from the outside, by another character. These presentations also create ambiguity by emphasizing unflattering aspects of the man which he would not himself reveal.

Alain is as passive as Camille is active. His preference for the leisurely, secluded life within the garden contrasts with Camille's energy. As Forde observes (p. 361), Alain is often seen lying down, looking up at Camille (p. 45, pp. 97-99), or looking up at his mother in the garden (p. 103). I have already mentioned Alain's gradual loss of physical vigor, represented by fatigue and weight loss. While Camille's interest lies in the future, Alain longs to return to the garden and the companion of his adolescence, i.e., the cat. He views change with terror and treasures all that is unchanging, as represented by the cat, the garden, his mother: "Que j'aime votre gros peignoir blanc, maman, toujours le même, toujours le même . . ." (p. 168). Alain longs to abolish time entirely, to remain static, fixed at an ideal moment in his childhood: "Entre la chatte, le rosier, les mésanges par couples et les derniers hannetons, Alain goûta les moments qui échappent à la durée humaine, l'angoisse et l'illusion de s'égarer dans son enfance" (p. 34).

Camille's ready speech has been seen as, among other things, a willingness to reveal herself. Alain repeatedly refuses to speak to Camille; in fact he deliberately impedes communication between them (pp. 121, 150, 180). Camille's open eye is an obsessive image for Alain. It determines the decor of his dreams, where it prevents him from attaining the protective darkness of the shadows (p. 28). He finds a visual reference to it in the light cast by the headlights of his car (p. 117) and in the fireworks seen from the window of the "Quart de Brie" apartment (p. 141). Despite its openness, Alain cannot decipher Camille's eye, and he reacts with fear to it, attempting to hide. Here as throughout Colette's work the woman's eye and her glance serve to establish her dominance in a relationship.[7] Thus Alain's dream describes his fear of Camille's power over him and his fear of being seen, or revealed.

Chéri is passive to the point of idleness (pp. 50-51). He spends much of his time waiting, rather than causing anything to happen. He is also recumbent much of the time, as when he talks with Edmée, who is upright (pp. 34, 125, 171), or when he reclines on the couch in the Copine's apartment. Chéri also grows weaker as the novel progresses and no longer nourishes himself, thereby hastening his decline. This of course contrasts sharply with the healthy appetites of Edmée and Léa and becomes as elsewhere in Colette's works "the basic symbol of moral as well as physical decay."[8] Unable to endure a poignant evocation of the Norman countryside where he had once been happy with Léa, Chéri faints. Léa notices that he is ailing (p. 88), as does Edmée (p. 122). A mysterious force is at work in his features (pp. 76, 121), undermining his youth and beauty and prefiguring his death: "Edmée se sentit soudain rassasiée du spectacle que l'ombre des rideaux, la pâleur du dormeur et le lit blanc teignaient aux couleurs romantiques de la nuit et de la mort" (p. 124).

Chéri also resembles Alain in his passionate dislike of change, and in his quest for permanence. His fundamental problem is the emptiness of a life that had been given meaning only by his attachment to Léa, a maternal figure. But the war served in his case to create a temporal awareness, putting his sense of loss into sharp relief. If he cannot endure the changes in the women around him it is because they point to the passing of time, which Chéri, like Alain, would like to arrest at a point in his adolescence. Thus he is able to appreciate his mother, precisely because she has not changed: "'Un fléau, quoi' se dit-il. 'Un fléau mais pas une étrangère'" (p. 131). The present holds no attraction for him, and when Desmond speaks to him of the future, Chéri sees nothing but the harsh sunlight beating down on the roof (p. 53).

Fearing revelation of his secrets, Chéri protects himself in sleep, and he hides from Edmée in various ways, even spying on her from behind the window (p. 41). Like Alain, Chéri prefers silence—"Il aimait le silence et la sournoiserie" (p. 40)—and is also deliberately uncommunicative in his conversations with Edmée (pp. 36, 171) so as not to expose himself.

Phil also lacks the energy of his female companion and is relatively inactive. In comparison with the vivid colors that express Vinca's vitality, Phil's coloring is moderate, pale by contrast. As Phil becomes involved with Mme Dalleray, he weakens, is increasingly tired, and generally displays signs of ill health. He grows morbidly sensitive in response to his sexual experience, wincing when Vinca steps on a crab (p. 111), flinching under the hot sun (p. 113), and actually sobbing when Vinca spears a fish (p. 113). Like Chéri, he faints during a painful conversation (p. 145). He sleeps late and dreams each morning; he is often recumbent, from the first scene of the novel (p. 32) to the last, when he looks up at Vinca, happy and radiant in her window (p. 187).

Despite his youth, Phil is already nostalgic for his childhood relationship with Vinca, the uncomplicated, fraternal love of two androgynous beings. His attitude toward the future changes from anxious impatience (pp. 45-48) to traumatic fear, as revealed by the fact that he faints precisely as his father is speaking to him about his future (p. 150). He seeks like the others to protect his secrets, and like the others he comes to prefer darkness and night to the bright light of daytime.

The series of contrasts outlined above can be summarized by the following binary pairs:

Active vs. Passive
strong/healthy vs. weak
upright vs. recumbent

Present/Future vs. Past
changing vs. unchanging

Exposure vs. Self-Protection
self-revelation vs. dissimulation
articulate vs. inarticulate
open vs. closed
light vs. darkness

In each pair, the first term, which is conventionally the positive one, applies to the young woman. The second term, which usually carries a negative connotation, characterizes Alain, Chéri, and Phil. Ambiguity, as explained above, results from the fact that as focalizor and principal character, the man has nevertheless gained much of the reader's sympathy. A clue to the ultimate nature and significance of this textual ambiguity lies in the kind of textual space which both men and women, but especially the men, create for themselves.

Textual space in Colette's novels is literally defined by the textual body of the woman, as Yannick Resch has pointed out: "La comparaison du corps à certains moments de la journée illustre un des principes qui régit la construction d'un personnage féminin: le corps de la femme est avant tout un milieu, une atmosphère. Localisé temporellement, le corps l'est aussi spatialement. Le corps est cet espace dans lequel il se meut."[9]

The textual space of both the men and the women in these novels, i.e., the space which they choose and with which they are associated, is in fact described by semantic components of the terms of the binary pairs listed above. Thus Camille feels at ease in the triangular rooms of the high-rise apartment, the "Quart de Brie," which are full of glass and windows, open to the light. This space is defined by its "openness," its modernity, and its height. Camille herself is defined by her openness and willingness to reveal herself. The apartment's modernity relates to Camille's orientation towards the present and future. The height of the apartment refers to the upright vs. recumbent pair; the upward component seems to be a spatial correlative of Camille's dynamism and upward mobility. Edmée's activity also suggests an open space; she moves freely between her home and the world outside. Edmée too is "open" to other people. She talks on the telephone and is eager to entertain guests. Edmée is often dressed in white. Chéri regularly associates her white-clad body with the white spaces which Edmée likes. In the hospital where Edmée works, Chéri pities the patients who must endure so much white (pp. 57-58). He explodes during a family dinner in the stark light of the dining room, "dépouillé de toute ombre par la lumière . . . [qui] tombait sans ménagement du plafond," and where "une constellation de cristal bougeait à chaque mouvement de la robe d'Edmée" (p. 127). Vinca's space is the outdoors, and often the sea, where her eyes reflect the blue of the sea or refuse to do so according to the nuances of her relationship with Phil (e.g., p. 95).

The spaces defined by Alain, Chéri, and Phil are all strikingly similar. In each case, the man's space plays a determining role in the development of the character and the narrative. Alain's space is of course his mother's garden in Neuilly, enclosed and claustral, which he inhabits in solitude with the cat, a mother substitute who embodies an ideal of love for Alain. It is significant that when Alain is living in the Quart de Brie, he seeks refuge from its openness on a divan in a narrow, enclosed hallway, which he shares with the cat. His mother is also present in the garden, though unobtrusively. The garden has never changed; it represents Alain's past, and in it he often regresses to childlike behavior: "Quand il déjeunait seul, il n'avait pas à rougir de certains gestes élaborés par le vœu inconscient de l'âge maniaque, entre la quatrième et la septième année" (p. 31). Frequent reference is made to the dead tree which stands in the center, as well as to other plants evocative of death, such as laburnum (Forde, p. 364). The servants are old and moribund. Numerous configurations of the garden plants point downward (Forde, p. 364), and Alain is seen lying down in the final scene. The garden, which is closed off from the rest of the world, provides the shadowy refuge in Alain's recurring dream. Alain's space is thus defined by Alain himself, providing a spatial actualization of the "recumbent," "past," "unchanging," "closed," and "darkness" members of the descriptive binary pairs. Alain's solitude within his space is part of "self-protection," as is the relative silence of all of its inhabitants.

La Fin de Chéri can be seen as Chéri's search for a space in which to flee from the stressful relationships of the present: "il n'avait songé qu'à une chose: posséder une retraite dont la porte s'ouvrirait, se refermerait pour lui seul, sur un lieu ignoré d'Edmée, de Charlotte, de tous . . ."(p. 144). Early in the novel, Chéri confines himself to the bedroom and systematically avoids contact with Edmée's guests. Traumatized by his visit to Léa's new apartment, which lacks the rose-colored, erotic charm of her old one, Chéri daydreams: "Ah, une chambre d'hôtel, une bonne chambre rose, bien banale et bien rose" (p. 139). The bar in which Chéri meets La Copine prefigures the space he will soon find: enclosed, without specific dimensions or form, it is "rougeâtre, démodé, invariable et pareil à lui-même depuis que Chéri, garçonnet, y avait sucé du bout d'une paille ses premiers barbotages . . . Le barman lui-même ne changeait pas, et si la femme assise en face de Chéri était une femme flétrie, du moins ne l'avait-il jamais connue belle, ni jeune" (p. 145). He finds his ideal space in La Copine's apartment, "une pièce basse" (p. 146). The furnishings and the inhabitant are old, as are the photographs of the Léa of long ago which transport him into the past. La Copine, a substitute for Léa, who was herself the maternal presence in Chéri's life, ministers to his needs as he lies recumbent upon a couch. Chéri's space, like Alain's, actualizes Chéri's characteristics as "passive," "recumbent," oriented toward the "past," and "unchanging." "Closed," "dark," and "dissimulation" (the apartment is a secret from everyone else) are components of "self-protection."

Phil's space, the Villa Ker-Anna of Mme Dalleray, is also prefigured, in a dream: "Il dépassa une grotte—un hamac de fibres creuse sous une forme nue, un feu rougeoyant qui battait de l'aile à ras de terre—puis perdit son sens divinatoire, sa puissance de vol, chavira, et toucha le fond moelleux du plus noir repos" (p. 71). The entire villa is enclosed by a wall, which Phil in his initial terror thinks of scaling (p. 83); once inside, he falls, as in his dream. He undergoes a physical trauma, symbolic of his emotional state, which is ostensibly caused by the cold, dark, cavelike interior, but which announces the physical weakness which will worsen from this point until the end of the novel. In this "abîme nocturne" (p. 109), images of fire and ice transcode the intensity of Phil's experience (p. 83). During subsequent visits to the secret place, the traumatic aspect lessens, and the villa becomes sumptuously comfortable. Phil's preference for the night begins as he returns from these rendezvous (pp. 101-07). The road to this place inhabited by the mother figure is "blanche dans la nuit laiteuse" (p. 102); the weather is "un doux temps breton qui . . . mêlait à la mer un lait immatériel" (p. 89). When Mme Dalleray leaves, Phil is stricken with nostalgia. The entire experience has the effect of orienting him toward the past. As in the other novels, the masculine space is one of "passivity," "weakness," and "recumbency." It is secret, closed, and dark, actualizing "self-protection."

In each case, this intimate space is inhabited by the mother or mother substitute, and is informed by the young man's feelings about her. It excludes the younger woman, who is representative of adult connections in the present, and it appears to the young man as a refuge from the inadequacies of his relationship to the young woman and from the strain of negotiating with the present and the future. In the case of Alain, the space is actually figured as a garden, but I believe that in all three novels this space is in fact a particular negative variant of Sido's garden as it appears throughout Colette's works. Usually the place of origin and of the comforting maternal presence, the garden elsewhere restores strength and lucidity. But here the garden fosters dependency and eventually inertia. It serves to detach the character from reality, as represented symbolically by dreamlike imagery and oneiric references. Alain's garden is the shadowy place of which he dreams. Chéri experiences a total loss of reality as the Copine's voice carries him back forty years and her coffee transports him to an "island paradise" (p. 159). Phil is obsessed by a "bad dream" of Ker-Anna, which haunts his waking hours with its unreal, dreamlike colors (p. 88).

The maternal refuge also fosters a tendency toward excessive devotion to an ideal, which is also a refusal of reality. For Alain, the cat embodies the ideal of the love relationship. Chéri has of course idealized Léa, who is further idealized by the highly flattering photos selected by the Copine: "Moi je suis pour les portraits flatteurs . . . un portrait comme celui-ci, voyons, en conscience, est-ce que ce n'est pas à joindre les mains et croire en Dieu?" (p. 147). Phil idealizes the "gift" made by Mme Dalleray (his sexual initiation) and is also encouraged by his experience to idealize Vinca, as a virginal young girl (p. 172). In Phil's case as in the others this idealization is dangerous; it is reflected in the narrative by the characters' progressive inability to associate their ideal with sexual desire. And, of course, in Chéri's case idealization ultimately leads to death.

It is also noteworthy that the maternal relationship provides each character with a role which he considers to be an ideal self: Alain identifies with his cat and feels that Camille interferes with this mode of existence (p. 122). Both Chéri and Phil take pleasure in imagining themselves as they were with Léa and Mme Dalleray, and accordingly each is surprised by his image in the mirror, which does not confirm the reality of this self. Chéri repeatedly fails to understand that he is no longer a young man of twenty-four (p. 45). Phil expects to see a man's face in the mirror, and sees instead the face of a tormented young girl (p. 107). The maternal relationship here precludes self-awareness and actually alienates these characters from their most profound reality.

What is most striking to even the casual reader of Colette is the radical difference between this variant of the garden, or maternal space, and those found elsewhere in her works. Typically, a young female character returns to the garden, i.e., her place of origin, after a disappointing experience with love and sensuality. She seeks legitimately to abolish time by returning to the origin to prepare the "rebirth" that Sido accomplished throughout her life at the break of day. From Claudine to Julie de Carneilhan, the "retraite sentimentale" is a valid refuge and a viable alternative, either in the short run, as in *Claudine en Ménage,* or in the long run, as in *Le Toutounier* or *Julie de Carneilhan.*

In *La Chatte, La Fin de Chéri,* and *Le Blé en Herbe,* the claustral space and indeed the entire symbolic system which describes the men point instead to the need for the character to move beyond the garden. If the itinerary that leads back to Sido is a circle, or, especially, a "full circle," it must in its first move depart from the space inhabited by Sido. The female self must be constituted with reference to the mother, certainly, but she also requires a broader experience. Michèle Sarde integrates several of the stories in *La Maison de Claudine* into her biography of Colette, in order to show that the need to depart is already present in the close connection to the mother.[10] In **"La Petite,"** Gabrielle (Colette) dreams of leaving home to become a sailor, an adventurous, masculine career that would also mean escape from a traditional female existence, symbolized at that same moment by Sido glimpsed through the window as

she prepares a meal. Gabrielle also dreams of being kidnapped and removed from her mother's home in **"L'Enlèvement."** In *Sido* as well, the garden is the place to which she returns, but only after "tasting in the two springs the intoxicating brew of her first freedom" (Sarde, p. 40).

It is important to realize that the spaces which women create for themselves in Colette's fiction are not in all respects the same as the place of origin, although in several novels and short stories female space, as distinguished from "patriarchal space," is represented by a garden. The new female space is necessarily different, just as the new female self must be distinct from Sido, even while remaining deeply faithful to Sido's precepts for living. In these three novels "female space," limitless and rich with possibility, lies beyond the claustral space of the garden, signifying a distinction between the self and the mother. For if "all of Colette's work can be seen as an exodus from patriarchal space," as Mari McCarty observes,[11] it is also an exodus, at least initially, from matriarchal space, as Colette tells us in *Les Vrilles de la Vigne*: "Je regrette aujourd'hui quelqu'un qui me posséda avant tous, . . . avant que je fusse une femme. J'appartiens à un pays que j'ai quitté" (p. 222).[12]

Camille, Edmée, and Vinca are realistic and adaptive, as was Sido. They represent the counterweight which Colette found to the need to return to the origin: the ability to adapt to life, a fundamental feminine strength in Colette's universe. But readers admire Alain's cat, and they understand his longing for the restful tranquility of the garden. They share the pain that Chéri feels when he sees that Léa is no longer beautiful, and Phil reminds them that passion does indeed immobilize its victims. The reader's ambivalence, and the resulting ambiguity in these novels, is finally related to feelings about the garden space. Nostalgia for the peace and tenderness of the garden are natural and inevitable. It is the tension between allegiance to and difference from the mother that ultimately creates ambiguity. It is interesting that between 1922 and 1933 Colette wrote not only these three novels, but also the three works that describe in unqualified terms her mother's house and Sido as the model for her own conduct: *La Maison de Claudine* (1922), *La Naissance du Jour* (1928), and *Sido* (1930).

It is also possible to connect the ambiguity in these novels with Colette's biographical experience as a young, provincial girl faced not only with her exploitative husband Willy, but with the shock of living in the patriarchal, capitalist society of turn-of-the-century Paris. Suzanne Relyea offers an illuminating discussion of Colette's loss of identity in leaving her village, and the difficulties she faced in forging a new identity: "In giving up her girlhood, she also gives up the maternal line, the symbol set where woman and full being coincide, to enter a whole new set of power relations within which she holds no title to existence except with respect to men. While restoring her to the world of Saint-Sauveur (Chatillon) her own ultimate choice (of name), "Colette," reflects the degree to which she viewed the loss as irreversible."[13] Forced by Willy to write fiction, Colette slowly, after much struggle, negotiated successfully with patriarchal relations and their embodiment in the symbolic order, i.e., in language. She became a writing subject with "full being," a new kind of female self.

In *L'Etoile Vesper* she reminds us of the extent to which her writing finally differentiated her life from her mother's, even when she became a mother herself: "Mon brin de virilité me sauva du danger qui expose l'écrivain, promu parent heureux et tendre, à tourner auteur médiocre, à préférer désormais ce qui récompense une visible et matérielle croissance: le culte des enfants, des plantes, des élevages, sous leurs formes diverses. Un vieux garçon de quarante ans, sous la femme encore jeune que j'étais, veilla au salut d'une partie peut-être précieuse" (p. 329). Here, Colette identifies with the (virile) "confirmed bachelor" and simultaneously rejects the maternal role model. This would appear to be at odds with the three novels I have discussed, in which it is the male who is unable to dissociate himself from the mother, whereas the woman has had little problem with differentiation. An explanation of this apparent discrepancy and a clue to Colette's reversal of the sex of the three protagonists may be found in the facts of her early life as they related to men and to writing. Although Willy had aspirations as a writer, he was totally incapable of writing, as was her father, Captain Colette. (At the death of her father, Colette found many bound volumes of the Captain's "works" in the family library, all dedicated to Sido: the pages were completely blank). Thus both men may have been perceived as lacking in a certain virility, and both were also highly dependent upon women. Their lack of virility may have served as a model for several of Colette's male characters, i.e., those who had not moved beyond the mother's space, and as a negative model for herself of dependency and passivity coupled with "castration." Colette was to claim this virility for herself as essential to her identity as a writer, thereby differentiating herself from both parents at once. It also seems probable that the more general fluidity of sex-role definition in her work is related to her dilemma of differentiating herself from her mother, but also from her father, in order to be able to write[14]

La Chatte, La Fin de Chéri, and ***Le Blé en Herbe*** point to a significant nuance in the privileged relationship between mother and daughter that is everywhere present in Colette's fiction. While the daughter must refer at all times to the values transmitted by the mother, she must also leave the garden; the "full circle" back can and should only be traced over a lifetime. It is striking that in these novels the familiar Colettian binary pair associated with Sido, abstention vs consummation, receives a somewhat different treatment. Camille, Edmée, and Vinca embrace life eagerly and sensually, while the excessive idealism and exacerbated sensitivity of Alain, Chéri, and Phil create varying degrees of difficulty in relating sensually to the young woman and to reality. Strength is derived not from abstention as an approach to life, but from a posture of attempted possession. "Tout va s'évanouir, si tu l'effleures seulement": Sido's precept in ***La Naissance du Jour*** (p. 24) is honored by Colette, who understands the impossibility of possession in love. Yet her own sensuality, "qui eut toujours, Dieu merci, les yeux plus grands que le ventre" (p. 27) irresistibly urges her to attempt sensual possession through writing. While the men in these novels protect themselves in silence, the women all expose themselves in their words, which are also a source of strength and dominance. The reader feels that they, like Colette, attain full being with possession of language. The necessity of writing is affirmed, even as the futility of communication reminds the reader of the ambiguous status of language in these novels.

Notes

1. Mieke Bal explains the role of focalization in creating the reader's complicity in *Narratology: Introduction to the Theory of Narrative* (University of Toronto Press, 1985), p. 104. Bal explains that "the agent that sees must be given a status other than that of the agent that narrates" (p. 101). The "agent that sees" is the *focalizor,* who may or may not coincide with a character: "If the focalizor coincides with [a] character, that character will have a technical advantage over the other characters. The reader watches with the character's eyes and will, in principle, be inclined to accept the vision presented by that character" (p. 104). Alain, Chéri, and Phil are consistent focalizors in these novels. There are occasional shifts to external focalization, i.e., to a narrator-focalizor, in all three, but only rarely does the focus of narration reside within another character. In *La Chatte,* Alain is the only true focalizor/character, while in *La Fin de Chéri* and *Le Blé en herbe* there are two or three brief shifts of a focalization to other characters (Edmée, Charlotte; Vinca, Mme Dalleray).

2. Marianna Forde, "Spatial Structures in *La Chatte,*" *French Review* 58, (1985), 363.

3. For several reasons, I have not included *Chéri* in this discussion. The principal character in *Chéri* is not Chéri but Léa, who is most often the focalizor. In addition, Edmée differs in *Chéri* from *La Fin de Chéri* in a way that excludes the triangular situation I have described. She is a shadowy, col-

orless figure in *Chéri,* pretty but not threatening to Léa except by virtue of her youth, and in no way compelling to Chéri. Chéri's final departure from Léa's apartment "comme un évadé" also indicates a different significance in his relationship with her. For reasons that will become apparent, these facts point to a different interpretation of the text.

4. For page references in *La Chatte,* I have used Le Livre de Poche (Paris: Hachette, 1960). For *La Fin de Chéri* and *Le Blé en herbe,* see the Garner-Flammarion editions (Paris, 1983 and Paris, 1969 respectively). All other quotations from Colette's works are from her *Œuvres complètes* (Paris: Flammarion, 1960).

5. Yannick Resch, *Corps féminin, corps textuel* (Paris: Klincksieck, 1973), p. 85.

6. One such critical study was made by Silvie Romanowski, "A Typology of Women in Colette's Novels," in *Colette: The Woman, the Writer,* E. M. Ersinger and M. W. McCarty, eds. (Pennsylvania State University Press, 1981).

7. "La dominance par le regard qui est généralement attribuée à la femme est décrite différemment suivant que ce pouvoir décrit ou non un code compréhensible; en d'autres termes, l'auteur utilise un procédé stylistique qui rend compte de la lisibilité du message en se servant de *La couleur.* Une couleur précise rendra intelligible le message tandis que l'absence de couleur servira à décrire l'illisibilité du regard . . . Nous avons vu dans *La Chatte* le peu de référence aux couleurs et parallèlement l'impossibilité pour Alain de comprendre ces yeux . . ." (Resch, p. 59).

8. Ilene Olken, "Imagery in *Chéri* and *La Fin de Chéri:* Taste and Smell," *French Studies* 16 (July 1961), 251.

9. Resch, p. 23. This very useful insight helps to explain that much of the imagery in all three novels can be seen as an extension by the man's consciousness of the woman's physical attributes to the environment. The man's body and sentiments as the narrator presents them are also projected onto the surroundings, as in the following passage from *La Chatte.* Alain, suffering in the stifling heat in the Quart de Brie apartment, is figured as an aged tree, a dying remnant of a lost garden: "Trois peupliers âgés, épaves d'un beau jardin détruit, balançaient leurs cimes à la hauteur de la terrasse, et le vaste soleil de Paris, rouge sombre, étouffé de vapeurs, descendait derrière leurs têtes maigres d'où la sève se retirait" (p. 79).

10. Michele Sarde, *Colette Free and Fettered* (New York: Morrow, 1980), p. 57.

11. Mari McCarty, "Possessing Female Space," *Women's Studies* 8 (1981), 285.

12. In fact, Sido's space as it appears in *La Maison de Claudine* and *Sido* differs from Colette's garden space in *La Naissance du Jour,* despite the fact that Colette as a character saw her Provençal home as a way back to Sido. Jean-Pierre Richard describes this distinction pair. In Sido's garden, there are strategies for escape: lateral, upward, and inward. Sido herself has strategies for keeping at a distance from what is close and for apprehending what is far. She is receptive to the four winds, which bring her information. She commands, brings order, controls. In *La Naissance du Jour,* the Provençal outside seeks violently to enter the closed house; the wind and now the sun cause discomfort. No longer is there mastery of what is inside and "divination of an horizon": there is instead withdrawal and self-defense. Jean-Pierre Richard, "L'Ail et la grenouille," *NRF* 308 (1978), 99-109.

13. Suzanne Relyea, "The Symbolic in the Family Factory," *Women's Studies* 8 (1981), 285.

14. In psychoanalytic terms, Colette's problem of differentiation with respect to her mother can be seen as a manifestation of a more universal feminine problem of individuation. Nancy Chodorow describes the way "girls come to experience themselves as less differentiated than boys, as more continuous with and related to the external object-world, and as differently oriented to their inner object-world as well" (Nancy Chodorow: *The Reproduction of Mothering,* University of California Press, 1978, p. 167). More fluid ego boundaries lead to feeling connectedness and empathy with the mother and with the outside world, but they can also create a need in certain instances to determine the boundaries of the self and the other. Both of these feelings inform Colette's works, but in the three novels discussed here it is the ambiguity created by the need for individuation that predominates. More research is needed on the issues described by Chodorow as they appear in the relationship between Sido and Colette, particularly as it concerns writing. And as I have indicated, differentiation from the father also seems to have played a role in Colette's achievement of identity as a writer.

Diana Holmes (essay date 1991)

SOURCE: Holmes, Diana. "Green Sealing Wax: Language, Style, and Gender." In *Colette,* pp. 92-111. New York: St. Martin's Press, 1991.

[*In the following excerpt, Holmes explores language and gender in Colette's short fiction as it relates to theme and form.*]

The relationship between gender and language is a crucial question for feminist literary theory, and has been particularly central to the writing of French theorists. For Jacques Lacan, whose interpretations of and commentaries on the writings of Freud provide a starting point for the work of Hélène Cixous and Julia Kristeva, the child becomes a human subject precisely at the point of language acquisition, when s/he distinguishes between the self and what is not the self, and thus takes up a position within the Symbolic code (language). The recognition of the self as located within an external code, as "I", "you" or "s/he", is termed the "mirror stage", and coincides with the establishment of specifically human identity. The Symbolic code operates by distinguishing between one thing and another, by the principle of difference, and in this process the original term, or the primary signifier, is the phallus.

According to Lacan's theory the function of the phallus as primary signifier means that from the moment of becoming a subject the human being is gendered, because the relationship of the male and female child to the phallus is inevitably different. Though it is difficult to establish precisely what relationship Lacan assumes between the physical penis and the symbolic phallus, Lacanian theory certainly appears to establish a primary gender difference in that the very principle of language defines the masculine as the positive term, the feminine as the negative, as that which is not the phallus. On this theory, women's relationship to the Symbolic code must always and inherently be problematic, in that they speak from the position of the negative, of that which is silenced or repressed. It is clearly quite possible to move from this psychoanalytical theory to a theory of cultural exclusion, and we are not far from Dale Spender's "man-made language"[1] and the identification of a need to find linguistic modes of expression for the feminine and to challenge a linguistic formulation of the world that privileges the masculine. However, on Lacan's theory, this presents an insuperable theoretical problem, for there is no pre-discursive truth, no position from which to contest a linguistic code which does not merely signify a pre-existing reality but creates reality.

Kristeva presents a possible way forward in that she posits the existence of a space, or a time, which precedes the entry into the Symbolic but which may continue to have meaning for the subject. This pre-verbal stage, marked by identification with the mother's body, "previous and necessary to the acquisition of language but not identical to language", is termed the "semiotic", and its traces may appear in the text in the form of "a space, underlying the written . . . rhythmic, unfettered, irreducible to its intelligible, verbal translation".[2]

Whilst the "semiotic" would not be the exclusive realm of the woman writer, since all human subjects share the same fundamental drama of identification with and separation from the maternal body, it could be associated particularly with the feminine, both because it precedes the Symbolic's assignment of the feminine to the negative term, and because it brings the maternal body into the signifying process. If, as Terry Eagleton explains it, the "semiotic" is "a process *within* our conventional sign systems, which questions and transgresses their limits" and challenges "the phallus (as) symbol of sure, self-identical truth"[3] then the "semiotic" may be a useful category through which to consider the inscription of the feminine in women's writing.

The implication of Kristeva's theory here is that an articulation of the feminine may mean the disruption of both linguistic and literary forms, that the Symbolic code itself is, as Annie Leclerc termed it "man's word"[4] and that the semiotic may provide the formal possibility of articulating a "woman's word". Hélène Cixous writes of women writing "from 'without', from the heath where witches are kept alive; from below, from beyond 'culture'; from their childhood which men have been trying desperately to make them forget . . . .".[5]

Both in language itself and in the codes of meaning that are produced by literary genres, a recurring feminist argument identifies the articulation of the feminine with disruption, subversion, a necessary flight from convention. If there is a danger here, it is that of a return to the gender essentialism which feminism began by contesting: women's writing would be identified with incoherence, disorder and uncontrolled emotionality to the exclusion of those qualities which bespeak control of the Symbolic code: formal precision, humour, varied modulation of tone and meaning.

The positive point of such theories, however, is that they provide a critical framework within which to examine specific relationships between sexual and textual politics (as Toril Moi's title nicely phrased it).[6] In Colette's case, this means examining language and gender in the texts in terms of both theme and form. Colette's writing itself thematises the relationship between language and gender, so that the nature of the Symbolic code, and the different places occupied by men and women in relation to language, may be explored as a recurring preoccupation in her work. But also, whilst it would be inappropriate to try to define such a skilled manipulator of language primarily in terms of the "semiotic", Colette's characteristic style does have distinct elements of the disruptive, for it disturbs comfortable relationships between signifier and signified and between the terms of those "scrupulous binary oppositions"[7] on which the Symbolic order is founded.

The theme of language takes the form of a recurring distinction between male and female discourse. Male characters in Colette's texts tend to assume a linguistic authority, a confident ability to name and categorise the world, that may operate at the level of speech or of the written word. Their confidence rests implicitly on the knowledge that their codes of meaning are those of the dominant discourse: the power to name means the power to define, to bring into existence or conversely, to silence and repress. Women are named by men, their social identity bestowed by husband or lover. The "Colette" of *Break of Day* (**BD**) refers to the author's own succession of linguistic identities before she achieved the freedom to name herself: first concealed completely in her texts behind the name "Willy", then Colette Willy, then Colette de Jouvenel, and at last "it came about that both legally and familiarly, as well as in my books, I now have only one name, which is my own. Did it take only thirty years of my life to reach that point, or rather to get back to it?" (**BD,** 19).

Marco in **"The Képi"** is called Marco because her name was Leonie before she married an artist: "Leonie wasn't the right sort of name for V's wife" (**CSC** [*Collected Stories of Colette*], 507). Mitsou's only name is given by the man who keeps her, and represents an acronym of the two companies he manages ("Minoteries Italo-Tarbaises" and "Scieries Orléanaises Unifieés", flour-mills and sawmills). Thus Mitsou's name signifies that she is her lover's property, though the text itself not only narrates Mitsou's accession to language through the writing of letters to the "Blue Lieutenant", it also refuses the Namer his "proper name" by designating him only as *"L'Homme Bien"* or the "Well-to-do Man".

Gigi's education, in the story of the same name, is an exercise in repression: Gigi is taught that if she is to survive economically, she must not attempt to express herself outside those codes of language, dress and behaviour which, in the dominant discourse, signify "femininity". Gigi's inclination to articulate spontaneous feeling and to clearly describe the career for which she is being groomed must be curbed, for "Calling people and things by their name has never done anyone any good" (**G** [*Gigi*], 22) insists her grandmother, functioning here as representative and teacher of the patriarchal code which has determined her own identity.[8]

Men's control of language is envied and coveted by female characters, but is also undermined and contested within the text as inadequate to a complex, plural reality. The story **"Green Sealing Wax"** (**"La Cire verte"**, 1943) presents this ambivalent view of language in humorously figurative form. Narrated by the author's textual alter ego "Colette", set in the family home when she was fifteen-years-old, this story weaves together a narrative of murder and forgery with the themes of female adolescence and maternal protection, but foregrounds the process of writing itself.

The "green sealing wax" of the title is just one of the desirable objects displayed on the desk of the narrator's father, who collects there all the paraphernalia of the writing process, from pens with nibs of varied sizes to "a lacquer bowl filled with a golden powder to dry the wet page" (**CSC,** 388), to early gadgets for making multiple copies. His daughter covets this wealth of tantalising objects and braves her father's possessive wrath to steal objects to add to her own collection or, in the case of sealing wafers, to eat, but whilst she thus attempts to share her father's figurative access to the written word, she also recognises the void that this conceals. Equipped with all the ceremonial signs of writing, the father rarely puts pen to paper, whereas Sido dispenses with all formal signs of linguistic production but produces texts whose close association with everyday reality is signified by the circumstances of their writing:

> sitting at any old table, pushing aside an invading cat, a basket of plums, a pile of linen, or else just putting a dictionary on her lap by way of a desk—Sido really did write. A hundred enchanting letters prove that she did.
>
> (**CSC,** 389)

Paternal access to language here is both enviable as a rich, varied resource, equipped with all that is necessary for the production of texts, and seen as ultimately empty, possessing less substance than the private, scribbled but communicative discourse of the mother. Perhaps it is significant too that Madame Hervouet, the story's murderess, tries to authenticate her forgery of her husband's will—a very bad forgery, in her woman's writing, wildly improbable in legal terms—by sealing it with the green sealing wax taken from Captain Colette's desk. The text comments ironically on the understandable but ultimately self-defeating temptation to simply appropriate male discourse.

The contrast between an authoritative, categorising male language and a more plural, tentative female voice recurs in several novels and stories. Max, in *The Vagabond* (**V**) with his "prescriptive sense of normality"[9] is a black and white figure not only in terms of his physical characterisation, but also in his straightforwardly dualist vision of the world. When Renée packs her underclothes next to those of her male partner to save luggage space on tour it is "contemptible . . . sordid . . . promiscuous" (**V,** 142-3) and two women embracing are a "depraved couple" (161). Marriage, on the other hand, represents an appropriate destiny for a woman that can replace mere stop-gap careers "But, darling, you no longer need the music-hall now that I am there . . ." (**V,** 122). Renée's problem in coming to terms with Max is posed in specifically linguistic terms: "I don't know how to talk to you, poor Dufferein-Chautel. I hesitate between my own personal language . . . and the slovenly, lively idiom . . . which one learns in the music-hall . . . Unable to decide, I choose silence" (**V,** 70).

Farou of *The Other One* (**OO**) proposes his definitions of femininity and relationships not only in private but publicly on the stage, as a popular playwright, and his wife winces at the inaccurate simplicity of his version of a dialogue between two women.

> This time, Fanny listened, irreverently. "Perhaps he really thinks that's how it would be. He makes me laugh".
>
> *(OO,* 144)

Michel of **Duo** shocks Alice with the platitudinous certainties through which he attempts to understand her infidelity: "The funniest thing of all is that he believes it; he thinks he knows what a woman's desire is like" (*Duo,* 53). In **"The Képi"** the "Colette" narrator opposes her own sympathetic and complex characterisation of Marco to the crudely reductionist wit of Masson and Willy who greet her late discovery of the pleasures of love with cold cynicism: "Probably, like many women, our worthy Marco imagines she is the bride of Satan. It's the phase of infernal joys" comments Masson.

> I thought it detestable that either of her two friends should call Madame V. "our worthy Marco". Nor was I any more favourably impressed by the icily critical comments of these two disillusioned men, especially on anything concerning friendship, esteem or love."
>
> *(CSC,* 520)

These female responses to male discourse tend to be quietly ironic, to question the self-importance implicit in the male speaker/writer's representation of masculinity, and to question the accuracy of his characterisation of the feminine. The technique of the unspoken critique, scarcely articulated but sufficiently indicated to throw a perspective of female irony over the text, is carried to its logical conclusion in the "dialogues for one voice", texts in which the presence of "Colette" as silent participant in the conversation is indicated only by a row of dots or by the speaker's appeals to her. Thus in **"An Interview"** "Colette's" hostile reaction to the pompous journalist who interviews her without ever allowing her to speak, and reads his own assumptions into her enforced silence, is signified by his responses:

> What do you mean, you haven't opened your mouth? Except that in that expression there are a hundred lines of psychology. Isn't a woman entirely in what she doesn't say?
>
> *(CSC,* 44)

The same technique serves to challenge the masculine complacency of Chaveriat in **"The Tender Shoot"**. Once the narration of his story is begun, the "Colette" who has elicited it by direct invitation and by loosening the speaker's tongue with best brandy, remains silent— but her critical response to Chaveriat's tactics as a seducer and to his way of defining his own behaviour is indicated in the text by Chaveriat's "Excuse me, what

were you saying, my dear? That it was a horrid proceeding and a classical one?" (*CSC,* 427), and his "Begging your pardon, I am not a brute" (*CSC,* 436).

Men speak and write with the authority of the dominant culture: the least articulate of Colette's male characters are those, like Chéri, who have failed to properly assimilate the codes of masculine behaviour. Women's language, it is suggested, is less public, less rhetorical, more exploratory. There is, of course, a very fundamental contradiction here in that by their very presence the books demonstrate the existence of female-authored texts within the public world of discourse: the daughter "Colette" may have taken her mother's writing as "model" as she emphasises in **Break of Day** ("She gave me life and the mission to pursue those things which she, a poet, seized and cast aside as one snatches a fragment of a floating melody drifting through space" [**BD***,* 25]), but she has also appropriated her father's writing equipment by bringing her texts into the public realm.

This dual relationship to language is acknowledged within the fiction, where despite the critical perspective on a public language largely identified as masculine, the imperative to write, and thus to assume the role of subject within the Symbolic code, is frequently a female concern. If Renée "the vagabond" rejects the very real temptation to seek fulfilment in Max's love, it is partly because love here is incompatible with writing "as if the one dominating anxiety in my life were to seek for words, words to express how yellow the sun is, how blue the sea, and how brilliant the salt like a fringe of white jet" (*V,* 176).

The "Colette" narrators of the stories **"Bella Vista"** and **"Rainy Moon"**, like the narrator of **Break of Day,** are writers by profession as well as by their position in the text, motivated by what Renée defines as "a need, sharp as thirst in summer, to note and to describe" and engage in "the perilous and elusive task of seizing and pinning down . . . the many-hued, fugitive, thrilling adjective" (*V,* 13).

Even Colette's detractors have tended to acknowledge the quality of her style: she was, wrote the celebrated critic Gustave Lanson "one of the great stylists of the age".[10] What this means from the reader's point of view is that the pleasure of reading Colette lies less in the thrill of suspense and satisfaction provided by narrative, than in the contemplative, almost sensual delight of language itself. Colette's practice as a writer corresponds to her thematic treatment of language. She is both a skilful manipulator of the Symbolic code within its own terms, using language to name, represent, evoke a world as thrillingly varied as the articles on her father's desk, and she employs stylistic devices which correspond to Kristeva's "semiotic" in that they produce language "irreducible" to an intelligible signified, which accentuate the sensual pleasure of speech that precedes acquisition of the Symbolic for the infant. As the quotation from *The Vagabond* above suggests, Colette's writing is founded both on the principle of representation, the desire to "note and describe" and thus to achieve linguistic form for experience, and on the intratextual pleasures of playing with language as a system of sound and meaning.

There is a consistent element of what we might term successful realism in Colette's style, in the sense that her descriptions of place, character and objects produce in the reader that shock of recognition that greets the precise articulation of a known, or of an acutely plausible, reality. Though, in the fiction at least, description always has a thematic and/or narrative function, rather than simply providing a backdrop or reinforcing a sense of the real, it does create the illusion of the text as "mere transcription of reality".[11] When in *Ripening Seed*:

> An off-shore breeze wafted the scent of the new-mown after-crop, farmyard smells, and the fragrance of bruised mint; little by little, along the level of the sea, a dusty pink was usurping the domain of blue unchallenged since the early morning.
>
> (*Ripening Seed* [*RS*], 21)

the heady odours of the breeze and the gradual replacement of the colour blue by pink connote Phil's state of vulnerable sensuality, and herald the theme of alternative forms of love, but the precise sensory images also verbally represent a Breton seascape. In both *The Vagabond* and the much later **"Rainy Moon"**, an urban street scene represents, for the narrator, the splendid variety of life outside the confines of obsessive love. In the earlier novel Renée is on tour in Marseilles and watches the happy, idle passersby on a quay side street:

> there are fresh flowers, carnations tied up in stiff bunches, like leeks, soaking in green pails: there is a street-stall loaded with black bananas smelling of ether, violets, clams, blue mussels and cockles, dotted about with lemons and little flasks of pink vinegar.
>
> (*V,* 162-3)

whilst the narrator of **"Rainy Moon"** observes a busy shopping street that slopes up to Montmartre in Paris, and sees amongst the hung chickens and the false hair pieces:

> oranges piled up in formation like cannon-balls for ancient artillery, withered apples, unripe bananas, anemic chicory, glutinous wads of dates, daffodils, pink panties, bloomers encrusted with imitation Chantilly . . .

as well as "shapeless housewives . . . blondes in down-at-heel shoes and brunettes in curlers . . . mother-of-pearl smelts", "butcher boys with cherubic faces" (*CSC,*

361). Structured as lists that accumulate disparate objects, jumbling together colours, shapes, tastes and smells, both descriptions elide the banal with the beautiful, the inanimate with the human, in a celebration of what is termed elsewhere "the marvellous commonplace" (*CSC,* 366). At one level these passages function through classically realist techniques of accumulated detail and appeal to the senses, though their absence of any aesthetic hierarchy that would separate flowers from bloomers, and the emphasis on plurality and variety rather than unity, are typical of Colette.

It is already apparent in these passages that the device of analogy is central to Colette's descriptive style: the carnations are "tied up in stiff bunches like leeks", the bananas smell of ether, the oranges are piled like cannon-balls and the butcher-boys' faces are like those of cherubs. Figures of speech based on analogy are features of standard linguistic practice, and offer a rich set of signifying possibilities. Colette employs simile and metaphor as devices which enhance descriptive precision—the visual image of the oranges is less exact without the analogy of cannon-balls—and which signify beyond the descriptive: the carnations "like leeks", the "mother-of-pearl" fish, contribute to an overall refusal to distinguish between objects of beauty and objects for use.

This extensive use of analogy is equally important in the construction of characters, where again the function of the simile or metaphor tends to be both visually descriptive and indicative of thematic concerns. Analogy can condense meaning, providing in an economical way both a vivid indication of physical appearance and a signifier of the character's function in the text's system of meaning: it is thus of particular value in the short story, where character must be rapidly established, and in the case of minor characters who again, need to be constructed for the reader with a relative economy of means. Thus Madame Hervouet of **"Green Sealing Wax"** owes her clear visual characterisation to her "resemblance to a black-and-yellow wasp" (*CSC,* 392), an image which also establishes the repressed anger and passion that will lead to her final undoing.

In the story **"Toutouque"** in *My Mother's House* (*MMH*), the central character is a dog, but a dog whose transformation from equable, affectionate family pet to wild fury under the influence of sexual passion, clearly has a human significance. The sensitive and wholly charming character of Toutouque is established through a rapid series of similes and metaphors: she is "broad and squat as a four-months pigling", but has delicate "shell-like" ears, with warm eyes "the color of old Madeira" like those of "a mulatto woman", and she displays a "nanny-like" amiability. Thus the shock of seeing Toutouque as a "kind of bristling yellow monster" (*MMH,* 98) is prepared.

Odette of **"The Rendez-vous"** with her strong white teeth and cruel wit is a "cannibal"; the grotesque old woman in **"The Burglar"** (**"Le Cambrioleur"**, 1924) who still dresses and acts like a beautiful young girl has a face like "a death's head in make-up", "pink as a piece of cracked wax fruit" (*CSC,* 271), images which establish the hideous visual contrast between decay and artifice. The same strongly visualised contrast occurs in the minor character of old Lili in **Chéri** (**C**): the embodiment of Léa's worst fears about aging, but also a member of the cast of characters representing the *demimonde* of 1900, Lili's disturbing concealment of an aging body beneath signifiers of youthful sexuality is expressed partly through analogies: she has "the corpulence of a eunuch", "a skinny bosom crinkled like the wattles of a turkey-cock" a neck "the shape of a flower-pot and the size of a belly" (*C,* 56).

In the case of the novels and of the major characters, the system of analogy tends to extend beyond the level of the individual simile or metaphor, and to become an integral part of the texts' system of meaning, taking us to another level of analysis. Chéri, for example, is associated throughout the novel with a cluster of non-human images: demon, god, blackbird, Asiatic prince, savage which establish the form and the impact of his beauty whilst signifying his alienation from the dominant culture, just as the consistent comparison of Farou (**The Other One**) to a wild animal establishes both his sexual magnetism and his human inadequacy.

Several novels set up internal metaphors, where a system of mutual comparison refers character to setting, and setting back to character. Léa is partially constructed as a character through the image of her welcoming, well-tended household with its dominant shade of pink but the house, in turn, and the colour pink, come to signify Léa even in her absence. The great indestructible leather sofa "le toutounier" is the place where Alice and her sisters talk, sleep, offer mutual love and support, but it then comes to mean all of these things, and the promise of their renewal, when Alice is left alone. Vinca with her "periwinkle eyes" and blonde hair "like stiff corn-stalks glinting in the sun" (*RS,* 5) is both a strongly visualised character and, through her identification with the natural world, part of a complex network of figurative meanings that unify the novel. Colette's use of the "indirect discourse"[12] of the image, and particularly of colour imagery, has been thoroughly analysed elsewhere and does not need lengthy discussion here.[13]

The purpose above has been to identify the referential qualities of Colette's style, those qualities which produce a convincing evocation of a world both tangible and suffused with meanings, through the use of familiar linguistic techniques of accumulated sensory detail and of analogy. This imples some optimism about existing

forms of language as a resource for the woman writer: that rigidity and reductionism that Colette associates thematically with male discourse would seem not to be a feature of language itself, but merely a particular, and avoidable, style of language. "The round material world, crammed with savours" (*BD,* 111) may be experienced and communicated within the medium of the Symbolic code. There are, nonetheless, two crucial features of Colette's style which invite discussion in terms of Kristeva's category of the "semiotic", and both of them lead towards the figure of the mother, of "Sido", that lies at the heart of Colette's work.

Though Colette's analogies are very frequently unexpected, like the Swiss lake in **The Captive** (**Cap**) "the colour of a sick pearl" (*Cap,* 59) or the cat's "yawn like a flower" (*BD,* 15) in **Break of Day,** the rational basis for the analogy can generally be deduced. Occasionally the frontier of logic is passed and an image produces, instead of a sudden perception of resemblance, that spark of incongruity sought by the Surrealists,[14] as when Fanny is described by Farou as "white as a coloured girl" (*OO,* 38), or the shadow of white trees is as "blue as young corn".[15]

Colette's writing favours the paradoxical, the disturbance, through apparently contradictory associations of words, of meanings which our culture holds to be rational and self-evident. Stupidity, in Colette's texts, may be "sublime" (*CSC,* 206), Chéri's lack of intelligence or education gives him "majesty" (*LC* [**The Last of Chéri**], 211), he is "magnificent and inferior" (*LC,* 211). The parents in **Ripening Seed** have the "childishness" and "faith in a rosy future" (*RS* [**Ripening Seed**], 40) which Phil and Vinca in their adolescent wisdom, envy, and Camille is never so pitiable a character as when she has just tried to murder Saha in **The Cat,** "poor little murderess" (*Cat,* 132). "Impetuosity" in **"The Képi"** has its own peculiar rituals (*CSC,* 527) and the **"The Hidden Woman"** ends her story in a glorious state of "immodest innocence" (*CSC,* 238).

The most frequent forms of linguistic paradox are those which involve the transposition of gender signs. From Phil's "traits . . . of a violated girl" (*RS,* 61), Vinca's "virile contempt" (*RS,* 66) and Camille's "soft, masculine voice" (*RS,* 45) in **Ripening Seed,** a novel that operates a constant exchange of gender signs between the three central characters, to Julie de Carneilhan's "shocking and masculine gesture(s)" (**Julie de Carneilhan** [**JC,**] 182) and her lover Coco's resemblance to "one of those old fashioned French girls" (*JC,* 116), Colette's writing is characterised by a deliberate and playful displacement of the signifiers of masculinity and femininity.

The questioning of accepted meanings through paradox and contradiction is particularly associated with Sido. The style of speech and writing that Colette attributes to her "model" Sido in *Break of Day* is paradoxical because it denies the most fundamental dualities in the name of a celebratory sense of wholeness and unity. Faithful, monogamous heterosexual love is one of the major positive values of our culture but "So great a love!" writes Sido of her husband's life-long devotion to her, "What frivolity!" (*BD*, 127), and in another letter evoked in the same text "Love is not a sentiment worthy of respect" (*BD*, 22). For love, as her daughter comments, "suppresses and condemns everything around it" (*BD*, 133). Sido also "knew that one possesses through abstaining, and only through abstaining" (*BD*, 24) and refused the distinction between good and evil for "evil and good can be equally resplendent and fruitful" (*BD*, 27). Youth and age cease to be opposites: "Seventy-five? . . . it's not true is it? Must one really soon give up being young?" writes Sido.

No, no, of course not, don't give it up yet—I've never known you anything but young, your death saves you from growing old and even from dying, you who are always with me.

(*BD*, 91)

The structure of *Break of Day* echoes the paradox, for Sido who was Colette's point of origin becomes in turn her destination, and the distinction between birth and death is itself questioned by the placing of the mother at the end as well as at the beginning. This refusal of the most fundamental dualities of language, particularly in its correspondence with a powerful image of the mother as source of a re-found unity, seems to belong with the "semiotic" as that force which "questions and transgresses . . . the limits of our conventional sign systems". In the words of Nicole Ward-Jouve "Difference is no longer the absolute corner-stone."[16]

There is another sense too in which the "semiotic" is relevant to Colette's writing. The Symbolic code works through an assumption of clear and fixed relationships between verbal signifier and the signified: though the relationship between sound and sense is in fact, on the whole arbitrary, a functional use of language requires that we suppress awareness of that arbitrary coding and proceed as if "dog" meant, in some immutable way, "dog". The semiotic, in as far as it originates in that pre-verbal period when sounds were pleasurable without fixed meanings, could be said to free the signifier from the signified, as in certain forms of poetry.

There is a distinct preoccupation in Colette's texts with the word as sensual experience, with the materiality of language or what the writer herself calls "phonetic rapture" (*Journey for Myself* [*JM*], 83). The child astride the garden wall plays with the multiple possibilities of the word "presbytery" "with its harsh and spiky beginning and the brisk trot of its final syllables" (*MMH*, 45), shouting it at invisible outlaws "Begone! you are

all presbyteries!", and then deciding that it "might very possibly be the scientific term for a certain little yellow-and-black striped snail". To learn that the word is limited to the sole signified of "a priest's house" can only be a disappointment. It is a child too who, in the story **"The Sick Child"** (**"L'Enfant malade"**, 1944) frees words from their functional limits to experience them as sound, smell, or image, so that his robust cousin Charlie's use of the word "boy-scout" is "half-steel, half India-rubber" (*CSC*, 336), and when he hears his mother and the doctor discussing his possibly salutary "crisis":

Sometimes it entered ceremoniously, like a lady dressed up to give away prizes with an h behind its ear and a y tucked into its bodice: Chrysis, Chrysis Wilby-Sallatry . . .

(*CSC*, 339)

The sick child rides on words, meets them as monsters "pointed sounds with muzzles like mongooses" (*CSC*, 341), hears their music, and since good health will restore him to a structured life and a functional perception of language, the story's "happy ending" is only qualified and he falls asleep "assenting, cured and disappointed" (*CSC*, 346). The adult narrator of *Break of Day* retains some sense of the sensual variety of words:

Solitary . . . it's a beautiful-looking word, beginning with its capital S rearing like a protective serpent. I can't entirely isolate it from the fierce glitter it receives from the solitaire diamond . . .

(*BD*, 67)

and the narrator of *Journey for Myself: Selfish Memories* (*Le Voyage egoiste*, 1922) feverishly hot, delights not just in the thought but in the word "frost" (*givre* in French): "When I repeat that sparkling word, I feel that I'm biting into a crunchy ball of snow" (*JM*, 20). Chéri's incantatory use of the name "Nounoune" for Léa is surely also based on the sensual pleasure of the repeated syllable, and resembles the first sounds that babies make, intensifying the sense that for Chéri loving Léa means a return to the semiotic.

The "semiotic" means the carrying forward, into adult life and adult discourse, of a lost unity preceding identity, preceding difference. If the Symbolic code is identified with the masculine, because of the status of the phallus as positive term, then the semiotic can well be seen as the potentially disruptive power of the suppressed feminine. The problem is that this locates the feminine in a backward-looking search for total fusion with the mother, when the achievement of adult identity requires both identification and differentiation. To see the semiotic as the only authentic source of a "woman's word" seems to exclude women from the realm of written language, except where writing is at the very frontiers of intelligible meaning.

Colette's writing demonstrates a woman's highly competent, and confident, assumption of the role of subject within the Symbolic code, whilst thematically addressing the issue of male control of language, and whilst introducing a dimension that could usefully be related to the "semiotic". Particularly through the figure of Sido, but also through consistent aspects of her style, Colette disturbs the comfortable polarities of language and the unquestioned relationship of signifier to signified. Sido does not represent only the nostalgic reality of a presymbolic past, but also represents a movement forwards, which integrates and transcends the rational world identified with the father. It is Sido who first takes the green sealing wax from her husband's desk and offers it to her daughter; it is Sido who, in her daughter's recreation, writes letters which are both intelligible and suffused with an interrogation of standard meanings, and it is she who in her final letter before her death leaves the constrictions of language behind not to regress, but to advance. The two sheets she addressed to her daughter (in **Break of Day**) contain few words, only "joyful signs" and embryonic sketches which echo the book's dominant metaphor of blossoming, shining outwards: "arrows emerging from an embryo word, little rays" (**BD,** 142). These represent:

> messages from a hand that was trying to transmit to me a new alphabet or the sketch of some ground-plan envisaged at dawn under rays that would never attain the sad zenith.

and if her daughter can pursue the signs then she will gain access to the disparate, wonderfully various plurality of meaning signified by the book's closing images: "a quickset hedge, spindrift, meteors, an open and unending book, a cluster of grapes, a ship, an oasis . . ." (**BD,** 143).

Notes

1. Dale Spender, *Man-Made Language* (London: Routledge & Kegan Paul, 1980).

2. From Julia Kristeva's *Revolution in Poetic Language* in Toril Moi, *The Kristeva Reader* (Oxford: Blackwell, 1986), p. 97.

3. Terry Eagleton, *Literary Theory: an Introduction* in Mary Eagleton (ed.) *Feminist Literary Theory* (Oxford: Blackwell, 1986), p. 215.

4. Annie Leclerc, *Parole de femme* (Paris: Grasset, 1974).

5. Hélène Cixous, "The Laugh of the Medusa" in Mary Eagleton, op. cit., p. 227.

6. Toril Moi, *Sexual/Textual Politics* (London: Methuen, 1985).

7. Terry Eagleton, op. cit., pp. 214-15.

8. For an analysis of *Gigi* as a story about linguistic repression see Susan D. Cohen, "An Onomastic Double Bind: Colette's *Gigi* and the Politics of Naming" (*PMLA,* October 1985).

9. Jacob Stockinger, "The Test of Love and Nature: Colette and Lesbians" in E. M. Eisinger and M. W. McCarty, *Colette: The Woman, The Writer* (Pennsylvania State University Press, 1981), p. 85.

10. Gustave Lanson, *Histoire de la littérature française* (Paris: Hachette, 1951), p. 1235.

11. Suzanne Relyea, "Polymorphic Perversity: Colette's Illusory 'Real'" in Eisinger and McCarty, op. cit., p. 154.

12. André Joubert, *Colette et Chéri* (Paris: Nizet, 1972), p. 165.

13. For example, see the article by I. T. Olken, "Aspects of Imagery in Colette: Color and Light" (*PMLA,* LXXVII, March 1962), pp. 140-8.

14. The Surrealist poets, writing in France in the 1920s and 30s, took as one of their central techniques the creation of images based on incongruity rather than similarity e.g. Paul Éluard's "The world is blue as an orange".

15. Colette, in *Notes de tournées* (Tour Notes), *Oeuvres II,* p. 203.

16. Nicole Ward-Jouve, *Colette* (Brighton: Harvester, 1987), p. 140.

Bibliography

Here my aim is to provide a complete list of those texts referred to in my study: these are listed in order of original publication, with the titles in English first where references are to the English edition, and in French first where the translations are my own. Wherever possible, references are to English translations in paperback editions.

Claudine à l'école [1900] (*Claudine at School*), in *Oeuvres I* (Paris: Gallimard, Bibliothèque de la Pléaidé, 1984).

Claudine à Paris [1901] (*Claudine in Paris*), in *Oeuvres I,* as above.

Claudine en ménage [1902] (*Claudine Married*), in *Oeuvres I,* as above.

Claudine s'en va [1903] (*Claudine and Annie*), in *Oeuvres I,* as above.

La Retraite sentimentale [1907] (*The Retreat from Love*), in *Oeuvres I,* as above.

Les Vrilles de la vigne [1908] (*The Tendrils of the Vine*), in *Oeuvres I,* as above.

The Innocent Libertine [1909] (*L'Ingénue libertine*) (London: Penguin, 1972).

The Vagabond [1910] (*La Vagabonde*), (London: Penguin, 1960).

"L'Enfant de Bastienne" [1912] ("Bastienne's Child"), in *The Collected Stories of Colette* (ed.) Robert Phelps (London: Penguin, 1985), henceforth referred to as *CSC*.

L'Envers du music-hall [1913] (*Music-hall Sidelights*), in *Oeuvres II* (Paris: Gallimard, Bibliothèque de la Pléaide, 1986).

The Captive [1913] (*L'Entrave*) (London: Penguin, 1970).

La Paix chez les bêtes [1916] and *Autres Bêtes* [1916] (*Creatures Great and Small*), in *Oeuvres II*, as above.

Les Heures longues [1917] (*The Long Hours*), in *Oeuvres II*, as above.

Dans la foule [1918] (*In the Crowd*), in *Oeuvres II*, as above.

Mitsou ou comment l'esprit vient aux filles [1918] (*Mitsou*), in *Oeuvres II*, as above.

Chéri and *The Last of Chéri* [1920 & 1926] (London: Penguin, 1954).

My Mother's House and *Sido* [1922 & 1929] (*La Maison de Claudine* and *Sido*) (London: Penguin, 1966).

Journey for Myself: Selfish Memories [1922] (*Le Voyage egoiste*) (London: Peter Owen, 1971).

Ripening Seed [1923] (*Le Blé en herbe*) (London: Penguin, 1959).

"The Hidden Woman" [1924] ("La Femme cachée"), in *The Collected Stories of Colette* (ed.) Robert Phelps (London: Penguin, 1985), henceforth referred to as *CSC*.

Aventures quotidiennes [1924] (*Everyday Adventures*), selections in *Journey for Myself: Selfish Memories*, above.

Break of Day [1928] (*La Naissance du jour*) (London: The Women's Press, 1979).

The Other One [1929] (*La Seconde*) (London: Penguin, 1972).

The Pure and the Impure [1932 under the title *Ces Plaisirs,* changed in 1941 to *Le Pur et l'impur*] (London: Penguin, 1971).

The Cat [1933] (*La Chatte*), in *Gigi* and *The Cat* (London: Penguin, 1958).

Duo and *Le Toutounier* [1934 & 1939] (London: The Women's Press, 1979).

La Jumelle noire [1934-38] (*The Black Opera-Glasses*: volume of theatre criticism) in *Oeuvres Complètes*, vol. x (Paris: Editions le Fleuron, 1948-50).

Mes Apprentissages [1936] (*My Apprenticeships*) (Paris: Frenczi et fils, 1936).

"Bella Vista" [1937] in *CSC,* see above.

"Gribiche" [1937] in *CSC,* see above.

Chance Acquaintances [1940] (*Chambre d'hotel*) (London: Penguin, 1957).

Looking Backwards [1941] (*Journal à rebours*) (London: The Women's Press, 1987).

Julie de Carneilhan [1941] (London: Penguin, 1957).

Mes cahiers (Paris: Aux Armes de France, 1941).

"Le Képi" [1943], in *CSC,* see above.

"Green Sealing Wax" [1943] ("La Cire verte") in *CSC,* see above.

"The Tender Shoot" [1943] ("The Tendron") in *CSC,* see above.

Gigi [1944] in *Gigi* and *The Cat* (London: Penguin, 1958).

"The Sick Child" [1944] ("L'Enfant malade") in *CSC,* see above.

Belles Saisons [1945] (Paris: Flammarion, 1945).

The Evening Star [1946] (*L'Etoile vesper*) (London: The Women's Press, 1987).

The Blue Lantern [1949] (*Le Fanal bleu*) (London: Secker & Warburg, 1963).

The following editions of texts by Colette were also particularly useful in this study:

Colette: au cinema edited by Alain and Odette Virmaux (Paris: Flammarion, 1975).

Colette/Sido: Letters (Paris: Editions des femmes, 1984).

Dana Strand (essay date fall 1992)

SOURCE: Strand, Dana. "The 'Third Woman' in Colette's 'Chance Acquaintances.'" *Studies in Short Fiction* 29, no. 4 (fall 1992): 499-508.

[*In the following essay, Strand maintains that despite its resemblance to trite nineteenth-century stories about sexual indiscretion, "Chance Acquaintances" is a complex and unconventionally structured examination of gender differences.*]

A distraught husband, confined to a resort hotel where his wife is taking the cure, prevails upon a fellow vacationer, whom he has met quite by chance, to visit his mistress in Paris in order to find out why he has not heard from her in over two weeks. When the acquaintance, a woman writer and part-time music hall performer, returns with the news that the mistress has disappeared without a trace, the philandering husband is so shaken that he attempts suicide. Bungling the affair badly by taking a massive dose of an emetic poison, he survives only to become involved in another romantic liaison, this time with an opportunistic "dancer" to whom he has been introduced by the writer. Meanwhile, despite her husband's flagrant infidelities, the wife, occupied alternately by her profligate spouse, her illness and her intricate needlework, remains a paragon of feminine virtue.

Thus summarized, Colette's short story, **"Chance Acquaintances"** is, if truth be told, decidedly pedestrian. At first glance, the story's events and characters present little more than a reworking of a plot line that, by the end of the nineteenth century, had become a trite commonplace. In fact, the plot of this tale of sexual indiscretion calls to mind any number of turn-of-the-century novels that were the product of a collaborative effort of the group of hack writers deftly managed by Colette's first husband, Willy. The narrative lines of such novels as *Une Passade* or *Maîtresse d'esthètes* trace the amorous adventures of naïve or inexperienced men who fall victim to what Claude Pichois refers to, in his introduction to Colette's collected works, as "vampire women," a uniformly rapacious lot, no doubt direct descendants of the destructive women who haunted the creative imaginations of Flaubert, Zola and the decadents (1: lxxvi). The prototypical predatory woman, represented in Colette's story by both mistresses of the male character, Gérard Haume, finds her opposite in Haume's wife, an exemplary model of the saintly female whose most noteworthy quality is a silent passivity in the face of adversity.

In recent years, literary critics have come to view the tendency among male authors either to exalt or denigrate female characters as a manifestation of psychosexual phenomena that are the direct outgrowth of the limitations imposed by rigidly determined gender definitions. Isabelle de Courtivron, for example, basing her arguments on the theories of Karen Horney, suggests that a sublimated struggle between fear of and wish for castration leads to a deep-rooted ambivalence in men toward their own and female sexuality (223). In playing out his "wish to be a woman," an impulse toward androgyny that is thwarted by narrowly defined sex roles in patriarchal societies, the male writer thus creates the cruel, sadistic woman as a check on what he recognizes as a dangerous fantasy.

Object-relations theorists, stressing the primacy of the mother-child relationship in both male and female ego formation, hold that the particular circumstances in which the masculine personality is formed produce an unavoidable ambivalence toward women.[1] According to this account, the male child must establish his identity through a breaking of the pre-oedipal bond with the mother, a separation that, during the Oedipal stage, necessarily involves a simultaneous reinforcement and repression of the infantile love turned heterosexual. As a result, in order to reaffirm their independent identities, men must strive at all costs to deny their connections with femininity, continuing all the while to harbor nostalgic fantasies of their "lost union with mother-as-flesh" (Kahn 77).

Whatever the explanation for the predilection among male writers to depict women as either passively angelic or aggressively malevolent, it is clear that in **"Chance Acquaintances"** Colette fashions a narrative that, despite a plot structure and characterizations drawn from a vision that is gendered male, manages to veer significantly from the model. Using the stock plot elements and characters as a springboard for exploring issues that, from the earliest collections of her short stories to those published toward the end of her literary career, have been central to her enterprise, she diverts the course of the conventional plot by cleverly manipulating the role the narrator plays in the story and its structuring. For the writer who becomes the reluctant confidant of the wayward husband is the narrator Colette, whose complex relation to the events (and of the events) opens the way to a consideration of such fundamental issues as the inadequacies of generally accepted gender differences and the multiplicity of the female self.

If in the novels signed by Willy, his narrator (also a double for the author) is often an experienced man of a rigidly defined world in which males are invariably victimized by scheming, unscrupulous females, the Colette character in **"Chance Acquaintances"** is revealed to be an equally experienced woman of a world where such easy, unambiguous categories no longer hold sway. Through the interventions of Colette, who, in the guise of intermediary (she refers to herself as a "proxy" [291]) participates in the action, and, in the role of narrator, both discloses and decodes other characters and events, the strict adherence to literary stereotypes, on which the plot seems at first to be founded, gradually crumbles away. By her reworking of past practices, Colette exposes her particular, if not idiosyncratic, vision of the world, introducing a perspective that in many ways resists essentialist psychoanalytic explanations.

From the outset, the narrator establishes the fundamental design of the text, when she explains her reasons for writing the story by reproducing brief notes that she made after first meeting the Haumes:

> Fear of strangers. Contrariwise, the fear of displeasing strangers whose reaction has been amiable, whether or not with a hidden purpose. I tiptoe past a closed door,

to avoid being obliged to say good morning if the door should be opened. Contrariwise, the need to send Mme Haume a big bunch of the yellow irises that grow beside the mountain streams. The desire to place the illustrated weeklies alongside Mme Haume's white suede shoes outside her door. Withdrawals . . . Advances.

(243)

This auto-citation, portraying the narrator in the grips of opposing forces, motivated alternately to advance and then to retreat by an almost simultaneous fear of indifference and involvement, functions as an intertextual *mise en abîme,* prefiguring a similar oscillation in Colette's role as interpreter of her own narrative. As her judgments of others shift from sympathy to antipathy and back again, the portraits of the three central characters that gradually emerge are subtly modified in such a way as to dismantle the fixed triangle in which we might expect to find a victimized and thus largely sympathetic male balanced precariously between a "good" and a "bad" woman.

Colette opens the story with a description of Lucette d'Orgeville, a marginal theatrical performer rejected by the true music hall artists who scorn her lack of professionalism. In her initial appearance, Lucette conforms to the model of the destructive Eve figure. Compared by the narrator to a parasitic mollusk, she represents a human type Colette disdainfully refers to as "envoys from the nether world" (225), who through the exercise of mysterious powers of attraction, succeed in luring their victims into unpleasant situations and relationships. Quixotic ("her mood would vary with her luck" [226]) and self-centered, Lucette awaits only a suitably enticing monetary incentive to abandon one lover for another.

The image of a self-absorbed, autonomous Lucette is, however, modulated by the observations of the narrator, whose reading of the woman brings to the surface the hidden dangers of her situation. In describing Lucette adorned with the jewels lavished upon her by her current lover, the narrator notes: "she raised both her arms together as though they were handcuffed" (230) and remembers her later "weakly raising her fetters of diamonds . . ." (291). Through her interpretive interventions in the text, the narrator stresses the high personal cost to Lucette of the role she has been assigned. The manipulative fortune hunter is unmasked to reveal a woman imprisoned by a situation that forces her to surrender her own love interests in return for economic dependence upon men to whom she remains sentimentally indifferent.

Although, in **"Chance Acquaintances,"** Colette claims that her narrative has little to do with Lucette ("It is quite unnecessary for the purposes of this story to dwell for long on the subject of Mlle d'Orgeville" [226]), she nevertheless carefully develops her largely unsympathetic portrait over several pages of the text. Now it is almost always the case in Colette's short fiction that apparently gratuitous digressions, even when labeled as such by a disingenuous narrator, serve to reinforce the overall narrative design. Colette's strategic showcasing of a parasitic woman, prone to easy liaisons for which she is more often than not materially rewarded, is an illustration of this general rule. The text begins with Lucette's description and ends with her sordid death. The account of Gérard Haume's misadventures, regularly punctuated by reminders of his wife's stoic passivity, is thus framed by Lucette's story, with which it eventually becomes entangled. As the plot unfolds, in fact, the focus of interest shifts from the romantic foibles of the male protagonist (Haume = *homme*?) to the constellation of exemplary women (Luc*ette,* Antoin*ette* and of course Col*ette*) whose complexly drawn characters stand in sharp contrast to the rather dull, undifferentiated Gérard.

Lucette's central position in the story is justified toward the end of the narrative, when she responds to Colette's complaints about her involvement with a married man. The defense she mounts, completely devoid of moral considerations, is based on the claim that for her, Gérard is an example of "the chap at the end of the wire." She then explains:

> The wire of the electric bell. Haven't you ever been tempted by the button of a door-bell, when you're in a strange place? I am, often, I say to myself, 'I'd like to know what's at the end of that wire. Suppose I press that button? Perhaps it'll bring the police or cause an explosion, or a peal of God's thunder. . . .'

(306)

Colette admits that, were it not for the poor Antoinette, she would be amused by Lucette's liaison with Gérard Haume, since she no doubt realizes that, in her dealings with chance acquaintances, she has fallen victim to a similar curiosity. The two women, daughters of Eve to the extent that they are both seekers of truth, disregard the risks they may encounter in their pursuit of knowledge. Although Colette characterizes her decision to remain at the hotel after Antoinette's recovery as a perverse response to Gérard's bitterness about the role she played as messenger in his abortive love affair ("I decided to leave for Paris, but I stayed on because Gérard Haume wished me ill" [289]), her unconvincing explanation does not appear to justify her actions. What is important for our understanding of the structuring principle underlying the text is that, as the narrator hesitates between withdrawal and advance, she establishes an underlying pattern that constantly varies the distance between narrator and character, keeping the reader off-balance as narrative perspective slips sometimes imperceptibly from that of disinterested, casual observer to that of a woman who strongly identifies with a particular character.

In the slowly evolving portrait of Antoinette that the narrator sketches throughout "Chance Acquaintances," is inscribed a similar pattern of approach followed by avoidance, of approval laced with censure. As a representative of the "eternal feminine" (45), Antoinette is, for better or for worse, in sickness or in health, ever patient and silent. The sort of woman who, according to the narrator, is inclined to suffer from heat in the summer and cold in the winter, she is given to frivolous and unproductive preoccupations with fashion and needlepoint. In her rather mundane interests as well as in her lackluster conversation, the narrator finds her singularly unremarkable.

Yet, there is another side to Antoinette that the narrator also carefully observes. Struck from their first meeting by her masculine physical characteristics ("a husky, virile voice" and "powerful wrists"), the narrator is impressed by the woman's courage and strength in the face of illness and her husband's infidelity:

> She never complained. I like courage in women. I like to watch the ingenuity it gives rise to in organising a life of suffering. I admired Antoinette's patience and the way she would sit without speaking, wrapped up against the wind in a little shawl of patterned satin, edged with mink, which I thought atrocious, while she cut the pages of a novel. Her wisdom appealed to me in much the same way as her powerful wrists, her strong and by no means ugly mouth, her firm, thick neck—a smooth column instinct with exceptional power.
>
> (247)

Colette openly admits that in many respects, she is no match for her friend, who is "endowed with great and good qualities in which I am lacking: patience, a gift of observation that put mine in the shade, and courage, beside which my bold gestures were hardly more than temporary whims" (308-09).

By linking virility to patience, to the capacity to endure life's injustices without complaint, Colette suggests a realignment of the traditionally accepted views of the feminine and the masculine. In contrast to her husband, whose high voice and delicate hands are signs of his fragility and inconstancy, Antoinette displays remarkable resilience and strength. Gérard Haume is, in fact, perhaps one of the best examples in Colette's fiction of her particular view of the "eternal masculine."[2] Weak in character, narcissistic, indecisive, he fails in his only attempt at independently initiated action, his suicide. The narrator, irritated by his phlegmatic posture, has no sympathy for his plight: "Men who are too exclusively taken up with women receive their punishment, in due course, from the women themselves" (281).

But, if the narrator paints a predominantly unfavorable picture of Gérard, the reader must be careful not to put too much faith in her judgments, for she gives fair warn-ing that she is not a consistently reliable witness. Initially attracted to Haume because of his physical appearance (she notes his habit of drawing attention to his blue eyes by wearing clothing of the same color), Colette is disappointed to discover that he remains indifferent to her: "I could read no actual hostility into Gérard Haume's look; but then again, no desire to please. There can hardly exist a woman who would not be faintly offended at such swift and silent proof of her own harmlessness" (248). She subsequently acknowledges that her objectivity may be compromised by her pride: "Women are quick to attribute such signs of indifference to the cause of mental deficiency" (249).

At several key points, the narrator openly calls into question the validity of her own judgments, drawing upon a lucidity that time has afforded her. Her occasional reflections on her unavoidable partiality introduce into an otherwise straightforward relation of events the ambiguity that makes this and other texts by Colette a great deal more complex than many critics have acknowledged. As Mieke Bal demonstrates in her thorough analysis of the novel, *The Cat*, Colette manipulates narrative perspective in such a way as to systematically prevent the reader from identifying too closely with any one character. Her adroit shifts in point of view make definitive interpretations of characters and events problematic.

The narrator's uncertainty in sorting out what she observes is underscored by a recurrent motif that casts her in the role of a decipherer, who tries unsuccessfully to penetrate the mysteries of others. Antoinette's needlework, with which she is continually occupied both during and after her illness, is the first of these motifs to test Colette's decoding skills. Although she asks her friend several times to repeat the specific name of the embroidery she is working on, Colette seems unable to retain it. The embroidery comes to represent Antoinette's infinite patience, a quality that the narrator admits, here as well as in her autobiographical novel, *Break of Day*, is foreign to her realm of experience:

> The jobs I don't like are those that need patience. It takes patience to write a book and also to win over a man when he's feeling savage, to mend worn linen and to sort the raisins for a plum cake. I would never have made either a good cook or a good wife, and I nearly always cut string instead of untying knots.
>
> (88-89)

While acknowledging that Antoinette possesses a patience superior to her own, the narrator nevertheless seems perplexed by her friend's silent passivity. As symbol of the stoic woman's implacable nature, her needlework reminds Colette of her half-sister Juliette, who also engaged frequently in what she calls this "frivolous activity." The reference to Juliette is revealing, since in *My Mother's House,* Colette presents her older sister as an enigmatic figure whose secrets cannot be easily discerned even by her own family members: "she would sometimes turn towards me an unseeing glance, that sexless, ageless glance of the obsessed, full of obscure defiance and an incomprehensible irony" (79).

Expressing both the admiration and the incomprehension that Antoinette's patience evokes in her, Colette exploits all the contradictory metaphorical implications of sewing as they have been developed in literature. Tied to domestic confinement, needlework can be seen as a trivialized feminine occupation or the activity of powerful women who, like Penelope, "exercise their art subversively and quietly in order to control the lives of men" (Gilbert and Gubar 521). The theme of sewing, in fact, surfaces frequently in Colette's short stories, affording her the opportunity to examine the unexplored signification of this female art. In **"The Sempstress,"** a chapter of *My Mother's House,* she confesses that she would have preferred that her daughter not learn how to sew, for she recognizes the disruptive currents that can be tapped by a mind left free to think: "it would seem that with this needle-play she has discovered the perfect means of adventuring, stitch by stitch, point by point, along a road of risks and temptations" (132).

In another short piece entitled **"If I Had a Daughter . . . ,"** Colette debates the importance of needlework with her "friend Valentine," who maintains that teaching young girls how to sew is a way of reaffirming old-fashioned moral values. While Valentine views sewing as a means of taming the female spirit ("a young lady who plies her needle isn't looking for trouble, believe me" [**"If I Had . . ."** 57]), Colette sees it as a potentially seditious activity, affording the young girl the opportunity to give free rein to her lively imagination:

> For a solitary little girl, what immoral book can equal the long silence, the unbridled reverie over the open-work muslin or the rosewood loom? Overly precise, a bad book might frighten, or disappoint. But the bold daydream soars up, sly, impudent, varied to the rhythm of the needle as it bites the silk; it grows, beats the silence with burning wings, inflames the pale little hand, the cheek where the shadow of the eyelashes flutters.
>
> (60)

Through the play between appearance and reality, the calm and quietly conciliatory posture of the sewing woman is undermined by the suggestion that an unfettered spirit pulsates beneath her serene exterior. Colette's inability to understand her friend's embroidery, which represents, at one and the same time, feminine passivity and courage, serves to suggest that the intricate needlework is to be taken as a token of the complex intricacy of the female self.

In her hesitation to attach a fixed identity to her female acquaintances, Colette underscores not only her own reluctance to intervene, but what is no doubt more important, the fundamental "undecidability" of the female self. The choice of the term is particularly significant because it is one called upon by Freud in his attempts to account for feminine sexuality. According to Sarah Kofman, Freud's inability to lay to rest his fears of the unfathomable mystery that woman represented for him, led him to formulate the "castration complex" as a means of stabilizing what he recognized as woman's inevitable movement between opposites, her underlying bisexuality (248). As Elizabeth Berg points out in an article entitled "The Third Woman," Kofman rejects the notion of the castration complex, that "reduces woman to a lesser version of man" (12), arguing that woman's resistance to any essentialist notion of her femininity lies precisely in her irresolvable oscillation between her passive and active tendencies.

In a reprise of the movement furnishing the basic pattern of the narrative, Colette's evolving portraits of the three female characters in **"Chance Acquaintances"** trace the same swing between opposing forces. Lucette balances between independent, affirmative action and a dependency induced, at least in part, by economic necessity. Antoinette, although a model of female passivity, reveals an inner reserve of resilience. And finally, Colette, in spite of her aversion for initiating action, is ultimately directly or indirectly responsible for everything that takes place: it is she who tells Gérard of his mistress's disappearance, precipitating his suicide attempt, it is she who introduces him to Lucette, and of course it is she who, after all, has generated the narrative. Incontestable proof of her creative powers, the story (and not just the narrating) is clearly of her own making: "Ghosts, even flesh and blood ghosts, do not appear unless they are summoned up" (254).

In a discussion of the variety of sexual types that figure in the pages of *The Pure and the Impure,* Ann Cothran convincingly argues,

> to many readers these portraits seem separate and distinct, a reaction no doubt due to the general social tendency to classify human sexuality in rigid, polarized categories. However, a close textual analysis of the ways in which meaning is communicated and organized . . . reveals that Colette has altered our conventional perceptions by breaking down and reassembling these categories.
>
> (335-36)

Similarly, the ultimate effect of the fluid portraits of women that dominate **"Chance Acquaintances"** is to undermine any reading of the story that would allow sexual stereotypes to remain intact. Fulfilling a threefold function as observer, character, and writer, Colette intervenes in all three capacities to call into question rigidly drawn gender boundaries.

"Chance Acquaintances" is one of several short stories by Colette that examine gender roles either by exploring what is often depicted as the treacherous area separating male and female experience or by subtly blurring fixed and immutable boundaries that wall off those experiences from one another.[3] In fact, it could be argued that the vast majority of her short fiction focuses on one or another kind of frontier experience, making forays into the uncharted terrain that marks the dividing line between, for example, past and present versions of the self, youth and adulthood, economic security and poverty. In each case, Colette's story provides fertile ground for a systematic interrogation of boundary zones, often detailing the exciting, if dangerous consequences of flirting with forbidden frontiers.

If we return to the plot summary with which this essay begins, we can now modify it to reflect the actual impact of Colette's complexly drawn portraits on the reader in the following way: Challenging the peril-ridden domain of phallocentric representation, an "affirmative" woman (to use Kofman's term), tells a story that posits woman as fundamentally multiple, resisting all attempts to fix her image. By embracing such indeterminacy as a positive reflection of the polymorphous nature of the female self, the portraits she creates combat the social and literary tendencies of the time to view gender differences and definitions as static and unchanging. Instead, the story offers a highly nuanced vision that systematically deconstructs sexual stereotypes by subsuming categorical opposites under the inclusive rubrique of the eternal(ly protean) feminine.

Notes

1. The most often cited proponent of object-relations theory is Chodorow (*Reproducing of Mothering*). For a cogent critique of the deterministic grounding of Chodorow's theoretical assumptions, see Baym.

2. See Biolley-Godino for a full examination of this issue. Biolley-Godino frequently refers to Gérard Haume as a representative male character in Colette's fiction.

3. Among Colette's other stories exploring gender roles and relations are "The Other Woman," "Armande," and "The Photographer's Wife."

Works Cited

Bal, Mieke. *Complexité d'un roman populaire.* Paris: La Pensée universelle, 1981.

Baym, Nina. "The Madwoman and Her Languages: Why I Don't Do Feminist Literary Theory." *Feminist Issues in Literary Scholarship.* Ed. Shari Benstock. Bloomington: Indiana UP, 1987. 45-61.

Berg, Elizabeth. "The Third Woman." *Diacritics* 12 (Summer 1982): 11-21.

Biolley-Godino, Marcelle. *L'Homme objet chez Colette.* Paris: Klincksieck, 1972.

Chodorow, Nancy. *The Reproducing of Mothering: Psychoanalysis and the Sociology of Gender.* Berkeley: U of California P, 1978.

Colette. "Chance Acquaintances." *Three Short Novels* 225-315.

———. *The Collected Stories of Colette.* Ed. Robert Phelps. New York: Farrar, 1983.

———. "If I Had a Daughter . . ." *Collected Stories* 56-58.

———. *My Mother's House and Sido.* Trans. Una Vincenzo Troubridge and Enid McLeod. New York: Penguin, 1966.

———. *Three Short Novels by Colette.* Trans. Patrick Leigh Fermor. New York: Farrar, 1952.

Cothran, Ann. "*The Pure and the Impure:* Codes and Constructs." *Women Studies* 8 (1981): 335-57.

Courtivron, Isabelle de. "Weak Men and Fatal Women: The Sand Image." *Homosexualities and French Literature.* Ed. Elaine Marks and George Stambolian. Ithaca, NY: Cornell UP, 1979. 210-27.

Gilbert, Sandra, and Susan Gubar. *The Madwoman in the Attic: The Woman Writer and the Nineteenth-Century Literary Imagination.* New Haven, CT: Yale UP, 1979.

Kahn, Coppélia. "The Hand that Rocks the Cradle: Recent Gender Theories and Their Implications." *The (M)other Tongue: Essays in Feminist Psychoanalytic Interpretations.* Ed. Shirley Nelson Garner, Claire Kahane and Madelon Sprengnether. Ithaca, NY: Cornell UP, 1985. 72-88.

Kofman, Sarah. *L'énigme de la femme dans les textes de Freud.* Paris: Galilée, 1980.

Pichois, Claude. Preface. *Oeuvres.* By Colette. 2 vols. Paris: Editions de la Pléiade, 1984. 1: ix-cxxii.

Willy. *Une Passade.* Paris: Calmann-Lévy, 1894.

———. *Maîtresse d'esthètes.* Paris: Simonis Empis, 1897.

Dana Strand (essay date 1995)

SOURCE: Strand, Dana. "Mothers and Daughters" and "The Narrator as Quick-Change Artist." In *Colette: A Study of the Short Fiction,* pp. 14-24, 80-94. New York: Twayne Publishers, 1995.

[*In the following excerpt from her study of Colette's short fiction, Strand examines Colette's use of the mother figure in her later stories before turning to the shifting narrative perspectives in her work.*]

Infused with vivid reminiscences of Sido, the almost mythical mother figure whose portrait evolves in several volumes of memoirs as well as fiction, Colette's entire opus serves as testimony to the prevailing influence of the maternal image in her writing. Portrayed alternatively as a "beneficent goddess," or a "primal source,"[1] Sido was above all a model whose literary presence her daughter carefully molded over the years. As Mari McCarty warns, "we cannot take Sido to mean Colette's flesh and blood mother, but rather Colette's idea and reconstruction of her mother in the text. After creating herself, Colette created her own mentor."[2] Although in Colette's earliest works, maternal figures were curiously absent, as her writing became more blatantly autobiographical she began to reserve a growing place for the literalized "Sido." Yet, because in these later stories the narrative voice gathers strength and confidence from the mother image it evokes, what Robert Phelps calls the "savory and magnetic presence"[3] of the narrator is brought into clearer focus as her poeticized model takes form.

An early story that appeared in the collection ***The Other Woman,*** entitled **"Secrets,"** serves as a useful introduction to the complex boundary that both separates and unites the mother / daughter pair in Colette's short fiction. The story is told from the perspective of Madame Grey, the 50-year-old mother of the young Claudie, who is on the verge of announcing her engagement to André Donat, with whom she is clearly infatuated. Observing her daughter as she dances at a social gathering, Madame Grey finds that her resemblance to the girl she herself was at the same age is disarming. Struck by Claudie's loveliness, she is nevertheless still able to maintain a distance view, feeling what the narrator identifies as "expert tenderness for her daughter, a tenderness incapable of blindness, the sort of critical devotion that ties the trainer to the champion" (**CS** [***The Collected Stories of Colette***], 291). Throughout Colette's writing, oxymorons such as "expert tenderness" and "critical devotion" serve to underscore the lucidity that so often accompanies the deep emotional attachment of the female characters in her fictional universe. In this instance, rather than preventing the mother from assessing her daughter's situation objectively, her devotion to her daughter demands the tough stance of the trainer whose goal is to prepare his fighter for the difficult battles that inevitably lie ahead. The image, borrowed from an exclusively male domain, dispels any notion of the conventional weak and sentimental woman whose judgment is likely to be compromised by her maternal feelings.

Madame Grey draws upon her personal experience in envisioning the battles her daughter will no doubt face. As she watches her future son-in-law, she notices signs of the disappointment that awaits Claudie. For example, she sees in André's insistence upon order, on "arrang-ing his books according to the color of their spines" (**CS,** 292), the same obsession with precision her own husband revealed to her with alarming candor early in their marriage. Recalling her horror when her spouse declared his inability to sleep if the fringes on the towels hanging from the rack were not lined up with each other and her revulsion at his habit of running his thumbnail over his lip, she decides not to tell Claudie about her disillusionment in marriage, but instead to keep secrets about "the mold that grows on married life, the refuse a man's character leaves behind at the border between childishness and dementia . . ." (**CS,** 293). Resigned to her daughter's fate and her own, as if they were one, she keeps her silence, sits down beside her husband, "and her hand, that of a good wife, admonished, with a meaningful squeeze, the unconscious hand which had been running back and forth, back and forth over his lip . . ." (**CS,** 293).

Madame Grey's negative view of the relations between the sexes finds its reflection in other stories of this and subsequent collections eventually establishing a recurrent pattern that, through the force of repetition, takes on the guise of the universal. Yet, her closely guarded secrets do not constitute the sign of solidarity between women, which is viewed in other texts as the product of shared experiences. Registering exclusively the reactions of the mother, who recasts her daughter's experiences as a dim reflection of her own, the narrative presents Madame Grey's reticence as a manifestation of the older woman's subordination of the younger through the withholding of knowledge, which ultimately serves to erect a barrier between the two. Colored by the mother's cynicism towards love and marriage, the daughter's life is all but assimilated into her mother's past. Convinced Claudie's fate can and will be no different from her own, Madame Grey resigns herself anew to humiliation and disappointment, as if to insure that, when the time comes, she will be able to pass the standard of submission on to her offspring.

In the mother-daughter relationships that characterize the majority of Colette's stories, shared and sometimes secret knowledge (often reinforced by anticipation of the young girl's inevitable loss of autonomy upon passing into adulthood) is depicted as a source of renewable strength for the daughter. The mother comes to represent a refuge, providing support and sustenance to the child, particularly in moments of temporary retreat from the male-dominated world. The first short stories in which this important relationship begins to emerge clearly are those that appear in ***My Mother's House,*** published in 1922.

A loosely organized collection of vignettes based primarily on childhood reminiscences, this work inaugurates the literary image of "Sido," while clearly establishing the authoritative presence of the narrative voice that links present to past as well as mother to daughter. In one of these stories, **"The Abduction,"** Colette sets out a fundamental pattern for the mother-daughter relationship that will reappear with variations throughout her work. The anecdote recounts Sido's instinctively protective response when the nine-year-old Minet-Chéri moves into the room recently vacated by her older sister, who has married. Because the room is far-removed from her own, Sido is apprehensive, fearing the kidnapping of her only remaining daughter. The child, on the other hand, is excited by the prospect of the move, her curiosity aroused no doubt by an engraving hanging in the hallway of her parents' home: "It represented a post-chaise, harnessed to two queer horses with necks like fabulous beasts'. In front of the gaping coach door a young man, dressed in taffeta, was carrying on one arm with the greatest of ease a fainting young woman. Her little mouth forming an O, and the ruffled petticoats framing her charming legs, strove to express extreme terror. The Abduction! My innocent imagination was pleasantly stirred by the word and the picture."[4]

Even a casual acquaintance with Western mythology will suggest the conventional connotations attached to the word "abduction": adventure and romance, yes, but also the threat of violence and sexual violation dreaded by the fiercely protective mother. And yet the child is blind to the darker side of the concept, so captivated is she by her own innocent vision of the image and the word, which both lay claim to her youthful imagination. In fact, her intuition is born out. One windy night, two strong arms lift her from her bed and, cradled in what she cannot know to be their maternal embrace, she is spirited away. The next morning, she awakens in the safety of her former room and, recalling her dream of a dashing figure in taffeta, calls out, "Mama, come quick! I've been abducted!" (*MH* [*My Mother's House,*] 43). She has learned from this experience that "abduction" signifies an exciting adventure, free from danger, bathed in maternal warmth and tenderness. The word and the image coincide, if only within the enclosed female space of the childhood haven, a domain ordered by a lexicon that blithely ignores the signifying system of the world beyond.

The power that mother and daughter derive from their complicity in this adventure is undermined by the distance separating the narrator, the mature Colette, from the events she is relating, a distance succinctly conveyed by the use of the adjective "innocent" to describe the child's fantasies. The gap between the two irreconcilable moments in time corresponds to the space separating the conventional meaning of the word "abduction" from the one the child, with the help of her mother, claims as her own. Laced with gentle humor, the story locates its narrative interest in the ironic play between the lost world of childhood, in which a titillating abduction is transformed into a mother's embrace,

and the very real world of threatening dangers that the imposing presence of the narrator never allows the reader to forget. The tone of knowing indulgence that the narrator adopts as she relates this tale is essential to the overall effect of the story, for the reader can only perceive this unresolved narrative tension when constantly reminded of the inescapable force of the signifying system that is being challenged from within.

A similar complicity and strong sense of continuity between mother and daughter pervade the later story, **"Green Sealing Wax,"** set in the village in which Colette grew up.[5] The autobiographical axis of the narrative is established in the introductory paragraphs, when the young Colette, caught up in the turbulence of adolescence, responds alternatively to the lure of two opposing vices. The first of these she characterizes as her "craze to be glamorous" (*CS,* 391), literally her "crisis of flirtatiousness," initiating her inevitable passage into womanhood. While Colette seems oblivious to the dangers of crossing this frontier, her mother is only too aware of the threat that coming-of-age poses to the female child. When she finds her daughter at play under the designing gaze of an older man, Sido observes that the girl seems prettier than she was at home: "That is how girls blossom in the warmth of a man's desire, whether they are fifteen or thirty" (*CS,* 387). Sido speedily whisks her child out of danger's way.

Colette's growing awareness of her own sexuality is counterbalanced by an intense fascination with writing tools. Attracted to the jealously guarded supply of pens, paper, letter openers, and the like, which her father has amassed in the vain hope of literary creation, the child finally yields to temptation and steals from her father's worktable "a little mahogany set square that smelled like a cigar box, then a white metal ruler." Upon discovering his daughter's transgression, Colette's father severely reprimands her for trespassing into the patriarchal domain. "I received full in my face the glare of a small, blazing gray eye, the eye of a rival" *CS,* 388).

Although Sido does not fully grasp the attraction that desk paraphernalia hold for her daughter, she actively encourages Colette's acquisitiveness as a welcome alternative to the competing seductions of adolescence with their attendant dangers. As a final diversionary gesture, she takes a stick of green sealing wax flecked with gold from her husband's desk and gives it to the grateful Colette. When the child asks if her father, her "rival," has willingly given up the wax or if her mother has stolen it, the latter replies enigmatically, "Let's say your father's lending it to you and leave it at that" (*CS,* 390). Through this act of complicity, Sido reaffirms the dual relationship between mother and child that so marks what Freud calls the pre-Oedipal period of the early childhood years, while at the same time fostering in her daughter "ambitious wishes," expressed by the narrator as "the glory . . . of a mental power" (**CS**, 389).⁶ By actively encouraging Colette's retreat to the library, safely nestled within the maternal space, Sido intervenes to arrest or at least forestall Colette's passage to womanhood along the prescribed pathway, while at the same time indirectly supporting her daughter's ambitious drives.

Into this highly personal narrative of the family triangle, Colette inserts the shocking tale in which a former postal worker, Mme Hervouët, coldheartedly poisons her husband and forges a will in her favor. Following M. Hervouët's unexpected demise, his niece, claiming to have seen a will sealed with green, gold-flecked sealing wax at her uncle's home some time before his death, contests the widow's assertion that her husband died intestate. About this time, a visibly distraught Mme Hervouët pays a visit to the Colette home, seeks out the wide-eyed Minet-Chéri in her library lair, and sends the girl off for a few moments in search of her mother. All the threads of the narrative are woven together in the final scene. Having produced at the last minute a second, blatantly contrived false will, bearing the stamp of the telltale green wax, the widow is confronted with her duplicity and flies into a delirious frenzy. Confessing to the double crime of murder and forgery, she is carried off to an asylum. Soon after, caught up in the spirit of confession, Colette reveals to her mother that her stick of green wax disappeared on the very day of Mme Hervouët's visit.

At first glance, the only link between the inquisitive, well-adjusted adolescent girl and the passionate, unbalanced murderess seems to be the sealing wax, a symbol of access to almost mystical cerebral powers for the former, an agent of treachery and deceit for the latter. Yet, on closer examination, it becomes clear that both characters are transgressors against accepted social codes, the one institutionalized by the legal system, the other reified by strictly defined gender roles. The reaction of Sido and Colette to Mme Hervouët's crime underscores their unconscious recognition of shared experience. When they take up the widow's defense, the frustrated Captain Colette exclaims, "There you go, the two of you! Already siding with the bull against the bullfighter!" to which Sido pointedly replies, "Exactly! Bullfighters are usually men with large buttocks and that's enough to put me against them!" (**CS**, 394). Sido thus establishes, in no uncertain terms, the need for female solidarity as a defense against "fat landowners" like M. Hervouët, calling into question the legitimacy of their claim to privilege, which is derived primarily from the wealth to which their gender has given them access.

When the facts are finally revealed, Sido revises but does not reverse her opinion of the crime and its perpetrator, reproaching the widow only for her failure to

recognize her own limitations: "Poisoning poor old Hervouët with extremely bitter herbal concoctions, right, that wasn't difficult. Inept murderer, stupid victim, it's tit for tat. But to try and imitate a handwriting without having the slightest gift for forgery, to trust to a special, rare kind of sealing wax, what petty ruses, great heavens, what fatuous conceit" (**CS**, 398).

I will postpone considering the implications of the ethical values Sido proposes in **"Green Sealing Wax"** as a counter to the moral code that prevails in patriarchal society until my discussion of Colette's treatment of the boundary between acceptable social behavior and that judged "deviant" by community standards. Here I would like to stress the importance of Colette's emphasis on the maternal source of the tale. Locating the origins of the story in matrilinear lore, the narrator admits that what little order she has captured in its retelling she owes to Sido, "thanks to the the extraordinary 'presence' I still have of the sound of her voice" (**CS**, 396). Imbued with the presence of Sido's wise, authoritative voice, the narrative itself stands as palpable proof of the salutary consequences of female-generated discourse.

Colette's account of her own coming-of-age, intricately interwoven with her initial flirtation with writing, is thus played out against a backdrop that affirms her storytelling skills as a maternal legacy, suggesting her natural right to the pen. Yet, in order to fully understand the magic wrought through the literary transformation of both mother and daughter, we must remember that, although Sido's aura may pervade the text, both her voice and her presence have been passed through the same kaleidoscopic lens of memory and imagination at work in **"The Abduction."** Claude Pichois notes that, driven by the need both to tell a story and to achieve autonomy, Colette eventually replaces Sidonie, her real mother, with a character who becomes her own reflection.⁷ As the invented "Sido" is gradually transformed into a theme to be renewed, enriched, and exploited, the mother-daughter boundary becomes increasingly blurred. By recasting her mother in her own image, Colette quietly assimilates Sido's narrative authority into her own, all the while preserving the illusion of stereoptic vision that contributes so effectively to the success of the stories written about her childhood.

In **"The Abduction,"** mother and daughter occupy a protective maternal space so firmly delineated as to create an almost closed border, setting them off from the world beyond. Mari McCarty sees the pattern of conscious marginality as fundamental to Colette's work, in which female space becomes a locus of empowerment for those who take refuge there.⁸ This theme is further developed in the framed story, **"The Tender Shoot,"** originally included in **The Kepi,** published in 1943. Unlike the two stories mentioned above, this one is not directly narrated by Colette, although her subtle presence in the guise of the person to whom the story is told is central to the narrative's design.

The story begins when Colette receives a visit from an old friend, Albin Chaveriat, whom she describes as a white-haired 70-year-old with the reputation of an aging roué. Having loosened Chaveriat's inhibitions and his tongue with a fine dinner and brandy, Colette persuades him to reveal the circumstances that led him to renounce his passion for young girls.[9] He explains that, 20 years earlier, he came across a "well-rounded" 15-year-old peasant girl, Louisette, while taking a walk on his friend's estate in Franche-Comté. Her ripe, frank sensuality aroused his desire enough that he returned several times to see her.

Chevariat notes that, although she eagerly accepted physical intimacy with him, she nevertheless took great precautions to prevent her mother from finding out about their trysts. In fact, as he recalls, he found it curious that she insisted upon keeping him at a safe distance, never letting him proceed beyond the crumbling wall that separated the dilapidated "château" in which she lived alone with her mother from his friend's property on the other side. One evening, he continues, when a sudden cloudburst sent the two lovers scurrying for shelter, Louisette led Albin across the forbidden threshold of her home, where they waited for the storm to abate. Suddenly, the girl's mother appeared and, discovering her daughter nestled in the arms of a man, surveyed the scene with "a wide, magnificent gaze . . . that was not upturned in anguish but that imperiously insisted on seeing everything, knowing everything" (*CS,* 442). Abruptly switching allegiances, Louisette turned the full force of her adolescent rage on Chaveriat, finally joining forces with her mother to hurl stones at his retreating head. Albin admits that, upon his return to his friend's home, he was struck down with a bout of fever probably brought on, at least in part, by emotional stress. He ends his story with a reference to its salutary consequences, for after being nursed back to health by his agreeable host, he left Franche-Comté, cured forever of "all the Louisettes in this world" (*CS,* 447).

This brief plot summary does not take into account the nuances introduced by the circumstances of narration. While we are kept aware of the narrator's presence by asides, direct remarks to his listener, and minor digressions (often referring to events that preceded or followed those being related), he never asserts the same authority over his story as does the "Colette" narrator in the other stories discussed thus far. Because his audience is an old friend, an experienced woman who knows him perhaps too well, he feels obliged to monitor her responses to what he is saying. At times, he self-consciously interrupts himself in order to offer a defense in response to a raised eyebrow or slight frown that he takes as a sign of his listener's disapproval. So,

for example, when he is explaining his fascination with young maidens, he asks the rhetorical question, "What is there in a young girl that is so ripe and ready and eager to be exploited except her sensuality?" Then, no doubt sensing Colette is on the verge of objecting, he quickly interjects, "No, don't let's argue about that, I know you don't agree with me" (*CS,* 424).

At other times, he will interpret events in such a way as to cast himself in the best possible light, or, under the direst of circumstances, simply to save face. When Louisette and her mother chase him from their domain by stoning him as he hurries down the steep path, he finally turns on his attackers, seized by "a good honest rage, the rage of an injured man," and advances towards them. As he explains, "No doubt they too suddenly recovered their reason and remembered that they were females, and I was a male, for after hesitating, they fled and disappeared into the neglected garden behind some pyramid fruit trees and a feathery clump of asparagus" (*CS,* 446). The ferocity with which the mother and daughter pursue Albin and the terror that their relentless attack arouses in him are at odds with his self-serving analysis of their retreat, which conveniently ignores the fact that they have accomplished their goal and so can triumphantly return to their own domain, having expelled the interloper from their garden. Colette's silent interventions (through facial expressions and gestures), often in response to Albin's all-too-obvious editing of the facts he presents, constantly undermine what Mari McCarty refers to as the narrator's "patriarchal assumptions,"[10] providing a textual reflection of the physical challenge to male dominion launched by the mother-daughter pair.

There are, in fact, two superimposed readings of this story. The first, perhaps a bit too overtly orchestrated by the narrator, terminates with the moral that Albin articulates: young peasant girls can be hazardous to the health and well-being of a would-be Don Juan. The second, pieced together by the reader from intermittent unmediated access to certain passages of the text in which the voice of Albin is temporarily muted, as well as from the addressee's silent commentary, conveys a vastly different message: young peasant girls, whose closeness to nature makes their innocent sensuality a weapon rather than a weakness, can escape male domination and sexual exploitation through a fortifying alliance with a powerful mother.

The relationship between Louisette and her mother bears further consideration, since the principal surprise in the story results from Louisette's swift betrayal of Albin when confronted with a choice between her "lover" and her mother. The narrator does supply a number of hints suggesting that Louisette's attachment to her mother is decidedly different from that of the typical young girls he has encountered in his previous escapades. Despite her obvious poverty, she refuses the bead necklace he buys to replace the string of wild berries hanging around her neck, protesting, "I can't take it because of Mamma. Whatever would Mamma say if she saw me with a necklace" (*CS,* 428). When he continues to press her into accepting the gift, asking, "Are you so very frightened of your mother?" her reply is revealing, "No. I'm afraid she'll think badly of me" (*CS,* 429).

In refusing the necklace, Louisette makes no reference to community standards determining the code of behavior for a 15-year-old girl, nor does she cite the threat of parental punishment, that might deter other adolescents from yielding to temptation. Instead, she bases her decision on the personal relationship she has with her mother, grounded in mutual respect and esteem. The mother's scathing exchange with Chaveriat, when she confronts him in her cottage, is further indication that her moral judgments, like those of Sido in **"Green Sealing Wax,"** do not necessarily reflect those of the larger society. Perfectly lucid and remarkably free from the anguish the narrator expects to see in a mother who fears her daughter's honor has been compromised, she berates Louisette, not simply for becoming sexually involved, but for forming a liaison with a man old enough to be her father. Exhorting Louisette to take a close look at Albin, she screams at her, "Do you see what he's got on his temples? White hairs, Louise, white hairs, just like me! And those wrinkles he's got under his eyes! All over him, wherever you look, he's got the stamp of ancience, my girl, yes, ancience" (*CS,* 445). No mention here of moral virtue, of preserving girlhood innocence, but an uncomplicated appeal to common sense and practicality, summed up in the mother's brutally frank reproach, "That man who would have been 50 years older than his child, suppose you had been pregnant by him, Louise!"

At the story's end, as Louisette and her mother unite to drive out the intruder threatening the tranquillity of their realm, the boundary between the two, at least in Albin's mind, has been all but effaced. When the narrator is confronted by their combined fury, in the blinding light of an unshaded lamp, he is struck by their resemblance: "Their two heads, close together and so terribly alike, stared me out of countenance" (*CS,* 445). And again, as they join together to protect their own borders, he describes them as if they were moving in unison: "Two heads, close side by side, followed my movement; they must be starting off again in pursuit of me. I was only too right; the two heads reappeared farther on, waiting for me. White hairs and gold hairs fluttered in the air like poplar seeds" (*CS,* 446).

All three of these stories, despite their great diversity, trace a similar gesture on the part of the mother figure. Sido's "abduction" of her daughter to the safety of the maternal inner sanctuary, her "surgical intervention"

(*CS,* 388) to save Colette from a brush with burgeoning adolescence in the opening pages of **"Green Sealing Wax,"** and the mother's fierce protection of the sanctity of the domain she shares with her daughter in **"The Tender Shoot,"** represent attempts, futile though they may ultimately be, to stave off their children's inevitable passage to womanhood by creating a temporary haven from patriarchal space. In each case, strengthening the mother-daughter bond emphasizes the continuity between the two while at the same time widening the gap between women and the male-dominated world from which they take refuge.

. . . . .

In Colette's short fiction, objective reality is repeatedly subordinated to knowledge gained through the collaborative effort of the senses. In the process the object, whether a garden-variety snail or a handsome yet vacuous lover, is reduced to the role of supporting the subject's desire, longing, pleasure, or anguish. In **"Flora and Pomona,"** published in the same volume as **"The Photographer's Wife"** and **"The Sick Child,"** Colette claims that the orchids she describes defy scientific labels, for they are "creatures mad for imitation, disguised as birds, hymenoptera, open wounds, sex organs."[11] Seduced into questioning an easy allegiance to "reality" by this highly evocative and suggestive set of images, the reader is at the same time not permitted to forget the existence of the actual flowers thus "disguised." Their material immutability, lying outside of the charmed circle inscribed by the writer's eroticized gaze, is affirmed through the litany of their scientific names ("miltonia," "aristolochia," etc.).

The gap separating the technical terms for flowers from their polysemic poetic images, or the accepted sense of "presbytery" from the meaning conjured up by the untrammeled imagination of a young child, is inhabited by a desire or longing that transforms objects without, however, completely abolishing their material models. The nagging resistance of those models to the attack launched by the perceiving subject is accomplished on a narrative level by a shifting perspective, which places the narrator (and the reader) simultaneously in two positions that are nevertheless separated by an insuperable distance.[12] In **"The Abduction,"** discussed in the section devoted to mother / daughter relations, the narrator declares herself to be a mother recounting her experiences as a little girl. She therefore identifies with both the small child whose erotic dream of abduction excludes its implicit dangers, and the mother with whom she shares an understanding gained from adult knowledge of the world. Her tone, her choice of language, her subtly shifting voice, allow her to speak at once for both the rebellious child, who stubbornly defends her right to an existence (and a language) outside the Symbolic order (the world "out there" threatening to coerce her into submission to the codes and constraints of culture), and the gently mocking alter ego of the maternal law enforcer.

Gliding effortlessly between the roles of object and observer, the narrator of Colette's short stories often ably negotiates between these two poles without identifying exclusively with either one. In the texts cited above, the positions of subject and object are clearly delineated in recognizable roles (mother, child, mature and authoritative writer) as well as by the "real life" author's relation to each. In other stories, in which the tie between subject and alter ego is less obvious, or the position of the narrator more elusive, the "cat-and-mouse" game of shifting perspectives and doubled voices leaves the reader uncertain about how to establish meaning.

One such story, whose complex narrative perspective has encouraged varying and often contradictory interpretations since it was first published in the collection entitled ***Bella-Vista*** in 1937, is **"The Rendezvous,"** one of the rare third-person narratives among Colette's longer works of short fiction. The story, set in Morocco, is ostensibly told from the point of view of Bernard Bonnemains, an architect vacationing with Cyril and Odette Bessier and their recently widowed sister-in-law, Rose. Bernard, who is "exactly thirty, [with] no rich clients and not much money" (***CS***, 471), has an amorous liaison with Rose which, out of fear of family opposition, he is struggling to keep secret, hoping that Cyril will ask him to become his partner, thus taking the place of the deceased younger Bessier. His seething antagonism towards the Bessiers, particularly towards Odette, whom he views as an aggressive interfering "female," is surpassed only by his reluctance to compromise his position by offending them.

Frustrated in his efforts to pursue his affair with Rose, Bernard finally arranges, through a series of subterfuges whose success is dependent on Rose's complete complicity, for a late-night assignation. The two slip out of their hotel rooms and, trembling with pent-up desire, hasten to a clearing chosen earlier in the day by Bernard. While inspecting the ground before spreading out Rose's raincoat, Bernard comes across the body of a man bleeding from a knife wound to the arm. On closer inspection, he discovers Ahmed, a young Arab boy employed at their hotel, who has apparently had a fight with a rival over the affections of a local woman.

After bandaging the injured man's wounds with strips of cloth torn from his shirt, Bernard tries to convince Rose to go for help. By refusing to risk exposing her indiscretion for fear of scandal, Rose provokes Bernard's anger, and with an embittered outburst directed at both Rose and the "bourgeois" Bessiers, he sends her packing. The story ends with an apparently complacent Bernard "[watching] the morning dawn and [tasting] a contentment, a surprise as fresh as love but less restricted and totally detached from sex" (***CS***, 496). As he waits beside a sleeping Ahmed for help to arrive, he dismisses the woman he desired so fervently with the thought, "She was my woman but this one here is my counterpart. It's queer that I had to come all the way to Tangiers to find my counterpart, the only person to make me proud of him and proud of myself. With a woman, it's so easy to be a little ashamed, either of her or of oneself. My wonderful counterpart! He had only to appear . . ." (***CS***, 496).

Judging from review articles written in 1937 and 1938, most of Colette's contemporaries were considerably less puzzled by the story than modern-day readers, for they naively assumed a perfect concordance between the protagonist, narrator and author. Lauding Colette's accurate depiction of recognizable female types, one critic characterized Odette as a "vulgar woman" of the sort encountered all too frequently "in Paris and elsewhere," while another found Rose representative of the "incredible stupidity and monstrous selfishness of the infatuated European woman, who would rather leave an Arab to die than risk soiling her coat or her reputation." For yet another, Colette's negative portraits of the two sisters-in-law confirmed her underlying misogyny.

The story's denouement was often viewed as championing the superiority of "fraternity" over less rewarding romantic liaisons with frivolous or vulgar women. Witness the following summary of the story's message: "A handsome chap suddenly discovers that the woman whom he desired, and even thought he loved, is much less important to him than the combined comradery, fraternity, devotion, and charity that he encounters under circumstances in which, finally delivered from sensuality, he has the opportunity to dedicate himself to another man." The redemptive quality of Bernard's decision was generally underscored, as critics contrasted the purity of his gesture with the baseness and mediocrity of the two women.[13]

Among the readers emphasizing the theme of homosociality was Colette's third husband, Maurice Goudeket, who rhapsodized about his wife's success in painting so accurate a picture of male bonding.

> This short story has, within Colette's work, a unique resonance. At the site of a rendezvous, at the very moment when between a man and a woman the ritual of love-making is about to take place, a weak cry reveals the presence of a young native, wounded during a fight. This single cry suspends all desires in the man's heart except the urge to come to the aid of his fellow man in distress, even if he is only an insignificant youth. And so, he lets his female companion take off, in a rage.
>
> I wasn't the only one to admire the fact that a woman could write such a virile story. This secret between men, this strong solidarity which is fostered by war and the rallying of troops, this complicity, which we imagine to be beyond women's understanding, was not sheltered from Colette's penetrating gaze.[14]

Other readers, attributing more self-interested motives to Bernard's supposedly humanitarian gesture, deplored the signs of a veiled homosexuality they found in the story. For example, in his review for *Mercure de France* in 1938, John Carpentier remarked "If the hero of **'The Rendezvous'** accomplishes an act of humanity which releases him from a degrading passion, he only frees himself through sensuality. The escape proposed to him by his guardian angel, so to speak, is on a par with animality."[15] Carpentier's reference to the story's homoerotic overtones signals his implicit understanding that the exotic North African setting, suggesting all that the "Orient" had symbolized for centuries in the imagination of the average French reader, would have an inevitable erotic appeal. Serving as a reminder of the beautiful, young Arab boys that awaken the protagonist of Gide's *The Immoralist* to the possibilities of physical pleasure, Ahmed is an inseparable element of the sensual phantasm that the Moroccan decor calls forth. Carpentier's moral outrage notwithstanding, his reading certainly builds upon well-known literary commonplaces.

Given the certainty with which her contemporaries approached this story, in spite of their often diametrically opposed conclusions, a reader attuned to Colette's careful manipulation of narrative perspective may be less certain of interpreting **"The Rendezvous"** correctly. My own initial notes are peppered with questions. "Do the insights into Bernard's thoughts, the only subjectivity the story allows for, invite sympathy with his denigration of women? Is the story to be read as a transposition into male terms of the positive female bonding experience that figures so prominently in other Colette stories? And what of the class and racial implications of **'The Rendezvous'**"?

The difficulty of answering these questions definitively was brought home to me when, in trying to write an objective plot summary of the story, I discovered its unstable perspective; the indeterminacy of both characters and events made even this straightforward task problematic. For example, the reference to Bernard's financial circumstances is taken from a passage relating Odette's frequent reminders of his inferior social and economic status: "'Bernard had better not count his chickens before they are hatched,' Odette was in the habit of saying, whenever she thought it expedient to recall the fact that Bonnemains was exactly thirty, had no rich clients and not much money." The only information about Bernard's background supplied by the narrative is thus colored by the caustic irony of a character who is herself presented, for the most part, negatively *and* from the protagonist's limited viewpoint.

The complex handling of the story's narrative perspective encourages multiple readings, undermining the assumptions of unitary point of view that guided Colette's

contemporaries. For example, despite Bernard's humane act and defiant dismissal of the bourgeois prejudices and crass self-interest of his traveling companions, he seems unlikely as a self-sacrificing hero, able to achieve a certain transcendence through solidarity with other men. There are too many inconsistencies between Bernard's final gesture, described in his own words and thoughts, which stress its sincerity and egalitarian thrust, and the occasional glimpses of a less appealing side to his personality.

For example, Bonnemains only permits his suppressed anger to surface in rare, unexpected outbursts that, because they are not explained, make him seem like a small child in the throes of a temper tantrum. On more than one occasion, his unrealized fantasies highlight his reticence to take any action that might compromise his financial stability. Speculating about what might happen if he were to unleash the fury of his sexual frustration on the insensitive Odette, he thinks, "'If I didn't control myself, I'd remind her there was such a thing as decency.' But he did control himself, wincing like a starving man reminded of food" (*CS*, 471). Bernard's recurring daydreams of taking a stand, speaking his mind to the Bessiers, overpowering Rose as a means of seeking revenge on "the others," never materialize, leaving an overall impression of weakness and impotence that is never fully effaced by his last, defiant act.

The hint of self-delusion that emerges from the scene in which Bernard exchanges a passionate glance with Rose under the watchful eye of Odette, and then turns away from her "with a cowardice which he told himself was discretion" (*CS*, 474), serves to raise the specter of doubt about the motivations underlying Bernard's surprising choice at the end of the story. High-minded and noble as his gesture may appear, the parting image is that of Bernard, liberated from the chafing role of frustrated suitor and subservient fortune seeker, eager to assume the dominant position in a self-declared alliance with his unlikely "counterpart."

The last paragraph brings together the contradictory motives animating Bernard, leaving the reader the difficult task of sorting through them. "Before lifting Ahmed, Bonnemains tested the knots of his amateur dressing. Then he wrapped his arms around the sleeping boy, inhaled the sandalwood scent of his black hair, and clumsily kissed his cheek, which was already virile and rough. He estimated the young man's weight as he might have done that of a child of his own flesh or that of a quarry one kills only once in a lifetime" (*CS*, 497). Although the second sentence of the passage cited above conveys a suggestion of homoerotic desire, it also appears to contradict Bernard's assertion that his attraction to his "counterpart" (in French, the word is *semblable*, meaning literally "fellow," or "equal") is based on the bond of similarity. In fact, Ahmed's odor of sandalwood and his black hair, both evoking the exotic, call attention to his otherness as the main feature of his appeal. Furthermore, the two analogies in the last sentence conjure up vastly different images, the first evoking protective tenderness and selfless love (that of a parent for a defenseless child, or that of a lover enthralled by the touch and smell of his cherished loved one), the other suggesting control, conquest, and domination (of hunter over prey).

If the insights into Bernard's character provided by the narrative favor the second image, making his gesture a self-serving quest for power by an ineffectual man, parallels with other Colette short stories support the first image, in which escape from adversity is achieved through solidarity with fellow women. Bernard's retreat from love recalls the novella, *The Toutounier* (1939) and the collection of vignettes, *The Tendrils of the Vine* (1908), in which female characters assuage the pain they have suffered in heterosexual relations gone awry by establishing intimacy with other women. In short, Colette's story leaves unanswered the question of whether Bernard is a good Samaritan who finds comfort in identifying with his "counterpart," a dissatisfied middle-class Frenchman who discovers, in the stereotypical "sensuality" of an African setting, the pleasures of either homosocial or homosexual relations, or, as Marie-Christine Bellosta would have it, "a failed painter, an unsuccessful architect," whose sudden commitment to male solidarity is his way of compensating for feelings of frustration and powerlessness.[16]

As one of a collection of stories that interrogate community attitudes towards gender and sexuality (**"Bella-Vista"**), incest (**"The Patriarch"**), and abortion (**"Gribiche"**), **"The Rendezvous,"** while flirting with such potentially controversial issues as homosexuality, colonial myths of the Orient, and bourgeois complacency, resists espousing any particular moral position. The reader cannot comfortably seek answers to the questions that have been posed from an authoritative narrative voice, since its position has been effectively destabilized. As a result, the very openness of the text, its polysemic ambiguity, serves as a challenge to the rigid social codes upon which a linear reading of the story might otherwise be predicated.

In **"Rainy Moon,"** published in 1940 in the volume entitled *Chance Acquaintances,* the image of the narrator's past self is revived through the introduction of a textual alter ego, a technique that results in a proliferation of narrative "I's." Here, the doubling effect leads to an intermingling of the self (or selves, since the ghost of the younger Colette is called forth) and the other. As narrator / protagonist, Colette is forced to confront painful memories when she discovers Rosita Barberet, the typist whom she has recently hired, lives in the same apartment that she, Colette, occupied following the

breakup of a romantic relationship. The coincidence is compounded after Colette meets Rosita's sister, Délia, who is nursing emotional wounds inflicted by an unfaithful husband. Colette is immediately drawn to Délia, whom she envisions at times as a reflection of her younger self. Her attraction for this eerie reminder of her past is tempered by her reluctance to relive the suffering with which it is inextricably allied.

When Colette arrives one day at the Barberet apartment and finds Délia lying inert before the front door, Rosita accounts for her sister's bizarre behavior with oblique references to black magic and the occult. She finally confesses to Colette that Délia is plotting to kill her husband, Eugène. Having attempted to "summon" him by repeating his name, she has taken to weaving an evil spell (Rosita hints darkly at sharp needles dipped in foul substances). Unsettled by these strange occurrences, Colette renounces further contact with the troubling, yet strangely fascinating sisters, vowing to turn them into a memory. Despite her decision to avoid the Barberets, she catches a glimpse of Délia quite by chance on several occasions, looking "pale and diminished, like a convalescent who is out too soon" (*CS*, 386). At the story's end, the narrator runs across a visibly restored Délia, devouring a large bag of fried potatoes with obvious gusto. Her apparently calm and complacent demeanor is in contrast to her apparel, a black dress and hat, adorned with the unmistakable white crepe band of a widow.

Colette prefaces the story by calling attention to her role as writer, comparing her own affinity for the past to the preferences of Proust. "Marcel Proust, gasping with asthma amid the bluish haze of fumigations and the shower of pages dropping from him one by one, pursued a bygone and completed time. It is neither the true concern nor the natural inclination of writers to love the future. They have quite enough to do with being incessantly forced to invent their characters' future, which, in any case, they draw from the well of their own past. Mine, whenever I plunge into it, makes me dizzy." In light of Colette's self-proclaimed aversion for theoretical pronouncements (or for pronouncements of any kind, for that matter) on the craft of writing, this brief passage, in which she casually aligns herself with one of the most accomplished French writers of her time, should give the reader pause. For Colette is foregrounding at once both the autobiographical (conventionally understood as referential) underpinnings of the tale she is about to tell and its status as invention, by calling attention to herself as a writer who creates characters and their futures.

Referentiality is emphasized here, as in many of the stories previously discussed, by liberally incorporating elements of verifiable reality into the fictional narrative. For example, the Colette character prepares stories for publication in periodicals the names of which would be immediately recognizable to the reading public of her time, and she goes on carefree picnics in the Bois de Boulogne with her real friend, Annie de Pène. Historical grounding is further reinforced by passing references to Colette's contemporaries, Proust, Francis Carco, and Pierre Veber.

On the other hand, several passages counteract easy referentiality with reminders of the artifice of fiction, stressing the act of writing. Remarking that, despite her efforts, she was never able to complete the serial novelette she had initially asked Rosita to type, Colette admits to a loathing for the "'action' and swift adventure" that are requisite elements of successful popular fiction. The unwritten story to which she alludes stands in sharp contrast to the written one, "Rainy Moon," with its rambling, disjointed structure, its discursive insouciance, and its penchant for subtle detail. The implicit comparison heightens the reader's awareness of the story's divergence from established convention, suggesting that an alternative reading approach may be needed. In a passage that modestly plays down her literary imagination, Colette confesses that her "rational view of things" makes her cling to the distinction "between fact and possibility, between an event and the narration of it" (*CS,* 358). Her praise for those writers who succeed in conflating these seemingly contradictory terms serves ironically to direct attention to boundaries that, in the majority of her stories, are carefully and cleverly concealed.

If self-reflexivity is clearly not a hallmark of Colette's short fiction, neither are black magic and the occult. Yet interestingly, the intersection of these two apparently anomalous features of **"Rainy Moon,"** when considered in the light of Freudian psychoanalytic theory, furnishes one key to approaching the story.[17] In a 1919 article, Freud used the German word *"unheimlich,"* literally "not of the home," to define a phenomenon he described as "that class of the frightening which leads back to what is known of old and long familiar."[18] Since the word's opposite, *"heimlich,"* can signify both "familiar, agreeable" and "concealed, out of sight, or unfamiliar," Freud notes that the term, which in its positive form suggests the familiar, may contain within it hidden, fear-provoking dangers. The uncanny, as the phenomenon has come to be called in English translations of Freud, is therefore "something which is familiar and old-established in the mind and which has become alienated from it only through the process of repression."[19] One important characteristic of repressed material is that, while it is subject to the repulsion of the consciousness, it also exercises a counter-balancing attraction "upon everything with which it can establish a connection,"[20] thus accounting for the involuntary recurrence of uncanny effects.

There are two other points in Freud's essay that help elucidate **"Rainy Moon."** First, in enumerating the categories of the uncanny, among the most prominent themes that emerge is the figure of the double, possessing "knowledge, feelings and experience" in common with the subject. By identifying with another, Freud explains, the self seeks protection from the threatening effects of the operations of the conscience, a critical agency capable of treating the rest of the ego like an object. By ascribing unrealized, and potentially dangerous, fantasies to the figure of the double, the self takes a protective measure that allows it to project outward that which has been repressed. Second, in evaluating the functioning of the uncanny in literature, Freud maintains that only works that profess to "move in the world of common reality" can have uncanny effects, resulting from the shock created when the imaginary is inserted into a realistic setting.[21] Thus purely fantastic literature, such as fairy tales, cannot produce uncanny effects.

The implications of Freud's essay for **"Rainy Moon"** are suggestive. It would be hard to imagine a more *"heimlich"* atmosphere, in the full and contradictory sense of the term, than the one that pervades "Rainy Moon," from the moment the narrator arrives at the Barberets' apartment. Although Colette used to live in the same neighborhood, she is so disoriented by the changes that have taken place since her departure that she cannot even locate her street, which has either disappeared or changed its name. As she looks out the window in an attempt to get her bearings, her hand falls upon its unmistakably familiar hasp, shaped like a mermaid, and the unanticipated jolt of memory elicits "the rather pleasant giddiness that accompanies dreams of falling and flying" (*CS,* 348). From then on, the past continues "to raise its dripping mermaid's head" (*CS,* 351), reinforcing the alienating homeliness of the place: the wallpaper with its "ghost of a bunch of flowers, repeated a hundred times all over the walls" (*CS,* 348), the ceiling rose, and the "rainy moon," the narrator's fond name for a prism of rainbow colors projected on the wall by sunlight passing through a flaw in the windowpane.

The impression of unfamiliar familiarity intensifies when Colette leaves the apartment after her first visit: "From the pavement, I studied my house, unrecognizable under a heavy makeup of mortar. The hall, too, was well disguised and now, with its dado of pink and green tiles, reminded me of the baleful chilliness of those mass-produced villas on the Riviera" (*CS,* 350). Exuding pungent memories of a poorly buried past, the apartment and its environs are disguised not only by the changes introduced over time but also, undoubtedly, by the imperfect veiling of repression. In the dreamlike state brought on by the confused messages she is receiving, Colette's estrangement surfaces with a textual "*frisson*," expressed in the "baleful chilliness" of those undifferentiated Provençal houses that are devoid of both memories and meaning.

The uncanniness of the experience is heightened when Colette finally meets Rosita's sister, whose mirroring function is presaged when Rosita remarks that Délia has changed her name, roughly inverting the syllables of her christened name, Adèle.[22] Entering the bedroom she recognizes as formerly hers, Colette is taken aback, "For a second, I had that experience only dreams dare conjure up: I saw before me, hostile, hurt, stubbornly hoping, the young self I should never be again, whom I never ceased disowning and regretting" (*CS,* 360). Colette's response reenacts the dual movement of repression, as she at once disavows and yearns for this vision of her former self, "that sad form stuck like a petal between two pages, to the walls of an ill-starred refuge" (*CS,* 367). Admitting that she has been continually haunted by the nightmare of coming face-to-face with her alter ego, Colette explicitly acknowledges what she most fears: dredging up old disappointments in love. "They are the least worthy of being brought back to mind, but sometimes they behave just like a cut in which a fragment of hair is hidden; they heal badly" (*CS,* 352). The comparison is an apt image for the nagging return of the repressed. Colette's description of her state of mind when she met the Barberets suggests the concealed presence of that "sad form" from her past, which continues to worry the wound inflicted by her own painful love affair: "a private life that was clouded and uncertain, a solitude that bore no resemblance to peace . . ." (*CS,* 362).

Délia is further allied with the uncanny when it becomes clear that she is engaging in the practice of witchcraft. According to Freud, techniques of magic are linked to that which is "familiar and old-established" because they revive residues of the previously surmounted animistic belief in the omnipotence of thought and imagination (i.e., the idea that wishing something can make it happen) (Freud, 240). When an exasperated Colette criticizes Délia for her apparent indolence, she protests that the "work" she is doing in her head is every bit as grueling as her sister's. Pressed to explain the exact nature of her work, she replies enigmatically that she is creating something "a bit like a novel, only better" (*CS,* 368).

Using supernatural powers to summon her husband, casting a spell on him, causing him to weaken and finally die, Délia expresses primitive, or perhaps infantile beliefs in the individual's mastery of the universe. There is not such a great distance, after all, separating Délia's (fictionlike) control of her husband's fate and the young Colette's (fanciful) victory over threats to the free exercise of her imagination (and her will) posed by the adult world. Like the child's dream of abduction, the story Délia is conjuring up asserts its creator's fervent desire to rewrite the drama in which she participates.

That drama is rewritten with the help of the most unlikely fatal instruments: sewing needles contaminated with poisonous substances, materializing Délia's vengeful feelings towards her husband. To reiterate a point made earlier in my discussion of **"Chance Acquaintances,"** although needlework is traditionally a symbol of feminine domesticity and docility, in Colette's short fiction this seemingly innocuous activity more often than not masks subversive, or even, unlawful thoughts. In the case of **"Rainy Moon,"** they are spectacularly realized. Here, Délia's handiwork proves to be a good deal more than the clever talent of an idle woman; Délia's self-declared "profession," her bead work, aided and abetted by her ritualistic repetition of her husband's name, succeeds in killing him.

As narrator / protagonist, Colette is particularly implicated in the tale of her character's exploits, since she so clearly acknowledges her undeniable link with Délia. Despite the narrator's efforts to maintain a distanced attitude towards the disturbing young woman during periods of wakefulness, her dreams divulge the extent to which her life is intermingled with Délia's on the level of the unconscious. "I kept relapsing into a nightmare in which I was now my real self, now identified with Délia. Half reclining like her on our own divan-bed, in the dark part of our room, I 'convoked' with a powerful summons, with a thousand repetitions of his name, a man who was not called Eugène" (*CS,* 385).

To fully explore the complex implications of the Colette / Délia connection, as well as its central importance in the story, I will need to return briefly to Freud, and specifically to his 1917 essay entitled "Mourning and Melancholia." In comparing the two complexes, Freud notes that in melancholia "the occasions which give rise to the illness extend for the most part beyond the clear case of a loss by death, and include all those situations of being slighted, neglected or disappointed."[23] In this account of the neurotic functioning of melancholia, the subject shifts reproaches against the loved object onto its own ego through narcissistic identification. Although a similar libidinal investment in the lost object also occurs during the mourning process, the subject in mourning can usually free its libido from the lost object, eventually mending the ego that was divided against itself by self-reproaches. With melancholia, recuperation is arrested by the subject's inability to resolve ambivalent feelings towards the (not fully) lost object. Thus, as Flieger concludes, "successful mourning seems to result in an identification that heals the ego, assimilating and integrating the fantoms that haunt it, while melancholia exacerbates the split in the ego, the internal warfare among ghosts, fraught with guilt and anguish."[24]

Freud illustrates the pernicious effects of this essentially negative process with an analogy particularly pertinent to **"Rainy Moon"** when he writes that "the complex of melancholia behaves like an open wound."[25] The narrator's explicit acknowledgment of her agitated state (a life "clouded and uncertain," a solitude that bears "no resemblance to peace"), the comparison of disappointments in love with "cuts that heal badly," her nightmares centering around the lost love object, and her immediate identification with an alter ego whose anguish "uncannily" mirrors and magnifies her own, paint a picture faithful to Freud's description of the melancholic subject. If the story is interpreted as a case study in melancholia, then the murder of the absent loved one opens the door for the healing of the injured ego, for with his death and utter disappearance, the true mourning process can begin. But, the question remains, what does Délia's rehabilitation, so clearly signalled by her robust appearance and healthy appetite in the final scene, have to do with the narrator? Is the reader to conclude that Eugène's death lays to rest the unnamed *revenant* from the narrator's past? If so, by what black (and white?) magic is the double murder accomplished?

By the end of the story, the attentive reader will discover that failed relationships are not the only thing the two central characters have in common. Just as Délia conquers the phantoms of her past, using the magical powers of the spoken word to seduce her errant husband into her web of witchcraft and deadly needles to sew up his sorry fate, the narrator exorcises the specter "not called Eugène" by weaving a text with her own tools of seduction: the written word and the pen. The therapeutic value of the story becomes explicit when the narrator places it in the category of "a particular kind of unremarkable and soothing event," reminiscent of "the dressing of wet clay and bits of twig, the marvelous little splint the snipe binds around its foot when a shot has broken it" (**CS,** 357). While this second reference to the narrator's painful wound is further proof that, like her counterpart, she still suffers from the "internal warfare among ghosts" characteristic of melancholia, the soothing effect that the story has on her implies a healing process that parallels Délia's.

Since the work of mourning is an active labor (remember that Délia contends she calls upon all her energies to achieve her goal), the narrator's role as storyteller must be asserted, so that she can reap the psychic benefits of her own creative act. In other words, for the narrator's story to serve her as a "snipe's bandage," she must affirm her authority over its production and in a sense, exposing the text's unconscious. By interspersing gentle reminders of the story's status as fiction into a narrative that nevertheless makes manifest its referential underpinnings, the narrator cleverly manages to preserve the conditions necessary for the uncanny to perform its work, while at the same time dropping tantalizing hints of her own collusion in inventing the events she describes.

Despite the detailed alibi the narrator offers to absolve herself from responsibility for the plot that unfolds, she occasionally allows the reader to see through her veil of innocence. For example, she remarks offhandedly that she refrained from telling Annie de Pène about the "Barberet story," for fear that her wise friend might guess the reason for her interest in the young women: "Would not Annie's subtle ear and lively bronze eyes have weighed and condemned everything in my narrative that revealed no more than the craving to go over old ground again, to deck out what was over and done with a new coat of paint?" (**CS,** 357). Furthermore, although the narrator staunchly clings to her rational skepticism in the face of the supernatural happenings with which she is confronted, she infiltrates the uncanny effects into the text in such a way as to lull the reader into accepting them, strange though they may seem. From the eerie projection of refracted light to the proliferation of coincidences, the narrative provides an accumulation of evidence that ultimately undermines the storyteller's level-headed rejection of the unexplained.

The narrator first creates a character who acts as her surrogate, and then, by cagily positioning herself in relation to the double's story, furnishes a "novellike" conclusion to her own pain and suffering. Although she cautiously disassociates herself from Délia's darker side, she is, in fact, the unindicted coconspirator of Délia's crime, chasing her own personal demons while shirking responsibility for her character's unlawful act. In a stunning demonstration of what Freud calls the storyteller's "peculiarly directive power,"[26] the law-abiding narrator exorcises the ghosts from her own past by telling the daring story of her fictional character's bold, defiant gesture.

The reader will recall that in **"Green Sealing Wax"** there is a similar doubling of the narrator with a female character whose personal account complements the autobiographical story line. While the Colette / Délia rapport is more clearly articulated than the link between the adolescent girl and the impetuous widow of **"Green Sealing Wax,"** their shared circumstances should be evident from the previous discussion. In both stories, the deviant, sinister, and distinctly aggressive actions of the double, an unmistakable transgressor against the Law, provide a contrasting backdrop for the more conventional behavior of the narrator, whose discretion and common sense keep her safely within the bounds of accepted feminine conduct. Challenging the increasingly elusive dividing line between autobiography and fiction, author and character, subject and object, self and other, woman and writer, past and present, **"Rainy Moon"** is perhaps one of the most exemplary short stories in Colette's extraordinarily rich repertoire.

Notes

1. Michèle Sarde *Colette, Free and Fettered,* trans. Richard Miller (New York: Willam Morrow and Co., 1980) 22, 39.

2. Mari McCarty, "Possessing Female Space: 'The Tender Shoot,'" *Women's Studies* 8 (1981): 368.

3. *The Collected Stories of Colette,* ed. Robert Phelps (New York: Farrar, Straus, Giroux, 1983), xii. Hereafter referred to as CS.

4. "The Abduction," in *My Mother's House* (England: Penguin Books, 1966), 42-43. Hereafter referred to as MH.

5. The analysis that follows represents a revised version of my article, "Colette's 'La Cire verte': Breaking the Law," *Modern Language Studies* (Winter 1991), 37-44. Copyright © Northeast Modern Language Association 1991. Reproduced by permission of the publisher.

6. Sigmund Freud, "The Relationship of the Poet to Daydreaming," (1908) in *On Creativity and the Unconscious,* trans. I. F. Grant Duff (New York: Harper, 1958), 47.

7. *Oeuvres* II (Paris: Editions de la Pléiade, 1986), lii-liii.

8. McCarty, 367.

9. The title of the story in French is *"Le Tendron,"* which can be translated as both "tender shoot" and "young girl."

10. McCarty, 373.

11. In *Gigi* (Paris: Hachette, 1960), 146 (my translation).

12. Among the critics who have examined the importance of shifting perspective in Colette's writing are Jerry Aline Flieger in *Colette and the Fantom Subject of Autobiography* (Ithaca: Cornell University Press, 1992) and Marie-Christine Bellosta in her introduction to "The Rendezvous" in *Oeuvres* III, 1881-91.

13. François Porché, "La Vie littéraire: L'art infaillible de Colette," *Le Jour,* 15 décembre 1937, 2; Robert Kemp, "Les Livres," *La Liberté,* 28 décembre 1937, 4; Pierre Loewen, "La Vie littéraire: 'Bella-Vista' par Colette," *L'Ordre,* 27 décembre 1937, 2; Robert Brasillach, "Causerie littéraire: Colette, 'Bella-Vista' [. . .]," *L'Action française,* 9 décembre 1937, 5, (my translations). For a complete summary of critical reaction to "The Rendezvous," from which I have selected the preceding references, see Marie-Christine Bellosta's introduction to the story, in *Oeuvres* III, 1881-91.

14. Maurice Goudeket, preface to *Fleurs du désert* (Flowers of the Desert), as cited in *Oeuvres* III, 1888 (my translation).

15. As cited in *Oeuvres* III, 1887 (my translation).

16. Marie-Christine Bellosta, in her introduction to "The Rendezvous," *Oeuvre* III, 1890.

17. Jerry Aline Flieger's cogent analysis of the relevance of Freudian theory to selected autobiographical works by Colette has contributed significantly to my analysis of "Rainy Moon." See her *Colette and the Fantom Subject of Autobiography.*

18. Sigmund Freud, "The Uncanny," in *The Complete Psychological Works of Sigmund Freud,* trans. James Strachey, 17 (London: The Hogarth Press, 1955), 220.

19. *Ibid.,* 241.

20. Sigmund Freud, "Repression," *The Freud Reader,* ed. Peter Gay (New York: W. W. Norton and Co. 1989) 570.

21. Sigmund Freud, "The Uncanny," in *The Complete Psychological Works of Sigmund Freud,* 250.

22. Several critics have noted the rapport between the reflexive name of another Colette character, Renée Néré, the protagonist of the novel *The Vagabond* and her project of self-analysis. See, for example, Joan Hinde Stewart, *Colette* (Boston: Twayne Publishers, 1983), 47. In this story, of course, Délia gives the narrator the same opportunity for self-appraisal afforded other Colette women characters by their reflections in mirrors.

23. Sigmund Freud, "Mourning and Melancholia," in Gay, *The Freud Reader,* 588.

24. Flieger, 201. Flieger convincingly presents this line of reasoning in much greater detail in tracing the mourning process of Colette's autobiographical subject, who must overcome melancholic identification with her lost parents.

25. Sigmund Freud, "Mourning and Melancholia," in Gay, *The Freud Reader,* 589.

26. Sigmund Freud, "The Uncanny," in *The Complete Psychological Works of Sigmund Freud,* 251.

Bibliography

Unless otherwise specified, English translations are cited from *The Collected Stories of Colette.* Edited by Robert Phelps. New York: Farrar, Straus, and Giroux, 1983.

Works by Colette

The definitive edition of Colette's complete works is currently in progress. The first three volumes, covering works published through 1939, have already been published as *Oeuvres.* Edited by Claude Pichois. vols. I, II, III. Paris: Editions de la Pléiade, 1984-1991.

Paysages et portraits. Paris: Flammarion, 1958. ("A Letter," "The Sémiramis Bar," "If I Had a Daughter . . . ," "Rites," "Newly Shorn," "Grape Harvest," "In the Boudoir," "Alix's Refusal" included in *The Collected Stories of Colette*.)

Mes Apprentissages. Paris: Ferenczi et fils, 1936. (*My Apprenticeships*. Translated by Helen Beauclerk. New York: Farrar, Straus and Giroux, 1978.)

CRITICISM

Butler, Judith. *Gender Trouble: Feminism and the Subversion of Identity.* New York: Routledge, 1990.

Flieger, Jerry Aline. *Colette and the Fantom Subject of Autobiography.* Ithaca: Cornell University Press, 1992.

Juliette M. Rogers (essay date summer 1996)

SOURCE: Rogers, Juliette M. "Addressing Success: Fame and Narrative Strategies in Colette's *La Naissance du jour*." *Studies in Twentieth Century Literature* 20, no. 2 (summer 1996): 505-20.

[*In the following essay, Rogers explores the melding of autobiography and fiction in Colette's writing and argues that the author developed a relationship with her readers in order to fashion their reception of her.*]

> To be talked about is to be part of a story, and to be part of a story is to be at the mercy of storytellers—the media and their audience. The famous person is thus not so much a person as a story about a person.
>
> —Braudy, *The Frenzy of Renown* (592)

Colette, as one of France's most well-known *femmes de lettres* of the twentieth century, rebelled from Braudy's definition of a famous person. Although she is obviously "part of the story" of twentieth-century French literature, Colette struggled publicly with the images that her "storytellers" produced of her and made direct contributions to change those stories about herself. Her fame thus went through many phases over the course of her literary career and while she was sometimes left at the "mercy" of the media and her reading public, she made concerted efforts to shape her own fame. It has been difficult for critics of the past to discuss an author's urge to fame or even her desire to shape the type of fame that she enjoys without encountering a certain amount of uneasiness or resistance on the part of either the author, her public, or other critics. The urge to fame has often been viewed in a negative light, that is, as selfish, egotistical, and greedy, or as evidence of an uncontrollable hunger for power, money, and prestige, all of which have been conceived to be especially unattractive qualities for women. This cultural attitude explains in part the surfeit of gushing admiration that character-

izes almost all Colette biographies, or "hagiographies," as Elaine Marks has aptly named them (Marks xi), and the careful sidestepping of the issue of fame in most psychoanalytical or theoretical works on Colette.

It is possible that the negative facets of fame may have influenced Colette's writings, but they are not retraceable elements in her works, nor are they relevant to my project here. On the other hand, there are many positive ways of interpreting the urge to fame, such as an individual's vision for improving her position in society, or for legitimizing a particular group's role in that society. I have chosen to study Colette's attempts to reshape her fame because of the positive impacts that they had for herself, as a woman writer of the early twentieth century in France, and for her relationship to her readers, both popular and critical.

Colette's particular combination of literary reputation and public recognition is fascinating because of its crossover between the domains of "low" popular culture and "high" aesthetic movements, and because of the transition it underwent, from the naughty schoolgirl "Claudine," to the independent "Vagabonde," to the wise and respected "mother of modern French letters," as she was finally remembered. I will be studying here the techniques that Colette employed to purposefully alter her audience's reception of her, and will be focusing mainly on the complex mélange of autobiographical and fictional elements in her writing.

I do not wish to imply that Colette single-handedly produced her own literary reputation, exclusive of all influences from critics and her reading public. The construction of a literary reputation is not only based on a writer's work. As John Rodden notes, "Not only the quality or 'genius' of a writer's work earns him and it a literary reputation, but also an institutional network of production, distribution, and reception which circulates and values his achievement" (Rodden 4). Colette found avenues to mold her own famous persona through this institutional network, either through publicity stunts or through her reputation as a critic and journalist. Thus, during her earliest years in the limelight, Colette's manipulation of the media and their audience did not always involve writing. In her first promotional appearance in 1900, when, as a twenty-seven-year-old woman, she dressed up as her fifteen-year-old fictional schoolgirl character Claudine, Colette offered to the public a series of images that would contribute to her renown. In the particular case of the Claudine publicity poses, Colette later announced that she had been reluctant to appear as Claudine, but had felt forced to do so by her ex-husband Willy, who had been responsible for publishing the novel *Claudine à l'École*. In this instance of author-character identification, Colette the author had been squeezed to fit into the image of Claudine the fictional character, apparently against her will and without any real control over her husband's or the media's interpretation of her.

Whether it was her husband or Colette herself who invented the idea, the publicity stunt was highly successful and produced a fad for many Claudine products—Claudine cigarettes, perfume, soap, and hats, not to mention Claudine novels. For much of her early career, the story of Colette was written not only by "the media and their audience," as Braudy states, but by herself and her husband Willy.[1] When she separated from Willy around 1910 and began writing for magazines such as *Le Matin*, Colette regained much of the power to tell her own story about herself. Her role as a reviewer and journalist would put Colette in the role of "storyteller," allowing her to form other authors' reputations and to begin undermining the power that outsiders had maintained on forming her public image.

Aside from publicity stunts and journalism, Colette's main sources of reputation production came through her novels, and principally through her semi-autobiographical narratives, both of which would reshape the public images of herself in the forms that she chose. It may be objected that the use of autobiographical confession to change one's reputation is nothing new in French literary history. Rousseau's now classic example, *Les Confessions*, could be interpreted as an authorial attempt to explain his life, to justify his perceived failings as a writer, and to manipulate the public reception of his work. However common it may be in general French literary history, Colette's urge to fame and her urge to shape that fame are two topics that have not been discussed until very recently in Colette criticism.[2] To study these particular aspects of Colette's persona production, I have chosen to explore one of her most well-known texts, *La Naissance du Jour* (1928), because it contains narrative techniques specifically designed to manipulate her readers' reception of her.

La Naissance du Jour is probably most renowned as Colette's ultimate work on the complex mother/daughter relations between her mother Sido and herself. Written between *La Maison de Claudine* (1922) and *Sido* (1929), this text sustains the nostalgia for the mother that Colette had begun to develop in *La Maison de Claudine* and that she would continue to explore in the *Sido* essays.[3] At the same time, however, it justifies her efforts during this period to take new paths in her writing career. I use the term "new" paths, because the daughter's story here is an attempt to narrate a new set of power relations not only within the private realm of the family but also in the very public arena of the celebrity writer and her admirers. By the time this work was published, Colette was a well-established novelist and popular cultural figure and she had learned early on

how to market herself, first as a fictional character, then as a writer. Yet the public attention that she received during the first twenty years of her literary career was mostly popular, whether in the form of the book review or the gossip column.

Notable exceptions to the generally positive reception of the texts were the three full-length critical biographies that had been published on Colette by 1928.[4] These critical exceptions eventually became the rule in Colette criticism. The way in which this autobiographical novel would mark a turning point for Colette's career is itself exceptional: she addressed the specific problems of her own reception within the pages of the book itself. In *La Naissance du Jour,* Colette cites Anna de Noailles' incredulous question, "Vous n'aimez donc pas la gloire?" 'You don't like fame?', As a metaphorical response, Colette announces clearly her desire for renown among her "frères et complices" 'brothers and peers' and "autres créatures vivantes" 'other living creatures': "Mais si. Je voudrais laisser un grand renom parmi les êtres qui, ayant gardé sur leur pelage, dans leur âme, la trace de mon passage, ont pu follement espérer, un seul moment, que je leur appartenais" 'Yes of course I do. I would like to have made a name for myself among those creatures who, having kept, upon their fur and within their soul, a trace of my passage, might have hoped, just for a moment, that I belonged to them' (*Naissance* 304). This passage is preceded by a section on the narrator's love for animals, thus perhaps limiting her desire for fame to the animal kingdom. However, the ambiguity of *frères et complices* leaves her declaration open to readers or other human beings, among whom she might also wish to leave "un grand renom."

The Colette character's efforts to change her readers' impressions of her in *La Naissance du Jour* (1928) provide a clear break from Colette's earlier heroines. For example, in *Claudine à l'École,* the entire narrative is written from the point of view of the main character Claudine in the form of a personal diary. Claudine may complain that her father or her teachers do not understand her, but she remains silent on the possibility of a response (negative or positive) from an outside critic or audience. *La Vagabonde,* written ten years later (1910), was also in the first-person singular, but the main character Renée begins to show a perceptive awareness of her music-hall spectators. However, even though she writes constantly about her performances, she speaks uncritically of her audience, thankful to have an admiring public. She does not attempt to change their one-sided impressions of her. In the same vein, when speaking of the book reviews of her first three novels, Renée disagrees completely with the critics, but she does not try to change her readers' views, and is content with simply stating her own personal preferences for the third text, generally considered a failure by the public (*La Vagabonde* 1084). In contrast, the Colette character of *La Naissance du Jour* both directly and indirectly addresses her readers in order to shape their reception of her work. How does the text succeed in performing such a task? And why has its "mission" been understood as an autobiographical mother/daughter memoir? Both of these questions are essential for a new interpretation of *La Naissance du Jour* and for a better understanding of Colette's narrative strategies with regard to the shaping of her own fame. It is these two questions that I will undertake to answer in this essay.

To begin our discussion, we must look at the dual message in *La Naissance du Jour.* The text perpetuates the fame that Colette had gained up until the publication of this text, which could be summarized as the image of the daughter, whether in the form of an impish ingénue, an independent divorcée, or a seductive older woman. The novel also works to shape a different type of fame, one that Colette would enjoy more and more after the appearance of this work. This image could be characterized as the "mother of twentieth-century French literature," whose wisdom and maturity are reflected in her complex writing style. These two competing elements of authorial fame are promoted in *La Naissance du Jour* through the development of a dual plot rivalry.

On the one hand, Colette writes a memoir-styled monologue in response to an epistolary "dialogue" between Sido and herself. Although there is no actual dialogue here (her mother died sixteen years before Colette started writing *La Naissance du Jour*), her mother's letters act as catalysts that produce Colette's monologic discourse on aging and renunciation. The narrative concerning Sido and Colette appears to be primarily "autobiographical": personal memories, reflections on growing older, and the transcription of letters from Sido.[5] It has usually been considered the primary text of *La Naissance du Jour.* Indeed, the text begins and ends with this narrative, which I will call the "Sido-Colette story."

On the other hand, Colette writes about a conventional romantic triangle that includes Vial, Hélène, and herself. Vial and Hélène are two of Colette's young neighbors in Saint-Tropez, where she is currently spending the summer in her newly acquired villa, "La Treille Muscate." Vial desires an affair with Colette, while Hélène secretly loves Vial. Colette, older than both, tries to turn Vial's attentions from herself to Hélène. This fictional love story, which I will call the "Saint-Tropez story," emerges only in the fifth chapter of the book and is written in a more traditionally fictional style: introduction of the conflict, then its development, crisis, dénouement, and, finally, conclusion; all centered on a heterosexual love triangle. Furthermore, the main characters of the triangle, Hélène and Vial, are both invented; that is, Colette's circle of friends in Saint-

Tropez did not actually include persons named Hélène Clément or Valère Vial.[6]

These two plots are not neatly divided into separate sections of the book. In fact, Colette weaves the two together using the same narrator ("Madame Colette") for both the Sido-Colette story and the Saint-Tropez story, and the same first-person singular narration for both storylines. Yet there remains a clearly defined competition between the two plot lines for the reader's attention. The memoirs are presented first, thus establishing the reader's expectations for an autobiographical set of memories rather than a traditional, "novelistic" plot. Although it may be easier to follow the fictional plot of the love story, the lyrical style of the memoirs makes the Sido-Colette story remarkably powerful. Not surprisingly, it is the mother-daughter story that most Colette critics have prioritized.

Questions about the love-triangle plot arose as soon as *La Naissance du Jour* appeared in 1928. In spite of them, or perhaps because of them, the work became an instant bestseller, an indication that the Saint-Tropez story did not bother her readers, but was seen as an entertaining distraction from the "main" plot of the text. Critical reviews of the book forecast its wide success particularly because of Colette's beautiful style and her portrait of Sido. However, the praise was accompanied by perplexed comments as to what should be done with the "other" component of the text (the love story). André Billy's 1928 book review gives the following description of the Saint-Tropez story: "Une ombre de roman se situe là . . . où la romancière semble ne vouloir tenir qu'un rôle de témoin. . . . Pourtant, l'autobiographie—la 'fatale autobiographie' des oeuvres de la femme—reprend, ici et là, ses droits" 'There is the shadow of a novel here . . . in which the novelist seems to want to act only as a witness. . . . Nevertheless, autobiography—the "inevitable autobiography" of women's writing—now and then rears its head' (n. pag.).

Over the next sixty years, questions about *La Naissance du Jour*'s dual narratives would not disappear. In 1968, Anne Ketchum claimed that Colette wrote a fictional section into *La Naissance du Jour* only to appease editors who insisted that she write a novel, not another autobiographical text (Ketchum 224-25). In 1981, Nancy K. Miller suggested that the fictional Saint-Tropez narrative was written as an example of the principles that Colette established in the autobiographical Sido-Colette narrative (Miller 168). In 1992, Lynne Huffer labeled the Saint-Tropez love story a "response," explaining that the daughter Colette "organized a spectacle of her own" in mimicry of "the mother's epistolary model" which would allow the daughter to "recover the maternal matrix." Thus, again, the primary text remained the Sido-Colette story (Huffer 38). It seems, then, that there is a consensus among critics that the love-triangle narrative is secondary, banal, and subsumed by the main "dialogue" between the mother and daughter. However, certain questions remain. Critics cannot agree on why the love story was included: was it essentially imposed by the editors or did it represent a choice made by Colette? Nor can they agree on how the Saint-Tropez narrative functions in the work: is it an example of or in opposition to the Sido-Colette narrative? A discussion of how the two stories interact narratively and/or stylistically has been completely neglected, except for suggestions such as Miller's or Huffer's that the Saint-Tropez narrative may be interpreted as an example of the principles of renunciation established in the Sido-Colette narrative. However, by working through the position of the narrator in each plot, I will uncover hidden narrative strategies that Colette employed to perpetuate the fame that she already enjoyed while at the same time shaping that fame into a different form of recognition. These narrative strategies will not only upset the established primacy of the Sido-Colette story, but also open up a new view of the Colette-reader relationship.

FICTIONAL AUTOBIOGRAPHY: PERPETUATING FAME

Recent Colette critics have produced enlightening studies of the representations of the maternal figure and of its effect on Colette's tone and voice throughout *La Naissance du Jour.*[7] Their studies focus mainly on Colette's literary connection to Sido (the maternal letter-writer, muse, and model) and on psychoanalytical approaches to the muse-pupil relationship. I will mention only in passing the now (in)famous letter from Sido about her pink cactus, located on page one of *La Naissance du Jour,* and the alterations that Colette made to the original letter to create a maternal character that would suit her needs for the tone of this work. Colette biographer Michèle Sarde was one of the first to point out that Colette changed several of her mother's letters before including them in the work, thereby producing a textual maternal muse who would embody the ideals of renunciation and independence that Colette herself was embracing in *La Naissance du Jour* (Sarde 286-87). In Philippe Lejeune's canonical definition of autobiography, the process of alteration and reconstruction is normally considered an infringement of the "autobiographical" pact, especially when the altered text is presented to the reader as true. However, as autobiography has always contained elements of fiction, by nature of its form and structure, the Sido-Colette plot, including the altered letters from Sido, continues to be understood as the more autobiographical section of *La Naissance du Jour.*

Colette rewrites her mother's letters so that Sido will appear as her maternal muse, and she informs the reader that she will not include any information about her own maternal relationship with her own daughter, Colette de Jouvenel. Thus, the only maternal images that the reader encounters in *La Naissance du Jour* are those found in the "Sido" character, and the altered or censored maternal texts are designed to accentuate only the similarities between Colette and her mother. Clearly, then, the images of Colette that are created in these sections of the Sido-Colette plot are designed to perpetuate the previously established public images of Colette as an inspired daughter-figure, one who imitates her maternal muse.

However, if we look closely, there are also differences between Sido and Colette that Colette suggests indirectly within the text. One that I will emphasize, because of its relevance to the subject of fame, is the difference in class or social standing that has grown between her mother and herself. Colette now belongs to a privileged leisure class; the novel describes her summer on the French Riviera writing novels and entertaining friends. Her mother Sido, on the other hand, lived her entire adult life in a downwardly mobile, petty bourgeois environment, and her letters describe a life of hardship.[8] Leisure and independence in her small provincial village are rare.

The narrator describes the movements of the two women in very different modes. Sido runs from house to house in snow and wind begging for a poor neighbor's newborn child: "elle courut sous la neige fouettée de vent crier de porte en porte, chez des riches, qu'un enfant, près d'un âtre indigent, venait de naître sans langes, nu sur de défaillantes mains nues . . ." 'she ran through the wind-driven snow from door to door, in rich neighborhoods, crying out that a child, in an indigent household, had just been born with nothing to wear, naked and in weak, naked hands . . .' (*Naissance* 278). In contrast, Colette and her friends enjoy their eleven o'clock swims in the Mediterranean and prolonged afternoon meals: "Segonzac, Carco, Régis Gignoux et Thérèse Dorny devaient quitter les hauteurs d'une colline, et manger ici un déjeuner méridional, salades, rascasse farcie et beignets d'aubergines, ordinaire que je corsais de quelque oiseau rôti" 'Segonzac, Carco, Régis Gignoux, and Thérèse Dorny were to leave the hilltop, and eat a southern lunch, salads, stuffed scorpion fish, and fried eggplant, an everyday meal which I spiced up with a roast bird' (297); "mes camarades d'été, au nombre d'une dizaine, fêtaient le temps léger et le bain tiède . . ." 'my summer friends, ten or so of them, celebrated the mild weather and the warm water . . .' (330). The urgency of Sido's visit to her neighbors in the cold winter contrasts starkly with Colette's lazy rendezvous with her neighbors to indulge in leisure activities. Sido also writes to say that she is still feeling young, and to prove it she has just finished chopping up six bundles of wood to provide for the coming winter: "J'ai aussi scié du bois et fait six petits fagots. . . . Et puis, en somme, je n'ai que soixante-seize ans!" 'I also cut wood, and made six little bundles of it . . . after all, I'm only 67 years old' (296). Colette, in comparison, "returns" to nature by planting a tropical mandarin tree in her backyard, expecting to reap its benefits in ten years: "Ce tout petit mandarinier en boule, crois-tu qu'il a un bon style, déjà? . . . Dans dix ans, Vial, on cueillera de belles mandarines sur ce petit arbre" 'This tiny mandarin tree, don't you think it looks nice already? . . . In ten years, Vial, we'll pick beautiful mandarins off that little tree' (327). Colette may glorify her humble background by glorifying her mother's image, but there is no question of her returning to that lifestyle.

While her mother ended her life in comparatively impoverished surroundings, Colette has been successful and remains firmly grounded in her newly acquired status as writer, celebrity, and member of the artistic leisure class of France. Even though they may appear similar in spiritual or emotional terms (due to the narrator's alteration of her mother's letters), in material terms, they lead very different lives. Both through these indirect comparisons made by the narrator and through her fictionalized autobiography in the Sido-Colette plot, Colette signals to her readers that the relationship between her mother and herself is not always one of muse-pupil, nor even one of equality. Through a close reading of Colette's "autobiographical" narrative, we find a model of mother-daughter relations that weaves together both real and fictional differences. These differences undermine the images of Colette as inspired daughter and of Sido as muse-mother that critics and readers have usually emphasized. They also begin to reveal the first part of the new claims that Colette was trying to make about herself as a successful writer. The second part, that of her status in the public realm, comes to the fore in the Saint-Tropez story of *La Naissance du Jour.*

Autobiographical Fiction: Shaping Fame

On a first reading, the "fictional" Saint-Tropez plot is, in form at least, a traditionally "autobiographical" narrative. That is, the narration continues in the first person singular, and the narrator has the same name as the author, Madame Colette. The setting is in Colette's actual home, "La Treille Muscate" in Saint-Tropez, and some of the characters are people who actually existed—Luc-Albert Moreau, Dunoyer de Segonzac, Thérèse Dorny, Régis Gignoux, Francis Carco, and Villeboeuf were all artists, writers, and actors who knew Colette and who were in southern France while she was living there. However, the main characters of the romantic triangle, Hélène and Vial, and the triangle itself are all fictional,

not based on events in Colette's life. Colette chose to narrate the story with a classic, novelistic plot, and, in great contrast to the Sido-Colette sections of the text, she retells events in progressive, chronological order.

Not only are the content and structure different in the Saint-Tropez plot; we find that the voice of the narrator, Madame Colette, changes considerably in the love-triangle narrative. Instead of searching for a higher, maternal authority or a literary muse, in the Saint-Tropez narrative sections of the work, Colette openly portrays herself as a respected literary author and authority on love, relationships, and life. In other words, she has become the muse in the Saint-Tropez narrative of *La Naissance du Jour.*

For a French reader of the 1920s, this image of Colette as the muse and authority was not surprising: the name "Colette" immediately conjured up images of the well-known figure and novelist. At the time that *La Naissance du Jour* was published, she had many best-sellers circulating; she was a regular contributor to *Vogue, Le Figaro,* and *Le Journal,* and had performed in numerous mime shows in Paris and all over France. Yet even for a casual reader of the 1990s, the idea of the narrator as muse and authority is fully supported through details included within the text. No external knowledge of Colette's life and previous literary successes is necessary, because the narrator, in traditional autobiographical form, mentions past works and fictional characters: "je consignais, incorrigible, quelque chapitre dédié à l'amour, au regret de l'amour, un chapitre tout aveuglé d'amour. Je m'y nommais Renée Néré, ou bien, prémonitoire, j'agençais une Léa" 'incorrigibly, I would set forth a chapter dedicated to love, to regrets about love, a chapter blinded by love. I would name myself Renée Néré, or else, as if by premonition, I would sketch out a Léa' (*Naissance* 286). She alludes to both her critics' comments and her summer friends' admiration for her work: "Vous ne mesurerez que plus tard, me disait Mendès peu avant sa mort, la force du type littéraire que vous avez créé" '"Only later will you realize," Mendès told me a little before he died, "the force of the literary type you have created"' (316).

In the Saint-Tropez narrative, then, we find a narrator who is also a celebrity; it is through the use of this new voice that she establishes a muse-pupil relationship with her fictional neighbors. In contrast to the Sido-Colette relationship, where Sido was placed in the position of authority/author of letters and Colette in the role of admirer/reader of letters, the relationship between Colette and her fictional neighbors turns Colette into the author/authority and places her neighbors in the subordinate position of reader/admirers.

For the author-reader relationship, Colette thus provides a number of possible authorial models and influences within the text of *La Naissance du Jour:* her mother's letters, her previous literary successes, and her popular image at that time in France. However, she also describes the other side of the relationship—the elements that are needed for a model reader. In the Saint-Tropez sections especially, the narrator enumerates different types of readers that she has encountered during her literary career, including what she considers poor readers, usually those readers who identify the author with the narrator of a work. Colette notes with annoyance that both her summer acquaintances and her anonymous public often end up associating her, the author, with the narrator of her novels. She refers to the adolescent readers who write letters to her about the *Claudine* novels that they have just finished reading, where they assume that Colette the author (approximately age fifty-five at the time of *La Naissance du Jour*) is still the same age as Claudine the narrator (fifteen): "Il y a des jeunes filles—trop jeunes pour prendre garde aux dates des éditions—qui m'écrivent qu'elles ont lu les *Claudine* en cachette, qu'elles attendent ma réponse à la poste restante . . . à moins qu'elles ne me donnent rendez-vous dans un 'thé.' Elles me voient peut-être en sarrau d'écolière, qui sait?" 'There are young girls—too young to pay attention to copyright dates—who write me to say that they have read the *Claudine* books in secret, that they are awaiting an answer from me . . . or else they expect me to meet them in a tearoom. They might imagine me wearing a schoolgirl's smock, who knows?' (316). Here she uses humor to point out the absurdity of linking a narrator to the author of a text, and thus denies to some extent her connection with the book and with the reader on this level. She is not comfortable with being treated as peer to a fifteen-year-old reader and resists efforts made by her younger readers to turn her fictional character into a "real" person.

She also finds that some of her close summer friends look to her novels for clues to understanding her thoughts. She rebukes Vial promptly when he remarks that he does not remember having read a comment that she just made in any of her novels: "'Nous n'avons que faire de mes livres ici, Vial.' Je ne pus lui dissimuler le découragement jaloux, l'injuste hostilité qui s'emparent de moi quand je comprends qu'on me cherche toute vive entre les pages de mes romans" "'This isn't about my books, Vial." I could not hide from him the jealous discouragement, the unjust hostility that come hold of me when I realize that someone is trying to find me between the pages of my novels' (341). Vial also tries to connect the narrator of the text to the author, but instead of assuming that she is a fifteen-year-old Claudine, he assigns her a superstar status, placed on a pedestal above ordinary, mortal friendships. Colette's reprimand is perhaps more pronounced because of this particular reader's (Vial's) proximity to herself; he should know her better than a fifteen-year old reader of *Claudine* novels. She also feels more "unjust hostility" towards him because he insists on reading her as a fic-

tional character, not as a person. Vial's reading claims the opposite of the teenaged reader's in that he has tried to fictionalize his real-life neighbor by assimilating her to one of her novel's heroines, rather than trying to make a fictional heroine become a living human being. He will not treat "Madame Colette" simply as a friend and neighbor (and possible lover), but as a literary figure and a fictional character.

Colette does not limit her portrayal of bad readers to popular readings of her: within *La Naissance du Jour,* she also mentions two of her critics, Motherlant (304) and Mendès (316), and even takes on the criticisms of one of her ex-husbands. But rather than allowing their words and opinions to have the final say in forming public impressions of her, she critiques their short-sighted views of her works and herself, thus reappropriating the power of image production into her own hands. In response to her husband's remonstrance that she never writes about anything but love, Colette replies with irony, "Si le temps ne l'eût pressé de courir—car il était beau et charmant—vers des rendez-vous amoureux, il m'aurait peut-être enseigné ce qui a licence de tenir, dans un roman et hors du roman, la place de l'amour . . ." 'If he had not been pressed for time—for he was handsome and charming—by amorous rendezvous, he might perhaps have taught me what, in the novel and outside the novel, should take the place of love . . .' (285-86). She also mentions her male readers' amazement by the fact that Colette can divulge private feelings and emotions in a published work (315). The misunderstandings that arise between Madame Colette and her various readers bring out not only the difficulties confronted by a writer when her autobiography becomes subject to public interpretation, but the autobiographer's warning to future readers not to follow the same misguided paths that past readers have.

To find an example of a good reader, on the other hand, we must return to the Sido-Colette plot of *La Naissance du Jour* where Colette portrays herself as the model reader. She reads, interprets, and understands her mother's letters in such a way that her mother need never correct her daughter's interpretations. Furthermore, Colette is able to learn lessons from her readings and apply them to her own writing and life. Colette admits that her mother is obviously a better writer than she (370) and that she could never imagine or invent what her mother would have said in certain situations, given her mother's linguistic genius (336). These comments demonstrate what the model reader's response should be and how they contrast with the obstinate and poor readers' responses.

Are we to learn from the negative examples of poor readers given in *La Naissance du Jour*? Perhaps yes, but the ambiguity of the narrator in Colette's autobiographical fiction makes it difficult to do so. Most Colette biographers and critics have been tempted to identify the narrator with the author of the work, just as Vial and the Claudine-reader did. The more important point here is that Colette had gained the authority to tell her readers how she felt about them and their readings of her, and would do so openly in her texts. This newly found narrative authority was expressed both in her deviations from the muse-pupil paradigm in the Sido-Colette story and in her claims to fame in the Saint-Tropez story. If we look specifically at the effects produced by her voice of authority, rather than those produced by her admirative daughter-narrative that has been emphasized over the years, we see that they produce new readings of her. These passages are written in a style that is clearly conscious of her readers' preconceived notions of her persona and one that is clearly aimed at reshaping that fame. Through the act of authorizing her success, both in the descriptions of her life of leisure at Saint-Tropez and in the references to her literary fame, Colette in fact developed an author-reader relationship designed to shape the reception that she enjoyed and to enable her to become part of the French literary canon of her day.

Notes

1. Although Braudy's notion of renown as the "story about a person" was written with twentieth-century performers in mind, it is also well suited for writers, and particularly for writers whose subject matter often centers around their own lives. In France, the star system has always included not only actors, musicians, and politicians, but also writers and even literary critics.

2. See for example Michèle Sarde's "The First Steps in a Writer's Career" (1981) or Michel Mercier's "Notice" in Colette's *Oeuvres* (1991). Both articles offer explanations for some of Colette's more infamous statements about her writing and her public image. Sarde, for example, explores Colette's statement of denial: "No, I don't know how to write. In my youth, I never, never wanted to write" (16).

3. I prefer Lynne Huffer's name for these three Colette works: her "maternal cycle" (9).

4. The three full-length works include one biography: Robert Sigl's *Colette* (1924), and two works that combined critical study with biography: Paul Reboux's *Colette ou le génie du style* (1925) and Jean Larnac's *Colette, sa vie, son oeuvre* (1927). All three tend toward the hagiographic.

5. Although it may be problematic, I use the term "autobiographical" here in a canonical sense; that is, that the work is true, that it quotes accurately from real life documents, is personal and written in the first person, that it fulfills the "autobio-

graphical pact" with the reader that Philippe Lejeune speaks of in his article "Le pacte autobiographique." As I will demonstrate further, Colette's own particular brand of autobiographical novel does not adhere to these oversimplistic prescriptions and constantly mixes fiction with autobiography.

6. It may appear that there is an autobiographical basis for the narrator's relationship to the thirty-five-year-old Vial in *La Naissance du jour,* especially if one considers the fact that Colette's relationship with her third husband (thirty-five-year-old Maurice Goudeket) first developed during a summer vacation in Saint-Tropez. However, Colette herself, as well as Maurice Goudeket and numerous biographers and critics, have openly stated that Vial was not based on Goudeket, but rather on a young antique dealer in Saint Tropez who did not know Colette personally and who only indirectly influenced Colette's life.

7. In the collection of essays entitled *Colette: The Woman, the Writer,* Colette critics Nancy K. Miller (164-75), Joan Hinde Stewart (43-53), Erica Eisinger (85-103), and Suzanne Relyea (150-63) all develop new conceptual models that have been excellent tools for rereading Colette. More recently, Nicole Ward Jouve, in her 1987 monograph *Colette,* Marianne Hirsch, in *The Mother/ Daughter Plot: Narrative, Psychoanalysis, Feminism* (Hirsch 103-08), and Lynne Huffer in *Another Colette* study the maternal figure of Sido in Colette's mother-daughter works.

8. After her husband had squandered her family's fortune, Sido was forced to live a simple, rural life. During her last years, as a widow, she had no means of financial support and moved in with her son's family.

Works Cited

Billy, André. Rev. of *La Naissance du jour. Illustration* 28 April 1928. N. pag.

Braudy, Leo. *The Frenzy of Renown.* Oxford: Oxford UP, 1986.

Colette. *Claudine à l'école. Oeuvres.* 3 vols. Paris: Gallimard, 1983-91. 1: 3-218.

———. *La Naissance du jour. Oeuvres.* 3 vols. Paris: Gallimard, 1983-91. 3: 277-371.

———. *La Vagabonde. Oeuvres.* 3 vols. Paris: Gallimard, 1983-91. 1: 1067-1232.

Eisinger, Erica and McCarty, Mari, eds. *Colette: The Woman, the Writer.* University Park: Pennsylvania State UP, 1981.

Hirsch, Marianne. *The Mother/Daughter Plot: Narrative, Psychoanalysis, Feminism.* Bloomington: Indiana UP, 1989.

Huffer, Lynne. *Another Colette: The Question of Gendered Writing.* Ann Arbor: University of Michigan Press, 1992.

Jouve, Nicole Ward. *Colette.* Bloomington: Indiana UP, 1987.

Ketchum, Anne. *Colette ou la naissance du jour: Etude d'un malentendu.* Paris: Minard, 1968.

Lejeune, Philippe. "Le pacte autobiographique." *Poétique* 14 (1973): 137-62.

Marks, Elaine. "Foreword: Celebrating Colette." *Colette: The Woman, the Writer.* Eds. Erica Eisinger and Mari McCarty. University Park: Pennsylvania State UP, 1981. ix-xi.

Miller, Nancy K. "The Anamnesis of a Female 'I': In the Margins of Self-portrayal." *Colette: The Woman, the Writer.* Eds. Erica Eisinger and Mari McCarty. University Park: Pennsylvania State UP, 1981. 164-75.

Rodden, John. *The Politics of Literary Reputation: The Making and Claiming of 'St. George' Orwell.* Oxford: Oxford UP, 1989.

Sarde, Michèle. *Colette: Free and Fettered.* Trans. Richard Miller. New York: William Morrow, 1980.

———. "The First Steps in a Writer's Career." *Colette: The Woman, the Writer.* Eds. Erica Eisinger and Marci McCarty. University Park: Pennsylvania State UP, 1981. 16-21.

Joan Hinde Stewart (essay date 1996)

SOURCE: Stewart, Joan Hinde. "Dialogues" and "Chance Acquaintances." In *Colette*, pp. 60-81, 99-121. New York: Twayne Publishers, 1996.

[*In the following excerpt from her study of Colette, Stewart examines the novella* Gigi—*which she calls "a small masterpiece of stylish humor and meticulous execution"— and offers detailed analyses of Colette's major volumes of short works, focusing on the author's narrative voice and methods.*]

Gigi

Gigi, which appeared in periodical form in 1941 and as the title story of a collection of short pieces in 1944, is Colette's last major work of fiction, and the locus of several contradictions. While the heroines of her later years are mostly mature (Julie de Carneilhan, for example, is 45), Gigi is an adolescent, created when Colette was nearing 70. She worked on the novelette during the war years, which were among her life's bleakest. Paris was occupied; Maurice Goudeket was arrested in 1941 and sent to a prison camp, and after his release spent months in hiding. Colette was already suffering from the lesion which would become crippling arthritis. But *Gigi* is extraordinarily optimistic for a Colette story. The title character has reached an enormous public. Americans have heard of her, seen the movie with Maurice Chevalier, and can hum the title song—but few know that Colette wrote the book. *Gigi* is such a bright, breezy story that one may incline to dismiss it as just adequate for a musical. In fact, this is a small masterpiece of stylish humor and meticulous execution. Its source is an anecdote Colette had heard in the 1920s (it occurred around 1918), but she sets her version in 1899, so that her last heroine lives in the same era as Claudine and at the time when Colette herself, under Willy's guidance, was becoming intimate with Paris and the demimonde.

The story is well known. The guileless 15-year-old product of several generations of hard-working courtesans is being groomed to follow the profession of her grandmother and great-aunt. Their efforts are about to be crowned with a lucrative arrangement. Thirty-three-year-old Gaston Lachaille, sugar tycoon and family friend (Gigi's grandmother seems to have once been the mistress of Gaston's father), wants to make Gigi his mistress. To the consternation of all, Gigi at first rejects the proposition, which strikes her as sordid. And then, just when her love for Gaston has brought her to the point of accepting, he offers her his hand in marriage instead.[1]

One of Colette's most ironic works, *Gigi* is exceptionally spare of lyricism. The constant source of humor is the contrast between her family's consecrated moral laxity, on the one hand, and on the other its rigid adherence to established codes, unvarying confidence in the reliability of signs, and enforcement of principles of order, cleanliness, and "correct" behavior. Paradoxically, their modest home without men gives proof of energetic compliance with bourgeois standards. Bed linens are changed every 10 days, meals are served at regular hours, and Madame Alvarez, the *mater familias,* rises punctually at 7:30 to wage a daily war against impropriety. She has especially inculcated in her progeny dedication to a certain ideal of bodily cleanliness: "You can, at a pinch, leave the face till the morning when traveling or pressed for time. For a woman, attention to the lower parts is the first law of self-respect" (literally, "is a woman's dignity" [142]). The reassignment of dignity from face to sexual organs is part of the code governing this society. It valorizes sex as a survival strategy: cleanliness (*propreté*) is the necessary propriety and the route to prosperity, to property (*propriété*).

When Gigi assures her great-aunt Alicia, "I understand that we don't marry" (151), she seems to endorse this sexual but nonmarital system of exchange. The operative deemphasis of marriage is so complete that, for Aunt Alicia at least, married people are by definition "ordinary" and "useless." Yet the rules for acceptable liaisons are as severe as any bourgeois rules of engagement and marriage, and Gigi understands that she must keep herself inviolate—not until her wedding day, but until her first official liaison. In preparation for her role as a wealthy man's mistress, she must watch her figure, learn to eat lobster properly, and choose cigars and evaluate jewels critically. The liaison is a transaction of paramount importance to an economy in which the family is exclusively matrilinear. Gigi is in fact related only to her mother, grandmother, and great-aunt, with Gaston (the novel's only man) in a tantalizingly ambiguous posture. His early relation to Gigi is avuncular, and the familiar French word for "uncle" that she uses to address him ("Tonton") even resonates with his name. This surrogate uncle eventually tries to withdraw from this role and become a lover. Gigi wins a victory and realigns the family when she makes of him a husband instead.

In redesigning her family tree, she transcends a social order built on scrupulous observance of an imperious sign system. For example, when Gigi wants to wear her everyday coat for the weekly call on Aunt Alicia, her grandmother declares: "That wouldn't show it's Sunday." Gigi arrives at her Aunt's to find her "wearing her little lace cap to show she had a headache" ("en signe de migraine" [138]). And when Gigi's mother opines that there is nothing extraordinary about Liane d'Exelmans, Gaston's most recent mistress: "You're wrong," retorts Madame Alvarez, "she is extraordinary. Otherwise she would not be so famous" (142). She protests again when Aunt Alicia calls Gigi a little brat: "A young girl who has held the attention of Monsieur Lachaille is not a little brat" (169). The family's faith in the appropriateness of wearing a Sunday coat on Sundays and a lace cap for migraines dovetails with their subscription to a code where appearances constitute essence and reputation is truth.

"Calling people and things by their names never did anyone any good," another of Madame Alvarez's maxims, indicates the parameters of the family's pedagogy: certain lexical items are unutterable. In the opening scene, Gigi protests wearing her skirts short on the grounds that they oblige her to be forever thinking of her "you-know-what" ("ceque-je-pense"), which she must conceal with a minimum of fabric. Her grandmother's response:

> "Silence! Aren't you ashamed to call it your you-know-what?"
>
> "I don't mind calling it by any other name, only—"
>
> Madame Alvarez blew out the spirit lamp, looked at the reflection of her heavy Spanish face in the looking

glass above the mantelpiece, and then laid down the law: "There is no other name."

> (127)

In a patrilinear society, the father's voice gives names, whereas Gigi's matrilinear community attempts to discredit or annihilate them. Custodian of language and sexual knowledge, her grandmother adopts a strategy that makes the female space a linguistic absence. But Gigi's sex is constantly on the verge of surfacing, and every other consideration is measured according to it. It is, in fact, the most present and powerful of signifieds, and the very refusal to name it provokes conversations foregrounding its importance. In like manner, Gaston's essential financial identity subtly surfaces in the name of the candies that he eats during his visit to her home: *agents de change.*

Madame Alvarez's mirroring of "her heavy Spanish face" is the most curious example of wordplay and the ramifications of naming, for Madame Alvarez is not Spanish. "Alvarez" is adopted, the Spanish name of a deceased lover. Her appearance has accommodated itself to the name and given the bearer pale and creamy fleshiness and lustrous, oily hair. And not only does she acquire a physiognomy to match the surname; these looks attract, in turn, a suitable Christian name: "eventually she took to calling herself Inez" (128). "Alvarez" undergoes a transformation in the next generation, for her daughter (who, to Madame Alvarez's exasperation, prefers singing to a life of gallantry), is called Andrée Alvar, "in small type on the Opéra-Comique playbills" (139). The playbill typography defines and confines Andrée, just as the Spanish suffix does her mother. The family surname will change more radically still with Gigi's acquisition of a legitimate one through marriage.

Gigi's education involves learning to acknowledge the power of the sociolect in which her mother and grandmother live their lives. Her backwardness is evidenced on the one hand by her bold invocation of the prohibited nonname—her you-know-what—and on the other by her failure to recognize and use correctly terms and names in public currency. To Gaston's astonishment, she has never heard of the playwright Feydeau. And when she has finally assimilated the fact that a demimondaine does not die when she routinely "commits suicide" at the end of an affair, Gigi still cannot sort out the social histories that give her mother and grandmother no trouble. Of Gaston's notorious ex-mistress, Liane:

> "The last time she killed herself, Grandmama, was for the sake of Prince Georgevitch, wasn't it?"
>
> "Where are your brains, my darling? It was for Count Berthou de Sauveterre."

> (143)

While those around her are deliberately ambiguous at times, they are consummately precise at others. "Let us talk briefly and to the point" (162), declares Gaston to Madame Alvarez, when he comes to say he wants Gigi for a mistress; and so they do. The terms of their negotiation are relayed only vaguely to Gigi, however, translated by her grandmother into Gaston's altruistic desire to "make Gigi's fortune." She is expected to acquiesce docilely to the euphemized scheme, but at her confrontation with Gaston, she pointedly announces, "They've drummed into my ears that I am backward for my age, but all the same I know the meaning of words" (166). Shattering the family's plans, she refuses to subscribe to a code which, by eliminating denotation, encourages sexual exploitation, and she delineates her understanding of what it means to have her "fortune" made: like all his previous mistresses, she must sleep in his bed until the day when, with great notoriety, she passes into someone else's. To Gaston's embarrassed, "Gigi, I beg of you," she counters: "But, Tonton, why should I mind speaking of it to you? You didn't mind speaking of it to Grandmama" (166).

There is, of course, no answer to Gigi's question. Why *should* she mind speaking of it? Why the ominous verbal prohibitions surrounding a transparent arrangement? Gigi's you-know-what is the elusive, problematic center of a network of financial and sexual exchange. It is simultaneously concealed (under a short skirt and a nonname) and valorized (sold intact to Gaston Lachaille); unnamed and unnamable, it is nonetheless continually evoked. Her refusal of the circumlocutions, substitutions, and silences that her family demands is the rejection of a system by which they have lived for generations, and which grants centrality to the you-know-what. Gigi is, in fact, from the start, somewhat off center, eccentric. The expression is Madame Alvarez's, who refuses in the first scene to wave Gigi's hair, maintaining that ringlets at the ends are "the maximum of eccentricity permissible for a girl your age" (my translation). Asserting finally that she will have her own "word," Gigi lays claim to a different social configuration. Her verbal and sexual triumph over Gaston rewrites the code: she imposes her own terms of exchange. Her successful attempt to communicate recreates a family that is no longer matrilinear, and a new center emerges: love replaces commercial exchange.

The fiction of Colette's maturity, from *The Other One* to *Gigi,* is similarly eccentric, deviating from traditional fiction into a new feminocentric orbit, whose axis is a subtle investigation of sexual dialogue.

Colette's major volumes of short pieces include *Bella-Vista* (1937), *Chambre d'hôtel* (1940), *Le Képi* (1943), and *Gigi* (1944). The beguiling stories within their pages deserve study for their ambiguities of form and problematics of narration. Some are traditional third-person narrative, like **"The Sick Child,"** an almost surrealistic account of a little boy's affliction with polio. But the greater number are in the first person; narrated by a woman called "Colette," they have filiations with autobiography as well as fiction, and include some of Colette's most experimental and most original pieces.[2]

THE STORIES OF "COLETTE"

Elaine Marks counts 33 of the 57 titles of the complete works (*Oeuvres complètes*) as narrated in the first person.[3] The later and longer stories that concern us here are related to the Claudine novels, to **"The Tendrils of the Vine,"** *The Pure and the Impure, My Apprenticeships,* and *Break of Day*—to name only the most illustrious antecedents. But in these stories there is no obvious fictional transposition, as from Colette to Claudine; and unlike *My Apprenticeships,* most of them are not explicitly the author's own story. They have a lot in common with sections of **"The Tendrils of the Vine,"** where Colette describes visits from her "friend Valentine." In certain of the later pieces, however, it is less a question of friends than, as the title of one proclaims, of "chance acquaintances," passers-by whose dramas she witnesses. In a passage at the beginning of *My Apprenticeships,* Colette notes that, paradoxically, those features most deeply engraved in her memory "are not of people who have played decisive parts in my life. I have it in me to keep a cherished corner for the chance acquaintance as well as for the husband or relation, for the unexpected as fondly as for the everyday" (4). Throughout the short stories, she gives us to understand that fleeting encounters enriched her as woman and as writer.

Structured by the play of coincidence and only partial explanation, these pieces tend more toward anecdote than rigorously articulated narratives. Deliberate, digressive, meditative, they are internally nourished and linked to each other by their settings, and by the predominance of a single voice. In spite of a variety of incidents from the trivial to the criminal, the pieces are curiously reiterative; situations, characterizations, and obsessions reflect the historical Colette's preoccupations. They illustrate—may we say they prove?—certain of her convictions about sexuality, memory, the past, men and women. The heroines are memorable, sometimes attaining what Colette labeled in *Mitsou* a "banal heroism," and their vitality echoes the narrator's own vigor while it shapes the stories.

The tone is somewhere between journalistic and autobiographical, while the fabulations are subtle and difficult to delimit. They are all supposed to be authentic accounts of true experiences in which Colette plays the double role of observer and protagonist. The ambiguous mixture of fiction and autobiography makes for a special effect, a genre I am calling "autography," and of which ***The Pure and the Impure*** is another important example. The idea is bewitchingly simple: Colette tells stories about herself, only the stories are not quite true. She toys with the formal generic distinction that the twentieth century generally respects by fictionalizing *in her own name,* re-creating a self who lives a series of imagined events. Her narrator shares the writer's history as country girl, dancer, novelist, and divorcée, and the characters this "Colette" encounters allude to her past, both personal and literary—to Sido and Achille, to Claudine, Minne, and Toby-Dog. But these references are principally symbols intended to sustain credibility; they are not elaborated, their meanings rarely expanded. They are less revelations of the author than part of a codified aesthetic structure. Colette seems to enjoy the prerogative of rewriting her past by setting her stories against a detailed background of factual autobiography, while being apparently as fanciful as she pleases in the creation of character and plot. The narrator Colette, who mimics and embellishes her creator's biography, emerges as quintessentially feminine and sensitive, immensely experienced and a wise interpreter of experience. It is difficult in the final analysis to assess the overlap between *her* history and the real Colette's, to determine the precise point at which imagination begins to supplement biographical data.

"BELLA-VISTA"

Published in 1937 in the volume of the same name, **"Bella-Vista"** is dated "thirteen years ago." It presumably belongs therefore to the period after Colette's 1923 separation from Henry de Jouvenel, about the time she was discovering the attractions of Provence as a vacation spot (she bought her Saint-Tropez house, La Treille Muscate, in 1926). The psychological dating of the story is more rigorous and pertinent than the chronological:

> It is absurd to suppose that periods empty of love are blank pages in a woman's life. The truth is just the reverse. . . . When I was younger, I did not realize the importance of these "blank pages." The anecdotes with which they furnished me—those impassioned, misguided, simple or inscrutable human beings who plucked me by the sleeve, made me their witness for a moment and then let me go—provided more "romantic" subjects than my private personal drama. I shall not finish my task as a writer without attempting, as I want to do here, to draw them out of the shadows to which the shameless necessity of speaking of love in my own name has consigned them.
>
> (7)

Major first-person novels like ***The Vagabond*** and ***The Shackle,*** whose autobiographical inspiration is perceptible, may be assimilated to Colette's romances. But she insists that the short pieces she came to favor in the end reveal an equally crucial aspect of a "woman's life."

Love blinds one to the fascinating discoveries that can be made in periods free of passion. Colette takes as her task both to address the subject of love and to set its limits; part of her mission is to redeem those "empty" periods of female experience that might be considered insignificant because they take no account of love. She fills in the blanks with stories about events in some ways more enthralling and more romantic than those of the novels.

In **"Bella-Vista,"** the narrator has just purchased a modest vineyard in Provence. While the house is being modernized, she and her dog Pati spend a few weeks in a nearby hotel, the "Bella-Vista." Its middle-aged owners are Madame Suzanne, winsome but not very intelligent, and Madame Ruby, who has a thick American accent, thicker fingers, a heavy-set neck, and a T-shaped torso. There is one other guest, the sinister M. Daste, whom animals especially find antipathetic. One night Colette overhears a quarrel in the next room and discovers the owners' secret: Ruby is really Richard, a man in hiding for some reason and masquerading as a woman. And he has recently stepped so far out of his role as to get the maid pregnant. The apparently eccentric pair of lesbians who had charmed Colette are in fact just an old heterosexual couple. That same night Daste inexplicably murders all of Suzanne's parakeets and secretly moves out. As the proprietor accompanies an exasperated Colette to the train station next morning, her predominant sentiment is annoyance: "I was on the verge of reproaching myself for ever having been taken in by this tough fellow whose walk, whose whole appearance was that of an old Irish sergeant who had dressed himself up as a woman for a joke on St. Patrick's day" (66).

Hotel life, Colette maintains, tends rapidly to become demoralizing. "The main reason for this is that people who really mean nothing to us acquire an artificial importance" (33). Daste, Suzanne, and Ruby preoccupy her unnaturally by dint of their proximity and her own isolation from normal routine. But the sociability into which they force her foregrounds an inner tension; her neighbors simultaneously attract and repel her. Her articulated misanthropy (she reiterates her preference for the company of animals to that of humans) belies an instinctive fascination with strangers. As the days draw on, she notes, "My only idea was to get away yet, against my will, I was growing used to the place. That mysterious attraction of what we do not like is always dangerous. It is fatally easy to go on staying in a place which has no soul, provided that every morning offers us the chance to escape" (35). "Fatally easy," but fatal to whom? Certainly not to Colette herself, who acts on her "keen and slightly cowardly desire to leave Bella-Vista" the very day she learns the truth about Ruby. But very likely fatal to Richard, who comes close to being discovered by Daste; and certainly fatal to the parakeets. Perhaps the ultimate fatality resides in the inevitable inscription of the story: "If the idle looker-on in me exclaimed delightedly 'What a story!,' my honourable side warned me to keep the story to myself. I have done so for a very long time" (63).

Colette intimates that seemingly ordinary people like Ruby and Suzanne appear quite extraordinary if the observer is willing to take time for careful study. But does every apparently anodine existence conceal a drama? At least three other stories, the lengthy *Chance Acquaintances,* "The Rainy Moon," and "The Photographer's Missus" ("La Dame du Photographe"), suggest an affirmative answer.

Chance Acquaintances

I did not acquire my habitual mistrust of nonentities over a period of years. Instinctively, I have always held them in contempt for clinging like limpets to any chance acquaintance more robust than themselves. . . . [They] are, in fact, envoys from the nether-world, deputised to act as a liaison between ourselves and beings with no other means of approach.

(141)

These curious affirmations appear at the beginning of *Chance Acquaintances* (*Chambre d'Hôtel,* in a volume by that name, 1940). Colette illustrates her meaning with an anecdote from her music-hall days. Half prostitute, half actress, Lucette d'Orgeville would cross Colette's path every year or so. Now she would appear draped in sable and emeralds, now impoverished. They meet on one particular occasion when she is in the latter state. Lucette has retained a summer chalet in a mountain thermal resort in the Dauphiné, for herself and her favorite lover, the faithful Luigi. But financial wisdom forces her to change her plans and accept instead the proposition of a wealthier suitor; regretfully, she is off to America. She persuades Colette to enjoy the chalet in her stead. Colette goes but dislikes the dust and assembly-line construction, and takes a room in a nearby hotel instead, intending to return to Paris the next day.

She is hardly settled in the hotel when, through the offices of her cat, who strays across the balcony, she makes the acquaintance of Antoinette and Gérard Haume. Their voices reach her before she catches sight of the pair, and she is surprised to discover that the rasping voice is Gérard's, while the huskier, more pleasant and more virile tones are his wife's. This schematic gender reversal on the one hand recalls the more dramatic example of "Madame Ruby" in "Bella-Vista" and, on the other, reiterates numerous situations of Colette's fiction where an apparently masculine dimension in women characters formulaically connotes moral strength. It also finds an internal echo in Colette's cat, who wears "the masculine look of a she-cat who has decided to make frequent evasions of her gender" (160).

Like Lucette, the Haumes latch on to Colette. In spite of Antoinette's excessive familiarity, impersonal stylish looks and clichéd speech, Colette is drawn by the kindness of her neighbor and her courageous determination to triumph over the illness that brought the couple to the thermal waters of "X-les-Bains." From day to day, then week to week, Colette postpones her departure. Gérard remains for some time a mystery. Colette's initial assumption is that *he* must be the sick one, and her misprision is based on an accurate assessment of his weakness and propensity to self-indulgence. Eventually he confides (virtually all the characters in Colette's short fiction sooner or later confide in the narrator) that he is in despair over the silence of his Parisian mistress, Madame Leyrisse, who has not answered his letters for 18 days. He persuades Colette to return briefly to Paris at his expense to check on her, for Gérard himself cannot decently leave Antoinette. Colette reports back that his mistress has moved out, leaving no forwarding address. The distraught lover attempts suicide, broods for weeks, and perks up only when Colette introduces him to Lucette. She has returned from her transatlantic expedition raped, beaten, and with a nasty untreated wound on the nape of the neck, but still nonchalant. She and Luigi have come to occupy the villa near the hotel. A new affair begins: Luigi is still her true love, but they need money, so Lucette accommodates Gérard. But not for long. One day a terse note from Luigi brings the hotel news of Lucette's death from blood poisoning.

These "nonentities" whom the narrator condemns in fact reveal themselves as both consequential and significant, since beneath their colorless exterior lurk dangerous susceptibilities, immense reserves of energy, and inclinations to high romance and despair. Gérard's aborted suicide, of course, recalls Chéri's and Michel's successful attempts in *The Last of Chéri* and *Duo.* His charm and vanity disguise both his moral pallor and his flair for drama. Antoinette is equally contradictory, her thoughtlessness and vulgarity of dress concealing an essential superiority, just as Madame Suzanne in "Bella-Vista" turns out to be morally superior, even though intellectually inferior, to her male companion. In the short stories, like the novels, the women—strong, generous, and self-effacing—are heroic.

The narrator's own role is the most complicated aspect of *Chance Acquaintances.* Her connivance in the story takes two forms: first, she acts (grudgingly) as Gérard's intermediary with Madame Leyrisse and (unwittingly) with Lucette d'Orgeville; and, secondly, she isolates and thereby elevates to the level of story a cycle of events that would not otherwise be identified as such. All the connections between the villa and the hotel, Luigi and Gérard, and Lucette and Madame Leyrisse, are visible from no vantage point other than Colette's. Her own situation and feelings provide, moreover, a partial and problematic explanation of her role as go-between. For Colette stresses her own attitudes: her fear of strangers, on the one hand; her loneliness, impecuniousness, uneasiness, and "vague longing to be happy," on the other. She admits being piqued at Gérard Haume, who shows no interest in her as a woman. A blatant womanizer, Gérard never flirts with Colette, whom he apparently does not find attractive. Does she avenge herself by involving him in a double adventure with desertion and death? In fact, she verbalizes both her pleasure in returning from Paris with bad news about Madame Leyrisse, and her later temptation to tell Antoinette the truth about the Lucette affair. Her prolonged stay at X-les-Bains itself invites as explanation an obscure pleasure in Gérard's suffering. Her attention to him is not without consequences, as she notes: "Ghosts, even flesh and blood ghosts, do not appear unless they are summoned up. The fact of spying on your neighbor is enough to turn him into an evil-doer" (169). Obliquely, she absolves him and reproaches herself at the end: "No doubt all that was wrong with them [the Haumes] was that it had been their lot to be caught up by and steeped in their desire to become my friends" (228).

Chance Acquaintances crystallizes obscure tensions. Drama is the under surface of ordinariness, the latter thereby containing something like its own denial. And Colette's very "fear of strangers" and "fear of displeasing strangers" paradoxically produce minatory friendships based on entrapment. There is, finally, the opposition between the narrator's articulated boredom and desire to distance herself from the events, and her involvement in the story she creates. Colette defines herself as the intermediary who lures chance acquaintances from the abyss of their nonentity, the initial allusion to the nether-world and its shadowy beings suggesting that these beings adumbrate a mysterious, and perhaps maleficent force in Colette herself.

"The Rainy Moon"

Through the most apparently ordinary acquaintance imaginable, Colette discovers the sensational event she recounts in **"The Rainy Moon"** (**"La Lune de Pluie,"** also in the volume *Chambre d'Hôtel*). Rosita Barberet is a typist, shortsighted, and prematurely withered. She has the solicitous appearance of "a well-trained nurse or a fashionable dentist's receptionist or one of those women of uncertain age who do vague odd jobs in beauty-parlors" (162-63). But this inoffensive young woman inhabits a murky world where devilry and witchcraft operate. Near the beginning of her narrative, Colette offhandedly recalls the astrologers, card readers, and palmists she has often consulted, only to discount their powers: "Among fortune-tellers, there are very few whom out presence momentarily endows with second sight" (160). Only much later in the story does it become clear that the point of **"The Rainy Moon"** is the efficacy of at least one kind of occultism.

The narrator's typist quits to get married and recommends a replacement. Colette takes her a manuscript and discovers that her Montmartre flat is one Colette herself once occupied: "it had fallen to my lot when I was alone and very far from happy" (158). Rosita Barberet lives there now with her younger and prettier sister, Délia Essendier, a semirecluse who waits day and night for the return of the husband who abandoned her. Colette does not tell them that the flat was once hers, nor does she immediately learn much about the Barberets. But her curiosity takes her obsessively back to "the scene of [her] unhappy, fascinating past" (184), where she searches for clues to the mystery of these sisters, and especially for traces of her own passage. She resolves to decipher what she terms the "enigma" of Délia—a young woman "pretending, out of sheer obstinacy and jealousy, to relive a moment of [Colette's] own life" (190). Rosita at last confides that Délia is planning her husband's death by witchcraft, and has secluded herself to cast a spell on poor Eugène, "convoking" him to die by endless repetitions of his name. Distaste supplants Colette's initial interest—"I am frightened of harmless lunatics, of people who deliver long monologues in the street without seeing us, of purple-faced drunks who shake their fists at empty space and walk zigzag" (194)—and she returns no more to the Barberet flat. But in spite of this effort to trivialize the event, she begins running into Délia in the street, "by pure chance," as it were. And the last time she spots her, Délia Essendier is wearing the black dress and white neck band of mourning.

Colette meets the Barberet sisters during one of those "empty" periods in her life. During just such a period she sojourned at the Bella-Vista, and she clearly alludes to that story when she writes in **"The Rainy Moon,"**

> Does one imagine those periods, during which anodynes conquer an illness one believed serious at the time, fade easily from one's memory? I have already compared them, elsewhere, to the "blanks" that introduce space and order between the chapters of a book. I should very much like—late in life, it is true—to call them "merciful blanks," those days in which work and sauntering and friendship played the major part, to the detriment of love.
>
> (165)

She notes a few pages later, "I have never had less notice taken of me by men than during those particular years whose date I dissemble here" (176). Like the narrator of *Break of Day,* she subordinates specifically sexual involvement with men to a more general interest in humanity and nature.

Among the experiences of such periods of idleness, relaxation, and virtual sexlessness, this particular anecdote is prepotent, because it is at one and the same time the story of chance acquaintances and—if not historically, then potentially and perhaps morally—her own. The play of coincidence is more personal here than in **"Bella-Vista"** or *Chance Acquaintances,* because it brings her face to face with an avatar of her former self, interweaving her present state, a problematic past, and someone else's drama.

In the old building, Colette finds the familiar stairs, and in the apartment, the same window latch that spontaneously responds to her knowing grip, the same style of faded wallpaper, and the same bedroom furniture arrangement. On a daybed in one corner, Délia half reclines. Just so did an anxious Colette in lonely years past. Her entrance into the flat is a return home, a descent into her past, and her fascination with those melancholy sisters an attraction toward the young woman she was:

> To my cost, I have proved from long experience that the past is a far more violent temptation to me than the craving to know the future. Breaking with the present, retracing my steps, the sudden apparition of a new, unpublished slice of the past is accompanied by a shock utterly unlike anything else and which I cannot lucidly describe. . . . It is neither the true concern nor the natural inclination of writers to love the future. They have quite enough to do with being incessantly forced to invent their characters' future which, in any case, they draw up from the well of their own past. Mine, whenever I plunge into it, turns me dizzy. . . . Besides the person I once was, it reveals to me the one I would have liked to be.
>
> (160)

The past is the writer's obsession, then, and the woman's, too, while **"The Rainy Moon"** is a fable about its dangerous seductions. Colette's entire opus, from *Claudine at School* to *The Blue Lantern,* testifies to the magic of the past, to her tendency to look inward and downward. The liminary piece in *"Landscapes and Portraits"* (*Paysages et Portraits*)—a posthumous collection of previously unpublished essays—reads like a gloss on **"The Rainy Moon."** In five pages Colette lyrically describes the irresistible attraction exerted on her by her own past and, specifically, her anguished fascination each time she drives by an apartment she once inhabited (and there were quite a few!). How she would love to resurrect the woman she was, to relive even a single hour among all those she has lived. She savors her past like a streaming cup exhaling memory, illusion, and regret (her metaphor).

What, in fact, is Délia's relation to Colette? Does the apartment autonomously breed unhappiness, or did Colette herself plant the seeds of Délia's drama? The last possibility emerges most clearly when Colette explains how a blister of glass in a windowpane catches a ray of sun and projects a tiny rainbow onto the wall opposite. During her residence there, she used to call the little

planet with its seven colors her "rainy moon," and it charmed her solitude. But Délia, according to Rosita, dubs the refracted light her sad little sun: "she says it only shines to warn her something bad is going to happen" (167). Colette silently wonders, "Whatever can I have bequeathed to that reflection?" (168).

Does Délia, in her murderous design, realize a proclivity of the younger Colette? After her last visit with Rosita, Colette goes to bed early: "I kept relapsing into a nightmare in which I was now my real self, now identified with Délia. Half-reclining like her on *our* divanbed, in the dark part of our room, I 'convoked' with a powerful summons, with a thousand repetitions of his name, a man who was not called Eugène" (209-10). The dream association links the end of the story to the beginning, for her very first visit to the apartment also entails a dream image. After climbing first the hill to Montmartre and then the stairs to the mezzanine apartment, Colette looks out of the window and down into the street: "Immediately, I was conscious of the faint, rather pleasant giddiness that accompanies dreams of falling and flying" (155). Is her return to this apartment a dream of revenge for past abandonment? Her first sight of Délia jolts her, and she compares the vision, which is at once numinous and fearsome, to a dream: "I had that experience only dreams dare conjure up; I saw before me, hostile, hurt, stubbornly hoping, the young self I should never be again, whom I never ceased disowning and regretting" (173). The movements of ascent (going up to Montmartre, walking up to the mezzanine, flying) and descent (going back to her younger days, looking down into the street, falling) parallel those of "disowning and regretting." The double movement of rejection and nostalgia in a general way describes the relation to her past that characterizes Colette's work and particularly structures this story. She harbors the extravagant dream/anecdote of these passing acquaintances not in her unconscious, but in her writer's memory. Its inscription completes its exorcism.

"The Photographer's Missus"

For her suicide, Madame Armand, "the photographer's missus," goes to bed in silk stockings and black satin shoes in order to conceal her corns and crooked third toe, takes an overdose of drugs and leaves two notes. One says, "My darling Geo, don't scold me. Forgive me for leaving you. In death, as in life, I remain your faithful Georgina." A second scrap of paper, also intended for her husband, reads: "Everything is paid except the washerwoman who had no change on Wednesday" (387). But her attempt to die fails.

The narrator's acquaintance with the unhappy woman is slim. Colette gets to know her a bit only because the studio/flat of a photographer nicknamed "Big Eyes," "Geo," or "Exo," is across the hall from that of Mademoiselle Devoidy, a pearl stringer to whom Colette goes to have her necklace rethreaded. (Madame Armand's story is, like that of another of Colette's suicidal characters, Chéri, under the sign of the pearl.) Occasionally Colette notices Madame Armand encamped on the landing, with an "air of vague expectancy" (369). One day she arrives to find the building in commotion, guesses that Madame Armand is the cause, and reacts precisely as she did at the Bella-Vista and at X-les-Bains with the Haumes: "Desire to escape, slight nausea and idle curiosity struggled within me, but in the end they gave way to a strange resignation. I knew perfectly well—already out of breath before I had begun to run—I knew perfectly well that I should not stop until I reached the top landing" (385). Mademoiselle Devoidy gives her client a scaled-down version of the attempted suicide, and a few days later Colette visits the convalescent Madame Armand and hears the story from her—a story both funny and moving in its schematic evocation of a simple female existence. Madame Armand wanted to die because her life was trivial.

Structurally, **"The Photographer's Missus"** (**"La Dame du Photographe,"** which appeared in 1944 in the collection *Gigi*) resembles **"The Rainy Moon."** Its setting is a working-class Parisian apartment house where Colette goes on business, and it involves three women and one man who, although crucial to the story, appears only once or twice. It too recounts disappointment and desperate resolution. In both, Colette meets the principal character through the mediation of a respectable tradeswoman. Like Rosita Barberet, Mademoiselle Devoidy is dry, unmarried, neither young nor old, and superlatively practices a humble trade.

Here as in **"The Rainy Moon,"** Colette transcribes her ambivalence toward the actors and events. As she inevitably becomes disenchanted with Délia and Rosita, judging them, respectively, dangerous and colorless, and their home a "desert," so the moment arrives when a harsh judgment of Madame Armand and Mademoiselle Devoidy corrects a previously favorable one: the former is merely a "stale, insipid mystery," while Mademoiselle Devoidy presents only "the attraction of the void" (394). Yet Colette writes the story, as she did the Barberets', and with the same reservations about the importance to be accorded to such passers-by:

> Do those transient figures who featured in long-past periods of my life, deserve to live again in a handful of pages as I here compel them to? They were important enough for me to keep them secret, at least during the time I was involved with them. For example, my husband, at home, did not know of the existence of Mademoiselle Devoidy. . . .
>
> (384)

It is the same temporary secrecy she lavished on the Barberets: "'I'm going to tell the Barberet story to Annie de Pène,' I mentally began. And then I told nothing

at all" (**"The Rainy Moon,"** 169); "[Sido] liked to hear the news of my men and women friends, and of any newly-formed acquaintances. I omitted however to tell her the Barberet story" (**"The Rainy Moon,"** 191). By emphasizing that neither her mother, nor her husband, nor her friend knew anything about these "stories" at the time they occurred, Colette seems to divorce them from the material of her "real" autobiography, reminding us that neither Sido, nor Annie, nor Jouvenel could confer external authentification on events harbored in her writer's memory.

The concluding passage in **"The Photographer's Missus"** is interesting as part of the same problematics of "autographical" narration. When Colette relates, at the story's end, Madame Armand's own explanation of the "suicide" (the photographer's missus gives it the status of an accomplished fact), she accords the oral narrative about eight pages of almost uninterrupted direct discourse. We read pretty much what Madame Armand is supposed to have said—with an important reservation:

> It is easy to relate what is of no importance. . . . But, beginning with the words, "I have always had a very trivial life . . ." I feel absolved from the tiresome meticulousness imposed on a writer, such as carefully noting the over-many reiterations of "in one way" and "what poor creatures we are" that rose like bubbles to the surface of Madame Armand's story. Though they helped her to tell it, it is for me to remove them. It is my duty as a writer to abridge our conversation and also to suppress my own unimportant contribution to it.
>
> (396)

The writer Colette impinges here on her own persona. Her short fiction beguiles in large measure because of the interweaving of styles—autobiographical, journalistic, novelistic. Passages like these (there is a similar notation in **"The Kepi,"** 253) underscore the tension resulting from Colette's multiplicity of roles as participant, observer, narrator, and writer. The invocation of the writer's duty obliquely reminds us that the principal function is doubtless the last.

With simplicity, Madame Armand recites the concerns of her life as "photographer's missus": the cleaning, washing, ironing, menu-planning (she can't serve breast of veal again; they had it just last Sunday), shopping, jam-making. She insists that she never despised these tasks; but still, one day she asked herself, "Is that all? Is that the whole of my day, today, yesterday, tomorrow?" (398). She struggled against her "mania for something big," reminding herself that she had a "perfect" husband, but finally concluded that only in death would she find the desired "apotheosis" (it is her auditor, Colette, who suggests the word). So she dressed, wrote her notes, took the drug, went to bed, waited and had the "fidgets," worrying, for example, that her husband would have only a cold supper when he came in that night. Death fails her, but unlike Gérard Haume in **Chance Acquaintances,** Madame Armand does not pout. Quite the contrary, she learns an invaluable lesson: "What I am sure of is that never, never again will I commit suicide. I know now that suicide can't be the slightest use to me, I'm staying here" (404).

In her apparent frailty, in the very triviality of her life and concerns, Madame Armand, thin and solitary on her dark landing, has the solidity and grandeur of Colette's women, and is perhaps the most heroic of them all. The moral at the end is explicit: "Whenever I think of her, I always see her shored up by those scruples she modestly called fidgets and sustained by the sheer force of humble, everyday feminine greatness; that unrecognized greatness she had misnamed 'a very trivial life'" (404).

"The Kepi"

Its setting seems to attach **"The Kepi"** (**"Le Képi,"** in the volume by the same name, 1944) to an earlier period than **"Bella-Vista," Chance Acquaintances, "The Rainy Moon,"** or **"The Photographer's Missus."** Here Colette is the young wife of Willy, and the episode takes place around 1897. Thematically, it belongs, with **Chéri, The Last of Chéri,** and **Break of Day,** to the cycle of books about renunciation, suggesting that a woman's body ages tragically faster than her emotions. Marco is a middle-aged woman who is separated from her husband and earns a meager living as a ghostwriter. All day long she pores over dusty volumes at the Bibliothèque Nationale to produce manuscripts for which she gets one sou a line from a man who gets two sous a line from a chap who gets four from a fellow who gets ten. One day Marco answers, in jest, a personal ad: "Lieutenant (regular army), garrisoned near Paris, warm-hearted, cultured, wishes to maintain correspondence with intelligent, affectionate woman" (229), and it develops into a love affair, miraculously rejuvenating her. But after an idyll of under a year with Lieutenant Trallard, her 45 years catch up with her. Cavorting in bed one afternoon, she plants her young lieutenant's cap on her own head in a roguish gesture which, according to Colette's superior wisdom, only a younger woman could allow herself. Colette's message is by no means reassuring. Marco forgets for an instant, like Léa in **Chéri,** that the aging mistress of a young man must constantly monitor her looks. Relaxing her vigilance, she acts the young woman she feels like but no longer resembles. With its visor and its flat top sloping toward the eyes, the kepi throws into fearful relief all Marco's age marks, and the indiscretion costs her the lover.[4]

What has Colette to do with all this? Counselor and confidante, she follows from a lesser or greater distance the vagaries of Marco's romance. But for her, Marco is a "story" even before they meet. This is how **"The Kepi"** begins:

> If I remember rightly, I have now and then mentioned Paul Masson, known as Lemice-Térieux on account of his delight—and his dangerous efficiency—in creating mysteries. As ex-President of the Law Courts of Pondichéry, he was attached to the cataloguing section of the Bibliothèque Nationale. It was through him and through the Library that I came to know the woman, the story of whose one and only romantic adventure I am about to tell.
>
> (212)

My Apprenticeships is the principal intertext to speak of Masson, his friendship with the Willys, and his taste for mystification. In it, Colette describes how, one day at the shore, Masson begins to make notations on cards, explaining that he is "saving the honor of the Catalogue," by remedying lacunae and providing the titles of Latin and early Italian works "that ought to have been written." But why, she objects, if the books don't exist? "He waved an airy hand. 'Ah!' said he. 'I can't do everything'" (**My Apprenticeships,** 42-43).

In **"The Kepi,"** she explains how Masson would visit the housebound young wife she was then, with a view to cheering her up. She appreciates his caustic wit and marvelous stories. One such story is "the lady of the Library," who writes for one sou a line, and leads a poor and chaste existence, having never had a real romance. "Her Christian name is Marco, as you might have guessed," observes Masson. "Women of a certain age, when they belong to the artistic world, have only a few names to choose from, such as Marco, Léo, Ludo, Aldo. It's a legacy from the excellent Madame Sand" (214). Intrigued to discover that the story of Marco is no mere fabulation, Colette wants to meet her. She finds her sensitive and well bred, with a "perfect voice" and "impeccable table-manners." So much so that Willy regards her as a desirable companion for his wife. Marco vacations with the Willys, and the two women become "great friends," a phrase Colette nuances to exclude serious intimacy: they talk a lot about clothes.

One day Masson proposes that he, Colette, and Marco compete at producing the best answer to an ad in the personals column. It is thus as a literary pastime that the second phase of Marco's story begins. Already a professional ghostwriter, Marco was already a part of Masson's repertory. With the sexual act, she becomes one of *Colette*'s stories, a part of *her* written text in addition to Masson's oral one. Colette narrates what she saw of the affair and what Marco told her, depending on Marco's account for the episode of the kepi. And here Colette edits and abridges Marco's words, underscoring her interference, just as she did in the suicide recital in **"The Photographer's Missus"**: "In putting down the story that I heard, I am obliged to cut out all that made it, in Marco's version, so confused and so terribly clear" (253).

Few of Colette's narratives so starkly differentiate masculine and feminine. Exquisitely symbolic, **"The Kepi"** is constellated with discourse, objects, and events that are generically charged. Marco, like Délia Essendier in **"The Rainy Moon,"** is one of Colette's doubles, for Marco and Colette share not only a profession, but the same complicated status of underling. Both write books for men to sign, both are exploited economically and professionally. Colette by no means dwells here on her victimization by Willy, but there are allusions to the unhappiness and loneliness that she glosses in *My Apprenticeships.*

Many of the conversations between Colette and Marco center on traditionally feminine concerns: fashions, makeup, interior decoration. Both as narrator and as protagonist, Colette is especially preoccupied by women's fashion, and her lines on turn-of-the-century styles are fetching and precise, echoing numerous remarks in *My Apprenticeships* on the styles of 1900. She censures Marco for betraying by her preference for ruffles and frills the fact that she "naturally belonged" to an earlier period. Although only half Marco's age, Colette plays the maternal role, counsels her on frocks and fabrics, arranges her hair, shadows her eyes, and colors her cheeks. When Marco gets a windfall from her estranged husband, Colette advises her on stylish acquisitions, and Marco becomes attractive enough to seduce a young officer.

Colette's secondhand account of the affair is striking for its precision, a woman's analysis of the changes wrought by passion in another woman. She speaks of her friend's "belated puberty," comparing her also to a "traveller who was setting off on a dangerous voyage, with no ballast but a pair of silk stockings, some pink makeup, some fruit and a bottle of champagne" (241). Marco's calm becomes fear, fever, then blissful immolation and satiety.

The last phase does her in. Marco's original beauty is discreet, firm, and slender, masculine in a word, like her name: "She looked less like a pretty woman than like one of those chiselled, clear-cut aristocratic men who adorned the eighteenth century and were not ashamed of being handsome" (217). Like those of Camile in *The Cat,* her sexual cravings arouse other desires, and satisfied love makes her grow heavier: "Her romantic love affair had already been going on for eight months. She looked so much fatter to me that the proud carriage of her head no longer preserved her chin line and her waist, visibly compressed, no longer moved flexibly inside the petersham belt, as it had done last year" (245). Her modesty and restraint disappear as well, and remarks like "A little extra flesh does make one's breasts so pretty" (245) embarrass Colette, who secretly judges moreover that her friend has "breasts like jellyfish, very broad and decidedly flabby" (247).

Her changes in weight, symbol of an active sexuality, incur the mockery of Masson and Willy. "Madame Dracula" is how Willy describes her during the early stage, when she is still thin. Colette, whose own judgments are none too favorable, nonetheless feels her "blood boil" at the critical comments of two "disillusioned" men, who make fun of her friend "as if the romance that lit up Marco's Indian summer were no more than some stale bit of gossip" (249). Masson reacts with humor and disgust to Marco's new fleshy femininity, which he dubs the phase of the dray-horse: "Marco's first, most urgent duty was to remain slender, charming, elusive, a twilight creature beaded with raindrops, not to be bursting with health and frightening people in the streets by shouting: 'I've done it! I've done it!'" (250). When she was a dry little library mouse, Masson deemed Marco colorful, good material for his tales; when she was still a stranger to impulsiveness and indiscretion, Willy, too, found her appealing. But when Marco's sexuality is emphasized, she in some way emasculates them and their horror finds expression in cynicism. Her own severity toward the changes in Marco notwithstanding, Colette is ready to exculpate her in the face of a male onslaught.

The new and sexual Marco is *Colette*'s story—a feminine story turning on feminine words, acts, and destiny. Vestimentary concerns, traditionally female, shape Marco's fate, and an object of clothing ultimately betrays her. Not just any object of clothing but one typically masculine, military, and not subject to fashion: the kepi. Marco only confusedly perceives that the military cap is her undoing, confiding to Colette, "I can't get rid of the idea that the kepi was fatal to me. Did it bring back some unpleasant memory? I'd like to know what *you* think" (255). Colette understands instantly and replies silently:

> I saw you just as Alexis Trallard had seen you. My contemptuous eyes took in the slack breasts and the slipped shoulder-straps of the crumpled chemise. And the leathery, furrowed neck, the red patches on the skin below the ears, the chin left to its own devices and long past hope. . . . And, crowning all that, the kepi! The kepi—with its stiff lining and its jaunty peak, slanted over one roguishly-winked eye.
>
> (256)

From a man's story (Masson's) of professionalism and exploitation, Marco becomes a woman's (Colette's), the thread of which is sexuality—nascent, betrayed, moribund. "If I stick to facts," Colette notes, "the story of Marco is ended. Marco had had a lover; Marco no longer had a lover" (257). Once the kepi has put an end to the affair, Colette quickly loses touch: it is difficult, she metaphorically remarks, to hold onto someone who is losing weight fast. Marco ceases to be the subject of passion or the object of desire, and her desexing is symbolized by her weight loss and by her reentry into Masson's repertory. She is again simply "the lady of the Library," and Colette becomes again dependent on Masson for news. The concluding lines of the story, a conversation between the two principal storytellers, signify Marco's return from the sexual to the economic sphere:

> "So she's taken up her old life again," I said thoughtfully. "Exactly as it was before Lieutenant Trallard . . ."
>
> "Oh no," said Masson. "There's a tremendous change in her existence!"
>
> "What change? Really, one positively has to drag things out of you!"
>
> "Nowadays," said Masson, "Marco gets paid two sous a line."
>
> (260)

"THE TENDER SHOOT"

"The Tender Shoot" (**"Le Tendron,"** which also appeared in *Le Képi*) gives its name to the volume of English translations of Colette's short stories. It illustrates Colette's constant theme of female alliance against the male. But while in *The Other One, Duo,* and *Le Toutounier* the bond between women is associated with images of healing, renewal, and renaissance, here it has rather more violent overtones.

In May 1940 an elderly Colette urges her old friend Albin Chaveriat, who is also nearing 70, to leave Paris for the duration of the war, and suggests a resort in Normandy teeming with girls. Chaveriat replies that this is the very thing to put him off; by way of explanation, he tells her about an episode that took place some 17 years earlier, curing him of his taste for young flesh.

During an extended summer holiday on the country estate of a friend, Chaveriat happened across a peasant called Louisette who was herding goats nearby. She was 15 and a half years old—precisely the age of Vinca in *The Ripening Seed* and of Gigi. "I saw she was ripe for dissimulation, for forbidden collusion, in other words, for sin" (274). Sensually, their nocturnal rendezvous in the fields and bushes satisfied him completely; emotionally, much less. Louisette willingly gave her body, but rejected his gifts and refused her debonair lover the signs of affection and dependence he would normally expect from so unsophisticated a girl. At their second meeting, she tossed him neither a kiss nor a flower, but a pebble, and he reproached her for her lack of poetry. Her one overriding concern was to keep the affair secret from the mother she feared and worshiped, and Chaveriat began "getting impatient at being com-

pletely unable to understand a girl who roamed the woods at night, with [him], but sprang up as if she had been shot, turned pale and trembled at the knees if she heard the step or the voice of her mother" (287). After several weeks came a stunning climax: a downpour one night sent the lovers scurrying for refuge to Louisette's house, where they made no noise so as not to wake the mother sleeping upstairs. Chaveriat wanted only to escape as soon as possible, but Louisette fell asleep in his arms and he dared not move. Suddenly he was aware of a light shining on them and sprang to his feet at the appearance of a small woman. "Her resemblance to Louisette left me no doubt, no hope. Same frizzy hair, but already almost completely white, and faded features that would one day be Louisette's. And the same eyes, but with a wide, magnificent gaze Louisette perhaps would never have" (292). As for Louisette, she did "the only thing she could," she screamed for help: "Mamma!"

Far more certainly her mother's daughter than her lover's mistress, Louisette listened transfixed while the old woman pronounced no ordinary moral lesson, speaking neither of virtue, nor folly, nor maternal disappointment, but harping on the seducer's age: "Do you see what he's got on his temples? White hairs, Louise, white hairs just like me! And those wrinkles he's got under his eyes!" (296). The two women, the "screaming shrew" and the "adorable idiot," chased him out of their house and back toward his friend's property. When Chaveriat got to a narrow path skirting a dilapidated wall that marked the limits of his host's domain, he thought he had safely outdistanced his tormentors. But they were above the wall and heaved a large stone which grazed his shoulder. A few steps later, a second stone skinned his ear and injured his toe. Finally he retaliated, brandishing a vine-branch. (The weapon seems suited to his bacchanalian role as libertine and to his age: if Louisette is the tender shoot, Chaveriat is the hoary bough.) The aftermath of his adventure, fever and delirium, eventually passed, but Chaveriat retained, as a fitting punishment, the fear of nubile maidens.[5]

His story is a confidence he makes to Colette one night after dinner. In some sense, it perfects their friendship—a friendship, as Colette describes it, "limited by the closely-guarded secrets of Albin Chaveriat's love-life" (262). After three pages of introduction, **"The Tender Shoot"** is related in Chaveriat's own words, neither edited nor paraphrased by the hearer. Even the last words are Chaveriat's; Colette does not take the floor again at the end to sum up or point out a moral, as in **"The Photographer's Missus."** But the quotation marks that begin each paragraph are evidence of her silent role, for Chaveriat tells his story *to* her. He repeatedly invokes her presence, moreover, and responds to the objections he alone hears:

No, don't let's argue about that, I know you don't agree with me. (265)

Excuse me, what were you saying, my dear? That it was a horrid proceeding, and a classic one? Allow me to defend myself. (270)

But I observe you're looking apprehensive, not to say disapproving.

(280)

Numerous asides like this translate the authorial point of view and suggest strategies for reading the text. Chaveriat tries to portray his young prey as a girl both stupid and vicious, but his allusions to the interventions of the first narrator subvert his design. Directly, Colette says nothing, but she apparently forces Chaveriat into a defensive posture that suggests another view of Louisette: as a victimized child. Indeed, as we know her, Colette cannot fail to understand the "consuming sensual audacity" (the phrase is from *My Apprenticeships*, 56) of young girls like Louisette, and to condemn old lechers who take advantage of them with geniality. The heroine of *My Apprenticeships* is just such a girl and Willy just such a man.

Apart from this filiation with Colette herself, however, Louisette is related especially to Colette's men. Her color is not the blue associated with the favored heroines, but the red and gold of young Phil in *The Ripening Seed*. Louisette has a "face like a ripe peach" (283), golden hair almost red, pink tendrils on her neck, and a body "tinged with pink" (271). Chaveriat first finds her wearing a necklace of wild pink berries, and at their second encounter offers her one of coral (which Louisette rejects with violence). They meet under a pink moon and clouds "rimmed with fire" (289). In rage she becomes red "as a nectarine, as a dahlia, as the most divinely red thing in the world" (286). And her mouth tastes of raspberries. Louisette's mother, an older version of Louisette herself, is fittingly dressed in mauve.

While red suggests here the passion and blood that Colette also associates with it elsewhere, and while the sexual initiation occurs, as elsewhere in her works, between a young partner and a much older one, still, in Louisette's case, this is no routine initiation. Chaveriat deems himself neither "ordinary" nor "careless" as a lover, for he never takes Louisette "like a straightforward normal animal, like a man who knows only one way to possess the woman he desires" (289). When he tries to exculpate himself by explaining to the mother his care not to impregnate Louisette, she asks ironically if she is supposed to say thank you. Louisette and her mother are no ordinary Colette heroines; nor is the lesson that emerges typical of Colette's works.

If the maiden shares the color associations of Phil, she is indecipherable like another male, the Willy of *My Apprenticeships*. Even her plumpness recalls Willy's

rotundity. Chaveriat delights in her lack of angularity: "The expression 'well-rounded,' so long out of fashion, describes a type of beauty which, believe me, is positively intoxicating when that beauty is adolescent" (269). She is, finally, like Willy in still another way, her exploitation of her partner. There can be more than one lecher in a story of lechery, and in the last third of the narrative, Chaveriat voices the idea that has already occurred to the reader: "I used to wonder now and then whether Louisette were not exploiting me like a lecherous man who's found a willing girl" (287).

Chaveriat's insight into his own exploitation by his Lolita-like mistress is one aspect of the theme of knowledge that structures "The Tender Shoot," where the important symbols are eyes, light, and the gaze. The old woman's arrival in the room where Louisette dozes in Chaveriat's arms is heralded by the appearance of a light which he at first takes for the moon. Her look insists "on seeing everything, knowing everything" (292), and she stares at the anxious lover: "The unshaded lamp shone straight in her eyes but she did not blink" (293). Chaveriat, on the other hand, is nearly blinded by it. But it is not really to Chaveriat that she speaks—except scornfully to ask his age. Her gaze and her words are all for the daughter who is trying to hide her eyes, metaphorically trying to avoid seeing what has happened. Chaveriat is excluded from the mother's conversation (like Farou who happens to come in during the confrontation between Jane and Fanny in *The Other One*), and almost reified. Imprisoned in this female domain, he is treated like a thing Louisette must be forced at last to *see:* "Yes, now you don't want to see him any more, high time too, Louise! All the same, you've *got* to look at him! Yes, look at him, the man who was born the same year as your own father!" (296). This peasant mother can readily understand the sexual urge, and says she would condone intercourse with a *young* man. Her humiliation of Chaveriat is excruciating, for she does not judge his sexuality to be fearsome, merely ridiculous. She holds her daughter by the hair so tightly that "the little thing's eyes [are] drawn up slantwise." Louisette has no choice and does "indeed begin to look at [him]" (296). The sight seals her alliance with her mother.

"The Tender Shoot" deals with two kinds of knowledge: the first, sexual, the second and more important, intellectual and emotional. This is the knowledge forced on Louisette by her mother, and by both of them on Chaveriat. Colette's fiction frequently concerns itself with aging and with recognition of bodily limits: Léa's wrinkled neck loses her Chéri, and Renée Néré's incipient middle age causes her constant self-doubt, not to mention poor Marco in **"The Kepi."** But **"The Tender Shoot"** stands apart as the story of a *man,* a myth of male ridicule and punishment. Here for once it is the male whose vanity suffers from an accumulation of years, who finds his sexuality discredited by his wrinkles, his economic and intellectual superiority compromised by the sight and insight of a peasant woman. Chaveriat lacks what Colette calls in **Break of Day** "the supreme elegance of knowing how to diminish" (142). He goes off from his last encounter with Louisette marked by her color, red. Thanks to the rock that bloodied his ear, he wears, like Phil in **The Ripening Seed,** a red facial smudge suggesting violent initiation.

FEMALE AUTONOMY

As discrete tales, these stories are haunting, while the persona who emerges from their accumulation is one of Colette's major accomplishments. The narrator is a clear, lyric voice which the reader comes to associate with wisdom, vigor, and femininity, and which suggests the sense of her opus.

The interest of the pieces is thematic as well as formal, and they are also marked by the predominance of strong female characters who write a new self-definition for women, one of the constitutive elements of which is an outright or implicit dissociation from men. Most of the heroines decline to derive identity exclusively from sexuality or from relations with men; they claim dominance over their destinies rather than allow their lives to be shaped by masculine criminality, sensuality, triviality, and fickleness. And even those whom sexuality rules are bound neither by convention nor habit, but forge responses that are consistently unexpected. When polite, reserved Marco in **"The Kepi"** finally has a romance, neither prudence nor decorum deters her from a total commitment to sex that can only amaze and amuse her jaded male friends. Masson, Gérard Haume, Albin Chaveriat, and Lieutenant Trallard are predictable and easily astonished, but the women are full of surprises and hard to surprise. Their analyses of situations and determined rejection of traditional perspectives serve to redistribute normal textual emphasis and to clarify and demystify male-female relations. Louisette in "The Tender Shoot" mutely spurns the role of adoring adolescent mistress, choosing and using her lover (like Lucette in **Chance Acquaintances**) and unsentimentally repudiating him at the opportune moment. Madame Armand in **"The Photographer's Missus"** opts for an attempt at "apotheosis" over permanent definition as a man's "missus"; it does not succeed and she returns to her housewifely chores, but her "suicide" changes her life, and her situation becomes one she consciously chooses. Délia Essendier comes out of seclusion when she has definitely eliminated her husband; the widow's band signifies successful refusal of the role of abandoned wife. Most important, the Colette of **"Bella-Vista,"** **Chance Acquaintances,** and **"The Rainy Moon"** colludes with passers-by and immensely enriches her writer's memory storehouse during the periods when she has no confining entanglements with men.

Hotel-keepers, typists, pearl-stringers, goat-herds, the women are capable and productive, displaying a taste for survival and most effectively functioning as creative agents when they have established autonomy—whatever effort and anguish the process costs. They are independent signifiers in these stories, with clusters of meaning centering on them rather than on the male characters whom they surpass in almost every conceivable way. It is not simply that Antoinette's strength dwarfs Gérard's in **Chance Acquaintances,** as Suzanne's does Ruby/Richard's in **"Bella-Vista,"** and Louisette's does Chaveriat's in **"The Tender Shoot."** Colette's women seem to usurp the traditionally male privilege of originating action and significance. And a woman, the narrating Colette, is of course the central figure in all the stories she discovers, glosses, and frames. The plot of **"The Kepi"** provides an interesting commentary on this schema, for there the young Colette's profession as writer (doubled by that of Marco as ghostwriter) contrasts with Masson's function: he inspires Colette, arousing the initial interest in "the lady of the Library," but he never makes a real (written) story of the oral anecdote. Woman-as-writer and woman-as-story thus stand in opposition to man-as-muse (or gossip), and that important paradigmatic relation traced in **My Apprenticeships** between a writing Colette and an ingenious but impotent Willy finds its echo here.

Notes

1. Gigi's sexual appeal is the ambiguous boyish charm of Colette's earlier female adolescents, Claudine and Vinca: "At times she looked like Robin Hood, at others like a stone angel, or again like a boy in skirts; but she seldom resembled a nearly grown-up girl" (*Gigi,* translated by Roger Senhouse. In *Gigi and Selected Writings.* New York: New American Library [Signet], 1963. See p. 128).

2. Their sheer number makes it impossible to deal with all of Colette's short pieces. My selection of half a dozen is somewhat arbitrary, but they are among the longer stories and those I consider formally most interesting. With the exception of *Chance Acquaintances,* all those I deal with appear in *The Tender Shoot and Other Stories,* translated by Antonia White (New York: Farrar, Straus and Giroux, 1958). *Chance Acquaintances* is in the volume entitled *Julie de Carneilhan and Chance Acquaintances,* translated by Patrick Leigh Fermor (London: Secker and Warburg, 1952). My references are to those volumes. (Except for *Chance Acquaintances,* these stories are also included in *The Collected Stories of Colette,* ed. Robert Phelps, translated by Matthew Ward, Antonia White, Anne-Marie Callimachi, and others [New York: Farrar, Straus and Giroux, 1983]. Here

"The Photographer's Missus" is retitled "The Photograper's Wife.")

3. Elaine Marks, *Colette* (New Brunswick: Rutgers University Press, 1960), p. 174. Marks's chapter 14, containing a discussion of Colette's first-person narratives, was useful to my thinking.

4. Colette must have had the idea in mind for a long time. In *The Vagabond,* which she published in 1911, Renée Néré writes: "I have seen satisfied, amorous women in whom, for a few brief and dangerous minutes, the affected ingénue reappears and allows herself girlish tricks which make her rich and heavy flesh quiver. I have shuddered at the lack of awareness of a friend in her forties who, unclothed and all breathless with love, clapped on her head the cap [*le képi*] of her lover, a lieutenant of Hussars" (*The Vagabond.* Translated by Enid McLeod. New York: Farrar, Straus and Giroux, 1955; pp. 199-200).

5. For some compelling comments on the use of space in this story, see Mari McCarty, "Possessing Female Space: 'The Tender Shoot,'" *Women's Studies* 8: 3 (1981), 367-74.

Hope Christiansen (essay date fall 1998)

SOURCE: Christiansen, Hope. "Finding a Room of Her Own in Colette's *La Vagabonde.*" *Dalhousie French Studies* 44 (fall 1998): 81-96.

[*In the following essay, Christiansen maintains that Colette's novella* La Vagabonde *is a fictional expression of Virginia Woolf's theory that women need their own space to write.*]

In her 1929 essay, *A Room of One's Own* (which is based on two papers read to the Arts Society at Newnham and the Odtaa at Girton the previous year), Virginia Woolf explores the question of women's writing. She wonders, for example, why women wrote so few great works of literature during the Elizabethan period, and attempts to pinpoint the obstacles to their creativity. Her answer is cast in the form of a striking image, that of the spider web:

> [. . .] it is a perennial puzzle why no woman wrote a word of that extraordinary literature when every other man, it seemed, was capable of song or sonnet. What were the conditions in which women lived, I asked myself; for fiction, imaginative work that is, is not dropped like a pebble upon the ground, as science may be; fiction is like a spider's web, attached ever so lightly perhaps, but still attached to life at all four corners [. . .]. But when the web is pulled askew, hooked up at the edge, torn in the middle, one remembers that these webs are not spun in midair by incorporeal creatures,

but are the works of suffering human beings, and are attached to grossly material things, like health and money and the houses we live in.

(43-44)

In short, she concludes later in the essay,

> Intellectual freedom depends upon material things. Poetry depends upon intellectual freedom. And women have always been poor, not for two hundred years merely, but from the beginning of time. Women have had less intellectual freedom than the sons of Athenian slaves. Women, then, have not had a dog's chance of writing poetry. That is why I have laid so much stress on money and a room of one's own.

(112)

Eighteen years earlier, Colette had published *La Vagabonde,* a first-person novel which tells the story of an independent thirty-three year old divorcée who, like Colette herself, not only earns a living as a music-hall performer, but also loves to write. While the demanding career of the heroine, Renée Néré, is certainly fulfilling in two respects—financially and personally—it leaves little time and energy for other pursuits, such as writing and love relationships. Colette's novel can thus be read as an exploration of the quandary of the working woman who must balance career and personal life, each of which brings a different kind of satisfaction. "Renée is perhaps one of the first career women in literature," notes Erica M. Eisinger, "a new creature for whom love and work are equal pulls" (101). In that sense, *La Vagabonde* might be considered a sort of fictional "case study," *avant la lettre,* of Woolf's essay topic.[1] It is an account of Renée's arduous search for the space to write—for a room of her own.[2]

In the opening pages of *La Vagabonde,* several key aspects of Renée's life quickly come to the fore: her work, her solitude, and her writing. All of these elements are interconnected and sometimes set in opposition to one another. That the notion of space—Renée's "room"[3]—is tied to each of these factors only complicates the matter further. Indeed, the very structure of the novel is determined by how the heroine defines and tests the boundaries imposed by those different aspects of her life. The Renée of Part I is a working woman who may have the physical room to write, but who lacks the time and energy, because of her career, to do so. The tension is thus initially between work and writing—the demands of the first more or less preclude the opportunity for the second. Part II reveals a Renée whose domestic and professional space have been invaded by a man; here, then, love and work are at odds, and, as we shall see, the suitor shows signs of limiting further—by his physical appropriation of her room, as well as by his apparent failure to recognize Renée as a writer—the possibility (as well as the space) of writing. It is only in the final section, Part III, that Renée discovers a means, by reconfiguring her space, of resolving the conflicts among these elements that shape her life.

From the very start it is clear that Renée's attitude toward her room is deeply ambivalent, as is revealed by the initial account of her return home after work:

> Comme d'habitude, c'est avec un grand soupir que je referme derrière moi la porte de mon rez-de-chaussée. Soupir de fatigue, de détente, de soulagement, ou l'angoisse de la solitude? Ne cherchons pas, ne cherchons pas!
>
> (1071)

She refers to her apartment as a shelter, "un abri suffisamment confortable à des 'dames seules' comme moi" (1071), a place of repose after grueling music-hall rehearsals and performances. But it is obvious that for Renée, at least at this point, possessing this space also implies an absence, for she occupies it alone. Solitude, in her eyes, is bittersweet, at once "un vin grisant qui vous saoule de liberté" and "un poison qui vous jette la tête aux murs" (1073). Renée's conception of her room at the outset, then, is not so much a place where she can write, but rather, a place where she can recover, albeit alone, from her exhausting work as a performer.

If there can be no "room" in her life for writing as long as Renée must work, writing is nonetheless a preoccupation that is, curiously, a consequence of her solitude; since she has only her dog, Fossette, and her image in the mirror with whom to converse, she is obligated to talk to herself: "Et si je me parle en dedans, c'est par besoin littéraire de rythmer, de rédiger ma pensée" (1073). The need and the desire to write are clearly present, even if the other conditions necessary for its realization are not. Hence Renée's definition of herself as "[u]ne femme de lettres qui a mal tourné. Voilà ce que je dois, pour tous, demeurer, moi qui n'écris plus, moi qui me refuse le plaisir, le luxe d'écrire" (1074). As Nancy K. Miller aptly puts it, for Renée at this stage, "being a performer means unbecoming a writer" (232).

Yet just how important writing is to Renée is underscored by a lengthy, very lyrical passage in the opening pages of the novel:

> Écrire! pouvoir écrire! cela signifie la longue rêverie devant la feuille blanche, le griffonnage inconscient, les jeux de la plume qui tourne en rond autour d'une tache d'encre, qui mordille le mot imparfait, le griffe, le hérisse de fléchettes, l'orne d'antennes, de pattes, jusqu'à ce qu'il perde sa figure lisible de mot, mué en insecte fantastique, envolé de papillon-fée [. . .]. Cela veut dire aussi l'oubli de l'heure, la paresse au creux du divan, la débauche d'invention d'où l'on sort courbatu, abêti, mais déjà récompensé [. . .]. Écrire! plaisir et souffrance d'oisifs!
>
> (1074)

For Renée, that is, writing requires not only creative energy, but also solitude and precious time to dream and await the muse. Significantly, this quote announces the

sense of the novel's title—that is, that true or authentic writing is a kind of *vagabondage*. Woolf will emphasize those same elements:

> There must be freedom and there must be peace. Not a wheel must grate, not a light glimmer. The curtains must be close drawn. The writer [. . .] once his experience is over, must lie back and let his mind celebrate its nuptials in darkness. He must not look or question what is being done. Rather, he must pluck the petals from a rose or watch the swans float calmly down the river.
>
> (108)

In short, the space of the writer's room must be sealed off from the "real" world, as Renée, too, suggests, in a strikingly similar passage: "Il faut trop de temps pour écrire! Et puis, je ne suis pas Balzac, moi . . .[4] Le conte fragile que j'édifie s'émiette quand le fournisseur sonne, quand le bottier présente sa facture, quand l'avoué téléphone" (1074). Unlike Balzac, Renée feels incapable of writing while juggling everyday tasks, or of writing quickly under pressure.

Shortly after the passages quoted above, we discover exactly why writing is of such importance to Renée and why she has had to abandon an activity that brings her so much satisfaction. In a flashback which occurs, not coincidentally, after the suitor, Maxime Dufferein-Chautel, begins to show interest in her, we learn that Renée began writing only after the breakup of her marriage. Writing served initially as an antidote to her pain[5]; for Renée, in fact, writing and suffering would appear to go hand in hand: "Après les premières trahisons, après les révoltes et les soumissions d'un jeune amour qui s'opiniâtrait à espérer et à vivre, je m'étais mise à souffrir avec un orgueil et un entêtement intraitables, et à faire de la littérature" (1083-84).[6]

But while writing initially served as a means of purging herself of anger and sorrow, it quickly proves to have a broader impact on Renée's life. Writing, she discovers, can be a way of making contact with a reading public; however, the idea of achieving celebrity through writing has little appeal for Renée. The turning point is reached when she realizes that writing can be in itself an utterly private, intensely pleasurable activity. The heroine characterizes her first novel, which was extremely successful, as "un petit roman provincial, [. . .] souriant, plat et clair comme les étangs de mon pays, un peu serin, très gentil" (1084); the tenor of the appraisal seems somewhat self-disparaging, as if she were not entirely satisfied with the subject or tone of that book. A different attitude appears, however, in Renée's description of her second novel which, although less successful commercially, brought her a great deal of personal satisfaction:

> Mon second livre [. . .] se vendit beaucoup moins. Pourtant j'avais savouré, en mettant celui-là au monde, la volupté d'écrire, la lutte patiente contre la phrase qui

s'assouplit, s'assoit en rond comme une bête apprivoisée, l'attente immobile, l'affût qui finit par *charmer* le mot.

(1084)

With her third novel, Renée came to realize that what matters most is what she, not her public, thinks of her work:

Quant au troisième [. . .] il tomba à plat et ne se releva pas. Celui-là, c'est mon préféré, mon 'chef-d'œuvre inconnu' à moi . . . On le trouva diffus et confus, et incompréhensible, et long . . . Encore à présent, quand je l'ouvre, je l'aime, je m'y aime de tout mon cœur. Incompréhensible? pour vous, peut-être. Mais, pour moi, sa chaude obscurité s'éclaire; pour moi, tel mot suffit à recréer l'odeur, la couleur des heures vécues, il est sonore et plein et mystérieux comme une coquille où chante la mer, et je l'aimerais moins, je crois, si vous l'aimiez aussi . . . Rassurez-vous! je n'en écrirai pas un autre comme celui-là, je ne pourrais plus.

(1084)

Indeed, as Martha Noel Evans has suggested, Renée's aim may have been precisely that of remaining unrecognized by her reader, "while enjoying meeting and loving herself in her own language" (48). Writing has the potential, then, to be a self-directed act that brings its own intrinsic fulfillment. Renée's reflections on her first three novels suggest that there is indeed a difference between writing for others and "authentic" writing, the kind of writing that characterized her third book, and the kind that she will eventually rediscover in Part III.

It is particularly noteworthy, in light of Woolf's thesis, that Renée had effectively to abandon the room in which she wrote after her divorce, because as a single woman, she has to work in order to survive: "D'autres travaux, d'autres soucis me réclament à présent, et surtout celui de gagner ma vie" (1084). Ironically, then, being able to keep the physical space to write implies depriving herself of the very time and energy necessary to write. It is in that sense, as Miller observes, that *La Vagabonde* "as the fiction of a return to writing materializes the rhetoric of *A Room of One's Own:* Renée's performing career enacts the fragility of being without the five hundred pounds and room of her own that would permit a woman to write" (234). Although her work as a dancer and mime involves a form of self-expression which might itself be considered a kind of "writing," work and writing are most often described at this early point in the novel as if they were mutually exclusive activities, the former satisfying her immediate material needs, the latter her more personal ones.[7]

This situation only becomes more complicated when the suitor, Max, enters the picture, because he will increasingly come to occupy some of the precious space in Renée's room; his intrusion could, one suspects, further delay any "return to writing" on her part. Her initial reaction to Max's penetration of the dressing room, which is, by extension, part of her more general room, is to refer to him as "cet envahisseur" (1079) and to force him to leave. She states, rather matter-of-factly, that "[i]l n'y a rien de nouveau dans ma vie, qu'un homme patient qui me guette" (1106). Before long, it is obvious not only that Max has no intention of abandoning his efforts to get closer to Renée, but that Renée may even allow him into her space: "Et puis, il y a cet homme—le Grand-Serin[8]—qui s'arrange pour vivre dans mon ombre, pour mettre ses pas dans l'empreinte des miens, avec une obstination de chien" (1109).

From the very start, then, Renée views Max as a usurper of her space: her shadow and footprints are in effect appropriated by his. That she nevertheless gradually accepts this invasion is manifested in her neutral account of the things that magically seem to have materialized in her apartment or her dressing room: flowers, a dog dish for Fossette, even three tiny "animaux fétiches" set on her writing table as if to replace the instruments typically used for writing. In addition, Max forges relationships with her closest allies, with Hamond, a friend who is allowed—even welcomed—in Renée's space, as well as with Fossette, who betrays her mistress by "smiling" at Max (1114). Although Renée confides to Hamond that "[l]e Grand Serin s'insinue chez moi plus que je ne lui ai permis" (1115), she seems loath to put an end to the invasions.

The emergence of love as a focus in Renée's life corresponds to the conclusion of Part I, which also coincides with a welcome break in the heroine's music-hall schedule. This "délivrance" (1115), as Renée herself describes it, means that she is free once again to turn her attention to that long-neglected "room of her own." As Part I comes to a close, Renée is eagerly anticipating the opportunity to "vivre chez moi le soir" (1115-16) and even to embellish and redefine her home space. When Brague, a friend and co-worker, intimates that she must be redecorating because of the new man in her life, she insists that she is doing so only for herself. That emphasis on self reappears in the final paragraphs, when Renée contemplates the possibility of leaving on tour, which would entail leaving her room for an extended period of time. The ambivalence that characterizes Renée's attitude toward so many facets of her life could not be more obvious than in the passage which brings Part I to a dramatic close:

Mon goût tardif,—acquis, un peu artificiel,—des déplacements et du voyage fait bon ménage avec un fatalisme foncier et paisible de petite bourgeoise. Bohème, désormais, oui, et que les tournées ont menée de ville en ville, mais bohème ordonnée [. . .] Vagabonde, soit, mais qui se résigne à tourner en rond, sur place, comme ceux-ci, mes compagnons, mes frères . . . Les départs m'attristent et m'enivrent, c'est vrai, et quelque chose de moi se suspend à tout ce que je traverse,—pays nouveaux, ciels purs ou nuageux, mers sous la pluie couleur de perle grise,—s'y accroche si passionnément qu'il me semble laisser derrière moi mille petits fantômes à ma ressemblance, roulés dans le flot, bercés sur la feuille, dispersés dans le nuage . . . Mais un dernier petit fantôme, le plus pareil de tous à moi-même, ne demeure-t-il pas assis au coin de ma cheminée, rêveur et sage, penché sur un livre qu'il oublie de lire?

(1119)

The opening paragraphs of Part II reveal a renewed emphasis on Renée's room, but from the perspective of Max (to whom she now refers as "mon amoureux" [1120]). He seems fascinated by the striking contrast between her warm, cozy apartment, which he characterizes as "un joli coin intime" (1120), and her music-hall existence. This view of her space filtered through Max's eyes is followed by an account of Renée's response to his appraisal. She seems to step back and observe her living space objectively, musing about the conclusions that "le passant" (who may or may not be Max, the text remains ambiguous) might draw upon glancing at her lamp, crystal vase, armchair, and sofa. That observer would, in her opinion, necessarily surmise that the occupant leads "une vie retirée, pensive et studieuse, de femme supérieure" (1120). One could consider this the image of an *active* writer, not of a music-hall performer—the very woman Renée might be if her career did not consume all of her time and energy.

More importantly, Renée then goes on to call attention to what the "passant" apparently *fails* to notice: the dusty inkpot and dry pen, the very tools of writing, which have been abandoned because their owner has to work; working appears once again intertwined with work and space. This incomplete perception of an aspect of Renée's life which is so important to her, leads one to speculate: if the "passant" and Max *are* one and the same, she could indeed risk becoming even further distanced from her writing should she admit Max into her space, at the very moment when the freedom from work might otherwise lead to a resumption of writing. We are left with the impression, then, that Max is about to replace work in the work/writing opposition that governed Part I; in other words, a relationship with Max threatens to keep Renée from writing in much the same way that work has done since her divorce.

It is perhaps not surprising, therefore, that Renée's own appraisal of her room should change: "Cela sent l'indifférence, l'abandon, l' 'à quoi bon ', presque le départ" (1121). It is as if, because of Max's intrusion, her space were in a state of neglect, or were somehow less inviting to her. Moreover, she seems mystified at the ease with which Max has managed to enter her room: "J'ai un amoureux. Pourquoi celui-là, et non un autre? Je n'en sais rien. Je regarde, étonnée, cet homme qui a réussi à pénétrer chez moi. Parbleu! il le voulait tellement!" (1121). Indeed, she finds his presence "aussi insolite qu'un piano dans une cuisine" (1122), and avoids both visual and verbal communication with him, preferring to maintain a distance between them, incredulous that "le même rayon de soleil glisse sur sa joue et sur la mienne [. . .]. Il n'est pas là, il est à mille lieues! À tout moment, je veux me lever et lui dire: 'Pourquoi êtes-vous ici? Allez-vous-en!' Et je n'en fais rien" (1122).

Max's constant presence affects Renée at more than one level. First of all, he has awakened her sensual self, making her yearn to love and be loved for the first time since her divorce. Renée's independent, self-sufficient side wants desperately to fight this desire, for giving in to it means running the risk of being hurt once again. Secondly, Max's physical presence, which she finds both alluring and unsettling, threatens to limit her space in her own room, which in turn makes her want to abandon what has always served as her refuge, albeit a solitary one. It makes sense, then, that Renée might turn her attention to the possibility of resuming her work rather than to reveling in her "chez moi," as she initially intended to do at the start of her hiatus from performing. Faced with the greater menace of being "domesticated" by Max, Renée no longer sees work and writing as two antithetical concerns, as she had before: "je me sens joyeusement reprise de la fièvre active, du besoin de *travailler* . . . un besoin mystérieux et indéfini, que je dépenserais à danser aussi bien qu'à écrire, courir, jouer la comédie ou tirer une voiture à bras" (1131). That *écrire* is included among the verbs which fall under the general category of work, and more importantly, that it appears on equal footing with *danser* and *jouer la comédie,* which are, of course, activities in which she engages as a music-hall performer, seems to indicate that writing and work can co-exist. As we shall see—particularly in Part III—they can indeed, but only if Renée is able to map out a new space of her own.

The more Max threatens to drive her out of her room, both by his physical presence and by the threat to her independence and individuality that he represents, the more Renée comes to embrace the idea of going on tour with her music-hall troupe: "Oh! oui, partir, repartir, oublier qui je suis et le nom de la ville qui m'abrita hier" (1132). The fact that she is willing to go so far as to forfeit both her personal ("qui je suis") and spatial identity ("le nom de la ville qui m'abrita") shows just how threatened she feels. Commenting on the paradoxical circumstances in which Renée finds herself, Ann Cothran explains:

> When she allows Max to enter her life, solitude ceases to be a problem. However, now that she is no longer alone, she is also no longer in control of her own exist-

ence. Instead she is, figuratively speaking, a prisoner. In order to regain control of her existence, she will have to free herself from possessed spaces and find new ones.

(32)⁹

The extent to which Renée finds herself effectively excluded from space which once was hers alone, can be illustrated by a scene in which she returns home to discover Hamond, Fossette, and Max in her apartment, gaily playing *écarté*. It is only because her departure is imminent that she is able to overcome her anger and take part in the festivities; uncharacteristically, she even lets herself go, drinking too much and falling asleep. When she awakens, she is startled to find herself alone with Max, who physically crowds her and constricts her space: "Debout contre moi, le Grand-Serin barre toute la hauteur de la chambre" (1141). Angry ("j'en avais assez de le voir si haut, si près de moi" [1142]), she forces him to depart through the window, as if to punish and demean him. Yet paradoxically, as in so many other scenes, she then gazes out the window, "accoudée, comme une amante" (1147), as he leaves. Once again unable to reconcile her desire for love with her desire for space, she seems to yearn at once for absence and for presence.

Renée's ambivalence toward Max's sharing of her space is nowhere more evident than in the account of the couple's first successful kiss. The qualifier "successful" is necessary as there was a previous kiss, which was deemed "raté" by Renée (1152), perhaps because it occurred in Max's space (his car) where Renée felt imprisoned. When his face nears hers on this second try, she initially experiences a feeling of suffocation: "Il n'y a presque plus d'espace, presque plus d'air entre nos deux visages, et je respire brusquement, comme si je me noyais, avec un sursaut pour me dégager" (1159). But gradually she becomes an active participant who seeks—and finds—pleasure in the kiss:

> Je laisse l'homme qui m'a réveillée boire au fruit qu'il presse. Mes mains [. . .] s'abandonnent chaudes et molles dans sa main, et mon corps renversé cherche à épouser son corps. Pliée sur le bras qui me tient, je creuse son épaule un peu plus, je me serre contre lui, attentive à ne pas disjoindre nos lèvres [. . .].
>
> (1160)

This striking image of a languid and sensuous woman vanishes almost as quickly as it materialized, however, giving way to that of the submissive dog which awaits its master's next command:

> Maxime est demeuré sur le divan, et son muet appel reçoit la plus flatteuse réponse: mon regard de chienne soumise, un peu penaude, un peu battue, très choyée, et qui accepte tout, la laisse, le collier, la place aux pieds de son maître . . .
>
> (1160)

In the pages that follow, what Renée emphasizes is not the pleasure which could be enjoyed through intimacy with Max, but rather what she stands to lose if she does give herself physically to this man who is somehow, despite the many flaws she perceives in him, tantalizing. Such a sacrifice would mean losing her self and yielding full authority over her space, her thoughts: "il m'entraîne, m'étourdit de sa présence, m'empêche de penser. Il décide, il ordonne presque, et je lui fais, en même temps que l'hommage de ma liberté, celui de mon orgueil" (1162).

It is, finally, when Max expresses dissatisfaction with her chosen profession—"'Mais, chérie, vous n'avez plus besoin de music-hall'," he declares, "'puisque je suis là [. . .]'" (1173)—that Renée experiences a sudden flash of lucidity, realizing that Max, who is wealthy, has never had to work. In contrast to Renée, who finds personal and financial freedom in earning her own living, Max enjoys what she calls a "liberté d'oisif" (1170).¹⁰ He clearly sees himself as a substitute for the music hall—both the profession and the space.

In this long middle section devoted to the evolving relationship with Max, writing, one of Renée's constant preoccupations in the opening pages of the novel, virtually disappears. To put it simply, using the terms so critical to Renée's situation, there is no "room" for writing and a man in the same space. Renée's friend, Hamond, views the situation in a positive light; if she marries Max, he muses, "Vous pourrez, grâce à Maxime, vivre confortablement, luxueusement même, et . . . reprendre, nous l'espérons tous, cette plume spirituelle qui se rouille . . ." (1179). Hamond implies not only that Renée is dependent upon Max to live comfortably, but—despite the fact that the text provides evidence to the contrary—that her freedom to be able to write is equally tied to him. Oddly enough, Max is capable of providing, if only in the eyes of Hamond, the two essential conditions put forward by Woolf: the room and the money.

As Part II of the novel comes to a close, it is not the heroine, but a sentimental Max who is reluctant to leave the objects in her apartment—the divan, the portraits, the ray of sunshine. Eager to appropriate those items for himself, he pleads with her to give him her furnishings once they are together, after the tour, and promises to have others made for her. Renée's reaction, not surprisingly, is to minimize the importance of these things, now that they are no longer solely hers:

> Mobilier hanté, où je m'éveillai souvent avec la peur folle que ma liberté ne fût un songe . . . Singulier cadeau de noces à un nouvel amant! Un abri et non un home, c'est tout ce que je laisse derrière moi: les boîtes roulantes de seconde et première classe, et les hôtels de tout ordre, et les sordides loges des music-halls de Paris, de la province et de l'étranger, me furent plus

familiers, plus tutélaires que ceci, nommé par mon ami
"un joli coin intime "!

(1194)

Renée is clearly in the process of redefining her room,
substituting tour space for home space; she can no
longer claim the latter for her own because Max intends
to occupy and possess it. While her attitude toward the
separation is characteristically ambivalent, the final,
most striking image of Part II is one of movement—in
time and in space—and of metamorphosis: "je pars ag-
itée, débordante de regret et d'espoir, pressée de reve-
nir, tendue vers mon sort nouveau avec l'élan brillant
du serpent qui se délivre de sa peau morte" (1194).[11]
The heroine is ready, like the snake, to shed her old
skin, to be reborn, "renée."

The third and final part of the novel chronicles the process by which Renée comes to terms with the tensions
among the three elements (work, love, writing) which
define her life. That writing itself plays a fundamental
role in this process is suggested by the unique form of
Part III, which consists largely of letters that Renée has
written to Max during her tour, interspersed with blocks
of first-person narration as in the rest of the novel. Writing and work thus come to co-exist peacefully in the
new room—the space of travel, of *vagabondage*—which
Renée now claims as her own. Although Miller reads
Part III as "an epistolary novel revised" (248), one of
the usual ingredients of this sub-genre—the multiplicity
of voices—is absent: Max's voice is largely excluded
from the narrative space. Hence Stewart's comment that
Part III is "essentially a monologue. Max's very words
are subordinated to Renée's, filtered through her consciousness" (37). Writing letters to Max is, it seems, the
first step in the process of rediscovering herself as a
writer. Michel Baude notes that

> la rupture devient possible, non pas parce que Max est
> resté à Paris, mais parce que Renée écrit de nouveau—
> elle rédige des lettres. Ou plutôt, l'éloignement ne suf-
> firait pas s'il ne donnait l'occasion à Renée de retrou-
> ver sa véritable raison de vivre: le métier d'écrivain
> qui, abolissant et transcendant toutes les formes de dis-
> tance, lui permet enfin d'adhérer à elle-même et au
> monde, et de conquérir une certaine unité. *La vaga-
> bonde* serait en définitive un roman qui retrace la des-
> tinée d'un écrivain sauvé par l'écriture. L'écriture, elle,
> n'est pas vagabonde: elle sait où elle va.

(115-16)

It is as if Renée needed the separation, the physical
space between herself and Max, combined with the resumption of her work, to be able to express herself. Not
long after her departure, she writes: "Mon Dieu, comme
je vous écris! Je passerais tout mon temps à vous écrire,
j'y ai moins d'effort, je crois, qu'à vous parler" (1202).
Just how selfishly she wants to maintain that distance is
apparent when Max shows an interest in joining her on

tour. Alarmed that he would now invade her space and
her work as a performer, she writes: "Laissez-moi toute
seule à mon métier, que vous n'aimez pas!" (1207). Although Renée has made it clear in earlier episodes that
it is the music-hall work to which Max objects, she
may be referring as well to her *métier* as writer, for indeed, his physical presence would put an end to the
letter-writing which, while clearly not the "authentic"
writing that characterized her third novel, nonetheless
represents a critical first step in her rebirth as an author.
Writing, as Woolf tells us, requires not only a room and
money, but the sort of solitude which at the beginning
of the novel seemed so bittersweet to the heroine.

Just as Renée gradually begins to realize that Max has
no real place in the spatial framework which permits
her development as a writer, Max offers his own conception of what she needs in terms of space and what
she will become as a result. He writes, for example:
"Vous aimez le voyage, ma femme chérie? Vous en aurez jusqu'à vous lasser; vous aurez à vous toute la terre,
jusqu'à ne plus aimer qu'un petit coin à nous, où vous
ne serez plus Renée Néré, mais Madame Ma Femme!"
(1209). In other words, he—or, more specifically, his
wealth—will allow her to travel until all she needs is
the "petit coin" which will not be hers, of course, but
theirs; in losing her own room, she will also lose her
identity, becoming no more than one of Max's possessions, "Madame Ma Femme." The word "coin" here
brings to mind Max's earlier characterization of Renée's
apartment as a "joli coin intime" (1120), by which he
effectively destroyed its privileged quality as her private
space. The repetition of the word is indicative of the
struggle between Renée and Max to define her space:
while Renée seems to desire a vast space, essentially
without walls, Max would like to reduce it, to confine
her to a "small corner." Recognizing the danger in accepting Max's terms, Renée asks herself: "Oui, qu'est-ce
que je deviens dans tout ça?" (1209), and finds that she
is unable to respond honestly to his proposal: "Que
faire? . . . Pour aujourd'hui, écrire, brièvement, car
l'heure presse, et mentir . . ." (1212).

"[É]crire [..] et mentir": the juxtaposition of the two
verbs indicates just how quickly the heroine is moving
from mundane writing to a more authentic mode of
writing, that of fiction, for lying to Max entails creating
a persona that is no longer the real Renée. This could
not be more evident than in Renée's reaction to a photograph sent by Max, a photograph which shows him
playing tennis with another woman. Though Renée evidently feels a twinge of jealousy, she will not express
that feeling to Max:

> Non, je ne lui dirais rien. Mais écrire, c'est si facile!
> Écrire, écrire, lancer à travers des pages blanches
> l'écriture rapide, inégale, qu'il compare à mon visage
> mobile, surmené par l'excès d'expression. Écrire sin-

cèrement, presque sincèrement! J'en espère un soulage-
ment, cette sorte de silence intérieur qui suit un cri, un
aveu . . .

(1214)

This passage reveals the extent to which Renée's writing has evolved since her tour began: *dire,* which clearly
implies the telling of the truth, and *écrire* are now as
distinct in her mind as *écrire* and *mentir* are connected.
Renée's description of the writing process here bears an
uncanny—and telling—resemblance to the long passage
at the beginning of the novel (1074), where it was not
at all a question of writing letters, but of a more authentic writing, the kind that takes on its own life, ener-
gizes and excites the writer, leaving her spent but satisfied.[12] The difference, of course, is that in the earlier
passage such writing figured only as a part of Renée's
past (since she had to give it up in order to work),
whereas here it defines her present and future.

The pivotal moment in the conflict between writing and
love occurs when Renée writes Max a highly ambiguous letter which she herself finds incomprehensible, as
her own commentary shows:

> Quatre grandes feuilles, sur la table, témoignent de ma
> hâte à écrire, non moins que le désordre du manuscrit,
> où l'écriture monte et descend, se dilate et se contracte,
> sensible . . . Va-t-il me reconnaître dans ce désordre?
> Non. Je m'y dissimule encore. Dire la vérité, oui, mais
> toute la vérité, on ne peut pas, on ne doit pas.

(1216)

Increasingly, Renée lets herself be carried away by the
creative aspect of writing—she refers here to what she
has just written, significantly, as a "manuscrit"—ne-
glecting its communicative function (which is more often than not, of course, the primary aim of letter
writing).[13] Indeed, the unintelligibility of Renée's letters
brings to mind her description of her third novel, considered a failure by everyone but Renée herself, and
whose incomprehensibility—"Incompréhensible? pour
vous, peut-être. Mais pour moi [. . .]" (1084)—made it
all the more precious to her.

As Renée ceases to use writing to communicate her true
feelings to Max, she gradually discovers its ability to
capture the beauty of the natural world. Just after she
writes the enigmatic letter to Max, she decides to leave
the confines of her hotel room and visit what she calls
her "refuge élyséen" (1216), the Jardins de la Fontaine
in Nîmes, whose beauty overwhelms her: "Tout ceci est
encore mon royaume, un petit morceau des biens magnifiques que Dieu dispense aux passants, aux nomades,
aux solitaires. La terre appartient à celui qui s'arrête un
instant, contemple et s'en va" (1217). Nowhere is the
disparity more striking between the space that Renée
wishes to appropriate for herself and that which Max
envisions for her. Renée's conception of her room seems

to have no limitations; it is the expansive space of the
"passant," of the "nomade," of the *vagabonde.* The
room that Max intends to offer her is just the opposite.
Ironically, it has taken Max's persistent invasion of her
now-abandoned room—her dressing room, her apartment—to make Renée realize just how broad and open
her spatial horizons truly need to be.[14]

Renée's epiphany, the realization that she could settle
for Max and the restricted space that he represents only
"si je ne pouvais pas faire autrement" (1217), is, not
surprisingly, expressed in terms of writing: "Cette fois,
la formule est nette! Je l'ai lue écrite dans ma pensée,
je l'y vois encore imprimée comme une sentence en petites capitales grasses . . . Ah! je viens de jauger mon
piètre amour et de libérer mon véritable espoir:
l'évasion" (1217). The link between writing and the
new definition of her room is now unmistakable:

> j'écris, avec une abondance, une liberté inexplicables.
> J'écris sur des guéridons boiteux [. . .] j'écris, un pied
> chaussé et l'autre nu, mon papier logé entre le plateau
> du petit déjeuner et mon sac à main ouvert [. . .] j'écris
> devant la fenêtre qui encadre un fond de cour, ou les
> plus délicieux jardins, ou des montagnes vaporeuses
> . . . Je me sens chez moi, parmi ce désordre de campe-
> ment, ce n'importe où et ce n'importe comment [. . .].

(1222)

"Chez moi" is no longer defined as an apartment, nor a
dressing room, but rather as "n'importe où," wherever
Renée can write authentically.

Max, "mon ennemi, [. . .] le pillard qui me vole à moi-
même" (1226), will necessarily be excluded from this
"n'importe où," just as he will, simultaneously, cease to
be the recipient of her letters. Letter writing has served
its purpose, enabling Renée to disengage herself from
love and to become reengaged in the kind of writing
which characterized her third novel. Max's "pillaging"
of her former space and identity is so complete, in fact,
that in the account of her return to her apartment for the
last time, Renée now envisions herself in the role of intruder ("Au petit jour, j'entrerai chez moi, sans bruit,
comme une voleuse" [1229]). What used to be her own
room is now a place where she does not rightfully belong; as Evans suggests, "[t]he woman who lived there
is no more. Truly now she is a vagabond" (66). It is in
her old apartment that Renée writes Max one final letter, a painfully honest *lettre de rupture,* in which she
admits her feelings for him, but ultimately rejects him
in favor of her freedom, the freedom to be a vagabond,
to have space, to write. In the passage following the letter, Renée acknowledges that her choice is not without
risks, for she will sometimes yearn for those walls represented by Max's limitations on her freedom: "Vagabonde, et libre, je souhaiterai parfois l'ombre de tes
murs . . . Combien de fois vais-je retourner à toi, cher
appui où je me repose et me blesse? [. . .] Ah! tu seras
longtemps une des soifs de ma route!" (1232).

That Renée remains ambivalent about her choice even while knowing that it is the right one indicates the complexity of the dynamic between women and writing; it is that very complexity that Virginia Woolf will highlight:

> But, you may say, we asked you to speak about women and fiction—what has that got to do with a room of one's own? I will try to explain [. . .]. The title "women and fiction" might mean [. . .] women and what they are like; or [. . .] women and the fiction that they write; or [. . .] women and the fiction that is written about them; or it might mean that somehow all three are inextricably mixed together [. . .]. But when I began to consider the subject in this last way [. . .] I soon saw that it had one fatal drawback. I should never be able to come to a conclusion [. . .]. All I could do was to offer you an opinion upon one minor point—a woman must have money and a room of her own if she is to write fiction; and that, as you will see, leaves the great problem of the true nature of woman and the true nature of fiction unsolved. I have shirked the duty of coming to a conclusion upon these two questions—women and fiction remain, so far as I am concerned, unsolved problems.
>
> (3-4)

Colette's heroine provides one possible model for the hypothetical woman writer imagined by Woolf, one who grapples, in a concrete situation, with the very questions Woolf will pose in a more abstract way some twenty years later. Having rejected love and redefined her room, Renée Néré can now turn, once and for all, to her writing, "comme s'il n'y avait pas de soin plus impérieux, dans ma vie, que de chercher des mots, des mots pour dire combien le soleil est jaune, et bleue la mer, et brillant le sel en frange de jais blanc . . ." (1220). Will she be a working woman who writes, or a writing woman who works? In the final analysis, it matters not, because she has created space for both in a room that is, this time, truly her own.

Notes

1. Critics have noted, in passing, parallels between *La vagabonde* and *A Room of One's Own:* Miller mentions the two together (230-31, 234-36), as does Becker, who, in her brief synopsis of the novel's plot, calls the stage "the only space in which Renée feels fulfilled, secure, and forgetful of male tyranny and betrayal; it is her 'room of her own'" (7). Our analysis will show, however, that Renée's "room" is not limited to the workplace, but rather consists of a space that is at once broadly circumscribed and private. Finally, other critics have compared different pairings of works by the two authors: Stewart links Woolf's essay to *Le pur et l'impur* (86); Ladimer juxtaposes *La vagabonde* and Woolf's *The Years* (244-45).

2. Two studies are particularly noteworthy in this context. Cothran looks at space from a structuralist perspective; although the subject of writing is not one of her primary interests, she affirms, in a note, that "[t]he relationship between writing and female space in *La vagabonde* [. . .] is of great significance and warrants further study. Writing [. . .] represents true freedom—economic freedom, the freedom to (re)create the self" (35). Miller's focus, on the other hand, is not space, but writing.

3. I have adopted Woolf's term, "room," which she seems to use most often in a literal sense. In the context of Colette's novel, however, the word carries a figurative sense as well: it indicates a literal "room" (meaning a space surrounded by four walls, a home) as well as a more general "space." Cothran makes a distinction between "literal" and "figurative" space, and characterizes the representation and function of the more general "female space" as "the creation of a real or imaginary location whose function is to offer a refuge in which women can exist as whole, independent beings" (27).

4. Renée makes frequent use of suspension points. Evans comments that those placed after "je ne suis pas Balzac, moi" in this passage "tell a long story. A sigh of resignation, of hopelessness: a lapse into silence. I'm not a great man, I'm not a great writer. I can't measure up, so why should I try? The presence of a powerful male predecessor is felt by Renée to be so overwhelming that it drowns her own desire to write" (43). See also Miller's discussion of Renée's declaration that she is no Balzac (232-33).

5. Although it may seem logical to assume that Renée began writing after the breakup of her marriage in order to earn money (because she no longer had a husband to support her), there is no evidence in the text that this was what motivated her to take up her pen. What is emphasized is Renée's desire to ease her pain.

6. Goodhand's Nietzschean reading of the novel offers the following appraisal of the link between the heroine's suffering and her writing: "Renée's attitude is crucial because it strikes me as precisely what Nietzsche meant by transcendence of the threat of a paralyzing pessimism through Dionysian delight both in life and art: the prodding of grief is a catalyst for creativity, and affirmation involves both pain and joy. Far from yielding to despair, Renée plunges into her career as music hall performer after feeling obliged to abandon literature" (201).

7. Cottrell, on the other hand, emphasizes the similarity, rather than the tension, between Renée's work and her writing: "Renée affirms that the pleasure of writing is in seizing and fixing words, that

is to say, in arranging them in an immutable order. In a world she perceives as unstable, she satisfies her 'need' [. . .] for order by creating a new, artistic order of reality in her novels and in her dancing" (72).

8. It is significant that the adjective "serin," used here in an ironic or mocking tone, also served to characterize Renée's first novel—the one that was the most successful in the eyes of the public, but the least worthy of admiration in her own eyes.

9. Viti looks at Renée's dilemma through the prism of existentialism: "Although her departure from Paris in Part Three might suggest an act of *mauvaise foi,* an attempt to circumvent the circumstances in which she finds herself, in fact, it allows her to confront her choices and to assume the responsibility of an *acte authentique*" (82).

10. Angelfors, in her study of "la prise de conscience féminine," argues that "[l]e travail est un domaine où Colette [. . .] renverse les rôles traditionnels de l'homme et de la femme. Dans ses romans, ce sont donc les femmes qui travaillent, alors que les hommes sont des oisifs vivant de leurs rentes ou des revenus d'une affaire familiale. Il est certes possible de voir dans ce renversement des rôles l'expression d'une révolte contre le contexte social de l'époque confinant encore, dans une large mesure, la femme à la maison" (63). A number of other critics (such as Cothran, Eisinger, Evans, Viti, Picard) also adopt, to one degree or another, a feminist stance. More generally, Flieger and Huffer employ psychoanalytic and feminist approaches in their discussion of such issues as autobiography, gender, and representation in Colette's work; *La vagabonde* is not under scrutiny in either study, however.

11. Eisinger explains Renée's decision to renounce love by stating that "Renée's project can be viewed as the struggle to establish an androgynous identity after an intense experience of sexual polarization: her choice of *vagabondage* becomes a specific rejection of the traditional female sphere of house and family for the androgynous world of freedom and creativity" (95).

12. Ladimer mentions the dynamic between Renée's creation of an "independent self" and her discovery of "an alternative sensuality in writing" (244).

13. In her broad analysis of Part III, Miller offers the following interpretation of Renée's progression from writing letters to Max to writing literature (which I have called writing "authentically"): "[. . .] by letter writing Renée returns herself to literature, to the older mastery of a hand moving across a page [. . .]. The return to writing begins

with letter writing about returning to Max, but the return to writing will also require the displacement and transformation of that epistolary fiction through letter writing. How does this happen? The process of writing itself undoes the structure of destination: just as Renée suddenly finds herself at home [. . .] on the move, in the same way, movement itself takes her past the notion of return" (248).

14. Strikingly, *L'entrave,* the sequel to *La vagabonde,* represents a blatant reversal of the earlier work, although it manifests the same basic structure and themes. Having received an inheritance from her ex-sister-in-law, Renée abandons not only her career but her writing. Renée's trademark independence and strength give way, in her relationship with a new lover, Jean, to what Viti terms an "abdication of autonomy" (91). The heroine even relinquishes her space; Stewart marvels that "[d]ispossessed of originality, Renée is even dispossessed of a home; while in *The Vagabond* she trysted with Max in her own apartment, the affair with Jean takes place in *his* houses. She puts her furniture in storage, moves into his Paris house, and continues to live there even after he has moved out!" (46). In the end, Jean, not Renée, is the "eager vagabond" (Stewart 47). The Renée of *L'entrave* is thus everything that her counterpart in *La vagabonde* was not—or, more precisely, she is not everything that her counterpart was. It is noteworthy that Colette eventually renounced her conclusion.

References

Angelfors, Christina. *La double conscience: la prise de conscience féminine chez Colette, Simone de Beauvoir et Marie Cardinal.* Lund: Lund University Press, 1989.

Baude, Michel. "La distance dans *La vagabonde:* techniques et thèmes romanesques." *Colette: nouvelles approches critiques (actes du colloque de Sarrebruck [22-23 juin 1984]).* Ed. Bernard Bray. Paris: Nizet, 1984. 109-16.

Becker, Lucille Frackman. *Twentieth-Century French Women Novelists.* Boston: G. K. Hall, 1989.

Colette, *La vagabonde.* Vol. I of *Œuvres.* Bibliothèque de la Pléiade. Paris: Gallimard, 1984.

Cothran, Ann. "The Dryad's Escape: Female Space in *La vagabonde.*" *Modern Language Studies* 21 (1991):27-35.

Cottrell, Robert D. *Colette.* New York: Frederick Ungar, 1974.

Eisinger, Erica M. "*The Vagabond:* A Vision of Androgyny." *Colette: The Woman, the Writer.* Ed. Erica M. Eisinger and Mari Ward McCarty. University Park: Pennsylvania State University Press, 1981. 95-103.

Evans, Martha Noel. *Masks of Tradition: Women and the Politics of Writing in Twentieth-Century France.* Ithaca: Cornell University Press, 1987.

Flieger, Jerry Aline. *Colette and the Fantom Subject of Autobiography.* Ithaca: Cornell University Press, 1992.

Goodhand, Robert. "Apollo and Dionysus: Bedfellows of Colette's *Vagabond." Contemporary Literature* 24 (1983):190-203.

Huffer, Lynne. *Another Colette: The Question of Gendered Writing.* Ann Arbor: University of Michigan Press, 1992.

Ladimer, Bethany. "Colette: Rewriting the Script for the Aging Woman." *Aging and Gender in Literature: Studies in Creativity.* Ed. Anne M. Wyatt-Brown and Janice Rossen. Charlottesville: University Press of Virginia, 1993. 242-57.

Miller, Nancy K. *Subject to Change: Reading Feminist Writing.* New York: Columbia University Press, 1988.

Picard, Anne-Marie. "Le nom du corps: lecture du manque et savoir de son sexe dans *La vagabonde." Études littéraires* 26 (1993):33-46.

Stewart, Joan Hinde. *Colette: Updated Edition.* Boston: Simon & Schuster Macmillan, 1996.

Viti, Elizabeth Richardson. "Colette's Renée Néré: Simone de Beauvoir's Existential Heroine?" *French Forum* 21 (1996):79-94.

Woolf, Virginia. *A Room of One's Own.* San Diego: Harcourt Brace Jovanovich, 1929.

Stephanie Schechner (essay date summer 2004)

SOURCE: Schechner, Stephanie. "A Delicate Balance: Becoming a Woman and a Writer in Colette's *Claudine à l'École* and *La Maison de Claudine." Dalhousie French Studies* 67 (summer 2004): 75-87.

[*In the following essay, Schechner examines the novel* Claudine à l'École *and the novella* La Maison de Claudine *to understand how Colette turned to writing and then came to accept herself as a writer.*]

I. LA VENUE À L'ÉCRITURE

"Mais dans ma jeunesse, je n'ai jamais, *jamais* désiré écrire. Non, je ne me suis pas levée la nuit en cachette pour écrire des vers au crayon sur le couvercle d'une boîte à chaussures! Non, je n'ai jamais jeté au vent d'Ouest et au clair de lune des paroles inspirées! Non, je n'ai pas eu 19 ou 20 pour un devoir de style, entre douze et quinze ans! Car je sentais, chaque jour mieux, je sentaïs que j'étais justement faite pour ne *pas* écrire."

(*Journal à Rebours* 144-5)

"Un an, dix-huit mois après notre mariage, M. Willy me dit:—Vous devriez jeter sur le papier des souvenirs de l'école primaire. N'ayez pas peur des détails piquants, je pourrais peut-être en tirer quelque chose . . . Les fonds sont bas."

(*Mes Apprentissages* 177)

In these two oft-cited remarks by Colette, we find her denying any ambition to write. This is Colette's public explanation of how she became a writer: Willy locked her in a room and told her to write. In spite of Colette's repeated insistence that she lacked any sense of literary vocation, the question of how Colette came to write, or more precisely, to continue writing is still worth asking. In particular, if one seeks to understand *how* Colette explicitly reconciled her lack of desire to write with the fact of her prodigious literary œuvre, one finds that Colette worked almost systematically to resolve the inner conflict felt by many women writers of her generation.

Colette began writing at a time when women were slowly making progress toward achieving equality with men in French society. During her lifetime, women began to demand and receive new freedoms[1], however, the question of how to live as a woman and to work as a writer was far from being answered. For Colette, a young woman educated to become a traditional housewife and who found herself uncomfortably compelled to write by her husband, the contradictions must have been daunting. As her biographers have shown, the paradox at the center of Colette's life story is that though her education, both formal and informal, taught her to be one kind of woman, a housewife and mother, she spent most of her adult life working as a writer and renouncing the more traditional roles which others expected of her.[2] This tension was one that presumably marked the lives of most women writers of her generation. What makes Colette's situation different is that she began writing not because she wanted to do so (in fact she repeatedly denied such a desire), but because her husband demanded this of her. When asked why she wrote, Colette often fell back on this excuse. However, this response and her denial of any desire to write do not explain why she continued to write long after her relationship with Willy ended.

What seems to have been forbidden to Colette was not so much writing as such (a good number of women managed to overcome the societal interdiction against women writing), but rather her desire. This prohibition was not an external one, but a self-imposed one. Some authors have chosen to focus on the issue of desire in order to understand why Colette spent her life writing.[3] Even though the underpinnings of Colette's drive to create remain largely obscured to the reader due to their subconscious nature, what the reader can trace on the surface of her texts is how Colette came to justify her work. Among Colette's many books, two of her novels,

Claudine à l'École and *La Maison de Claudine,* are especially well-suited to such an analysis. Joan Hinde Stewart recognized the important connections between the two texts in her article titled "The School and the Home" when she stated, ". . . the curious and scabrous 'autofiction' of *Claudine à l'École* is both origin and prophecy of the much admired autobiographical content of *La Maison de Claudine*" (260). These novels, which both treat the childhood education of the character Claudine/Colette, give us insight into how Colette learned about literature. In addition, since the novels were published approximately twenty years apart (and yet both explore the same period of Claudine's/Colette's life), we can see how Colette's understanding of her own development as a future artist changed over time. If we focus on these two novels, we find something very special, namely, how she came to writing in spite of her internal sense of prohibition against a desire to write and how she carefully rationalized her wish in a way which made it acceptable to her. Colette accomplished both of these feats by first validating the experiential as opposed to reflection and art. Secondly, Colette inscribed her work as an author in the realm of the experiential as a domestic art. An examination of how Colette represents education in *Claudine à l'École* and *La Maison de Claudine* ultimately gives us the opportunity to observe how she faced her internal contradictions by developing an understanding of herself as a writer/woman, one which allowed her to marry the often opposed terms of "writing" and "experience."[4]

II. Le Fruit de L'Expérience

To begin an exploration of how Colette came to write and to accept herself as a writer, one should first examine the representation of education in both *Claudine à l'École* and *La Maison de Claudine* because it is here that one finds stories of Colette's early intellectual formation. Although these novels do not explain in a direct manner how Colette began to write, they do provide ample evidence of Colette's educational process and, most importantly, of her notion that successful pedagogy involves learning through experience. In these novels, which describe her childhood and adolescence, direct, living proves to be a better teacher than abstract or mediated teachings. This validation of experience is Colette's first step in her quest to accept herself as a writer.

In both novels, formal education (i.e. lessons taught in a classroom by a teacher, and lessons practiced by a student through the more traditional mechanisms of reading or writing) is held up for our mockery over and over again. In *Claudine à l'École,* the lessons presented entail little more than memorization and regurgitation. Recitations, dictations and translations abound while creative work is virtually nonexistent. Even subjects which might appear to necessitate creativity, such as

drawing or essay writing, are circumscribed by rules and forms to which the students must adhere. The schoolmistresses seem concerned only that the girls appear to work and to learn. A typical aside from Claudine regarding her schoolwork is: "Il faut prendre un porte-plume et faire semblant au moins de travailler" (28)! One can easily conjure up the image of a young girl gazing dreamily out the window of her classroom. When called to attention, the girls heaves a great sigh, bites her lip and endeavors to give the impression of earnest concentration. About an essay assignment, Colette writes, "Après avoir bâillé un quart d'heure, je me décide, et j'écris tout de suite sur le 'cahier-journal' sans brouillon, ce qui indigne les autres" (72). Here, Colette takes pains to make apparent her careless attitude toward writing. Schoolwork, even writing, is not worthy of either hard work or close attention.

Her teachers become especially concerned with the appearance of learning at two moments in particular during the novel: during the visits of inspectors and at the final examination which determines who will receive the *brevet élémentaire.* Claudine remarks on the new-found seriousness of her instructors as the date of the exam draws near, "Adieu le repos! L'approche des examens, l'honneur qui doit rejaillir sur cette belle école neuve, de nos succès possibles, ont enfin tiré nos institutrices de leur doux isolement" (141). Formal education is thus presented as a joke, something to live through, to escape from whenever possible, and certainly not to be taken seriously.

Similarly, in *La Maison de Claudine,* we find a certain suspicion toward "formal learning." To begin with, even though this novel ostensibly treats some of the same periods of Claudine/Colette's life as were treated in *Claudine à l'École,* there is virtually no mention of schooling. Classmates are only mentioned when they are encountered at home or in the village. Perhaps, Colette felt that she had already sufficiently described her school days. However, one might also conclude that, when revisiting the material of her childhood twenty years after the publication of *Claudine à l'École,* school appeared so insignificant to Colette that it could be virtually erased. Whatever her reason, the result is the same: school is almost nowhere to be found in the lyrical set of remembrances which constitute *La Maison de Claudine.*

In spite of the lack of schoolroom scenes, we do find Claudine participating in some activities that are associated with formal learning. Most strikingly, several reading scenes are presented. These scenes strongly convey the idea that reading can be dangerous. Two cautionary tales are related. The first "Ma mère et les livres" recounts Claudine's reading of Zola. Her mother has permitted her to read certain novels by Zola which she judged appropriate, but it is the ones her mother has refused her which interest Claudine enough to steal them away in secret. One novel in question begins innocently enough, but at one point abruptly embarks on a description of childbirth. "Elle lui donnait le jour soudain, avee un luxe brusque et cru de détails, une minutie anatomique [. . .] où je ne reconnus rien de ma tranquille compétence de jeune fille des champs" (356). Claudine's reaction is to faint promptly upon reading the scene. Claudine's mother, after resuscitating her, reassures her:

> Ce n'est pas si terrible, va, c'est loin d'être terrible, l'arrivée d'un enfant. Et c'est beaucoup plus beau dans la réalité. La peine qu'on y prend s'oublie si vite, tu verras! . . . La preuve que toutes les femmes l'oublient, c'est qu'il n'y a jamais que les hommes— est-ce que ça le regardait, voyons, ce Zola?—qui en font des histoires . . .
>
> (36)

This short vignette gives the impression that the problem with Zola is not *what* he writes about (what could be more natural than childbirth?), but that he *writes*. Writing itself is inadequate to its subject here (the arrival of a child is "much more beautiful in reality") and it is this inadequacy which can damage a young person during her formative years. Here, as elsewhere, Claudine's mother marks her preference for direct, lived experience over the second-hand witnessing of a writer.

A second story which reinforces the idea that reading can be harmful is "Ma sœur aux longs cheveux." In this story, Claudine's sister becomes cut off from the world around her as she reads too much. "Ma sœur aux longs cheveux ne parlait plus, mangeait à peine, nous rencontrait avec surprise dans la maison, s'éveillait en sursaut si l'on sonnait" (69). What is unhealthy is the fact that Claudine's sister has become completely absorbed in the act of reading. In the end, this leads to illness and to exile. Claudine's sister eventually marries and moves next door to her parents, but has only limited contact with them. The conclusion one can draw here seems to be that an excess of reading causes an imbalance for a young woman. In order to live a good life, as we will see represented by Claudine's mother, one can read, but should do so in moderation thereby demonstrating a realization that "real life," or lived experience, must take precedence.

Comparing *Claudine à l'École* to two similar novels of the period which feature young, female protagonists, Juliette Rogers writes, "These education novels mirror the shared experiences of the writers and their readers. However, they are not merely reflections of the pedagogical history of French women in the Belle Epoque. Instead, [they] each develop a critique of the national educational system for girls . . ." (323). What Rogers highlights for us is that Colette did not merely describe

her experiences. Instead, she offered a critical appraisal of her learning experiences which included suggestions for how education is best achieved. As a result, *Claudine à l'École* is structured in such a way as to diminish the importance of Claudine's formal education in order to highlight the more significant lessons imparted by her observations of others and by her own interpersonal experiences. If Claudine's formal education was lacking in rigor and in depth, what I would call her "informal education" was a pedagogical model filled with ample opportunities to practice what was learned. These lessons form the majority of Claudine's education as she tells it. From all of this Claudine learns to flirt, to manipulate, to blackmail, to deceive, to wield power, and to form intimate relationships with men and women. As she herself sums up, her school is in a state of "désordre" marked by:

> [. . .] le tripotage des grandes filles par le délégué cantonal et ses visites prolongées à nos institutrices, l'abandon fréquent des classes par ces deux demoiselles, tout occupées à échanger des câlineries à huis clos, les lectures plutôt libres de mademoiselle Sergent, (*Journal Amusant*, Zolas malpropres et pis encore), le beau sous-maître gallant et barytonneur qui flirte avec les demoiselles du brevet [. . .]
>
> (80)

With all of these examples of (mis)conduct before her, Claudine learns well to be a consummate flirt and manipulator. Claudine learns by observing the behavior of her schoolmistresses and her classmates. In addition, when left alone by their teachers, the girls have the opportunity to discuss what they have observed. Finally, when men enter the scene (local officials and the boys' school teacher), the girls all get to practice their flirting. These men not only flirt with the girls, but attempt to take advantage of them physically. All in all, Claudine's lessons in seduction are quite successful as one can see in the later novels in the Claudine series. In these books, Claudine not only finds a husband, but seduces many men and women along the way.

Claudine à la Maison also presents informal lessons which can serve as a comprehensive primer for the education of a young girl in the domestic realm. In this work, we find careful descriptions of lessons learned by both girls and women in the course of their lives. Girls are to develop and to enjoy domestic skills as well as an intimate relationship with the natural world of plants and animals. The positive lessons which are described in the novel are ones which involve doing things, acquiring skills, participating in practices such as sewing, cooking, and gardening.

On the side of experience, we always find Colette's mother Sido who lived a rich life, one which found its center in domesticity. As Elaine Marks put it in her first work on Colette: "Raised by her mother, Sido, to look at and to marvel at the daily miracles of nature, Colette felt no estrangement from the world around her, no anxiety, but rather delight before natural objects" (8). Sido's great passions were plants, animals, her children and domestic tasks. In a telling passage from *La Maison de Claudine* in the chapter titled "Ma mère et le fruit défendu," we find the aged and weakened mother of Claudine who still has flashes of her prior vitality. When she feels such a surge of energy, her mother will set to work at strenuous domestic tasks such as chopping wood or moving furniture. In her mother's world, doing these sorts of activities represents the best that life has to offer.

Having reflected on how education and lessons are explicitly presented in these two novels, one can see that Colette presents both positive and negative lessons. Like other writers, Colette seems to have had an underlying theory, albeit an unconscious one, of how one best assimilated the lessons one had to learn in life. If we briefly revisit her treatment of lessons, one can see that the teaching that was mocked as ineffective was accomplished through rote repetition and through reading or writing. We can almost hear Michel de Montaigne's echo: "Savoir par coeur n'est pas savoir (c'est tenir ce qu'on a donné en garde à sa mémoire)" (264). This type of learning was presented as ridiculous at best and dangerous at worst. In contrast, we find that the lessons Claudine learns best she learns through doing or observing others doing, through experiential contact with the world around her. In this respect, Colette seems to fully embrace the pedagogical model of learning through practice that Montaigne endorsed several centuries before her time. What Colette offers us then is a practical pedagogy, one which insists that one learns best by doing. One can see that in *Claudine à l'École* and *La Maison de Claudine* learning through experience has been privileged over any formal or abstract education. In this way, Colette has begun the process of making sense of her identity as a woman and a writer.

III. Telle Mère, Telle Fille

Although the question of Colette's motivation for privileging experience is not at the center of our current inquiry which focuses instead on how she accomplishes this, it is worth exploring briefly why Colette felt the need to justify her desire to write in the first place. To be sure, many authors during this time were critical of the rote memorization and regimented classrooms of the period; however, this does not fully account for Colette's personal investment in valorizing an alternative learning practice.

For Colette, mediated knowledge such as one gains through reading and writing was often negatively opposed to direct, sensual experience. Though many might argue that this is a false opposition, that there is no experience which is not mediated by language in some form, Colette herself sets up this conflict and ultimately seems to find a way to resolve it. One example of how Colette established the difference between mediated and direct knowledge can be found in the first chapter of *La Maison de Claudine.* In the middle of a description of her childhood home, Colette writes:

> Le reste vaut-il que je le peigne, à l'aide de pauvres mots? Je n'aiderai personne à contempler ce qui s'attache de splendeur, dans mon souvenir, aux cordons rouges d'une vigne d'automne que ruinait son propre poids, cramponnée, au cours de sa chute, à quelques bras de pin.
>
> (6)

It appears that, for Colette, words were adequate neither to the lived experience of her life nor even to her memories of it. Experience seems to carry with it an intangible quality, a "splendor," which can not be fully communicated in language. A little further along in this passage, Colette marks not only her language but also her adult self as unworthy of her childhood:

> Maison et jardin vivent encore, je le sais, mais qu'importe si la magie les a quittés, si le secret est perdu qui ouvrait,—lumière, odeurs, harmonie d'arbres et d'oiseaux, murmure de voix humaines qu'a déjà suspendu la mort,—un monde dont j'ai cessé d'être digne? . . .
>
> (6)

For Colette, one's direct connection to the natural world of experience is strongest during childhood. Writing about her own daughter, she closes *La Maison de Claudine* with this idea: "Mais peut-être ne retrouvera-t-elle pas sa subtilité d'enfant, et la supériorité de ses sens qui savent goûter un parfum sur la langue, palper une couleur et voir—'fine comme un cheveu, fine comme une herbe'—la ligne d'une chant imaginaire . . ." (159). In this passage, Colette firmly establishes both the elevated status of children, endowed as they are with "superior senses," and the rupture that occurs as one develops into an adult. She worries that Bel-Gazou may lose her sensual capacities in the course of just one year. In these final lines, Colette reiterates her belief in an unbridgeable chasm which separates the child's imaginary world of experience and that of the adult who can only struggle to remember the past by means of language.[5]

For Colette to put herself on the side of mediated knowledge, of reading and writing, she would have had to separate herself from experience and from her mother, Sido. As we have seen, it is Colette's mother who is consistently described in terms of lived experience as defined by contact with others and with nature. To enter the abstract world of words, either through reading or writing seems to have represented an impossible break with Sido. François Mallet-Joris explains that, for Colette, writing was associated with masculinity.[6] Colette's father led his family to believe that he was a writer, going so far as to have blank books bound and inscribed with titles and his name as author. It was not until much later that the family learned the books were blank. Colette's first husband was a writer of sorts, employing a large number of ghost writers to produce works he published under his name. In spite of both men's failed attempts to write, Colette came to see writing as the province of men. This link between masculinity and writing is made explicit much later in Colette's **Derniers Écrits.** In the chapter titled, "Gîte d'écrivain," Colette asks about the origin of her desire to write. She answers herself, "Il m'arriva de voir, dans une trêve, la longue ressemblance et l'imitation volontaire de la trompeuse et dernière nonchalence qui ne détachait plus guère de mon père, Jules-Joseph Colette, que des lambeaux de versification facile, brillants de banalité . . ." (61). Here, Colette reveals an unconscious attempt to imitate her father's careless attitude toward writing. Mallet-Joris writes, "This feeling that she is not, at some particular point, wholly a woman, this nostalgia which touches almost on guilt—is it not precisely the act of writing, her writer's career, her man's career, which she takes so much care to present as fortuitous" (9)? Here Mallet-Joris demonstrates why Colette would hesitate to define herself as a writer, as doing so would separate her from the realm of the feminine as exemplified by her mother.

There is ample evidence to show that the idea of leaving her mother caused her some anxiety. In **La Maison de Claudine** we find several passages which describe the separation of a mother and daughter and the fear this provokes. In the chapter titled "L'enlèvement," Claudine's mother develops a phobia that her daughter will be kidnapped after she moves into a bedroom in the house that is farther away from her parents' room than her previous one. This fear is communicated to Claudine who shares it, but who also senses a sort of positive anticipation at the thought of being taken forcibly from her mother. This scene seems to prefigure Colette's own "kidnapping" by Willy. Despite the fact that Colette married Willy by choice, the imbalances of power in their relationship (Willy was older, Willy forced Colette to write) suggest a sort of taking by force. (Here one might consider once again the fate of Claudine's sister who read too much and who, though living next door, remained fundamentally separated from her mother.) This symbolic separation from her mother carried great weight for Colette as evidenced by her continuing effort to avoid such a rupture. Laurie Corbin argues that this anxiety finds its origin in Sido herself:

> . . . in her treatment of Sido as an instrument of the patriarchy who must form her daughters into suitable women, the reader is given two views of this function:

through the child 'Gabrielle's' eyes we see a dutiful wife and mother combing her daughters' long hair and reassuring them about childbirth. However narrative distance shows a woman who is unhappy when it is time for her daughters to marry and who finds the institutions of love and marriage ignoble and untrustworthy. Colette splits her narrative representation into different points of view and thus portrays a woman divided against herself . . .

(16-17)

Sido's inner conflict was shared by Colette who, as an alternative to breaking completely with the feminine, opted to find a middle ground, a way to reconcile writing with experience. This was not accomplished in a single stroke but rather was an on-going process for Colette. Having seen how Colette privileged experience in both **Claudine à l'École** and **La Maison de Claudine,** we should now focus our attention on how Colette inscribed both reading and writing on the side of experience in **La Maison de Claudine.** It is here, in this later novel, that Colette gives the reader some clues as to how she began to accept her work.

IV. Les Arts de la Lecture et de L'Écriture

As was noted earlier, reading, in spite of its dangers, did have a role to play in Colette's mother's world. Christiane Makward confirms that one can not simply designate Sido as "unlettered:" "The association of [. . .] the mother with irrational or non-verbal communication does not fully account for Colette's portrayal of her parents' relation to communication and signs" (189). On the contrary, Sido encouraged her children to read, even when she did not understand their choice of material. At one point, she complains, "—Pourquoi ne lis-tu pas Saint-Simon? me demandait-elle. C'est curieux de voir le temps qu'il faut à des enfants pour adopter des livres intéressants" (33)! As this comment and the passage regarding Zola illustrate, Sido had strong ideas about which works were most appropriate for her children.

Interestingly, though, what seems to have made the deepest impression on the young Claudine is not so much the content of any of these books as their physical presence as objects to be appreciated. Colette writes, "Des livres, des livres, des livres. Ce n'est pas que je lusse beaucoup. Je lisais et relisais les mêmes. Mais tous m'étaient nécessaires. Leur présence, leur odeur, les lettres de leurs titres et le grain de leur cuir . . ." (32). Colette insists upon the significance of the physical interaction with books which takes place during reading and re-reading. She underscores the material aspects of the book: its cover, its print, even its smell. A page later she continues, "Beaux livres que je lisais, beaux livres que je ne lisais pas, chaud revêtement des murs du logis natal, tapisserie dont mes yeux initiés flattaient la bigarrure cachée . . ." (33). This comparison is important for two reasons. First, Colette is aligning books and reading with her home. She is emphasizing that, although books can be construed in terms of their content and abstract ideas, for her, it is their presence, regardless of whether she had read them or not, which was essential. Furthermore, her comparison highlights the idea that books are the product of physical work, woven like fabric. This initial understanding of the experience of reading and the physicality of books foreshadows the way in which Colette will later figure writing as a "domestic art."

Having examined how Colette described the role of reading in her childhood, let us now turn to the domain of writing. Even though she does not explicitly treat the process of writing in *La Maison de Claudine,* her descriptions of Bel-Gazou's silent reflection while sewing evoke the creative mental processes that are often associated, by Colette and others, with writing. Hence, it is here that we find a relatively early example of how Colette came to meld her two worlds into one. A brief analysis of the vignette titled **"La Couseuse"** will allow us to demonstrate the sophistication of Colette's later work, and hence to sketch out some of the traces of her development as a writer. More importantly, however, we will see how she carefully offers us an indirect description of writing as an experience. She does this by presenting travel and navigation, two physical actions, as metaphors for reflection and mental discovery. In this way, Colette manages to "physicalize" what would otherwise be a purely psychological moment in her young daughter's development and, by extension, in the work of a writer.

This story explains how and why Colette's daughter, Bel-Gazou, learned to sew at the age of nine. The story opens with several of Colette's friends expressing surprise: "—Votre fille a neuf ans, m'a dit une amie, et elle ne sait pas coudre? Il faut qu'elle apprenne à coudre. Et par mauvais temps il vaut mieux, pour une enfant de cet âge, un ouvrage de couture qu'un livre romanesque" (153). Like Sido, this friend of Colette prefers a domestic task like sewing for young girls as opposed to reading. By privileging a domestic task, the story reminds one of many other passages in the book which deal with reading and housework.

Throughout this chapter, Colette develops an extended metaphor in which she compares Bel-Gazou's activities, both reading and sewing, to voyages. Near the beginning, Bel-Gazou, in spite of her lady-like task, is described as follows: "elle ressemble davantage[. . .] à *un mousse ravaudant un filet* qu'à une petite fille appliquée . . ." (153).[7] This choice of metaphor is a significant one since it marks Bel-Gazou as masculine. This is interesting when considered in light of Colette's understanding of writing and creative work as the province of men which we noted earlier.

Despite Bel-Gazou's effort to conform to some degree to societal expectations of how she should spend her time, she is not entirely successful. Colette writes, ". . . ses mains[. . .] ourlent en dépit du bon sens: le simple 'point devant', par leurs soins, rappelle *le pointillé zigzaguant d'une carte routière* [. . .]" (153-4). For her mother, these stitches come to represent steps on a path which will lead away from her.

Colette goes on to establish a difference between the kind of (mental) traveling that Bel-Gazou does when she reads and when she sews. Colette, as opposed to her friends, is clearly in favor of reading: "Sa maman ne dit rien—il faut maîtriser les grandes joies. Mais faut-il les simuler? J'écrirai la vérité: je n'aime pas beaucoup que ma fille couse" (154). In spite of the approval of her friends, Colette is not pleased. She explains why immediately: "Quand elle lit, elle *revient* [. . .]"(154). Reading is "un poison éprouvé, traditionnel, dont les effets sont dès longtemps connus" (154). So, in spite of the fact that reading involves distancing herself from her mother, this route can be retraced since it is a well-worn path that others have taken by reading the same books.[8]

The route traveled while sewing is a different one. When she sews, Bel-Gazou is silent and she thinks. Colette explains,". . . elle ait justement découvert le moyen de descendre, point à point, piqûre à piqûre, *un chemin* de risques et de tentations" (154-5). In this sentence, Colette draws the clearest connection thus far between sewing, navigation and writing. The words "point à point" can be interpreted in three different ways. First, they mean literally "stitch by stitch" in order to describe the task which Bel-Gazou is completing. Secondly, though, the word "point" can refer to a navigational point used by sailors. Hence, Colette reiterates the image of Bel-Gazou as ship's boy traveling by sea, carefully navigating her perilous route. Finally, a "point" is a period, the punctuation mark which ends a sentence. As Bel-Gazou descends from "point à point" she is moving from sentence to sentence, slowly shaping ideas in her head. It is this act of mental creation which seems to be dangerous and to evoke writing most directly.[9] Bel-Gazou will not be stopped: "Le bras armé du dard d'acier va et vient . . . Rien n'arrête la petite exploratrice effrénée" (155). As she sews, Bel-Gazou performs a mental activity which one might compare to writing: "Elle coud et superpose, à son œuvre qu'elle néglige, des images, des associations de noms et de personnes, tous les résultats d'une patiente observation" (156). Instead of focusing on the task in her hand, Bel-Gazou embroiders a second, but no less important, mental pattern.

Because she is relatively uninterested in sewing, Bel-Gazou's mind drifts away from her work. This mental wandering is made patent by her errant stitches which can not be kept straight without her full concentration and by the questions she asks her mother from time to time. Near the end of the chapter, Colette recounts a scene in which Bel-Gazou asks a series of questions which ultimately reveal that she understands, or is beginning to understand, that an affair is going on between a married man and a divorced woman. As Bel-Gazou approaches knowledge of the "truth" of this situation, i.e. love between a man and woman, Colette feels unable to explain or even respond to her questions. Here, communication is blocked by the sort of interference that Yannick Resch described in his study *Corps féminin, corps textuel:* "L'étude des expressions visuelles, verbales et gestuelles a mis en lumière le rôle du masque dans la communication. Regards ensommeillés, chantonnement, sourire sont autant de barrières qui entravent le dialogue et déforment le message" (197). Bel-Gazou's focus on an activity, i.e. sewing, allows her to avert her eyes from her mother's gaze. By looking away, she effectively severs the contact that Colette desires. As a result, we find mother and daughter together yet as fundamentally separated as two ships passing in the night.

This mental wandering is ultimately what Colette fears for her daughter because it is what lead her, Colette, away from her own mother. As she exlains. "L'autorité maternelle les liait là des années, des années, elles ne se levaient que pour changer l'écheveau de soie, ou fuir avec un passant . . ." (155). This bond will inevitably be cut however as a young woman falls in love or begins to think like a writer, and it is to this rupture that Colette seems to allude at the close of the story: "Mais elle est trop *près* de la vérité, et trop naturelle pour ne pas connaître, de naissance, que toute la nature hésite *devant* l'instinct le plus majestueux et le plus trouble, et qu'il convient de trembler, de se taire et de mentir lorsqu'on *approche* de lui" (156). Even in this last passage. Colette recalls the theme of a voyage which she has established, using spatial metaphors to describe what is a passage in time, in maturation. She says that Bel-Gazou is "near" the truth, she finds herself "before" an instinct which she "approaches." This vignette, with its spatial metaphor of travel developed so meticulously, gives a sense of the depth of Colette's talent as a writer. This passage devoted to sewing, to the decoration of a fabric, is itself an elaborately woven text.

In this passage, the most important element is the physical metaphor which Colette constructs in order to elucidate the moment of developmental discovery through which Bel-Gazou is passing. This trope is significant because it is here that Colette finds a way to bridge the gap between the concrete and the abstract, between direct and mediated knowledge, between Sido's world and her own. While Colette's life was very different from her mother's, she never really gave up Sido's world. Instead, she found a way to describe her work as a writer as something akin to her mother's work as a homemaker.

Some fourteen years after the publication of *La Maison de Claudine,* Colette offered a brief explanation of her "art." In general, Colette made a practice of not commenting on her work as a writer, so this passage has become an important one for many Colette scholars. In this passage, Colette describes once again how Willy "forced" her to write. She compares her work to that of a "raccommodeuse de porcelaines:"

> . . . mon art le plus certain, qui n'est pas celui d'écrïre, mais l'art domestique de savoir attendre, dissimuler, de ramasser des miettes, reconstruire, recoller, redorer, changer en mieux-aller le pis-aller, perdre et regagner dans le même instant le goût frivole de vivre . . .
>
> (118)

Even as Colette explicitly denies that she is describing her writing, she offers us insight into what she understood as her greatest accomplishment. In this brief citation, Colette suggests an interesting idea which ironically has been echoed by many seeking to describe and account for women's writing: namely, that women's art is a domestic art. The question that Colette's whole œuvre seems to ask is: "What is writing if it is not the patient waiting, observing and recollecting of experience?" As a result, although Colette was offering an explanation of the art of her survival in Willy's "jail," it makes sense to conclude that Colette's writing was the result of similar gathering and refashioning. For Colette, any art with which she would associate was a concrete experience not an abstract, intellectual process. This passage calls to mind, albeit indirectly, the earlier one in *La Maison de Claudine* in which books are compared to tapestries, to domestic objects.

The connection which Colette established in *La Maison de Claudine* and in *Mes Apprentissages* between writing and domesticity is echoed elsewhere in her work. Another illuminating passage is found in *Journal à Rebours* in the chapter titled "La Chaufferette." Here, Colette's approach to discussing her career is more direct. She begins by marking the origin of her career: "Vocation, signes sacrés, poésie enfantine, prédestination? . . . Je ne retrouve rien de tel dans ma mémoire. Au commencement de ma carrière fut une chaufferette . . ." (141). Colette again denies that there were any early signs that she would become a writer. In place of juvenalia, we find instead a domestic object: the footwarmer. Colette goes on to detail the uses of the footwarmer in the home. Each female seems to have one: the cook, the ladies' maid, her mother and Claudine herself.

At school, the "chaufferette" serves triple duty: weapon for schoolyard fights, footwarmer, and source of amusement (for, when a little girl would sit on one to stay warm, she might subsequently burn her "petit derrière.") It is from such an object that Colette learns about writing. Even as she mocks the lessons of Mademoiselle Fanny who teaches reading in a ridiculously exaggerated manner, Colette draws a beautiful "image rustique" of winter during her youth, all inspired by the humble footwarmer. This domestic object has served as the touchstone for her work in this chapter.[10]

Later in the chapter, Colette explains how she spent her childhood and adolescence. She recalls, "Mon enfance, ma libre et solitaire adolescence, toutes deux préservées du souci de m'exprimer, furent toutes deux occurées uniquement de diriger leurs subtiles antennes vers ce qui se contemple, s'écoute, se palpe et se respire" (145). Once again, Colette emphasizes the importance of the encounter between her senses and the world around her. She goes so far as to ask whether her true "école" was the "rude paradis" of her "pays natal." The effect of this reflection inspired by the footwarmer is to suggest that, although Colette did not want to write as a young girl, she was preparing for a life as a writer in the best way possible: by observing the world around her. Sido's exhortations to make and maintain contact with the natural world seem to have served Colette, the writer, well, giving her an endless source of inspiration and ideas for her writing.

By writing, Colette ultimately learned how to be herself, how to wed the disparate parts of her personality into one written self. This discovery of how to "make herself through writing," to borrow Jerry Flieger's formulation, was the ultimate fruit of Colette's lifelong education as a writer.[11] When trying to understand how Colette reconciled her work with the values of her mother, I have found that, in addition to focusing on descriptions of Colette's education, it is essential to examine as well those moments when Colette explores the development of the self outside the classroom. As a result, we can find traces of Colette's coming to writing in places such as the vignettes I have discussed. It is in passages such as these that we can see most clearly how Colette explained and resolved the inner conflict she felt as a writer. In spite of all Colette's protests that she did not want to write and that she did not have a theory of writing, these passages give us a sense of Colette's aesthetic vision, ultimately a subtle yet complex intermingling of life and writing, of the feminine and the masculine, and of doing and reflecting.

Notes

1. In Colette's lifetime (1873-1954), France saw a number of gains for women including the extension of secondary education to young girls (1880), the right for married women to dispose of their own salary (1907), and the right to vote (1944).

2. Two excellent biographies which have articulated the internal and external conflicts. Colette faced as she came to writing are Michèle Sarde's *Colette: Free and Unfettered* and Judith Thurman's *Secrets of the Flesh: A Life of Colette.*

3. For example, Mary Lydon has written in her essay titled "Homework" of this inner conflict which Colette experienced: "the wish 'to see herself' as a writer had to be (doubly) veiled in order to slip pass the censor (internal and external) unobserved" (18). Colette repeatedly denied her desire to become or to be a writer, and yet this desire to write comes through not just in the fact of her writing, but in its substance as she demonstrates her pleasure in writing.

4. Although these two novels have been studied by many scholars, few have focused on the question of Colette's education. Instead, the majority of all Colette scholarship has focused on several issues which can be roughly organized into the following five categories autobiography, the construction of gender, mother-daughter relationships, the representation of women's experiences and, finally, women's writing. By far the two most popular "approaches" to Colette are via auto-biography and gender. These two categories account for approximately a quarter of the research done on Colette to date.

Among the large number of important studies of Colette on these topics, I would highlight the following as particularly useful ones: on autobiography: Jerry Aline Flieger's *Colette and the Fantom Subject of Autobiography* and Nancy K. Miller's "Writing Fictions: Women's Autobiography in France," in *Life/lines,* on gender: *Colette: The Woman, The Writer* edited by Erica Mendelson Eisinger and Mari Ward McCarty, on mother/daughter relationships: Laurie Corbin's *The Mother Mirror: Self Representation and the Mother Daughter Relationship in Colette, Simone de Beauvoir and Marguerite Duras.* Other areas which have received considerable attention are psychoanalytic approaches to Colette's work, examinations of her narrative techniques and structures, questions of intertextuality and explorations of space in her novels. There are a few studies of Colette in terms of education or pedagogy including the work of Joan Hinde Stewart, who has written on the parallels between *Claudine à l'école* and *La Maison de Claudine* in terms of education, and the work of Juliette Rogers, who has written articles which provide an excellent historical contextualization of the representation of women's education in Colette's novels.

5. I have chosen to refer to the child's world of experience as "imaginary" here because the idea that children have direct contact with the world around them seems to be an illusion created by Colette

(and other authors) as a way to account for their own nostalgia for childhood. In light of the teachings of Lacanian psychoanalysis. I would suggest that once children begin to understand language, all their experiences are in fact mediated by the language they use to make sense of them. In this way, children are more like adults then Colette may care to recognize. I would agree with Colette that children do seem to be more in tune with their other senses (smell, taste, touch) than adults. In this way, perhaps, their experience of the world is qualitatively different than that of adults. However, I would stop short of claims that children have an unmediated experience of the world around them.

6. Throughout *La Maison de Claudine* we find many instances in which reading and writing are linked with men. In one early chapter, Claudine's father is annoyed by the lack of respect his children have for "papier imprimé" (16). Later, Colette recalls that her nickname, "Bel-Gazou", which means "beau langue" in patois, was given to her by her father. Throughout the text, the father's domain is the library. It is to this room that he retires in one scene to salvage the scraps of a moth-eaten cape which belonged to Claudine's mother. He emerges triumphantly hours later with the cape transformed, not insignificantly, into a very chic "essuie-plume." Even in scenes such as this one which do not contain any explicit discussion of literature, the father is repeatedly associated with the written word. It is worth highlighting that Colette chooses her father's family name as her *nom de plume*.

7. This evocation of the sea and of travel recalls an earlier episode in the book, "La Petite," in which the young Claudine/Colette tells her friends she wants to be a sailor when she grows up. Like "La Couseuse," "La Petite" treats the issues of both separation from and return to the mother.

8. As we saw in the other passages, reading, though dangerous, can be counterbalanced by experience. Reading, unlike writing, does not necessarily represent an irreparable break with the mother.

9. Again, this passage evokes an earlier one titled "Le curé sur le mur." Here, Colette/Claudine asks her daughter what the is thinking. The young Bel-Gazou replies, "A nen, maman" and Colette/Claudine remarks approvingly, "C'est bien répondu. Je ne répondais pas autrement quand j'avais son age [. . .] Il n'est pas mauvais que les enfants remettent de temps en temps, avec politesse, les parents à leut place. Tout temple est sacré" (28).

10. Yet another passage which identifies her source of inspiration as domestic is the chapter titled "Au coin du feu" found in *En Pays connu*. Here, we find Colette seated by her fire which serves as her medium to recall ". . . des images qui sont lointaines, heureuses, grave profondément, qui dépendent du feu" (285). At the end of this chapter, she explains that although her mother taught her that she could not return to the past, she still pays attention to sparks that fly from her fire as though they might be signals or connectors to her past.

11. In an effort to explain how Colette resolved this conflict, Jerry Aline Flieger argues, "here the writing subject is a self-made woman, fabricated by the transaction of writing itself . . ." (10). This citation suggests that it is by writing that Colette, as we know her, came to be.

Works Cited

Colette. *Derniers écrits* in *Œuvres complètes de Colette: Tome 14*. Paris: Flammarion, 1973.

———. *En pays connu* in *Œuvres complètes de Colette: Tome 11*. Paris: Flammarion, 1973.

———. *Journal à rebours*. Paris: Ferenczi, 1936.

———. *La Maison de Claudine*. Paris: Le Livre de Poche, 1960.

———. *Mes Apprentissages* in *Œuvres complètes de Colette: Tome 8*. Paris: Flammarion, 1973.

Corbin, Laurie. *The Mother Mirror: Self-Representation and the Mother-Daughter Relation in Colette, Simone de Beauvoir, and Marguerite Duras*. New York: Peter Lang, 1996.

Eisinger, Erica Mendelson and Mari Ward McCarty eds. *Colette: The Woman, The Writer*. University Park, PA: Pennsylvania State UP, 1981.

Flieger, Jerry Aline. *Colette and the Fantom Subject of Autobiography*. Ithaca, NY: Cornell UP, 1992.

Lydon, Mary. *Skirting the Issue: Essays in Literary Theory*. Madison, WI: University of Wisconsin Press, 1995.

Makward, Christiane. "Colette and Signs: A Partial Reading of a Writer 'Born *Not* to Write'" in *Colette: The Woman, The Writer*. Erica Mendelson Eisinger and Mari Ward McCarty eds. University Park, PA: Pennsylvania State UP, 1981.

Mallet-Joris, Françoise. "A Womanly Vocation" Eleanor Reid Gibbard trans. *Colette: The Woman, The Writer*. Erica Mendelson Eisinger and Mari Ward McCarty eds. University Park, PA: Pennsylvania State UP, 1981.

Marks, Elaine. *Colette*. New Brunswick, NJ: Rutgers UP, 1960.

Miller, Nancy K. "Writing Fictions: Women's Autobiography in France." *Life/lines*. Bella Brodzki and Celeste Schenk eds. Ithaca, NY: Cornell UP, 1988.

Montaigne, Michel de. *Essais: Volume I,* André Tournon ed. Paris: Imprimérie Nationale Editions, 1998.

Resch, Yannick. *Corps féminin, corps textuel: Essai sur le personnage féminin dans l'œuvre de Colette.* Paris: Librairie C. Klincksieck, 1973.

Rodgers, Juliette. "Educating the Heroine: Turn-of-the-Century Feminism and French Women's Education Novels." *Women's Studies: An Interdisciplinary Journal.* New York: 1994 23:4 321-334.

Sarde, Michèle. *Colette: Free and Unfettered,* Richard Miller trans. New York: William Morris and Company, Inc., 1980.

Stewart, Joan Hinde. "The School and the Home." *Women's Studies: An Interdisciplinary Journal.* New York: 1981 8:3 259-272.

Thurman, Judith. *Secrets of the Flesh: A Life of Colette.* New York: Knopf, 1999.

Willy and Colette. *Claudine à l'école.* Paris: Le Livre de Poche, 1997.

Julie Solomon (essay date summer 2004)

SOURCE: Solomon, Julie. "*Feuille à Feuille*: The Coming of Spring in Colette's *La Vagabonde.*" *Nottingham French Studies* 43, no. 2 (summer 2004): 24-33.

[*In the following essay, Solomon discusses the image of the rose and the implications of ageing for a woman's sexuality in the novella* La Vagabonde.]

I. Winter to Spring

In *La Vagabonde,* Colette uses changes of place and climate to distort her experience of the passage of time. The story takes place over a period of several months, from December to May. Renée, whose very name suggests rebirth, is thirty-three years old and sees herself as hesitating between the autumn and the spring of her life. Can she blossom again, or, according to the relentless logic of femininity, is she beyond youth, and therefore beyond beauty and love? We will see that in the end it is a Ronsardian perspective that prevails, but that Colette gives it a new twist. By reworking the Ronsardian image of the rose Colette attempts to come to terms with the meaning of ageing for a woman and for her sexuality.

The novel begins in Paris, in the depths of winter. The narrator-heroine's life as a dancer and mime is described in terms of death and loneliness. The cold, the month of December, and the time of day—evening—all suggest old age. In the context of this paper, which reads *La Vagabonde* against Ronsard's *carpe diem* poems, this overdetermination of age and death imagery recalls the first lines of his famous 'Quand vous serez bien vieille'. Several of Renée's fellow performers are ill: Stéphane-le-danseur has tuberculosis, and Bouty suffers from gastric complaints. Bouty always has with him a little bottle of medicinal milk to treat his 'entérite chronique' (1077).[1] This liquid is not given the usual symbolic value of milk: fertile, nourishing, maternal. 'Il lampe à petites gorgées son verre de lait, un lait bleuâtre, comme de l'amidon' (1077). The dressing rooms are unheated. Everything is cold, grubby, dark, but Renée describes these bitter rigours of theatrical life with a certain relish that seems to grow from her sense of independence and her pride in her work. When she returns home after the performance, we find that she lives in a rather sterile, new area of Paris. Her building does not look like a solid home, but an unconvincing stage set: 'Ma maison [. . .] a 'l'air que ce n'est pas vrai' (1071). Emerging from the foggy night, her 'quartier' is described as empty, a sugary dessert: 'ce quartier neuf que j'habite, surgi tout blanc derrière les Ternes, décourage le regard et l'esprit. [. . . M]a rue, à cette heure, est un gâchis crémeux, praliné, marron-moka et jaune caramel, un dessert éboulé, fondu, où surnage le nougat des moellons' (1071). Again, this sickly sweet confection presents whiteness as sullied and nauseating rather than nourishing or pure.

Very quickly, the symbolism changes, apparently in response to the arrival on the scene of Max, Renée's new suitor. She goes for a Sunday morning walk in the *bois de Boulogne* with her god, Fossette, and even though the weather is still very cold, the time of day, the *joie de vivre* of the little dog, and the pink sunlight filtering through the fog suggest warmth and life. In the same way, we are now told that her modest apartment does boast a precious shaft of direct sunshine that lights up the bedroom all morning, making the ceiling glow pink. Not only is Renée's winter relieved of its harshness, but signs of the coming spring are already discernible as January begins. After another morning walk with Fossette she notices with pleasure 'une si surprenante et si molle douceur d'avant-printemps' (1113) in the air. The hint of warmth is the backdrop for her arrival home to meet her old friend Hamond for lunch. Hamond, an ageing portrait painter, is, like Renée, bitter about his failed marriage. He contributes a bunch of winter grapes to their meal: 'du beau raisin noir de décembre, d'un bleu de prune, dont chaque grain est une petite outre pleine d'eau insipide et douce' (1096). Hamond represents winter, a winter which is not without its compensations, but winter nonetheless: passion and its pain are only a memory for him. Renée thinks of herself in the same way, but is of course much younger. Hamond himself will in fact attempt to encourage her in the new relationship that offers itself in the person of Maxime Dufferein-Chautel. For a second lunch, on a slightly warmer morning, he arrives with Max in tow, pressuring Renée to accept the courtship of the young aristo-crat who has admired her at the music hall.

In the second part of the novel, as Max's courtship seems to be succeeding, the opposition between cold and warmth continues to carry the same rather unsur-prising values. Max is warmth, the heat of passion. The colours of sexuality are pink and deep red. Renée is ini-tially cold and contracted, 'rétractile' (1124-5). Max has warm, masculine hands, smells of tobacco, is big and comforting to embrace. With the approach of spring, Renée will find herself unable to resist the animal (as she sees it) force of sexual desire. And when she finally gives in to the pleasure of his embrace, she is a long way from Hamond's winter grapes. The kiss is de-scribed with the summery image of squeezing the juice from an overripe plum: 'malgré moi, ma bouche s'est laissé ouvrir, s'est ouverte, aussi irrésistiblement qu'une prune mûre se fend au soleil. [. . .] Je laisse l'homme qui m'a réveillée boire au fruit qu'il presse' (1159). Here, then, we are in the traditional territory of the *carpe diem*. Sexuality and beauty come to fruition and very quickly to decomposition. A woman should, and really can only, enjoy her beauty and the pleasures it both gives to others and makes available to her when she is a young rosebud. Roses and plums bloom, ripen and then die.

However, what seems at first to be an unproblematic use of a classic binary opposition soon becomes more complicated. If Max seems to represent the heat of pas-sion and summer's delicious but damaging languor he is also identified with a landscape of the north. His family home is in the Ardennes, a place of cool, dark, ancestral forests, protected by an explicitly castrating mother, 'la mère coupe-toujours'. Max's mother man-ages the 'patrimoine' of the family's forests as a 'maîtresse-femme': 'Elle coupe, elle coupe, et elle scie, et elle vend. [. . .] Mais elle n'abîme pas, vous savez! Elle sait ce que c'est que le bois, elle s'y entend comme un homme' (1145). Later, Max will chillingly evoke his ability to master her. She had objected to Renée as a daughter-in-law: 'Ma mère a bien crié un peu, mais je la laisse crier. Elle a toujours fait ce que j'ai voulu' (1208-9). Madame Coupe-Toujours is faithful and sub-servient to the patriarchal order she supports with such masculine strength. And this, of course, is the rôle that Renée would be expected to fill as Max's wife. Max's mastery over his mother and the family domain makes Renée uneasy. It reminds her of her first husband's power over her and over women in general, and makes her hesitate to give herself to this new love. The prop-erty in the Ardennes is the northernmost landscape de-scribed in **La Vagabonde**. Finally, even though Renée's sensuality is reawakened as a result of her nascent feel-ings for Max, this rebirth will in fact lead her away from him towards the south, the 'midi' and beyond, to South America.

Max, Renée and Hamond are walking in a wood near Paris, the *bois de Meudon*. It is a wintry landscape (mid-March, though). The woods are not frozen but wet with rain and cold. The damp smell of fallen leaves evokes different associations for the three characters. For Hamond, 'Ça sent l'automne' (1151). Renée on the other hand perceives the approach of spring in the sweet dampness of the forest: 'le clair jour gris, très doux, printanier' (1150); 'je me penchais pour boire un peu le vent faible, chargé du musc amer des anciennes feuilles décomposées' (1151). Both she and Max are also re-minded of the smell of the forest in their childhood homes: 'Ça sent comme chez nous' (1151). But their at-tachment to these wooded places does not bring them together.

Max's grand northern forests represent patriarchal sta-bility and staidness, while Renée's childhood home is more magical and feminine, filled with rainbows, dark waters and brambles: 'Vos forêts d'Ardennes humili-eraient, dans votre souvenir, mes taillis de chênes, de ronces, d'alisiers [. . .]' (1198). During her theatrical tour later in the novel, Renée passes through this re-gion. It is located between Dijon and Lorraine, and no doubt corresponds to Saint-Sauveur-en-Puisaye where Colette herself grew up. Colette and her biographers describe it as a small village in a poor region of Bur-gundy, about which such humility would be appropri-ate: 'Saint-Sauveur est construit à l'est d'une colline entourée des marécages et des vastes forêts de la 'Bour-gogne pauvre' qui a toutes les raisons d'envier la riche Bourgogne et ses vignobles aux noms chantants: Beau-jolais, Beaune, Chablis . . .'.[2]

For Renée, it is also the place that represents her virgin-ity and the first stirrings of desire before her marriage to Taillandy. At her apartment window, thinking of Max, Renée is reminded of an evening long ago, not a winter night in an *invraisemblable* Paris apartment, but a sum-mer night when as an adolescent she had discovered the certainty of love. Alive with innocence and exaltation, the young girl had leaned out into a perfumed and moonlit garden, 'cette nuit triomphale et solitaire, cou-ronnée de glycines et de roses! . . .' (1148). The femi-ninity of this warm, nocturnal garden contrasts with the diurnal and vertical order of the ancestral forests.

In the *bois de Meudon,* then, Renée and Max seem to be united by the damp, dead leaves as each is reminded of the smell of 'chez nous'. But the heroine's 'chez nous' must in fact be protected from Max and his kind. As Max's wife, she would be taken care of, husbanded, as we say in English, like the forests. She would bear his child and, as he reminds her with simple joy, 'tu ne pourrais plus me quitter, ni courir toute seule les grands chemins, hein? tu serais prise!' (1180). When they en-counter a doe during one of their forest walks Renée asks if he would have killed it while hunting: '"tuer une biche? Pourquoi pas une femme?" répondit-il simplement' (1186). Max's gallantry reminds Renée—and the reader—of the practical reasons behind chivalrous avoidance of doing violence to the female of the species.

In the third and final part of the novel Renée leaves Max behind in Paris while she undertakes a theatrical tour, having promised to become his mistress on her return. As their exchange of letters progresses, he finds himself asking her to marry him. But for Renée, this proposed marriage comes to represent a sunny, warm enclosure, a comfortable, safe and boring prison: 'Que vas-tu faire dans cette galère,' she asks herself, 'pas même! dans ce bateau-lavoir, solidement amarré, où l'on blanchit une lessive patriarcale?' (1223). The enclosed, stable place, and in particular the sun-warmed stone wall, figure on several occasions in the symbolic landscapes of **La Vagabonde**. Renée prefers adventure, uncertainty, constant motion. While she sometimes dreams of having a stable home, she in fact prefers her temporary apartment, her hotel rooms, making herself comfortable in a train compartment, launching herself on the uncertain and distinctly feminine waters of the ocean, and, finally, she prefers to be alone.

During the first days of her theatrical tour, Renée's letters to Max describe a cold and comfortless landscape, and beg him to warm her with his love. From Dijon:

> Il a plu sur mes deux premières stations, pour que je savoure mieux mon abominable abandon, entre des murs d'hôtel tendus de chocolat et de beige. [. . .] Il fait beau sur Dijon, d'ailleurs, et j'accueille timidement ce soleil, comme un cadeau qu'on va me reprendre tout de suite. [. . .] Quel froid crépuscule, si vous saviez! . . . Le ciel est vert et pur comme en janvier, lorsqu'il gèle très fort. Ecrivez-moi, aimez-moi, réchauffez votre Renée.
>
> (1197-8)

But Max's replies are not able to warm her as his presence does: 'Sa chaude sollicitude m'arrive, il s'en doute, toute refroidie sur ce papier, traduite en une écriture bien équilibrée' (1201). Max is unable to exert his attraction at a distance, in part because he is an indifferent writer. For reasons she does not yet understand, Renée wishes to complete her theatrical engagements before committing herself to a relationship with Max. She uses the letters she writes to him both to reassure him of the strength of her feelings, and to prevent him from attempting to join her on the trip. She writes love-letters promising that she is not dying from his absence but simply hibernating: 'Mon beau paysan, je n'en suis qu'endormie, j'hiverne. [. . .] Embrassez-moi bien serré, bien serré!' (1202).

As the tour continues southwards, this reassurance disappears. Renée sends descriptions of burgeoning, blossoming spring. Lyons is already 'doux, mou, gris' (1202). Travelling south in April and May creates an impression of accelerated Spring.

Je m'éloigne, c'est vrai, mon ami. Nous venons de dépasser Avignon et j'ai pu croire hier, en m'éveillant dans le train après un somme de deux heures, que j'avais dormi deux mois; le printemps était venu sur ma route, le printemps comme on l'imagine dans les contes de fées, l'exubérant, l'éphémère, l'irrésistible printemps du Midi, gras, frais, jailli en brusques verdures, en herbes déjà longues que le vent balance et moire, en arbres de Judée mauves, en paulownias couleur de pervenche grise, en faux ébéniers, en glycines, en roses!

(1205)

Renée is intoxicated by the heady rapidity with which spring rises to greet her. It seems at first to mirror her sexual reawakening. But the physical separation and Max's lack of prowess as a letter-writer gradually undo his masculine power. The extravagant and sudden spring advances as she moves away from her rich suitor until finally the choice between Max and solitude inverses the values established in the first part of the novel. While he waits for her in the northern climes of the Ardennes, the warmth of his sexual talents becomes associated with a stifling and enclosing stasis. The sensual reawakening linked to wisteria and roses, and to the delicious *midi*, can only be appreciated in solitude; its variety and intensity available to Renée if she travels alone, free to open herself to different experiences and emotions and to put them into words: 'le bonheur des solitaires' (1214) is expressed more and more clearly as she reacts, in Marseilles and other towns in the south of France, to his precipitous proposal of marriage.

Finally, in a pivotal scene which takes place in the *jardins de la fontaine* in Nîmes, she sees that 'tout ceci est encore mon royaume, un petit morceau des biens magnifiques que Dieu dispense aux passants, aux nomades, aux solitaires' (1217). Opposing her own definition of riches to that which would make the propertied gentleman's proposal so attractive, she affirms that 'La terre appartient à celui qui s'arrête un instant, contemple et s'en va; tout le soleil est au lézard nu qui s'y chauffe' (1217). Nudity, sensuality, warmth have clearly changed sides. Furthermore, the correspondence with Max has reawakened her pleasure in writing: 'comme s'il n'y avait pas de soin plus impérieux, dans ma vie, que de chercher des mots, des mots pour dire combien le soleil est jaune, et bleue la mer, et brillant le sel en frange de jais blanc . . .' (1220).

In Lyons Renée had been exhilarated by a cold wind that smelled of the sea:

> [J]'écoute le vent noir qui se lève et remonte le quai du Rhône avec un ronflement marin. D'où vient que je me balance ce soir sur une houle invisible, comme un navire que renfloue la mer? C'est un soir à voguer jusqu'à l'autre côté du monde. J'ai les joues froides, les oreilles glacées, le nez humide: tout mon animal se sent dispos, solide, aventureux . . .
>
> (1204)

Linked with the earlier evocations of animal pleasure in running through the winter forests with Fossette, this passage reminds us that even while Renée considers her female sexuality to be a simple animal instinct, it is not the only pleasure that her body seeks. Her desire to escape from Max is also about the wish to be sad, cold and uncomfortable at times, and not to limit her experience to warmth and safe pleasures.

II. VANITAS VANITATIS . . .

The term *vanitas* refers to *Ecclesiastes* 1,2: 'Vanity of vanities, saith the preacher; all is vanity.' ('Vanité des vanités, dit l'Ecclésiaste, vanité des vanités, tout est vanité.') A tradition of *vanitas* painting exists from the Renaissance, and was a particularly favoured theme in seventeenth-century Dutch art. Commonly still-life paintings, the images used to depict the transitory nature of life include abundant flowers, overripe fruits, snuffed candles, skulls, timepieces, and, of course, beautiful young women contemplating their image in a mirror. In fact, the *carpe diem* theme and the *vanitas* are remarkably close to each other in their representation of the fleeting nature of worldly pleasures. The difference is of course in the injunction: to despise the world, or to enjoy it while one may. In the third part of *La Vagabonde* the 'overripe plum' and its avatars tip over from the *carpe diem* to the imagery of the *vanitas*.

Roses figure prominently in *La Vagabonde*. Max sends a large bunch of flowers to her dressing room after their second meeting, and Renée's fellow music-hall artist, the young singer Jadin, immediately appreciates their value: 'Sa main rapide de chapardeuse [. . .] a saisi une grosse rose pourpre, avant que j'aie seulement ouvert la petite enveloppe [. . .]. J'ose dire que c'est des fleurs! dit Jadin [. . .] C'est votre ami?' (1103-4). Early in the tour, writing of the explosion of spring in Avignon, she describes the roses she has bought for herself: 'Les premières roses, mon ami aimé! [. . .] Elles embaument l'abricot, la vanille, le très fin cigare, la brume soignée, c'est l'odeur même, Max, de vos mains sèches et foncées . . .' (1205-6).

Ronsard's classic, and paradigmatic, use of the rose to figure feminine beauty in its brief perfection is, I think, an intertextual undercurrent in the imagery of *La Vagabonde,* particularly in the third part of the novel.

Comme on voit sur la branche au mois de mai la rose
En sa belle jeunesse, en sa première fleur,
Rendre le ciel jaloux de sa vive couleur,
Quand l'Aube de ses pleurs au point du jour l'arrose;
La grâce dans sa feuille, et l'amour se repose,
Embâmant les jardins et les arbres d'odeur;

I do not wish to claim that Colette's text consciously rewrites this particular sonnet, but it is an apt example of the discourse of the loss of beauty which Colette redefines in her novel. Renée's theatrical tour takes place

from the fifth of April to the fifteenth of May. The descriptions of spring and its flowers, roses in particular, underline, as does Ronsard, the symbolic value of the month of May, the dawn sky, the perfume and colour of the flowers.

In Nîmes, Renée writes that she is worried about younger rivals. Both she and Max are aged thirty-three, 'l'âge christique' of course, which adds further ironies to the question mark over the possibility of rebirth for the heroine of *La Vagabonde*. Renée is in any case aware that being in her early thirties, and unattached, is a vastly different position for a woman in 1911 than for a man:

> Nous avons le même âge, je ne suis plus une jeune femme. Imagine, ô mon amour, ta maturité de bel homme, dans quelques années, auprès de la mienne! Imagine-moi belle encore et désespérée, enragée dans mon armure de corset et de robe, sous mon fard et mes poudres, sous mes fragiles et jeunes couleurs . . . Imagine-moi belle comme une rose mûre qu'on ne doit pas toucher! Un regard de toi, appuyé sur une jeune femme, suffira à prolonger sur ma joue, le pli triste qu'y a creusé le sourire, mais une nuit heureuse dans tes bras coûtera davantage à ma beauté qui s'en va . . . J'atteins—tu le sais!—l'âge de l'ardeur.

(1215)

For Nancy Miller this expression to Max of her fear of losing him as she ages reads largely as an excuse: 'Renée rehearses a refusal comprehensible to Max's masculinity; a classically feminine insecurity about appearance'.[3] This argument of course has merit, but Renée is also very much concerned about the role of ageing and appearance in heterosexual love scenarios. Her rewriting of the story and her desire for freedom are real, but so is her acknowledgment of the social meaning of an ageing woman's face and body. She does not oppose the idea that women's beauty is fleeting. Ronsard continues:

> Mais battue ou de pluie, ou d'excessive ardeur,
> Languissante elle meurt, feuille à feuille déclose.

The heat of the sun and the fire of passion are damaging to the delicate rose, as are the tears of excessive emotion. Renée could almost be playing with this metaphor when she writes to Max in response to his marriage proposal. Attempting to hide her indecision, her desire to flee, she claims that: 'c'est trop de soleil, trop de lumière à la fois' (1212).

After describing herself as a 'rose mûre', then, Renée takes refuge in the *jardins de la fontaine*. These gardens are described as 'mon refuge élyséen' (1216), and the antique landscape is rich with evocations of mythology. Renée is Diana at her bath, not to be disturbed by curious hunters. The garden is outside time, as though last year's spring had endured, waiting for her. It is *féerique*, 'le printemps immobile et suspendu sur toutes choses' (1216). There are stone walls warming silently in the sun. But these walls do not enclose. They are ruins of a temple, an old tower; harmless vestiges of a long-gone empire. Diana's solitude and freedom are protected by them.

She is also protected by the weather. A storm approaches, the brisk wind has dropped and all is still and expectant. 'L'approche de l'orage a chassé tout intrus, et la grêle, l'ouragan, montent lentement de l'horizon, dans les flancs ballonnés d'un épais nuage ourlé de feu blanc' (1216). Waiting to be 'battue de pluie', she finally confesses to herself that she does not want to marry Max. Furthermore, she is afraid: 'Toute la vérité, que j'ai dû taire à Max, je me la dois. [. . .] "Je ne veux pas . . . il ne faut pas . . . j'ai peur!"' (1217). As she thinks through the ramifications of this *prise de conscience,* the storm approaches, 'versant goutte à goutte une eau paresseuse et parfumée. Une étoile de pluie s'écrase au coin de ma lèvre et je la bois, tiède, sucrée d'une poussière à goût de jonquille . . .' (1218). The rain is not only cleansing but nourishing. It is good milk, like that evoked in an earlier reverie, when she still imagined that Max offered this kind of renewal:

> Ne plus penser, Hamond, se terrer quelque part, avec lui, dans un pays qui me tendrait, à portée de ma bouche et de mes mains, tout ce qui s'offre et se dérobe à moi derrière la vitre du wagon [. . .]. A midi, dans les prés, les filles de fermes trayaient les vaches: je voyais, dans l'herbe profonde, les seaux de cuivre fourbi, où le lait mousseux giele en jets fins et raides. Quelle soif, quel douloureux désir j'avais de ce lait tiède, couronnée d'écume!
>
> (1178).[4]

The sweet spring rain belongs to the feminine, the maternal, the pre-symbolic. Renée no longer feels cut off from this life-giving power by her dancing career.

This rose is not destroyed by the heat and the rain. The storm itself is sensual. Renée is revivified, but the rebirth takes her away from the masculine fire of sexual passion and on to other experiences and to writing. Her rather dour friend and ex-sister-in-law, Margot, had predicted that she would be out of the frying pan of her marriage and back into the fire of some new relationship: 'chatte échaudée tu retourneras à la chaudière' (1108).[5] Instead, she is tempted by the ocean and the south. She gazes at the sea from her train window, early one morning, and finds that she has actually forgotten the existence of Max for a certain length of time. 'La mer! [. . .] Le soleil de sept heures, bas encore, ne la pénétrait point; elle refusait de se laisser posséder, gardant, mal éveillée, une teinte nocturne d'encre bleue, crêtée de blanc . . .' (1220). This is a feminine, nocturnal, dangerous sea. Like Diana, like the sea, Renée will not be possessed. She desires rather to possess all the riches of the earth through her own eyes and words. All the rest, she thinks, is ashes (1221). Where Ronsard's

rose is reduced to ashes by the violence of the rain and sun ('La parque t'a tuée et cendre tu reposes'), Renée revels in these experiences, leaves passion behind and is interested in anything but repose.

Brague, her fellow mime, asks whether she will be available for a theatrical tour to South America and she reacts with enthusiasm: 'L'Amérique du Sud! J'ai eu, à ces trois mots-là, un éblouissement d'illettrée qui voit le Nouveau Monde à travers une féerie d'étoiles en pluie, de fleurs géantes, de pierres précieuses et d'oiseaux mouches' (1223). Suddenly, Max is simply in the way. 'Et Max! Et Max! Encore! Jusqu'à quand le trouverai-je dans mes jambes, celui-là? [. . .] Alors moi, je n'existe que pour me soucier de cet encombrant rentier' (1223). In this passage, Max is for all the world like a demanding child, unable to look after himself, and tied to her apron strings. And returning to the safety of marriage becomes a symbolic return to the womb, a regressive flight from life. Christina Angelfors has shown that, in this novel, freedom is aligned with cold, loneliness and death, but that death is coded as positive. Symmetrically, passion is associated with life and warmth but the life-giving qualities of love are cloying, regressive, and, of course, illusory.[6] Here, then, Max is at once Renée's tyranical child and her suffocating mother in this symbolic regime. Even though she still finds herself dreaming of the comfort of his shoulder the decision is in reality already made.

As the month of May advances, Renée's tour brings her back towards the north, and very reluctantly towards Max.

> Le printemps craintif fuit devant nous. Il rajeunit d'heure en heure et se referme feuille à feuille, fleur à fleur, à mesure que nous regagnons le Nord. [. . .] L'azur plus pâle, l'herbe plus courte, une humidité acide de l'air créent l'illusion de rajeunir et de remonter le temps . . .
>
> (1225)[7]

Feuille à feuille. Ronsard uses the same phrase to describes the rose losing its petals one by one under the beating sun and rain. In **La Vagabonde** flowers close, returning to the state of virginal buds. Renée recognizes it as an illusion. She cannot recuperate the spring of her beauty or her virginity. But she can act upon the understanding gained during her magical parenthesis outside time. As she travels northward she retreats from the relationship with Max. 'Si je pouvais dévider à rebours les mois échus, jusqu'au jour d'hiver où Max entra dans ma loge . . .' (1225). This relationship was 'une manque', a mistake in knitting, a dropped stitch. The knitting must be undone and started again from the point of the mistake. 'Une "manque"! voilà donc ce qu'aura été dans ma vie, mon pauvre second amour, celui que je nommais ma chère chaleur, ma lumière . . .' (1225). A symbol of the mother-daughter dyad, this knitting image proposes an alternate warmth and sensuality to that she could have with Max.[8]

Finally, she embraces the chill northern air and leaves Max behind. Renée is no more than a shadow, alone and unremarked on a cold and dark train station. 'Un timbre fêlé grelotte timidement dans l'ombre, comme suspendu au cou d'un chien transi. [. . .] J'entends, là-bas, l'appel des sirènes sur la mer' (1228). She knows that she will sometimes wish for the pleasures she has foregone in leaving Max: 'Vagabonde et libre, je souhaiterai parfois l'ombre de tes murs' (1232). The petals, which Ronsard describes falling from the dying rose, fall too from Renée, one by one, as her desires and her eyes alight on the ceaseless variety of experiences that construct and will continue to be her life. For Colette, these petals, leaves, and small shadows, are not merely signs of loss, but traces of her presence and her passage that she leaves behind as she lives her life and grows older. The return to the world is a return to life and to a mortality unencumbered by the injunctions that a woman's value lies only in her brief moments as a rosebud.

> Je laisse, à chaque lieu de mes désirs errants, mille et mille ombres à ma ressemblance, effeuillées de moi, celle-ci sur la pierre chaude et bleue des combes de mon pays, celle-là au creux moite d'un vallon sans soleil, et cette autre qui suit l'oiseau, la voile, le vent et la vague.
>
> (1232)

The last petal to fall will indeed signal her death: 'jusqu'au jour où mes pas s'arrêteront et où s'envolera de moi une dernière petite ombre . . .' (1232).

This symbolism is indeed already present at the end of part one of the three-part novel. Renée describes her feelings about travel in the same terms: 'Les départs m'attristent et m'enivrent, c'est vrai, et quelque chose de moi se suspend à tout ce que je traverse [. . .] s'y accroche si passionnément qu'il me semble laisser derrière moi mille et mille petits fantômes à ma ressemblance [. . .]' (1119). *Partir,* of course, *c'est mourir un peu.* At the end of part one Renée wonders if the last little ghost, the one that is most truly her, is not the one that stays home, reading a book beside the fire. Now, at the end of the novel, as she looks forward to a life unencumbered by Max, revelling in her solitude and freedom, these 'fantômes' become shadows, and finally leaves and petals. The image suggests an acceptance of the loss of youth and beauty and indeed of mortality. And the return to writing that has taken place during the third part of the novel adds a further layer. Not only is Renée losing her petals like Ronsard's rose, but each becomes a leaf of paper, and will be preserved through her work as a writer.

It should not be forgotten that the Marie of 'Comme on voit sur la branche' dies very young. Ronsard underlines her youth, cut down in the first blush of her beauty:

> Ainsi en ta première et jeune nouveauté,
> Quand la Terre et le Ciel honoraient ta beauté,
> La Parque t'a tuée, et cendre tu reposes.

What is threatened in 'Mignonne allons voir' and 'Quand vous serez bien vieille' has actually occurred here. With the drooping of the rose comes a tragic death, rather than the humiliating loss of beauty and desirability (much less the fruition that in fact follows flowering). In fact, according to the Ronsardian perspective, this outcome is preferable, in that the young woman's body is preserved for eternal beauty by the poet's words. The fact that Renée is older is thus a part of her rethinking of the rose topos.

Renée, then, is at once the rose and the poet. Reborn to sensuality, to writing and to the world, she is not reborn to her youth. As she sheds her leaves and petals, they become texts. *Vagabondage* is not simply a way of fleeing sexuality for Renée. For in Colette's terms, the return to sexuality entails belief in the possibility of cyclic renewal of human life, a second spring. The choice of *vagabondage* means accepting the linearity of life, and the inevitability of ageing. Colette agrees with Ronsard that women's beauty is fleeting, that passion accelerates its destruction, and that only a poet's text can conserve it.

Ronsard's poem concludes:

> Pour obsèques reçois mes larmes et mes pleurs,
> Ce vase plein de lait, ce panier plein de fleurs,
> Afin que vif et mort ton corps ne soit que roses.

The milk and flowers Renée describes do not embalm her youthful body, but fill her with life and energy, a healthy desire for movement, freedom and solitude, and the capacity to nourish her own senses. Furthermore, and most importantly, it is Renée herself who seizes the pen, and writes for herself the experience of beauty and its loss. Her act of writing demonstrates that a text such as Ronsard's, rather than preserving the woman's body as an eternally fresh rose-bud, is actually a 'vanity' whose subject is ageing and mortality.

Notes

1. Colette, *La Vagabonde* (1910), in *Œuvres,* edited by Claude Pichois (Paris: Gallimard [Bibliothèque de la Pleiade], 1984). References to this edition will be given in parentheses in the text.

2. Claude Francis and Fernande Gontier, *Colette* (Paris: Perrin 1997), p. 30.

3. Nancy Miller, 'Woman of Letters: The Return to Writing in Colette's *The Vagabond*', in *Subject to Change: Reading Feminist Writing,* (New York: Columbia University Press, 1988), 229-64 (p. 253).

4. See also Nancy Miller's reading of this symbolically dense passage (op. cit., p. 247).

5. Of course, readers of Colette know that in the sequel to *La Vagabonde, L'Entrave* (1913), Renée will in fact return to be burnt again.

6. Angelfors, C., *La Double conscience. La prise de conscience féminine chez Colette, Simone de Beauvoir et Marie Cardinal,* (Lund: Lund University Press, 1989), p. 89.

7. Colette is not the only French author to exploit this topos. A more recent example is Michel Tournier short story 'L'air du muguet', in *Le coq de bruyère* (Paris: Gallimard, 1978).

8. See Miller, op. cit. p. 251

FURTHER READING

Bibliography

Norell, Donna M. *Colette: An Annotated Primary and Secondary Bibliography.* New York: Garland Publishing, Inc., 1993, 562 p.
  Thorough listing of primary and secondary sources through 1993.

Biographies

Francis, Claude Fernande Gontier. *Creating Colette: Vol. 1, From Ingenue to Libertine 1873-1913.* South Royalton, Vt.: Steerforth Press, 1998, 367 p.
  Focuses on Colette's life in Belle Époche France.

————. *Creating Colette: Vol. 2, From Baroness to Woman of Letters 1912-1954.* South Royalton, Vt.: Steerforth Press, 1998, 298 p.
  Covers Colette's later years.

Kristeva, Julia. *Colette.* New York: Columbia University Press, 2004, 521 p.
  Examines the life and work of Colette with an eye toward her autobiographical themes.

Thurman, Judith. *Secrets of the Flesh: A Life of Colette.* New York: Alfred A. Knopf, 1999, 579 p.
  Detailed academic biography that presents the author in the social milieu of early-twentieth-century Paris and highlights her unconventional morality.

Criticism

Holmes, Diana. "Disguise and Paradox in Colette's 'La Femme cachée.'" *Essays in French Literature* 23 (November 1986): 29-37.
  Considers the story "La Femme cachée" as an encapsulation of some of Colette's principal themes.

Jouve, Nicole Ward. "The Mother's Houses." In *Colette,* pp. 117-32. Sussex, United Kingdom: The Harvester Press, 1987.
  Explores the mother-daughter relationship in *Sido.*

McCarty, Mari. "Possessing Female Space: 'The Tender Shoot.'" *Women's Studies* 8 (1981): 367-74.
  Examines Colette's view of female space, which the critic characterizes as a refuge from patriarchy and phallic contracts, as depicted in the story "The Tender Shoot."

Phelps, Robert. "Introduction." In *The Collected Stories of Colette,* edited by Robert Phelps, pp. xi-xiii. New York: Farrar, Strauss, and Giroux, 1983.
  Maintains that Colette's primary interest as a writer was the joy and pain found in the private lives of individuals, and asserts that she strove to share her personal observations and perceptions of life with her readers.

Stockinger, Jacob. "Impurity and Sexual Politics in the Provinces: Colette's Anti-Idyll in 'The Patriarch.'" *Women's Studies* 8 (1981): 359-66.
  Examines the story "The Patriarch," asserting that Colette's focus on incest and male dominance was an expression of social criticism—thus refuting critics who view the author as an apolitical libertine.

Additional coverage of Colette's life and career is contained in the following sources published by Thomson Gale: *Contemporary Authors,* **Vol. 131;** *Contemporary Authors—Brief Entry,* **Vol. 104;** *Dictionary of Literary Biography,* **Vol. 65;** *DISCovering Authors 3.0; DISCovering Authors Modules,* **Eds. NOV;** *Encyclopedia of World Literature in the 20th Century,* **Ed. 3;** *European Writers,* **Vol. 9;** *Guide to French Literature,* **Vol. 1789 to the Present;** *Literary Resource Center; Major 20th-Century Writers,* **Eds. 1 and 2;** *Major 21st-Century Writers,* **Ed. 2005;** *Reference Guide to World Literature,* **Eds. 2 and 3;** *Short Story Criticism,* **Vol. 10;** *Twayne's World Authors;* **and** *Twentieth-Century Literary Criticism,* **Vols. 1, 5, and 16.**

Wilkie Collins
1824-1889

(Full name William Wilkie Collins.) English novelist, short story writer, travel writer, and playwright.

INTRODUCTION

Collins is remembered as a principal founder of English detective fiction, an early master of the mystery story, and one of the first writers of psychological thrillers. In addition to producing novels, plays, and journalism, Collins published a dozen novellas and fifty short stories. He often collaborated with his friend and mentor, Charles Dickens, co-writing serialized novels and stories for Dickens's magazine *Household Words*. Collins's stories were enormously popular in his day, but critics often dismissed his work as sensationalist. By the twentieth century, Collins began to receive recognition for his innovations in the detective and mystery genres. Some of his best-known short fiction includes "The Terribly Strange Bed" (1852), a story in which a gambler is almost suffocated by a bed canopy; "A Stolen Letter" (1855), a tale reminiscent of Edgar Allan Poe's "Purloined Letter"; the novella *The Haunted Hotel* (1878), whose highlight is a severed head; and the novella *The Frozen Deep* (1874), based on the ill-fated 1845 Franklin expedition to discover the Northwest Passage. Criticism of Collins's short fiction has focused on his early stories in the mystery genre, the writer's interest in the supernatural, and his collaborative efforts with Dickens.

BIOGRAPHICAL INFORMATION

Collins was born in London on 8 January 1824, the son of the renowned landscape painter William Collins. He was named for his father and his godfather, the artist Sir David Wilkie. Raised among artists and writers, Collins rebelled against the routine at the tea-broker's firm where, at the age of seventeen, he'd been placed by his father. He subsequently studied law at Lincoln's Inn and was called to the Bar in 1851, but was to use his legal expertise only when writing fiction. After his father's death in 1847, Collins wrote *Memoirs of the Life of William Collins, Esq., R.A.* (1848), and two years later published a lengthy novel, *Antonina; or, The Fall of Rome.* Soon after the publication of his first novel, Collins met Dickens, and the two became close friends, working together on Dickens's magazines, traveling to-

gether, and collaborating on stories. Collins achieved immense popularity after the publication of his sensation novel *The Woman in White* in 1860, which spawned a literary vogue for such fiction that peaked in 1868 with the appearance of his highly successful *The Moonstone*. Collins made dramatic adaptations of these and several of his other works of fiction, which were produced in England and the United States with fair success. After rising to fame, Collins became the subject of considerable scrutiny due to his unconventional personal life. Collins lived with his mistress—said to have been the model for the "woman in white"—and supported, in addition, another woman by whom he had three illegitimate children. Although Collins was accepted by literary friends, he was often ostracized by society at large. His rage at hypocrisy and perhaps his desire to emulate Dickens inspired Collins to compose the didactic novels and stories of his later years. He died in London in September of 1889.

MAJOR WORKS OF SHORT FICTION

Collins began writing short fiction after he met Dickens in 1851. In April of 1852 he wrote the story "A Terribly Strange Bed" for Dickens's periodical *Household Words*, and later that year, inspired by the success of Dickens's Christmas books, produced the story "Mr. Wray's Cash-Box." Collins soon became Dickens's most valued literary associate. He produced many stories and serialized novellas for Dickens's journal (of which he was co-editor), and in 1855 the pair produced a volume of Christmas stories together, entitled *The Holly Tree Inn*. The following year Collins joined the staff of *Household Words*, collaborating in earnest with Dickens on pieces for the magazine. Collins aided Dickens with the planning of the novella *The Wreck of the Golden Mary* (1856), for which he helped compose the frame narrative. Collins's own stories published in the magazine, which were often set in exotic locales and involved strong heroines, charlatans, and physical or psychological afflictions, became hugely popular with the reading public. In 1856 Collins's early stories were collected in his first solo volume, *After Dark*, which was enthusiastically received. This was followed in 1859 by *The Queen of Hearts*, a collection of stories told by three old brothers to a young girl, which also received favorable reviews. With the 1860 publication of his novel *The Woman in White*, Collins's fame grew. He produced a novel a year after that but also continued publishing stories in magazines, which were collected in *Miss or Mrs.?: And Other Stories in Outline* (1873) and in *Frozen Deep and Other Stories*. These later stories, however, are considered far inferior to his earlier short fiction. Collins produced six novellas in his later years, the best of which are *John Iago's Ghost* (1873-74), about a man who is thought to have been murdered but who returns after his accusers have been sentenced to death, and *The Haunted Hotel*, a sensational work about a group of friends who meet in an Italian castle-turned-hotel that they discover is haunted by a countess.

CRITICAL RECEPTION

Most criticism of Collins's work focuses on his longer works, particularly *The Woman in White* and *The Moonstone*, which are considered his best novels. Many critics writing about Collins's short stories view them as good entertainment—grippingly readable but lacking depth and psychological horror. Critics who have studied Collins's shorter works have emphasized his important place as one of the progenitors of the mystery story. They have also admired the writer's ability to amuse and his skill at handling the ingredients of "sensationist" fiction, using situations characteristic of Gothicism but then sublimating the appeal of fear in a rational atmosphere of suspense. Scholars have written extensively about Collins's collaboration with Dickens, viewing his time with the older novelist as his literary apprenticeship. They agree, too, that Collins's stories written after the late 1860s, which begin to reflect his views about the social problems in Victorian society, are far inferior to his earlier work. His reputation as a writer of short fiction rests solidly on the stories and novellas he wrote in the 1850s and 60s, in which he uses intricate plots and unexpected storylines to shock readers as well as to delight and amuse them.

PRINCIPAL WORKS

Short Fiction

"Mr. Wray's Cash-Box; or, The Mask and the Mystery: A Christmas Sketch" (short story) 1852; republished as "The Stolen Mask; or, The Mysterious Cash-Box" 1864

The Holly-Tree Inn [with Charles Dickens] (short stories) 1855

After Dark (short stories) 1856

The Wreck of the Golden Mary [with Charles Dickens] (novella) 1856

The Queen of Hearts (short stories) 1859

Miss or Mrs.?: and Other Stories in Outline (short stories) 1873; revised 1877

The Frozen Deep and Other Stories (short stories) 1874

The Haunted Hotel, a Mystery of Modern Venice (novella) 1878; republished as *The Haunted Hotel, a Mystery of Modern Venice, to Which Is Added: My Lady's Money.* (short stories) 1879

Little Novels. 3 vols. (novellas) 1887

Other Major Works

Memoirs of the Life of William Collins, Esq., R.A., with Selections from His Journals and Correspondence (biography) 1848

A Court Duel (play) 1850

Antonina; or, The Fall of Rome: A Romance of the Fifth Century (novel) 1850

Rambles beyond Railways; or, Notes in Cornwall Taken A-Foot (travelogue) 1851

Basil: A Story of Modern Life (novel) 1852

Hide and Seek (novel) 1854; revised as *Hide and Seek; or, The Mystery of Mary Grice* 1861

The Lighthouse [with Charles Dickens] (play) 1855

The Frozen Deep [with Charles Dickens] (play) 1857

The Two Apprentices: With a History of Their Lazy Tour [with Charles Dickens] (travel narratives) 1857

The Red Vial (play) 1858

The Woman in White (novel) 1860

A Message from the Sea: A Drama in Three Acts [with Charles Dickens and others] (play) 1861

No Name (novel) 1862

No Name: A Drama in Five Acts (play) 1863

Armadale (novel) 1866

Armadale: A Drama in Three Acts (play) 1866

No Thoroughfare: A Drama in Five Acts [with Charles Dickens and Charles Fechter] (play) 1867

The Moonstone (novel) 1868

Black and White: A Love Story in Three Acts [with Charles Fechter] (play) 1869

Man and Wife (novel) 1870

The Woman in White (play) 1871

Poor Miss Finch (novel) 1872

The New Magdalen (novel) 1873

The Law and the Lady (novel) 1875

The Two Destinies: A Romance 1876

The Moonstone (play) 1877

The Fallen Leaves (novel) 1879

A Rogue's Life: From His Birth to His Marriage (novel) 1879

Jezebel's Daughter (novel) 1880

The Black Robe (novel) 1881

Heart and Science: A Story of the Present Time (novel) 1883

Rags and Riches (play) 1883

The Evil Genius: A Domestic Story (novel) 1886

The Guilty River: A Story (novel) 1886

The Legacy of Cain (novel) 1889

Blind Love (unfinished novel) 1890

*The Lazy Tour of Two Idle Apprentices; No Thorough-
    fare; The Perils of Certain English Prisoners* [with
    Charles Dickens] (travel narratives) 1890
The Dead Secret (novel) 1899

CRITICISM

Saturday Review (review date 1859)

SOURCE: *"Saturday Review."* In *Wilkie Collins: The
Critical Heritage,* edited by Norman Page, pp. 74-77.
London: Routledge & Kegan Paul, 1974.

[*In the following 1859 review of* The Queen of Hearts,
*the critic asserts that Collins is a storyteller who seeks
to amuse rather than instruct, and finds that the author's tales are well written and cleverly contrived.*]

Both in his preface and in the body of his work, Mr.
Collins invites the reader to observe what is the object
which the author has set before him in composing the
series of tales collected under the name of the *Queen of
Hearts.* What Mr. Collins aims at is being a story-teller.
He wishes to construct a narrative the effect of which
shall be to awake, sustain, and satisfy the interest of the
reader. There are plenty of novels written in these days
to unfold the philosophy or to instil the instruction
which finds favour with the writer. There are novels in
which the author attempts to elaborate character, and to
show how certain vices or virtues are revealed or fostered by the circumstances in which the actors of the
fiction are placed. There are, again, novels intended to
describe states of society which have passed away, or
ways of life unfamiliar to the English public, or scen-
ery, customs, and institutions foreign to our usual habits
of thought. Mr. Collins considers that all these attempts
are divergencies from the proper duty of a novelist. A
story-teller should have a story to tell, and should tell
it. It is his business not to improve or to instruct mankind, but to amuse. Common life is full of strange incidents. If these are related disjointedly and unmethodi-
cally, the attention of a reader or hearer is only
momentarily arrested. But here lies the field for a novelist's skill. He can so arrange the story that the interest
shall be prolonged. He can devise a number of minute
incidents, all converging in a central point. He can bring
constantly home to the conviction of his reader that this
central point exists, and yet can conceal what it is. He
can manage that, when this central point is revealed, all
that before seemed obscure shall seem clear, and every
main incident shall appear to have occurred independently and naturally, though conducing to the evolution
of the final mystery. A story thus becomes a well-
managed puzzle. First of all, the narrator has to find the
right sort of puzzle to set. It must be something nearly
connected with common life, or the final explication
will appear forced. At the same time, it must be something removed from every-day experience, or the theatre of action will seem too mean or obscure. Then,
when the right species of puzzle has been hit on, the
storyteller must set it in the right way, using none but
legitimate contrivances, and coming to an end when the
facts of which he makes use naturally lead him to do
so. Mr. Collins asks his readers and critics to observe
that this is by no means an easy thing to do, and he
claims that he shall have due credit for any success he
may have achieved in carrying out his conception of his
art.

There are ten stories in the three volumes which bear
the title of the *Queen of Hearts.* They are held together
by a device which is at least as good as such devices
generally are. A young lady comes to stay with three
old brothers in a lonely Welsh valley, and the son of
one of these brothers is in love with her. The lover is
away from home, and in order to detain her till he
comes, the old men agree to read a story in the evenings. These separate stories are exceedingly well told.
They are possible, interesting, and natural, and have the
great merit that they stop when it is probable in real life
they would have stopped. We may take as a specimen a
story called **'The Dead Hand.'** A young man going to
Doncaster in the race week is obliged to sleep in a
double-bedded room, and finds that the occupant of the
other bed is a corpse. He strikes a light in the middle of
the night, and to his horror sees that the hand of the
corpse has moved. He awakens the house; medical aid
is obtained, and the dead man is restored from his trance
to life. The young stranger does not learn who the person is whom he has resuscitated, but the doctor, who is
acquainted with the family, discovers that the supposed
dead man is an illegitimate brother of the young man.
Some years afterwards, a stranger arrives at the doctor's
surgery, and bringing a recommendation with him applies, under an assumed name, to be the doctor's assistant. He is received on this footing, and stays with the
doctor several years. The doctor strongly suspects that
the stranger is the man who had been laid out as dead,
but he never can make himself quite sure. Here the
story ends, and it is slight enough to make its chief interest centre in the manner of its treatment. The moving
of the limbs of a supposed corpse is one of those incidents which we know to be possible, for evidence is
abundant that the circumstance has often happened, but
it is uncommon, and horrible enough to thrill the nerves
of readers. Of course, the art of the story chiefly consists in the manner in which we are prepared for the
moving of the hand. We are told how the young man
came to hire the room—how he was persuaded to stay
in the room when he found that he had a dead man beside him—and how the thought of his room-fellow fas-

cinated him, until he could not avoid watching the dead body closely. But although our interest is thus worked up, it is worked up in a legitimate manner. This young man is not represented as a peculiarly nervous or fanciful person. He does not undergo the excitement which might befall a mind of unusual timidity or strength of imagination. He feels merely what an ordinary young man would feel. After the dead man is recovered, the interest is sustained by the suggestion that the two are brothers; but the complication of circumstances is not more curious or more wonderfully unravelled than is customary in real life, and at the end of the story we are left in uncertainty whether the dead man revisited the doctor or not. This is evidently a contrivance of the artist to bring us to the level of the uncertainties of daily experience, for it might be objected that the point could scarcely be left in doubt between persons who were for years in constant intercourse. Mr. Collins is willing to run the risk of this being considered slightly improbable in order that he may finish without any excessive wonder of a catastrophe. There can be no doubt that the contrivance succeeds, and an air of reality is thus imparted to the narrative.

Occasionally, however, we have to complain of incidents in these stories which are too poor and thin for the occasion. . . .

We notice, too, in all the stories a very great similarity of talking, thinking, and acting. Everybody, whatever may be his or her sex, age, or education, uses precisely the same language and entertains precisely the same views of right and wrong, of what is expedient, customary, and practical. The whole group of stories, therefore, seems worse than any one does when taken by itself.

Still, the stories are well written and very cleverly contrived. According to Mr. Collins' views of a storyteller's duty, his success has been great. It requires much thought, much patient elaboration, great practice, and considerable native power to tell a tale as he tells it. Very few people could tell a story founded on the incidents selected by Mr. Collins, so well as he does. But we cannot agree with him that this art of setting and solving a puzzle is anything like the ideal of a novelist. It is an ingenious trick, and produces a very good marketable novel. But it is by no means a great performance. If we compare the work of a great master with these stories of Mr. Collins, we perceive at once how very small a thing it is to keep the interest of the reader alive in the same way, although in a higher degree, as it is sustained by a newspaper anecdote. The story of the *Bride of Lammermoor* is exactly the story which Mr. Collins would like to tell. But the *Bride of Lammermoor* is a masterpiece, not because it leads us naturally to a fearful catastrophe, but because in doing so it un-

folds to us the characters of Lucy Ashton, Caleb Balderstone, and the Master of Ravenswood. We read on without the sense of an ingenious puzzle, and yet at the end the story seems almost painfully real. Mr. Collins constructs his machinery well, but he never rises above a machinist. He avoids entirely drawing character. There is no more interest about the people of whom he tells us in themselves than there is about the sufferer when we read in a newspaper that a farmer was robbed, a lady knocked down, or a clergyman assaulted. There is some interest in the fact that persons of this description sustained the calamities mentioned, but the interest is in the fact, not in the individual. If Mr. Collins were to tell the story of the Bride of Lammermoor, he would, on his principle of setting us a puzzling plot, merely have to tell us that Lucy Ashton was a young Scotch lady. We need scarcely go into the reasons which have long ago decided great artists to believe that it is in the combination of characters which appeal to our feelings, with a good machinery, that the ideal of fiction lies. As compared with the host of foolish novels that are written every year, Mr. Collins' stories are good—for the ordinary novel has no character and no plot. But although, by careful attention to his machinery, Mr. Collins achieves a definite success, this success is a small one.

William H. Marshall (essay date 1970)

SOURCE: Marshall, William H. "The Shorter Works through 1870" and "Uneven Shadows." In *Wilkie Collins*, pp. 40-50, 108-12. New York: Twayne Publishers, Inc., 1970.

[*In the following excerpt, Marshall offers brief analyses of Collins's novellas and short stories written prior to 1870, then of the short fiction he published in his last years, which the critic notes is of far less merit than Collins's earlier work.*]

I. THE NOVELETTES

Any discussion of Wilkie Collins' shorter fiction initially runs the risk of floundering upon the question of definition. The obvious imprecision of the terms *novelette* and *short story* is compounded by the fact that, whatever the first form of publication might have been (often in *Household Words* or *All the Year Round*), a number of the shorter pieces of fiction were indiscriminantly collected as "stories" in *After Dark* (1856) and in *The Queen of Hearts* (1859). In general, the division employed in this study, between the novelettes and the short stories, has been set forth by those previously concerned with Collins and his work; though it is not always borne out by significant differences in lengths.

Qualitatively, the differences may be even less discernible. So long as Collins restricted himself to an incident or at most a brief episode, as in **"A Terribly Strange Bed,"** success in the short story was likely. But to protract the narrative to a series of events or to attain the *sursis indefini* supporting certain kinds of dramatic effect, he required greater length than the short story allowed. Most of his novelettes are well constructed and filled with characters of credible and significant motivation, but the novel offered the opportunity most suited to Collins' abilities. Aside from the restrictions placed upon him by ill health and by his work as an editorial associate during the early years of *All the Year Round* (established by Dickens on April 30, 1859),[1] there may be other significance in the fact that during his major period—from the appearance of *The Woman in White* in 1860 through the publication of *Man and Wife* in 1870—Collins published neither novelettes nor short stories; certainly, the amount of work required to create the five major novels is a principal cause, but the degree to which they satisfied his creative demands remains at least a possibility.

Mr. Wray's Cash Box, Collins' first novelette, was published in one volume by Bentley as a Christmas book in December, 1851. A work of slight intrinsic merit, it came between *Antonina* and *Basil*; it marks, therefore, Collins' departure from the model set forth by Bulwer Lytton to the "actual." Although the influence of Dickens (and particularly of the Dickens of Christmas stories and plum pudding) is easily discernible, certain subjects and techniques which become familiar in Collins' later fiction are apparent here: the lack of action and mobility, the use of dreams, the concern with shock and alternating psychological states, types such as the country squire and the parson, and art used as a symbol of identity.

Mr. Reuben Wray, in *Mr. Wray's Cash Box,* a retired player of small parts under John Kemble, makes a living for his granddaughter Annie by giving elocution lessons and by directing amateur private theatricals (all in the manner of the adored Kemble). At Stratford-on-Avon, Reuben secretly takes a mold and makes a cast of the famous Shakespeare bust; afraid of discovery, he quickly leaves Stratford and goes to Tidbury-on-the-Marsh, with the mask in his otherwise empty cash box. Chummy Dick and Benjamin Grimes steal Reuben's box, expectedly believing that it contains cash; in the course of their flight, they shatter the mask and with it Reuben Wray's symbol of identity. The old man falls into shock and hovers near insanity. Annie, knowing that the mold was left at Stratford, returns secretly, and retrieves it. Thereafter, repressing all recent recollections by accepting their content as a dream, Reuben is able to join his granddaughter and his Tidbury friends for a huge and jolly Christmas dinner.

Gabriel's Marriage (1853) reveals a significant improvement in the control of materials and the penetration of a character's state of mind. Set in Brittany during the suppression of the Church by the French Revolution, the story concerns a young man's suspicions that his father has committed murder, which he regards as a moral barrier to his own planned marriage. Only after Gabriel has seen his simple world shattered by these suspicions, which are themselves ultimately resolved, can he begin to build a new kind of faith—one sustained by the image of Father Paul, the messianic priest who defies the Revolution—and then to look forward to happiness with his betrothed, Perrine. Although the theme of expiation, to become central in much of Collins' later work, has been implicit in Numerian's guilt over misjudgment of Antonina and in Basil's writing the story of his terrible error, it is first made explicit in the task that Gabriel's father assumes in payment for his crime: rebuilding wayside crosses destroyed during the Revolution.

Sister Rose (1855), a tale of the French Terror, involves the sentencing of the innocent and the momentary triumph of the guilty. It sustains suspense until the dénouement; yet, by dividing the story into parts, between which action can be assumed to occur and time to pass, Collins was able to avoid the direct report of action that in this case would have detracted from the state of psychological tension through which the narrative survives. The structure of the novelette rests upon the principle of duplexity, the struggle of wits between the treacherous former aristocrat, Charles Danville—who betrays his brother-in-law and his wife to the Terror—and Lomaque, once the land-steward for Danville and now an official of the Revolution. Lomaque finally wins, of course; while, in a memorable scene, Danville is exposed as the hypocrite that he is. Because of the intensity of the action and mood, the relief that the conclusion brings—with death for Danville and secluded peace for Rose—far outweighs any incredulity felt about the means by which Lomaque saves the lives of Rose Danville and her brother during the resultant confusion as Robespierre goes to the guillotine.

That Rose is saved marks an emerging characteristic of Collins' work, which, for better or worse, was to be exploited in a number of ways—the return to life of those presumed by someone to be dead. In Collins' first novel Antonina herself was left for dead by the Huns and later stabbed almost fatally by Goisvintha; in *Basil,* Mannion recovers from the beating which the protagonist fears has been fatal; the grandfather of young Gabriel makes a deathbed confession and glides into the darkening shadows, but before they have become opaque, he momentarily emerges to retract his words; and in the same narrative the victim of "murder" rises to walk again. In each instance revival is essential for the furtherance of the narrative beyond a specific point; in *Sister Rose* the return to life and freedom of those presumed to have died becomes the central point on which all action and the resolution of the narrative must rest.

In *The Yellow Mask* (1855)—a work firmly in the Protestant middle-class tradition, akin to Matthew Gregory Lewis' novel *The Monk* (1796)—Father Rocco, a Pisan priest and the brother of the master-sculptor Luca Lomi, schemes that Luca's daughter Maddalena might marry Fabio, a wealthy nobleman studying under Luca. Having learned that Fabio's family acquired much of its wealth during the confiscation of Church lands, Rocco hopes by his scheme to restore what he feels rightfully belongs to the Church. But Fabio falls in love with Nanina, a poor young girl modelling in the studio, whom Father Rocco subsequently persuades to disappear to Florence, where he places her in a family that can spy on her for him. Fabio marries Maddalena, who dies in childbirth, leaving a daughter, whom Rocco must now plan to train in order to influence Fabio to restore the Church's wealth.

Nanina, discovering that Father Rocco has arranged to have her watched, quietly returns to Pisa, where she obtains work serving at a masked ball at which, it is rumored, Fabio will make his first social appearance following the death of his wife. At the ball, Fabio is persistently annoyed by a woman in a yellow mask, who, finally alone with him, removes the mask and reveals what appears to be the face of his wife. In the shock that follows, Fabio hangs near death but is slowly nursed to health by Nanina. By accident, she discovers that the woman was Brigida, once hopeful of marrying Fabio and acquiring his wealth, who has been in the employ of Father Rocco; hoping to frighten Fabio and thereby prevent his marriage to Nanina, Rocco had taken a mask of Maddalena from a statue in Luca's studio. Discovered, Rocco makes a confession to Rome; he is soon summoned there and is heard of no more. Brigida leaves Pisa, "alone and penniless." And, completing the moral tidiness of the conclusion, Fabio and Nanina find happiness, rearing Fabio's daughter by his first marriage.

Collins wrote *Mad Monkton* in February 1852, but—first rejected by Dickens, on the grounds that its subject, hereditary insanity, might distress the readers of *Household Words*[2]—it was not published until late in 1855 in *Fraser's Magazine*. The narrative concerns one episode, recalled in a straightforward fashion by the speaker, a friend to Alfred (sometimes called "Mad") Monkton; its effects depend largely upon language and situations calculated to protract uncertainty and to intensify suspense:

> At the head of the staircase my friend the *attaché* met me.

"What! going away already?" said he.

"Yes; and on a very curious expedition. I am going to Monkton's rooms, by his own invitation."

"You don't mean it! Upon my honor, you're a bold fellow to trust yourself alone with 'Mad Monkton' when the moon is at the full."

"He is ill, poor fellow. Besides, I don't think him half as mad as you do."

"We won't dispute about that; but mark my words, he has not asked you to go where no visitor has ever been admitted before without a special purpose. I predict that you will see or hear something to-night which you will remember for the rest of your life."

We parted. When I knocked at the court-yard gate of the house where Monkton lived, my friend's last words on the palace staircase recurred to me, and, though I had laughed at him when he spoke them, I began to suspect even then that his prediction would be fulfilled.

(Chapter II)

As it turns out, Alfred Monkton is not at all dangerous. The survivor of an ancient Roman Catholic family, he is presumed to carry the family curse of insanity, to which others attribute any unusual behavior on his part. Actually, it is quite a different curse that Monkton feels himself bearing; for this reason he has postponed his marriage and made the present journey to Naples. An ancient family prophecy, written on the blank leaf of one of the manuscripts at Wincot Abbey, foretells that at the time one of the Monktons lies unburied under a foreign sky, "Monkton's race shall pass away." Alfred Monkton wishes, therefore, to locate the resting place of his scapegrace uncle, Stephen Monkton, reportedly killed in a duel, and seeks the narrator's help in his search.

Slowly, guided by the rational conclusions on the part of the narrator, they move closer to the location of the body. The narrator approaches a monastery, of which the description, equalling anything else in Collins' work, illustrates one way that Collins, using a single episode, sustained interest in his narratives. It begins:

> It was a dark, low, sinister-looking place. Not a sign of life or movement was visible any where about it. Green stains streaked the once white façade of the chapel in all directions. Moss clustered thick in every crevice of the heavy scowling wall that surrounded the convent. Long lank weeds grew out of the fissures of roof and parapet, and, drooping far downward, waved wearily in and out of the barred dormitory windows. The very cross opposite the entrance-gate, with a shocking life-sized figure in wood nailed to it, was so beset at the base with crawling creatures, and looked so slimy, green, and rotten all the way up, that I absolutely shrank from it.

(Chapter V)

The speaker proceeds, however, and discovers the body of the slain Monkton, unburied and rotting in an outbuilding of the monastery. In time, after various kinds of negotiation, Alfred Monkton prepares to return with the body to the vaults of Wincot Abbey. He thus believes that, if the curse someday is worked out effectively, it at least will not do so through his agency or neglect. But the body remains *outside* the vaults of the Abbey, and the prophecy *is* fulfilled. The storm that sinks the boat is not in any way extrarational, a fact that is of some structural significance; the narrative itself, cast in the words of a highly rational speaker, is primarily concerned with the natural means by which an essentially supernatural prediction is fulfilled.

The Dream Woman (1855), a straightforward story, has some of the qualities of the ballad narrative. An ostler, "Unlucky Isaac" Scatchard, spending a night away from home in an inn, is attacked with a knife by a "dream woman," who is fair and fine and has a slight droop in her left eyelid. In the years that follow this incident, he encounters the woman of the dream once more, marries her in sympathy, but discovers her to be a drunkard who indeed attempts to murder him with the same knife. The preoccupation with the apparition and what it foretells for the protagonist is an early instance of Collins' use of the prophetic dream, a device appearing with increasing frequency in his later works. Here, as in the novel *Armadale* (1866), a character gives a full account of a dream, in this instance Isaac to his mother, that she might record it as a warning against events of the future.

As in most of Collins' other works, two sensibilities are operating in *The Dream Woman.* By one, that of Isaac Scatchard and his mother, the dream is regarded as at least supernaturally revelational, a prophecy; by the other, ironically informing the narrative from a point outside it, recording the events in the episode, the association between dream and reality is seen as coincidental but in no way necessary. The presence of the two sensibilities is far less obvious than in *Mad Monkton,* in which the tone of the narrative is explicitly rational. As in the case of determining the real nature of Sarah Leeson's "dead secret," the reader is allowed a choice of what to believe; and by his choice he does not judge the story so much as the story reveals *his* sensibility.

A Rogue's Life (*Household Words,* 1856; 1879) represents a departure from Collins' characteristic mode. In the manner of Thackeray's *The Memoirs of Barry Lyndon Esq.* (1884), the outlaw tells his own story, thereby passing significant judgment upon the society that has superficially judged him. Thus, the work becomes the first full instance of Collins' fiction of social purpose, though here it is cast in a facetious tone that on occasion may seem overbearing. Collins did not return to this type of fiction, in which an outlaw is sympathetically portrayed as the central character. However, in *No Name* (1862) Captain Wragge dominates much of the action, accumulating sympathy for his roguery as he

continues to act. As in much picaresque storytelling, the rogue himself is extraordinarily likeable.

The son of a physician who is kept poor because he must live up to his own position as son-in-law to a Lady, the narrator of *A Rogue's Life* is soon forced to earn his way in the world by his own devices. These always assume the form of fraud—copying "Old Masters," which are then sold as authentic; serving as secretary to a Literary and Scientific Institution in the town of Duskydale; and finally, counterfeiting coins. In each case, by his deception of society he judges the very people who through their laws would claim to judge him. Ultimately, of course, he must triumph, for the society in which he operates is essentially false and will in time find a place for a man of consummate fraudulence.

In Australia, to which he has been transported, he is able, by the adroitness of his maneuvers, to become, two years before the expiration of his sentence, "a convict aristocrat—a prosperous, wealthy, highly respectable mercantile man. . . . I have a barouche and two bay horses, a coachman and a page in neat liveries, three charming children, and a French governess, a boudoir and lady's-maid for my wife. She is as handsome as ever, but getting a little fat. So am I, as a worthy friend remarked when I recently appeared holding the plate, at our last charity sermon" (Postscript). Presumably, a prosperous reader of *Household Words* would be amused at the narrator's evil doings or at the chase of the counterfeiters by the Bow Street Runners; he would see not himself in the concluding portrait but a rather dreadful fellow who had managed to prosper in Australia, where the laws were not very firm and where society was not founded on sound business principles.

The final novelette during this period, *A Plot in Private Life* (1858), offers little in comparison with its predecessors. It concerns the marriage of a wealthy widow to an enterprising man, Mr. James Smith, who soon becomes his wife's foil, just as Josephine, an unfaithful maid to Mrs. Smith, becomes the foil to Mrs. Smith's faithful servant and confidant, William. Despite Smith's attempts at extortion, his bigamy, and Josephine's having Mrs. Smith and William prosecuted for Smith's murder, the principal villain is found to be living—in that kind of revival that Collins often used—and all ends well.

Clearly, during this period Collins' attainments in the novelette were as uneven as his subjects were varied.

II. THE SHORT STORIES

Aside from the short stories in the Christmas numbers of *Household Words,* in which Collins collaborated with Dickens to an undetermined extent, before 1860 Wilkie

Collins wrote and published ten short stories. Of these, the most celebrated among Collins' shorter pieces and the one most frequently anthologized is **"A Terribly Strange Bed"** (1852). In it, two young Englishmen in Paris decide to visit a blackguard gambling house, where the narrator breaks the bank at *rouge et noir*. Made drunk in celebration by those who own the house and persuaded to pass the night, the narrator soon realizes that he has been drugged; fighting his impulse to sleep, he finally lies down but becomes aware, barely in time, that the top of the canopy of the bed is descending to crush him. In the narrative there is little conflict, except between the narrator himself and the forces of evil which momentarily he is unable to explain. As he learns later, the canopy is controlled not by any force beyond comprehension but by a simple mechanism operated through the ceiling from the room above. The effect of this story derives from the sustained tension created by the struggle between the man and the unknown force.

In **"The Stolen Letter"** (1854), a trivial piece, the son of a haughty squire, about to marry a governess, is victimized by a blackmailer; when he is saved by a benign lawyer—a familiar Collins type—the story ends on a happy note. More successful is **"The Lady of Glenwith Grange,"** written especially for publication in *After Dark.* Suggesting Miss Havisham of Dickens' later novel *Great Expectations* (1859), Ida Welwyn, a spinster, retains Glenwith Grange as a macabre monument to her own dead past and to the younger sister whose tragic marriage had destroyed her. The story has sufficient incident, credibly recorded, to sustain it.

"The Diary of Anne Rodway" (1856) is both Collins' first use of the epistolary method—to become one of his most important devices—and his first murder mystery. Anne, a miserably poor young woman, supports herself by needlework. Her close friend Mary Mallinson, the daughter of a brutal drunkard and a woman even more desperate than Anne, is an addict to laudanum. One night Mary is brought home unconscious from a blow on the head, from which she dies. Though the inquest rules her death accidental, Anne refuses to accept this verdict; tracing the murderer by a clue found on Mary's person, Anne solves the crime.

"The Siege of the Black Cottage" (1857) is an undistinguished recounting of a young girl's bravery in saving a sum of money belonging to others from the grasp of two petty outlaws. **"Uncle George; or the Family Mystery"** (1857) concerns a young man's discovery of the reason for the disappearance of a favorite uncle many years before. **"The Dead Hand"** (1857) is, perhaps more than any other of the short stories, an incident deprived of external conflict. The story rests upon the protagonist's opposing responses to the situation in which he finds himself when he shares a room with twin beds in an inn with a person whom he soon presumes to be dead.

In Collins' **"The Biter Bit"** (1858), usually regarded as the first humorous detective story,[3] Matthew Sharpin, a somewhat too confident young man who is forced by others upon the Detective Police, is given his first case; he incredibly mismanages it with what amounts to a travesty of the rational process. The absurdity of his activities in the fulfillment of his role is intensified by the epistolary form that the story assumes, with the majority of the letters coming immodestly but revealingly from Sharpin himself. "I am now comfortably established next door to Mr. Jay, and I am delighted to say that I have two holes in the partition instead of one," Sharpin writes, characteristically, to Chief Inspector Theakstone of the suspect he is pursuing:

> My natural sense of humor has led me into the pardonable extravagance of giving them both appropriate names. One I call my peep-hole, and the other my pipe-hole. The name of the first explains itself; the name of the second refers to a small tin pipe or tube inserted in the hole, and twisted so that the mouth of it comes close to my ear while I am standing at my post of observation. Thus, while I am looking at Mr. Jay through my peep-hole, I can hear every word that may be spoken in his room through my pipe-hole.

If **"The Biter Bit"** is the most amusing of this group of stories, **"Fauntleroy"** (1858) is clearly the warmest. Based upon the life and death of Henry Fauntleroy (1785-1824), hanged for forgery,[4] the story is told by one man who, though recognizing fully the evil in Fauntleroy's act, nevertheless defends him as a man with strong loyalties and personal integrity. Like so many of Wilkie Collins' other characters, the protagonist emerges as one who is tempered in his worst moments by a strong flame of good.

Following **"Fauntleroy,"** **"The Parson's Scruple"** (1859) comes as an anticlimax. In this story a fundamentalist preacher who marries a young "widow" discovers that she is really a divorcée, and leaves her. Represented is an early form of Collins' protest against the unfairness of marriage laws in the United Kingdom.

The majority of Collins' short stories, while not outright failures, probably have little to recommend them either on esthetic grounds or for the needs of the modern reader. Of the ten published before 1860, **"A Terribly Strange Bed"** might be joined in the anthologies by **"The Dead Hand,"** **"The Biter Bit,"** and **"Fauntleroy,"** each bringing to the collection its own particular appeal. But, beyond these, each of the others probably best serves the student of literature in revealing an analogue with a major element in one of Dickens' principal novels or in displaying the growth in Collins' own work.

In 1856 Collins brought together three of his novelettes and three short stories in the two volumes which Smith and Elder published as *After Dark.* He made some attempt at imposing cohesiveness upon the collection by casting it as a volume dictated to Mrs. Leah Kerby by her husband, a travelling portrait painter whose ailing eyes force him to rest from his accustomed work and to find another means to support his family—the production of a collection of the stories that he has heard during his professional travels.

In 1859, when Hurst and Blackett published his second collection, *The Queen of Hearts,* Collins was more persuasive in the frame that he imposed upon the work. Three old brothers who have retired to their ancient house, the Glen Tower, are, by the terms of an oddly conceived will, paid a visit of six weeks by a young girl named Jessie Yelverton. In order to amuse her, and to prolong her stay until the son of one of the old men can arrive at Glen Tower to propose to her, the old men conceive the idea of telling stories, each drawn from the experiences of one of them, during the evenings near the end of her visit. Though the framing narrative hardly maintains suspense about the outcome—whether the young man will arrive in time and succeed in winning the girl—it establishes a cohesive background in mood that derives from the setting of the marvelous old house itself and from Collins' exploitation of the varying potential that the weather offers. . . .

III. OTHER WORKS, 1870-89

Of the six novelettes which Collins published during his final years, four can lay some claim to literary merit, and then unevenly. Of these probably the weakest is *The Frozen Deep* (1874), an adaptation of the drama of 1857 and 1866. The story is strikingly simple: Richard Wardour, replaced in the affections of Clara Burnham by an unknown man, vows revenge; on an Arctic expedition, Wardour learns that Clara's fiancé is one of his peers, Francis Aldersley, with whom, by accident, Wardour is separated from the rest of the group. He now has the power to attain revenge, but, undergoing a spiritual transformation, he leads Aldersley back to civilization—and to Clara—where, his expiation fulfilled, Wardour dies in exhaustion. One of Collins' most melodramatic accomplishments, *The Frozen Deep* is also one of his most celebrated—a fact which impinges upon any attempt to make a literary judgment of it. By any standard the work is deficient: the plot is hopelessly contrived, resting entirely upon a major coincidence, and the central character's principal decision, on which the only significant action turns, is incredibly motivated. Yet these conclusions may be obscured, or at least assimilated, by the image handed down through book and tradition of the play's production at Tavistock House in 1857, with Dickens' performance as Richard Wardour, passionate but exhausted, to Wilkie Collins' Francis Aldersley.

Miss or Mrs? (1873) has no tradition of dramatic performance either to confuse judgments of its literary merits or to emphasize its absurdities. At the center of the story stands Richard Turlington, a highly successful merchant of early middle age and, it is firmly suggested, of dubious past. As suitor to Natalie Graybrooke, daughter of the incredibly wealthy Sir Joseph, Turlington hesitates at nothing to bring the girl, with her wealth, to an early marriage; when he realizes that his schemes have been checked, he becomes savage in a way that is unparalleled in Collins' work, firing a pistol through a door in an effort to kill Sir Joseph. Unlike most of Collins' villains, Richard Turlington has in his past life only darkness, nothing to explain or mitigate the evil that is his. He becomes totally sinister, and with his absolute villainy binds together the elements of what in all other respects is an extraordinarily weak piece of fiction.

In *John Jago's Ghost* (1873-74) the achievement is somewhat more remarkable, resting upon a greater variety of characters, generally well motivated and integrated with their stark rural American background. Based upon a legal episode which had occurred in Vermont in 1819,[5] Collins' novelette uses the theme of the presumed dead returning to life. Found in earlier works, most strikingly in *Sister Rose* and "**The Dead Hand,**" it was here put to credible use in the case of John Jago, for whose supposed murder the Meadowcroft brothers are convicted on the basis of massive circumstantial evidence. Only after the young men have been sentenced to death is Jago, who has fled the Meadowcroft farm in bitterness and anger, induced to return and then captured.

Aiding credibility and imposing a cohesiveness upon the narrative elements is the very mood permeating the farmhouse and all its world, from which only two beings are exempt, and they are the least compelling characters in the novelette: Philip Lefrank, a visiting Englishman, the narrator trying to impose a somewhat objective order on what he relates; Naomi Colebrook, the orphaned cousin of the Meadowcrofts, bright amidst their darkness. All else is the stark Puritan American setting, with its social suppression and personal frustration, in which brother betrays brother and the living are committed to the endurance until death of life's work and pain.

Miss Meadowcroft, the daughter of the invalid farmer Isaac Meadowcroft, though clearly an extreme instance, is representative of the spirit creating the atmosphere at the farm: "She was a melancholy, middle-aged woman, without visible attractions of any sort—one of those persons who appear to accept the obligation of living under protest, as a burden which they never would have consented to bear if they had only been consulted first" (Chapter II). If Collins essentially misinterpreted his

American materials,[6] he used them with extraordinary skill to create an atmosphere that permeates and sustains the narrative.

Countering those who insist upon a steady decline in Collins' abilities is the fact that for its kind *The Haunted Hotel: A Mystery of Modern Venice* (1879) was one of his most successful undertakings. The question may arise about the worth of the *kind* itself, the sensation narrative, of which this is an almost pure example. With a highly complex and to no purpose plot—contrived around mysterious experiments, secrets from the past, the substitution of one man for another in death, and the shadowy barrier between sanity and madness—*The Haunted Hotel* moves toward one climactic scene, in which all the possibilities of sensation are realized. Agnes Lockwood, the female protagonist, awakens in the haunted room to find the evil Countess Narona sitting in a stupor beside her; "midway between her [own] face and the ceiling" hovers "a human head—severed at the neck, like a head struck from the body by a guillotine." Agnes, captured by the terror of the apparition, sees nothing else:

> The flesh of the face was gone. The shriveled skin was darkened in hue, like the skin of an Egyptian mummy—except at the neck. There it was of a lighter color; there it showed spots and splashes of the hue of that brown spot on the ceiling, which the child's fanciful terror had distorted into the likeness of a spot of blood. Thin remains of a discolored mustache and whiskers, hanging over the upper lip, and over the hollows where the cheeks had once been, made the head just recognizable as the head of a man. Over all the features death and time had done their obliterating work. The eyelids were closed. The hair on the skull, discolored like the hair on the face, had been burned away in places. The bluish lips, parted in a fixed grin, showed the double row of teeth. By slow degrees, the hovering head (perfectly still when she first saw it) began to descend toward Agnes as she lay beneath. By slow degrees, that strange doubly-blended odor, which the Commissioners had discovered in the vaults of the old palace—which had sickened Francis Westwick in the bed-chamber of the new hotel—spread its fetid exhalations over the room. Downward and downward the hideous apparition made its slow progress, until it stopped close over Agnes—stopped, and turned slowly, so that the face of it confronted the upturned face of the woman in the chair.

(Chapter XXII)

Mitigating the purity of this novelette as sensation fiction is the moral conflict that is taking place in the mind of Countess Narona, who sees herself compelled by fate to commit acts of evil and thereby bring on her own destruction. Thus she assimilates the fatality of the story into her own motivation, causing the incidents that would otherwise be considered fatal; as T. S. Eliot emphasized, the melodramatic therefore becomes a quality of her character rather than of the work itself in which that character occurs.[7]

In the last years Collins wrote some short stories, but few of significance. **"The Fatal Fortune"** (1874) is a more pointed attack upon the system of private asylums and their abuse by the unscrupulous than Collins had made in *The Woman in White*; here, painfully illustrating the most striking fault others were to find with his fiction of social criticism, he concluded with a frank statement of the "moral" of his story: "Assisted by a doctor, whose honesty and capacity must be taken on trust, these interested persons [the covetous relatives of a wealthy Englishman], in this nineteenth century of progress, can lawfully imprison their relative for life, in a country which calls itself free, and which declares that its justice is equally administered to all alike."

In 1887 Chatto and Windus published fourteen short stories in three volumes under the title *Little Novels.* Collected from Collins' periodical publication during the 1870's and the first half of the 1880's, these were retitled so that each bears the name of two characters, such as **"Mrs. Zant and the Ghost"** or **"Miss Mina and the Groom."** Contrived in their plots and in their happy conclusions, they illustrate nothing so much as the degree to which Collins was unevenly losing control of his materials; in each story there are perhaps several of the characteristics marking the earlier and finer work, but in none of these was the informing spirit active. . . .

Notes

1. See Johnson, II, 944 ff.

2. Robinson, p. 73.

3. Ashley, *Wilkie Collins,* p. 55.

4. See Pierce Egan, *Account of the Trial of Mr. Fauntleroy* (London, 1824); *Encyclopedia Britannica* (11th Edition).

5. See Robert Ashley, "Wilkie Collins and a Vermont Murder Trial," *New England Quarterly,* XXI (1948), 368-73.

6. *Ibid.,* 373.

7. Eliot, *Selected Essays,* p. 380.

Selected Bibliography

PRIMARY SOURCES

I. BOOKS

Memoirs of the Life of William Collins, Esq., R. A. with Selections from His Journals and Correspondence. 2 vols. London: Longman, Brown, Green, and Longmans, 1848.

Antonina; or, The Fall of Rome. A Romance of the Fifth Century. 3 vols. London: Bentley, 1850.

Rambles Beyond Railways, or, Notes in Cornwall Taken A-foot. London: Bentley, 1851.

Mr. Wray's Cash-Box; or, the Mask and the Mystery. A Christmas Sketch. London: Bentley, 1852.

Basil: A Story of Modern Life. 3 vols. London: Bentley, 1852.

Hide and Seek. 3 vols. London: Bentley, 1854.

After Dark. 2 vols. London: Smith & Elder, 1856. Connected by "Leaves from Leah's Diary" are six narratives, of which five were published previously in *Household Words:* "A Terribly Strange Bed" (*HW,* April 24, 1852), "A Stolen Letter" (*HW,* Christmas number for 1854, entitled *The Seven Poor Travellers*), "Sister Rose" (*HW,* April 7-28, 1855), "The Lady of Glenwith Grange" (first publication), "Gabriel's Marriage" (*HW,* April 16-23, 1853), "The Yellow Mask" (*HW,* July 7-28, 1855).

The Dead Secret. 2 vols. London: Bradbury & Evans, 1857. (First published serially, in *Household Words,* January 3-June 13, 1857.)

The Queen of Hearts. 3 vols. London: Hurst & Blackett, 1859. Within connecting narrative are ten fictional pieces previously published: "The Siege of the Black Cottage" (*Harper's New Monthly Magazine,* February 1857), "The Family Secret" (as "Uncle George; or the Family Mystery," *The National Magazine* [New York], May 1857), "The Dream-Woman" (as "The Ostler," *Household Words,* Christmas number for 1855, entitled *The Holly-Tree Inn*), "Mad Monkton" (as "The Monktons of Wincot Abbey," *Fraser's Magazine,* November-December 1855), "The Dead Hand" (*HW,* October 10, 1857), "The Biter Bit" (as "Who is the Thief?" *The Atlantic Monthly,* April 1858), "The Parson's Scruple" (as "A New Mind," *HW,* January 1, 1859), "A Plot in Private Life" (as "A Marriage Tragedy," *Harper's New Monthly Magazine,* February 1858), "Fauntleroy" (as "A Paradoxical Experience," *HW,* November 13, 1858), "Anne Rodway" (as "The Diary of Anne Rodway," *HW,* July 19-26, 1856).

The Woman in White. 3 vols. London: Sampson Low, 1860. (First published serially, in *All the Year Round,* November 26, 1859-August 25, 1860.)

No Name. 3 vols. London: Sampson Low, 1862. (First published serially, in *All the Year Round,* March 15, 1862-January 17, 1863.)

My Miscellanies. 2 vols. London: Sampson Low, 1863. Selected and revised by Collins himself are essays previously published in *Household Words* and *All the Year Round:* "Talk-Stoppers" (*HW,* October 25, 1856), "A Journey in Search of Nothing" (*HW,* September 5, 1857), "A Queen's Revenge" (*HW,* August 15, 1857), "A Petition to the Novel-Writers" (*HW,* December 6, 1856), "Laid Up In Lodgings" (*HW,* June 7-14, 1856),

"A Shockingly Rude Article" (*HW,* August 28, 1858), "The Great (Forgotten) Invasion" (*HW,* March 12, 1859), "The Unknown Public" (*HW,* August 21, 1858), "Give Us Room!" (*HW,* February 13, 1858), "Portrait of An Author, Painted by His Publisher" (*AYR,* June 18-25, 1859), "My Black Mirror" (*HW,* September 6, 1856), "Mrs. Badgery" (*HW,* September 26, 1857), "Memoirs of an Adopted Son" (*AYR,* April 20, 1861), "The Bachelor Bedroom" (*AYR,* August 6, 1859), "A Remarkable Revolution" (*HW,* August 1, 1857), "Douglas Jerrold" (*HW,* February 5, 1859), "Pray Employ Major Namby!" (*AYR,* June 4, 1859), "The Poisoned Meal" (*HW,* September 18-October 2, 1858), "My Spinsters" (*HW,* August 23, 1856), "Dramatic Grub Street" (*HW,* March 6, 1858), "To Think, or Be Thought For?" (*HW,* September 13, 1856), "Save Me from My Friends" (*HW,* January 16, 1858), "The Caldron of Oil" (*AYR,* May 11, 1861), "Bold Words by A Bachelor" (*HW,* December 13, 1856), "Mrs. Bullwinkle" (*HW,* April 17, 1858).

Armadale. 2 vols. London: Smith & Elder, 1866. (First published serially, in *The Cornhill Magazine,* November, 1864-June, 1866.)

The Moonstone. A Romance. 3 vols. London: Tinsley, 1868. (First published serially, in *All the Year Round,* January 4-August 8, 1868.)

Man and Wife. A Novel. 3 vols. London: F. S. Ellis, 1870. (First published serially, in *Cassell's Magazine,* January-September, 1870.)

Poor Miss Finch. A Novel. 3 vols. London: Bentley, 1872. (First published serially, in *Cassell's Magazine,* October, 1871-March, 1872.)

The New Magdalen. A Novel. 2 vols. London: Bentley, 1873. (First published serially, in *Temple Bar,* January-December, 1872.)

Miss or Mrs? and Other Stories in Outline. London: Bentley, 1873. Reprinted are three pieces of fiction, though four in 1875 edition of the volume: "Miss or Mrs?" (first published, *The London Graphic Illustrated Newspaper,* December 13, 1871); "Blow Up with the Brig!" (as "The Ghost in the Cupboard Room," *AYR,* Christmas number for 1859, entitled *The Haunted House*); "The Fatal Cradle" (as "Picking Up Waifs at Sea," *AYR,* Christmas number for 1861, entitled *Tom Tiddler's Ground*); "A Mad Marriage" (as "A Fatal Fortune," *AYR,* October 17-24, 1874).

The Frozen Deep and Other Tales. 2 vols. London: Bentley, 1874. Republished are three narratives: "The Frozen Deep" (adapted from the play, first published serially, in *Temple Bar,* August-October, 1874), "The Dream Woman" (revised for public readings in America: see *Queen of Hearts,* above), "John Jago's Ghost" (first published serially, in *The Home Journal* [London], December, 1873-February, 1874).

The Law and the Lady. 3 vols. London: Chatto & Windus, 1875. (First published serially, in *The London Graphic Illustrated Newspaper,* early 1875 [files not available].)

The Two Destinies. A Romance. 2 vols. London: Chatto & Windus, 1876. (First published serially in *Temple Bar,* January-August, 1876.)

The Haunted Hotel, a Mystery of Modern Venice; to which is added My Lady's Money, 2 vols. London: Chatto & Windus, 1879. Each narrative was previously published: *The Haunted Hotel* in *Belgravia Magazine,* June-November, 1878; *My Lady's Money* in *The London Illustrated News,* December, 1877.

A Rogue's Life. From His Birth to His Marriage. London: Bentley, 1879. (First published serially, in *Household Words,* March 1-29, 1856.)

The Fallen Leaves—First Series. 3 vols. London: Chatto & Windus, 1879. (First published serially, in *The World,* January 1-July 23, 1879.)

Jezebel's Daughter. 3 vols. London: Chatto & Windus, 1880. (First published serially, in *The Bolton Weekly Journal* and other syndicated newspapers during 1879 [files not available].)

The Black Robe. 3 vols. London: Chatto & Windus, 1881. (First published serially, in *The Canadian Monthly,* November, 1880-June, 1881.)

Heart and Science. A Story of the Present Time. 3 vols. London: Chatto & Windus, 1883. (First published serially, in *Belgravia Magazine,* August, 1882-June, 1883.)

I Say No. 3 vols. London: Chatto & Windus, 1884. (First published serially, in *Harper's Weekly,* December 22, 1883-July 12, 1884.)

The Evil Genius. A Dramatic Story. 3 vols. London: Chatto & Windus, 1886. (First published serially, in *The Leigh Journal and Times,* December 11, 1885-May 11, 1886.)

The Guilty River. A Story. Bristol: Arrowsmith, 1886.

Little Novels. 3 vols. London: Chatto & Windus, 1887. Reprinted are fourteen stories: "Mrs. Zant and the Ghost" (first published as "The Ghost's Touch," *Harper's Weekly,* October 23, 1885), "Miss Morris and the Stranger" (as "How I Married Him," *The Spirit of the Times,* December 24, 1881), "Mr. Cosway and the Landlady" (as "Your Money or Your Life," *The People's Library,* December 17, 1881), "Mr. Medhurst and the Princess" (as "Royal Love," *Longman's Magazine,* Christmas 1884), "Mr. Lismore and the Widow" (as "She Loves and Lies," *The Spirit of the Times,* December 22, 1883), "Miss Jéromette and the Clergyman" (as "The Clergyman's Confession," *The Canadian Monthly,* August-September, 1875), "Miss Mina and the Groom"

(as "A Shocking Story," *The International Review* [New York], November 2, 1878), "Mr. Lepel and the Housekeeper" (as "The Girl at the Gate," *The Spirit of the Times,* December 6, 1884), "Mr. Captain and the Nymph" (as "The Captain's Last Love," *The Spirit of the Times,* December 23, 1876), "Mr. Marmaduke and the Minister" (as "The Mystery of Marmaduke," *The Spirit of the Times,* December 28, 1878), "Mr. Percy and the Prophet" (as "Percy and the Prophet," *All the Year Round,* July 2, 1877), "Miss Bertha and the Yankee" (as "The Duel in Herne Wood," *The Spirit of the Times,* December 22, 1877), "Miss Dulane and My Lord" (as "An Old Maid's Husband," *The Spirit of the Times,* December 25, 1886), "Mr. Policeman and the Cook" (as "Who Killed Zebedee?" *The Seaside Library,* January 26, 1881).

The Legacy of Cain. 3 vols. London: Chatto & Windus, 1889.

Blind Love. (Completed by Walter Besant) 3 vols. London: Chatto & Windus, 1890. (First published serially, in *The Illustrated London News,* July-December, 1889.)

The Lazy Tour of Two Idle Apprentices and Other Stories. (In collaboration with Charles Dickens) Reprinted are three pieces: "The Lazy Tour of Two Idle Apprentices" (*Household Words,* October 3-31, 1857), "No Thoroughfare" (*All the Year Round,* Christmas number for 1867), "The Perils of Certain English Prisoners (*HW,* Christmas number for 1857).

II. UNCOLLECTED PIECES

"The Last Stage Coachman," *Illuminated Magazine* (August, 1843).

"The Twin Sisters," *Bentley's Miscellany* (March, 1851).

"A Passage in the Life of Perugino Potts," *Bentley's Miscellany* (February, 1852).

"The Cruise of the Tom-Tit," *Household Words* (December 22, 1855).

"The National Gallery and the Old Masters," *HW* (October 25, 1856).

The Wreck of the Golden Mary (in collaboration with Charles Dickens), *HW* (Christmas number for 1856).

"A Fair Penitent," *HW* (July 18, 1857).

"The Yellow Tiger," *HW* (August 8, 1857).

"The Debtor's Best Friend," *HW* (September 19, 1857).

"A Deep Design on Society," *HW* (January 2, 1858).

"The Little Huguenot," *HW* (January 9, 1858).

"Thanks to Dr. Livingstone," *HW* (January 23, 1858).

"Strike," *HW* (February 6, 1858).

"A Sermon for Sepoys," *HW* (February 27, 1858).

"A Shy Scheme," *HW* (March 20, 1858).

"Awful Warning to Bachelors," *HW* (March 27, 1858).

"Sea Breezes with a London Smack," *HW* (September 4, 1858).

"Highly Proper!" *HW* (October 2, 1858).

"A Clause for the New Reform Bill" (in collaboration with Charles Dickens), *HW* (October 9, 1858).

"Doctor Dulcamara, M.P." (in collaboration with Charles Dickens), *HW* (December 18, 1858).

A House to Let (in collaboration with Charles Dickens), *HW* (Christmas number for 1858).

"Pity a Poor Prince," *HW* (January 15, 1859).

"Burns Viewed as a Hat-Peg," *HW* (February 12, 1859).

"A Column to Burns," *HW* (February 26, 1859).

"A Breach of British Privilege," *HW* (March 19, 1859).

"Sure To Be Healthy, Wealthy, and Wise," *All the Year Round* (April 30, 1859).

"A Dramatic Author," *HW* (May 28, 1859).

"The Royal Academy in Bed," *AYR* (May 28, 1859).

"New View of Society," *AYR* (August 20, 1859).

"Cooks at College," *AYR* (October 29, 1859).

"My Boys," *AYR* (January 28, 1860).

"My Girls," *AYR* (February 11, 1860).

"Boxing Day," *AYR* (December 22, 1860).

A Message from the Sea (in collaboration with Charles Dickens), *AYR* (Christmas number for 1860).

"A Night in the Jungle," *AYR* (August 3, 1861).

"An Unreported Speech," *AYR* (November 16, 1861).

"A Trial at Toulouse," *AYR* (February 15, 1862).

"Suggestions from a Maniac," *AYR* (February 13, 1864).

"To Let," *AYR* (June 18, 1864).

"Going into Housekeeping," *AYR* (July 8, 1865).

"The Devil's Spectacles," *The Spirit of the Times* (December 20, 1879).

"Considerations on the Copyright Question. Addressed to an American Friend," *The International Review* (New York), (June, 1880).

"Fie! Fie! or the Fair Physician," *The Spirit of the Times* and *The Pictorial World Christmas Supplement* (December 23, 1882).

"The Poetry Did It: An Event in the Life of Major Evergreen," *The Spirit of the Times* (December 26, 1885).

"Victims of Circumstances, Discovered in Records of Old Trials," *Youth's Companion* (August 19, 1886).

"The First Officer's Confession," *The Spirit of the Times* (December 24, 1887).

"Reminiscences of a Story-Teller," *The Universal Review* (May-August, 1888).

SECONDARY SOURCES

Ashley, Robert. *Wilkie Collins.* New York: Roy Publishers, 1952.

Eliot, T. S. "Wilkie Collins and Dickens," (London) *Times Literary Supplement,* August 4, 1927, pp. 525-26. An important critical article, stressing the melodramatic elements in Collins and their significance, this was reprinted in *Selected Essays, 1917-1932* (New York: Harcourt, Brace, 1947). The article also became the basis for the introduction to *The Moonstone,* which Eliot wrote for the Oxford University Press publication in 1928.

Johnson, Edgar, *Charles Dickens. His Tragedy and Triumph.* 2 vols. New York: Simon & Schuster, 1952. An excellent biography, this reveals Collins, through its many references to him, as a whole and sympathetic human being and as Dickens' close friends.

Robinson, Kenneth. *Wilkie Collins. A Biography.* London: The Bodley Head, 1951. The first biography; an admirable piece of work, it presents Collins in full perspective.

C. H. Muller (essay date March 1973)

SOURCE: Muller, C. H. "Victorian Sensationalism: The Short Stories of Wilkie Collins." *Unisa English Studies* 11, no. 1 (March 1973): 12-24.

[*In the following essay, Muller argues that while Collins's early stories display a consummate skill in the construction and handling of "sensationist" ingredients—tracing the various stages of the protagonist's mental state and using situations characteristic of Gothicism—they downplay fear in a rational atmosphere of suspense.*]

Wilkie Collins wrote during the mid-nineteenth century, when the vogue of the sensation novel was at its highest. This period following the Industrial Revolution saw the emergence of a new reading public. With the new bourgeois middle classes, literature was no longer restricted to the gentry and professional classes; instead, it became an article of mass production, and therefore had to appeal to popular tastes and provide amusement.

Dickens appreciated this, observing in a letter to Charles Knight that the English are 'the hardest-worked people on whom the sun shines', adding, 'Be content if, in their wretched intervals of pleasure, they read for amusement and do no worse'.[1] The critics, however, were disturbed that such amusement was frequently provided by the horror and crime story with its emphasis on suspense and startling incidents; like the melodramatic pieces of the Transpontine theatres, sensational fiction depended primarily on the appeal of fear and excitement, and there was generally an avoidance of psychological exposition. It is not surprising that whereas the appeal of the sensational was tremendous, to the critics it was disquieting and a symptom of deterioration in literary tastes. They regarded the new vogue as 'sensation-mongering', the writing of stories which, according to a *Daily News* reviewer, were full of 'violent improbable incidents, and . . . situations laid on with a thick brush'.[2] This prevailing critical attitude was adequately expressed in an anonymous satirical poem entitled 'The "Sensation" Mania', which appeared in *Sharpe's Magazine* in 1864:[3]

> Here and there and everywhere is some
> powerful sensation,
> And nothing seems to go down but a
> startling situation,
> Which to our heart oft doth impart
> unpleasant palpitation,
> And leaves one in a state of universal
> trepidation. . . .

Although disparaging criticism was generally levelled at inferior women purveyors of popular fiction like Miss Braddon and Mrs Henry Wood, it was inevitable that conservative journals like the *Edinburgh Review* and *Quarterly Review* should have regarded Wilkie Collins, and even Dickens, as being responsible for the collapse of literary taste. Whereas James Fitzjames Stephen, writing in the *Edinburgh Review,* attacked Dickens and Charles Reade for 'suppressing all that is dull, all that does not contribute to dramatic effect'[4] in their respective novels *Little Dorrit* and *Never to late to Mend,* H. L. Mansel, writing in the *Quarterly Review,* classified Wilkie Collins's *No Name* with works like Miss Braddon's *Lady Audley's Secret* and Mrs Wood's *Danesbury House,* drawing attention to the 'class of literature [that] has grown up around us' which played 'no inconsiderate part in moulding the minds and forming the habits and tastes of its generation . . . by "preaching to the nerves"'.[5] According to Mansel, 'excitement, and excitement alone, seems to be the great end' at which these writers aimed; their fiction was 'called into existence to supply the cravings of a deseased appetite'.

It is unfortunate that Wilkie Collins should have been so easily confused with the mediocre sensationists of the time, since even his early short stories which preceded such masterpieces of the 'sixties as *The Woman in White* and *The Moonstone* display a consummate skill in construction and the handling of the 'sensation' ingredients. (It is necessary to observe that nineteenth-century sensationism was an offshoot of the earlier Gothic tradition wherein novels like Walpole's *Castle of Otranto* and Mrs Radcliffe's *Mysteries of Udolpho* depended on the appeal of fear and crude melodrama for violent emotional thrills.) Collins cannot be contemptuously dismissed as a mere sensationist because he succeeded in elevating the Gothic tradition to the level of serious fiction. In Gothicism, as in the sensationism of the mid-century, the emphasis was on melodrama and not on dramatic intensity: the crude appeal of the supernatural, terrifying incidents, and strong passions pictorially represented, were more important than the skilful evocation of dramatic tension which Wilkie Collins achieved by making the narrative work dramatically and by evoking awe-inspiring 'atmosphere'. In Collins's fiction the fear-inspiring situations are not merely theatrical but dramatic in the profounder sense. This is a natural outcome of Collins's creed—that the novel and play, according to his preface in *Basil,* are 'twin sisters in the family of Fiction', the one being 'a drama narrated' and the other 'a drama acted'. Although the early novels before *The Woman in White* are inferior in dramatic instinct and construction, the real genesis of Wilkie Collins's dramatic fiction is his short-story fiction wherein he rationalizes and renders more credible the characteristically supernatural melodrama of the Terrorist tradition. In stories like *A Terribly Strange Bed* (1852), *The Double-Bedded Room* (1857) and *Blow up with the Brig!* (1859) Collins clearly uses the type of situation characteristic of Gothicism, but sublimates the Terrorists' appeal of fear (usually associated with the supernatural) in a rational atmosphere of suspense that arises from dramatic suggestion and a remarkable blend of melodrama with realism.

A Terribly Strange Bed was Wilkie Collins's first contribution to Dickens's *Household Words* Although it appeared in April, 1852, only six months before *Basil,* his second novel, this tale of the macabre is remarkable for the creation of tense atmosphere, and is generally regarded as the most exciting short story that Collins wrote. The narrative tells how an artist named Faulkner, after winning heavily at *rouge et noir,* is persuaded by the proprietor of a gambling house to spend the night on the premises rather than risk the danger of carrying his winnings through the dark streets of Paris. The four-poster bed in which Faulkner sleeps turns out to be a monstrous murder-device: the canopy top, operated by mechanism above, descends upon the sleeper; paralysed with fear, Faulkner is unable to move, but at the last moment escapes suffocation by rolling on to the floor.

The prototype of this story is the conventional Gothic 'ghost story' in which a traveller is obliged to spend the night in a haunted chamber. In these the Gothic castle, or sinister house, and the midnight occurence of ghostly noises and visions constitute the traditional machinery of crude terror. Although the 'haunted chamber' theme is utilized by Collins, he is able to achieve by rational means effects of atmosphere more arresting than most writers could achieve by calling upon the whole paraphernalia of the supernatural. In the gambling house a sinister atmosphere full of dramatic tension is created by means of realistic characters etched with a few easy strokes of the pen:

> The quiet in the room was horrible. The thin, haggard, long-haired young man, whose sunken eyes fiercely watched the turning up of the cards, never spoke; the flabby, fat-faced, pimply player, who pricked his piece of pasteboard perseveringly, to register how often black won, and how often red—never spoke; the dirty, wrinkled old man, with the vulture eyes and the darned greatcoat, who had lost his last *sou*, and still looked on desperately, after he could play no longer—never spoke. Even the voice of the croupier sounded as if it were strangely dulled and thickened in the atmosphere of the room. I had entered the place to laugh, but the spectacle before me was something to weep over.

Though admitedly caricatures in the Dickens sense, the characters described comprise the sinister *milieu* of the story and emerge naturally from the flow of the narrative. It was a premise of Collins's art that emphasis be placed on the telling of the story, and that characters should evolve of their own accord from the story. The figures described here are intended primarily to enhance the tense atmosphere, each giving added emphasis to the 'quiet in the room'; the artful repetition of the phrase 'never spoke', and finally the croupier's 'strangely dulled and thickened' voice, build up an uncanny effect of silence which engenders in the reader expectations of mystery and impending scenes of sensation. All this is conveyed by means of a sober and clear flowing narrative style, engaging in its simplicity and sincerity. Collins's style is necessarily devoid of the touches of whimsicality and humour Dickens employs in his ghost stories, since these would detract from the tense atmosphere. His serious tone not only evokes the reader's sympathy, but engages his credulity for the strange events to follow.

Although the influence of Dickens on Collins is recognized, the methods employed by each writer are different. In *The Bagman's Story* (part of *Pickwick Papers*) and *The Haunted House*, Dickens makes similar use of the traditional ghost story setting and the 'sinister house' motif; but whereas Wilkie Collins places greater emphasis on suspense and the description of the protagonist's human sensations and reactions, Dickens devotes more attention to idiosyncrasy of character and bizarre phantasy verging on the farcical. *The Bagman's Story*, for example, is told in a semi-mock-heroic vein which burlesques the Gothic tradition. In the rustic figure of Tom Smart who takes refuge from a storm in an old public house, Dickens creates an amusing character much given to punch; the traditional ghost-story ingredients of a howling wind and creaking timbers are described, but the chatty and conversational style dispels the usual sinister effects:

> Hot punch is a pleasant thing, gentlemen—an extremely pleasant thing under any circumstances—but in that snug old parlour, before the roaring fire, with the wind blowing outside till every timber in the old house creaked again, Tom Smart found it perfectly delightful. He ordered another tumbler, and then another—I am not quite certain whether he didn't order another. . . .

Dickens's unobtrusive manner of addressing an imaginary audience engenders intimacy and sympathy between narrator and reader, and evokes the intimate atmosphere, not of the suspense story, but of the Christmas story with all the feelings of conviviality characteristic of the Christmas season. Sympathy for Tom is created by the author's confiding tone and humour, and the reader shares the author's mirth at Tom's sluggish and intemperate nature. The treatment of the 'haunted chamber' theme is itself highly amusing, and is in no way calculated to inspire fear. In contrast, Wilkie Collins's story achieves compelling fascination in the description of a face in an old picture which, in the feeble light of the candle, is suddenly obscured by a 'dusky object'—the slowly descending canopy of the bed. The situation described by Dickens, on the other hand, is fraught with laughter-provoking fun when the same serious attention is applied to a grim-looking, high-backed chair with 'Gothic' connotations, but which gradually assumes the lineaments of an old man who insists on winking and leering at the befuddled Tom. The same brand of light-hearted fun is evident in *The Haunted House*, where the vivid picturesqueness of character and felicity of expression—incongruous in a ghost story—do much to dispel the dramatic tension; thus Dickens describes the housemaid who, like the other servants, is full of trepidation in consequence of the 'supernatural' tendencies of the house:

> I am unable to say whether she was of an unusually lymphatic temperament, or what else was the matter with her, but this young woman became a mere Distillery for the production of the largest and most transparent tears I ever met with.

Although Dickens is capable of creating situations that are pregnant with mood and atmosphere such as the appearance of Magwitch in Pip's chambers in London amidst a violent storm, his short stories reveal a great mind working within very narrow limits. When the protagonist in *The Haunted House* awakens in a haunted room to find himself not only sharing the bed with the skeleton of its previous occupant, but followed by that skeleton about the room, the effect is purely ridiculous; the good-humoured discussion with the spectre which follows, and the pervasive humour which impregnates the narrative, obliterates the sensations of terror which are characteristic of Collins's stories. Dickens, more concerned with revealing his protagonist's mental state in all its nuances and processes of association at a particular moment, suggests, in *The Haunted House,* that the skeleton that haunts the protagonist is the ghost of his younger self. But, to achieve this, the story tends to become too phantasmagorical, the pure fantasy leaving the reader incredulous with little real suspense to sustain his interest.

Collins, unlike Dickens, is successful in sustaining interest by tracing the various stages of his protagonist's mental state, and by telling the story swiftly and economically. Thus his story moves forward at an incredible pace, forcibly engaging the attention and interest of the reader who becomes increasingly anxious to learn what fate has in store for the protagonist. Collins, supremely successful in blending romantic or at least melodramatic incident with realism of setting, creates a breathless interest in spite of the absence of supernaturalism when he depicts his hero playing recklessly at *rouge et noir,* increasing his stakes as his winnings increase; as the other gamblers gradually withdraw from the game, breathlessly watching the reckless player amidst a tense silence broken by 'a deep-muttered chorus of oaths and exclamations', the intangible excitement, mounting to fever pitch, is communicated to the reader who feels a growing concern for the young man's safety. The dramatic tension is enhanced by the repeated warnings and entreaties of the young man's friend to stop playing. These warnings, together with the dire intimations of imminent danger when the suspicious landlord is described (a typical specimen of the melodramatic villain, with 'goggling bloodshot eyes, mangy mustachios, and a broken nose') create a sense of fatality, a device frequently used by Collins to heighten the suspense.

Collins's faculty for dramatic suggestion is further evident in his use of dramatic narrative. When the story is continued by the dialogue between the landlord and the narrator who express themselves in vivid, colloquial speech which conveys the mad excitement and reckless triumph of the young man, it achieves vivacity and verisimilitude. As Faulkner becomes more and more intoxicated with champagne, the narrative becomes more and more reckless with a liberal sprinkling of exclamations; while this expresses Faulkner's mad state of exhilaration, the repetition of the rhetorical question heightens the dramatic tension:

'. . . *Your* bottle last time; *my* bottle this. Behold it! Toast away! The French Army!—the great Napoleon!—the present company! . . .'

. . . No excess in wine had ever had this effect on me before . . . Was it the result of a stimulant acting upon my system when I was in a highly excited state? Was my stomach in a particularly disordered condition? Or was the champagne amazingly strong?

It has been argued that the lack of profound character-analysis in Collins's fiction corresponds with the over-emphasis placed on the story. Although it is true that Faulkner exists chiefly for the purposes of the action itself with the result that his character remains static with a limited range of feeling, the very intensity of that narrow range imparts psychological realism. The reader's emotional identification with the protagonist is made possible through the very realistic human sensations of Faulkner. The effects of a drugged cup of coffee are described:

The room whirled round and round furiously; the old soldier seemed to be regularly bobbing up and down before me like the piston of a steam-engine. I was half deafened by a violent singing in my ears; a feeling of utter bewilderment, helplessness, idiocy, overcame me.

Here the deliberately exaggerated similes express the weird sensations of complete intoxication as well as the sense of losing touch with reality, while the wild, sporadic rhythm conveys the utter bewilderment and confusion of the young man. The minutely described physical sensations give his experiences a quality of acute reality, as when he describes his insomnia and heightened nervous excitement as he tosses and turns restlessly, perserveringly seeking out the cold corners of the four-poster bed. Even the setting and contents of the room are conveyed through the narrator's experience, and not described in full upon the protagonist's first entrance into the room, as in Scott's story *The Tapestried Chamber.* Scott, a keen analyst of terror, employed the same setting of an old-fashioned bed in a room rife with the usual atmosphere of gloom and moaning wind without; described as the visitor to Woodville Castle (the 'Gothic' castle) enters the chamber, the setting is contrived to inspire immediate mounting uneasiness and mild suspense in the reader. Collins's method, however, is less in the traditional vein and has more of the ring of truth, since when Faulkner first enters the room he is naturally too preoccupied with his own feelings of discomfort after the champagne and drugged coffee to notice details; it is only when he is lying restlessly awake that the realistic details of his surroundings impress themselves on his mind, and the effect, altogether more convincing and sinister, underlines the nervous, unsettled state of his mind. By not describing setting as though it were a stage-property, Collins uses the narrator's art rather than the dramatist's, and yet the effect is more truly dramatic as well as psychologically convincing.

Because Wilkie Collins places greater emphasis on the description of the narrator's human sensations and reactions, and since he is more preoccupied with suggestion and imaginative excitement than the actual presentation of the supernatural, he is more successful than writers like Scott or Bulwer Lytton in creating an atmosphere charged with suspense. In Lytton's story *The Haunted and the Haunters,* as in Scott's *The Tapestried Chamber,* the detailed descriptions of phantoms minimize the terror of the ghastly sights. Whereas Lytton's story is rife with floating globules of light, opalescent ghostly forms and chairs which move about the room of their own accord, Scott's vivid description of an apparition whose face had 'the fixed features of a corpse' and bore the imprint of 'the vilest and most hideous passions' is an attempt at undiluted horror and terror, calculated to evoke a violent emotional thrill in the reader. Collins, however, eschews the crude appeal of fear in favour of the thrilling sensations of suspense that are communicated to the reader by means of subtle atmospheric effects and the realistic experience of the protagonist. Bathed in moonlight, the scene Collins describes has something of the lighting effects of a Transpontine theatre, but a tense atmosphere is created simply by the sound of water dripping which emphasises the silence of the room; and the moonlight itself is a means of evoking a somnambulent strain of retrospection as the narrator recalls a certain moonlight night with all its associations of sublime beauty. The reader is carefully prepared by this preceding mood for the shock of suspense which takes place when the narrator's retrospection is abruptly broken by his sudden realisation that the bed is moving. The silent, sinister descent of the bed-top is more terrifying, the paralizing effect of the narrator's panic more acutely felt, than the terror and weird ghosts in the stories of Scott and Lytton:

> I looked up, motionless, speechless, breathless. The candle, fully spent, went out; but the moonlight still brightened the room. Down and down, without pausing and without sounding, came the bed-top, and still my panic-terror seemed to bind me faster and faster to the mattress on which I lay—down and down it sank, till the dusty odour from the lining of the canopy came stealing into my nostrils.

> *At that final moment the instinct of self-preservation startled me out of my trance, and I moved at last. There was just room for me to roll myself sideways off the bed. As I dropped noiselessly to the floor, the edge of the murderous canopy touched me on the shoulder.*

Suspense is created by the compact structure of sentences and the slow but inevitable descent of the canopy. Emotional identification with the protagonist is made possible through the reactions of Faulkner, who under the stimulus of fear reacts in accordance with the stereotyped but very real patterns of human behaviour. Although paralytic with terror, all his senses are alert; and the 'dustry odour', the touch of the canopy on the shoulder, are quite as spine-chilling as the dank odour, the touch of death, characteristic of conventional ghost stories. It is because of the suspense, the intensity of the melodrama, that the reader is compelled to share the narrator's sensations, and the situation is perhaps more vivid than a similar situation in the tale of *The Pit and the Pendulum* in which Poe describes the gradual, in-

evitable descent of a razor-sharp scimitar which, swinging from side to side, threatens to slice the bound victim's body. Collins may well have been unconsciously influenced by Poe, since some of his phrases are counterpointed in Poe's story (cf. Poe's wording, 'The odour of the sharp steel forced itself into my nostrils', and Collins's wording, '. . . the dusty odour from the lining of the canopy came stealing into my nostrils . . .'). Although the description of the descending pendulum has a poetic force, Poe does not achieve the same tension which fully involves the reader in the protagonist's terror, since he is too detached, too philosophically analytic in his objective treatment of the protagonist's sensations of frantic madness and despair.

Collins's ability to evoke in his reader an intensity of mental and emotional involvement, a characteristic of popular melodrama, is seen at its best in his terrifying tale of *The Double-Bedded Room,*[6] which also derives its strength from the dramatic qualities of the more refined drama. A first-rate terror story, its basic appeal lies in the strong melodramatic element without which, according to T. S. Eliot,[7] no drama has ever been greatly and permanently successful. The melodrama is certainly responsible for the masterly evocation of what a contemporary critic called 'the creepy effect, as of pounded ice dropped down the back'[8] when the protagonist, Arthur, discovers that his roommate in a desolate inn is a corpse, while portentious atmospheric effects of rain pattering drearily against the window pane and the distant sound of a church clock striking reinforce the dramatic graveyard atmosphere.

The reader is prepared for the scene by the landlord's suspicious mannerisms and mysterious behaviour, by the grim humour and double meanings in his assurances that Arthur's roommate is a sound sleeper, and by the irony in his wishing the young man a good night's rest; while these mysterious hints pique the reader's curiosity, they thrill him with expectations of something fearful and mysterious to be revealed. The gradual increase of terror and suspense is effected by the compelling fascination of horror which the corpse has for Arthur. Attempting to while away the night by walking restlessly to and fro, he cannot keep his eyes away from the dead man; he repeatedly advances to the curtained bed, attempting to dispel his fear by recognising the reality of the corpse, and when he attempts to distract himself by staring out of the window, he again becomes 'conscious that his eyes were fixed on it'. There is considerable psychological realism in this inner conflict, as well as in the mingling of involuntary feelings of compassion for the dead man with the instinctive feelings of repugnance and horror. The same effective method Collins uses in *A Terribly Strange Bed* to describe the bleak setting is used in this story. Too uneasy to sleep, Arthur employs his mind by studying the contents of the room. The story is thus given verisimilitude, since at first his fascination for the corpse naturally prevents him from noticing details; the observation, at this moment, of the dingy surroundings—suggestive of decay and very like the interior of Satis House in *Great Expectations*—is more dramatic and chilling in its effect.

The story achieves more psychological realism and dramatic intensity as the thought of the corpse becomes more persistent, gradually taking possession, as it were, of Arthur's mind. When he attempts to study a card with riddles printed upon it, he feels 'as if a shadow from the curtained bed had got between his mind and the gaily printed letters'. Arthur is not haunted by an actual ghost, but by the mere presence of the corpse. By such rational means Collins achieves a psychological tension which the Terrorists, appealing to the supernatural, were incapable of. The dramatic intensity of Arthur's experience becomes portentious when he is confronted by the spectre of the dead man's face:

> The darkness forced his mind back upon itself, and set his memory at work, reviving, with a painfully-vivid distinctness, the momentary impression it had received from the first sight of the corpse. Before long the face seemed to be hovering out in the middle of the darkness, confronting him through the window, with the paleness whiter, with the dreadful dull line of light between the imperfectly-closed eyelids broader than he had seen it—with the parted lips slowly dropping farther and farther away from each other—with the features growing larger and moving closer, till they seemed to fill the window and to silence the rain, and to shut out the night.

Here the atmospheric effects, with the reiteration of darkness and the vision of the spectre, are very like those used by Dickens. The scene portrayed by Collins is, in fact, very reminiscent of a similar scene in *Bleak House* when Mr Tulkinghorn discovers the corpse of Nemo, the law-writer, in a dingy room with the 'gaunt eyes' of the dead man staring—as it seemed—from the shutters of the window:

> No curtain veils the darkness of the night, but the discoloured shutters are drawn together; and through the two gaunt holes pierced in them, famine might be staring in—the Banshee of the man upon the bed.
>
> (Ch. X)

Dickens's scene, like Collins's, is lit by the ghostly light of a tallow candle—lighting effects which reinforce the atmosphere of desolation which, in each case, haunts the scene and emphasises the solemn presence of the corpse. Collins, however, is more consciously dramatic than Dickens, and makes use of the dead-alive motif in describing how the spectre apparently grows and fills the window, the parted lips slowly moving further apart, to suggest how Arthur becomes obsessed and fascinated by the presence of the corpse.

The story's chief appeal lies, in fact, in the sensationally effective use of the dead-alive motif, and it reaches its highest pitch of interest when, looking towards the corpse again, Arthur suddenly realises that it has moved. Like *A Terribly Strange Bed,* the story's climax is concerned with a man seized by an overwhelming fear, and this is effectively conveyed by the short, dramatic paragraphs, the economy of words which merely suggest Arthur's state of being transfixed with horror, his eyes dilated and unblinking, and by the dramatic repetition of the phrase most weighted with sinister implications—the 'long white hand'—which becomes the visual focus of the scene:

> When he looked at the bed now, he saw, hanging over the side of it, a long white hand.
>
> It lay perfectly motionless, midway on the side of the bed, where the curtain at the head and the curtain at the floor met. Nothing more was visible. The clinging curtains hid everything but the long white hand.
>
> He stood looking at it unable to stir, unable to call out; feeling nothing, knowing nothing, every faculty he possessed gathered up and lost in the one seeing faculty.

In *The Double-Bedded Room* much of the suspense is created by the tallow candle which dimly lights the room, since Arthur dreads the moment when it will be completely burnt out, leaving him with the corpse in complete darkness. This is the principal means of evoking suspense in a later story, *Blow up with the Brig!,* which has for its main situation a unique variant of the 'haunted chamber' theme. Instead of having to pass the night in some form of sinister house, the protagonist, in this story, is bound and gagged by a villainous Spanish pilot who shuts him in a ship's hold, surrounded by kegs of gunpowder. A length of cotton-yarn rubbed with gunpowder is attached, at one end, to the kegs, and at the other to a point mid-way along the length of a slow-burning candle placed in close proximity to the protagonist's face. As he stares transfixedly at the candle, at one moment petrified, the next struggling violently as he waits to be blown up, the protagonist experiences the same type of mental agony described by Poe in *The Pit and the Pendulum.* Written at about the same time that his first masterpiece, *The Woman in White,* began to appear in serialised form, this story presents a demonstration of Collins's most mature powers of creating suspense in combination with psychological realism. The story is, in fact, a masterly study of the slow disintegration of the human mind under pressure of extreme fear, progressing from rationality to the verge of insanity. The story is told in the quaint nautical language of an old sea-dog, and the narrator's physical sensations, at first described by his colloquial speech full of hyperbolic imagery and exaggerated similes, have the paradoxical effect of simultaneously evoking the reader's amusement and horror:

> I lay in the dark for a little while, with my heart thumping as if it was going to jump out of me . . . The horrors laid hold of me from head to foot, and the sweat poured off my face like water.

When the narrator realises the full implications of his horrid plight, his language becomes less picturesque and more direct and forceful, conveying his sheer terror. As he watches, at first in a hypnotic trance, the small flame, the symbol of his own life, inevitably, inexorably, reaching the point of termination, the reader becomes increasingly conscious of his mental torture, seeing his rational mind give way to mad panic, wild physical struggles and desperate attempts to breathe due to the suffocating effect of the gag. The psychological realism is undeniable when the protagonist, haunted by the certainty of death and the uncertainty of what it will be like to be blown up, experiences mental frenzy interspersed with moments of lucid rationality. While the dramatic tension is reinforced, not by the conventional rain and wind, but by the methodical creaking of the old spars, the wick of the candle achieves a fascination of horror akin to that of the corpse in *The Double-Bedded Room*. Collins's reliance on the solid foundation of factual realism to inspire fear instead of supernaturalism is seen in his graphic description of so mundane an object as the broadening, reddening wick, which is his substitution for the actual visualisation of an apparition. The effect is more terrible and dramatic as the reader shares the protagonist's sensations of despair and horror, his eyes rivetted on the wick that threatens to fall upon the fuse:

> An hour and a quarter. The wick grew terribly as the quarter slipped away, and the charred top of it began to thicken and spread out mushroom-shape. It would fall soon.

By means of the powerful metaphorical language ('the flame of the candle flew . . . all over me, and burned up the rest of my thoughts', and '. . . the sweat of my own death agony on my face . . .') a vivid impression of the narrator's agony is conveyed as the flame literally conquers his rational mind and obliterates all thought and senses, bar the sense of sight which becomes concentrated the more intensely on the wick. The psychological drama is intense when the wick, at length, falls harmlessly into the bottom of the candlestick, and the protagonist finds himself laughing hysterically from sheer relief. Again the metaphorical language ('the light of the candle leaped in through my eyes, and licked up the laughter, and burned it out of me . . .') expresses the exact nature of the torment as the flame burns away his rational mind, reducing it, finally, to a state of wild delirium. When the images of his mother and sister take on physical form, and hallucinations dance before his eyes in a horrible kaleidoscope of fire and mist together with disintegrated thoughts and flashes of sanity, Collins achieves a psychological truthfulness almost entirely by means of the sheer intensity of melodrama. The depiction of a mind that becomes increasingly unhinged by means of an internal conflict, conveyed by the perfect control of heightened dramatic tension resulting from the impera-

tive fascination for an inanimate object, is an achievement few writers were capable of. Collins's story, however, anticipates something of the marvellous tension of nerve and brain in a similar story by Ambrose Bierce,[9] where the protagonist, trapped beneath a pile of rubble, is driven to suicide by the intense mental anguish caused by the menacing stare of a gun barrel—his gaze fixed on 'the little ring of metal with its black interior'.

It is because of the dramatic tension which keeps the reader constantly on tenterhooks in the three stories considered above, that these stories fulfil the prime requisite of sensation fiction—the maintenance of suspense. And it is because of their suspense and skilfully controlled melodrama that these stories look forward to Collins's greatest novels. It is surprising, however, that the features which distinguish his greatest novels are anticipated in one of Collins's earliest attempts at fiction, *Mad Monckton,* which Dickens rejected for publication in *Household Words* in February, 1853, on the grounds that its chief theme was hereditary insanity, a subject which the editor felt would cause distress 'among those numerous families in which there is such a taint'.[10] The story looks forward to novels like *The Woman in White* and *Armadale* in so far as the leading character, Alfred Monckton, is a highly individualised creation whose mental and emotional abnormality makes him particularly suitable for the purposes of the sensation story. In the portrayal of Monckton, whose character is internally melodramatic, Collins employs every advantage of dramatic effect. This is particularly evident in Monckton's extraordinary habit of fixing his eyes intensely on vacant space, in a manner possibly intended to recall Macbeth. But again there is no direct appeal to the supernatural, since the startling vision which Monckton sees of his dead uncle is put forward as a projection of his nervous state of mind. His vacant stare recurs throughout the story like a *leitmotif,* always at crucial and dramatic moments. The description of his eyes, wandering 'slowly, inch by inch . . . , until they stopped at a certain point', is carefully calculated to evoke suspense and an atmosphere charged with uncanny feeling. The scene derives its power purely from Collins's dramatic techniques. While the narrator's dismissal of the apparition as a mere figment of Monckton's diseased imagination engages the reader's credulity in the scene, the dramatic techniques actually reinforce the presence of the apparition. This is effected by the theatrical technique of dumb play, since Collins meticulously describes the facial expressions and dramatic gestures of the leading actor to suggest the horrific experience of seeing the apparition, instead of actually describing the apparition. Consequently sentences like 'his face whitened horribly, and the perspiration broke out all over it', and 'His eyes flashed and dilated; his voice deepened; a fanatic ecstasy shone in his expression . . .', enable the reader to enter fully into the emotional involvement, while the narrator, minutely describing his own terror, serves as the reader's own centre of consciousness, reacting in much the same way as the reader might be expected to react:

> I felt my blood curdling as he spoke, and I knew in my own heart, as I sat there speechless, that I dare not turn round and look where he was still pointing . . . My own nerves were more shaken than I could have thought possible . . . A vague dread of being near him in his present mood came over me . . .

Another means whereby Collins employs melodrama to portray the character of Monckton is found in the idea of an ineluctable fate. In his novels, particularly *Armadale,* the dream is used as a device of foreshadowing and foreboding, creating suspense through expectation. In *Mad Monckton* suspense is built around the gradual, inevitable fulfilment, not of a dream, but of an old family prophecy which states that the Monckton line will be extinguished when a Monckton lies 'graveless under open sky'. Fatality, in this story, is not merely a mechanical device to heighten the suspense of a sensational tale but a means of enhancing the dramatic struggle within Monckton. Obsessed by the idea of fatality, and goaded by the vision of his dead uncle, his motives themselves are melodramatic when he tries to avert the decree of fate in a desperate search for his uncle's body.

It is by means of the fatality motif, too, that Collins successfully creates a sense of mounting terror as the reader waits for the discovery of the gruesome body for which the prophecy has prepared him. This is sustained, as the moment of discovery approaches, by the oppressive atmosphere, the sinister 'Gothic' connotations of a decaying Campanian monastery streaked with green stains, and by the claustrophobic effect of a dark, stifling wood with rotting vegatation—an atmosphere remarkably similar to that described by Poe, which 'had reeked up from the decayed trees, and the grey wall, and the silent tarn' in *The Fall of the House of Usher.* While the gloomy setting serves to conjure up thrilling expectations of gruesome horror, it underlines the protagonist's intense feelings of dendrophobia and vague uneasiness; consequently a perfect setting and atmosphere is created for the discovery of the rotting corpse, when the narrator peers into the dark interior of a deserted out-house:

> The sight of horror that met my eyes the instant I looked through the hole, is as present to my memory now as if I had beheld it yesterday . . .

> The first impression conveyed to me . . . was of a long recumbent object, tinged with a lightish blue colour all over, extended on trestles, and bearing a certain hideous, half-formed resemblance to the human face and figure . . . My eyes got accustomed to the dim light streaming in through the broken roof; and I satisfied myself . . . that I was looking at the corpse of a

man—a corpse that had apparently once had a sheet spread over it—and that had lain rotting on the trestles under the open sky long enough for the linen to take the livid, light-blue tinge of mildew and decay which now covered it.

Although the reader is at first titillated by the expectation of horror caused by the writer's deliberate attempt to procrastinate the actual fact of seeing the corpse, he is led into a mental ambuscade, and taken almost by surprise when the narrator's precise and controlled language unexpectedly presents him with the garish, charnel-house details. The shock, the thrill of horror experienced by the reader, exactly expresses the protagonist's own sensations—'the hideous spectacle unexpectedly offered to my eyes . . . had shaken my nerves . . .'. This is the type of sensational shock which H. L. Mansel, in his article on 'Sensation Novels', compared to the effect of the galvanic battery that 'carries the whole nervous system by steam'.[11] Horror-stricken, the reader, like the protagonist, is stunned by the sudden revelation; but unlike the protagonist, the reader is intended to enjoy a thrilling sensation, an exhilaration that comes from contemplating the scene of garish realism—a scene comprised of the same sensational stuff as that in which Hugo describes a half-decayed corpse suspended from the gallows in *L'Homme qui rit,* or the scene of repulsive horror described by Charles Reade in *It is Never too late to Mend* when a body is discovered in the Australian bush, the flesh lacerated, the eyes picked out by crows. While garishness of this sort is not the excrescence of immaturity, but a deliberate quality aimed at energising the sensational scenes with the traditional appeal to fear and terror, reliance on such material, as W. C. Philips[12] has pointed out, was a canon of art for Collins as well as for Reade and Dickens—they had tolerably definite formulas regarding the grotesque, the violent and theatrical, since they wrote not exclusively for the cultivated or sophisticated, but for the whole public.

Although Wilkie Collins is in danger of melodramatic overemphasis in his climax of horrific effect, the admirable handling of the fatality motif rescues the story from moments of sheer melodramatics. There is considerable psychological insight, for example, in Monckton's frenzied exultation when, on hearing from his friend that his uncle's body has been found, he believes that he has thwarted the old prophecy. This mental frenzy, counterpointed by the narrator's vague melancholy forebodings and unaccountable depression, creates a sense of inevitability against which it is impossible to struggle. It is by means of this sense of inevitability, which corresponds to life itself, that Collins gives his story verisimilitude, and realises Dickens's dictum, that 'the business of art is . . . to *suggest,* until the fulfilment comes'. Such, according to Dickens, are 'the ways of Providence, of which all art is but a little imitation'.[13] A master of mystification, Collins uses the fatality motif in the early stages of the story as a means of darkly foreshadowing the future, the aura of mystery creating a mild atmosphere of suspense. Monckton, with his strange behaviour and inexplicable behaviour of staring into vacancy, is himself a mystified character and the proto-type of many enigmatical personages that people the later novels. In this story, however, Collins is not concerned merely with the progressive deepening, and ultimate solution, of a mystery,[14] as is Poe in *The Oblong Box*. The concluding portion of Collins's story substantially corresponds with Poe's story, since both writers describe a sea journey in which a corpse is carried as baggage with the ultimate loss of the ship; and in either case a person of dubious sanity, susceptible to 'fits of moody misanthropy',[15] is unwilling to abandon the corpse, and dies soon afterwards. But whereas in Poe's story the main events constitute a puzzle-formula that excites the reader's curiosity about the grizzly contents of the wooden box, in Collins's tale the events are the inevitable, if not natural, outcome of an ineluctable fate which gives the story an organised unity and a final totality of effect.

Apart from the psychological melodrama, the fatality motif and the Pre-Raphaelite-theatre type of realism, there are other incidental characteristics of *Mad Monckton* which anticipate features of Collins's best work. There is the delectable humour, for example, in the very realistic picture of a senile Capuchin monk who takes a child-like delight in snuff—a picture conceived in the same humorous vein as the child-like Mrs Wragge, and a Scotch fly-driver excessively fond of whisky, both in *No Name*. Furthermore, there is the technique of furthering the plot by means of a newspaper report (an account of the duel in which Monckton's uncle is killed) which enhances the verisimilitude of the story by giving it an air of documentary fact. This technique looks forward to Collins's use of various legal documents that form an integral part of the plot in novels like *The Woman in White* and *No Name,* and to some extent also anticipates the epistolary technique which constitutes the basic narrative form of these works.

Although none of the short stories considered in this article actually make use of the epistolary technique, it is perhaps not unfeasible that the early short stories were the genesis of Collins's multi-narrational method whereby character is more intimately revealed through letters and documents written in the first-person. All the short stories considered are, in fact, written in the first person singular, and each story presents a distinct and separate personality in the narrator. These stories may well constitute the basis of Collins's apprenticeship in the technique of adapting each narrative to its narrator; by projecting himself into different characters, he achieves variety of style and tone, and affords his char-

acters a means of dramatic self-revelation. Thus whereas in *The Double-Bedded Room* the conversational style of an elderly medical practitioner has an authoritative and moralising tone, allowing the main figure, Arthur, to be seen objectively, the easy conversational style of *A Terribly Strange Bed* is more pronounced, revealing the protagonist as an excitable, impetuous young man. The semi-serious tone and colloquial, unpedantic style of *Blow up with the Brig!,* on the other hand, is in keeping with the character of an old sailor who, never quite sure of his facts, tends to ramble, and admits his lack of learning—'I am not a scholar myself'. The style and narrative technique of *Mad Monckton* are akin to the methods of Sheridan Le Fanu in his story *Green Tea*. In the first chapter the narrator is concerned with 'hearsay evidence', describing what he saw and heard of Monckton as an intelligent observer, but relies, in the second chapter, on his 'own personal experience'. While something of the analytic mind of the lawyer emerges in the systematic presentation of facts, later chapters reveal the narrator as an adventurous, though conscientious young man with a genuine concern for his friend, when he becomes personally involved in the events of the narrative. Thus the first-person narrative achieves a three-dimensional effect, not only in the portrayal of the narrator, but also in the portrayal of Monckton. It makes it possible for the story to give a step-by-step penetration into the character of Monckton—first from a distance, then through the account of a friend of the narrator, and ultimately by means of personal contact and friendship—with the result that Monckton becomes progressively less distanced from the reader. Such, then, is the nature of Collins's early narrative methods which undoubtedly perfected his effective technique of the multiple-first-person point of view in novels like *The Woman in White* and *The Moonstone.* By means of this technique, character is revealed dramatically, the result being that his great masterpieces of fiction, like his early short stories, are not merely melodramatic, since they are given the intimate immediacy of true drama.

The influence of Collins's early short stories, with their concentration of imagination and economy of stroke in achieving effect, on his later fictional career cannot be underestimated, since Collins began to write at a time when the three-volume serialised novel was a shapeless, sprawling form with little unity. It is not surprising that his novels before 1860, like the over-elaborate historical romance *Antonina,* offered little more than the narrative sprawl and chaos characteristic of mid-nineteenth century novels which Henry James described as 'large loose baggy monsters'. Although Collins was initially unable to sustain interest and suspense over the wide span of the three-decker novel, the concise structure, the close unity, the narrower range of intense experience and the concentration of sensational effect in the short story popularised by Poe undoubtedly assisted him in achieving the sustained vitality and the remarkable adroitness of narrative manipulation evident in **The Woman in White.** It is not surprising that the most eminent creator of popular fiction of the day should have recognised the early manifestation of Collins's talent; although Dickens did not consider **Mad Monckton** suitable for the readers of *Household Words,* he nevertheless informed Wills, his sub-editor, that there was much evidence in the story of 'many things, both in the inventive and descriptive way, that [Collins] could do for us . . .'.[16] It was undoubtedly Collins's inventive genius in the dramatic portrayal of character, and his descriptive power in the evocation of dramatic atmosphere, which that other eminent sensationist, Charles Reade, recognised when, in his diary, he penned his terse eulogium: 'Wilkie Collins. An artist of the pen. There are terribly few among writers'.[17]

Notes

1. Letter to Charles Knight, 17 March 1854, *Letters of Charles Dickens,* ed. Walter Dexter (London: Nonesuch Dickens, 1938), II, 548.

2. *Daily News* (4 Oct., 1865), 2.

3. *Sharpe's London Magazine,* XXIV (May, 1864), 276.

4. [Fitzjames Stephen], 'The Licence of Modern Novelists', *Edinburgh Review,* CVI (July, 1857), 125.

5. [H. L. Mansel], 'Sensation Novels', *Quarterly Review,* CXIII (Apr., 1863), 482. It is not surprising that Mansel, who was a strong Tory and Oxford don with high church principles, whose interest lay in the English divines and ecclesiastical history, should have been averse to the new 'sensational' trend in literature.

6. This story appears as part of *The Lazy Tour of Two Idle Apprentices,* in which Dickens and Collins collaborated.

7. T. S. Eliot, 'Wilkie Collins and Dickens', *Selected Essays* (London: Faber & Faber, 1966), p. 468.

8. Quoted by Kenneth Robinson, *Wilkie Collins: A Biography* (New York: MacMillan, 1952), p. 152.

9. 'One of the Missing'. Bierce, a later Victorian and American writer, wrote short stories similar to those of Edgar Allan Poe.

10. Letter to W. H. Wills, 8 February 1853, *Charles Dickens as Editor,* ed. R. C. Lehmann (London: Smith, Elder & Co., 1912), p. 97.

11. [Mansel], op. cit., p. 487.

12. W. C. Philips, *Dickens, Reade, and Collins: Sensation Novelists* (New York: Russel & Russel, 1962), pp. 11-12.

13. Letter to Wilkie Collins *re A Tale of Two Cities,* 6 October 1859, *Letters of Charles Dickens,* ed. cit., III, 125.

14. Collins is, of course, best known for his literary ingenuity in the creation of intricate plots invested with mystery, and for this reason is generally considered the father of the English detective story. The detective novel, however, was a *genre* unknown to Collins, and he was foremostly a master sensationist whose main concern lay in the serious fictional treatment of popular melodrama—as his early short-story fiction, written before his masterpieces of mystery and intrigue, would seem to testify.

15. Poe: 'The Oblong Box'.

16. Letter to W. H. Wills, 8 February 1853, *Charles Dickens as Editor,* ed. cit., p. 98.

17. Quoted by Charles L. Reade and Rev. Compton Reade, *Charles Reade, Dramatist, Novelist, Journalist: A Memoir* (London: Chapman & Hall, 1887), II, 277.

R. V. Andrew (essay date 1979)

SOURCE: Andrew, R. V. "Two Good Short Stories; and a Poor One." In *Wilkie Collins: A Critical Survey of His Prose Fiction with a Bibliography,* pp. 282-86. New York: Garland Publishing, Inc., 1979.

[*In the following excerpt, Andrew discusses the stories "Who Killed Zebedee?," "How I Married Him," and "Your Money or Your Life," the last of which, the critic suggests, displays the triteness characteristic of Collins's later fiction.*]

> "Yes, sir, I am to caution the persons that whatever they may say will be taken down, and may be used in evidence against them."

> "I removed the key from the street door after locking it; and I said to the landlady: 'Nobody must leave the house, or enter the house, till the Inspector comes.'"

Who Killed Zebedee? is an exciting short story of detection. Collins includes features which have, once again, provided with subsequent writers with techniques without which they seem ill-equipped to write a detective story. We are introduced to regular routine police procedure: The doors are locked, windows checked for security, enquiries are made about visitors and the times of their arrival and departure, and the histories of the residents are checked. These residents all have characteristics which make them possible candidates for the role of murderer, and the person who admits to being guilty is obviously innocent. The murder weapon is photographed and advertised widely in every police station in the country. Several most satisfactory red herrings are included.

Who Killed Zebedee? was first published in *The Seaside Library* on the 26th January, 1881 and was included in the **Little Novels** collection as **Mr Policeman and the Cook.**

Mr Zebedee, who is on his way with his wife to Australia, is found murdered in a lodging-house in London. Mrs Zebedee believes that she has murdered her husband in his sleep. The murder weapon is a knife bearing the inscription "To Zebedee from. . . .". One of the residents, Mr Deluc, a Creole from Martinique, is suspect. He had made advances to Mrs Zebedee and, upon being repulsed, had said "Madam, you may live to regret this." He is watched, but nothing suspicious is discovered. A description of the knife is circulated, but to no purpose. The case is filed, but the young policeman cannot take his mind off the problem. In the course of his investigations he has fallen in love with the cook at the lodging-house, and arranges a visit to her parents. She has preceded him and he misses the train when seeking refreshment at the station previous to his destination. Whiling away the time until he can catch the next train, he wanders about the town. On the off-chance, he makes enquiries about the knife at a cutlor's shop. The unfinished engraving on the knife is explained: it should have read "To Zebedee. From Priscilla Thirby"—that is the cook's name. Once he has completed his journey, he makes enquiries of the local parson and learns that Zebedee had worked in that area, had been engaged to the cook, but had left after the banns had been called and after attempting unsuccessfully to seduce her. The cook had reclaimed the knife from the engraver before the inscription had been completed and had gone to London to seek a position. When Zebedee had turned up at the lodging-house bound for Australia with another wife, the cook had seized her opportunity and had plunged the knife into him.

This is one of Collins's best short stories and certainly his best short detective story. The construction is excellent, the leat-likely-person motif is cleverly exploited and the red herrings are most satisfactory. There are two small points of adverse criticism: Collins departs from the fair-play rule when he withholds from us information obtained from the cook as regards Deluc; and chance plays rather too large a part in bringing the constable to the cutler's shop.

Your Money or Your Life, published in *The People's Library* on the 17th December, 1881, and in **Little Novels** as **Mr Cosway and the Landlady,** is a flimsy story of two naval officers who run into debt at an inn while waiting for their ship to sail. The landlady suggests that she will take no steps against them if one of them will marry her. Though the marriage is not to be consummated, it will give her status and protection in her position as landlady. Mr Cosway marries her, spends four years at sea, leaves the navy, inherits a fortune and learns that his wife is dead. He falls in love with a young lady far above him in station, but the course of true love does not run at all smoothly. A senior shareholder in his prospective father-in-law's business, a Miss Benshaw, turns out to be his wife. Reports of her death had been false. Upon inheriting her father's estate she had given up the inn and had resumed her maiden name.

Two years later Cosway learns that his wife has been drowned in a boating accident and that her fortune has been bequeathed to the girl he loves, provided she does not marry Cosway. She does, nevertheless.

Collins informs us that the strange marriage is based on fact and is taken from an anecdote in Lockhart's *Life of Scott* which concerns one of Scott's cousins who married the proprietress of an inn under similar circumstances.

Collins writes with skill and fluency, but there is in this story a triteness which is to become increasingly evident in later stories.

How I Married Him, published in *The Spirit of the Times* on the 24th December, 1881 and included in **Little Novels** as **Miss Morris and the Stranger,** is written with lightness and charm and a fine understanding of a young woman's mind. We find in this short story an excellent example of that strange secret language which only women understand, a language which seems perfectly innocuous to men, but with which women can wound each other deeply. There is a touch of malice in Miss Morris. When a gentleman says that her rival sings so well that she should be on the stage, she places on record:

> "I thought so too. Big as it was, our drawing room was not large enough for her."

Nancy Morris, a friendless, poor orphan, is provided with an education by Sir Gervase. She shows her gratitude in such a becoming manner that he becomes truly fond of her. Upon taking up a position as governess, she meets Mr Sax. They love each other, but Sax is so shy that he is easily rebuffed. Upon Sir Gervase's death Nancy inherits seventy thousand pounds, but the executor suggests that Sir Gervase's nephew has more right to the money. Nancy refuses the bequest and then learns that the nephew is Mr Sax. When he refuses to accept the money, she drops her maidenly reserve and suggests that they solve the difficulty by marrying.

Collins has obviously written this story for a special market: the light magazine. Yet there are some delightful touches of character: Mrs Fosdyke has an easy competent way with children, Mr Sax's shyness leads him deeper into the mire whenever he tries to extricate himself from a predicament. The story flows smoothly, the difficulties are created and resolved with aplomb, and a delicate vein of humour flows through all. This is a first-person narrative in which Nancy Morris emerges as a natural and sweet young woman with a well-developed sense of humour—provided she is not in the presence of a rival.

Julian Thompson (essay date 1995)

SOURCE: Thompson, Julian. Introduction to *Wilkie Collins: The Complete Shorter Fiction*, edited by Julian Thompson, pp. vii-xi. New York: Carroll & Graff Publishers, Inc., 1995.

[*In the following essay, Thompson presents an overview of Collins's short fiction, discussing characterization, themes, and Collins's interest in the occult.*]

Collins is surely the most readable of all major English writers. As T. S. Eliot pointed out he has the 'immense merit . . . of being never dull.'[1] Whether he is offering up a slight jest, a glorified potboiler, or a striking tour-de-force, there is always a confidence that the eye will be propelled profitably from page to page (Collins after all believed that 'the primary object of a work of fiction should be to tell a story'), and that the plants Collins puts down will all be taken up. His rich gifts for characterisation and the sustenance of narrative constitute a major part of his appeal.

Not the whole of it, however. As a sensational writer Collins delights in extraordinary events and peculiar states of mind. Life in the small hours, hereditary madness, violent abductions, the sufferings of women: Collins permits us to glimpse areas of Victorian society usually hidden from fictional consideration, as befits a man with two mistresses, two households and a lifelong disinclination for marriage. He knows his nether world well—Collins's healthy rakishness was a major part of his appeal for the more conventional Dickens—and insinuates something of its arduousness and strangeness into our memory of his most bustling stories.

Collins is probably best known for his tales of the occult. His ghosts are extraordinarily convincing. As G. K. Chesterton points out,[2] they sidle softly and solidly as Count Fosco, and disturb and satisfy the reader in the same weightily insouciant way. Collins's repeated use of the double is striking, too—but it is grounded much more firmly in the actual, and is much less theoretic than the conventional Gothic *doppelganger,* which stiffly allegorises the human soul. In Godwin's *Caleb Williams* (1794), Falkland's guilt and Caleb's fear are

recto and verso of the same emotion. Similarly, Poe's William Wilson must acknowledge his shadowy persecutor, Frankenstein struggle to regain his lost monster-self, Jekyll take responsibility for Hyde. The effect may be complex, but the intention is clear: 'This thing of darkness I acknowledge mine.'[3] By contrast the moral fable in Collins's stories such as '**The Dead Hand**' or the original version of '**The Dream Woman**' seems much less articulate. This is partly because Collins is not as serious as his rivals: his motive is more openly to entertain. But it is also because Collins refuses the portentousness that can so easily overtake Romantic-Gothic gestures: he is in some ways closer than his masters to that canny accommodation of mystery and uncertainty that Keats called negative capability. None of Collins's stories seems to work better in this way than the very early *Mad Monkton* (1852), where the ghost of a dead profligate uncle is superimposed on the living figure of the hero's fiancée: 'Think of the calm angel-face and the tortured spectre-face being always together, whenever my eyes meet hers!' The contortion of sexuality and personal obsession in Monkton's imagination is appalling and naked; the uncle's festering sensuality, drifting for ever about the hero's consciousness as his unburied corpse drifts along the ocean tides, is a fearful reality for Monkton, and becomes one both for the story's sceptical narrator and eventually for the reader. It is quite unnecessary to raise the whole thing to an abstract plane, and mutter about ineluctable dualism. Collins was capable at his best of 'a sort of involuntary mysticism which dealt wholly with the darker side of the human soul' (Chesterton again).[4] Robert Aickman suggests that the story seems to be written 'by the light of gas-flares.'[5]

Throughout his career Collins continues to brush the nerves with a thrill of the *unheimlich*. As the clergyman discovers when the spectre of Miss Jéromette hardens like guilt out of his past, 'the chill of the mist was in the wine'. The effect often seems to hinge on the audacity with which Collins juxtaposes the mysterious and the everyday. Catherine Peters has brilliantly pointed out a moment of compelling subtlety in the undervalued story '**Nine o'Clock!**': 'A young man, standing beside his brother, sees the brother's projection or shadow-self simultaneously walking in the garden with their father. The father, though sympathetically presented, cannot tell the shadow from the real son: a fleeting but effective image of parental obtuseness.'[6] Even where the component parts seem to vibrate uncomfortably, the stories have a still centre where powerful effects are achieved. In '**Gabriel's Marriage**' the white spectre women riding the waves seem to create the taste by which the story's vision of atonement is relished. The grisly glamour of Notman's Arctic experience emphasises rather than overpowers the moralistic fable in '**The Devil's Spectacles**'. The sensation of the young man's panic in '**A Terribly Strange Bed**' is wonderfully involved with the description of the apparently dissolving picture on the wall. Most striking of all is the effect in **'The Black Cottage'**. This is Collins's most brutal story: the persecution of the lonely wife in her isolated homestead is carried on so luridly as to resemble melodrama or even pantomime. And yet even here Collins achieves a fabular grandeur—despite the coarseness of the treatment, the story becomes an embodied nightmare, and recognisably a mythic presentation of a woman's worst fears.

But Collins did not only confine his attentions to ghost stories and psychological fables. His best-known novels, *The Woman in White* (1860) and *The Moonstone* (1868), eschew supernatural machinery, and Collins's 'daylight work' retains its power to shock and energise, or at the very least to keep us turning the pages. As an untried author he felt the need to display a range of wares. His first surviving fiction, **'The Last Stage Coachman'** (1843), is a piece of magic realism; his second published story, **'The Twin Sisters'** (1851), is a study in the incorrigibility of sexual choice; his third, **'A Passage in the Life of Perugino Potts'** (1852), is a skit on artistic egotism; his fourth is the brazenly sensational **'A Terribly Strange Bed'** (1852). The variety is impressive but some of Collins's early stories are (by the standards of the time) also formidably inventive: almost singlehanded he effected the importation into England of the detective story on Poe's model, but with an unassuming control of humour (for instance, in **'The Biter Bit'**) and character (the private investigator in **'A Plot in Private Life'**) that seems quite beyond the range of Poe. By the mid 1850s Collins had accumulated sufficient short stories to want to preserve some of them in book form, and his ability to produce page-turning copy (especially early in his career) is wonderfully illustrated by the framing-narratives he concocted to support this republication. It is beyond the scope of the present volume to reproduce these, but the reader is urged to seek out both *After Dark* (1856) and *The Queen of Hearts* (1859) to see how neatly Collins wove very disparate stories into sustained omnibus entertainment. In *After Dark* the device is that a portrait painter has suffered an eye infection and cannot paint. At his wife's instigation he turns instead to telling stories—and the stories he tells are those told to him in the course of the protracted sittings that make up his working life. In *The Queen of Hearts* the framing-narrative is if anything even more colourful. Three crusty old bachelors, living in a Peacock-like hermitage on the Welsh borders, have to keep a spry young girl from quitting them for the delights of the town—the arrival of the eligible son of one of them is imminent. Like Scheherazade they hit on the idea of telling her stories, and the stories they tell are those Collins had been purveying in *Household Words* and elsewhere in the previous three or four years. Both

After Dark and *The Queen of Hearts* are highly readable collections: the plays-without-the-play being quite as good as the main entertainment.

Part of the secret of Collins's charm lies in his skill in creating and sustaining serviceable characters. In the great novels, Frederick Fairlie's hypochondria and the imperturbability of Sergeant Cuff take plenty of time to assert themselves. In the short story Collins must work faster, and he does. The old Capuchin in **'Mad Monkton'** is as vivid a time-waster as the vestry clerk at Welmingham in *The Woman in White*. The bitter baroness in **'Mr Medhurst and the Princess'** deprecates English modesty with Fosco-like brio. In **'Mr Percy and the Prophet'** the egoistic Mr Bowmore fusses that his speeches must be delivered correctly in his absence (an objective correlative for the one right of man this radical reserves above all others, 'the right of using his tongue'). Equally well done (among many other examples) are the Galt-like prissiness of the Minister of Cauldkirk in **'Mr Marmaduke and the Minister'**, and the brittle feistiness of the young governess in **'Miss Morris and the Stranger'**.

Collins's stories show other aspects of his command of characterisation. What Miss Mina in **'Miss Mina and the Groom'** calls 'the influence that men have on women *because* they are men' was no mystery to Collins. As J. I. M. Stewart has pointed out, Collins is 'able to portray women with a fidelity much in advance of some more famous Victorian novelists. Perhaps because he himself lived . . . outside the ring-fence of Victorian convention, he was more willing to endow women with intellect, passion and strength-of-will than were many of his more famous contemporaries.'[7] Not only does he deal sympathetically and fully with disadvantaged women—governesses (**'Miss Morris and the Stranger'**), work-girls (**'Anne Rodway'**), serving-girls (**'Mr Policeman and the Cook'**), the daughters of stone-cutters (**'The Black Cottage'**) and lodge-keepers (**'Mr Lepel and the Housekeeper'**).[8] He is also never slow to signal female sexuality (much quicker than Dickens), though strictly within the bounds of magazine propriety. Miss Mina's glands have not yet been activated, as her rather striking confession illustrates: 'When a man pressed my hand, I felt it in my rings, instead of my heart.' The South-Sea island girl in **'Mr Captain and the Nymph'**, on the other hand, has the 'fearless candour of a child. "Squeeze me again. I like it!"' Nancy Morris, in **'Miss Morris and the Stranger'** has the temerity to cut through her suitor's plot-bound scruples, and demand to be taken with her money; whereas Salome Skirton, in **'Fie! Fie! or, The Fair Physician'** has all the Byronic languor of a sofa-bound Dudu. But despite the confidence with which Collins portrays women as sexual beings, it would be unreasonable to claim him as an unqualified champion of women's rights. The medical examinations of **'Fie! Fie! or,** the Fair Physician' are full of male chauvinist double entendre: '[The female doctor's] pretty hand grasped his shoulder, and her little rosy ear pressed (medically pressed) Sir John's broad back.' The story seems brusquely unaware that if female doctors are subject to universal flirtatiousness, the problem lies not in feminism, but in unreconstructed male sexuality. But then, as **'Miss Dulane and My Lord'** makes clear, Collins believed that 'very few women . . . mean No when they say No.'

It is often pointed out that Collins's later stories are thinner in texture than his early ones, and show the scars of having been wrung from an ailing mind and body. Certainly some of them leave possibilities unfulfilled. Hardy, for instance, would have made so much of the quasi-mythic ironies and ambiguities that mark the situation in **'Mr Lismore and the Widow'**, where the sexually eligible young woman impersonates an aged woman to secure her marriage contract, and then seduces her husband in the persona of her younger self. The denouement of Collins's story is striking, certainly, but the interest springs (in a manner familiar with Collins when his imagination is not wholly engaged) more from the extraordinary situation than its psychological convolution and suggestiveness. Similarly **'Mr Captain and the Nymph'**, a tale of the South Seas, despite purple sub-Coleridgean visions of volcanic fires, burning skies and 'empty and endless seas', never aspires to the tragic resonance which Stevenson or Conrad might tease out of similar material, nor to the racial allegories of Melville's *Typee* or *Omoo*.

Some of the late stories also show evidence of reworking of old themes in a lower key, or with a more perfunctory treatment. **'Miss Jéromette and the Clergyman'**, in bringing the false lover and the timid clergyman together (both have led lives of sexual irregularity), recalls Collins's favourite 'double' motif— and also reworks in somewhat jaded fashion the 'pursuer as nemesis' theme that had done such sterling service in his early novel **Basil**. The ghostly duellist in **'Miss Bertha and the Yankee'** brings us back to familiar territory from **'Mad Monkton'**, but this time Collins injures the effect (as in **'Miss Dulane and My Lord'**) with a somewhat stretched rational explanation. Although individual stories (and parts of stories) from the last decade or so of Collins's career have a kind of desperate flair and power—as of a candle guttering in the socket—reading them collectively one does get the impression of narrative weariness, and of involuntary repetition. By the mid 1880s the short story was moving on, and leaving Collins behind. Kipling had published his collection of life-histories in three pages, *Plain Tales From the Hills* (1886). In comparison Collins looks leisurely and old-fashioned: a writer of the mid-century increasingly out of the swing of the literary world. But the best of his short stories withstand the test of time. In conclusion I shall quote (as many have quoted) the literary creed of the hard-to-please young lady who listens to the yarns of the old men in **The Queen of Hearts.** In many ways it precisely expresses Collins's own:

> 'I'm sick to death of novels with an earnest purpose. I'm sick to death of outbursts of eloquence, and large-minded philanthropy, and graphic descriptions, and unsparing anatomy of the human heart, and all that sort of thing. Good gracious me! isn't it the original intention or purpose, or whatever you call it, of a work of fiction to set out distinctly by telling a story? . . . Oh, dear me! what I want is something that seizes hold of my interest, and makes me forget when it is time to dress for dinner; something that keeps me reading, reading, reading, in a breathless state to find out the end.'⁹

Notes

1. T. S. Eliot, *Selected Essays* (1932; Faber, 1951), p. 468.

2. G. K. Chesterton, *The Victorian Age in Literature* (London: Williams and Norgate, 1913), p. 132.

3. *The Tempest*, V. i. 275-6.

4. *The Victorian Age in Literature*, p. 130.

5. Introduction to Robert Aickman, ed. *The Fourth Fontana Book of Great Ghost Stories* (1967), p. 10.

6. Catherine Peters, *The King of Inventors* (London: Secker and Warburg, 1991), p. 112.

7. J. I. M. Stewart, Introducion to *The Moonstone* (Harmondsworth: Penguin, 1966), pp. 9-10.

8. Collins's championship of marginal women has led to feminist studies of his work in recent years. See Tamar Heller's *Dead Secrets: Wilkie Collins and the Female Gothic* (1992).

9. Wilkie Collins, *The Queen of Hearts* (London: Hurst and Blackett, 1859), Vol. I, pp. 94-5.

Ira B. Nadel (essay date 1995)

SOURCE: Nadel, Ira B. "Wilkie Collins and His Illustrators." In *Wilkie Collins to the Forefront: Some Reassessments,* edited by Nelson Smith and R. C. Terry, pp. 149-64. New York: AMS Press, 1995.

[*In the following excerpt, Nadel focuses on the illustrations accompanying Collins's works, from the sketches illuminating his short stories in magazines to the wood engravings accompanying his longer works, concluding that Collins sought to retain a connection between verbal and visual elements.*]

Response to the account of John Everett Millais' mid-1850s journey through the dimly lit streets of north London in the company of Charles and Wilkie Collins after a party at 17 Hanover Terrace, the home of Mrs. William Collins, has concentrated on the encounter and pursuit of Caroline Graves by Wilkie Collins. Yet another aspect of the evening is its confirmation of the friendship between Millais and Wilkie Collins marked by three artistic events: the 1850 portrait of Collins by the 21-year-old painter; the publication of Millais' first book illustration in Collins' fourth book, *Mr. Wray's Cash-Box*; and the printing of a Millais engraving as the frontispiece in the 1864 one-volume edition of *No Name.*

Collins, in turn, promoted Millais' work and supported him in his crisis with Ruskin which concluded with Millais' marriage to Effie Gray Ruskin; Collins, incidently, gave the farewell dinner for Millais the night before he left for Scotland to be with Effie just before their wedding in 1855. But more importantly, the Millais-Collins relationship emphasizes Collins' long-term association with illustrators and illustrations for his fiction. Throughout Collins' career, Hablot Brown ("Phiz"), Sir John Gilbert, Luke Fildes, George du Maurier, and Millais, among others, illustrated his work. But my purpose is not to survey the work of these artists but to consider their contributions in the broader context of the meaning of illustration for Victorian fiction.

One begins with a simple question: what is the function of illustration in a Victorian novel? The obvious answers include commercial appeal, visual enhancement, and lengthening the text. Illustrations accompanying the periodical publication of a novel, such as George du Maurier's eighteen engravings for Mrs. Gaskell's *Wives and Daughters* in the *Cornhill,* often created visual appeal for otherwise conservatively designed periodicals. Such illustrations also extended the tradition of illustrated journalism which originated in fashion magazines of the late eighteenth century, satirical papers of the 1820s and pictorial news magazines such as *The Illustrated London News* which began on 14 May 1842. That most "triple deckers" or one-volume editions of these novels failed to reproduce such illustrations has made reading such works today incomplete. Nonetheless, the theoretical significance of illustrations for the Victorian novel, and Collins' work in particular, needs to be addressed.

An illustration is a sign encoding cultural and narrative values embedded in the language of the text. It establishes a frame for the reader's entrance into the work, creating a structure as well as an image through which he views the text. Although critics have suggested that an illustration might be "dangerous" because it could easily be identified with the thing or being it represents, or become a mere token of the text, a successful illustration extends the writing through symbolizing values and connotations not evident in the base text. The semiotic properties of the illustration nevertheless provide both an immediate image and a conceptual system for understanding the work.

Illustrations, in short, are complementary forms of writing that may correspond to, or confuse, reality. Over time, figured writing in the form of hieroglyphics or the Chinese ideogram diminished as the linear power of prose divorced the signified from the represented. The dissociation of sign and resemblance, originating in the seventeenth century, continued to make readers skeptical of illustrations because they realized that a "sign can be more or less probable, more or less distant from what it signifies [because] the relation of the sign to its content is not guaranteed by the order of things in themselves."[1] In the nineteenth century, however, there was an effort to eliminate the division between signifier and signified confirmed by the flourishing of illustrations in the Victorian novel.

The effort to unite image and text, however, also generated objections originating in the supposed reduction of the symbolic resonance of the text which obscured such important qualities as point of view. George Eliot expressed this in terms of the author/artist split in 1862. To Frederick Leighton, illustrating *Romola* in the *Cornhill,* she wrote "I feel for you as well as for myself in this inevitable difficulty—nay impossibility of producing perfect correspondence between my intention and the illustrations." "I am convinced", she added, "that illustrations can only form a sort of overture to the text."[2] Handicapping the reader's visual imagination or competing with the verbal text (as James warned could happen, in the Preface to the *Golden Bowl*) are additional reasons for rejecting illustrations.[3] But the desire to reclaim the unity between the represented and the signified through the union of image and text remained a goal of the nineteenth-century reader, as well as author and illustrator.

Initiating a visual reference point for every reader is the frontispiece which competes with the title page for control over the text. The illustration functions to visualize hermeneutical elements of the text, inscribing or confirming what the language suggests. This may, of course, be limiting since a definite image replaces the ambiguity of the verbal title. But when the novelist and artist collaborate, or lacking that, when the illustrations enhance the text thematically, narratively or structurally, as has been argued occurs in the work of Dickens, the importance of illustration exceeds that of decoration, ornament, or device.[4]

Wilkie Collins, the son of a painter and himself a student of art, was well aware of this. In preparing for the publication of *Mr. Wray's Cash-Box,* he told Richard

Bentley that he desired illustrations in the text and provided specific instructions:

> My idea is that Frontispiece, Vignette and Tail Piece would be quite enough—*well* done—ordinary mediocre work won't do—work by the famous men is only to be had at a high price. . . . I should propose that the three illustrations should be done by three young gentlemen who have been making an immense stir in the world of art, and earned the distinction of being attacked by the Times (any notice *there* is a distinction)—and defended in a special pamphlet—the redoubtable *Pre-Raphaelite* Brotherhood! One of these "Brothers" happens to by *my* brother as well—the other two, Millais and Hunt, are intimate friends. For my sake as well as their own they would work their best and do something striking, no matter on how small a scale—I could be constantly at their elbows, and get them to be ready as soon as I should. . . .[5]

William Holman Hunt, too involved with completing his important painting "The Light of the World," and Charles Collins, too indecisive and unable to begin an illustration, failed to contribute to his brother's work; but Millais enthusiastically contributed the frontispiece . . . which shows the comic carpenter and stage-hand Martin Blunt, aka Julius Caesar, having his tie tied by Annie Wray, the protagonist's granddaughter.[6] In the novella Collins refers to the frontispiece and its importance when, following a lengthy apology on his inability to describe in words the beauty of Annie Wray, he writes, "I prefer leaving the reader (assisted by a striking likeness in the frontispiece) to form his own realisation of the personal appearance of the customer at Messrs. Dunball and Dark's" (6). This statement is symptomatic of Collins' allegiance to illustration—encouraging, instructing, and approving such work because he understood the critical importance of a visualized text as an aid in conceptualizing and understanding his prose. Notwithstanding Collins' objection to the title of the frontispiece—in a letter to Bentley's assistant manager, Marsh, several days after the volume appeared, Collins requested that the lettering under the illustration be "*stamped out*" because the image did not relate to the title-caption, "Mr. Wray's Cash-box"—the frontispiece itself is essential. His own suggested caption was "*The New Neck-cloth.*" A further letter of 1852 tells Marsh of Millais' wish to remove his name from directly beneath the two figures to the side since its present location spoils the design. Collins concludes his note with this exasperated declaration: "'The difficulty of writing a book is nothing to the difficulty of lettering a *plate*!'" (Davis 110). Characteristically, Bentley refused all requests for change (including Wilkie Collins' wish to add gilt edges to the edition!).

Seventeen years later, Collins continued to take a proprietary interest in the illustrations to his work. Writing to Harper and Brothers in New York, who were preparing the American edition of *The Moonstone,* he notes that the illustrations in the first number "are very picturesque—the three Indians and the boy being expecialy good, as I think." However, he goes on to complain that "in the second number, there is the mistake (as we should call it in England) of presenting 'Gabriel Betteredge' in *livery*. As head servant he would wear plain black clothes—and would look, with his white cravat and grey hair, like an old clergyman." Collins then explains his concern with this detail: "I only mention this for future illustrations—and because I see the dramatic effect of the story (in the first number) conveyed with such real intelligence by the artist that I want to see him taking the right direction, even in the smallest technical details.'"[7] The first American edition of *The Moonstone* (NY: Harper & Brothers, 1868) contained 66 wood engravings.

From Collins' earliest publication, **"The Last Stage Coachman"** which appeared in Douglas Jerrold's *Illuminated Magazine* for August 1843, to his last, the unfinished *Blind Love* (1890) which began in the *Illustrated London News,* he was conscious of the value of illustrations. His prose style, of course, encouraged this emphasis because of its descriptive detail and scenic construction inherited from his family's involvement with art. Not only was his father a successful landscape painter and member of the Royal Academy, and his mother a cousin of one of the best known nineteenth-century Scottish painters, Andrew Geddes, but his aunt Margaret Carpenter was a distinguished portrait painter. Among Collins' youthful acquaintances were John Constable, Sir David Wilkie, Joseph Severn, John Ruskin, and Augustus Egg, who introduced him to Dickens in 1851. Collins' brother Charles, of course, became a painter of minor reputation and an associate of the Pre-Raphaelites. In the biography of his father, the pictorial elements that later distinguished Collins' writing appear in the detailed descriptions of William Collins' paintings. The son's account of the pictures for 1829, for example, includes a lengthy analysis of five works his father completed for exhibition that year.[8]

Publishers, of course, capitalized on Wilkie Collins' prose talent, recognizing the ease with which illustrators could convey his descriptions of place and character. Illustrators, in turn, realized the guidance Collins provided them. Whether it was the 1861 new edition of *Antonina* with its vignette engraving by "Phiz" inserted before the title, or Sir John Gilbert's illustrations to the reissues of *Basil* and *Hide and Seek,* or Luke Fildes' illustrations to *After Dark and Other Stories* (1856) or du Maurier's 1875 steel engravings for *The New Magdalen, The Moonstone,* or *Poor Miss Finch,* all published by Chatto and Windus, artists of renown found Collins' work challenging and satisfying to illustrate. But among these many figures, Millais stands out, with the frontispiece to *No Name* his most important contribution.

Millais was an acknowledged force on the art scene by 1864, the year Sampson and Low published the one-volume edition of *No Name*. A founder of the Pre-Raphaelite Brotherhood and later president of the Royal Academy, he established his reputation as an illustrator through his contributions to the Moxon *Tennyson* (1857), his six illustrations to *Framley Parsonage* (1861), and his forty to *Orley Farm* (1862); such striking paintings as "Christ in the House of his Parents" (1849), "Mariana" (1851), "Ophelia" (1851-52), "Ruskin" (1854), "Autumn Leaves" (1856) and "Sir Isumbras at the Ford" (1857) made him a dominant figure. Sampson and Low recognized his importance by tipping in a slip to the 1864 edition of *No Name* which read *"NOTICE.—To meet the wishes of Collectors of Mr. Millais' works, a very small number of proof impressions of the Illustration of 'No Name' have been taken, price 10s 6d."*⁹ In 1864-65 Collins wanted Millais to illustrate **Armadale,** but other commitments prevented him from contributing to the novel.

The frontispiece to **No Name** is complex. . . . Readers familiar with the novel will immediately recognize its reference to chapter 12 of the "Fourth Scene" where Magdalen Vanstone's choice between life and death rests on the number of even or odd ships that pass in the distance. Readers unfamiliar with the text would find in the image an anxious figure straining under pressure to settle a crisis, alone and cut off from the world around her. But to view the frontispiece without knowledge of the story does not in any fundamental way negate the novel; indeed, the reverse is true since the image complements, in a puzzling but as yet unknown way, the title since among other things, there is no caption and we do not yet know the name of the figure. A hermeneutical space emerges for the reader between the engraving and the title-page which are viewed almost simultaneously. The uninitiated reader queries the connections that might be established between the image and the title, prompting a series of critical questions about the text which the haunting image constantly echoes. The frontispiece, in other words, initiates a critical vocabulary and image which the text seeks to confirm.

That Millais selected this scene to illustrate and treats it in such an enigmatic manner, emphasizing the contrast between darkness and light, the rigidity of the furniture with the curved figure of Magdalen, the sterility of the surroundings with the sensuous folds of her skirt, with all darkly illuminated by the off-center light, intensifies the alienation and loss of identity evoked by the title. Furthermore, the dark crosshatching of the engraving emphasizes the restriction of the room with the desk and, presumably, the letter of Magdalen to her sister, in opposition to the natural light highlighting her face from the outside. Bisecting the dark-light division is the pull from the window shade, in its singular manner a sinister sign of the fragile border between life and death.

The time is 4 A.M., dawn, a new beginning, but with her right hand about to clasp the laudanum and her left clutching the watch, Magdalen and the viewer know her life is in the balance.

The perspective of the viewer is unique since we stand unknown before Magdalen intruding on her monumental decision. The frontispiece functions as a thematic and even structural emblem for the condition of the heroine throughout the novel, while positioning the reader as an intrusive figure, emphasized later by the reader's privileged position as reader of highly personal letters between Mrs. Lecount and Mr. De Bleriot, or as witness to Mrs. Lecount's dictation of Noel Vanstone's letter to Admiral Bartram (ch. 3, "The Fifth Scene"). The title of the "Between the Scenes" section, separating the fourth and fifth scenes of the novel, is "Progress of the Story Through the Post." The prominence of the watch with its artificial time in Millais' frontispiece, in contrast to the flow of natural time represented by the passage of the boats in the distance, marks the disjunction between artificial boundaries such as the law and natural ties such as love and family which the novel explores. The frontispiece becomes an allegory of the spirit balancing life against death with time and the sea represented as traditional archetypes. What Millais chose *not* to illustrate is equally significant for as Magdalen waits for ships two and three (the text indicates they appear at close intervals), he focuses on her anxiety and dilemma rather than her action as the half-hour ends without the eight ship at first appearing and her clutching the laudanum.¹⁰ Millais avoids the melodrama of the scene's end when, overcome with thankfulness that the eight ship has appeared, Magdalen falls on her knees in thanksgiving (369). What the frontispiece conveys is suspense, perhaps the most consistent attribute of Collins' sensation fiction.¹¹ The importance of the engraving as a frontispiece can be compared to its appearance in the edition of **No Name** published in New York by Peter Fenelon Collier in 1900. In that edition, the identical image appears unattributed in volume 2, two pages later than the action in the chapter with the caption "One Half Hour." Its placement seriously alters its impact.

A comparison with the frontispiece of another edition of **No Name,** that of the Harpers Illustrated Library version, published in London and New York in 1889, indicates the significance of the Millais frontispiece as a conceit for the text. Reprinting the 1873 edition, the Harpers edition presents a scene from "The Third Scene, Chapter IV" as the frontispiece . . . drawn by John McLenan and which originally appeared in *Harper's Weekly* for 19 July 1862 (Vol. VI, No. 290: 461). The text describes a deceptive, coquettish Magdalen seated before her mirror without her disguise confronting her satisfied self with a mixture of emotions from the conniving to the abused (223). By contrast, the engraving shows a bewildered young woman adjusting her hair and admiring her good looks. This *gentile* woman is in sharp contrast with both the text and Millais' woman of conflict and despair.

The American artist John McLenan did the engraving, having done the illustrations for the first American publication of *No Name* which began in *Harper's Illustrated Weekly* on 15 March 1862. His line drawings are more comic than dramatic, although the publication of the second number of the novel, which contained chapters 3 and 4, established the iconography of Collins as well as the work in a dramatically-designed full-page layout. . . . Accompanying the nearly half-page oval portrait of Collins was not only his signature validating his authorial presence but a brief biography which reported in part that the subject of his first work, "Antonina," was "ill chosen" but that his later novels, especially "The Woman in White . . . have placed him in the first rank of contemporaneous Novel writers." The final paragraph of one sentence suggestively adds, "Mr. Collins is allied to the family of Mr. Charles Dickens" (*Harpers Weekly* [Vol. VI, No. 273: 189]).

The variety of visual interpretations of Collins' fiction makes any pattern of treatment difficult to discern. His two best-known novels, *The Woman in White* and *The Moonstone,* suffer from their very popularity and a frenzy of visual excesses. In the first American edition of *The Woman in White* (New York: Harper and Brothers, 1860), illustrated with seventy-four wood engravings by John McLenan, Count Fosco appears almost cherubic; he becomes more sinister, however, in the New York edition of 1900, grotesquely looming over Percival Glyde, Laura Halcomb, and Mrs. Fosco. Nothing, it seems, can hide his bulk, an embodiment of his overpowering evil. But melodrama tinged with the Gothic seems to grip the illustrator of the same edition when he presents the reappearance of Laura at her supposed grave at the conclusion of Part the First, the 26th Number of the novel. However, a 1984 Russian edition of the novel with eleven illustrations is not to be outdone as the front and back covers suggest in their collage of images from the drawings within. Promoting the *risquée* (note the popular off the shoulder style of Laura to the right and slightly above the title) and the horrific, the Russian illustrator feels at home with a Byronic Walter Hartright and a somewhat aged Count Fosco. . . .

The Moonstone suffers from equally diverse treatment. The frontispiece to volume 1 of the 1900 New York edition shows a corpulent statue resplendent with the jewel and supplicating followers, while volume 2 reveals a pensive Ezra Jennings evoking Durer's "St. Jerome in His Study." With his medical texts strewn about, Jennings appears as a brooding figure of mystery, his pen and potions at the ready. The most intriguing image in the edition is that of the moonstone itself, an abstract mystical eye resting on a strange sea with a temple in the background and the moon above. . . . The source is the opening of chapter 11 in the "First Period," when Rachel remembers that "the Diamond might take to shining of itself, with its awful moony light, in the dark—and that would terrify her in the dead of night."[12] Franklin Blake and Rachel are themselves depicted in an elegant manner in the same edition, stylistically posing in the midst of artistic composition. . . . A *fin-de-siècle* air pervades the engraving with a suggestive foot placed by Rachel on the rung of the stool. The scene contrasts with the impressionistic style of John Sloan who illustrated a 1909 Scribner's edition of *The Moonstone,* or William Sharp who over-dramatized the work in a 1948 edition. Increasingly, illustrators of the novel blended the dramatic with the romantic, as Sharp's illustration of Cuff on the Cliff demonstrates.

But a discussion of Collins's illustrations requires more than a summary, although the study of art in Victorian fiction has so far been characterized and circumscribed by cataloguing and enumeration rather than interpretation. We lack what Evelyn Goldsmith, for example, has attempted in her study *Research into Illustration*: a model of analysis based on the division of pictorial signs into semantic, syntactic, and pragmatic units originating in the sign theory of Charles W. Morris. The study of Victorian illustrations has so far remained historical and descriptive because we have failed to confront the critical questions that emerge from works that so dramatically embody the dynamic of figure and discourse.

And yet, in its effort to reclaim the union between picture and text, the Victorian novel suggests the parallelism of image and text often found in the illuminated manuscript. There, illumination is the manifestation of the text; ironically, in *The Moonstone* Collins uses an illuminated Oriental manuscript as a plot device to tempt both Godfrey Ablewhite and Mr. Luker into the clutches of the Indians (239, 242). In opposition to the fragmentation of Victorian society and culture, illustrations reaffirm a unified, pre-lapsarian world where what language states is what we see and what we see resides in what we say. This is the world before the fall which pictures without words could express.

The pictorial prose of Collins, which illustrators, publishers, and readers celebrated at almost every opportunity, reflects a fundamental desire to retain the coherence between the verbal and the visual. But for Collins, the impetus is not that of Alice who in wonderland confesses to being bored with "a book without pictures," nor Emma Bovary's who "thrilled as she blew back the tissue paper over the prints" which "rose in a half-fold and sank gently down on the opposite page."[13] The impetus for Collins is that of one who recognized the affirmative bond between resemblance and affirmation. And as he sought to unite the world of science with that of fiction, the world of romance with that of reality, Collins also sought the union of the image with the text through the illustrations to his novels.

Notes

1. Michel Foucault, *The Order of Things* (1966; NY: Vintage, 1973) 63.

2. George Eliot, *Letters* IV, ed. Gordon Haight (New Haven: Yale UP, 1955) 40-41.

3. See Marianna Torgovnick, *The Visual Arts, Pictorialism and the Novel* (Princeton: Princeton UP 1985) 105-6.

4. See Michael Steig, "Dickens, Hablot Browne and The Tradition of English Caricature," *Criticism* 11 (1969): 219-33; Steig, "The Critic and The Illustrated Novel: Mr. Turveydrop from Gillray to *Bleak House*," *Huntington Library Quarterly* 36 (1972): 55-67; Robert Patten, "The Art of Pickwick's Interpolated Tales," *ELH* 34 (1967): 349-66.

5. Collins in Nuel Pharr Davis, *The Life of Wilkie Collins* (Urbana: U of Illinois P, 1956) 105-6.

6. W. Wilkie Collins, *Mr. Wray's Cash-Box* (London: Richard Bentley, 1852), 37. All further references to this edition published between 13-29 December 1851 according to Parrish. For access to this edition I am indebted to Professor W. E. Fredeman.

7. Collins in M. L. Parrish, *Wilkie Collins and Charles Reade, First Editions Described with Notes* (London: Constable, 1940; New York: Burt Franklin, 1968) 74-75.

8. W. Wilkie Collins, *Memoirs of the Life of William Collins, Esq., R.A.* I (London: Longman, Brown, Green and Longmans, 1848) 314-17.

9. Cited in M. L. Parrish, *Collins and Reade* 49.

10. Wilkie Collins, *No Name,* ed. Virginia Blain (1862; Oxford: World's Classics, 1986) 368. All further references are to this edition which uses the one-volume 1864 version of the text.

11. *Mr. Wray's Cash-Box* is again an early example of Collins' wish to generate suspense in his fiction. Immediately after publication, Collins wrote to Bentley requesting that the "Introduction" be dropped since it impeded the story and indicated his "secret"—what was in the cash-box—too early. Bentley refused. See Collins in Davis, 100-12.

12. Wilkie Collins, *The Moonstone,* ed. J. I. M. Stewart (1868; Harmondsworth: Penguin, 1968) 112.

13. Lewis Carroll, *Alice in Wonderland,* ed. Donald J. Gray (New York: Norton, 1971); Gustave Flaubert, *Madame Bovary,* tr. Alan Russell (Harmondsworth: Penguin, 1972) 51.

Lillian Nayder (essay date 1997)

SOURCE: Nayder, Lillian. "Literary Apprenticeship." In *Wilkie Collins,* pp. 15-40. Boston: Twayne Publishers, 1997.

[*In the following excerpt, Nayder discusses Collins's apprenticeship with Charles Dickens.*]

DICKENS AND COLLINS

With its sensational and sexually explicit content, **Basil** received mostly hostile reviews when it appeared in November 1852. Complaining of Collins's "unfortunate selection of material," a number of critics found the novel "absolutely disgusting."[1] While admiring Collins's artistic skill, they objected in particular to his treatment of adulterous passion and betrayal: "There are some subjects on which it is not possible to dwell without offence; and Mr. Collins . . . has rather increased the displeasure it excited, by his resolution to spare us no revolting details."[2] "**Basil** is a tale of criminality, almost revolting from its domestic horrors," another reviewer complained. "The vicious atmosphere in which the drama of the tale is enveloped, weighs on us like a nightmare."[3]

Yet in the midst of these objections, Collins received praise from a new and valuable acquaintance, Charles Dickens, whom he had met the previous year, and to whom some critics believe he was indebted for the style and subject matter of **Mr. Wray's Cash Box.**[4] Thanking Collins for a copy of **Basil** in a letter written on 20 December 1852, Dickens assures him that he has "read the book with very great interest, and with a very thorough conviction that you have a call to this same art of fiction." "I think the probabilities here and there require a little more respect than you are disposed to show them," Dickens writes:

> But the story contains admirable writing, and many clear evidences of a very delicate discrimination of character. It is delightful to find throughout that you have taken great pains with it besides, and have "gone at it" with a perfect knowledge of the jolter-headedness of the conceited idiots who suppose that volumes are to be tossed off like pancakes, and that any writing can be done without the utmost application, the greatest patience, and the steadiest energy of which the writer is capable.
>
> For all these reasons I have made **Basil**'s acquaintance with great gratification, and entertain a high respect for him. And I hope that I shall become intimate with many worthy descendants of his, who are yet in the limbo of creatures waiting to be born.
>
> (*Letters*, 2:435-36)

Dickens had reason to admire **Basil,** a suspenseful novel written in a less-stilted prose style than **Antonina** and complicated by the inclusion of fictive newspaper accounts and letters written by characters from different social classes, a narrative strategy that anticipates such multivoiced novels as *The Moonstone* and *Armadale.* Even before the publication of *Basil,* Dickens had shown his approval of Collins's writing by accepting **"A Terribly Strange Bed"** for *Household Words* A bizarre tale of attempted murder by means of a collapsing four-poster bed in a low gambling house in Paris, this story shows signs of Collins's growing interest in "the nervous . . . state of mind"[5] and was the first of dozens of his works to be published by Dickens in *Household Words* and *All the Year Round.*[6]

The first years of Collins's literary apprenticeship were dominated by his relationship with Richard Bentley, who published *Antonina* (1850), *Mr. Wray's Cash Box* (1851), *Rambles beyond Railways* (1851), and *Basil* (1852) as well as a number of short stories. But Bentley was quickly displaced by Dickens, who serialized four of Collins's major novels in a little over 10 years: *The Dead Secret* in *Household Words* (1857); and *The Woman in White, No Name,* and *The Moonstone* in *All the Year Round* in 1859-1860, 1862-1863, and 1868, respectively. While publishing Collins's works, Dickens also collaborated with him on a number of stories that appeared in his journals, usually as special Christmas Numbers, including **"The Wreck of the Golden Mary"** (1856), **"The Lazy Tour of Two Idle Apprentices"** (1857), **"The Perils of Certain English Prisoners"** (1857), **"A Message from the Sea"** (1860), and **"No Thoroughfare"** (1867). Although Bentley published four of Collins's short stories in his *Miscellany* in 1851 and 1852,[7] and *Hide and Seek* in 1854, and was an influential figure whose list of "Standard Novels" was well known (*King,* 86), Dickens became what Bentley simply could not: the young writer's mentor.

Yet Dickens's role in Collins's life was not simply that of a teacher and guide. In his own ways, Collins gave support to Dickens, offering him companionship during his stormy marital separation, providing an unconventional example of domestic life, accompanying him on late nights out in Paris and London, and influencing a number of his novels as well. At the same time, Dickens's attitude toward the work of his protégé was sometimes more critical than admiring. Although he generally approved of Collins's writing, Dickens was wary of his subversive attitudes and served as Collins's censor as well as his guide. "I mark this note 'Immediate,' because I forgot to mention that I particularly wish you to look well to Wilkie's article about the Wigan schoolmaster, and not to leave anything in it that may be sweeping, and unnecessarily offensive to the middle class," Dickens wrote to W. H. Wills, his subeditor, in September 1858, about Collins's **"Highly Proper."** "He has always a tendency to overdo that" (*Letters,* 3:58). Although Collins's decision to write for *Household Words* and to become a salaried member of Dickens's

staff seems to suggest his willingness to compromise his political principles to succeed as a professional writer,[8] Collins did not simply subordinate his views to those of Dickens, but tested the political limits of his editor and sometime collaborator.

Their work on **"The Perils of Certain English Prisoners"** amply illustrates this point and shows that Collins, while collaborating with Dickens, did not necessarily adopt his views or help to realize his intentions. Dickens conceived of **"The Perils,"** the 1857 Christmas Number of *Household Words,* in reaction to the Indian Mutiny, which began in May of that year. The Indian sepoys who rebelled against their British officers were animated by economic and political grievances, but the immediate reason for their revolt was religious. Enfield rifles had been introduced into the army, and the sepoys believed that the new cartridges, which had to be bitten off for loading, were greased with pig and cow fat. The sepoys thus felt that the British were forcing them to commit sacrilege, and rebelled. British officers, as well as their wives and children, were killed, and a number of Englishwomen were allegedly raped by the Indians. Daily accounts of atrocities committed by the sepoys appeared in the British press and generated "calls for repression and revenge." "No episode in British imperial history raised public excitement to a higher pitch than the Indian Mutiny," Patrick Brantlinger notes.[9]

Sharing in this "excitement," Dickens called for the "extermination" of the Indian race and decided to write a story "commemorating . . . the best qualities of the English character that have been shown in India" (*Letters,* 2:894). Asking Collins to write the middle chapter of this story, Dickens wrote the first and third. He set the narrative in an English colony in Central America, an island where the silver taken from a mine in Honduras is temporarily stored, and represented the Mutiny as an assault on English men, women, and children by a band of pirates, who raid the island for the silver store. Dickens's first chapter portrays the leisurely life of the island before the attack and ends with the victory of the pirates over the colonists; Collins's chapter recounts the imprisonment of the British in the jungle; and Dickens's final chapter describes their escape and eventual victory over their captors.

What is most striking about **"The Perils"** are its inconsistencies in tone and characterization, which suggest that the intentions of the two writers are at odds. In the first chapter, Dickens reinforces racist stereotypes of the sepoys when he describes the martyrdom of the Englishwomen in the colony, who prefer death to sexual violation: "I want you to make me a promise," Miss Maryon tells Private Davis, "that if we are defeated, and you are absolutely sure of my being taken, you will kill me." "I shall not be alive to do it, Miss," Davis replies. "I shall have died in your defense before it comes to that."[10] But in the chapter that follows, Collins deflates Dickens's melodramatic account of British heroism, portraying the English prisoners struggling to suppress their laughter at the comic antics of the pirate chief, who plays his guitar "in a languishing attitude," "with his nose conceitedly turned up in the air" (281).

Whereas Dickens represents the pirate chief as an exotic figure, Collins highlights his English qualities, using him to depict imperial abuses rather than native treachery. Dickens models the pirate leader on the stereotype of the sadistic sepoy and shows him "playfully" mutilating his English captives with his cutlass (267). By contrast, Collins models him on the dandified British officers in India, known for their extravagant living and their inhumanity toward their native servants. Collins's pirate chief parades among his camp followers like one of "the dandies in the Mall in London" (269), in stiffened coat-skirts and a lace cravat. He abuses the natives under his command, using their backs as writing desks, and complaining of their stench, while covering his nose with "a fine cambric handkerchief," scented and edged with lace (270-71). Dickens adheres to the racist patterns of Mutiny literature in his portions of **"The Perils,"** defining the evil natives against their innocent British victims. But Collins complicates matters by calling attention to the underlying abuses of power that generated the Mutiny in the first place.

Although Collins's attitude toward British imperialism is not consistently critical, and combines his sense of imperial wrongdoing with his fear of savagery among natives, he is considerably more wary of empire building than Dickens proves to be, and he defends colonized peoples against a host of racist allegations in his fiction and journalism. His political differences with Dickens over such matters may well have contributed to the increasing coolness between them in the 1860s, as did the marriage of Collins's brother, Charles, to Dickens's daughter Kate, a union of which Dickens disapproved. By the time of Dickens's death in 1870, he and Collins saw one another rarely. Although Dickens helped to launch Collins's literary career, and was for years his nearly constant companion, the relationship between mentor and protégé had been soured by their differences of opinion and their literary rivalry, for Collins had long since come into his own as one of the most popular writers of the day, a master of mystery and detection.

Notes

1. *Dublin University Magazine* (January 1853); and *Westminster Review* (October 1853); reprinted by Page, 50, 52.

2. *Westminster Review* (October 1853); reprinted by Page, 52.

3. [D. O. Maddyn], *Athenaeum* (4 December 1852); reprinted by Page, 48.

4. In *Wilkie Collins: A Biography* (New York: Macmillan; 1952), Kenneth Robinson sees this work as a "successful imitation of the Dickens' model" (68), and Peters notes that John Ruskin found it "'a gross imitation of Dickens,'" "'a mere stew of old cooked meats,'" a view she finds too harsh (*King*, 111).

5. Wilkie Collins, "A Terribly Strange Bed," *Household Words* 5 (24 April 1852); reprinted in *Mad Monkton and Other Stories,* ed. Norman Page, 1-20, 11.

6. By the middle of September 1856, when Dickens offered Collins a salaried position on the staff of *Household Words,* he had already published 13 of Collins's pieces in his weekly journal. These include "A Terribly Strange Bed" (24 April 1852); "Gabriel's Marriage" (16-23 April 1853); "The Fourth Poor Traveller," a portion of the 1854 Christmas Number entitled "The Seven Poor Travellers" (December 1854); "Sister Rose" (7-28 April 1855); "The Yellow Mask" (7-28 July 1855); "The Cruise of the Tomtit" (22 December 1855); "The Ostler," a portion of the 1855 Christmas Number entitled "The Holly-Tree Inn" (December 1855); "A Rogue's Life" (1-29 March 1856); "Laid Up in Two Lodgings" (7-14 June 1856); "The Diary of Anne Rodway" (19-26 July 1856); "My Spinsters" (23 August 1856); "My Black Mirror" (6 September 1856); and "To Think, or Be Thought For?" (13 September 1856).

7. These stories include "The Twin Sisters" and "A Pictorial Tour to St. George Bosherville," published in *Bentley's Miscellany* in 1851; and "A Passage in the Life of Perugino Potts" and "Nine O'Clock," published in *Bentley's Miscellany* in 1852.

8. "The very act of writing for Dickens on the staff of *Household Words* . . . represented a political choice on Collins' part," Tamar Heller in *Dead Secrets: Wilkie Collins and the Female Gothic* (New Haven: Yale University Press, 1992), argues. Compromising those "elements in his fiction that a predominantly middle-class readership would find subversive," he "affirm[ed] his identity as part of the bourgeoisie" (92-93).

9. Patrick Brantlinger, *Rule of Darkness: British Literature and Imperialism, 1830-1914* (Ithaca: Cornell University Press, 1988), 199; hereafter cited in text. For other discussions of the Mutiny, see Pratul Chandra Gupta, *Nana Sahib and the Rising at Cawnpore* (Oxford: Clarendon Press, 1963); Christopher Hibbert, *The Great Mutiny: India 1857* (New York: Penguin, 1980); and Thomas Metcalf, *The Aftermath of Revolt: India, 1857-1870* (Princeton: Princeton University Press, 1964).

10. Charles Dickens and Wilkie Collins, "The Perils of Certain English Prisoners," *Household Words,* Extra Christmas Number, 1857; reprinted in *The Lazy Tour of Two Idle Apprentices and Other Stories* (London: Chapman and Hall, 1890), 237-327, 260; hereafter cited in text.

Anthea Trodd (essay date autumn 2001)

SOURCE: Trodd, Anthea. "Messages in Bottles and Collins's 'Seafaring Man.'" *Studies in English Literature 1500-1900* 41, no. 4 (autumn 2001): 751-64.

[*In the following essay, Trodd discusses Collins's narrative strategy in his story "The Seafaring Man," a chapter from* A Message from the Sea, *written in collaboration with Dickens.*]

In November 1860 Charles Dickens and Wilkie Collins visited Devon and Cornwall together to gather ideas for the nautical story, *A Message from the Sea,* the 1860 Christmas number for *All The Year Round,* which would prove to be their penultimate collaboration.[1] They "arranged and parcelled out" the sections for the story before they returned, and wrote it in London during the next fortnight.[2] The fourth chapter, **"The Seafaring Man,"** was Collins's prime responsibility, and Dickens responded with irritation to Collins's original beginning for this section, writing to Georgina Hogarth: "Wilkie brought the beginning of his part of the Xmas No. to dinner yesterday. I hope it will be good. But is it not a most extraordinary thing that it began: 'I have undertaken to take pen in hand, to set down in writing—& c. & c—' like the W in W narratives? Of course, I at once pointed out the necessity of cancelling that, 'off,' as Carlyle would say 'for evermore from the face of the teeming earth where the universal Dayvle stalks at large.'"[3] **"The Seafaring Man"** is a first person narrative framed by a story in the third person written predominantly by Dickens.[4] It was Collins's first contribution to a collaboration with Dickens since the publication earlier that year of *The Woman in White,* and, even after Dickens's intervention, further develops the method of Collins's first major success. It is a personal testimony, an eyewitness account, whose effect depends upon its insistence on the speaker's entire individuality and the limitations of his point of view. Further, its authenticity is assured to the reader by the speaker's proclaimed and demonstrated diffidence and inadequacy in ordering his memories into narrative form.

A Message from the Sea is a story about the healthful circulation of information and sympathy on which the progress of society depends, and of which the collaboration of Dickens and Collins was itself affirmation.

"The Seafaring Man," however, written by a Collins increasingly confident after the success of *The Woman in White,* departs conspicuously from the narrative methods of the frame. In this penultimate joint work we can see his path diverging markedly from his senior partner. In the frame, genial American ship owner Captain Jorgan brings a message in a bottle, retrieved from the southern ocean, to Alfred Raybrock, the Devonshire fisherman brother of the lost sailor who wrote it. Their attempts to solve the mystery of this partly erased message take them to a Cornish pub, where a local club is engaged in communal storytelling. Hugh, the missing sailor, appears and tells his story, the longest piece of continuous narrative in the number.

In **"The Seafaring Man,"** Collins constructs Hugh's ordinary individuality by distinguishing him from the archetypal figure suggested in the title, and by disappointing expectations of a yarn in the tradition that credits the sailor, as in Walter Benjamin's "The Storyteller," with skill in creating a fiction based on experience and travel, with the purpose of communicating practical wisdom.[5] In the nautical fictions of the post-Napoleonic decades, a common enthusiasm for Dickens and Collins, this archetype was propagated by a Romantic nostalgia for a community that had preserved the archaic skills of traditional storytelling.[6] In Captain Frederick Marryat's novels such as *Peter Simple* (1836) and *Masterman Ready* (1840), a deep understanding of the principles of storytelling is the sailor's dominant characteristic.[7] The club subscribes to this tradition and invites Hugh to join them in their cozy parlor on the strength of it. They are incredulous of his claims of narrative incompetence: "A sailor without a story! Who ever heard of such a thing?" Hugh is precisely not the common sailor his story's title suggests. He responds to the proffered archetype by insisting on his more-elevated status: "A man likes his true quality to be known."[8] If his anxiety that they should understand his professional identity as second mate seems a little prickly, this is probably because it was notoriously a job of dubious status, so described in R. H. Dana's immensely popular *Two Years before the Mast* (1840), which both Dickens and Collins admired: "The second mate's is proverbially a dog's berth. He is neither officer nor man . . . The crew call him the 'sailor's waiter.'"[9] A modern seaman, preoccupied with status, Hugh then confirms his departure from the archetype by a spectacular display of narrative incompetence. He does not, like Marryat's sailors, understand the delicate borderline between fiction and fact: "as I take it . . . a story is bound to be something which is not true" (p. 378). He does not understand his responsibilities as storyteller to his listeners, nor does he understand narrative closure; upon reaching a difficult point in his narrative, he simply stops there, and is surprised when "these curious men all howled and groaned at me directly, as if I had done them some grievous injury" (p. 378).

Hugh's lack of narrative skills, his ordinariness, his difference from the fictional Tar, are offered as guarantees of the authenticity of his narrative.

Hugh's desert island story itself departs ostentatiously from the possibilities explored by other fictional versions of the genre, from *Robinson Crusoe* itself to its various popular nineteenth-century descendants. The common motif of the disembarking of the stores from the wrecked ship is present in the narrative, but Hugh, unlike his predecessors, fails to get adequate supplies off the ship before it sinks. The island itself, a scrubland waste, offers almost no resources in vegetation or animal life. Instead of Crusoe's solitude, or the congenial and cooperative company enjoyed by the castaways of Johann Wyss's *The Swiss Family Robinson* (1813), Marryat's *Masterman Ready,* and W. H. Ballantyne's *The Coral Island* (1857), Hugh has one companion, Clissold, a malevolent, elderly alcoholic who knows a dark secret about his father. The usual promise of privacy offered by the island is absent; Clissold's presence makes the island a nightmare.[10] When, one morning, Hugh sees a footprint outside his cave, it is not a promise of companionship but a reminder that Clissold is spying on him. His southern beach offers none of the possibilities commonly encountered by British heroes, luxuriant natural resources for intelligent exploitation, or exciting new forms of colonial community to establish. The natives who rescue him when Clissold incinerates the island are neither noble savages nor cannibals, but a practical group who make use of his "general handiness" until a British ship picks him up (p. 405). By this time, Hugh, whose disinterest in racial hierarchies is also uncharacteristic of fictional castaways, "could hardly talk my own language," following the example not of Crusoe, but of his real-life model, Alexander Selkirk (p. 405).

Collins thus disassociates Hugh both from the archetype of the yarning seaman and from the best-known desert island fictions. There is yet another aspect in which Hugh departs from the usual attributes of the Tar; he lacks the capacity for open spontaneous expression of feeling with which sailors were identified in the fiction and stage melodrama of the period, an attribution founded in the belief that "as close reflections of the elements, they seem to have escaped the process of restraining and interiorizing standards."[11] To melodrama which was organized, as Peter Brooks argues, around "the admiration of virtue" and belief in its "expressive transparency," sailors credited with absolute transparency of feeling were figures of especially potent moral presence.[12] The first thing that we learn about Hugh, from his brother, is that he "was not a quick man (anything but that)" (p. 349). Hugh links this slowness to his emotional inarticulacy. When he finds himself in the same pub bedroom with his sleeping brother he does not know how to make himself known to him—

whether he should wake him or let him sleep. When he finally gets around to waking Alfred, he is unable to show his feelings: "The poor lad burst out crying—and got vent that way. I kept my hold of his hands, and waited a bit before I spoke to him again. I think I was worst off, now, of the two—no tears came to help *me*—I haven't got my brother's quickness any way" (p. 380). The natural facility of seamen with strong emotions was a given for melodrama; Hugh's behavioral uncertainties and inexpressiveness disrupt expectations for a scene of fraternal reunion.

The archetype of the yarning seaman imagines a perfect fit of teller and audience; everyone is hungry for stories, and sailors' life experiences make them appropriate tellers. Hugh, however, seems to belong to a more modern category, as a member of that "Unknown Public," whom Collins had analyzed in his most famous article. **"The Unknown Public"** (1858) suggests that there are many people who, in the transition from oral to written fiction, have lost all understanding of the principles of storytelling. These are the estimated three million who read the penny journals, people out of reach of mainstream fiction. They have heard of Robinson Crusoe, but believe his story to be real rather than a novel by Daniel Defoe. Confronted with a serial reprint of the masterpiece of feuilleton narrative, Alexander Dumas's *The Count of Monte Cristo,* they are unable to grasp the narrative principles on which "that consummate specimen of the rare and difficult art of storytelling" is constructed.[13]

Hugh clearly belongs to this "Unknown Public," and like them would not be able to understand the stories of Crusoe or Monte Cristo—both, as it happens, fictions of ordinary sailors who recreate themselves as heroes on desert islands. Collins's article was a call to novelists to reach out toward this lost readership; in Hugh he incorporates their unheard voice into his fiction, imagining the story of someone who does not understand stories. *The Moonstone* (1868) again invoked the Robinson Crusoe test—Gabriel Betteredge has read it but does not recognize it as fiction. Again, ignorance of fiction is offered as guarantee of authenticity of testimony. **"The Seafaring Man"** pursues the method of *The Woman in White*: narrative as limited personal testimony used "to present the truth always in its most direct and most intelligible aspect."[14] The truth of Hugh's eyewitness testimony is authenticated by his ignorance of narrative.

Dickens's irritation with the original beginning of **"The Seafaring Man"** was directed at Collins's shaping of Hugh's story as written testimony rather than oral storytelling. The frame narrative celebrated the values of oral storytelling, while Collins directed his section according to his very different interest in the awkward individuality of those unfamiliar with reading or writing. Dickens's expressed enthusiasm for *The Woman in*

White had not centered on the narrative method it employed. He admired the characterization and a new "tenderness" he observed in the writing, but he had reservations about the multiple narration: "you know that I always contest your disposition to give an audience credit for nothing—which necessarily involves the forcing of points on their attention—and which I have always observed them to resent when they find it out—as they always will and do . . . Perhaps I express my meaning best when I say that the three people who write the narratives in these proofs, have a DISSECTIVE property in common, which is essentially not theirs but yours."[15] Dickens had no great faith in Collins's ability to create the appearance of entire individuality on which his fictional method depended, and distrusted Collins's judgment of his readers. In this 1860 irritation with Collins's narrative method we can see the famous 1868 condemnation of *The Moonstone* beginning to form: "The construction is wearisome beyond endurance, and there is a vein of obstinate conceit in it that makes enemies of readers."[16]

The frame narrative of *A Message from the Sea* is dominated by another sailor who embodies all the qualities of the archetypal Tar from which Hugh departs. Captain Jorgan, based on Dickens's American friend, Captain Morgan, and on a benign interpretation of New World dynamism, has the Tar's instant identifiableness. This, in a modern world of reserve and secrecy, where it was increasingly difficult to ascertain the occupation or identity of persons encountered, was associated with openness, honesty, and emotional facility. "'*He*'s a sailor!' said one to another, as they looked after the captain moving away. That he was; and so outspeaking was the sailor in him, that although his dress had nothing nautical about it . . . a glimpse of his sagacious weather-beaten face or his strong brown hand would have established the captain's calling" (pp. 345-6). Captain Jorgan's frequent slapping of his leg when gratified by evidences of good in human nature is a sign of this openness of feeling. Unlike the diffident Hugh, he engages in "converse with everybody within speaking distance" (p. 343).

Captain Jorgan also preserves the Tar's skills in storytelling. Where Hugh's account of rounding the Horn uses nautical technicalities, and worries about the ship's deficiencies in laying to, Jorgan's story of how his ship drifted "out of all the ordinary tracks and courses of ships" draws on metaphor, exaggeration, and narrative suspense (p. 351). His account of "the identical storms that blew the devil's horns and tail off, and led to the horns being worked up into toothpicks for the plantation overseers in my country" takes the story insidiously into fantasy (p. 351). His arrival at an uncharted island assumes the narrative clarity of fairytale: "There was a reef outside it, and, floating in a corner of the smooth water within the reef, was a heap of seaweed,

and entangled in that seaweed was this bottle" (p. 352). Captain Jorgan, like Marryat's Tars, understands the delicate balance of experience and fiction that is the seaman's specialty, and later episodes demonstrate his ease with narrative. During the club's storytelling session he takes over the chairman's role of facilitating the transition between stories, comments on each narrative, and produces one himself. In chapter 5, in what reads like a covert comment on Collins's narrative method, he is reported as giving a précis of Hugh's narrative: "the captain recounted, very tersely and plainly, the nature of Clissold's wanderings on the barren island, as he had condensed them in his mind from the seafaring man" (p. 410). The story's conclusion grants him a grand apotheosis as storyteller. In the darkening post office at evening, as he prepares Hugh's wife for the return of the husband she believes to be lost at sea, he claims an extraordinary regenerative power for his yarns:

> "Yes," said the captain, still looking at the fire, "I make up stories and tell 'em to that child. Stories of shipwreck on desert island and long delay in getting back to civilised lands. It is to stories the like of that, mostly, that
>
> Silas Jorgan
>
> Plays the organ.
>
> . . . I make up stories of brothers brought together by the good providence of GOD. Of sons brought back to mothers—husbands brought back to wives—fathers raised from the deep, for little children like herself."
>
> (p. 415)

The story awards him the stature of a Prospero or a Paulina—as he uses his arts to reunite dispersed families, and to return the lost from the dead—and it ends in a claim for the regenerative powers of fiction embodied in the figure of the yarning Tar.

The different attitudes of the two seamen toward storytelling are further exemplified in the treatment of the message. Dickens's narrative concerns are for delivery and decipherment, Collins's for the original circumstances of writing. Both parts of the story emphasize the vital importance of maintaining connections. *A Message from the Sea* is about the restoration of a family across wide spaces through the telling of stories and the sending and delivery of a message—for example, Jorgan who has crossed the world to deliver the message he found in the southern ocean. In 1850 in the first number of *Household Words* Dickens had celebrated the reach, speed, and efficiency with which the post office kept private and public communications in circulation.[17] David Trotter has discussed how this article illuminates Dickens's fascination with maintaining the flow of information. "Semantic stoppage engrossed Dickens. The metaphor of circulation which had catalyzed his imaginings of social process made unintelligibility (or mystery) an object of compelling horror. The worst and most exciting evil was that which kept people apart by obscuring what they said to one another."[18] Captain Jorgan exemplifies the same kind of life-maintaining efficiency of circulation as the post office. He comes from the southern ocean to the quaint village of Steepways, which seems tucked away from the great world around which the Captain circulates, but which does have a post office. It may indeed be taken as a sign of instantly identifiable virtue that Hugh's mother runs a post office. Jorgan brings a message from an island far more "out of the ordinary tracks and courses" than Steepways. He chases the message's secret across Devon and Cornwall, and, in a final whirl of activity in chapter 5, divests it of all mystery, and transforms it into information. By this time the secret has been very thoroughly aired, taken from London, where it began, to the southern ocean, reformulated and written down as the message on a desert island, and returned to be walked around Devon and Cornwall until finally deciphered. It is as if the constant exercise in the open air itself dispels the horror of the secret.

Hugh entirely shares Jorgan's views on the importance of keeping information in circulation. When he hears from Clissold that there is a dark secret associated with his father's past, his immediate anxiety is to find some way to get this secret into circulation: "That secret had father's good name mixed up with it—and here was I, instead of clearing the villainous darkness from off of it, carrying it with me, black as ever, into my grave. It was out of my horror I felt at doing that, and out of the yearning of my heart towards you, Alfred, when I thought of it, that the notion came to comfort me of writing the Message at the top of the paper, and of committing it in the bottle to the sea" (pp. 402-3). Hugh and Clissold are facing imminent death by starvation, and the secret of Hugh's father's alleged disgrace will presumably die with them. Some devoted sons might settle for that probability, but Hugh is overcome with "horror" at the thought that the secret will remain a secret, be taken out of circulation forever, and not be clarified into information. Only the possibility of passing it on offers comfort.

The message that Captain Jorgan, as super postman, transmits is an especially vulnerable form of communication, the message in a bottle. Messages in bottles are inherently poignant; the writer is possibly in danger, and is certainly outside the normal channels of communication. Their delivery is exceptionally subject to chance and the good will of the finder. In an age self-conscious about the rapid extension of communications, they were strikingly archaic, but at the same time were used to fill in the crucial gaps still existing in more modern forms of communication. The Admiralty distributed printed forms to British ships to be used in emergency for messages in bottles, with requests in six languages that the message be returned to the Admiralty or the nearest British Consul.[19] (In *Armadale* [1866] the plot turns at one point on a British Consul receiving a fake message in a bottle.)[20] The most up-to-the-minute form of communication in the 1860s, Reuter's News Agency, employed messages in bottles to fill a vital gap before the transatlantic telegraph was finally laid in 1866. Reuter's financed the extension of the telegraph line from Cork to the southwest tip of Ireland. The devoted staff of the telegraph office Reuter's established there could fish from the sea the messages in cylinders thrown from passing ships carrying the latest news from America. Thus Reuter's could scoop the American news and be several hours ahead of its competitors.[21]

The most famous message in a bottle of the period, however, was found in 1859 at Victory Point, King William's Island, in the high Arctic, by the last of the search parties looking for traces of Sir John Franklin's lost 1845 expedition to find the Northwest Passage. This message was written in the margins of one of the Admiralty's printed forms, in the spaces left by an earlier message recording the explorers' achievements, and reported the expedition's disintegration after its leader's early death.[22] Since 1854 there had been public anxiety about the expedition's reported descent into cannibalism, as described by Inuit to Dr. John Rae of the Hudson Bay Company. Dickens's *Household Words* series, "The Lost Arctic Voyagers" (1854), and his two Christmas collaborations with Collins for 1856, *The Wreck of the Golden Mary* and *The Frozen Deep,* had addressed themselves to this anxiety, and especially to whether the great explorer and naval hero had himself been implicated in the descent. Now he was cleared; Franklin, the message revealed, had died early in the expedition, before supplies ran out.

Curiously, *All The Year Round* did not respond to this conclusive evidence on Franklin's behalf, despite Dickens's long identification with the campaign to defend the lost hero.[23] *A Message from the Sea* may be seen as a kind of response; just as the Victory Point message cleared the name of the patriarch of Arctic exploration, so the message Jorgan brings home to Devon clears Hugh's father's name. Indeed, such is its redemptive potential for patriarchal reputations, that it also happens to vindicate Alfred's prospective father-in-law, old Mr. Tregarthan, who also turns out to have been living under the darkness of the secret. The elderly Franklin, Trafalgar veteran and seasoned explorer, had been accorded the status of moral icon. "The name of Franklin alone is, indeed, a national guarantee," said Sir Roderick Murchison, President of the Royal Geographic Society, when the expedition sailed.[24] This "national guarantee" had sailed out of the ordinary tracks of ships, and, it was feared, out of the ordinary tracks of civilized men, to descend, like Saturn, to eating his children.

Raybrock Senior, as a Barnstaple tradesman, had gone out of his ordinary track in one foray in speculation, and Hugh, on his desert island, discovers that his father's recovered money may be tainted, and his father's name not be the guarantee on which his sense of self is founded. The solution of the secret restores that guarantee.

The parallels between the father's dangerous voyage into financial speculation and his son's into uncharted seas address fears of how, in the accelerated pace of modern life, one may stray out of safe, accustomed paths—the quaint old-fashioned nooks of Steepways—and lose altogether what has traditionally constituted identity. Hugh's island fears about the stability of paternal reputation are a version of the anxiety realized in several fictions around 1860 by the motif of the sailor who returns home to find his place at his own hearth filled by another. The motif was most famously treated by Alfred. Lord Tennyson in *Enoch Arden* (1864), but in two previous Christmas numbers, for which Dickens and Collins had collaborated on the frame, there were also stories using the motif: Adelaide Procter's "The Old Sailor's Story" in *The Wreck of the Golden Mary* (1856), and Elizabeth Gaskell's "A Manchester Marriage" in *A House to Let* (1858). In *Sylvia's Lovers* (1863), Gaskell provided another variant on the themes of the returning sailor, the usurped hearth, and the lost home seen from without.

These stories evoked fears of being twice lost—of embarking on a dangerous speculative voyage out and losing one's identity, only to return and, in an agonizing repeated displacement, find the old place taken. Those who failed to find a place in the dynamic modern world might seek in vain to resume the security of their old niche. Hugh on his island clings to his few remaining supports. He has his professional status. He has his wife's letters; going back to retrieve them saves him from the fate of his crewmates in the swamped lifeboat. He fears he may not have the guarantee of his father's good name, but the letters save him a second time, providing means for the message. His hearth is still waiting. Enoch Arden and his immediate predecessors have an especial pathos; they are victims because they are in the gaps not reached by the great modern advance in communications. *A Message from the Sea,* like its emblematic bottled message, is all about filling in those gaps; Hugh, a true son of the post office, in maintaining his attachment to retaining and sending letters, preserves his identity.

Dickens and Collins shared a fascination in the extension of communication through society. For Dickens it is the efficiency of the process that fascinates. In his 1850 article, "Valentine's Day at the Post-Office," documents of intense personal interest to individuals are processed with exemplary dispatch, "parcelled out, car-ried about, knocked down, cut, shuffled, dealt, played, gathered up again and passed from hand to hand, in an apparently interminable and hopeless confusion, but really in a system of admirable order, certainty and simplicity, pursued six nights every week, all through the rolling year."[25] *A Message from the Sea* offers another example of this marvel of modern communication. The message is carried around the civilized—even the uncivilized—earth until it yields its secrets, and Captain Jorgan is the dynamic facilitator, deciphering, processing, controlling. To him, nowhere is out of the "ordinary tracks and courses." Hugh's partly erased message, the report of a man in delirium tremens transmitted by a man slow of understanding, is difficult to decipher. It might easily become a dead letter but, as in the post office, there is an expert at hand to ensure that its meaning is decoded. In "Valentine's Day at the Post-Office" there is a reproduction of a particularly badly scrawled and incompetently directed address, to illustrate the description of the post office's keen-eyed employees who decipher such scrawls and ensure that even they reach their destination. Dickens's admiration for these detectives of bad handwriting and semiliteracy resembles his admiration for the equally keen-eyed detective police. In both cases he celebrates an expert surveillance, an ability to pore over incompetent traces and extract meaning necessary to the healthy continuance of society, just as Jorgan deciphers Hugh's incompetent message. He is indeed an image of the editor, as Dickens practiced the role, and the club episode, where he cajoles and facilitates others in storytelling, resembles Dickens's complaints about his never-ending problems with the contributors to his Christmas numbers.[26] Jorgan even locates a vital missing document in his steward's hat brim, as if plucking unsuspected value from unlikely heads.

For Collins it is not the process, but individual testimony—the expression of specific experience—that is interesting. He imaged collaboration not as the managed communal exchange of yarns but, as in *The Woman in White* and *The Moonstone,* as the juxtaposition of individual testimonies, each making their limited contribution to what becomes the revelation of truth "in its most direct and most intelligible aspect." Alexander Welsh has argued that *The Moonstone* anticipates modernism in its redirection of fiction from the narrative of managed circumstantial evidence to a "renewed interest in experience that can be captured only through testimony," as the personal testimonies of several characters expose the flaws in Cuff's adroitly managed case.[27] Hugh's story, with its insistence on the speaker's narrative incompetence, and his unlikeness to the archetypal Tar, attempts to create a distinctively individual voice, a very limited individual perception, within the managed frame of *A Message from the Sea,* with its dynamic agent of the "good Providence of God" in Captain Jorgan.

Dickens and Collins agreed that social health and stability urgently required involvement of the "Unknown
Public" in the values of storytelling, but disagreed profoundly on the method of that involvement. For Dickens it meant assiduous attention to the best means of
putting good storytelling in the public's way and trust-
ing them to receive it appropriately; everyone is grateful for Jorgan's interventions. Dickens's public readings, which began in December 1853, explored the
possibilities of extending readership through personal
performance, and *A Message from the Sea* endorses the
importance of oral storytelling. Collins's narrative
method attempted to extend storytelling to the "Unknown Public" by mimicking their supposed modes of
thought and expression. Hugh's wary ignorance of fiction, banality of expression, intellectual limitations, and
professional bias might be familiar and therefore attractive to such readers. Dickens's running irritation with
this approach, and the distrust of the readership he read
in it, eventually exploded over *The Moonstone.*

In **"The Seafaring Man."** Collins's writing is clearly
the product of collaboration with Dickens, especially on
the Christmas numbers. Both as collaborator on the
frame narrative, and contributor of interpolated stories,
his role had been to work within strictly assigned limits, to fill in the gaps left by Dickens—usually in advancing the action between predetermined points or
elaborating the experience or quirks of individual narrators. The interpolated stories in the numbers were usually in the first person. The writer who emerged from
these five years of collaboration from 1855 to 1860 had
unsurprisingly evolved a narrative method in which first
person testimonies made their limited contribution to
the overall design. The doggedly awkward Hugh is the
product of the collaboration; by filling in the gaps in
Dickens's communications, Collins had found his distinctive method.

Notes

I am grateful to the Leverhulme Trust for their support,
which enabled me to research on the collections of
Charles Dickens and Wilkie Collins.

1. By 1860 Dickens and Collins had collaborated on
   three Christmas numbers (*The Wreck of the Golden
   Mary* [1856], *The Perils of Certain English Prisoners* [1857], and *A House to Let* [1858]) and on
   the travel series, *The Lazy Tour of Two Idle Apprentices* (1857). Dickens had intervened heavily
   in Collins's plays, *The Lighthouse* (1855) and *The
   Frozen Deep* (1856), and in a number of his articles for *Household Words* and *All The Year
   Round.* Their final collaboration was another
   Christmas number, *No Thoroughfare* (1867).

2. Charles Dickens, *The Letters of Charles Dickens,*
   ed. Madeline House, Graham Storey, and Kathleen Tillotson, Pilgrim edn., 11 vols. (Oxford:
   Clarendon Press, 1965-), 9:336.

3. Dickens, *Letters,* 9:339.

4. There are some disagreements about attribution of
   sections in *A Message from the Sea.* The problem,
   which centers on chapter 3, is outlined by Harry
   Stone in "Dickens Rediscovered: Some Lost Writings Retrieved," *NCF* 24, 3 (Winter 1969-70):
   527-48. Dickens intervened in chapter 4; the Cornish material in the frame partly derives from Collins's *Rambles beyond Railways* (1851). There is,
   however, no argument that chapter 4 is largely
   Collins's.

5. Walter Benjamin, "The Storyteller," in *Illuminations,* trans. Harry Zohn (London: Collins, 1973),
   pp. 83-109.

6. See Alain Corbin, *The Lure of the Sea: The Discovery of the Seaside,* trans. Jocelyn Phelps (1994;
   rprt. Harmondsworth: Penguin, 1995). pp. 219-20.

7. On Frederick Marryat's influence in fiction, see
   Patrick Brantlinger, *Rule of Darkness: British Literature and Imperialism, 1830-1914* (Ithaca: Cornell Univ. Press, 1988), pp. 47-70, and on Dickens's admiration for him, see Donald Hawes,
   "Marryat and Dickens: A Personal and Literary
   Relationship," *DSA* 2 (1972): 39-68.

8. Dickens, *A Message from the Sea* in *Dickens: The
   Christmas Stories,* ed. Ruth Glancy (London: Everyman, 1996), p. 377. All subsequent references
   will be to this edition and will be cited parenthetically within the text.

9. Richard Henry Dana, *Two Years before the Mast*
   (Ware: Wordsworth, 1996), p. 10.

10. On the privacy theme in island romances see
    Corbin, pp. 179-81, 180-1.

11. Corbin, p. 349 n. 70.

12. Peter Brooks, *The Melodramatic Imagination:
    Balzac, Henry James, Melodrama and the Mode
    of Excess* (New Haven: Yale University Press,
    1995), pp. 25, 47. On the Tar as melodrama icon
    see J. S. Bratton et al., *Acts of Supremacy: The
    British Empire and the Stage. 1790-1930*
    (Manchester: Manchester Univ. Press, 1991), pp.
    18-61.

13. Wilkie Collins, "The Unknown Public," *House-
    hold Words* 18 (21 August 1858): 217-22.

14. Wilkie Collins, *The Woman in White* (Boston:
    Houghton Mifflin, 1969), p. 1.

15. Dickens, *Letters,* 9:194-5.

16. *The Letters of Charles Dickens,* ed. Walter Dexter,
    Nonesuch edn., 3 vols. (London: Nonesuch Press,
    1938), 3:660.

17. Dickens and W. H. Wills, "Valentine's Day at the Post-Office," *Household Words* 1 (30 March 1850): 6-12.

18. David Trotter, *Circulation: Defoe, Dickens, and the Economies of the Novel* (London: Macmillan, 1988), p. 109. See also, on Dickens's fascination with the postal principle: John Bowen, "Posts, Ghosts and *Pickwick*," in *Neo-Formalist Papers,* ed. Joe Andrew and Robert Reid (Amsterdam: Rodopi, 1998), pp. 65-77.

19. See Roderic Owen, *The Fate of Franklin* (London: Hutchinson, 1978), p. 386.

20. Wilkie Collins, *Armadale* (Oxford: Oxford Univ. Press, 1989), p. 568.

21. See Donald Read, *The Power of News: The History of Reuter's, 1849-1989* (Oxford: Oxford Univ. Press, 1992), pp. 33-5.

22. There is a facsimile reproduction of the message in Owen Beattie and John Geiger, *Frozen in Time: The Fate of the Franklin Expedition* (London: Grafton, 1989), p. 37.

23. See James E. Marlow, "English Cannibalism: Dickens after 1859," *SEL* 23, 4 (Autumn 1983): 647-66.

24. Quoted in Beattie and Geiger, p. 16.

25. Dickens and Wills, "Valentine's Day at the Post-Office," p. 9.

26. See, for instance, Dickens, *Letters*, 9:172.

27. Alexander Welsh, *Strong Representations: Narrative and Circumstantial Evidence* (Baltimore: Johns Hopkins Univ. Press, 1992), pp. 198, 216-35.

Lillian Nayder (essay date 2002)

SOURCE: Nayder, Lillian. "Class Consciousness and the Indian Mutiny: The Collaborative Fiction of 1857." In *Unequal Partners: Charles Dickens, Wilkie Collins, and Victorian Authorship,* pp. 100-28. Ithaca, N.Y.: Cornell University Press, 2002.

[*In the following excerpt, Nayder points out that Collins and Dickens held different political opinions, particularly about India and Indians, which are clearly revealed in their shared stories of 1857.*]

Toward the end of November 1857, three months after his last performance as Richard Wardour in **The Frozen Deep,** Dickens wrote to Angela Burdett-Coutts describing the Christmas Number he and Collins had just finished writing for *Household Words*: "It is all one story this time, of which I have written the greater part (Mr. Collins has written one chapter), and which I have planned with great care in the hope of commemorating, without any vulgar catchpenny connexion or application, some of the best qualities of the English character that have been shewn in India" (Pilgrim, 8:482-83). In speaking of the "best qualities" shown by the English in India, Dickens refers to their "heroic" resistance against the native sepoys, who had begun to mutiny in May of that year. The sepoys had political and economic grievances, but the immediate cause of their revolt was religious. The British had introduced Enfield rifles into the army, and the sepoys had to bite off the ends of the greased cartridges before they were loaded. Suspecting that the cartridges were greased with cow and pig fat, and hence sacrilegious to Hindus and Muslims, the sepoys concluded that the British were forcing them to commit sacrilege and rebelled. Some murdered their officers as well as English women and children.[1] Every day, accounts of Indian atrocities and examples of British martyrdom were reported in the British press: the sale of Englishwomen to Indians in the streets of Cawnpore, for example.[2] Predictably enough, these accounts elicited calls for repression and retribution. "No episode in British imperial history raised public excitement to a higher pitch than the Indian Mutiny," Brantlinger observes.[3]

Dickens shared in this so-called "excitement." Like many of his contemporaries in 1857, he called for the extermination of the Indian race. His genocidal response to the mutiny is recorded in a letter written to Burdett-Coutts on 4 October 1857. But as this letter makes clear, Dickens's racism was generated by domestic as well as imperial anxieties, since class tensions in England, not only racial hostilities in India, were brought to the fore by the mutiny:

> When I see people writing letters in the *Times* day after day, about this class and that class not joining the Army and having no interest in arms—and when I think how we all know that we have suffered a system to go on, which has blighted generous ambition, and put reward out of the common man's reach—and how our gentry have disarmed our Peasantry—I become Demoniacal.
>
> And I wish I were Commander in Chief in India. The first thing I would do to strike that Oriental race with amazement (not in the least regarding them as if they lived in the Strand, London, or at Camden Town), should be to proclaim to them, in their language, that I considered my holding that appointment by the leave of God, to mean that I should do my utmost to exterminate the Race upon whom the stain of the late cruelties rested; and that I begged them to do me the favor to observe that I was there for that purpose and no other, and was proceeding, with all convenient dispatch and merciful swiftness of execution, to blot it out of mankind and raze it off the face of the Earth.
>
> (Pilgrim, 8:459)

Dickens addresses what appear to be two separate concerns in this letter—the disinterest of working-class men in joining the army and the need to punish the sepoys for their "cruelties." Yet these two concerns are inseparable in his thinking. Not only did racial conflict in India expose class differences in England; the image of the treacherous sepoy enabled Dickens to imaginatively resolve those very differences. In the summer and fall of 1857, the London *Times* had printed letters complaining of the reluctance of working-class men to join the fight against the sepoys as well as letters justifying their reluctance and calling for easier promotion from the ranks. If one out of three commissions went to non-commissioned officers or privates, a writer argued on 2 October, the "prospect of promotion would be added to the motive from righteous indignation at atrocities greater than any which are known to have been perpetrated since the world began."[4] Addressing this problem in his letter to Burdett-Coutts, Dickens justifies the resentment of "the common man" and his reticence to fight the sepoys, since the army system reinforces class differences by "blight[ing] . . . ambition" and "put[ting] reward out of . . . reach." He then goes on to attack the Indian mutineers in a way that resolves these differences—by defining the otherness of the "Oriental" against the sameness of all Englishmen, regardless of their class: the Indians are "not in the least" to be viewed "as if they lived in the Strand, London, or at Camden Town." Conveying his sense of English solidarity rhetorically, Dickens puts himself in the shoes of the common man and wishes for a promotion himself ("I wish I were Commander in Chief").

Like Dickens, Collins was interested in the relationship between class identity and nationalism, and understood that representations of racial difference often serve a unifying and nationalistic end. From nearly the start of his literary career, he considered the tension between class and national allegiances and its consequences for imperialism. Drawing on a number of historical sources in *Antonina; or, The Fall of Rome*, Collins attributes Rome's fall to class divisions at the heart of the ancient empire. Rather than joining the fight against the invading barbarians, the discontented character Probus, angered by the political and economic abuses of the aristocrats ruling his own country, welcomes them to Rome:

> Goths! . . . Is there one among us to whom this report of their advance upon Rome does not speak of hope rather than of dread? Have we a chance of rising from the degradation forced on us by our superiors until this den of heartless triflers and shameless cowards is swept from the very earth that it pollutes? . . . Do you wonder now that . . . I say to the Goths—with thousands who suffer the same tribulation that I now undergo—"Enter our gates! Level our palaces to the ground! Confound, if you will, in one common slaughter, we that are victims with those that are tyrants!"[5]

Although Collins's novel is set in antiquity, its recurring refrain—"in Ancient Rome, as in Modern London"—makes it a warning parable for those governing the British Empire in the 1850s.[6] Indeed, Collins's image of citizens failing to defend "their" empire from barbarians because they feel "exile[d]" from their own "country's privileges" recurs in Dickens's letter to Burdett-Coutts as well as those written to the *Times* in 1857.[7] Without the promise of promotion from the ranks, the common man in Victorian England, like Collins's ancient Probus, will never feel the "righteous indignation" necessary to fight the sepoys and may identify with the mutinous barbarians instead.

The problem of the army system and the disaffection of the common man inform the two stories conceived by Dickens and coauthored by Collins in 1857—**"The Lazy Tour of Two Idle Apprentices,"** serialized in *Household Words* in October, and **"The Perils of Certain English Prisoners,"** published in December as the Christmas Number. While **"The Perils"** has been identified as Dickens's story about the Indian Mutiny, **"The Lazy Tour"** has not. Yet Dickens responds to the mutiny in both works, although in a rather surprising way: by seeking to repair class relations. In fact, the class divisions revealed by recruitment efforts in England during the mutiny prove to be a more pressing concern for Dickens than race relations themselves, and he uses racial conflict as one of several ways in which to overcome the class differences and class resentment that were exposed to view by events in India. In **"The Lazy Tour,"** Dickens elides class differences by imagining an England in which all labor is suspended, in which "all degrees of men, from peers to paupers," are members of an idle class.[8] In **"The Perils,"** he displaces the class resentment of English privates with racism, transforming their socially subversive feelings of class injury into a socially quiescent hatred of natives.

In his own contributions to these stories, Collins both complies with and resists Dickens's aims; his response marks the political differences between the two writers as well as the changing terms of their relationship. Since the publication of Nuel Pharr Davis's *Life of Wilkie Collins*, critics have noted that Collins's response to the mutiny differed markedly from Dickens's and that the virulent racism that characterizes Dickens's remarks about Hindus—"low, treacherous, murderous, tigerous villains . . . who would rend you to pieces at half an hour's notice" (Pilgrim, 8:473)—is notably absent from Collins's writing, or expressed by figures we are meant to distrust. In **"A Sermon for Sepoys,"** published in *Household Words* in 1858, Collins points to "the excellent moral lessons" provided by "Oriental literature" and advocates the moral reform of Indians rather than their extermination.[9] Less anxious to elide class differences than Dickens, Collins has no *need* for the virulent racism that Dickens expresses. As his portrait of Probus in *Antonina* suggests, Collins is willing to imagine—and justify—an alliance between the members of an imperial underclass and those of a subject race, and he does so in the works that follow the Indian Mutiny as well as in those that precede it.

In the 1857 stories, Collins more clearly stakes out his own position and questions that of Dickens than he had in such works as **"The Seven Poor Travellers"** and **"The Wreck of the Golden Mary."** He was encouraged to do so by his growing professional success and by his increasingly important role as Dickens's companion and confidante. In 1857, Dickens's marital unhappiness and his romantic pursuit of the young actress Ellen Ternan left him in a state of "restlessness" (Pilgrim, 8:423), and he often sought the companionship and support of the younger writer, whose own unconventional relationship with Caroline Graves dates from that year: "Any mad proposal you please, will find a wildly insane response in. Yours Ever," Dickens concludes his letter of 11 May 1857 (Pilgrim, 8:323). "On Wednesday Sir—on Wednesday, if the mind can devise any thing sufficiently in the style of Sybarite Rome in the days of its culminating voluptuousness," Dickens tells Collins on 22 May, "I am your man" (Pilgrim, 8:330). A staff member rewarded for his "devot[ion]" and "great service" to *Household Words* with an annual pay raise of fifty pounds (Pilgrim, 8:440, 457), Collins remained well aware of the value placed on his "submission" to Dickens, but he was also newly conscious of Dickens's vulnerability to public opinion and of his own crucial importance to his famous friend.

Thus when Catherine Peters describes Collins in 1857 as "a willing instrument and extension of Dickens" (*King,* 168), her portrait is incomplete. In **"The Lazy Tour"** and **"The Perils,"** Collins proves considerably less compliant than Peters suggests and challenges as well as supports Dickens's strategies and aims. Writing as Thomas Idle in **"The Lazy Tour,"** Collins accepts a role that obscures his subordination to Dickens at *Household Words,* playing the part of a fellow apprentice whose obscurity is due to a disinclination for work, not to the suppression of his name in publications. But while embracing the idleness that Dickens ascribes to his fictional persona, Collins also identifies it as a mark of Idle's gentility and develops its meaning as a class privilege in his interpolated tale. Using the 1857 mutiny to ally the apprentices, whatever their differences may be, Dickens refers to India as a place "which Idle and Goodchild did not [like]" (6). By contrast, Collins parodies the rhetoric intended to unify Englishmen against threatening others, comically deriding the "smouldering treachery" of "equine nature" (102) rather than that of the "Oriental race."

In his chapter of **"The Perils,"** similarly, Collins deflates the elevated tone of Dickens's narrative, debunking the martyrdom allegedly suffered by the English at

Indian hands. Dickens seeks to "commemorat[e] . . . the best qualities of the English character shewn in India," but Collins takes a more equivocal position. He treats the rebel leader as a mirror image of "dandies . . . in London," reminding his readers that the mutiny was caused, in part, by the excesses of English officers who abused their Indian subordinates.[10] Allying the English privates and sailors with the natives alongside whom they labor, Collins suggests that working-class Englishmen may have more in common with mutinous sepoys than Dickens allows. In a story about mutiny, Collins exhibits his own penchant for insubordination, although his resistance to Dickens often takes subtle and compromised forms.

I

Drawing the names of their protagonists from William Hogarth's sequence of engravings entitled *Industry and Idleness* (1747) in **"The Lazy Tour of Two Idle Apprentices,"** Dickens and Collins describe the adventures of Francis Goodchild and Thomas Idle as they travel into the north of England in September 1857, with Dickens writing from Goodchild's perspective and Collins from that of Idle. In the opening section, Dickens explains that the apprentices, "exhausted by the long, hot summer, and the long, hot work it had brought with it," have run away from their employer—whom he identifies as "lady . . . Literature"—in the hopes of "making a perfectly idle trip, in any direction" (3). In the first chapter, Dickens recounts their departure from London and their stay in Carlisle and Heske, while Collins describes their ascent of Carrock Fell, on which Idle sprains his ankle. In the second chapter, Dickens brings the apprentices to Wigton and then to an unnamed Cumberland town, where they meet Dr. Speddie and his assistant Mr. Lorn. Taking up the narrative, Collins writes an interpolated tale related by Dr. Speddie, in which a poor young man pronounced dead one afternoon returns to life that evening. In chapter 3, Dickens describes the apprentices' arrival in Allonby, while Collins recounts the disasters caused by Idle's attempts at industry. Dickens concludes the chapter by taking the characters from Allonby to an intermediate railway station, and on to Lancaster. Chapter 4, written solely by Dickens and set in Lancaster, is largely taken up with an interpolated tale narrated by a ghost who describes forcing his young bride to die by the power of his will and murdering her male defender, and who confesses to being hanged for his crimes in the previous century. In the final chapter, Dickens describes the apprentices as they travel through Leeds to Doncaster, arriving during race week for the running of the St. Leger, while Collins explains Idle's dislike of "equine nature."[11]

As Dickens's letters from September 1857 make clear, the plotline of **"The Lazy Tour"** generally follows the itinerary of the two writers as they made their way

from London to Doncaster, composing weekly install-
ments of the story as they went from place to place,
and each of the chapters selectively describes events
they experienced on their travels. Collins badly sprained
his ankle on Carrock Fell, for example, and Dickens
went to the St. Leger in Doncaster, although the fact
that he accompanied Ellen Ternan to the races goes un-
mentioned in the story.[12]

Dickens first refers to the story that became **"The Lazy
Tour"** in a letter written to Collins on 29 August 1857,
soon after his last performance in *The Frozen Deep*:

> Partly in the grim despair and restlessness of this sub-
> sidence from excitement, and partly for the sake of
> Household Words, I want to cast about whether you
> and I can go anywhere—take any tour—see any
> thing—whereon we could write something together.
> Have you any idea, tending to any place in the world?
> Will you rattle your head and see if there is any pebble
> in it which we could wander away and play at Marbles
> with? We want something for Household Words, and I
> want to escape from myself.
>
> (Pilgrim, 8:423)

Citing this letter, critics and biographers discuss Dickens's need to "escape from [him]self" in the fall of
1857—or, rather, his desire to escape from his wife
Catherine—arguing that his growing sense of marital
unhappiness and his interest in Ellen Ternan lay "behind his ostensibly 'lazy tour' with Collins."[13] Wishing
for a separation from Catherine, but fearing "it is impossible" (Pilgrim, 8:434), Dickens planned a trip that
would bring him to Doncaster when Ellen and her family members were scheduled to perform at the Theatre
Royal, traveling with Collins, whom he knew would
not find his extramarital interests at all offensive. Indeed, Dickens refers to Collins's own aversion to matri-
mony in his portion of chapter 3—when he describes
Idle's desire to "eat Bride-cake without the trouble of
being married" (64-65)—and both writers complain of
the caprices and difficulties of women in their interpolated tales.

But if Dickens's tour enabled him to escape from the
confinement of his marriage, the story itself is escapist
in another sense. Deborah Thomas notes that **"The Lazy
Tour"** can be read as "a kind of creative game" that
Dickens and Collins played together, a work that expresses a "holiday *jeux d'esprit*."[14] Yet this holiday spirit
serves a serious social end. Representing his characters
as the members of an all-inclusive idle class, a nation
gone on holiday, Dickens solves the problem of resentment in the rank and file.

The social anxieties that underlie **"The Lazy Tour"** are
suggested by the context in which the story first appeared as well as by its own treatment of class relations. Its first installment in *Household Words* was im-

mediately followed by "Indian Recruits and Indian
English," an article describing the "lesson written in
fire and blood" by the treacherous sepoys, "a horde of
blood-thirsty enemies," but that begins by acknowledging the scarcity of army volunteers back home: "In Europe, the task of recruiting-sergeant is anything but a si-
necure. In fact, scarcely any nation relies on any other
than forced conscription to replenish its armies. England alone seems able to furnish an adequate number
of volunteers, and even in England, the demand is often
much beyond the supply."[15]

In Dickens's opening section of **"The Lazy Tour,"** as
in this *Household Words* article, the recruiting-sergeant
makes his appearance, in a scene reminding us that volunteers are scarce. "Through all the . . . bargains and
blessings" offered during market morning in Carlisle,
Dickens observes, "the recruiting-sergeant watchfully
elbowed his way, a thread of War in the peaceful skein.
Likewise on the walls were printed hints that the Oxford Blues might not be indisposed to hear of a few fine
active young men; and that whereas the standard of that
distinguished corps is full six feet, 'growing lads of five
feet eleven' need not absolutely despair of being accepted" (8). To Dickens's original readers, his passing
references to the recruiting sergeant, on the one hand,
and to the Oxford Blues (or Royal Horse Guards), on
the other, would have brought to mind the problem of
the army system as he describes it to Burdett-Coutts.
Directed by the commander in chief of the army and
headed by aging aristocrats who had last fought at Wa-
terloo, the Horse Guards were notoriously elitist and
anachronistic in the 1850s. "The spirit of persistence in
old blunders is certainly not national, but is of the Horse
Guards, local, and only of the old school military," an
article later published by Dickens explained.[16] Because
commissions in the Horse Guards were among the most
expensive, the regiment made the class divisions in the
army and the elitism of its officers particularly apparent.
Whereas a commission in the infantry cost £450 in
1821, the purchase price for a commission in the Horse
Guards was £1,200.[17] By the time **"The Lazy Tour"**
was published, the elitism of cavalry officers had become a familiar subject of political cartoons, which represented them as "wasp-waisted" dandies.[18] Although
the "hints" printed on Carlisle's market walls in **"The
Lazy Tour"** suggest that those "few . . . fine men"
who wish to join the Horse Guards "need not absolutely
despair of being accepted," Dickens's readers understood that the common man, pursued by the recruiting-
sergeant, had little interest in joining the ranks.

Having alluded to the class tensions underlying his
story, Dickens goes on to relieve them—not by advocating reform in the army system but by eliding class
distinctions. Transforming industry into idleness and
work into play, Dickens represents Englishmen as members of a leisure class, whether they are high or low

born, wealthy or impoverished. For example, "the working young men" of Carlyle idle about town with "their hands in their pockets" and "nothing else to do" (7). The fishermen in Allonby "never fish," but "g[e]t their living entirely by looking at the ocean" (53). Although the appearance of workers in Wigton is "partly of a mining, partly of a ploughing, partly of a stable character," they do not labor in mines, fields, or stables. Instead they "look . . . at nothing—very hard": "Their backs are slouched, and their legs are curved with much standing about. Their pockets are loose and dog's-eared, on account of their hands being always in them" (23).

In **"The Lazy Tour,"** such idleness is not a symptom of economic depression or unemployment but a feature of an idyll in which men earn their keep without labor and in which objects themselves deny their use value. Thus in the drawing room of the inn at Heske, as Dickens describes it, the furniture and dishes pass themselves off as purely ornamental, as "nick-nack[s]" rather than tools. "The copper tea-kettle . . . took his station on a stand of his own at the greatest possible distance from the fire-place, and said: 'By your leave, not a kittle, but a bijou.' The Staffordshire-ware butter-dish . . . got upon a little round occasional table in a window, with a worked top, and announced itself . . . as an aid to polite conversation, a graceful trifle in china to be chatted over by callers, as they airily trifled away the visiting moments of a butterfly existence" (10). In Dickens's portions of **"The Lazy Tour,"** virtually everyone shares this "butterfly existence." The apprentices travel "deep in the manufacturing bosom of Yorkshire" but see no signs of factory life, and they soon arrive at Doncaster during race week to find "all work but race-work at a stand-still; all men at a stand-still" (89). It is September, and harvest time, but the crops are "still unreaped" (8): "No labourers [are] working in the fields" (91) because the business of play engages "all degrees of men, from peers to paupers" (89).

This suspension of labor is all the more striking when **"The Lazy Tour"** is compared to the story that Nuel Pharr Davis identifies as its literary source—Collins's **"A Journey in Search of Nothing,"** published in *Household Words* on 5 September 1857.[19] In this story, Collins's narrator is a professional author whose "weary right hand ache[s] . . . with driving the ceaseless pen."[20] Told that he has "been working too hard" by his doctor, who orders him to "do nothing" as a cure, he travels to retired country villages but discovers that he cannot escape from labor.[21] Each town to which he travels, no matter how remote or leisurely it appears, reminds him of the "necessities of work."[22] Observing "the sons of labor" in these villages, "cadaverous savages, drinking gloomily from brown mugs," he contrasts romantic depictions of such figures with "modern reality," debunking the pastoral idealizations of workers in the poetry of Keats and the paintings of Claude and Poussin: "Where

are the pipe and tabor that I have seen in so many pictures; where are the simple songs that I have read about in so many poems?"[23]

In **"A Journey in Search of Nothing,"** Collins restores the realities of labor to the poetry and paintings of the romantics, but in **"The Lazy Tour"** Dickens asks him to do the reverse—to imagine the English as members of a nationalized leisure class. Dickens's escape from material realities takes its most personal form in his representation of himself and Collins as Goodchild and Idle—"misguided young men" who have run away from their "employer," "a highly meritorious lady (named Literature), of fair credit and repute" (3). As the conductor of *Household Words,* Dickens and not "lady . . . Literature" was Collins's employer, and the two writers set off for Cumberland, in part, because copy was needed for the journal. But Dickens identifies Goodchild and Idle as fellow apprentices on vacation, obscuring the authority he wields in their working relationship as well as the labor they performed during their tour. In his letters from Doncaster, Dickens speaks of "fall[ing] to work for HW," and recounts the daily routine that he and Collins followed in order to produce the necessary amount of copy (Pilgrim, 8:448). "Collins is sticking a little with his story," Dickens told Wills on 17 September, "but I hope will come through it tomorrow" (Pilgrim, 8:448). Such difficulties are eliminated in **"The Lazy Tour,"** however, in which the vacationing apprentices produce only "lazy sheets" from "lazy notes" (70).

If any work is accomplished on the tour, Dickens claims, it is performed by Goodchild, who has no real idea of idleness. "You *can't* play," Idle complains to Goodchild in Dickens's narrative: "You make work of everything" (66). Whereas "Goodchild was laboriously idle," Dickens explains, and "had no better idea of idleness than that it was useless industry," Idle "was an idler of the unmixed Irish or Neapolitan type; a passive idler, a born-and-bred idler, a consistent idler, who practices what he would have preached if he had not been too idle to preach" (4). Justifying the inequities between himself and his staff member and the discrepancies in their recognition and rewards, Dickens models Goodchild on the "industrious apprentice" of Hogarth's series and Collins's Idle on his foil, while also suggesting that *true* idleness—the "born-and-bred" variety—is not English but "Irish or Neapolitan."

Whereas Dickens attributes idleness, in its purest form, to racial others, Collins identifies it as English—and upper class. Like his aristocratic taste for "sedan-chair[s]" (100), the idleness embraced by Collins's Idle is the sign of a specific class identity. In Collins's narrative, Idle lies on the sofa, crippled by his exertions on Carrock Fell, and wistfully remembers "that the current of his life had hitherto oozed along in one smooth stream of laziness, occasionally troubled on the surface by a slight passing ripple of industry" (56). Resolving "never to be industrious again" (60), he recounts the "disasters" that resulted from his "activity and industry" in the past, efforts that he made at public school, on the cricket field, and in the legal profession: places that define his class identity. Idle's industry results in disaster, Collins suggests, because it violates what he facetiously describes as "the great do-nothing principle" of English gentlemen (59). Playing the part of Idle, Collins undoubtedly enjoyed imagining himself as a "do-nothing" gentleman defined against a hopelessly industrious Dickens. While enjoying this fantasy, however, Collins also used it to a subversive end: to illustrate class privilege in a story designed to obscure class differences.

Collins more fully develops the social meaning of idleness in the interpolated tale he contributed to chapter 2 of **"The Lazy Tour,"** a short story later anthologized in *The Queen of Hearts* (1859) as **"The Dead Hand."** Narrated by Dr. Speddie, who is called in to treat Idle's sprained ankle, the tale recounts the experiences of an impoverished man pronounced dead in an inn one afternoon but brought back to life that night by the doctor, in the presence of the young man occupying the same double-bedded chamber as the "corpse." Compared to Collins's melodrama *The Red Vial* (1858), in which a body in a morgue is revitalized, **"The Dead Hand"** is generally disparaged as an exercise in the macabre or as a way in which Collins "padded out" his contribution to *Household Words*.[24] But in portraying the privileged figure who discovers signs of life in his roommate—a wealthy gentleman of leisure named (appropriately) Arthur Holliday—Collins reworks the central theme of **"The Lazy Tour,"** undermining the social idyll constructed in the larger story.

Like the workers in Carlyle and the fishermen in Allonby, whom Dickens describes in his portions of **"The Lazy Tour,"** Collins's Arthur Holliday has no need to work for a living. Unlike the leisure of Dickens's idle figures, however, Holliday's idleness marks his class privilege. The son of a wealthy manufacturer, he is "comfortably conscious of his own well-filled pockets" (31). Sauntering into Doncaster during race week without having troubled to reserve a room, he is amused by "the novelty of being turned away into the street, like a penniless vagabond" (29). But instead of endorsing Arthur's "holiday" spirits, Collins attributes them to the callous complacency of the leisure class and contrasts them with the bitterness of the poor man brought back to life only to perform whatever work "will put bread into [his] mouth" (42).

The interpolated tale that Dickens contributed to **"The Lazy Tour"** also calls attention to the sufferings of those who labor but does so in a safely distanced way, by criticizing the slave trade of Lancaster merchants in

the previous century.[25] Having inherited the wealth of his dead bride, the ghostly narrator of Dickens's tale invests it in the "dark trade" at "Twelve Hundred Per Cent" (80). But like the slave merchants to whom Dickens refers when he first describes Lancaster, the narrator fails to benefit from profits derived from "wretched slaves":

> Mr. Goodchild concedes Lancaster to be a pleasant place. A place . . . possessing staid old houses richly fitted with old Honduras mahogany, which has grown so dark with time that it seems to have got something of a retrospective mirror-quality into itself, and to show the visitor, in the depth of its grain, through all its polish, the hue of the wretched slaves who groaned long ago under old Lancaster merchants.
>
> (65)

In this passage, Dickens assumes the role of a social critic who exposes hidden wrongs—the past sufferings of the "wretched slaves" whose labor brought wealth to Lancaster but whose exploitation is largely invisible and forgotten. However, Dickens obscures as much as he exposes here: perhaps most notably, the industrial "slavery" of the Lancashire operatives who are themselves hidden from view in **"The Lazy Tour,"** yet compared to slaves of African descent by Victorian social reformers.[26] In *The Pickwick Papers,* published twenty years earlier, Dickens himself complains that the people of Muggleton condemn slavery abroad while condoning its practice in the English mills; they have presented "no fewer than one thousand four hundred and twenty petitions against the continuance of Negro slavery abroad, and an equal number against any interference with the factory system at home."[27] But in **"The Lazy Tour,"** Dickens avoids such analogies; the factory workers themselves never appear in the story, and the Lancaster slave merchants of the eighteenth century are compared not to the mill owners of Dickens's own day but to the mythical Eastern oppressors who figure in *The Arabian Nights* and whose "money turned to leaves" (65).

Furthermore, Dickens's "retrospective" look at the slaves who "groaned long ago" under Lancaster merchants implies that England's history of racial exploitation is just that: a thing of the past. Referring to "Uncle Tom" and "Miss Eva" in **"The Lazy Tour"** (9), Dickens reminds his readers that slavery is practiced by Americans in 1857, not by the English, whose role is to liberate rather than enslave. As one *Household Words* article asserts, "It is England's proudest boast that wherever her flag is unfurled, wherever her supremacy is established, there she carries the blessings of liberal institutions: she conquers but to set free. The same justice which is provided for the proudest son of Albion, is sent forth across the waters to attend on the meanest swarthy subject of Her Majesty, in distant India."[28]

In 1857, such claims about the "blessings" of English liberalism and the freedom bestowed through conquest were challenged on two fronts: by common men unwilling to join the army and by sepoys in open revolt. In **"The Lazy Tour,"** Dickens responds to this crisis by evading it, imagining working men as gentlemen of leisure and referring to India only briefly, to dismiss the subject: "There was a lecture on India for those who liked it," he notes, "which Idle and Goodchild did not" (6). While Collins does not defend the sepoys in his portions of **"The Lazy Tour,"** he proves less evasive in his treatment of the mutiny than Dickens does and suggests that the exploitation of the "subject races" by the English is hardly a thing of the past.

Writing at a time when calls for retribution against the sepoys were commonplace, Collins parodies the rhetoric used to describe them in his final section of the story, which represents the comic musings of Idle on the "treachery" of "equine nature." Idle's stereotype of the horse echoes that of the mutinous Indian, satirizing the racist hysteria that reduced the sepoys to ungrateful and dangerous beasts:

> I prefer coming at once to my last charge against the horse, which is the most serious of all, because it affects his moral character. I accuse him boldly, in his capacity of servant to man, of slyness and treachery. I brand him publicly, no matter how mild he may look about the eyes, or how sleek he may be about the coat, as a systematic betrayer, whenever he can get the chance, of the confidence reposed in him. . . . When he had made quite sure of my friendly confidence . . . the smouldering treachery and ingratitude of the equine nature blazed out in an instant. . . . What would be said of a Man who had requited my kindness in that way?
>
> (99, 102)

Informing this passage is the standard British explanation of the mutiny, which reduced a religious and political movement to yet another example of the innate treachery of "that Oriental race." A number of the articles that Dickens published on the subject of the mutiny explain it in this way: "Hindoo Law," for instance, describes the "savage cruelty" of the seemingly "mild" Hindus, which has broken out "like a long-smouldering flame," and Dickens himself defines "the Oriental character" for Emile de la Rue as "low, treacherous, murderous, tigerous" in a letter of 23 October 1857 (Pilgrim, 8:473).[29]

Using this language in his account of "equine nature" to describe a pony that fell while carrying Idle and a horse that shied, Collins makes it sound grossly overblown and suggests its failure to explain the sepoys' behavior. His comic account of the "revolt" of various animal species "overtaxed" by humankind suggests, too, that the sepoys have reason to rebel; "the cow that kicks

down the milk-pail," for example, "may think herself taxed too heavily to contribute to the dilution of human tea and the greasing of human bread" (102). Even more pointedly, Collins repeatedly speaks of Idle's fears of "losing caste" at public school (56-57), referring to what those sympathetic to the sepoys understood to be the immediate cause of their revolt—not the innate treachery of their race but their fear that the British were forcing them to commit sacrilege. "You will soon lose your caste altogether," a low-caste Hindu allegedly told the first sepoy mutineer; "the Europeans are going to make you bite cartridges soaked in cow and pork fat."[30]

Collins's parody of mutiny rhetoric in **"The Lazy Tour,"** and his suggestion that the English as well as the Hindus have a "caste" system, look ahead to his treatment of the sepoy revolt in **"The Perils of Certain English Prisoners"**—and, later, in *The Moonstone* as well. While Dickens uses the image of the treacherous sepoy to elide class differences in **"The Perils,"** Collins puts English privates and sailors in the position usually occupied by those subject to colonial rule, acknowledging the social inequities obscured by his collaborator.

II

While **"The Lazy Tour"** was running in *Household Words*, Dickens began to conduct research for the upcoming Christmas Number, which Collins agreed to coauthor. On 18 October, Dickens wrote to Morley, whose articles often focused on South and Central America. Explaining that he "particularly want[s] a little piece of information, with a view to the construction of something for Household Words," Dickens asks him to "consider and reply to the following question":

> Whether, at any time within a hundred years or so, we were in such amicable relations with South America as would have rendered it reasonably *possible* for us to have made, either a public treaty, or a private bargain, with a South American Government, empowering a little English Colony . . . to work a Silver-Mine (on purchase of the right). And whether, in that supposititious case, it is reasonably *possible* that our English Government at home would have sent out a small force, of a few Marines or so, for that little Colony's protection; or (which is the same thing), would have drafted them off from the nearest English Military Station.
>
> Or, can you suggest, from your remembrance, any more probable set of circumstances, in which a few English people—gentlemen, ladies and children—and a few English soldiers, would find themselves alone in a strange wild place and liable to hostile attack?
>
> I wish to avoid India itself; but I want to shadow out in what I do, the bravery of our ladies in India.
>
> (Pilgrim, 8:468-69)

Morley responded by sending Dickens Carl Scherzer's *Travels in the Free States of Central America: Nicaragua, Honduras, and San Salvador* (1857). Forwarding the book to Collins on 22 October, Dickens referred him to specific passages on silver mining, told him that they must "come to some conclusion, right or wrong," about their story, and scheduled a meeting with him for the next afternoon (Pilgrim, 8:470).

Although Dickens tells Collins that the material he has received "complicates" his plans for the story (Pilgrim, 8:470), his conception of its plot and aims, as described to Morley, is largely realized in the finished work, which he and Collins completed by the end of November. Consisting of three chapters—the first and third by Dickens and the second by Collins—**"The Perils"** brings together English gentlefolk and English soldiers in "a strange wild place." Narrated by Gill Davis, a private in the Royal Marines, it describes an attack on a "very small English colony" in Central America; the colony is an island off the coast of Honduras, where the silver taken from a mine on the mainland is temporarily stored. The British governor of Belize, acting on orders from home, sends twenty-four marines stationed in his settlement to "Silver-Store" to protect it against a "cruel gang of pirates." Along with a crew of sailors, they arrive there on the *Christopher Columbus,* a sloop that brings supplies to the island once a year, and then transports the annual accumulation of silver to Jamaica for sale and distribution "all over the world" (240). After a large party of marines and sailors is lured out to sea, the pirates raid the island for the silver, attacking English women and children as well as soldiers and male civilians, and killing some of them. These mutineers are a heterogeneous band and include "Malays, . . . Dutch, Maltese, Greeks, Sambos, Negroes, and Convict Englishmen from the West India Islands . . . some Portuguese, too, and a few Spaniards" (264). They are aided by a character named Christian George King, a composite of a black "sambo" and an American Indian, who betrays his English benefactors and is ultimately killed by them in reprisal. In the first chapter, Dickens depicts the leisurely life on the island before the attack and ends with the victory of the pirates over the colonists and their defenders, who are transported to the mainland. In the second, Collins recounts the difficult six-day march of the English through the forest, where they are imprisoned in a crumbling Indian ruin but eventually escape. In the third, Dickens describes their moonlit journey on rafts down a dangerous river and their eventual victory over their captors.

Dickens sets **"The Perils"** in Central America in 1744 rather than India in 1857, but many of its characters and events have obvious mutiny prototypes, and its earliest reviewers read it in the way that Dickens hoped they would—as a patriotic story "commemorating . . . some of the best qualities of the English character . . . shewn in India" (Pilgrim, 8:482-83). The reviewer in

the London *Times* of 24 December, for example, felt that Dickens had captured "the salient traits so recently displayed by his countrymen and countrywomen":

> Their intrepidity and self-confidence, their habit of grumbling at each other without occasion and of helping each other ungrudgingly when occasion arises, the promptitude with which they accommodate themselves to any emergency and the practical ability with which they surmount every embarrassment . . . in short, the spirit of mutual reliance, of reciprocal service and sacrifice, which they have exhibited in fact Mr. Dickens has striven to reproduce in fiction.[31]

Recent critical approaches to **"The Perils"** call the reputed heroism and sacrifice of the English colonists into question, but they too emphasize the story's connection to the Indian Mutiny. The treacherous "sambo" Christian George King, critics point out, is based on Nana Sahib, an Indian leader responsible for massacres at Cawnpore, and the bureaucratic bumbler Commissioner Pordage on "Clemency Canning," the lenient lieutenant governor of India in 1857.[32]

In their readings of **"The Perils,"** critics emphasize Dickens's concern with imperial affairs. Brantlinger notes that Dickens "was deeply disturbed by the news from India," and Oddie argues that the mutiny made such "a deep . . . impression" on him that it inspired *A Tale of Two Cities* as well as **"The Perils."**[33] In Oddie's view, the representation of class revolution in *A Tale of Two Cities* is informed by the sepoy rebellion: "Behind the fevered intensity of Dickens's evocations of French atrocities must lie also his feelings about the massacre of English victims in India."[34] Yet it is equally true that Dickens's fear of class conflict informs his treatment of the mutiny—that his representation of native insurrection in **"The Perils"** both disguises and resolves the anxieties about class relations that underlie his portions of the story. His two chapters are characterized by a series of displacements that enable the narrator, an illiterate private in the Royal Marines, to abandon his feelings of class hatred and to recognize his *real* enemies—his racial "inferiors" rather than his social superiors.

When Gill Davis first arrives at the English colony, Dickens characterizes him as a man consumed by feelings of class consciousness and animosity toward his social superiors. A "foundling child" starved and beaten by his father and neglected by the parish beadle, Davis resents the "idle class" living on the island and criticizes what he sees as the unjust separation of capital and labor:

> I had had a hard life, and the life of the English on the Island seemed too easy and too gay to please me. "Here you are," I thought to myself, "good scholars and good livers; able to read what you like, able to write what you like, able to eat and drink what you like, and spend what you like, and do what you like; and much *you*

care for a poor, ignorant Private in the Royal Marines! Yet it's hard, too, I think, that you should have all the halfpence, and I all the kicks; you all the smooth, and I all the rough; you all the oil, and I all the vinegar."

(241)

As his portrait of the dissatisfied private reveals, Dickens writes **"The Perils"** with the topical issue of the unjust army system in mind; he begins the story by presenting a common man who feels that the system has cheated him and put reward out of his reach. Davis is conscious of his merits and feels that they go unrecognized and unrewarded. He asserts that *he*, the private, deserves to be officer rather than such "delicate" gentlemen as Lieutenant Linderwood and Captain Maryon: "I thought I was much fitter for the work than they were, and that if all of us had our deserts, I should be both of them rolled into one" (241).

Furthermore, Dickens repeatedly distinguishes between the commissioned and the noncommissioned officers, revealing the inequities between them, and implicitly criticizing the elitism of the army system. Unlike Lieutenant Linderwood and Captain Maryon, Corporal Charker and Serjeant Drooce have risen from the ranks. But even as officers who have demonstrated their merit, they remain subordinates. When it is believed that the pirates are hiding on the mainland, Drooce and Charker are excluded from the pursuit by their commissioned superiors and left to supervise the presumably compliant native population on the island: "Because it was considered that the friendly sambos would only want to be commanded in case of any danger (though none at all was apprehended there), the officers were in favour of leaving the two non-commissioned officers, Drooce and Charker. It was a heavy disappointment to them" (253).[35]

In spite of such inequities and disappointments, however, these characters do not act on their feelings of resentment in Dickens's chapters and claim their "deserts." Instead, their class consciousness is assaulted—first by the nationalism of Miss Maryon, the sister of Captain Maryon, and then by the "mutiny" itself. Miss Maryon appeals to the Englishness of Davis and Charker, implicitly asking them to put aside their sense of class consciousness in the name of national brotherhood and sisterhood. Defining herself as "an English soldier's daughter" rather than as a "lady," Miss Maryon suggests that she and they have a common genealogy. Offering to show the "English soldiers how their countrymen and countrywomen fared, so far away from England" (242), she takes them on a tour of the living quarters in the colony.

Shortly after Miss Maryon identifies private Davis and Corporal Charker as Englishmen rather than as members of the working class, the pirate attack occurs. The most striking and curious feature of this attack is that it more closely resembles a class revolt than it does the Indian Mutiny. In **"The Perils,"** Dickens uses the treacherous Christian George King and the band of pirates to represent the Indian mutineers. Like the allegedly merciless sepoys, they lay siege to the English fort and commit atrocities, killing English women and children. Yet the pirate band is made up of Europeans as well as the members of "subject races," and their motives as well as their origins set them apart from the mutinous sepoys as Dickens elsewhere describes them. In *Household Words*, the mutiny is generally attributed to the "tigerish" and "treacherous" nature of the Oriental, but Dickens's pirates act for economic reasons, attacking the colonists because they want the silver in their possession. Like a proletarian mob—Dickens describes them as the "scum of all nations" (317)—they seize the capital of the colony, a treasure produced by a labor force that is never identified or described in Dickens's narrative. In effect, the pirates take the place of this absent labor force, their attack substituting for the mutiny threatened by Davis and his sense of class injury.

As the colonists and privates defend themselves against the pirates in chapter I, the distinctions among them dissolve. Dickens unites Davis with his officers—in part, by underscoring their common manhood as they protect the treasure of the island, which includes the sexual resources of the Englishwomen as well as the mineral resources of the colony, as Dickens's full title reveals: **"The Perils of Certain English Prisoners, and Their Treasure in Women, Children, Silver, and Jewels."** Like other works of mutiny fiction, Dickens's narrative represents the mutineers as rapists and Englishmen as chivalric defenders of an imperiled female virtue.[36] "I want you to make me a promise," Miss Maryon tells Davis: "That if we are defeated, and you are absolutely sure of my being taken, you will kill me." "I shall not be alive to do it, Miss," Davis replies. "I shall have died in your defence before it comes to that" (260).

As this image of the chivalric English private suggests, Dickens unites Davis with his superiors by obscuring their class differences as well as highlighting their common manhood. During the siege, the lower-class private demonstrates his nobility while the gentlefolk demonstrate their ability to labor. In **"The Lazy Tour,"** Dickens elides class differences by representing the English as members of a nationalized idle class, but in **"The Perils"** he does so by identifying them all as workers. The English ladies and gentlemen whom Davis had disdained for their delicacy prove to be determined and effective laborers rather than members of the idle class:

> What I noticed with the greatest pleasure was, the determined eyes with which those men of the Mine that I had thought fine gentlemen, came round me with what

arms they had: to the full as cool and resolute as I could be, for my life—ay, and for my soul, too, into the bargain! . . . Steady and busy behind where I stood . . . beautiful and delicate young women fell to handling the guns, hammering the flints, looking to the locks, and quietly directing others to pass up powder and bullets from hand to hand, as unflinching as the best of tried soldiers.

(259, 261)

While class distinctions are weakened during the attack, racial differences are strengthened and defined by Dickens in their threefold character: Christian George King, Dickens tells us, is "no more a Christian than he [is] a King or a George" (241). In aiding the pirates, the ostensibly faithful native proves to be not only un-Christian, un-aristocratic, and un-English—he is subhuman as well. While the pirate attack illuminates the nobility of the private and the energy and endurance of English gentlefolk, it also exposes the bestiality of the native. At the outset of the story, the English colonists accept Christian George King as one of their own. Miss Maryon tells Davis that King is "very much attached" to the colonists and "would die" for them (243), and he cries "in English fashion" when the ship springs a leak (245). But in the third chapter, Dickens unmasks him as an ungrateful and vicious animal, when he is shot in the jungle:

Some lithe but heavy creature sprang into the air, and fell forward, head down, over the muddy bank.

"What is it?" cries Captain Maryon from his boat. . . .

"It is a Traitor and a Spy," said Captain Carton. . . . "And I think the other name of the animal is Christian George King!"

(324)

Throughout **"The Perils,"** Davis is troubled by his sense of being other than the gentlefolk around him, and he repeatedly tells Miss Maryon that "England is nothing to [him]": "England is not much to me, Miss, except as a name" (315). But just as Dickens displaces Davis's mutinous feelings onto the pirates, so he displaces his otherness onto Christian George King. In exposing the native as a false Englishman, Dickens identifies the private as a true one, a point underscored when King is shot through the combined efforts of Davis and his superior, Captain Carton; although the captain pulls the trigger, the private loads the gun. Appealing to the racial hatred generated by the Indian Mutiny and demonstrating the need to "exterminate" the treacherous "animals," Dickens unifies the English characters in his chapters of the story and thus solves the problem of class resentment in the rank and file. At the expense of the native, he compensates the common man, who has been alienated by a system that promotes class differences and puts reward out of his reach.

Collins offers the common man a different sort of compensation in his portion of **"The Perils,"** however, and proposes a more radical solution to the problem of class conflict than Dickens does. In his chapter of the story, Collins reworks the allegiances established by Dickens in the opening section, highlighting class differences among the English characters, associating the privates and sailors with native laborers, and criticizing imperial practices instead of defending them.

In their discussions of **"The Perils,"** Collins's critics and biographers contrast the high seriousness of Dickens's chapters with the facetiousness of his own, noting that the younger writer did not share Dickens's racist view of the mutiny. Nuel Pharr Davis argues that Collins makes "a burlesque out of Dickens' philippic against the sepoys," and Nicolas Rance reiterates the point: "Collins was unable to rise to the hysterical pitch of the editor of *Household Words*. The cool and sardonic tone of the part of the narrative by Collins is not conducive to identifying with the prisoners in their plight."[37] In chapter I, Dickens presents the pirate captain as a sadistic figure who threatens to sexually violate the Englishwomen and who takes pleasure in mutilating his prisoners. By contrast, Collins compares his "flourish with his sword" to "the sort that a stage-player would give at the head of a mock army" (279) and portrays the English prisoners struggling to suppress their laughter as "the Don" plays his guitar "in a languishing attitude . . . with his nose conceitedly turned up in the air" (231). "As for the seamen," Collins writes, "no stranger who looked at their jolly brown faces would ever have imagined that they were prisoners, and in peril of their lives" (277).

Unlike Dickens, Collins approaches the mutiny and the imprisonment of the English as a comic rather than a tragic subject, and he reworks Dickens's opening chapter in other ways as well, redefining prototypes and dramatizing the plight of native laborers. While identifying the pirate captain as a Portuguese ruffian, Dickens models himon on the stereotype of the sadistic sepoy; he speaks in broken English and "laugh[s] in a cool way" as he commits violent acts, hitting Davis crosswise with his cutlass "as if [the private] was the bough of a tree that he played with: first on the face, and then across the chest and the wounded arm" (267). Collins, too, depicts the pirate captain in racially charged terms—as "lean, wiry, brown" and "cat-like" (269, 271). But he also describes him speaking English "as if it was natural" to him (270) and dressing in "the finest-made clothes," like one of "the dandies in the Mall in London" (269). Portrayed by Collins as a "gentleman-buccanier," he parades among his camp followers in stiffened coat-skirts and lace cravat, recalling the arrogant English officers notorious for their extravagant living and their inhumanity toward their Indian servants. Abusing the natives, the pirate captain in Collins's chapter speaks of "Indian beasts" whose "dirty hides shall suffer" for burning his food (304), and he uses the back of a "nigger" under his command as a writing desk, complaining of the man's stench, and covering his nose with "a fine cambric handkerchief" scented and edged with lace (270-71).[38] A parodic mirror image of dandified English officers, Collins's pirate leader conflates their abuses with the lawlessness attributed to the sepoys. At times, Collins uses racist language in his narrative—when he refers to the "black bullock bodies" of the "Sambos" (270), for example. But he also declines to make martyrs of the English colonists and instead suggests that their wrongdoing was partly responsible for the mutiny.

Furthermore, Collins questions the celebrated unity of the English by developing the tie between the "Sambos" and Indians on the one hand, and the English privates and sailors on the other. Thus Collins puts Davis in much the same position as the "nigger" used by the pirate captain as a writing desk, as Miss Maryon "place[s a] paper on [his] breast, sign[s] it, and hand[s] it back to the Pirate Captain" (274). Facing forward rather than backward, Davis seems less dehumanized than the native, yet the connection between them is clear. It is reinforced during the march through Honduras, when the pirates eat meat from a store of provisions they have brought from the English colony, but Davis and his companions eat beans and tortillas, "shar-[ing] the miserable starvation diet . . . with the Indians and the Sambos" (281). Instead of considering the natives their enemies, as they do in Dickens's chapters, the English prisoners see them as allies. "Dread the Pirate Captain, Davis, for the slightest caprice of his may ruin all our hopes," Collins's Miss Maryon proclaims, "but never dread the Indians" (302).

Indeed, the working-class Englishmen and the Central American Indians prove to have much in common in Collins's chapter. Despite their racial differences, both groups constitute a labor force that the pirate captain hopes to command and exploit in restoring the ruined Mayan palace he claims as his headquarters. As Davis and his companions prepare to enter the forest, the private is surprised to see "a large bundle of new axes," which he assumes the natives will use to cut through overgrown forest paths. But when the group arrives at the edge of the woods, the Indians use their machetes instead, and the sight of the axes, as yet unused, begins to "weigh . . . heavily" on Davis's mind (286). We soon learn that Davis has good cause for his anxieties, since the captain has only kept the soldiers alive because he wants "[their] arms to work for [him]," chopping down a forest of trees and making planks "to roof the Palace again, and to lay new floors over the rubbish of stones" (295). By having the English privates perform the manual labor assigned to "Negroes" and "Caribs" in the colonies of Central America,[39] Collins points to the regressive social ends of empire building. Whereas the resentful Probus welcomes the Goths to the gates of Rome in *Antonina,* hoping they will "level

our palaces to the ground," Collins's English privates are forced to restore a dilapidated palace and, in the process, to rebuild the ruins of an ancient empire.

Collins brings us from the flourishing English colony of Silver-Store to the ruins of the Mayan empire; in so doing, he raises pressing questions about imperial decline and fall. In Collins's chapter, Davis finds himself in a "mysterious ruined city" built "by a lost race of people" (288), a place that Collins models on the ancient Mayan ruin of Copan, first explored by an Englishman in 1839:[40]

> A wilderness of ruins spread out before me, overrun by a forest of trees. In every direction . . . a frightful confusion of idols, pillars, blocks of stone, heavy walls, and flights of steps, met my eye; some, whole and upright; others, broken and scattered on the ground; and all, whatever their condition, overgrown and clasped about by roots, branches, and curling vines. . . . High in the midst of this desolation . . . was the dismal ruin which was called the Palace; and this was the Prison in the Woods which was to be the place of our captivity.
>
> (289)

Among Victorians, the discovery and excavation of the ruins of ancient empires, whether Egyptian, Greek, Roman, or Mayan, brought the stability of their own to mind and suggested that no empire is invulnerable. "Comparisons have often been drawn between the Roman and the British empires," one article in *All the Year Round* notes, "and the question asked: Will Britain lose its strength and fade away, as Rome faded?"[41] This question seemed especially troubling in 1857, when the hitherto faithful sepoys revealed their allegedly treacherous nature. Rather than holding unruly natives responsible for imperial decline, however, Collins suggests that social inequities among the colonizers themselves may bring about an empire's fall. He conveys this point by staging scenes in which English privates and sailors are forced to labor like Indians and plot their own rebellion among the "dismal ruin[s]" of a once-powerful empire.

Whereas Dickens resolves the problem of class resentment in the rank and file by pitting privates against natives, Collins, in a scene that mirrors the pirate raid but casts the thieves as heroes, represents English workers seizing the goods they have produced. Davis and his companions are industrious in felling trees but only because they mean to profit from their own labor. As the sailor Short explains, they can use the timber for their own purposes, to build rafts and escape captivity:

> When we began to use the axes, greatly to my astonishment, [Short] buckled to at his work like a man who had his whole heart in it; chuckling to himself at every chop. . . . "What are we cutting down these here trees for?" says he.
>
> "Roofs and floors for the Pirate Captain's castle," says I.

"*Rafts for ourselves!*" says he, with another tremendous chop at the tree, which brought it to the ground—the first that had fallen. . . . "Pass the word on in a whisper to the nearest of our men to work with a will; and say, with a wink of your eye, there's a good reason for it."

(296-97)

In Dickens's two chapters, Davis is angered by the separation of capital from labor but learns to see such distinctions as insignificant. Having defined those who "have all the half-pence" against those who have "all the kicks" (241) in the first chapter, he declines to accept the "purse of money" he is offered by his superiors in the third. By the time Mr. Fisher, one of the English mine owners, tells Davis that he "heartily wish[es] all the silver on our old Island was yours" (314), Davis no longer wants to possess it, and the wealth of Silver-Store is not redistributed when the treasure hoard is finally recovered at the end of the story. In Collins's narrative, by contrast, the English soldiers and sailors seize what they produce, even though the dandified pirate captain claims to own it all.

The subversive implications of their act of seizure in Collins's chapter are wholly muted by Dickens in the third, which rewards Davis for his bravery but does so by putting him in his proper place. Having proved his nobility, the private is rewarded, though not with a share of the silver he has helped to protect nor with a promotion to the rank of sergeant; instead, he is transformed into a subservient vassal, who pledges himself to his lady, Miss Maryon, in chivalric fashion:

"I think it would break my heart to accept of money. But if you could condescend to give to a man so ignorant and common as myself, any little thing you have worn—such as a bit of ribbon—"

She took a ring from her finger, and put it in my hand. And she rested her hand in mine, while she said these words:

"The brave gentlemen of old—but not one of them was braver, or had a nobler nature than you—took such gifts from ladies, and did all their good actions for the givers' sakes. If you will do yours for mine, I shall think with pride that I continue to have some share in the life of a gallant and generous man."

(325)

Despite the reference to Davis's "noble . . . nature," Dickens's narrative valorizes his feudal subordination and conforms to the dual pattern of imperial literature as Brantlinger describes it, justifying both aristocratic and imperial rule.[42] At the end of **"The Perils,"** Dickens places the common man in a state of utter dependence on his social superiors. After his return to England, Davis becomes the object of their charity, living on the estate of Admiral Carton and his wife, the former Miss Maryon. Although Dickens initially contrasts the noble

private with the bestial native, he brings them into an analogous relationship with the English ruling class. Offering a socially regressive solution to the problem of the army system and the class divisions it promotes, Dickens places the private in the position reserved for the faithful native at the beginning of the story; the difference between the two is that Davis deserves the charity of the gentlefolk while Christian George King does not.

In proving his nobility, Davis paradoxically learns to accept his state of dependence and see himself as an "ignorant and common" man: "It may be imagined what sort of an officer of marines I should have made, without the power of reading a written order," he says in Dickens's narrative, thinking back on his earlier social presumption. "And as to any knowledge how to command the sloop—Lord! I should have sunk her in a quarter of an hour!" (241-42). While Captain Carton is promoted and becomes "Admiral Sir George Carton, Baronet," Davis is not. Yet Dickens makes it clear that the private has not been unfairly overlooked. Davis is not promoted because he, like the native, has inherent limitations, and not because he is oppressed by the system: "I was recommended for promotion, and everything was done to reward me that could be done; but my total want of all learning stood in my way. . . . I could not conquer any learning, though I tried" (326). In Collins's chapter, Davis watches as a native, forced to his knees, serves as a desk upon which the pirate captain writes, and then provides a similar service for Miss Maryon; "knowing how to write" (271) thus appears a class privilege and illiteracy a mark of class injury. But in Dickens's portions of **"The Perils,"** illiteracy is innate, and Davis cannot learn, although he is given the chance. Unable to read or write, he needs Lady Carton's help to tell his story. As she puts his oral account of the pirate attack into writing, Dickens inscribes the regressive social ideal of "The Perils" into its narrative form.

At the conclusion of **"The Perils,"** Davis appears wholly dependent on the former Miss Maryon for support and expression, yet she, too, has been put in her proper place. Dickens's treatment of Miss Maryon demonstrates that imperial fiction, like chivalric romance, idealizes the subordination of women while seeming to dramatize their strength. Resembling the mutiny novels discussed by Nancy L. Paxton, which "mobilize" chivalry to conservative social ends, Dickens's narrative naturalizes Victorian gender norms as well as imperial relations, countering "demands for women's greater political and social equality."[43] Although Dickens claims that his story will "shadow out . . . the bravery of our ladies in India" (Pilgrim, 8:469), their bravery, as he represents it, consists largely of endurance. Miss Maryon "handl[es] the guns, hammer[s] the flints, [and] look[s] to the locks" during the siege (261), but her primary function is maternal in Dickens's narrative: "Miss Maryon had been from the first with all the children, soothing them, and dressing them . . . and making them believe that it was a game of play, so that some of them were now even laughing" (259). Rather than taking up arms herself, she gives Davis "the strength of half a dozen men" through her dependence, encouragement, and praise of the "brave soldier" (260).

Dickens justifies Miss Maryon's dependence by illustrating the dangers of letting her think for herself. He holds her womanly misperception of the natives partly responsible for the imperial crisis at hand and in so doing models her on the English ladies of whom he complained to Emile de la Rue in October 1857; these women "know nothing of the Hindoo character" yet unwisely "rush[ed] after" visiting "Indian Princes" three years before: "Again and again, I have said to Ladies, spirited enough and handsome enough and clever enough to have known better[,] . . . 'what on earth do you see in those men to go mad about? You know faces, when they are not brown; you know common expressions when they are not under turbans; Look at the dogs—low, treacherous, murderous, tigerous villains who despise you while you pay court to them, and who would rend you to pieces at half an hour's notice'" (Pilgrim, 8:472-73). Like these ladies, Miss Maryon "pay[s] court" to "treacherous" natives in Dickens's portion of **"The Perils,"** much to Davis's surprise:

> "Under your favor, and with your leave, ma'am," said I, "are [the Sambos] trustworthy?"
>
> "Perfectly! We are all very kind to them, and they are very grateful to us."
>
> "Indeed, ma'am? Now—Christian George King?—"
>
> "Very much attached to us all. Would die for us."
>
> She was, as in my uneducated way I have observed very beautiful women almost always to be, so composed, that her composure gave great weight to what she said, and I believed it.
>
> (243)

When it comes to natives, Dickens suggests, the knowledge of "uneducated" Englishmen exceeds that of Englishwomen, however well born.

In his collaborations with Collins, stereotypes of women and their failings sometimes serve Dickens well, providing common ground for the two writers—when they joke about the female contributors to *Household Words,* for example, or jointly illustrate the dangers of female emancipation in **"The Wreck of the Golden Mary."** But increasingly, gender issues became a source of contention for the two writers, as the history of *The Frozen Deep* makes clear, and their portraits of Miss Maryon, like those of Nurse Esther, diverge. Without minimizing the class privileges enjoyed by Miss

Maryon, Collins suggests that gender norms unduly restrict her. Like Davis, she demands her own fair share—not of wealth or property but of "work" and "risk": "It is time that the women, for whom you have suffered and ventured so much, should take their share," she tells the private in Collins's narrative (302). Unlike the ill-judging woman who fails to see the natives for what they are in Dickens's first chapter, Collins's Miss Maryon carefully observes the pirate guards and their routine, discovering the means of drugging their food and making possible the prisoners' escape. "I have resolved that no hands but mine shall be charged with the work of kneading [the poison] into the dough," she asserts (302).

In such passages, Collins gives new meaning to women's work, using Miss Maryon to subvert the gender norms that his characters generally accept but that Davis comes to question:

> "How can a woman help us?" says Short, breaking in on me.
>
> "A woman with a clear head and a high courage and a patient resolution—all of which Miss Maryon has got, above all the world—may do more to help us, in our present strait, than any man of our company," says I.
>
> (298-99)

Courageous and resolved as well as patient—perhaps more effective "than any man"—Collins's Miss Maryon looks back to Lucy Crayford in his draft of *The Frozen Deep* and ahead to Marian Halcombe in *The Woman in White.* But she also anticipates the mountaineering heroine who figures in the next and final work that Collins and Dickens coauthored, **"No Thoroughfare,"** in which the dangers of female autonomy and strength again prove a subject of debate between the two writers.

Notes

1. For discussions of the Indian Mutiny from different vantage points, see Wayne G. Broehl Jr., *Crisis of the Raj: The Revolt of 1857 through British Lieutenants' Eyes* (Hanover, N.H.: University Press of New England, 1986); Pratul Chandra Gupta, *Nana Sahib and the Rising at Cawnpore* (Oxford: Clarendon Press, 1963); Christopher Hibbert, *The Great Mutiny: India 1857* (New York: Penguin, 1980); Thomas Metcalf, *The Aftermath of Revolt: India, 1857-1870* (Princeton, N.J.: Princeton University Press, 1964); and Vinayak Savarkar, *The Indian War of Independence, 1857* (Bombay: Phoenix Press, 1947).

2. *Examiner* (5 September 1857); quoted by William Oddie, "Dickens and the Indian Mutiny," *Dickensian* 68 (January 1972): 4.

3. Patrick Brantlinger, *Rule of Darkness: British Literature and Imperialism, 1830-1914* (Ithaca, N.Y.: Cornell University Press, 1988), p. 199.

4. *Times* (London), 2 October 1857, 4. Shortly before the mutiny, Dickens himself published an article criticizing the "snail-like" pace of "promotion from the ranks" during the Crimean War and contrasting the English army system with the French system of "promotion by merit": "Once in the ranks, always in the ranks, is the maxim in the English army; and the man who accepts the shilling from the recruiting-sergeant . . . bids adieu to all hope of rising in the military profession." See [Reeves], "Promotion, French and English," *Household Words* 15 (24 January 1857): 91. Similarly, "Why We Can't Get Recruits" argues that no "educated man of the English working classes" will join the army because he "hope[s] to better himself" (*All the Year Round* 14 [9 December 1865]: 464). Dickens continued to publish articles on the English army system, criticizing the priority given to "money" over "merit." See, for example, "Money or Merit?" *All the Year Round* 3 (21 April 1860): 30-32; and "Pay For Your Places," *All the Year Round* 4 (27 October 1860): 67-69. Brian Bond discusses the Indian Mutiny and the problem of army recruitment in the 1850s, as well as the reforms to which the crisis gave rise, in "Prelude to the Cardwell Reforms, 1856-68," *Journal of the Royal United Service Institution* 106 (1961): 229-36, and "Recruiting the Victorian Army, 1870-92," *Victorian Studies* 5 (June 1962): 331-38.

5. Wilkie Collins, *Antonina; or, the Fall of Rome,* vol. 17 of *The Works of Wilkie Collins,* 30 vols. (New York: AMS Press, 1970), pp. 81-82.

6. Ibid., p. 481.

7. Ibid., p. 80.

8. Charles Dickens and Wilkie Collins, "The Lazy Tour of Two Idle Apprentices," in *The Lazy Tour of Two Idle Apprentices and Other Stories* (London: Chapman and Hall, 1890), p. 89; subsequent references to "The Lazy Tour" are cited parenthetically in the text.

9. [Wilkie Collins], "A Sermon for Sepoys," *Household Words* 17 (27 February 1858): 244.

10. Charles Dickens and Wilkie Collins, "The Perils of Certain English Prisoners," in *The Lazy Tour of Two Idle Apprentices and Other Stories,* p. 269; subsequent references to "The Perils" are cited parenthetically in the text.

11. Generally speaking, critics agree on how to divide the literary labors of Dickens and Collins in "The Lazy Tour." Using the 1890 Chapman and Hall edition of the story, Nuel Pharr Davis attributes its authorship as follows: chapter 1, Dickens, pp. 1-11, Collins, pp. 11-19; chapter 2, Dickens, pp. 20-28, Collins, pp. 28-49; chapter 3, Dickens, pp. 50-55, Collins, pp. 55-65; chapter 4, Dickens, pp. 66-86; chapter 5, Dickens, pp. 87-96, Collins, pp. 97-103, Dickens, pp. 103-4. Davis mistakenly attributes a portion of chapter 3 to Collins (the description of the railway station, which Dickens authored [see Pilgrim, 8:454]), but otherwise his attributions agree with my own. Frederic G. Kitton is less accurate in his analysis of "The Lazy Tour"; citing Forster, he mistakenly attributes all of chapter 5 to Collins. Yet as the Pilgrim editors explain, Forster purposely misattributed chapter 5 to Collins to "avert . . . attention from the revealing passages" that describe Goodchild's infatuation with a young woman modeled on Ellen Ternan (Pilgrim, 8:448 n. 1). See Davis, *The Life of Wilkie Collins* (Urbana: University of Illinois Press, 1956), p. 326 n. 24; and Kitton, *The Minor Writings of Charles Dickens* (London: Elliot Stock, 1900), p. 134.

12. Claire Tomalin discusses Dickens's meetings with Ellen Ternan in Doncaster, noting that Dickens chose it as his destination because he knew that the Ternans were scheduled to perform there. See *The Invisible Woman: The Story of Nelly Ternan and Charles Dickens* (New York: Knopf, 1991), pp. 102-5.

13. Deborah A. Thomas, *Dickens and the Short Story* (Philadelphia: University of Pennsylvania Press, 1982), p. 113. Like Thomas, Harry Stone reads "The Lazy Tour" as an "intensely and avowedly autobiographic" work that registers "Dickens' troubled flight away from self." See *Dickens and the Invisible World: Fairy Tales, Fantasy, and Novel-Making* (Bloomington: Indiana University Press, 1979), pp. 288, 291.

14. D. Thomas, *Dickens and the Short Story,* pp. 80-81.

15. [E. Townsend and Alexander Henry Abercromby Hamilton], "Indian Recruits and Indian English," *Household Words* 16 (3 October 1857): 320, 319.

16. "Tape at the Horse Guards," *All the Year Round* 6 (6 March 1862): 568. "Soldier's Law," similarly, speaks of the "brute inert opposition [to reform] on the part of the ancient generals at the Horse Guards" (*All the Year Round* 16 [28 July 1866]: 55), as does "The Horse Guards Rampant" ([Henry Morley], *Household Words* 8 [31 December 1853]: 428-31). "At the horse guards," the military historian Correlli Barnett notes, "old men . . . stultified progress" (*Britain and Her Army, 1509-1970* [New York: William Morrow, 1970], p. 282).

17. Edward M. Spiers, *The Army and Society, 1815-1914* (London: Longman, 1980), p. 11.

18. Jerome J. McGann, *The Beauty of Inflections: Literary Investigations in Historical Method and Theory* (Oxford: Clarendon Press, 1988), p. 195.

19. Davis, *Life of Wilkie Collins,* p. 204.

20. Wilkie Collins, "A Journey in Search of Nothing," *Household Words* 16 (5 September 1857): 217-23; *My Miscellanies,* vol. 20 of *The Works of Wilkie Collins,* p. 26.

21. Ibid., pp. 24-25.

22. Ibid., p. 46.

23. Ibid., pp. 39, 29-30.

24. Kenneth Robinson, *Wilkie Collins: A Biography* (New York: Macmillan, 1952), p. 116.

25. A story in which an older man forces his young wife to die by the power of his will, Dickens's interpolated tale usually interests critics because of its disturbing autobiographical elements and the way it conflates hostility toward an "encumbering wife" with the desire to shape and control a young woman named "Ellen" in the narrative (D. Thomas, *Dickens and the Short Story,* p. 113). See Stone, *Dickens and the Invisible World,* pp. 288-94; and Michael Slater, *Dickens and Women* (London: J. M. Dent, 1983), pp. 142-43.

26. For a discussion of this analogy as it was developed by chartists and abolitionists in the 1830s, see Betty Fladeland, "'Our Cause being One and the Same': Abolitionists and Chartism," in *Slavery and British Society, 1776-1846,* ed. James Walvin (Baton Rouge: Louisiana State University Press, 1982), pp. 69-99.

27. Charles Dickens, *The Pickwick Papers,* ed. Robert L. Patten (1972; reprint, Harmondsworth: Penguin, 1981), p. 161.

28. [John Capper], "Law in the East," *Household Words* 5 (26 June 1852): 347.

29. [Henry Richard Fox Bourne], "Hindoo Law," *Household Words* 18 (25 September 1858): 337. See also Brantlinger, *Rule of Darkness,* pp. 202-3.

30. Hibbert, *Great Mutiny,* p. 63.

31. *Times* (London), 24 December 1857, 4.

32. Oddie, "Dickens and the Indian Mutiny," 7-9. In the most recent study of "The Perils" to date, Laura Peters examines Dickens's debt to press coverage of the mutiny in the *Illustrated London News,* considers the ways in which he "stoke[s] the fires of empire" (126) in his portions of the story, and discusses his "imperial role" as editor of *Household Words.* See "'Double-dyed Traitors and Infernal Villains': *Illustrated London News,*

Household Words, Charles Dickens and the Indian Rebellion," in *Negotiating India in the Nineteenth-Century Media,* ed. David Finkelstein and Douglas M. Peers (New York: St. Martin's Press, 2000), pp. 110-34.

33. Brantlinger, *Rule of Darkness,* p. 206; Oddie, "Dickens and the Indian Mutiny," 15.

34. Oddie, "Dickens and the Indian Mutiny," 15.

35. As the writer of "Why We Can't Get Recruits" notes, officers "have an intense dislike to any scheme which narrows the gulf between the commissioned and non-commissioned ranks" (466).

36. For a detailed analysis of "the colonial rape narrative" generated by the Indian Mutiny, and the political functions it served, see Nancy L. Paxton, "Mobilizing Chivalry: Rape in British Novels About the Indian Uprising of 1857," *Victorian Studies* 36, 1 (fall 1992): 5-30.

37. Davis, *Life of Wilkie Collins,* pp. 207-8; Nicholas Rance, *Wilkie Collins and Other Sensation Novelists: Walking the Moral Hospital* (Rutherford, N.J.: Fairleigh Dickinson University Press, 1991), p. 131.

38. Hibbert briefly discusses the physical and verbal abuse of Indian servants by the English in *The Great Mutiny,* pp. 30-31. In using the term "nigger" to describe his native subordinates, Collins's pirate captain resembles the young officers criticized in the *Illustrated London News* in August 1857 and held accountable for the mutiny. Ignorant and arrogant, these officers referred to "proud and sensitive high-caste Brahmins as 'niggers' with whom it was degrading to associate" (quoted by L. Peters, "'Double-dyed Traitors,'" 113).

39. E. G. Squier, *The States of Central America; Their Geography, Topography, Climate, Population, Resources, Productions, Commerce, Political Organization, Aborigines, Etc., Etc.* (New York: Harper and Brothers, 1858), p. 199.

40. As a source for his descriptions, Collins probably relied on the well-known account of the Mayan ruins provided by John Lloyd Stephens in *Incidents of Travel in Central America,* a work first published in 1841. Stephens visited Copan in the company of the English artist Frederick Catherwood in 1839.

41. "Touching Englishmen's Lives," *All the Year Round* 15 (30 June 1866): 582.

42. Brantlinger discusses the "regressive" patterns of imperial literature throughout *Rule of Darkness,* but see pp. 35-39 in particular. See also Abdul R. JanMohamed's analysis of "racial romance,"

which serves "to justify the social function of the dominant class and to idealize its acts of protection and responsibility" (72), in "The Economy of Manichean Allegory: The Function of Racial Difference in Colonialist Literature," *Critical Inquiry* 12, 1 (autumn 1985): 59-87.

43. Paxton, "Mobilizing Chivalry," 6.

Works Cited

Brantlinger, Patrick. *Rule of Darkness: British Literature and Imperialism, 1830-1914.* Ithaca, N.Y.: Cornell University Press, 1988.

Collins, Wilkie. "Laid Up in Lodgings." In *My Miscellanies.* Vol. 20 of *The Works of Wilkie Collins.* 30 vols. New York: AMS Press, 1970. 85-125.

Davis, Nuel Pharr. *The Life of Wilkie Collins.* Urbana: University of Illinois Press, 1956.

Hibbert, Christopher. *The Great Mutiny: India 1857.* New York: Penguin, 1980.

Oddie, William. "Dickens and the Indian Mutiny." *Dickensian* 68 (January 1972): 3-15.

Paxton, Nancy L. "Mobilizing Chivalry: Rape in British Novels about the Indian Uprising of 1857." *Victorian Studies* 36, 1 (fall 1992): 5-30.

Peters, Laura. "'Double-dyed Traitors and Infernal Villains': *Illustrated London News, Household Words,* Charles Dickens and the Indian Rebellion." In *Negotiating India in the Nineteenth-Century Media,* edited by David Finkelstein and Douglas M. Peers. New York: St. Martin's Press, 2000. 110-34.

Stone, Harry. *Dickens and the Invisible World: Fairy Tales, Fantasy, and Novel-Making.* Bloomington: Indiana University Press, 1979.

Thomas, Deborah A. *Dickens and the Short Story.* Philadelphia: University of Pennsylvania Press, 1982.

Peter Haining (essay date 2004)

SOURCE: Haining, Peter. "Introduction." In *Sensation Stories: Tales of Mystery and Suspense,* by Wilkie Collins, edited by Peter Haining, pp. 7-23. London: Peter Owen, 2004.

[*In the following essay, Haining explores the beginnings and development of the sensation story, which he credits Collins with founding, making him an important progenitor of the modern mystery tale.*]

Wilkie Collins is regarded as the founding father of the "Sensation Novel", a literary phenomenon generally agreed to have been inaugurated in 1860 by his best-seller *The Woman in White,* although he had already been writing realistic stories of suspense laced with mystery and thrills for at least a decade previously. In dramatic plots that revolved around hidden secrets, bloody crimes, villainous schemes and clever detective work, all occurring in everyday settings, he helped to shape a new genre that was different from anything being written by his contemporaries—and one that was to have a far-reaching influence.

If this literary development can be said to have a birth-place, then the honour belongs to the isolated hamlet of Winterton on the wind-swept coast of East Anglia. Wilkie Collins had first been taken there as a child by his artist father, and the bleak landscape and grim legends of the desolate Norfolk community at once filled his imagination with thoughts of mystery and suspense that would later inspire his fiction. It was at Winterton, too, that he met a young woman who would become his mistress and an important part of his life and work.

Situated in a bay just north of Yarmouth, Winterton is an ancient fishing village with a wide sweep of beach and sand dunes that David Yaxley in his *Portrait of Norfolk* (1977) describes as having in winter "all the odd attractiveness of a deserted site like a ghost town of the Gold Rush". It is sheltered on the north-east by a promontory, Winterton Ness, the most easterly spot on the coast of Britain and was, according to William White in his *Gazetteer of Norfolk* (1845), "famous to mariners as the most fatal headland between Scotland and London". Daniel Defoe, who passed through in 1724, was just one of many visitors who have testified to the dangers of sailing along this coast:

> The farmers and country people had scarce a barn or a shed or a stable, nay not the pales of their yards and gardens, not a hogstye, not a necessary-house, but what was built of old planks, beams and timbers, etc., the wrecks of ships and ruins of mariners' and merchants' fortunes, and in some places were whole yards filled and piled up very high with the same stuff.

Defoe also mentioned that over two hundred colliers and corn ships had been lost at sea during a storm in a single night in 1692 and described how the huge waves that crashed on the sands were regularly throwing up mysterious fragments of wood and bone that bore witness to drama and death at sea. Not surprisingly, the area around Winterton has for centuries suffered from erosion by the sea, and in December 1791, for example, what William White described as a "monstrous" high tide actually breached the sandhills and flooded land all the way to Yarmouth and Beccles.

The buttressed stone tower of Winterton's Holy Trinity Church stands nearly 130 feet high and can be seen for miles around on land and at sea. Wilkie Collins may well have climbed to the top during one of his visit—

many tourists do—although whether he experienced the strange sensation described by W. G. Clarke in *Norfolk & Suffolk* (1921) is not recorded: "This prominent landmark is said to sway backwards and forwards in a gale to such an extent that a tombstone at the base is alternately visible and obscured to an observer on the summit."

Collins's interest in the locality had been made all the greater because of his love of the works of Defoe, in particular *Robinson Crusoe*. Ever since he had read the classic, the fact that Crusoe's first voyage had ended in disaster at Winterton Ness was for ever etched in his memory. On several occasions during his life Collins sailed in the same waters as his literary hero—although always when the sea was calm.

In all probability he heard about other sea tragedies from some of the 150 fishermen who lived among Winterton's population of eight hundred souls in the middle of the nineteenth century. Probably, too, he would have heard about a number of huge bones found near the ness. The largest of these, weighing fifty-seven pounds and measuring three feet by two inches, "was pronounced by the faculty to be the leg-bone of a man", according to a contemporary report. What *kind* of man, no one could be sure.

Small wonder, then, that such a unique spot should have proved irresistible to someone with Collins's imagination, and specific references to the area can be found in his novels *Armadale* (1866), a mystery drama set on the Norfolk Broads, *The Moonstone* (1868), in which Gabriel Betteridge shares his author's passion for *Robinson Crusoe,* as well as several of his essays and short stories. Collins's sexual emotions were equally aroused when he first saw the attractive and independently minded local girl Martha Rudd, probably in 1860. Indeed, there are those in Winterton who have suggested that their first encounter—and its implications—might just have inspired some episodes in *The Woman in White.*

Martha was one of eight children of a shepherd, James Rudd, and his wife, Mary, who lived in a tiny, squalid cottage in Black Street. Although it is probable that she received a basic education at the National School, by the age of sixteen she was working as a barmaid in a local inn, the Fisherman's Return. With her dark, smouldering eyes, high cheek-bones and full red mouth, she caught the eye of many a customer—not the least of them, it seems, the successful author up from London on holiday. She was then nineteen years old. Catherine Peters in her biography of Collins, *The King of Inventors* (1991), says that Martha appears to have drifted into Collins's life "as casually as a stray kitten" but that her determination and strong character and his idiosyncratic if caring sense of responsibility propelled them

into a relationship that would last throughout the author's life. Peters adds:

> If Wilkie had been writing his life, instead of living it, he would have married Martha Rudd. Her archetype was, after all, the Wronged Maid rather than the Dream Woman. But the King of Inventors who did not hesitate in the didactic fiction of his later years to arrange marriage for prostitutes (one of them to a clergyman), or to match an elderly aristocrat with the mother of a (stillborn) illegitimate baby and a well-born young man with a lively country girl much like Martha, was himself content with a "morganatic family". It was his own phrase for Martha and the three children [two daughters and a son] she bore him.

Theirs was a partnership guaranteed to shock in prudish Victorian times. Yet this combination of a single-minded young girl from a poor backwoods family and a writer from a prosperous city background driven by a curiosity about the strange and the mysterious was to form a unique element in the creation of the Sensation Novel—a genre short-lived in itself but ultimately the inspiration of the modern story of mystery, detection and suspense.

William Wilkie Collins was born in 1824 in London, the son of William Collins, a noted landscape painter and member of the Royal Academy. It is evident that Collins senior had an abiding love for East Anglia, and, indeed, his artistic fame dated from 1818 when his main exhibit at the academy's annual show, *Scene on the Coast of Norfolk,* was bought by the Prince Regent and became part of the Royal Collection at Windsor.

Collins began his education at the Maida Hill Academy, but when his father was urged to visit Europe to broaden his knowledge of art for his work the youngster spent two years with his parents in France and Italy. In Rome Collins never forgot his father employing several models for his paintings, including a beautiful young man who posed as either a cupid or an angel and yet—in Collins's own words—"was in private life one of the most consummate rascals: a gambler, thief and a stiletto-wearer, at twelve years of age!"

From childhood, Collins was an avid reader—and soon proved to be a born storyteller, too. After his Grand Tour of Europe he was sent to a private boarding-school in Highbury and there often entertained the other boys with stories based on his travels or drawn from his imagination. This budding talent enabled him to save himself from beatings by the school bully, whom he amused each night with a story. One of the most popular of these tales apparently concerned a boy "who made a business out of swallowing spiders". Collins's ability to come up with entertaining stories at short notice would later stand him in good stead.

Collins left school in 1840, just before his seventeenth birthday. Not interested in going to university or entering the Church—his father's preferred options—he settled instead for an apprenticeship with a London firm of tea importers. The job was undemanding and scarcely fulfilling, and Wilkie admitted that instead of concentrating on bills of lading and invoices he wrote a string of "tragedies, comedies, epic poems and the usual literary rubbish accumulated about themselves by young beginners".

Collins's long-suffering father tried instead to encourage him to enter the legal profession. Wilkie sat the customary examinations and was called to the Bar at Lincoln's Inn but never practised. The ambition to be a writer was already burning in him too strongly to be ignored.

In fact, not all of the compositions he had written during these years were "rubbish". In 1843, when he was just nineteen, one of his stories, **"The Last Stage Coachman"**, was accepted by *The Illuminated Magazine* and published in the August issue. The magazine was edited by Douglas Jerrold, author of the great theatrical success *Black-Eyed Susan* and a prolific contributor to *Punch.* He was evidently impressed by the story of a phantom stagecoach with its hapless passengers and, in particular, its author's ability to conjure up an engrossing macabre situation.

There are certainly several influences at work in this story, which has never been reprinted. Collins had ridden on the Winterton stage-coach to Yarmouth several times and regretted the demise of this form of transport in the face of the ever-growing competition from the railways. He had also endured a terrifying trip with a surly conductor on a diligence between Paris and Chalon-sur-Saône during his travels in Europe with his father. **"The Last Stage Coachman"** bears traces, too, of "The Story of the Bagman's Uncle" from *Pickwick Papers* by Charles Dickens, another of Collins's literary idols and soon to become one of his closest friends.

Exactly a year after the publication of this story Collins went on holiday to Paris and there gathered the details for what would become one of his most famous short stories, **"A Terribly Strange Bed"**. An artist he knew named William Herrick told him about a den in Paris where the proprietor kept a mechanized bed that smothered anyone who slept in it. The account had the feel of an urban myth about it, but Wilkie busied himself around the back streets of the city looking for authentic detail to use in the story, which would again display his reading of other writers, namely the French author Erkmann-Chatrian and Sir Walter Scott.

In the story Collins mingles the fantastic and the realistic in a manner that lays the foundations for the Sensation Novel, as N. P. Davis has written in *The Life of Wilkie Collins* (1956):

His purpose was to impart a new sensation to his readers by a combination of the startling and the familiar, to lay before them a situation as weird as anything that might have occurred "in the lonely inns of the Hartz Mountains" but to build it up out of absolutely commonplace and convincing properties that any one could actually see for himself "in the nineteenth century, in the civilised capital of France".

"A Terribly Strange Bed" was not only a groundbreaking story, it was also the first of Collins's tales to be published by Charles Dickens in his magazine *Household Words,* in the issue of 24 April 1852. Subsequently, critics have described it as "almost a throwback to the Gothic story of terrors with its machine of torture" or, alternately, a pioneer of the "locked room mystery".

Collins had met Dickens in 1851 through their shared love of amateur dramatics. Wilkie joined the circle of admirers surrounding Dickens—then enjoying the acclaim for *David Copperfield*—to appear in the satire *Not So Bad As We Seem* to raise money for the Guild of Literature and Art. The two men appeared in several more productions—notably the "petite comedy" *Used Up* (1852)—became firm friends and began a literary association writing stories and essays for Dickens's magazines that would last until the great man's death in 1870.

With the publication of **"A Terribly Strange Bed"** Collins at last began to feel confident that he could be a successful writer. In the interim his pen had been busy with other contributions, notably with a trio of stories for the popular magazine *Bentley's Miscellany*. These were a romance, **"The Twin Sisters"** (March 1851), a Dickens-inspired comic saga, **"A Passage in the Life of Perugino Potts"** (February 1852), and a gruesome mystery, **"Nine O'Clock"** (July 1852), that was another significant step for Collins, although, surprisingly, it, too, has never been reprinted.

"Nine O'Clock" is essentially a story of precognition and out-of-body experience set during the French Revolution. It had been inspired partly by Collins's visits to Paris and more especially by his interest in the new craze for hypnotism and clairvoyance. The previous winter he had attended a number of gatherings in London and contributed a series of articles, **"Magnetic Evenings at Home"**, to *The Leader* newspaper. From these interests he wove the story of a curse that condemns the members of a family to certain death at the fateful hour.

Despite Dickens's enthusiasm for **"A Terribly Strange Bed"**, he was not an editor easily satisfied. When, the following spring of 1853, Collins's offered him a second story, **"Mad Monkton"**, it was rejected. Dickens explained that he could not publish the tale of hereditary madness as it might cause distress to those of his readers "in the numerous families in which there is such a taint". (As a result of this rejection, Collins put the story to one side, and it was not printed until 1855 in *Fraser's Magazine,* since when it has been endlessly anthologized.)

Dickens was, though, at pains to encourage his new friend and invited him to submit a story to the interlinked series of tales he was preparing for the special Christmas 1854 issue of *Household Words.* The series was called *The Seven Poor Travellers,* and Collins broke new ground again with **"The Fourth Poor Traveller"** in which a clever lawyer-detective recounts to an artist who is painting his portrait how he went about recovering a stolen letter from a man intent on blackmailing one of his clients. Robert Ashley, author of *Wilkie Collins* (1955), claims the tale is the first *British* detective story and has commented: "It utilises more successfully than any other Collins's narrative of the fifties his favourite theme of hide and seek and employs many of the devices of the modern detective story."

Collins followed this success with **"The Dream Woman"** for the next Christmas number of *Household Words* in 1855. It was the first time he used a technique of foreshadowing events and creating an atmosphere of suspense through expectation that would become such a feature of his later major novels. The story is also a daring departure with its description of a middle-aged man who has a nightmare about a murderous female and then becomes infatuated with and marries the ladylike Rebecca Murdoch, while remaining completely unaware of her real intent. It proved uncomfortable fireside reading and was later described by a critic of the *New York Herald* as "a mixture of voluptuousness, cruelty and horror". In 1874 Wilkie expanded the original version to three times its length as **"A Mystery in Four Narratives"** and changed the thought-provoking ending for a finale of mayhem and murder which is far less satisfying.

On 19 July 1856 Wilkie added another first to his literary achievements with **"The Diary of Anne Rodway"** for *Household Words* A remarkable first-person tale, it relates in diary form a young working-class girl's attempt to hunt down the killer of her friend, making her *the* pioneer female detective. The narrative had an extraordinary effect on Dickens, and as soon as he had finished the manuscript he scribbled a hasty note to his friend:

> I cannot tell you what a high opinion I have of **"Anne Rodway"**. I read the first part at the office with strong admiration and read the second part on the railway. My behaviour before my fellow passengers was weak in the extreme, for I cried as much as you could possibly desire. I think it is excellent, feel a personal pride in it which is a delightful sensation, and know no one else who could have done it.

Curiously, the significance of the story as both a new step in detective fiction and for accurately describing the emotions of a simple but whole-hearted young working-class girl—perhaps subconsciously revealing Collins's own feelings towards females such as Martha Rudd who he would soon meet in Winterton—had to wait years to be recognized. For the author's part, he had latched on to an idea that he would soon develop further.

If there is ever a short story in a writer's life that can later be seen to presage one of his great works, then Collins's **"A Marriage Tragedy"**—which was first published in the USA in *Harper's Monthly Magazine* in February 1858—fits the description perfectly. Apart from being one of his best mystery stories, it is written in a similar style and with similar revelations about the characters as his novel *The Woman in White,* which would appear two years later.

There have been many suggestions about the inspiration for *The Woman in White,* a book acknowledged as a classic and one that has never been out of print and which has been translated into every major language. One source is said to have been his meeting with Martha Rudd; another a chance purchase of some old books in France, about which he wrote to a friend many years later:

> I was in Paris wandering about the streets with Charles Dickens amusing ourselves by looking into the shops. We came to an old bookstall—half shop and half store—and I found some dilapidated volumes with records of French crime—a sort of French Newgate Calendar. I said to Dickens, "Here is a prize!" So it turned out to be. In them I found some of my best plots.

The books were entitled *Recueil des Causes Célèbres* by Maurice Méjan and, according to Collins's definitive biographer, Kenneth Robinson, in *Wilkie Collins* (1951), the tattered old volumes remained on his library shelves until his death. "But for them," says Robinson, "*The Woman in White* would probably never have been written."

A still more dramatic source was said to be the events when Collins was walking down a darkened lane in north London one night and he saw a beautiful, terrified young woman dressed all in white running for her life. When he stopped the girl and calmed her she revealed a terrible story of having been imprisoned by a man against her will for months on end. Wilkie combined this dramatic encounter with one of the cases from Méjan's book to create the novel of an heiress, Laura Fairlie, who becomes the victim of a plot to declare her mad by her debt-ridden husband and the villainous Count Fosco in order to seize her property rights.

The Woman in White was first serialized by Dickens in his new magazine *All The Year Round* and in the USA by *Harper's Weekly.* Such was its immediate popularity that on the day of publication of each new weekly episode huge crowds thronged outside the publisher's offices in London. A cult quickly grew up around the story, as the social historian S. M. Ellis has written in *Wilkie Collins, Le Fanu and Others* (1931):

> All through 1860 every possible commodity was labelled "Woman in White". There were "Woman in White" cloaks and bonnets, "Woman in White" perfumes and all manner of toilet requisites, "Woman in White" waltzes and quadrilles. There were also a host of imitators with stories of women in black, grey, green, yellow, blue and everything else, and so the "Sensation Novel" was born.

The circulation figures of *All The Year Round* exceeded even those for the serialization of Dickens's *A Tale of Two Cities* which had preceded it, and Wilkie Collins found himself being praised by leading writers—including William Thackeray and Edward Fitzgerald, who reread it four times—while the story was known to be a favourite of both Prince Albert and Prime Minister William Gladstone. With *The Woman in White* Collins found himself on a par with his mentor.

It was only a matter of time before the novel was being adapted for the other forms of entertainment. Collins himself was commissioned to write the theatrical version that was first staged at the Olympic Theatre, London, in October 1871, opening a year later on Broadway. This adaptation has been produced on numerous occasions, most recently in December 1988 when Helena Bonham Carter took the title role in the Greenwich Theatre production in London.

The story was first filmed as a silent movie by Pathe in 1917, and in 1929 Herbert Wilcox directed Blanche Sweet, Cecil Humphreys and Frank Perfitt as the three main protagonists in the British and Dominions Film Corporation version. The British master of melodrama, Tod Slaughter, starred in a 1940 adaptation for Ambassador Films retitled *Crimes at the Dark House,* and this was followed by the lavish 1948 Warner Brothers version with Eleanor Parker, John Emery and Sidney Greenstreet playing the oily and loathsome Count Fosco.

The Woman in White has also been adapted for television in both Britain and the USA, notably in April 1982 when Ray Jenkins scripted a five-episode series for the BBC starring Diana Quick, John Shrapnel and Alan Badel. It was again serialized by the BBC in November 1997 with Susan Vidler, Ian Richardson and Simon Callow. Now Collins's masterwork is to be adapted as a musical by Andrew Lloyd Webber who believes the plot has all the originality and theatricality of his greatest triumph *The Phantom of the Opera,* which was also based on a nineteenth-century classic novel, *Le Fantôme de l'Opéra* by Gaston Leroux.

Several authorities on Wilkie Collins have drawn parallels between the short story **"A Marriage Tragedy"** and *The Woman in White.* In both, the plot is activated by a complicated family conspiracy, and the villain in the short story, James Smith, bears a striking resemblance to the evil-hearted husband, Percival Glyde, of the novel. **"A Marriage Tragedy"** also has its private investigator, the sharp-witted, tireless Mr. Dark, who foreshadows the hawk-like Sergeant Cuff, and whose battle of wits with the sinister Josephine resembles that between the heroine of *The Woman in White* and her scheming husband and Count Fosco.

Collins also adapted the incident of the bloodstained nightgown in **"A Marriage Tragedy"** to a paint-stained gown in his second great Sensation Novel *The Moonstone,* published in 1868. This, according to T. S. Eliot, is "the first, the longest and the best of modern English detective novels", and, while this claim is open to dispute, the Sergeant is unquestionably the first and most significant detective in English literature. Few who have read the book would argue with Dorothy L. Sayers's verdict that it is "probably the very finest detective story ever written".

Again *The Moonstone* had a basis in fact—the case of 21-year-old Constance Kent acquitted of murdering her half-brother in Wiltshire in 1860 and which she later confessed to having committed—plus a complex plot featuring a priceless Indian diamond stolen from a religious idol and now the object of a relentless search by a trio of fanatical worshippers determined to retrieve it from the young woman to whom it has been given. Anxious to see justice done is, once again, the intrepid Sergeant Cuff whom Collins based on Jonathan Whicher, the Scotland Yard inspector who investigated the Constance Kent case and whose reputation was ruined by the not-guilty verdict.

Like *The Woman in White,* the story was hailed by the reading public and critics alike, an anonymous reviewer in *The Times* declaring that "*The Moonstone* will remain, as long as sensation novels are read, as a model of all that is most sensational, most thrilling, and most ingeniously probable in the midst of improbability." The novel also introduced a number of classic features to the novel of detection: a country-house robbery, false suspects, a final twist in the plot and an eccentric, celebrated detective to solve the mystery.

This novel, too, has been filmed several times. First in 1915 as a silent movie by Pathe, then in Monogram's 1934 version starring Charles Irwin as a very correct Cuff and again in 1972 by Columbia Pictures, with Maurice Denham interpreting the Sergeant as a fidgety and rather garrulous officer of the law.

Some ten years before writing *The Moonstone* Collins had demonstrated that crime could be amusing as well as deadly serious in a little tale entitled **"Who Is the**

Thief?" published in April 1858 in a newly launched US magazine, *The Atlantic Monthly*. The story recounts the mishaps of a bungling new detective tracking some suspects through London and is noteworthy on two counts: as the first humorous or satirical detective story and the first detective story to be written in the form of letters exchanged by the policemen involved in the case. **"Who Is the Thief"** again contains a number of the elements found in the Sensation Novel before it was established as such.

Although Wilkie Collins wrote several ghost stories as well his tales of sensation, they are not among the best of his work. The supernatural is to be found in **"Mad Monkton"** (1855), **"John Jago's Ghost"** (1873) and **"Mrs. Zant and the Ghost"** (1887), but probably the most accomplished is **"The Clergyman's Confession"**, written in 1875 and originally published in *Canadian Monthly,* which had been reprinting the author's earlier work. The story of a ghost who helps to solve a murder, it stirred up controversy because of the sensual elements in the plot. Indeed, the theme may well have made Collins's usual British publishers nervous about publishing it.

The clergyman of the title is tormented by an affair he had as a young man with a petite Frenchwoman, Miss Jéromette, despite the fact she admitted to him she was the "love slave" of another man who deserted her. Some years later her ghost appears to the man of the cloth revealing that her other lover has murdered her, leaving him with a dilemma to resolve. What makes the story unique among supernatural stories of the time is that Collins describes a seamy, physical side to erotic relationships, all the more powerful in the character of a student of divinity.

Three years after the publication of this story Collins returned to the supernatural again, albeit rationalized, in *The Haunted Hotel* (1878), which most critics agree was probably his last good novel. His health had been poor for years and by this stage of his life he was heavily dependent on opium: "Laudanum—divine laudanum—was my only friend", he was to confess in his diary. Later still, in a "note made on a spring morning" in 1883, he professed his addiction ever more forcefully:

> Who was the man who invented opium? I thank him from the bottom of my heart. I have had six delicious hours of oblivion. I have woken up with my mind composed and dawdled over my morning toilet with an exquisite sense of relief—and all through the modest little bottle of drops which I see on my bedroom chimney-piece at the moment. Drops, you are a darling! If I love nothing else, I love you!

There was a price to pay for his addiction, however. As the doses grew larger so did Collins's grip on reality diminish. He claimed to see a green woman with tusks waiting to bite a piece out of his shoulder, and one visitor to his home in 1885—four yers before his death—said that his eyes had become "enormous bags of blood".

Collins's last years were, indeed, a sad climax after the ground-breaking achievements of his early stories and the success of his two great novels. Indeed, as the Sensation Novel gave way to the story of mystery and suspense, so his own reputation declined. Where once he had been compared with his friend Charles Dickens, Collins would now have to wait for years to be recognized as a great writer. It was as late as 1976 that his qualities began to be reappraised when Chris Steinbrunner and Otto Penzler in their *Encyclopedia of Mystery and Detection* awarded Collins the following accolade:

> He ranks with Dickens as the best popular novelist of his time, and, although his characterisations do not approach those of his friend, his carefully worked-out plots, complete with red herrings, cliff-hanging miniclimaxes, multitudinous suspicions and evasive alibis, are superior to those of any novelist of the nineteenth century.

Collins continued writing to the bitter end, however, and found his most ready sales to American magazines with stories such as **"The Magic Spectacles"** (*The Seaside Library,* June 1880), concerning the mysterious powers of a pair of glasses, a romance, **"The Fair Physician"** (*Pictorial World, 23* December 1882), and one final mystery story, **"Love's Random Shot"** (*The Seaside Library,* August 1884). This is a rather melancholy account of a Scottish police officer's last case, and it reads as if both the detective and his creator are aware that their best days are behind them. None the less, it provided the title story for the last collection of Wilkie Collins's work, *Love's Random Shot & Other Stories,* issued posthumously in New York in 1894 by George Munro's Sons and reprinted here for the first time since.

Wilkie Collins once asked that his epitaph should read "Author of *The Woman in White* and other works of fiction". Such a statement, though, ignores his major contribution to the Sensation Novel as well as the pioneering nature of the best of his short fiction. Without either, the modern mystery story might have been years—even decades—later in its development.

FURTHER READING

Bibliography

Beetz, Kirk H. *Wilkie Collins: An Annotated Bibliography.* Metuchen, N.J.: The Scarecrow Press, Inc., 1978, 167 p.

Thorough bibliography of Collins's works and secondary studies.

Biographies

Clarke, William M. *The Secret Life of Wilkie Collins.* London: Allison & Busby, 1988, 239 p.

Discusses Collins's mistresses and the more scandalous aspects of his life.

Davis, Nuel Pharr. *The Life of Wilkie Collins.* Urbana: University of Illinois Press, 1956, 360 p.

Conventional biography of Collins.

Robinson, Kenneth. *Wilkie Collins: A Biography.* London: The Bodley Head, 1951, 348 p.

The first thorough biography of Collins that presents the author in full perspective.

Sayers, Dorothy L. *Wilkie Collins: A Critical and Biographical Study,* edited by E. R. Gregory. Toledo, Oh.: The Friends of the University of Toledo Libraries, 1977, 120 p.

A concise, mostly biographical study of Collins.

Criticism

Ashley, Robert. "Journeyman Novelist." In *Wilkie Collins,* pp. 32-58. London: Arthur Baker, Ltd., 1952.

Discusses Collins's collaboration with Dickens on the magazine *Household Words* and other works, then examins the early stories collected in *After Dark.*

Grinstein, Alexander. "The Tellers of Tales." In *Wilkie Collins: Man of Mystery and Imagination,* pp. 95-103. Madison, Conn.: International Universities Press, Inc., 2003.

Comments on the collaboration between Collins and Dickens, Collins's stance toward women, and his stories that deal with marriage.

Lonoff, Sue. *Wilkie Collins and His Victorian Readers: A Study in the Rhetoric of Authorship.* New York: AMS Press, Inc., 1982, 294 p.

Examines the ways in which Collins attempted to both manipulate and appease his audience.

Watson, Graeme. "A Rather Strange Proustian." *Australian Journal of French Studies* 18, no. 1 (January-April 1981): 35-38.

Suggests that "A Terribly Strange Bed" simulates a passage in Marcel Proust's *Combray.*

Additional coverage of Collins's life and career is contained in the following sources published by Thomson Gale: *British Writers Supplement,* **Vols. 6;** *Concise Dictionary of British Literary Biography,* **Vol. 1832-1890;** *Dictionary of Literary Biography,* **Vols. 18, 70, and 159;** *Gothic Literature: A Gale Critical Companion,* **Ed. 2;** *Literature Resource Center;* *Mystery and Suspense Writers;* *Nineteenth-Century Literature Criticism,* **Vols. 1, 18, and 93;** *Reference Guide to English Literature* **Ed. 2;** *Reference Guide to Short Fiction,* **Ed. 2;** *St. James Guide to Crime & Mystery Writers,* **Vol. 4;** *Supernatural Fiction Writers,* **Vol. 1; and** *World Literature and Its Times,* **Ed. 4.**

M. R. James
1862-1936

(Full name Montague Rhodes James.) English short story writer, translator, and nonfiction writer. For additional information on James's short fiction, see *Short Story Criticism,* Volume 16.

INTRODUCTION

James is considered the creator and foremost craftsman of the modern ghost story. Writing in the tradition of Joseph Sheridan Le Fanu, who he thought "stood in the first rank as a writer of ghost stories," James avoided the atmospheric Gothicism of his predecessor's work and instead employed a simple narrative style designed to heighten the terrifying effect of his tales. In the works of Le Fanu and other Gothic writers, terror arises from both psychological and supernatural sources, but in James the agent of fear is entirely an objective phenomenon outside character psychology. As critics have pointed out, his characters are pursued to their unpleasant doom for no apparent reason aside from their being in the wrong place at the wrong time. James originally delivered his stories orally, to entertain his friends. A well-respected scholar of archaeology, paleography, and antiques, James set his stories in the dusty halls of academia and his protagonists are antiquaries or scholars who are often quite literally haunted by the past. This is seen in his best-known stories, "Oh, Whistle, and 'll Come to You, My Lad" (1904), which features a professor pursued into the darkness of a strange bedroom in which the bedclothes are possessed, and "Casting the Runes" (1911), about a scholar's occult revenge against those who have not appreciated his literary achievements. Although James's stories are widely seen as lacking the depth or complexity of other masters of horror tales, they are admired for their careful craftsmanship and atmospheric intensity.

BIOGRAPHICAL INFORMATION

James was born in 1862 in Wingham, Kent, the youngest son of a rector in the Suffolk village of Livermere. He was raised an Evangelical Christian, and maintained his childhood faith with complete orthodoxy throughout his life. An intensely studious child, he spent more time in the library than with friends. He was educated at Eton and then King's College, Cambridge, where he devoted himself to studying apocryphal documents con-nected with the Old and New Testaments and cataloguing medieval manuscripts. He soon became a world-renowned authority in his field and progressed rapidly in his academic career, holding the posts of fellow, provost, tutor, dean, and vice-chancellor at King's College, and provost of Eton. His first ghost stories were read at meetings of the Chitchat Society, a Cambridge literary club organized "for the promotion of rational conversation." Urged by club members to produce more stories, he did so and eventually published *Ghost-Stories of an Antiquary* (1904). Collections of James's ghost stories were immensely popular and his candlelight readings at Cambridge became a Christmas Eve tradition. James never married. He died in his lodge at Eton in 1936.

MAJOR WORKS OF SHORT FICTION

James published four volumes of original tales between 1904 and 1925; these were republished in 1931 as *The Collected Ghost Stories of M. R. James.* Though not a professional or even frequent writer of fiction, James was a self-conscious artist who followed specific literary guidelines in his tales of terror. "Canon Alberic's Scrapbook," first read to friends in 1893, then published in the *National Review* in 1895, set the pattern for his later stories, which generally begin in familiar, realistic settings with characters involved in ordinary pursuits, often of an academic nature. The inevitable intrusion of malevolent supernatural forces does not detract from—and indeed seems to intensify—the aura of believability established from the start. Rather than mobilizing the familiar wispy apparition, James's ghost stories commonly feature such substantial horrors as the-hairy-handed thing in "Canon Alberic's Scrapbook," the demonic cat in "The Stalls of Barchester Cathedral" (1911), and the tentacled companion in "Count Magnus" (1904). In addition to writing short stories, James translated fairy tales and edited a volume of Le Fanu's mysteries.

CRITICAL RECEPTION

James has been admired by fans of the horror genre for his ability to engage readers by introducing the unexpected in the most ordinary situations. The horror novelist H. P. Lovecraft said that James was "gifted with an almost diabolic power of calling horror by gentle steps from the midst of prosaic daily life," and knew how to "apportion statement, imagery, and subtle suggestions in order to secure the best results with his readers." While critics generally consider James a master of the ghost story, citing as evidence his realistic settings and plausible plots, some commentators have suggested that his restrained prose limits, rather than explores, the supernatural possibilities introduced in his tales. For James himself, critical acceptance was a less valid measure of his success than was a story's ability to make his reader "feel pleasantly uncomfortable when walking along a solitary road at nightfall, or sitting over a dying fire in the small hours." Although scholars do not regard James as a writer in the ranks of Edgar Allan Poe or Mary Shelley, several detailed studies of his works have appeared. Critics have paid particular attention to the author's indebtedness to Le Fanu; the timeless moral messages in his stories; his interest in antiquaries, folklore, and living history; the themes of sexuality and gender equality in his work; the recurring motif of golf as a game that displaces the past; and similarities between James's outlook and that of Sigmund Freud. James's *Collected Ghost Stories* has never been out of print and he continues to attract a loyal following among readers of the horror and supernatural genres.

PRINCIPAL WORKS

Short Fiction

Ghost-Stories of an Antiquary 1904

More Ghost-Stories of an Antiquary 1911

A Thin Ghost, and Others (short stories) 1919

A Warning to the Curious, and Other Ghost Stories 1925

The Collected Ghost Stories of M. R. James 1931

"The Experiment: A New Year's Eve Ghost Story" 1931

"The Malice of Inanimate Objects" (short story) 1933

"A Vignette" (short story) 1936

Other Major Works

Guide to the Windows of King's College Chapel, Cambridge (nonfiction) 1899

Old Testament Legends, Being Stories out of Some of the Less-Known Apocryphal Books (nonfiction) 1913

The Wanderings and Homes of Manuscripts (nonfiction) 1919

The Lost Apocrypha of the Old Testament (nonfiction) [translator] 1920

The Five Jars (juvenilia) 1922

"Madam Crowl's Ghost" and Other Tales of Mystery by Joseph Sheridan Le Fanu [editor and translator] (short stories) 1923

The Apocryphal New Testament, Being the Apocryphal Gospels, Acts, Epistles, and Apocalypses, with Other Narratives and Fragments [translator] 1924

Eton and King's: Recollections, Mostly Trivial, 1875-1925 (memoir) 1926

Hans Andersen: Forty Stories [translator] (short stories) 1930; enlarged and published as *Forty-Two Stories*, 1953

CRITICISM

M. R. James (essay date 1931)

SOURCE: James, M. R. "Preface." In *The Collected Ghost Stories of M. R. James*, pp. vii-x. London: Edward Arnold (Publishers) Ltd., 1931.

[*In the following introduction to a collection of four volumes of his ghost stories, James answers several questions that have been posed to him, including whether his stories are inspired by his own experiences or those of others; whether his stories are grounded in particular places; whether he has any theories of writing ghost stories; and whether he believes in ghosts.*]

In accordance with a fashion which has recently become common, I am issuing my four volumes of ghost stories under one cover, and appending to them some matter of the same kind.

I am told they have given pleasure of a certain sort to my readers: if so, my whole object in writing them has been attained, and there does not seem to be much reason for prefacing them by a disquisition upon how I came to write them. Still, a preface is demanded by my publishers, and it may as well be devoted to answering questions which I have been asked.

First, whether the stories are based on my own experience? To this the answer is No: except in one case, specified in the text, where a dream furnished a suggestion. Or again, whether they are versions of other people's experiences? No. Or suggested by books? This is more difficult to answer concisely. Other people have written of dreadful spiders—for instance, Erckmann-Chatrian in an admirable story called *L'Araignée Crabe*—and of pictures which came alive: the State Trials give the language of Judge Jeffreys and the courts at the end of the seventeenth century: and so on. Places have been more prolific in suggestion: if anyone is curious about my local settings, let it be recorded that S. Bertrand de Comminges and Viborg are real places: that in *Oh, Whistle, and I'll Come to You,* I had Felixstowe in mind; in *A School Story,* Temple Grove, East Sheen; in *The Tractate Middoth,* Cambridge University Library; in *Martin's Close,* Sampford Courtenay in Devon: that the cathedrals of Barchester and Southminster were blends of Canterbury, Salisbury, and Hereford: that Herefordshire was the imagined scene of *A View from a Hill,* and Seaburgh in *A Warning to the Curious* is Aldeburgh in Suffolk.

I am not conscious of other obligations to literature or local legend, written or oral, except in so far as I have tried to make my ghosts act in ways not inconsistent with the rules of folklore. As for the fragments of ostensible erudition which are scattered about my pages, hardly anything in them is not pure invention; there never was, naturally, any such book as that which I quote in the *Treasure of Abbot Thomas.*

Other questioners ask if I have any theories as to the writing of ghost stories. None that are worthy of the name or need to be repeated here: some thoughts on the subject are in a preface to *Ghosts and Marvels.* [*The World's Classics,* Oxford, 1924.] There is no receipt for success in this form of fiction more than in any other. The public, as Dr. Johnson said, are the ultimate judges: if they are pleased, it is well; if not, it is no use to tell them why they ought to have been pleased.

Supplementary questions are: Do I believe in ghosts? To which I answer that I am prepared to consider evidence and accept it if it satisfies me. And lastly, Am I going to write any more ghost stories? To which I fear I must answer, Probably not.

Since we are nothing if not bibliographical nowadays, I add a paragraph or two setting forth the facts about the several collections and their contents.

"Ghost Stories of an Antiquary" was published (like the rest) by Messrs. Arnold in 1904. The first issue had four illustrations by the late James McBryde. In this volume *Canon Alberic's Scrap-Book* was written in 1894 and printed soon after in the *National Review: Lost Hearts* appeared in the *Pall Mall Magazine.* Of the next five stories, most of which were read to friends at Christmas-time at King's College, Cambridge, I only recollect that I wrote *Number 13* in 1899, while *The Treasure of Abbot Thomas* was composed in summer 1904.

The second volume, **"More Ghost Stories,"** appeared in 1911. The first six of the seven tales it contains were Christmas productions, the very first (*A School Story*) having been made up for the benefit of the King's Col-

lege Choir School. *The Stalls of Barchester Cathedral* was printed in the *Contemporary Review: Mr. Humphreys and His Inheritance* was written to fill up the volume.

"A Thin Ghost and Others" was the third collection, containing five stories and published in 1919. In it, *An Episode of Cathedral History* and *The Story of a Disappearance and an Appearance* were contributed to the *Cambridge Review.*

Of six stories in **"A Warning to the Curious,"** published in 1925, the first, *The Haunted Dolls' House,* was written for the library of Her Majesty the Queen's Dolls' House, and subsequently appeared in the *Empire Review. The Uncommon Prayer-Book* saw the light in the *Atlantic Monthly,* the title-story in the *London Mercury,* and another, I think *A Neighbour's Landmark,* in an ephemeral called *The Eton Chronic.* Similar ephemerals were responsible for all but one of the appended pieces (not all of them strictly stories), whereof one, *Rats,* composed for *At Random,* was included by Lady Cynthia Asquith in a collection entitled *Shudders.* The exception, *Wailing Well,* was written for the Eton College troop of Boy Scouts, and read at their camp-fire at Worbarrow Bay in August, 1927. It was then printed by itself in a limited edition by Robert Gathorne Hardy and Kyrle Leng at the Mill House Press, Stanford Dingley.

Four or five of the stories have appeared in collections of such things in recent years, and a Norse version of four from my first volume, by Ragnhild Undset, was issued in 1919 under the title of *Aander og Trolddom.*

Jack Sullivan (essay date 1978)

SOURCE: Sullivan, Jack. "The Antiquarian Ghost Story: Montague Rhodes James." In *Elegant Nightmares: The English Ghost Story from Le Fanu to Blackwood,* pp. 69-90. Athens: Ohio University Press, 1978.

[*In the following essay, Sullivan examines James's ghost stories about collectors and antiquarians, focusing on the author's indebtedness to the writer Sheridan Le Fanu.*]

"Count Magnus," from M. R. James's *Ghost Stories of an Antiquary,* is haunted not only by its own ghosts, but by the ghost of Sheridan Le Fanu. Mr. Wraxall, the hero of the tale, dooms himself by peering at a terrifying sarcophagus engraving which should have remained unseen and opening an obscure alchemy volume which should have remained closed. By doing these things, he inadvertently summons the author of the alchemy treatise, the dreaded Count Magnus, from the sarcophagus.

To make matters worse, he also summons the count's hooded, tentacled companion. Anyone who has read Le Fanu's "Green Tea" knows that such creatures are easier summoned than eluded. Mr. Wraxall flees across the Continent, but his pursuers are always close behind. They arrive at his remote country house in England before he does and wait for him there. Not surprisingly, he is found dead. At the inquest, seven jurors faint at the sight of the body. The verdict is "visitation of God," but the reader knows that he has been visited by something else.

In both incident and vision, **"Count Magnus"** is darkened by the shadow of Le Fanu. The basic dynamic of the story, the hunt, is symbolized by the sarcophagus engraving:

> Among trees, was a man running at full speed, with flying hair and outstretched hands. After him followed a strange form; it would be hard to say whether the artist had intended it for a man, and was unable to give the requisite similitude, or whether it was intentionally made as monstrous as it looked. In view of the skill with which the rest of the drawing was done, Mr. Wraxall felt inclined to adopt the latter idea.[1]

Upon reading this insidiously understated passage, the reader who is familiar with Le Fanu immediately knows two things: that the fleeing figure will soon be Mr. Wraxall himself and that the outcome of the pursuit will be fatal for him. Such a reader will not be surprised by the mysterious illogic of the plot, the absence of any moral connection between the hunter and the hunted. Mr. Wraxall is no Gothic villain or Fatal Man; he is a singularly unremarkable, almost anonymous character. He resembles several Le Fanu characters (especially in "Green Tea" and "Schalken the Painter") in that he is a pure victim, having done nothing amiss other than reading the wrong book and looking at the wrong picture. We are told in an ironic passage that "his besetting fault was clearly that of over-inquisitiveness, possibly a good fault in a traveler, certainly a fault for which this traveler paid dearly in the end" (100). We are not told why he is any more overly inquisitive than James's other antiquaries, many of whom are never pursued. The narrator sums up the problem near the end of the story: "He is expecting a visit from his pursuers—how or when he knows not—and his constant cry is 'What has he done?' and 'Is there no hope?' Doctors, he knows, would call him mad, policemen would laugh at him. The parson is away. What can he do but lock his door and cry to God?" (118). This fragmented summary of Mr. Wraxall's final entries in his journal suggests that the horror of the situation is in the chasm between action and consequence. In the fictional world of Le Fanu and James, one does not have to be a Faust, a Melmoth, or even a Huckleberry Finn to be damned. The strategy of both writers is the same: to make the reader glance nervously around the room and say, "If this could happen to him, it could happen to me."

The style also owes much to Le Fanu. In an odd sense, **"Count Magnus"** is more in the Le Fanu manner than Le Fanu. James's use of innuendo and indirection is so rigorous that it hides more than it reveals. Le Fanu creates a balance between uneasy vagueness and grisly clarity. But James tilts the balance in favor of the unseen. Tiny, unsettling flashes of clarity emerge from the obscurity, but usually in an indirect context. We are allowed to see the protruding tentacle of one of the robed pursuers, for example—but only in the engraving, not in the actual pursuit. In the most literal sense, these are nameless horrors.

James also follows Le Fanu's example in his use of narrative distance, again transcending his model. Le Fanu separates himself from his material through the use of elaborate, sometimes awkward prologues and epilogues which filter the stories through a series of editors and narrators. Sometimes, as in **"Mr. Justice Harbottle,"** the network of tales within tales results in a narrative fabric of considerable complexity. In "Count Magnus," the narrator is an anonymous editor who has access to the papers Mr. Wraxall was compiling for a travelogue. The story consists of paraphrases and direct quotations from these papers, a device which gives the narrative a strong aura of authenticity. The transitions from one document to the other, occurring organically within the text, are smooth and unobtrusive. They are also strangely impersonal, as if the teller in no way wishes to commit himself to his tale.

James's reticence probably relates as much to personal temperament as to the aesthetic problem of how to write a proper ghost story. It is commonly accepted, largely because of the work of James and Le Fanu, that indirection, ambiguity, and narrative distance are appropriate techniques for ghostly fiction.[2] (Material horror tales, such as Wells's "The Cone" and Alexander Woollcott's "Moonlight Sonata," are another matter.) Supernatural horror is usually more convincing when suggested or evoked than when explicitly documented. But James's understated subtlety is so obsessive, so paradoxically unrestrained that it feels like an inversion of the hyperbole of Poe or Maturin. I find his late work increasingly ambiguous and puzzling, sometimes to the point of almost total mystification. It is as if James is increasingly unwilling to deal with the implications of his stories. What begins as a way of making supernatural horror more potent becomes a way of repressing or avoiding it. Often he appears to be doing both at once, creating a unique chill and tension.

Although he claimed to be merely a follower of Le Fanu, his work has a different feel, despite the obvious similarities in vision and style. Indeed, he unwittingly created his own "school," a surprisingly large accumulation of tales for which James serves as a paradigm. At least two of his more talented admirers, E. G. Swain and R. H. Malden, are far closer to James than James imagined himself to Le Fanu.

James published four volumes of ghost stories during his lifetime (1862-1936): *Ghost Stories of an Antiquary* (1904), *More Ghost Stories* (1911), *A Thin Ghost and Others* (1919), and *A Warning to the Curious* (1925). He was originally a teller, rather than a writer, of ghost stories. His first two stories, **"Lost Hearts"** and **"Canon Alberic's Scrapbook,"** were written down to be read aloud at an 1897 meeting of the Chitchat Society, a literary gathering which met for "the promotion of rational conversation."[3] The readings were intended to enliven what had become a listless, apathetic (if "rational") group. They must not have been entirely successful, for although the readings continued, the group dissolved in 1897; as James put it, in his typical phraseology, the society "expired of inanition."[4] Nevertheless, the meeting marked the beginning of a yearly ritual in which James would deliver 11 p.m. Christmas readings to friends, first at King's and later at Cambridge. At some of these meetings, James read Le Fanu (with "great relish," according to one of his friends), thus beginning the Le Fanu revival which culminated in James's edition of rare Le Fanu ghost stories.[5] Some of the listeners, like A. C. and E. F. Benson, were connoisseurs of the weird and became ghost story writers themselves. Partly because of their prodding, and partly because James's friend James MacBryde agreed to be his illustrator, James published his first and most famous collection, *Ghost Stories of an Antiquary.* As the prodding continued, so did the other collections, even though MacBryde (who, according to James, was the main reason he decided to publish anything at all), died suddenly before completing the illustrations for *Ghost Stories.* The climax of this curiously reluctant career was the publication of the *Collected Ghost Stories* in 1931. By then, in its review of the collected stories, the *Spectator Literary Supplement* was able to refer to James as "long" having "been an acknowledged master of his craft."[6]

Other than a lifetime fondness for oldness, James's life demonstrates little direct connection to his fiction. His reputation rests not on his fiction, still relatively unknown, but on his contribution to medieval scholarship (though this situation is rapidly changing).[7] James prepared an estimated fifteen to twenty thousand bibliographic descriptions of medieval manuscripts, as well as the *Apocryphal New Testaments.* Unlike Le Fanu, he did not steep himself in Swedenborg or any other esoteric doctrines, but remained, according to the obituary notice of the British Academy, "a devoted son of the Church of England."[8] Nevertheless, his prodigious scholarly activities provided him with the learned tone

and much of the content of his stories. Though largely fabricated, the names of churches, manuscripts, villages, and allusive scholarly minutiae in his stories always sound unerringly authentic. In all outward respects, his life was conservative, the perfect embodiment of a successful post-Victorian man of letters: he was a Fellow of King's College, Provost and Vice-Chancellor at Cambridge, Director of the Fitzwilliam Museum, and finally Provost of Eton. Although Protestant, "he liked a grave and dignified ceremonial." In politics, he was "uninterested but faintly conservative."[9]

James once described the ghost story as an inherently "old-fashioned" form.[10] Yet in the context of his life, the writing of ghost stories seemed eccentric and unorthodox, almost a blemish on an otherwise spotless career. Sir Stephen Gaselee refers with embarrassment to the "pile of 'shockers' in his room."[11] (The "shockers" included, among others, Conan Doyle, Blackwood and, of course, Le Fanu.) Gaselee doesn't like James's "or any other ghost stories," but adds condescendingly that "experts tell me they are among the best of their kind." James's biographer and lifelong friend, S. G. Lubbock, devotes only a single page to the ghost stories.[12]

But the most stubbornly unhelpful commentator on James's fiction is James himself. In his odd preface to his *Collected Ghost Stories,* James states that the only reason he is yielding any commentary at all is that "a preface is demanded by my publishers."[13] Given the demand, the preface "may as well be devoted to answering questions which I have been asked."[14] The answers, to put it mildly, are brief: "First, whether the stories are based on my own experience? To this, the answer is No. . . . Or again, whether they are versions of other people's experiences? No. . . . Other questioners ask if I have any theories as to the writing of ghost stories. None that are worthy of the name or need be repeated here: some thoughts on the subject are in a preface to *Ghosts and Marvels.* . . . Supplementary questions are: Do I believe in ghosts? To which I am prepared to consider evidence and accept it if it satisfies me."[15] This delightful evasiveness represents a consistent effort on James's part to dissociate himself from the clichés which usually dominate discussions of ghost stories. But it also represents an oblique refusal to comment on the craft of ghost story writing (a subject which Edith Wharton, L. P. Hartley, Robert Aickman, and others have always been eager to discuss). The reference to James's supernatural fiction anthology, *Ghosts and Marvels,* is as sneaky and underhanded as any of James's apparitions. If, as James suggests, we search out that rare volume for enlightenment, we find this statement: "Often I have been asked to formulate my views about ghost stories. . . . Never have I been able to find out whether I had any views that could be formulated."[16]

This is more than simple modesty. James's aggressively deflationary attitude toward himself and his material is part of the mystique of his fiction. The stories use every available verbal resource to avoid calling attention to themselves, as if the otherworldly phenomena are creepy enough on their own not to require a loud voice for their exposition.

Moreover, the stories fit thematically into this context, for they often imply a kind of emptiness and restlessness on the part of the characters. It is not "overinquisitiveness" that gets Mr. Wraxall into trouble so much as ennui. James's stories assume a radical breakdown of the work ethic in which the forces of evil take advantage of idleness. Mr. Wraxall is like most of James's heroes in that he is a roving antiquary, a bachelor who is wealthy and cultivated but seems to have no fixed place in society: "He had, it seemed, no settled abode in England, but was a denizen of hotels and boarding houses. It is probable that he entertained the idea of settling down at some future time which never came" (100). Though James does not make much out of the idea, the supernatural in his stories has a way of materializing out of a void in people's lives. In **"The Uncommon Prayer Book"** (one of his happiest titles), Mr. Davidson spends a week researching the tombs of Leventhorp House because "his nearest relations were enjoying winter sports abroad and the friends who had been kindly anxious to replace them had an infectious complaint in the house" (490). Even those who have a "settled abode" are curiously unsettled.

There is thus an implicit "Waste Land" ambiance to these stories. The characters are antiquaries, not merely because the past enthralls them, but because the present is a near vacuum. They surround themselves with rarefied paraphernalia from the past—engravings, rare books, altars, tombs, coins, and even such things as doll's houses and ancient whistles—seemingly because they cannot connect with anything in the present. The endless process of collecting and arranging gives the characters an illusory sense of order and stability, illusory because it is precisely this process which evokes the demon or the vampire. With the single exception of Mr. Abney in **"Lost Hearts,"** James's men of leisure are not villainous, merely bored. Their adventures represent a sophisticated version of the old warning that idleness is the devil's workshop.

This is a crucial difference between James and Le Fanu. In Le Fanu, supernatural horror is peculiarly militant—it can emerge anytime it pleases. In James's antiquarian tales, horror is ever-present, but it is not actually threatening or lethal until inadvertently invoked. For Le Fanu's characters, reality is inherently dark and deadly; for James's antiquaries, darkness must be sought out through research and discovery.

It is true that the final discovery is always accidental: James's stories are distinctly different from the more visionary stories of Blackwood and Machen, stories with characters who are not bored, but stifled, and who consciously seek out weirdness and horror. Nevertheless, there is a half-conscious sense in which the antiquary knows he may be heading for trouble but persists in what he is doing. An example is Mr. Parkins in the (again) wonderfully titled **"Oh, Whistle and I'll Come to You, My Lad,"** a man whose bed clothes become possessed. Parkins brings this singularly unpleasant fate on himself by digging up a dreadful whistle and having the poor sense to blow it. He doesn't *have* to blow it. He is given ample warning—certainly more than any of Le Fanu's victims ever get—from a Latin inscription on the whistle: "Quis est iste qui venit?" ("Who is this who is coming?") "Well," says Parkins with a nice simplicity, "The best way to find out is evidently to whistle for him" (132).

Another aspect of James which separates him from Le Fanu is the radical economy of his style. Although he hides more than Le Fanu, he etches what he chooses to reveal in brief but telling detail. An example is the apparition (of a man burned at the stake) in **"The Rose Garden"**:

> It was not a mask. It was a face—large, smooth, and pink. She remembers the minute drops of perspiration which were starting from its forehead: she remembers how the jaws were clean-shaven and the eyes shut. She remembers also, and with an accuracy which makes the thought intolerable to her, how the mouth was open and a single tooth appeared below the upper lip. As she looked the face receded into the darkness of the bush. The shelter of the house was gained and the door shut before she collapsed.
>
> (206)

Another, more colloquially rendered, is the library apparition in **"The Tractate Middoth"**:

> This time, if you please—ten o'clock in the morning, remember, and as much light as ever you get in those classes, and there was my parson again, back to me, looking at the books on the shelf I wanted. His hat was on the table, and he had a bald head. I waited a second or two looking at him rather particularly. I tell you, he had a very nasty bald head. It looked to me dry, and it looked dusty, and the streaks of hair across it were much less like hair than cobwebs. Well, I made a bit of noise on purpose, coughed and moved my feet. He turned round and let me see his face—which I hadn't seen before. I tell you again, I'm not mistaken. Though, for one reason or another I didn't take in the lower part of his face, I did see the upper part; and it was perfectly dry, and the eyes were very deep-sunk; and over them, from the eyebrows to the cheek-bone, there were *cobwebs*—thick. Now that closed me up, as they say, and I can't tell you anything more.
>
> (217)

Le Fanu would not have cut either scene off as quickly, nor would he have been as prosaic. Compared to the stateliness of Le Fanu's prose, James's seems spare and unadorned. Terse and controlled, his stories give the sense of a ruthless paring down of incidents and characters, a constant editing out of anything which might clutter up the supernatural experience or the antiquarian setting. But the scheme is not rigid enough to exclude a frequent light touch, as the **"Tractate Middoth"** scene amply demonstrates. Indeed, the editing itself is often accomplished with droll humor: "Tea was taken to the accompaniment of a discussion which golfing persons can imagine for themselves, but which the conscientious writer has no right to inflict upon any non-golfing persons" (**"The Mezzotint,"** page 40). There is also a frequent impatience with the inevitable stereotypical horror scene: "Next day Sir Matthew Fell was not downstairs at six in the morning, as was his custom, nor at seven, nor yet at eight. Hereupon, the servants went and knocked at his chamber door. I need not prolong the description of their anxious listenings and renewed batterings on the panels. The door was opened at last from the outside, and they found their master dead and black. So much you have guessed" (**"The Ash Tree,"** page 59). Assuming the reader knows the basics, James is ever-anxious to move ahead toward his own variations.[17]

This implicit understanding between writer and reader is a phenomenon common to much post-Le Fanu ghostly fiction. We know basically what is going to happen, and (if the writer is reasonably sophisticated) the writer knows that we know: the interest lies in how he is going to bring it off, in whether he can play a spooky enough variation on the basic theme to make us turn up the lights. Thus the concern with technique in Le Fanu becomes almost an obsession in James, who makes a programmatic, somewhat artificial use of understatement, innuendo, and precisely orchestrated crescendo.

But it would be a mistake to think that James is concerned solely with performance. The premises themselves are frequently startling and imaginative. His contribution is to demonstrate that the old forms of supernatural evil are still respectable, still viable, if seen through different glasses. It is as if the reader were looking through the haunted binoculars in **"A View from a Hill,"** watching a familiar landscape transform itself in sinister, ever-changing ways. Vampires, for example, are familiar enough by the twentieth century, but in **"An Episode of Cathedral History"** James creates a vampire posing as a saintly relic in a fifteenth-century cathedral altar-tomb. The church renovators, surprised at finding a full-length coffin in the altar, are more than surprised when the red-eyed inhabitant of the coffin, annoyed at being disturbed, leaps out in their faces. Witches are also commonplace in fiction, but James's witch (who inhabits **"The Ash Tree"**) has some uniquely unsavory traits, among them the ability to breed gigantic spiders. In all cases, James moves from

the traditional concept to his own variation with such swiftness and conciseness that the reader almost forgets he is reading a reworked version of old, sometimes trite material.

On rare occasions, James makes manifesto-like statements about the need for linguistic economy. The Ezra Pound of ghost story writers, James once criticized Poe for his "vagueness"; for his lack of toughness and specific detail; for the "unreal" quality of his prose.[18] The charge is similar to Pound's denigration of Yeats's early poems. Actually, Poe and James were attempting very different things. Poe's tales are not ghostly but surreal. They immerse themselves in the irrational, whereas James's tales only flirt with it. The power of James lies in his ability to set up a barrier between the empirical and the supernatural and then gradually knock it down—to move subtly from the real to the unreal and sometimes back again. The distinction between the two is much more solid than in Poe, where nightmare and reality constantly melt into one another. James's stories assume a strong grounding in empirical reality. In this context, his refusal to accept the existence of ghosts until he encounters "conclusive evidence" is consistent with the attitude of his stories. The stories are consciously addressed to skeptical readers, readers with a twentieth (or eighteenth) century frame of reference. In making us momentarily accept what we instinctively disbelieve, the burden falls heavily on the language. The way to reach such a reader, James implies, is through clarity and restraint: the hyperbole and verbal effusiveness of the Gothic writers are to be strictly avoided, as are the "trivial and melodramatic" natural explanations of Lord Lytton and the neo-Gothic Victorians.[19] To James, both overwriting and natural explanations in ghost stories are related forms of cheating. Although James usually avoids issuing these anti-Gothic manifestoes, he indirectly pans the Gothic tradition in the introduction to the *Collected Ghost Stories* by refusing to acknowledge any literary debt to it.

To James, only Le Fanu is worth imitating: "He stands absolutely in the first rank as a writer of ghost stories. This is my deliberate verdict, after reading all the supernatural tales I have been able to get hold of. Nobody sets the scene better than he, nobody touches in the effective detail more deftly."[20] Interestingly, James's use of detail is far more selective, small scaled, and particular than Le Fanu's. For all his "deliberateness" and "leisureliness,"[21] Le Fanu's vision frequently opens out onto a large canvas which depicts nameless energies sweeping across the cosmos. The gigantic blob-like entity which hurtles through the trees in **"Ultor de Lacy"** could not inhabit the cramped world of a James story: there would be no room for it. Instead, such creatures invade the more accomodating outdoor stories of Blackwood and Lovecraft.

In James, even the visionary scenes seem almost pro-saic—yet strangely effective for being so. When Parkins, for example, blows his ill-omened whistle, he has the most compact of visions:

> He blew tentatively and stopped suddenly, startled and yet pleased by the note he had elicited. It had a quality of infinite distance in it, and, soft as it was, he some-how felt it must be audible for miles round. It was a sound, too, that seemed to have the power (which many scents possess) of forming pictures in the brain. He saw quite clearly for a moment a vision of a wide, dark expanse at night, with a fresh wind blowing, and in the midst a lonely figure—how employed, he could not tell. Perhaps he would have seen more had not the pic-ture been broken by the sudden surge of a gust of wind against his casement, so sudden that it made him look up, just in time to see the white glint of a seabird's wing somewhere outside the dark panes.

(132)

If Blackwood had written this passage, he would have used the "quality of infinite distance" as the tenor for a series of elaborate visual metaphors, converting sound into several layers of perception. But James opts for di-rect images, indeed a single "picture" seen "quite clearly for a moment." The combination of momentariness and clarity make for a kind of ghostly epiphany. Yet though the outlines of the vision are sharply drawn, the center is obscure. Lonely, anonymous, and mysteriously threat-ening, the central figure remains an enigma throughout the story. We never know who he is (or what he was)—or why he is so fond of Parkins's whistle.

One exception to James's habitual terseness can be found in the descriptions of some of his settings. If the present is lacking, the past is always alive. Whenever James describes the antiquarian lore which provides the settings for all of his stories, his prose instantly be-comes crowded with historical or scholarly detail. The opening paragraphs in **"Lost Hearts"** and **"The Ash Tree"** are learned, graceful little essays on styles of ar-chitecture in the early and late eighteenth centuries as they relate to the houses in the stories. They provide no "atmosphere," at least not in the Gothic sense which James so despised, and no ominous forebodings (which come later). Indeed the narrator of **"The Ash Tree"** ad-mits that the entire opening section is a "digression." These stories are saturated with nostalgia, yet never in a propagandistic context. In contrast to the stories of Ma-chen and Blackwood, there are no Yeatsian spokesmen for the glories of the past. The emptiness of the present and richness of the past are implied by the distinct ab-sence of the one and overwhelming presence of the other, but James never forces his fetish for the old down the reader's throat.

The paradox in James is that this very oldness is invari-ably a deadly trap. If antiquarian pursuits provide the only contact with life, they also provide an immediate contact with death. Even in tales where there is no dra-matic coffin-opening scene, there is always an implicit analogy between digging up an art object and digging up a corpse. In the antiquarian tale, evil is something old, something which should have died. Old books are especially dangerous as talismanic summoners of this evil. The danger is trickier in James than in similar evil-book tales by James's contemporaries in that nei-ther the nature nor titles of the books necessarily be-trays their lethal potential. Chambers's *The King in Yel-low* Yeats's *Alchemical Rose,* and Lovecraft's *Necronomicon* (all imaginary books) are works with spectacularly demonic histories which the collector in a given story opens at his own risk. But James's collec-tors are liable to get in trouble by opening almost any-thing. In **"The Uncommon Prayer Book,"** a remark-able rag-like monstrosity is summoned by a psalm (admittedly a "very savage psalm") in an eighteenth-century prayerbook. For James's antiquaries, even the Holy Scriptures can become a demonic text. Undermin-ing the very thing they celebrate, the plots seem to symbolize, perhaps unconsciously, the futility of the en-tire antiquarian enterprise.

In a curious way, the style reinforces this contradiction. The most striking aspect of this style, even more strik-ing than its ascetic brevity and clarity, is the gap be-tween tone and story. This gap is especially telling in the more gruesome tales. In **"Wailing Well,"** a small boy is tackled and brought down, much as in a football game, by an entire field of vampires. He is found hang-ing from a tree with the blood drained from his body, but he later becomes a vampire himself, hiding out with his new friends in a haunted well. (James wrote this cheerful tale for the Eton College troop of Boy Scouts.) More gruesome yet is **"Lost Hearts,"** which tells of an antiquary who, in following an ancient prescription, seeks an "enlightenment of the spiritual faculties" through eating the hearts of young children while they are kept alive. (James is as unsparing of children as Le Fanu.) In the end, the children rise from the grave to wreak a bloody, predictably poetic justice. In both sto-ries, the style is distinguished by a detachment, an ur-banity, and a certain amount of Edwardian stuffiness which are entirely at odds with the nastiness of the plots. The narrators seem determined to maintain good manners, even when presenting material they know to be in irredeemably bad taste. Alternating between casu-alness and stiffness, chattiness and pedantry, James's narrators maintain an almost pathological distance from the horrors they recount. This contradiction between scholarly reticence and fiendish perversity becomes the authenticating mark of the antiquarian ghost story. For James's narrators, sophisticated literary techniques are a form of exorcism in a world filled with hidden menace. To stare the menace in the face is unthinkable; to con-vert it into a pleasant ghost story is to momentarily banish it. The reader, however, experiences an inversion of this process: the very unwillingness of the narrators to face up to implied horrors makes the stories all the more chilling and convincing.

James disguises unpleasantness in several ingenious ways. Narrative coolness is one disguise, but he sometimes builds others directly into the plot. There is a whole class of stories in which the dark center is enclosed, and occasionally buried, by several layers of supernatural apparatus. These stories move toward a gradual uncovering of the layers, but the anticipated climax, the final revelation, is less compelling than the means of arriving at it. The disguises do not appear in the form of occult mystification, as in the *Mythologies* of Yeats—James almost never uses elaborate occult material; nor do they appear in the form of complex visionary mechanisms, as in the Georgian fantasies of Dunsany and de la Mare. Like everything in James, the device is disarmingly straightforward rather than metaphysical. It involves the re-evoking, not of an actual supernatural being, as in **"Count Magnus,"** but of a supernatural melodrama from the past. The twist in these stories is that the art object acts not as a mere catalyst, but as the substance of the experience. Although the scene itself is invariably grotesque and horrifying, the interest lies in the eccentricity of the mode of perception. Moreover, the antiquary is not physically threatened: he is a mortified, though by no means unwilling, spectator.

James first tried this method in **"The Mezzotint"** (1904), a story which became a paradigm not only of several later James stories, but of several efforts by R. H. Malden and E. G. Swain.[22] **"The Mezzotint"** is James's most original creation. In many of his stories, such as **"Canon Alberic's Scrapbook"** and **"Count Magnus,"** old engravings serve as the prelude to an apparition. Meticulously described, they seem almost to come alive, and they are sometimes more frightening than the spectres they prefigure. In **"The Mezzotint,"** James gives us a picture which really does come alive: the picture itself is the apparition. Initially only a mediocre topographical engraving of a house, it undergoes a series of transformations which are all the more startling for their inexplicability. The collector, Mr. Williams, observes a skeletal, shroudlike figure who mysteriously materializes on the lawn in the mezzotint, crawls into the house and emerges later with a baby in its arms. The final view of the picture is James at his best:

> There was the house, as before, under the waning moon and the drifting clouds. The window that had been open was shut, and the figure was once more on the lawn: but not this time crawling cautiously on hands and knees. Now it was erect and stepping swiftly, with long strides, towards the front of the picture. The moon was behind it, and the black drapery hung down over its face so that only hints of that could be seen, and what was visible made the spectators profoundly thankful

> that they could see no more than a white dome-like forehead and a few straggling hairs. The head was bent down, and the arms were tightly clasped over an object which could be dimly seen and identified as a child, whether dead or living it was not possible to say. The legs of the appearance alone could be plainly discerned, and they were horribly thin.

> (50)

The passage is an ideal example of James's art. What we see, we see clearly, as in an etching: what we don't see, we are "profoundly thankful" for not seeing.

There are two layers of supernatural storytelling here: the transformation of the picture and the scene it recreates, itself a supernatural tale. The former is far more mysterious than the latter. The ghost at least has a reason for coming back to life: Williams discovers that the house belonged to an extinct family, the last heir of which "disappeared mysteriously in infancy" shortly after the father had a man hanged for poaching. But the picture has no such reason. Only James could have written a tale at once so sophisticated and so lacking in metaphysical, symbolic, or even causal connections. His weird pictures are utterly unlike those of his predecessors: the picture of Chief Justice Harbottle in Le Fanu's "An Account of Some Strange Disturbances in Aungier Street" is chilling because it reminds us of the evil Harbottle; that of Hawthorne's Edward Randolph in "Edward Randolph's Portrait" because of its symbolic associations. But James's mezzotint is intrinsically spooky. There is no reason for it to change—it simply does. And to make matters stranger, it never changes again.

We take it for granted in James that art objects are inherently demonic—or at least have the potential for being so. Here we must assume that more mechanical phenomena can be haunted as well. As lean and as calculated as James seems as a writer, he nevertheless possesses the romantic impulse, investing even chemical processes with spiritual powers. Gadgetry and machinery can be as talismanic as art.[23]

Yet James is a closet romantic at best. If we decide that the ghostly power of mezzotints is the theme of the story, we are left with curiously little to say, for James is not interested in expounding romantic or occult theories. The wry, typically understated conclusion discourages the reader from using the story as a brief for any demonic precept:

> The facts were communicated by Williams to Dennistoun, and by him to a mixed company, of which I was one, and the Sadducean Professor of Ophiology another. I am sorry to say that the latter, when asked what he thought of it, only remarked: "Oh, those Bridgeford people will say anything"—a sentiment which met with the reception it deserved.

I have only to add that the picture is now in the Ashle-ian Museum; that it has been treated with a view to discovering whether sympathetic ink has been used in it, but without effect; that Mr. Britnell knew nothing of it save that he was sure it was uncommon; and that, though carefully watched, it has never been known to change again.

(53)

The brisk parallelism of the syntax in the final paragraph moves us out of the story before we have a chance to speculate on metaphysical ramifications. James's fiction is self-enclosed in that it rarely refers to any system of ideas or values outside the confines of the plot. Mystery writer Gerald Heard's statement that "the good ghost story must have for its base some clear premise as to the character of human existence—some theological assumption," can refer only to a class of stories (Kipling's are a good example) to which James's are opposed.[24] If there is any theological "premise" in James, it is never developed—and is certainly not "clear." James himself, in the preface to *Ghost Stories of an Antiquary,* is careful to deflate any "exalted" notions of ghost story writing: "The stories themselves do not make any very exalted claim. If any of them succeed in causing their readers to feel pleasantly uncomfortable when walking along a solitary road at nightfall, or sitting over a dying fire in the small hours, my purpose in writing them will have been attained."[25] What is attractive about James's stories is precisely that they succeed in maintaining this weird balance between the pleasant and the uncomfortable.

Other **"Mezzotint"** stories include **"The Rose Garden," "A View From a Hill,"** and (the most fanciful variation) **"The Haunted Doll's House,"** all of which involve visions within visions which tie themselves into mysterious knots while seeming to unravel. These are the most radically distanced of James's works. In **"The Mezzotint,"** the narrative is a third hand account of a story which itself concerns something never directly experienced. And the character with whom the story is ultimately concerned—the occupant of the house in the mezzotint—is entirely invisible.

Another device James uses to disguise or distance his horrors is humor. Humor and horror, as we have seen in Le Fanu's case, are often two sides of the same coin. Eliot's famous reference to "the alliance of levity and seriousness (by which the seriousness is intensified)" is useful, for James's humor does not defuse horror so much as intensify it by making it manageable and accessible. Without James's deadpan wit, these stories might seem unreal and "Gothic" to a sophisticated reader.

James's use of humor is more conscious, sophisticated, and programmatic than Le Fanu's, whose humor seems more spontaneous (and occasionally unintentional). Of-

ten, James will concoct a situation which is inherently funny. An example is Mr. Somerton's encounter with a toad-like creature in **"The Treasure of Abbot Thomas"**:

"Well, I felt to the right, and my fingers touched something curved, that felt—yes—more or less like a heavy, full thing. There was nothing, I must say, to alarm one. I grew bolder, and putting both hands in as well as I could, I pulled it to me, and it came. It was heavy, but moved more easily than I had expected. As I pulled it towards the entrance, my left elbow knocked over and extinguished the candle. I got the thing fairly in front of the mouth and began drawing it out. Just then Brown gave a sharp ejaculation and ran quickly up the steps with the lantern. He will tell you why in a moment. Startled as I was, I looked round after him, and saw him stand for a minute at the top and then walk away a few yards. Then I heard him call softly, 'All right, sir,' and went on pulling out the great bag, in complete darkness. It hung for an instant on the edge of the hold, then slipped forward on my chest, and *put its arms round my neck.*

(175)

The jolt we experience on reaching the italics springs as much from the absurdity of the situation as from the horror: it scarcely matters whether we shudder or laugh. Ideally, we should do both.

James frequently entrusts major scenes to colloquial, clownish narrators—usually cockney servants. The servant's account of Mr. Potwitch's death in **"The Uncommon Prayer Book"** is both ghoulish and comic:

"And then, sir, I see what looked to be like a great roll of old shabby white flannel, about four to five feet high, fall for-ards out of the inside of the safe right against Mr. Potwitch's shoulder as he was stooping over; and Mr. Potwitch, he raised himself up as it were, resting on his hands on the package, and gave a exclamation. And I can't hardly expect you should take what I says, but as true as I stand here I see this roll had a kind of a face in the upper end of it, sir. You can't be more surprised than what I was, I can assure you, and I've seen a lot in me time. Yes, I can describe it if you wish it, sir; it was very much the same as this wall here in colour (the wall had an earth-coloured distemper) and it had a bit of a band tied round underneath. And the eyes, well they was dry-like, and much as if there was two big spiders' bodies in the holes. Hair? no, I don't know as there was much hair to be seen; the flannel-stuff was over the top of the 'ead. I'm sure it warn't what it should have been. No, I only see it in a flash, but I took it in like a photograft—wish I hadn't. Yes, sir, it fell right over on to Mr. Potwitch's shoulder, and this face hid in his neck—yes, sir, about where the injury was,—more like a ferret going for a rabbit than anythink else."

(511)

Though James's rendering of dialect is skillful and idiomatic, he tends to overuse these servant recapitulations of horror scenes. After a while, the cockney narrators—in **"A View from a Hill,"** and **"An Episode of Cathedral History,"** among others—become an annoying mannerism.

In some stories, James's use of humor has little to do with the basic premise, but seems an end in itself. This deliciously sardonic digression in **"Wailing Well"** could almost have been written by Evelyn Waugh or Roald Dahl:

> The practice, as you know, was to throw a selected lower boy, of suitable dimensions, fully dressed, with his hands and feet tied together, into the deepest part of Cuckoo Weir, and to time the Scout whose turn it was to rescue him. On every occasion when he was entered for this competition, Stanley Judkins was seized, at the critical moment, with a severe fit of cramp, which caused him to roll on the ground and utter alarming cries. This naturally distracted the attention of those present from the boy in the water, and had it not been for the presence of Arthur Wilcox the death-toll would have been a heavy one. As it was, the Lower Master found it necessary to take a firm line and say that the competition must be discontinued. It was in vain that Mr. Beasley Robinson represented to him that in five competitions only four lower boys had actually succumbed. The Lower Master said that he would be the last to interfere in any way with the work of the Scouts; but that three of these boys had been valued members of his choir, and both he and Dr. Ley felt that the inconvenience caused by the losses outweighed the advantages of the competitions. Besides, the correspondence with the parents of these boys had become annoying, and even distressing: they were no longer satisfied with the printed form which he was in the habit of sending out, and more than one of them had actually visited Eton and taken up much of his valuable time with complaints. So the life-saving competition is now a thing of the past.
>
> (630)

Although the passage is irrelevant to the plot, it is highly relevant to the relationship of the narrator to his materials. The understated savagery of the humor establishes a context which trivializes the value of life and death, removing the narrator from the suffering and cruelty he is about to recount by allowing him to treat it all as a grim joke.

A more underhanded means that James uses to create distance is deliberate obscurity. Occasionally he moves so far in the direction of mystification that he runs the risk of leaving us completely behind. This device, James's ultimate disguise, occurs with increasing frequency in the later stories. **"The Story of a Disappearance and an Appearance,"** **"Two Doctors,"** **"Mr. Humphreys and His Inheritance"** and **"Rats"** read more like dark enigmas than finished works of fiction. The narrators often seem aware of the problematic nature of this material, even to the point of sometimes warning the reader in the opening paragraph. The narra-

tor of **"Two Doctors,"** for example, describes his tale as an incomplete *dossier,* "a riddle in which the supernatural appears to play a part. You must see what you can make of it." (459) James ungraciously provides only the outline of a gruesome tale in which one doctor uses an unexplained supernatural device to do in another. The tale is densely packed with fascinating hints: a rifled mausoleum; a reference to Milton ("Millions of spiritual creatures walk the earth/Unseen both when we wake and when we sleep."); a haunted pillow which enfolds the head of the sleeping victim like a strange cloud; a recurring dream of a gigantic moth chrysalis disclosing "a head covered with a smooth pink skin, which breaking as the creature stirred, showed him his own face in a state of death" (467). Since there are so many ways to piece together the information, the tale becomes more ominous with each reading. The initial reading is curiously empty and frustrating, almost as if James demands that we try again.

Furthermore, he takes it for granted that we know his earlier stories which, for all their nonrational connections, are easier to fathom. The structure of **"Two Doctors"**—a sketchy presentation of lawyers' documents—is so fragmented that whatever piecing together we do must be based, at least in part, on patterns from *Ghost Stories of an Antiquary.* **"Death by the Visitation of God,"** the surgeon's verdict, makes little sense unless we see it as a reference to the same verdict in the earlier **"Count Magnus,"** a story which has its own stubborn mysteries, but which is clearly a tale of demonic pursuit. Once this connection is made, **"Two Doctors"** becomes thematically related to a whole class of Le Fanuesque pursuit tales by James: **"Count Magnus,"** **"Lost Hearts,"** **"A School Story,"** **"The Tractate Middoth,"** **"Casting the Runes,"** **"The Stalls of Barchester Cathedral,"** and **"The Uncommon Prayer Book."** But seen in isolation, the ending of **"Two Doctors"** makes almost no sense.

These sly cross references are another indication of the self-referential character of James's fictional world. His narrative posture, at least in the late tales, assumes an audience of connoisseurs, an elect readership which can extrapolate a plot from a sentence. The demands James makes on his readers are somewhat at odds with his determination to present himself as an aggressively "popular" writer whose sole function is to entertain and amuse in as undemanding a way as possible. This is minor fiction to be sure, but fiction which nevertheless succeeds in creating a universe of its own which can be apprehended only through careful, thoughtful reading. Like so much quality ghostly fiction from this period, James's stories fall into the uniquely alienated category of being too controlled and sophisticated for "horror" fans, yet too lightweight for academics. In his relation to twentieth-century culture, James is very much a ghost himself, or very much like his own Mr. Humphreys in

"Mr. Humphreys and His Inheritance," a man lost in a haunted maze.

If James is not a major writer, he nevertheless deserves a larger audience than he currently enjoys.[26] His fictional palate is admittedly restricted, even in comparison with other writers of ghostly tales. His stories have considerable power, but only muffled reverberation. He exhibits little of Henry James's psychological probity, none of Poe's Gothic extravagance, none of Yeats's passion—but he delivers a higher percentage of mystery and terror than any of these. If he is merely a sophisticated "popular" writer, content with manipulating surfaces, those very surfaces are potent and suggestive.

James is far more innovative than he pretends to be. In R. H. Malden's preface to *Nine Ghosts,* he reminds us that James "always regarded" Le Fanu as "The Master."[27] Yet Malden also speaks of a distinct James "tradition," implying that James refined, modified, and transgressed Le Fanu's precepts in ways profound enough to set James apart as an original. He brought to the ghost story not only a new antiquarian paradigm of setting and incident, but also a new urbanity, suaveness, and economy. To a contemporary audience, conditioned by the monotonous brutality of so many occult novels and films, James's use of subtlety to evoke ghostly horror is likely to seem as radical and puzzling as ever. Both academics and popular readers tend to associate supernatural horror in fiction with hyperbole, capitals, promiscuous exclamation marks, and bloated adjectives. Yet the field is crowded with undeservedly obscure writers—L. T. C. Rolt, E. G. Swain, R. H. Malden, Ramsey Campbell, H. R. Wakefield, Russell Kirk, Arthur Gray, Elizabeth Bowen, and Robert Aickman, among many others—who follow James's example.

James also gave the ghost story a new theme. His ghosts materialize not so much from inner darkness or outer conspiracies as from a kind of antiquarian malaise. Remaining modestly within the confines of popular entertainment, his fiction nevertheless shows how nostalgia has a habit of turning into horror. This is a distinct departure from Poe, where antiquarian pursuits are tied to sensationally deranged psyches such as Roderick Usher's. In James, the antiquaries are stolidly normal, and their ghosts are real. Above all, James's collectors clearly enjoy what they are doing: those who survive these stories would not dream of giving up their arcane pursuits simply because they were almost swallowed up by unearthly presences.

But the real enjoyment is ours. As readers, we can immerse ourselves in the process of discovery without taking any risks. We can even indulge in expecting the worst. Alfred Hitchcock has often said that terror and suspense grow not out of shock and surprise, but out of thickening inevitability.[28] James, who had already

learned this lesson from Le Fanu, is careful to keep us one step ahead of the character so that the dreams and premonitions are as eerie as the apparitions they announce. This is the delightful paradox of James's ghost stories: the more of his stories we read and reread, the more we know what to expect, but that very reservoir of expectations infuses each reading with added menace. The sheer pleasure of these gentlemanly horror tales continually rejuvenates itself.

Notes

1. M. R. James, *Collected Ghost Stories* (1931; rpt. New York, 1974), pp. 112-113. Further quotations from James's stories will be documented by citing page numbers from the text.

2. Even H. P. Lovecraft comments on the appropriateness of these techniques, despite his failure to use them in his own fiction. See Lovecraft, *Supernatural Horror in Fiction.*

3. S. G. Lubbock, *A Memoir of Montague Rhodes James* (Cambridge, 1939), p. 37.

4. *Ibid.*

5. *Madam Crowl's Ghost and Other Tales of Mystery* (1923).

6. Peter Fleming, "The Stuff of Nightmares." *Spectator Literary Supplement,* 18 April 1931, p. 633.

7. The new, handsome St. Martin's Press edition of James's collected stories was reviewed enthusiastically in the 7 July 1975 edition of the *Village Voice.*

8. Stephen Gaselee, *Proceedings of the British Academy,* 1936, XXII, 424.

9. *Ibid.*

10. James, "Prologue," Sheridan Le Fanu, *Madam Crowl's Ghost,* p. vii.

11. Gaselee, p. 430.

12. Lubbock, p. 39.

13. James, p. vii.

14. *Ibid.*

15. *Ibid.,* p. 9.

16. James, "Introduction," *Ghosts and Marvels,* p. vi.

17. L. P. Hartley, Ramsey Campbell, and Walter de la Mare are similar to James in this respect. But many writers in the genre—including Arthur Machen, H. P. Lovecraft, and Algernon Blackwood—feel a tiresome obligation to treat hackneyed situations and tropes as if the reader had never encountered them before.

18. From an interview with James included in a review of *Madam Crowl's Ghost* published in the Morning Post, 9 October 1923, p. 11.

19. *Ibid.*

20. James, *Madam Crowl's Ghost,* p. vii.

21. *Ibid.*

22. See Malden's "The Thirteenth Tree" in *Nine Ghosts* (London, 1943). See also Swain's "The Man with the Roller" in *Stoneground Ghost Tales* (Cambridge, 1912). Stylistically as well as conceptually, Swain and Malden are closer to James than to any other writers in the field.

23. For a further development of this motif, see the stories in L. T. C. Rolt's superb *Sleep No More* (London, 1948). An engineer by profession, Rolt is a master of situations involving haunted mines, canals and various kinds of machinery. Especially effective is "Hawley Bank Foundry," a tale which demonstrates that terror can emerge from the most unlikely settings.

24. Quoted by Russell Kirk in the epilogue to his collection of ghost stories, *The Surly Sullen Bell* (New York, 1964), p. 157.

25. M. R. James, "Preface," *Ghost Stories of an Antiquary* (1904; rpt. New York, 1971), p. 8.

26. Though interest in James appears to be growing (see note 7), it is still nowhere near as large as interest in the Lovecraft circle or in contemporary writers such as William Blatty, Thomas Tryon, and Stephen King.

27. Malden, p. 5.

28. Alfred Hitchcock, "Preface," *Fourteen of My Favorites in Suspense,* ed. Alfred Hitchcock (New York, 1959), p. 9.

A Selected Bibliography of Ghostly Fiction

James, M. R. *The Collected Ghost Stories of M. R. James.* London: Arnold, 1931. St. Martin's edition, 1974.

———. *Ghost Stories of an Antiquary.* Ed. E. F. Bleiler. 1904; rpt. New York: Dover, 1971. (See also the 1974 Penguin edition, which contains *More Ghost Stories of an Antiquary* in the same edition.)

Kirk, Russell. *The Surly Sullen Bell.* New York: Fleet, 1962.

Malden, R. H. *Nine Ghosts.* London: Arnold, 1943.

Rolt, L. T. C. *Sleep No More.* London, Constable, 1948.

Swain, E. G. *The Stoneground Ghost Tales.* Cambridge: W. Heffer and Sons, 1912.

Secondary Sources

Gaselee, Stephen. M. R. James Obituary. *Proceedings of the British Academy.* XXII (1936), 424.

Hitchcock, Alfred. "Preface." *Fourteen of My Favorites in Suspense.* New York: Dell, 1959.

James, M. R. "Introduction." *Ghosts and Marvels.* London: Oxford University Press, 1927.

———. "Introduction." Joseph Sheridan Le Fanu. *Madam Crowl's Ghost.* London: G. Bell, 1923.

Lovecraft, H. P. *Supernatural Horror in Literature.* 1927; rpt. New York: Dover, 1973.

Lubbock, S. G. *A Memoir of Montague Rhodes James.* Cambridge: Cambridge University Press, 1939.

Michael A. Mason (essay date summer 1982)

SOURCE: Mason, Michael A. "On Not Letting Them Lie: Moral Significance in the Ghost Stories of M. R. James." *Studies in Short Fiction* 19, no. 3 (summer 1982): 253-60.

[*In the following essay, Mason discusses the "historical distance" of James's stories, noting their timeless themes and the fact that they have never gone out of print.*]

In her study of stories about the uncanny, a study entitled *Night Visitors: The Rise and Fall of the English Ghost Story,* Julia Briggs has reminded us that the ghost stories of M. R. James have never fallen out of public favor.[1] They have remained in print ever since he first published them. The apparent moral purpose of his doing so may be worth investigating, although the moral force of these stories is unlikely to be the main reason for their popularity.

By 1894, when James began to publish the ghost stories which were to bring him a far wider fame than all his scholarly researches, educated readers could feel perfectly safe in dismissing his apparitions as entirely without objective existence. Anyone could experience ghosts if he deliberately cultivated the state that Tennyson had got himself into by re-reading Hallam's letters to him; just as, two or three generations into the twentieth century, anyone who stares at the sky for long enough can discover flying objects, whether or not he can identify them. From time to time, the sanity of people who described their own strange experiences might be in question; but otherwise freak weather conditions or indigestion could provide a sufficient explanation for an age as far above the vulgar errors of its ancestors as electric power could raise it. However, since this new unbelief did not seem to make the world more tolerable, perhaps tales of the uncanny might, in a limited way, minister to psychological necessities inherited by modern man from his ignorant forefathers. Besides, there is a peculiar pleasure in being terrified vicariously.

Montague Rhodes James (1862-1936) wrote his ghost stories over a period of some forty years. "I never cared," he tells us in an epilogue to his **Collected Ghost Stories,** "to try any other kind."[2] Researchers into mediaeval and other documents helped to inspire in his imagination a host of demons that might irrupt into the human dimension. His difficulty, of course, is to persuade us that they could; to give them a reason, or at least an excuse, for doing so; and to make them behave interestingly when they arrive. The first of these he achieves by the use of time, tradition, and a sense of reality.

James believes in setting a discreet barrier of time between the event and the reader. "The detective story," he says with authority, for he had read a great many of these, "cannot be too much up-to-date. . . . For the ghost story a slight haze of distance is desirable. 'Thirty years ago,' 'Not long before the war,' are very proper openings. If a really remote date be chosen, there is more than one way of bringing the reader in contact with it. The finding of documents about it can be made plausible; or you may begin with your apparition and go back over the years to tell the cause of it; or . . . you may set the scene directly in the desired epoch, which I think is hardest to do with success. On the whole . . . I think that a setting so modern that the ordinary reader can judge of its naturalness for himself is preferable to anything antique. For some degree of actuality is the charm of the best ghost stories; not a very insistent actuality, but one strong enough to allow the reader to identify himself with the patient; while it is almost inevitable that the reader of an antique story should fall into the position of the mere spectator."[3] By "actuality" James means sense of present time fully as much as realism. Some of his own settings are quite remote, but he counters an effect of too much distance by precision in dating. Two periods far apart, neither of them contemporary, may be exactly given, and both events clearly described: in **"The Residence at Whitminster"** these are 1730 and 1823-4. That the present time is the viewpoint is scarcely hinted. If there is a midway period, the latest time being the present, the remotest period may be shadowy and the origin of ghosts. **"An Episode of Cathedral History"** is one of the best examples of this telescopic technique. It has a very obscure foundation in the fifteenth century, when considerable trouble since lost to history must have been experienced. When, however, the satyr escaped from its tomb in the summer of 1840, a number of people were able to guess at the nature of what had happened before. That summer of 1840 is the story's narrative area, told to "a learned gentleman" by the elderly Head

Verger, who remembers in 1890 that particular adventure of his boyhood. More than twenty years later, the learned gentleman hands the story to our narrator; and now, beyond his time, the modern reader adds yet another perspective to what already had so much of the mysterious haze of distance.

A true impression of historical distance can be achieved only by a writer with a real sense of historical time, including an idea of the kind of English spoken for instance in the criminal courts in which Judge Jeffreys distorted justice in the 1680s. James's reading of the *State Trials* helped him here. So did the immense scholarship of his work as an antiquary and manuscript editor, for this kind of learning gave him an authentic fictional context for the discovery by some of his characters of those manuscripts and inscriptions which left them wiser and far more wary—if they survived— than they had been before. His use of Latin, usually translated at some point, is a particular feature of James's stories. If the teacher of Latin wants to ensure that his students remember the genitive case after *memini,* or the construction of a conditional sentence with a future consequence, he cannot do better than read them **"A School Story."** *Si tu non veneris ad me, ego veniam ad te* comes through with sinister force. A ghost of a feeling persists that Latin, the legal, political, religious, and linguistic root of so much of western history, is the proper tongue in which to conjure and dismiss apparitions, and there is about it a certain solidity and conciseness that gives authority to the stories about them.

The sense of reality resides in James's power to create the ordinary, normal rhythm of life. His adventurers are intelligent people and, for most purposes, sensible. They are not complex characters, and are therefore, in their outlined form, all the easier for the reader or listener to identify with. A number resemble James himself in being university dons with enough freedom—in terms of seventy or eighty years ago—to go on short-range expeditions out of England as far as to Southern France or Scandinavia. Within their reach are the resources of local wisdom or of level-headed friends whose advice they would have done better to follow. It is safer, at times, to be humble and ignorant.[4] Indeed, this is the happy state of all those people who pass on oral tradition about bygone people and places and comment occasionally on what is happening in the cathedral, the distant woods, or the quiet country mansion. Through the normality of these people—innkeepers and housekeepers, gardeners and butlers, cathedral vergers, retired colonels, and so forth—the reader keeps in touch with the everyday world at the same time as he follows his intrepid hero into a confrontation with the uncanny. The general public of the countryside accordingly act as guarantors of the reality of the supernatural, in which they can believe without any difficulty.

When we come to consider the reasons for the intrusion of the supernatural into ordinary life, we find that they can be summed up in one word: disturbance. Some kind of sensitive environment has been violated by an act of thoughtlessness, often in defiance of good advice as well as good sense; and it is then that the question of provocation arises. Provocation on the part of the disturber makes him vulnerable to some act of malice roughly classifiable as revenge.

At this point we should note that, in certain professions, encounters with the supernatural are occupational hazards. The clergy are particularly vulnerable; professors and scholars may also find themselves in strange company, as may travellers, amateur archaeologists, experimenters of many kinds, and even medical men. The reasons for vulnerability often amount to the single trouble of ambition. "That last infirmity of noble mind" it may well be, but its range—in James's stories, at least—encompasses a very wide spectrum from the simplest unnecessary curiosity to overweening vanity and uncompromising arrogance. This kind of motivation will lead a man to investigate a locked room at the inn where he is staying; or to hasten into the next world some elderly relative or superior who seems to be reluctant to remove himself from the surface of this one; or to improve his own status by deliberately seeking what certain powers of the unseen world can do for him, in return—presumably—for access through him to the physical universe. Through this channel there then passes an illicit two-way traffic, which has, however, its penalties.

We therefore often find ourselves observing a living person who has awakened trouble for himself by his temerity or even by his criminal actions. In the latter event, the kind of retribution he suffers may be no more than his just, if unmerciful, punishment. More often, what occurs is a kind of wild justice visiting any offence with death, or at least with the fear of it. The predicament of the victim is naturally the one with which the reader identifies; it is, in mundane terms, an insoluble one. It cannot be avoided. It must, like a typhoon at sea, be encountered head on and, if possible, survived. As for identification with the avenger itself, this is—by its very nature—impossible.

Although the reader feels more at ease, if this expression may be allowable in such a context, with the spirits of dead people rather than with spiritual entities of which he can have no understanding, the dead have often been those who have isolated themselves so effectually in life as to have alienated the sympathy of other people even then. James bestows upon the dead the fate of haunting their old homes for some evil action committed in life. It seems as if his earthbound spirits have chosen to keep for themselves a treasure or power of some kind in their earthly existence, and have thus

bound themselves, or some part of themselves, whether voluntarily or not, to the safeguarding of it. No fruitful contact with them seems to be possible. In fact, it is essential, for James's narrative purposes, that no contact of either a prolonged or an intelligent kind ever be established.[5] The ghost is to have all the disconcerting advantages of appearance and disappearance—rather like the ghost of Banquo—but without the chance of presenting its case for reprieve, if it has one. Prolonged contact would weaken the unfamiliarity and therefore the mystery of the supernatural, and—if intelligent as well—could easily bring the story down to the colloquial level of Scrooge and Marley in *A Christmas Carol*: with Marley—it will be recalled—presenting his former business partner with a whole battery of unpaid professional consultants for Scrooge's eternal benefit. James's tales are as cautionary as Marley's advice to Scrooge, but his ghosts are all inimical. His advice can therefore take only one course: leave them alone by not tempting them out. They are powerful forces rather than individual personalities, and probably cannot do anything but whatever they are programmed, robot-like, to do. One might as well try to argue with Grendel.

Unfortunately, by the time this has become evident to the victim of such an entity's attentions, and to his friends, it may be too late for any action but a final conflict. If the enemy itself is of such a nature as to have forfeited forgiveness for sins committed, it cannot be expected to forgive any offence against itself. It is also solid enough to inflict considerable damage; James seems to prefer the tangible Scandinavian entities to be met with in saga and folklore. In his preface to the collected edition he claims to "have tried to make my ghosts act in ways not inconsistent with the rules of folklore."[6] He edited the Latin texts of "Twelve Medieval Ghost-Stories" for the *English Historical Review* in July, 1922, and found these to be "redolent of Denmark."[7] They were local to Yorkshire and included ghosts with those powers of attacking and grappling with humans that he introduces into his own stories.

The motivation of his own spirits is, however, James's personal invention. We have noted the vanity or self-seeking of some potential victims, as well as the greed or avarice which has condemned people of former times to undergo whatever eternal trouble they are now in. Still alive or long dead, such human principals in the stories have been tainted by pride and must endure the penalty for selfish independence. No satisfying exorcism, as in Kingsley Amis's *The Green Man*,[8] no outright defeat of supernatural evil by straightforward human means, will occur in James's stories; for it does not seem to be his purpose to offer remedies, but rather to point out the risks.

However, in James's mysterious world there are many variations. It may be possible to divert the intending attacker of Mr. Goodman on to another target. If so, what target more suitable than the Mr. Badman who has been directing his supernatural agent against Mr. Goodman? One of James's better-known tales is called **"Casting the Runes."** Mr. Badman is an authority on the occult and resents an unfavourable review that someone has written about a book of his. Authorities may, of course, be of different kinds, just as a winegrower and an alcoholic may both claim with some authority to be experts about the same product. Mr. Karswell, the Mr. Badman in this affair, has taken some kind of apprenticeship in order to become an authority. It is not scholarly authority in the usual sense that he has, but practical experience of the occult. Regrettably, Mr. Karswell also desires to be recognised as a scholar, which he is not; and he takes such great personal offence against a certain adverse critic of his scholarship as to ensure that one of his own unusual friends shall make away with the critic. To repeat this success, which he ultimately designs to do with another offender, he chooses, reasonably enough, to employ the same technique: one of its vital preliminaries being the delivery to the victim of a slip of writing which he must freely accept, though he will not be able to comprehend the writing. The slip is duly given to the second victim; but, before Mr. Badman's familiar can operate, the brother of the first victim is contacted for advice and assistance. Second victim and brother of first victim then co-operate in returning the slip of writing to Mr. Badman; and he, having freely accepted it as part of a larger package, becomes in turn the victim and is deservedly eliminated.

I have referred to the non-human entities as powerful forces rather than personalities. James's emphasis on their impact deprives their behavior of subtlety, and requires that they call attention to themselves by sheer unpleasantness. In James's first published story, **"Canon Alberic's Scrapbook,"** written in 1894, the intrusive demon is described as having "intelligence beyond that of a beast, below that of man."[9] This artistic precision is less admirable than a little more artistic restraint would have been, and James would not again venture a comment of this kind on a supernatural character's IQ. A concentration of evil might indeed have some such disastrous effect on a former human being, whose behavior might in consequence become interestingly bizarre. In **"Number 13,"** written in 1899, a human being has apparently become a demon. At any rate, Mr. Anderson, a Church historian visiting Denmark to examine archives of the sixteenth century, finds that the inn at which he has Room Number 12 also has a Room Number 13, but only at night. This interesting discovery coincides with his reading of archival correspondence about the alleged activities of a certain Magister Nicolas Francken in the time of the last Bishop to hold the see under the Church of Rome. What Magister Nicolas Francken had done had not been set down in any surviving detail, but could be summed up in the expression "secret and wicked arts" which appeared in the accusa-

tions against him. The matter was apparently never brought to trial, as the Bishop referred to the defendant's having been "suddenly removed from among us," and this ended the documentation.

Mr. Anderson abruptly found himself able to continue it, after a fashion, when the occupant of the neighbouring room began that same night to dance and sing. The dancing, though surprisingly vigorous—as revealed by the antics of his shadow against the blank street-wall opposite his room—was silent. His singing was not, besides being of such a disturbing quality as to bring to his door a reluctant deputation armed with crowbars and a desperate determination to discover what manner of thing this was. It is at this moment of truth that the test of the writer also comes. James cannot allow a meeting, so he compromises. While the weapons are being fetched, the occupants of Rooms 12 and 14 are on guard outside the door of Room 13. While the nearer man has his head turned from it in order to address his companion, "the door opened, and an arm came out and clawed at his shoulder." If James takes the event that far, he must go a little further. "It was clad in ragged, yellowish linen, and the bare skin, where it could be seen, had long grey hair upon it." This is as far as James will go. Anderson pulls Jensen out of the way, the door shuts again, "and a low laugh was heard." This incident is enough to alarm the witnesses; to demoralise the reinforcements who hear of it when they arrive soon afterwards; to impel Mr. Anderson to encourage and organise them for the attack; and, in fact, to allow a sufficiently plausible time to elapse between the incident and the eventual attack on the door: so that, as the attack is delivered, the moment of dawn arrives and Number 13 disappears. Before the next sunset, the discovery of relics under the floorboards removes the chance of its reappearance.

The living characters in the story of **"Number 13"** are merely witnesses of what had apparently been happening for some time: the Faustian figure of Nicolas Francken had been translated into something extremely unpleasant, and certainly much less human than he had been in life. It is, however, when we come to consider the behavior of a demon without human origin, that we appreciate all the more the wisdom of letting them lie. **"An Episode of Cathedral History"** describes the architectural ambitions of a reforming Dean of the Cathedral of Southminster in the summer of 1840. James takes the opportunity to show that some architectural reforms can amount to desecration. However, the demolition revealed "many interesting features of older work," as James's narrator expresses it. The most interesting feature of all was an altar-tomb of the fifteenth century, quite plain, but with a defect in the form of a slight gap between two slabs on the north side.

The cathedral renovations most unfortunately coincide with a wave of ill health among the local residents. Unpleasant dreams disturb them and sickness actually carries some of them off. The boy who, as an elderly man, tells the story to James's narrator remembers especially the nocturnal phenomenon known as "the crying"—as this was the time when he and his dog would, by mutual agreement, share his bed until it had stopped for that night, as the dog would know. The reader's identification with a boy and his dog is, of course, strong—and almost as strong with the boy and his friend who, being members of the choir, had easy access to the cathedral and to the attempts being made to plug up the hole in the altar-tomb. After listening to an argument between foreman and plasterer about a failure to do this, the boys are alone by the tomb. One of them has looked into the gap, and seen something. "I says to Evans, 'Did you really see anything in there?' 'Yes,' he says, 'I did indeed.' So then I says, 'Let's shove something in and stir it up.'" So they roll up a music sheet and shove it in, and then, when nothing happens, Worby—our informant—whistles. Inside, something moves; the roll of music, shoved in again, is held fast and has to be torn free; and the boys, having certainly stirred up something, take fright and run. A night or two later the crying is worse than ever before, and the day after that the cathedral authorities, duly armed with crowbars, assemble in force and watch while a bar is used upon the gap in the north side of the altar-tomb. The demon emerges, though only Worby's father seems to have been favored with a view of it, and it escapes by the north door, never to be seen again. At the end of such a sickly season as that had proved to be to the residents of Southminster, it is unfortunate to have to report that the reforming Dean was none the wiser for the trouble he had initiated, and none the worse either, except for having been bowled over by the emerging demon—and even that he had managed to identify as the Canon in residence.

For ghosts as gothic as these are, as normal a setting as possible is very suitable. Everyday normality does not negate the likelihood of other dimensions. The folk wisdom of those people in James's stories who are consulted on local history seems to confirm this. In **"The Rose Garden"** an old man is remembered who had advised a lady's father many years before against the removal of certain garden furniture, or perhaps particularly a single post: "he's fast enough in there without no one don't take and let him out." But oral tradition is not always passed on to newcomers, and the point of this advice is not understood until the removal of the post makes it clear. We may, if we wish, discover in James's stories of such phenomena forces that exist within the human heart rather than in the universe outside us, and we can believe in them easily enough when we survey the realities of terror and horror that human beings daily inflict upon one another. Of the consequences of such actions upon the evildoers themselves as well as upon their victims we also see something.

If—to keep to literary examples—Banquo's trust in Macbeth as his host leads to Banquo's murder, that murder itself has its retribution in the despair and eventual killing of Macbeth, lured to his fate by the evil forces on the heath.

But the evil forces themselves as objective existences are harder for us to accept. In James's stories they may to some extent even be useful, performing upon human evildoers the work of sharks or scavengers. Persuading us to believe that there are superhuman powers of evil may be James's oblique way of convincing us also of the strength of their opposites, though these seem to rely on human agents alone to battle against the enemy. If the healing touch is less evident in these stories than is the touch that withers, let us recall that James, for many years Provost of Eton School, must have found that the cautionary tale worked very well upon creatures of wild nature such as boys.[10] If a class in school were told the story of **"There Was a Man Dwelt by a Churchyard,"** and the chief masculine genius in obstreperousness were fixed on in good time as the target, it might be possible to position oneself in readiness for the climax, and then to drop on him with the most gratifying effect. This, however, may be found merely to illustrate how easy the temptation can be to imitate the punitive forces in James's stories rather than those of toleration and understanding.

Notes

1. Julia Briggs, *Night Visitors: The Rise and Fall of the English Ghost Story* (London: Faber, 1977), p. 125.

2. *The Collected Ghost Stories of M. R. James* (London: Arnold, 1942), p. 643.

3. Introduction to *Ghosts and Marvels. A Selection of Uncanny Tales from Daniel Defoe to Algernon Blackwood,* ed. V. H. Collins (London: Oxford University Press, 1927), pp. vi-vii.

4. Advocated by William Beckford at the end of *Vathek* as the wise alternative to "blind curiosity" and "restless ambition:" one of *Three Gothic Novels,* ed. E. F. Bleiler (New York: Dover, 1966), p. 194.

5. Contact of both kinds may be inferred from a number of James's stories, but the contact between the narrator, as distinct from the central character, and the spirits is either minimal or nonexistent. Non-human entities in particular never make verbal or other intelligent contact with the narrator.

6. *The Collected Ghost Stories,* p. viii.

7. "Twelve Medieval Ghost-Stories," *English Historical Review,* 37 (July 1922), 414.

8. Kingsley Amis's novel describes prolonged and intelligent contact between the chief character and the ghost, which is of human origin, subtle and malignant.

9. *The Collected Ghost Stories*, p. 16.

10. The identification is James's own: "some boy or other creature *ferae naturae*," *The Collected Ghost Stories*, p. 127.

Martin Hughes (essay date January 1993)

SOURCE: Hughes, Martin. "A Maze of Secrets in a Story by M. R. James." *Durham University Journal* 85, no. 1 (January 1993): 81-93.

[*In the following essay, Martin analyzes "Mr. H. and His Inheritance," contending that in addition to the physical maze depicted in the story, James incorporated an intellectual maze that contains a philosophically interesting message.*]

In M. R. James's story **'Mr. Humphreys and His Inheritance'**[1] Mr. Humphreys, the central character, arrives to take over an eighteenth-century estate, whose most prominent feature is a maze. The maze was designed to protect the religious secrets of the man who created it. The painful revelation to Humphreys of these secrets is the theme of the story. The reader encounters another kind of maze, created by the allusions and symbols which James uses: the aim of this paper is to show that, if explored, this maze too contains a message: an interesting one and one written from a philosophically interesting position.

The Interpretation of M. R. James's
Stories and of 'Mr. Humphreys' in
Particular: Some Recent Opinions

How should James's ghost stories be approached? R. W. Pfaff, a recent biographer of James, tells us that 'writers on ghost stories . . . fall not so much in praising MRJ's stories too little . . . but in paying little or no attention to the really remarkable thing about them, the brilliance of the antiquarian background'.[2] He quotes a colleague of James who remarks that the material of the ghost stories is 'suggested by some line of learned research and worked out with minute accuracy of detail, and at the same time with an ease and lightness of touch which can communicate . . . to the . . . reader guiltless of commerce with manuscripts'.[3] The antiquarian references in **'Mr. Humphreys'** bear out the correctness of this comment; they are certainly worked out with minute accuracy of detail. Even without examining these references we can still find a good story, written indeed with a light touch. But by examining them we find not only a good story but also James's reflections

on certain esoteric and unorthodox spiritual and theological movements—their roots, their persistence and the dangers inherent in them.

Another recent biographer, Michael Cox, warns us against treating the stories as if they were on the highest literary plane and against trying to make them bear an undue weight of speculation. In particular he warns us against 'dwelling on them as vehicles of unconscious psychological revelation'.[4] These are wise warnings. The antiquarian style, which gives the stories their special character, also sets firm limits to their scope. It is a style which normally places records and relics, things whose existence the modern world may not notice and whose meaning it cannot easily see, in the foreground of the story: so the things which everyone notices, such as sexual passion and political commitment, are absent from the foreground; and this absence limits the scope of the stories severely and so keeps them from attaining to the highest literary plane. But this is not to say that the stories take a narrow view of human life or are merely escapist. On the contrary, the premise of antiquarian stories is that records and relics are very important: when properly studied they are extremely revealing of all aspects of life in the past; moreover what they reveal is still important now. Accordingly, antiquarian stories—at least those stories which contain, as **'Mr. Humphreys'** does, detailed and copious references to people and ideas of the past—are, in a way, puzzles: not puzzles which we solve by finding out what the author thought unconsciously but puzzles which we solve by finding out, through study of the antiquarian clues, what the author consciously intended to convey.

'Mr. Humphreys' conveys some of its author's knowledge not only of esoteric thought but of the ability of the mind to be hooked or fascinated. The idea of finding abandoned traces of the past, relics of strange or dangerous forms of thought, has a certain power to hook the mind. Humphreys is linked to his ancestor because both of them experience this power. James himself had experienced one adolescent episode of unbalanced fascination.[5] This episode did not arise out of his antiquarian interests but from the popular press: he became absurdly fascinated with the events surrounding a royal wedding and with the person of the Queen. This episode does not suggest that James suffered from abnormality of mind, quite the contrary: he was like the millions who respond to the publicity machines of today, finding that the royal family provides a pleasant and (on the whole) harmless focus for sexual feeling. But the experience was no doubt a lesson to James about fascination; he would have understood that the attendant feelings might, in other circumstances, be morbid.

If James learnt something about fascination from his experience, he learnt about esoteric religion from his studies. There is no doubt that James regarded esoteric religion, at least in most of its forms, as unpleasant and dangerous. His stories more than once portray people who make the transition from antiquarian studies to the practice of magic: that is, they use what they learn in an attempt to gain supernatural power for themselves. We should notice that all these portraits are strongly negative,[6] just as we might expect from James's dislike of ghost stories which seemed to give credence to occultism.[7]

Here I refer to Jack Sullivan's comments on the ghost story tradition. His view is that that the general effect of ghost stories is to create in the reader's mind the sense that we are not free of menace even when the story is over: 'the deadly apparition is still at large'.[8] He adds that ghost stories are enigmatic stories, suggesting the presence of a dominant enigma in the whole universe. These are stories, he says, which 'relate to an inexplicable, irrational whole'.[9] To my mind, James's stories are for the most part designed to have an effect somewhat different from the one Sullivan describes: they aim to make us 'pleasantly uncomfortable'[10] rather than seriously alarmed; they are indeed enigmatic, but not quite in Sullivan's sense. The facts that James's deadly apparitions usually influence the world through a fixed point of contact and that the point of contact can sometimes be sealed off negates the idea that the deadly apparition is always still at large. The enigma lies in the problem of understanding the apparition so that we can be careful not to admit it to the world all over again. The antiquarian information plays an ambivalent part: on the one hand, the source of the dangers in which the characters in the stories find themselves; on the other hand, the only available means of understanding those dangers.

James writes disturbing stories but, because his characters sometimes escape the traps he sets for them, he balances fear and hope. I agree with Sullivan, whose analysis of James's style I find very valuable, that the presence of both fear and hope, horror and the avoidance of horror, create a 'unique chill and tension'.[11] Tension is conveyed by the fact that, though James's characters sometimes escape from horror by a fortunate turn of events, their good fortune gives us no comforting sense of a watchful providence. Humphreys's stroke of luck is his concussion when the demonic apparition approaches: the idea of divine providence, if we think of it here, turns sour. The suggestion of being saved by concussion is, after all, close to a sarcastic parody of the belief that God sustains and enlightens us. But, for all the hints of pessimism, the stories are not without hope. The existence of an enigma in Sullivan's sense, 'an irrational whole', is hinted at by James but not conceded.

In **'Mr. Humphreys'** the hint is conveyed by Cooper, Humphreys's bailiff, a vividly realised character with a distinctive way of talking. He is entirely supportive but has no understanding of the problems Humphreys has to face. His final suggestion to Humphreys is placed so as to constitute a kind of concluding observation within the whole series of **More Ghost Stories**: 'All these many solemn events have a meaning for us, if our limited intelligence permitted of our disintegrating it.' James has Cooper use the word 'disintegrate' when you would expect 'comprehend' or 'understand' and thereby suggests that the rational universe has been shattered, leaving only an enigma which defies understanding. But the suggestion is made in a gentle way by a comic character, indicating that James is not committed to it.

The same suggestion is made more forcibly and grimly in some other stories, such as **'Count Magnus'** and **'The Stalls of Barchester Cathedral'**,[12] which I have no space to discuss here. But the fact that these stories are untypically bleak again indicates that the suggestion was not fully accepted in James's mind. The bleaker stories are certainly enough to show that James understood that the Church and the tradition for which it stands sometimes inspire very little confidence. But the general tenor of his stories reflects a mind whose confidence in the Christian tradition was under pressure but had not quite broken. It is philosophically interesting to see how the imagination develops in a mind which has reached this position.[13]

The warning, not merely frightening, quality of James's stories illustrates where he stands. The stories follow those of Le Fanu, James's principal exemplar, by offering vivid glimpses of horrors extremely hard to reconcile with the orthodox idea of a benign God bestowing a rational order on the world. In Le Fanu, these horrors may befall anyone; in James they befall those who invoke them:[14] the rest of us are thereby warned.[15] Warning is worth while only if precautions are possible, so only in a world where some signs of rational order are found. But James's warnings contain tensions of their own, helping to keep the stories tense. He uses his antiquarian research to warn us of dangers but these often turn out to be the dangers of antiquarian research: the warning and the danger fuse. Sometimes the only way to prevent the release of demons into the present world is to destroy the very relics of the past on which antiquarian science and its power to warn depend.[16] It may seem surprising that antiquarian stories should sometimes celebrate the obliteration of the relics of the past: but obliteration is only an extreme, dramatic form of the censorship which James himself sometimes applied to aspects of the past which he found unpleasant. The most interesting example of censorship by him comes from his work on Walter Map's *De Nugis Curialium*.[17]

But from the same evidence we see that his attitude to what he found unpleasant was certainly not one of bitter intolerance. Some of *De Nugis* was, he thought, 'too odious to translate': hence he resorted to omission and disguise of meaning, itself a way of misrepresenting the facts of the past. But James saw that this practice needed some justification, which he offered in moderate terms: 'Map was not a great offender for his age but his public were amused at things which do not amuse us.' Cox comments that we should not think of this as showing that James was affected by '"Victorian" prudery': certainly post-Victorian editors share some of James's reticence.[18] Indeed, the tone of James's explanation of his treatment of Map suggests rational thought rather than prudery: thought with two aspects. In the first place he tries to use his antiquarian knowledge, in this case his knowledge of the medieval attitude to obscenity, to excuse Map. To do this he must have studied other examples of medieval obscenity, moved by the enquiring antiquarian spirit which the ghost stories repeatedly celebrate,[19] for all that it sometimes has bad consequences. In the second place he removes the genuine record of the past because that is the only way to remove something offensive from the world. The same two aspects of James's thought are developed in **'Mr. Humphreys'**, to whose text I now turn.

THE FIRST INSCRIPTIONS: AN ALTERED
PROPHECY

On first arrival at the estate designed by his ancestor, Humphreys notices the unfinished appearance of the house. His ancestor had unfinished business, whose nature the story reveals.

On first arrival at the maze, Humphreys finds an inscription written over the gates: *'Secretum meum mihi et filiis domus meae'*. He wonders for a moment what the origin of the words is but the story does not say whether he discovered that it is adapted from the Vulgate version of Isaiah.[20] In all versions of this passage Isaiah hears cries of triumph but, despite the fact that these cries are echoed everywhere, finds that his personal feelings are, for some reason, discordant with the feelings of the majority.[21] In the Vulgate the reason for his trouble is his possession of a secret: *'Secretum meum mihi, secretum meum mihi, uae mihi'*—'My secret is for me, my secret is for me, alas for me!' There is nothing in English translations from the Hebrew (and nothing in the Septuagint) to echo the reference to a secret, so Humphreys was unlikely to think readily of the real origin of these words. Wilson, Humphreys's ancestor who developed the estate, had, in any case, changed his original, so that it now reads, 'My secret for myself and the children of my house'. Wilson has put new words in place of the lament *'uae mihi'*; the amendment appears to give the prophecy a new and benign form, suggesting that the pain of secrecy can be avoided if the secret is shared within a family or a small group. But if this suggestion turns out to be wrong then the true meaning of the prophecy in its new form must be 'My secret for myself and the children of my house—alas for me and

for them'. If this is the new form of the prophecy it is not benign but more distressing than its original.

The inscription also suggests a theological idea: Isaiah must have kept his secret to himself because he believed it was his duty to God to keep it; so it may be right to keep theological secrets, that is those pertaining to God or to the next world. So the secrets of the maze, which Humphreys is urged to keep, must be of this kind. The idea of secrets which it is God's will we should keep, a foundational idea for those who hold an esoteric religious belief, may develop into the more disturbing idea that God wishes us to keep our own true nature a secret between us and Him. According to this idea we can express our true relationship with God only in secret forms of worship and devotion—these forms others might find repugnant. So the words of the inscription, because they raise this idea, are a warning: the person who enters runs a very serious risk, the risk of losing contact with the ordinary understanding of right and wrong.

The warning is apt because the whole idea of secret devotion contrasts strongly with other ideas which are more popular, for instance with the basic ideas of the Delphic Oracle, 'Know yourself' and 'Nothing too much': these two precepts are linked in a fashion which presupposes that self-knowledge is linked to self-control, so that we can make our real selves, our real faces, as acceptable to others in public as they are to ourselves in private. Wilson's other construction, apart from the house and the maze, is a classical temple,[22] something which suggests sympathy with the Delphic ideal and whose pleasant appearance, at one or two points of the story, duly gives Humphreys a false sense of reassurance. The suggestion of sympathy with reassuring forms of paganism must, considering the contents of the maze, be merely a blind. The blind must mask his rejection of the Delphic idea that we must make our real face into an acceptable face. Hence the repulsiveness of his face when it appears.

The idea that God may allow us freely and unashamedly to express in our secret devotions aspects of our nature which our fellow human beings would condemn morally if they were expressed in public is even more suspect from an orthodox Christian than from a Delphic point of view. After all, orthodox Christianity believes that God has publicly decreed a moral law which we should observe in all aspects of our life. The unpleasant resonance which surrounded the word 'heresy' in former times and surrounds the words 'sect' and 'cult' in modern days indicates how strong within Christian ways of thought moral suspicion of unorthodox groups is. If this suspicion is at all justified—and James suggests that it is—we might argue that those who try to express their true nature under cover of secrecy are in constant moral danger. From this point we might argue, much more intolerantly and dangerously, that the true nature of such people does not deserve any expression at all: instead it deserves to be detested and shunned.

But if this line of thought, which is firmly hostile to religious and moral esotericism, is strongly held by the majority it leads to stern demands for conformity and puts those whose real thoughts make conformity impossible into a very painful position. Because they cannot conform with real commitment they have in their minds something like a complex sealed maze, cut off from the public gaze. Their self-examination becomes painful: if they look into the complex maze concealed in their own minds the isolation of their position, cherishing a secret which they cannot discuss, may strike them hard: Isaiah's '*uae mihi*' applies. To relieve their isolation and to hedge themselves against the hostility of the majority they may strive, discreetly but vigorously, to draw a few others into their way of thinking. Thus plain hostility towards sects helps to perpetuate sects: the more people are frightened of speaking openly the more desperately they will try to influence a few others and to do so in secret. In the story, Wilson tries desperately to influence the children of his house.

So the inscription is a warning to the child of the house that, when he enters the maze, he risks the hostility of the rest of the human race: at the same time it is an invitation to enter and therefore the promise of something desirable to be found within, a *secretum* which no longer causes its possessor to cry '*uae mihi*'. But Humphreys does not recognise the origin of the inscription and therefore neither recalls the warning implied by '*uae mihi*' nor appreciates that the changed words make him a promise. So he neither thinks how to protect himself nor considers whether the promise is really attractive.

But the reader is in a position to see, even at this stage, one root of esoteric religion: the idea of a secret worth having which, though it might shock the majority, may be kept by its initiates without pain or guilt. This idea implies that the secrecy exists not because the initiates have something to be ashamed of but because the majority is unworthy to know the secret: conventional morality, symbolised by the temple, is inferior to the secret morality symbolised by the maze.

THE SECOND INSCRIPTION: AN ALTERED PROVERB, DEFACED AND RESTORED

Humphreys, the child of the house, never finds any difficulty in getting to the centre of the maze, where he finds the inscribed and engraved copper globe which is part of Wilson's message to him. But the inscriptions on the copper globe were not meant by Wilson to be the next written message received by Humphreys after he had read the first, the altered oracle of Isaiah. He should have read, letter by letter, a message on a series of stones.

The message on the stones has been defaced by an intermediate heir. This was the younger Wilson, the older Wilson's grandson. Cooper tells Humphreys that the younger Wilson was a man of shattered health and spirits—'a valetudinarian'—and that he cherished a deep dislike of his grandfather. He expressed this dislike by destroying his grandfather's papers and by removing the stones, part of the record of his grandfather's unpleasant religion, to another building and keeping them out of order. But he did not destroy the maze. By his time, evidently, mazes were coming to be seen as attractive curiosities and destruction might have led to unwanted local publicity and protest. In recent years the protests would have been led by Lady Wardrop, a forceful personality who intends to serve local conservationist sentiment by writing a guidebook to mazes. Her surprise and regret at the destruction of mazes are exactly the sentiments expressed by a real guidebook, *The Earthworks of England*,[23] published in 1908: 'It is marvellous that the memory of such things, once prominent features of rural life, can die out so rapidly as it does.'

It is Wardrop who eventually explains to Humphreys how to restore the series of stones and so recover the message carved on them. She initially becomes friendly with Humphreys because he gives her access to the maze, something which the younger Wilson had always refused: he kept the maze intact but unexplored. Accordingly, he found himself obeying his hated grandfather's command to keep the *secretum domus meae*: being forced into this position must have contributed to his depressive state. This fact points to the power of secrets, which James would have us notice, to entangle those who would never have wished to create them. The secret destroyed the younger Wilson: this fact shows that events have already given the revised form of Isaiah's words the more ominous of their two possible meanings—'Alas for the children of the house!'

On this showing the older Wilson was an evil man who left a corrupt legacy. Most other details of the story support this negative view of him. His deviousness is manifest in the confusing nature of the maze, which makes it impossible for Humphreys to show ordinary visitors around. His contact with infernal powers is shown by the unnatural heat which repels Cooper when he touches the copper globe. The insidious nature of his presence is so borne in on Lady Wardrop that her wish to preserve the maze is quickly and remarkably changed. She soon makes it clear that she would consent to its destruction.

'Wardrop' is an older form of 'wardrobe': we are perhaps to imagine her as sturdily built and with a sound, well-stocked mind. But an upper-class Englishwoman's wardrobe is, perhaps, not very receptive to anything which shocks and surprises: neither is Lady Wardrop's mind. She fulfills the role, known elsewhere in James's work, of helper and adviser to the central character. It is often a feature of these secondary characters that they are more robust or resourceful than the central character himself,[24] and this feature suggests that the central character, by contrast, has weaknesses which dark forces can exploit. The dark forces find Humphreys's weak point because he becomes fascinated with the secrets of the past incautiously, before he understands their true nature. This must have been the weakness which originally snared the older Wilson when he first investigated the half-forgotten religions of the ancient world. Something of Wilson survives in Humphreys: perhaps his eventual marriage to the niece of the solid and sound Lady Wardrop is a useful correction.

When the inscription on the stones is restored on Wardrop's instructions it does indeed turn out to be rather shocking: it reads *'penetrans ad interiora mortis'*—'pressing on into the inner places of death'. Here again the phrase is a slightly amended Biblical quotation, this time from the Book of Proverbs.[25] It is worth looking at the context of this phrase. The author of *Proverbs*, purportedly King Solomon, warns his young hearer against someone who is called in the King James version 'the strange woman' and in the Vulgate *'mulier extranea et aliena'*—'the foreign, alien woman'—and his warning ends with the words, *'Viae inferi domus eius, penetrantes ad interiora mortis'*—'Her dwellings are paths to hell, leading to the inner places of death'. I suggest 'pressing on' for Wilson's amended motto partly because it expresses the lonely quality of his determination, a loneliness signified by his use of the singular *'penetrans'* for the plural *'penetrantes'*; he is determined, however much he is alienated from the rest of humanity, to survive even in the inner places of death. Moreover, 'pressing on' recalls the sexual meaning of *'penetrans'*, a meaning abundantly suggested by its Biblical context. Whether the emphasis of the Hebrew original falls on the woman's sexuality and prostitute trickery or else on her foreignness and pagan sexual freedom (the foreignness seems to be emphasised by the Vulgate's use of two adjectives, *'extranea et aliena'*, where the English version uses one, 'strange') is disputed among the commentators.[26] Whatever the truth of that dispute we shall see that both an interest in forbidden pleasure, born of reaction against puritan preaching, and an interest in ideas alien to his native culture are important aspects of Wilson's personality.

At any rate, reference to the seventh chapter of *Proverbs* is reference to the kind of sexual freedom which that chapter condemns on behalf of orthodox religion. Wilson must have considered that condemnation from his unorthodox point of view. Just as 'Solomon' imputes extreme sexual irresponsibility to those who reject his religion, Wilson would impute extreme sexual repressiveness to those who accept it. So we can note that hope of liberation from irksome sexual restrictions is another root from which esoteric religion can grow. But how could the contrary advice and urgent warnings of orthodox religion be answered? How can the esoterics' claim to moral superiority be sustained? Something of an answer to these questions is conveyed by the inscriptions on the copper globe.

THE GLOBE

The copper globe adds substantially to the message delivered by Wilson to Humphreys. The globe turns out both to be a map of another world and to contain Wilson's ashes. By locating his ashes in a map Wilson indicates the place where he is determined that his spirit will survive. The globe is a parody of a celestial globe. The parody begins by putting Draco, the Serpent, who would be in the northern hemisphere of a celestial globe, around the equator; the pole is occupied by *Princeps Tenebrarum,* the Prince of Darkness. Where Humphreys might have expected Hercules he finds Cain; where he might have expected Ophiuchus, the Serpent-Holder, he finds Chore, plunged into the earth. Chore is presumably Korah,[27] who was swallowed up by the earth for attempting to usurp Aaron's priesthood. The absence of Ophiucus suggests that there is no one in the world represented by this globe who can restrain the Serpent: and it is a 'snaky' tree which is shown holding Absalom by his hair. The globe depicts the underworld not only as a place of dangerous serpents but as a place where there is sometimes darkness—*'umbra mortis'* 'shadow of death' and sometimes fire—*'Vallis Filiorum Hinnom'*, 'Gehenna', the place of unquenched burning. But, despite all their hideous surroundings, Cain and other characters are not extinguished but alive in the world depicted by the globe. Before looking further at the clue provided by Cain, Korah and Absalom we should notice the final character depicted on the globe, the Magus Hostanes, whom Humphreys does not recognise. He is a figure of authority, robed and conversing with demons: in fact, the only figure on the globe whose existence is attested by sources outside the Bible and Christian tradition.

Ancient and medieval references to Hostanes, running with commentary to eighty-nine pages, are collected by Bidez and Cumont,[28] beginning with the notice in the Elder Pliny's *Natural History,* where we read that Hostanes accompanied Xerxes, King of Persia, on his invasion of Greece in 480 BC. The magus had more success than his king, because, according to Pliny, leading Greek thinkers flocked to talk with him: 'he sowed the seeds of his pestilential art, leaving on his way an infected world everywhere he wandered.'[29] The second or third century Christian apologist Minucius Felix recognised as Hostanes 'the foremost of the Magi both in word and deed', and accepted his belief in 'wandering and malevolent demons'[30]—his companions in Wilson's engraving. Wilson evidently knew the byways of ancient literature well enough to encounter the record of Hostanes; but to Humphreys, though he was an educated man and though the record is extensive, the name of Hostanes meant nothing. By his time, education concentrated on the central, most rational exponents of ancient culture: the eccentrics and outsiders of the ancient world were being forgotten and thus the rank growths started by Hostanes were at last enfeebled.

James presents the dank, overgrown maze as the place where Hostanes' name is preserved: in doing this he was surely thinking of Pliny's testimony and of his reference to the evil seed and the infected ground—also of the bad reputation in the Roman world of the yew trees of which the maze is formed.[31] The dense, obstructive vegetation of the maze—which Humphreys tries in vain to clear for the benefit of visitors—represents the power of some unpleasant ideas to detain and entangle our minds. Humphreys's more modern education is one of the causes which frustrate Wilson's effort to create 'a secret for the children of my house': after a few generations, the secret could hardly be understood. But the evil seed has, for all that, much power. This power is marked by the fact that when Humphreys becomes aware of something malevolent advancing to meet him he sees it as the offspring of evil seed, that is as trees and bushes which contain a hostile presence.[32]

The combination of figures on the globe goes a long way towards explaining Wilson's theology. Cain was the hero of a minute Gnostic sect, the Cainites, denounced by Irenaeus.[33] It seems to have been the theory of the Cainites that the Old Testament was an arcane text, revealing between the lines that the world was temporarily not in the hands of the true God but of a witch (called Hystera—'the Womb') who pretended to be God and whose demand for blood sacrifices was, presumably, the undeserved downfall of Cain, who had at first, unlike his brother Abel, attempted to advance civilisation by tilling the land and by offering a sacrifice which contained no blood. Other losers in the struggles recorded by the Old Testament, such as Korah and Absalom, were regarded by the Cainites as heroes or victims, not as evildoers justly punished. Anyone who wished to take the Cainites' part could argue that Absalom was the victim of treachery and that Korah's claim that 'all the people are holy'[34] is morally superior to the exclusivism of Aaron—that is to say, could argue that a morally sensitive reading exposes the arcane message.

The Magi, whom Hostanes represents, were not so interested in interpreting the Old Testament but their ideas bore comparison to those of the Cainites at two points. First, the idea of pretended Gods, that is malevolent demons who would appear to *nescii*, those not skilled in magic, and offer them false guidance, was an idea stressed by the Magi to reveal their own usefulness to the human race. James writes with some irony here. The Magi claimed to be helpful to the *nescii*: after all they knew about demons. But James shows their foremost representative, Hostanes, as a netherworld figure and companion of demons: this suggests that the science of the Magi was not a help but a threat. Can the same suggestion be made about his own antiquarian science which often, in the stories, plays a dangerous part? The point is gently made at the end of the story, where we discover that the evil magician and the author who imagined him have a common name: he is James Wilson.

We also find within the religion of the Magi the idea that God does not demand blood sacrifice and that demons do demand it:[35] an idea which might be used both to unmask the deceitful demons and to confirm the Cainites' view of the Old Testament God.

Wilson's choice of figures for the globe which contained his ashes demonstrates that his theology was formed by the intersection of Cainism and Magianism. Hence he would have believed that he was morally superior to the bloodthirsty witch who pretends to be God and that he had wisdom and strength enough both to expose her deceptions and to survive her revenge. What is the way to that wisdom? The answer to this question must be part of the secret left to the children of his house. Since it is a secret it must be revealed discreetly, and since it is for the children of the house it is fitting that the key to the secret be within the house.

Before turning to the house and its library, note how a third root of esoteric religion has been suggested by the inscriptions on the infernal globe: that root is fascination, clearly felt by Wilson, with the hidden face of the past, the face which modern education may increasingly obscure. This fascination—certainly shared by James, the great student of apocrypha—cannot be wholly wrong: in so far as it expresses the rational desire not to let the prejudices of the present distort the past it is laudable. But it becomes wrong if it encourages us to revive and take seriously the illusions and moral excesses of previous generations.

At the same time the theology implied by the inscriptions on the globe shows how esoteric religion tries to overcome the problem mentioned above in connection with its second root. Faced with the urgent moral advice of orthodox religion, it replies with claims to moral superiority in spite of appearances. Orthodoxy, it says, is a systematic misunderstanding of God; moreover, if we read the sacred texts in a morally sensitive way, we will see through the misunderstanding. Faced with the threats of orthodox religion, even with the threat of death, it replies that these threats come not from the true ruler of the universe but from usurping powers and therefore can be endured: Wilson grimly claims that he can endure even the inner places of death. These replies show us how esoteric religion is an act of personal will: a determination not to accept objections which everyone else finds insurmountable. We may find this grossly irrational but we should note that, in comparison with orthodox ways of thought, esoteric religion expresses personal autonomy. We may think that the word 'ingenious', if applied to those who read the Bible as an arcane text, is too flattering: but at any rate they show a certain agility and resourcefulness of mind beside which orthodox minds may seem ponderous.

The Sermon on Pleasure and Death

The setting of the story alternates between the garden and the house, especially Wilson's library. Humphreys begins his survey of the library by reflecting on how unreadable many old books now are. The only named book which he thinks might be readable is Picart's *Religious Ceremonies,* a book whose possession hints discreetly at the owner's unorthodoxy, more plainly at his interest in religious ideas which belong outside his native culture.[36] But looking at the books and pamphlets he initially thinks unreadable,[37] he comes upon one, an old sermon called *A Parable of this Unhappy Condition,* which he finds himself reading with interest.[38]

A Parable is the centrepiece of **'Mr. Humphreys'** because it is a story in itself, beautifully elaborated—'one of Monty's best parodies, his pseudo-seventeenth-century meditation on mazes'.[39] Note that it reflects the spiritual climate of the seventeenth century, even though it is found in an eighteenth-century library. Literary reflections on mazes were not uncommon; Matthews collected examples, some puritanically gloomy, going back to 1496.[40] *A Parable* is a reflection on what we might call the logic of mazes. Mazes are structures which are inviting but also threatening: the threat is that we may get lost (with unforeseeable consequences) but the maze is none the less inviting because it will (for some reason—we may not clearly see what the reason is) be satisfying to get to the structure's heart. The sermon represents the view, quite contrary to Wilson's, that the inescapable threat far outweighs the uncertain promise. Its author correctly perceives that the maze is a model for the world as puritans see it, full of dangers. So the emotion with which he surrounds his story is fear of unknown hazards and the title states his overriding conviction, which is that this life is an unhappy condition.

The sermon refuses to be part of Humphreys's plan for a catalogue of the library:[41] when he has read it once, he can never find it again. The preacher's parable—James captures an antique style in an astonishingly convincing way—concerns a man who enters a maze and there finds a jewel of great price, just as Humphreys had found the copper globe. The man in the parable escapes with the jewel but is subject, after nightfall, to certain

terrors, especially to the sense of pursuers who never quite face or catch up with him but always stop when he stops, always move when he moves. The biblical reference to the night as the time 'when all the beasts of the forest do move'[42] is used to remarkable effect, creating a compelling picture of fear. The preacher claims that the jewel corresponds to the pleasures of this world and the terrors to the price which we must pay for seeking those pleasures.

The fact that the sermon vanishes when the relics of Wilson's strange religion are destroyed indicates that it has a connection with him, though it is wholly orthodox and therefore survived the younger Wilson's censorship. Old Wilson, the eighteenth-century heretic, cannot have agreed with seventeenth-century puritanism, though it must have influenced his upbringing: so his connection with the sermon must lie in the fact that the puritan spirit was the genesis of his unorthodoxy. He attempted to escape from it and this attempt was understandable because it was a religion dominated by intense fear of the pleasures of life: not that this justifies his choice of an escape route which has the opposite fault, spiritual recklessness marked by the readiness to venture *ad interiora mortis.*

But a chink of sympathy for Wilson is opened up and can be closed only if we agree with the sermon that life here on earth is, inescapably and by the set providence of God, an unhappy condition. James would not have expected such agreement from twentieth-century readers; nor do his stories, which suggest that demonic dangers can often be overcome, uge his readers to abandon their comparatively confident view in favour of the old puritan fears. To James personally the evangelical religion, which is the descendant of puritanism, had become somewhat alien.[43]

The preacher, who speaks for orthodox Christianity, would have it that the precious object found in the maze is mere transitory pleasure, bought at a terrible price, and that the maze should, accordingly, be shunned. But precious, hidden objects may symbolise arcane knowledge;[44] and what Humphreys found in the maze was not in itself sensuously pleasant but rather a reminder of Wilson's religious beliefs and ethics. The foundation of Wilson's ethics must be the rejection of the preacher's doctrine that total commitment to pleasure brings only death and is therefore to be shunned. This doctrine is powerful and may be salutary, instilling a prudent fear. But it is also dangerous: it may actually lead us to embrace what we fear.

The power inherent in this doctrine is manifest whenever the human race faces certain moral predicaments: the association between pleasure and death seems to lie in the human mind waiting to be invoked. The predicament faced by 'Solomon' was created by the departure of young people from traditional morality, something which he pictured as seduction by a strange woman. This problem for ever takes new forms. We find one contemporary form if we consider the warnings produced by the British Government when it undertook to inform us about AIDS. The first series of television warnings used pictures of bleak gravestones and the sound of the *Dies Irae*. A later series showed a seductive woman and the message was that, though she was outwardly beautiful, she carried death in the inner places of her body. This modern televison icon, whom we might call the casual partner, corresponds remarkably to the word-painted icon whom the *Book of Proverbs* calls 'the strange woman'. If television advertisements used Latin mottos then '*penetrans ad interiora mortis*' would have been highly apt, with the puritan meaning that in the search of sexual pleasure we find only death. The sermon left by Wilson for Humphreys could reasonably be taken as a commentary on Solomon's warning phrase.

But the danger inherent in the doctrine and in all the dramatic warnings which the doctrine inspires is that the warnings may increase our fascination with the dangerous thing. This is what happens to Humphreys: the reading of the sermon seems only to increase the interest he feels in the maze and in the secrets associated with it. Therefore he is drawn towards Wilson, who stands for a secret ethic in which the preacher's doctrines and warnings are all discarded. The result, of course, is fascination in Humphreys's mind which leads to the climactic scene and to the encounter with Wilson: though whether Humphreys meets Wilson in reality or in his overwrought imagination we cannot be quite sure. Wilson struggles 'like a wasp from a rotten apple' out of a black hole which appears in Humphreys's plan of the maze, a hole which both repels and fascinates Humphreys and which turns out to be a gateway to hell. When Wilson, with his face repulsively burnt in the unquenched fire, tries to seize him, Humphreys falls back and is concussed. When he returns to consciousness he acts drastically to break his link with Wilson. He destroys the globe and grubs up the maze.

In the encounter scene, the sexual symbolism of forbidden depths is vigorously used. Wilson's attempted contact with Humphreys is a kind of embrace and arouses Humphreys's strongest spasm of disgust. But it is obvious from the narrative of the encounter that fascination as well as repulsion is present in Humphreys's mind. The existence of fascination is all the more emphasised if we read the encounter not as a real event but as the product of Humphreys's imagination, unable until the last minute to tear itself away from Wilson and the mysterious theology for which Wilson stands.

The story encourages us to share Humphreys's disgust because of the loathsome nature of Wilson's appearance. Does it encourage us to approve his decision to destroy the maze? The acceptance of the decision by Lady Wardrop shows that it reflects orthodox thinking. But orthodox thinking may be too ready to overlook the more unpleasant aspects of human history and to substitute a bland fiction for the truth. Moreover, if something unpleasant and hitherto secret is, like the maze, obliterated from the record by conscious decision, then those who take the decision find they still have a secret: they know something which the record does not show. Humphreys's entanglement in secrecy is not entirely ended, though the secret has taken a new form.

Still, the lightening of the atmosphere at the end of the story makes it clear that Humphreys did the right thing: he had, in all the circumstances, to take drastic action against the inheritance he received from Wilson. I mentioned above that other ghost stories, as well as the translation of Walter Map, show that the decision to rewrite or censor the record of history was, in James's opinion, sometimes inevitable; but also that this option has another and more positive aspect. It is not an opinion which springs from any bitter form of intolerance or disgust: these would be alien to the antiquarian temper, whose purpose is to discover the past in a spirit which is objective and free of distorting emotion. And if we are not to be bitter towards what we condemn we have to seek some understanding of it. This dual view is developed through the warning aspect of James's stories, including **'Mr. Humphreys'**.

NEW DANGERS

Wilson's claim to our understanding lies in the fact that his strange and reckless form of religion was a reaction against the fear-laden and oppressive religion of the puritans. Humphreys can claim that he was rightly afraid of the dangerous, demon-releasing relics which he inherited from Wilson. But the danger is that an excessively fear-laden reaction to strange ways of thought merely turns the cycle again, causing yet another reaction against an orthodoxy which has become cautious and joyless. Did Humphreys do the right thing but under the spur of an excessive fear?

The story suggests that Humphreys's specific fears of Wilson and Wilson's influence, the fears which led him to grub up the maze, were indeed exaggerated; but there is a sting in the tail of this suggestion. We need not really be afraid of those forms of esoteric religion which cannot survive except in conditions which were possible only in the past; Wilson's religion was one of those forms. The car which brings Lady Wardrop (and brings her from a residence named Bentley!) is not just a sign of her modernity but also a sign that the reclusiveness and isolation of the Wilson demesne is less and less possible; that spiritual experiments cannot be conducted in the twentieth century behind screens made in the eighteenth. This point is re-emphasised by Wardrop's observation that very few mazes are left. Moreover, Wilson's arrogant attempt to rewrite Isaiah's prophecy has led only to the fulfilment of the prophecy in the bleakest possible way: not only the founder of the secret but also the children of his house have been severely troubled. The words of scripture stand; the esoteric variant vanishes.

The sting in the tail arises because these considerations are not wholly comforting: therefore there was at least some justification for Humphreys's fears. Specific forms of esoteric thought do indeed come and go. But desire for secrecy, impatience with sexual restriction and fascination with what is strange, the roots from which these changing forms grow, still survive. The story, if I have interpreted it correctly, reminds us that these roots spread wide and deep in human nature; that the esoterics appeal to our natural desire for a truly personal, autonomously chosen belief or way of life; that the agility of mind which supports strange beliefs will always find admirers. So the fact that the words of scripture concerning secrecy and secret beliefs have not been discredited and that efforts to modify them have been in vain is not a fact which provides reassurance to the modern world. As ever, the words convey a warning. That this warning still matters is the message at the centre of James's maze of allusions.

Warnings have a dual nature: in the first place they cause fear, in this case fear of secret experiments which go too far; in the second place they call for understanding of what we fear. Someone in James's philosophical position is able, for all that he has not abandoned orthodoxy, to see the side of orthodoxy which inspires least confidence: accordingly he is well-placed to understand the perennial, therefore modern, attractiveness of rival, heretical ways of thought. Warning stories are the natural imaginative product of a mind which is aware of an attraction which it does not, in the end, follow. **'Mr. Humphreys'** is a warning story springing from this understanding. The story is written in the antiquarian manner and so makes no specific predictions of how twentieth-century technology, which it glimpses, will deliver its impact on moral and spiritual life. The story does not foresee the specific spiritual climate of our time, the age of contraception—hence of freer experiment in sexual relationships—and of mind-bending drugs, whereby people experiment on themselves. But it does, through its contrast between the heretic Wilson and the orthodox preacher, help us to see why some people are driven to secretive spiritual experiment, into which others are then drawn by fascination: alas for them and for us.

Notes

1. M. R. James, *More Ghost Stories of an Antiquary* (London: Edward Arnold, 1911), sequel to *Ghost Stories of an Antiquary,* produced by the same publisher in 1904.

2. R. W. Pfaff, *Montague Rhodes James* (London: Scolar Press, 1980), p. 415.

3. A. Hamilton Thompson in his biographical note of M. R. James, *Leicestershire Archaeological Society Transactions,* 19 (1936-37), pp. 113-117. See Pfaff, p. 323.

4. M. Cox, *M. R. James, an Informal Portrait* (Oxford: 1983), p. 149n.

5. Cox, p. 32.

6. Cf. 'Lost Hearts' (in *Ghost Stories*) and 'Casting the Runes' (in *More Ghost Stories*). The clerical ghost in 'The Tractate Middoth' (*More Ghost Stories*) may not be entirely malevolent but is certainly unpleasant enough to support my point: he has the horrifying face characteristic of James' magicians.

7. Cox, p. 148, referring to the Introduction to *More Ghost Stories*.

8. J. Sullivan, *Elegant Nightmares, the English Ghost Story from Le Fanu to Blackwood* (Athens, Ohio: 1978), p. 10.

9. Sullivan, p. 134.

10. According to James's stated purpose in the Preface to *Ghost Stories*.

11. Sullivan, p. 71.

12. In 'Count Magnus' (*Ghost Stories*) the central character is persecuted for reasons which remain enigmatic; he tries to 'cry to God' but in vain. 'The Stalls of Barchester Cathedral' (*More Ghost Stories*), the story of a murderous Archdeacon, prompts certain cynical reflections on the Church.

13. James's public commitment to the Church of England never wavered (Sullivan, p. 73). Cox records James's pleasure in what was 'pedestrian and Anglican and Victorian' (p. 134) and Lytton Strachey's view of James's autobiography as suggesting a vapid, childlike character (p. 220). But it is inconceivable that the real truth about such a lively mind was that it had never grown up or that it was really content with pedestrian forms of thought. His deeper thoughts are in the ghost stories.

14. Sullivan, pp. 70, 75.

15. *A Warning to the Curious* is the title of another of James's collections of ghost stories. One story in *More Ghost Stories,* 'The Rose Garden', ends on a warning motto: '*Quieta non movere*'.

16. Cf. 'Canon Alberic's Scrapbook' and 'Oh, Whistle, and I'll Come to You, my Lad' (*Ghost Stories*); also 'The Stalls of Barchester Cathedral' (*More Ghost Stories*).

17. Walter Map was a twelfth-century Archdeacon of Welsh origin. James first edited the Latin text of *De Nugis Curialium* (Oxford: 1914) and later produced an English translation (Volume 9 of the Record Series of the Honourable Society of Cymmrodorion: 1923). A new and revised edition, with Latin and English in parallel, was prepared by C. N. L. Brooke and R. A. B. Mynors for the Clarendon Press (Oxford, 1983).

18. Cox, p. 222. It is clear that James treated as 'odious' many passages of Map which are explicitly, but only mildly, erotic. But this fact does not show that he was prudish to any special degree. If we look at Map's words in some detail we see, firstly, where James drew the line and, secondly, how Brooke and Mynors, scholars of a later generation, tend in their revised edition to draw the same line in the same place. The methods used by James are disguised translation, complete omission and reproduction in the English text of untranslated Latin. Cox briefly notes these methods and refers us to *De Nugis Curialium* III 2, a story about Galo, a knight who diverts his scheming Queen from her plan to seduce him by planting a story that he has a serious sexual problem: '*cum omnia possit a mulieribus evincere, vacuum se penitus fatetur ab opere*'. James (p. 121) puts this into reticent English—'He could extort every favour from women [but] confesses . . . that he cannot'. This is deliberately to make the translation imperfect: something of the tone of the story is lost unless a phrase like 'for the job, he is deeply lacking' is used; all the same, James's censored words reappear in the revised edition (p. 215). James now resorts to total omission. The Queen sends one of her servants to check the rumour about Galo: '*docet aditum, quo possit in Galonis amplexus illabi, nudamque se nudo iungere*'. James substitutes dots for this instruction; his revisers are prepared only to advance from omission to disguised translation: they have the woman 'insinuate herself into Galo's good graces, with no holds barred', instead of 'slip into his embraces, naked woman with naked man'. Only once, as far as I can see, does James put untranslated Latin into his English text: this is a joke made by a scurrilous nun in II 17 (p. 91): '*Domnus Cunnanus nihil est nisi cunnus et anus*', which the revisers also (p. 169) quote but do no translate. It means 'Lord Cunnanus is nothing but cunt and anus' and is a play on the Celtic name Conan (see the Introduction to the revised edition, p. xl). This joke is incidental to the story and could easily be omitted by a prudish editor but James did not omit it. Indeed in his Latin edition he accepts the suggestion of the previous editor (Thomas Wright, 1850) that '*est*' should be introduced editorially, making the phrase into a line of verse. It would be fair to say that, because Map is not really odious or pornographic, James is oversentitive; also fair to say that he shows a dislike of vulgarity which other scholars manifestly share. Moreover, a translator commissioned by the Honourable Society of Cymmrodorion would bear in mind that an important section of his intended readership would be people of a strict nonconformist background, shocked by the least bad language. Hence it would be unfair to say that the attitudes revealed by James's work on Map amount to prudery on James's part. The question of 'Victorian prudery' is important because, if we attribute that quality to James, we would feel more justified in regarding him as repressed and accordingly in searching his work for meanings of which he was unconscious: a search for which I have little sympathy.

19. Cf. Sullivan, p. 90.

20. Study of the Latin Bible is much assisted by the remarkably clear *Novae Concordantiae* of B. Fischer (Stuttgart: Fromann-Holboog, 1977).

21. *The Book of the Prophet Isaiah*, chapter 24, verse 16.

22. Actually modelled on the Temple of the Sybil at Tivoli. The Sybil did have connections with the underworld but, even so, was fully acceptable to mainstream paganism, as the Sixth Book of the *Aeneid* shows.

23. The author, A. H. Allcroft, is cited in W. H. Matthews, *Mazes and Labyrinths* (London: Longmans, 1922), p. 213.

24. Compare the military man in 'Oh, Whistle, and I'll Come to You, My Lad' (*Ghost Stories*) and the brother of the former victim who supports Dunning against Karswell in 'Casting the Runes' (*More Ghost Stories*). Wilson and Karswell are very similar characters, both having a secret religion and, in due accord with the Le Fanu tradition, a dreadful face. James seems to think that there had been a decline in the standards of esoterics since the eighteenth century in that Wilson was clearly very well educated and Karswell is semi-literate—moreover Karswell, living as the story reminds us in the age of mass advertisement, sometimes ventures out of his secrecy and seclusion in the attempt to give his powerful magic a degree of publicity, both academic and commercial. The presence of effective and helpful secondary characters in James departs from the Le Fanu tradition, where, as Sullivan points out, the victims get no more help from human than from divine sources (p. 43).

25. *The Book of Proverbs,* chapter 7, verse 27.

26. Cf. W. McKane, *Proverbs* (London: SPCK, 1970), p. 139.

27. *The Book of Numbers,* chapter 16. The name in the Vulgate is 'Core'; there seems to be a pun on the Greek 'chora', 'earth', perhaps unintentional. James sometimes misspelt names with which he was familiar, for instance that of Judge Jeffreys—cf. Cox, p. 144.

28. J. Bidez and F. Cumont, *Les Mages Hellénisés,* Paris: 1938), Vol. II, p. 266 ff.

29. Pliny, *Natural History,* Book XXX, ch. 8.

30. Minucius Felix, *Octavius* ch. 26. This work, all that survives of its author, is translated in the *Ante-Nicene Christian Library* (Edinburgh: 1869) Vol. 13. M. Sage in *Cyprian* (Philadelphia: 1975), p. 47 ff, argues that *Octavius* was written between AD 197 and AD 250.

31. Virgil (*Georgics,* II 257) refers to yews as noxious—'taxi nocentes'. That to the Romans the yew was *'ein damonischer, den Todesgöttern geweihter Baum'* is confirmed in F. Bömer's comments on Ovid's *Metamorphoses* IV 432 (Heidelberg: Carl Winter, 1976). Wilson would have been familiar with the Italian term *'albero della morte'* for yew. But we can see from Matthews (p. 115 and p. 140) that there are both practical and aesthetic reasons for the use of yew (*taxus baccata*) in mazes.

32. Sinister Irish yew trees appear both in 'Mr. Humphreys' and in 'A School Story', where the murderer, a teacher of classics, sees fit to dispose of his victim among the yews, the trees of death, only to find that the victim is less dead than he would have liked. Other oppressive foilage appears in 'The Rose Garden'—all these are found in *More Ghost Stories.*

33. Irenaeus, *Adversus Haereses,* Book I, chapter 31, to be found in the *Ante-Nicene Christian Library* (Edinburgh, 1868), Vol. V, p. 113.

34. *Numbers,* chapter 16 verse 3.

35. The attribution of this idea to the Magi is not beyond question but is convincingly supported by F. Cumont, *The Oriental Religions in Roman Paganism* (Chicago: 1911), p. 268.

36. Information about Bernard Picart (1673-1733) may be found in several works of reference. The *Biographie Universelle* (inspired by L.-G. Michaud and completed in Paris in 1854) akes a rather dim view of Picart; a more favourable view is found in E. and E. Haag, *La France Protestante*

(Geneva: 1966) and in Roth and Wigoder's *Encyclopaedia Judaica* (Jerusalem: 1972). Picart was a great engraver and his principal work was entitled *Cérémonies et coûtumes religieuses de tous les peuples du monde,* whose six-volume English edition appeared in 1733. His work was continued by others after his death; these others wrote about religion in a more and more sceptical and scathing manner.

37. The two supposedly unreadable authors mentioned are the fifteenth century Bishop Tostado of Avila and the sixteenth century Jesuit Pineda. Tostado was at one stage forced to retract heretical opinions and Pineda, represented in the Library by his commentary on *Job,* also wrote *De rebus Salamonis*—'curieux et savant' according to the *Biographie Universelle:* Solomon has, of course, an important place in the occult tradition. Tostado and Pineda are mentioned in the *New Catholic Encyclopaedia.*

38. The sequence is: discovery of the globe, reading of the sermon, examination of the globe.

39. Cox, p. 143.

40. Matthews, pp. 193-199.

41. Humphreys is like Wilson in many ways: both can be fascinated with strange relics of the past. But Wilson unreservedly guards his secrets: Humphreys, at least initially, wants not only to examine the contents of the house but to publish what he finds and also to collaborate with Lady Wardrop's plans for a guidebook, describing the maze to the general public.

42. Psalm 104 (in the Vulgate 103) verse 20.

43. Cox, p. 72.

44. An ancient example of this imagery is provided by the Gnostic *Acts of Thomas,* which contains a long passage named by modern scholars 'the Hymn of the Pearl': cf. B. Layton, *The Gnostic Scriptures* (London: SPCK, 1987), pp. 366-375.

Cyndy Hendershot (essay date 1993-95)

SOURCE: Hendershot, Cyndy. "The Return of the Repressed in M. R. James's *Martin's Close." University of Mississippi Studies in English* 11-12 (1993-95): 134-37.

[*In the following essay, Hendershot examines "Martin's Close" as an example of a tale in which the repressed memory returns as the imaginary mother in monstrous form.*]

In "Dialectic of Fear," Franco Moretti suggests that within the literature of terror, the repressed memory of the imaginary phase returns "disguised as a monster."[1]

Therefore, terror literature, or Gothic literature, "*expresses* the unconscious content and at the same time *hides* it" (Moretti 103). Moretti further argues that to represent the monster as a female means little distortion of the unconscious content (104). Within the imaginary phase it is the mother who represents the values which the symbolic order forces the subject to repress. Thus "the return of the repressed" Moretti discusses is the return of the imaginary mother (98). Moretti discusses this theory in relation to *Dracula* and *Frankenstein:* I submit that this theory may be applied to most supernatural beings which haunt Gothic texts. "The return of the repressed" may thus be applied to ghosts as well as to the monsters which manifest themselves in *Dracula* and *Frankenstein.*

In this essay I will examine M. R. James's ghost story **"Martin's Close"** as an example of "the return of the repressed." Within this story imaginary experience is embodied in Ann Clark, a woman who returns from the dead after being murdered by her lover, George Martin. I propose that both Ann and her ghost represent imaginary experience repressed by both Martin and the seventeenth-century English society in which he lives. Although the story reveals imaginary experience in Ann, Ann's ghost, and Ann and Martin's relationship, it also conceals the threat posed by imaginary experience to the symbolic order because the imaginary mother is portrayed as a threat only to those who attempt to transgress symbolic law.

Several aspects of Ann Clark's character make it possible to read her as a representative of the imaginary order. Ann is described as retarded, "one to whom Providence had not given the full use of her intellects."[2] In Lacanian theory, the imaginary phase is an experience prior to language, an experience dominated by identification and duality. The imaginary is a time when the libidinal flow is directed towards everything, and the child is incapable of making distinctions between itself and its mother's body, or itself and any objects around it. The imaginary order offers an alternative to symbolic culture because it posits a radical androgyny and bisexuality. The imaginary infant has no concept of sexual difference, or any type of difference. Because the imaginary continues to coexist along with the symbolic when the infant enters the symbolic, it continues to exist as an alternative to phallocentric culture.

Although the imaginary continues to exist, it is repressed in the subject and, as Julliet Mitchell notes, "can only be secondarily acquired in a distorted form."[3] Thus if we read Ann Clark as a representative of imaginary experience, her mental retardation may be read as a symbolic interpretation of the imaginary. To the symbolic order, which is structured by language and institutions, Ann may appear retarded. Because psychoanalytic theory describes the imaginary in the trope of a

"prehistoric era" which exists prior to the culture of the oedipus complex, Ann Clark's inability to express herself in appropriate symbolic language links her with the imaginary order.

The inability of Ann to express herself in symbolic terms extends to the story itself. The story of Ann's murder and return as a ghost is something which seems to defy language. At the beginning of the story, the narrator asks what he should be told about Ann's story. His friend, the rector, replies: "I haven't the slightest idea" (72). Furthermore, the account of Martin's trial is not published until a century later, and even then only in longhand form. Therefore, the difficulty of expressing the story in language is emphasized and links Ann's story to the imaginary because imaginary experience is prelanguage and can be only unsatisfactorily expressed in language.

Ann's appearance further links her with the repressed memory of imaginary experience. She is described as being "very uncomely in her appearance" (78). Furthermore, a boy called to testify at Martin's trial describes Ann in monstrous terms: "she would stand and jump up and down and clap her arms like a goose . . . she was of such a shape that it could not be no one else" (87). Ann's monstrous appearance, both before her death and after, connects her with Moretti's theory of "the return of the repressed." Because the imaginary order poses a threat to the symbolic, it must be portrayed as monstrous. It must, as Moretti argues, literally frighten the reader into accepting the dominant values of the society (107). Thus Ann's monstrous appearance combined with her supposed retardation provoke fear and disgust in the reader rather than attraction and identification.

Furthermore, the threat of Ann's ghost is presented as being a threat only to Martin, a subject who attempts to transgress symbolic law in his relationship with Ann. The story links Martin and Ann's relationship to imaginary experience in several ways. Martin and Ann communicate through music rather than spoken language. The prosecuting attorney at Martin's trial comments that Martin and Ann had a signal for their meetings. He states that Martin "should whistle the tune that was played at the tavern: it is a tune, as I am informed, well known in that country, and has a burden, '*Madam, will you walk, will you talk with me?*'" (78). Thus even though the content of the song has symbolic signification, Martin and Ann rely on music to communicate. This coincides with Silverman's contention that music "images the fusion of mother and child" and thus recalls imaginary experience.[4] Therefore, Martin and Ann's relationship may be said to invoke imaginary pleasure in that it eschews language, the cornerstone of the symbolic order.

Martin and Ann's relationship further suggests the imaginary because it undermines conventional hierarchical relationships. In the symbolic the subject is encouraged to identify with one position; in the imaginary the infant identifies with a variety of positions. Martin and Ann ignore class hierarchies in their relationship. Within the symbolic their relationship would be one of master/slave. Martin, a gentleman, would never meet Ann, a poor, retarded woman, on equal terms. The story, however, suggests that Ann and Martin's relationship is one of equals. Martin asks Ann to dance at a public party, and their meetings appear to be well known to everyone in the village. Therefore, their relationship undermines the master/slave hierarchy and posits equality between men and women and between people of different social classes.

Ultimately, however, Martin succumbs to the pressures of the symbolic order. He ends his relationship with Ann in order to enter into an arranged marriage with "a young gentlewoman of that country, one suitable every way to his own condition . . . such an arrangement was on foot that seemed to promise him a happy and a reputable living" (79). Martin thus decides to abandon his desire for imaginary pleasure (embodied in his relationship with Ann) for a position fully within the symbolic. He gives up his notion of woman as equal and opts for woman as commodity, the view of woman encouraged by the symbolic order. The arranged marriage posits a woman as "pure exchange value," what Luce Irigaray calls the virginal woman in phallocentric society.[5] In Martin and Ann's relationship, the phallocentric economy does not intrude on their pleasure, but with Martin's decision to be a "respectable citizen," he begins to view women only as commodities.

Martin tries to murder his attraction to the imaginary through the murder of Ann. However, his repressed desire for imaginary experience comes back to haunt him. Ann's ghost does not threaten him physically, it only reminds him of his desire by singing the song which served as their signal. Ultimately, however, Ann's ghost does destroy Martin because it is used as evidence in his murder trial. But although other people see and hear Ann's voice, its threat is directed only at Martin. Martin is thus condemned by the symbolic order for flirting with imaginary experience. His executed body is interned in "Martin's Close," a bit of land "with quickset on all sides, and without any gates or gap leading into it" (72). Martin is thus presented as an example of what flirting with imaginary desire will lead to, death and isolation from the community. The story to some extent supports this interpretation of Martin and Ann's story through its title: **"Martin's Close"** suggests the "moral" lesson to be learned from Ann and Martin's actions.

"Martin's Close" thus both reveals and cloaks imaginary experience. The imaginary returns, but in a monstrous form. Although, as Moretti suggests, the supernatural female is more threatening because it recalls more directly the imaginary mother, the subversive qualities associated with Ann are undermined because they threaten only Martin. The danger of Ann's ghost lies in the "evidence" it provides for symbolic law. Thus, to a certain extent, the radical alternative posited in the imaginary is co-opted by the symbolic. This co-option is evident in the judge's pronouncement to Martin that "I hope to God . . . that she [Ann's ghost] *will* be with you by day and by night till an end is made of you" (89). Ann returns embodying repressed imaginary experience, but ultimately she is transformed into a weapon in the arsenal of symbolic law.

Notes

1. Franco Moretti, "Dialectic of Fear," *Signs Taken for Wonders: Essays in the Sociology of Literary Forms,* trans. Susan Fischer, et al. (New York, 1988), p. 103.

2. M. R. James, "Martin's Close," *More Ghost Stories of an Antiquary* (New York, 1988), p. 77.

3. Julliet Mitchell, *Psychoanalysis and Feminism: Freud, Reich, Laing and Women* (New York, 1974), p. 404.

4. Kaja Silverman, *The Acoustic Mirror: The Female Voice in Psychoanalysis and Cinema* (Indianapolis, 1988), p. 96.

5. Luce Irigaray, *This Sex Which is Not One,* trans, Catherine Porter. (Ithaca, 1985), p. 186.

Martin Hughes (essay date January 1995)

SOURCE: Hughes, Martin. "Murder of the Cathedral: A Story by M. R. James." *Durham University Journal* 87, no. 1 (January 1995): 73-98.

[*In the following essay, Hughes discusses the complex moral history explored by the central character in "The Stalls of Barchester Cathedral."*]

Introduction

Can the Church—or any institution which claims to possess *episcope* or moral authority—be genuinely reconstructed and renewed to face new challenges? Or do those who attempt reconstruction really murder the institution to which they are supposedly committed? They may be accused of murder in one of two ways: either because they welcome warmly too many outside ideas, that is ideas which the institution did not create; or else because, by contrast, their view of authority is so exclusive and narrow-minded that outside ideas are rigorously purged, even though they are needed. One strong influence which drew James into the problem of Christian authority and classical ideas, ideas which were both new and old, was Charles Reade's *The Cloister and the Hearth;* James's own views form a more reflective version of the fierce pro-classical rhetoric which Reade puts into the mouth of Fra Colonna.[1]

Church reconstructions[2] of the classical period attract accusations of the first kind: pagan ideas seem to be welcomed too warmly. Church reconstructions of the Gothic Revival attract accusations of the second kind: conformity is exalted too much and significant works of art are destroyed if they do not conform to the Revival's authoritarian ideals. This range of problems, which had been canvassed much in architectural debate,[3] is addressed and put into wider moral context in M. R. James's story **'The Stalls of Barchester Cathedral'**, published as part of **More Ghost Stories** in 1911. This story splendidly fulfils one of the functions of antiquarian stories, which is to illustrate moral history. One of my purposes is to display the complex moral history which the central character explores.

A degree of factual accuracy was claimed by James for the physical reconstructions he describes—the Cathedrals of his imagination are, he says, 'blends of Canterbury, Salisbury and Hereford'.[4] But it is significant that this claim is not quite accurate.

This is a story about a scholar—one of James's collection of other selves—who, under the influence of the ideas he studies, resorts to murder; the destruction of his victim reflects the extensive destruction to be wrought in the Cathedral. The scholarship for which James stands has both its risks and its uses.[5] Kenneth Clark makes clear how scholarship was, in the early days of the Revival,[6] tangled up with fantasy in the retrieval and resurrection of ideas which seemed to have been abandoned for good. Heine's definition of Romanticism[7]—*die Wiedererweckung der Poesie des Mittelalters, wie sie sich in dessen Liedern, Bild-und Bauwerken, in Kunst und Leben manifestiert hatte*—is cited by Clark: *mutatis mutandis*,[8] it fits the Gothic movement in Britain fairly well, reminding us that this was a resurrection of ideas which had moral as well as aesthetic impact; and therefore badly needed the restraint and balance of mind which comes from genuine scholarship.[9]

It is also a story about moral authority in decline. At the beginning of the story the Church stands as a great but weakened institution: Dr Haynes, the central character, is trying in his writing to defend Episcopacy—the system by which the Church exercises authority over its members; and also, by desperate measures, attempting to rescue *episcope,* the authority of the Church, from the threat posed to it by long-standing habits of inaction among the Church's own leaders. The story's portrait of the Church, as an institution alternating between useless inertia and desperate efforts at reconstruction, contrasts

very sharply with the ideas of Victorian piety,[10] whereby the Church and its worship bring heaven, with its freedom from change and death, down to earth. The authority of the Church's scripture does survive, though it survives in a disturbing form: the story meditates on some words of St Paul about failure of restraint.

Haynes—the name means 'enclosures' and suits one who lives and works in a Cathedral Close;[11] perhaps there is also some hint of a mind trapped—is destroyed in his turn and by his destruction the flaws in *episcope* are exposed even more painfully. But in the end of this bitter story a ray of hope appears.

Murderous Thoughts and Significant Names

The name 'Barchester' is significant because it invites a comparison with the Church of Trollope's Barchester, where the same problem of long-standing inertia challenged by suspect forms of activism appears; from this comparison the bitter aspect of James's attitude to the Church begins to merge. Moreover, the critical situation which exists in Barchester is illustrated by the name of Haynes's victim.

Trollope deals with many episodes of ambition but one such episode, towards the beginning of *Barchester Towers,* is especially relevant. Here Archdeacon Grantly discovers in himself something like a longing for the death of his sick father, whom he hopes to succeed as Bishop. Since he is not without moral qualities, he is immediately distressed by his discovery: and eventually distressed because, since his father does not die before the government changes, he loses his preferment by a matter of a short time. Grantly's self-discovery is recalled by the problem facing Haynes towards the beginning of **'The Stalls of Barchester Cathedral'**, set in the same place some forty years earlier. Haynes's predicament is very like Grantly's: believing with good reason that he would do a good job if he became Archdeacon, he finds the job held obstinately by a much older and quite incompetent incumbent; moreover he himself is no longer young and might be passed over if he canot get the job soon. Taking desperate measures, he not only murders his predecessor but also founds the system which we encounter at the opening of Trollope's chronicles, whereby the ineffectuality of the Bishop (perhaps already the elder Grantly) in the affairs of Barchester is partly remedied by the energy of the Archdeacon. His display of energy allows him to convince himself that by arranging a murder he had 'acted for the best'—a key phrase in his diary (though the phrase appears half scratched-out: in the end he could not believe it).

Trollope's Church has grown complacent amidst its riches but has not been corrupted finally: its better members, like Harding and Arabin, begin to recover the higher moral ground; and even the worldly and aggressive Archdeacon Grantly has not, as the scene mentioned shows, really lost his conscience or his sensitivity. By comparison, James's Church is one where Haynes, one of its leading members, solves his problem by resort to murder. The bitterness of James's story is the greater because there is no recovery or advance to higher ground: Haynes never repents; and if the Churchmen of later days take note of his crime they merely conceal it.

It is worth observing the nature of the moral damage which threatens both Grantly and Haynes, especially worth observing that its nature is difficult to explain. There is nothing wrong with hoping that someone who is plainly dying, or who has pathetically lost many faculties, will die soon. Again, there is nothing wrong with hoping that a cherished ambition for personal advancement will be achieved. But it is hard to explain, from a balanced and rational point of view, why these two hopes should not be combined in the same mind at the same time, supposing that the death will lead to the ambition's achievement: it seems, from this point of view, quite logical to let anyone hope for an acceptable means to an acceptable end. But, as Grantly instinctively knew and as Haynes could not understand, the truth of the situation is more subtle than this point of view suggests. There is something wrong with the two hopes in combination even when there is nothing wrong with them by themselves. It would have been implausible to have Grantly, in a tense and emotional moment, think this point out by a rational process: instead he resorts to prayer—this being one of the few moments where one of Trollope's clerics prays from the heart. At such a moment there is a risk that someone who used purely rational processes would go severely wrong, as Haynes did.

It is important to note that Haynes's estimate of himself, that he is a strong-minded man, not one to be misled by emotion or imagination, is implicitly accepted by the story. The implication, a very disturbing one, is that his strength has become a weakness and that it is possible to be misled, in some very significant sense, by the strict and unaided operation of reason.

His victim's name is Pulteney, the name of a leading eighteenth century politician and antagonist of Robert Walpole. This historical Pulteney[12] had scholary interests and lived to be eighty, looking 'like an old raven'; but his political career had been effectively finished when, at a moment in 1742 when he might have succeeded Walpole, he permitted himself to be 'kicked upstairs' into the House of Lords. His reputation suffered badly: according to his detractors he had seemed to be a 'patriot' and a reformer but had forgotten his principles once an earldom was on offer.

So the name which James chooses recalls the immobilism, the refusal to implement or seriously to consider change, which blights the Church in those earlier part of Trollope's Barchester Chronicles; at one point Trollope, like James, uses a play on names to underline the survival of questionable features of the eighteenth century: the obnoxious Obadiah Slope is a descendant of Tristram Shandy's Dr Slop,[13] the family having used the interval to make its name more genteel. Much more savagely, James uses Pulteney's name to suggest that the eighteenth-century system, where people could be removed from power but left with some honour, has broken down into something far worse. The real Pulteney was kicked upstairs; James's fictional Pulteney is thrown downstairs by a conspiracy between Haynes and a sinister servant.

Pulteney's very name tells us something of what he represents. But to see what Haynes represents we have to turn to the intellectual pursuits which he has used to distract himself before his career advanced. These pursuits show that he was rooted—just like Pulteney himself, presumably—in the education system of the eighteenth century, which was based on classical literature. But Haynes, like James, was an explorer of unfamiliar areas of that literature: perhaps his response to what he found moved him, more than it would have moved anyone of Pulteney's generation, away from his roots and towards new modes of thought.

The narrator records the obituary to Haynes in the *Gentleman's Magazine*.[14] At the time of his death he was trying without success to find a publisher for his *Defence of Episcopacy;* but he had already published a study of Joshua's life and a translation of Valerius Flaccus.

HAYNES'S SCHOLARLY PURSUITS: THE HERO ALLIED WITH A WOMAN

The two ancient books on which Haynes worked both concern heroes, the Israelite Joshua and the Minyan Jason, who achieved important work for their people in a violent clash with people of other cultures, against extreme odds and with the co-operation of women, Rahab and Medea, at crucial points. The Book of Joshua concerns the fulfilment of God's marvellous promises to Israel and opens with an exhortation to Joshua and the Israelites in which God three times insists that they must be strong and of good courage. The Vulgate, which Haynes no doubt consulted, seems to capture the message well with the words '*Confortare et esto robustus*'.[15] This means that not only must they face great odds but also they must be robust, indeed ruthless, in their treatment of those who bar their way. Just as the Romans' reflection on the expansion of their empire founded the idea of just war, so the Israelites' reflection on their expansion into the Promised Land, a reflection expressed in the Books of Joshua and Deuteronomy, is the true foundation of the idea of holy war: that is of the suspension of normal ethical relations at the express command of God and for a profound ethical purpose. This makes *Joshua* morally disturbing, one of the most disturbing parts of biblical literature. Haynes became a morally disturbed man.

That Joshua should have advanced his cause with the aid of Rahab the harlot raises certain difficulties which were felt in ancient times. A modern commentator[16] remarks that she is merely one of several Old Testament characters who do good work though they begin from a 'despicable' occupation: for instance, King David had been a shepherd. But this remark is an unconvincing attempt to minimise the difficulty caused by Rahab's function in the story: prostitution may not be the only occupation which is despised but on conventional views of morality, ancient or modern, prostitution surely contaminates the personality of those engaged in it and so makes them personally despicable in a way that few other occupations could. If Haynes appreciated the difficulty in this passage of scripture and came, by his reflections upon it, to the conclusion that good work— God's work, perhaps—could be done not only through people of despicable occupation but through despicable people, then he might have felt himself warranted to approach the sinister Jane Lee, Pulteney's servant.

Haynes's acting as he supposes out of loyalty to God's Church, which cannot stand much more of Pulteney's incompetence, recreates or at least parodies the co-operation of Joshua with Rahab and of Jason with Medea by suborning Lee, who removes a stair rod and so causes Pulteney's fatal fall. Everyone believes it was an accident and Lee secretly collects money from Haynes, sending a blackmailing letter which the narrator finds. Lee has no love for Haynes but she claims to be concerned for someone else, 'her man': concern for her man was Medea's motive; and Rahab sheltered Joshua's spies in return for the protection of her family.

Medea is a figure of classical legend and, as the furniture of the Cathedral is to show, Haynes was brought up in a kind of Christianity which was profoundly influenced by classical literature; he was drawn to the byways of that literature, particularly to the story of Jason and Medea contained in Valerius Flaccus' sole work, *Argonautica*. What would the moral influence of this neglected but impressive poem be?[17]

WITHOUT FEAR OR SHAME: THE HERO ON THE VERGE OF CRIME

Valerius's personal thinking about his famous subject are best revealed—as far as the unfinished state of his story permits[18]—in his many revisions of his principal source, the Greek *Argonautica* of Apollonius Rhodius,

revisions which throw light on the moral history of paganism. The development of moral thought which appears from a comparison between Valerius and Apollonius is one of the features which would have interested Haynes, who was, according to his obituary, a 'spirited and scholarly' translator. Valerius approves of those who refuse to fear dangers; senses that the gods and our prayers to the gods may be vain or misleading, may even add to the moral complexity which the universe already has; treats with sympathy those caught in moral dilemmas and suggests that they may sometimes, if they are only on the verge of crime, rightly avoid retribution.

To begin with the refusal to fear: Apollonius has the seer Idmon join the crew of Argo even though he knew from the omens that he would not return from the voyage; his motive is to avoid the bad opinion of his people. Valerius gives him a more properly moral reason: '*turpe viro timuisse futura*—for a man to have become fearful of what will happen is a disgrace'. The refusal to fear then extends into the realm of morally dangerous actions. In both versions of the story, Jason addresses his crew on arrival in Cochis, where King Aeetes guards the golden fleece which he has come to reclaim. In Apollonius he asks his crew to put their trust in the moral law—a very misplaced trust, considering Aeetes' nature—and the speech shows something of the weakness which makes him constantly dependent on being rescued by others. In Valerius the speech is much shorter and stronger:[19]

> . . . Mens experienda tyranni.
> Adnuet ipse, reor: neque inexorabile certe
> quod petimus: sin vero preces et dicta superbus
> respuerit, iam nunc animos firmate repulsae,
> quaque via patriis referamus vellera terris
> stet potius: rebus semper pudor absit in artis.

> The King's mind must be tested. I think he will agree; what we ask is surely not unreasonable. However, if he is arrogant, if he scorns our requests and all we have to say, begin now to set your minds firm: we are not to be refused. Rather: whatever the way may be to bring the Fleece back to our native land, let that way stand before us. In tight corners there is never room for shame!

The exhortation '*animos firmate*!' is echoed in one of Haynes's most frequent diary entries 'I must be firm'; and the phrases '*turpe viro timuisse futura*' and '*pudor absit rebus in artis*' both fit very precisely the state of mind which Haynes must have been in when he became determined to act against Pulteney.

These passages in Valerius represent not an amoral attitude but a sense of the complexity of moral life. Like most pagan poets Valerius has his gods add to that complexity rather than resolve it easily. His Medea becomes so angry (VII, 294) with (the disguised) Venus for plunging her into insoluble difficulties that she wants to scratch her face.[20] Valerius' positive moral belief is that courage to fight our way out of our problems is a primary virtue. The example of this virtue which he most has in mind can be seen from his opening passage, where he praises the new Flavian regime in Rome. This had been established by a *coup d'état* which was to set a terrible precedent: but the *coup* also destroyed a previous regime which had made Rome's claim to moral and religious leadership of the world seem utterly preposterous. Valerius presumably valued this leadership, since he was an officer of the national religion.[21] Presumably he accepted that the nation and its position in the world had to be restored, *rebus in artis,* by drastic means.

Medea, Aeetes' daughter and a drastic character, is the key to Jason's success in all versions of the story. Apollonius motivates her solely with passion; the tragedy which we foresee is that love becomes murderous hatred. Apollonius' portrayal of Medea is extremely powerful and vivid. But, conformably to the traditional view of Medea, he uses the power of his portrait to make the moral questions which his story raises less pressing. It is Medea's passionate and sometimes ruthless actions which move the story forward but the decisions she takes are not of a moral character, both because she is so fiercely in love and because she has lost her own moral roots in her fascination with the alien Greeks: she refers to morality only to expose the fact that she is not guided by it.[22] She is not so much faced with a moral dilemma as captured by forces stronger than herself.

By contrast, Valerius' Medea involves his readers in genuine moral dilemmas, both those faced by his characters and those raised by his theology. His main achievement is to give Medea not just an overwhelming passion but a love which grows slowly and grows partly for moral reasons, as she becomes alienated from the cruelty and treachery of her father Aeetes, a '*trux tyrannus*', and cannot face seeing Jason die. The tragedy which we foresee is that a partership built on foundations with which we have moral sympathy ends in moral evil, as Medea murders her children after Jason divorces her. The problems of the characters merge into problems with the gods: there is something distressingly ambivalent about Jupiter's denunciations of Medea's disloyalty: he, the guardian of the moral order, decrees that her disloyal plans will succeed.[23]

And we are not reassured by a fact known to us but not to Jason and typical of Valerius' complicated moral universe; that some of Aeetes' truculence is caused by the appearance in a dream[24] of the very being to whom Jason prays for assistance, the ghost of his cousin Phrixus on whose account the Minyans first lost the golden fleece and on whose helpfulness he counts. Valerius, the pillar of Roman religion, has an attitude to prayer very unfamiliar to Christians: it is often wasted breath, 'scat-

tered to the winds';[25] and the gods sometimes deceive. It is interesting (partly by contrast with Grantly) that Haynes, who has studied this pagan work so closely, resorts to serious prayer solely in his last and most desperate days—and unavailingly. By this time the sentence has been passed upon him that, in the horrifying words of Psalm 109, his prayer should be turned to sin.

The final scene in Valerius' unfinished work has Jason in trouble as the Argonauts demand that Medea be surrendered to her pursuing brother Apsyrtus. To his credit, Jason's principal emotion in this tight place is, despite his earlier insistence, '*pudor*'—shame at the thought of betraying Medea: the moral basis of his relationship with her is thus acknowledged. But we know from common versions of the story that the only way which Jason and Medea could find to express their loyalty to each other was a way which involved the treacherous murder of Apsyrtus. In Apollonius the murder is another expression of Medea's magnificently ruthless nature. Valerius' text ends when Apsyrtus has made his demand and where we expect him to pay with his life: and it seems as if Valerius is about to present his murder as the only means for Jason and Medea to show their mutual loyalty. That loyalty is reemphasised in the poem's final (rather moving) lines:[26]

> Haeret, et hinc prasens pudor, hinc decreta suorum
> dura premunt. utcumque tamen mulcere gementem
> temptat et ipse gemens et dictis temperat iras:
> 'mene aliquid metuisse putas? me talia velle?'

> He hesitated; from one side innermost conscience, from the other the relentless insistence of his companions press in upon him. But somehow he tries to calm her passion with passion of his own and with his words he soothes her anger. 'Do you think that I was afraid of anything? That I would agree to any such thing?'

The death of Apsyrtus, presented not as a ruthless act by the barbarian Medea but as the result of Jason's desperate effort to show Medea the loyalty and love which she deserves, would be very different from its counterpart in Apollonius' story—something of more real-life importance to civilised readers like Haynes and of much more concern to philosophers. It illustrates the idea that our very efforts to preserve our moral integrity can actually lead us to break our normal ethical bonds: which is perhaps even more disturbing than either the suggestion of Apollonius that there can be something superb about those who do break them, or the suggestion of *Joshua* that they may be broken legitimately, for the deep purposes of God.

Valerius has his own ideas, interesting in their own right for the purposes of moral history, about divine purposes and divine justice. As part of this justice, the worst murderers are haunted and tormented by their victims. Mopsus, the other Argonaut seer, explains these matters after the night-battle in which the Argonauts have, by misunderstanding, killed their friend King Cyzicus and his men: but, by contrast with his counterpart in Apollonius, he explains them in a philosophical manner; in Apollonius Mopsus simply reads the signs which the gods send.[27] In Valerius's account we hear that the dead have the right to take revenge but that those who kill unwillingly or by savage mischance can be paralysed not so much by the revenge of the dead as by their own remorse, remorse which the Argonauts now suffer: but really they were only 'on the verge of crime', *proxima culpae*.[28] In this situation the pangs of conscience can be quieted and must be quieted when there is necessary work to be done: and in order to quiet them Mopsus leads a ceremony in which the regretful killers offer gifts which the gentle snakes who serve the dead collect; with this demonstration that peace between the two groups is restored, remorse is dissipated. The impact of Mopsus' philosophy on someone in a tight corner could be quite powerful. Haynes, insisting that he 'acted for the best' and remembering what he had read and translated, must have assured himself both that he had killed very unwillingly and that the situation which necessitated Pulteney's death was really a kind of appalling bad luck or mischance, a *fors saeva*. At any rate he was able, like the Argonauts, to put remorse aside and to dedicate himself to his necessary work.

The *Book of Joshua* may have convinced Haynes that God sometimes, in matters of importance to His government of the world, sets our ethical obligations aside. But at the time of the murder he acts more in the self-reliant spirit of the Argonauts, abandoning conscience or shame, once he is in a tight corner, and disdaining to fear what might happen; only as his determined spirit is tested to destruction does he, by contrast with Grantly, begin, unavailingly, to pray. He has seized on pagan ideas of self-reliance and sought to use them for the needs of the Church. His job as a scholar was to sympathise with his subject: but sympathy has become a kind of conversion.

After the Archdeaconry papers are in order, Haynes discovers a new enthusiasm: the Cathedral itself. It is difficult to see what could have come from this enthusiasm on the part of a dedicated administrator with a restless passion for work other than reconstruction: and reconstruction at that time would have had to be Gothic. All we know of his plans is that they extended to music and were obstructed by the organist, who had been in place since 1786 and was presumably too old (like Dr Ayloff in 'An Episode') to favour changes; but it is likely that Haynes was interested in the fabric as well as the music and that some of the changes which had befallen Barchester by the narrator's time had been set in motion by Haynes. But has Haynes's own career shown that, at all events, these changes were necessary

to avoid the spread to others of the corruption which afflicted him? Was Haynes's embrace of pagan ideas about self-reliant action partly to be blamed on the classical Cathedral, which had been furnished so as to tell all comers that pagan ideas are not dead? The story suggests these questions as it moves on from Haynes's private scholarship to the Cathedral itself and so to the arena of long-running, highly-charged public debates.

THE CLASSICAL CATHEDRAL AND THE LONG DEBATE

In James's time many would have believed that classical Cathedral furnishing embodied moral dangers. The zeal of many nineteenth-century people, 'fired by Evangelicals and Tractarians alike, and fuelled by Macaulay, deplored the corrupt, easy-going spiritual outlook of the Georgian Church in whose tangible legacy they all too readily saw classical paganism'.[29] This tangible legacy was certainly denounced: for instance, in John Britton's survey of Winchester Cathedral we read:

> Nearly facing the pulpit is the Bishop's stall, a very incongruous and absurd piece of workmanship: like the screen, it is formed in Roman or classical style and *therefore* becomes an unsightly object.

The emphasis is mine: still, Britton's strength of feeling against classical work within a Christian context—'barbarous disfigurement' as he calls it a few pages later,[30] in a turn of phrase comparable to the Prince of Wales's 'monstrous carbuncle'—is unmistakeable. James in his turn sees barbarity in the way distinguished classical work was (as a later writer says) 'unceremoniously ejected',[31] broken and degraded so that its pieces were made into cupboards and the like.

Before agreeing too readily with James's view of the Revival, we should note that drastic reconstructions were sometimes unavoidable because the previous period had been one of sheer neglect.[32] But for the Victorians' efforts major parts of our church heritage would, by this century, have fallen into disuse or even ruin: and lack of commitment to the buildings implies lack of commitment to the religion in whose name cathedrals are built. The nineteenth-century reaction was based on renewed commitment, moral as well as aesthetic: it was a return to the Gothic, feudal value of unreserved faith and loyalty.

Neglect of Gothic buildings had been based on dislike and fear of Gothic values: unreserved faith had seemed like unrestrained fanaticism. The existence of this fear showed how moral and aesthetic questions had begun to mingle well before the Gothic Revival: James was contributing to a long-running debate. England in the Caroline and Georgian periods had for the second time—the first was the Perpendicular period—turned away from the decoration and elaboration of Continental styles; and for a second time this was a statement both of political isolation—created first by the Hundred Years' War and then by the Reformation—and also of moral superiority over those who would not accept English ideas of order and restraint. When John Evelyn called Gothic architecture 'fantastical and licentious'[33] he was evidently accusing it of encouraging departure both from truth and from moral restraint: so of posing a moral threat.

To people of that epoch Gothic seemed to be 'licentious' and morally threatening because it seemed to follow no set rules of the kind which Vitruvius laid down for classical architecture. Some might suppose that without explicit, rationalised rules the idea of restraint fails even to make sense: in the absence of explicit rules how can we know when restraint is required of us? The counterpart to the idea of licentiousness is the idea of chastity, a kind of restraint: and the word 'chaste' was indeed used in the same epoch as a term of aesthetic approval.[34] The sense of moral threat, of danger to good customs posed by a strong alien force, was increased by the fact that the hostile monarchies of Catholic Europe seemed to have replaced Gothic with even more licentious forms of display in the style we call Baroque. According to one modern account, Baroque churches were theatrical, meant to arouse emotion centring round the cult of saints: but later, 'when, in due time, the Catholic countries experienced a reaction against the emotional extravagances of Baroque, the two sides drew together again architecturally'.[35] This account faces us once again with the opposition between extravagance and restraint: James's story has more to say about restraint, as the scriptural passages it uses will show.

Not that the mingling of moral and artistic questions, the mingling which helps to make antiquarian stories into moral histories, is confined to church buildings or of interest only to Christians. Lord Palmerston's comments[36] on the long duration and high passions of architectural debates—though he was thinking of debates which concerned Government buildings, not churches—rings just as true in our time (when so much controversy has centred on the Prince of Wales's architectural commitments) as in his. In time, political passions began to overshadow religious ones: Gothic, which had once been praised because it was Catholic, began to be praised because it was old enough to have escaped contamination by the spirit of capitalism.[37]

James's own dislike of the Gothic Revival is clear enough. This dislike has to be set against his respect for genuinely medieval art. Perhaps he would, considering his antiquarian bent, have agreed with the modern comment that 'medieval art is a script'[38] and have thought that enthusiasts were so carried away by their plans to use the script in their own cause that they forgot to read it. There is every difference between the antiquarian

view, where the past is simply to be studied and understood, and the revivalist view, which makes an attempt to give the past a new lease of life: and manages, according to James, to produce ugly and incongruous results. These results have appeared in Barchester since Haynes's time:

> When you enter the choir of Barchester Cathedral now, you pass through a screen of metal and coloured marbles, designed by Sir Gilbert Scott, and find yourself in what I must call a very bare and odiously furnished place. The stalls are modern, without canopies. The places of the dignitaries and the names of the prebends have fortunately been allowed to survive and are to be seen inscribed on small brass plates affixed to the stalls. The organ is in the triforium and what is seen of the case is Gothic. The reredos and its surroundings are like every other.
>
> Careful engravings of 100 years ago show a very different state of things. The organ is on a massive classical screen. The stalls are also classical and very massive. There is a baldacchino of wood over the altar, with urns upon its corners. Further east is a solid altar screen, classical in design, of wood, with a pediment, in which is a triangle surrounded by rays, enclosing certain Hebrew letters in gold. Cherubs contemplate these. There is a pulpit with a great sounding-board at the eastern end of the stalls on the north side and there is a black and white marble pavement.

The pulpit, and ideas associated with it, are to play a major part in **'An Episode of Cathedral History'**, James's second treatment of the themes of **'Barchester'**, where his satire on the Gothic Revival is even more bitter. Even in **'Barchester'** the unusually scathing toe of the usually urbane narrator's voice in all its references to the Revival is plain enough, as is the emphatic, triple and favourable use of the word 'classical'. James's evident belief that it is possible to create harmonious classical effects in a Christian setting contradicts the suspicion that classical Cathedrals were channels for vicious pagan ideas. But what is the evidence for his belief? Do the examples which he refers to in his Introduction bear him out?

In the next section I examine James's examples and consider the agents of Haynes's punishment. These are works of art which were incorporated into the Cathedral at the same time as the classical furniture but whose style is not classical but Dutch.

THE GOLDEN LETTERS AND THE GROTESQUE
CARVINGS: REALITY AND EXAGGERATION

These agents are certain carvings in the grotesque style, which were commissioned or accepted by Dean West, whose ideas gave a coherent plan to Barchester in its classical days. Around West's time in Barchester one element of barbaric local tradition evidently came to an end: that was the use of a specific tree, the Hanging Oak in the Holywood, as a public gibbet for murderers.

A local carver, John Austin, made some figures from the wood of the Hanging Oak: and these West, according to the record which Haynes finds, agreed to buy. The figures represent a cat and two demons, one in the state of a decomposing corpse and carrying a halter,[39] and one seated as if in judgement. These disquieting figures are complementary in West's system to the serene and reassuring golden letters, which must have formed the Name of God. The letters and the figures represent opposite poles, good and evil, heaven and hell. The story's overstatements exist to make that opposition stark and to suggest how, from the point of view of Christian classical art, that stark opposition is interestingly, perhaps truthfully, dealt with.

Haynes himself provides a rather mannered description of the figures for the *Gentleman's Magazine:* at this stage he regards them just as part of the Cathedral and he is entirely and complacently comfortable with them. The idea of living without uneasiness in the presence of demonic forms can take a less complacent and more thoughtful form, that which West presumably intended and which James himself offers in **'An Episode of Cathedral History'**: evil is contained by being organised into the system which is dominated by the Name and presence of God. In 'An Episode' the disease-bearing demon is trapped beneath the great pulpit—*'ibi cubavit lamia'*—harmless under the weight of rational preaching until the Revivalists release it.

James states that Barchester is a blend of Canterbury, Salisbury and Hereford. This statement can be borne out in several ways, but not borne out perfectly. The 'unceremonious ejection' of the beautiful classical choir stalls from Canterbury has been mentioned: work from the office of Sir Gilbert Scott, whose name James mentions with such distaste, replaced them. But revolutions in taste have continued: at Hereford 'the former screen, designed by Scott and made from wrought iron, brass, copper and cut stones, was in 1966 sent to Coventry, i.e. the basement of the Museum there . . . a great loss to Hereford.'[40] At Salisbury, Scott left the stalls—some of which are medieval, but have been described as 'largely new'[41] without canopies, as in Barchester (the present canopies were added in 1913-14); and he created a reredos and another of his metal choir-screens, which have now in their turn been ejected. At Hereford, the stalls of 1375 survive, though reduced in number; nineteenth-century brass plates, such as James mentions, have been added. Both Hereford and Salisbury had black and white marble floors during their classical period; Canterbury had contrasting shades of grey.[42]

But the way James transforms fact into fiction—his models into Barchester—has an element of overstatement. The most important feature of Barchester which does not come from any of the three named sources is the organ-bearing classical screen: in all three real Ca-

thedrals the medieval screen either still survives, as at Canterbury, or survived until the Gothic Revival, as at Salisbury and Hereford.[43]

The relationship of the altar area at Barchester with its sources is a matter of judgement. Urns appear on the early eighteenth century baldacchino at Canterbury and on the reredos in eighteenth-century Hereford; moreover during most of the eighteeth century at Hereford and some of the eighteenth century at Canterbury there had been a 'glory' of rays above the altar, with the motif IHS (for Jesus).[44] It is clear that at Hereford there was also a dove (for the Holy Spirit) and that these symbols were on a rectangular background, which in turn was on an arc-shaped wooden pediment. Barchester uses the Name of God motif—which certainly was used in some real places with classical and Baroque furnishings—and encloses it, with its glory, in the triangle so characteristic of Greek temples, with cherubs to admire the effect. Neither Barchester's specific motif nor its triangle nor its cherubs come from any of the three stated sources. We may judge that this degree of departure from the sources is merely trivial; or that James deliberately chose to improve on his sources in order to emphasise the harmonious co-presence of themes deeply characteristic of Old Testament and of Greek culture. Because of the departure from sources in respect of the screen, I incline to the second of these judgements.

James goes beyond his sources to create the serenity of the system which the golden letters complete; and beyond them again, I think, to create—beyond what was really acceptable in Cathedral architecture—the infernal atmosphere surrounding the grotesque figures. Animal and demonic figures are common enough in the misericord carvings of the Middle Ages and sometimes appear in Cathdral churches where these 'forms of beasts and human heads [were] reminders of the surviving, if veiled, presence of the Germanic gods whose formal abandonment the Romanesque churches were intended to declare.'[45] But as the Middle Ages progressed the carved forms created in churches developed, at least in England, a strongly secular[46] and so more lighthearted nature—though Cathedral art continued to accept emaciated figures and skeletons: Britton mentions two at Salisbury and dwells on one at Winchester as an example of Christian humility.[47] But the specially horrific feature, the representation not just of emaciation but of putrescence, points, as the Barchester people understood, to a foreign, specifically to a Low Countries, style which in reality never quite influenced any real English church artist—as far as it influenced Austin, James's fictional artist. But no one seems to think that this foreign-influenced work is out of place: the infernal nature of the figures only adds to the impression of a completely realised classical whole and of a triumphant harmony which not even the evil embodied in the carved figures can overcome.

This impression is absolutely the reverse of Garbett's impression that strongly classical work could be admired only 'in another situation', outside the Cathedral; still more the reverse of Britton's impression that classical work in a medieval building results in a clash, amounting to 'barbarous disfigurement'. But in all the named Cathedrals there was less of a classical whole and therefore more possibility of a disfiguring clash than there was at Barchester: so was a Gothic Revival necessary, in the real world, to sweep the disfigurements away and to prevent pagan imagery from giving continuing life to the whole range of pagan ideas, including the pagan kind of self-reliance into which Haynes lurches? For James, the answer to this question is No: the attempt to sweep away all suspect ideas results in odious bareness.

If we are to exclude all imagery which is pagan or in any way dangerous, the exclusion must be enforced by an authority which is always vigilant against, one might say always at war with, images and ideas which are not reliably orthodox. At the aesthetic level, the result will surely be both the odious bareness of the Victorian Barchester Quire and the conventionality of the reredos: the works of art which are permitted will indeed be 'like every other'. The moral analogy to these works of art is an odious conformism.

The underlying and confidently Christian idea of Dean West's Barchester is that the opposite poles of good and evil belong to one universe, with the evil somehow subsumed into the good: even the carved demons fit into that universe, existing in their proper place under the symbol of God's presence. The import of this idea is that no other idea is irretrievably an enemy; symbols and imagery which have some evil in their origin are not necessarily cast out and may be treated gently: they can be, at any rate with due care and restraint, considered and adapted. Thus the spirit of classical Christian art may take the pleasantly relaxed form which James recalls (in **'An Episode'**) with his regretful reference to Wren's long-destroyed floral motifs at Salisbury. This spirit will lead to the indiscriminate and licentious acceptance of dangerous ideas only if some force corrupts it. In its pristine condition it is, as the story presents it, morally not vicious or destructive but confident and gentle; aesthetically not barbarous and clashing but pleasing and coherent. In this presentation we find the story's answer to the accusations, moral and aesthetic, which were raised against classical art in Christian contexts.

The force which produces corruption is the readiness, found in Haynes's desperate action against Pulteney, to abandon the classical demand for restraint. Restraint is a pagan virtue of which Haynes is reminded by a passage of Christian scripture.

'ONLY LET THE RESTRAINER BE OUT OF THE WAY!'

A letter congratulating Haynes on taking over from Pulteney refers to Pulteney as ὁκατέχων, a rather cruel reference (says the narrator) to the Restrainer 'who now letteth' in the *Second Epistle to the Thessalonians* ii, 1-8:

> Now we beseech you . . . that ye be not soon shaken in mind . . . as that the day of Christ is at hand . . . : for that day shall not come, except there be a falling away first, and that man of sin be revealed, the son of perdition; who opposeth and exalteth himself above all that is called God, or that is worshipped; so that he as God sitteth in the temple of God, showing himself that he is God. Remember ye not, that, when I was yet with you, I told you these things? And now ye know what witholdeth that he might be revealed in his time. For the mystery of iniquity doth already work: only he who now letteth will let until he be taken out of the way. And then shall that Wicked be revealed whom the Lord shall consume with the spirit of His mouth and shall destroy with the brightness of His coming.

The English of the Authorised Version—'he who now letteth will let until he be taken out of the way'—has rather too many words and slightly underestimates the sense of imminent doom which is in the Greek 'μόνον ὁκατέχων ἄρτι ἕως εκ μὲσου γένηται': 'only let the Restrainer, present now, be out of the way!' Though Paul is trying to calm his readers and to persuade them that the end of the age has not yet begun, he sets his discussion amid alarming references to tribulation and apostasy.

The quotation does not initiate the complete, dramatic fulfilment of Paul's prophecy but it is cruel and revealing in more ways than the letter-writer intended. The intended cruelty is to Pulteney: his only function, in the writer's opinion, was 'to let'—i.e. to restrain or impede; this opinion reassures Haynes and prompts him to keep the letter. But unintentionally the letter contains a suggestion cruel to Haynes, that he might resemble the wicked man, who 'sitteth in the temple' and practices deception—recall how well he impressed his colleagues. Though he had not, like Paul's Wicked Man, claimed to be God, he had not shrunk from sharing God's right to take life. There is an underlying cruelty or desperation in the way James prompts us, by his use of this passage, to think about the Church: perhaps the day when the wicked will deceive and possess it is steadily coming nearer, as the mystery of iniquity corrupts *episcope* at its heart.

The passage serves James's purposes because it originally prophesied the fall of the first classical civilisation and in this story points to the fall of the second. Paul accepts that the old order had contained important forces of restraint; the slow failure of these forces will, he believes, open the way for disaster extending well beyond the Christian community. Nor did events promptly refute him: within twenty years crisis of Nero's reign has unfolded; the Jews had been scattered by a fierce imperial war, the rule of law had been breached shockingly by the first persecution of the Christians[48] and government had changed hands in a convulsive series of *coups*.

Restraint is certainly a virtue whose roots in classical civilisation are deep. The mysterious, deceptive nature of the pagan oracles makes restraint, in the form of personal care and caution, necessary, even in the presence of divine guidance: for instance, Plato surely intends us, having surveyed the arguments of *Euthyphro* and *The Apology of Socrates,* to conclude that the questioning Socrates, with his inner voice of restraint,[49] was not only wiser than the forward Euthyphro but also more pious. And without powerful forces of restraint no one could look with confidence on the open-minded, philosophical aspect of classical civilisation: without restraint, speculative philosophy would, in practice, activate dangerous forms of fanaticism.

The virtue of restraint, since it has these roots, may seem to be linked profoundly with paganism. But the story suggests that it is still a needful virtue, and exactly the virtue which Haynes lacks. The classical Cathedral, by my arrangement above, stands, by contrast with the conformism of its successor, for openness of mind combined with confidence. This combination still depends, by the same logic as in ancient times, on powerful forces of restraint. And restraint still implies an element of personal care and caution in religious matters: but in the second classical age this care was exercised not because the oracles were deceptive but because, while the degenerate forms of Christian *episcope* were disgracefully inert, the prevailing form was simply moderate: itself an example of restraint.

Paul writes cryptically:[50] we can't be sure where he lays blame for the failure of restraint. But in the story, with its implied parallel between Pulteney's destruction by Haynes and the Cathedral's destruction by the Revivalists, the failure of restraint and the blame for it lies clearly within the Church itself. In the minds of the new, nineteenth-century leaders both in the Catholic and in the Protestant worlds, moderate forms of *episcope* were connected with laxity taken to the point of apostasy[51] and with liberalism taken to the point of paganism. So their purpose was to create a visibly renewed authority: itself a rejection of restraint—a rejection which invited conflict, drove doubters towards extremism and left the Christian consciousness (like Haynes's consciousness) intensely troubled. The Revival, whose overriding motive was to create church buildings which visibly proclaimed the authority of the Church,[52] served the purposes of the new leadership.

The story proceeds to argue that even divine justice, once restraint has failed, takes harsh and grotesque forms. Thus the belief of *II Thessalonians* in a visitation ('visitation' is one of the meanings of '*episcope*') which destroys the guilty is not rejected: but the 'brightness' of the visitation is that of a flame, not that of a new dawn. Paul probably hoped for a new dawn but this kind of hope is one which all subsequent Christians have had to moderate. But if the new dawn is not yet how do we avoid the harsher forms of justice? Surely we need to consider restoring the restraints of the old order: bringing classicism back.

I turn again to the grotesque persecutors which Haynes encounters.

EMBLEMS, CANTICLES, AND CATS

The people of Barchester see the Dutch style in Austin's carvings: and there is a Dutch genre whose central subject is divine love, but which often displays that love in grotesque guises.

Mario Praz, in his work on seventeenth century symbolism, mentions and evidently endorses the judgement that 'love poems and emblems are genuine national products, both literary and pictorial, of the Low Countries . . . a closer study of Dutch emblems would be worthwhile.'[53] Emblems are a combination of words (most often Latin verses) and pictures, often depicting animals. Emblem books—which came to deal with love as a religious theme and hence to deal more widely with religion and morals—were, for a time in the seventeenth century, quite popular in England, though little of the best work was home-grown. 'It was only during the last century', writes Praz, 'that the emblems of divine love found in England an illustrator who could equal the Flemish and Dutch artists, the last of whom was Jan Luyken.' Note 'Flemish and Dutch'—the genre was popular in Catholic Flanders as well as in Protestant Holland. Luyken published in Amsterdam in 1714: interestingly for our purposes, Praz notes that Luykens 'knows the foulness of the flabby flesh of bestial Body [and] the horror of the decomposition of tissues'[54]— though he usually concerned himself with more pleasant expressions of divine love.

The English illustrator Praz mentions here is Robert Cruikshank, who helped—his is already the humour of *Punch,* says Praz—to transmute the religious emblem into the modern political cartoon. Despite the use of learned languages emblems were, like the cartoons descended from them, a popular form, not intended only for those of high education.

The publishers of emblem books must have given employment to woodworkers (both woodcuts and copperplates were used) to produce their pictures: Austin was a woodcarver and might well have studied them, both for business and for edification. So here is the influence which gave those people of nineteenth-century Barchester people who knew about popular religious art of previous times the sense that the carvings were of Dutch workmanship. Austin evidently shared Luykens's interest in the 'decomposition of tissues'!

Praz remarks that the visual nature of emblems was meant to give them immediate impact but, on the other hand, 'emblematics, following in the track of hieroglyphics, aims at establishing . . . an esoteric language', a point taken up by Francis Quarles, the only English emblematist of any note, who calls his work 'Egyptian'.[55] This aspect of emblematics is highlighted when the verbal part of the message is concealed: Austin conceals his inside one of the figures which Haynes touches; and this aspect of Austin's work heightens our awareness that Haynes lives the last part of his life surrounded by a mystery which he cannot understand,[56] asking himself what his persecutor is 'trying to say'. His scholarship does not resolve his perplexity.[57]

The first contact with the persecutors comes in a scene of some comedy when Haynes is dozing through the *Magnificat.* Haynes's sleepiness indicates how comfortable he is, at least in the daytime when he can apply the anaesthetic of work, with the memory of his crime. Indeed, he has told himself in his diary—the narrator refers us back to this entry—that he awaits his *Nunc dimittis,* by which he means God's acknowledgement of his good work. (His treatment of Pulteney could be summed up by the words *'Nunc te dimisi',* 'Now I have let you go!'—Pulteney has been dismissed first from the world and then from conscience.) In his slightly pompous way he wishes that people would pronounce this canticle sincerely; though perhaps he should have thought of the context, where Simeon refers to the fall and rise of many and the revelation of the thoughts of many hearts, something which Haynes for one could scarcely afford. On the contrary, his relaxed and sleepy state during the *Magnificat,* the canticle which, in the order of Evensong, precedes the Bible reading which precedes *Nunc dimittis,* indicates his complacent daytime expectation that, for him, *Nunc dimittis* is only a matter of time. But in a sleepy moment half like a dream, when his rational consciousness is unable to preserve the lie he has come to believe in, the carved cat on his stall seems to respond to his touch with movements of attack. And so he begins to learn his lesson from an appropriate canticle: the *Magnificat* refers to the ejection of the powerful from their seat; in this case the seat itself begins to eject the complacent office-holder. This passage in the *Magnificat* had just been pre-echoed in Psalm 84, which is set for the seventeenth evening and which refers (vs. 44) to a throne cast down: we are reminded that, at Barchester, the seat of office is as much doomed as its occupant. The Psalms

whose days correspond to Haynes' diary entries have already begun to pick up his insecurity and fear of the dark, that is of the quiet night hours when his dedication to his work was failing to protect his mind from guilt. On the evening of the fifteenth day (when sister Letitia, whose name means 'happiness', had just left him)[58] Psalm 77 (vss. 6-7) complains: 'In the night I commune with mine own heart and search out my spirits. Will the Lord . . . be no more intreated?'

The teacher he encounters in daylight is not a representative of moral integrity but an animal of notorious ambivalence, well fitted to convey an esoteric message. Or perhaps better fitted to frighten than to inform: note Umberto Eco's comment[59] that

> the night of the Middle Ages seems to be haunted by a crowd of barking dogs and crying, sick people . . . In this landscape hens and parrots sometimes scratch about but as far as I know no cats show up. They are probably reserved for more intimate sorcery parties and could not be required as usual inhabitants of the official city.

On the other hand, this comment should be balanced by reference to more pleasant themes, for instance the cat and fiddle found in church carvings and associated by the nursery rhyme not with sorcery but with fun.[60] The dual nature of cats is reflected in English folklore: cats assist witches in their sorcery but bring good luck. In real life cats are, on the one hand, attractive and playful animals who bring fun to our houses but are, on the other hand, disturbingly cruel and moved by purposes of their own.

This dual nature is material for moralistic reflection. An example of this reflection is an emblem of 1564, published in Flemish Antwerp by the German artist Johannes Sambucus[61] entitled *Imprudens Facinus*—'Crime without counting the cost'. The text reads:

> Insidiis captat mures, sequiturque nocentres
>   Triticeo, felis pellat ut a cumulo.
> Fecit at interdum furem malesuada cupido,
>   Murmure sed furtum prodidit ipse suum.
> Non minus ingenio vitium, quam recta teguntur:
>   In cruce supplicium non bene cautus habet.
> Illicitae et quamvis lateant nos saepe rapinae,
>   Serior at duplici poena dolenda venit.

> The cat lies in wait for mice and pursues the wretched creatures to drive them from their hoards of food. But perverse desire sometimes makes him too into a thief— but he himself, by his purring, reveals his theft. Our failings are hidden by no less cleverness than our good deeds: but it takes a lot of cleverness to avoid a crucifying punishment. Wrongful and violent acts may lie hidden from our view for a time: the punishment comes later but in double measure.

Like Sambucus' emblem, James's story both makes the cat ambivalent—it pursues a wretched and guilty man but does so with perverse malevolence—and also takes up the idea of a payment more terrible for having been postponed. Clearly, I have no reason to be sure that James was thinking of this particular work. But he does mean us, I think, to recall the harsh moral tone of certain Low Countries art.

The Low Countries emblem-style produces pictures with inscriptions: and Austin duly provides an inscription, concealed in a carving and found only after Haynes's death:

> When I grew in the wood
> I was watered with Blood
> Now in the Church I stand
> Who that touches me with his Hand
> If a Bloody hand he bear
> I councell him to be ware
> Lest he be fecht away
> Whether by night or day
> But chiefly when the wind blows high
> In a night of February.
> This I drempt 26 Febr. Ao 1699 John Austin.

The carvings drawn from the Holywood seem to suit the worship of an implacable god; and an implacable god would be an inadequate and barbarous foundation for any moral authority: so the authority of the Church still remains in question. Indeed, if the story does, as I have argued, commend the cardinal virtue of restraint or temperance, then the story might seem also to condemn all religion and the emotion associated with it, emotion which is always capable, as we so well know, of taking barbarous, grotesque forms. Jack Sullivan's opinion,[62] that James's stories express the inadequacy of all religion to deal with the enigma of the universe, is plausible: we might suppose that the endless reconstructions of the Cathedral are really an admission by the religious consciousness of its own incurable frailty. But I seek in the next section to develop a view rather different from Sullivan's.

THE UNJUST JUDGE

To make the question over authority yet more pressing, another scriptural passage intervenes in the story: one of the curses which may support the traditional atheist case that religion depends on superstitious terror: and thus makes the enigma of the universe deeper and more painful.

The choir (accompanied, no doubt, by the hostile organist) sings the verse from Psalm 109: 'Set an ungodly man over him and let Satan stand at his right hand'; at the same moment the figure in friar's robes stirs in Haynes's hand, revealing the dampness and decay which he will encounter again when the demon visits his house and whispers beside his bed. Haynes would, in connection with his projected book on Episcopacy—that is, on office and authority in the Church—have studied this passage because it is a curse on the

holder of an office and contains, in the Greek version, one of the Old Testament occurrences of the word *episcope*. So he would have laid to heart the full extent of the curse of Psalm 109, including loss of office, fewness of days and the turning of prayer into sin. From the first of his diary entries the shortening of days in the sense of seasonal change had frightened him, doubtless by reminding him of the shortening of days in the sense of days made few, of early death.

James uses this Psalm twice, once here and once in **'An Uncommon Prayer Book'**, where it is the favourite of Lady Sadleir, a political enthusiast. His attitude to the Psalm may be compared to that of another populist writer, C. S. Lewis, who regards it as 'the worst' of the psalms of cursing. Lewis's general method, in his discussion of this and other awkward features of the Psalms, is to allegorise: he suggests a deflection of anger from the sinner to the sin. James sees more realistically that a corrupt office-holder must be cursed personally: he must fall painfully from the office he coveted. James has the curse fulfilled against Haynes with a certain cruel exactness: note the appearance of 'the extortioner' later in the story: again, it is realistic to suppose that corruption attracts blackmailers. Both the pathos of Haynes's predicament and the story's fear of destructive forms of religion are emphasised if we both recall his unavailing prayers and also note that Psalm 109, while warning us that prayer may be turned to sin, encourages us to trust in prayer.[63] Thus encouraged, Lady Sadleir puts her trust in a form of 'uncommon prayer' which endlessly inflames her cherished hatred.

The Satan who stirs at Haynes's touch is a Satan in the original meaning of the word, an accuser: his whisperings accuse Haynes before his own conscience. Corresponding to the 'accuser standing at his right hand'[64] is the seated figure with its royal trappings and long talons, the ungodly judge to whom the accusation is addressed. Haynes seem never to touch this third and most fearsome figure, the figure whose appearance in the last of his dreams may well have driven him in the February darkness from the comparative safety of his bedroom to the stairway of whose dangers he was so well aware; and the judge's taloned hands were there to play their part, along with the cat's claws, in the mutilation of Haynes's face. The retribution visited on Haynes is almost as disquieting, particularly because the judge who judges Haynes does not stand for justice, as are the fierce retributions of pagan stories where civilised justice gives way to barbaric revenge, as when Pelias is dismembered at Medea's prompting.

In *Ghost Stories of an Antiquary* the evil spirits usually stir because someone, usually one of James's scholarly other selves, stumbles on their lair by accident;[65] in *More Ghost Stories* the visitation is as likely to be a punishment as an accident. The punishments of *More*

Ghost Stories may be authorised, as *II Thessalonians* suggests, by the sublimely authoritative Mouth of God: but they are often mediated through some remarkably unjust judges. Perhaps the most disturbing appearance of the theme of the Unjust Judge[66] is in **'Martin's Close'**, where the brutal and undignified Judge Jeffreys compares himself with God: God has the keys of hell, Jeffreys has the keys of Newgate. The idea that sublime justice might be mediated through such vicious creatures is the more disturbing if we identify ourselves with the victims, as James to some extent identifies himself with Haynes: a scholar used to administration (James was Head of a Cambridge College and later on Vice-Chancellor) but versed in the byways of literature and interested in the subject of *episcope*. James's own interest in episcope may be suggested by the appearance in *More Ghost Stories* of two of the passages in the Old Testament where the word 'ἐπισκοπή' occurs in the Greek version. This was familiar territory for James, who had won the Jeremie Septuagint Prize as an undergraduate.[67]

The key characteristic of the persecutors of **'Barchester'** is the degree to which they, even though they belong to a mysterious emblem-style work of art, are activated by canticles and Psalms, the public scriptures of the Church. They are really the scriptures come to life, taking a mysterious form in order to slip into Haynes's dreams and so to pierce the armour of his workaday consciousness. The story is no less horrific if we deny their supernatural reality and accept the 'natural explanation' at which James usually liked to hint: perhaps Haynes's tormented conscience produced, in response to the scriptural passages which he encountered every day, delusions about damp, whispering lips and fierce cats (whispering enemies are, as I mentioned, a common theme of the Psalms, which he heard so regularly). After all, the torments inflicted by a conscience which cannot be silenced and so tears the personality inwardly into an accusing and a guilty part do not have to be supernatural in order to be terrifying and in order to pose a problem. All moral authorities, not just religious ones, depend on the consciences of their followers: and therefore depend on the unpleasant, perhaps unworthy, threat of releasing the torments of conscience on those who do not conform.

A story where the scriptures, which are supposed to be holy, themselves people our minds with demons, real or imaginary, must come close to accepting, and to accepting in vivid form, the traditional atheist idea that religion is at its root a kind of mental illness, based on illegitimate, dreamlike terrors:—*tantum religio potuit suadere malorum*. This slogan of Lucretian atheism is mentioned, with a slight hint of amused sympathy, by James in one of his protests against the destruction of art—this time medieval[68] rather than classical. I argue that the story may come close, but still does not take the finalstep, to acceptance of the slogan.

After all, it is important to note that the passages of scripture which James chooses to feature in his story convey not only a hint of terror but also a coherent theme. The demons of Psalm 109 are invoked by a progression from the prophecy of *II Thessalonians:* and this progression represents not mental illness but a morally necessary logic. If those in authority have followed the prediction of *II Thessalonians* by a significant abandonment of restraint then their authority is corrupted: they will be demoralised and another will, by the working of Psalm 109, take over their office—perhaps take it over too late, for Psalm 84 may also be right to envisage that the seat of office will itself be cast down. A strict and logical process of retribution may seem little different from a barbarous and implacable process. But really there is a difference, which will be clearly seen on one crucial condition: that a working form of *episcope* coexists with the logical process of retribution, so that they form parts of the same system. The function of *episcope* is surely to warn and to guide before mistakes are made and, if mistakes have been made, to expiate guilt.

So only if *episcope* has ceased to function will retribution necessarily take its harshest form, administered by a judge who is implacable and 'will be no more intreated'. A judge of that kind is to some extent unjust, to some extent an indispensable avenger in an extreme situation when evils have gone too far. Even Jeffreys appears, in James's treatment, to be necessary in a certain kind of crisis: his brutality, being undiscriminating, prevents George Martin from using his social privilege to avoid punishment. It is, of course, highly desirable to moderate and civilise the grotesque forms of justice for which these unjust judges stand: but this moderation may not be possible in the immediate aftermath of the collapse of restraint.

Haynes had studied the Argonauts' story, with its elaborate scenes of expiation. If he had had any chance of expiating his guilt then the behaviour of the persecutors would have a certain integrity: they keep to their mission of 'councell' and leave time for their counsel to be understood, while the scriptures which accompany their work do at first leave room for hope. Psalm 73, vs. 2: 'My feet were almost gone; my treadings were well nigh slipt' corresponds to Haynes's diary entry for the same (fourteenth) evening, 'I had as near as possible fallen', when he encounters the cat on his stair. Because the fatal fall has just been avoided recovery still seems to be possible, though it would surely require repentance, which is essential to the Christian form of expiation. And Psalm 78, vs. 39, set for the following (fifteenth) evening, reminds us that God may delay retribution: 'Many a time turned he his wrath away and would not suffer his whole displeasure to arise'. But, because Haynes never withdraws (though he scratches out) his claim to have acted for the best, he never repents: and the atmosphere set by the scriptures grows, accordingly, bleaker. Haynes may have found the Gospel at his last Communion service very bleak: it contains Jesus' famous reference to a failed exorcism, where seven devils worse than the first take over.[69] True *episcope* is what Haynes needed in the meanwhile but never found.

I suggest in the next section that he never found it because, to his misfortune, the authority to which he looked combined the worst of both worlds, both the inertia of Pulteney's time and also the self-serving determination to maintain itself which is characteristic of Revivalism. This misfortune may well show the frailties of religious leaders but does not necessarily show either that religion is incurably frail or that it survives only *suadendis malis,* by superstition and terror. Sometimes the scriptures may plant terrors in our minds but these terrors will not reflect mere superstition but something better, that is the inner coherence, the moral logic which the scriptures or any system which gains widespread authority must surely have. Because its events reflect this logic, the story, though its view of the leaders of religion is indeed very bitter by comparison with Trollope's, refuses to take the final step towards the Lucretian, atheist view of religious culture. I think it glimpses the truer, more general view—a view which antiquarians should properly take and which Lucretius, in this famous verse, glimpses only partially: that there is something inescapable about an established culture, and therefore, to those who live with it, something threatening.

The Defence of Episcopacy: Misplaced Trust?

Haynes is working on a book, his *Defence of Episcopacy;* and he praises to the *Gentleman's Magazine,* with some fulsomeness, the prelate who now occupies the Bishop's throne; this may well be Bishop Grantly (particularly if 'now' indicates a recent arrival), whose neglectfulness and lack of achievement we know about from Trollope: another Pulteney. His trust in this particular Bishop is misplaced: so, evidently, is his trust in the whole system. After all, this was the system which gave the Bishop no means, even if he had the will, legitimately to replace a colleague who had become useless.

Moreover, there is sarcasm and sadness in the fact that Haynes is defending the Church's system of supervision and is in close contact with those who should exercise it but is unable (perhaps because scandal is unthinkable) to make the least use of the system when

he desperately needs its help: in his hour of need, the Church is still as useless as Pulteney was. Haynes needs to put his personality, torn apart by the tension between his reasoned sense of having acted for the best and his inescapable sense of guilt, together again. But his final state, with his face (his public mask) torn away by the hellcat to expose his inner wound, shows how absolutely his need failed to be met.

The Church failed or chose to fail to detect that anything was wrong behind Haynes's mask: and this failure connects with a second failure, less catastrophic but more persistent, to examine his papers (which told the full story) after his death; or at least to act on what they reveal. The obituarist (who knows something of Haynes's work on Episcopacy and so, very likely, is cousin Allen, Haynes's sole visitor) certainly senses that something has gone very wrong: were enemies of the established order (he deplores the influence of Voltaire and Byron) at work?

It seems that an investigation was begun, since Haynes's correspondence was reassembled; perhaps the fact that Haynes's papers were unwelcome at his old College suggests that the College had been warned by the Bishop about a possible scandal—(recall how bishop Proudie was later to consult with Lazarus College, Oxford). Allen, if it was he who reassembled the papers, would have seen at last through Haynes's mask, and probably guessed that the drab, whispering figures whom he had encountered in the corridor were in fact Jane Lee and her man; that they had fled when they found that Haynes was not alone but had returned a few nights later; and that Haynes had been attacked with a knife and thrown downstairs in a sordid quarrel over money. But by James's rules[70] this natural explanation of Haynes's death would have run into difficulties, perhaps a surprisingly good alibi for the suspects. These difficulties would have been enough for the Bishop, not knowing whether to dread natural or supernatural explanations more, to persuade Allen, in consideration of Letitia's interests, to abandon the enquiry. At all events, the papers were effectively hidden for ninety years: even the narrator is allowed to use them only on the understanding that the College—still an institution allied to the Church—suffers no discredit from any publication; hence the 'disguise of identities' which he promises.[71]

So the story tells us that throughout the century of the Gothic Revival the Church is never reconstructed so that it is capable of self-understanding, able to face up to the evils within itself. And this is surely because revivalism, with its fierce insistence on an institution's authority, has its own logic; a logic which makes it difficult even to understand that the institution, which is there to correct faults, might itself be at fault; and the difficulty only grows with the fervour of the Revival.

The *episcope* of the Church thus takes, as I suggested, very faulty forms, partly inert and partly self-serving. By contrast with Trollope's Barchester, there is no sign that the traditional authority is regaining the high moral ground: and the absence of any such sign favours the scepticism about all authority, hence about all religion, which Sullivan's interpretation implies.

But it is crucial to note that the story balances that scepticism about moral authority with the sense that all human beings have a deep need for *episcope,* for a moral authority which supplements our own resources: the prelude to Haynes's mutilation is the increasingly intense isolation in which his own resources, originally great, run out. This balance within the story amounts to a refusal to press sceptical feeling to extremes; my interpretation differs from Sullivan's by laying emphasis on this refusal.

Catastrophe occurs, by the suggestion of the story, when *episcope* fails. Then how can *episcope* be restored? Certainly not by the sheer determination to create a new order dominated by a revived form of traditional authority: this determination was the mark of Haynes himself and of the Gothic Revival. So the only chance for renewed *episcope* is to restore the old order and with it the old form of restraint. The return of restraint implies the removal of the grotesque forces which were released when restraint failed: and indeed the grotesque figures of the story have been, as the last sentence tells us, in their turn destroyed.

RAYS OF HOPE

The figures are burnt after their removal from the Cathedral because they frighten some small children. The manner of their destruction may offer a ray of hope at the end of the story: the demons which destroy the guilty may in their turn be destroyed by the innocent; so we may hope that new generations can evade the tensions of old times and makes a fresh start. The ray of hope was the last theme mentioned in my introduction and in this section I briefly survey those themes again. First I note that the ray is not dazzlingly bright: original innocence does not prevent eventual corruption if *episcope* is lacking.

The fresh start has to be made in a modern world where the relics of ancient authority may have become, as the story reminds us towards its end, little more than museum pieces: therefore it is a world full of novelty, restlessness and scepticism with no source of *episcope* available within the story's purview other than the new successor to ancient authority, that is the unprepossessing religion symbolised by the bare and odiously furnished Cathedral.

Physical reconstruction of the older Cathedral may be beyond our powers. But there is another element of hope in the very fact that the Barchester of James's educated imagination was more perfectly classical than any real Cathedral to which James could refer. Thus the religious and philosophical beliefs for which classical Barchester stood—including the belief in confident but peaceful treatment of difficult or alien ideas—can still be restored in our minds, just as they were restored in James's mind and in his fiction, by the action of an educated imagination. This kind of educated imagination needs a culture in which a deep tincture of classicism is present so that, contrary to many forces in the modern world, powerful symbols of restraint can form in individual minds, opening those minds to the gentle form of *episcope* for which the classical Cathedrals once stood.

The story shows us how restraint is not always maintained, can indeed be subverted, by strength of mind and by a reasoned commitment to what is best; restraint, therefore, does not spring from the full domination of reason over the mind: so it must depend partly on our emotions and on how our culture trains our emotions. If the culture of new generations is right we may hope that they need never resort to and need never suffer the harsher, more grotesque forms of justice and that they may recover the purer, less odious forms of religion.

The needful kind of culture depends on the kind of scholarship for which James's real self stood and which some of his other, fictional selves misuse. James was a scholar who constructed fantasies partly in order to warn us against scholars—more generally, intellectuals—who ruthlessly and without restraint pursue fantasies which have gained power over their minds; it is their kind of scholarship whose risks outweigh its uses and whose risks the scholars, by a further corruption of their scholarship, refuse or fail to see: as Haynes responded to the demonic warnings only with perplexity. Contrasting himself and his like with these people, James asks us to accept that his literary fantasies are rooted in genuine knowledge. Theodore Roosevelt was exaggerating when he said that James knew 'all about everything'[72] but he had taken much of James's intended message.

The story presents us with what the author considered to be a true account of moral history. According to this account, Paul's warning about the failure of restraint marked the beginning of the fall of the original classical world, a beginning which Valerius, a pagan contemporary, observed anxiously. But the march of time brought not a new world, whose one foundation was Christianity purged of all paganism, but one in which Christianity had been renewed, for a long time and with great success, by building classical elements and ideas of pagan origin into its foundations. So the story's answer to the question from which I started is that genuine renewal is possible, provided it is of the right, more open-minded sort.

But a new failure of restraint, symbolised by the indiscriminate destructiveness of the Gothic Revival—which was a reconstruction of the wrong sort, dominated by the determination of activists to maintain their authority—produced the fall, the murder, of the second classical world and many of its great buildings; and James returns to the theme in **'An Episode'**, where the image of murder is replaced by that of sickness. The story advises us to educate ourselves so that, as far as may be possible, we can *in Kunst und Leben* restore that damaged world.

Notes

1. *The Cloister and the Hearth* was first published in 1867; it appears on one of James's very short lists of favourite reading (Lubbock, *A Memoir of Montague Rhodes James,* Cambridge University Press, 1939, p. 13). Reade writes with great sympathy of those who were trying to introduce classical learning into the Church and makes the defenders of the old intellectual order seem narrow-minded to the point of fanaticism; Colonna and his like have by far the greater vitality (chapter 74; see the Collins edition, London, 1953, pp. 495 ff.). The picture of the medieval world on the brink of modernity is powerfully drawn in Reade's work; it seems that steps which might have prevented the Reformation, the split in the Church produced by the stressful impact of modern knowledge, could have been but were not taken.

2. Reade thinks of Europe, while James's story directly concerns only the English scene, with its distinctive architectural and cultural style—his comments on the parallel problems of the French Church, for which he had an affection (Lubbock, p. 36), would have been welcome. For European Catholics the Gothic style is, quite rightly, associated with Gallican, rather than with pure Roman tradition (see E. Norman, *The House of God* (London: Thames and Hudson, 1990), p. 276; for the intense royalism of early French Gothic see O. von Simson, *The Gothic Cathedral,* second edition, Princeton, 1962, p. 89). Thus the most important buildings of the ultramontane Catholic Church in England sought, at least after Pugin's influence had waned, to bring into England styles which were neither classical nor Gothic. Westminster Cathedral, whose Byzantine interior is 'one of the most moving of any church in London' (N. Pevsner and P. Metcalf, *English Cathedrals: Southern England* (London: Viking, 1985, p. 211), suggests (as Reade had suggested) that we should go back deeper in history to a point before all the distressing controversies of modern times had arisen; Liverpool Metropolitan Cathedral, with its modern ecumenical appearance, suggests that we should start again from a new synthesis. I suggest

towards the end of this essay that James did believe, but very guardedly, in the possibility of a fresh start.

3. Restoration is 'the most total destruction which a building can suffer', according to John Ruskin, *Seven Lamps of Architecture* (Collected Works, Vol. 8, edited by E. T. Cook and A. Wedderburn, London: Allen, 1903), pp. 242 ff. Ruskin's idea that buildings should be propped up for as long as possible and then destroyed is plainly ridiculous: but he was trying to prevent the kind of wildly destructive restoration described by Kenneth Clark in *The Gothic Revival* (London: Constable, 1928), p. 225. For controversies about restoration see Norman, *The House of God,* p. 275.

4. I am grateful for correspondence from Mrs Margaret Sparks, editor of the Canterbury Cathedral History, Miss Suzanne Eward, Librarian of Salisbury Cathedral and Miss Joan Williams, Librarian of Hereford Cathedral.

5. Lubbock (*Memoir,* p. 20) states that James's interest in the more obscure parts of ancient literature began in his schooldays; also that he knew the Psalms by heart. He replied to the question, 'Monty, what's the good . . . of these old manuscripts?' with 'What's the good of anything?' Lubbock takes this remark as meaning only that questions about usefulness are the mark of a second-rate mind. I think it means also that human activities may be both more and less useful than we hastily suppose; and that James thought seriously about both the usefulness and the dangers (see following note) of his absorption in the past. In his children's story *The Five Jars* (London: Edward Arnold, 1922, p. 33) he insists defiantly that learning Latin was among the most useful things he ever did.

6. Kenneth Clark, *Revival,* p. 68. Horace Walpole made sure that exact drawings of medieval work were made for the benefit of his house at Strawberry Hill; on the other hand the Gothic movement created buildings like Fonthill Abbey (ibid., p. 108) which were almost fantastic parodies of medieval work and, in its reconstructions of churches, allowed ruthless expression of the restorer's will at the expense of genuine relics of the medieval past, for instance Wyatt's relocation of the medieval pulpitum at Salisbury Cathedral (ibid., p. 103). Evidently Wyatt disclaimed responsibility for 'destructions' at Salisbury and Durham. Clark's citation of Heine is on p. 76.

7. Heine, *Die Romantische Schule,* published in 1836; *Werke und Briefe* (Berlin: Aufbau Verlag, 1961-4), V, p. 15.

8. Heine and like-minded Romantics did not share the enthusiasm for traditional religion which char-

acterised the Gothic Revival. H. Spence, *Heine* (Boston: Twayne, 1982) remarks (p. 52) that Heine 'implies that Romanticism, along with Christian orthodoxy, is now obsolete and must give way to a literature that is committed to political involvement'. Heine thus anticipates (at least in this phase of his thought) the switch within architectural and artistic ideology from religion to politics which occurred later in Britain—see D. Watkin, *Morality and Architecure* (Oxford University Press, 1977). No more than Ruskin or anyone else does Heine solve the paradox of warmly welcoming the *Wiedererweckung* of medieval influence while fiercely rejecting Catholicism.

9. The foolish Dean in 'An Episiode in Cathedral History' (James's other attack on this subject) who asserts so depressingly that he is 'an educated man' is an exemplar—James probaby knew the type quite well—of an unbalanced attitude created by shallow enthusiasm.

10. I am grateful to my colleague Professor D. M. Knight for referring me to M. Wheeler, *Death and the Future Life in Victorian Literature and Theology* (Cambridge, 1990), who discusses the idea of heaven in ch. 3, p. 15 *et passim*.

11. Wyatt's idea of surrounding a Cathedral with a Close was pioneered, perhaps perfected, at Salisbury and remains much more popular than many other ideas associated with Wyatt, that much reviled man. For 'Haynes', E. Ekwall, *Oxford Dictionary of Place Names* (fourth edition, 1969) suggests the meaning 'enclosures'. Somewhat different accounts of the name are given by A. Room, *Dictionary of Place Names in the British Isles* (London: Bloomsbury, 1988), by P. Hanley and F. Hodges, *A Dictionary of Surnames* (Oxford: OUP, 1988) and by M. H. Reaney and R. M. Wilson, *A Dictionary of British Place Names* (Routledge, 1976): these authorities favour the meanings 'clearing', 'mean person' and 'hawthorn'. but a clearing is a kind of enclosure; and the idea of a mean person is not out of place in the story. That James was thinking primarily of 'enclosures' is really proved by Haynes's middle name, 'Benwell', which (see Ekwall, op. cit.) means 'place within the wall'. (The only Benwell in Britain is on Tyneside: was Haynes a Northumbrian of unprivileged background who despised the aristocratic Pulteney?) The names 'John Haynes' and 'Jane Lee' (belonging to the two accomplices in Pulteney's murder) have closely similar meanings: beneath the differences of sex and class, they were one and the same spirit. 'John' and 'Jane' are variants on the same Hebrew name, which in turn reflects the Name of God which dominated the Cathedral. 'Lee' echoes 'Haynes' by referring to 'a dweller by the wood or clearing' (Reaney and Wilson; Hanley and Hodges, op. cit.); moreover, since the dregs of wine are 'lees' there is an echo of the idea of 'mean person' in 'Haynes'. John Benwell Haynes, with his loyalty to the Church and his scholarly spirit, should have been the better self of the barely literate Jane Lee, whose only loyalty was to a worthless man. As things turned out she was corrupted by him and was the means of expressing the worst side of the determined and resourceful character which they both shared; and the mark which God had set on both their names was defaced.

12. See article on Pulteney (the first Earl of Bath) in the *Dictionary of National Biography;* also P. Langford, *A Polite and Commercial People* (Oxford: Clarendon Press, 1989) and A. S. Foord, *His Majesty's Opposition* (Oxford: Clarendon Press, 1964). These authorities explain sympathetically Pulteney's predicament in the crisis created by Walpole's resignation in 1742: he needed power but was hampered by previous promises not to take office (Foord, p. 225); moreover he was looking for a way of reforming the existing system without purging it too violently of its existing personnel and, in the end, 'could not bear the psychological pressures exerted on him' (Langford, p. 188). We don't know James's detailed view of the historical Pulteney, who assured George II that 'he was not a man of blood', but was widely suspected of having sold the cause of reform for an earldom: for the phrase 'kicked upstairs', that is into the House of Lords, see Brewer's *Dictionary of Phrase and Fable.* But evidently James uses Pulteney's name to suggest the kind of person who becomes the victim of drastic action because he would never take drastic action himself. James was no doubt aware that Pulteney's influence remained important, even years later, particularly in the area of ecclesiastical appointments (Langford, p. 187): no doubt it is that influence which, in James's fictional world, benefited an obscure cousin, who became Archdeacon of Barchester. The '-ey' element in the name 'Pulteney' means 'island': perhaps both the real statesman and the fictional cleric were somewhat marooned.

13. Trollope, *Barchester Towers,* chapter 4. Slope himself is probably responsible for the 'euphony' of the change; Trollope cannot discover at what point the family changed its religion (since Dr Slop was a Catholic). Slope's rigorous, unprepossessing evangelicalism seems to be not a sincere change from, but a cosmetic overcompensation for, both Slop's religion and his sloppy professional behaviour.

14. Kenneth Clark (*Revival*, p. 23) remarks on the extensive interest in Gothic architecture shown by this journal at the period where James's story is set: it was the principal vehicle for debate over Wyatt's restorations of Salisbury and Hereford Cathedrals (models for James's Barchester). It is appropriate that at one point in the story Haynes drafts a letter to Sylvanus Urban: 'Sylvanus Urban' was the name used by successive editors of the *Magazine*.

15. *Joshua* I, 7, 9, 18.

16. A. Soggin, *Joshua* (London: SCM, 1972) *ad loc.* For the transformation of Rahab into an innkeeper by the ancient paraphrases called the Targums, see Boling and Wright, *Joshua* (New York: Doubleday, 1982). The commentators I mention all dismiss the idea that Rahab was not an ordinary prostitute but one of the 'cultic prostitutes' of Canaanite religion.

17. That Valerius belongs to the byways of literature, where James himself often moved, is shown by the fact that for centuries no one did what James imagines Haynes to have done, that is publish a complete English translation of his work: see A. Schulte, *Index Verborum Valerianus* (Iowa: 1934), p. 8. R. R. Bolgar, *The Classical Heritage and its Beneficiaries* (Cambridge: CUP, 1963), p. 536, mentions N. Whyte's translation of 1565 (which was perhaps the last before Mozley's Loeb translation of 1934 and which Schulte appears to have overlooked), but indicates that there were no pre-1600 translations into any other modern language. Schulte praises an 1808 translation of Valerius's first book, published under the strange title *Blackheath and other Poems*. R. J. Getty, in the 1949 *Oxford Classical Dictionary*, praises Valerius both absolutely and by comparison with his contemporaries in the Silver Age.

18. He does not reach the last and saddest episodes of the story. We do not know whether Valerius would have used these episodes to show the survival or the collapse of Jason's moral commitment to do what must be done for the good of his people.

19. Valerius I, 67 for Idmon's morality; V, 319-24 for Jason's speech—compare Apollonius III, 171-93. E. V. Rieu, *The Voyage of Argo* (London: Penguin, 1971) notes (p. 15) that Apollonius frequently applies the unheroic description ἀμήχανος—'helpless'—to Jason.

20. Medea does not recognise Venus but still believes that she is conversing with someone of supernatural powers. Venus is disguised as Medea's aunt Circe, magician and daughter of the Sun.

21. He was a *Quindecimvir Sacris Faciundis*. Mozley's Introduction to the Loeb (1934) edition of *Argonautica* tells us what little is known of Valerius' life. See also Walter C. Summers, *A Study of Valerius Flaccus* (Cambridge, 1894).

22. Francis Vian (*Argonautiques* III, Budé, 1980, p. 47) collects several passages where she condemns herself forthrightly: but still she is not deflected from her chosen course of action. Her cold, resolute planning of her brother's murder (IV, 411 ff.) is one of literature's best brief portraits of ruthlessness. Apollonius suggests that passion was all along her dominant motive (IV, 445), though his character argues with him (IV, 1018). For the clash of cultures, Asiatic and Greek, in Medea's personality see Vian's comments (ibid., p. 21, p. 35 ff).

23. Valerius, *Argonautica* VII, 128-40, 158-70, 198-209, for Medea's douts and their resolution. These are discussed by Summers, *A Study*. Medea has resisted Juno's blandishments and has resolved not to help Jason: only can she find a way to avoid seeing him die? Her resolution, which of course contains the seeds of her relenting, is described compellingly, so that we incline to disagree with Jupiter and consider that she has made the right choice. But the right choice is backed up by moral argument of a cruelly spurious kind, offered by the disguised Venus, who praises European civilisation and ends with a scornful reference to polygamy among the Sauromatian and Gelonian princes of the Black Sea region; we are likely to think of this argument as spurious, since we know that Jason will divorce Medea and that Medea will return to Asia with her last son, Medus, the founder of the Kingdom of the Medes. The deceptive nature of the gods is important in moral history, since it is bound up (see next two notes) in the pagan conception of faith. For Jupiter's denunciations of Medea, see *Argonautica* V, 14 and VI, 86.

24. V, 233-40; for this scene there is no parallel in Apollonius. Polytheism encourages faith but admits that faith in a particular supernatural being may be misplaced. Apollonius (III, 586) says that Phrixus was the kindest and most godfearing of men; Valerius's Jason knows Phrixus's character but underestimates his loyalty to Aeetes.

25. Virgil uses this idea (*Aeneid* IX, 312-13) when the Trojans, convinced (in the end, rightly) that the gods have not abandoned them, surround the doomed heroes Nisus and Euryalus with prayers and good wishes and when (*Aeneid* XI, 795) the sinister Arruns prays that he will get away with killing the admirable Camilla. Valerius recalls it when Tiphys the helmsman dies (*Argonautica* V, 20). Both he and Apollonius refer to a double tomb, that of Tiphys and that of Idmon: presumably two 'tombs of Argonauts' were shown on the

Black Sea coast. In both versions Idmon has prophesied that he will not return from the voyage. Apollonius makes the scene of Idmon's death, on the tusks of a vicious boar, very dramatic; Valerius has Idmon die much less dramatically—of a disease which then carries off Tiphys also. Why did Valerius sacrifice one of Apollonius' best scenes? Perhaps it did not suit his narrative structure: but in any case he uses his less dramatic account of Idmon's death to shift the theological emphasis. In Apollonius that emphasis falls on the inexorable fulfilment of inspired prophecy, even at the expense of the prophet himself; in Valerius it falls on the pointless nature of some of our fervent prayer. Idmon, in close contact with the gods, does not even try to intercede for himself; the Argonauts do attempt to intercede by prayer for Tiphys, who seems essential to their task—but 'they give their words to the wind': the words recall Arruns and remind us that it is not only bad people who may find their words of prayer scattered. The point that our contact with the gods may be worse than vain—even deceptive—has been made by Valerius' Jason when a portent encourages his attempt to pass the Clashing Rocks: *'Sequor, o quicumque deorum'* Aesonides *'vel fallis!' ait*—'Whoever among the gods you are and even if you cheat me' said Aeson's son 'I follow!': a pagan kind of faith in which there is no full assurance of the goodness of the god. J. E. Shelton, *A Narrative Commentary on the Argonautica of Valerius Flaccus* (unpublished doctoral dissertation, Nashville, 1971) comments *ad loc.* that Jason acquires and deserves divine favour only because he takes the risk and shows confidence not only in the god but in himself: the tincture of aggressive self-confidence gives Jason's faith a further pagan flavour which may have appealed to Haynes.

26. Whether these really are the final lines is in dispute among editors. I accept the placement of them by Mozley and others. Langen for one (Berlin: Calvary, 1900) thinks that they might well belong elsewhere.

27. The traditional story contains two principal scenes of expiation, that following the death of Cyzicus and that following the death of Apsyrtus. Apollonius, known as a learned poet, tried, perhaps with some success, to capture the genuine moral atmosphere of the heroic age. Cyzicus's death is an accident. The city named after him stood at the narrow neck of the wide and mountainous peninsula of Dindyme, the principal home of Rhea, the reclusive mother of the gods to whom, says Apollonius, Zeus himself defers when she visits the heavens, ὅτ' ἐξ ὀρέων μέγαν οὐρανὸν εἰσαναβαίνῃ (I, 1100). The Argonauts are unfamiliar with these waters and they do not understand, when they have rounded the peninsula at night, that they are returning to the same city from the opposite side (see Vian's endpaper map; Valerius makes the fact that they returned from a new direction clear by his reference to the river Rhyndacus (III, 34), which is well to the east of Cyzicus). Cyzicus's death and the angry suicide of his young wife provoke the great forces of nature which are embodied in Rhea and the Argonauts are subject to storms which make progress impossible. But after a few days a kingfisher hovers over Jason and Mopsus reads the sign: Rhea will now accept a ceremony of placation. The underlying symbolism of the scene seems to contain the idea that accidental destruction is part of the order of nature, which is disturbed by it, but only for a time: Rhea and the forces embodied in her will always fulfil their fundamental role, which is to ensure that life goes on. Vian explains at length (*Argonautiques*, Vol. I, p. 35) that the ceremony described by Apollonius centres on the regeneration of nature, not on a moral act of apology and restitution. Cyzicus's people are still wailing over his death but the Argonauts clash their weapons against their armour and drown the mournful sound: in a ceremony which treats the fatal accident as an interruption in life, rather like a hard winter, the forces of life, symbolised by the rejoicing animals of the mountain, gather and sweep away everything to do with death. On the other hand the death of Apsyrtus is a crime and is dealt with by Zeus, who, in his dual nature, both resents and helps the guilty: ὃς μέγα μὲν κοτέει, μέγα δ' ανδροφόνοισιν ἀρήγει (Apollonius, *Argonautica* IV, 701). But the ceremony of purification seems to have a purely religious significance—the god turns the avenging ghost from its pursuit—and not a moral one: Circe, who performs the ceremony on behalf of Zeus, condemns Medea bitterly after the ceremony is over. She is Aeetes's sister and has some right to feel aggrieved: but it is noteworthy that the purifier does not by any means forgive and that Medea, though purified, is not reformed. Pelias, Jason's wicked uncle, is about to find, just as Apsyrtus did, that those who are in contact with Medea do not always get away in one piece; and though Pelias is a bad man, his death, just like that of Apsyrtus, is surrounded by treachery. This version of Medea's purification shows how early religion tried to grapple with the difficult fact that to fix punishment is often to restrict punishment within limits which may seem highly arbitrary.

28. Valerius, *Argonautica* III, 362. How Valerius was going to deal with Apsyrtus's death and Medea's purification we do not know: clearly he decided to

introduce a much more moral element—and thus new problems—into the ritual surrounding Cyzicus's death. His ritual introduces, by contrast with that in Apollonius, elements of apology and restitution: in response, the snakes who serve the dead in the underworld come peaceably to receive the offerings. He also introduces both the moral problem of deciding how someone qualifies for being merely 'on the verge' of crime and the religious problem of maintaining the seriousness of the ritual of expiation when the most intelligent people already understand that they are really innocent, having not yet crossed the verge of crime. It is interesting how Jason, the dynamic leader, and Mopsus, the philosophical seer, seem, while the ceremony is planned, already to be immune the pangs of remorse which demoralise the other Argonauts. Mopsus is serenely confident that his professional skill—*nostra cura,* founded on profound religious experience—will 'find a way' even when morale is shattered. Haynes, the scholarly translator and dedicated Christian who craves a position of leadership, comes, like Mopsus before him, to suppress remorse by thinking only of work and by exercising his professional skill.

29. Randall, *English Church Furnishing,* p. 28.

30. J. Britton, *Cathedral Antiquities,* Vol. II, pp. 76, 81 of the section on Winchester, edition of 1836. This was a very influential work in its time and is widely quoted in modern books on the subject. Britton's engravings are very important evidence for the state of the buildings at their date. The section on Winchester was completed before the removal of the classical screen in 1820. Note that Britton begins his page sequence a new as he moves on to describe a new Cathedral and that the 1836 publication bundles together, rather than merges, his studies of individual buildings.

31. Woodman, *An Architectural History of Canterbury Cathedral* (London: Routledge, 1981), p. 236. At Canterbury, some seventeenth-century stalls were made into cupboards in the crypt.

32. Clifton-Taylor, *Cathedrals,* p. 236.

33. For the divergence of island and continent, see Clifton-Taylor, p. 195. Norman, *House of God,* p. 172, says of Perpendicular that 'there is a certain austerity about the style, perhaps in reaction to contemporaneous French Flamboyant modes'. For the quotation from Evelyn, see Clifton-Taylor, p. 11. Compare John Summerson, *Georgian London* (London: Barrie and Jenkins, 1988), p. 64, for the importance of rules in the aesthetics of the time and Kenneth Clark, *Revival,* pp. 58-9, for the much-abused attempt by Batty Langley to write rules for the Gothic style.

34. Examples in the OED.

35. Norman, *House of God,* for reference to Bernini's term *theatrum sanctum,* p. 211; for the central role of the cult of saints in Baroque, p. 221; for the reaction, p. 232. Norman's suggestion that the convergence occurred from both Catholic and Protestant sides and was not simply a matter of a one-sided and sinister *Wiedererweckug des Mittelalters* in Protestant England is interesting: something of a corrective to James's views.

36. Quoted, with further information, by Kenneth Clark. Palmerston thought that these debates exceeded in passion any others of the Big-Ender versus Little-Ender kind. The 'cynicism and humour' which Clark attributes to Palmerston are evident in these remarks: but there is an element of serious commitment too. That cynicism and humour (and a licentious personal life) should characterise an intelligent, aristocratic opponent of the Gothic cause is interesting in itself; as is the fact that capitalists immediately gave Sir Gilbert Scott, smarting at the Prime Minister's rejection of his Gothic designs, the balm he needed: the mighty St Pancras Station is the result.

37. Watkin, *Morality and Architecture* (Oxford: Clarendon Press, 1977). Kenneth Clark (*Revival,* p. 185) says that Pugin, the fierce convert to Catholicism, began to sow the seeds of Christian socialism and that Ruskin, who loathed Catholicism and despised Pugin, put the discussion of the Gothic style on a wholly new footing which was intensely confused but in which the social element, taken up by William Morris, tended to prevail against the religious. Watkin, who contributes (p. 51 ff.) an interesting critique of Pugin from a Catholic point of view, goes on to note the growth of the politically-inspired fiction that Gothic art was socially rather than individually created and the continuing use of art history to press religious points of view. Sir Nickolaus Pevsner is, on Watkin's account, both an author of the myth and a partisan of Protestantism (p. 77).

38. Emile Male, cited in A. Martindale, *Gothic Art* (London: Thames and Hudson, 1967), p. 13. A script depends on definite rules for conveying meaning: certainly Abbot Suger, one of the founders of the Gothic, claims proudly that his work made use of rules and was constructed *geometricis et arithmeticis instrumentis:* clearly, Suger would have been surprised by later assertions that Gothic is 'licentious' or rule-free. For these claims by Suger see von Simson. *Gothic Cathedral,* p. 101. For the supposed connection between rules of this sort and divine order, see E. Panofsky, *Gothic Architecture and Scholasticism* (New York: Meridian, 1957), p. 45. On the other hand W. Wor-

ringer's *Form in Gothic* (English translation published in London by Putnam's, 1927) argues (p. 64) that Gothic was always hybrid, with discipline and fantasy co-existing. Worringer is commended by his translator, the distinguished theorist Sir Herbert Read, for transcending amateurishly romantic views of Gothic (p. xii).

39. Suzanne Eward, in a dissertation on James which she wrote as an undergraduate and which I have benefited from reading, notes that this figure is 'muffled in a long mantle' and so recalls the appearance of Samuel 'covered with a mantle' when the Witch of Endor invokes him (*I Samuel* xxviii, 14). Samuel is no demon but the allusion to him once again reminds us of the deposition of an office-holder amidst the anger of God. James explicitly uses the Witch of Endor story in 'The Residence at Whitminster'.

40. For the Canterbury stalls, see Woodman, *Architectural History*, p. 326; Pevsner, *English Cathedrals (Southern)*, p. 75; for the sending to Coventry, Pevsner, *English Cathedrals (Midlands etc.)*, p. 176.

41. G. Cobb, *English Cathedrals, the Forgotten Years* (Batsford, 1980), pp. 110-11. Cobb's account leaves many questions unanswered. How extensive was Wren's work? How many stalls were due to him? It is clear that he put in some 'vulgar Grecian screens'—in the words of detractors who praised Wyatt's wholesale removal of them. But these did not include the main pulpitum, which Wren evidently left in place: Wyatt, claiming to restore, actually got away with exiling this excellent and genuine medieval monument—a large part of it 'splendidly unrestored', according to Pevsner, still stands elsewhere in the Cathedral—and substituting a pastiche of his own. Cobb is very scathing about all this, but Pevsner refers to Wyatt as 'tidying up'. For the canopies, see Pevsner, *English Cathedrals (Southern)*, p. 279. Some of those whom I have consulted in the different Cathedrals go further than I do in rejecting James's claim to have used them as models: Suzanne Eward considers that Barchester is like no representation of Salisbury Cathedral known to her; she considers that Wren may have played much less part in Salisbury's architecture than scholars have come to believe. Margaret Sparks considers that the only two features unquestionably drawn from Canterbury are the screen behind the altar and the name Austin, since a family of that name served Canterbury Cathedral. On the other hand, Joan Williams notes several points of resemblance between Barchester and Hereford (screen, pavement, wooden wainscotting round the altar, urns, rays, position of organ and pulpit).

42. For Salisbury, see Cobb, *Forgotten Centuries, loc. cit.*; for Hereford, there is an illustration, showing the East End of the Choir in 1841, in A. W. Fisher, *The Cathedral Church of Hereford*, part of Bell's Cathedral Series (to which James refers) published in 1898 (no page number). Joan Williams informs me that there are other prints which confirm the impression given by Fisher. Margaret Sparks informs me of the colours of the Canterbury pavement.

43. For Hereford, G. Marshall, *Hereford Cathedral, its Evolution and Growth* (Worcester, 1951), p. 125. For Salisbury, Pevsner, *English Cathedrals (South)*. For Canterbury, Woodman, *Architectural History*, has a controversial essay on the pulpitum.

44. For Canterbury, see illustration in Woodman, *Architectural History*, p. 237; Margaret Sparks confirms the existence of the 'IHS' motif. The urns and the motif at Hereford are shown in Fisher's illustration for Bell's Cathedral Series.

45. Norman, *House of God*, p. 130. R. Sheridan and A. Ross, *Grotesques and Gargoyles* (Newton Abbott: David Clare, 1975) note the terrifying nature of some of church art, notably (p. 55 etc.) the roof bosses of Canterbury Cathedral (which James may have had in mind); on p. 40 they illustrate a carving of a cat (from outside England). Norman comments further on the role of demons in the Romanesque crypt at Canterbury (pp. 124, 131).

46. See Pevsner, *Cathedrals of England (Middle, Eastern and Northern)*, p. 174 for the fact that at Hereford, a Cathedral which was one of James's models for Barchester, the numerous misericords have exclusively secular subjects. Remnant's *A Catalogue of Misericords in Great Britain* (Oxford: OUP, 1969) shows that secular subjects who appear in these carvings do not seem to be shocking intruders on normal life, but to belong, not too uncomfortably, to its edges; thus they have an entertaining rather than a terrifying nature.

47. Britton, *Antiquities II: Salisbury*, p. 49; *Winchester*, p. 94. In the Winchester scene the pelican which formed the crest of Bishop Fox, who died in 1528, is also present and this leads Britton to believe that the figure is that of Fox himself, represented as near or in the hour of his death, so that we may have a lesson in humility.

48. The Christians certainly attracted some sympathy at the time but it may seem anachronistic to attribute this to shock and dismay at atrocious and lawless government. T. D. Barnes, *Tertullian* (Oxford University Press, 1972), strives to paint a picture of the persecutions in which they were basically constitutional. There was certainly no law

against Christianity, but Barnes assimilates the persecution to normal peacekeeping: the Christians, he considers, were unpopular and their unpopularity could lead to disorder. But 'illegal in the absence of law' was surely a contradiction in ancient just as much as in modern terms. If the lynch mobs and kangaroo courts of Barnes's picture really belonged to normal Roman life then the result is not to assimilate the persecutions to legitimate peacekeeping but to assimilate normal Roman life to the anomaly and atrocity of the persecutions. The widely accepted saying that the blood of the martyrs was the seed of the Church reflects the belief that contemporaries too recognised something atrocious in the persecutions: and, after all, the Roman Empire was supposed to provide peace and law. Valerius's comment that the common people often have better sentiments than their violent kings (*melior vulgi nam saepe voluntas,* IV, 158) may not have been written with the Christians in mind but surely was written with Nero in mind and does acknowledge that the *vulgus* was alarmed by atrocious government.

49. See T. C. Brickhouse and N. D. Smith, *Socrates on Trial* (Cambridge University Press, 1989), p. 35 and p. 237 ff.

50. See Rigaux, *Les Epitres aux Thessaloniciens* (Paris, 1956) and Best, *A Commentary on the First and Second Epistles to the Thessalonians* (London, 1977). L. Morris, *The First and Second Epistles to the Thessalonians* (Grand Rapids: Eerdman, 1991), p. 226 ff., discusses the meaning of the passage at length and gives mild support to the idea, which he associates with Dietrich Bonhoeffer, that 'it is when law is taken out of the way that the Lawless One will rule'. The interepretation which I attribute to James is quite like this, acknowledging that there had been genuine forces of law and restraint in pagan society, but expecting these forces to fail amid general crisis. Morris dates both letters (whose authorship is not beyond dispute) to around AD 50: the author does not have detailed foresight of Nero's policy but surely foresees that suffering will come to the Christians in the course of a wider crisis.

51. 'National apostasy' was the title of the sermon by John Keble which started the Oxford Movement: the most important danger, to the supporters of this movement, was liberalism in all its forms (S. L. Ollard, 'The Oxford Movement', in Hasting's *Encyclopaedia of Religion and Ethics* (Vol. IX, 1917)). One of the 'lamps' described in Ruskins's *Seven Lamps of Architecture* is the Lamp of Obedience: this part of Ruskin's work attacks the basic idea of personal liberty.

52. Clark, *Revival,* pp. 196, 201. 'Purely fashionable medievalism' is contrasted with the instructions given by those who wanted to build so that 'every part proclaims the House of God'. Gilbert Scott's comment on the religious motives of the Revivalists is cited on p. 281. (Not that all exponents of religious authority were Revivalists in architecture—*ibid.,* p. 197, with reference to Newman and Keble.)

53. M. Praz, *Studies in Seventeenth Century Imagery* (Rome, Edizione di Studi e Letteratura, 1964). The judgment he quotes (in his foreword, with no page number) is that of C. P. Burge in 1924.

54. Praz, *op. cit.,* pp. 166, 168.

55. Quarles published his *Emblems* in 1635 and *Hieroglyphicks* in 1638. In the 1669 edition of these two works we find, in the letter to the Reader (p. 'A3') the remark that emblems are silent parables (which the carvings on Haynes's stall certainly were) and, on p. 321, the description of his work as an 'Aegyptian dish, drest on the English manner'.

56. His understanding fails because of his moral blindness. The idea that moral weakness corrupts our understanding and our scholarship is somewhat trite and moralistic but it is part of what James is trying to say. Haynes seems in his latter days to be ignoring several clues which point to his destruction on the morning or on the evening of the 26th February, 1818: after all, the night of the 26th February, 1817, was the night of his most frightening encounter of the previous winter. That was when he 'committed the error' of saying 'come in' when the demon spoke in a low, disguised voice outside the door of his bedroom, where he had previously been safe. (The idea that even a very powerful demon cannot enter without an invitation is also used by Bram Stoker in *Dracula.*) Moreover, the cycle of Psalms leaves Psalm 119, with its streak of distress, behind on the 26th evening; the 27th day introduces Psalms of a more exalted mood, a mood which on the whole continues until the end of the month—even the famous *De Profundis* (Psalm 130) ends on that note of reassurance which Psalm 119 appears to lack. Dahood, *Psalms,* assures us that careful study of the Hebrew of Psalm 119 has convinced him, contrary even to some modern commentators, that there is a genuine train of thought in the Psalm as a whole. But the Book of Common Prayer translation both makes it look like a mosaic of different ideas and also makes it seem to end on a painful, ambiguous note: 'I have gone astray as a sheep that is lost . . . I do not forget thy commandment' (vs. 176). This was the Psalm which Haynes heard just before his terrifying, but still perhaps not irre-

deemable, experience of February 26th, 1817. The last service of his life was evensong on February 25th, 1818: and the last verse set for that evening (vs. 104) suggests not painful ambiguity but a clear claim to virtue, 'I hate all evil ways', corresponding to Haynes's refusal clearly to acknowledge his fault even to himself or his diary. This refusal seems to blind him to all warnings; if he had appreciated their urgency he might have been shocked into repentance.

57. A further clue should have come from the status of late February in Roman religion (which he would have studied in order to translate Valerius, the pious pagan, with due scholarship). The old-style Roman year began in March (just as the old-style English year began on March 25th, not in imitation of the Romans, but because that was supposed to be the day of Jesus' conception). 'February' comes from *februum,* an instrument of purification: 'this was the period in which the living were made ready for the civil and religious work of the coming year and in which the yearly duties to the dead were performed' (W. Warde Fowler on 'Calendar, Roman', in Hastings's *Encyclopaedia of Religion and Ethics,* Vol. III, 1910). Sir James Frazer in his edition of Ovid's *Fasti* (London: Macmillan, 1929) explains that the intercalary days between the 23rd (the Terminalia) and the 24th (the Regifugium) marked a period when normal rules were suspended; H. H. Scullard, *Festivals and Ceremonies of the Roman Republic* (London: Thames and Hudson, 1981) confirms (p. 81) the association of the Regifugium with the intercalary days and with a sense of guilt. Ovid and Frazer between them offer several explanations of the ritual of the Regifugium, when the priest-king fled from the sacrifice. All their explanations recognise that, on this date, some sort of end is reached: the festival by recalling the end of the monarchy marks the limited nature of republican office; or it marks the end of the tenure for the individual priest; or it demonstrates his fitness for renewed office; or it marks the sacrifice of an exceptionally sacred or (what is the same thing) an exceptionally purifying victim, thus completing the February rituals emphatically. The new beginning comes with the first festival which refers to the new campaigning season, which is the Horse Festival (the Equirria), falling not on 1st March but on 27th February: the atmosphere of the new year spread forward for a few days. Thus there was reason within paganism for Haynes to foresee that, if he was forbidden to see the start of the new year, he would not see dawn on the 27th. So when the demon on the night of 31st Decem-

ber, 1816, wished Haynes a happy new year, he was conceding another complete cycle within the old-style pagan meaning.

58. For *laetitia* and for Haynes's state of mind, Dr Fitzpatrick points out a pagan parallel, where Catullus (poem 76) likens the trouble in his mind to a pest, a plague, a dread disease (*pestis, pernicies, taeter morbus*) and considers that the gods should release him from his trouble as a reward for his *pietas,* his religious fidelity; his trouble has deprived him of all forms of happiness—*expulit ex omni pectore laetitias* (line 22).

59. U. Eco, *The Limits of Interpretation* (Indiana, 1990), p. 122.

60. Remnant's *Catalogue,* pp. 62, 137, 174.

61. *Emblemata,* edited by A. Henkel and A. Schöne (Stuttgart, Mezlersche, 1967).

62. J. Sullivan, *Elegant Nightmares, the English Ghost Story from Le Fanu to Blackwood* (Athens, Ohio: 1978), pp. 10, 35.

63. Compare C. S. Lewis, *Reflections on the Psalms* (London: Bles, 1958), p. 20. The reference to an extortioner is in verse 11, the references to prayer in verses 4 and 7. In the Septuagint this is Psalm 108.

64. Dahood, *Psalms,* reminds us that 'at the right hand' is where God is asked to stand to defend the poor at the end of Psalm 109 and also where the accuser stands in *Zechariah* iii, 1 (a reflection of Israelite court procedure?). Dahood regards Satan and the evil one in authority as the same figure, rather than two as the story makes them: the Hebrew habit of double reference to the same thing has often caused problems to speakers of other languages.

65. James himself, as Michael Cox notes, is the model for his illustrator when he depicts Dennistoun, who is the hero of James's first story and who stumbles on a Demon of the Night *qui diu volebat strangulare homines.* This inadvertent encounter is a slight variation on the theme of Sheridan Le Fanu (James's principal influence in ghost-story writing) in *Green Tea*—though Le Fanu makes the intrusion on the world of evil spirits even more accidental than it is in James, produced as it is by green tea, a seemingly harmless drug. Sullivan discusses the way in which 'Count Magnus'— James's most terrifying story—makes its amateur antiquarian the helpless victim of forces he scarcely understands. My essay on 'Mr. Humphreys' mentions the discreet link, noted by my colleague Dr Fitzpatrick, established between the magician Wilson and his creator, since his first

name is finally revealed to be James. But in a way 'Mr. Humphreys' is untypical of *More Ghost Stories* in that it revives the *Stories* theme of inadvertent entry on the domain of evil (the maze). *More Ghost Stories* makes more use (see next note) of the theme of unjust judges, persecutors who are malicious but have some reason to seek out their victims. This takes up the theme suggested by Le Fanu in *Mr. Justice Harbottle.* This theme is not absent from *Stories,* certainly not from 'Lost Hearts', where the scholar is so convinced of his own value that he resorts to murder to prolong his life.

66. 'The Rose Garden' mixes the theme of inadvertent stumbling and the theme of the Unjust Judge: the evil spirit on whose lair Mary Anstruther stumbles is that of Sir William Scroggs, the judicial murderer of many of the Popish Plot victims—James tries to capture his physical appearance (cf. J. P. Kenyon, *The Popish Plot* (London: Heinemann, 1972), p. 117.) Scrogg's 'disgrace', as the story calls it, is just the kind of murky episode which would have interested James. It was an important event, though some accounts (Kenyon, p. 204) pass over it perfunctorily; but see *Dictionary of National Biography* and F. S. Ronalds, *The Attempted Whig Revolution of 1678* (Urbana: Illinois, 1937), p. 50. K. D. H. Haley, *The First Earl of Shaftesbury* (Oxford: OUP, 1968), p. 543, shows Scroggs angrily defending himself at a dinner party after he had, seemingly on second thoughts, withdrawn support from the perjured informer Titus Oates. Scroggs, particularly if James shared the *DNB* view of him as a man of blood who had second thoughts, becomes an interesting counterpart to Pulteney, the man who shrank from blood. 'Martin's Close' takes up the theme of the Unjust Judge because it is a courtroom story, dominated by Jeffreys. In 'Casting the Runes' Karswell gives himself judicial airs (mocking the quasi-judicial behaviour of his academic victim, a referee who had prevented the publication of his work): Karswell, in his pretentious way, pronounces a sentence and suspends its execution for six months. In 'The Tractate Middoth' the Reverend Mr Rant, a student of Talmudic law, acts both as *agent provocateur,* judge and executioner. The theme of unjust judgement is close to theme of revenge, which appears both in 'Martin's Close', 'Casting the Runes' and 'A School Story'.

67. Lubbock, *Memoir,* p. 15. The two passages are Psalm 109 (see vs. 8) in this story and *Book of Numbers* xvi (see vs. 29) in 'Mr. Humphreys', where the word is used in its frequent sense of 'visitation' on Korah, one of the characters depicted on Wilson's infernal globe. (So Haynes was in a way writing in defence of divine visitation upon evildoers: perhaps he sensed the irony; certainly he was very much in the position described in *Luke* xix, 44, of 'not knowing the time of his visitation'.) The appearance of these two passages may indicate that James had been thinking about the idea of *episcope,* since research into that idea would certainly involve looking up the Old Testament uses of the appropriate word. (There are, according to Hatch and Redpath's *Concordance to the Septuagint,* 34 uses in the canonical Old Testament, plus 13 in the Apocrypha.) But Haynes's status as one of James's other scholarly selves makes him unusual among the victim characters of *More Ghost Stories,* most of whom have no established status in University or Church: Sampson ('A School Story') is a schoolmaster, Mary Anstruther ('The Rose Garden') the domineering wife of a well-off man, Garrett ('The Tractate Middoth') a junior librarian, Martin ('Martin's Close') an empty-headed Cambridge graduate. On the other hand Harrington ('Casting the Runes') is a scholarly referee for learned journals, though in underestimating Karswell he makes a bad mistake.

68. M. R. James, 'The Wall-paintings in Wickhampton Church', in *Supplement to Blomefield's Norfolk,* edited and published by Clement Ingleby (London, 1929), p. 125 ff. Blomefield was an eighteenth-century incumbent of a Norfolk parish; one of the reasons why his work needed supplementation was that he had left it unfinished. A colleague had tried to complete the work but his pet magpie had seized all his notes on Great Yarmouth and scattered them over a wide area; though most of them were retrieved the reverend gentleman never recovered his composure. Another reason was that new discoveries had been made, including the wall paintings of Wickhampton, which show three princes encountering, during a hunt, three dead men whose words (though they are now illegible) may be presumed from the parallels which James cites to have conveyed pious warnings. The paintings had been uncovered during the 1850s and careful drawings had been made. James comments on them and then adds that they had been covered again, this time with limewash, which had damaged them severely by the time another attempt had been made to rescue them. '*Tantum religio potuit suadere malorum*', says James, 'is the most parliamentary comment that occurs'. It is interesting as a sidelight on 'Barchester' to see that James (writing, I admit, much later) attributes this destructiveness to religious fanaticism, not to unthinking vandalism. It is also important to remember that the Gothic Revivalists sometimes devastated genuinely medieval work, either throwing it away (Cobb, *Forgotten Centuries,* p. 110, quotes a letter, most distressing to read,

from a Salisbury merchant who was disposing of medieval stained and painted glass in job lots) or substituting their own pastiche.

69. *Gospel of Matthew* xii, 45; cf. *Luke* xi, 26. Dr P. J. Fitzpatrick has kindly investigated the calendar for 1818 and identified the Gospel passage. The fourteenth night seems to play a substantial part in Haynes's experiences: and Psalm 74, vs. 5 contains a pointer to the message of the carvings, since Haynes knew of their origin in the Holywood: 'He that hewed timber afore out of the thick trees was known to bring it to an excellent work'. (This is the translation of the *Book of Common Prayer;* the Authorised and other versions are substantially different.)

70. I am indebted to Suzanne Eward's dissertation for its discussion of natural explanations. James, in his Introduction to the anthology *Ghosts and Marvels* (London: 1924) says (p. vi) that the natural explanation should not be 'quite practicable'.

71. This promise might raise the suggestion that James is playing a game of disguises with his readers and really has some Cathedral in mind other than those he mentions in the Introduction. But I do not think this suggestion is correct. Worcester is still a very complete Gothic Revival Cathedral and it did have a seventeenth-century organ screen, dated to 1613. But perhaps James regarded it as Mannerist rather than classical: it is certainly not as unmistakably classical as the Winchester screen, created by Inigo Jones about a decade later. Worcester is fully described in Cobb, *Forgotten Centuries.* But I cannot see why James failed to mention Worcester in the Introduction unless he simply believed that Worcester was less close to Barchester than the Cathedrals which he did name. Winchester raises further problems, in that James may have had a reason for thinking of it but not mentioning it. There is a possibility that James had some personal involvement in the transfer of the remains of the Jones screen to Cambridge and had some reason of tact for not wanting to mention the matter. In the winter of 1908-9 this screen (taken down in 1820 by Garbett) was removed from the Cathedral by the architect, T. G. Jackson, and placed under a covering of straw. In *Country Life* for May 1909 H. Avray Tipping ridiculed the Dean and Chapter for regarding the screen as 'a horrid nuisance' and the City for allocating it to the Recreation Grounds Committee. Early in 1910 it was decided to 'build the screen in'—it was still a very substantial structure, even after much damage—to the new Museum of Archaeology and Ethnography at Cambridge, which Jackson was also building: all this attracted much attention, for in February 1910 we find Jackson telegraphing in response to 'congratulations' from an internationally distinguished writer, Baron von Hügel. The screen now leads from the New Guinea to the Pacific section of the Museum. James's 'Barchester' was published by the *Contemporary Review* in 1910 and so presumably, since the Introduction tells us that these were Christmas stories, written in the autumn of 1909. It is hard to believe, though I know of no documentation, that Cambridge University did not consult James on this matter or that the topic of the Winchester screen was out of his mind at the time of writing. On the other hand the descriptions of Winchester in Pevsner's *Cathedrals* and elsewhere do not lead me to think that overall, which is what matters, it corresponded to Barchester more closely than the named source-Cathedrals. My information about the Winchester screen comes from an article by J. M. G. Blakiston, *Cambridge University Record 47,* kindly supplied to me, along with a copy of the telegraphed letter to von Hügel, by Dr Anita C. Herle of the Cambridge Museum of Archaeology and Anthropology, to whom I am most grateful.

72. Pfaff, *M. R. James,* p. 229. Sullivan (*Elegant Nightmares,* p. 6) mentions another American admirer of James. This was H. P. Lovecraft, a central figure in the American genre of popular horror writing. This genre sometimes includes scenes, inconceivable in James's work, where the demon's intended victims face and defeat him. For an effectively written example, see the demonic Gaunt's defeat at the hands of Alan and Polly in Stephen King's *Needful Things* (London: New English Library edition, 1992), p. 779. Alan's magic weapon, with its coalescing beams of light, symbolises the integrity of his character and explains why he can resist the spirit of selfishness and strife which Gaunt has used to subvert the good people of America. Polly, standing at Alan's side, delivers both the crucial attack on Gaunt's clawlike hand and also the words which finally defeat his lying rhetoric. Thus King's characters can gather together their moral and rational powers, intensify them by sexual feeling for each other, and use them in a supreme struggle. By contrast, James's characters never find any such raw strength: perhaps because the scholarship which distinguishes most of them also inflicts on them certain kinds of doubt and weakness or even (as with Haynes) helps to corrupt them. None of James's heroes would feel Alan's delight at the discovery that he can surprise Gaunt with the weapons of Gaunt's own supernatural world, and still less would express their feelings with Alan's battlecry of 'Abracadabra, you lying fuck!'. By contrast Dunning, in 'Casting the Runes', still feels compunction after he has, by a ruse, turned

Karswell's lethal runes against Karswell. This is partly a very British compunction about annihilating an enemy and partly a scholar's ambivalent feeling about turning knowledge into power. Still, James has had some influence on a mainly American tradition which certainly shares his fear of moral decline but suggests, as he never does, both that force may play a part in bringing decline to an end and also that there are at least some ordinary people who can, because of their profound integrity, be trusted to use extreme force well. Thus this tradition answers warnings of the kind which James conveys and answers them by calling on certain virtues which are supposed to flourish in a society which is, like the United States, democratic. But these are virtues upon which James, whose life was dedicated to educating the traditional British elite, would not have relied with confidence: his uneducated characters are usually good people (Jane Lee is an exception) who are bewildered and ineffectual in the presence of evil; for instance the well-meaning servants in 'Lost Hearts'. But Roosevelt, the twenty-sixth President of the United States, was surely able to sense that James's discussion of moral decline does raise some political questions.

Robert Michalski (essay date spring 1996)

SOURCE: Michalski, Robert. "The Malice of Inanimate Objects." *Extrapolation* 37, no. 1 (spring 1996): 46-62.

[*In the following essay, Michalski asserts that James's sense of the living past of objects portrayed in his stories differs from the modern view of objects as commodities.*]

If an interest in the supernatural or the occult betrays a fundamental nostalgia for times past and for superseded modes of thinking, M. R. James (1862-1936) is an anachronism even among writers interested in the supernatural.[1] Unlike other practitioners of the ghost story such as Henry James and Algernon Blackwood, M. R. James had little interest in the contemporary occult phenomena of spiritualism and psychic research (Briggs 124).[2] The plots of James's stories rely more on a reflection on the religious beliefs and superstitions of the past than on an engagement with the spiritual controversies of his own time.

Despite (and perhaps because of) their studied anachronism, James's ghost stories provide a unique glimpse into and critique of modernity. Like the occult fiction of Arthur Machen, with its evocations of a mythic Celtic past, James's stories partake of a process of cultural layering that critiques modern society by contrasting it

with times past. The portrayals of modern society in James's fiction, however, are often only implicit and usually very incomplete. Unlike Machen, who explicitly deals with modern medical science in "The Great God Pan" (1894), with the new "science" of ethnology in "The Three Imposters" (1895), and with a burgeoning consumer-oriented society in "A Fragment of Life" (1906), James uses the modern world as the almost unnoticed background against which the picturesque and exotic intrusions of the supernatural appear.[3] The "contemporary" in James's fiction generally inhabits the span of time including the reign of Victoria and the three decades following it; it consists primarily of the privileged society of academic gentlemen of "independent means" or of a marginal and residual religious order populated by such eccentric creatures as deans, vergers, and prebendaries.

The most familiar modern aspects of this academic and clerical world are skepticism toward the supernatural, an increasing departmentalization of knowledge, and the declining prominence of organized religion in society (a fact to which the ghost stories attest by their abundance of empty chapels and unread devotional writings). James's decidedly biased (and backward-looking) vision of "modern" society lacks any explicit recognition of either the material achievements of British industry in the nineteenth century or the social changes this expansion of capitalism helped bring about—developments on which any "objective" history of nineteenth-century society would likely focus. Only by inference may we contrast the values and beliefs of the religious and academic milieus of the ghost stories with the dominant values and beliefs of late-nineteenth- and early-twentieth-century culture, a culture increasingly dominated by the production, consumption, and exchange of commodities.

Although the scrupulous detail of James's ghost stories does not include a description of the expansion and development of the system of commodity production in the nineteenth century or a description of the newly developing "consumer culture" of the twentieth, his ghost stories do comprise a discourse about objects and their exchange, whether by gift or theft. Objects in James's tales seldom directly take part in commodity exchange, yet the relationship between the supernatural and material objects in these tales suggests a similarity between them and Marx's theory of commodity fetishism, in which "a commodity is . . . a mysterious thing, simply because in it the social character of men's labour appears to them as an objective character stamped upon the product of that labour; because the relation of the producers to the sum total of their own labour is presented to them as a social relation, existing not between themselves, but between the products of their labour" (77). Although the objects in the world of James's fiction are not usually commodities, they nonetheless possess hidden spiritual powers that implicitly comment not only on the exchange of objects in the modern capitalist world but on the social relations that underly that exchange.

James's 1925 short story, **"A View from a Hill,"** provides a relatively uncomplicated example of the occult power of things. Mr. Fanshawe, an academic, borrows a pair of field glasses while visiting his friend Squire Richards. Fanshawe peers through the glasses and sees a church tower that does not really exist and a gallows on a hilltop that in actuality is covered only by a thick grove of trees. After an uncanny experience in the grove, during which the trees appear to grab and clutch at him, Fanshawe returns to the Squire's estate to learn the history of these strange field glasses. Through both Richards and his servant Patten, Fanshawe discovers that a local watchmaker, Baxter, constructed the glasses after conducting some suspicious experiments with the remains of criminals hanged at the long-since-transformed hilltop. These experiments enable Baxter to see through the eyes of the dead and thus establish himself as an amateur archaeologist celebrated for his discovery of a Roman villa and for the accumulation of interesting artifacts dating from various periods of the county's history. Baxter's final and greatest achievement, however, was the discovery of a process to distill the bones of the dead and concentrate the extract in his pair of glasses. This ultimate degradation and desecration of the unhallowed remains eventually leads to Baxter's death at the hands of the enfuriated spirits.

The means of acquiring possession of an object in **"A View from a Hill"** are various. The Squire's purchase of Baxter's archaeological collection after the latter's demise and his subsequent presentation of the collection as a gift to the town museum represent relatively unproblematical modes of exchange in the story. Likewise, Fanshawe's borrowing of the glasses in order to replace a pair that he in turn had lent to a colleague figures in the story as motivation for the retrieval of Baxter's glasses from their state of disuse in the Squire's cupboard. More important to the disastrous outcome of the tale, however, are the concepts of discovery and creation as means of acquiring possession of an object. Baxter's necromantic techniques for ferreting out the hidden cultural treasures of the past provide the only title of ownership for his collection of ancient pots and medieval implements. Indeed, although the discovery of the villa does not give the old watchmaker legal ownership, the Squire refers to it as "Baxter's Roman villa" (537). The right of discovery also provides the foundation for Baxter's growing reputation in archeology, a field outside his original calling.

A part-time antiquary, Baxter remains on the safe side of sacrilege only as long as he confines his activities to the accumulation of "found objects." Once he makes the transition from the role of the relatively passive discoverer of cultural artifacts to the role of active creator, his effrontery to the spirits of the dead becomes too great for these spirits to bear. Baxter creates the field glasses from the remains of the dead and intends to use his possession of them for profit. As Patten, the Squire's old servant, reports in the description of his conversation with Baxter, the watchmaker does not intend to sell the glasses: "I [Patten] says, 'might I have a look at them?' 'No, no,' he says, 'I've put 'em to bed for tonight, and when I do show 'em you, you'll have to pay for peepin', so I tell you.' And that gentlemen, were the last words I heard that man say" (556-57). Instead of renouncing claim to the glasses by selling them, Baxter hopes to make a profit from them by renting them out, perhaps for their diversionary interest, perhaps for the historical knowledge they could reveal. In any case, Baxter's plans do not reach fruition. Compelled to join forces by being imprisoned in the field glasses, the ghosts acquire a power they were unable to achieve while scattered about amidst the fragments of their earthly remains; they in turn "take possession" of Mr. Baxter, drag him around town, and ultimately kill him on Gallows Hill. Baxter's proprietary claim over the spirits by right of discovering their remains backfires, and his potential as a creator remains unrealized.

The implications of this revolt of the spirits of the dead jeopardize the status of Baxter's only other "imaginative" creation—a "reconstructive" drawing of the tower of Fulnaker Priory, a local landmark that had lost its tower many years before. Baxter made his drawing during the one week between the completion of the field glasses and his death. In Fanshawe's opinion, the drawing offers suggestive evidence that Baxter had the potential for becoming "a very respectable artist" (545). Fanshawe's appreciation of the picture is so great that at the very end of the tale he implies that the aesthetic value of the drawing outweighs the desecration necessary to produce it and the hideous punishment required to atone for the sacrilege. The recognition that the conception and execution of a "respectable" artwork depends on the involuntary collaboration of the most despised stratum of society—condemned criminals—complicates more, however, than just the question of creative authority, control, and possession. It invites the consideration that the original Fulnaker Priory as well as Baxter's Roman villa and the other cultural artifacts unearthed by archaeologists are founded on a similarly coercive relationship between "creators" and menial laborers without whom such creation is impossible.

The supernatural status of the glasses in **"A View from a Hill"** resembles that of the gift in primitive societies as described by anthropologist Marcel Mauss. In *The Gift* (1925), Mauss claims that in Maori culture the thing given possesses part of the spirit of the person from whom it originated:

The obligation attached to a gift itself is not inert. Even when abandoned by the giver, it still forms a part of him. Through it he has a hold over the recipient, just as he had while its owner, a hold over anyone who stole it. For the *taonga* [object] is animated with the *hau* [spirit] of its forest, its soil, its homeland, and the *hau* pursues him who holds it. . . .

But for the moment it is clear that in Maori custom this bond created by things is in fact a bond between persons, since the thing itself is a person or pertains to a person. Hence it follows that to give something is to give a part of oneself. . . . It follows clearly from what we have seen that in this system of ideas one gives away what is in reality a part of one's nature and substance, while to receive something is to receive a part of someone's spiritual essence.

(9-10)

Mauss's gift differs from the capitalist commodity by retaining the "memory" of where it originates, of who created it, and of the social obligations its exchange creates. As Michael Taussig points out in *The Devil and Commodity Fetishism in South America,* conceiving of labor as a commodity that is paid for by a wage "exorcises" the product of any personal embodiment, and thus the product attains "an autonomy apart from human social activities" (28). The haunted field glasses of **"A View from a Hill,"** according to this view, inhabit the realm of precapitalist economic relations—but not completely. Although, like the *hau* in relation to the recipient of a Maori gift, the spirits of the haunted field glasses pursue Baxter and in fact obtain a "hold over" him, the tragedy enacted in the ghost story could not occur without Baxter's misguided belief that he could alienate a single faculty—vision—from the collective spirit embodied in the skeletal remains and concentrate it in the field glasses. Indeed, for the narrator to pause and recount the events surrounding this experience as events worthy of notice—for Fanshawe and Squire Richards to imagine that Baxter's glasses do contain a mystery—in part depends on a worldview that sees binoculars, Roman villas, and broken pots as ordinarily autonomous of the human beings who make and use them.

The complete "exorcism" of person from product does not, however, exist in the world of **"A View from a Hill."** What does exist are suggestions of an alternative way of conceiving the relationship between people and things that does not provoke the same disorder and disruption of the everyday "modern" world as do the more obviously supernatural modes of possession. This intermediate form of relationship is represented by both Baxter's status as an artisan and his part-time amateur pursuits. As a watchmaker and skilled workman, Baxter has a position in the general economy of modern society that is somewhat marginal, at least when contrasted with the predominant form of unskilled wage labor. He owns his own shop, but it does not appear that anyone works for him; the entire business seems to be in his

hands alone. Therefore, it would not be strange to say that Baxter, as an artisan, is responsible for his product, or that the watches he makes (like his achievements as an amateur archaeologist or artist) are "Baxter's" even when no notion of legal ownership is implied.

This limited right of possession that Baxter enjoys over the products of his craftsmanship and over the results of his archaeological skill help explain why, despite the disturbance of the field glasses from their place of rest, Baxter himself never makes a supernatural appearance in the story. The recovery of an object intimately connected to such traumatic events might, in any number of other ghost stories, provoke the ghostly return of the person fatally involved in those events. But in **"A View from a Hill,"** Baxter's spirit remains quiet. His ghost does not return because, in the world of the story, it is quite *natural* for the products of Baxter's knowledge and skill to retain a "memory" of him; it is quite natural for the world of Fanshawe and Richards to remember Baxter for his achievements. The anonymous slaves, thieves, and murderers executed on Gallows Hill were never given proper burials or cemetery headstones by which to remember their names. For this reason, the extraordinary attempt of these bones of the dead to "remember" their former owners is a supernatural event. Baxter's spirit hovers about the mysterious glasses only in the figurative sense that the field glasses inspire those with memories of Baxter to tell his history.

Two figures that appear prominently in James's ghost stories—the antiquary (or collector) and the storyteller—also appear in the work of the German cultural critic Walter Benjamin. A brief look at Benjamin's ruminations concerning the collector and the storyteller can help illuminate the role that the possession and exchange of objects play in James's fiction. Benjamin's essays "Unpacking My Library" (1931) and "The Storyteller" (1936) describe the collector and the storyteller as apparently antithetical figures. "Unpacking My Library" emphasizes the collector's acquisitive ego: as Benjamin states at the beginning of the essay, his purpose is to give "some insight into the relationship of a book collector to his possessions." The collector in "Unpacking My Library" assumes the shape of private property personified: for him an object realizes its true "freedom" only once it has entered into *his* possession. Benjamin claims, similarly, that "the phenomenon of collecting loses its meaning as it loses its personal owner" (67). Not surprisingly, therefore, the collector is the fetishist *par excellence:* "For inside him there are spirits, or at least little genii, which have seen to it that for a collector—and I mean a real collector, a collector as he ought to be—ownership is the most intimate relationship that one can have to objects. Not that they come alive in him; it is he who lives in them" (67). Not only do the possessions of a collector have a life of their own, but these same objects animate the collector himself: the objects themselves are the source of the little genii who inspire the passion of acquisition. Paradoxically, Benjamin implies, the fetishist is a fetish of his own possessions. Rich in things, the acquisitive ego is nonetheless impoverished—not by the revelation that things mediate his relationships with other people but by the realization that he is merely the mediator of a relationship among things.

Benjamin describes the *storyteller*, on the other hand, as one embedded in and conscious of social relations: "A great storyteller will always be rooted in the people, primarily in a milieu of craftsmen" (101). In contradistinction to the solitary, isolated collector of artifacts, the storyteller is a practitioner of a craft, an artisan whose product, the telling of stories, is simultaneously a distribution among a "community of listeners" (91). This involvement in an active practice is what most distinguishes the storyteller from the collector of objects d'art; not surprisingly, therefore, Benjamin finds the storyteller's origins in an oral culture where voice and gesture aid in his attempts to directly communicate experiences to his listeners. The collector, in contrast, accumulates the already-finished artifacts of an exclusively material culture, for there is little space in the collector's cramped quarters for the performing arts. Finally, where Benjamin claims that all "real" stories contain something useful (it may be a moral or even a bit of practical advice), he asserts that the rare editions and manuscripts of the book collector attain a value wholly independent of their use value; in fact, according to Benjamin, sheer possession of a book often outweighs any desire to read it as motive for its acquisition. Benjamin, in short, describes the storyteller as the dispenser of wisdom and practical advice and the collector as the storyteller's opposite, the solitary accumulator of objects.

Nonetheless, as Terry Eagleton has suggested in *Walter Benjamin or Towards a Revolutionary Criticism,* the Benjaminian (and, for my purposes, the Jamesian) storyteller himself mediates social relations. Eagleton argues that, as a recollector and recounter of experiences, the storyteller is embedded in social relations; he stands midway between his listeners and those other storytellers from whom he has acquired the experiences out of which he crafts his own tales. In such a way, Eagleton points out, storytelling is a collective practice, and the storyteller is a collector of experiences (60-61).

The distinction between these two figures blurs when one takes a closer look at the collector as well. In his study of James's contemporary and fellow fantasist Arthur Machen, Donald M. Hassler, for example, argues that a "small community of devoted book collectors" (118) helped provide Machen and other "antimodernists" with the basis for a "filial alternative" (124) to modernism. Hassler suggests that the collector, like the

storyteller, is embedded in a social community intimately related to the activity of collecting. Even Benjamin states, with only a hint of facetiousness, that the most praiseworthy method of acquiring books is by writing them. In this most demanding way of becoming a book collector, we see how it may, from a particular perspective, be impossible to distinguish the collector from the storyteller. Even in less extreme situations, the true collector is a collector of stories, the histories of objects he owns: "Everything remembered and thought, everything conscious, becomes the pedestal, the frame, the base, the lock of his [the collector's] property. The period, the region, the craftsmanship, the former ownership—for a true collector the whole background of an item adds up to a magic encyclopedia whose quintessence is the fate of his object. . . . As he holds them in his hands, he seems to be seeing through them into their distant past as though inspired" (60-61).

Like Baxter the archaeologist, Benjamin's collector founds his right of possession not on the narrow basis of legal ownership but on his knowledge of the history of objects. For the collector, knowledge of the history of an object is his title of ownership—the collector, too, is a collector of stories. Paradoxically, by only truly living through his objects, by being the fetish of his fetishes, the seemingly egoistical collector opens himself up to the people whose histories have also been touched by the same object. By recollecting, by giving life to the histories of his possessions, the collector asserts his membership in the community of craftsmen and former owners that is the history of the object.

Like the possessions of Benjamin's collector, the field glasses of **"A View from a Hill"** are not as inert as they initially appear to be; rather, they represent a nexus of active exchanges. These exchanges are not merely the movement of an object from the collection of one antiquarian to that of another; primarily, the binoculars mark an exchange of experiences between storytellers—between the Squire and Fanshawe and between the narrator and his listeners/readers. Most importantly, the glasses represent an exchange between the dead and the living, an exchange that illustrates how dangerous memories of superseded cultural orders may be for the dehistoricized, naturalized conception of the present order of things. Unlike the exchange of commodities in Marx's view of the marketplace, the exchange of objects and experiences in M. R. James's ghost stories occasions not the occulation of the social history of the production of cultural artifacts but its revelation.

In order to illustrate more fully this transformation of inert objects into active practices in James's ghost stories, it will be necessary to take a look at two tales from early in James's ghost story writing career: **"The Treasure of Abbot Thomas"** (1904) and **"Casting the Runes"** (1911). **"The Treasure of Abbot Thomas"** has a simple enough plot. Set in 1859, the tale recounts the adventures of Mr. Somerton, a squire with antiquarian interests, who decides to write a book about a series of sixteenth century painted windows. Brought to England after the confiscation of much Church land during the German Reformation, the windows that interest Somerton originated at the Abbey Church of Steinfeld, "the most considerable of these involuntary contributors to our artistic possessions" (153). In his research, Somerton discovers a 1712 history of the abbey that refers to an Abbot Thomas, who had supposedly hidden a cache of gold somewhere in the monastery. When the other monks asked Thomas about the treasure, the Abbot, according to the history, replied, "Job, John, and Zechariah will tell either you or your successors" (152). Somerton eventually runs across one of the Steinfeld windows at the chapel of a Lord D; the windows depict the three prophets Job, John, and Zechariah. Each figure holds a scroll that bears a passage from the Vulgate version of their respective inspired writings. The rest of the story concerns Somerton's deciphering of the messages hidden in these writings, his discovery of the treasure's location (at the bottom of the Steinfeld Abbey well), and his attempt to retrieve the treasure. However, when Somerton finally gets to the bottom of the monastery well, he manages only to bring to the surface the guardian demon stationed over the treasure by Abbot Thomas. Shaken by Thomas's practical joke, Somerton summons Gregory, the rector of his parish, to Steinfeld in order to assist the former's personal servant in replacing the stone over the hole where the gold is, an operation that Somerton hopes will prevent the demon from keeping his close watch on the squire.

In **"The Treasure of Abbot Thomas,"** as in **"A View from a Hill,"** an antiquarian disturbs a haunted object, the spirit of which subsequently comes to torment the disturber. Compared with **"A View from a Hill,"** however, **"The Treasure of Abbot Thomas"** presents a situation in which objects and their relationships to people are much more complicated. The problem that **"The Treasure of Abbot Thomas"** presents is that the haunted gold, as it functions in the tale, is not really a valuable material artifact but a symbol for abstract value itself. The Roman villa and the medieval implements of **"A View from a Hill"** possess value because of what they tell us about the cultures in which they originated. If they possess a spirit, they possess it because of the specificity and individuality both of the people who made them and of the time and place of their creation. Abbot Thomas's gold, however, does not possess any of the specificity of such cultural artifacts. Although coins may be of historical or aesthetic interest, nowhere does **"The Treasure of Abbot Thomas"** identify the specific form of this gold. In spite of Somerton's sensitivity to antiquarian and artistic detail, he never gets close enough to the treasure to determine whether it takes the shape of coins, objects d'art or just shapeless

heaps of metal. The gold is less an identifiable object than a symbol of abstract value. The reader of this tale must look elsewhere for the specificity that the treasure of Abbot Thomas lacks.

"The Treasure of Abbot Thomas" locates the cultural and historical specificity that the gold lacks in the textual and pictorial representations that hover "around" the treasure of abstract value. The most obvious example of these representations is the series of windows depicting Job, John, and Zechariah. Even without the treasure's incentive, the windows apparently possess enough aesthetic and historical interest to warrant Somerton's writing a guidebook about them. In the process of unraveling Abbot Thomas's riddle, Somerton provides a fairly detailed description of the windows as well as an evaluation of the paintings' style and technique that confirms the place and time of their making. The narrator provides us with other cultural representations that surround the treasure including a portion of the early-eighteenth-century Latin text that first sets Somerton in search of the treasure. Thus, both Somerton's correct "reading" of the Abbot's scattered hints and the narrator's authentic rendering of this process of discovery depend on a sensitivity to detail—aesthetic, historical, and linguistic—which in the end fails to grasp the supposed object of the tale, the gold itself.

Unlike **"A View from a Hill,"** which illustrates the inseparability of objects and the spirits of the people who created them, **"The Treasure of Abbot Thomas"** demonstrates more clearly that what may appear as the supernatural power or spirit of inert objects is actually the result of a performance or practice requiring the active participation of both "producers" and the "consumers." The deceptive autonomy of objects obscures the fact that they are always embedded in such social processes, and it leads to the notion that the "consumption" of a cultural artifact is a relatively passive affair. Even persistent scrutiny of the representations of Abbot Thomas's treasure fails to appropriate the fabled treasure. Somerton's "failure of vision" suggests that the "real object" of the story is that the "consumption" of a cultural artifact is an active participation in and recreation of that artifact.

As in **"A View from a Hill,"** the predominant mode of discovery and appropriation in **"The Treasure of Abbot Thomas"** is vision. As if to emphasize this, Abbot Thomas has inscribed on one of his windows the Vulgate passage, "'Oculos habent, et non videbunt' (They have eyes, and shall not see)" (169) and has the prophet Zechariah offer as a clue to the whereabouts of the gold the cryptical "Super lapidem unum setem oculi sunt," "Upon one stone are seven eyes" (154). Somerton sets off on his quest for the treasure after first reading about the Steinfeld legend; significantly, the legend leads him to a series of painted windows the importance of which only he is able to "see." Nowhere is there any indication in the story that Somerton intends to share his discovery with either Lord D, the owner of the windows, or the current owners of Steinfeld Abbey, the actual location of the treasure. Having eyes *and* being able to see is claim enough for the possession of the gold. For Somerton, moreover, vision is not merely a means of appropriating objects but also of consuming them. Once he has extracted all of the information that he needs from the painted windows, all thought of the windows vanishes from Somerton's mind. Despite his extensive knowledge of art, the correct reading of the windows fails to contribute to their aesthetic appreciation; rather, in comparison with Somerton's interest in the treasure, it impoverishes them.

Confident in the knowledge that he possesses the appropriating gaze, Somerton receives a violent shock when he dislodges the stone with seven eyes, the penultimate obstacle to his possession of the gold. All of Somerton's ingenuity of perception comes to naught with the release of the guardian demon and Somerton's subsequent realization that the laughing, ghoulish figure at the top of the well was the ghost of Abbot Thomas himself. As Parson Gregory explains the affairs of that night, "the person who set the trap might have come to see the success of his plan" (177). Indeed, the Abbot seems to have written the script for a drama that the all-too-perceptive reader Somerton could not help but perform. The "real object" of **"The Treasure of Abbot Thomas,"** therefore, turns out not to be an object at all but the process of working through the Abbot's puzzle. From this perspective, the seemingly inert object once again reveals itself as the crossroads of a living interaction between the past and the present.

This description of the transformation of a passive observer of an action into an active participant needs some qualification. In **"The Treasure of Abbot Thomas,"** an alternative form of looking translates itself into an active "doing" without the trauma of supernatural terror. This transformation, as Somerton's account of the discovery of a hidden cypher in the windows suggests, may as accurately be described as the translation of doing into looking as of looking into doing: "But it so happened that there was a good deal of dust on the surface of the glass, and Lord D happening to come in, noticed my blackened hands, and kindly insisted on sending for a Turk's head broom to clean down the window. There must, I suppose, have been a rough piece in the broom; anyhow, as it passed over the border of one of the mantles, I noticed that it left a long scratch, and that some yellow stain instantly showed up. I asked the man to stop his work for a moment, and ran up the ladder to examine the place" (163). Somerton's description of this small incident seems innocent enough—until we reach the last sentence. His blackened hands and the description of the brush's movements imply that Som-

erton's hand holds the brush, when, in fact, an unnamed servant wields it. (In rereading the passage I had to hesitate over the second sentence. It almost appears to describe the brush acting autonomously of both the servant and Somerton!) Somerton, we finally realize, merely supervises the work of the anonymous servant. In a similar way, Lord D's inadvertent supervision of his social inferior, Somerton, precipitates the cleaning of the window and the ensuing action of the story.

These acts of supervision, however, are not confined to this seemingly trivial scene of the story; they are a historical echo of the social relations existing between Abbot Thomas and his subordinates. As the Latin history of the Abbey relates, "Among other works carried out by this Abbot [Thomas] I may specially mention his filling the great window at the east end of the south aisle of the church with figures admirably painted on glass, as his effigy and arms in the window attest. He also restored almost the whole of the Abbot's lodging, and dug a well in the court of it, which he adorned with beautiful carvings in marble" (152). Grammatically, this description makes it appear that Thomas himself filled the windows and renovated the abbey, but, of course, he achieved these things only in the sense that a patron commissions an artist to paint a window or sculpt a figure. As a patron of the arts, Thomas is the one whose vision or imagination provides the impetus for the creation of the windows, whose supervision ensures that the artist correctly encodes the clues to the treasure, and whose observation of the events of that night in 1859 makes him the "consumer" of the resulting spectacle. Thus, through the concept of supervision—the subordination of execution to conception—**"The Treasure of Abbot Thomas"** provides a decidedly unsupernatural way in which a passive vision transforms itself into action.

In recognition of the relationship between the supernatural and the "natural" methods of transforming vision into action, James provides a twist in class relationships at the very end of his tale, a twist that combines the supervisory character of the "natural" form with the reciprocal, interactive "looking" across time of the supernatural mode. Where, hitherto in the story, all the characters who possess the appropriating gaze generally supervise the activities of their subordinates, the climactic scene of Somerton's experience allows master and subordinate to finally meet face to face. In the fateful scene at the abbey well, James gives William Brown, Somerton's servant, a more active role in the narrative than other subordinate figures have had thus far. Standing near the mouth of the well, Brown notices and draws Somerton's attention to the seven-eyed stone that marks the location of the gold. Given his spatial position in relation to Somerton, Brown does literally supervise the actions of his master at the bottom of the well. This places him, as it turns out, on the same footing as Abbot Thomas as a spectator of the un-folding drama. Indeed, if a literal exchange of looks oc-curs in the story, it transpires between Abbot Thomas and William Brown, who describes the ghostly cleric as "a holdish man, and the face very much fell in, and lar-fin, as I thought" (177). Despite his leading role in the solution of the Abbot's puzzle, Somerton does not see Thomas himself; instead he only catches a glimpse of the malformed guardian demon, the Abbot's servant, who will, subsequent to the violation of the treasure's hiding place, keep his menacing watch over Somerton. As in **"A View from a Hill,"** the supernaturalism of **"The Treasure of Abbot Thomas"** represents the inter-action of the past with the present. More so than in the former ghost story, this engagement with the past takes the form of an interaction between classes.

Like **"The Treasure of Abbot Thomas," "Casting the Runes"** involves the obtaining and the subsequent re-turn of a cursed object. In **"Casting the Runes,"** how-ever, the nature of the object and its means of exchange differ greatly from the cache of gold in **"The Treasure of Abbot Thomas."** More "modern" than most of James's stories, the setting of **"Casting the Runes"** is contemporary, 1911 London. The central figure is Mr. Karswell, the mysterious and wealthy owner of Lufford Abbey and, as it becomes apparent through the course of the story, a practitioner of the black arts. Unlike the practical joker, Abbot Thomas, Karswell uses his magic not for frivolous reasons but to achieve literary and scholarly respectability. This craving manifests itself in two works that Karswell writes, his *History of Witch-craft* and *The Truth of Alchemy,* neither of which is well received by the academic community. The rest of **"Cast-ing the Runes"** recounts Karswell's occult revenge against the people responsible for the poor reception of his scholarly achievements.

Edward Dunning, the alchemical expert who causes a prestigious association to reject Karswell's latest paper on the medieval "science," learns of the history of a predecessor in Karswell's "bad books" (240) in a curi-ous way. While idly gazing at the advertisements pasted to the windows of the electric tram in which he is trav-eling, Dunning spies an unusual example of this infor-mative genre: "In memory of John Harrington, F.S.A. [Fellow of the Society of Antiquaries], of The Laurels, Ashbrooke. Died Sept. 18th, 1889. Three months were allowed" (244). Several days later, on his way to the British Museum, Dunning encounters a distributor of advertising leaflets who thrusts into his hands a paper with a similar announcement of Mr. Harrington's death twenty years before. Intrigued by this series of coinci-dences and oppressed by a foreboding feeling "that something ill-defined and impalpable had stepped in be-tween him and his fellow-men—had taken him in charge, as it were" (250), Dunning begins to make in-quiries about the mysterious John Harrington. In his

pursuit of the mystery, Dunning discovers that Har-rington had written a scathing review of Karswell's first book and that Harrington's brother Henry was familiar with the events of the dead scholar's last months.

With a knowledge of John Harrington's unfortunate his-tory, the younger Harrington and Dunning are able to sift through the events of the previous days and piece together Karswell's modus operandi. Like the older Harrington twenty years before, Dunning, in a seem-ingly trivial occurrence, lost a sheaf of papers that he subsequently recovered through the aid of a "civil man" (259), who turns out to have been Karswell. Upon in-spection, the sheaf reveals a slip of paper with unintelli-gible runic markings on it. The two conclude that the Runes must contain a "message or commission" that has "the effect of bringing its possessors into very un-desirable company" (260), possibly an evil spirit. As in **"The Treasure of Abbot Thomas,"** Dunning can only remove the curse if he returns the object in question (the slip of paper) to its original home, Karswell's pos-session.

As the story progresses, Dunning and Harrington, with some difficulty, manage to follow Karswell on the first leg of the occultist's journey to the Continent. On a train headed for Dover, Karswell drops his ticket case; Dunning retrieves it, secrets the paper in the case, and proffers it to Karswell. The case is accepted and the circle completed. With their mission accomplished and Karswell safely in France, Dunning and Harrington de-velop uneasy consciences and decide to telegraph a warning to the magician. This effort, however, is to no avail. While Karswell inspects the design of a French cathedral, a stone dislodges and crushes him.

As in **"The Treasure of Abbot Thomas,"** the status of the spirit-possessed object in **"Casting the Runes"** is uncertain. With this tale, however, we need not pause too long in describing how the seeming stability of ob-jects gives way to reveal itself as an active relationship among people. The slip of paper that passes between Karswell and his intended victims lacks supernatural power, a fact made clear by a comparison of the respec-tive fates of Harrington's runic writings and Dunning's. Shortly after John Harrington receives Karswell's runic curse, the mysterious paper, seemingly of its own ac-cord, flutters into Harrington's fireplace and is con-sumed by flames. But the destruction of the paper has no effect on the curse's fatal intent. Conversely, with the aid of Henry Harrington's knowledge of his broth-er's fate, Dunning and the younger Harrington make sure to preserve the slip of paper, yet "both hesitated to copy them [the Runes], for fear, as they confessed, of perpetuating whatever evil purpose they might conceal" (260). The paper itself, as these events suggests, har-bors no evil spirit; on the contrary, the Runes express the "curious message or commission" (260) that contains the supernatural. More important for the effective-ness of Karswell's curse than the continued possession of its material trace is the voluntary acceptance (if only in a disguised form) of this enigmatic message. The tale's supernaturalism hovers around the activities of giving and receiving, not necessarily around the material thing given and accepted.

If any "thing" is under contention between Karswell and his more respectable academic opponents, it is the intangible (but to Karswell, very real) reputation of a scholar that only membership in their community can give him. Karswell's bid for acceptance in this community, his books, and his revenge against the people who frustrate this attempt, the Runic curse, bear an inverse relationship to each other. Karswell presents both to the representatives of the community he wishes to join, but while Harrington and Dunning reject the merit of the works, they unwittingly accept the concealed curse. Readers of Karswell's two types of discourse, the scholarly and the runic, describe the one as "hopeless" (242) and the other as "not decipherable" (260). The inability to understand the first "unintelligible discourse" prevents Karswell from joining the academic community, while the unwitting acceptance of the second "brings its possessors into very undesirable company" (260).

Karswell's maliciousness should not blind us to this desire for community. Although this need for acceptance manifests itself in an unforgiving "literary ambition" (242), Karswell employs his more potent means of practical magic only after Harrington and Dunning have dealt unsympathetically with Karswell's prosaic attempts to elucidate witchcraft and alchemy. Karswell, Harrington, and Dunning join a host of James's other lonely scholars, antiquarians, and clerics whose supernatural encounters do not represent a breakdown of psychic stability and the impending threat of madness (the subject matter of so many fantastic tales of the nineteenth century) but rather represent the last faint possibility for a community based on values other than those of the dominant ideology of individualism. The clerical and academic settings of James's stories manifest this anti-individualism in their appeal to the Middle Ages and its supposed unity of purpose. His semi-monastic academic life as a don at Cambridge and later as provost of Eton perhaps represented to James one of the last residues of the communitarian aspects of the Middle Ages.

As in **"A View from a Hill"** and **"The Treasure of Abbot Thomas,"** the portrayal of the animate powers of inanimate objects in **"Casting the Runes"** gradually reveals itself to be not a discourse about objects per se but a discourse about active relationships among people, relationships that only come to light through the exchange of a "possessed" object. In **"Casting the Runes,"** however, James takes this presentation one step further by creating a situation in which the supernatural "object," the runes, is a discourse. The essential property of any kind of discourse in this tale is its power to bring one into some sort of community with other beings—either fellow antiquarians or vengeful demons. In James's tales objects cease to be autonomous, inert entities and become the active elements of a discourse that reveals the nature of the relationship between its producers and its "consumers."

The question of the relationship between objects and discourses in James's ghost stories suggests consideration of another discourse about objects that makes a brief appearance in **"Casting the Runes"**: advertising. After a busy day at the British Museum, Dunning idly peruses the advertisements pasted to the windows of his tram car: "As was not unnatural, the advertisements in this particular line of cars were objects of his frequent contemplation, and, with the possible exception of the brilliant and convincing dialogue between Mr. Lamplough and an eminent K.C. [King's Counsel] on the subject of Pyretic Saline, none of them afforded much scope to his imagination" (244). The narrator is incorrect, of course, for Dunning then spies the peculiar announcement of John Harrington's death. Although Harrington may not have been "an eminent K.C.," his personal acquaintance with Karswell's occult powers surely qualifies his history as sufficient testimony both to the authenticity of Karswell's *History of Witchcraft* and to the effectiveness of Karswell's practical knowledge of magic. Unlike "the brilliant and convincing dialogue" concerning Pyretic Saline, this advertisement refers not to a specific object but to a practice, a ritual exchange of words that leads to the recipient's death.

This brief intrusion of advertising, one of the most salient features of modern culture, into the nostalgic world of James's ghost stories is suggestive. Although the clumsy hawking of Pyretic Saline seems to bear no resemblance to the enigmatic advertisement of Karswell's magical knowledge and abilities, advertisements during the late nineteenth and early twentieth centuries (and after), like James's ghost stories, testify to the strangely animate power of inanimate objects. Before the period beginning in the 1890s, advertisements in both the United States and Great Britain tended to portray commodities as if they were completely autonomous of the human beings who created and used them. The text constituting most advertisements in the mid-nineteenth century, as Richard Ohmann points out in *Politics and Letters,* described the remarkable powers and uses of commodities as if these qualities were the inherent properties of the objects themselves—no attempt made to contextualize their production or use.

With the consolidation of "corporate" capitalism and the establishment of national markets beginning in the 1880s, Ohmann identifies a dramatic transformation of advertising techniques in the United States. Among other significant changes, Ohmann especially notes the receding of the product from its former prominence in the advertisement. Pictorial images, which now dominate the advertisement's printed text, may still portray the commodity, but usually the material qualities of the product are no longer emphasized. Instead, as Ohmann notes, "the product is embedded in a whole way of life, full of social meaning" (153). The object is now contextualized in a scene of consumption that emphasizes the social and economic status of its consumers. Raymond Williams, in a study of the history of British advertising, likewise locates the crucial transformation of the organization and importance of British advertising in the period beginning with the 1880s. Williams similarly describes the world of modern advertising as "a cultural pattern in which the objects are not enough but must be validated, if only in fantasy, by association with social and personal meanings which in a different cultural pattern might be more directly available" (185).

This expansion of the commodity's role, from simple saleable object to gateway to a "whole way of life," parallels the course that the meaning of objects take in the ghost stories of M. R. James. Objects both in James's stories and in the consumer culture lose their self-sufficiency and expose their embeddedness in a system of social relations. In the words of Michael Schudson, objects "do not have value in themselves but only relationally, as part of a language of values, in a socially constituted and situated vocabulary of meanings" (135).

The two discourses about objects, advertising in consumer culture, and James's ghost stories, however, differ in crucial ways. Although in both discourses objects may form part of a language (to continue with Schudson's analogy), James's supernatural objects, like the runic writing of **"Casting the Runes,"** represent the intrusion of unintelligible words into the language of goods in a consumer culture—words that bring their "possessors into very undesirable company" (260). Where advertisements in the post-1890 period attempt to place commodities in the context of a desirable socioeconomic life-style, supernatural objects in the world of M. R. James are separated from their original cultural context. The medieval implements discovered through Baxter's use of a "dead man's eyes" (555) and the various artistic and monetary treasures of Abbot Thomas have all outlived the cultures that produced them. When the Baxters and Sumertons of James's fiction attempt to use or appropriate these newly rediscovered cultural artifacts, they learn that these artifacts cannot be assimilated by the modern world without the shock and terror of the supernatural. Unlike the products of turn-of-the-century advertising, the animate objects of M. R. James cannot be easily integrated into the "whole way of life" of modern society, nor do these

enigmatic and puzzling objects readily reveal their "social meaning."

In a sense, James's discourse about objects differs most from advertising in that it is a discourse about the history of objects. What characterizes the supernaturalism of James's objects and makes them difficult to integrate into the modern world is the sense of the living past inherent in them. It is this "sense of the past" (to borrow a phrase from one of Henry James's occult fictions) that modern commodity culture lacks. As Ohmann suggests in a discussion of 1890s advertisements for name-brand cereals, description of the product's past, its production, recedes from prominence in the advertisement and gives way to an emphasis on the social conditions of its consumption. With "modern man," the Jamesian antiquarian shares the same skepticism toward the belief that the dead are still with us. Like Benjamin's collector, he is a marginal figure in the modern world who cannot help imbuing himself in the pasts of objects—their previous owners, their makers, their workmanship, and sometimes, as Baxter discovers, the social implications of their production.

Notes

1. Recent commentators on the ghost stories of M. R. James include S. T. Joshi, who criticizes what he sees as the "ultimately thin and insubstantial nature" (142) of James's work, as well as Julia Briggs and Jack Sullivan, who admire both "the power that [his] classically well-made tale[s] . . . exert over . . . modern reader[s]" (Briggs 139) and the "radical" nature of "James's use of subtlety to evoke ghostly horror" (Sullivan 90).

2. Sullivan takes this sentiment a step further by claiming that, "In his relation to twentieth-century culture, James is very much a ghost himself" (89).

3. For a discussion of Machen's nostalgia for times past and his antimodernism, see Hassler.

Works Cited

Benjamin, Walter. *Illuminations*. Ed. Hannah Arendt. Trans. Harry Zohn. New York: Schocken Books, 1969.

Briggs, Julia. *Night Visitors: The Rise and Fall of the English Ghost Story*. London: Faber, 1977.

Eagleton, Terry. *Walter Benjamin, or, Towards a Revolutionary Criticism*. London: NLB, 1981.

Hassler, Donald M. "Arthur Machen and Genre: Filial and Fannish Alternatives." *Extrapolation* 33 (Summer 1992): 115-27.

James, M. R. *The Collected Ghost Stories of M. R. James*. London: Edward Arnold, 1931.

Joshi, S. T. *The Weird Tale: Arthur Machen, Lord Dunsany, Algernon Blackwood, M. R. James, Ambrose Bierce, H. P. Lovecraft*. Austin: U of Texas P, 1990.

Machen, Arthur. "A Fragment of Life." 1906. In *The House of Souls*. New York: Knopf, 1928. 1-110.

———. "The Great God Pan." 1894. In *The House of Souls*. New York: Knopf, 1928. 167-243.

———. *The Three Imposters*. 1895. New York: Knopf, 1930.

Marx, Karl. *Capital: A Critique of Political Economy*. 1867. Ed. Frederick Engels. Trans. Samuel Moore and Edward Aveling. New York: International Publishers, 1967.

Mauss, Marcel. *The Gift: Forms and Functions of Exchange in Archaic Societies*. 1925. Trans. Ian Cunnison. New York: Norton, 1967.

Ohmann, Richard. *The Politics of Letters*. Middletown, CT: Wesleyan UP, 1987.

Schudson, Michael. *Advertising the Uneasy Persuasion*. New York: Basic Books, 1984.

Sullivan, Jack. *Elegant Nightmares: The English Ghost Story from Le Fanu to Blackwood*. Athens: Ohio UP, 1978.

Taussig, Michael. *The Devil and Commodity Fetishism in South America*. Chapel Hill: U of North Carolina P, 1980.

Williams, Raymond. *Problems in Materialism and Culture*. London: Verso, 1980.

Jacqeline Simpson (essay date 1997)

SOURCE: Simpson, Jacqeline. "'The Rules of Folklore' in the Ghost Stories of M. R. James." *Folklore* 108 (1997): 9-18.

[*In the following essay, Simpson explores how James's ghost stories are informed by his knowledge of folklore.*]

When Dr Montague Rhodes James of King's College, Cambridge, published in 1904 the first volume of the elegant but alarming tales with which his name is now always associated, he called it ***Ghost Stories of an Antiquary***; in 1911 he followed it with ***More Ghost Stories of an Antiquary***. The word "antiquary" already had an old-fashioned charm about it, and was appropriate for a scholar whose work revolved round medieval manuscripts, biblical Apocrypha, library catalogues, church iconography and the like.[1] But he was something of a folklorist too (more so than his self-deprecating remarks on the topic imply), with a particular interest in the development and persistence of local legends and historical memories, a good knowledge of traditional beliefs, and an interest in oral narration.

This does not mean, however, that he was in sympathy with the dominant group among folklorists of his time, the comparative anthropologists and mythologists, with their sweeping theories and universalist explanations. They are lampooned in the person of the sinister Mr Karswell in **"Casting the Runes,"** who is author of a *History of Witchcraft* and a paper on "The Truth of Alchemy," about whom one of the other characters in the story comments:

> There was nothing that the man didn't swallow: mixing up classical myths, and stories out of the *Golden Legend* with reports of savage customs today—all very proper, no doubt, if you know how to use them, but he didn't; he seemed to put the *Golden Legend* and the *Golden Bough* exactly on a par, and to believe both: a pitiable exhibition, in short.
>
> (James 1970, 258-9)

That is fiction, written in 1911; in 1917 James raised the same issues in all seriousness against no less a scholar than Jane Harrison, when she wrote a paper linking the dance of Salome and the beheading of John the Baptist to the dance of Agave with the head of Pentheus in the *Bacchae* as "the dance of the daimon of the New Year with the head of the Old Year, past and slain." After countering Harrison's arguments, James commented:

> I have often viewed with very grave suspicion the way in which comparative mythologists treat their evidence . . . I regret to see that a researcher of her experience can allow herself to make public crude and inconsequential speculations of this kind, which go far to justify those who deny to Comparative Mythology the name and dignity of a science. I believe it to be a science, but only in the making. I also believe that one of the worst services that anyone responsible for the direction of young students can do them is to encourage them to make it the subject of dissertations, or to propound any theory concerning it. Loose thinking, exaggeration of resemblances, ignoring of differences, and downright falsification of evidence, are only a few of the evils which a premature handling of it fosters in its votaries.
>
> (James 1917; cf. Pfaff 1980, 255-6)

These are stern criticisms, which went against the intellectual fashions of the day but which we can now see were largely justified. If that was "the science of folklore," then James certainly had no wish to call himself a "folklorist." At the same time, he knew that a practical knowledge of folklore was useful when reading old texts. He was quite willing to explain the curious way that in Scandinavia and Germany the feastday of St Stephen was linked to horse-fights and racing as reminiscent of the cult of Frey (Pfaff 1980, 133). When he edited Walter Map's *De Nugis Curialum* in 1914 he regretted his lack of expertise on "romance and folk-lore" which prevented him from offering an explanatory commentary, while for his translation of the same work in 1923 he enlisted the help of the folklorist E. S. Hartland as editor and annotator. In 1922 he published some fascinating accounts of ghostly encounters which he had discovered as addenda (in Latin) in a medieval manuscript from Byland Abbey in Yorkshire, using comparisons with nineteenth-century Danish beliefs to explain certain obscure points (James 1922). Towards the end of his life, he translated some of Hans Andersen's fairytales (James 1930). He described one of his fictional narrators (who, as usual, seems to be a self-portrait) as one who had "dabbled a good deal in works of folk-lore" (James 1970, 517). And most significantly, he declared in the Preface to the collected volume of his ghost stories that, although he was not conscious of being indebted to any specific local legend whether written or oral, yet he had "tried to make my ghosts act in ways consistent with the rules of folklore" (James 1970, viii). This is the aspect of his work which I wish to explore here.

It is not, however, the most immediately obvious aspect. A reader who sets out to analyse the flavour of an M. R. James story will surely always be first conscious of the antiquarianism to which his titles drew attention—the easy familiarity with a world of college libraries, old manuscripts, rare books, cathedrals, private chapels, and so forth. Allied to this is the skill in literary pastiche, producing such delights as the sermon on mazes in **"Mr Humphreys and His Inheritance,"** the transcript of a supposed trial by Judge Jeffreys in **"Martin's Close,"** and several similar though briefer passages. Underlying this, one can glimpse personal susceptibilities to particular aspects of the horrific—spiders, thinness, hairiness, hooded figures and linen drapery are recurrent motifs. James himself gave one deliberate piece of information as to the origins of his ideas. As a child he had seen a toy Punch and Judy set with a cardboard Ghost:

> It was a tall figure habited in white with an unnaturally long and narrow head, also surrounded with white, and a dismal visage. Upon this my conceptions of a ghost were based, and for years it permeated my dreams.
>
> (James 1931)

A related clue can be gleaned from a posthumously published story entitled **"A Vignette,"** which he sent to the *London Mercury,* but with the comment that he was "ill satisfied" with it. It is a first-person narrative where the narrator himself experiences the horror (unlike most of his others) and its setting is his own childhood home, giving it, as Michael Cox points out, "an autobiographical flavour" (Cox 1986, 151). In it he speaks of a gate with a square hole cut in it, and how one afternoon, looking from the house towards that gate:

> through that hole I could see—and it struck like a blow on the diaphragm—something white or partly white. Now this I could not bear, and with an access of some-

thing like courage—only it was more like desperation, like determining that I must know the worst—I did steal down and, quite uselessly, of course, taking cover behind bushes as I went, I made progress until I was within range of the gate and the hole. Things were, alas!, worse than I had feared. Through that hole a face was looking my way. It was not monstrous, not pale, fleshless, spectral. Malevolent I thought and think it was; at any rate the eyes were large and open and fixed. It was pink and, I thought, hot, and just above the eyes the border of a white linen drapery hung down from the brows . . . I fled, but at what I thought must be a safe distance inside my own precincts I could not but halt and look back. There was no white thing framed in the hole of the gate, but there was a draped form shambling away among the trees . . . Why I make a lame effort to [describe it] now I cannot very well explain; it undoubtedly has had some formidable power of clinging through many years to my imagination.

> (James 1987, 297-8)

Such experiences, and the childhood nightmare to which James alludes in **"Oh Whistle and I'll Come to You, My Lad,"** clearly left a lasting mark on his imagination. Indeed, throughout his life there are occasional signs that, in spite of his strong Christian faith, he could not shake off a lurking fear that ghosts might exist, though his public remarks on the matter were always resolutely neutral (Cox 1986, 194; James 1987, xvi-xvii).

As well as his childhood capacity to feel and recall horror, the young Monty James soon displayed the other essential gift he would be needing—the narrative and dramatic skills to convey horror to others. At Eton, aged sixteen, he found himself "rather popular" for what he called a "dark seance," i.e. a telling of ghost stories, though whether these were stories he had himself devised he unfortunately does not say. At seventeen, he addressed the Literary Society on "The Occult Sciences," particularly black magic and demonology, for which he used Collin de Plancy's *Dictionnaire Infernal;* and at eighteen he wrote two essays for the *Eton Rambler* on ghost stories, including an anecdote of his own which already shows typical features of his later material, though the handling lacks subtlety. At about the same age, he wrote another paper on fabulous animals; these activities caused his Eton tutor to comment that "He dredges the deeps of literature for refuse" (Cox 1986, 38-40). Throughout his life, he enjoyed reading his own stories aloud to small groups of friends, often as Christmas entertainment; some were composed especially for this purpose, and others to entertain the choristers of King's College (ibid. 1986, 132-5).

He was fully aware that the literary ghost story, as practised by himself and his admired forerunners Dickens and Le Fanu, was only a recent offshoot from the older custom of oral storytelling, to which he pays tribute in the framing of two of his lesser tales, **"An Evening's**

Entertainment" and "There Was a Man Dwelt by a Churchyard." The former begins:

> Nothing is more common form in old-fashioned books than the description of the winter fireside, where the aged grandam narrates to the circle of children that hangs on her lips story after story of ghosts and fairies, and inspires her audience with a pleasing terror. But we are never allowed to know what the stories were. We hear, indeed, of sheeted spectres with saucer eyes, and—still more intriguing—of "Rawhead and Bloody Bones" (an expression which the Oxford Dictionary traces back to 1550), but the context of these striking images eludes us.
>
> Here, then, is a problem which has long obsessed me; but I see no means of solving it finally. The aged grandams are gone, and the collectors of folklore began their work in England too late to save most of the actual stories which the grandams told. Yet such things do not easily die quite out, and imagination, working on scattered hints, may be able to devise a picture of an evening's entertainment . . . in some such terms as these. . . .

(James 1970, 588)

The story which follows on from this preamble turns out to be a gruesome fragment of local history, told by a granny to two children, partly so that they should not wake their bad-tempered father from his after-dinner nap, but mainly to warn them against picking blackberries in a certain lane. It is an account of the horrible deaths of two men who had shown a sinister interest in prehistoric burial mounds and heathen worship, how they were refused Christian burial and laid at a crossroads, and how the ruins of their former cottage are still infested with stinging flies—flies that had first been seen thickly clustered on the "great patches of blood" where the corpses had been carried along the lane. James presents this in a convincing pastiche of oral storytelling methods; the grandmother is telling of things that happened "before I was born or thought of," but her information comes from her own father, who had witnessed them, and is bolstered up with topographical details and appeals to current rumours—"They say horses don't like the spot even now, and I've heard there was something of a mist or a light hung about for a long time after, but I don't know the truth of that" (ibid., 600). She herself had once been bitten by one of the "horrid" flies and had had to send for "the wise man over at Bascombe"—"but what it was he bound on my arm and what he said over it he wouldn't tell us" (ibid., 603-4).

The other story to which I have referred, **"There Was a Man Dwelt by a Churchyard,"** takes its title from Shakespeare. In *The Winter's Tale* (Act 2 scene 1) the queen's young son Mamillius declares that "A sad tale's best for winter: I have one / Of sprites and goblins," and begins "There was a man dwelt by a churchyard . . ." As James says:

> There is no more of the story; Mamillius died soon after without having a chance of finishing it. Now what was it going to have been? Shakespeare knew, no doubt, and I will be bold to say that I do. It was not going to be a new story; it was to be one which you have most likely heard, and even told. Everybody may set it in what frame he likes best. Here is mine.

(ibid., 609)

It turns out to be a variation on what is indeed a well-known type of tale (AT 366)—the man who steals something from the dead (in this case, a bag of money from a grave), and how a revenant comes to seek it, and draws gradually closer, closer, until:

> The figure whipped round, stood for an instant at the side of the bed, raised its arms, and with a hoarse scream of "YOU'VE GOT IT!"—at this point H.R.H. Prince Mamillius flung himself upon the youngest of the court ladies present, who responded with an equally piercing cry.

(ibid.)

Many children have relished stories of this kind, told as gruesome jokes, and complete with the final, unexpected, blood-curdling scream. James may well have used them himself in childhood, perhaps on his sister, or on boys in his prep school.

Although James was skilled in reproducing the tone of English conversational narratives, he took for granted that the art of formal storytelling was dead in England, or very nearly so. In **"Martin's Close"** he shows the folk memory of a local murder as surviving for some two hundred years, but only in obscure and fragmentary form, and only in one man's recollection. However, James discovered for himself that other countries were more fortunate. In 1892 he visited Ireland, where he was told some stories about fairies (Cox 1986, 107), but more significant were the repeated cycling holidays in Denmark and Sweden with various friends—in 1899, 1900, 1901, 1906 and 1923 (Pfaff 1980, 149-50, 222 and 405; Cox 1986, 109-10, 124 and 219).

Even before the first visit he had read "Hans Andersen and the old ballads,"[2] and so was prepared to regard Denmark as "a land of romance"; in the course of that visit he and his two companions, James McBryde and Will Stone, became "much engrossed with the folklore of Jutland, which peoples its wide and lonely heaths with many strange beings." They examined standing stones and old churches, James being especially amused by a fresco at Roskilde illustrating the medieval *exemplum* of the devil noting names of those who chatter in church. During the visit to Sweden in 1901, James saw in the University Library at Uppsala "two contracts with the devil written (and signed in blood) in 1718 by Daniel Salthenius, who was condemned to death for writing them. He escaped that and died professor of divinity at Konigsberg."[3] Two stories from James's first collection are set in Scandinavian places he had visited—**"Number 13"** at Viborg in Denmark, and **"Count Magnus"** at Råbäck in Sweden—while his friend McBryde created a series of cartoons, *The Story of a Troll-Hunt,* in which the three Englishmen in search of trolls are clearly intended to be himself, Monty James and Will Stone.

Tucked away in one of James's learned articles lies a crucial clue to the extent and source of his knowledge of Scandinavian folklore. As I mentioned above, in 1922 he published the Latin texts of some ghost stories inserted into a medieval manuscript, with the following brief introductory comment:

> On blank pages . . . a monk of Byland [Abbey] has written down a series of ghost-stories of which the scenes are laid in his own neighbourhood. They are strong in local colour, and though occasionally confused, incoherent and unduly compressed, evidently represent the words of the narrators with some approach to fidelity.
>
> To me they are redolent of Denmark. Any one who is lucky enough to possess E. T. Kristensen's delightful collections of *Sagan frå Jylland* will be reminded again and again of traits which occur there. Little as I can claim the quality of "folklorist" I am fairly confident that the Scandinavian element is really prominent in these tales.
>
> (James 1922, 414)

We do not know by what happy chance James came upon the works of Kristensen, who is now regarded as one of the foremost folklorists of his age, though in his lifetime he was given little financial or scholarly support. But he clearly studied him in detail. In one footnote he cites three volumes of Kristensen's Jutland legends (1883; 1886[4]; 1888) to explain an obscure point in his own text, namely that it is dangerous for someone who has seen a ghost to look at a lamp unless he has first looked at a fire; two more notes give Danish parallels on other matters (James 1922, 415, 419 and 420). Further proof of James's appreciation of Kristensen is the fact that some years later, when translating a selection of Hans Andersen's fairytales, he inserted a couple of tales on the theme of "The Grateful Dead" from Kristensen's collections alongside Andersen's version of this tale-type, "The Travelling Companion"—presumably so that readers might compare the oral tellings with the literary treatment (James 1930, 16). Whether either Andersen or Kristensen would have been pleased at the juxtaposition is another matter.

One question which immediately arises is, when and where did James acquire these Kristensen volumes of the 1880s? It would be natural to assume that he bought them in Denmark itself, in the enthusiasm for Jutland folklore which marked his first holiday there in 1899,

and possibly influenced by the publicity Sir William Craigie had recently given to Kristensen's work.[5] On the other hand, the heart-eating motif inspiring one of his earliest tales, **"Lost Hearts"** (written in 1893), suggests that he had read them even earlier.[6] If so, he must have encountered them in England. Dr Benedik Benedikz has pointed out to me that James would certainly have known Eiríkur Magnusson, an Icelander who was Under Librarian at Cambridge University Library from 1871 onwards, with special responsibility for the purchase of European materials. Eiríkur's interests included Scandinavian folklore; he was tireless in introducing younger scholars to the relatively unknown delights of Nordic culture, and could well have been James's initiator in this field.

The two tales to which James gave Scandinavian settings (**"Number 13"** and **"Count Magnus"**) date from 1899-1900 and 1901-2 respectively (Cox 1986, 136), but I hope to show that the Danish influence continued throughout his years as a ghost-story writer.

It is instructive to consider why Evald Tang Kristensen was so exceptional among folklorists of the nineteenth and early twentieth century, for this helps to explain his importance to James. First, his material included a vast number of local legends (*sagn*) and personal-experience narratives, many of them concerned with the supernatural and firmly rooted in actual beliefs. It was to these that James went when seeking parallels for his medieval Yorkshire manuscript, and they could have supplied many of the "rules of folklore" which he wished his own ghosts to follow, confirming the authenticity of the more fragmented British material. Secondly, unlike most folklorists of his time, Kristensen insisted on publishing tales in the plain language his informants used, without embellishments; true, he smoothed out the broken sentences and false starts which surely occurred, but he kept close to the Jutland idiom, including turns of phrase which jarred on the sensibilities of the educated classes, and pleading with his readers to accept "this simple and true-hearted quality" in regional speech (Kristensen 1876, iv-v).

This must have appealed to James, who appreciated vernacular styles. One reason he relished the records of seventeenth-century State Trials was that there alone, in his view, one could find "the unadorned common speech of Englishmen" of that period (Cox 1986, 144); he would have recognised the same quality in Kristensen. **"Count Magnus"** includes an inset anecdote told by the Swedish innkeeper to the English hero, which is a superb imitation of Scandinavian oral narrative style (besides being, to my taste at least, one of the most impressively grim passages he ever wrote). The Jutland style is spare, bleak, understated, swift-moving, and given to a species of sinister imprecision at moments of crisis which can sound astonishingly Jamesian—"something was scrabbling at the door and fumbling with the handle"—"sometimes people would see something come running from that field and down to the farm at night" are phrases from Kristensen (1897, 471 and 419), to set alongside James's "Mr Gregory woke once or twice during the small hours and fancied he heard a fumbling across the lower part of his locked door" (**"The Treasure of Abbot Thomas,"** James 1970, 161) or "she thought she saw something all in tatters with the two arms held out in front of it coming on very fast, and at that she ran for the stile, and tore her gown all to flinders getting over it" (**"A Neighbour's Landmark."** ibid., 529).

One of the most striking features of James's style is the interplay between the leisurely, mildly pedantic phrasing of the preliminary narrative and descriptions, reflecting the persona of the donnish "antiquary," and the rapid glimpses of horrific concrete details at the climax, vividly but tersely expressed, and never over-explained. Kristensen's volumes could have supplied many models for the latter kind of effect, and the technique for achieving it, at a time when other folklore collectors almost always smothered their material in verbiage.

Kristensen's content would have been equally congenial. Jutland ghosts are not remote historic personages, nor are they vague psychic manifestations. They are very commonly revengeful or arbitrarily malevolent, or doomed to "walk" for their past sins; they often manifest themselves in physical ways, by chasing or attacking people or, at the least, by noise and commotion in the farms. No sophisticated psychic or occult explanations are offered for their existence; Kristensen's informants—and indeed Kristensen himself—accepted them without needing to theorise about them. All this fits well with James's general concept of the revenant (palpably physical, menacing, evil or vengeful, often allied to demons) and his dislike of abstract "quasi-scientific" speculations.

As regards individual motifs, there are of course a great many that are common to British and to Danish lore—that ghosts come at dusk, but that candle-light keeps them at bay; the ghost or fiend in the form of a dog; ghosts that enter only when invited; storms at the deaths of evil men; ghosts or demonic animals guarding buried treasure; the revenge of the dead on those who steal from them or maltreat their bodies; witches that turn into hares; the learned black magician, with his satanic pact and his devilish familiars. All these are ideas that James uses, and though one can unhesitatingly say that they are folkloric, they are too widespread to trace to specific sources. The ghosts that creep slowly and stealthily towards their target in **"The Mezzotint"** and **"Mr Humphreys and His Inheritance"** recall those in certain West of England legends, and also in Danish ones, who after having been once exorcised are return-

ing home from their place of banishment by the length of one cock's stride, or one hen's feather or one straw, every year (Brown 1979, 26, 32, 33, 36, 62 and 78; Kristensen 1886, 245 and 247; 1897, 151). In Denmark these "cockstride ghosts" are seen as malevolent, whereas the British ones are penitential, which may make Danish influence slightly more likely here.

Other elements, however, are definitely British or Irish. The songs used to such sinister effect in **"Oh Whistle . . ."** and in **"Martin's Close"** are well-known Scottish and English ones; Ireland is said to be the source for the belief that ash trees are sinister, which runs counter to English ideas[7] (**"The Ash Tree"**). In **"A Warning to the Curious"** (1925) James uses the heraldic arms of East Anglia, which show three crowns, as basis for a convincingly "traditional"-looking claim that three crowns buried on the coast guard England from invasion. This is now often taken as a genuine legend, and was told as such by "several Suffolk residents" to the folklorist Enid Porter, who seems to have accepted it as authentic (Porter 1974, 131-2 and 181). One local writer says that a sexton named Eade, living at Blythburgh in the 1950s, "believed implicitly" that the last remaining crown had saved England from a Nazi invasion (Forrest 1961, 134-5). However, no source earlier than James has yet been found. I believe he simply wove his own story round the heraldic crowns according to the "rules of folklore," possibly modelled on the spurious but popular legend of Drake's Drum or on the tale about the head of Bendigeidfran in the *Mabinogion*. I also suspect that the remark embedded in his story that "it is rather surprising" that the legend "has not made its way into print before" (James 1970, 567) is a sly hint that he himself invented it.

One motif can be definitely identified as Danish, for it has no equivalent in British lore—even though James, with characteristic cleverness, has transplanted it into a wholly English setting which conceals its origins. The story in question is **"The Rose Garden,"** in his second collection (1911), and my attention was first drawn to its Danishness some years ago by Joan Rockwell, author of a major biography of Kristensen (Rockwell 1981). In this story, a woman is planning to have an old summerhouse pulled down to make way for a rose garden; a relative of the previous owners tells her of an odd experience she had had there in childhood:

> All at once I became conscious that someone was whispering to me inside the arbour. The only words I could distinguish, or thought I could, were "Pull, pull. I'll push, you pull" . . . And—this sounds very foolish, but still it is the fact—I made sure it was strongest when I put my ear to an old post which was part of the end of the seat.
>
> (James 1970, 199)

Despite this alarming information, the new owner goes ahead with her plan; the summerhouse is demolished, the old post uprooted. There follow sinister dreams, sounds of strange calls by night and owls hooting, and eventually the woman is horrified by glimpsing what she at first takes to be a mask but is in fact "a face— large, smooth and pink," with eyes closed, among the branches of her shrubbery. It turns out that an evil seventeenth-century judge had died in the house, but his ghost had troubled the parish till several parsons assembled to lay him, and "the stake is in a field adjoining to the churchyard" (ibid., 207).[8]

There are of course ghost-laying stories in British tradition, but generally the revenant is forced into a bottle which is then thrown into water, or else banished to the Red Sea. The idea that it is pinned under a stake which must never be moved is typically Danish, as are also the phrases "You pull, I'll push" or "Pull, pull!" or "Shake it! Pull it!" heard coming from the ground; these have no British parallels, but frequently occur as an "epic formula" at the core of Danish legends. Examples are plentiful in Kristensen (1876, 245 and 248; 1880, 171-2; 1883, 118; 1897, 217-19). In Danish belief, if the ghost is released by uprooting its stake, it may manifest itself as a sinister "night-raven" (a nightjar?); hence, possibly, the owl in James's story. It may be worth noting that in one of Kristensen's versions the removal of the stake is due to the foolish obstinacy of a priest's domineering wife, who wants to turn part of the orchard into her personal garden, and secretly uproots the post, which she had promised never to disturb; with a terrifying din, a fiery ghost leaps out and chases her back to the house (cf. "the shelter of the house was gained and the door shut before she collapsed." James 1970, 206). After that, she is a reformed character (Kristensen 1880, 171-2). The similarity to the nagging wife in James's story may be no coincidence.

Similarly, **"A Neighbour's Landmark"** transplants a characteristically Danish motif, the so-called "boundary ghost" whose sin is to have wrongfully acquired a neighbour's land, either by literally shifting a boundary stone, or by a false oath, and whose doom is to walk round it forever. It is of course true that the biblical text "Cursed be he that removeth his neighbour's landmark" was familiar in England through its use in the Anglican Commination Service on Ash Wednesday; nevertheless, land-theft is not a usual theme in English ghost legends, whereas it is common in Danish collections, including the ones which James owned (Kristensen 1876, 205-10; 1883, 115-18). There, the "boundary ghosts" are often described as shouting, screaming or wailing as they patrol their ill-gotten land; sometimes, one can hear them coming nearer and nearer (Kristensen 1897, 104-5), just as in James; in one story, a man foolishly taunts the invisible ghost to "Shout now, man!", only to have it yell right beside him (Kristensen 1886, 199). James was certainly aware of this motif, for he alludes to it in a footnote to his paper on the **"Medieval Ghost Stories,"**

one of which concerns a spirit that yelled "Ho, hoo, hoo!" in the night (James 1922, 419). His own story must have been taking shape in his mind at about this same period (it was first published in 1924); the story and the article both allude to a line from Sir Walter Scott ("Where walks, they say, the shrieking ghost"). Since we also know that he identified the "heroine" of this tale with a real-life English villainess (Lady Ivie, tried for forging deeds to some land at Shadwell. James 1970, 532), we can appreciate how skilfully he combined elements from varied sources—and how cunningly he covered his tracks.

The two tales that do have Scandinavian settings, **"Number 13"** and **"Count Magnus,"** both deal with an evil magus or black magician, a topic to which James returned again and again, perhaps because the quest for secret knowledge represented a temptation which he as a scholar could readily understand, involving "the ability of the mind to be hooked or fascinated" (Hughes 1993, 81-2 and 87; cf. Weighell 1984; MacCulloch 1995). There are many such Faustian figures in Scandinavia and of course in British traditions too; they are often said to be priests, but that is one motif James never uses, presumably finding it offensive to his Christian convictions. Many are said to have acquired their arts by studying in the "Black School," always alleged to be in some distant university town, and presided over by the devil himself. James offers us a variation which seems to be his own invention: Count Magnus had gone on a "Black Pilgrimage" to the accursed city of Chorazin to salute the Prince of the Air (i.e. Satan— *Ephesians* 2:2), in order "to obtain a faithful messenger and see the blood of his enemies" (James 1970, 107).[9]

One striking detail in **"Count Magnus"** is the padlocked tomb. The count lies in a copper sarcophagus with sinister engravings (but no crucifix), secured by "finely worked and massive padlocks, three in number" (ibid., 113). Three times the hero, moved by some half-conscious impulse, finds himself saying aloud that he wishes he could see the Count. Each time, a padlock opens and falls off, and the third time, the lid moves. Hunted down by the Count and his monstrous hooded "messenger," the hero comes to a bad end. This is a magnificent example of a Jamesian ghost behaving in accordance with "the rules of folklore." I have not found anything so crude as a direct source of these padlocks, Bengt af Klintberg having kindly confirmed for me that there is none in Swedish legend, though the general idea that if a buried person is mockingly greeted he will emerge in a frightful shape is common there. However, as regards the padlocks, I can point to one English tale and a cluster of Danish ones which could have provided stimulating guidance for James's creative imagination.

The English legend is one James certainly knew: that of the Witch of Berkeley, as told by William of Malmesbury (on whom James once lectured). She asked that her corpse should be sewn up in the skin of a stag and laid in a stone coffin fastened with three chains, which should be left unburied for three nights; in vain—for each night devils came and snapped one chain, and on the third night Satan kicked the coffin to pieces and carried her off (Westwood 1986, 244-5). But these chains have no padlocks. In Danish tradition, on the other hand, there are indeed padlocks, but they are rarely on coffins, the only example I have found so far being the following reminiscence about a Cunning Man:

> Knud the Smith in Elsborg claimed to be a good deal cleverer than most people, and he was a bit peculiar too. For instance, while he was still alive he had a coffin made and painted red, with a padlock to it, and he declared that he wanted to be buried in that when he died, as was indeed done.

> (Kristensen 1880, 205)

Elsewhere, the padlocks are linked with ghost-laying; in some cases they symbolise the power which the exorcist achieves over the revenant, and in others the stages by which the latter draws closer to the house where the exorcist awaits him. The motif is regularly found in the legend of how a man named Bertel the Unborn (like Macduff, he had been cut from his mother's womb) laid the ghost of a landowner named Gyldenstjaerne, who had been haunting the manorhouse of Stubbergaard. In one version, it is said that Bertel set three lights and one padlock on a table, and told a girl to watch the padlock carefully, "for by that she would know if he had won the mastery, for if the lock closed properly he would have succeeded, but if it couldn't or wouldn't, then Peder Gyldenstjaerne had mastered him" (Kristensen 1876, 240). James delicately hints at this symbolism when he notes that his hero tries to re-close the first two padlocks, but fails.

In another version of the same legend, the ghost has been appearing in the form of a dog and four priests have failed to lay it:

> Then Bertel takes a padlock from his pocket, which he sets down in five separate pieces on the table in front of the four priests, and he tells them that if the padlock slides together they must do nothing to hinder it—"I'll deal with the matter myself; but if any of the pieces fall to the ground, you must come at once to save me." So the five priests remained sitting there, each with his book in front of him, and so Bertel and the dog went off together and came to the boggy pit on Ellemose Heath . . . and there he began to conjure him down. When some time had passed, the padlock began sliding about on the table back at home, time after time, time after time, and finally it snaps shut with a clang. At that very moment it was all over, the ghost gave a shriek, and so he was laid.

> (Kristensen 1880, 166-7; cf. 1886, 244-5)

In his 1886 volume, Kristensen gives two variants. In the first, the exorcising priest (here called Jørgen the Unborn) "took a padlock and opened it and laid it on the table, saying this would be a token for the girl that he had overcome the ghost, for the padlock would close up bit by bit"; and so it does, for when the priest returns safely from his exorcism "the girl was sitting quietly, and the padlock was shut" (Kristensen 1886, 244-5). The second illustrates the other type of symbolism. Here, the exorciser (Knud the Unborn) sets seven candles and one padlock on the table, and he and the girl keep watch. "Then the padlock on the table gave a hop, and the priest said: 'Now Gyldenstjaerne has jumped up out of his grave in Viborg.' At the second hop of the padlock he was at Hagebro, and at the third, at Stubbergaard" (Kristensen 1886, 246; cf. 252-3, where the lock and its hasp draw nearer to one another at each stage of the ghost's approach). There are also variations on this idea where the exorcist sets up three wooden pegs, which fall one by one as the ghost draws nearer. I have even found one where there are three closed padlocks lying on the table, and they spring open one by one at each stage of the ghost's journey, which is the closest to James's plot—but, frustratingly, this comes from Kristensen's last collection, published in 1934, far too late for James to have used it.

Other echoes of Danish lore can be found in certain details in **"The Residence at Whitminster,"** alongside allusions to Irish witchcraft, satanic sacrifices, scrying and demonic dogs. The first is when one of the characters finds that a book he is carrying is struck, or rather twitched, out of his hand in the dark (James 1970, 382), for Danish ghosts commonly knock the Bible or prayerbook out of the hand of the exorcist trying to lay them (e.g. Kristensen 1883, 147-8; 1886, 247). The second is the housekeeper's comment about the young magician's familiars: "Them that was with him, why they were such as would strip the skin from a child in its grave," for the Jutlanders believed that the Devil would steal the skin from a corpse and wrap himself in it to masquerade as a ghost (Kristensen 1886, 322).[10] The collapse of a revenant into a pile of dust once its mission is accomplished (**"The Tractate Middoth," "An Uncommon Prayerbook"**) also has Danish parallels which James would have known (Kristensen 1876, 163-4).

On the other hand, one thing in James that looks Scandinavian probably is not—there is no precedent for the way runes are used in his story **"Casting the Runes,"** where a strip of paper "with some very odd writing on it in red and black [which] looked more like Runic letters than anything else" carries a curse to the person unwittingly receiving it. True, Tacitus tells how ancient Germans quite literally cast slivers of wood on the ground as a form of divination, and many scholars assume these were inscribed with runes; true, there are references in medieval Icelandic texts to runes as protective magic, so one could logically deduce that they could be harmful too; true, carved runes were sometimes coloured red. But there is nothing in archaeology or in medieval texts which corresponds at all closely to the way the evil Mr Karswell uses runes in this story; there might of course be something relevant in the later Scandinavian grimoires, which James might have happened upon, but if so I have not yet found it.

"An Episode of Cathedral History" is rich in motifs with Danish parallels. The story centres on the discovery of an old altar tomb in the choir (on the north side, significantly) which had long been concealed under the structure of the pulpit—and "on the north side of it there was what looked like an injury: a gap between two of the slabs composing the side. It might be two or three inches across" (James 1970, 422). Once this tomb is uncovered, trouble begins; people fall ill, horrific wails and shrieks are heard by night, occasionally something with dully glowing red eyes is glimpsed in the dark. A woman who sits on the tomb finds the hem of her dress torn away. It proves impossible to repair the gap between the slabs, for the plaster is violently blown out again. A choirboy stoops near the chink, puts two fingers in his mouth and whistles, and at that he thinks he hears something stirring; his friend sticks a rolled-up sheet of music in, and something catches it and pulls the end off, leaving the torn end wet and black (ibid., 427-9).

All these can be seen as adaptations of Danish motifs. It is very common for a Danish haunting to manifest itself as noises rather than sights, and to cause sickness of humans or animals; the red-eyed church-dwelling ghost appears in a widespread migratory legend (e.g. Kristensen 1876, 290-2; 1897, 233-5); and the crack or hole through which a ghost regularly passes is common too, as for example in this anecdote:

> Once he was dead, he haunted the place dreadfully. As for his grave, which was the type that is built of bricks and has oak palings round it, they never could keep it bricked up as it ought to be; the eastern end of it was constantly falling down, because it was through there he used to come out. I've often gone past that grave, and always seen it in that state—perfectly all right all round, except just at the east end.
>
> (Kristensen 1880, 112-13; cf. 1897, 119, 246 and 451)

Sometimes, it is said that if one tries to stop up such holes in graves, the stones will get drawn down into the grave overnight and disappear (Kristensen 1897, 241-2). Other things may get dragged in too. One rather grotesque legend concerns the ghost of a Madam Vissing who was partly but not completely laid, so that her head and shoulders remained sticking up out of the ground, "so they set an upturned barrel over her"; years later, when the barrel was beginning to rot, a child jokingly poked a whip into a hole in it, "and then she snatched the whip away from him" (Kristensen 1897, 313-14).

The damage to the music sheet and to the hem of the woman's dress has no exact parallel in either British or Danish lore, as far as I recall, but there is one Danish motif which is fairly similar—namely, that a malevolent ghost demands that a living person should clasp his hand in token of some pledge, but the latter prudently offers a kerchief or apron instead; the ghost rips the end off, and the torn edge is then seen to be blackened and scorched.

As for whistling, particularly at night, the consequences could be quite horrific, according to Jutland beliefs. It could summon up a ghost, who might then chase you; or the will-o-the-wisp; or the Wild Hunt; or a demonic dog; or the Devil himself, especially if you had whistled through the keyhole of a church door (Kristensen 1876, 293; 1883, 288 and 289; 1886, 195 and 290).

And this of course leads us to the most famous story James wrote, which many recall with a particular shudder: **"Oh Whistle and I'll Come to You, My Lad."** As ever, the elements are admirably blended. There is the East Anglian setting; the antiquarian mystery of the whistle itself, found in the ruins of a Templar chapel, with its puzzling inscription FUR-FLA-FLE-BIS; the theme of the pursuing ghost; the artful gradations of horror, conveyed in hints and brief perceptions; the touches drawn from folklore, such as the power of candlelight and the taboo on "whistling for the wind" (about which one of the characters comments that "they believe in it all over Denmark and Norway, as well as on the Yorkshire coast"). But the most memorable feature of this particular ghost is the way it invades the unfortunate hero's hotel room and takes possession of the spare bed, so that "the clothes were bundled up and twisted together in the most tortuous confusion"; from these sheets it fashions itself a body of fluttering linen draperies. A child glimpses it by daylight, "waving" at the window; by night, it rises and attacks its victim, revealing "a horrible, an intensely horrible, face *of crumpled linen*" (James 1970, 148; his emphasis).

It does not take much detective work to relate this climax to James's personal fears—to the face, draped in white, peering through the hole in the gate in **"A Vignette,"** or the sheeted ghost of the Punch and Judy show. Indeed, making a rare personal comment within the text of **"Oh Whistle . . ."** itself, he tells the reader, at the moment when the hero first sees the ghost sit up in an empty bed, that "I have in a dream thirty years back seen the same thing happen"; and in his Preface he confirms that this is the one case when he based a story on his own experience, since "a dream furnished the suggestion" (ibid., vii). Though James does not say so explicitly, it must have been a childhood dream; thirty years previous to the date of publication (1904), he was only twelve.

As he read through his volumes of Kristensen, James would have come upon quite a number of tales with details that would have recalled his nightmare, for one of Kristensen's regular subdivisions is "Haunted Bedrooms," and the haunting often takes the form of dragging the sleeper's quilt or sheets off him (e.g. Kristensen 1886, 227). Still more horrible, there are ghosts that actually get inside the bed—not a spare bed, but one already occupied. The human sleeper at first rolls over to make room for the newcomer (sharing beds was quite commonplace, especially for farm-workers), but then realises it is a revenant, and flees (Kristensen 1876, 187; 1886, 224).[11] Sometimes a prayer will drive such ghosts away (Kristensen 1880, 113). In one case there is a tussle in the dark, won by the living man; it turns out that the ghost came to claim the sheets because they should have been put in the grave (Kristensen 1897, 486). Of haunted rooms in certain great houses it is said that they stand empty, but "the bed has to be remade every day" because a white lady haunts the room and "every night a little dog lies on that bed," or that the bed "always has signs on it in the morning that someone has slept in it all night" (ibid., 491 and 512).

Nothing in all this, of course, equals the horror of James's conception of the creature with the face of crumpled linen, let alone the skill with which this horror is conveyed. By pointing to partial parallels in folklore for this and others among his tales, I do not mean to detract from his originality, but simply to show how the driving force of his powerful imagination allied itself to plots and motifs from traditional storytelling. The literary "rules" of a ghost story, he once wrote, are merely those of any short story (James 1987, 339); maybe so, but he also knew the "rules of folklore," and obeyed them too, with superbly effective results.

Notes

1. Two biographies are available. That by R. W. Pfaff (1980) concentrates on James's vast output of scholarly work; that by Michael Cox (first published 1983, reprinted 1986) is a more rounded and vivid portrait, with plenty of personal detail, to which I am much indebted. Cox has also written the prefaces and notes to two recent selections of James's stories, relating them to their biographical contexts (James 1986; 1987). The latter includes three texts omitted from the Collected Edition (James 1970), namely "The Experiment," "The Malice of Inanimate Objects" and "A Vignette"; also, as an appendix, James's various comments on the craft of writing ghost stories. An article by Norman Scarfe (1986) describes the Suffolk settings used in some of the tales (my thanks to Jennifer Chandler for giving me this reference); further identifications will be found in Cox's notes to James (1987).

2. Probably in the original. He had a great facility in acquiring languages, and was capable of reading a six-volume history of Sweden in Swedish (Pfaff 1980, 134).

3. The document can still be seen there, and is translated in Lindow 1978, 45. At the end of "Number 13" James says, more accurately, that Salthenius became Professor of Hebrew.

4. The article gives the reference as "*Sagn og Overtro,* 1866," but this date is a misprint for "1886."

5. A selection of eighty-six legends from Kristensen had been included in Sir William Craigie's *Scandinavian Folklore* of 1896, though only five are about ghosts. James might also have noticed an appreciation of Kristensen which Craigie had just written in *Folk-Lore,* with the comment that "The Danish ghost is not so impressive as the Icelandic, but its doings often have an uncomfortable touch of the horrible about them" (Craigie 1898, 213). By the time James visited Denmark the prolific Kristensen had published, not merely the *Jyske Folkeminder* series to which James alluded in 1922, but also most of his *Danske Sagn* series, of which volume 5 (1897) contains ghost legends.

6. In this story, the villain hopes to obtain magic powers of flight and invisibility by eating the hearts of "not less than three human beings below the age of twenty-one years," having found this recipe "in considerable detail in the works of Hermes Trismegistus." The many writings attributed to "Hermes" are treatises on alchemy, the invocation of angels, and allegedly ancient philosophical wisdom; heretical they may be, but they do not include crude cannibalism (I am grateful to Mr R. Weighell for confirmation on this point). James had read some of them while still a schoolboy (Pfaff 1980, 36); later, as a scholar specialising in apocrypha of the early Christian centuries, he would surely have had further occasion to explore them. It seems strange that he should blacken their reputation in this way. However, there was a genuine Danish folk belief that magic powers of flight could be got by eating the hearts of seven (or twelve) foetuses cut from their mothers' bodies, and James could have learnt this in Kristensen's 1883 volume (Kristensen 1883, 108-9 no. 156 and note) and adopted it in a bowdlerised form. *Die Handwörterbuch des Deutschen Aberglaubens* (2:16) attests to the belief in Germany too, giving as reference Carl Meyer, *Der Aberglaube des Mittelalters und der nächtsfolgenden Jahrhunderte* (Basel 1884, 279). I suspect James of indulging in mystification here, misdirecting the reader to the impressive Hermes Trismegistus, but actually using folklore—probably Danish, but just possibly German.

7. In England, ash trees are credited with healing, divinatory and protective powers. I have found one Scottish story and two from the Fens where ghosts are seen near ashes (Briggs 1971, 1:478-80, 482-4 and 489-91), but this hardly seems significant. Scarfe suggests that the allusion is to actual trees, including ash trees, round Livermere Hall in the village where James grew up (Scarfe 1986, 1418); the unusual surname "Mothersole," given to the witch in this tale, occurs on gravestones in Livermere churchyard.

8. In an unfinished story, recently published under the title "John Humphreys," there is "a tall post newly covered with black and glistening tar" seen by the hero in fields which were "ancient pastures"; next day it has disappeared, and a farm worker assures him that there had never been any such thing there. This incident is the first in a series of threatening events involving black magic; James may have intended to reveal that a "ghost-post" of the Danish type had indeed once stood in the pasture and had been moved, releasing an evil spectre, or (equally possibly) the post may be one of a series of manifestations of the shape-changing ghost itself (James 1993). This story is an early draft for "Mr Humphreys and his Inheritance," and it may well be relevant that at the climax of the latter there is a hole, seeming infinitely deep, out of which a ghost comes crawling up to attack the hero (James 1970, 355-6). The preceding imagery of the story does nothing to prepare readers for this hole; possibly James was still half consciously recalling the ghost-posts of Denmark.

9. Bengt af Klintberg kindly informs me that no "Black Pilgrimage" is known in Sweden, though the "Black School" is known there as elsewhere. Michael Cox suggests a link with a curious report in 1815 (in the *Monthly Repository of Theology and General Literature* 10:110 [1815]:121) that "the late King of Sweden" (i.e. the deposed and exiled Gustavus IV) meant to go on pilgrimage to the Holy Land with ten companions, all to be clad in black robes and calling themselves the "Black Brethren" (James 1987, 310-11).

10. There is an English variant which James might have known in *Choice Notes from "Notes and Queries": Folklore* (London 1859, 170), about a man who sold his soul to the Devil on condition the Devil might strip his skin from him after death (reprinted in Briggs 1971, 1:56, as "A Cock Scares the Fiend").

11. In the 1886 volume, Kristensen gave titles to individual tales (a practice he later dropped), and this one he called "The Ghost in the Bed"—a title sure to catch James's eye and recall his own nightmare fear.

References Cited

Briggs, Julia. *Night Visitors: The Rise and Fall of the English Ghost Story*. London: Faber and Faber, 1977.

Briggs, K. M. *A Dictionary of British Folk-Tales in the English Language*. Part B, *Folk Legends*. London: Routledge and Kegan Paul, 1971.

Brown, Theo. *The Fate of the Dead: Folk Eschatology in the West Country after the Reformation*. Ipswich: D.S. Brewer, 1979.

Cox, Michael. *M. R. James: An Informal Portrait*. Oxford and New York: Oxford University Press, 1983; 1986.

Craigie, W. A. "Evald Tang Kristensen: A Danish Folklorist." *Folk-Lore* 9 (1898):194-224.

Forrest, A. J. *Under Three Crowns*. Ipswich: Norman Adlard and Co., 1961.

Hughes, Martin. "A Maze of Secrets in a Story by M. R. James." *Durham University Journal* 85 (1993):81-93.

James, M. R. "Some Remarks on 'The Head of John the Baptist'." *Classical Review* 31 (1917):255-6.

———. "Twelve Medieval Ghost Stories." *English Historical Review* 37 (1922):413-22.

———. "Ghosts—Treat Them Gently!" *Evening News* (17 April 1931).

———. "A Vignette." *London Mercury* 35 (1936):18-22. Reprinted in James 1987:293-8.

———. *The Collected Ghost Stories of M. R. James*. London: Edward Arnold, 1931; 1970.

———. *The Ghost Stories of M. R. James*. Introduced by Michael Cox. Oxford: Oxford University Press, 1986.

———. *M. R. James: "Casting the Runes" and Other Stories*. Introduction and notes by Michael Cox. Oxford: The World's Classics, 1987.

———. "John Humphreys." Edited by Rosemary Pardoe. *Ghosts and Scholars* 16 (1993):1-10.

———, trans. *Forty Stories by Hans Andersen*. London: Faber and Faber, 1930.

Kristensen, E. T. *Jyske Folkesagn (= Jyske Folkeminder III)*. Copenhagen: Gyldendalske Boghandel, 1876.

———. *Sagn frå Jylland (= Jyske Folkeminder IV)*. Copenhagen: Karl Schonbergs Forlag, 1880.

———. *Sagn og Overtro frå Jylland (= Jyske Folkeminder VI)*. Copenhagen: Karl Schonbergs Boghandel, 1883.

———. *Sagn og Overtro frå Jylland (= Jyske Folkeminder VIII)*. Copenhagen: Karl Schonbergs Boghandel, 1886.

————. *Sagn og Overtro frå Jylland (= Jyske Folke-minder* IX*)*. Copenhagen: Karl Schonbergs Boghandel, 1888.

————. *Danske Sagn* V. Århus: Jakob Zeuners Bogtryk-keri, 1897.

————. *Danske Sagn: Ny Raekke V.* Copenhagen: C.A. Reitzels Forlag, 1934.

Lindow, John. *Swedish Legends and Folktale.* Berkeley, Los Angeles and London: University of California Press, 1978.

MacCulloch, Simon. "The Toad in the Study: M. R. James, H. P. Lovecraft and Forbidden Knowledge (Part One)." *Ghosts and Scholars* 20 (1995):38-44.

Pfaff, R. W. *Montague Rhodes James.* London: Scolar Press, 1980.

Porter, Enid. *The Folklore of East Anglia.* London: Bats-ford, 1974.

Rockwell, Joan. *Evald Tang Kristensen: A Lifelong Adventure in Folklore.* Aalborg and Copenhagen: Aalborg University Press, 1981.

Scarfe, Norman. "The Strangeness Present: M. R. James's Suffolk." *Country Life* 230 (November 6 1986):1416-19.

Weighell, Ron. "Dark Devotions: M. R. James and the Magical Tradition." *Ghosts and Scholars* 6 (1984):20-4.

Westwood, Jennifer. *Albion: A Guide to Legendary Britain.* London: Book Club Associates, 1986.

Brian Cowlishaw (essay date fall 1998)

SOURCE: Cowlishaw, Brian. "'A Warning to the Curious': Victorian Science and the Awful Unconscious in M. R. James's Ghost Stories." *Victorian Newsletter,* no. 94 (fall 1998): 36-42.

[*In the following essay, Cowlishaw contends that James's conception of civilization, influenced by prominent Victorian scientists, closely resembles Freud's, except for his attitude toward the unconscious.*]

M. R. James, who published four collections of ghost stories between 1904 and 1925,[1] was "the perfect embodiment of a successful post-Victorian man of letters" (Sullivan 73): he was a graduate fellow, museum director, and finally Vice Chancellor of Cambridge, as well as a respected medievalist and biblical scholar. The standard critical approach to his stories has been to focus upon the "man of letters"—to seek the sources of the historical and archaeological details that crowd his ghost stories in his academic/antiquarian occupations.[2] That this should be the *standard* approach is a bit

strange, though, considering James's own assertions that the stories are definitely not "based on my own experience" (*Stories* [*The Penguin Complete Stories of M. R. James*] 5), that both the settings and the legends attaching to them are mostly imaginary, and that "the fragments of ostensible erudition which are scattered about my pages" are almost completely "pure invention" (5-6). Authors' statements about their work cannot always be trusted, but statements as direct as these should be taken more seriously than they have been.

One more fruitful approach to his stories can be found in the *first* half of Jack Sullivan's characterization: James as "post-Victorian." James might accurately say of himself the words he gives the narrator of **"A Neighbour's Landmark"**: "Remember, if you please . . . that I am a Victorian by birth and education, and that the Victorian tree may not unreasonably be expected to bear Victorian fruit" (*Stories* 289). James was born in 1862, only twenty-five years into Victoria's sixty-four-year reign, and he graduated from Cambridge in 1886. His roots, then, are solidly Victorian, as is his "fruit," his stories.

From this point of view, the stories prove quite revealing. What they reveal is a particularly Victorian set of assumptions about history, historical records, evolution, and human civilization that closely resembles Sigmund Freud's, but that seeks to bury what Freud seeks to uncover and decode. That is: James's stories reproduce Victorian reconstructive science's[3] assumption that history and civilization are readable, though generally only with difficulty and with uncertainty as to results. James also reproduces the Victorian doctrine of evolution— that *homo sapiens* descended from simpler organisms, some of which still survive in the present in primitive, unevolved form. In James's stories, as in Victorian reconstructive science, human existence can be conceived of in levels of development or civilization, with the most "civilized" and recent level lying nearest the top (in terms of both quality and accessibility). Earlier, lower, more "savage" levels survive below; one cannot ordinarily see them, but with the right kind of "digging" one can locate, reconstruct, and read them. James's conception of human civilization, borrowed from influential Victorian scientists, thus closely resembles Freud's. In effect, then, if not in intention, when James reproduces in his stories the views of Victorian reconstructive science, he is writing about what Freud would call "the unconscious." However, James differs radically from Freud in his attitude toward the unconscious. Whereas the Victorians and Freud saw the unearthing and reading of the past "as an important practical guide to the understanding of the present and the shaping of the future" (Tylor 1:24), James's stories suggest that the reading of the past is actually dangerous—that to unearth the savage past is to summon it to the more civilized present, with frightening, destructive results. Whereas Freud sought to read the unconscious much as Victorian scientists sought to read fossils, the geological record, and human cultures, James wants to keep the unconscious buried. Freud sought to relieve repression; James encourages it.

I. READING THE PAST

In M. R. James's ghost stories, the past is always readable, if with difficulty. In this belief James follows the lead of Charles Lyell and Charles Darwin. Lyell, a very influential early-Victorian geologist,[4] first published *Principles of Geology* in 1830. In that text, Lyell writes of "reading" the geological evidence; he envisions the world as a text, its fossils and geological formations being the "handwriting." His task as geologist is to interpret this handwriting accurately. But Lyell, "a student of Nature" recognizes he can at best become "acquainted only with one-tenth part of the processes *now* going on upon or far below the surface, or in the depths of the sea" (1:462, emphasis added), let alone the processes that occurred millennia ago. This renders all attempts to read the earth's distant past in the geological record sketchy and uncertain; geologists find themselves in much the same position as readers of human language "acquainted with just one-tenth part of the words of some living language," and then "presented with several books purporting to be written in the same tongue ten centuries ago" (1:461). Provided with such a fragmented text, a geologist could easily "declare without hesitation that the ancient laws of nature have been subverted" (1:462)—and be completely wrong. Charles Darwin, too, employs Lyell's reading metaphor, in addition to echoing Lyell's warnings. In *The Origin of Species,* published in 1859, Darwin writes:

> For my part, following out Lyell's metaphor, I look at the natural geological record, as a history of the world imperfectly kept, and written in a changing dialect; of this history we possess the last volume alone, relating only to two or three countries. Of this volume, only here and there a short chapter has been preserved; and of each page, only here and there a few lines. Each word of the slowly-changing language, in which the history is supposed to be written, being more or less different in the interrupted succession of chapters, may represent the apparently abruptly changed forms of life, entombed in our consecutive, but widely separated formations.

(316)

With such fragmentary evidence to interpret, the geologist can gather a sense of the past, but can make no complete or certain readings. For Lyell and Darwin, then, the geological-historical record is readable but only with considerable difficulty and uncertainty.

James imbibes both elements of the Victorians' attitude toward the historical record: confidence in the possibility of reconstructing and reading the past, and caution that the results may not be complete or accurate. Like the narratives of Darwin and Lyell, James's ghost stories center around reconstruction of the past by means of the available evidence. The person performing this historical reconstruction generally does that sort of work habitually, being an amateur antiquary, an academic, or both. He (there are no female investigators in James's stories) sets out to reconstruct a history, usually of an old church or of another decrepit building. Often, significantly, this place of research is a site of ruins, suggestive perhaps of the Temple of Jupiter Serapis (see Lyell 1:449-59), which mysterious ruins Lyell used to illustrate his "reading" techniques. Or at any rate, ruins in James definitely indicate a long human history waiting to be read. Ruins provide a physical location for the act of reading human history, in much the same way geological formations provided a physical location for reconstructive scientists' acts of reading geological history. While investigating the history of the ruin or building, James's investigator accidentally discovers another, secret history; the piecing-together of this secret history is the focus of the story. His investigators connect evidence from physical artifacts with fragments of private letters and journals, published histories, reference books, parish records, and other official documents, to form the narrative of the secret history. Again, this method, piecing together narratives by means of physical evidence and written texts, was precisely that of Victorian scientists.[5] Sometimes, in James's stories, part of the evidence is in another language, generally Latin; or it is written in secret code. And finally, the stories are narrated in such a way that the reader must do some of the reconstructive work; James never provides a complete, confident, explicit explanation of events in the manner of, say, a Sherlock Holmes mystery. By coding some of the evidence and leaving histories more or less incomplete and implicit, James thus emphasizes the *difficulties* in reading history as much as the *possibility* of it.

An extended example should illustrate these generalizations. In "'**Oh, Whistle, and I'll Come to You, My Lad,**'" a "Professor of Ontography" (*Stories* 75), one Mr. Parkins, decides to find, examine, and sketch a ruined Templar church he has read about. Note Parkins's occupation, Professor of Ontography. No such position actually existed at an English university; the invented title suggests he studies what-writing-is, which indicates his investment in words, reading, writing, and investigation in general. At the site of the ruins, he sees among mysterious mounds and eminences a bare patch of earth, where the turf has been "removed by some boy or other creature *ferae naturae* [of a wild nature]" (79). (That James equates a boy with a wild creature is significant, as should be apparent in the second section of this essay.) Digging below the bare spot, Parkins finds "a small cavity" containing an object "of man's making—a metal tube about four inches long, and evidently of some considerable age" (79) This turns out to be a whistle, with inscriptions on front—

FLA

FUR   BIS

FLE

and back:

QUIS EST ISTE QUI VENIT

(81)

He translates the latter inscription to read, "Who is this who is coming?" It should be noted that the Latin word "iste," the word "this" in the translation, connotes disgust. Also, in Latin grammar, "quis" and "qui," "who," can refer either to a person or a creature; there is not the "who/that" distinction that exists in English. Parkins, however, never deciphers the meaning or significance of the four three-letter words. (Or are they even words?) Nor does he decipher the swastika-like symbols. (The story was written and is set a few decades before the advent of the Nazis.) Thus he is able to make only a partial reading of this artifact—just enough to gather a cryptic warning that something dreadful is coming.

In his curiosity, Parkins blows the whistle twice; that night he experiences all sorts of frights—fears he will die, nightmares, and awful sounds in the wind. In the morning he shows the whistle and its inscriptions, and relates his experiences, to a fellow lodger at his hotel, a Colonel just back from India. Putting together the written and physical evidence, the Colonel decides that Parkins's blowing the whistle has caused bad experiences, though the Colonel can't say exactly why or how that is so. He suspects the whistle's being found at a Templar ruin probably indicates some sort of evil magic: "he should himself be careful about using a thing that had belonged to a set of Papists, of whom, speaking generally, it might be affirmed that you never knew what they might not have been up to" (86). More specifically, the Templars, who some believe to be the precursory organization to the Freemasons (see Robinson and many, many others), have long figured in conspiracy theories both supernatural and secular. However, the Colonel can only suspect; he cannot reconstruct the entire history. Nor can he explain satisfactorily what happens to Parkins the next night: Parkins is attacked by "a horrible, an intensely horrible, face *of crumpled linen*" (90) that arises from his supposedly empty spare bed. The Colonel bursts in and saves Parkins, taking away the whistle, "which he cast[s] as far into the sea as a very brawny arm could send it" (90), returning the artifact back to the oblivion whence it came. The whistle seems to have summoned the mysterious creature, but no one—including the reader, who is only told as much as the Colonel—can determine exactly what the creature was, what its powers might be,[6] why the whistle summons it, what the Templars have to do with the creature and the whistle, or what might have happened had Parkins blown the whistle once more.

Such methods and understandings of reconstructing history are typical of James's stories in general. James's characters and readers, like Victorian reconstructive scientists, can always draw connections between certain significant fragments of physical and written evidence, always construct some *sense* of what happened. However, no one can progress from there on to total explanation or to absolute certainty. And teleology—*why* certain events happen—generally remains shrouded in mystery, just as the teleology of the earth's or animals' evolution remained obscure to Darwin and Lyell.

II. Evolution and Civilization

M. R. James ghost stories also reproduce Victorian science's beliefs regarding evolution and human civilization. Specifically, the stories reveal the position first advanced by Robert Chambers and furthered later by Charles Darwin, that *homo sapiens* descended genealogically from simpler organisms. Also, one can see behind James's stories E. B. Tylor's (and, earlier, Darwin's) doctrine of survivals.

In *Vestiges of the Natural History of Creation*, first published in 1844, Chambers placed all living creatures in a hierarchy: "The vegetable and animal kingdoms are arranged upon a scale, starting from simply organized forms, and going on to the more complex, each of these forms being but slightly different from those next to it on both sides" (236). Atop the scale in the animal kingdom is "man," for humans belong to the most complex "sub-kingdom" (239), the vertebrata; and human beings are the "typical" vertebrate—that is, the "best" of that type or sub-kingdom.

Chambers argued not only that humankind is the best representative of the best sub-kingdom, but also that humankind descended genealogically from the "lower animals": "[T]he simplest and most primitive type, under a law to which that of like-production is subordinate, gave birth to the type next above it . . . this again produced the next higher, and so on to the very highest" (222, emphasis in the original), from one-celled animals all the way up to human beings. As evidence Chambers observes that "every individual amongst us actually passes through the characters of the insect, the fish, and reptile, (to speak nothing of others,) before he is permitted to breathe the breath of life!" (234-35). (Note the word "characters" here, suggestive not only of bodily forms but also of written, readable language.) Furthermore, he claims, once the fetus reaches a recognizably human state, "the varieties of his race are represented in the progressive development of an individual of the highest, before we see the adult Caucasian, the highest point yet attained in the animal scale" (199). The developing Caucasian fetus passes through the form of the "lower" races in ascending to that of the "highest": "it passes through the characters in which it appears, in the Negro, Malay, American, and Mongolian nations, and finally is Caucasian" (306). (Here again appears that important word "characters.")

For Chambers, then—not surprisingly, a Caucasian himself—the Caucasian is both the most recently evolved and the best of all creatures in the animal kingdom. But its status is not assured, for regression, and other races' progression, always remain possible. Chambers cites the example of an American Indian tribe, the Mandans, who he claims "cultivated the arts of manufacture, realized comforts and luxuries, and had attained to a remarkable refinement of manners. . . . They were also more than usually elegant in their persons, and of every variety of complexion between that of their compatriots and a pure white."[7] Supposedly the more "civilized" they became, the whiter they grew, even as individuals, which suggests that white skin is a result and signifier of "civilization." It also indicates that levels of civilization need not be congential—they can be earned. But if they can be earned, they can be lost, too; Caucasians can easily revert to barbarism and consequently grow darker. Thus, "the varieties of mankind . . . are simply the result of so many advances and retrogressions. . . . According to this view, the greater part of the human race must be considered as having lapsed or declined from the original type. In the Caucasian or Indo-European family alone has the primitive organization been improved upon" (308-309). Skin color becomes for Chambers a reliable index of civilization, at the levels of the tribe and the individual.

Here Chambers's views on human evolution coincide with Tylor's. Tylor arranges human cultures in a hierarchy according to their levels of "civilization," a term he never really defines. By reading a culture as a "complex whole" (1:1), and assigning that whole a place in his hierarchy, he hopes to "draw a picture where there shall be scarce a hand's breadth difference between an English ploughman and a negro of Central Africa" (1:7)—just as Chambers ought to arrange all organisms into a virtually seamless hierarchy.

Key to understanding James's stories, too, is Tylor's concept of "survivals." Tylor writes that even within the most civilized societies, there are "processes, customs, opinions, and so forth, which have been carried on by force of habit into a new state of society different from that in which they had their original home, and they thus remain as proofs and examples of an older condition of culture out of which a new has been evolved" (1:16). These he calls "survivals." Not only discrete phenomena observable within particular cultures, but whole societies, "modern savage tribes," can be considered survivals or "remains of an early state of the human race at large," people whose culture does not change despite "the main tendency of culture . . . [to move] from savagery towards civilization" (1:21).

The concept of survivals constitutes an anthropological version of Darwin's "Tree of Life," drawn in *The Origin of Species*. Tylor himself likens his study of cultures to Darwin's work: "What this task is like, may be almost perfectly illustrated by comparing these details of culture with the species of plants and animals as studied by the naturalist" (1:8). Darwin's "Tree of Life" illustrates his conception of the genealogy of species: one species ramifies into many, some of which become extinct; some branches die out altogether; and some species do not ramify at all, but instead continue to exist unchanged, unadapted, while other originally contemporary species change and ramify greatly (*Origin* 160-61). Thus, according to Darwin and, later, to Tylor, many levels or periods of evolution—both human and animal—exist simultaneously in the present.

James reproduces in his ghost stories the theories of Chambers, Darwin, and Tylor outlined above. One way James does this is in the making physical form of his "ghosts" resemble humans at earlier stages of evolution. Unlike most other English writers' ghosts, James's have tangible bodies. As Michael A. Mason observes, the typical Jamesian ghost is "solid enough to inflict considerable damage" (256). And these solid, tangible forms resemble the human form as it might have appeared in an earlier time. For example, James describes the ghost of **"Canon Alberic's Scrap-Book"** thus:

> At first you saw only a mass of coarse, matted black hair; presently it was seen that this covered a body of fearful thinness, almost a skeleton, but with the muscles standing out like wires. The hands were of a dusky pallor, covered, like the body, with long, coarse hairs, and hideously taloned. The eyes, touched in with a burning yellow, had intensely black pupils. . . . Imagine one of the awful bird-catching spiders of South America translated into human form, and endowed with intelligence just less than human, and you will have some faint conception. . . .
>
> (16-17)

The avenging creature in **"The Haunted Dolls' House"** "might be described as a frog—the size of a man—but it had scanty white hair about its head" (272). Note the explicit linking of these humanoid creatures with other, "lower" animals: the links go beyond mere comparison (humanoid creature = spider or frog) to suggest unevolved states of *homo sapiens*, human beings as they might have looked when humans still resembled, or might have resembled, frogs or spiders. Note in the first example, too, the excessive hair as a signifier of subhumanity. According to Richard Pfaff, hair is "one of MRJ's favourite motifs" (410). Many of James's creatures resemble humans but are too hairy to *be* human; see, for example, **"The Diary of Mr. Poynter," "An Episode of Cathedral History,"** and **"A View from a Hill."** In all his stories James's "ghosts" occupy places below modern *homo sapiens* in a Chambersian/ Darwinian evolutionary hierarchy. Some creatures are very much subhuman: for instance, the creature menacing **"The Residence at Whitminster"** possesses "long thin arms, or legs, or feelers" (218), while in **"Count Magnus,"** the "unduly short" figure "muffled in a hooded garment" (71) brandishes tentacles. The creatures always prove dangerous to the antiquarians who unearth them; sometimes the investigator escapes alive, and sometimes he does not, but he is always threatened and horrified. The creatures appear to be survivals, loathsome living fossils of earlier, less evolved states of humankind, come from the past into the present to destroy.

The other important way James reproduces Victorian beliefs regarding human evolution and civilization is in making the very appearance of the supernatural a kind of regression to an earlier, less civilized stage in humanity. For James, "civilized" and "skeptical" are synonyms. His investigators are all Caucasian, well-educated, upper-class, refined in manners and speech, and disinclined to believe in ghosts and similar rubbish. For people like this—people at the very acme of Chambers, Darwin, and Tylor's hierarchies—to experience firsthand and be forced to attest to the reality of the supernatural is for them to return to "a world which only a few generations ago would have been our own—a world of witchcraft and black magic, fairies and goblins, when the supernatural was too much a reality to be reasoned away" (Search 20). James's urban antiquarians move backward in time to the world of servants and rural folk. It is not the polished investigators but the "lower orders"—working-class, country, and serving people—who know the local legends and superstitions, who are most closely in touch with supernatural forces. James has them relate their information to the investigator, and thereby, to the reader, in exaggeratedly illiterate accents that highlight their death of civilization. **"Martin's Close"** describes one character, a country boy, so backward that when he gives testimony in court regarding an experience with the supernatural, "my lord could not well apprehend him, and so asked if there was anyone that could interpret him" (180); the parson, apparently more civilized than the boy but less civilized than the judge, has to translate. By connecting the supernatural with the uncivilized, James implies a cause-and-effect relationship: if the uncivilized were not to tell what they know about the supernatural, or were to become more civilized and so forget it, the truly civilized would never discover it. The supernatural would disappear; humankind would evolve beyond it. Tylor writes that "most of what we call superstition is included within survival" (1:17); James suggests that

these particular survivals would *not* survive if not for the cultural foot-dragging of certain low-class types.

III. THE UNCONSCIOUS

Thus, in writing his ghost stories, M. R. James reproduces the assumptions of Victorian geological, evolutionary, and anthropological science. To use a Lyellian geological metaphor, James's stories portray human civilization as a thin, recently developed crust riding uncertainly atop a restless mass of older formations threatening at every moment to destroy the crust and break through to the top. One can partially, tentatively reconstruct the history of the formations by digging through and examining various strata or layers, then assembling the bits of evidence.

This conception of human civilization, of course, closely resembles that of a famous contemporary of James's: Sigmund Freud. Freud, too, writes of the human mind in terms of genealogical development and survivals, and conceives of consciousness as a recently formed, relatively complex, and highly evolved formation residing uneasily atop older, simpler ones. In *Civilization and Its Discontents,* Freud writes, much in the vein of Chambers, Darwin, Tylor, and James, "In the animal kingdom we hold to the view that the most highly developed species have proceeded from the lowest; and yet we find all the simple forms still in existence to-day" (15-16). As in the animal kingdom, in the

> realm of the mind, . . . what is primitive is so commonly preserved alongside of the transformed version which has arisen from it that it is unnecessary to give instances as evidence. When this happens . . . one portion . . . of an attitude or instinctual impulse has remained unaltered, while another portion has undergone further development. . . . [I]n mental life nothing which has once been formed can perish . . . everything is somehow preserved and . . . in suitable circumstances (when, for instance, regression goes back far enough) it can once more be brought to light.
>
> (*Civilization* 16-17)

The mind's "primitive" and "simple forms" survive along with more complex, more highly civilized forms, just as, for James and Victorian scientists, less evolved organisms survive along with their more highly evolved descendants. More highly civilized forms of the mind reside in consciousness, comprising only a small portion of the mind, the "top"; the former remain in the unconscious, constituting most of the mind, "deeper down." As Freud explains in "The Unconscious," "at any given moment consciousness includes only a small content, so that the greater part of what we call conscious knowledge must in any case be for very considerable periods of time in a state of latency, that is to say, of being psychically unconscious" (167).[8]

In psychoanalysis, the analyst's work is a work of historical reconstruction, much like that of James's antiquaries. The analyst assembles the fragments of evidence dug up from the unconscious in an effort to reconstruct the history of the mind, as Freud explains in "Constructions in Analysis":

> His task is to make out what has been forgotten from the traces which it has left behind or, more correctly, to *construct* it. . . . His work of construction, or, if it is preferred, of reconstruction, resembles to a great extent an archaeologist's excavation of some dwelling-place that has been destroyed and buried or of some ancient edifice.[9]
>
> (259)

The task proves complicated, however, and the results necessarily inconclusive, for the analyst is working only with "traces," and, too, "if an object makes its appearance in some particular level, it often remains to be decided whether it belongs to that level or whether it was carried down to that level owing to some subsequent disturbance" (259). Only fragments of the record remain, and they cannot always be arranged chronologically. Still, a dogged analyst can generally reconstruct at least a sense of the patient's psychic history—much like James's determined investigators, or the Victorian reconstructive scientists they emulate, can assemble some sense of the historical narrative in their respective fields.

Clearly, then, James's conception of human civilization bears close resemblance to Freud's. Given the close similarity of their understandings of civilization and the human mind, James can be seen as, in effect, writing about the unconscious. James does not refer directly to "the unconscious," but his stories posit its existence metaphorically: the subhuman, the uncivilized, the superstitious, the supernatural—all the horrifying phenomena unearthed by his antiquarian investigators may be considered "the unconscious," for James views these phenomena in much the same light as Freud regarded the unconscious. That is, the ghastly/the unconscious is old, unevolved, uncivilized, and large; the rational/the conscious is new, evolved, civilized, and small.

While James might be understood to be writing metaphorically about the unconscious, his plans for what to *do* with the unconscious differ radically from Freud's. Freud sought actively to dig down through the layers of memory, uncover repressed memories, reconstruct the history stored in the unconscious fragments, and use that history, once brought to the patient's consciousness, to facilitate psychoanalytic cure. James, in contrast, indicates that digging into the past/the unconscious is a mistake: the results are invariably horrifying and sometimes even fatal. To dig into the past is to transport oneself back in time to a more superstitious, savage state of humanity, and to uncover terrible things better left buried. If James's antiquarians would only let sleeping ruins lie, they would remain safe. True, the un-

earthed horrors belong to secret histories *other* than the ones being investigated directly, but with the past/the unconscious that is precisely the point—one never knows *what* one will dig up. James suggests that our minds work more of less like Mrs. Maple's, the Old-yes' maid in **"The Residence at Whitminster"**:

> "How will Miss Oldys manage to make [Mrs. Maple] remember about the box?" I asked.
>
> "Mary? Oh, she'll make her sit down and ask her about her aunt's illness, or who gave her the china dog on the mantelpiece—something quite off the point. Then, as Maple says, one thing brings up another, and the right one will come round sooner that you could suppose."
>
> (*Stories* 221)[10]

To think of one thing, all one need do is think of another. To summon a vengeful demon, all one need do is poke around a picturesque ruin. It is the *act* of delving into the past, not the precise subject, that James finds dangerous.

Sometimes James warns directly against investigativeness. For instance, of Mr. Wraxall, protagonist of **"Count Magnus,"** he writes, "His besetting fault was pretty clearly that of over-inquisitiveness, possibly a good fault in a traveller, certainly a fault for which this traveller paid dearly enough in the end" (65). Wraxall's "price" was to be haunted, harried, and eventually slaughtered by the Count, after inadvertently raising him from the dead. And all Wraxall originally *intended* to investigate was materials for a travel book. In **"Rats,"** Mr. Thomson, "in a mood of quite indefensible curiosity, and feeling confident that there could be no damaging secrets in a place [the hotel room next door] so easily got at" (343), finds a dead man, or rather an undead man, and barely escapes with his life. History/the unconscious is for James a kind of Bluebeard's chamber,[11] and he warns his readers of the dangers of opening it.

Besides providing such direct warnings, he also models repression metaphorically. His stories include example after example of some secret and/or enclosed space that is opened, reveals some horror, and is hurriedly sealed back up. In **"The Treasure of Abbot Thomas,"** for instance, Mr. Somerton interprets a secret code that leads him to a treasure buried in an abbey well. Trouble is, sealed up with the treasure is a supernatural guardian; therefore, Somerton and his servant and friend seal up the well again. The title character of **"Mr. Humphreys and His Inheritance"** discovers, at the center of his newly inherited hedge maze, "a face—a human face—a *burnt* human face . . . waving black arms prepared to clasp the head that was bending over them" (204). Humphreys barely escapes the humanoid creature with his life, and immediately has the maze destroyed. And in **"An Episode of Cathedral History,"** the repressed actively tries to escape. While renovating the Cathedral at

Southminster, workmen lay bare a tomb below the altar, and worse, make a small breach in the tomb's wall. Every day a mason fills the hole with a brick—and every day the brick is pushed out again by the ghost living inside. Finally the tomb is destroyed, and out of it rushes a "thing like a man, all over hair, and two great eyes to it" (247). These secret/enclosed spaces represent the unconscious mind; the horrible creatures inside, repressed memories and desires. James shows that when one has opened those spaces/the unconscious, the best and safest thing to do is to seal them up again quickly. Otherwise, the hidden horrors will have their revenge, like the creature of **"Martin's Close,"** who, sealed in a small cupboard for many years, immediately commits a gruesome murder once set free. The typical ghost story by James, then, offers a "Warning to the Curious"[12]: do not investigate the past/the unconscious, for what you find will frighten and probably harm you. James is the ultimate Enlightenment figure, warning against even *looking* into the dark.

Thus, James, imbued with the tenets of Victorian reconstructive science, constructs in his ghost stories a model of human evolution, civilization, and mind which is strikingly Freudian. In effect, he posits both the existence of the unconscious and its readability. The attitude Julia Briggs ascribes to English ghost story writers in general is particularly true in James: "as a descendant [sic] of the beasts, [man] had a bestial inheritance within him which he must learn to sublimate and restrain" (20). Better to sublimate and restrain, for James, than to dig up, piece together and work through. To repress is to progress, both as an individual and as a species.

Notes

1. The contents of these four volumes, plus the story "Wailing Wall," are collected in *The Penguin Complete Stories of M. R. James,* as well as in the Wordsworth Classics edition of *Collected Ghost Stories.* References in this essay are to the Penguin edition.

2. In addition to Sullivan, see Pfaff, J. Randolph Cox, and Michael Cox.

3. The "reconstructive sciences" included primarily biology, geology, and anthropology—branches of science which construct narratives accounting for the past out of available physical evidence.

4. To give one index of Lyell's influence: Charles Dickens mentions Lyell in *Martin Chuzzlewit,* Chapter 22. La Fayette Kettle, an American, invites Martin Chuzzlewit to speak to the Young Men's Watertoast Association "upon the Tower of London," or, if he prefers, "upon the Elements of Geology" (363). The *Elements of Geology,* published in 1838, was a simplified recasting of the third volume of the *Principles,* cited here. Apparently the *Elements* was a book an American could expect an educated Englishman to know in 1843-44, when *Martin Chuzzlewit* was published.

5. Lyell, for example, cites copious texts dating back hundreds of years as evidence of the geological conditions of various parts of Europe at those times, in addition to his analyses of physical evidence.

6. The Colonel is "of opinion that . . . its one power was that of frightening" (90-91), but Parkins has other ideas.

7. (298-99). Chambers did not do this research himself. He uncritically cites one "Mr. [George] Catlin" on the subject of the Mandans.

8. The dwarfing of consciousness by the unconscious parallels the way that, for Chambers, the uncivilized greatly outnumber the civilized.

9. Recall that James's investigators generally do their investigating at a site of ruins or another decrepit building.

10. As I argue above, for James, servants such as Mrs. Maple are more in touch with the supernatural unconscious than more "civilized" people. For Freud and James, all minds work essentially like hers; hers is just *closer* to those hidden forces than, say, the mind of her master, Mr. Oldys, an urbane clergyman.

11. James himself uses the phrase "Bluebeard's chamber" in "The Residence at Whitminster," to describe the room containing a box that holds fatal magical artifacts (*Stories* 224).

12. This is the title of a story by James and of his fourth published collection of stories.

Works Cited

Briggs, Julia. *Night Visitors: The Rise and Fall of the English Ghost Story.* London: Faber, 1977.

Chambers, Robert. *Vestiges of the Natural History of Creation and Other Evolutionary Writings.* Ed. James A. Secord. Chicago, London: U of Chicago P, 1994.

Cox, J. Randolph. "Ghostly Antiquary: The Stories of Montague Rhodes James." *ELT* 12 (1969): 197-202.

Cox, Michael. *M. R. James: An Informal Portrait.* Oxford, New York: Oxford UP, 1983.

Darwin, Charles. *The Origin of Species by Means of Natural Selection.* 1859. Ed. J. W. Burrow. London: Penguin, 1985.

Dickens, Charles. *The Life and Adventures of Martin Chuzzlewit.* 1844. The Oxford Illustrated Dickens, Oxford, New York: Oxford UP, 1987.

Freud, Sigmund. *Civilization and Its Discontents.* Trans. and ed. James Strachey. New York & London: W.W. Norton, 1961.

———. "Constructions in Analysis." *The Standard Edition of the Complete Psychological Works of Sigmund Freud.* Trans. James Strachey. Eds. James Strachey and Anna Freud. 24 vols. Vol. 23. London: Hogarth P, The Institute of Psycho-Analysis, 1964. 255-69.

———. *The Unconscious. The Standard Edition of the Complete Psychological Works of Sigmund Freud.* Trans. James Strachey. Eds. James Strachey and Anna Freud. 24 vols. Vol. 14. London: Hogarth P, The Institute of Psycho-Analysis, 1957. 159-215.

James, M. R. *The Penguin Complete Ghost Stories of M. R. James.* Harmondsworth: Penguin, 1984.

Lyell, Charles. *Principles of Geology.* 1830. 3 vols. Chicago, London: U of Chicago P, 1990.

Mason, Michael A. "On Not Letting Them Lie: Moral Significance in the Ghost Stories of M. R. James." *Studies in Short Fiction* 19 (1982): 253-60.

Pfaff, Richard William. *Montague Rhodes James.* London: Scolar P, 1980.

Robinson, John J. *Born in Blood: The Lost Secrets of Freemasonry.* New York: M. Evans, 1989.

Search, Pamela, ed. *The Supernatural in the English Short Story.* London: Bernard Hanison, 1959.

Sullivan, Jack. *Elegant Nightmares: The English Ghost Story from Le Fanu to Blackwood.* Athens: Ohio UP, 1978.

Tylor, E. B. *Primitive Culture: Researches into the Development of Mythology, Philosophy, Religion, Language, Art, and Custom.* 7th ed. 2 vols. New York: Brentano's, 1924.

Peter Erlsbacher (essay date March 1999)

SOURCE: Erlsbacher, Peter. "Riddling the Runes." *Baker Street Journal* 49, no. 1 (March 1999): 52-7.

[*In the following essay, Erlsbacher claims that James's story "Casting the Runes" features Dr. Watson of Sherlock Holmes fame.*]

One of the most frustrating facts for a Canonician must certainly be the lack of corroborative evidence concerning the life and exploits of Mr. Sherlock Holmes and Dr. Watson outside the accounts published under the name of Arthur Conan Doyle. As there are no external sources to warrant even their existence, the whole proud building of Higher Canonical Study rests on simple belief in the authenticity of Dr. Doyle's stories. That, we

hasten to add, is not to imply that the lack of evidence in any way diminishes the plausibility of the Canon, rather it ennobles it with a truly pious *credo quia absurdam.* Still, in the footsteps of the Master, we should not be content with the simple faith of our forefathers, but put all our energy, our knowledge and imagination into the search for clues. A lucky find thus enables us to expand our knowledge of Dr. Watson, based upon an objective and independent source. ***The Ghost Stories*** by Mr. M. R. James[1] (first published in collected form in 1931) contain the story **"Casting the Runes,"** which should be of paramount interest to Sherlockians. In short, it concerns the alarming experiences of Mr. Dunning, the expert for alchemistical manuscripts. His negative evaluation prevents publication of the article "The Truth of Alchemy" by M. Karswell, an occultist. Thereupon Mr. Dunning receives perplexing threats and a hint concerning the death under mysterious circumstances of Mr. Harrington in 1889, who likewise severely criticized Mr. Karswell's book *A History of Witchcraft.* Finally, Mr. Dunning receives a piece of paper with rune-like signs from Mr. Karswell. Luckily, he is informed that Mr. Harrington likewise received such a paper shortly before his death. Just in time, Mr. Dunning is able to plant these runes on Mr. Karswell himself, who promptly expires in a curious and satisfying manner.

For the Sherlockian, this story (very readable in its own right) has to be of the greatest importance, containing as it does a short conversation between Mr. Dunning and his "medical man," for this Doctor is named Watson. Naturally everybody with an interest in the Canon will start to ponder whether this Dr. Watson could be "our" Dr. Watson of Baker Street fame. Could it be possible, chronologically, geographically?

"Casting the Runes" is rather neatly dated. The story opens with three letters, dated the 15th, 18th and 20th April 190-, the last one of which has just been brought in by the typist. So the year could be any between 1900 and 1909.[2] Mr. Dunning first appears "on an evening rather later in this week" returning home from his research in the British Museum. Five days later he meets Dr. Watson. Let us try to narrow down the year. We can conclude from the text that a year in the first lustrum of this century is implied. Mr. Harrington died on 18 September 1889, shortly after reviewing *A History of Witchcraft.* This book, we learn, was published "ten years or more" before the events of the story. 1889 plus 10 is 1899, too early as the letters show. It seems to us that the expression "ten or more years" cannot cover more than 15 years, which gives 1904. So we are looking at the years 1900 to 1904. We should now be able, considering the weekdays and the words "rather later in this week," to be more exact. April 20 cannot be a Sunday, there being office work. Monday the 20th means the letter of the 18th was written on Saturday; Tuesday however would mean that the 18th was Sunday, so it's out. Wednesday is a definite possibility. Thursday would mean that "an evening rather later in this week" was Saturday, when Mr. Dunning was doing research at the British Museum, quite improbable. Therefore Friday and Saturday are out too, there being not enough days left in the week. Let us now look on which day the April 20 falls in the relevant years. In 1900 it is a Friday, 1901 a Saturday, 1902 a Sunday, 1903 a Monday, 1904 (a leap-year) a Wednesday, 1905 a Thursday and so on. Only 1908 (Monday) would be possible again (but too late by our fifteen-years-maximum), 1909 (Tuesday) would be out again and 1910 is excluded by the letters. So 1903 or 1904 can be assumed confidently to be the year of **"Casting the Runes,"** with a strong bias towards 1903, as will be shown later on. The place is clearly London; at lunch on the 20th a certain Mrs. Bennett[3] remarks that she has seen Mr. Karswell leave the British Museum. Mr. Dunning works there also, but he lives in a comfortable house in a suburb. "A train took him to within a mile or two of his house, an electric tram a stage further and ended three hundred yards from his home." It is in all probability impossible to identify the suburb, since we do not know from which railway station he started, though—should his physician Dr. Watson live there also, which seems probable—it would teach us even more about the post-Baker Street life of Dr. Watson, should the two Watsons be really only one.

Is this evidence compatible with the Canon? What do we know about Dr. Watson in 1903 (perhaps 1904)?

According to William S. Baring-Gould's *Sherlock Holmes,* Dr. Watson took new lodgings in Queen Anne Street in July 1902.[4] On 4 October 1902 he married for the third time,[5] shortly after he had started practicing again. On 26 May 1903 he visited Holmes in Baker Street, in September 1903 he wrote of his practice.[6] 1904 is *terra incognita;* we do not have any records for that year. What conclusions can we draw?

In autumn 1902 Dr. Watson was already practicing, therefore he could have been Mr. Dunning's "medical man" by April 1903. It is true that his own rooms in the summer 1902 were in Queen Anne Street, but this does not necessarily imply that he stayed there. It would be quite plausible that as soon as he became betrothed he left Baker Street (Holmes would certainly not be amused by frequent visits of the fair sex and the concomitant billings and cooings) in order to arrange his marriage and look for a place for his family and practice. Mr. Dunning mentions that Dr. Watson is a rather recent settler and in April 1903 this would be perfectly correct (in April 1904 however it would be out of date).

All of this proves that the Canon does not pose objections to our identifying Dr. Watson of **"Casting the Runes"** with Dr. John H. Watson from Baker Street.

This being just an *argumentam ex nihilo,* which proves nothing, it cannot satisfy the stringent logical principles of Sherlock Holmes which we try to emulate. We have to look for positive proof in the dialogue between Mr. Dunning and Dr. Watson. We will cite this conversation *in extenso;* it being perhaps the only known external piece of Watsoniana passed on to us, these words should be cherished as a unique treasure:

> On arriving at his house he [Mr. Dunning] found Dr. Watson, his medical man, on his doorstop. "I've had to upset your household arrangements, I'm sorry to say, Dunning. Both your servants hors de combat. In fact, I've had to send them to the Nursing Home." "Good heavens! What's the matter?"
>
> "Its something like Ptomaine poisoning, I should think. You've not suffered yourself, I can see, or you wouldn't be walking about. I think they'll pull through all right."
>
> "Dear, dear! Do you have any idea what brought it on?"
>
> "Well, they tell me they bought some shell-fish from a hawker at their dinner-time. It's odd. I've made inquiries, but I can't find that any hawker has been to any other houses in the street. I couldn't send word to you; they won't be back for a bit yet. You come and dine with me tonight anyway, and we can make arrangements for going on. Eight o'clock. Don't be too anxious."

A bit later it is said that "Mr. Dunning spent the time pleasantly enough with the doctor (a rather recent settler)."

What does the dialogue tell us about this Dr. Watson?

The first thing to strike us is the poisoning.[7] ("Ptomaine—kinds of poisonous alkaloids found in putrefying matter" *Pocket Oxford Dictionary,* 1925). We know that Mr. Holmes was very interested in poisons and their effects. It would be surprising if Dr. Watson had not picked up a certain expertise about such things which a common practitioner would never need to have. This allowed him the quick diagnosis of what must have looked (after the short time elapsed) like a simple, if severe, case of indigestion.

Secondly of interest is the expression *"hors de combat."* The phrase, common as it is, nonetheless implies a military context. It seems implausible that this phrase should be uttered so casually by a peaceful physician of London's Suburbia.

Further remarkable is the Doctor's reaction of immediately inquiring whether the suspect hawker had been noticed at the other houses. Again this would in our opinion imply a way of thinking far removed from the everyday experiences of a suburban G.P.

Putting all this together we arrive at a Doctor named Watson who opened a practice in a London suburb shortly before 1903, who is experienced with poisons, has a military background and tends to think like a detective. To identify this man with the Dr. John H. Watson whom we all know and love is in our view compelling.

Thus it should sadden us the more when we learn from the dialogue that Dr. Watson's third marriage also seems to have ended after a few months, probably by the death of Mrs. Watson.[8] For as we are told, Dr. Watson invites Mr. Dunning to "come and dine with me" (not us), that he intends to make arrangements for going on (to invite him), and that Mr. Dunning spends the evening pleasantly enough with the doctor and makes no mention of a Mrs. Watson.[9] Moreover, would Dr. Watson, being married only a few months, have been so eager to invite Mr. Dunning, a quite recent neighbor (resp. patient), if his loving wife had been expecting him? On the other hand, had Dr. Watson been widowed only a short time ago, it would be perfectly understandable for him to invite somebody so as not to have to spend a lonely evening in his solitary home.[10]

We hope to have proved beyond doubt that **"Casting the Runes"** contains the single (to our knowledge) eye-witness account of a meeting with John H. Watson, M.D. from an independent source outside the Canonical cycle. It allows us to view Dr. Watson in a quite different light than he uses to present himself—humble, restrained, self-effacing. Here, seen by a stranger, he appears decisive, at ease in his profession, self-assured, in command of the situation; in short a wise and good man to have at your side in a crisis. Thus it becomes understandable that this man was for almost twenty years the companion of the best and wisest man in England.

Notes

Authors note: This piece was written before the author became aware that Mr. Robert A. Emery in his essay "Dr. James and Dr. Watson" (BSJ NS Vol. 38 No.2/June 1988) had already published the relevant material. Mr. Emery reached, insofar as he drew conclusions, in some instances similar insights. Without wishing to belittle the merits of Mr. Emery's s work, it must be said that he presents his finding without analyzing it as it deserves. The author certainly regrets that this matter is not his singular discovery (which would be rather surprising anyhow with him living in Austria far removed from the centers of learned Sherlockian discourse); still he begs indulgence to present his considerations and conclusions arrived at without benefit of Mr. Emery's work. Corrections of obvious errors or omissions by Mr. Emery have, however, been included.

1. Montague Rhodes James (1862-1936): "Medievalist and Provost of Eton. Editor of numerous bibliographical and paleographical works . . . his

"Ghost Stories" are well known and have been collected "*Concise Oxford Dictionary of English Literature,* 1939)

2. Not, however, 1910, as Mr. Emery states.

3. It would be tempting to see in her the mother or aunt of Mr. Trevor Bennett, the Assistant to Professor Presbury of CREE, but, unless further sources turn up, this must remain speculative.

4. ILLU: "I was living in my own rooms in Queen Anne Street then."

5. BLAN: "The good Watson had at that time left me for a wife" writes Holmes in January 1903. 3GAB: "I had not seen Holmes for some days."

6. CREE: "As my practice was not inconsiderable by that time."

7. We cannot concur with Mr. Emery's opinion that this was a demonic poisoning and a demonic hawker. "The world is big enough for us. No ghosts need apply" (SUSS). It is possible to explain the obvious persecution mania suffered by Mr. Dunning (and, lethally by Mr. Harrington) by the application of a slow acting hallucinatory contact poison in the paper or ink of the runes. Mr. Karswell, having occasionally used this substance, was already sensitized and suffered a massive, acute and fatal fit on exposure.

8. Probably by February 1903, since nothing is said about it in January—*vide* 5.

9. Mr. Emery also notes the curious incident of Mrs. Watson at dinnertime, but lets matters rest there. His remarks on the relationship between Dr. Watson and Mr. Dunning are surely wrong. To imply that Dr. Watson inclined toward Alchemy and Demonology and managed to fool Mr. Holmes all those years (CREE: "Good, Watson! You always keep us flatfooted on the ground") is simply unacceptable. Mr. Emery states correctly that Mr. Dunning had "lots of hobbies." A convivial evening with Dr. Watson and his colorful experiences would be ensured. (We certainly wish we could have joined them).

10. Why did Dr. Watson not return to Baker Street? Could it be possible that Mr. Holmes drove him to this marriage? We must keep in mind that in October 1903 Holmes left Baker Street to take up bee-keeping and violin-playing in the Sussex downs. Knowing Mr. Holmes we cannot believe that this was a sudden impulse. It is quite probable that he began to plan his retirement already in 1902, with finding a fitting residence and so on. Dr. Watson strikes us as a typical metropolitan dweller, in spite of being settled and bourgeois. It is rather hard to imagine him frequenting the

downs except on holidays. His options were scant, should Holmes move. Should he stay in Baker Street, where every door-handle reminded him of the exciting adventures with Holmes? Should he start to look for other dwellings? Or should he start all over, with a marriage, a practice, new surroundings? This, obviously, is the course he set. That his marriage should end tragically after a short time he could not anticipate. We would like to think that contacts with neighbors like Benning helped him to overcome the loneliness and the memories.

Penny Fielding (essay date fall 2000)

SOURCE: Fielding, Penny. "Reading Rooms: M. R. James and the Library of Modernity." *Modern Fiction Studies* 46, no. 3 (fall 2000): 749-71.

[*In the following excerpt, Fielding discusses the prominence of libraries in James's stories, examining how the author uses this motif to explore themes of sexuality, gender identity, and social intersubjectivity.*]

If we were to read the development of Gothic fiction through its objects of terror, from giant helmets to serial killers, then M. R. James would be hard to place. While he occasionally does make use of traditional Gothic conventions—two of his stories, **"Count Magnus"** and **"Wailing Well,"** are populated by that familiar monster of Victorian horror, the vampire; in other stories he includes a number of troglodytic characters resembling Robert Louis Stevenson's Mr. Hyde; and some monstrous spiders appear in **"The Ash Tree"**—usually James's creatures are more difficult to categorize. Sometimes they lurk in the uncanny objects of the everyday: curtains, prayer books, rolls of linen, and bedclothes all take on a ghostly animation. More often it is hard to say precisely of what the phobic objects consist, as they rarely take on material form. James is a master of the unexplained supernatural, not so much in luring the reader into a bewildering and impossible choice of explanations, as Henry James does in *The Turn of the Screw*, but in seeming almost willfully unconcerned with the provision of any explanation at all. In **"Rats,"** a short story from his **Collected Ghost Stories** (1931), James draws attention to this tendency by opening with an epigraph from Charles Dickens's story "Tom Tiddler's Ground": "'And if you was to walk through the bedrooms now, you'd see the ragged, mouldy bedclothes a-heaving and a-heaving like seas.' 'And a-heaving and a-heaving with what?' he says. 'Why, with the rats under 'em.'" But in line with the perverse anti-logic of James's later tales, when the story itself commences it turns out not to be about the **"Rats"** of the title at all: "But was it with the rats? I ask, because in another case

it was not. I cannot put a date to the story, but I was young when I heard it, and the teller was old. It is an ill-proportioned tale, but that is my fault not his" (341). And, contrary to the reception of James as a master of the "well-made tale," **"Rats"** *is* ill-proportioned, with an extensive and somewhat repetitive buildup to a conventional "what's behind the locked door?" plot, followed by a cursory explanation about an executed murderer whose animated corpse may have been spotted.[1]

Thus James's stories—particularly his later ones—show a marked disregard for any kind of conventional plotting. Many stories are oddly shaped, containing large sections of description only related to the plot by proximity, and others, like the confusing **"Two Doctors,"** do not bother with any explanation at all. An interesting case in this respect is the Freudian-entitled **"The Malice of Inanimate Objects."** The story begins as Mr. Manners tells Mr. Burton of the suicide by throat-cutting of George Wilkins, a man they both knew, and with whom Burton had been in legal dispute (expressed only in the vaguest of terms in the story). The two men then take a walk and Burton destroys a kite imprinted with the letters "I.C.U." Burton continues through the day experiencing all sorts of minor accidents until he apparently has his own throat cut on a train, the words "Geo. W." being inscribed in blood near the body. With typically misleading confidence, the narrator ends the story by remarking, "Do not these facts—if facts they are—bear out my suggestion that there is something not inanimate behind the Malice of Inanimate Objects?" (**"Casting"** 292). Of course, they do not: the story provocatively fails to establish a connection between the various annoying but trivial objects of Burton's day, including the kite, and the supposed ghost of "Geo. W. Feci," who never turns up in person. This uneasy relationship between objects and their ordering in the cause-and-effect narration of the ghost story characterizes James, and it is this relationship, rather than the nature of the objects themselves, that helps us to understand his position in Gothic modernism.

James is known as a conservative writer whose frissons are carefully contained by the comfortable world of the antiquarians and historians who populate his stories. But to reverse this relationship is to reveal a world in which the antiquarian past returns to trouble a fragile and alienated sense of modern life. In some ways, James continues a tendency in Victorian and fin-de-siècle Gothic to move the sites of horror away from the otherness of sublime landscapes and foreign castles and into the more familiar world of the modern town or bourgeois home. The phobic objects of such tales enact a double role in that they are both sensationally alien to modern life yet also produced by it. Thus Dracula arrives from feudal Transylvania to awaken Lucy's already excessive sexuality, while Dorian Gray's picture enacts both an attempt to transcend materiality, and the inevitable consequences of modern decadence. In other ways, James conjures up a more radically alienated modernity that marks the inability of his heroes either to live in the present or to process the epistemological lessons of the past. Jack Sullivan has deftly tied James's heroes to the modernism of T. S. Eliot, arguing that "[t]here is [. . .] an implicit 'Waste Land' ambiance to these stories. The characters are antiquaries, not merely because the past enthralls them, but because the present is a near vacuum" (75). And if we pursue this in greater detail, we can see how the empty spaces of James's antiquarian heroes become haunted by the very fears about modern life that they seek to avoid.

James's stories, like a number of the late nineteenth-century Gothic tales that immediately precede them, seem concerned with problems of gender identity and social intersubjectivity. His heroes are exclusively male and usually bachelors, but they rarely participate in the all-male coterie of *The Strange Case of Dr. Jekyll and Mr. Hyde* or in *Dracula*'s vampire-hunting band of brothers. Instead, James gives us a world of isolated single men who holiday alone in quiet hotels or take golf-playing vacations. Free, it seems, from engagement with social complexities, they are able to devote themselves to the pursuits of reading and collecting. Yet the repression of social and gender relations, unsurprisingly, occasions the Gothic return of these determinants. Over and over again in James's stories, the objects sought by his professional and amateur antiquarians enact the Gothic's violent irruption of the past into the present, but this is a past whose monstrosities are summoned up in the very attempt to contain, process or understand them. More specifically, we can see how James's isolated male heroes, as they try to preserve their singular, masculine pursuits, become overtaken by precisely those complexities of gender and sexuality that they originally feared.

The Library of Horrors

As befits their solitary lifestyles, the most common habitat for James's heroes is the library. Before looking in detail at the apparitions that haunt these libraries, I will examine the library itself and the ways in which it organizes and delimits knowledge in history, particularly in terms of the intense competition over the very term "library" before and during the publication of James's stories. The nature of the library is a pressing concern for modernism, and Walter Benjamin usefully introduces the subject when speaking of his own extensive collection of books:

> Every passion borders on the chaotic, but the collector's passion borders on the chaos of memories. More than that: the chance, the fate, that suffuse the past before my eyes are conspicuously present in the accustomed confusion of these books. For what else is this collection but a disorder to which habit has accommo-

dated itself to such an extent that it can appear as order? You have all heard of people whom the loss of their books has turned into invalids, or of those who in order to acquire them became criminals. These are the very areas in which any order is a balancing act of extreme precariousness.

(59)

Benjamin's relationship with his collection reflects his pervasive concerns about the place of tradition in modernity. Here, as in other essays, he attempts to secure the individual in the face of alienating and disintegrating cultural values through the personal archaeology of experience and memory. Yet he simultaneously acknowledges how unstable are the defenses of the collection, how easily broken down by psychosomatic illness and criminality. Benjamin acknowledges that collecting is an expression of his own subjectivity: "the phenomenon of collecting loses its meaning as it loses its personal owner" (67). Equally, he recognizes the precariousness of this kind of personal collection in the midst of an alienating historical process where private libraries were giving way to public ones: "Even though public collections may be less objectionable socially and more useful academically than private collections, the objects get their due only in the latter" (67). Benjamin's predicament speaks to the particular dilemmas of modernity that are my subject. The library's metonymic position as a signifier of "culture," at a time when that very word was a contested issue, allowed it to become a repository not only of books but also of competing social fears and desires. And in the midst of these, as Benjamin observes, were anxieties about subjectivity in a period when psychoanalysis was turning its attention to our relationship to objects such as books.

Two illustrations give us contrasting images of the late-nineteenth-century library. [One] is the frontispiece to Andrew Lang's study, *The Library* (1881), a guide to book collecting for wealthy bibliophiles. This defining illustration represents the library as a condition of stasis and equilibrium that harks back to a version of a medieval, or at least premodern, ideal of scholarship. To be more accurate, this library is a historical composite—the globe and the proliferation of printed books suggest a Renaissance setting, but the characters are wearing vaguely medieval dress, and scrolls are also in evidence. Despite—or perhaps because of—its competing historical representations, this library is also dehistoricized, as if drawing on that particular brand of nineteenth-century medievalism that becomes a generalized past in contradistinction to the present. Such a broad perspective shades into other ideas about general conceptions of space and time: the globe reinforces the idea that in an era of limited literacy, the library can contain all there is to know about the world. And this is true of the picture's temporal vista as well: the gaze of the two figures is directed inwards towards a metonymic pile of books that conjures up the idea of the library as a self-contained space. Yet if we glance at the lower part of the frame, we notice that this self-containment is bounded only by infinitude. The hourglass at the bottom rests upon the symbols of alpha and omega, and the design calls up the intersection of time and eternity, infusing the whole image with the suggestion that the library is *all* time, that it is bounded only by timelessness. This library, then, is not a collection, a representative selection of culture, but culture itself.

Yet although the frame seems designed to foreground the conceptualization of the library as I have outlined above, there remain other, more troubling items in the picture. The old and young men might further signify the timelessness of libraries but there is also a hint of the homoerotic in the way the picture is arranged to show off the young man's legs. Perhaps underscoring such a suggestion, one of the naked figures at the top has its back to us, concealing its gender. Is this pair Adam and Eve, tasting the fruit of the tree of knowledge of good and evil and introducing a serpentine evil into the edenic library? Or are they the same sex, narcissistic mirror images of each other that reinforce the homoeroticism of the library in a covert manner? What is their relationship to the texts in the library? Are they there to signify Adamic language, the absolute correspondence of names and things, or is their fruit consumption a reminder that they brought absence into the world and all our poststructuralist language theories?

Again, these cryptic signs may prove to be more worrying, and more culturally specific, than the limitless values that the images declare, . . . The illustration from an anonymous 1895 pamphlet entitled *The Truth about Giving Readers Free Access to the Books in a Public Lending Library* clearly suggests that a whole nest of alarming serpents has invaded the library space. At one side, with his back to us, an elderly man sits reading quietly in the manner of a bygone age; at the other side, a cloth-capped working-class man lurks in a sinister fashion round the back of a bookcase, pocketing a book. The most prominent image, in the center of the picture, is a woman standing on a ladder who knocks off the top hat of a gentleman standing below. To her left, two men fight over a book. Some fairly clear conclusions can be drawn from this scene. No longer is the library an ideal space touching the atemporal and the universal: troubling social phenomena have already invaded in the form of tense class and gender relations. Taking both pictures together, we have two ways of figuring the library: one lays claim to an ahistorical universalism, while the other announces the effects of social divisions. We might see this as a visualization of certain developments both in the social history of the library in the late nineteenth century, and in the function of the library as a site of cultural negotiation. Driving such negotiations is the idea of the collection. Many recent theories of collection that I draw on have concentrated on the museum or the private collection of objects, but we can also see the library as a special, and sometimes awkward, case. The library is both space and system: the term is commonly applied both to a building, for example the British Library, and to a method of publication such as the Everyman's Library. Michel de Certeau, writing of the origins of national archives, adds an important third dimension: in his terms, the archive is "the combination of *group* (the 'erudite'), *places* ('libraries'), and *practices* (of copying, printing, communication, classification etc)" (73). If we introduce these concepts into the economy of the library, cracks appear in its edifice; while remaining distinctive as a collection, the library differs from other forms of collection because of the unstable relationship between de Certeau's terms. In the ideal library, . . . these are imagined in perfect harmony. The medieval connotations are pressed into the service of such an idyll: the users of the library are those capable of understanding its texts, but as those texts constitute the whole world, its readers are an epistemological repository for *all* knowledge of the world. The space of the library is contained, yet timeless, and the systems it generates are all geared to the preservation of the collection-as-world. However, the inability of the library to live up to the demands of such a model has given it a divided history unlike that of the museum. The ideal library is always haunted by its more subversive and socialized doppelgänger. While museums are generally regarded as socially enlightening, libraries have not always been so well esteemed.

We can see this double existence in operation in the nineteenth-century library. On the one hand, the library aspires to a condition of expansion, plenitude, or even completion. Although I do not wish to subsume the library entirely under the general umbrella of the collection, we can see how the building up of civic collections fits into a more general pattern of nineteenth-century collecting. Underpinned by an anglocentric—and often imperialist—universalism, manifested in collections from the Great Exhibition of 1851 to such great textual assemblies of anthropology as James George Frazer's *Golden Bough,* the collection seeks to encompass a totality of knowledge. Susan Stewart has commented usefully on this phenomenon:

> The collection is often about containment on the level of its content and on the level of a series, but it is also about containment in a more abstract sense. Like Noah's Ark, those great civic collections, the library and the museum, seek to represent experience within a mode of control and confinement. One cannot know everything about the world, but one can at least approach closed knowledge through the collection.
>
> (161)

Yet the growth of the civic library also marks the institutionalizing of the public library and already the collection becomes riven internally. During the period between the two Public Libraries Acts, that of 1850 (which allowed for the first time the levying by borough councils of a 1/2 d. rate for the maintenance of a town library) and that of 1919 (which enabled counties to provide library services and removed the limitation on rates), the identity of a library in England was particularly unstable (Kelly 1-15, 319). The new public libraries had to be classified among the already existing uses of the term: commercial subscription libraries, national collections, university libraries, or private libraries. Libraries had been used for a long time as the focus for class distinctions based upon reading habits. Circulating libraries, for instance, had been in operation since the eighteenth century and had been famously looked on with suspicion as the site of middle-class romance reading and novel procuring. As working-class literacy increased in the nineteenth century, new kinds of libraries sprang up both to cater to the desires of this new reading public and to control that desire by ensuring that "suitable" reading matter was provided for working-class readers. Parish libraries had existed in Scotland since the early nineteenth century, funded by subscription and sponsorship; in England, libraries attached to mechanics' institutes catered to an industrialized population. Both these kinds of libraries were typically stocked with improving literature: religious texts and repositories of "useful knowledge" in the form of popular science, all illustrating the harmony of a divinely-created universe. The new public libraries were often seen, despite contemporary librarians' fervent claims to the contrary, as providers of reading matter to the working class. It soon became apparent that readers were more interested in fiction than in the improving factual works that the libraries had been intended to supply.[2]

As a policy for regulating social reading practices, the libraries did not quite succeed, because the habits they were supposed to control continued to subvert the ideal model. While attempting to maintain their original aim of providing social order and enlightenment, libraries were also commonly regarded as the scene of the dark forces of disorder as evinced in the "Chaos in the Lending Library" illustration. Women not only were evident in the lending libraries but also assaulted the more traditionally male reading rooms. As Judith Walkowitz identifies in her study of gender roles played out in the late Victorian city, great national collections were no longer safe: "Advanced women not only invaded governmental bodies and assumed a commanding presence in the streets, they encroached on other male preserves as well. One prime target was the British Museum Reading Room. The Reading Room became the stomping ground of the 'bohemian set,' a place where trysts were made between heterodox men and women" (69).

Readers of both sexes increasingly wanted to take books out of lending libraries, a desire that had a different aim from that of the expansion of the collection, and that was tangential to its aspiration to completeness. Readers introduced a disorderly subjectivity into the pure objects contained by the library and disrupted its systems. Even if they did not break up the collection by borrowing, they were liable to disturb principles of classification if open access was permitted. Classification, which Susan Stewart calls "order beyond the reach of temporality" (151), attempts to stave off alterity by freezing historical process in synchronic states, replacing narrative with lists or tables. Furthermore, the suspicion of bad reading could be contained by the classification not simply of books but of space and, by extension, of the bodies of readers themselves. Ephemeral reading, for example, could be confined to a periodicals reading room to minimize frivolous reading habits in the main reading room.[3] Libraries could classify their readers in tables catalogued by occupation. All these systems are threatened in figure 2, where the act of readerly choice is dramatized. The author of the pamphlet cautions, "As the majority of the visitors to public libraries possess very little knowledge of books, direct access really encourages a desultory kind of reading and means, with rare exceptions, wandering aimlessly about the shelves, scanning book after book for the pictures" (4). With the introduction of open access, boundaries are transgressed, readers become agents rather than passive recipients of a prescribed "knowledge," and thus the perpetrators of social impropriety or of criminal acts.

Against this background of the reading public as criminally irresponsible, Andrew Lang constructs his ideal library, which exists to fulfill the desire of only one reader: himself. Lang's perfect library . . . is an attempt to evade the problematic doubleness of the civic/lending library altogether by the conjuring up of the neo-medieval private library described earlier. Like many collectors, Lang wants the individual elements of his collection to stand in synecdochal relation not only to the collection as a whole, but also to an ideal world outside the collection. Like artifacts from a distant culture that are included in exhibitions not only to represent that culture, but also to function as part of it, Lang minimizes the difference between the world and knowledge of the world.

Lang's library indulges in a fantasy of totality that it can never make real. The private library operates on the principles of inclusion of books and exclusion of anything that might interrupt the carefully controlled environment in which Lang's temporality and classification can stand for the universal. Not surprisingly, this campaign is doomed from the start. Lang's first move is to get rid of the monsters brought into circulation by the lending library: women and the working class. He refers to himself and fellow bibliophiles as "bookmen" and he means it. Women can have the honorary position

of "lady booklovers" but even so are not highly regarded. Lang is pleased to define his library space as
rigorously exclusive to middle-class men and thus "remote from the interruptions of servants, wife, and children" (*Library* 34). *The Library* is virtually a manual of
war against the foes of the library, yet his construction
of the library space becomes infused by the very forces
which Lang attempts to repress. In a classic strategy,
the cultural agenda of which famously has been exposed by the anthropologist Mary Douglas, Lang seeks
to expel dirt from his library, warning that "[t]here is
nothing so hideous as a dirty thumb mark on a white
page" (58). Douglas points out that the successful management of dirt is essential to cultural value systems:
"Where ever there is system there is dirt. Dirt is the by-
product of a systematic ordering and classification of
matter, in so far as ordering involves rejecting inappropriate elements" (36). Yet Lang finds dirt a difficult
thing to reject as it lurks around the shelves in the form
of an almost intangible dust. This sets up an anxiety in
his writing. In a move later to be theorized by Julia
Kristeva, Lang warns the reader that if he (Lang is addressing other men) does not abject dirt, dirt will abject
him. Dirt, Lang explains, attracts book-worms that bore
through the frame of the book, attacking both its physical integrity and its status as an object in which Lang
has invested his subjectivity. This phenomenon of the
dissolution of the object is mirrored by echoes of the
lending library—the activity of books entering and leaving the library space. Lang is generally unhappy about
the conjunction of space and movement in the library.
He is distressed equally by thieves and by "compulsive
lenders" who disturb his control over the collection. In
fact these two library foes—dirt and theft/lending—are
really part of the same phenomenon. As Kristeva reminds us, the aspiration to keep the body clean is com-
mensurate with the desire to keep it proper; the clean
and proper body is the illusion of our integrity as subjects. The proper body is distinguished both as the self-
ownership of the body, and the discrete nature of the
owned body. And in turn, this ideal of the proper body
is contained by its frame. If we refer back to the frontispiece of Lang's *The Library,* we remark again on the
weak spots of this defensive frame: the intrusion of a
concealed—and thus unspeakable—sexuality. And not
surprisingly, the return of this repressed invasion of
cleanliness by the horrific is present metatextually in
Lang's narrative.

The most worrying of all the invaders of the library is
the "Book-Ghoul." This creature immediately projects
us into the Gothic horror of the James stories, but before I make that link, I will expand upon Lang's own
monstrously transgressing creation. The Book-Ghoul attacks the book as synecdoche for the library as a whole
and all that it represents:

> The Book-Ghoul is he who combines the larceny of the
> biblioklept with the abominable wickedness of break-

ing up and mutilating the volumes from which he steals.
He is a collector of title-pages, frontispieces, illustrations, and book-plates. He prowls furtively among public and private libraries, inserting wetted threads, which
slowly eat away the illustrations he covets; and he
broods, like the obscene demon of Arabian superstition,
over the fragments of the mighty dead. His disgusting
tastes vary.

(56)

The sheer revulsion engendered by the Book-Ghoul
links the two strands of my argument, for in his horrified yet strangely intimate knowledge of the ghoul's activities, Lang testifies to the fragility of the private library as totality. That totality is both a creation and
reflection of the collector's subjectivity. As Jean Baudrillard points out, "the collection or the series is what
underpins the possession of the object, which is to say,
the reciprocal integration of object with person." That
is, the state of being of an object in the collection derives from the subjectivity of the collector and vice
versa: "its absolute singularity as an object depends entirely upon the fact that it is / who possess it—which,
in turn, allows me to recognize myself in it as an absolutely singular being" (12). As the Book-Ghoul fragments and rearranges Lang's collection it disturbs his
own subjectivity by inducing horror and loathing: the
signs—or rather the non-signs—of Kristevan abjection.
Ghouls can be recognized by their disgusting looks,
which will inspire revulsion as they are "generally
snuffy and foul in appearance" (61).

The Book-Ghoul has a further connotation that exposes
the economic realities that Lang's library seeks to expel. The ghoul is a literalization of the collection as the
reader's digest, a monstrous incorporation of texts and
the cheapening of them in the terms of a cultural value
predicated on economics. The late nineteenth century is
characterized partly by a shift in the beliefs about the
purpose of an economy. The perception of a new consumerism based on abundance, shopping, and the pursuit of pleasure across classes moved economic theory
from production-based models to consumption-based
ones. This economy of pleasure and desire of course
needed to be regulated. David Trotter, who sees these
phenomena behind the novels of the period, points to
concerns about nutrition in a population which was eating itself into unhealthiness, and, more alarmingly,
about the control of sexual desires through eugenics
(12-15). Lang goes to great lengths to keep his library
free from economics or sexual forces, sublimating the
economic value of his books into an aesthetic one. But
the Book-Ghoul is consumerism run riot, literalizing the
term in its treatment of books but also underscoring
their status as commodity. The stolen sections, Lang informs us, are to be reassembled and sold in American
markets.

THE MONSTERS IN THE LIBRARY

The sexualizing of the library is played out in M. R. James's spooky stories, which allow Lang's Book-Ghoul to enact in various guises the problematizing of the library space. James was himself a medievalist, antiquarian, and book-collector; but if his *Collected Ghost Stories* collect anything, it is a set of ideas that push the collection towards its most extreme limits. James's stories offer a canvas on which some of the most common social phobias of the period loom large: irresponsible science, degeneration, recidivism, racial difference, homosexuality, sexually dangerous women. A few examples should fill in this picture: in **"The Residence at Whitminster,"** the scion of an Anglo-Irish family is pursued to his death by some unseen and unnamed supernatural things which "he brought with him from Ireland" (223). In **"Oh, Whistle, and I'll Come to You, My Lad,"** a don is attacked by animated bedclothes from a bed that was to be occupied by an unwanted male companion. In **"A School Story,"** a schoolmaster is enticed to his death by a "beastly thin" man who appears to inhabit a well. Years later, two male bodies are discovered in the same well and "[o]ne body had the arms tight round the other" (113). In **"The Mezzotint,"** the figure that moves across the picture to snatch a baby is a horrifying and remarkable vision both of speeded-up evolution and its descent into a Wellsian future of physical degeneracy:

> The window that had been open was shut, and the figure was once more on the lawn; but not this time crawling cautiously on hands and knees. Now it was erect and stepping swiftly, with long strides, towards the front of the picture. The moon was behind it, and the black drapery hung down over its face so that only hints of that could be seen, and what was visible made the spectators profoundly thankful that they could see no more than a white dome-like forehead and a few straggling hairs.
>
> (37)

The white, dome-like head emblematizes fears of a "Coming Man," the product of reversed or perverted evolutionary progress, who might, in Andrew Lang's words, be "'bald' and 'toothless'" ("Realism" 689) unless a more fit and healthy human destiny can be established.[4] Alternatively, the apparitions in many of the stories are (like Stevenson's Mr. Hyde) hairy and bestial: the criminal monsters of degenerate recidivism. In short, James's tales feature an astonishing variety of the social neuroses of the fin de siècle and the early twentieth century.[5] Interesting as this collection is, it is also an anti-collection, turning itself inward on the dynamics of collecting itself. As I mentioned earlier, it is comparatively difficult to be precise in attaching the objects of James's stories to narrative signifiers. More properly, it is the process of combining or ordering these objects that gives rise to a breakdown in social signification itself.

In James's first story, **"Canon Alberic's Scrap-Book,"** the protagonist, Dennistoun, hopes to "fill a note-book" (11), but the title itself reminds us of problems inherent in the library as collection. A scrap-book is a collection that brings together and integrates disparate items, yet, as its name reminds us, is also an assemblage of bits of texts: scraps. As a metonym for the private library, the scrap-book reminds us that this institution also is heterogeneous and fragmentary and that its project of establishing a complete *collection* will always be thwarted by the dynamics of *collecting*. Thus Lang's Book-Ghoul is not really very different from Lang himself and, as if to prove it, **"Canon Alberic's Scrap-Book"** has its *"amateur des vieux livres"* (13) pursued by a genuine Book-Ghoul that emanates from the scrap-book of the title (a collection of pieces of illuminated manuscripts) to terrorize the book-hunting protagonist. The aspiration to collect is interrupted by the threat of disintegration contained within it.

The terrors of the collection are closely linked in James's stories with a socialized topography that maps out a world of libraries. As in many turn-of-the-century ghost and horror stories, the topology of the haunted house gives clues to the signification of the apparitions found within it. The task of how to read rooms in working out the structures and dynamics governing nineteenth-century culture has now become important in analyses of the period and its texts. Throughout the century, Gothic terrors move from the crypts of castles and abbeys to alarm urban bourgeois professionals in their own homes, hiding out in attics, appearing in bedrooms and drawing rooms, and leading up to the terrifying domesticity of Charlotte Perkins Gilman's *Yellow Wallpaper* (1892). In James's stories, this social topology appears in the haunted library. James's libraries are in a state of crisis as the distinctions between private collection and lending library are broken down, creating a condition in which knowledge and its social function are uncertain and frightening. As James's bachelor heroes wander through their precarious world of hotels and golf-playing holidays, the Langian library, with its refusal to admit social change, is a dangerous place to be. The hero of **"The Tractate Middoth,"** a librarian named Garrett, is rescued from the confines of the library by his marriage to Miss Simpson, his landlady's daughter (an unusual turn of events in a James story). Garrett's name is important in a story that invites us to read the significance of rooms, as he moves from the isolation of the attic to the female space of the parlor. Other rooms take on a more sinister role: the tale involves the missing will of Dr. Rant, a man so annoyed by the marriage of his niece (Mrs Simpson), that he emblematizes his aspirations at everlasting bachelorhood by having himself buried "sitting at a table in his ordinary clothes, in a brick room that he'd made underground in a field near his house" (129). From this isolated personal library space, the now-dead Rant wreaks havoc with the lives of his surviving relatives, having written his will, which leaves everything to Mrs. Simpson, in a book deposited in the unnamed but "famous" library (124) where Garrett is employed. The exact status of this library is not specified by the text; it seems to be a university library but Garrett refers to it as a "public place" (131), and the story opens with a discussion of borrowing rights, focusing on the distinguishing characteristic of a lending library. Mrs. Simpson's devious cousin works out the location of the book and borrows it from the lending library, causing Garrett protracted anxiety at the apparent failure of the classification system. But as the villain begins to tear out and destroy the will, he is done to death by a mysterious dark shape lacking any precise form. Although all turns out well for Garrett and the Simpsons, and a happy domesticity prevails, we are nevertheless made aware of the sinister forces at work in libraries; as one character remarks with ominous prescience: "there's something wrong in the atmosphere of the library" (127). Classification breaks down; Book-Ghouls lurk round every shelf ready to deface the collection. The supposedly neutral, asocial space of the library becomes the site for economic gain, its authenticity open to swindling and theft.

Another sustained example of the library as Gothic horror is provided by James's most famous story, **"Casting the Runes."** This tale establishes even more clearly the circulation of books as something to be afraid of, and in this tale the principle of the returning of texts acts as a kind of Gothic horror in itself. In *Night of the Demon*, the 1958 film based on this story, the runes summon up a physical (and rather impressive) fiery demon to carry off the villain, a detail which serves to emphasize that in the original tale no monster is called for, as it is the return itself of the runes that does the damage. The villainous Karswell, a man who is introduced to us "coming out of the British Museum" (139) is, according to the brother of his last victim, an aspiring bookman but a deeply flawed example. He abuses the British Museum by introducing into it the demonic principles of the lending library that reclaims the books that leave it. Karswell has discovered a means of condemning his enemies to death by planting strips of runic writing on them. Because the runes must be willingly accepted by the victim, they are hidden in something as it is returned: a dropped theatre program or a mislaid coat, or, most significantly for the returning texts motif, some disturbed papers handed back to the hero in the British Museum Reading Room. Needless to say, the runes are eventually returned by the hero to Karswell himself, inevitably resulting in his death. One of a number of bookish villains in James's tales, Karswell is killed by the action of the lending library that compels the return of its possessions.

All of James's stories are haunted by sexual danger for men. Sometimes this is the threat of homosexuality, as in **"A School Story"** or **"Whistle, and I'll Come to You."** More often it is a deadly female sexuality. Not surprisingly, given the fate of collectors' desires for fullness, the most terrifying and repeated threat occurring in James's stories is that of an imagined female sexuality that constitutes a direct threat to the potential wholeness of the library. Female sexuality—culturally defined by absence and lack—is in direct contravention of the rules of collection and, in a number of James's stories, it strikes at the heart of library culture. Try as they might to keep women out of the picture, James's largely bachelor heroes are continually confronted with sexual imagery which, though disguised, is familiar to the reader by virtue of its adoption of visual forms which render it both hidden and customary. Of the collection of topographical drawings in a Cambridge museum, a space similar to the library in many respects, the narrator of **"The Mezzotint"** remarks, "even a department so homely and familiar as this may have its dark corners" (30). The close connection of the frightening and strange with the apparently homely and familiar is, of course, just what Freud's *unheimliche* identifies as a symptom of repression, and the libraries of James's stories prove to be uncanny indeed. It is as if the library, a site of the impulse towards completeness and classification, reveals its fragility under the assault of the very sexual forces it had attempted to deny or repress. Many of James's protagonists are bookmen attracted to "accumulations of books" (289). But if the masculine library is characterized by the hopes of completion and plenitude, it is not surprising that the greatest threat to it should be a correspondingly "female" emptiness or lack. Women do not feature greatly as characters in James's stories other than as barely noticed wives and servants, yet the presence—or rather the easily discernible absence—of their sexuality is everywhere, turning up with a kind of gleeful frequency. In **"Wailing Well,"** the skeletal vampires who prey on the Scout Troop apparently inhabit a well situated within "a sort of clump" (352) marked on the map by a red ring; even the Boy Scout, Baden Powell's epitome of a pure, uncorrupted masculinity, cannot withstand the strange holes that open up everywhere in James's tales. Other boys are rather more fortunate, but their instructors are not: Mr. Sampson, the schoolmaster of **"A School Story,"** is found dead at the bottom of a well covered by a yew thicket. Another well, in **"The Treasure of Abbot Thomas,"** contains a bag which, according to its finder, "slipped forward on to [his] chest and *put its arms round [his] neck*" (105). In **"The Ash-Tree,"** the hollow trunk of the tree is found to contain not only a nest of loathsome spiders, but also the remains of the suggestively-named witch Mrs. Mothersole, implying, in both the image and the name, that the female is rotten at the core.

The equation of monstrous sexuality and demonic libraries is not difficult to establish. In didn't take long before the sexual implications of collecting, implicit in Freud, himself something of a collector, were made explicit by Ernest Jones who writes of "[t]he refusal to give and the desire to gather, [. . .] collect and hoard": "All collectors are anal erotics, and the objects collected are nearly always typical copro-symbols. [. . .] Not to speak of the fond care that may be lavished on a given collection—a trait of obvious value in custodians of museums and libraries" (430). This basic position is echoed by Baudrillard, and expanded by him into theories of the collection as fetishized object and narcissistic image. Like Andrew Lang, Baudrillard identifies collecting as a peculiarly male concern and a facet of phallic signification. The collector subject constructs himself in relation to the objects he possesses, which form a metonymic chain. The fear of castration, the absence that calls male subjectivity into being, is endlessly deferred along the series of the collection, each item becoming an object of desire by virtue of its momentarily filling up the absence for which it was acquired. This Lacanian reading is put more blatantly by Baudrillard in a discussion of the possessive nature of the collector: "If it is true that one is hardly inclined to lend another person one's car, one's pen, one's wife, this is because these objects are, within the jealousy system, the narcissistic image of oneself: and were such an object to be lost or damaged, this would mean symbolic castration. When all is said and done, one never lends out one's phallus" (18). Such a phallocentric assertion underscores how collecting, for Baudrillard, Lang, and James, is associated with a masculine sexual identity. In James's stories this is very fragile. The sexuality of the femme fatale, reduced to images of her terrifying and sometimes lethal female genitalia, everywhere invades the masculine territory so carefully mapped out by the heroes and antiheroes of the stories.

The most extended example of the demonic gendering and sexualization of the collection is **"Mr. Humphreys and His Inheritance."** This story enacts Derrida's concept that "the archiviolithic drive is never present in person [. . .].As inheritance, it leaves only its erotic simulacrum" (11). It is also a story that demonstrates the extent to which, in Derrida's phrase (though not, of course, his original idea) the archive is "patriarchic"— like many of James's story it threatens its bachelor hero with the terrifying absence of female sexuality that wipes out the plenitude embodied by the library space. The story is about the dissolution of the library—a process which it itself enacts by throwing up a succession of synechdocal models for the library, as if the collection were continually falling backwards into its metonymic fragments. **"Mr. Humphreys"** operates in two overlapping strata—as social critique of the Langian private library, and as a study of the fragility of language enacted by the library in general. Humphreys, the story's bachelor hero, is clearly a Langian bookman who considers himself lucky to inherit a house with a well-developed library. The library strikes him as a good place for the exercise of consignment: "He had all the predisposition to take interest in an old library, and there was every opportunity for him here to make a systematic acquaintance with one [. . .]. The drawing up of a *catalogue raisonné* would be a delicious occupation for winter" (194). Humphreys wants to go over the objects in his collection, to establish his ownership of them by representing them in series form and thereby establishing his own subjectivity. At this point, however, the story itself seems to fall into a parody of this very seriality, throwing up more and more examples of libraries in various states of confusion. First, Humphreys is tempted out of his library into a maze in the grounds. The maze is the library's evil twin: while the library openly displays its aspiration to order by providing shelf-mark sign posts, the maze lures us in with its promise of a hidden order there for us to discover if we can.

Uncertain about the maze, Humphreys returns to the library to conduct some research. The purpose of library research tends, in the experience of scholars, to exceed the simple convenience of being able to have access to a number of books. The library reinforces that familiar impression that the scholar is contributing to a mythical "body of knowledge," and however circumscribed, provisional, or partial his or her own efforts may be, they will nevertheless be put to rights when they join that great totality which the library appears to represent. Eventually Humphreys finds an old book that gives a cryptic account of the maze's history: it is reputed to contain "a Jewel of such Price and Rarity that would enrich the Finder thereof for his life" (195). The Jewel once recovered, the Finder in fact finds himself pursued by strange noises and "the constant fear of falling into some Pit or Trap, of which he had heard, and indeed seen with his own Eyes that there were several" (196). In a movement frequently repeated in the text, the library's mnemonic function is illusory, its status as the bearer of history leads, literally, to nothing.

The mysterious book is itself in pieces. Indeed it seems as if a Book-Ghoul has been at work here: the small quarto volume is "loose in the binding," its label has fallen off, and although described as a "collection" of other texts it is "mutilated at that, for the first sheet [is] gone" (194). The little book is the library set in reverse or into dissolution. Nevertheless, Humphreys decides to repeat his cataloguing activities in the library by making a plan of the maze, as if its troublesome interiority could be cured by its exterior representation. No sooner has he embarked on this perilous mission than he is troubled by various sexualized images of an unspecified nature. There is some vague description of dark and dank undergrowth and a strategically placed "bush-thing under the library window" (202). These nonobjects are worrying enough, but most significantly, holes open up in Humphreys's map of the maze. At the center of the maze is a four-foot column, yet even this reassuringly phallic object is less secure than it might at first seem. Most fearful of all is the suspicion that, by some specular sleight-of-hand, the library may be turned inside out, and the phallus itself may contain the terrifying absence of imagined female sexuality. As Humphreys studies the plan of his maze, his attempts to map it out are thwarted by the emergence of "a very odd hole" in the paper, marking the spot of the column, which seems to lure his gaze into it: "For some reason it was hateful to him from the first, but he had gazed at it for some moments before any feeling of anxiety came upon him; and then it did come, stronger and stronger—a horror lest something might emerge from it, and a really agonizing conviction that a terror was on its way, from the sight of which he would not be able to escape" (203-04).

The hole in the map turns into the *vagina dentata* common to many horror stories of the period (notably *Dracula*), threatening to draw in and destroy Humphreys's phallocentric gaze. The objectified female turns into a dangerous, predatory subject. But more importantly, the story offers a parody of the whole impulse of collecting as a means of dealing with castration anxieties. Even Humphreys's cataloguing and ordering activities cannot resist the implications of a lethal female sexuality A marble temple on the grounds contains random lettered tiles that have been removed from the column in the maze; when rearranged, they read in Latin "penetrans ad interiora mortis" ("penetrating into the heart of death"; 204). The tiles, like the sections of the scrap-book or the books in a library, refuse to represent completion and fullness even, in fact especially, when they are collected together. This seems to be the final nightmare that lurks within the collection: that the already embattled systems of collection and representation might fail at the very point at which they are brought into being, that the apparently endless and thus timeless system of substitution may end, not so much moving beyond the pleasure principle as outwitting it, in premature and undesired death. In Humphreys's great cataloguing scheme, language itself, not surprisingly, turns out to be the most fatal collection of them all.

Notes

1. Julia Briggs characterizes James in this way: "Without being in any sense experimental or exploratory, his stories demonstrate the power that the classically well made tale may still exert over a modern reader" (139).

2. This was the finding of Andrew Lang, who in a 1901 survey of books borrowed from lending libraries, conducted with the ghostly assistance of the unnamed "'X,' A Working Man," concludes that they cater for identifiably lower-class tastes; See "The Reading Public" 794.

3. For library design see Edwards, *Free Town Libraries*. Edwards explicitly extends the classification of books to the management of bodies: "An additional and smaller Reading Room in the Free Libraries of large towns would better meet the peculiar wants of real workers. Such an arrangement would 'class' the readers in a way which is entirely unobjectionable" (57).

4. This degenerate physical feature recurs to distress the hero of "The Tractate Middoth": "he had a bald head [. . .]. I tell you he had a very nasty bald head" (128).

5. My argument is thus at odds with a recent essay, "M. R. James and His Fiction," by Clive Bloom, who writes that "[y]ou cannot undermine the literary nature of James's work with a 'political' reading for the *subversive* and politically sophisticated reading of the modern critic is met with by the ironic, bland and sophisticated refusal of any of the stories to yield to such a subversion: the tales do not open to reveal the contradictions of the bourgeois age" (67).

Works Cited

Baudrillard, Jean. "The System of Collecting." *The Cultures of Collecting*. Ed. John Elsner and Roger Cardinal. London: Reaktion, 1994. 7-24.

Benjamin, Walter. "Unpacking My Library: A Talk About Book Collecting." *Illuminations*. Trans. Harry Zohn. Ed. Hannah Arendt. New York: Schocken, 1969. 59-67.

Bloom, Clive. "M. R. James and His Fiction." *Creepers: British Horror and Fantasy in the Twentieth Century*. Ed. Clive Bloom. London, Colorado: Pluto, 1993. 64-71.

Briggs, Julia. *Night Visitors: The Rise and Fall of the English Ghost Story*. London: Faber, 1977.

de Certeau, Michel. *The Writing of History*. Trans. Tom Conley. New York: Columbia UP, 1988.

Derrida, Jacques. *Archive Fever: A Freudian Impression*. Trans. Eric Prenowitz. Chicago: U of Chicago P, 1996.

Douglas, Mary. *Purity and Danger: An Analysis of the Concepts of Pollution and Taboo*. 1966. London: Routledge, 1991.

Edward Edwards. *Free Town Libraries*. London: Trubner, 1869.

James, M. R. *The Collected Ghost Stories of M. R. James*. 1931. Harmondsworth: Penguin, 1984.

———. *"Casting the Runes" and Other Ghost Stories.* Ed. Michael Cox. Oxford: Oxford UP, 1987.

Jones, Ernest. *Papers in Psychoanalysis.* 5th ed. 1948. Boston: Beacon Books, 1961.

Kelly, Thomas. *A History of Public Libraries in Great Britain 1845-1975.* London: The Library Association, 1977.

Lang, Andrew. *The Library.* London: Macmillan, 1881.

———. "The Reading Public." *The Cornhill Magazine* N.S. 11 (1901): 783-95.

———. "Realism and Romance." *The Contemporary Review* 52 (1887): 683-93.

Stewart, Susan. *On Longing.* 1984. Durham: Duke UP, 1993.

Sullivan, Jack. *Elegant Nightmares: the English Ghost Story from le Fanu to Blackwood.* Athens: Athens UP, 1978.

The Truth about Giving Readers Free Access to the Books in a Public Lending Library. London: n.p., 1895.

Trotter, David. *The English Novel in History 1895-1920.* London: Routledge, 1993.

Walkowitz, Judith. *City of Dreadful Delight: Narratives of Sexual Danger in Late-Victorian London.* Chicago: U of Chicago P, 1992.

Terry W. Thompson (essay date summer 2001)

SOURCE: Thompson, Terry W. "M. R. James's 'Oh, Whistle, and I'll Come to You, My Lad.'" *The Explicator* 59, no. 4 (summer 2001): 193-95.

[*In the following essay, Thompson suggests that the game of golf in "Oh Whistle and I'll Come to You, My Lad" is a metaphor for what gets the professor in trouble with the restless spirit in the story.*]

The last few decades of the nineteenth century and the first two of the twentieth have frequently been called the golden age of the English ghost story. Authors on both sides of the Atlantic—but especially in Great Britain—produced supernatural tales at an unprecedented pace and of unmatched subtlety and style. Writers such as Sheridan Le Fanu, M. E. Braddon, F. Marion Crawford, Oliver Onions, and Algernon Blackwood gained tremendous popularity by tapping into the seemingly insatiable public appetite, at the turn of the century, for stories about the otherworldly, the mysterious, and the unexplained. Even such well-established, mainstream authors as Henry James, Edith Wharton, Arthur Conan Doyle, and H. G. Wells dabbled in the genre, as had Charles Dickens before them.

For many devotees of the end-of-the-century renaissance in supernatural tales, Montague Rhodes (M. R.) James is considered the Father Abraham of ghost literature. The quietly prolific and distinguished English scholar (he served as provost for both Eton College and King's College, Cambridge) produced an impressive body of finely crafted, character-rich ghost stories during a long and respected career in the genre. His supernatural tales "have never been out of print and have been adapted for cinema, radio, television, and cassette recordings, making him known to a host of readers to whom his scholarly writings mean little or nothing" (Cox 37). Of James's many fine stories, his widely anthologized tale **"Oh, Whistle, and I'll Come to You, My Lad"** (1904) is viewed by many as his masterpiece. Indeed, many aficionados of ghost literature consider this dark, understated, yet thoroughly terrifying narrative to be the greatest ghost story ever written in English. In it an arrogant young professor—who believes only in what is real and concrete and provable—learns a terrifying midnight lesson about the power of the supernatural during a visit to a coastal lodge far away from the ivory-towered safety of his logical and neatly ordered university campus.

As the story opens, the progressive, modern, and superbly educated professor—Parkins, by name—is described as "young, neat, and precise in speech" as well as "rather henlike [. . .] in his little ways," qualities that permeate every facet of his personality and demeanor (James 106, 108). Poised at the beginning of the twentieth century, Parkins represents the apex of modern civilized man. Empirical, rational, scientific, unhindered by superstition, and free of all folkloric fear, he is the very model of British domination of the world, when the vast Victorian empire was the sole superpower on earth. Early in the tale, when questioned about ghosts and spirits, Parkins boasts to his colleagues, "'I hold that any semblance, any appearance of concession to the view that such things might exist is equivalent to the renunciation of all that I hold most sacred'" (109). However, true to the conventions of the genre, the self-satisfied Parkins will later endure a dark night of the soul, which will first challenge and then change his belief that cold science is at the very center of all existence. His "orderly and prudent life," so cultivated and so sheltered, will be rent asunder by a ghastly visitor from beyond the grave (James 119). He learns through a terrifying ordeal that there are "primitive powers of evil which are always waiting to be summoned up by reckless" moderns who scoff at what they cannot validate with reason and experiment (Wise and Fraser 516).

Besides reading and studying in the peace and isolation of a private room in an out-of-the-way sea lodge, Parkins plans to improve his golf game during his vacation getaway to the channel coast. James's choice of golf as the professor's avocation is an interesting one and deserves discussion. More than just an excuse to get the haughty young pedant into a haunted spot for a frightening lesson in the occult, it is very important symbolically. That genteel sport, so trendy with English bon vivants at the turn of the century, becomes an important metaphor for what gets the professor into trouble with a restless spirit in the first place. Golf is a relatively modern game; it is not ancient, was not played by the Celts or the Jutes or the Picts. It is fitting that the new sport appeals to the elitist streak in Parkins. Furthermore, golf is a decidedly British game, invented in Scotland and invested with the cool, measured demeanor for which inhabitants of Great Britain are so well known. Because the professor believes in order and safety above all else, it is fitting that he makes golf his passion: It is an eminently "safe" and structured pastime; there is no contact, no violence, and no injury—save for an occasional backache the next day. The sport is also individualistic and does not require a team effort. It fits in perfectly with the professor's smug disdain for the local inhabitants of the village—the ignorant, backward, and uneducated people who do not have the good professor's erudition and breeding. Further, golf is about the physical, not the metaphysical. The game involves an understanding of angles, velocities, trajectories, wind resistance, drag, and so on, all topics that would appeal to a man of reason and science.

In *Elegant Nightmares: The English Ghost Story From Le Fanu to Blackwood,* Jack Sullivan writes that "the endless process of collecting and arranging gives the characters an illusory sense of order and stability, illusory because it is precisely this process which evokes the demon or vampire" (75). And nothing better represents modern man's desire to force order and stability upon nature's wildness than a golf course. Perhaps even more important to the main theme of the story—that the local inhabitants of an ancient area often have oral generational knowledge that an outsider, no matter how learned or well read, simply cannot fathom—is that the golf course on which the professor plays is an affront to the primeval spirits that inhabit the area. The course is built on sacred ground, amid the ancient ruins and graves of a medieval Templars' church. The building of it ignores nature, history, and tradition and insults the mystical and the mysterious. A golf course turns nature into a commodity; folklore, local culture, superstition, and even religion are cast aside for the sake of profit and recreation. Nature is remade to fit an artificially imposed pattern, and the pristine golf course becomes cold and soulless.

Ever since the earliest ghostly tales were shared around prehistoric campfires, humans have taken "a peculiar pleasure in being terrified vicariously" (Mason 253). In **"Oh, Whistle, and I'll Come to You, My Lad,"** M. R. James's masterly use of "circumstantial detail, believable living characters, economy of style, and the power

of suggestion all create the necessary atmosphere for a successful ghost story" (Cox and Gilbert x). The integral use of golf and the main character's fascination with it help to move the plot along, and this, in turn, elevates the tale, giving it a depth and resonance that transcend a frequently dismissed genre. This brief tale says something important about respect for the oral tradition and the belief that not all things in the great and mysterious universe can be measured, weighed, or observed with the limited senses of even the most educated of humans.

Works Cited

Cox, Michael. Introduction. *The Ghost Stories of M. R. James.* Oxford: Oxford UP, 1986.

Cox, Michael, and R. A. Gilbert. Introduction. *The Oxford Book of English Ghost Stories.* Oxford: Oxford UP, 1986.

James, M. R. "Oh, Whistle, and I'll Come to You, My Lad." *Ghost Stories of an Antiquary.* New York: Dover, 1971.

Mason, Michael A. "On Not Letting Them Lie: Moral Significance in the Ghost Stories of M. R. James." *Studies in Short Fiction* 19.4 (1982): 253-60.

Sullivan, Jack. *Elegant Nightmares: The English Ghost Story from Le Fanu to Blackwood.* Athens: Ohio UP, 1978.

Wise, Herbert A., and Phyllis Fraser, eds. *Great Tales of Terror and the Supernatural.* New York: Modern Library, 1972.

Ramsey Campbell (essay date 2001)

SOURCE: Campbell, Ramsey. "Introduction." In *Meddling with Ghosts: Stories in the Tradition of M. R. James,* pp. vii-x. London: The British Library, 2001.

[*In the following essay, Campbell offers a brief history of the composition and publication of James's short fiction and comments on his enduring influence on the genre of the ghost story.*]

M. R. James is the most influential British writer of supernatural fiction. This anthology is designed to represent the tradition he refined and to demonstrate his influence.

Montague Rhodes James was born in Kent in 1862, but moved with his family to Great Livermere outside Bury St Edmunds three years later. His childhood love of church architecture and of the Suffolk landscape would be crucial to his adult writing, both fiction and nonfiction. He won a scholarship to Eton, where he distinguished himself in classics, divinity and French. He became provost of King's College, Cambridge, for thirteen years, then took up that position at Eton for a further eighteen until his death. His published books include *Old Testament Legends, The Apocryphal New Testament, Abbeys, Suffolk and Norfolk* (which includes, as the reader of the present anthology will discover, a tang of the macabre) and *The Wanderings and Homes of Manuscripts*. Best known, however, are his four books of ghost stories: ***Ghost-Stories of an Antiquary*** (1904), ***More Ghost Stories of an Antiquary*** (1911), ***A Thin Ghost and Others*** (1919), and ***A Warning to the Curious and Other Ghost Stories*** (1925), all included in ***The Collected Ghost Stories of M. R. James*** (1931, frequently reprinted since). A few stories were subsequently published but have never been included in the omnibus.

His writings on the ghost story were sparse but valuable, though sometimes his own practice contradicts them. The most substantial as a survey appeared in the December 1929 issue of *The Bookman*, where James demonstrates his familiarity with the genre, even tracing the roots of *Dracula* to (apparently) a skeptical article on vampirism from the November 1856 issue of *Chamber's Repository*. He clearly made it his business to read widely in the field. Some of his tales refer explicitly to its established tropes and clichés before building on them or subverting them (not, despite the view of some critics, that art need subvert its chosen form). While the Victorian spectre was often ethereal or simply kept its distance, James's apparitions tend to be grisly and physical, though a glimpse of them is frequently enough to provoke a shudder. The sheet had pretty well become the uniform of the traditional ghost, and so (in **'Oh, Whistle, and I'll Come to You, My Lad'**) James imagines its ultimate manifestation: a sly black joke, perhaps, but memorably horrible.

Many of his stories were written for reading aloud. Some were composed to frighten children: the first audience of **'A School Story'** was the King's College Choir School, while **'Wailing Well'** was heard at a camp fire by the Eton College Boy Scout troop. Most, however, were initially performed to adult friends at King's as an annual Christmas treat. In this James clearly meant to align himself with the tradition of the festive ghost story and indeed of oral storytelling, and he remarks in the introduction to his collected stories that he has 'tried to make my ghosts act in ways not inconsistent with the rules of folklore'. All this may suggest a certain cosiness, which would be confirmed by the standard view that the most important Jamesian attribute is his antiquarianism. Of course that is crucial to the verisimilitude of many of the stories, and many of them deal with scholars whose comfortable world is invaded by the malign supernatural. Nevertheless I maintain that the essence of James is to be found less in his

characters and settings than in his technique. The quality that makes his best tales—which is to say most of them—unforgettable is his wit in communicating horror.

I hope it is not presumptuous of me to suggest he would have taken this as praise. In his *Bookman* essay he calls for 'malevolence and terror . . . and a modicum of blood' and two years later, in the *Evening News,* wrote 'I say you must have horror and also malevolence. Not less necessary, however, is reticence.' He had no time for fiction that sought to be nauseating, but story after story demonstrates his willingness to be as frightening as possible. Nor was his definition of the ghostly confined to revenants. His tales swarm with spiders either giant or multitudinous, immense half-glimpsed insects, tentacled demons and even worse familiars to be found down wells or, most nightmarish of all, under your pillow. Even the returned dead tend to be, in his own words, ugly and thin. He had a genius for the telling phrase, into which he could compress more supernatural dread than most of us can manage in a paragraph. It's hardly surprising that on Peter Nicholls' tribute to the ghost story on Radio 4's *Kaleidoscope,* Kingsley Amis (author of *The Green Man,* one of the very few successful Jamesian novels) was able to quote verbatim from memory a gruesome passage from the provost's **'Count Magnus'**.

The present book seeks to place James in the tradition he developed and to demonstrate his continuing influence. Let me suggest one possible source of his method. The reader is invited to consider this, from 1871:

> . . . when Irene, who had been lost in thought, looked up, she saw it was nearly dark, and at the same moment caught sight of a pair of eyes, bright with a green light, glowering at her through the open window. The next instant, something leaped into the room. It was like a cat, with legs as long as a horse's, Irene said, but its body no bigger and its legs no thicker than those of a cat . . .

That is to be found in George MacDonald's *The Princess and the Goblin,* a children's novel James might conceivably have read. Reticence and terror are certainly present in this passage and in others such as

> But at that instant the something in the middle of the way, which had looked like a great lump of earth brought down by the rain, began to move. One after another it shot out four long things, like two arms and two legs, but it was now too dark to tell what they were . . .

and

> . . . while yet in the shadow, he caught sight of a creature standing on its hind legs in the moonlight, with its fore feet upon a window ledge, staring in at the window. Its body might have been that of a dog or

wolf—he thought, but he declared on his honour that its head was twice the size it ought to have been for the size of its body, and as round as a ball, while the face, which it turned upon him as it fled, was more like one carved upon a turnip inside which he is going to put a candle, than anything else he could think of . . .

Soon 'a score of creatures' is seen:

> The supernatural or rather subnatural ugliness of their faces, the length of necks and legs in some, the apparent absence of both or either in others . . . such creatures as I have not attempted to describe except in the vaguest manner—the various parts of their bodies assuming, in an apparently arbitrary and self-willed manner, the most abnormal developments . . .

I find the last passage suggestive of Lovecraft as much as of James. Lovecraft is one of the writers whose debt to James is seldom remarked. In 'The Call of Cthulhu', however—written a year after his reading of James—he has surely learned from **'Canon Alberic's Scrap-Book'** the effectiveness of describing a portrait of the monster early in the tale so that its actual manifestation can be less explicitly shown, and a line from the same James story ('It was drawn from the life') is echoed at the end of 'Pickman's Model', Lovecraft's next tale. Sadly, the admiration wasn't mutual: James's only recorded response to finding himself praised in Lovecraft's *Supernatural Horror in Literature* was to bemoan the prose style.

Perhaps it's best that Lovecraft is not reprinted herein, but James might have been surprised by other occurrences of his own influence: in L. P. Hartley, in some of the detective novels of John Dickson Carr and his *alter ego* Carter Dickson, in a ghostly tale embedded in Penelope Fitzgerald's splendid novel *The Gate of Angels* . . . Opinions remain divided over various attempts to film James; certainly Jacques Tourneur, director of three supremely reticent RKO horror films of the forties, was the man to do it, and *Night* (or *Curse*) *of the Demon,* loosely based on **'Casting the Runes'**, is one of the most accomplished examples of British horror cinema. The most authentic tribute on celluloid so far may well be the 1997 Japanese film *Ringu* (*Ring*), a modern retelling of more than one Jamesian episode. Its restraint bodes well for the future of the genre. Whenever the field rediscovers subtlety and suggestiveness, in prose or in film, the example of M. R. James should prove vital.

Terry W. Thompson (essay date June 2004)

SOURCE: Thompson, Terry W. "Revenge of the Matriarchy: M. R. James's 'The Ash-Tree.'" *English Language Notes* 41, no. 4 (June 2004): 64-70.

[*In the following essay, Thompson maintains that "The Ash-Tree" can be interpreted as a subtle representation of the archetypal conflict between ancient pagan matriarchy and the male-dominated Christianity that displaced it.*]

In his excellent introduction to the 1971 Dover edition of *Ghost Stories of an Antiquary,* E. F. Bleiler writes that Montague Rhodes James "is generally considered to have been the finest twentieth-century writer of ghost stories. No anthology of supernatural fiction can be considered quite complete without one of his stories, and no serious discussion of ghost stories of the past would be possible without a tribute to his work."[1] Originally printed in 1904 at the persistent urging of his many friends and admirers, *Antiquary* was the first published collection of the author's erudite, understated, and disarmingly enigmatic ghost stories. Prior to that year, James's elegant tales had been composed to be read aloud—by the light of a single candle—to a close circle of friends and family at Christmastime. The numerous subsequent editions of this modest collection—only eight stories in all—testify heartily to the continued popularity of the author's dark but deliciously inviting vision of the unknown.

If the aim of a good ghost story "should be to make us afraid, or at the very least less sure of ourselves and our condition," then clearly one of the most successful entries in this collection is **"The Ash-Tree."**[2] Although not nearly as well-known or as widely anthologized as some of the author's other supernatural efforts, this story nonetheless displays James's celebrated fondness for "the antiquarian details and the scholarly background material that lend authenticity to" his ghostly tales.[3] However, there is something deeper going on in this brooding narrative than just the hanging of a seventeenth-century English witch. While usually read and enjoyed as an atmospheric tale of a widow who is executed for sorcery and then buried in unhallowed ground, only to conjure up a ghastly revenge upon her enemies, this story can also be interpreted as a subtle representation of the archetypal conflict between the ancient pagan matriarchy—so popular in late Victorian social and religious thought—and the male-dominated Christian patriarchy that displaced it. In short, it is a tale that resonates with the primeval female-versus-male dynamic as played out symbolically on the green fields of East Anglia.

According to Jack Sullivan in *Elegant Nightmares,* the most effective ghost stories always commence with "elegant surfaces that gradually imply or reveal something not so elegant."[4] Rich with James's trademark description—sentence upon sentence filled with local color and historical reference—the introductory paragraph of **"The Ash-Tree"** provides just such a refined and nonthreatening beginning. But then this long paragraph is quickly dismissed by the narrator in the first sentence of the second paragraph. He labels his own meticulously detailed introduction as nothing more than a wasteful and unimportant "digression."[5] This is, however, quite the red herring. Indeed, the first paragraph, which seemingly has little if anything to do with the rest of the tale other than to affirm the geography, provides the historical background for the basic conflict that drives the entire narrative: the female view of nature as a creative force to be venerated as opposed to the male view of nature as simply a source of raw materials to be exploited for the sake of progress and power.

For example, in the opening, the narrator praises the beautiful estates and grand game preserves carved out of the forest by the powerful squire classes of eastern England. He describes the lush beauty of the well-groomed country estates in Suffolk, "with parks of some eighty to a hundred acres," surrounded by rolling hills and luxuriant pastures (James 52). In particular, the narrator speaks glowingly of Castringham Hall, the ancestral home of the Fell clan. He admires the sharp, angular charm of the "split oak" fences encompassing the land, the many blue "meres with their reed-beds," and, far away from the lovely country estate, the hazy "line of distant woods" (52). In other words, the narrator, an English male and citizen of an expanding empire, relishes the open, sweeping vistas of an ordered and structured nature, one that has been fenced in, dotted with manmade ponds, and cleared of all the primeval oaks and yews and ashes that covered the landscape in ancient pagan times. Only in the faint far distance is there a tiny line of trees that have been spared the English broadaxe. In essence, the narrator defends a masculine restructuring of Mother Nature: it has been brought to heel, subdued, mastered, enclosed, overcome, conquered. The dark primordial woods, filled with mist and mystery, have been pushed back like a rejected paramour, and nature is now neatly trimmed, crisply bordered, aggressively manicured, and, above all, carefully planned. It may, indeed, be beautiful, even striking, but it is no more "natural" than a soccer field. The deep and sibylline groves of towering, old-growth hardwoods, so sacred to the ancient pagan Britons, have been removed to make the land more productive and accessible, while the rolling, naked hills have been stocked with game animals—for the shooting pleasure of the squire classes.

By 1690, the time of the story, there is only one tree left anywhere near Castringham Hall, and that is the giant, stately ash of the title. This majestic, centuries-old tree—the lone remnant of the profound and glorious forests that once blanketed all of eastern England—stands on the western side of the estate house, just a few feet away from the second-floor bedroom of Sir Matthew Fell, the powerful squire of Castringham Hall. In addition to being a wealthy and influential landowner, Sir Matthew is also the Deputy-Sheriff, and he accuses a local woman, Mrs. Mothersole, of being a witch. He testifies under oath that on three separate nights he looked out his bedroom window and saw her climbing about the limbs of his ash tree in the light of a full moon, "cutting off small twigs with a peculiarly curved knife," but when he ran downstairs and tried to apprehend the trespasser, all he ever saw was a single wild hare fleeing across his carefully tended yards (James 54). In a century rife with executions for even the mildest of accusations, this testimony from a leading citizen of Suffolk County is more than enough to convict the woman and earn her a quick death on the gibbet. She is executed on a damp and miserable morning in March, the month named for Mars, the male deity of war, destruction, and blood. As Mrs. Mothersole is led to the noose, her last words are a strange and ambiguous threat directed toward Sir Matthew: "'There will be guests at the hall'" (55).

Three months later in May—symbolically appropriate since this month is named for Maia, a powerful earth goddess—Sir Matthew Fell dies mysteriously in his own bed. The servants discover him cold, stiff, black, and swollen, with no marks of violence on his horribly contorted corpse, only a few minuscule prick marks where some deadly toxin may have been introduced. Ominously, his bedroom window had been left open all night. And just outside looms the great ash tree, standing like a mute guardian of the primeval darkness. Sir Matthew's son inherits title and estate, but, in marked contrast to his father, the new squire chooses to live a quiet and sedate life, a life of peace and harmony and seclusion. He sleeps in a different bedroom of the rambling manor house—far away from the old tree—and shows no interest whatsoever in disrupting the land or the many mysteries that dwell beneath it. The son of the witch killer lives to old age and dies a natural death: the mysterious curse of Mrs. Mothersole skips a blameless generation.

However, the next squire of Castringham Hall—Sir Matthew's grandson—inherits the genes of impatience and bad decision making that doomed his grandfather. When Sir Richard, who is described by the narrator as "a pestilent innovator" (60), "systematic" (61), obsessed with "alterations and improvements" (64), takes over the Hall and its attendant power, he will not leave the land alone. Even more importantly, he will not let the dead rest in peace. He dreams up the scheme of grandly enlarging the parish chapel to add a "great family pew on the north side of the church" (60). But to erect this imposing bit of ego-architecture, the unhallowed grave of Mrs. Mothersole must be disturbed. When her coffin is exhumed after forty-five years and pried open, there is nothing inside—no bones, no dust, not even a strand of the witch's black hair. Impatient to a fault, completely unconcerned with what unseen powers he might be offending, Sir Richard stupidly orders that "the coffin should be burnt" as so much rubbish, an affront to the living as well as the dead (60). The proud and overweening new squire will live to regret his rash and dis-respectful attitude, for the forces of darkness "are easier summoned than eluded" (Sullivan 69).

Shortly after the grave desecration episode, Sir Richard begins to suffer from insomnia, a very bad case of it, and eventually declares that he must find another bedroom in Castringham Hall, one that will allow him some quality slumber. He finally settles on his grandfather's bedchamber—the one where the old squire was discovered dead decades before. It has been sealed tightly since his horrific and inexplicable death. When a female servant is ordered to unseal the room and air it out, she, rich in feminine intuition, tries to warn the headstrong young squire. "'Oh, Sir Richard, but no one has slept there these forty years. The air has hardly changed since Sir Matthew died there'" (62). Arrogantly, foolishly, condescendingly, he ignores her sound and insightful advice: "'No, I do not wish to listen to any more. Make no difficulties, I beg. You have your orders—go'" (63).

Not long after moving into the "close and earthy" death chamber of his late grandfather, Sir Richard is also found dead—black and swollen and twisted, exactly like his witch-hanging grandfather (James 62). The killers are later discovered in the hollow of the old ash tree: giant black spiders, plump and furry, that had crept silently, under cover of "the terrible dark," into Sir Richard's bedroom through the open casement window and bit the belligerent, coffin-burning squire about the head, injecting him with enough poison to kill half a village.[6] Friends and neighbors set fire to the old tree and watch as the huge black spiders scamper out ablaze, sputtering and clawing across the yard in their death throes. The ultimate horror awaits, however. When the old tree has burned down to the stump, a cavern is discovered beneath its ancient roots, and in that dank, black hole, resting mummified against an earthen wall, is the missing corpse of Mrs. Mothersole. Like furious Greek daughters, her black children of the night have avenged the wrongs done her by two generations of Fell patriarchs.

According to some critics, "the ghost story" almost always "deals with power," who has it and how they obtained it (Cox and Gilbert xiii). If the diurnal Sir Matthew and Sir Richard represent the male desire to dominate nature, to saddle and bridle it like a recalcitrant mare and control its wild spirit, then the nocturnal Mrs. Mothersole is the embodiment of the female creative power in nature—unfettered and unconquered, as free as Diana's wild heart, as untamed as Medea's flowing hair. In life, the old witch practiced her matriarchal religion, ancient and pagan, millennia older than the Christian faith that vanquished it and drove it underground, destroyed its sacred groves and its dark places, supplanting them with sunny pastures and spacious parks, with hunting preserves and formalized gardens.

When she is spotted by Sir Matthew clambering about the limbs of his ash tree with her strangely curved knife (much like those used by the Druids), she may be gathering mistletoe from the ancient branches since this evergreen parasite was considered sacred by many of Europe's pagan religions. Or she may be amputating the mistletoe to save the old ash since the parasitical growth, although a powerful fetish in pagan magic, was, over a period of time, fatal to the host tree. On the other hand, a much more plausible and satisfying explanation is that Mrs. Mothersole is simply gathering cuttings from the tree itself because, according to folkloric tradition, ash branches made the best magic wands for witches. Since she is doing her work by the light of a full moon—and the two revenge killings likewise occur during full lunar cycles—Hecate and Artemis, the twin goddesses of witchcraft and the moon, become players in the drama. Both were protectors of women, guardians of the darkness and the deep woods, defenders of the matriarchal mysteries. And both ancient goddesses were worshiped by secretive female cults from Asia Minor to the Baltic Sea, thus providing, according to some, the very origins of witchcraft itself.

A carefully designed and artificially shaped landscape as a metaphor for man's arrogance towards nature is found in other supernatural tales by James. For example, golf courses appear in several of his stories, such as **"The Mezzotint," "The Rose Garden,"** and the peerless **"'Oh, Whistle, and I'll Come to You, My Lad.'"** Such manmade, manicured, and precisely laid out structures symbolize the male drive to control and circumscribe the land and its features, to transform wild nature into something modern and measured and bright, but appallingly cold, sterile, and artificial. In short, Mother Nature itself, in the hands of ambitious landowners like the Fell squires, is turned into mere commodity, a source of profit, a masculine measure of wealth and power, a way of keeping score by acres and hectares. However, all of this alpha-male effort to force order upon the environment provides merely "an illusory sense of order and stability, illusory because it is precisely this" false sense of control that makes the sudden appearance of the supernatural so jarring, so threatening (Sullivan 75).

In their introduction to *The Oxford Book of English Ghost Stories,* Michael Cox and R. A. Gilbert maintain that "Circumstantial detail, believable living characters, economy of style, and the power of suggestion all create the necessary atmosphere for a successful ghost story" (x). In **"The Ash-Tree,"** M. R. James provides all four of these necessities in a most deft and sophisticated rendering of the eternal human struggle over how best to relate to the land and its bounty: whether to live in attempted harmony amidst the green, the brown, and the blue; or to treat nature as an adversary to be overcome with brute force and subdued into the role that the powerful choose for it. Sir Matthew Fell, tragically, chooses the latter. He sins against nature—in the night-loving, tree-climbing, grudge-holding persona of Mrs. Mothersole—and then pays an awful price for his great affront. The squire's original blunder, although seen by him as merely doing his sworn duty, inspires the curse that causes two gruesome deaths in the earthy, redolent bedroom with the open window. The pagan matriarchy, at least in this little corner of East Anglia, wins a small victory against the male usurper, who is, of course, too busy to see the forest for the ash-tree.

Notes

1. E. F. Bleiler, introduction, *Ghost Stories of an Antiquary,* by M. R. James (New York: Dover, 1971) 3. For the sake of consistency, American style punctuation is used in all quotations.

2. Michael Cox and R. A. Gilbert, introduction, *The Oxford Book of English Ghost Stories* (Oxford: Oxford UP, 1986) xi.

3. Michael Cox, *M. R. James: An Informal Portrait* (Oxford: Oxford UP, 1983) 142.

4. Jack Sullivan, *Elegant Nightmares: The English Ghost Story From Le Fanu to Blackwood* (Athens: Ohio UP, 1978) 8.

5. M. R. James, "The Ash-tree," *Ghost Stories of an Antiquary* (New York: Dover, 1971) 54.

6. Phyllis Cerf Wagner and Herbert A. Wise, introduction, *Great Tales of Terror and the Supernatural* (New York: Modern Library, 1994) xiii.

Terry W. Thompson (essay date fall 2004)

SOURCE: Thompson, Terry W. "'I Shall Most Likely Be out on the Links': Golf as Metaphor in the Ghost Stories of M. R. James." *Papers on Language and Literature* 40, no. 4 (fall 2004): 339-52.

[*In the following essay, Thompson examines the role of golf in James's stories, pointing out that it is a metaphor for safety, modernity, security, predictability, order, and dominance over nature.*]

Celebrated author, medievalist, wit, raconteur, Provost of both Cambridge University and Eton College, Montague Rhodes James is described by E. F. Bleiler in his introduction to the Dover edition of **Ghost Stories of an Antiquary** as "in many ways the epitome of the brilliant but slightly eccentric British scholar," a genuine Renaissance man who produced some of the most popular ghost stories of his or any other generation (5). Distinguished by their nonpareil "urbanity, suaveness, and economy" (Sullivan 90) and found in practically every

anthology of the supernatural published on either side of the Atlantic for the last hundred years, James's elegant and measured turn-of-the-century narratives usually recount the tribulations of well-educated Victorian and Edwardian elites who stumble into contact with the otherworldly and then have to cope somehow with the irrational, non-intellectual horrors they have unwittingly, often stupidly, unleashed.

In his wonderfully crafted and harmonious tales, James frequently makes use of man-modified landscapes to append meaning to his stories, to layer, enrich, and deepen their import, in short, to give them "larger reverberations" and render them more than mere pulp thrillers (Sullivan 8). For instance, in **"The Ash-Tree,"** easily one of the author's most gruesome and macabre efforts, the powerful English squire class has cleared the primeval forests of East Anglia and turned the virgin wilderness into vast estates and private hunting preserves, with open rolling pastures and rich grazing lands. The towering old-growth forests of ash and oak and elm that once dominated the region have been eliminated, while the land has been partitioned into precisely measured parcels: acres and hectares to be bought and sold as commodities. Thus, in surface appearance at least, the ancient land—once so dark and shadowy, so mystical and inviolate—appears conquered and docile, bludgeoned into submission by the mighty English broadaxe and the muscular backs of the yeomanry until there is nothing left but an insignificant "fringe of woods" surrounding the clear-cut landscape (James, **"The Ash-Tree"** 40). That placidity is all illusory, however, for beneath the surface of this sunny and ordered land lurk what Herbert A. Wise and Phyllis Cerf Wagner describe as "the old fears," the displaced pagan beliefs—Celtic and Druid and Wiccan—which once dominated the dark green forests of ancient Britain (Introduction xiv). And, in the end, those primordial powers—long dormant beneath the surface facade of order and control—rise up to destroy the prideful English squires who had so abused the land, had sought to subdue and dominate and reconfigure it to their own narrow ends.

In similar manner, in many of his other ghostly tales, M. R. James deftly employs the genteel sport of golf—and the open, verdant courses upon which this supremely patrician and strictly ruled game is played—to foster a false sense of security, of quiet order, in a tranquil locale into which something paranormal, illogical, and uncontrollable is about to be suddenly and horribly unleashed, summoned by accident from "among the primeval shadows" or conjured up on a foolish whim (Wharton 8).

For example, in the masterfully executed **"Oh, Whistle, and I'll Come to You, My Lad"**—arguably the finest ghost story ever written in English and certainly the best titled—a haughty and pedantic college professor named Parkins, a modern man of science and fact and empirical thinking, goes away to the English seacoast for a well-deserved holiday. Like many of James's protagonists, Parkins is a self-satisfied scholar, a heavily starched and formally lettered man who enjoys a cloistered and cliquish existence. His is an "orderly and prudent life" far removed from the lives of regular folk whom he casually dismisses due to their backward beliefs and unscientific attitudes (James, **"Oh, Whistle"** 83). In a quaint village on the east coast of Britain—a world away from the tidy, tome-lined halls of the College of Saint James—this smug, no-nonsense academician plans to read a few good books and, in his own sweet time, compose a scholarly monograph or two. As for the majority of his much-anticipated fortnight by the sea, he smilingly informs his colleagues, "'When I'm not writing I shall most likely be out on the links'"—enjoying eighteen holes of carefree distraction amid wide-open fairways and carefully maintained putting greens (76).

When Professor Parkins, the very trope of logic and rationalism, is out on the golf course with his beloved niblicks and mashies, the winds may blow and the mists may come, but otherwise, nature is controlled, is bent to man's indomitable will. The Bermuda grass has been laid out in precise and pleasing patterns, then cut to fit some modern idea of perfection, while the flawless greens are smoothly manicured and crisply bordered. The various manmade hazards—sand traps and roughs and duck ponds—are, like the golf course itself, painstakingly designed and thoroughly planned. Nothing, not a blade of grass nor a stray tulip, is left out of place. It is nature strained through the sieve of modern sporting desire. What was once an ancient grove of lofty sacred oaks protected by devout Druids and fervent Celts is now the rigidly controlled domain of weekend duffers and their deferential caddies. In short, the modern golf course is nature presented in a way that is acceptable to those who have the power and influence to crimp, shape, and mold the natural environment to fit their concepts of what is attractive and, above all else, what is profitable. Before the coming of the broadaxe, those primordial stands of colossal hardwoods offered only shade and mystery. Now, however, with their decimation, a large golf course with all of its accouterments offers recreation for players as well as bulging coffers for investors.

One of the main reasons golf is so appealing to Professor Parkins—a very cerebral and otherwise non-athletic man—is its rigid code of rules. In this highly structured game, players must obey precise regulations to the letter, and those regulations, as constant as the laws of physics, are put down in a code of conduct dating back to the game's Scottish origins in the fifteenth century. Little if any spontaneity, creativity, or deviation is al-

lowed. With its strict score keeping—its bogies and pars, birdies and eagles—golf is a sport flush with mathematical absolutes and scientific exactitude; it is a contest of accurate angles and proper trajectories, of perfect club speed and precise ball placement. In fine, it is just as much a game of the intellect as of the body, requiring a knowledge of physics and geometry, of lift and drag, of inertia and wind-speed ratios. Finesse and strategy, not brute animal force, earn one victory out on the links. Golf is thus the perfect hobby for the vacationing Professor Parkins, a man who is, according to the narrator, invariably meticulous, "neat, and precise" in all of his endeavors (75), so much so that even his everyday conversations ring with the donnish "tone of a lecturer" addressing a room full of unenlightened undergraduates (85).

Another reason the bookish Parkins loves the game of golf and the land it is played on is simple class snobbery. Unlike today when almost anyone can enjoy a few rounds on a publicly owned course, at the turn of the century, this tranquil sport was largely the domain of the upper crust. Well-to-do patricians were the usual patrons on the exclusive courses in England and America, partly because equipment was so expensive, but also due to the rigid caste system. Professor Parkins, like almost all of James's main characters, is of the socially elite class, extremely well-educated and toppingly articulate, a sophisticated bon vivant who oozes culture, poise, and refinement from his very pores. Accustomed to private clubs, upper-class friends, and sophisticated functions, the Professor naturally seeks the same elevated status in his sporting pursuits. Sweaty, raucous, and plebeian team sports, like rugby or soccer, are far beneath his stature and breeding, whereas golf is an avocation for proper gentlemen, sporting types who are well-dressed, well-bred, urbane, and stylish. When the cosmopolitan Parkins goes to the links, he knows that the only people of lower social rank he will encounter are the caddies and the grounds keepers; and they shall be only too happy to accommodate his every whim and need.

When all things are considered, only those enterprises that are concrete and summative, solid and controllable, appeal to the fussy pedagogue from Saint James's, whether in the classroom or out on the windswept links. Before leaving his hotel to enjoy a leisurely round, the Professor, ever the finicky, foppish dresser, labors long to put "the finishing touches to his golfing costume" (84). And each evening, just before retiring, he is likewise compelled "to arrange his materials for work" the next morning "in apple-pie order upon a commodious table" across from his bed (77). If he does not perform this nightly ritual, then he cannot sleep for thinking that a pen or notebook might be somehow out of place or otherwise askew. In the opinion of the narrator, the obsessive Professor Parkins is "something of an old woman—rather hen-like, perhaps, in his little ways; totally destitute, alas! of the sense of humour, but at the same time dauntless and sincere in his convictions" that only the physical, the measurable, and the rational are subjects worthy of consideration by a civilized and order-loving Englishman (77). Whenever someone, even in jest, mentions the supernatural or the transcendental—topics that do not fit into the Professor's neatly structured and perfectly logical universe—he curtly dismisses such nonsense. When softly teased by one of his colleagues that he is about to vacation in a part of England that is famous for its haunted castles and specter-filled graveyards, Parkins responds testily, "'I hold that any semblance, any appearance of concession to the view that such things might exist is equivalent to a renunciation of all that I hold most sacred'" (77).

Once unpacked at the venerable Globe Inn in Burnstow, the Professor spends "the greater part of the day following his arrival" out on the golf course "improving his game," but on his leisurely walk back from the links that afternoon, his precisely laid plans for a quiet and relaxing fortnight of reading, writing, and golfing take an unscheduled—and terrifying—detour (78). While strolling among some ancient ruins near the course, he discovers a bronze whistle, "about four inches long, and evidently of some considerable age," hidden deep in a hole among the decayed remains of what was once a sacred place to the extinct Knights Templar as well as to thousands of years' worth of Britain's earlier inhabitants, barbarians all to the Professor—untutored, quasi-literate people who did not know of modern science and rational inquiry and critical thought (79). Ever the fearless investigator, the sober empiricist, and the self-appointed debunker of puerile superstition, Parkins eschews all dire warnings from the locals and keeps and cleans the curious whistle. On one side of it, after some scraping, he discovers the ominous phrase "'Who is this who is coming?'" written in block Latin (81).

Although "it may not be quite prudent" to meddle in the supernatural realm lest some "formidable visitants" be aroused (James, **"Stories I Have Tried to Write"** 362), eventually Professor Parkins cannot resist the temptation. He blows the whistle and thereby summons forth a horrifying being, a spirit of something long dead, something dark and dreadful and untempered by reason, logic, science, modernism, or cutting-edge theory in any discipline. The thing that is animated by the careless blast on the whistle is neither man nor god, flesh nor blood, Victorian nor Edwardian. It is a ghastly and primal "figure in pale, fluttering draperies," some frightfully "ill-defined" being from the nether-world of dreams and nightmares, dark places where hard science has no purchase and modern theory is irrelevant (**"Oh, Whistle"** 83). All the rational thought in the material world will not deter this unwittingly evoked avatar of "some stubbornly unexpunged faith," will not return the

sinister wraith to its clammy resting place amid the ancient Templar ruins (Leithauser 13). The headstrong Professor learns the hard way that "such creatures are easier summoned than eluded" (Sullivan 69).

When the horrid specter corners him in his room at midnight and all seems lost, Parkins is delivered at the last moment by a fellow guest at the lodge, a retired army officer named Colonel Wilson, a gruff man of the world who has seen the occult at work in the dusky places of the globe, has seen firsthand the dire powers that sometimes dwell in darkness. The non-cloistered, non-academic Colonel rescues the hapless pedagogue from his otherworldly tormenter and sends the dark specter back to its resting place; the Colonel—a man of action, not theory—then goes down to the beach and hurls the offending whistle "as far into the sea as a brawny arm could send it" (James, **"Oh, Whistle"** 90).

By the end of his seaside holiday, the windswept coast of England proves not quite as restful and simple as the good Professor had anticipated, proves not nearly as tame and safe and ordered as a beautifully manicured golf course. When he recovers from his queasy supernatural encounter—an encounter that has shattered his once comprehensible universe—he returns to the ivory-towered, neatly structured environment of Saint James a wiser and more modest man, for now he knows that there is far more to the universe than can be manipulated, classified, or controlled by human ego: "the Professor's views on certain points are less clear cut than they used to be [. . .] and the spectacle of a scarecrow in a field late on a winter afternoon has cost him more than one sleepless night" (91). Or as Michael A. Mason asserts in "On Not Letting Them Lie: Moral Significance in the Ghost Stories of M. R. James," sometimes "It is safer [. . .] to be humble and ignorant" than proud and vainglorious (255).

In **"The Mezzotint,"** one of the most widely anthologized and frequently imitated ghost stories in the English language, James again references the gentlemanly sport of golf in a meaningful and symbolic way, thus providing an extra bit of layering to this "characteristically urbane and learned" narrative of an antique picture that will not stop changing, will not stop terrifying any and all who dare to look upon it (Cox 142). In the tale, a confident young scholar named Williams works for the museum at Cambridge, and thus he is always in pursuit of objects and artifacts to add to the University's collection. This scholar's particular antiquarian metier is "engravings, plans, and old sketches of mansions, churches, and towns in England and Wales" (James, **"The Mezzotint"** 30).

On an otherwise uneventful February morning, there appears on Williams's desk at the museum a catalog listing some items that might be of interest to a man in his profession, and one item, number 978, has been pointed out by a fellow antiquary for special attention: "Interesting mezzotint; View of a manor-house, early part of the century. 15 by 10 inches; black frame" (31). The purchase price is listed at two pounds and two shillings. Young Williams is not particularly taken with the description of this "interesting" mezzotint, and furthermore, he feels that the piece is somewhat overpriced. Nevertheless, he asks "for the article to be sent on approval, along with some other engravings and sketches which appeared in the same catalog" (31). When it arrives, he declares the mezzotint a "rather indifferent" piece of work since it offers only a commonplace, even amateurish-looking, "full-face view of a not very large manor-house of the last century, with three rows of plain sashed windows with rusticated masonry about them, a parapet with balls or vases at the angles and a small portico in the centre" (31-32). On either side of the strikingly nondescript country house "were trees, and in front a considerable expanse of lawn" (32).

Disappointed with the ordinariness of the antique mezzotint, Williams tosses it aside, and later, when some academic companions arrive, he and his friends begin to address one of Williams's other intellectual passions: namely, "playing golf" (32). These well-to-do English scholars debate "what other strokes might have been better" during their recent trip to the links as they all enjoy what the narrator describes as "a discussion which golfing persons can imagine for themselves" (32). And when the same scholars gather regularly for "Sunday morning breakfast," hardly a topic is "left unchallenged, from golf to lawn-tennis" (34). Just as in **"Oh, Whistle, and I'll Come to You, My Lad,"** golf appeals to these young academicians because it is almost scientific in its design and intent. It is mathematically challenging, as precise as an algebraic formula, as clean as a geometric form, as concrete and understandable as a ledger page. Plus, the exclusionary nature of golf's class appeal is another attraction for them, just as it was for the haughty Professor Parkins.

After the mezzotint has been in his office for some hours, Williams examines it again, thinking that perhaps he had been too hasty in his earlier dismissal of it. He notices that an odd looking figure has appeared where he is certain there was no figure, odd or otherwise, before. He quickly summons his friends to bear witness to what they see, and, ever the methodical investigator, he even goes so far as to get them to write down what they observe and then sign their affidavits. Over the next several hours, the figure in the picture moves closer and closer to the manor-house—always without any human eye seeing the actual movement—until it disappears into the old manse through an open first-floor window. The skeletal figure, dressed in tattered black clothing, emerges later from the house "erect and stepping swiftly, with long strides, towards the

front of the picture. [. . . W]hat was visible made the spectators profoundly thankful that they could see no more than a white dome-like forehead and a few straggling hairs" (**"Mezzotint"** 37). The wan countenance of the ghostly mezzotint figure "was bent down, and the arms were tightly clasped over an object which could be dimly seen and identified as a child, whether dead or living it was not possible to say" (37).

During the horror of the changing of the mezzotint—as the dark and ominous figure creeps closer and closer to the house to thieve, Rumpelstiltskin-like, an infant from its parents—the scholars who watch the unfolding crime regularly return to the subject of golf and its welcome respite from the strange events taking place in the two-dimensional world of the cursed mezzotint. The young men invariably play "golf during the afternoon," and they frequently bandy about "words with which [others] have no concern [. . .] mere golfing words" (33). Like so many of "the authorities of the University [they] indulge in that pursuit by way of relaxation," for in the tangible world of golf, there is order; there is sanity, concreteness, logic, predictability, continuity, surety (32). In the phantasmal world of a bewitched mezzotint that reenacts a terrible crime committed over a century before, there is no such assurance of logic and coherence, of an orderly and fathomable universe that can be quantified, toted, diagramed, or even clearly explained. Thus, after being so "unexpectedly introduced" to the supernatural, a trip to the pleasantly green and logically structured links—or even a calming conversation about the gentlemanly sport—is a welcome return to normalcy, to the known, the rational, the easily understood (30).

In the innocuously entitled **"The Rose Garden,"** once again the waggishly erudite James uses the pastoral and controlled sport of golf to counterbalance, with a subtle touch of humor, an incredible horror that patiently waits to be summoned, this time by a well-to-do couple freshly moved to "the county of Essex," where they have purchased "Westfield Hall" and are in the process of restoring the antique country estate after some years of neglect and disrepair (114). Behind their old manor house, Mr. and Mrs. Anstruther have grand plans for a new flower garden in a "small clearing just off the shrubbery path that goes towards the church" (114). This chosen patch of ground is "bounded on one side by a path, and on the other by thick box-bushes, laurels, and other evergreens," yet the middle of what should be a fertile clearing is curiously "bare of grass and dark of aspect" (115). Plus, the location is cluttered by the ruins of what seems a very decayed summer-house or gazebo of some sort. The rot is so advanced that it is hard to tell much about the structure save for its approximate dimensions. There are badly decomposed "remains of rustic seats," and most peculiar of all, there is "an old and corrugated oak post" standing right in the center of the clearing (115). Neither the husband nor the wife can figure out just what the isolated wooden post is doing in the middle of the grassless spot. They logically assume that perhaps it once held up a roof of some kind, long rotted away in the moist Essex clime.

Whatever the function of the weathered pole looming obtrusively in the midst of Mrs. Anstruther's new rose garden site, some great effort will be required to remove it as well as the ruined seats and the surrounding shrubbery; in short, heavy manual lifting lies ahead. Only then can the industrious new chatelaine of Westfield Hall commence planting her favorite Bonicas and Lagerfelds. Her husband—much less ambitious and far less energetic about yard work—peppers their conversation with references to golfing, explaining that he simply cannot help with the manual labor at present because "'I had half arranged to play a round with Geoffrey Williamson this morning'" (114). To the husband, golf is his escape, his way of evading the unpleasantness of heavy outdoor labor, of sweat and strain. His wife finally agrees that "'After luncheon [. . .] you can go over to the links'" and relax with friends, to which the shirking spouse responds cheerily, "'I should be glad of a round'" (115).

According to Jack Sullivan in *Elegant Nightmares: The English Ghost Story From Le Fanu to Blackwood,* in most supernatural tales, "The endless process of collecting and arranging gives the characters an illusory sense of order and stability, illusory because it is precisely this process which evokes the demon or vampire" (75). Such was the case with Professor Parkins and his logically ordered desk and carefully matched golfing attire. Such was the case with young Williams and his clinical observations and signed affidavits. Thus it is with Mrs. Mary Anstruther and her plans for a perfectly arranged, logically plotted rose garden. After she has "dismissed her husband to his golf" and assigned Collins, her groundskeeper, to begin ripping up the old rotted ruins, strange emotions begin to perturb her (James, **"Rose Garden"** 116). Something is wrong in the new garden site, something inexplicable and dark, something sinister, vague, unpleasant—"'one of those things that can hardly be put into words'" (117). Bizarre dreams and haunting images suddenly plague her as, once again, a Jamesian main character stumbles upon the "various residues [. . .] of some stubbornly unexpunged" primal force (Leithauser 13).

When Mrs. Anstruther's husband eventually deigns to join in the clearing of the strange patch of earth, he, too, experiences eldritch occurrences, sensing rightly that "'a most horrible villain'" is somehow associated with this small lea of sour ground (James, **"Rose Garden"** 120). When the two share their misgivings with each other over these singular events, Mr. Anstruther hits upon the perfect solution, at least for him: "'I think

I *will* go over to the Lodge and see if I can get a game with any of them'" (121). For the lethargic and frightened husband, unused to things that cannot be seen or touched or logically defined, the routine normalcy of a good eighteen holes on a sunny day will cure most ills short of death itself. For the upper crust Mr. Anstruther—as for Professor Parkins and Mr. Williams before him—in the slow, measured tedium of golf there is tranquility and solace, while fear, worry, and the unexplained are left far behind.

Only much later, after many disquieting occurrences, do the two sophisticated newcomers to rural Essex come to learn what really took place on that dark spot of dead ground just off the path to the church. In the very clearing selected for the new rose garden, a "malicious evil" has been preserved "through the centuries" only to be "decanted with terrifying effect" in modern times (Wise and Wagner, "Note" 495). In that unhallowed place centuries before, show trials were held, unjust and corrupt, and many innocents were sentenced to slow, twitching deaths on the gibbet. At bottom, the sterile clearing is cursed and poisoned because it is haunted by the toxic ghost of the "Lord Chief Justice under Charles II," a tyrannical magistrate who sent many an Englishman to an early grave on false charges of treason or sedition (James, **"Rose Garden"** 122). Under the gnarled and rotted central post his wicked body lies interred forever, unmourned and unremembered, without stone or monument to acknowledge his passing. As punishment for his many and heinous sins against God and man, the ghost of the evil Lord Chief Justice must haunt the blighted and infertile spot, never to be given peace because of his foul crimes: the weathered upright beam is like a giant vampire's stake pinning him to that denuded piece of ground. Plans for the new rose garden are immediately abandoned, and the dead spot, a cold place where "elemental forces are loose" (Stern ix), is given wide berth whenever the couple pass through that particular part of their property. Since both Mr. and Mrs. Anstruther are avid golfers and are of the leisure class, however, they can escape to their beloved links and leave behind the ephemeral and shadowy world of the spirits in favor of the tangible, the solid, and the real. Although frightened and somewhat "uncentered" (Leithauser 21) by their unsought brush with the supernatural, wide fairways, fast greens, and stubby pencils will soon soothe their frayed nerves and salve their rattled psyches; baggy plus-fours and the welcome heft of a good six-iron on a Saturday morning will soon palliate most all their fears of the unknown.

In the "brief but densely detailed" (Leithauser 12) ghost stories of Montague Rhodes James, there is important symbolic meaning borne in the various methods by which humans—especially the wealthy and well-educated classes—attempt to control nature. Golf and the carefully laid-out, neatly manicured courses upon which this most civilized of sports is played are used by the author to show man's implacable drive to tame his surroundings, to tailor nature, by fence and survey, by deed and title, by border and marker, to fit his narrow ends, thus inducing an inflated and quixotic sense of his own grandeur, his own power. When finally compared with the vast natural energies it claims to dominate and rule, however, that human power is shown—by the end of James's wonderfully chilling tales—to be weak, fallible, inferior, and temporal, as insignificant as a single shriek in a howling whirlwind.

Works Cited

Bleiler, E. F. Introduction. *Ghost Stories of an Antiquary*. By M. R. James. New York: Dover, 1971. 3-6.

Cox, Michael. *M. R. James: An Informal Portrait*. Oxford: Oxford UP, 1983.

James, M. R. "The Ash-tree." *The Penguin Complete Ghost Stories of M. R. James*. Harmondsworth, Middlesex, UK: Penguin, 1984. 40-50. All quotations from James come from this edition of his collected ghost stories. For the sake of consistency, all punctuation has been converted to American usage.

———. "The Mezzotint." 30-39.

———. "Oh, Whistle, and I'll Come to You, My Lad." 75-91.

———. "The Rose Garden." 114-123.

———. "Stories I Have Tried to Write." 360-362.

Leithauser, Brad. Introduction. *The Norton Book of Ghost Stories*. New York: Norton, 1994. 9-21.

Mason, Michael A. "On Not Letting Them Lie: Moral Significance in the Ghost Stories of M. R. James." *Studies in Short Fiction* 19.4 (1982): 253-260.

Stern, Philip Van Doren. Introduction. *Great Ghost Stories*. New York: Washington Square, 1964. ix-xxvi.

Sullivan, Jack. *Elegant Nightmares: The English Ghost Story from Le Fanu to Blackwood*. Athens: Ohio UP, 1978.

Wise, Herbert A., and Phyllis Cerf Wagner. Introduction. *Great Tales of Terror and the Supernatural*. New York: Modern Library, 1994. xiii-xviii.

———. "A Note on M. R. James." *Great Tales of Terror and the Supernatural*. 495.

Wharton, Edith. Preface. *The Ghost Stories of Edith Wharton*. New York: Scribner, 1997. 7-11.

FURTHER READING

Biographies

Cox, Michael. *M. R. James: An Informal Portrait*. Oxford: Oxford University Press, 1983, 264 p.
> Detailed biography of James that concentrates on his character, personal life, and relationships; includes photographs.

Pfaff, Richard William. *Montague Rhodes James*. London: Scolar Press, 1980, 466 p.
> Considered the most accurate and detailed study of James's life.

Criticism

Adair, Gerald. "A Specter Is Haunting Fritz Leiber: The Influence of M. R. James on 'The Pale Brown Thing.'" *Extrapolation* 40, no. 3 (fall 1999): 224-32.
> Considers the influence on James's theories of ghost stories on a work by Fritz Leiber.

Johnson, William C., Jr.. "On the Literary Use of Myth." In *The Power of Myth in Literature and Film*, pp. 24-34. Tallahassee: University Presses of Florida, 1980.
> Examines James's "The Ash-Tree" as an example of the appropriation of myths in ghost stories.

John Morrison
1904-1998

(Full name James Gordon Morrison) Australian short story writer, novelist, and nonfiction writer.

INTRODUCTION

Although he also published two novels and numerous essays, Morrison is best known as a writer of short fiction. He wrote most of his stories while earning his living as a manual laborer, working variously as a station hand in the Australian outback, a longshoreman, and a gardener. Writing in the social realist tradition, Morrison devoted himself to reflecting his experiences, telling of the economic hardships suffered by working-class men through the difficult years of the Depression and then during and after the Second World War. A committed Marxist, Morrison in his stories highlights workers' struggles in the face of a changing economic and social landscape, pointing out the difficulty of maintaining a sense of dignity under harsh conditions. Morrison's best-known stories take place on the Melbourne dock, where he worked for a decade; his tales of dock workers, or "wharfies," look at the lives of longshoremen with humor, describing the ludicrous in human nature while drawing attention to urgent social problems. Although never a popular success, Morrison was recognized during his life as one of the finest writers of short stories in his adopted home of Australia, and he is still regarded as having produced that country's most finely observed stories of working life.

BIOGRAPHICAL INFORMATION

Morrison was born in Sunderland, England, in 1904, to a working-class family. He read widely as a child, and he frequented his public library to study books on travel and natural history. He also read fiction, and was particularly affected by Joseph Conrad's *Lord Jim*; it planted in him a yearning for adventure on the seas, and he began to spend time at the docks near his home. Morrison left school at fourteen to begin work, initially at the Sunderland Museum, which fostered his interest in wildflowers and butterflies, and later as a gardener at the estate of a ship owner. At nineteen, Morrison sailed to Australia as a government-assisted migrant. In the 1920s he worked in New South Wales in sheep stations and in the outback, sometimes drifting and often leaving jobs to escape exploitation by his employers. Dur-

ing this period he began to write. In 1927 Morrison returned to England briefly, where he tried unsuccessfully to have his work published. He met his first wife, Frances Rosina Jones, on the ship back to Australia. They married in 1928.

After marrying, Morrison settled in Melbourne. During the Depression of the 1930s he worked as a jobbing gardener and then on the waterfront as a dock worker. He worked as a "wharfie" on the docks from the late 1930s through World War II, becoming politically active in the Waterside Workers' Federation (WWF) and the Communist Party. Morrison's experiences both as a gardener and a longshoreman provided him with vivid material for the short stories he began to write in the 1930s. By the mid-1940s, Morrison had earned some exposure as a writer, having published stories in journals and literary anthologies, and in 1947 he received a Commonwealth Literary Fund Grant; he received another two years later. This allowed him to take time off and write two novels. In the 1950s he was an active member of the Realist Writers Group and began to establish his reputation as an important young writer with two volumes of short stories. Morrison worked as a gardener until 1963, when he suffered a heart attack. He then retired from manual labor but continued writing. Morrison's first wife died in 1967, and he married again two years later. He published five more volumes of stories as well as two volumes of nonfiction before his death in 1998.

MAJOR WORKS OF SHORT FICTION

Although he began writing in earnest as a teenager, shortly after moving to Australia, Morrison only began to be published in his thirties, while working as a dockworker. As an active member of the WWF and the outlawed Communist Party of Australia, Morrison highlighted in his stories the plight of men looking for work—and dignity—during the Depression. The finest expression of this is found in the 1944 story "The Compound," which describes dockworkers competing for jobs and openly criticizes the Waterside Workers' Labour Bureau in Melbourne. Morrison wrote a number of stories for the *Communist Review* during the 1940s as well, which reflect one of his major themes: the dilemma of remaining a decent and productive human being in a world of haves and have-nots, where money or the lack of it has the power to debase and divide. Morrison's stories were first collected in *Sailors Belong Ships* (1947), a volume concerned with class division, racism, working conditions, and the isolation of life as a ship worker. The collection includes Morrison best-known story, "Nightshift," a narrative that chronicles the death of a fellow "wharfie." His next collection, *Black Cargo* (1955), is also made up predominantly of waterside stories. The stories in that volume make parallels between the black slave trade and industrial working conditions.

Morrison's next collection of stories was published while he worked as a gardener. Because he lived a far distance from his place of employment, Morrison had to spend long hours commuting by train, and the setting of a railway compartment is used in many pieces of the *Twenty-Three Stories* of 1962. That collection won the Gold Medal of the Australian Literature Society in 1963. The dominating themes of the *Selected Stories* of 1972, which includes reprints of previously published work, are loneliness and isolation. In 1982 Morrison published the collection *North Wind,* which included previously published and new works. Some of the themes explored in these stories include greed, economics, and the elusive nature of love. *Stories of the Waterfront,* which appeared in 1984, includes dockside stories printed in earlier collections, and 1985's *This Freedom* includes reprints of older stories as well as some previously uncollected pieces. It contains his well-known pro-union stories "Lena" and "The Ticket," as well as the "wharfie" stories "The Welcome" and "To Margaret." A compilation of Morrison's most highly regarded short fiction appeared in 1988.

CRITICAL RECEPTION

Morrison spent his entire working life—save for two years when he was writing his novels while living on a grant from the Commonwealth Literary Fund—doing manual labor. He found time to write around his work commitments, and indeed his work served as the major inspiration for his fiction and nonfiction. Morrison first started gaining recognition as a writer while working as a longshoreman in the mid-1940s. His work was published in respected Australian literary journals as well as in Communist Party of Australia publications. Even after he became disenchanted with some aspects of Communism, Morrison was viewed by many intellectuals within the party as well as the writers of the Australian Realist movement as an exemplar because of his working-class background, and many of his stories were translated for Communist publications in the Soviet Union, Poland, Hungary, and Romania. Morrison's reputation grew steadily in the 1950s and while his output was relatively modest, he won an important national literary prize, the Gold Medal of the Australian

Literature Society, in 1963. Thereafter he was recognized by critics as one of Australia's best short story writers, although he never achieved much popular success. In 1986 Morrison won the Patrick White Award for Writers of Distinction. The award, set up by White from the proceeds of his Nobel Prize, is awarded to an older Australian writer who has received insufficient critical attention.

While many critics maintain that Morrison is one of the finest writers of short stories that Australia has produced, his work has generated little critical commentary beyond reviews and introductions to his published works. Some critics have argued that because his stories focus on white Australian men and their economic and social problems during a particular time period, his work is dated and lacks appeal for modern readers. Those who have commented on Morrison's work have discussed why he favored the short story as a genre, with some suggesting that he wrote short fiction because his time was constrained by his work. Other topics of interest have included Morrison's "old-fashioned" writing style, his proletarian politics, his moralistic themes, and his particular brand of realism. Critics in general have praised Morrison's economical, understated style, his ear for dialogue, and his subtle use of detail to illuminate character. They regard his stories as simple, unaffected, and natural yet moving and highly readable. Morrison's stories continue to be popular in Australian high-school curricula, and "The Night-Shift" is included in every collection of Australia's best short stories.

PRINCIPAL WORKS

Short Fiction

Sailors Belong Ships (short stories) 1947
Black Cargo and Other Stories 1955
Twenty-Three: Stories 1962
Selected Stories 1972
North Wind (short stories) 1982; revised and enlarged
    as *The Best Stories of John Morrison* 1988
Stories of the Waterfront 1984
This Freedom (short stories) 1985
The Best Stories of John Morrison 1988

Other Major Works

The Creeping City (novel) 1949
Port of Call (novel) 1950
Australian by Choice (essays) 1973

The Happy Warrior: Literary Essays on the Giants of Australian Literature (essays) 1987

CRITICISM

A. A. Phillips (essay date winter 1974)

SOURCE: Phillips, A. A. "The Short Stories of John Morrison." *Overland* 58 (winter 1974): 31-5.

[*In the following essay, Phillips comments on Morrison's highly realistic proletarian fiction, maintaining that it reveals the author as holding old-fashioned, even conservative, values while advocating adventure and freedom of self-expression.*]

John Morrison began his march towards becoming an Australian writer when he rebelled against employment in the English north-country museum of which his Presbyterian father was curator, and took to the sea. That life-accepting initiative explains much in his writing, but I believe that nearly as much is explained by the nature of his background; for the values which Morrison's writings assume and express are often the values of certain conformisms, positively accepted and practised with strength. That is also the tradition, on its best side, of those whom we call Nonconformists; and that best side is often best achieved in the northern sections of the United Kingdom.

Such a statement about the practitioner of an art must seem derogatory and is likely to be resented by Morrison's admirers—who could produce apparently convincing evidence in its refutation. But I believe it is neither unjust nor derogatory.

So improbable an assertion demands the wariness of an oblique approach to its justification. Let me begin, then, with a proposition that cannot arouse argument—that Morrison was certainly no conformist to the fashionable trends in the writing of his time. He adopted old-fashioned methods of story-writing, and there was a certain square-jawed determination about his rejection of modernisms.

Lying behind his acceptance of old-fashioned methods is a conception of the nature of literature which strongly influences his work. He saw it as a way of commenting on the lives of men; he did not see it as a way of revealing the nature of the Life of Man (with certain important exceptions to this principle I shall deal later). That, of course, implies a real limitation; but it also refreshingly separates Morrison from the ruck of writers who insist upon attempting what only the greatest can achieve. In defence of his position, he might claim: "If I can get my observation of the lives of men accurate and honest, something about the Life of Man will emerge; that must be left to take its chance".

Such an attitude inevitably affects his approach to technique. He does not see story-writing as the achievement of Significant Form. What the story has to tell about men and their lives is what alone matters. Form is important only in helping that purpose. That does not mean that his technique is off-hand or sloppy. It is carefully carpentered, with a particularly alert awareness of the value of the evocative ending. It is easy to miss the degree of skill which Morrison has often expended on his structuring. In **"The Nightshift"**, for instance, the description of the river crossing seems merely matter-of-fact, without memorable phrase or hint of fine writing. But it not only accurately conveys the scene, it communicates the mood of the romantic adolescent through whose eyes we are looking. But, where no such special need calls forth a special engagement in method, Morrison is quite content to let the stories clump along in working-boots.

How far he carries his principle of the supremacy of the comment on life can best be seen in the early stories of the wharfside. They are thinly represented in the recently issued paper-back of his selected stories, presumably because most of them are not "stories" by any acceptable formal definition of the term. They exist in a no-man's-land lying somewhere between documentary and fiction. Their rejection might therefore seem reasonable; but it ignores the truth that the hybrid nature of the form there employed is rightly conceived for the kind of comment which these pieces make.

Primarily Morrison wants here to speak for the wharfies, to bring to his readers an understanding of their problems and a justification of their approach to industrial politics. But straight documentary or political argument could not achieve his purpose, because it was the human situation creating the political attitudes which he wanted to illuminate. For that he needed the intimacy of created dialogue and individualised characters. The hybrid method which results ignores theories of "artistry", but the result justifies the means. As a commentator has said, "after reading them one will never again glance at a newspaper report about a waterside dispute or a rationalisation plan without a new life starting between the dull lines".

That illumination works most effectively when the impulses of the fiction-writer predominate over the insistences of political engagement. **"Nine O'Clock Shift"**, for example, is a simple account of a gang's resistance to a decision to continue work over the week-end; but it probes the nature of sea-front industrial politics probably better than **"Black Cargo"**, which traces the course of a famous confrontation between left and right Labor Party cliques, accurately recording the historical facts. Nevertheless **"Black Cargo"** probably tells the uninformed more about how Labor politics in the post-war era really worked than most economic historians are likely to convey (or know), despite some distortions through partisan emphases.

In the best known of these stories, **"Going Through"**, it is again the deployment of an artistic mode which communicates most effectively. Morrison here wants to convey the pride of solidarity built about membership of the Waterside Workers' Federation, the frontline infantry brigade of the ports' industrial battles. The detail of the account of the admission of new members to the WWF is rather less humanly informing than is usual in a Morrison story, always built on the meticulous observation and selection of detail. The vigor of the pride is rather conveyed in the rhythms which the narrative achieves. One wonders, if one has the intrusive curiosity of the critic, how far Morrison conceived this rhythmic method as a deliberated ploy and how far it ran unsummoned from his mind's engagement with his theme to his pen.

These stories, which in some respects stand apart from most of Morrison's work, particularly well illustrate one of its persistent characteristics. The men with whom he is concerned are those placed in the lower half of the economic scale. "Upper class" figures appear usually in response to a plot-demand, and are shallowly conceived. Most of them, indeed, are variants of the same figure: rigid of mind, formal of manners, deep-frozen in feeling and ridden by a harsh and egoistic possessiveness. They are the creations of a Socialist Realist writer rather than of a social realist—and usually Morrison can justly claim the more honorable title.

Any fiction-writer of good sense is likely to stand on the social ground where he feels most at home, most capable of achieving sympathy with his characters. But Morrison achieves something rarer in a writer than sympathy: he stands not merely on the side of his proletarians but among them. He responds to life as they do—or at least he successfully creates that impression. There is no trace in him of the artist's usual claim to membership of the élite of special sensitivity or superior imaginative vitality (a confrontation between him and Norman Lindsay, that propagandist for the aristocracy of the artist, might have been fun, unless Norman had borne him down by the sheer impetus of his volubility turned against a personality with little taste for verbal pyrotechnics). His work implies that men are most men (and, perhaps, most Man) when they are most ordinary.

He determinedly restricts his art to the sphere of the actual—and once almost truculently declares for it. **"The Man in the Night"** is a slight and peaceful sketch of a child's experience. Unusually, Morrison's first-person narrator is here the central figure in the story, which suggests that it is autobiographic. At the end of this tranquil piece of relaxed reminiscing, Morrison suddenly leaps to his feet and hurls a hand-grenade:

> That was the day that I learned for all time that the creatures of fable and fantasy are never half as nice as the creatures of real life.

That would seem sheer treason to whole tribes of writers who believe that the aim of art is to achieve the fables which will reveal truth—and with them stands their archetype, the great artist myth-maker of ancient Athens who held that Reality lies outside our cave of shadows. Morrison takes a stand opposing Plato, only in part because he enlisted with Marx.

In conformity with his view he uses a largely objective approach, save when he feels called to battle in support of a temperately militant leftism. For him, the story-writer's duty is to observe and report. Strangely, at first thought, his objectivity is indicated by his preference for first-person narrative; for his narrators are usually observers stationed on the fringe of the action, noting its course. Such a viewing-point denies the writer the opportunity to move inside the head of a character and report his thinking—a resource almost essential to a fiction-writer who is really writing about his own extraordinariness, or assaying to illuminate the Life of Man (which is, in the practice of the less great, often much the same thing). As I have said, that indicates a limitation to the degree of Morrison's penetration—it is perhaps significant that two of his most humanly revealing stories—**"The Nightshift"** and **"Morning Glory"**—discard the first-person method. But if Morrison's acceptance of a limited aim and a limiting method keep him out of the more exciting oceanic depths, they also help to create a sense of unpretentious honesty in his work.

However objective the methods which Morrison quietistically adopts, that honesty prevents him from draining out of his stories a necessary measure of subjectivity. He is too direct, too square-jawed a writer, to assume an attitude of ironic agnosticism, to conceal his values or refuse to place the sympathy as those values demand.

In these values, I believe, one can sense the north-country Presbyterian still working within him. It is apparent in the kind of theme which he finds worth writing about. The point of conflict in his stories is usually a moral point. He is indifferent to the attractions of ingenious twists of plot, and is quite prepared to let the reader see where the story is heading after the first few paragraphs. The fascinations of emotional intricacies, of the devastations of passion, leave him unstirred. He is antipathetic to the whine over the dismal fate of modern man—I doubt if he believes there is any such subdivision of the eternally human species. What pins his aroused attention is the moment when one of his plain men is faced with a decision about conduct; and while he regards human weakness with understanding and compassion, the rightness or wrongness of the character's decision is firmly implied—not that he is the kind of bore who subjects fiction to a moral didacticism, save occasionally in a piece of political propagandism. Simply, for him the moments that really matter are the moments of moral decision, so that acceptance of the doctrine of the amorality of art would mean, from his view, a denial of any reality of interest in life. An elder of the kirk who read him might seldom accept his judgments, but nonetheless feel a concordant direction of interest.

The judgments which underlie these studies are, with certain important modifications, judgments on the side of conformity with the simpler moral verities. A hostile amorality-of-art man might, with some show of justice, accuse him of respectability, despite his contempt for primness, hypocrisy, and the wrong kind of submissiveness; for his work implies an unhesitating acceptance of the simple but rigorous demands of a sense of duty. One can feel it in his attitude in **"The Drunk"**. The conflict here lies between the demands of loyalty to a mate, which is almost the religion of the watersider, and the duty of condemning a man who compromises everyone's safety by getting drunk on the job. No-one has extolled the values of solidarity more convincingly than Morrison; but his disapproval of the men who want to cover up the drunkard's offence is firm. Again, in his portrait of **"The Sleeping Doll"**, when he writes, "Boyd looked as if he'd never raised a sweat or a blister since the day he was born", one can sense the rejecting twist of his lip. That is partly, of course, an expression of Morrison's sympathy with the "working man" against the possessors and the manipulators; but it is more an abiding preference for the man who accepts the duty of work over the drone (although the story ends with enjoyment of the sleeping doll's victory over the hard-working, and hard-driving, boss; no writing which humanely relishes life can afford the luxury of a schematic consistency).

Perhaps the most expressive indication of Morrison's valuation of moral toughness is a word dropped into **"The Incense Burner"**. He is describing a Salvation Army refuge and the 'trusties' who assure themselves comfortable jobs on the staff by going through the ritual of being "saved":

> And if you weren't anxious to move on, and were sufficiently unscrupulous, you could be one of the running brigade.

Observe the strength of contempt conveyed by the choice of so emphatic a term as "unscrupulous". It is,

of course, partly conveying a Marxist's scorn for the opium of the people; but it also reveals a moral conviction which the elders of the kirk would understand. That conviction does not exclude the tenderness; it is tempered by the tolerance implicit in a humorous approach and by the writer's duty of compassion; but ultimately it stands pat on the belief that a man shows his strength through his fidelity to the simpler moral imperatives.

There is one strand in Morrison's writing which seems to run counter to this essential Puritanism. A scatter of stories approve the rebels who desert suburbanism in a search for the horizons of adventure and freedom. Rory O'Mahony is the fullest study of this type of rebel, though the story ends ambiguously—rightly enough, for Such is Life. The theme is perhaps better illustrated in **"The Door"**, despite its slightness. A drunk at the genial stage of beeriness finds himself in a railway carriage with two prim respectables who disapprove both his beery expansiveness and a trio of kids who slam the door. So the drunk hoists his little red flag by a super-slam which smashes the window. It is significant that the narrator of the story for once deserts the neutral stance. He does a little slamming too.

Yet even here there is a betraying survival from the tradition of the north-country kirk. The paragraph describing the narrator's slam contains the phrase "even the most disciplined of us" and the assertion that, having been challenged by the drunk with whom he has revealed his sympathy "he had to go through with it for the sake of his blessed self-respect". Door-slammers should be inspired by more pagan motives.

I doubt if there is a real contraction between the two themes which I have been discussing, though the one sympathises with the emancipation of vitality from the bondage of social responsibility and the other admires fidelity to moral imperatives: for each is a way by which a man may find and test his strength. When Morrison deserted the museum for the sea, was he drawn by a thirst for romance or by the desire to test his strength against the challenge of tough demand? It is a silly question; for the adolescent who thus adventures feels both these impulses and does not nicely discriminate between them.

The easy mating of the themes can be seen in another which is the most persistent in Morrison's writing, revealed in a series of studies of the debilitating influence of possessions. Of the seventeen stories in *Selected Stories*,[1] six are centred on this theme, and it is a contributing element in two others. There are for example the two mates who win Tatts and, quarrelling about the division of the spoils, destroy their mateship, thus coming out losers. There is Abbs of **"This Freedom"**, who cannot blossom into meaningful living until he has broken the drought of his house-pride. There is the fine story **"Morning Glory"**, in which a man accepts the primacy of possessions and ends by accepting a killing as a proper penalty for the invasion of his property rights.

In some of these stories the bondage to possessions destroys, or threatens, the victim's freedom and the vitality which it can bestow. In some it erodes his fidelity to moral demands. But the implication behind these variants is the same. "The imp of avarice", as Morrison once calls it, has damned the victim by stealing his strength. The man who lets his vitality rot and the man who evades moral demand have both lost the ability to stand sturdy on firmly-planted feet.

A different dimension of this recognition is presented in **"Pioneers"**, one of Morrison's most mature stories, in quality as well as dating (1964). Like **"Morning Glory"**, belonging to the same late period, it follows a technical method first successfully exploited in the early **"The Nightshift"** (1944). The well-carpentered evolvement of a narrative is supplemented by a more atmospheric, and imaginatively involved, process, the juxtaposing of pictures which will cumulatively convey the story's inward significance. In these stories, as in **"Goyai"** and a few others, that significance is less exclusively concerned with observation of the process of living, more intent on suggesting the element of mystery in human existence. It is significant that in both these late stories, and in **"The Nightshift"**, death is an important element, with all that implies about the view of life. The atmosphere is darker-hued; "wuthering" is perhaps the right word to describe it, although Morrison in this mood is closer to Hardy than to Brontë.

The central figure in **"Pioneers"** is seen from a hostile point of view. Yet he has much in common with those neo-Puritans whom Morrison often admires. He has the sturdiness of stance. He has fidelity to his principles, such as they are; and he is efficient, a quality which Morrison normally approves. He is disqualified from sympathy because he is consumed by egotism. If he is in part a neo-Puritan, he is also a development from that upper-class stereotype whom Morrison has used when the plot-development demanded a near-villain. This variant has been demoted to the social status of a selector and promoted to a full individuality.

Unlike the upper-class villains and the central figure of **"Morning Glory"**, the selector has not been rotted by possessions, which he largely despises, preferring to indulge subtler forms of possessiveness, which he exercises against his wife and daughters. Here lies his essential criminality. He denies life and he has the power to destroy it in others. That he commits a murder is merely incidental to the deeper viciousness of his hostility to a warm and flowering vitality.

For if Morrison's sturdiness of stance, derived from his north-country Presbyterian forbears, gives his writing its special flavor, in the last resort he stands with the artists against the deniers of life—who frown upon exuberant slammers of railway-carriage doors and who would have shut a youth within the creaking doors of a museum.

Note

1. John Morrison: *Selected Stories* (Rigby, $1.75).

Stephen Murray-Smith (essay date 1982)

SOURCE: Murray-Smith, Stephen. "Introduction." In *The Best Stories of John Morrison*, pp. ix-xv. Ringwood, Victoria, Australia: Penguin Books, 1988.

[*In the following essay, originally published in 1982, Murray-Smith focuses on three aspects of Morrison's writing often discussed by critics: strong ethical content, the so-called "parable" style, and the author's "old-fashioned" story-writing technique.*]

The publication by Penguin Books of a new collection of the stories of John Morrison is of particular timeliness and significance. George Steiner has recently written in the London press of the new mood of humanist and social awareness that is growing in Europe, to displace the involuted and insulated literary theories and experiments of the last twenty years, and in Australia too there are signs, in film, drama and books, that the mode of the 1980s will be strongly influenced by a return to the Real, a departure from the artist as his own subject, a re-emphasis on continuity in human affairs.

Even if this does not prevail, there is no doubt that the stories and novels of John Morrison have shown a surprising historical vitality. The work of few Australian writers whose literary experience comes from the 1920s and 1930s, and whose writing is that of the 1940s and 1950s, has remained in print and grown in reputation in the past thirty years. John Morrison's work is likely to be part of the small proportion of the writing of its time that will survive indefinitely.

On the face of it, John Morrison's literary world is well removed from current literary fashion and social preoccupation. His waterside workers, once satisfying as heroes to the Left and as villains to the Right, are now a small and dwindling band. Perhaps in the 1980s air traffic controllers, with their white collars and swimming pools, will take their place as symbolic figures on the industrial scene. Morrison's backblocks 'hatters' have by now been placed in care by diligent social workers, his train- and tram-travellers have switched to Datsuns and Commodores, his Dandenongs pensioners have moved to the Gold Coast, and his farmers now rank higher in the social scale than their bank managers. Only the drunks remain.

The world of which John Morrison writes was remote even to me, when I was shanghaied into it in the 1950s. Not *quite,* actually. That world of Morrison's young manhood, on which hang many of his stories, was the world of my childhood. But I knew nothing of his hot inland, his clanging tramp-steamers, his mist-wreathed mountain forests. What I did know a little of was another of his celebrations: the middle-class suburban Melbourne of the one-day-a-week gardener, the 'nature-strip', and the bottomless gap between the 'worker' and the rest. When reading **'North Wind'** it is salutary to remind oneself that John Morrison, as a jobbing gardener, used to pedal his bicycle from Mentone to places like Kew every day for work—some twelve miles, perhaps against a north wind—and then home again after a long day. It is a world, this 'respectable' world, that he draws in delicate and damning touches: its affectations, its fear of common humanity, its shallow-rooted pretensions.

Jobbing gardeners may now be as rare a species as *Citriodora echeveria eugenoides* in **'The Haunting of Hungry Jimmy'**, but *that* world of John Morrison remains, though his **'Avalon'** and **'Elysia'**, and Mr Cameron's home in Hawthorn Road may long ago have become petrol stations. For, while it is true that on one level the writer is constructing a magnificent, moving, even nostalgic picture of a Melbourne about which (since we don't talk to old people) we now know little; and while it is important not to underrate this achievement—yet Morrison is read, and will continue to be read, for quite different reasons.

There have been acute and important discussions of John Morrison's art by David Martin, Arthur Phillips and Ian Reid, which I do not want to recapitulate, partly because they are readily accessible (sources are listed at the end of this introduction), and partly because I want to write, not so much about the totality of Morrison's work, as about what we can learn of it through the stories in this collection. But I do wish to discuss three aspects of Morrison's writing which these critics refer to.

One is the strong 'ethical' content in the writing. He likes to take his characters, says Phillips, at the moment of 'ethical decision'. It is, I think, an important point, and it clearly relates in part to Morrison's North Country background (Presbyterian, both parents Sunday-school teachers) and to his affiliations with that latter-day redemptionist institution, the Communist Party. He does believe that not only once, but many times, to every man and nation comes the moment to decide

> In the strife of truth with falsehood,
> For the good or evil side.

That a writer should have ethical considerations at the back of what he writes is not only, in my view, desirable, but inevitable. No statement or action by anyone is 'value-free', let alone those of artists, who all voluntarily elect to enter an arena. All artists are teachers, including those who deny that they are: *they* simply hold to a teaching or 'ethical' position which maintains that what they are doing is indeed 'value-free'. Since this is, I presume, generally conceded, the argument in Morrison's case must be that he strongly adheres to a perceptible ethical stance, one that colours his writing visibly.

Perhaps so. But I suggest that the interesting thing about much of Morrison's writing is that, within certain discernible 'ethical' considerations, he is so often able to suggest moral ambiguities. And the more fully fledged his stories are, the more firmly the reader rather than the writer is pushed into the judgement seat. In **'North Wind'** we are worried, whether Morrison realizes it or not, at a certain obsessiveness which governs both actors, the desperate husband and the recalcitrant mother-in-law. His triumph here is to suggest flaws in the stance of the husband even though it is the husband that is telling the story. At the end, as the flames consume the weather-board house, a black pall of uncertainty casts its shadow over all. Maybe we are expected to side whole-heartedly with Jim Thurgood, but it really isn't as simple as that. It's a strange and worrying tale.

'The Battle of Flowers' is another example. Here the moral dilemma of the gardener, caught in a malevolent helix, is explicitly one of the main points of the story, and it can easily be read as a parable, as the critics often suggest of so many of Morrison's stories. If it were to be read as a parable—and I take issue with this approach later on—it might be read as a religious parable, of the Devil leading man to damnation with mincing steps, or as a political parable, of the inability of humanity to order its world in a sane way.

No doubt somewhere or other in Morrison's consciousness or subconscious such considerations have something to do with it, but the story can be read otherwise as well, as an exercise in the genuine confusion that exists in the sphere of moral concerns, a refusal to accept an easy answer to the question Joseph Furphy posed in *Such is Life*—just which branch line do you take at what moment? (In fact, if one wanted to discuss symbols in Morrison, the place of the train and the tram in his stories would be important.) There are several moralities operating in this story, and one of them is an existentialist one. Existentialism in Morrison is discussed by David Martin in his article; for me, in relation to **'The Battle of Flowers'**, it is a strand in the story which admits the two gardeners, not as active agents in evil, but as observers or passive agents in a progression which is not only out of their control, but which—taking into account the vindictiveness of the Heavenly Twins—they should properly stand aside from. It is, of course, the strength of Morrison that he can deftly and economically weave so many layers of response into his work.

My third example is perhaps Morrison's greatest story, **'Pioneers'**, in my view a candidate for being the finest story written in this country since Lawson. Arthur Phillips has pointed out how Roy Davison, with his stern self-reliance, his disdain for 'show' and his utter competence (he himself is the only witness to it, but that is enough), 'has much in common with those neo-Puritans whom Morrison often admires'. He is destroyed, says Phillips, by 'egotism'; perhaps another way of saying it would be that Davison is destroyed by the reverse side of his own virtues: self-reliance becomes the immodesty, the brutality, which the primitive surrounds of his life have nurtured. Quite so, quite so. But over **'Pioneers'** lies another cloud, an elemental cloud, which enshrouds the whole story. Bob Johnson, the observer, makes his sympathies plain, but for all that he *is* an observer, an astronomer watching galaxies collide; and in my view we are left at least as much with the feeling of 'what right have we to be here?' as with the 'ethical' judgement that Roy Davison is a prime bastard.

I do not, in other words, accept the view that John Morrison is a preacher to any significant degree, and I think that he too is subtly making the same point by including in this collection gentle stories of observation and human feeling—**'Transit Passenger'** and **'Dog-box'**, for instance. Note that 'gentle' stories need not lack impact and meaning; the meaning is all the more puissant because (and one might even say, to the degree that) Morrison leaves the reader to work it out for himself. His view of humanity is seldom disapproving in a judgmental sense. It is distanced, regretful, sometimes sad. His overwhelming quality as a writer is a quiet capacity for detachment.

So I do not share—to take up my second point—a view of Morrison as writing 'parables'. I am sure he has no objection to his readers interpreting some or all of his stories this way, but I do not believe that he is setting out to 'write big'. I think he is too good a writer for this. He has a much less ambitious and at the same time a much more profound aim: to discuss human nature as he knows it, and to tell a good story reconstructed from bits and pieces garnered and thought about over many years. He has, in John Manifold's phrase, a 'queer affection' for the human race: never cynical, but sometimes sardonic; never resentful, though sometimes angry; never judging—or seldom judging—beyond the point to which his characters bring him.

It is the view of a gardener of men, for whom docks sprouting in the borders do not destroy a broader vision of potential beauty. It is the view of a writer who has said that 'An attitude which maintains that literature should be regarded as an instrument in the social struggle and nothing else' must lead 'straight to literary damnation'. The function of the artist, John Morrison maintains, 'is to move his audience emotionally'.

A third point the critics have sometimes advanced in discussing Morrison is the rough-hewn quality of his prose, his disdain for literary niceties, his concern that his words should be no more than hand-maidens of larger concerns. 'Old-fashioned methods of story-writing', Arthur Phillips has called them, though to be fair Phillips has also been careful to point to Morrison's 'carefully-carpentered' technique. None of the critics I have mentioned deny Morrison's literary skills, but the phrase 'old-fashioned' does keep cropping up, and it is a phrase with which I want to take issue. There are plenty of contemporary novelists and short-story writers of the highest rank who do not rely on experiment with literary *form* for part of their effects, though all, as does Morrison, tailor the choice, flow and arrangement of their words to the job in hand. It is important here to see what Morrison is doing—I nearly said 'what Morrison is aiming at', but there is a difference. He is working towards an unforced and relaxed style, not because he is in any way 'old-fashioned', but because only the achievement of such a style can carry the psychological realism which is his aim and his accomplishment.

Look, for instance, at **'The Haunting of Hungry Jimmy'**, where the initial aim is to reinforce the reader's understanding of the character of Hungry Jimmy, on which the rest of the story totally depends. Notice the *patience* with which Morrison rejects the natural impulse in a short-story writer to 'get on with it', and instead takes us quietly through a rehearsal of Jimmy's guttersnipe acuity. Notice, too, the quiet personal aside with which Morrison reminds us that the narrator of his first-person stories is also a participant: in **'Tinkle, Tinkle, Little Bell'**, where he writes, 'Not Carnation. He'd been outflanked, and he wasn't going to let me get away with it'. And observe the timing of such an interpolation, which carries with it an acute—and sometimes uncomfortable—sense of the narrator's position. And witness the ability to seize on a moment in order to set a scene and to heighten the senses of the reader, as in **'The Nightshift'**:

> The night is full of sounds. Little sounds, like the rattle of winches at the distant timber berths; big sounds, like the crash of the coal-grabs opposite the gasworks. All have the quality of a peculiar hollowness, so that one still senses the overwhelming silence on which they impinge.

This is not 'old-fashioned' writing. It is writing that knows what literary form is appropriate to the emotion that is being created. It is only old-fashioned in the sense that the paper from which this book is made is old-fashioned.

Questions of form and style apart, John Morrison has an importance to Australians which transcends a simple 'literary significance'. Like David Martin, but not perhaps a great many others, he is a creature from outside who has lived long and thoughtfully among us as a writer. His first interest is in a humanity common to all men and women, but his secondary interest, heightened of course by his coming to Australia as an adult, is in what our environment and our society have done to *us*. The experience of 'Australianness' has become a cliché in television soap-opera and in film, but serious writers have turned away from it, especially in the last two decades, for at least two reasons: because it seemed important to look at human experience in this continent in more individual terms, and (which is really part of the same) because of an increasing suspicion of, and hence incapacity to handle, generalization.

Morrison is not a generalizer, except in the sense that he will allow humanity to triumph in his stories if he can (**'Perhaps You've Got It'**) or, failing that, will engage his readers in moral considerations. But in his stories he has, for all that, sketched in and filled in a view of a specific people in a specific place. He has asked, and gone further perhaps than any other towards answering, the most important question of all: to what degree is this society one in which people may call their souls their own?

The question is as important as the answer.

References

David Martin: 'Three Realists in search of Reality', *Meanjin*, no. 3, 1959.

A. A. Phillips: 'Short Story Chronicle', *Meanjin*, no. 4, 1962.

Ian Reid: 'Introduction', in John Morrison, *Selected Stories* (Rigby, Seal Books, 1972).

A. A. Phillips: 'The Short Stories of John Morrison', *Overland*, no. 58, 1974.

John Morrison (essay date 1984)

SOURCE: Morrison, John. "Introduction." *Stories of the Waterfront*, pp. vii-x. Ringwood, Victoria, Australia: Penguin Books, 1984.

[*In the following essay, Morrison reflects on his experiences as a "wharfie," detailed in his stories of the waterfront.*]

This collection brings together for the first time in one cover all my stories of the Melbourne waterfront. All are firmly based on experiences during my own ten years as a Melbourne wharfie, the decade extending from the late 1930s to the late '40s. A decade that saw great changes on the waterfront, technical changes with the coming of the pallet and mobile forklift, humaniz-

ing changes in the conditions under which men in the industry worked. When I began there, the open pick-up system of engaging labour, known as the Bull system, was still in operation. Minimum period of engagement could be for as little as two hours; smokoes were limited to particularly strenuous or fast cargoes such as pig-iron and bagged flour; stevedoring companies had not yet established a centralized pay system, nor was payment of wages made at jobs distant from the Compound. Mess rooms were few and scruffy, and no protective clothing was provided for men working in refrigerated chambers. When I left the waterfront in 1949 all these long-standing grievances had been settled.

Then came containerization, with big reductions in labour costs for the stevedoring companies, and for the Federation some compensation in the form of redundancy payments to men no longer required. Further improvements in the 1950s were paid annual holidays, payment for attendance at pick-ups (work or no work), substantially improved first-aid services, more up-to-date diningrooms and call-ups by radio and newspaper. I have no experience of this later period and have not attempted to write about it.

Now, in the quiet years of retirement, I reflect often as a writer on those ten years in the waterfront industry and of the riches of the human material I got from the men I worked with, by far the staunchest community of men my lot was ever thrown among. Tough? Yes, of course they were tough. They were engaged in a tough industry. An industry casual in the fullest sense of the word, rarely anything but strenuous, always dirty, often unhealthy, and sometimes decidedly dangerous. Moreover, in the stevedoring companies we were faced with tough employers, who fiercely resisted most efforts to improve working conditions. Added to all this there was the persistent underlying irritation brought about by the public image of our kind which was promoted through the media—an image of a drunken, thieving, work-shy, socially irresponsible, industrial militant.

Thieves and vagabonds? Yes, of course we had them, but the villainy was individualistic, and petty indeed compared to the orchestrated within-the-law villainy radiating from the seats of economic power. In any event, the Federation membership had its own methods of enforcing discipline on the job. Two actual cases are personalized and examined in depth in these stories. One is **'The Drunk'** which deals also with the question of wildcat stoppages. The other is **'All through the Night'**, in which several problems are gone into, notably that of pillage. Charges of pillage, collectively and on an absurd scale, were always a sore point with wharfies. In these days of steel bulk containers it would be interesting to know to what degree—and allowing for the important element of inflation—insurance rates on cargoes have varied. Wharfies never even see the goodies now, much less touch them. Are the really big operators still in business?

In the 1930s, wharfies badly needed a spokesman to present their side of these apparently simple issues, and thanks to enlightened editors such as C. B. Christesen of the literary quarterly *Meanjin,* and the late George Farwell of the short-lived (five issues) *Australian New Writing,* I was able to raise one small voice for the defence. That, however, is not intended to lay stress on altruistic motivation. I'd been writing, although with only minimal success, for many years before I entered the industry. As a writer, my debt is to the men of the waterfront. The waterfront gave me new heart, and, more importantly, re-direction. It was a catalyst.

Catalyst? Explosion, rather. I'd been around quite a lot, but my introduction to a waterfront pick-up of labour was an emotional experience. I was, of course, aware that this was the notorious Outer, where men awaiting admission to the Federation assembled in the hope of picking up a job. I also knew that the scene in the Federation section at the rear of the great bleak shed was quite different. That morning I was a newcomer with only the promise of a nomination for membership of the ruling aristocracy. All I had was a brand-new blank Licence in my pocket entitling me to become one of these hundreds of men clamouring for work. I remember at the time recalling the famous declaration by Jean-Jacques Rousseau: 'Man was born free, and is everywhere in chains', and reflecting that he should see us now, two hundred years later, begging for the chains. It's all there in my story, **'The Compound'**, at the start of this collection.

Nevertheless, the initial reaction soon passed. It was a precarious way of earning a living, picking up the leftovers of work that came out from the Federation, but I was in good physical shape and rapidly discovered that it was possible to earn more here than I could anywhere else. There was an attraction even in the ever-present element of gambling. Coming in to a pick-up a man never knew if he would get a ship at all, if he would be working in the trunkway of a liner at Port Melbourne, or packing in live sheep as deck cargo on one of the little Bass Strait traders, if it would be nightshift or dayshift, if it would be just two hours topping up a 'tween-deck of a vessel on the point of departure, or ten days discharging timber from Canada, or loading bagged flour for the East Indies. Giving a bite to all this was the ever-present question of what would be the nature of the 'blue' that marked every job: a confrontation with a deck officer over the condition of the ship's gear, with an engineer over the temperature of a refrigerated

chamber, with an excessively keen foreman over the pace at which work was proceeding, or even with one of our own vigilant officers for not being available when required.

Ships still come and ships still go, but the waterfront as I knew it has gone forever. It was a hit-or-miss world, variable, lively, noisy and colourful, but I took to it like a duck to water. Born and bred in an ancient English port, where the docks were one of my playgrounds as a boy, being among ships again was like coming home.

Only in recent years has the study of grassroots industrial relations taken on its real importance to the social historian. My hope is that this collection of stories, the background authenticity of which no one need doubt, may be found of more than passing interest.

Ivor Indyk (essay date December 1987)

SOURCE: Indyk, Ivor. "The Economics of Realism: John Morrison." *Meanjin* 46, no. 4 (December 1987): 502-12.

[*In the following essay, Indyk describes Morrison's particular brand of realism and how it dignifies the people and situations it describes.*]

Australia boasts a very strong socialist realist tradition in literature, yet we are still a long way from being able to describe just how this realism works.

We might take as a starting-point the formula applied by A. A. Phillips to Lawson, Furphy and their successors in the tradition: 'They wrote of the people, for the people, and from the people.' For all its simplicity, the statement does serve as a guide to the subject matter, the style, and the points of view appropriate to realism. What it does not cover, though, is what we might call the economics of realism, the way it establishes the value of its material.

A sketch by John Morrison illustrates this aspect of realism. In **'Pastoral'** Morrison recalls observing, against the backdrop of a sunset in the Dandenongs, a large flock of swifts flying back and forth, forming a great oval in the sky several hundred yards long. The performance is an odd one: it is as if the birds were playing a game, clicking their beaks in greeting as they pass each other in the sky. Then the author, shifting his gaze to the roadside about him, notices that 'something odd was happening here also'. Out of a hole in the bare earth pours a stream of winged ants. Each one pauses, scurries away from the hole, then takes off into the sunset. Meditating on 'what extraordinary promise it was that drew them with such crazy haste into the evening sky', he follows their flight, into 'the fatal oval', where one by one they are snapped up by the wheeling swifts. 'There came a time when the little hole in the ground ceased to give forth, and within seconds the swifts also were gone.' The sketch ends with a moral application, which warns against upsetting the delicate economy of nature through the use of insecticides and the wanton shooting of birds. (*ABC* [*Australian by Choice*], 145-7)[1]

We may take this case as a paradigm. The significance of one event is established in relation to another occurring nearby, adjacent in time or place. The two events are related as parts within a larger context or whole, the economy of nature. At the end of the sketch, that context is subsumed within another, the moral and social economy of human concerns.

In a linguistic framework, this movement from part to part, and from part to whole, is known as metonymy. There have been several attempts to apply the concept of metonymy to the description of realist writing, beginning with Roman Jakobson's essay, 'Two Aspects of Language' in *Fundamentals of Language* (1956); a more recent example would be David Lodge's *The Modes of Modern Writing* (1977). But while the concept does justice to the contextual orientation of realism—the way it builds details into a larger sense of reality—metonymy nevertheless remains an essentially formal term, useful for tracing the movement from part to whole, but not for defining the nature of the whole, or the value conferred on its constituent parts. As our concern is with value, it would be more appropriate to think of the orientation of realism as economic rather than metonymic. This perspective is in any case more appropriate to the consideration of socialist realism, where the whole is defined primarily in economic terms, and where the centrality of labour ensures that the question of value is always to the fore.

Morrison's stories habitually move outwards from particular situations to the economies in which they occur. In his two novels, *The Creeping City* (1949) and *Port of Call* (1950), the question of value is heightened because the subject in each case is in transit between two competing economies, so that its value changes as it shifts from one to the other. In *The Creeping City* the hamlet of Mabooda in the Dandenongs is the setting for the passage from a pioneering economy which has brought the land under cultivation, to a middle-class economy which is rapidly transforming its orchards into weekenders for the wealthy of Melbourne. The shift in values is aptly summarised by Morrison: 'They didn't talk now of what they could get out of the land; they talked of what they could get *for* it.' (*CC*, 5) The changing features of the landscape testify to the change in economies. Now that the land has become too valuable

to cultivate, large parts of it revert to the bush from which it had been won over a generation of hard labour. The old people sell out, the children move to the city. As the weekenders and day-trippers move in, the local trappings of community life disappear; but there are new appearances too, 'metal roads instead of bush tracks, brick houses instead of wooden ones, electricity instead of kerosene, today's newspapers instead of yesterday's' (122). Public utilities give way to private enterprise, labour on the land to entrepreneurial ventures and the service industry. Properties are divided and subdivided, post and rail fences are replaced by palings and pickets, even the flowers in the garden change, camellias and standard roses for the old viburnums and weigelias, rowans and copper beeches in place of wattles and blackwoods.

One of Morrison's great strengths is his ability to trace the process of economic and social change, through all its implications and contradictions, in terms of the changes wrought on ordinary things, and ordinary lives. As the features of their landscape shift about them, so the characters are driven forward or cast aside by the current of change, their sense of authority and self-esteem waxing or waning as the old order gives way to the new. Bob Smith embodies the pioneering spirit: a hero of the old order, he watches the mantle of leadership pass to Mrs Terry, guest-house proprietress, the new power in the land. At home, his authority crumbles before the moral ascendancy of his wife, the product of his labour alienated by her 'gentle art of nagging and wrangling'. In defeat Smith is dignified and defiant: not so John Rae, upon whom the novel's focus finally settles. Presented as 'the victim of circumstance and environment', he is driven to murder by his bondage to a woman, and to the power of feminine sexuality.

Morrison's second novel *Port of Call* also takes the point of view of an outsider and victim, here the sailor Jim Boyd, who moves from a nautical to a land-based economy when he jumps ship in Melbourne. The period is again the mid-1920s, and Boyd struggles unsuccessfully to prove his worth in an economic order ruled by capital, where labour is now highly differentiated according to skills, and governed by a complex web of allegiances and rules of conduct. And again, it is a world in which women appear to be in the ascendancy. Boyd is ruled by feminine employers. The woman he loves, and who leaves him, is a strong, independent figure, whose confidence, assurance and dignity stand in marked contrast to his sense of worthlessness, estrangement and isolation. Indeed he seems to be surrounded by half-crazed masculine failures. Their habitual misogyny is perhaps best summed up in the rebuke one of them, a collector of butterflies, levels against his wife: 'She squashed my caterpillars!' (177). In Morrison's work women are sometimes seen to be as much at risk in the new order as men, but at other times they represent some of its worst aspects, particularly self-interest and the desire for possessions. Morrison's most valued women are mothers, bearing out the claim made by one of the characters—'They must have something to look after, something to nurse, something to hold in their arms, whether it's a baby or a man' (*ABC,* 69). When women do not play this role in what is apparently presented as a natural economy of the sexes, men are most likely to be at risk.

At the end of ***Port of Call*** Boyd retreats to the security of his ship, and although Morrison suggests that there will be a next time, when he will succeed, one is left with the clear impression that the contemporary economic order is not one in which a man will easily find a position of value. The same is true of ***The Creeping City*** even though Morrison has the philosopher Mishkin declare 'Mabooda was never greater than it is today'—the bourgeoisie may be in control, but tired workers are walking and singing in the forests, and the day will come when a liberated people will take over the mansions and guesthouses for the benefit of all. Morrison's assertions here about 'the stream of communal progress' are heavily qualified by the limited nature of the communities he does portray (the sense of isolation is often as strong within these as without, and particularly strong within the family), as also by his tendency to adopt the point of view of the outsider, the marginal, the eccentric and the anachronistic type.

This is to suggest that there are restrictions on the totalising tendency in Morrison's realism. Perhaps the most appropriate image of the social world evoked by Morrison's fiction is that presented in his train-carriage stories, including **'The Hold Up'**, **'Dog Box'** and **'Murder on the One-Thirty'**. In each case, a group of people who are strangers to each other bring their obsessions, discomforts, responsibilities and sympathies into a momentary conjunction before they part again to go their separate ways. In his stories of the waterfront and of gardening in particular, Morrison leads us into social realms the complexities of which we may have appreciated only dimly before. In certain stories—like **'Transit Passenger'**, which traces the courtship between a widower and a widow 'rather beyond middle age' from its inception over smoked fish, mash and green peas in a cafeteria in Walton's to its consummation after a long conversation about the felling of trees—he brings new areas of experience into Australian fiction.

On the whole, though, there is a thinness about Morrison's social world, an abbreviated sense of history or tradition, and very little sense of national or communal identity. We may think of this as characteristic of migrant, or of Australian writing (the two have much in common in this respect), though in Morrison's case there is also the political consideration that in a capitalist world, exploitation, self-interest and private property might have inhibited or weakened the bonds of community. As compensation for the withering of the social spirit, Australian socialist realist writers have often turned to the spirit of the land, to the consolation of the natural order—this recourse is also available to Morrison, but he uses it sparingly, and usually only as a background in his stories.

There is, however, a world within this unfriendly social world which does afford companionship and a sense of belonging. This is the community founded on physical labour, specifically labour on the waterfront. When Jim Boyd finally lands a job on the waterfront it fills him with strength and confidence. 'He was doing a man's work and receiving a man's wages . . . [in] a man's world, into which women could peep only with curiosity and envy' (*PC* [**Port of Call**], 224). The exclusion of women would seem to be one of the most important aspects of this world; mateship, clearly, is another. Morrison has a story, **'The Lonely One'**, in which a young Swede meets up with an old rabbiter suffering from 'wife trouble'. The title applies to both characters, and ironically, to the older man more thoroughly than to the younger. Evidently a man may feel as isolated in marriage as outside it, as isolated, in fact, as an immigrant in a strange land. You're damned if you have a family, and you're damned if you don't: it's as if isolation and loneliness were the inevitable consequences of being a man.

There aren't too many happy families in Morrison's stories, and generally speaking husband and wife inhabit two different worlds, the masculine world of physical labour and mateship set against the feminine world of domesticity and 'things'. In a way mateship is the chief benefit of labour: it allows a man to overcome his sense of isolation. Hence mateship is experienced as a physical sensation, as a feeling of warmth or intoxication. 'How good it is, the warm acclamation of one's fellow men!' exclaims the narrator of **'Going Through'** on his acceptance into the Waterside Workers' Federation. 'We feel suddenly rich. And not because of bigger pay envelopes to come. We've got ourselves three thousand mates' (*SW* [***Stories of the Waterfront***], 44). In **'Bo Abbott'** the narrator reacts with ecstatic joy when his mates show regard for his welfare—'It was exciting. Not one of those deep, melting moments when you feel your eyes fill, but one of those far better ones when all the life in you, from the tips of your toes to the roots of your hair, gives a great leap. What is it—the thrill of vindicated faith?' (*SW,* 33).

The masculine community offered by labour on the waterfront necessarily has a defensive character, set as it is against capitalist exploitation, women, and all the other forces which work to increase the masculine sense of isolation. It is a circumscribed world, but one ruled by complex lines of affiliation and obligation, and guarded by rituals of admission designed to enforce the loyalty and solidarity of its members. **'The Compound'** and **'Going Through'** provide cases in point: in the latter, the narrator seeking admission to the union is so revolted by the violent rejection of another candidate accused of scabbing, that he is moved to explain—'I've had to reason with myself, to tell myself that all this is not of their seeking. I am a witness not so much of a statement as of a response' (*SW*, 43).

Nevertheless, though its practices may have evolved as a response to external threat, within its limits this is a rich and evocative world, in which small details of conduct, the nuances of language, even the smell of soiled work clothes, may be heavy with implications and associations. Specific incidents—a dispute, a dangerous cargo—inevitably prompt discussion of other, related issues, and the memory of earlier incidents in the struggle for better working conditions. Although the action may be confined to the hold of a particular ship, the work of a particular gang, the loading and unloading of meat or timber or tea, the movement of these objects suggests much larger processes of exchange, on a national and an international scale. Having restricted his focus to a closed community of men, founded on a certain kind of labour, Morrison is then able to reach out, by implication at least, to the larger worlds beyond. This kind of extension through time and space allows Morrison to see, in the stacking of fifty thousand bags of flour in the hold of a ship, the expression of an 'ancient and significant urge' which takes us back to the very origins of human culture (*ABC*, 23; *SW*, 191).

But it is the moral issues which the men must confront in the course of their labour which open the largest perspectives in these waterfront stories. A. A. Phillips explains Morrison's 'moral toughness' in terms of his English North Country Presbyterian background, but in fact an intense preoccupation with the morality of conduct has been a hallmark of Australian realism from Lawson and Furphy on. The concern to establish the moral value of an action in the larger scheme of things is another aspect of that concern with value which marks the economic orientation of realism. In debating the rights and wrongs of a particular action, Morrison's workers map out the contours of their moral universe.

Hence in **'Nine O'Clock Finish'** the order to continue the shift until the cargo has been loaded leads to the suspension of work and the taking up of a conversation which ranges over the advantages of the gang-system as opposed to the voluntary pick-up, the use of night-gangs, the right to enjoy leisure and social activities, and the consequences of strike action, which in turn leads into history—

'What about the double-dumps blue?'

'And the black buses in the transport strike?'

'And the soda ash on the *Vito*?'

'And the '28 strike!'

And so it goes on, until the dissenting member of the gang complains '—drag in everything right back to the bloody ark, like you always do. What's all this got to do with working to a finish?' (*SW*, 77, 80). In **'Black Cargo'** the blacking of a ship manned by non-union labour sets the issue of international solidarity against that of intra-union rivalry, and then threatens to bring the state to a standstill as the conflict compounds, left-wing labour against right, union executives against rank and file, strike action against debate in council, the spirit of the people against the machinations of the press and the politicians. In **'Easy Money'** the prospect of being paid overtime for doing nothing stimulates a discussion which first considers the obligation a man has to his wife in these matters—

'A married man that taps his pay's a bastard,' says Clarrie.

'Depends what kind of missus he's got, doesn't it?' says Mick Anstey.

—before turning from the domestic economy to that of international capitalism—

'Stone the crows! I'm sitting here with fifty thousand bags of flour under my ginger. Who grew it? Who milled it? Who brought it here? Who put it into that hatch? And whose bloody flour is it? Don't ever talk to me about easy money! I know who gets the easy money _'

(*SW*, 192, 196)

Morrison's finest story in this vein is **'All through the Night'** which, in pursuing a night shift through its course, moves outwards through ever-widening perspectives, moral, political, economic, until at its farthest reach the labour of the night is set within the whole course of human history. 'To our own tiny portion of the great task we have been faithful. A tug has tied up just ahead of us, impatiently belching smoke. All other hatches have finished. We will not fail' (*SW*, 64). In this passage, as throughout the story, our attention shifts constantly, from context to detail and back again. The war against fascism is evoked through the narrator's encounter with an observing journalist who looks like Oswald Mosley; in his encounters with the Lascar seamen he discovers allies in the war against the Japanese, and larger identifications, the value of dignity, humility, optimism in the face of human suffering. Questions of moral principle are raised by an over-large case, an empty case, a case of sticking-plaster, by torn bags of soda ash. The significance of the ordinary detail is evident in the workers' new dining-room, recalling past struggles, projecting future aspirations: 'A dozen green tables, flanked by plain white forms; indirect lighting, and a hot-water service. We appreciate it as much for what it portends as for what it is. A sample of things to come. It took so long to get it.' (*SW*, 49) The action takes place at night, so that Morrison is able to weave a spell of enchantment over the proceedings, dignifying the rhythms of labour, enlarging and generalising its significance. The sense offered is very much that of labour as an expression of human value, as a humanising power reaching out to claim the world. The point is made at the end of the story as a new day dawns.

> Coode Island, laboriously emerging out of the dying night. Not much longer will it be an enchanted isle. Dark trees, ringed by a wreath of mist, as if smoke-streaming fairies had danced around them. Beloved Yarra, rippled only where a shag has just dived in. Cloudless Australian sky, steel-grey with an edge of rose and orange heralding the rising sun. It's just a little more our own since last night.
>
> (*SW*, 64)

Morrison describes gardening as 'the Cinderella of manual occupations' (*NW*, 40), and in the stories which deal with labour of this kind the sense of value is even more marked. Here there is little or no comfort in mateship, for the gardener is a solitary figure, and furthermore he is likely to be ruled by a feminine employer. But his labour causes the earth to flower, and in this way produces very visible tokens of human value. The best example is of course '**To Margaret**', where the whole garden speaks of the gardener's love for his employer's daughter, and where one bed declares this love by spelling out the daughter's name in linaria seedlings. This eloquence is in contrast to the employer's use of his wife's first name, which he mentions only when he wants to be nasty and pronounces as if it were a dirty word.

The same contrast between the expression and the denial of value is to be found in '**The Battle of the Flowers**', where the envy and selfishness of twin sisters turns two beautiful gardens into 'two little brown deserts', and the sisters themselves into spiteful old crones. Like the employer in '**To Margaret**', the two sisters clearly represent bourgeois self-interest; they are also isolated: 'from the shelter of an adequate independence they viewed the outside world without interest and without pity.' (*NW* [*North Wind*], 60) The two anti-social qualities go hand in hand, and are always known by their denials of value. A similar threat is posed by possession, private property. In '**Perhaps You've Got It**' a couple turn a vacant block at the back of their land to human use—their hens roam in it, it

provides apples and apricots for jam, kindling for their fire, a playground for children, it is a source of beauty, contemplation and relaxation. When the owner decides to sell, they purchase the block with their lottery winnings, thus paying to secure something which is in a sense already theirs by virtue of the good use to which they had put it.

Just as Morrison's concern for value manifests itself as a constant working outwards from the particular event or object to the economy in which it has a place, so the denial of value is seen in terms of the operation of a deranged economy. In the case of the 'bush-happy' Miss Taft in *Port of Call*, the derangement is evident in the collection of useless objects which clutter her house, and particularly her bedroom:

> a three-cornered boot-last with one foot missing, a sideboard with the veneer peeling off it in strips, a dressing-table with a smashed mirror, a splintered clock-case with no clock in it, a dressmaker's model bust, a policeman's helmet, an umbrella with bare ribs, a goldfish bowl full of corks, a parrot cage flattened by the weight of a broken spring mattress standing on top of it.
>
> (*PC* [*Port of Call*], 41)

No longer valuable, these objects await redeployment—they will wait forever—in Miss Taft's fantasy of a self-sufficient guesthouse. Miss Taft, by the way, was an expert on home economics: an educated woman, unmarried, her actual social position is little above that of a slave. The social criticism is more explicit in '**Christ, the Devil and the Lunatic**', in Morrison's portrait of an idiot son of a wealthy family indulged in his whims by an impoverished musician employed especially to buy things for him—

> Peter had the handle of the feather duster rammed down the front of his trousers, with the bunch of scarlet feathers ornamenting his chest. In one hand he held aloft a vivid and fully extended toy sunshade, in the other the mouthorgan on which he gave an occasional hideous blast. From one jacket pocket protruded a packet of lunchwraps, from the other a smelly bundle of firelighters. My share was the kewpie, a wooden Mickey Mouse on a swing, a bottle of turpentine, and the newspapers.
>
> (*SS* [*Selected Stories*], 131)

The story is set in the depression: the musician's comment—'Peter and I were Waste and Want parading hand in hand'—interprets the image as an emblem of the derangement at work in the capitalist economy.

The preceding examples present objects deprived of their use value in haphazard and arbitrary combinations. There's a second kind of derangement portrayed by Morrison, when objects are employed for their exchange value only in an endless series of transactions which return large profits to the operator and few benefits to anyone else. **'The Haunting of Hungry Jimmy'** is a fine illustration of the costs of the entrepreneurial spirit moving in the Australian economy in the 1960s (and since). Jimmy's opportunism is best observed in his penchant for cutting down trees. 'See the idea? The less trees, the more beds for his seedlings. Change over twice a year, and more labour for upkeep' (*NW*, 43). More profit, too, from grubbing out the stumps, and from the trees themselves, cut up into twelve-inch blocks for sale as firewood. The perspective here is very short—one of the points of the story is that objects may have a value in the long term which will not be realised in exchanging them for something else. As the something else in this case is usually money, the story also illustrates a third kind of derangement, where the elements which make up a varied economy are all made to perform the same function, or bear the same significance, thus in effect denying their individual values. In *Port of Call,* the pigment produced by the Magpie Chemical Company reduces everything to a weird yellow uniformity—

> It got through apron and overalls into his underclothing, it seeped into his shoes, it crusted his eyelids, it reached nostrils and throat through the cotton filter pad so that he coughed up yellow phlegm. He lived in a yellow world. He blew his nose on a yellow handkerchief, he lit a yellow cigarette with a match struck on a yellow box, fished money out of a yellow purse. It had a taste, too; a taste which, like the colour, went home with him at night. A taste that flavoured every meal he ate, and which was already in his mouth at the beginning of every day.
>
> (*PC,* 156-7)

Here it is an unregulated industrial economy that reduces everything to a poisoned sameness; elsewhere, it is obsession born of isolation and a sense of worthlessness. In **'Goyai'**, a recluse attempts to keep loneliness at bay by enlisting the number seventeen—his seventeen neighbours, the seventeen pines on the ridge, the seventeen calls of the podargus and so on—as evidence that his lost love is everywhere about him still. In **'Tinkle, Tinkle, Little Bell'** a child ringing a bell in innocent play reminds a man of a woman urinating into a specimen bottle. The man is 'a fixed-idea drunk', and there are many examples in Morrison's work of the fixed idea taking over, robbing things of their proper significance, and substituting its own self-serving meanings. The drunk is another of Morrison's misogynists—believing himself to be a victim of women's wiles, his obsessive devaluation of the feminine springs from his own sense of devaluation and impotence. Roy Davison in **'Pioneers'** has a similar fixation—'I've had women on me back all me married life'—though here the causes of obsession, in isolation and social dislocation, are more openly declared. The pioneer Davison is an anach-

ronistic type, cast aside by history. Having no place in the new order, he denies its existence by clinging to the old. The denial has turned him into a monster, sadistic, tyrannical, murderous. Morrison's obsessives attempt to fix the world to a single idea, but Davison has been consumed by the pioneering idea, fixed by it, and rendered inhuman.

Finally, in these and other stories, Morrison makes use of the Gothic mode to heighten the sense of disorder, placing ordinary details in a strange light, investing the scene with a bizarre intensity. In **'Morning Glory'** and **'North Wind'**, the two finest examples in this mode, a Gothic landscape becomes so charged with the characters' emotions that it seems the poison of their self-interest has deranged the very economy of nature. We usually think of Gothic as the preserve of the romantic writer, but one of the strengths of Australian realism has been its ability to reach out and find a use for the techniques of romanticism within its own domain.

Note

1. References to Morrison's work are identified here as follows: *ABC—Australian by Choice,* Adelaide, 1973; *CC—The Creeping City,* Hawthorn, 1972; *PC—Port of Call,* Melbourne, 1950; *SS—Selected Stories,* Adelaide, 1972; *NW—North Wind,* Ringwood, 1982; *SW—Stories of the Waterfront,* Ringwood, 1984.

Bibliographical Note

The statements by A. A. Phillips are from *The Australian Tradition,* Melbourne, 1958, p. 38 and 'The Short Stories of John Morrison', *Overland,* no. 58, 1974, pp. 31-5. Morrison's adoption of the outsider's point of view is discussed by Ian Reid in his introduction to Morrison's *Selected Stories,* pp. iii-iv.

John McLaren (essay date 1987)

SOURCE: McLaren, John. "Introduction." In *The Happy Warrior,* pp. 5-10. Fairfield, Australia: Pascoe Publishing Pty Ltd, 1987.

[*In the following essay, McLaren offers an overview of Morrison's short stories, discussing his interests, politics, techniques, influences, and thematic concerns.*]

John Morrison is a craftsman of words. Like one of his waterside workers building a wall of wheat bags, he lays every word with care for both its own weight and its place in the shape of the whole. Each story and essay attends to the details which construct a life and to the patterns of time and place he finds in the individual lives. As a craftsman, he has learned to give back to the people he has known and worked with the lives they themselves have built but have lost in the alienation of an industrial society. His writing is a part of the socialist creation to which he long ago dedicated his energies.

But while John Morrison is a socialist writer, he has never allowed the cause to dictate what he writes. He has gladly given his work to be published in union and political journals where it might be read by the people for whom he has written, but he has determined for himself what he will write, even at the cost of disagreement with his political colleagues. During the fifties, in correspondence with Frank Hardy, Morrison asserted his belief that only the communist movement stood between mankind and disaster, but at the same time argued that the party should 'leave the bloody writers alone,' and not dictate to them either their theme or their subject matter. In maintaining the right of the author to control his own product, he was in fact demonstrating a socialist ideal. He celebrates the lives of his workmates as he knows them and as they made them, not as any ideology would have them be.

Morrison's fundamental humanism places him in the tradition of British rather than European socialism. He speaks in **'Moving Waters'** of the dissenting atmosphere of North Britain which formed his ideals. These found fertile soil within the Australian labour movement, with its easy mateship and radical nationalist outlook. As this essay shows, however, the power of these ideals generate also contempt for those who, by greed or carelessness, destroy our capacity to live in harmony with both man and nature. He makes us realize the destruction of the North Sea beaches as a loss to us all. By contrast, the tributes he pays to his friend, Alan Marshall, show the kind of friendship which can enlarge the harmony and the people who share it. The clear waters of the North Sea that he recalls from youth and the friends he has enjoyed through life provide the standard by which he judges the world.

Many of Morrison's stories are told in the first person, either as an account of something that happened to the narrator, or as a story told to him by someone who figured in it. Even those that are not have an air of reportage about them. This can mislead the reader into thinking that the writer has merely written down what he has seen or been told, missing the art which the author has used to change fact into truth. The essays in this collection both show this art and make clear the sources from which Morrison has drawn its strength.

The essays are all written with the same craft which distinguishes Morrison's fiction, so that the slightest episode is polished until it reveals its true shape. For instance, the account of the rising of the Hattah Lakes,

The Big Drink, is pure record spiced with a plea for action, but it is also writing which allows us to share through our eyes and ears the hidden mysteries of the world about us.

Then again, many of the essays, particularly *How True Is That Story,* tell us of the origins of people and incidents which later found a place in the fiction. The accounts of these episodes reveal one truth in the pattern of the author's own life, and further truths about human behaviour in the patterns they combine to form in the fiction. Morrison traces these interweaving patterns in his account of the elements which came together in the story of *The Battle of the Flowers.* His discussion of how people and incidents grew into the shape of the story becomes a study in the nature of truth.

In this and other essays, Morrison gives us the privilege of sharing his craft. His *Author's Statement* written for *Australian Literary Studies,* explains his belief in the power of the short story, and in other places he discusses the importance of his own reading. But the main source of his work is reflection on the kind of episodes that come together in *The Battle of the Flowers.* In *The Big Drink* he talks about the way that memories combine to make fiction: they are the kind of things that do not usually stand up on their own, but which a writer treasures against the day they might give life and soul to a good story. In *English Is Good Enough,* he describes his efforts to learn the art of narrative, to overcome the intimidation of words and concentrate on the art of construction and selection which allows him to tell what he knows. In the whole collection, he demonstrates the art he describes, telling and retelling the stories which make his life.

I heard John Morrison speak about his writing many years ago in Wangaratta, when he and Alan Marshall were travelling together on one of their visits to the Murray Valley. Alan Marshall, who spoke first, said that he thought of life as a journey spent mainly in the swamps and valleys. But every now and then the journey takes you to a summit where you can see the whole countryside spread around you. Those moments are what he writes about. John Morrison several times in this book mentions Alan's idea of the special moment, but on that particular night he likened the writer to the man who comes across an interesting rock or stone and puts it in his pocket. For months, perhaps years, he carries it about, rolling it in his hands from time to time until it is polished. His stories, he said, were like these stones. The nuggets of his experience rolled around in his memory until they were polished into fiction. A major value of this book is that in its essays the author allows us to see the stones being gathered as well as polished.

Among the essays collected here we have a fragmentary autobiography of Morrison and a gallery of portraits of his friends and acquaintances. These include full studies of writers like Marshall, Judah Waten and Frank Dalby Davison, and sketches of characters like Joe the winchman (who was the original of Bo Abbott), of his early employers, and of the intimidating figures of his childhood. These recollections are shaped and rounded with the same skill that he shows in his fiction, which they complement rather than explain.

The greatest interest of the book is the portrait it gives us of Morrison himself. The autobiographical pieces are not particularly introspective, as from his earliest age he seems to have been interested in others rather than in the growth of his own consciousness. He recreates his childhood and youth with the slightly amused affection of the older man rather than through the eyes of the boy he then was. He tells us of his first kiss, but leaves us to infer his feelings from the little bit of doggerel he quotes from the time. He writes of his flights from home and the troubles they caused, and of the urge to venture which he got from the docks and seamen of Sunderland, but leaves us to guess at any deeper reasons that might have driven him around the world. He talks of his early wanderings about Australia, of the brief and innocent romance he found on a station and the events of his political education, but not directly of romance and politics. The essays include neither polemic or self-analysis. His stance towards himself is that of the detached, wry observer that he adopted for the narrator of so many of his stories.

But, for all the objectivity of his tone, a clear portrait of the writer emerges. The robust sense of egalitarian democracy, the sympathy for the vulnerable, and the anger at destruction and cruelty are what we might expect from the stories. But these prose pieces also reveal behind his apparent detachment a passionate identification with the world around him. In *The Big Drink,* he describes how Alan Marshall is so involved with the pelicans on the lake before him that he knows the moment they are about to go up in their soaring flight. Similarly, in *Singing Night Christmas,* he describes his friend holding his hands out to the songs of the birds and exclaiming that he can feel them on his skin. Morrison time and again shows this quality in himself. We see it in his description of the beaches around Sunderland, and in his absorption in the space and feel of Australia. He shows it in his feeling for the smell of dry eucalypt and moist bush mulch, in his love for the misty beauty of the Dandenongs, and in his observation of the flight of insects and the swifts who feed on them. He does not so much enter into the lives of others as allow them to enter into him, to shape their stories in his consciousness. The writer in these essays is not the romantic artist creating himself or the tyrant forcing the world into a shape of his choosing, but the craftsman who so gives himself to his materials that reveal their true shape. This is the ultimate generosity of both man and artist.

These qualities can all be seen in the essay *The Writer and the Swagman.* This is an account of the practical compassion Alan Marshall and his family extended to Albert, a destitute swagman whom Alan encountered on one of his journeys and later accommodated in a bush hut near Eltham. The narrative is perfectly shaped to lead us into an understanding both of Albert's lonely but eventually contented life and of the growth of his relationship with Alan. This relationship provides a frame through which we see also the little community of Eltham, the encroachments of the 'creeping city' which is converting it to another suburb—a common theme in his fiction. His account of the joint efforts to gain for Albert citizenship and a pension show the humanity which exists even in the tapebound recesses of bureaucracy. But underlying all this is Morrison's identification, not with Alan's charity, but with Albert's vulnerability. Albert comes, like the author, from the other side of the world, but unlike Morrison Australia has not given him the security of home and friends. The strength of Morrison's story comes from his recognition of this common need.

John Morrison remarks, in talking of Alan Marshall, that his books 'are concerned primarily with the only thing he loves more than his own country—the people who live in it.' The pieces in this book demonstrate that the same remark is true of Morrison himself.

John Morrison (essay date 1987)

SOURCE: Morrison, John. "John Morrison." In *The Happy Warrior,* pp. 137-41. Fairfield, Australia: Pascoe Publishing Pty Ltd, 1987.

[*In the following essay, Morrison explains why he is a short story writer and why other writers have chosen the form.*]

I think it's true to say that the majority of prose writers begin with the short story, but with dreams of ultimate success as novelists. To put it another way, inside and outside of the fraternity the short story has, by and large, been seen as the stepping-stone to the big time, the arena where newcomers to creative writing flex their literary muscles. Among writers themselves I doubt if the reasons for this are anything more subtle than the simple physical and economic facts of life. Not many beginners have the necessary stamina to stand up to the demands of a tale running to upwards of 70,000 words. The itch to write comes at an early age, and has of necessity to be indulged in whatever time can be spared from the pressures of study or the harsher immediate pressures of earning a living. With the short story the finishing line is in sight right from the beginning, and in a few days or weeks something is ready to offer in the market place. The sooner a young writer gets into print the better for his resolution, and the short story is usually the road in.

That brief preamble certainly applies to me, but is probably a fair generalisation. My two novels were both products of Commonwealth Literary Fund Fellowships; all the short stories were, let us say, written out of office hours. Perhaps if those novels had been substantially successful, giving me continued economic freedom, I may have gone on to others, but I doubt it. I knew by then exactly what was involved in tackling the novel: the strenuously sustained dedication, the endless road full of pitfalls and hurdles, the tight control needed for many characters and shifting scenes, time lapse and wordage in relation to action. And always the nagging fear that at the end it might all turn out to have been in vain. A fear which was not cancelled out by assurances from fellow-writers that a new novel of any reasonable promise was easier to place with a publisher than was a collection of stories, no matter how successful the latter may have been in their separate periodical runs. I was well into my forties when my own two novels were disposed of, full of experiences, of ideas, of reflections, all of which I wanted to embody in stories, and the long grind of two hundred thousand words had considerably developed my narrative skills. Short stories were almost frolics after such prolonged disciplines. I was back to the sprint, but with a difference. To sum up, my marriage to the short story was shot-gun, but I learned to love the bride, and have remained faithful.

In the short story so much can be said in so few words. Many would declare Balzac to be the greatest of all novelists, yet consider the terrific impact of his swiftly-told *El Verdugo,* in which a son is demanded in honour to execute his own family. Consider also *Two Friends,* Maupassant's sad little tragedy of the Franco-Prussian War of 1870: two uncomprehending French innocents going out for a day's fishing during the siege of Paris, and being taken and shot as spies. And Daudet's even more moving anecdote of the same war, *The Last Lesson* which tells, in only 3,000 words, of a whole community in ceded Alsace-Lorraine going along, children and adults all in their Sunday best, to a village school where an ageing teacher is to pronounce a benediction in and on a beloved language which is not likely ever to be taught there again. Anton Chekhov, holding the same high place in the short story as does Balzac in the

novel, gave himself plenty of room in his longer tales, but many of his most pungent pieces, such as *Woe, The Mask, Sergeant Pribisheyev,* were told in less than 3,000 words. And what of Australian Gavin Casey's thoughtful morsel, *The Thunderstorm* which, for me anyway, says more than his much longer and highly-rated *Short-Shift Saturday,* good as the latter also is. And Alan Marshall's hilarious story of his farting pony, *How I Met General Pau,* with its neatly integrated side-swipes at the tub-thumping pomposity of militarism.

From those chosen few of the really short masterpieces it's a far cry to the big fellows such as Maupassant's *Boule De Suif* and James Joyce's *The Dead,* but we're still in the accepted category of the short story. The dividing line between long short story and short novel cannot be other than arbitrary. *Boule De Suif* remains an anecdote, for all its far-ranging exploration of human nature. A single scene, and extending over only a few days, it has everything: lust of flesh and love of country, arrogance and humility, selfishness and generosity, cruelty and compassion. Yet, withal, a story which can be read just as an adventure, so packed with tension is the prolonged confrontation of the little Parisian prostitute and the Prussian officer. Weakness, like strength, can take many forms, and where will you find a more searching and sympathetic study of a struggle between love and jealousy than in James Joyce's highly elaborated and beautifully told *The Dead*? In the same length bracket there's Maxim Gorki's *Chelkash,* in which two men, a happy-go-lucky thief and a greedy convention-bound youth, isolated on a lonely beach, act out a powerful sermon on the curse of acquisitiveness. In wordage between these giants and those miniatures of Chekhov and Daudet lies a whole treasure-house of wonderful tales, such as Jack London's *The Apostate;* who can read it without a feeling of revulsion at the evils of child labour, and without a lift of the spirit when it comes to sharing the triumph of the little runaway?

I'm ready to agree that the greatest achievements in creative prose have been in the novel, but it's easy to hold a brief for the short story, for its power no less than for its entertainment value. Because I do take the stand that every writer worth his salt is moved, consciously or not, to do something more than just tell a diverting tale. Something of the inner self is always injected into it, something of abiding significance which has been picked up in his/her observations of the caperings, tragic and comic, of the human species. A cautious eye, however, needs always to be kept on this element lest it makes nonsense of the characters' motivations. In the short story everything must conform to plausibility, to dimension, to pace. Minor faults which would be missed in a novel will damn a short story.

The struggle is always for tidiness, for compactness, for brevity, and—no less than for the novelist—for a climax which, without the manipulated shock ending made fashionable by O. Henry, will, in the words of Katherine Susannah Prichard, leave the reader with a feeling of 'having passed through an emotional experience.'

Tolstoy's *Parables,* Balzac's *Droll Stories,* Boccacio's *Decameron, The Arabian Nights, Aesop's Fables,* the short story—sad, humorous, satirical, thrilling, illuminating, allegorical—has a long history, going right back to the primitives who, in their myths, also sought to explain as well as entertain.

To that history, hoary with age when the first novel was written, Australia has made its own distinctive contribution. A few years ago, in reviewing Frank Dalby Davison's novel *The White Thorntree,* I wrote that 'Australia has been a frontier country, a raw new world in which its writers found their material in Man's struggle to conquer and exist rather than in the subtleties of a settled and deeply rooted domesticated society.' In the last few decades that limitation has been widely breached. A new school of writers has increasingly come to grips with the ultimate business of Life, Man's struggle with himself instead of with his environment.

A few old-timers, including myself, have less trouble going along with changing attitudes than we have with changing narrative styles. There's a tendency to be preoccupied with odd-bods more than with the average man and woman, to lose the reader in a maze of imagery and symbolism, to mess about with spectacular word effects instead of taking the well-tried shortest possible route from one point to another. The overall picture, however, is promising enough. Pioneering/experimentation is as correct in literature as it is in other arts. No language ever does stand still, and as for subject matter, the best of our young writers are showing a healthy readiness to involve themselves in contemporary areas of social ferment: the loosening of traditional family relationships, the movement for the liberation of women, the consequences—unemployment among youth—of the frightening tide of technology, and the continuing influx of people from a wide range of cultures. The last is a specially rich field of human material which some newcomers themselves are ploughing with distinction.

Finally, there is the Literature Board of the Australia Council which, through supporting Grants, is doing much to encourage those who have, through periodicals and the many State and commercially funded competitions, demonstrated some claim to the joy of seeing their names on the spines of collections.

Strength to all their arms!

John McLaren (essay date May 2002)

SOURCE: McLaren, John. "The British Tradition in John Morrison's Radical Nationalism." *Australian Literary Studies* 20, no. 3 (May 2002): 215-24.

[*In the following essay, McLaren explores the English dissenting tradition as it informs Morrison's radical nationalist position in his adopted home.*]

Although historians have long known the importance of the British dissenting tradition in shaping Australian radicalism, it has been less considered by literary historians and critics. Peter Pierce (1988) characterises Australian literary history as a melodramatic assertion of Australia's distinctiveness that betrays its own fears that its distinctive system of values and allegiances is under threat from the source culture. Thirty years earlier, A. A. Phillips, in 'The Democratic Theme' (1958), had been intent on asserting the distinctiveness of Australian writing of the 1890s and later from its English and Australian British antecedents, and did not identify continuities.

John Morrison's work provides an exemplary case. The *Oxford Companion to Australian Literature* identifies his values as 'work, loyalty and self-discipline', but neither notes the tensions between loyalty and radicalism that run through his writing, nor relates it to other than its Australian context. David Carter (1988) relates his work to American radical contemporaries rather than Australian forebears, but does not mention the debt Morrison professed in particular to Joyce and Conrad (Morrison, *Australian by Choice* 171; *The Happy Warrior* 77-81). In a later essay, Phillips notes his indebtedness to north country dissent, but limits this influence to Morrison's insistence on the moral imperative of choice and his distrust of the corrupting power of possessions. Phillips finds a tension between his 'conformity' to old-fashioned Protestantism and his radicalism, which he sees as representing Morrison's liberation from the conformity of his childhood. Indyk explicitly disagrees with Phillips, placing Morrison firmly in the Australian radical tradition and its concern for moral issues. Loh (1987) likewise emphasizes Morrison's affinity for the Australian democratic tradition, and the sense of independence he welcomed when he first arrived in the country. On the contrary, I believe that Morrison's British dissenting background (it is revealing that Phillips uses the term 'conformism') produces the radicalism that he found a welcome for in his new country, an attitude to work that gives his fiction its distinctive quality, and gives a unity to his stories of the communal environment of the waterfront and of the more isolated work of gardening.

Morrison is properly recognised as a chronicler of the Australian working class, particularly of the waterfront and its ideals of mateship, and as a sensitive and appreciative observer of the Australian landscape. His narrative voice is that of a radical and a nationalist. His story **'The Incense Burner'** (***Black Cargo*** 99-114), fixes the scent of eucalyptus indelibly as an image of both home and absence. His earlier stories tell of the migrant coming to know Australia, and his later ones, based on his work as a jobbing gardener, give a worker's perspective on middle-class gentility and a caring account of the shaping of Australia's urban environment to meet human expectations. But these perspectives, while telling us about Morrison, ignore the depth of his roots in his family and the northern English working-class and dissenting tradition from which they came.

In **'The Moving Waters'** (in ***Australian by Choice***), Morrison talks of his religious origins.

> Ours was a strict Presbyterian home, with Father and Mother both Sunday-school teachers, and chapel again for the whole family every Sunday night. Nights which were horrors of boredom, and which no doubt laid firm foundations for my ultimate agnosticism.

Against these horrors of the church he sets the delights of nature, and particularly of the sea and seashore.

> . . . only rain or snow then kept us away from the beach. Soon after breakfast the dispensable five of us . . . would troop off . . .
>
> Winter and summer each had its own special attractions, as had low-tide and high-tide. . . . To my childish eyes the yellow sands were immense. Often we had it all to ourselves except for the screeching seagulls, and perhaps a stray dog whose excited barking echoed against the towering face of the columned and laminated cliffs. Father, a beach-rat himself, entered wholeheartedly into our games. We ran races, played leapfrog, constructed intricate irrigation systems in the firm wet sand. Sand which was sometimes rippled, sometimes, after a storm, strewn with straps of leathery kelp, but more often as smooth and unblemished as a vast sheet of pale brown paper.
>
> (89-96)

This passage is in part a characteristic of autobiography, the recall of a childhood Eden which in this case serves to emphasise the rhetorical point of the story—the subsequent destruction of this place of nature, and the global threat to the environment. But I want to draw attention to its significance in Morrison's personal formation. First, he presents the time at the beach as the alternative to the gloomy religion of his parents. Second, the passage celebrates not only nature, but the social joys he finds in nature. The young John Morrison and his companions do not merely contemplate the beauty of the scene, they actively interrupt it with their boisterous games and then learn to master it. 'Under father's watchful eye,' he continues, 'I also became a fairly good rough-water swimmer. "Broken water" he called it . . . in which he revelled' (92).

This essay contains two elements that persist through the writing drawn from his adult experiences. The first is the admiration for human mastery of nature, demonstrated here in his father's swimming, and persistently in the stories through the writer's delight in the skills of the wharfie, the gardener and the craftsman. The second is the delight in the harmony of human beings and nature, which heightens the tragedy of a story like **'The Night Shift'**, where this harmony is shattered by an avoidable death (***Sailors Belong Ships*** 19-28). The key to Morrison's politics is his disgust at the way human avarice destroys natural and social harmony, and so prevents individuals achieving full growth and recognition.

More generally, his politics arise from the convergence between his family's social background and his parents' specific beliefs and characters. Although both were committed Christians, neither religion nor politics was much discussed within the home. According to John's brother Alec, their mother would not have been interested, and their father was, if anything, Liberal. But he had a strong commitment both to his work and to the community. A foreman in the engineering branch of the Post Office, he worked mainly outdoors, and was gone before the family got up for breakfast. At night, he would spread out his worksheets on the kitchen table as he calculated the wages due. John, and later Alec, had the job of delivering these sheets to the Central Post Office.[1]

Alec said that the children's politics were determined by the conditions of their upbringing. The working classes lived in poor and overcrowded housing, lacking adequate food and fresh air, and tuberculosis was a constant presence. John and Alec received four years of elementary schooling, and when their school was taken over by the army during the war, they attended a neighbouring school for only half of each day. Although their father was fortunate to be in full-time employment, their parents were hard pressed to look after the youngest brother, Ronnie, who had only one leg. They had to find £40 plus insurance to buy him an artificial leg. Yet at the time of the Jarrow marches, when unemployment and misery were at their height, their father organised a life-saving club at Hendon as a form of community activity.

Both John and Alec testify to their father's importance in their lives. Their mother seems to have been heavily burdened with family duties and looking after an invalid son. But father was both a war hero and a hero to his family: he had during the Great War received a decoration from the French government for swimming out with a life-line to the crew of a sailing ship wrecked one night in a great storm (***Australian by Choice*** 92). On peace-time Sundays, while their mother cooked the roast dinner, he would take the family swimming near Grangetown. John describes the occasions.

. . . he had gathered around him a group of young men who idolised him, and who shared a common ambition to go out as far as he did. I recollect only one who ever did. Often we'd lose sight altogether of his bobbing dark head in the waste of tossing white-caps, and there would be rivalry amongst us as to who would be the first to glimpse him coming in. We could lose him for upwards of an hour, but were never touched by the anxiety of spectators . . . Father was Father, the best swimmer in the world, and more than a match for anything the sea could turn on.

(92-93)

John Morrison's parents were, in his words, 'both Presbyterian missioners, fanatical temperance evangelists', who around his tenth year 'waged a long struggle to save two once-wealthy people who came to live next door to us' (158). Morrison explains that this experience enabled him to understand what was happening in a household where he was engaged as a gardener in Australia many years later. This episode in turn gave him both the 'bibulous spouse' who appears in *Port of Call* and the caring housekeeper of 'To Margaret' (*Twenty-Three* 56-60). The notion of temperance, although not of abstention, remains a continuing theme in his life and work: he himself was a social drinker, who until nearly the end of his life enjoyed his beer and whisky. But, although in 'The Drunk' (*Twenty-Three* 137-46) he had described approvingly the way wharfies covered for a drunken mate in defiance of union discipline, he generally disapproved of excess. While this story endorses the loyalty of the men to each other, it recognises the conflicting ethical issues and disapproves of the behaviour of the man who causes the problem: '. . . a hundred men have stopped work not just because one man has come back drunk from lunch hour, but because of a sense of loyalty developed by legitimate struggle to a point where it has become an end in itself.' The two values of solidarity and work have come into conflict, not in this case because of the greed of the bosses, but because of the weakness of one individual. We can see in Morrison's story both the staunch morality and the compassion of his parents.

Morrison was equally moralistic in his attitudes to his own family, expressing to Stephen Murray-Smith at one stage his fears that his son was too convivial: 'The trouble—between ourselves, Stephen—is that he's too damn fond of parties, and has given me a lot of anxiety in the last year or two . . . maybe I'll let a bit of light on things when I see you next. John's misfortune is that he has inherited too many of my weaknesses and not enough of my disciplines.'[2] The emphasis on discipline again runs through his stories, which celebrate both the inherent discipline of work and the derived discipline of workmates, particularly in the solidarity of their unions. While he shares with his contemporary working-class

writer and comrade, Frank Hardy, an intense distrust of the bosses, individually and as a class, his writing almost totally lacks the larrikin sense of anarchic rebellion we find in Hardy's work.

At first reading, the story **'The Sleeping Doll'** (*Black Cargo* 52-70) seems an exception. In this story he tells of an almost totally unredeemable character whose laziness and self-absorption disrupt the smooth working of station life. Eventually, the man known as 'the Sleeping Doll' drives his boss to such fury that he is paid off there and then. However, while the boss hurries out to deal with an emergency on an outstation, he leaves the Doll with the last task of butchering the sheep for the station rations. But instead of killing the two sheep needed, the Doll interprets the boss's words literally and efficiently kills the entire flock. He leaves promptly the moment his time is up, leaving the neat carcasses and the mess for others to clean up. 'He said to keep going to five,' he explains. The narrator shakes his hand as he leaves: 'His clasp was unexpectedly hearty. Next to nothing had passed between us, but he knew very well he had my sympathy.' The story concludes as 'His short figure assumed heroic proportions as it melted into the darkness.' The narrator's admiration for the Doll's skill as a butcher, and the ingenuity with which he has turned the boss's hasty words, uttered in rage, against him, overcomes the strong distaste he has shown for him through the rest of the story. As author, Morrison for once has allowed his belief in loyalty to workmates, the issue behind the conflicts in **'The Drunk'**, to override his hostility to pointless indiscipline.

Yet the ending of the story sits uneasily with its body, which is an unequivocal condemnation of a man who contributes absolutely nothing, and who seems to value nothing, not even himself. Although Morrison heard the story first from a boundary rider he met, the character of the 'Doll' was based on 'a soporific swagman who fitted the part like a glove' and who 'dumped himself in my hut on Wainui Station in Western Victoria'. Morrison writes that this man had a 'genius for sleep' and 'a poisoned tongue'. The butcher's skill attributed to him in the last part of **'The Sleeping Doll'** seems inappropriate—it is as if the author has attributed this story to the wrong person. Morrison seems to have had this feeling himself. In a conversation towards the end of his life, he indicated that he himself was not happy with the ending: 'the ending is a shame on me—that man was a complete bastard and I made him out a hero—I don't know what made me do it—I allowed my political prejudices to get the better of me.'[3]

These qualities of Morrison's writing—the attention to the details of the actual work and its conditions, the emphasis on duty and loyalty to the job, although not necessarily to the boss, and the pride in workmanship—are quite distinctive in the Australian realist tradition. Lawson, for example, describes Australian workplaces, both urban and rural, and writes of men and women at work, but his emphasis falls on the way they endure their harsh conditions. Katharine Susannah Prichard admires the skills of timbermen, horsemen and miners, but she writes as an observer of the way they work rather than as someone who is inside with the work itself. Frank Hardy, Donald Stuart and Dorothy Hewett have all written about people at work, but again their interest is in the conditions of work rather than in the work itself. Among recent writers, Richard Flanagan has written most movingly of craftsmanship, but his character pursues his craft as a way of escaping from the conditions of his work rather than as work itself. Morrison not only describes the skills of the workmen, but lovingly crafts his stories from their idiom—the vernacular banter between them, the precise terms of their trades: winch and hawsehole; beams and hatch boards; combs, cutters and press. Morrison alone derives his politics—as well as his vocabulary—from the centrality of work in defining and fulfilling the worker. This, I would suggest, has its origins in a British, specifically Scottish, Presbyterian tradition that saw work as itself redemptive within a general framework of personal discipline and service to the community.

The tragedy of **'Battle of the Flowers'** (*Black Cargo* 115-48) arises when the work, of the sisters and of the gardener, is separated from its proper ends and turned in on itself. The role of the sisters in this story, however, represents a major element in the tradition from which he wrote. Their obsession with the garden is an outlet for what he refers to in **'The Blind Man's Story'** as 'the compassion that is in all women', and a source for their 'need of love and admiration and soothing' (*Australian by Choice* 51, 69). Denied an object for their instincts in the form of husband and children, they turn in on themselves, joined in a 'frigid harmony of mutual selfishness'. In *Australian by Choice*, Morrison tells us that this was an accurate description of the real-life models who had provided the source of his story (152). The sisters become part of that company of monsters and hags who appear regularly in his work—Miss Taft, the drunken Mrs Pye on 'Kulpinka' station, the stubborn mother-in-law of **'North Wind'**, the manipulatively tyrannical wife of **'The Blind Man's Story'**. Even Susan, Jim's love in *Port of Call*, casts a blight on his ambitions by her own determination to find independence.

Despite his clear distinction between men's and women's roles, Morrison shows as little sympathy for domestic tyrants, male or female, as he does for tyrannical bosses. His first novel, *The Creeping City*, opens with the picture of a man destroying his wife and children because he will not listen to them. *Port of Call* provides a bleak picture of men who are unable either to talk to their wives or to trust them, but the perspective remains stubbornly male. The location of Jim Boyd's ambitions may be in the bush rather than the city, but the ideal behind them remains the pattern that Morrison recalled from his own childhood, where the mother remained at home cooking the Sunday dinner while the father took his boys swimming. The measure of Jim's amatory failure is given by the glimpse we are afforded of Bo Abbott's domestic harmony, but Bo achieves this by letting his wife run the home while he solves the problems of work. Bo lets his wife organise him, but she allows him to be himself. 'And see youse put on old pants before you go', she admonishes him before they set off on their rabbiting excursion. 'I don't know what for they take the ferrets with them. Bo always finishes up crawling into the holes himself.' But the narrator adds that, 'For all her rough and ready ways, Mrs. Abbott kept a spick and span home' (199). When Jim, defeated, returns to his ship and leaves Melbourne, it is his memory of Mrs Abbott that offers him hope for his future. When, in a story like **'Pioneers'**, Morrison writes sympathetically of a woman dominated by a brutal husband, he locates the source of her tragedy in the husband's denial of her proper maternal and domestic role.

Women's performance of this domestic role is necessary if men are to fulfil their part as workers: the world of work depends on harmony at home. The picture of male solidarity in **'Nine O'Clock Finish'** is completed by the two old winchmen swapping gardening hints, bringing their domestic sphere into harmony with their world of work. But in **'A Man's World'** the two sets of values come into conflict, as the husband's honour and his loyalty to his mates prevent him keeping the lottery winnings they need literally to keep themselves in a house. Thus, women need to know their limitations as well as their duties. In **'This Freedom'**, **'The Blind Man's Story'** and **'The Busting of Rory O'Mahony'**, Morrison shows women whose passion for order makes their homes, in their men's eyes, into prisons. Their choice is either escape, like Rory, or surrender, like the blind man. In the autobiographical essay **'Escape'**, he claims that he first discovered this pattern in the lives of his own parents: his father, feeling that his wife had ceased to make the home 'a place where he could relax and recuperate', sought a brief escape in France. His mother, like the wife in **'Blind Man's Story'**, greeted her husband's eventual return 'with the smug smile of one nursing a secret joy'. In **'Escape'**, Morrison explains how his own father had once done something which, 'shrewdly exploited, would put him in the wrong with the neighbours' (*Happy Warrior* 151). It is easy in retrospect to see that Morrison's women seek such satisfaction in domestic power because they are denied any wider role. The judgement of his narrators, however, is clearly that they become domestic tyrants because they overstep their ordained role. Men must be at home in both spheres; women have only the domestic. This again is a legacy of Biblical Calvinism.

Without women, the men in his stories are as lonely and lost as the two sisters in **'The Battle of the Flowers'**. Bo Abbott's wife gives him the strength he needs as an active and outspoken unionist. Unlike his wharfies, the sailors on his ships and the bush workers in their station quarters are incomplete, trying to find in mateship a substitute for domestic fulfilment. They have a pride in their joint effort, in being part of a working unit, which Jim, in *Port of Call,* feels excluded from when he is on the house staff at 'Kulpinka': 'He wasn't a part of it, as the other men were, and as a sailor is part of the essential mechanism of a ship' (114). But being part of a whole is not enough. Jim tries to explain the sailor's predicament to Susan:

> You got anything from six to twenty mates, and you live with them all day and all night, every day and every night. . . . Ashore, when a feller finishes work he snaps right out of it. He goes home; he's got a wife and maybe kids. He gets in with other guys that have got different jobs and don't talk about one thing all the time. He can dress and go out. . . . Folks don't make up with sailors; they don't get time. . . . Now you see why it is sailors get drunk the minute they go ashore?

> (83-84)

Yet he later comes to realise, as he contemplates the sad figure of the station owner's alcoholic wife, that this loneliness is shared by all those who have not learned to integrate work and domestic life: 'for the first time he had come forward to take a closer look at the awful gulf he had imagined between sailors and the rest of humanity' (121). This is a purely Calvinist perception of the individual need for integration in the whole and the individual pride and stubbornness—his parents would have said sinfulness—that prevents it.

Yet, while Morrison brought these values—pride in work, male solidarity, female compassion and support, hatred of any tyranny—with him from England, his writing is thoroughly Australian in place and sentiment. He enjoyed the Australian expressions of British values, and the irreverence to authority that was at the heart of the creed of mateship that otherwise was at one with British working-class solidarity. His attachment to the bush as a place of beauty and nurture is evident both in his prose essays and in his two novels. Perhaps the best-known expression of this sentiment is in the story

already mentioned, **'The Incense Burner'**, about the old digger trapped in London who each month receives with a parcel of comforts a package of gum leaves that he takes off to the privacy of his room to soothe his cough. The story is framed with experiences of destitution that make Australia, by contrast, seem a promised land (*Black Cargo* 99-114).

But Morrison's experience of working there as an itinerant labourer ensured that his image of the bush was by no means romantic. Like Lawson, he knew too well the blight inflicted by poverty on hope. In **'Beyond the Picture'**, an apprentice work, published in *The Communist Review* in 1939 under the pseudonym 'Gordon', the narrator tells the reader of a portrait entitled **'The Cocky'**: 'An arresting picture . . . it was Australian to the very last stroke of the brush. Looking at it, one could almost smell burning gum leaves and hear the tinkle of magpies. Yet there was really little to it after all. Just a solitary horseman gazing out over a typical western Victorian landscape.' But he fills out the picture's emptiness with the catalogue's fulsome description of it as capturing the 'evasive, other-world spirit of Australia' and 'the virile unflinching spirit of its people'. Finally, however, he turns the story around by introducing the subject of the painting, a man defeated by hardship, poverty and the Closer Settlement Board. The story's concluding line, 'The free, independent spirit of our country', is undermined by the bush experience, locking into harsh irony the potential of a free people and their actual bondage. Even in this early work the outsider's romantic view is tempered by the insider's knowledge. Both the hope and the clarity come from that early experience of British working-class life where poverty was endured without allowing it either to extinguish idealism or to yield to sentimental illusion.

As the title of his autobiographical writings suggests, John Morrison fitted easily into Australia. Towards the end of his life, he asked me to visit him to record a message he wanted to leave the Australian people. Above all, he wanted to record his gratitude to Australia for the way it had supported and recognised him, through his membership of the Order of Australia, his pension from the Commonwealth Literary Fund, later the Australia Council, and the warmth with which his work had been received by readers and, above all, friends and fellow workers. He also wished to apologise because, despite his pension, he had not been able to write much in his later years. This, he said, was because he no longer mixed with the workers whose tales and language gave him his stories.[4]

He was above all a proud Australian, who, as he declares in **'English Is Good Enough'** placed his own writing in the tradition of Lawson (*Australian by Choice*

165-75). Yet, although he returned only twice, he retained his contacts with England. The strength of the reception of his writing in Australia as contributing to the tradition of radical nationalism in which he wrote shows, I believe, that this tradition, like the Labor movement to which it was allied, owed much to British working-class Protestantism and its sense of duty, solidarity, and egalitarianism. This is the spirit expressed in the concluding words to the story **'Black Cargo'**, when the workers have, after lengthy debate, successfully banned a ship crewed in defiance of union conditions:

> Coming into the cool night air a few minutes later, it seemed to him that it wasn't a deeper darkness that had settled over a befouled ship lying in the river—it was a light. A light that lit up not only the *Canadian Hector,* but all ships lying in all the rivers of the world, and all struggling, divided, tormented humanity. And the wide straight road to victory for those who had the faith and courage to tread it.
>
> (***Black Cargo*** 260)

The hard experience of work and struggle leads him to this deeply humanist vision of the potential he finds both in flawed men and women, and in the natural world they inhabit.

Notes

1. Information about the family is based on an interview with John's brother Alec by John and Shirley McLaren, at Haverhill, The Green, Catsfield, Battle, Sussex, 28.3.90, and with his niece, Ruth Greaves, by John McLaren, at Fulwell, Sunderland, 25.8.00. Notes of these interviews are held by the author.

2. Stephen Murray Smith papers, SLV ms 8727, Box 188/3-1, John Morrison to Stephen Murray-Smith, 5.1.58.

3. Notes of phone conversation between John Morrison and John McLaren, 16.7.95. Notes in possession of author.

4. The tape of this interview has been lodged with the Melbourne University archives.

Works Cited

WORKS BY JOHN MORRISON:

Sailors Belong Ships. Foreword by Frank Dalby Davison. Kensington, Vic.: Dolphin, 1947.

The Creeping City. Melbourne: Cassell, 1949.

Port of Call. Melbourne: Cassell, 1950.

Black Cargo and Other Stories. Melbourne: Australasian Book Society, 1955.

The Judge and the Shipowner. Melbourne: Australasian Book Society, 1955[?].

Twenty-Three. Sydney: Australasian Book Society, 1962.

John Morrison: Selected Stories. Adelaide: Rigby, 1972.

Australian by Choice. Adelaide: Rigby, 1973.

North Wind. Introduction by Stephen Murray-Smith. Ringwood, Vic.: Penguin, 1982.

Stories of the Waterfront. Introduction by the Author. Ringwood, Vic.: Penguin, 1984.

This Freedom. Ringwood, Vic.: Penguin, 1985.

The Best Stories of John Morrison. Introduction by Stephen Murray-Smith. Ringwood, Vic.: Penguin, 1988.

The Happy Warrior. Introduction by John McLaren. Fairfield, Vic.: Pascoe, 1987.

UNDER PSEUDONYM 'GORDON':

'Beyond the Picture.' *Communist Review* February 1939: 90-92.

As far as I know, the stories by 'Gordon' that appeared in this journal between 1939 and 1940 have not previously been attributed to Morrison, although Carter refers to his publishing work in radical magazines in the 1930s and 1940s. According to Alec Morrison, John was generally known in the family as Gordon, his middle name. He took care to include photocopies of all these stories among the papers he left to his son John. These have now been deposited in the University of Melbourne archives, but are yet to be listed.

OTHER WORKS CITED:

Carter, David. 'Documenting and Criticising Society.' *The Penguin New Literary History of Australia.* Ed. Laurie Hergenhan. Ringwood, Vic.: Penguin, 1988. 370-89, esp. 372-73.

Indyk, Ivor. 'The Economics of Realism.' *Meanjin* 46.4 (1987): 502-12.

Loh, Morag. 'John Morrison: Writers at Work.' *Meanjin* 46.4 (1987): 496-501.

Phillips, A. A. 'The Democratic Tradition.' *The Australian Tradition.* Melbourne: Cheshire, 1958. 35-57.

———. 'The Short Stories of John Morrison.' *Overland* 58 (1974): 31-35.

Pierce, Peter. 'Forms of Australian Literary History.' *The Penguin New Literary History of Australia.* Ed. Laurie Hergenhan. Ringwood, Vic.: Penguin, 1988. 82-87.

Wilde, William H. et al. *The Oxford Companion to Australian Literature.* 2nd ed. Melbourne: Oxford UP, 1994.

FURTHER READING

Criticism

Loh, Morag. "John Morrison: Writer at Work." *Meanjin* 46, no. 4 (December 1987): 496-501.

Surveys Morrison's career as a writer, focusing on his places of work as sources for his stories.

Reid, Ian. "Introduction." In *Selected Stories,* pp. i-vii. Sydney, Australia: Rigby, 1972.

Considers why Morrison favored the short story as a genre.

Roberts, Bev. "Writing about Reality: John Morrison, Amanda Lohrey, Conal Fitzpatrick." *Meanjin* 43, no. 3 (September 1984): 408-13.

Uses the theme of work to compare the writings of Morrison with those of two other Australian authors.

Additional coverage of Morrison's life and career is contained in the following sources published by Thomson Gale: *Contemporary Authors,* **Vol. 103;** *Contemporary Authors New Revision Series,* **Vol. 92;** *Dictionary of Literary Biography,* **Vol. 260; and** *Literature Resource Center.*

How to Use This Index

The main references

Calvino, Italo
1923-1985 .... CLC **5, 8, 11, 22, 33, 39,**
73; SSC 3, 48

---

list all author entries in the following Thomson Gale Literary Criticism series:

AAL = Asian American Literature
BG = The Beat Generation: A Gale Critical Companion
BLC = Black Literature Criticism
BLCS = Black Literature Criticism Supplement
CLC = Contemporary Literary Criticism
CLR = Children's Literature Review
CMLC = Classical and Medieval Literature Criticism
DC = Drama Criticism
FL = Feminism in Literature: A Gale Critical Companion
GL = Gothic Literature: A Gale Critical Companion
HLC = Hispanic Literature Criticism
HLCS = Hispanic Literature Criticism Supplement
HR = Harlem Renaissance: A Gale Critical Companion
LC = Literature Criticism from 1400 to 1800
NCLC = Nineteenth-Century Literature Criticism
NNAL = Native North American Literature
PC = Poetry Criticism
SSC = Short Story Criticism
TCLC = Twentieth-Century Literary Criticism
WLC = World Literature Criticism, 1500 to the Present
WLCS = World Literature Criticism Supplement

The cross-references

See also CA 85-88, 116; CANR 23, 61;
DAM NOV; DLB 196; EW 13; MTCW 1, 2;
RGSF 2; RGWL 2; SFW 4; SSFS 12

---

list all author entries in the following Thomson Gale biographical and literary sources:

AAYA = Authors & Artists for Young Adults
AFAW = African American Writers
AFW = African Writers
AITN = Authors in the News
AMW = American Writers
AMWR = American Writers Retrospective Supplement
AMWS = American Writers Supplement
ANW = American Nature Writers
AW = Ancient Writers
BEST = Bestsellers
BPFB = Beacham's Encyclopedia of Popular Fiction: Biography and Resources
BRW = British Writers
BRWS = British Writers Supplement
BW = Black Writers
BYA = Beacham's Guide to Literature for Young Adults
CA = Contemporary Authors
CAAS = Contemporary Authors Autobiography Series
CABS = Contemporary Authors Bibliographical Series
CAD = Contemporary American Dramatists
CANR = Contemporary Authors New Revision Series
CAP = Contemporary Authors Permanent Series
CBD = Contemporary British Dramatists
CCA = Contemporary Canadian Authors
CD = Contemporary Dramatists
CDALB = Concise Dictionary of American Literary Biography

CDALBS = Concise Dictionary of American Literary Biography Supplement
CDBLB = Concise Dictionary of British Literary Biography
CMW = St. James Guide to Crime & Mystery Writers
CN = Contemporary Novelists
CP = Contemporary Poets
CPW = Contemporary Popular Writers
CSW = Contemporary Southern Writers
CWD = Contemporary Women Dramatists
CWP = Contemporary Women Poets
CWRI = St. James Guide to Children's Writers
CWW = Contemporary World Writers
DA = DISCovering Authors
DA3 = DISCovering Authors 3.0
DAB = DISCovering Authors: British Edition
DAC = DISCovering Authors: Canadian Edition
DAM = DISCovering Authors: Modules
   DRAM: Dramatists Module; **MST:** Most-studied Authors Module;
   MULT: Multicultural Authors Module; **NOV:** Novelists Module;
   POET: Poets Module; **POP:** Popular Fiction and Genre Authors Module
DFS = Drama for Students
DLB = Dictionary of Literary Biography
DLBD = Dictionary of Literary Biography Documentary Series
DLBY = Dictionary of Literary Biography Yearbook
DNFS = Literature of Developing Nations for Students
EFS = Epics for Students
EXPN = Exploring Novels
EXPP = Exploring Poetry
EXPS = Exploring Short Stories
EW = European Writers
FANT = St. James Guide to Fantasy Writers
FW = Feminist Writers
GFL = Guide to French Literature, Beginnings to 1789, 1798 to the Present
GLL = Gay and Lesbian Literature
HGG = St. James Guide to Horror, Ghost & Gothic Writers
HW = Hispanic Writers
IDFW = International Dictionary of Films and Filmmakers: Writers and Production Artists
IDTP = International Dictionary of Theatre: Playwrights
LAIT = Literature and Its Times
LAW = Latin American Writers
JRDA = Junior DISCovering Authors
MAICYA = Major Authors and Illustrators for Children and Young Adults
MAICYAS = Major Authors and Illustrators for Children and Young Adults Supplement
MAWW = Modern American Women Writers
MJW = Modern Japanese Writers
MTCW = Major 20th-Century Writers
NCFS = Nonfiction Classics for Students
NFS = Novels for Students
PAB = Poets: American and British
PFS = Poetry for Students
RGAL = Reference Guide to American Literature
RGEL = Reference Guide to English Literature
RGSF = Reference Guide to Short Fiction
RGWL = Reference Guide to World Literature
RHW = Twentieth-Century Romance and Historical Writers
SAAS = Something about the Author Autobiography Series
SATA = Something about the Author
SFW = St. James Guide to Science Fiction Writers
SSFS = Short Stories for Students
TCWW = Twentieth-Century Western Writers
WLIT = World Literature and Its Times
WP = World Poets
YABC = Yesterday's Authors of Books for Children
YAW = St. James Guide to Young Adult Writers

Literary Criticism Series
Cumulative Author Index

Alexie, Sherman (Joseph, Jr.)
1966- .... **CLC 96, 154; NNAL; PC 53**
See also AAYA 28; BYA 15; CA 138;
CANR 65, 95, 133; CN 7; DA3; DAM
MULT; DLB 175, 206, 278; LATS 1:2;
MTCW 2; MTFW 2005; NFS 17; SSFS
18

al-Farabi 870(?)-950 .... **CMLC 58**
See also DLB 115

Alfau, Felipe 1902-1999 .... **CLC 66**
See also CA 137

Alfieri, Vittorio 1749-1803 .... **NCLC 101**
See also EW 4; RGWL 2, 3; WLIT 7

Alfonso X 1221-1284 .... **CMLC 78**

Alfred, Jean Gaston
See Ponge, Francis

Alger, Horatio, Jr. 1832-1899 .... **NCLC 8, 83**
See also CLR 87; DLB 42; LAIT 2; RGAL
4; SATA 16; TUS

Al-Ghazali, Muhammad ibn Muhammad
1058-1111 .... **CMLC 50**
See also DLB 115

Algren, Nelson 1909-1981 ..... **CLC 4, 10, 33;
SSC 33**
See also AMWS 9; BPFB 1; CA 13-16R;
103; CANR 20, 61; CDALB 1941-1968;
CN 1, 2; DLB 9; DLBY 1981, 1982,
2000; EWL 3; MAL 5; MTCW 1, 2;
MTFW 2005; RGAL 4; RGSF 2

**al-Hariri, al-Qasim ibn 'Ali Abu
Muhammad al-Basri**
1054-1122 .... **CMLC 63**
See also RGWL 3

Ali, Ahmed 1908-1998 .... **CLC 69**
See also CA 25-28R; CANR 15, 34; CN 1,
2, 3, 4, 5; DLB 323; EWL 3

Ali, Tariq 1943- .... **CLC 173**
See also CA 25-28R; CANR 10, 99

Alighieri, Dante
See Dante
See also WLIT 7

al-Kindi, Abu Yusuf Ya'qub ibn Ishaq c.
801-c. 873 .... **CMLC 80**

Allan, John B.
See Westlake, Donald E(dwin)

Allan, Sidney
See Hartmann, Sadakichi

Allan, Sydney
See Hartmann, Sadakichi

Allard, Janet .... **CLC 59**

Allen, Edward 1948- .... **CLC 59**

Allen, Fred 1894-1956 .... **TCLC 87**

Allen, Paula Gunn 1939- .... **CLC 84, 202;
NNAL**
See also AMWS 4; CA 112; 143; CANR
63, 130; CWP; DA3; DAM MULT; DLB
175; FW; MTCW 2; MTFW 2005; RGAL
4; TCWW 2

Allen, Roland
See Ayckbourn, Alan

Allen, Sarah A.
See Hopkins, Pauline Elizabeth

Allen, Sidney H.
See Hartmann, Sadakichi

Allen, Woody 1935- .... **CLC 16, 52, 195**
See also AAYA 10, 51; AMWS 15; CA 33-
36R; CANR 27, 38, 63, 128; DAM POP;
DLB 44; MTCW 1; SSFS 21

Allende, Isabel 1942- ... **CLC 39, 57, 97, 170;
HLC 1; SSC 65; WLCS**
See also AAYA 18, 70; CA 125; 130; CANR
51, 74, 129; CDWLB 3; CLR 99; CWW
2; DA3; DAM MULT, NOV; DLB 145;
DNFS 1; EWL 3; FL 1:5; FW; HW 1, 2;
INT CA-130; LAIT 5; LAWS 1; LMFS 2;
MTCW 1, 2; MTFW 2005; NCFS 1; NFS
6, 18; RGSF 2; RGWL 3; SATA 163;
SSFS 11, 16; WLIT 1

Alleyn, Ellen
See Rossetti, Christina

Alleyne, Carla D. .... **CLC 65**

Allingham, Margery (Louise)
1904-1966 .... **CLC 19**
See also CA 5-8R; 25-28R; CANR 4, 58;
CMW 4; DLB 77; MSW; MTCW 1, 2

Allingham, William 1824-1889 ...... **NCLC 25**
See also DLB 35; RGEL 2

Allison, Dorothy E. 1949- .... **CLC 78, 153**
See also AAYA 53; CA 140; CANR 66, 107;
CN 7; CSW; DA3; FW; MTCW 2; MTFW
2005; NFS 11; RGAL 4

Alloula, Malek .... **CLC 65**

Allston, Washington 1779-1843 .... **NCLC 2**
See also DLB 1, 235

Almedingen, E. M. .... **CLC 12**
See Almedingen, Martha Edith von
See also SATA 3

Almedingen, Martha Edith von 1898-1971
See Almedingen, E. M.
See also CA 1-4R; CANR 1

Almodovar, Pedro 1949(?)- .... **CLC 114;
HLCS 1**
See also CA 133; CANR 72, 151; HW 2

Almqvist, Carl Jonas Love
1793-1866 .... **NCLC 42**

**al-Mutanabbi, Ahmad ibn al-Husayn Abu
al-Tayyib al-Jufi al-Kindi**
915-965 .... **CMLC 66**
See Mutanabbi, Al-
See also RGWL 3

Alonso, Damaso 1898-1990 .... **CLC 14**
See also CA 110; 131; 130; CANR 72; DLB
108; EWL 3; HW 1, 2

Alov
See Gogol, Nikolai (Vasilyevich)

al'Sadaawi, Nawal
See El Saadawi, Nawal
See also FW

al-Shaykh, Hanan 1945- .... **CLC 218**
See Shaykh, al- Hanan
See also CA 135; CANR 111; WLIT 6

Al Siddik
See Rolfe, Frederick (William Serafino Aus-
tin Lewis Mary)
See also GLL 1; RGEL 2

Alta 1942- .... **CLC 19**
See also CA 57-60

Alter, Robert B(ernard) 1935- .... **CLC 34**
See also CA 49-52; CANR 1, 47, 100

Alther, Lisa 1944- .... **CLC 7, 41**
See also BPFB 1; CA 65-68; CAAS 30;
CANR 12, 30, 51; CN 4, 5, 6, 7; CSW;
GLL 2; MTCW 1

Althusser, L.
See Althusser, Louis

Althusser, Louis 1918-1990 .... **CLC 106**
See also CA 131; 132; CANR 102; DLB
242

Altman, Robert 1925- .... **CLC 16, 116**
See also CA 73-76; CANR 43

Alurista .... **HLCS 1; PC 34**
See Urista (Heredia), Alberto (Baltazar)
See also CA 45-48R; DLB 82; LLW

Alvarez, A(lfred) 1929- .... **CLC 5, 13**
See also CA 1-4R; CANR 3, 33, 63, 101,
134; CN 3, 4, 5, 6; CP 1, 2, 3, 4, 5, 6, 7;
DLB 14, 40; MTFW 2005

Alvarez, Alejandro Rodriguez 1903-1965
See Casona, Alejandro
See also CA 131; 93-96; HW 1

Alvarez, Julia 1950- .... **CLC 93; HLCS 1**
See also AAYA 25; AMWS 7; CA 147;
CANR 69, 101, 133; DA3; DLB 282;
LATS 1:2; LLW; MTCW 2; MTFW 2005;
NFS 5, 9; SATA 129; WLIT 1

Alvaro, Corrado 1896-1956 .... **TCLC 60**
See also CA 163; DLB 264; EWL 3

Amado, Jorge 1912-2001 ... **CLC 13, 40, 106;
HLC 1**
See also CA 77-80; 201; CANR 35, 74, 135;
CWW 2; DAM MULT, NOV; DLB 113,
307; EWL 3; HW 2; LAW; LAWS 1;
MTCW 1, 2; MTFW 2005; RGWL 2, 3;
TWA; WLIT 1

Ambler, Eric 1909-1998 .... **CLC 4, 6, 9**
See also BRWS 4; CA 9-12R; 171; CANR
7, 38, 74; CMW 4; CN 1, 2, 3, 4, 5, 6;
DLB 77; MSW; MTCW 1, 2; TEA

Ambrose, Stephen E(dward)
1936-2002 .... **CLC 145**
See also AAYA 44; CA 1-4R; 209; CANR
3, 43, 57, 83, 105; MTFW 2005; NCFS 2;
SATA 40, 138

Amichai, Yehuda 1924-2000 .. **CLC 9, 22, 57,
116; PC 38**
See also CA 85-88; 189; CANR 46, 60, 99,
132; CWW 2; EWL 3; MTCW 1, 2;
MTFW 2005; PFS 24; RGHL; WLIT 6

Amichai, Yehudah
See Amichai, Yehuda

Amiel, Henri Frederic 1821-1881 .... **NCLC 4**
See also DLB 217

Amis, Kingsley (William)
1922-1995 ...... **CLC 1, 2, 3, 5, 8, 13, 40,
44, 129**
See also AITN 2; BPFB 1; BRWS 2; CA
9-12R; 150; CANR 8, 28, 54; CDBLB
1945-1960; CN 1, 2, 3, 4, 5, 6; CP 1, 2,
3, 4; DA; DA3; DAB; DAC; DAM MST,
NOV; DLB 15, 27, 100, 139, 326; DLBY
1996; EWL 3; HGG; INT CANR-8;
MTCW 1, 2; MTFW 2005; RGEL 2;
RGSF 2; SFW 4

Amis, Martin (Louis) 1949- .... **CLC 4, 9, 38,
62, 101, 213**
See also BEST 90:3; BRWS 4; CA 65-68;
CANR 8, 27, 54, 73, 95, 132; CN 5, 6, 7;
DA3; DLB 14, 194; EWL 3; INT CANR-
27; MTCW 2; MTFW 2005

Ammianus Marcellinus c. 330-c.
395 .... **CMLC 60**
See also AW 2; DLB 211

Ammons, A(rchie) R(andolph)
1926-2001 ...... **CLC 2, 3, 5, 8, 9, 25, 57,
108; PC 16**
See also AITN 1; AMWS 7; CA 9-12R;
193; CANR 6, 36, 51, 73, 107; CP 1, 2,
3, 4, 5, 6, 7; CSW; DAM POET; DLB 5,
165; EWL 3; MAL 5; MTCW 1, 2; PFS
19; RGAL 4; TCLE 1:1

Amo, Tauraatua i
See Adams, Henry (Brooks)

Amory, Thomas 1691(?)-1788 .... **LC 48**
See also DLB 39

Anand, Mulk Raj 1905-2004 ...... **CLC 23, 93**
See also CA 65-68; 231; CANR 32, 64; CN
1, 2, 3, 4, 5, 6, 7; DAM NOV; DLB 323;
EWL 3; MTCW 1, 2; MTFW 2005; RGSF
2

Anatol
See Schnitzler, Arthur

Anaximander c. 611B.C.-c.
546B.C. .... **CMLC 22**

Anaya, Rudolfo A(lfonso) 1937- ...... **CLC 23,
148; HLC 1**
See also AAYA 20; BYA 13; CA 45-48;
CAAS 4; CANR 1, 32, 51, 124; CN 4, 5,
6, 7; DAM MULT, NOV; DLB 82, 206,
278; HW 1; LAIT 4; LLW; MAL 5;
MTCW 1, 2; MTFW 2005; NFS 12;
RGAL 4; RGSF 2; TCWW 2; WLIT 1

Andersen, Hans Christian
1805-1875 .... **NCLC 7, 79; SSC 6, 56;
WLC 1**
See also AAYA 57; CLR 6; DA; DA3;
DAB; DAC; DAM MST, POP; EW 6;
MAICYA 1, 2; RGSF 2; RGWL 2, 3;
SATA 100; TWA; WCH; YABC 1

Bakunin, Mikhail (Alexandrovich)
1814-1876 .... **NCLC 25, 58**
See also DLB 277

Baldwin, James (Arthur) 1924-1987 . **BLC 1;**
CLC 1, 2, 3, 4, 5, 8, 13, 15, 17, 42, 50,
67, 90, 127; DC 1; SSC 10, 33; WLC 1
See also AAYA 4, 34; AFAW 1, 2; AMWR
2; AMWS 1; BPFB 1; BW 1; CA 1-4R;
124; CABS 1; CAD; CANR 3, 24;
CDALB 1941-1968; CN 1, 2, 3, 4; CPW;
DA; DA3; DAB; DAC; DAM MST,
MULT, NOV, POP; DFS 11, 15; DLB 2,
7, 33, 249, 278; DLBY 1987; EWL 3;
EXPS; LAIT 5; MAL 5; MTCW 1, 2;
MTFW 2005; NCFS 4; NFS 4; RGAL 4;
RGSF 2; SATA 9; SATA-Obit 54; SSFS
2, 18; TUS

Baldwin, William c. 1515-1563 .... **LC 113**
See also DLB 132

Bale, John 1495-1563 .... **LC 62**
See also DLB 132; RGEL 2; TEA

Ball, Hugo 1886-1927 .... **TCLC 104**

Ballard, J(ames) G(raham) 1930- . **CLC 3, 6,**
14, 36, 137; SSC 1, 53
See also AAYA 3, 52; BRWS 5; CA 5-8R;
CANR 15, 39, 65, 107, 133; CN 1, 2, 3,
4, 5, 6, 7; DA3; DAM NOV, POP; DLB
14, 207, 261, 319; EWL 3; HGG; MTCW
1, 2; MTFW 2005; NFS 8; RGEL 2;
RGSF 2; SATA 93; SCFW 1, 2; SFW 4

Balmont, Konstantin (Dmitriyevich)
1867-1943 .... **TCLC 11**
See also CA 109; 155; DLB 295; EWL 3

Baltausis, Vincas 1847-1910
See Mikszath, Kalman

Balzac, Honore de 1799-1850 ... **NCLC 5, 35,**
53, 153; SSC 5, 59; WLC 1
See also DA; DA3; DAB; DAC; DAM
MST, NOV; DLB 119; EW 5; GFL 1789
to the Present; LMFS 1; RGSF 2; RGWL
2, 3; SSFS 10; SUFW; TWA

Bambara, Toni Cade 1939-1995 .... **BLC 1;**
CLC 19, 88; SSC 35; TCLC 116;
WLCS
See also AAYA 5, 49; AFAW 2; AMWS 11;
BW 2, 3; BYA 12, 14; CA 29-32R; 150;
CANR 24, 49, 81; CDALBS; DA; DA3;
DAC; DAM MST, MULT; DLB 38, 218;
EXPS; MAL 5; MTCW 1, 2; MTFW
2005; RGAL 4; RGSF 2; SATA 112; SSFS
4, 7, 12, 21

Bamdad, A.
See Shamlu, Ahmad

Bamdad, Alef
See Shamlu, Ahmad

Banat, D. R.
See Bradbury, Ray (Douglas)

Bancroft, Laura
See Baum, L(yman) Frank

Banim, John 1798-1842 .... **NCLC 13**
See also DLB 116, 158, 159; RGEL 2

Banim, Michael 1796-1874 .... **NCLC 13**
See also DLB 158, 159

Banjo, The
See Paterson, A(ndrew) B(arton)

Banks, Iain
See Banks, Iain M(enzies)
See also BRWS 11

Banks, Iain M(enzies) 1954- .... **CLC 34**
See Banks, Iain
See also CA 123; 128; CANR 61, 106; DLB
194, 261; EWL 3; HGG; INT CA-128;
MTFW 2005; SFW 4

Banks, Lynne Reid .... **CLC 23**
See Reid Banks, Lynne
See also AAYA 6; BYA 7; CLR 86; CN 4,
5, 6

Banks, Russell (Earl) 1940- .... **CLC 37, 72,**
187; SSC 42
See also AAYA 45; AMWS 5; CA 65-68;
CAAS 15; CANR 19, 52, 73, 118; CN 4,
5, 6, 7; DLB 130, 278; EWL 3; MAL 5;
MTCW 2; MTFW 2005; NFS 13

Banville, John 1945- .... **CLC 46, 118, 224**
See also CA 117; 128; CANR 104, 150; CN
4, 5, 6, 7; DLB 14, 271, 326; INT CA-
128

Banville, Theodore (Faullain) de
1832-1891 .... **NCLC 9**
See also DLB 217; GFL 1789 to the Present

Baraka, Amiri 1934- .... **BLC 1; CLC 1, 2, 3,**
5, 10, 14, 33, 115, 213; DC 6; PC 4;
WLCS
See Jones, LeRoi
See also AAYA 63; AFAW 1, 2; AMWS 2;
BW 2, 3; CA 21-24R; CABS 3; CAD;
CANR 27, 38, 61, 133; CD 3, 5, 6;
CDALB 1941-1968; CP 4, 5, 6, 7; CPW;
DA; DA3; DAC; DAM MST, MULT,
POET, POP; DFS 3, 11, 16; DLB 5, 7,
16, 38; DLBD 8; EWL 3; MAL 5; MTCW
1, 2; MTFW 2005; PFS 9; RGAL 4;
TCLE 1:1; TUS; WP

Baratynsky, Evgenii Abramovich
1800-1844 .... **NCLC 103**
See also DLB 205

Barbauld, Anna Laetitia
1743-1825 .... **NCLC 50**
See also DLB 107, 109, 142, 158; RGEL 2

Barbellion, W. N. P. .... **TCLC 24**
See Cummings, Bruce F(rederick)

Barber, Benjamin R. 1939- .... **CLC 141**
See also CA 29-32R; CANR 12, 32, 64, 119

Barbera, Jack (Vincent) 1945- .... **CLC 44**
See also CA 110; CANR 45

Barbey d'Aurevilly, Jules-Amedee
1808-1889 .... **NCLC 1; SSC 17**
See also DLB 119; GFL 1789 to the Present

Barbour, John c. 1316-1395 .... **CMLC 33**
See also DLB 146

Barbusse, Henri 1873-1935 .... **TCLC 5**
See also CA 105; 154; DLB 65; EWL 3;
RGWL 2, 3

Barclay, Alexander c. 1475-1552 .... **LC 109**
See also DLB 132

Barclay, Bill
See Moorcock, Michael

Barclay, William Ewert
See Moorcock, Michael

Barea, Arturo 1897-1957 .... **TCLC 14**
See also CA 111; 201

Barfoot, Joan 1946- .... **CLC 18**
See also CA 105; CANR 141

Barham, Richard Harris
1788-1845 .... **NCLC 77**
See also DLB 159

Baring, Maurice 1874-1945 .... **TCLC 8**
See also CA 105; 168; DLB 34; HGG

Baring-Gould, Sabine 1834-1924 ... **TCLC 88**
See also DLB 156, 190

Barker, Clive 1952- .... **CLC 52, 205; SSC 53**
See also AAYA 10, 54; BEST 90:3; BPFB
1; CA 121; 129; CANR 71, 111, 133;
CPW; DA3; DAM POP; DLB 261; HGG;
INT CA-129; MTCW 1, 2; MTFW 2005;
SUFW 2

Barker, George Granville
1913-1991 .... **CLC 8, 48**
See also CA 9-12R; 135; CANR 7, 38; CP
1, 2, 3, 4, 5; DAM POET; DLB 20; EWL
3; MTCW 1

Barker, Harley Granville
See Granville-Barker, Harley
See also DLB 10

Barker, Howard 1946- .... **CLC 37**
See also CA 102; CBD; CD 5, 6; DLB 13,
233

Barker, Jane 1652-1732 .... **LC 42, 82**
See also DLB 39, 131

Barker, Pat 1943- .... **CLC 32, 94, 146**
See also BRWS 4; CA 117; 122; CANR 50,
101, 148; CN 6, 7; DLB 271, 326; INT
CA-122

Barker, Patricia
See Barker, Pat

Barlach, Ernst (Heinrich)
1870-1938 .... **TCLC 84**
See also CA 178; DLB 56, 118; EWL 3

Barlow, Joel 1754-1812 .... **NCLC 23**
See also AMWS 2; DLB 37; RGAL 4

Barnard, Mary (Ethel) 1909- .... **CLC 48**
See also CA 21-22; CAP 2; CP 1

Barnes, Djuna 1892-1982 .... **CLC 3, 4, 8, 11,**
29, 127; SSC 3
See Steptoe, Lydia
See also AMWS 3; CA 9-12R; 107; CAD;
CANR 16, 55; CN 1, 2, 3; CWD; DLB 4,
9, 45; EWL 3; GLL 1; MAL 5; MTCW 1,
2; MTFW 2005; RGAL 4; TCLE 1:1;
TUS

Barnes, Jim 1933- .... **NNAL**
See also CA 108, 175; CAAE 175; CAAS
28; DLB 175

Barnes, Julian 1946- .... **CLC 42, 141**
See also BRWS 4; CA 102; CANR 19, 54,
115, 137; CN 4, 5, 6, 7; DAB; DLB 194;
DLBY 1993; EWL 3; MTCW 2; MTFW
2005

Barnes, Julian Patrick
See Barnes, Julian

Barnes, Peter 1931-2004 .... **CLC 5, 56**
See also CA 65-68; 230; CAAS 12; CANR
33, 34, 64, 113; CBD; CD 5, 6; DFS 6;
DLB 13, 233; MTCW 1

Barnes, William 1801-1886 .... **NCLC 75**
See also DLB 32

Baroja, Pio 1872-1956 .... **HLC 1; TCLC 8**
See also CA 104; 247; EW 9

Baroja y Nessi, Pio
See Baroja, Pio

Baron, David
See Pinter, Harold

Baron Corvo
See Rolfe, Frederick (William Serafino Austin Lewis Mary)

Barondess, Sue K(aufman)
1926-1977 .... **CLC 8**
See Kaufman, Sue
See also CA 1-4R; 69-72; CANR 1

Baron de Teive
See Pessoa, Fernando (Antonio Nogueira)

Baroness Von S.
See Zangwill, Israel

Barres, (Auguste-)Maurice
1862-1923 .... **TCLC 47**
See also CA 164; DLB 123; GFL 1789 to
the Present

Barreto, Afonso Henrique de Lima
See Lima Barreto, Afonso Henrique de

Barrett, Andrea 1954- .... **CLC 150**
See also CA 156; CANR 92; CN 7

Barrett, Michele .... **CLC 65**

Barrett, (Roger) Syd 1946-2006 .... **CLC 35**

Barrett, William (Christopher)
1913-1992 .... **CLC 27**
See also CA 13-16R; 139; CANR 11, 67;
INT CANR-11

Barrett Browning, Elizabeth
1806-1861 ...... **NCLC 1, 16, 61, 66, 170;**
PC 6, 62; WLC 1
See also AAYA 63; BRW 4; CDBLB 1832-
1890; DA; DA3; DAB; DAC; DAM MST,
POET; DLB 32, 199; EXPP; FL 1:2; PAB;
PFS 2, 16, 23; TEA; WLIT 4; WP

Bentley, E(dmund) C(lerihew)
1875-1956 .... **TCLC 12**
See also CA 108; 232; DLB 70; MSW
Bentley, Eric 1916- .... **CLC 24**
See also CA 5-8R; CAD; CANR 6, 67;
CBD; CD 5, 6; INT CANR-6
Bentley, Eric Russell
See Bentley, Eric
ben Uzair, Salem
See Horne, Richard Henry Hengist
Beranger, Pierre Jean de
1780-1857 .... **NCLC 34**
Berdyaev, Nicolas
See Berdyaev, Nikolai (Aleksandrovich)
Berdyaev, Nikolai (Aleksandrovich)
1874-1948 .... **TCLC 67**
See also CA 120; 157
Berdyayev, Nikolai (Aleksandrovich)
See Berdyaev, Nikolai (Aleksandrovich)
Berendt, John 1939- .... **CLC 86**
See also CA 146; CANR 75, 83, 151
Berendt, John Lawrence
See Berendt, John
Beresford, J(ohn) D(avys)
1873-1947 .... **TCLC 81**
See also CA 112; 155; DLB 162, 178, 197;
SFW 4; SUFW 1
Bergelson, David (Rafailovich)
1884-1952 .... **TCLC 81**
See Bergelson, Dovid
See also CA 220
Bergelson, Dovid
See Bergelson, David (Rafailovich)
See also EWL 3
Berger, Colonel
See Malraux, (Georges-)Andre
Berger, John (Peter) 1926- .... **CLC 2, 19**
See also BRWS 4; CA 81-84; CANR 51,
78, 117; CN 1, 2, 3, 4, 5, 6, 7; DLB 14,
207, 319, 326
Berger, Melvin H. 1927- .... **CLC 12**
See also CA 5-8R; CANR 4, 142; CLR 32;
SAAS 2; SATA 5, 88, 158; SATA-Essay
124
Berger, Thomas (Louis) 1924- .. **CLC 3, 5, 8,**
11, 18, 38
See also BPFB 1; CA 1-4R; CANR 5, 28,
51, 128; CN 1, 2, 3, 4, 5, 6, 7; DAM
NOV; DLB 2; DLBY 1980; EWL 3;
FANT; INT CANR-28; MAL 5; MTCW
1, 2; MTFW 2005; RHW; TCLE 1:1;
TCWW 1, 2
Bergman, (Ernst) Ingmar 1918- ...... **CLC 16,**
72, 210
See also AAYA 61; CA 81-84; CANR 33,
70; CWW 2; DLB 257; MTCW 2; MTFW
2005
Bergson, Henri(-Louis) 1859-1941 . **TCLC 32**
See also CA 164; EW 8; EWL 3; GFL 1789
to the Present
Bergstein, Eleanor 1938- .... **CLC 4**
See also CA 53-56; CANR 5
Berkeley, George 1685-1753 .... **LC 65**
See also DLB 31, 101, 252
Berkoff, Steven 1937- .... **CLC 56**
See also CA 104; CANR 72; CBD; CD 5, 6
Berlin, Isaiah 1909-1997 .... **TCLC 105**
See also CA 85-88; 162
Bermant, Chaim (Icyk) 1929-1998 ... **CLC 40**
See also CA 57-60; CANR 6, 31, 57, 105;
CN 2, 3, 4, 5, 6
Bern, Victoria
See Fisher, M(ary) F(rances) K(ennedy)
Bernanos, (Paul Louis) Georges
1888-1948 .... **TCLC 3**
See also CA 104; 130; CANR 94; DLB 72;
EWL 3; GFL 1789 to the Present; RGWL
2, 3

Bernard, April 1956- .... **CLC 59**
See also CA 131; CANR 144
Bernard, Mary Ann
See Soderbergh, Steven
Bernard of Clairvaux 1090-1153 .. **CMLC 71**
See also DLB 208
Berne, Victoria
See Fisher, M(ary) F(rances) K(ennedy)
Bernhard, Thomas 1931-1989 ..... **CLC 3, 32,**
61; DC 14; TCLC 165
See also CA 85-88; 127; CANR 32, 57; CD-
WLB 2; DLB 85, 124; EWL 3; MTCW 1;
RGHL; RGWL 2, 3
Bernhardt, Sarah (Henriette Rosine)
1844-1923 .... **TCLC 75**
See also CA 157
Bernstein, Charles 1950- .... **CLC 142,**
See also CA 129; CAAS 24; CANR 90; CP
4, 5, 6, 7; DLB 169
Bernstein, Ingrid
See Kirsch, Sarah
Beroul fl. c. 12th cent. - .... **CMLC 75**
Berriault, Gina 1926-1999 .... **CLC 54, 109;**
SSC 30
See also CA 116; 129; 185; CANR 66; DLB
130; SSFS 7,11
Berrigan, Daniel 1921- .... **CLC 4**
See also CA 33-36R, 187; CAAE 187;
CAAS 1; CANR 11, 43, 78; CP 1, 2, 3, 4,
5, 6, 7; DLB 5
Berrigan, Edmund Joseph Michael, Jr.
1934-1983
See Berrigan, Ted
See also CA 61-64; 110; CANR 14, 102
Berrigan, Ted .... **CLC 37**
See Berrigan, Edmund Joseph Michael, Jr.
See also CP 1, 2, 3; DLB 5, 169; WP
Berry, Charles Edward Anderson 1931-
See Berry, Chuck
See also CA 115
Berry, Chuck .... **CLC 17**
See Berry, Charles Edward Anderson
Berry, Jonas
See Ashbery, John (Lawrence)
See also GLL 1
Berry, Wendell (Erdman) 1934- ... **CLC 4, 6,**
8, 27, 46; PC 28
See also AITN 1; AMWS 10; ANW; CA
73-76; CANR 50, 73, 101, 132; CP 1, 2,
3, 4, 5, 6, 7; CSW; DAM POET; DLB 5,
6, 234, 275; MTCW 2; MTFW 2005;
TCLE 1:1
Berryman, John 1914-1972 ... **CLC 1, 2, 3, 4,**
6, 8, 10, 13, 25, 62; PC 64
See also AMW; CA 13-16; 33-36R; CABS
2; CANR 35; CAP 1; CDALB 1941-1968;
CP 1; DAM POET; DLB 48; EWL 3;
MAL 5; MTCW 1, 2; MTFW 2005; PAB;
RGAL 4; WP
Bertolucci, Bernardo 1940- ...... **CLC 16, 157**
See also CA 106; CANR 125
Berton, Pierre (Francis de Marigny)
1920-2004 .... **CLC 104**
See also CA 1-4R; 233; CANR 2, 56, 144;
CPW; DLB 68; SATA 99; SATA-Obit 158
Bertrand, Aloysius 1807-1841 .... **NCLC 31**
See Bertrand, Louis oAloysiusc
Bertrand, Louis oAloysiusc
See Bertrand, Aloysius
See also DLB 217
Bertran de Born c. 1140-1215 .... **CMLC 5**
Besant, Annie (Wood) 1847-1933 ..... **TCLC 9**
See also CA 105; 185
Bessie, Alvah 1904-1985 .... **CLC 23**
See also CA 5-8R; 116; CANR 2, 80; DLB
26
Bestuzhev, Aleksandr Aleksandrovich
1797-1837 .... **NCLC 131**
See also DLB 198

Bethlen, T. D.
See Silverberg, Robert
Beti, Mongo .... **BLC 1; CLC 27**
See Biyidi, Alexandre
See also AFW; CANR 79; DAM MULT;
EWL 3; WLIT 2
Betjeman, John 1906-1984 ...... **CLC 2, 6, 10,**
34, 43
See also BRW 7; CA 9-12R; 112; CANR
33, 56; CDBLB 1945-1960; CP 1, 2, 3;
DA3; DAB; DAM MST, POET; DLB 20;
DLBY 1984; EWL 3; MTCW 1, 2
Bettelheim, Bruno 1903-1990 .... **CLC 79;**
TCLC 143
See also CA 81-84; 131; CANR 23, 61;
DA3; MTCW 1, 2; RGHL
Betti, Ugo 1892-1953 .... **TCLC 5**
See also CA 104; 155; EWL 3; RGWL 2, 3
Betts, Doris (Waugh) 1932- ..... **CLC 3, 6, 28;**
SSC 45
See also CA 13-16R; CANR 9, 66, 77; CN
6, 7; CSW; DLB 218; DLBY 1982; INT
CANR-9; RGAL 4
Bevan, Alistair
See Roberts, Keith (John Kingston)
Bey, Pilaff
See Douglas, (George) Norman
Bialik, Chaim Nachman
1873-1934 .... **TCLC 25**
See Bialik, Hayyim Nahman
See also CA 170; EWL 3
Bialik, Hayyim Nahman
See Bialik, Chaim Nachman
See also WLIT 6
Bickerstaff, Isaac
See Swift, Jonathan
Bidart, Frank 1939- .... **CLC 33**
See also AMWS 15; CA 140; CANR 106;
CP 5, 6, 7
Bienek, Horst 1930- .... **CLC 7, 11**
See also CA 73-76; DLB 75
Bierce, Ambrose (Gwinett)
1842-1914(?) ..... **SSC 9, 72; TCLC 1, 7,**
44; WLC 1
See also AAYA 55; AMW; BYA 11; CA
104; 139; CANR 78; CDALB 1865-1917;
DA; DA3; DAC; DAM MST; DLB 11,
12, 23, 71, 74, 186; EWL 3; EXPS; HGG;
LAIT 2; MAL 5; RGAL 4; RGSF 2; SSFS
9; SUFW 1
Biggers, Earl Derr 1884-1933 .... **TCLC 65**
See also CA 108; 153; DLB 306
Billiken, Bud
See Motley, Willard (Francis)
Billings, Josh
See Shaw, Henry Wheeler
Billington, (Lady) Rachel (Mary)
1942- .... **CLC 43**
See also AITN 2; CA 33-36R; CANR 44;
CN 4, 5, 6, 7
Binchy, Maeve 1940- .... **CLC 153**
See also BEST 90:1; BPFB 1; CA 127; 134;
CANR 50, 96, 134; CN 5, 6, 7; CPW;
DA3; DAM POP; DLB 319; INT CA-134;
MTCW 2; MTFW 2005; RHW
Binyon, T(imothy) J(ohn)
1936-2004 .... **CLC 34**
See also CA 111; 232; CANR 28, 140
Bion 335B.C.-245B.C. .... **CMLC 39**
Bioy Casares, Adolfo 1914-1999 ... **CLC 4, 8,**
13, 88; HLC 1; SSC 17
See Casares, Adolfo Bioy; Miranda, Javier;
Sacastru, Martin
See also CA 29-32R; 177; CANR 19, 43,
66; CWW 2; DAM MULT; DLB 113;
EWL 3; HW 1, 2; LAW; MTCW 1, 2;
MTFW 2005

Birch, Allison .... CLC 65
Bird, Cordwainer
　　See Ellison, Harlan (Jay)
Bird, Robert Montgomery
　　1806-1854 .... NCLC 1
　　See also DLB 202; RGAL 4
Birkerts, Sven 1951- .... CLC 116
　　See also CA 128; 133, 176; CAAE 176;
　　CAAS 29; CANR 151; INT CA-133
Birney, (Alfred) Earle 1904-1995 .. CLC 1, 4,
　　6, 11; PC 52
　　See also CA 1-4R; CANR 5, 20; CN 1, 2,
　　3, 4; CP 1, 2, 3, 4, 5, 6; DAC; DAM MST,
　　POET; DLB 88; MTCW 1; PFS 8; RGEL 4
Biruni, al 973-1048(?) .... CMLC 28
Bishop, Elizabeth 1911-1979 ..... CLC 1, 4, 9,
　　13, 15, 32; PC 3, 34; TCLC 121
　　See also AMWR 2; AMWS 1; CA 5-8R;
　　89-92; CABS 2; CANR 26, 61, 108;
　　CDALB 1968-1988; CP 1, 2, 3; DA;
　　DA3; DAC; DAM MST, POET; DLB 5,
　　169; EWL 3; GLL 2; MAL 5; MAWW;
　　MTCW 1, 2; PAB; PFS 6, 12; RGAL 4;
　　SATA-Obit 24; TUS; WP
Bishop, John 1935- .... CLC 10
　　See also CA 105
Bishop, John Peale 1892-1944 ..... TCLC 103
　　See also CA 107; 155; DLB 4, 9, 45; MAL
　　5; RGAL 4
Bissett, Bill 1939- .... CLC 18; PC 14
　　See also CA 69-72; CAAS 19; CANR 15;
　　CCA 1; CP 1, 2, 3, 4, 5, 6; DLB 53;
　　MTCW 1
Bissoondath, Neil (Devindra)
　　1955- .... CLC 120
　　See also CA 136; CANR 123; CN 6, 7;
　　DAC
Bitov, Andrei (Georgievich) 1937- ... CLC 57
　　See also CA 142; DLB 302
Biyidi, Alexandre 1932-
　　See Beti, Mongo
　　See also BW 1, 3; CA 114; 124; CANR 81;
　　DA3; MTCW 1, 2
Bjarme, Brynjolf
　　See Ibsen, Henrik (Johan)
Bjoernson, Bjoernstjerne (Martinius)
　　1832-1910 .... TCLC 7, 37
　　See also CA 104
Black, Benjamin
　　See Banville, John
Black, Robert
　　See Holdstock, Robert P.
Blackburn, Paul 1926-1971 .... CLC 9, 43
　　See also BG 1:2; CA 81-84; 33-36R; CANR
　　34; CP 1; DLB 16; DLBY 1981
Black Elk 1863-1950 .... NNAL; TCLC 33
　　See also CA 144; DAM MULT; MTCW 2;
　　MTFW 2005; WP
Black Hawk 1767-1838 .... NNAL
Black Hobart
　　See Sanders, (James) Ed(ward)
Blacklin, Malcolm
　　See Chambers, Aidan
Blackmore, R(ichard) D(oddridge)
　　1825-1900 .... TCLC 27
　　See also CA 120; DLB 18; RGEL 2
Blackmur, R(ichard) P(almer)
　　1904-1965 .... CLC 2, 24
　　See also AMWS 2; CA 11-12; 25-28R;
　　CANR 71; CAP 1; DLB 63; EWL 3;
　　MAL 5
Black Tarantula
　　See Acker, Kathy
Blackwood, Algernon (Henry)
　　1869-1951 .... TCLC 5
　　See also CA 105; 150; DLB 153, 156, 178;
　　HGG; SUFW 1

Blackwood, Caroline (Maureen)
　　1931-1996 .... CLC 6, 9, 100
　　See also BRWS 9; CA 85-88; 151; CANR
　　32, 61, 65; CN 3, 4, 5, 6; DLB 14, 207;
　　HGG; MTCW 1
Blade, Alexander
　　See Hamilton, Edmond; Silverberg, Robert
Blaga, Lucian 1895-1961 .... CLC 75
　　See also CA 157; DLB 220; EWL 3
Blair, Eric (Arthur) 1903-1950 .... TCLC 123
　　See Orwell, George
　　See also CA 104; 132; DA; DA3; DAB;
　　DAC; DAM MST, NOV; MTCW 1, 2;
　　MTFW 2005; SATA 29
Blair, Hugh 1718-1800 .... NCLC 75
Blais, Marie-Claire 1939- .... CLC 2, 4, 6, 13,
　　22
　　See also CA 21-24R; CAAS 4; CANR 38,
　　75, 93; CWW 2; DAC; DAM MST; DLB
　　53; EWL 3; FW; MTCW 1, 2; MTFW
　　2005; TWA
Blaise, Clark 1940- .... CLC 29
　　See also AITN 2; CA 53-56, 231; CAAE
　　231; CAAS 3; CANR 5, 66, 106; CN 4,
　　5, 6, 7; DLB 53; RGSF 2
Blake, Fairley
　　See De Voto, Bernard (Augustine)
Blake, Nicholas
　　See Day Lewis, C(ecil)
　　See also DLB 77; MSW
Blake, Sterling
　　See Benford, Gregory (Albert)
Blake, William 1757-1827 . NCLC 13, 37, 57,
　　127; PC 12, 63; WLC 1
　　See also AAYA 47; BRW 3; BRWR 1; CD-
　　BLB 1789-1832; CLR 52; DA; DA3;
　　DAB; DAC; DAM MST, POET; DLB 93,
　　163; EXPP; LATS 1:1; LMFS 1; MAI-
　　CYA 1, 2; PAB; PFS 2, 12, 24; SATA 30;
　　TEA; WCH; WLIT 3; WP
Blanchot, Maurice 1907-2003 .... CLC 135
　　See also CA 117; 144; 213; CANR 138;
　　DLB 72, 296; EWL 3
Blasco Ibanez, Vicente 1867-1928 . TCLC 12
　　See Ibanez, Vicente Blasco
　　See also BPFB 1; CA 110; 131; CANR 81;
　　DA3; DAM NOV; EW 8; EWL 3; HW 1,
　　2; MTCW 1
Blatty, William Peter 1928- .... CLC 2
　　See also CA 5-8R; CANR 9, 124; DAM
　　POP; HGG
Bleeck, Oliver
　　See Thomas, Ross (Elmore)
Blessing, Lee (Knowlton) 1949- .... CLC 54
　　See also CA 236; CAD; CD 5, 6; DFS 23
Blight, Rose
　　See Greer, Germaine
Blish, James (Benjamin) 1921-1975 . CLC 14
　　See also BPFB 1; CA 1-4R; 57-60; CANR
　　3; CN 2; DLB 8; MTCW 1; SATA 66;
　　SCFW 1, 2; SFW 4
Bliss, Frederick
　　See Card, Orson Scott
Bliss, Reginald
　　See Wells, H(erbert) G(eorge)
Blixen, Karen (Christentze Dinesen)
　　1885-1962
　　See Dinesen, Isak
　　See also CA 25-28; CANR 22, 50; CAP 2;
　　DA3; DLB 214; LMFS 1; MTCW 1, 2;
　　SATA 44; SSFS 20
Bloch, Robert (Albert) 1917-1994 .... CLC 33
　　See also AAYA 29; CA 5-8R, 179; 146;
　　CAAE 179; CAAS 20; CANR 5, 78;
　　DA3; DLB 44; HGG; INT CANR-5;
　　MTCW 2; SATA 12; SATA-Obit 82; SFW
　　4; SUFW 1, 2

Blok, Alexander (Alexandrovich)
　　1880-1921 .... PC 21; TCLC 5
　　See also CA 104; 183; DLB 295; EW 9;
　　EWL 3; LMFS 2; RGWL 2, 3
Blom, Jan
　　See Breytenbach, Breyten
Bloom, Harold 1930- .... CLC 24, 103, 221
　　See also CA 13-16R; CANR 39, 75, 92,
　　133; DLB 67; EWL 3; MTCW 2; MTFW
　　2005; RGAL 4
Bloomfield, Aurelius
　　See Bourne, Randolph S(illiman)
Bloomfield, Robert 1766-1823 ..... NCLC 145
　　See also DLB 93
Blount, Roy (Alton), Jr. 1941- .... CLC 38
　　See also CA 53-56; CANR 10, 28, 61, 125;
　　CSW; INT CANR-28; MTCW 1, 2;
　　MTFW 2005
Blowsnake, Sam 1875-(?) .... NNAL
Bloy, Leon 1846-1917 .... TCLC 22
　　See also CA 121; 183; DLB 123; GFL 1789
　　to the Present
Blue Cloud, Peter (Aroniawenrate)
　　1933- .... NNAL
　　See also CA 117; CANR 40; DAM MULT
Bluggage, Oranthy
　　See Alcott, Louisa May
Blume, Judy (Sussman) 1938- .... CLC 12, 30
　　See also AAYA 3, 26; BYA 1, 8, 12; CA 29-
　　32R; CANR 13, 37, 66, 124; CLR 2, 15,
　　69; CPW; DA3; DAM NOV, POP; DLB
　　52; JRDA; MAICYA 1, 2; MAICYAS 1;
　　MTCW 1, 2; MTFW 2005; SATA 2, 31,
　　79, 142; WYA; YAW
Blunden, Edmund (Charles)
　　1896-1974 .... CLC 2, 56; PC 66
　　See also BRW 6; BRWS 11; CA 17-18; 45-
　　48; CANR 54; CAP 2; CP 1, 2; DLB 20,
　　100, 155; MTCW 1; PAB
Bly, Robert (Elwood) 1926- .... CLC 1, 2, 5,
　　10, 15, 38, 128; PC 39
　　See also AMWS 4; CA 5-8R; CANR 41,
　　73, 125; CP 1, 2, 3, 4, 5, 6, 7; DA3; DAM
　　POET; DLB 5; EWL 3; MAL 5; MTCW
　　1, 2; MTFW 2005; PFS 6, 17; RGAL 4
Boas, Franz 1858-1942 .... TCLC 56
　　See also CA 115; 181
Bobette
　　See Simenon, Georges (Jacques Christian)
Boccaccio, Giovanni 1313-1375 ... CMLC 13,
　　57; SSC 10, 87
　　See also EW 2; RGSF 2; RGWL 2, 3; TWA;
　　WLIT 7
Bochco, Steven 1943- .... CLC 35
　　See also AAYA 11, 71; CA 124; 138
Bode, Sigmund
　　See O'Doherty, Brian
Bodel, Jean 1167(?)-1210 .... CMLC 28
Bodenheim, Maxwell 1892-1954 .... TCLC 44
　　See also CA 110; 187; DLB 9, 45; MAL 5;
　　RGAL 4
Bodenheimer, Maxwell
　　See Bodenheim, Maxwell
Bodker, Cecil 1927-
　　See Bodker, Cecil
Bodker, Cecil 1927- .... CLC 21
　　See also CA 73-76; CANR 13, 44, 111;
　　CLR 23; MAICYA 1, 2; SATA 14, 133
Boell, Heinrich (Theodor)
　　1917-1985 ..... CLC 2, 3, 6, 9, 11, 15, 27,
　　32, 72; SSC 23; WLC 1
　　See Boll, Heinrich (Theodor)
　　See also CA 21-24R; 116; CANR 24; DA;
　　DA3; DAB; DAC; DAM MST, NOV;
　　DLB 69; DLBY 1985; MTCW 1, 2;
　　MTFW 2005; SSFS 20; TWA
Boerne, Alfred
　　See Doeblin, Alfred

Boyle, Mark
　　See Kienzle, William X(avier)
Boyle, Patrick 1905-1982 .... **CLC 19**
　　See also CA 127
Boyle, T. C.
　　See Boyle, T(homas) Coraghessan
　　See also AMWS 8
Boyle, T(homas) Coraghessan
　　1948- .... **CLC 36, 55, 90; SSC 16**
　　See Boyle, T. C.
　　See also AAYA 47; BEST 90:4; BPFB 1;
　　CA 120; CANR 44, 76, 89, 132; CN 6, 7;
　　CPW; DA3; DAM POP; DLB 218, 278;
　　DLBY 1986; EWL 3; MAL 5; MTCW 2;
　　MTFW 2005; SSFS 13, 19
Boz
　　See Dickens, Charles (John Huffam)
Brackenridge, Hugh Henry
　　1748-1816 .... **NCLC 7**
　　See also DLB 11, 37; RGAL 4
Bradbury, Edward P.
　　See Moorcock, Michael
　　See also MTCW 2
Bradbury, Malcolm (Stanley)
　　1932-2000 .... **CLC 32, 61**
　　See also CA 1-4R; CANR 1, 33, 91, 98,
　　137; CN 1, 2, 3, 4, 5, 6, 7; CP 1; DA3;
　　DAM NOV; DLB 14, 207; EWL 3;
　　MTCW 1, 2; MTFW 2005
Bradbury, Ray (Douglas) 1920- .... **CLC 1, 3,**
　　10, 15, 42, 98; SSC 29, 53; WLC 1
　　See also AAYA 15; AITN 1, 2; AMWS 4;
　　BPFB 1; BYA 4, 5, 11; CA 1-4R; CANR
　　2, 30, 75, 125; CDALB 1968-1988; CN
　　1, 2, 3, 4, 5, 6, 7; CPW; DA; DA3; DAB;
　　DAC; DAM MST, NOV, POP; DLB 2, 8;
　　EXPN; EXPS; HGG; LAIT 3, 5; LATS
　　1:2; LMFS 2; MAL 5; MTCW 1, 2;
　　MTFW 2005; NFS 1, 22; RGAL 4; RGSF
　　2; SATA 11, 64, 123; SCFW 1, 2; SFW 4;
　　SSFS 1, 20; SUFW 1, 2; TUS; YAW
Braddon, Mary Elizabeth
　　1837-1915 .... **TCLC 111**
　　See also BRWS 8; CA 108; 179; CMW 4;
　　DLB 18, 70, 156; HGG
Bradfield, Scott (Michael) 1955- .... **SSC 65**
　　See also CA 147; CANR 90; HGG; SUFW 2
Bradford, Gamaliel 1863-1932 .... **TCLC 36**
　　See also CA 160; DLB 17
Bradford, William 1590-1657 .... **LC 64**
　　See also DLB 24, 30; RGAL 4
Bradley, David (Henry), Jr. 1950- .... **BLC 1;**
　　CLC 23, 118
　　See also BW 1, 3; CA 104; CANR 26, 81;
　　CN 4, 5, 6, 7; DAM MULT; DLB 33
Bradley, John Ed(mund, Jr.) 1958- . **CLC 55**
　　See also CA 139; CANR 99; CN 6, 7; CSW
Bradley, Marion Zimmer
　　1930-1999 .... **CLC 30**
　　See Chapman, Lee; Dexter, John; Gardner,
　　Miriam; Ives, Morgan; Rivers, Elfrida
　　See also AAYA 40; BPFB 1; CA 57-60; 185;
　　CAAS 10; CANR 7, 31, 51, 75, 107;
　　CPW; DA3; DAM POP; DLB 8; FANT;
　　FW; MTCW 1, 2; MTFW 2005; SATA 90,
　　139; SATA-Obit 116; SFW 4; SUFW 2;
　　YAW
Bradshaw, John 1933- .... **CLC 70**
　　See also CA 138; CANR 61
Bradstreet, Anne 1612(?)-1672 ...... **LC 4, 30;**
　　PC 10
　　See also AMWS 1; CDALB 1640-1865;
　　DA; DA3; DAC; DAM MST, POET; DLB
　　24; EXPP; FW; PFS 6; RGAL 4; TUS;
　　WP
Brady, Joan 1939- .... **CLC 86**
　　See also CA 141

Bragg, Melvyn 1939- .... **CLC 10**
　　See also BEST 89:3; CA 57-60; CANR 10,
　　48, 89; CN 1, 2, 3, 4, 5, 6, 7; DLB 14,
　　271; RHW
Brahe, Tycho 1546-1601 .... **LC 45**
　　See also DLB 300
Braine, John (Gerard) 1922-1986 . **CLC 1, 3,**
　　41
　　See also CA 1-4R; 120; CANR 1, 33; CD-
　　BLB 1945-1960; CN 1, 2, 3, 4; DLB 15;
　　DLBY 1986; EWL 3; MTCW 1
Braithwaite, William Stanley (Beaumont)
　　1878-1962 .... **BLC 1; HR 1:2; PC 52**
　　See also BW 1; CA 125; DAM MULT; DLB
　　50, 54; MAL 5
Bramah, Ernest 1868-1942 .... **TCLC 72**
　　See also CA 156; CMW 4; DLB 70; FANT
Brammer, Billy Lee
　　See Brammer, William
Brammer, William 1929-1978 .... **CLC 31**
　　See also CA 235; 77-80
Brancati, Vitaliano 1907-1954 .... **TCLC 12**
　　See also CA 109; DLB 264; EWL 3
Brancato, Robin F(idler) 1936- .... **CLC 35**
　　See also AAYA 9, 68; BYA 6; CA 69-72;
　　CANR 11, 45; CLR 32; JRDA; MAICYA
　　2; MAICYAS 1; SAAS 9; SATA 97;
　　WYA; YAW
Brand, Dionne 1953- .... **CLC 192**
　　See also BW 2; CA 143; CANR 143; CWP
Brand, Max
　　See Faust, Frederick (Schiller)
　　See also BPFB 1; TCWW 1, 2
Brand, Millen 1906-1980 .... **CLC 7**
　　See also CA 21-24R; 97-100; CANR 72
Branden, Barbara .... **CLC 44**
　　See also CA 148
Brandes, Georg (Morris Cohen)
　　1842-1927 .... **TCLC 10**
　　See also CA 105; 189; DLB 300
Brandys, Kazimierz 1916-2000 .... **CLC 62**
　　See also CA 239; EWL 3
Branley, Franklyn M(ansfield)
　　1915-2002 .... **CLC 21**
　　See also CA 33-36R; 207; CANR 14, 39;
　　CLR 13; MAICYA 1, 2; SAAS 16; SATA
　　4, 68, 136
Brant, Beth (E.) 1941- .... **NNAL**
　　See also CA 144; FW
Brant, Sebastian 1457-1521 .... **LC 112**
　　See also DLB 179; RGWL 2, 3
Brathwaite, Edward Kamau
　　1930- .... **BLCS; CLC 11; PC 56**
　　See also BW 2, 3; CA 25-28R; CANR 11,
　　26, 47, 107; CDWLB 3; CP 1, 2, 3, 4, 5,
　　6, 7; DAM POET; DLB 125; EWL 3
Brathwaite, Kamau
　　See Brathwaite, Edward Kamau
Brautigan, Richard (Gary)
　　1935-1984 .... **CLC 1, 3, 5, 9, 12, 34, 42;**
　　TCLC 133
　　See also BPFB 1; CA 53-56; 113; CANR
　　34; CN 1, 2, 3; CP 1, 2, 3, 4; DA3; DAM
　　NOV; DLB 2, 5, 206; DLBY 1980, 1984;
　　FANT; MAL 5; MTCW 1; RGAL 4;
　　SATA 56
Brave Bird, Mary .... **NNAL**
　　See Crow Dog, Mary (Ellen)
Braverman, Kate 1950- .... **CLC 67**
　　See also CA 89-92; CANR 141
Brecht, (Eugen) Bertolt (Friedrich)
　　1898-1956 ..... **DC 3; TCLC 1, 6, 13, 35,**
　　169; WLC 1
　　See also CA 104; 133; CANR 62; CDWLB
　　2; DA; DA3; DAB; DAC; DAM DRAM,
　　MST; DFS 4, 5, 9; DLB 56, 124; EW 11;
　　EWL 3; IDTP; MTCW 1, 2; MTFW 2005;
　　RGHL; RGWL 2, 3; TWA

Brecht, Eugen Berthold Friedrich
　　See Brecht, (Eugen) Bertolt (Friedrich)
Bremer, Fredrika 1801-1865 .... **NCLC 11**
　　See also DLB 254
Brennan, Christopher John
　　1870-1932 .... **TCLC 17**
　　See also CA 117; 188; DLB 230; EWL 3
Brennan, Maeve 1917-1993 ... **CLC 5; TCLC**
　　124
　　See also CA 81-84; CANR 72, 100
Brenner, Jozef 1887-1919
　　See Csath, Geza
　　See also CA 240
Brent, Linda
　　See Jacobs, Harriet A(nn)
Brentano, Clemens (Maria)
　　1778-1842 .... **NCLC 1**
　　See also DLB 90; RGWL 2, 3
Brent of Bin Bin
　　See Franklin, (Stella Maria Sarah) Miles
　　(Lampe)
Brenton, Howard 1942- .... **CLC 31**
　　See also CA 69-72; CANR 33, 67; CBD;
　　CD 5, 6; DLB 13; MTCW 1
Breslin, James 1930-
　　See Breslin, Jimmy
　　See also CA 73-76; CANR 31, 75, 139;
　　DAM NOV; MTCW 1, 2; MTFW 2005
Breslin, Jimmy .... **CLC 4, 43**
　　See Breslin, James
　　See also AITN 1; DLB 185; MTCW 2
Bresson, Robert 1901(?)-1999 .... **CLC 16**
　　See also CA 110; 187; CANR 49
Breton, Andre 1896-1966 .. **CLC 2, 9, 15, 54;**
　　PC 15
　　See also CA 19-20; 25-28R; CANR 40, 60;
　　CAP 2; DLB 65, 258; EW 11; EWL 3;
　　GFL 1789 to the Present; LMFS 2;
　　MTCW 1, 2; MTFW 2005; RGWL 2, 3;
　　TWA; WP
Breytenbach, Breyten 1939(?)- .. **CLC 23, 37,**
　　126
　　See also CA 113; 129; CANR 61, 122;
　　CWW 2; DAM POET; DLB 225; EWL 3
Bridgers, Sue Ellen 1942- .... **CLC 26**
　　See also AAYA 8, 49; BYA 7, 8; CA 65-68;
　　CANR 11, 36; CLR 18; DLB 52; JRDA;
　　MAICYA 1, 2; SAAS 1; SATA 22, 90;
　　SATA-Essay 109; WYA; YAW
Bridges, Robert (Seymour)
　　1844-1930 .... **PC 28; TCLC 1**
　　See also BRW 6; CA 104; 152; CDBLB
　　1890-1914; DAM POET; DLB 19, 98
Bridie, James .... **TCLC 3**
　　See Mavor, Osborne Henry
　　See also DLB 10; EWL 3
Brin, David 1950- .... **CLC 34**
　　See also AAYA 21; CA 102; CANR 24, 70,
　　125, 127; INT CANR-24; SATA 65;
　　SCFW 2; SFW 4
Brink, Andre (Philippus) 1935- . **CLC 18, 36,**
　　106
　　See also AFW; BRWS 6; CA 104; CANR
　　39, 62, 109, 133; CN 4, 5, 6, 7; DLB 225;
　　EWL 3; INT CA-103; LATS 1:2; MTCW
　　1, 2; MTFW 2005; WLIT 2
Brinsmead, H. F(ay)
　　See Brinsmead, H(esba) F(ay)
Brinsmead, H. F.
　　See Brinsmead, H(esba) F(ay)
Brinsmead, H(esba) F(ay) 1922- ...... **CLC 21**
　　See also CA 21-24R; CANR 10; CLR 47;
　　CWRI 5; MAICYA 1, 2; SAAS 5; SATA
　　18, 78
Brittain, Vera (Mary) 1893(?)-1970 . **CLC 23**
　　See also BRWS 10; CA 13-16; 25-28R;
　　CANR 58; CAP 1; DLB 191; FW; MTCW
　　1, 2

Clarke, Shirley 1925-1997 .... **CLC 16**
See also CA 189

Clash, The
See Headon, (Nicky) Topper; Jones, Mick; Simonon, Paul; Strummer, Joe

Claudel, Paul (Louis Charles Marie)
1868-1955 .... **TCLC 2, 10**
See also CA 104; 165; DLB 192, 258, 321; EW 8; EWL 3; GFL 1789 to the Present; RGWL 2, 3; TWA

Claudian 370(?)-404(?) .... **CMLC 46**
See also RGWL 2, 3

Claudius, Matthias 1740-1815 .... **NCLC 75**
See also DLB 97

Clavell, James (duMaresq)
1925-1994 .... **CLC 6, 25, 87**
See also BPFB 1; CA 25-28R; 146; CANR 26, 48; CN 5; CPW; DA3; DAM NOV, POP; MTCW 1, 2; MTFW 2005; NFS 10; RHW

Clayman, Gregory .... **CLC 65**

Cleaver, (Leroy) Eldridge
1935-1998 .... **BLC 1; CLC 30, 119**
See also BW 1, 3; CA 21-24R; 167; CANR 16, 75; DA3; DAM MULT; MTCW 2; YAW

Cleese, John (Marwood) 1939- .... **CLC 21**
See Monty Python
See also CA 112; 116; CANR 35; MTCW 1

Cleishbotham, Jebediah
See Scott, Sir Walter

Cleland, John 1710-1789 .... **LC 2, 48**
See also DLB 39; RGEL 2

Clemens, Samuel Langhorne 1835-1910
See Twain, Mark
See also CA 104; 135; CDALB 1865-1917; DA; DA3; DAB; DAC; DAM MST, NOV; DLB 12, 23, 64, 74, 186, 189; JRDA; LMFS 1; MAICYA 1, 2; NCFS 4; NFS 20; SATA 100; YABC 2

Clement of Alexandria
150(?)-215(?) .... **CMLC 41**

Cleophil
See Congreve, William

Clerihew, E.
See Bentley, E(dmund) C(lerihew)

Clerk, N. W.
See Lewis, C.S.

Cleveland, John 1613-1658 .... **LC 106**
See also DLB 126; RGEL 2

Cliff, Jimmy .... **CLC 21**
See Chambers, James
See also CA 193

Cliff, Michelle 1946- .... **BLCS; CLC 120**
See also BW 2; CA 116; CANR 39, 72; CD-WLB 3; DLB 157; FW; GLL 2

Clifford, Lady Anne 1590-1676 .... **LC 76**
See also DLB 151

Clifton, (Thelma) Lucille 1936- .... **BLC 1;
CLC 19, 66, 162; PC 17**
See also AFAW 2; BW 2, 3; CA 49-52; CANR 2, 24, 42, 76, 97, 138; CLR 5; CP 2, 3, 4, 5, 6, 7; CSW; CWP; CWRI 5; DA3; DAM MULT, POET; DLB 5, 41; EXPP; MAICYA 1, 2; MTCW 1, 2; MTFW 2005; PFS 1, 14; SATA 20, 69, 128; WP

Clinton, Dirk
See Silverberg, Robert

Clough, Arthur Hugh 1819-1861 .. **NCLC 27,
163**
See also BRW 5; DLB 32; RGEL 2

Clutha, Janet Paterson Frame 1924-2004
See Frame, Janet
See also CA 1-4R; 224; CANR 2, 36, 76, 135; MTCW 1, 2; SATA 119

Clyne, Terence
See Blatty, William Peter

Cobalt, Martin
See Mayne, William (James Carter)

Cobb, Irvin S(hrewsbury)
1876-1944 .... **TCLC 77**
See also CA 175; DLB 11, 25, 86

Cobbett, William 1763-1835 .... **NCLC 49**
See also DLB 43, 107, 158; RGEL 2

Coburn, D(onald) L(ee) 1938- .... **CLC 10**
See also CA 89-92; DFS 23

Cocteau, Jean (Maurice Eugene Clement)
1889-1963 ...... **CLC 1, 8, 15, 16, 43; DC
17; TCLC 119; WLC 2**
See also CA 25-28; CANR 40; CAP 2; DA; DA3; DAB; DAC; DAM DRAM, MST, NOV; DLB 65, 258, 321; EW 10; EWL 3; GFL 1789 to the Present; MTCW 1, 2; RGWL 2, 3; TWA

Codrescu, Andrei 1946- .... **CLC 46, 121**
See also CA 33-36R; CAAS 19; CANR 13, 34, 53, 76, 125; CN 7; DA3; DAM POET; MAL 5; MTCW 2; MTFW 2005

Coe, Max
See Bourne, Randolph S(illiman)

Coe, Tucker
See Westlake, Donald E(dwin)

Coen, Ethan 1958- .... **CLC 108**
See also AAYA 54; CA 126; CANR 85

Coen, Joel 1955- .... **CLC 108**
See also AAYA 54; CA 126; CANR 119

The Coen Brothers
See Coen, Ethan; Coen, Joel

Coetzee, J. M. 1940- ..... **CLC 23, 33, 66, 117,
161, 162**
See also AAYA 37; AFW; BRWS 6; CA 77-80; CANR 41, 54, 74, 114, 133; CN 4, 5, 6, 7; DA3; DAM NOV; DLB 225, 326; EWL 3; LMFS 2; MTCW 1, 2; MTFW 2005; NFS 21; WLIT 2; WWE 1

Coetzee, John Maxwell
See Coetzee, J. M.

Coffey, Brian
See Koontz, Dean R.

Coffin, Robert P(eter) Tristram
1892-1955 .... **TCLC 95**
See also CA 123; 169; DLB 45

Cohan, George M. 1878-1942 .... **TCLC 60**
See also CA 157; DLB 249; RGAL 4

Cohan, George Michael
See Cohan, George M.

Cohen, Arthur A(llen) 1928-1986 ...... **CLC 7,
31**
See also CA 1-4R; 120; CANR 1, 17, 42; DLB 28; RGHL

Cohen, Leonard 1934- .... **CLC 3, 38**
See also CA 21-24R; CANR 14, 69; CN 1, 2, 3, 4, 5, 6; CP 1, 2, 3, 4, 5, 6, 7; DAC; DAM MST; DLB 53; EWL 3; MTCW 1

Cohen, Leonard Norman
See Cohen, Leonard

Cohen, Matt(hew) 1942-1999 .... **CLC 19**
See also CA 61-64; 187; CAAS 18; CANR 40; CN 1, 2, 3, 4, 5, 6; DAC; DLB 53

Cohen-Solal, Annie 1948- .... **CLC 50**
See also CA 239

Colegate, Isabel 1931- .... **CLC 36**
See also CA 17-20R; CANR 8, 22, 74; CN 4, 5, 6, 7; DLB 14, 231; INT CANR-22; MTCW 1

Coleman, Emmett
See Reed, Ishmael (Scott)

Coleridge, Hartley 1796-1849 .... **NCLC 90**
See also DLB 96

Coleridge, M. E.
See Coleridge, Mary E(lizabeth)

Coleridge, Mary E(lizabeth)
1861-1907 .... **TCLC 73**
See also CA 116; 166; DLB 19, 98

Coleridge, Samuel Taylor
1772-1834 ...... **NCLC 9, 54, 99, 111; PC
11, 39, 67; WLC 2**
See also AAYA 66; BRW 4; BRWR 2; BYA 4; CDBLB 1789-1832; DA; DA3; DAB; DAC; DAM MST, POET; DLB 93, 107; EXPP; LATS 1:1; LMFS 1; PAB; PFS 4, 5; RGEL 2; TEA; WLIT 3; WP

Coleridge, Sara 1802-1852 .... **NCLC 31**
See also DLB 199

Coles, Don 1928- .... **CLC 46**
See also CA 115; CANR 38; CP 5, 6, 7

Coles, Robert (Martin) 1929- .... **CLC 108**
See also CA 45-48; CANR 3, 32, 66, 70, 135; INT CANR-32; SATA 23

Colette, (Sidonie-Gabrielle)
1873-1954 .. **SSC 10, 93; TCLC 1, 5, 16**
See Willy, Colette
See also CA 104; 131; DA3; DAM NOV; DLB 65; EW 9; EWL 3; GFL 1789 to the Present; MTCW 1, 2; MTFW 2005; RGWL 2, 3; TWA

Collett, (Jacobine) Camilla (Wergeland)
1813-1895 .... **NCLC 22**

Collier, Christopher 1930- .... **CLC 30**
See also AAYA 13; BYA 2; CA 33-36R; CANR 13, 33, 102; JRDA; MAICYA 1, 2; SATA 16, 70; WYA; YAW 1

Collier, James Lincoln 1928- .... **CLC 30**
See also AAYA 13; BYA 2; CA 9-12R; CANR 4, 33, 60, 102; CLR 3; DAM POP; JRDA; MAICYA 1, 2; SAAS 21; SATA 8, 70, 166; WYA; YAW 1

Collier, Jeremy 1650-1726 .... **LC 6**

Collier, John 1901-1980 . **SSC 19; TCLC 127**
See also CA 65-68; 97-100; CANR 10; CN 1, 2; DLB 77, 255; FANT; SUFW 1

Collier, Mary 1690-1762 .... **LC 86**
See also DLB 95

Collingwood, R(obin) G(eorge)
1889(?)-1943 .... **TCLC 67**
See also CA 117; 155; DLB 262

Collins, Billy 1941- .... **PC 68**
See also AAYA 64; CA 151; CANR 92; CP 7; MTFW 2005; PFS 18

Collins, Hunt
See Hunter, Evan

Collins, Linda 1931- .... **CLC 44**
See also CA 125

Collins, Tom
See Furphy, Joseph
See also RGEL 2

Collins, (William) Wilkie
1824-1889 .... **NCLC 1, 18, 93; SSC 93**
See also BRWS 6; CDBLB 1832-1890; CMW 4; DLB 18, 70, 159; GL 2; MSW; RGEL 2; RGSF 2; SUFW 1; WLIT 4

Collins, William 1721-1759 ...... **LC 4, 40; PC
72**
See also BRW 3; DAM POET; DLB 109; RGEL 2

Collodi, Carlo .... **NCLC 54**
See Lorenzini, Carlo
See also CLR 5; WCH; WLIT 7

Colman, George
See Glassco, John

Colman, George, the Elder
1732-1794 .... **LC 98**
See also RGEL 2

Colonna, Vittoria 1492-1547 .... **LC 71**
See also RGWL 2, 3

Colt, Winchester Remington
See Hubbard, L. Ron

Colter, Cyrus J. 1910-2002 .... **CLC 58**
See also BW 1; CA 65-68; 205; CANR 10, 66; CN 2, 3, 4, 5, 6; DLB 33

Colton, James
See Hansen, Joseph
See also GLL 1

Corso, (Nunzio) Gregory 1930-2001 . **CLC 1, 11; PC 33**
See also AMWS 12; BG 1:2; CA 5-8R; 193; CANR 41, 76, 132; CP 1, 2, 3, 4, 5, 6, 7; DA3; DLB 5, 16, 237; LMFS 2; MAL 5; MTCW 1, 2; MTFW 2005; WP

Cortazar, Julio 1914-1984 ... **CLC 2, 3, 5, 10, 13, 15, 33, 34, 92; HLC 1; SSC 7, 76**
See also BPFB 1; CA 21-24R; CANR 12, 32, 81; CDWLB 3; DA3; DAM MULT, NOV; DLB 113; EWL 3; EXPS; HW 1, 2; LAW; MTCW 1, 2; MTFW 2005; RGSF 2; RGWL 2, 3; SSFS 3, 20; TWA; WLIT 1

Cortes, Hernan 1485-1547 .... **LC 31**

Corvinus, Jakob
See Raabe, Wilhelm (Karl)

Corwin, Cecil
See Kornbluth, C(yril) M.

Cosic, Dobrica 1921- .... **CLC 14**
See also CA 122; 138; CDWLB 4; CWW 2; DLB 181; EWL 3

Costain, Thomas B(ertram) 1885-1965 .... **CLC 30**
See also BYA 3; CA 5-8R; 25-28R; DLB 9; RHW

Costantini, Humberto 1924(?)-1987 . **CLC 49**
See also CA 131; 122; EWL 3; HW 1

Costello, Elvis 1954- .... **CLC 21**
See also CA 204

Costenoble, Philostene
See Ghelderode, Michel de

Cotes, Cecil V.
See Duncan, Sara Jeannette

Cotter, Joseph Seamon Sr. 1861-1949 .... **BLC 1; TCLC 28**
See also BW 1; CA 124; DAM MULT; DLB 50

Couch, Arthur Thomas Quiller
See Quiller-Couch, Sir Arthur (Thomas)

Coulton, James
See Hansen, Joseph

Couperus, Louis (Marie Anne) 1863-1923 .... **TCLC 15**
See also CA 115; EWL 3; RGWL 2, 3

Coupland, Douglas 1961- .... **CLC 85, 133**
See also AAYA 34; CA 142; CANR 57, 90, 130; CCA 1; CN 7; CPW; DAC; DAM POP

Court, Wesli
See Turco, Lewis (Putnam)

Courtenay, Bryce 1933- .... **CLC 59**
See also CA 138; CPW

Courtney, Robert
See Ellison, Harlan (Jay)

Cousteau, Jacques-Yves 1910-1997 .. **CLC 30**
See also CA 65-68; 159; CANR 15, 67; MTCW 1; SATA 38, 98

Coventry, Francis 1725-1754 .... **LC 46**

Coverdale, Miles c. 1487-1569 .... **LC 77**
See also DLB 167

Cowan, Peter (Walkinshaw) 1914-2002 .... **SSC 28**
See also CA 21-24R; CANR 9, 25, 50, 83; CN 1, 2, 3, 4, 5, 6, 7; DLB 260; RGSF 2

Coward, Noel (Peirce) 1899-1973 . **CLC 1, 9, 29, 51**
See also AITN 1; BRWS 2; CA 17-18; 41-44R; CANR 35, 132; CAP 2; CBD; CD-BLB 1914-1945; DA3; DAM DRAM; DFS 3, 6; DLB 10, 245; EWL 3; IDFW 3, 4; MTCW 1, 2; MTFW 2005; RGEL 2; TEA

Cowley, Abraham 1618-1667 .... **LC 43**
See also BRW 2; DLB 131, 151; PAB; RGEL 2

Cowley, Malcolm 1898-1989 .... **CLC 39**
See also AMWS 2; CA 5-8R; 128; CANR 3, 55; CP 1, 2, 3, 4; DLB 4, 48; DLBY 1981, 1989; EWL 3; MAL 5; MTCW 1, 2; MTFW 2005

Cowper, William 1731-1800 ..... **NCLC 8, 94; PC 40**
See also BRW 3; DA3; DAM POET; DLB 104, 109; RGEL 2

Cox, William Trevor 1928-
See Trevor, William
See also CA 9-12R; CANR 4, 37, 55, 76, 102, 139; DAM NOV; INT CANR-37; MTCW 1, 2; MTFW 2005; TEA

Coyne, P. J.
See Masters, Hilary

Cozzens, James Gould 1903-1978 . **CLC 1, 4, 11, 92**
See also AMW; BPFB 1; CA 9-12R; 81-84; CANR 19; CDALB 1941-1968; CN 1, 2; DLB 9, 294; DLBD 2; DLBY 1984, 1997; EWL 3; MAL 5; MTCW 1, 2; MTFW 2005; RGAL 4

Crabbe, George 1754-1832 .... **NCLC 26, 121**
See also BRW 3; DLB 93; RGEL 2

Crace, Jim 1946- .... **CLC 157; SSC 61**
See also CA 128; 135; CANR 55, 70, 123; CN 5, 6, 7; DLB 231; INT CA-135

Craddock, Charles Egbert
See Murfree, Mary Noailles

Craig, A. A.
See Anderson, Poul (William)

Craik, Mrs.
See Craik, Dinah Maria (Mulock)
See also RGEL 2

Craik, Dinah Maria (Mulock) 1826-1887 .... **NCLC 38**
See Craik, Mrs.; Mulock, Dinah Maria
See also DLB 35, 163; MAICYA 1, 2; SATA 34

Cram, Ralph Adams 1863-1942 ..... **TCLC 45**
See also CA 160

Cranch, Christopher Pearse 1813-1892 .... **NCLC 115**
See also DLB 1, 42, 243

Crane, (Harold) Hart 1899-1932 .... **PC 3; TCLC 2, 5, 80; WLC 2**
See also AMW; AMWR 2; CA 104; 127; CDALB 1917-1929; DA; DA3; DAB; DAC; DAM MST, POET; DLB 4, 48; EWL 3; MAL 5; MTCW 1, 2; MTFW 2005; RGAL 4; TUS

Crane, R(onald) S(almon) 1886-1967 .... **CLC 27**
See also CA 85-88; DLB 63

Crane, Stephen (Townley) 1871-1900 ...... **SSC 7, 56, 70; TCLC 11, 17, 32; WLC 2**
See also AAYA 21; AMW; AMWC 1; BPFB 1; BYA 3; CA 109; 140; CANR 84; CDALB 1865-1917; DA; DA3; DAB; DAC; DAM MST, NOV, POET; DLB 12, 54, 78; EXPN; EXPS; LAIT 2; LMFS 2; MAL 5; NFS 4, 20; PFS 9; RGAL 4; RGSF 2; SSFS 4; TUS; WYA; YABC 2

Cranmer, Thomas 1489-1556 .... **LC 95**
See also DLB 132, 213

Cranshaw, Stanley
See Fisher, Dorothy (Frances) Canfield

Crase, Douglas 1944- .... **CLC 58**
See also CA 106

Crashaw, Richard 1612(?)-1649 .... **LC 24**
See also BRW 2; DLB 126; PAB; RGEL 2

Cratinus c. 519B.C.-c. 422B.C. ..... **CMLC 54**
See also LMFS 1

Craven, Margaret 1901-1980 .... **CLC 17**
See also BYA 2; CA 103; CCA 1; DAC; LAIT 5

Crawford, F(rancis) Marion 1854-1909 .... **TCLC 10**
See also CA 107; 168; DLB 71; HGG; RGAL 4; SUFW 1

Crawford, Isabella Valancy 1850-1887 .... **NCLC 12, 127**
See also DLB 92; RGEL 2

Crayon, Geoffrey
See Irving, Washington

Creasey, John 1908-1973 .... **CLC 11**
See Marric, J. J.
See also CA 5-8R; 41-44R; CANR 8, 59; CMW 4; DLB 77; MTCW 1

Crebillon, Claude Prosper Jolyot de (fils) 1707-1777 .... **LC 1, 28**
See also DLB 313; GFL Beginnings to 1789

Credo
See Creasey, John

Credo, Alvaro J. de
See Prado (Calvo), Pedro

Creeley, Robert 1926-2005 .... **CLC 1, 2, 4, 8, 11, 15, 36, 78**
See also AMWS 4; CA 1-4R; 237; CAAS 10; CANR 23, 43, 89, 137; CP 1, 2, 3, 4, 5, 6, 7; DA3; DAM POET; DLB 5, 16, 169; DLBD 17; EWL 3; MAL 5; MTCW 1, 2; MTFW 2005; PFS 21; RGAL 4; WP

Creeley, Robert White
See Creeley, Robert

Crenne, Helisenne de 1510-1560 .... **LC 113**

Crevecoeur, Hector St. John de
See Crevecoeur, Michel Guillaume Jean de
See also ANW

Crevecoeur, Michel Guillaume Jean de 1735-1813 .... **NCLC 105**
See Crevecoeur, Hector St. John de
See also AMWS 1; DLB 37

Crevel, Rene 1900-1935 .... **TCLC 112**
See also GLL 2

Crews, Harry (Eugene) 1935- ..... **CLC 6, 23, 49**
See also AITN 1; AMWS 11; BPFB 1; CA 25-28R; CANR 20, 57; CN 3, 4, 5, 6, 7; CSW; DA3; DLB 6, 143, 185; MTCW 1, 2; MTFW 2005; RGAL 4

Crichton, (John) Michael 1942- ... **CLC 2, 6, 54, 90**
See also AAYA 10, 49; AITN 2; BPFB 1; CA 25-28R; CANR 13, 40, 54, 76, 127; CMW 4; CN 2, 3, 6, 7; CPW; DA3; DAM NOV, POP; DLB 292; DLBY 1981; INT CANR-13; JRDA; MTCW 1, 2; MTFW 2005; SATA 9, 88; SFW 4; YAW

Crispin, Edmund .... **CLC 22**
See Montgomery, (Robert) Bruce
See also DLB 87; MSW

Cristina of Sweden 1626-1689 .... **LC 124**

Cristofer, Michael 1945(?)- .... **CLC 28**
See also CA 110; 152; CAD; CANR 150; CD 5, 6; DAM DRAM; DFS 15; DLB 7

Cristofer, Michael Ivan
See Cristofer, Michael

Criton
See Alain

Croce, Benedetto 1866-1952 .... **TCLC 37**
See also CA 120; 155; EW 8; EWL 3; WLIT 7

Crockett, David 1786-1836 .... **NCLC 8**
See also DLB 3, 11, 183, 248

Crockett, Davy
See Crockett, David

Crofts, Freeman Wills 1879-1957 .. **TCLC 55**
See also CA 115; 195; CMW 4; DLB 77; MSW

Croker, John Wilson 1780-1857 .... **NCLC 10**
See also DLB 110

Crommelynck, Fernand 1885-1970 .. **CLC 75**
See also CA 189; 89-92; EWL 3

Danvers, Dennis 1947- .... **CLC 70**

Danziger, Paula 1944-2004 .... **CLC 21**
See also AAYA 4, 36; BYA 6, 7, 14; CA 112; 115; 229; CANR 37, 132; CLR 20; JRDA; MAICYA 1, 2; MTFW 2005; SATA 36, 63, 102, 149; SATA-Brief 30; SATA-Obit 155; WYA; YAW

Da Ponte, Lorenzo 1749-1838 .... **NCLC 50**

d'Aragona, Tullia 1510(?)-1556 .... **LC 121**

Dario, Ruben 1867-1916 .... **HLC 1; PC 15; TCLC 4**
See also CA 131; CANR 81; DAM MULT; DLB 290; EWL 3; HW 1, 2; LAW; MTCW 1, 2; MTFW 2005; RGWL 2, 3

Darley, George 1795-1846 .... **NCLC 2**
See also DLB 96; RGEL 2

Darrow, Clarence (Seward) 1857-1938 .... **TCLC 81**
See also CA 164; DLB 303

Darwin, Charles 1809-1882 .... **NCLC 57**
See also BRWS 7; DLB 57, 166; LATS 1:1; RGEL 2; TEA; WLIT 4

Darwin, Erasmus 1731-1802 .... **NCLC 106**
See also DLB 93; RGEL 2

Daryush, Elizabeth 1887-1977 ...... **CLC 6, 19**
See also CA 49-52; CANR 3, 81; DLB 20

Das, Kamala 1934- .... **CLC 191; PC 43**
See also CA 101; CANR 27, 59; CP 1, 2, 3, 4, 5, 6, 7; CWP; DLB 323; FW

Dasgupta, Surendranath 1887-1952 .... **TCLC 81**
See also CA 157

Dashwood, Edmee Elizabeth Monica de la Pasture 1890-1943
See Delafield, E. M.
See also CA 119; 154

da Silva, Antonio Jose 1705-1739 .... **NCLC 114**

Daudet, (Louis Marie) Alphonse 1840-1897 .... **NCLC 1**
See also DLB 123; GFL 1789 to the Present; RGSF 2

d'Aulnoy, Marie-Catherine c. 1650-1705 .... **LC 100**

Daumal, Rene 1908-1944 .... **TCLC 14**
See also CA 114; 247; EWL 3

Davenant, William 1606-1668 .... **LC 13**
See also DLB 58, 126; RGEL 2

Davenport, Guy (Mattison, Jr.) 1927-2005 .... **CLC 6, 14, 38; SSC 16**
See also CA 33-36R; 235; CANR 23, 73; CN 3, 4, 5, 6; CSW; DLB 130

David, Robert
See Nezval, Vitezslav

Davidson, Avram (James) 1923-1993
See Queen, Ellery
See also CA 101; 171; CANR 26; DLB 8; FANT; SFW 4; SUFW 1, 2

Davidson, Donald (Grady) 1893-1968 .... **CLC 2, 13, 19**
See also CA 5-8R; 25-28R; CANR 4, 84; DLB 45

Davidson, Hugh
See Hamilton, Edmond

Davidson, John 1857-1909 .... **TCLC 24**
See also CA 118; 217; DLB 19; RGEL 2

Davidson, Sara 1943- .... **CLC 9**
See also CA 81-84; CANR 44, 68; DLB 185

Davie, Donald (Alfred) 1922-1995 .... **CLC 5, 8, 10, 31; PC 29**
See also BRWS 6; CA 1-4R; 149; CAAS 3; CANR 1, 44; CP 1, 2, 3, 4, 5, 6; DLB 27; MTCW 1; RGEL 2

Davie, Elspeth 1918-1995 .... **SSC 52**
See also CA 120; 126; 150; CANR 141; DLB 139

Davies, Ray(mond Douglas) 1944- ... **CLC 21**
See also CA 116; 146; CANR 92

Davies, Rhys 1901-1978 .... **CLC 23**
See also CA 9-12R; 81-84; CANR 4; CN 1, 2; DLB 139, 191

Davies, (William) Robertson 1913-1995 .... **CLC 2, 7, 13, 25, 42, 75, 91; WLC 2**
See Marchbanks, Samuel
See also BEST 89:2; BPFB 1; CA 33-36R; 150; CANR 17, 42, 103; CN 1, 2, 3, 4, 5, 6; CPW; DA; DA3; DAB; DAC; DAM MST, NOV, POP; DLB 68; EWL 3; HGG; INT CANR-17; MTCW 1, 2; MTFW 2005; RGEL 2; TWA

Davies, Sir John 1569-1626 .... **LC 85**
See also DLB 172

Davies, Walter C.
See Kornbluth, C(yril) M.

Davies, William Henry 1871-1940 ... **TCLC 5**
See also BRWS 11; CA 104; 179; DLB 19, 174; EWL 3; RGEL 2

Da Vinci, Leonardo 1452-1519 ..... **LC 12, 57, 60**
See also AAYA 40

Davis, Angela (Yvonne) 1944- .... **CLC 77**
See also BW 2, 3; CA 57-60; CANR 10, 81; CSW; DA3; DAM MULT; FW

Davis, B. Lynch
See Bioy Casares, Adolfo; Borges, Jorge Luis

Davis, Frank Marshall 1905-1987 ...... **BLC 1**
See also BW 2, 3; CA 125; 123; CANR 42, 80; DAM MULT; DLB 51

Davis, Gordon
See Hunt, E(verette) Howard, (Jr.)

Davis, H(arold) L(enoir) 1896-1960 . **CLC 49**
See also ANW; CA 178; 89-92; DLB 9, 206; SATA 114; TCWW 1, 2

Davis, Natalie Zemon 1928- .... **CLC 204**
See also CA 53-56; CANR 58, 100

Davis, Rebecca (Blaine) Harding 1831-1910 .... **SSC 38; TCLC 6**
See also CA 104; 179; DLB 74, 239; FW; NFS 14; RGAL 4; TUS

Davis, Richard Harding 1864-1916 .... **TCLC 24**
See also CA 114; 179; DLB 12, 23, 78, 79, 189; DLBD 13; RGAL 4

Davison, Frank Dalby 1893-1970 ..... **CLC 15**
See also CA 217; 116; DLB 260

Davison, Lawrence H.
See Lawrence, D(avid) H(erbert Richards)

Davison, Peter (Hubert) 1928-2004 . **CLC 28**
See also CA 9-12R; 234; CAAS 4; CANR 3, 43, 84; CP 1, 2, 3, 4, 5, 6, 7; DLB 5

Davys, Mary 1674-1732 .... **LC 1, 46**
See also DLB 39

Dawson, (Guy) Fielding (Lewis) 1930-2002 .... **CLC 6**
See also CA 85-88; 202; CANR 108; DLB 130; DLBY 2002

Dawson, Peter
See Faust, Frederick (Schiller)
See also TCWW 1, 2

Day, Clarence (Shepard, Jr.) 1874-1935 .... **TCLC 25**
See also CA 108; 199; DLB 11

Day, John 1574(?)-1640(?) .... **LC 70**
See also DLB 62, 170; RGEL 2

Day, Thomas 1748-1789 .... **LC 1**
See also DLB 39; YABC 1

Day Lewis, C(ecil) 1904-1972 . **CLC 1, 6, 10; PC 11**
See Blake, Nicholas; Lewis, C. Day
See also BRWS 3; CA 13-16; 33-36R; CANR 34; CAP 1; CP 1; CWRI 5; DAM POET; DLB 15, 20; EWL 3; MTCW 1, 2; RGEL 2

Dazai Osamu .... **SSC 41; TCLC 11**
See Tsushima, Shuji
See also CA 164; DLB 182; EWL 3; MJW; RGSF 2; RGWL 2, 3; TWA

de Andrade, Carlos Drummond
See Drummond de Andrade, Carlos

de Andrade, Mario 1892(?)-1945
See Andrade, Mario de
See also CA 178; HW 2

Deane, Norman
See Creasey, John

Deane, Seamus (Francis) 1940- ...... **CLC 122**
See also CA 118; CANR 42

de Beauvoir, Simone
See Beauvoir, Simone de

de Beer, P.
See Bosman, Herman Charles

De Botton, Alain 1969- .... **CLC 203**
See also CA 159; CANR 96

de Brissac, Malcolm
See Dickinson, Peter (Malcolm de Brissac)

de Campos, Alvaro
See Pessoa, Fernando (Antonio Nogueira)

de Chardin, Pierre Teilhard
See Teilhard de Chardin, (Marie Joseph) Pierre

de Crenne, Helisenne c. 1510-c. 1560 .... **LC 113**

Dee, John 1527-1608 .... **LC 20**
See also DLB 136, 213

Deer, Sandra 1940- .... **CLC 45**
See also CA 186

De Ferrari, Gabriella 1941- .... **CLC 65**
See also CA 146

de Filippo, Eduardo 1900-1984 ... **TCLC 127**
See also CA 132; 114; EWL 3; MTCW 1; RGWL 2, 3

Defoe, Daniel 1660(?)-1731 .... **LC 1, 42, 108; WLC 2**
See also AAYA 27; BRW 3; BRWR 1; BYA 4; CDBLB 1660-1789; CLR 61; DA; DA3; DAB; DAC; DAM MST, NOV; DLB 39, 95, 101; JRDA; LAIT 1; LMFS 1; MAICYA 1, 2; NFS 9, 13; RGEL 2; SATA 22; TEA; WCH; WLIT 3

de Gouges, Olympe
See de Gouges, Olympe

de Gouges, Olympe 1748-1793 .... **LC 127**
See also DLB 313

de Gourmont, Remy(-Marie-Charles)
See Gourmont, Remy(-Marie-Charles) de

de Gournay, Marie le Jars 1566-1645 .... **LC 98**
See also FW

de Hartog, Jan 1914-2002 .... **CLC 19**
See also CA 1-4R; 210; CANR 1; DFS 12

de Hostos, E. M.
See Hostos (y Bonilla), Eugenio Maria de

de Hostos, Eugenio M.
See Hostos (y Bonilla), Eugenio Maria de

Deighton, Len .... **CLC 4, 7, 22, 46**
See Deighton, Leonard Cyril
See also AAYA 6; BEST 89:2; BPFB 1; CD-BLB 1960 to Present; CMW 4; CN 1, 2, 3, 4, 5, 6, 7; CPW; DLB 87

Deighton, Leonard Cyril 1929-
See Deighton, Len
See also AAYA 57; CA 9-12R; CANR 19, 33, 68; DA3; DAM NOV, POP; MTCW 1, 2; MTFW 2005

Dekker, Thomas 1572(?)-1632 ..... **DC 12; LC 22**
See also CDBLB Before 1660; DAM DRAM; DLB 62, 172; LMFS 1; RGEL 2

de Laclos, Pierre Ambroise Franois
See Laclos, Pierre-Ambroise Francois

Delacroix, (Ferdinand-Victor-)Eugene 1798-1863 .... **NCLC 133**
See also EW 5

Drummond, Walter
See Silverberg, Robert
Drummond, William Henry
1854-1907 .... **TCLC 25**
See also CA 160; DLB 92
Drummond de Andrade, Carlos
1902-1987 .... **CLC 18; TCLC 139**
See Andrade, Carlos Drummond de
See also CA 132; 123; DLB 307; LAW
Drummond of Hawthornden, William
1585-1649 .... **LC 83**
See also DLB 121, 213; RGEL 2
Drury, Allen (Stuart) 1918-1998 .... **CLC 37**
See also CA 57-60; 170; CANR 18, 52; CN
1, 2, 3, 4, 5, 6; INT CANR-18
Druse, Eleanor
See King, Stephen
Dryden, John 1631-1700 ..... **DC 3; LC 3, 21,
115; PC 25; WLC 2**
See also BRW 2; CDBLB 1660-1789; DA;
DAB; DAC; DAM DRAM, MST, POET;
DLB 80, 101, 131; EXPP; IDTP; LMFS
1; RGEL 2; TEA; WLIT 3
du Bellay, Joachim 1524-1560 .... **LC 92**
See also GFL Beginnings to 1789; RGWL
2, 3
Duberman, Martin (Bauml) 1930- ..... **CLC 8**
See also CA 1-4R; CAD; CANR 2, 63, 137;
CD 5, 6
Dubie, Norman (Evans) 1945- .... **CLC 36**
See also CA 69-72; CANR 12, 115; CP 3,
4, 5, 6, 7; DLB 120; PFS 12
Du Bois, W(illiam) E(dward) B(urghardt)
1868-1963 ..... **BLC 1; CLC 1, 2, 13, 64,
96; HR 1:2; TCLC 169; WLC 2**
See also AAYA 40; AFAW 1, 2; AMWC 1;
AMWS 2; BW 1, 3; CA 85-88; CANR
34, 82, 132; CDALB 1865-1917; DA;
DA3; DAC; DAM MST, MULT, NOV;
DLB 47, 50, 91, 246, 284; EWL 3; EXPP;
LAIT 2; LMFS 2; MAL 5; MTCW 1, 2;
MTFW 2005; NCFS 1; PFS 13; RGAL 4;
SATA 42
Dubus, Andre 1936-1999 ..... **CLC 13, 36, 97;
SSC 15**
See also AMWS 7; CA 21-24R; 177; CANR
17; CN 5, 6; CSW; DLB 130; INT CANR-
17; RGAL 4; SSFS 10; TCLE 1:1
Duca Minimo
See D'Annunzio, Gabriele
Ducharme, Rejean 1941- .... **CLC 74**
See also CA 165; DLB 60
du Chatelet, Emilie 1706-1749 .... **LC 96**
See Chatelet, Gabrielle-Emilie Du
Duchen, Claire .... **CLC 65**
Duclos, Charles Pinot- 1704-1772 .... **LC 1**
See also GFL Beginnings to 1789
Dudek, Louis 1918-2001 .... **CLC 11, 19**
See also CA 45-48; 215; CAAS 14; CANR
1; CP 1, 2, 3, 4, 5, 6, 7; DLB 88
Duerrenmatt, Friedrich 1921-1990 ... **CLC 1,
4, 8, 11, 15, 43, 102**
See Durrenmatt, Friedrich
See also CA 17-20R; CANR 33; CMW 4;
DAM DRAM; DLB 69, 124; MTCW 1, 2
Duffy, Bruce 1953(?)- .... **CLC 50**
See also CA 172
Duffy, Maureen (Patricia) 1933- ...... **CLC 37**
See also CA 25-28R; CANR 33, 68; CBD;
CN 1, 2, 3, 4, 5, 6, 7; CP 5, 6, 7; CWD;
CWP; DFS 15; DLB 14, 310; FW;
MTCW 1
Du Fu
See Tu Fu
See also RGWL 2, 3
Dugan, Alan 1923-2003 .... **CLC 2, 6**
See also CA 81-84; 220; CANR 119; CP 1,
2, 3, 4, 5, 6, 7; DLB 5; MAL 5; PFS 10

du Gard, Roger Martin
See Martin du Gard, Roger
Duhamel, Georges 1884-1966 .... **CLC 8**
See also CA 81-84; 25-28R; CANR 35;
DLB 65; EWL 3; GFL 1789 to the
Present; MTCW 1
Dujardin, Edouard (Emile Louis)
1861-1949 .... **TCLC 13**
See also CA 109; DLB 123
Duke, Raoul
See Thompson, Hunter S(tockton)
Dulles, John Foster 1888-1959 .... **TCLC 72**
See also CA 115; 149
Dumas, Alexandre (pere)
1802-1870 .... **NCLC 11, 71; WLC 2**
See also AAYA 22; BYA 3; DA; DA3;
DAB; DAC; DAM MST, NOV; DLB 119,
192; EW 6; GFL 1789 to the Present;
LAIT 2; NFS 14, 19; RGWL 2, 3;
SATA 18; TWA; WCH
Dumas, Alexandre (fils) 1824-1895 ...... **DC 1;
NCLC 9**
See also DLB 192; GFL 1789 to the Present;
RGWL 2, 3
Dumas, Claudine
See Malzberg, Barry N(athaniel)
Dumas, Henry L. 1934-1968 .... **CLC 6, 62**
See also BW 1; CA 85-88; DLB 41;
RGAL 4
du Maurier, Daphne 1907-1989 .. **CLC 6, 11,
59; SSC 18**
See also AAYA 37; BPFB 1; BRWS 3; CA
5-8R; 128; CANR 6, 55; CMW 4; CN 1,
2, 3, 4; CPW; DA3; DAB; DAC; DAM
MST, POP; DLB 191; GL 2; HGG; LAIT
3; MSW; MTCW 1, 2; NFS 12; RGEL 2;
RGSF 2; RHW; SATA 27; SATA-Obit 60;
SSFS 14, 16; TEA
Du Maurier, George 1834-1896 ..... **NCLC 86**
See also DLB 153, 178; RGEL 2
Dunbar, Paul Laurence 1872-1906 ... **BLC 1;
PC 5; SSC 8; TCLC 2, 12; WLC 2**
See also AFAW 1, 2; AMWS 2; BW 1, 3;
CA 104; 124; CANR 79; CDALB 1865-
1917; DA; DA3; DAC; DAM MST,
MULT, POET; DLB 50, 54, 78; EXPP;
MAL 5; RGAL 4; SATA 34
Dunbar, William 1460(?)-1520(?) .... **LC 20;
PC 67**
See also BRWS 8; DLB 132, 146; RGEL 2
Dunbar-Nelson, Alice .... **HR 1:2**
See Nelson, Alice Ruth Moore Dunbar
Duncan, Dora Angela
See Duncan, Isadora
Duncan, Isadora 1877(?)-1927 .... **TCLC 68**
See also CA 118; 149
Duncan, Lois 1934- .... **CLC 26**
See also AAYA 4, 34; BYA 6, 8; CA 1-4R;
CANR 2, 23, 36, 111; CLR 29; JRDA;
MAICYA 1, 2; MAICYAS 1; MTFW
2005; SAAS 2; SATA 1, 36, 75, 133, 141;
SATA-Essay 141; WYA; YAW
Duncan, Robert (Edward)
1919-1988 .... **CLC 1, 2, 4, 7, 15, 41, 55;
PC 2**
See also BG 1:2; CA 9-12R; 124; CANR
28, 62; CP 1, 2, 3, 4; DAM POET; DLB
5, 16, 193; EWL 3; MAL 5; MTCW 1, 2;
MTFW 2005; PFS 13; RGAL 4; WP
Duncan, Sara Jeannette
1861-1922 .... **TCLC 60**
See also CA 157; DLB 92
Dunlap, William 1766-1839 .... **NCLC 2**
See also DLB 30, 37, 59; RGAL 4
Dunn, Douglas (Eaglesham) 1942- .... **CLC 6,
40**
See also BRWS 10; CA 45-48; CANR 2,
33, 126; CP 1, 2, 3, 4, 5, 6, 7; DLB 40;
MTCW 1

Dunn, Katherine (Karen) 1945- .... **CLC 71**
See also CA 33-36R; CANR 72; HGG;
MTCW 2; MTFW 2005
Dunn, Stephen (Elliott) 1939- .. **CLC 36, 206**
See also AMWS 11; CA 33-36R; CANR
12, 48, 53, 105; CP 3, 4, 5, 6, 7; DLB
105; PFS 21
Dunne, Finley Peter 1867-1936 ...... **TCLC 28**
See also CA 108; 178; DLB 11, 23; RGAL 4
Dunne, John Gregory 1932-2003 ...... **CLC 28**
See also CA 25-28R; 222; CANR 14, 50;
CN 5, 6, 7; DLBY 1980
Dunsany, Lord .... **TCLC 2, 59**
See Dunsany, Edward John Moreton Drax
Plunkett
See also DLB 77, 153, 156, 255; FANT;
IDTP; RGEL 2; SFW 4; SUFW 1
**Dunsany, Edward John Moreton Drax
Plunkett** 1878-1957
See Dunsany, Lord
See also CA 104; 148; DLB 10; MTCW 2
Duns Scotus, John 1266(?)-1308 ... **CMLC 59**
See also DLB 115
du Perry, Jean
See Simenon, Georges (Jacques Christian)
Durang, Christopher 1949- .... **CLC 27, 38**
See also CA 105; CAD; CANR 50, 76, 130;
CD 5, 6; MTCW 2; MTFW 2005
Durang, Christopher Ferdinand
See Durang, Christopher
Duras, Claire de 1777-1832 .... **NCLC 154**
Duras, Marguerite 1914-1996 . **CLC 3, 6, 11,
20, 34, 40, 68, 100; SSC 40**
See also BPFB 1; CA 25-28R; 151; CANR
50; CWW 2; DFS 21; DLB 83, 321; EWL
3; FL 1:5; GFL 1789 to the Present; IDFW
4; MTCW 1, 2; RGWL 2, 3; TWA
Durban, (Rosa) Pam 1947- .... **CLC 39**
See also CA 123; CANR 98; CSW
Durcan, Paul 1944- .... **CLC 43, 70**
See also CA 134; CANR 123; CP 1, 5, 6, 7;
DAM POET; EWL 3
Durfey, Thomas 1653-1723 .... **LC 94**
See also DLB 80; RGEL 2
Durkheim, Emile 1858-1917 .... **TCLC 55**
Durrell, Lawrence (George)
1912-1990 ..... **CLC 1, 4, 6, 8, 13, 27, 41**
See also BPFB 1; BRWS 1; CA 9-12R; 132;
CANR 40, 77; CDBLB 1945-1960; CN 1,
2, 3, 4; CP 1, 2, 3, 4, 5; DAM NOV; DLB
15, 27, 204; DLBY 1990; EWL 3; MTCW
1, 2; RGEL 2; SFW 4; TEA
Durrenmatt, Friedrich
See Duerrenmatt, Friedrich
See also CDWLB 2; EW 13; EWL 3;
RGHL; RGWL 2, 3
Dutt, Michael Madhusudan
1824-1873 .... **NCLC 118**
Dutt, Toru 1856-1877 .... **NCLC 29**
See also DLB 240
Dwight, Timothy 1752-1817 .... **NCLC 13**
See also DLB 37; RGAL 4
Dworkin, Andrea 1946-2005 ..... **CLC 43, 123**
See also CA 77-80; 238; CAAS 21; CANR
16, 39, 76, 96; FL 1:5; FW; GLL 1; INT
CANR-16; MTCW 1, 2; MTFW 2005
Dwyer, Deanna
See Koontz, Dean R.
Dwyer, K. R.
See Koontz, Dean R.
Dybek, Stuart 1942- .... **CLC 114; SSC 55**
See also CA 97-100; CANR 39; DLB 130;
SSFS 23
Dye, Richard
See De Voto, Bernard (Augustine)
Dyer, Geoff 1958- .... **CLC 149**
See also CA 125; CANR 88

Eliot, T(homas) S(tearns)
1888-1965 ...... **CLC 1, 2, 3, 6, 9, 10, 13, 15, 24, 34, 41, 55, 57, 113; PC 5, 31; WLC 2**
See also AAYA 28; AMW; AMWC 1; AMWR 1; BRW 7; BRWR 2; CA 5-8R; 25-28R; CANR 41; CBD; CDALB 1929-1941; DA; DA3; DAB; DAC; DAM DRAM, MST, POET; DFS 4, 13; DLB 7, 10, 45, 63, 245; DLBY 1988; EWL 3; EXPP; LAIT 3; LATS 1:1; LMFS 2; MAL 5; MTCW 1, 2; MTFW 2005; NCFS 5; PAB; PFS 1, 7, 20; RGAL 4; RGEL 2; TUS; WLIT 4; WP

Elisabeth of Schonau c.
1129-1165 .... **CMLC 82**

Elizabeth 1866-1941 .... **TCLC 41**

Elizabeth I 1533-1603 .... **LC 118**
See also DLB 136

Elkin, Stanley L(awrence)
1930-1995 .. **CLC 4, 6, 9, 14, 27, 51, 91; SSC 12**
See also AMWS 6; BPFB 1; CA 9-12R; 148; CANR 8, 46; CN 1, 2, 3, 4, 5, 6; CPW; DAM NOV, POP; DLB 2, 28, 218, 278; DLBY 1980; EWL 3; INT CANR-8; MAL 5; MTCW 1, 2; MTFW 2005; RGAL 4; TCLE 1:1

Elledge, Scott .... **CLC 34**

Eller, Scott
See Shepard, James R.

Elliott, Don
See Silverberg, Robert

Elliott, George P(aul) 1918-1980 ...... **CLC 2**
See also CA 1-4R; 97-100; CANR 2; CN 1, 2; CP 3; DLB 244; MAL 5

Elliott, Janice 1931-1995 .... **CLC 47**
See also CA 13-16R; CANR 8, 29, 84; CN 5, 6, 7; DLB 14; SATA 119

Elliott, Sumner Locke 1917-1991 ..... **CLC 38**
See also CA 5-8R; 134; CANR 2, 21; DLB 289

Elliott, William
See Bradbury, Ray (Douglas)

Ellis, A. E. .... **CLC 7**

Ellis, Alice Thomas .... **CLC 40**
See Haycraft, Anna
See also CN 4, 5, 6; DLB 194

Ellis, Bret Easton 1964- ...... **CLC 39, 71, 117**
See also AAYA 2, 43; CA 118; 123; CANR 51, 74, 126; CN 6, 7; CPW; DA3; DAM POP; DLB 292; HGG; INT CA-123; MTCW 2; MTFW 2005; NFS 11

Ellis, (Henry) Havelock
1859-1939 .... **TCLC 14**
See also CA 109; 169; DLB 190

Ellis, Landon
See Ellison, Harlan (Jay)

Ellis, Trey 1962- .... **CLC 55**
See also CA 146; CANR 92; CN 7

Ellison, Harlan (Jay) 1934- ... **CLC 1, 13, 42, 139; SSC 14**
See also AAYA 29; BPFB 1; BYA 14; CA 5-8R; CANR 5, 46, 115; CPW; DAM POP; DLB 8; HGG; INT CANR-5; MTCW 1, 2; MTFW 2005; SCFW 2; SFW 4; SSFS 13, 14, 15, 21; SUFW 1, 2

Ellison, Ralph (Waldo) 1914-1994 .... **BLC 1; CLC 1, 3, 11, 54, 86, 114; SSC 26, 79; WLC 2**
See also AAYA 19; AFAW 1, 2; AMWC 2; AMWR 2; AMWS 2; BPFB 1; BW 1, 3; BYA 2; CA 9-12R; 145; CANR 24, 53; CDALB 1941-1968; CN 1, 2, 3, 4, 5; CSW; DA; DA3; DAB; DAC; DAM MST, MULT, NOV; DLB 2, 76, 227; DLBY 1994; EWL 3; EXPN; EXPS; LAIT 4; MAL 5; MTCW 1, 2; MTFW 2005; NCFS 3; NFS 2, 21; RGAL 4; RGSF 2; SSFS 1, 11; YAW

Ellmann, Lucy 1956- .... **CLC 61**
See also CA 128; CANR 154

Ellmann, Lucy Elizabeth
See Ellmann, Lucy

Ellmann, Richard (David)
1918-1987 .... **CLC 50**
See also BEST 89:2; CA 1-4R; 122; CANR 2, 28, 61; DLB 103; DLBY 1987; MTCW 1, 2; MTFW 2005

Elman, Richard (Martin)
1934-1997 .... **CLC 19**
See also CA 17-20R; 163; CAAS 3; CANR 47; TCLE 1:1

Elron
See Hubbard, L. Ron

El Saadawi, Nawal 1931- .... **CLC 196**
See al'Sadaawi, Nawal; Sa'adawi, al-Nawal; Saadawi, Nawal El; Sa'dawi, Nawal al-
See also CA 118; CAAS 11; CANR 44, 92

Eluard, Paul .... **PC 38; TCLC 7, 41**
See Grindel, Eugene
See also EWL 3; GFL 1789 to the Present; RGWL 2, 3

Elyot, Thomas 1490(?)-1546 .... **LC 11**
See also DLB 136; RGEL 2

Elytis, Odysseus 1911-1996 .... **CLC 15, 49, 100; PC 21**
See Alepoudelis, Odysseus
See also CA 102; 151; CANR 94; CWW 2; DAM POET; EW 13; EWL 3; MTCW 1, 2; RGWL 2, 3

Emecheta, (Florence Onye) Buchi
1944- ...... **BLC 2; CLC 14, 48, 128, 214**
See also AAYA 67; AFW; BW 2, 3; CA 81-84; CANR 27, 81, 126; CDWLB 3; CN 4, 5, 6, 7; CWRI 5; DA3; DAM MULT; DLB 117; EWL 3; FL 1:5; FW; MTCW 1, 2; MTFW 2005; NFS 12, 14; SATA 66; WLIT 2

Emerson, Mary Moody
1774-1863 .... **NCLC 66**

Emerson, Ralph Waldo 1803-1882 . **NCLC 1, 38, 98; PC 18; WLC 2**
See also AAYA 60; AMW; ANW; CDALB 1640-1865; DA; DA3; DAB; DAC; DAM MST, POET; DLB 1, 59, 73, 183, 223, 270; EXPP; LAIT 2; LMFS 1; NCFS 3; PFS 4, 17; RGAL 4; TUS; WP

Eminescu, Mihail 1850-1889 .. **NCLC 33, 131**

Empedocles 5th cent. B.C.- .... **CMLC 50**
See also DLB 176

Empson, William 1906-1984 ... **CLC 3, 8, 19, 33, 34**
See also BRWS 2; CA 17-20R; 112; CANR 31, 61; CP 1, 2, 3; DLB 20; EWL 3; MTCW 1, 2; RGEL 2

Enchi, Fumiko (Ueda) 1905-1986 ..... **CLC 31**
See Enchi Fumiko
See also CA 129; 121; FW; MJW

Enchi Fumiko
See Enchi, Fumiko (Ueda)
See also DLB 182; EWL 3

Ende, Michael (Andreas Helmuth)
1929-1995 .... **CLC 31**
See also BYA 5; CA 118; 124; 149; CANR 36, 110; CLR 14; DLB 75; MAICYA 1, 2; MAICYAS 1; SATA 61, 130; SATA-Brief 42; SATA-Obit 86

Endo, Shusaku 1923-1996 ..... **CLC 7, 14, 19, 54, 99; SSC 48; TCLC 152**
See Endo Shusaku
See also CA 29-32R; 153; CANR 21, 54, 131; DA3; DAM NOV; MTCW 1, 2; MTFW 2005; RGSF 2; RGWL 2, 3

Endo Shusaku
See Endo, Shusaku
See also CWW 2; DLB 182; EWL 3

Engel, Marian 1933-1985 .... **CLC 36; TCLC 137**
See also CA 25-28R; CANR 12; CN 2, 3; DLB 53; FW; INT CANR-12

Engelhardt, Frederick
See Hubbard, L. Ron

Engels, Friedrich 1820-1895 .. **NCLC 85, 114**
See also DLB 129; LATS 1:1

Enright, D(ennis) J(oseph)
1920-2002 .... **CLC 4, 8, 31**
See also CA 1-4R; 211; CANR 1, 42, 83; CN 1, 2; CP 1, 2, 3, 4, 5, 6, 7; DLB 27; EWL 3; SATA 25; SATA-Obit 140

Ensler, Eve 1953- .... **CLC 212**
See also CA 172; CANR 126; DFS 23

Enzensberger, Hans Magnus
1929- .... **CLC 43; PC 28**
See also CA 116; 119; CANR 103; CWW 2; EWL 3

Ephron, Nora 1941- .... **CLC 17, 31**
See also AAYA 35; AITN 2; CA 65-68; CANR 12, 39, 83; DFS 22

Epicurus 341B.C.-270B.C. .... **CMLC 21**
See also DLB 176

Epsilon
See Betjeman, John

Epstein, Daniel Mark 1948- .... **CLC 7**
See also CA 49-52; CANR 2, 53, 90

Epstein, Jacob 1956- .... **CLC 19**
See also CA 114

Epstein, Jean 1897-1953 .... **TCLC 92**

Epstein, Joseph 1937- .... **CLC 39, 204**
See also AMWS 14; CA 112; 119; CANR 50, 65, 117

Epstein, Leslie 1938- .... **CLC 27**
See also AMWS 12; CA 73-76, 215; CAAE 215; CAAS 12; CANR 23, 69; DLB 299; RGHL

Equiano, Olaudah 1745(?)-1797 . **BLC 2; LC 16**
See also AFAW 1, 2; CDWLB 3; DAM MULT; DLB 37, 50; WLIT 2

Erasmus, Desiderius 1469(?)-1536 ..... **LC 16, 93**
See also DLB 136; EW 2; LMFS 1; RGWL 2, 3; TWA

Erdman, Paul E(mil) 1932- .... **CLC 25**
See also AITN 1; CA 61-64; CANR 13, 43, 84

Erdrich, Karen Louise
See Erdrich, Louise

Erdrich, Louise 1954- .... **CLC 39, 54, 120, 176; NNAL; PC 52**
See also AAYA 10, 47; AMWS 4; BEST 89:1; BPFB 1; CA 114; CANR 41, 62, 118, 138; CDALBS; CN 5, 6, 7; CP 6, 7; CPW; CWP; DA3; DAM MULT, NOV, POP; DLB 152, 175, 206; EWL 3; EXPP; FL 1:5; LAIT 5; LATS 1:2; MAL 5; MTCW 1, 2; MTFW 2005; NFS 5; PFS 14; RGAL 4; SATA 94, 141; SSFS 14; TCWW 2

Erenburg, Ilya (Grigoryevich)
See Ehrenburg, Ilya (Grigoryevich)

Erickson, Stephen Michael 1950-
See Erickson, Steve
See also CA 129; SFW 4

Erickson, Steve .... **CLC 64**
See Erickson, Stephen Michael
See also CANR 60, 68, 136; MTFW 2005; SUFW 2

Erickson, Walter
See Fast, Howard (Melvin)

Ericson, Walter
See Fast, Howard (Melvin)

Eriksson, Buntel
See Bergman, (Ernst) Ingmar

Fauset, Jessie Redmon
1882(?)-1961 .. **BLC 2; CLC 19, 54; HR 1:2**
See also AFAW 2; BW 1; CA 109; CANR 83; DAM MULT; DLB 51; FW; LMFS 2; MAL 5; MAWW

Faust, Frederick (Schiller)
1892-1944 .... **TCLC 49**
See Brand, Max; Dawson, Peter; Frederick, John
See also CA 108; 152; CANR 143; DAM POP; DLB 256; TUS

Faust, Irvin 1924- .... **CLC 8**
See also CA 33-36R; CANR 28, 67; CN 1, 2, 3, 4, 5, 6, 7; DLB 2, 28, 218, 278; DLBY 1980

Fawkes, Guy
See Benchley, Robert (Charles)

Fearing, Kenneth (Flexner)
1902-1961 .... **CLC 51**
See also CA 93-96; CANR 59; CMW 4; DLB 9; MAL 5; RGAL 4

Fecamps, Elise
See Creasey, John

Federman, Raymond 1928- .... **CLC 6, 47**
See also CA 17-20R, 208; CAAE 208; CAAS 8; CANR 10, 43, 83, 108; CN 3, 4, 5, 6; DLBY 1980

Federspiel, J(uerg) F. 1931- .... **CLC 42**
See also CA 146

Feiffer, Jules (Ralph) 1929- ...... **CLC 2, 8, 64**
See also AAYA 3, 62; CA 17-20R; CAD; CANR 30, 59, 129; CD 5, 6; DAM DRAM; DLB 7, 44; INT CANR-30; MTCW 1; SATA 8, 61, 111, 157

Feige, Hermann Albert Otto Maximilian
See Traven, B.

Feinberg, David B. 1956-1994 .... **CLC 59**
See also CA 135; 147

Feinstein, Elaine 1930- .... **CLC 36**
See also CA 69-72; CAAS 1; CANR 31, 68, 121; CN 3, 4, 5, 6, 7; CP 2, 3, 4, 5, 6, 7; CWP; DLB 14, 40; MTCW 1

Feke, Gilbert David .... **CLC 65**

Feldman, Irving (Mordecai) 1928- ..... **CLC 7**
See also CA 1-4R; CANR 1; CP 1, 2, 3, 4, 5, 6, 7; DLB 169; TCLE 1:1

Felix-Tchicaya, Gerald
See Tchicaya, Gerald Felix

Fellini, Federico 1920-1993 .... **CLC 16, 85**
See also CA 65-68; 143; CANR 33

Felltham, Owen 1602(?)-1668 .... **LC 92**
See also DLB 126, 151

Felsen, Henry Gregor 1916-1995 ..... **CLC 17**
See also CA 1-4R; CANR 1; SAAS 2; SATA 1

Felski, Rita .... **CLC 65**

Fenno, Jack
See Calisher, Hortense

Fenollosa, Ernest (Francisco)
1853-1908 .... **TCLC 91**

Fenton, James Martin 1949- .... **CLC 32, 209**
See also CA 102; CANR 108; CP 2, 3, 4, 5, 6, 7; DLB 40; PFS 11

Ferber, Edna 1887-1968 .... **CLC 18, 93**
See also AITN 1; CA 5-8R; 25-28R; CANR 68, 105; DLB 9, 28, 86, 266; MAL 5; MTCW 1, 2; MTFW 2005; RGAL 4; RHW; SATA 7; TCWW 1, 2

Ferdowsi, Abu'l Qasem
940-1020(?) .... **CMLC 43**
See Firdawsi, Abu al-Qasim
See also RGWL 2, 3

Ferguson, Helen
See Kavan, Anna

Ferguson, Niall 1964- .... **CLC 134**
See also CA 190; CANR 154

Ferguson, Samuel 1810-1886 .... **NCLC 33**
See also DLB 32; RGEL 2

Fergusson, Robert 1750-1774 .... **LC 29**
See also DLB 109; RGEL 2

Ferling, Lawrence
See Ferlinghetti, Lawrence

Ferlinghetti, Lawrence 1919(?)- .... **CLC 2, 6, 10, 27, 111; PC 1**
See also BG 1:2; CA 5-8R; CAD; CANR 3, 41, 73, 125; CDALB 1941-1968; CP 1, 2, 3, 4, 5, 6, 7; DA3; DAM POET; DLB 5, 16; MAL 5; MTCW 1, 2; MTFW 2005; RGAL 4; WP

Ferlinghetti, Lawrence Monsanto
See Ferlinghetti, Lawrence

Fern, Fanny
See Parton, Sara Payson Willis

Fernandez, Vicente Garcia Huidobro
See Huidobro Fernandez, Vicente Garcia

Fernandez-Armesto, Felipe .... **CLC 70**
See Fernandez-Armesto, Felipe Fermin Ricardo
See also CANR 153

Fernandez-Armesto, Felipe Fermin Ricardo
1950-
See Fernandez-Armesto, Felipe
See also CA 142; CANR 93

Fernandez de Lizardi, Jose Joaquin
See Lizardi, Jose Joaquin Fernandez de

Ferre, Rosario 1938- ...... **CLC 139; HLCS 1; SSC 36**
See also CA 131; CANR 55, 81, 134; CWW 2; DLB 145; EWL 3; HW 1, 2; LAWS 1; MTCW 2; MTFW 2005; WLIT 1

Ferrer, Gabriel (Francisco Victor) Miro
See Miro (Ferrer), Gabriel (Francisco Victor)

Ferrier, Susan (Edmonstone)
1782-1854 .... **NCLC 8**
See also DLB 116; RGEL 2

Ferrigno, Robert 1948(?)- .... **CLC 65**
See also CA 140; CANR 125

Ferron, Jacques 1921-1985 .... **CLC 94**
See also CA 117; 129; CCA 1; DAC; DLB 60; EWL 3

Feuchtwanger, Lion 1884-1958 .... **TCLC 3**
See also CA 104; 187; DLB 66; EWL 3; RGHL

Feuerbach, Ludwig 1804-1872 ..... **NCLC 139**
See also DLB 133

Feuillet, Octave 1821-1890 .... **NCLC 45**
See also DLB 192

Feydeau, Georges (Leon Jules Marie)
1862-1921 .... **TCLC 22**
See also CA 113; 152; CANR 84; DAM DRAM; DLB 192; EWL 3; GFL 1789 to the Present; RGWL 2, 3

Fichte, Johann Gottlieb
1762-1814 .... **NCLC 62**
See also DLB 90

Ficino, Marsilio 1433-1499 .... **LC 12**
See also LMFS 1

Fiedeler, Hans
See Doeblin, Alfred

Fiedler, Leslie A(aron) 1917-2003 ..... **CLC 4, 13, 24**
See also AMWS 13; CA 9-12R; 212; CANR 7, 63; CN 1, 2, 3, 4, 5, 6; DLB 28, 67; EWL 3; MAL 5; MTCW 1, 2; RGAL 4; TUS

Field, Andrew 1938- .... **CLC 44**
See also CA 97-100; CANR 25

Field, Eugene 1850-1895 .... **NCLC 3**
See also DLB 23, 42, 140; DLBD 13; MAICYA 1, 2; RGAL 4; SATA 16

Field, Gans T.
See Wellman, Manly Wade

Field, Michael 1915-1971 .... **TCLC 43**
See also CA 29-32R

Fielding, Helen 1958- .... **CLC 146, 217**
See also AAYA 65; CA 172; CANR 127; DLB 231; MTFW 2005

Fielding, Henry 1707-1754 .... **LC 1, 46, 85; WLC 2**
See also BRW 3; BRWR 1; CDBLB 1660-1789; DA; DA3; DAB; DAC; DAM DRAM, MST, NOV; DLB 39, 84, 101; NFS 18; RGEL 2; TEA; WLIT 3

Fielding, Sarah 1710-1768 .... **LC 1, 44**
See also DLB 39; RGEL 2; TEA

Fields, W. C. 1880-1946 .... **TCLC 80**
See also DLB 44

Fierstein, Harvey (Forbes) 1954- ..... **CLC 33**
See also CA 123; 129; CAD; CD 5, 6; CPW; DA3; DAM DRAM, POP; DFS 6; DLB 266; GLL; MAL 5

Figes, Eva 1932- .... **CLC 31**
See also CA 53-56; CANR 4, 44, 83; CN 2, 3, 4, 5, 6, 7; DLB 14, 271; FW; RGHL

Filippo, Eduardo de
See de Filippo, Eduardo

Finch, Anne 1661-1720 .... **LC 3; PC 21**
See also BRWS 9; DLB 95

Finch, Robert (Duer Claydon)
1900-1995 .... **CLC 18**
See also CA 57-60; CANR 9, 24, 49; CP 1, 2, 3, 4, 5, 6; DLB 88

Findley, Timothy (Irving Frederick)
1930-2002 .... **CLC 27, 102**
See also CA 25-28R; 206; CANR 12, 42, 69, 109; CCA 1; CN 4, 5, 6, 7; DAC; DAM MST; DLB 53; FANT; RHW

Fink, William
See Mencken, H(enry) L(ouis)

Firbank, Louis 1942-
See Reed, Lou
See also CA 117

Firbank, (Arthur Annesley) Ronald
1886-1926 .... **TCLC 1**
See also BRWS 2; CA 104; 177; DLB 36; EWL 3; RGEL 2

Firdawsi, Abu al-Qasim
See Ferdowsi, Abu'l Qasem
See also WLIT 6

Fish, Stanley
See Fish, Stanley Eugene

Fish, Stanley E.
See Fish, Stanley Eugene

Fish, Stanley Eugene 1938- .... **CLC 142**
See also CA 112; 132; CANR 90; DLB 67

Fisher, Dorothy (Frances) Canfield
1879-1958 .... **TCLC 87**
See also CA 114; 136; CANR 80; CLR 71; CWRI 5; DLB 9, 102, 284; MAICYA 1, 2; MAL 5; YABC 1

Fisher, M(ary) F(rances) K(ennedy)
1908-1992 .... **CLC 76, 87**
See also CA 77-80; 138; CANR 44; MTCW 2

Fisher, Roy 1930- .... **CLC 25**
See also CA 81-84; CAAS 10; CANR 16; CP 1, 2, 3, 4, 5, 6, 7; DLB 40

Fisher, Rudolph 1897-1934 . **BLC 2; HR 1:2; SSC 25; TCLC 11**
See also BW 1, 3; CA 107; 124; CANR 80; DAM MULT; DLB 51, 102

Fisher, Vardis (Alvero) 1895-1968 .... **CLC 7; TCLC 140**
See also CA 5-8R; 25-28R; CANR 68; DLB 9, 206; MAL 5; RGAL 4; TCWW 1, 2

Fiske, Tarleton
See Bloch, Robert (Albert)

Fitch, Clarke
See Sinclair, Upton

Fitch, John IV
See Cormier, Robert (Edmund)

Fitzgerald, Captain Hugh
See Baum, L(yman) Frank

Gozzi, (Conte) Carlo 1720-1806 .... **NCLC 23**

Grabbe, Christian Dietrich
1801-1836 .... **NCLC 2**
See also DLB 133; RGWL 2, 3

Grace, Patricia Frances 1937- .... **CLC 56**
See also CA 176; CANR 118; CN 4, 5, 6,
7; EWL 3; RGSF 2

Gracian y Morales, Baltasar
1601-1658 .... **LC 15**

Gracq, Julien .... **CLC 11, 48**
See Poirier, Louis
See also CWW 2; DLB 83; GFL 1789 to
the Present

Grade, Chaim 1910-1982 .... **CLC 10**
See also CA 93-96; 107; EWL 3; RGHL

Graduate of Oxford, A
See Ruskin, John

Grafton, Garth
See Duncan, Sara Jeannette

Grafton, Sue 1940- .... **CLC 163**
See also AAYA 11, 49; BEST 90:3; CA 108;
CANR 31, 55, 111, 134; CMW 4; CPW;
CSW; DA3; DAM POP; DLB 226; FW;
MSW; MTFW 2005

Graham, John
See Phillips, David Graham

Graham, Jorie 1950- .... **CLC 48, 118; PC 59**
See also AAYA 67; CA 111; CANR 63, 118;
CP 4, 5, 6, 7; CWP; DLB 120; EWL 3;
MTFW 2005; PFS 10, 17; TCLE 1:1

Graham, R(obert) B(ontine) Cunninghame
See Cunninghame Graham, Robert
(Gallnigad) Bontine
See also DLB 98, 135, 174; RGEL 2;
RGSF 2

Graham, Robert
See Haldeman, Joe

Graham, Tom
See Lewis, (Harry) Sinclair

Graham, W(illiam) S(idney)
1918-1986 .... **CLC 29**
See also BRWS 7; CA 73-76; 118; CP 1, 2,
3, 4; DLB 20; RGEL 2

Graham, Winston (Mawdsley)
1910-2003 .... **CLC 23**
See also CA 49-52; 218; CANR 2, 22, 45,
66; CMW 4; CN 1, 2, 3, 4, 5, 6, 7; DLB
77; RHW

Grahame, Kenneth 1859-1932 ...... **TCLC 64,
136**
See also BYA 5; CA 108; 136; CANR 80;
CLR 5; CWRI 5; DA3; DAB; DLB 34,
141, 178; FANT; MAICYA 1, 2; MTCW
2; NFS 20; RGEL 2; SATA 100; TEA;
WCH; YABC 1

Granger, Darius John
See Marlowe, Stephen

Granin, Daniil 1918- .... **CLC 59**
See also DLB 302

Granovsky, Timofei Nikolaevich
1813-1855 .... **NCLC 75**
See also DLB 198

Grant, Skeeter
See Spiegelman, Art

Granville-Barker, Harley
1877-1946 .... **TCLC 2**
See Barker, Harley Granville
See also CA 104; 204; DAM DRAM;
RGEL 2

Granzotto, Gianni
See Granzotto, Giovanni Battista

Granzotto, Giovanni Battista
1914-1985 .... **CLC 70**
See also CA 166

Grass, Guenter (Wilhelm) 1927- ... **CLC 1, 2,
4, 6, 11, 15, 22, 32, 49, 88, 207; WLC 3**
See Grass, Gunter (Wilhelm)
See also BPFB 2; CA 13-16R; CANR 20,
75, 93, 133; CDWLB 2; DA; DA3; DAB;
DAC; DAM MST, NOV; DLB 75, 124;
EW 13; EWL 3; MTCW 1, 2; MTFW
2005; RGWL 2, 3; TWA

Grass, Gunter (Wilhelm)
See Grass, Guenter (Wilhelm)
See also CWW 2; RGHL

Gratton, Thomas
See Hulme, T(homas) E(rnest)

Grau, Shirley Ann 1929- .... **CLC 4, 9, 146;
SSC 15**
See also CA 89-92; CANR 22, 69; CN 1, 2,
3, 4, 5, 6, 7; CSW; DLB 2, 218; INT CA-
89-92; CANR-22; MTCW 1

Gravel, Fern
See Hall, James Norman

Graver, Elizabeth 1964- .... **CLC 70**
See also CA 135; CANR 71, 129

Graves, Richard Perceval
1895-1985 .... **CLC 44**
See also CA 65-68; CANR 9, 26, 51

Graves, Robert (von Ranke)
1895-1985 .. **CLC 1, 2, 6, 11, 39, 44, 45;
PC 6**
See also BPFB 2; BRW 7; BYA 4; CA 5-8R;
117; CANR 5, 36; CDBLB 1914-1945;
CN 1, 2, 3; CP 1, 2, 3, 4; DA3; DAB;
DAC; DAM MST, POET; DLB 20, 100,
191; DLBD 18; DLBY 1985; EWL 3;
LATS 1:1; MTCW 1, 2; MTFW 2005;
NCFS 2; NFS 21; RGEL 2; RHW; SATA
45; TEA

Graves, Valerie
See Bradley, Marion Zimmer

Gray, Alasdair (James) 1934- .... **CLC 41**
See also BRWS 9; CA 126; CANR 47, 69,
106, 140; CN 4, 5, 6, 7; DLB 194, 261,
319; HGG; INT CA-126; MTCW 1, 2;
MTFW 2005; RGSF 2; SUFW 2

Gray, Amlin 1946- .... **CLC 29**
See also CA 138

Gray, Francine du Plessix 1930- ..... **CLC 22,
153**
See also BEST 90:3; CA 61-64; CAAS 2;
CANR 11, 33, 75, 81; DAM NOV; INT
CANR-11; MTCW 1, 2; MTFW 2005

Gray, John (Henry) 1866-1934 ...... **TCLC 19**
See also CA 119; 162; RGEL 2

Gray, John Lee
See Jakes, John (William)

Gray, Simon (James Holliday)
1936- .... **CLC 9, 14, 36**
See also AITN 1; CA 21-24R; CAAS 3;
CANR 32, 69; CBD; CD 5, 6; CN 1, 2, 3;
DLB 13; EWL 3; MTCW 1; RGEL 2

Gray, Spalding 1941-2004 .... **CLC 49, 112;
DC 7**
See also AAYA 62; CA 128; 225; CAD;
CANR 74, 138; CD 5, 6; CPW; DAM
POP; MTCW 2; MTFW 2005

Gray, Thomas 1716-1771 .... **LC 4, 40; PC 2;
WLC 3**
See also BRW 3; CDBLB 1660-1789; DA;
DA3; DAB; DAC; DAM MST; DLB 109;
EXPP; PAB; PFS 9; RGEL 2; TEA; WP

Grayson, David
See Baker, Ray Stannard

Grayson, Richard (A.) 1951- .... **CLC 38**
See also CA 85-88; 210; CAAE 210; CANR
14, 31, 57; DLB 234

Greeley, Andrew M(oran) 1928- ...... **CLC 28**
See also BPFB 2; CA 5-8R; CAAS 7;
CANR 7, 43, 69, 104, 136; CMW 4;
CPW; DA3; DAM POP; MTCW 1, 2;
MTFW 2005

Green, Anna Katharine
1846-1935 .... **TCLC 63**
See also CA 112; 159; CMW 4; DLB 202,
221; MSW

Green, Brian
See Card, Orson Scott

Green, Hannah
See Greenberg, Joanne (Goldenberg)

Green, Hannah 1927(?)-1996 .... **CLC 3**
See also CA 73-76; CANR 59, 93; NFS 10

Green, Henry .... **CLC 2, 13, 97**
See Yorke, Henry Vincent
See also BRWS 2; CA 175; DLB 15; EWL
3; RGEL 2

Green, Julian .... **CLC 3, 11, 77**
See Green, Julien (Hartridge)
See also EWL 3; GFL 1789 to the Present;
MTCW 2

Green, Julien (Hartridge) 1900-1998
See Green, Julian
See also CA 21-24R; 169; CANR 33, 87;
CWW 2; DLB 4, 72; MTCW 1, 2; MTFW
2005

Green, Paul (Eliot) 1894-1981 .... **CLC 25**
See also AITN 1; CA 5-8R; 103; CAD;
CANR 3; DAM DRAM; DLB 7, 9, 249;
DLBY 1981; MAL 5; RGAL 4

Greenaway, Peter 1942- .... **CLC 159**
See also CA 127

Greenberg, Ivan 1908-1973
See Rahv, Philip
See also CA 85-88

Greenberg, Joanne (Goldenberg)
1932- .... **CLC 7, 30**
See also AAYA 12, 67; CA 5-8R; CANR
14, 32, 69; CN 6, 7; NFS 23; SATA 25;
YAW

Greenberg, Richard 1959(?)- .... **CLC 57**
See also CA 138; CAD; CD 5, 6

Greenblatt, Stephen J(ay) 1943- ...... **CLC 70**
See also CA 49-52; CANR 115

Greene, Bette 1934- .... **CLC 30**
See also AAYA 7, 69; BYA 3; CA 53-56;
CANR 4, 146; CLR 2; CWRI 5; JRDA;
LAIT 4; MAICYA 1, 2; NFS 10; SAAS
16; SATA 8, 102, 161; WYA; YAW

Greene, Gael .... **CLC 8**
See also CA 13-16R; CANR 10

Greene, Graham (Henry)
1904-1991 .... **CLC 1, 3, 6, 9, 14, 18, 27,
37, 70, 72, 125; SSC 29; WLC 3**
See also AAYA 61; AITN 2; BPFB 2;
BRWR 2; BRWS 1; BYA 3; CA 13-16R;
133; CANR 35, 61, 131; CBD; CDBLB
1945-1960; CMW 4; CN 1, 2, 3, 4; DA;
DA3; DAB; DAC; DAM MST, NOV;
DLB 13, 15, 77, 100, 162, 201, 204;
DLBY 1991; EWL 3; MSW; MTCW 1, 2;
MTFW 2005; NFS 16; RGEL 2; SATA
20; SSFS 14; TEA; WLIT 4

Greene, Robert 1558-1592 .... **LC 41**
See also BRWS 8; DLB 62, 167; IDTP;
RGEL 2; TEA

Greer, Germaine 1939- .... **CLC 131**
See also AITN 1; CA 81-84; CANR 33, 70,
115, 133; FW; MTCW 1, 2; MTFW 2005

Greer, Richard
See Silverberg, Robert

Gregor, Arthur 1923- .... **CLC 9**
See also CA 25-28R; CAAS 10; CANR 11;
CP 1, 2, 3, 4, 5, 6, 7; SATA 36

Gregor, Lee
See Pohl, Frederik

Gregory, Lady Isabella Augusta (Persse)
1852-1932 .... **TCLC 1, 176**
See also BRW 6; CA 104; 184; DLB 10;
IDTP; RGEL 2

Gregory, J. Dennis
See Williams, John A(lfred)

Gregory of Nazianzus, St.
  329-389 .... **CMLC 82**
Grekova, I. .... **CLC 59**
  See Ventsel, Elena Sergeevna
  See also CWW 2
Grendon, Stephen
  See Derleth, August (William)
Greve, Felix Paul (Berthold Friedrich)
  1879-1948
  See Grove, Frederick Philip
  See also CA 104; 141, 175; CANR 79;
  DAC; DAM MST
Greville, Fulke 1554-1628 .... **LC 79**
  See also BRWS 11; DLB 62, 172; RGEL 2
Grey, Lady Jane 1537-1554 .... **LC 93**
  See also DLB 132
Grey, Zane 1872-1939 .... **TCLC 6**
  See also BPFB 2; CA 104; 132; DA3; DAM
  POP; DLB 9, 212; MTCW 1, 2; MTFW
  2005; RGAL 4; TCWW 1, 2; TUS
Griboedov, Aleksandr Sergeevich
  1795(?)-1829 .... **NCLC 129**
  See also DLB 205; RGWL 2, 3
Grieg, (Johan) Nordahl (Brun)
  1902-1943 .... **TCLC 10**
  See also CA 107; 189; EWL 3
Grieve, C(hristopher) M(urray)
  1892-1978 .... **CLC 11, 19**
  See MacDiarmid, Hugh; Pteleon
  See also CA 5-8R; 85-88; CANR 33, 107;
  DAM POET; MTCW 1; RGEL 2
Griffin, Gerald 1803-1840 .... **NCLC 7**
  See also DLB 159; RGEL 2
Griffin, John Howard 1920-1980 ..... **CLC 68**
  See also AITN 1; CA 1-4R; 101; CANR 2
Griffin, Peter 1942- .... **CLC 39**
  See also CA 136
Griffith, D(avid Lewelyn) W(ark)
  1875(?)-1948 .... **TCLC 68**
  See also CA 119; 150; CANR 80
Griffith, Lawrence
  See Griffith, D(avid Lewelyn) W(ark)
Griffiths, Trevor 1935- .... **CLC 13, 52**
  See also CA 97-100; CANR 45; CBD; CD
  5, 6; DLB 13, 245
Griggs, Sutton (Elbert)
  1872-1930 .... **TCLC 77**
  See also CA 123; 186; DLB 50
Grigson, Geoffrey (Edward Harvey)
  1905-1985 .... **CLC 7, 39**
  See also CA 25-28R; 118; CANR 20, 33;
  CP 1, 2, 3, 4; DLB 27; MTCW 1, 2
Grile, Dod
  See Bierce, Ambrose (Gwinett)
Grillparzer, Franz 1791-1872 .... **DC 14;**
  NCLC 1, 102; SSC 37
  See also CDWLB 2; DLB 133; EW 5;
  RGWL 2, 3; TWA
Grimble, Reverend Charles James
  See Eliot, T(homas) S(tearns)
Grimke, Angelina (Emily) Weld
  1880-1958 .... **HR 1:2**
  See Weld, Angelina (Emily) Grimke
  See also BW 1; CA 124; DAM POET; DLB
  50, 54
Grimke, Charlotte L(ottie) Forten
  1837(?)-1914
  See Forten, Charlotte L.
  See also BW 1; CA 117; 124; DAM MULT,
  POET

Grimm, Jacob Ludwig Karl
  1785-1863 .... **NCLC 3, 77; SSC 36**
  See Grimm Brothers
  See also CLR 112; DLB 90; MAICYA 1, 2;
  RGSF 2; RGWL 2, 3; SATA 22; WCH
Grimm, Wilhelm Karl 1786-1859 .. **NCLC 3,**
  77; SSC 36
  See Grimm Brothers
  See also CDWLB 2; CLR 112; DLB 90;
  MAICYA 1, 2; RGSF 2; RGWL 2, 3;
  SATA 22; WCH
Grimm and Grim
  See Grimm, Jacob Ludwig Karl; Grimm,
  Wilhelm Karl
Grimm Brothers .... **SSC 88**
  See Grimm, Jacob Ludwig Karl; Grimm,
  Wilhelm Karl
  See also CLR 112
Grimmelshausen, Hans Jakob Christoffel
  von
  See Grimmelshausen, Johann Jakob Christ-
  offel von
  See also RGWL 2, 3
Grimmelshausen, Johann Jakob Christoffel
  von 1621-1676 .... **LC 6**
  See Grimmelshausen, Hans Jakob Christof-
  fel von
  See also CDWLB 2; DLB 168
Grindel, Eugene 1895-1952
  See Eluard, Paul
  See also CA 104; 193; LMFS 2
Grisham, John 1955- .... **CLC 84**
  See also AAYA 14, 47; BPFB 2; CA 138;
  CANR 47, 69, 114, 133; CMW 4; CN 6,
  7; CPW; CSW; DA3; DAM POP; MSW;
  MTCW 2; MTFW 2005
Grosseteste, Robert 1175(?)-1253 . **CMLC 62**
  See also DLB 115
Grossman, David 1954- .... **CLC 67**
  See also CA 138; CANR 114; CWW 2;
  DLB 299; EWL 3; RGHL; WLIT 6
Grossman, Vasilii Semenovich
  See Grossman, Vasily (Semenovich)
  See also DLB 272
Grossman, Vasily (Semenovich)
  1905-1964 .... **CLC 41**
  See Grossman, Vasilii Semenovich
  See also CA 124; 130; MTCW 1; RGHL
Grove, Frederick Philip .... **TCLC 4**
  See Greve, Felix Paul (Berthold Friedrich)
  See also DLB 92; RGEL 2; TCWW 1, 2
Grubb
  See Crumb, R.
Grumbach, Doris (Isaac) 1918- . **CLC 13, 22,**
  64
  See also CA 5-8R; CAAS 2; CANR 9, 42,
  70, 127; CN 6, 7; INT CANR-9; MTCW
  2; MTFW 2005
Grundtvig, Nikolai Frederik Severin
  1783-1872 .... **NCLC 1, 158**
  See also DLB 300
Grunge
  See Crumb, R.
Grunwald, Lisa 1959- .... **CLC 44**
  See also CA 120; CANR 148
Gryphius, Andreas 1616-1664 .... **LC 89**
  See also CDWLB 2; DLB 164; RGWL 2, 3
Guare, John 1938- .... **CLC 8, 14, 29, 67; DC**
  20
  See also CA 73-76; CAD; CANR 21, 69,
  118; CD 5, 6; DAM DRAM; DFS 8, 13;
  DLB 7, 249; EWL 3; MAL 5; MTCW 1,
  2; RGAL 4
Guarini, Battista 1537-1612 .... **LC 102**
Gubar, Susan (David) 1944- .... **CLC 145**
  See also CA 108; CANR 45, 70, 139; FW;
  MTCW 1; RGAL 4

Gudjonsson, Halldor Kiljan 1902-1998
  See Halldor Laxness
  See also CA 103; 164
Guenter, Erich
  See Eich, Gunter
Guest, Barbara 1920-2006 ... **CLC 34; PC 55**
  See also BG 1:2; CA 25-28R; 248; CANR
  11, 44, 84; CP 1, 2, 3, 4, 5, 6, 7; CWP;
  DLB 5, 193
Guest, Edgar A(lbert) 1881-1959 ... **TCLC 95**
  See also CA 112; 168
Guest, Judith (Ann) 1936- .... **CLC 8, 30**
  See also AAYA 7, 66; CA 77-80; CANR
  15, 75, 138; DA3; DAM NOV, POP;
  EXPN; INT CANR-15; LAIT 5; MTCW
  1, 2; MTFW 2005; NFS 1
Guevara, Che .... **CLC 87; HLC 1**
  See Guevara (Serna), Ernesto
Guevara (Serna), Ernesto
  1928-1967 .... **CLC 87; HLC 1**
  See Guevara, Che
  See also CA 127; 111; CANR 56; DAM
  MULT; HW 1
Guicciardini, Francesco 1483-1540 ..... **LC 49**
Guild, Nicholas M. 1944- .... **CLC 33**
  See also CA 93-96
Guillemin, Jacques
  See Sartre, Jean-Paul
Guillen, Jorge 1893-1984 . **CLC 11; HLCS 1;**
  PC 35
  See also CA 89-92; 112; DAM MULT,
  POET; DLB 108; EWL 3; HW 1; RGWL
  2, 3
Guillen, Nicolas (Cristobal)
  1902-1989 .... **BLC 2; CLC 48, 79; HLC**
  1; PC 23
  See also BW 2; CA 116; 125; 129; CANR
  84; DAM MST, MULT, POET; DLB 283;
  EWL 3; HW 1; LAW; RGWL 2, 3; WP
Guillen y Alvarez, Jorge
  See Guillen, Jorge
Guillevic, (Eugene) 1907-1997 .... **CLC 33**
  See also CA 93-96; CWW 2
Guillois
  See Desnos, Robert
Guillois, Valentin
  See Desnos, Robert
Guimaraes Rosa, Joao 1908-1967 .... **HLCS 2**
  See Rosa, Joao Guimaraes
  See also CA 175; LAW; RGSF 2; RGWL
  2, 3
Guiney, Louise Imogen
  1861-1920 .... **TCLC 41**
  See also CA 160; DLB 54; RGAL 4
Guinizelli, Guido c. 1230-1276 ...... **CMLC 49**
  See Guinizzelli, Guido
Guinizzelli, Guido
  See Guinizelli, Guido
  See also WLIT 7
Guiraldes, Ricardo (Guillermo)
  1886-1927 .... **TCLC 39**
  See also CA 131; EWL 3; HW 1; LAW;
  MTCW 1
Gumilev, Nikolai (Stepanovich)
  1886-1921 .... **TCLC 60**
  See Gumilyov, Nikolay Stepanovich
  See also CA 165
Gumilyov, Nikolay Stepanovich
  See Gumilev, Nikolai (Stepanovich)
  See also EWL 3
Gump, P. Q.
  See Card, Orson Scott
Gunesekera, Romesh 1954- .... **CLC 91**
  See also BRWS 10; CA 159; CANR 140;
  CN 6, 7; DLB 267, 323
Gunn, Bill .... **CLC 5**
  See Gunn, William Harrison
  See also DLB 38

Hamilton, (Robert) Ian 1938-2001 . **CLC 191**
See also CA 106; 203; CANR 41, 67; CP 1,
2, 3, 4, 5, 6, 7; DLB 40, 155
Hamilton, Jane 1957- .... **CLC 179**
See also CA 147; CANR 85, 128; CN 7;
MTFW 2005
Hamilton, Mollie
See Kaye, M(ary) M(argaret)
Hamilton, (Anthony Walter) Patrick
1904-1962 .... **CLC 51**
See also CA 176; 113; DLB 10, 191
Hamilton, Virginia (Esther)
1936-2002 .... **CLC 26**
See also AAYA 2, 21; BW 2, 3; BYA 1, 2,
8; CA 25-28R; 206; CANR 20, 37, 73,
126; CLR 1, 11, 40; DAM MULT; DLB
33, 52; DLBY 2001; INT CANR-20;
JRDA; LAIT 5; MAICYA 1, 2; MAIC-
YAS 1; MTCW 1, 2; MTFW 2005; SATA
4, 56, 79, 123; SATA-Obit 132; WYA;
YAW
Hammett, (Samuel) Dashiell
1894-1961 .... **CLC 3, 5, 10, 19, 47; SSC
17**
See also AAYA 59; AITN 1; AMWS 4;
BPFB 2; CA 81-84; CANR 42; CDALB
1929-1941; CMW 4; DA3; DLB 226, 280;
DLBD 6; DLBY 1996; EWL 3; LAIT 3;
MAL 5; MSW; MTCW 1, 2; MTFW
2005; NFS 21; RGAL 4; RGSF 2; TUS
Hammon, Jupiter 1720(?)-1800(?) .... **BLC 2;
NCLC 5; PC 16**
See also DAM MULT, POET; DLB 31, 50
Hammond, Keith
See Kuttner, Henry
Hamner, Earl (Henry), Jr. 1923- ...... **CLC 12**
See also AITN 2; CA 73-76; DLB 6
Hampton, Christopher 1946- .... **CLC 4**
See also CA 25-28R; CD 5, 6; DLB 13;
MTCW 1
Hampton, Christopher James
See Hampton, Christopher
Hamsun, Knut .... **TCLC 2, 14, 49, 151**
See Pedersen, Knut
See also DLB 297; EW 8; EWL 3; RGWL
2, 3
Handke, Peter 1942- .... **CLC 5, 8, 10, 15, 38,
134; DC 17**
See also CA 77-80; CANR 33, 75, 104, 133;
CWW 2; DAM DRAM, NOV; DLB 85,
124; EWL 3; MTCW 1, 2; MTFW 2005;
TWA
Handy, W(illiam) C(hristopher)
1873-1958 .... **TCLC 97**
See also BW 3; CA 121; 167
Hanley, James 1901-1985 ..... **CLC 3, 5, 8, 13**
See also CA 73-76; 117; CANR 36; CBD;
CN 1, 2, 3; DLB 191; EWL 3; MTCW 1;
RGEL 2
Hannah, Barry 1942- .... **CLC 23, 38, 90**
See also BPFB 2; CA 108; 110; CANR 43,
68, 113; CN 4, 5, 6, 7; CSW; DLB 6, 234;
INT CA-110; MTCW 1; RGSF 2
Hannon, Ezra
See Hunter, Evan
Hansberry, Lorraine (Vivian)
1930-1965 ... **BLC 2; CLC 17, 62; DC 2**
See also AAYA 25; AFAW 1, 2; AMWS 4;
BW 1, 3; CA 109; 25-28R; CABS 3;
CAD; CDALB 1941-1968; CWD;
CWD; DA; DA3; DAB; DAC; DAM
DRAM, MST, MULT; DFS 2; DLB 7, 38;
EWL 3; FL 1:6; FW; LAIT 4; MAL 5;
MTCW 1, 2; MTFW 2005; RGAL 4; TUS
Hansen, Joseph 1923-2004 .... **CLC 38**
See Brock, Rose; Colton, James
See also BPFB 2; CA 29-32R; 233; CAAS
17; CANR 16, 44, 66, 125; CMW 4; DLB
226; GLL 1; INT CANR-16

Hansen, Martin A(lfred)
1909-1955 .... **TCLC 32**
See also CA 167; DLB 214; EWL 3
Hansen and Philipson eds. .... **CLC 65**
Hanson, Kenneth O(stlin) 1922- .... **CLC 13**
See also CA 53-56; CANR 7; CP 1, 2, 3,
4, 5
Hardwick, Elizabeth (Bruce) 1916- . **CLC 13**
See also AMWS 3; CA 5-8R; CANR 3, 32,
70, 100, 139; CN 4, 5, 6; CSW; DA3;
DAM NOV; DLB 6; MAWW; MTCW 1,
2; MTFW 2005; TCLE 1:1
Hardy, Thomas 1840-1928 .... **PC 8; SSC 2,
60; TCLC 4, 10, 18, 32, 48, 53, 72, 143,
153; WLC 3**
See also AAYA 69; BRW 6; BRWC 1, 2;
BRWR 1; CA 104; 123; CDBLB 1890-
1914; DA; DA3; DAB; DAC; DAM MST,
NOV, POET; DLB 18, 19, 135, 284; EWL
3; EXPN; EXPP; LAIT 2; MTCW 1, 2;
MTFW 2005; NFS 3, 11, 15, 19; PFS 3,
4, 18; RGEL 2; RGSF 2; TEA; WLIT 4
Hare, David 1947- . **CLC 29, 58, 136; DC 26**
See also BRWS 4; CA 97-100; CANR 39,
91; CBD; CD 5, 6; DFS 4, 7, 16; DLB
13, 310; MTCW 1; TEA
Harewood, John
See Van Druten, John (William)
Harford, Henry
See Hudson, W(illiam) H(enry)
Hargrave, Leonie
See Disch, Thomas M(ichael)
**Hariri, Al- al-Qasim ibn 'Ali Abu
Muhammad al-Basri**
See al-Hariri, al-Qasim ibn 'Ali Abu Mu-
hammad al-Basri
Harjo, Joy 1951- ..... **CLC 83; NNAL; PC 27**
See also AMWS 12; CA 114; CANR 35,
67, 91, 129; CP 6, 7; CWP; DAM MULT;
DLB 120, 175; EWL 3; MTCW 2; MTFW
2005; PFS 15; RGAL 4
Harlan, Louis R(udolph) 1922- .... **CLC 34**
See also CA 21-24R; CANR 25, 55, 80
Harling, Robert 1951(?)- .... **CLC 53**
See also CA 147
Harmon, William (Ruth) 1938- .... **CLC 38**
See also CA 33-36R; CANR 14, 32, 35;
SATA 65
Harper, F. E. W.
See Harper, Frances Ellen Watkins
Harper, Frances E. W.
See Harper, Frances Ellen Watkins
Harper, Frances E. Watkins
See Harper, Frances Ellen Watkins
Harper, Frances Ellen
See Harper, Frances Ellen Watkins
Harper, Frances Ellen Watkins
1825-1911 ..... **BLC 2; PC 21; TCLC 14**
See also AFAW 1, 2; BW 1, 3; CA 111; 125;
CANR 79; DAM MULT, POET; DLB 50,
221; MAWW; RGAL 4
Harper, Michael S(teven) 1938- ... **CLC 7, 22**
See also AFAW 2; BW 1; CA 33-36R, 224;
CAAE 224; CANR 24, 108; CP 2, 3, 4, 5,
6, 7; DLB 41; RGAL 4; TCLE 1:1
Harper, Mrs. F. E. W.
See Harper, Frances Ellen Watkins
Harpur, Charles 1813-1868 .... **NCLC 114**
See also DLB 230; RGEL 2
Harris, Christie
See Harris, Christie (Lucy) Irwin
Harris, Christie (Lucy) Irwin
1907-2002 .... **CLC 12**
See also CA 5-8R; CANR 6, 83; CLR 47;
DLB 88; JRDA; MAICYA 1, 2; SAAS 10;
SATA 6, 74; SATA-Essay 116
Harris, Frank 1856-1931 .... **TCLC 24**
See also CA 109; 150; CANR 80; DLB 156,
197; RGEL 2

Harris, George Washington
1814-1869 .... **NCLC 23, 165**
See also DLB 3, 11, 248; RGAL 4
Harris, Joel Chandler 1848-1908 ..... **SSC 19;
TCLC 2**
See also CA 104; 137; CANR 80; CLR 49;
DLB 11, 23, 42, 78, 91; LAIT 2; MAI-
CYA 1, 2; RGSF 2; SATA 100; WCH;
YABC 1
**Harris, John (Wyndham Parkes Lucas)
Beynon** 1903-1969
See Wyndham, John
See also CA 102; 89-92; CANR 84; SATA
118; SFW 4
Harris, MacDonald .... **CLC 9**
See Heiney, Donald (William)
Harris, Mark 1922- .... **CLC 19**
See also CA 5-8R; CAAS 3; CANR 2, 55,
83; CN 1, 2, 3, 4, 5, 6, 7; DLB 2; DLBY
1980
Harris, Norman .... **CLC 65**
Harris, (Theodore) Wilson 1921- .... **CLC 25,
159**
See also BRWS 5; BW 2, 3; CA 65-68;
CAAS 16; CANR 11, 27, 69, 114; CD-
WLB 3; CN 1, 2, 3, 4, 5, 6, 7; CP 1, 2, 3,
4, 5, 6, 7; DLB 117; EWL 3; MTCW 1;
RGEL 2
Harrison, Barbara Grizzuti
1934-2002 .... **CLC 144**
See also CA 77-80; 205; CANR 15, 48; INT
CANR-15
Harrison, Elizabeth (Allen) Cavanna
1909-2001
See Cavanna, Betty
See also CA 9-12R; 200; CANR 6, 27, 85,
104, 121; MAICYA 2; SATA 142; YAW
Harrison, Harry (Max) 1925- .... **CLC 42**
See also CA 1-4R; CANR 5, 21, 84; DLB
8; SATA 4; SCFW 2; SFW 4
Harrison, James (Thomas) 1937- ...... **CLC 6,
14, 33, 66, 143; SSC 19**
See Harrison, Jim
See also CA 13-16R; CANR 8, 51, 79, 142;
DLBY 1982; INT CANR-8
Harrison, Jim
See Harrison, James (Thomas)
See also AMWS 8; CN 5, 6; CP 1, 2, 3, 4,
5, 6, 7; RGAL 4; TCWW 2; TUS
Harrison, Kathryn 1961- .... **CLC 70, 151**
See also CA 144; CANR 68, 122
Harrison, Tony 1937- .... **CLC 43, 129**
See also BRWS 5; CA 65-68; CANR 44,
98; CBD; CD 5, 6; CP 2, 3, 4, 5, 6, 7;
DLB 40, 245; MTCW 1; RGEL 2
Harriss, Will(ard Irvin) 1922- .... **CLC 34**
See also CA 111
Hart, Ellis
See Ellison, Harlan (Jay)
Hart, Josephine 1942(?)- .... **CLC 70**
See also CA 138; CANR 70, 149; CPW;
DAM POP
Hart, Moss 1904-1961 .... **CLC 66**
See also CA 109; 89-92; CANR 84; DAM
DRAM; DFS 1; DLB 7, 266; RGAL 4
Harte, (Francis) Bret(t)
1836(?)-1902 ... **SSC 8, 59; TCLC 1, 25;
WLC 3**
See also AMWS 2; CA 104; 140; CANR
80; CDALB 1865-1917; DA; DA3; DAC;
DAM MST; DLB 12, 64, 74, 79, 186;
EXPS; LAIT 2; RGAL 4; RGSF 2; SATA
26; SSFS 3; TUS
Hartley, L(eslie) P(oles) 1895-1972 ... **CLC 2,
22**
See also BRWS 7; CA 45-48; 37-40R;
CANR 33; CN 1; DLB 15, 139; EWL 3;
HGG; MTCW 1, 2; MTFW 2005; RGEL
2; RGSF 2; SUFW 1

Heliodorus fl. 3rd cent. - .... **CMLC 52**
　　See also WLIT 8
Hellenhofferu, Vojtech Kapristian z
　　See Hasek, Jaroslav (Matej Frantisek)
Heller, Joseph 1923-1999 . **CLC 1, 3, 5, 8, 11, 36, 63; TCLC 131, 151; WLC 3**
　　See also AAYA 24; AITN 1; AMWS 4; BPFB 2; BYA 1; CA 5-8R; 187; CABS 1; CANR 8, 42, 66, 126; CN 1, 2, 3, 4, 5, 6; CPW; DA; DA3; DAB; DAC; DAM MST, NOV, POP; DLB 2, 28, 227; DLBY 1980, 2002; EWL 3; EXPN; INT CANR-8; LAIT 4; MAL 5; MTCW 1, 2; MTFW 2005; NFS 1; RGAL 4; TUS; YAW
Hellman, Lillian (Florence) 1906-1984 .. **CLC 2, 4, 8, 14, 18, 34, 44, 52; DC 1; TCLC 119**
　　See also AAYA 47; AITN 1, 2; AMWS 1; CA 13-16R; 112; CAD; CANR 33; CWD; DA3; DAM DRAM; DFS 1, 3, 14; DLB 7, 228; DLBY 1984; EWL 3; FL 1:6; FW; LAIT 3; MAL 5; MAWW; MTCW 1, 2; MTFW 2005; RGAL 4; TUS
Helprin, Mark 1947- .... **CLC 7, 10, 22, 32**
　　See also CA 81-84; CANR 47, 64, 124; CDALBS; CN 7; CPW; DA3; DAM NOV, POP; DLBY 1985; FANT; MAL 5; MTCW 1, 2; MTFW 2005; SUFW 2
Helvetius, Claude-Adrien 1715-1771 .. **LC 26**
　　See also DLB 313
Helyar, Jane Penelope Josephine 1933-
　　See Poole, Josephine
　　See also CA 21-24R; CANR 10, 26; CWRI 5; SATA 82, 138; SATA-Essay 138
Hemans, Felicia 1793-1835 ...... **NCLC 29, 71**
　　See also DLB 96; RGEL 2
Hemingway, Ernest (Miller) 1899-1961 .... **CLC 1, 3, 6, 8, 10, 13, 19, 30, 34, 39, 41, 44, 50, 61, 80; SSC 1, 25, 36, 40, 63; TCLC 115; WLC 3**
　　See also AAYA 19; AMW; AMWC 1; AMWR 1; BPFB 2; BYA 2, 3, 13, 15; CA 77-80; CANR 34; CDALB 1917-1929; DA; DA3; DAB; DAC; DAM MST, NOV; DLB 4, 9, 102, 210, 308, 316; DLBD 1, 15, 16; DLBY 1981, 1987, 1996, 1998; EWL 3; EXPN; EXPS; LAIT 3, 4; LATS 1:1; MAL 5; MTCW 1, 2; MTFW 2005; NFS 1, 5, 6, 14; RGAL 4; RGSF 2; SSFS 17; TUS; WYA
Hempel, Amy 1951- .... **CLC 39**
　　See also CA 118; 137; CANR 70; DA3; DLB 218; EXPS; MTCW 2; MTFW 2005; SSFS 2
Henderson, F. C.
　　See Mencken, H(enry) L(ouis)
Henderson, Sylvia
　　See Ashton-Warner, Sylvia (Constance)
Henderson, Zenna (Chlarson) 1917-1983 .... **SSC 29**
　　See also CA 1-4R; 133; CANR 1, 84; DLB 8; SATA 5; SFW 4
Henkin, Joshua .... **CLC 119**
　　See also CA 161
Henley, Beth .... **CLC 23; DC 6, 14**
　　See Henley, Elizabeth Becker
　　See also AAYA 70; CABS 3; CAD; CD 5, 6; CSW; CWD; DFS 2, 21; DLBY 1986; FW
Henley, Elizabeth Becker 1952-
　　See Henley, Beth
　　See also CA 107; CANR 32, 73, 140; DA3; DAM DRAM, MST; MTCW 1, 2; MTFW 2005
Henley, William Ernest 1849-1903 .. **TCLC 8**
　　See also CA 105; 234; DLB 19; RGEL 2
Hennissart, Martha 1929-
　　See Lathen, Emma
　　See also CA 85-88; CANR 64

Henry VIII 1491-1547 .... **LC 10**
　　See also DLB 132
Henry, O. . **SSC 5, 49; TCLC 1, 19; WLC 3**
　　See Porter, William Sydney
　　See also AAYA 41; AMWS 2; EXPS; MAL 5; RGAL 4; RGSF 2; SSFS 2, 18; TCWW 1, 2
Henry, Patrick 1736-1799 .... **LC 25**
　　See also LAIT 1
Henryson, Robert 1430(?)-1506(?) ..... **LC 20, 110; PC 65**
　　See also BRWS 7; DLB 146; RGEL 2
Henschke, Alfred
　　See Klabund
Henson, Lance 1944- .... **NNAL**
　　See also CA 146; DLB 175
Hentoff, Nat(han Irving) 1925- .... **CLC 26**
　　See also AAYA 4, 42; BYA 6; CA 1-4R; CAAS 6; CANR 5, 25, 77, 114; CLR 1, 52; INT CANR-25; JRDA; MAICYA 1, 2; SATA 42, 69, 133; SATA-Brief 27; WYA; YAW
Heppenstall, (John) Rayner 1911-1981 .... **CLC 10**
　　See also CA 1-4R; 103; CANR 29; CN 1, 2; CP 1, 2, 3; EWL 3
Heraclitus c. 540B.C.-c. 450B.C. ... **CMLC 22**
　　See also DLB 176
Herbert, Frank (Patrick) 1920-1986 .... **CLC 12, 23, 35, 44, 85**
　　See also AAYA 21; BPFB 2; BYA 4, 14; CA 53-56; 118; CANR 5, 43; CDALBS; CPW; DAM POP; DLB 8; INT CANR-5; LAIT 5; MTCW 1, 2; MTFW 2005; NFS 17; SATA 9, 37; SATA-Obit 47; SCFW 1, 2; SFW 4; YAW
Herbert, George 1593-1633 . **LC 24, 121; PC 4**
　　See also BRW 2; BRWR 2; CDBLB Before 1660; DAB; DAM POET; DLB 126; EXPP; RGEL 2; TEA; WP
Herbert, Zbigniew 1924-1998 ..... **CLC 9, 43; PC 50; TCLC 168**
　　See also CA 89-92; 169; CANR 36, 74; CD-WLB 4; CWW 2; DAM POET; DLB 232; EWL 3; MTCW 1; PFS 22
Herbst, Josephine (Frey) 1897-1969 .... **CLC 34**
　　See also CA 5-8R; 25-28R; DLB 9
Herder, Johann Gottfried von 1744-1803 .... **NCLC 8**
　　See also DLB 97; EW 4; TWA
Heredia, Jose Maria 1803-1839 .... **HLCS 2**
　　See also LAW
Hergesheimer, Joseph 1880-1954 ... **TCLC 11**
　　See also CA 109; 194; DLB 102, 9; RGAL 4
Herlihy, James Leo 1927-1993 .... **CLC 6**
　　See also CA 1-4R; 143; CAD; CANR 2; CN 1, 2, 3, 4, 5
Herman, William
　　See Bierce, Ambrose (Gwinett)
Hermogenes fl. c. 175- .... **CMLC 6**
Hernandez, Jose 1834-1886 .... **NCLC 17**
　　See also LAW; RGWL 2, 3; WLIT 1
Herodotus c. 484B.C.-c. 420B.C. .. **CMLC 17**
　　See also AW 1; CDWLB 1; DLB 176; RGWL 2, 3; TWA; WLIT 8
Herrick, Robert 1591-1674 .... **LC 13; PC 9**
　　See also BRW 2; BRWC 2; DA; DAB; DAC; DAM MST, POP; DLB 126; EXPP; PFS 13; RGAL 4; RGEL 2; TEA; WP
Herring, Guilles
　　See Somerville, Edith Oenone
Herriot, James 1916-1995 .... **CLC 12**
　　See Wight, James Alfred
　　See also AAYA 1, 54; BPFB 2; CA 148; CANR 40; CLR 80; CPW; DAM POP; LAIT 3; MAICYA 2; MAICYAS 1; MTCW 2; SATA 86, 135; TEA; YAW

Herris, Violet
　　See Hunt, Violet
Herrmann, Dorothy 1941- .... **CLC 44**
　　See also CA 107
Herrmann, Taffy
　　See Herrmann, Dorothy
Hersey, John (Richard) 1914-1993 .... **CLC 1, 2, 7, 9, 40, 81, 97**
　　See also AAYA 29; BPFB 2; CA 17-20R; 140; CANR 33; CDALBS; CN 1, 2, 3, 4, 5; CPW; DAM POP; DLB 6, 185, 278, 299; MAL 5; MTCW 1, 2; MTFW 2005; RGHL; SATA 25; SATA-Obit 76; TUS
Herzen, Aleksandr Ivanovich 1812-1870 .... **NCLC 10, 61**
　　See Herzen, Alexander
Herzen, Alexander
　　See Herzen, Aleksandr Ivanovich
　　See also DLB 277
Herzl, Theodor 1860-1904 .... **TCLC 36**
　　See also CA 168
Herzog, Werner 1942- .... **CLC 16**
　　See also CA 89-92
Hesiod c. 8th cent. B.C.- .... **CMLC 5**
　　See also AW 1; DLB 176; RGWL 2, 3; WLIT 8
Hesse, Hermann 1877-1962 ... **CLC 1, 2, 3, 6, 11, 17, 25, 69; SSC 9, 49; TCLC 148; WLC 3**
　　See also AAYA 43; BPFB 2; CA 17-18; CAP 2; CDWLB 2; DA; DA3; DAB; DAC; DAM MST, NOV; DLB 66; EW 9; EWL 3; EXPN; LAIT 1; MTCW 1, 2; MTFW 2005; NFS 6, 15; RGWL 2, 3; SATA 50; TWA
Hewes, Cady
　　See De Voto, Bernard (Augustine)
Heyen, William 1940- .... **CLC 13, 18**
　　See also CA 33-36R; 220; CAAE 220; CAAS 9; CANR 98; CP 3, 4, 5, 6, 7; DLB 5; RGHL
Heyerdahl, Thor 1914-2002 .... **CLC 26**
　　See also CA 5-8R; 207; CANR 5, 22, 66, 73; LAIT 4; MTCW 1, 2; MTFW 2005; SATA 2, 52
Heym, Georg (Theodor Franz Arthur) 1887-1912 .... **TCLC 9**
　　See also CA 106; 181
Heym, Stefan 1913-2001 .... **CLC 41**
　　See also CA 9-12R; 203; CANR 4; CWW 2; DLB 69; EWL 3
Heyse, Paul (Johann Ludwig von) 1830-1914 .... **TCLC 8**
　　See also CA 104; 209; DLB 129
Heyward, (Edwin) DuBose 1885-1940 .... **HR 1:2; TCLC 59**
　　See also CA 108; 157; DLB 7, 9, 45, 249; MAL 5; SATA 21
Heywood, John 1497(?)-1580(?) .... **LC 65**
　　See also DLB 136; RGEL 2
Heywood, Thomas 1573(?)-1641 .... **LC 111**
　　See also DAM DRAM; DLB 62; LMFS 1; RGEL 2; TEA
Hibbert, Eleanor Alice Burford 1906-1993 .... **CLC 7**
　　See Holt, Victoria
　　See also BEST 90:4; CA 17-20R; 140; CANR 9, 28, 59; CMW 4; CPW; DAM POP; MTCW 2; MTFW 2005; RHW; SATA 2; SATA-Obit 74
Hichens, Robert (Smythe) 1864-1950 .... **TCLC 64**
　　See also CA 162; DLB 153; HGG; RHW; SUFW
Higgins, Aidan 1927- .... **SSC 68**
　　See also CA 9-12R; CANR 70, 115, 148; CN 1, 2, 3, 4, 5, 6, 7; DLB 14

Hogg, James 1770-1835 .... **NCLC 4, 109**
    See also BRWS 10; DLB 93, 116, 159; GL
    2; HGG; RGEL 2; SUFW 1

Holbach, Paul-Henri Thiry
    1723-1789 .... **LC 14**
    See also DLB 313

Holberg, Ludvig 1684-1754 .... **LC 6**
    See also DLB 300; RGWL 2, 3

Holcroft, Thomas 1745-1809 .... **NCLC 85**
    See also DLB 39, 89, 158; RGEL 2

Holden, Ursula 1921- .... **CLC 18**
    See also CA 101; CAAS 8; CANR 22

Holderlin, (Johann Christian) Friedrich
    1770-1843 .... **NCLC 16; PC 4**
    See also CDWLB 2; DLB 90; EW 5; RGWL
    2, 3

Holdstock, Robert
    See Holdstock, Robert P.

Holdstock, Robert P. 1948- .... **CLC 39**
    See also CA 131; CANR 81; DLB 261;
    FANT; HGG; SFW 4; SUFW 2

Holinshed, Raphael fl. 1580- .... **LC 69**
    See also DLB 167; RGEL 2

Holland, Isabelle (Christian)
    1920-2002 .... **CLC 21**
    See also AAYA 11, 64; CA 21-24R; 205;
    CAAE 181; CANR 10, 25, 47; CLR 57;
    CWRI 5; JRDA; LAIT 4; MAICYA 1, 2;
    SATA 8, 70; SATA-Essay 103; SATA-Obit
    132; WYA

Holland, Marcus
    See Caldwell, (Janet Miriam) Taylor
    (Holland)

Hollander, John 1929- .... **CLC 2, 5, 8, 14**
    See also CA 1-4R; CANR 1, 52, 136; CP 1,
    2, 3, 4, 5, 6, 7; DLB 5; MAL 5; SATA 13

Hollander, Paul
    See Silverberg, Robert

Holleran, Andrew .... **CLC 38**
    See Garber, Eric
    See also CA 144; GLL 1

Holley, Marietta 1836(?)-1926 .... **TCLC 99**
    See also CA 118; DLB 11; FL 1:3

Hollinghurst, Alan 1954- .... **CLC 55, 91**
    See also BRWS 10; CA 114; CN 5, 6, 7;
    DLB 207, 326; GLL 1

Hollis, Jim
    See Summers, Hollis (Spurgeon, Jr.)

Holly, Buddy 1936-1959 .... **TCLC 65**
    See also CA 213

Holmes, Gordon
    See Shiel, M(atthew) P(hipps)

Holmes, John
    See Souster, (Holmes) Raymond

Holmes, John Clellon 1926-1988 ...... **CLC 56**
    See also BG 1:2; CA 9-12R; 125; CANR 4;
    CN 1, 2, 3, 4; DLB 16, 237

Holmes, Oliver Wendell, Jr.
    1841-1935 .... **TCLC 77**
    See also CA 114; 186

Holmes, Oliver Wendell
    1809-1894 .... **NCLC 14, 81; PC 71**
    See also AMWS 1; CDALB 1640-1865;
    DLB 1, 189, 235; EXPP; PFS 24; RGAL
    4; SATA 34

Holmes, Raymond
    See Souster, (Holmes) Raymond

Holt, Victoria
    See Hibbert, Eleanor Alice Burford
    See also BPFB 2

Holub, Miroslav 1923-1998 .... **CLC 4**
    See also CA 21-24R; 169; CANR 10; CD-
    WLB 4; CWW 2; DLB 232; EWL 3;
    RGWL 3

Holz, Detlev
    See Benjamin, Walter

Homer c. 8th cent. B.C.- .... **CMLC 1, 16, 61;**
    PC 23; WLCS
    See also AW 1; CDWLB 1; DA; DA3;
    DAB; DAC; DAM MST, POET; DLB
    176; EFS 1; LAIT 1; LMFS 1; RGWL 2,
    3; TWA; WLIT 8; WP

Hongo, Garrett Kaoru 1951- .... **PC 23**
    See also CA 133; CAAS 22; CP 5, 6, 7;
    DLB 120, 312; EWL 3; EXPP; RGAL 4

Honig, Edwin 1919- .... **CLC 33**
    See also CA 5-8R; CAAS 8; CANR 4, 45,
    144; CP 1, 2, 3, 4, 5, 6, 7; DLB 5

Hood, Hugh (John Blagdon) 1928- . **CLC 15,**
    28; SSC 42
    See also CA 49-52; CAAS 17; CANR 1,
    33, 87; CN 1, 2, 3, 4, 5, 6, 7; DLB 53;
    RGSF 2

Hood, Thomas 1799-1845 .... **NCLC 16**
    See also BRW 4; DLB 96; RGEL 2

Hooker, (Peter) Jeremy 1941- .... **CLC 43**
    See also CA 77-80; CANR 22; CP 2, 3, 4,
    5, 6, 7; DLB 40

Hooker, Richard 1554-1600 .... **LC 95**
    See also BRW 1; DLB 132; RGEL 2

hooks, bell 1952(?)- .... **CLC 94**
    See also BW 2; CA 143; CANR 87, 126;
    DLB 246; MTCW 2; MTFW 2005; SATA
    115, 170

Hope, A(lec) D(erwent) 1907-2000 .... **CLC 3,**
    51; PC 56
    See also BRWS 7; CA 21-24R; 188; CANR
    33, 74; CP 1, 2, 3, 4, 5; DLB 289; EWL
    3; MTCW 1, 2; MTFW 2005; PFS 8;
    RGEL 2

Hope, Anthony 1863-1933 .... **TCLC 83**
    See also CA 157; DLB 153, 156; RGEL 2;
    RHW

Hope, Brian
    See Creasey, John

Hope, Christopher (David Tully)
    1944- .... **CLC 52**
    See also AFW; CA 106; CANR 47, 101;
    CN 4, 5, 6, 7; DLB 225; SATA 62

Hopkins, Gerard Manley
    1844-1889 .... **NCLC 17; PC 15; WLC 3**
    See also BRW 5; BRWR 2; CDBLB 1890-
    1914; DA; DA3; DAB; DAC; DAM MST,
    POET; DLB 35, 57; EXPP; PAB; RGEL
    2; TEA; WP

Hopkins, John (Richard) 1931-1998 .. **CLC 4**
    See also CA 85-88; 169; CBD; CD 5, 6

Hopkins, Pauline Elizabeth
    1859-1930 .... **BLC 2; TCLC 28**
    See also AFAW 2; BW 2, 3; CA 141; CANR
    82; DAM MULT; DLB 50

Hopkinson, Francis 1737-1791 .... **LC 25**
    See also DLB 31; RGAL 4

Hopley-Woolrich, Cornell George 1903-1968
    See Woolrich, Cornell
    See also CA 13-14; CANR 58; CAP 1;
    CMW 4; DLB 226; MTCW 2

Horace 65B.C.-8B.C. .... **CMLC 39; PC 46**
    See also AW 2; CDWLB 1; DLB 211;
    RGWL 2, 3; WLIT 8

Horatio
    See Proust, (Valentin-Louis-George-Eugene)
    Marcel

Horgan, Paul (George Vincent
    O'Shaughnessy) 1903-1995 .. **CLC 9, 53**
    See also BPFB 2; CA 13-16R; 147; CANR
    9, 35; CN 1, 2, 3, 4, 5; DAM NOV; DLB
    102, 212; DLBY 1985; INT CANR-9;
    MTCW 1, 2; MTFW 2005; SATA 13;
    SATA-Obit 84; TCWW 1, 2

Horkheimer, Max 1895-1973 .... **TCLC 132**
    See also CA 216; 41-44R; DLB 296

Horn, Peter
    See Kuttner, Henry

Horne, Frank (Smith) 1899-1974 ...... **HR 1:2**
    See also BW 1; CA 125; 53-56; DLB 51;
    WP

Horne, Richard Henry Hengist
    1802(?)-1884 .... **NCLC 127**
    See also DLB 32; SATA 29

Hornem, Horace Esq.
    See Byron, George Gordon (Noel)

Horney, Karen (Clementine Theodore
    Danielsen) 1885-1952 .... **TCLC 71**
    See also CA 114; 165; DLB 246; FW

Hornung, E(rnest) W(illiam)
    1866-1921 .... **TCLC 59**
    See also CA 108; 160; CMW 4; DLB 70

Horovitz, Israel (Arthur) 1939- .... **CLC 56**
    See also CA 33-36R; CAD; CANR 46, 59;
    CD 5, 6; DAM DRAM; DLB 7; MAL 5

Horton, George Moses
    1797(?)-1883(?) .... **NCLC 87**
    See also DLB 50

Horvath, odon von 1901-1938
    See von Horvath, Odon
    See also EWL 3

Horvath, Oedoen von -1938
    See von Horvath, Odon

Horwitz, Julius 1920-1986 .... **CLC 14**
    See also CA 9-12R; 119; CANR 12

Horwitz, Ronald
    See Harwood, Ronald

Hospital, Janette Turner 1942- .... **CLC 42,**
    145
    See also CA 108; CANR 48; CN 5, 6, 7;
    DLB 325; DLBY 2002; RGSF 2

Hostos, E. M. de
    See Hostos (y Bonilla), Eugenio Maria de

Hostos, Eugenio M. de
    See Hostos (y Bonilla), Eugenio Maria de

Hostos, Eugenio Maria
    See Hostos (y Bonilla), Eugenio Maria de

Hostos (y Bonilla), Eugenio Maria de
    1839-1903 .... **TCLC 24**
    See also CA 123; 131; HW 1

Houdini
    See Lovecraft, H. P.

Houellebecq, Michel 1958- .... **CLC 179**
    See also CA 185; CANR 140; MTFW 2005

Hougan, Carolyn 1943- .... **CLC 34**
    See also CA 139

Household, Geoffrey (Edward West)
    1900-1988 .... **CLC 11**
    See also CA 77-80; 126; CANR 58; CMW
    4; CN 1, 2, 3, 4; DLB 87; SATA 14;
    SATA-Obit 59

Housman, A(lfred) E(dward)
    1859-1936 .... **PC 2, 43; TCLC 1, 10;**
    WLCS
    See also AAYA 66; BRW 6; CA 104; 125;
    DA; DA3; DAB; DAC; DAM MST,
    POET; DLB 19, 284; EWL 3; EXPP;
    MTCW 1, 2; MTFW 2005; PAB; PFS 4,
    7; RGEL 2; TEA; WP

Housman, Laurence 1865-1959 .... **TCLC 7**
    See also CA 106; 155; DLB 10; FANT;
    RGEL 2; SATA 25

Houston, Jeanne Wakatsuki 1934- .... **AAL**
    See also AAYA 49; CA 103; 232; CAAE
    232; CAAS 16; CANR 29, 123; LAIT 4;
    SATA 78, 168; SATA-Essay 168

Howard, Elizabeth Jane 1923- ...... **CLC 7, 29**
    See also BRWS 11; CA 5-8R; CANR 8, 62,
    146; CN 1, 2, 3, 4, 5, 6, 7

Howard, Maureen 1930- .... **CLC 5, 14, 46,**
    151
    See also CA 53-56; CANR 31, 75, 140; CN
    4, 5, 6, 7; DLBY 1983; INT CANR-31;
    MTCW 1, 2; MTFW 2005

Huxley, Aldous (Leonard)
1894-1963 .... **CLC 1, 3, 4, 5, 8, 11, 18, 35, 79; SSC 39; WLC 3**
See also AAYA 11; BPFB 2; BRW 7; CA 85-88; CANR 44, 99; CDBLB 1914-1945; DA; DA3; DAB; DAC; DAM MST, NOV; DLB 36, 100, 162, 195, 255; EWL 3; EXPN; LAIT 5; LMFS 2; MTCW 1, 2; MTFW 2005; NFS 6; RGEL 2; SATA 63; SCFW 1, 2; SFW 4; TEA; YAW

Huxley, T(homas) H(enry)
1825-1895 .... **NCLC 67**
See also DLB 57; TEA

Huygens, Constantijn 1596-1687 .... **LC 114**
See also RGWL 2, 3

Huysmans, Joris-Karl 1848-1907 ... **TCLC 7, 69**
See also CA 104; 165; DLB 123; EW 7; GFL 1789 to the Present; LMFS 2; RGWL 2, 3

Hwang, David Henry 1957- .... **CLC 55, 196; DC 4, 23**
See also CA 127; 132; CAD; CANR 76, 124; CD 5, 6; DA3; DAM DRAM; DFS 11, 18; DLB 212, 228, 312; INT CA-132; MAL 5; MTCW 2; MTFW 2005; RGAL 4

Hyde, Anthony 1946- .... **CLC 42**
See Chase, Nicholas
See also CA 136; CCA 1

Hyde, Margaret O(ldroyd) 1917- ..... **CLC 21**
See also CA 1-4R; CANR 1, 36, 137; CLR 23; JRDA; MAICYA 1, 2; SAAS 8; SATA 1, 42, 76, 139

Hynes, James 1956(?)- .... **CLC 65**
See also CA 164; CANR 105

Hypatia c. 370-415 .... **CMLC 35**

Ian, Janis 1951- .... **CLC 21**
See also CA 105; 187

Ibanez, Vicente Blasco
See Blasco Ibanez, Vicente
See also DLB 322

Ibarbourou, Juana de
1895(?)-1979 .... **HLCS 2**
See also DLB 290; HW 1; LAW

Ibarguengoitia, Jorge 1928-1983 ..... **CLC 37; TCLC 148**
See also CA 124; 113; EWL 3; HW 1

Ibn Battuta, Abu Abdalla
1304-1368(?) .... **CMLC 57**
See also WLIT 2

Ibn Hazm 994-1064 .... **CMLC 64**

Ibsen, Henrik (Johan) 1828-1906 .... **DC 2; TCLC 2, 8, 16, 37, 52; WLC 3**
See also AAYA 46; CA 104; 141; DA; DA3; DAB; DAC; DAM DRAM, MST; DFS 1, 6, 8, 10, 11, 15, 16; EW 7; LAIT 2; LATS 1:1; MTFW 2005; RGWL 2, 3

Ibuse, Masuji 1898-1993 .... **CLC 22**
See Ibuse Masuji
See also CA 127; 141; MJW; RGWL 3

Ibuse Masuji
See Ibuse, Masuji
See also CWW 2; DLB 180; EWL 3

Ichikawa, Kon 1915- .... **CLC 20**
See also CA 121

Ichiyo, Higuchi 1872-1896 .... **NCLC 49**
See also MJW

Idle, Eric 1943- .... **CLC 21**
See Monty Python
See also CA 116; CANR 35, 91, 148

Idris, Yusuf 1927-1991 .... **SSC 74**
See also AFW; EWL 3; RGSF 2, 3; RGWL 3; WLIT 2

Ignatow, David 1914-1997 .... **CLC 4, 7, 14, 40; PC 34**
See also CA 9-12R; 162; CAAS 3; CANR 31, 57, 96; CP 1, 2, 3, 4, 5, 6; DLB 5; EWL 3; MAL 5

Ignotus
See Strachey, (Giles) Lytton

Ihimaera, Witi (Tame) 1944- .... **CLC 46**
See also CA 77-80; CANR 130; CN 2, 3, 4, 5, 6, 7; RGSF 2; SATA 148

Ilf, Ilya .... **TCLC 21**
See Fainzilberg, Ilya Arnoldovich
See also EWL 3

Illyes, Gyula 1902-1983 .... **PC 16**
See also CA 114; 109; CDWLB 4; DLB 215; EWL 3; RGWL 2, 3

Imalayen, Fatima-Zohra
See Djebar, Assia

Immermann, Karl (Lebrecht)
1796-1840 .... **NCLC 4, 49**
See also DLB 133

Ince, Thomas H. 1882-1924 .... **TCLC 89**
See also IDFW 3, 4

Inchbald, Elizabeth 1753-1821 ...... **NCLC 62**
See also DLB 39, 89; RGEL 2

Inclan, Ramon (Maria) del Valle
See Valle-Inclan, Ramon (Maria) del

Infante, G(uillermo) Cabrera
See Cabrera Infante, G(uillermo)

Ingalls, Rachel 1940- .... **CLC 42**
See also CA 123; 127; CANR 154

Ingalls, Rachel Holmes
See Ingalls, Rachel

Ingamells, Reginald Charles
See Ingamells, Rex

Ingamells, Rex 1913-1955 .... **TCLC 35**
See also CA 167; DLB 260

Inge, William (Motter) 1913-1973 ..... **CLC 1, 8, 19**
See also CA 9-12R; CAD; CDALB 1941-1968; DA3; DAM DRAM; DFS 1, 3, 5, 8; DLB 7, 249; EWL 3; MAL 5; MTCW 1, 2; MTFW 2005; RGAL 4; TUS

Ingelow, Jean 1820-1897 .... **NCLC 39, 107**
See also DLB 35, 163; FANT; SATA 33

Ingram, Willis J.
See Harris, Mark

Innaurato, Albert (F.) 1948(?)- ... **CLC 21, 60**
See also CA 115; 122; CAD; CANR 78; CD 5, 6; INT CA-122

Innes, Michael
See Stewart, J(ohn) I(nnes) M(ackintosh)
See also DLB 276; MSW

Innis, Harold Adams 1894-1952 .... **TCLC 77**
See also CA 181; DLB 88

Insluis, Alanus de
See Alain de Lille

Iola
See Wells-Barnett, Ida B(ell)

Ionesco, Eugene 1912-1994 ... **CLC 1, 4, 6, 9, 11, 15, 41, 86; DC 12; WLC 3**
See also CA 9-12R; 144; CANR 55, 132; CWW 2; DA; DA3; DAB; DAC; DAM DRAM, MST; DFS 4, 9; DLB 321; EW 13; EWL 3; GFL 1789 to the Present; LMFS 2; MTCW 1, 2; MTFW 2005; RGWL 2, 3; SATA 7; SATA-Obit 79; TWA

Iqbal, Muhammad 1877-1938 .... **TCLC 28**
See also CA 215; EWL 3

Ireland, Patrick
See O'Doherty, Brian

Irenaeus St. 130- .... **CMLC 42**

Irigaray, Luce 1930- .... **CLC 164**
See also CA 154; CANR 121; FW

Iron, Ralph
See Schreiner, Olive (Emilie Albertina)

Irving, John (Winslow) 1942- ... **CLC 13, 23, 38, 112, 175**
See also AAYA 8, 62; AMWS 6; BEST 89:3; BPFB 2; CA 25-28R; CANR 28, 73, 112, 133; CN 3, 4, 5, 6, 7; CPW; DA3;

DAM NOV, POP; DLB 6, 278; DLBY 1982; EWL 3; MAL 5; MTCW 1, 2; MTFW 2005; NFS 12, 14; RGAL 4; TUS

Irving, Washington 1783-1859 . **NCLC 2, 19, 95; SSC 2, 37; WLC 3**
See also AAYA 56; AMW; CDALB 1640-1865; CLR 97; DA; DA3; DAB; DAC; DAM MST; DLB 3, 11, 30, 59, 73, 74, 183, 186, 250, 254; EXPS; GL 2; LAIT 1; RGAL 4; RGSF 2; SSFS 1, 8, 16; SUFW 1; TUS; WCH; YABC 2

Irwin, P. K.
See Page, P(atricia) K(athleen)

Isaacs, Jorge Ricardo 1837-1895 ... **NCLC 70**
See also LAW

Isaacs, Susan 1943- .... **CLC 32**
See also BEST 89:1; BPFB 2; CA 89-92; CANR 20, 41, 65, 112, 134; CPW; DA3; DAM POP; INT CANR-20; MTCW 1, 2; MTFW 2005

Isherwood, Christopher (William Bradshaw)
1904-1986 .... **CLC 1, 9, 11, 14, 44; SSC 56**
See also AMWS 14; BRW 7; CA 13-16R; 117; CANR 35, 97, 133; CN 1, 2, 3; DA3; DAM DRAM, NOV; DLB 15, 195; DLBY 1986; EWL 3; IDTP; MTCW 1, 2; MTFW 2005; RGAL 4; RGEL 2; TUS; WLIT 4

Ishiguro, Kazuo 1954- . **CLC 27, 56, 59, 110, 119**
See also AAYA 58; BEST 90:2; BPFB 2; BRWS 4; CA 120; CANR 49, 95, 133; CN 5, 6, 7; DA3; DAM NOV; DLB 194, 326; EWL 3; MTCW 1, 2; MTFW 2005; NFS 13; WLIT 4; WWE 1

Ishikawa, Hakuhin
See Ishikawa, Takuboku

Ishikawa, Takuboku 1886(?)-1912 ..... **PC 10; TCLC 15**
See Ishikawa Takuboku
See also CA 113; 153; DAM POET

Iskander, Fazil (Abdulovich) 1929- .. **CLC 47**
See Iskander, Fazil' Abdulevich
See also CA 102; EWL 3

Iskander, Fazil' Abdulevich
See Iskander, Fazil (Abdulovich)
See also DLB 302

Isler, Alan (David) 1934- .... **CLC 91**
See also CA 156; CANR 105

Ivan IV 1530-1584 .... **LC 17**

Ivanov, Vyacheslav Ivanovich
1866-1949 .... **TCLC 33**
See also CA 122; EWL 3

Ivask, Ivar Vidrik 1927-1992 .... **CLC 14**
See also CA 37-40R; 139; CANR 24

Ives, Morgan
See Bradley, Marion Zimmer
See also GLL 1

Izumi Shikibu c. 973-c. 1034 .... **CMLC 33**

J. R. S.
See Gogarty, Oliver St. John

Jabran, Kahlil
See Gibran, Kahlil

Jabran, Khalil
See Gibran, Kahlil

Jackson, Daniel
See Wingrove, David (John)

Jackson, Helen Hunt 1830-1885 .... **NCLC 90**
See also DLB 42, 47, 186, 189; RGAL 4

Jackson, Jesse 1908-1983 .... **CLC 12**
See also BW 1; CA 25-28R; 109; CANR 27; CLR 28; CWRI 5; MAICYA 1, 2; SATA 2, 29; SATA-Obit 48

Jackson, Laura (Riding) 1901-1991 .... **PC 44**
See Riding, Laura
See also CA 65-68; 135; CANR 28, 89; DLB 48

Jackson, Sam
See Trumbo, Dalton

Jimenez (Mantecon), Juan Ramon
1881-1958 .... **HLC 1; PC 7; TCLC 4**
See also CA 104; 131; CANR 74; DAM
MULT, POET; DLB 134; EW 9; EWL 3;
HW 1; MTCW 1, 2; MTFW 2005; RGWL
2, 3

Jimenez, Ramon
See Jimenez (Mantecon), Juan Ramon

Jimenez Mantecon, Juan
See Jimenez (Mantecon), Juan Ramon

Jin, Ba 1904-2005
See Pa Chin
See also CA 244; CWW 2

Jin, Ha .... **CLC 109**
See Jin, Xuefei
See also CA 152; DLB 244, 292; SSFS 17

Jin, Xuefei 1956-
See Jin, Ha
See also CANR 91, 130; MTFW 2005;
SSFS 17

Jodelle, Etienne 1532-1573 .... **LC 119**
See also GFL Beginnings to 1789

Joel, Billy .... **CLC 26**
See Joel, William Martin

Joel, William Martin 1949-
See Joel, Billy
See also CA 108

John, Saint 10(?)-100 .... **CMLC 27, 63**

John of Salisbury c. 1115-1180 ..... **CMLC 63**

John of the Cross, St. 1542-1591 .... **LC 18**
See also RGWL 2, 3

John Paul II, Pope 1920-2005 .... **CLC 128**
See also CA 106; 133; 238

Johnson, B(ryan) S(tanley William)
1933-1973 .... **CLC 6, 9**
See also CA 9-12R; 53-56; CANR 9; CN 1;
CP 1, 2; DLB 14, 40; EWL 3; RGEL 2

Johnson, Benjamin F., of Boone
See Riley, James Whitcomb

Johnson, Charles (Richard) 1948- .... **BLC 2;**
CLC 7, 51, 65, 163
See also AFAW 2; AMWS 6; BW 2, 3; CA
116; CAAS 18; CANR 42, 66, 82, 129;
CN 5, 6, 7; DAM MULT; DLB 33, 278;
MAL 5; MTCW 2; MTFW 2005; RGAL
4; SSFS 16

Johnson, Charles S(purgeon)
1893-1956 .... **HR 1:3**
See also BW 1, 3; CA 125; CANR 82; DLB
51, 91

Johnson, Denis 1949- . **CLC 52, 160; SSC 56**
See also CA 117; 121; CANR 71, 99; CN
4, 5, 6, 7; DLB 120

Johnson, Diane 1934- .... **CLC 5, 13, 48**
See also BPFB 2; CA 41-44R; CANR 17,
40, 62, 95; CN 4, 5, 6, 7; DLBY 1980;
INT CANR-17; MTCW 1

Johnson, E(mily) Pauline 1861-1913 . **NNAL**
See also CA 150; CCA 1; DAC; DAM
MULT; DLB 92, 175; TCWW 2

Johnson, Eyvind (Olof Verner)
1900-1976 .... **CLC 14**
See also CA 73-76; 69-72; CANR 34, 101;
DLB 259; EW 12; EWL 3

Johnson, Fenton 1888-1958 .... **BLC 2**
See also BW 1; CA 118; 124; DAM MULT;
DLB 45, 50

Johnson, Georgia Douglas (Camp)
1880-1966 .... **HR 1:3**
See also BW 1; CA 125; DLB 51, 249; WP

Johnson, Helene 1907-1995 .... **HR 1:3**
See also CA 181; DLB 51; WP

Johnson, J. R.
See James, C(yril) L(ionel) R(obert)

Johnson, James Weldon 1871-1938 .. **BLC 2;**
HR 1:3; PC 24; TCLC 3, 19, 175
See also AFAW 1, 2; BW 1, 3; CA 104;
125; CANR 82; CDALB 1917-1929; CLR
32; DA3; DAM MULT, POET; DLB 51;
EWL 3; EXPP; LMFS 2; MAL 5; MTCW
1, 2; MTFW 2005; NFS 22; PFS 1; RGAL
4; SATA 31; TUS

Johnson, Joyce 1935- .... **CLC 58**
See also BG 1:3; CA 125; 129; CANR 102

Johnson, Judith (Emlyn) 1936- .... **CLC 7, 15**
See Sherwin, Judith Johnson
See also CA 25-28R, 153; CANR 34; CP 6,
7

Johnson, Lionel (Pigot)
1867-1902 .... **TCLC 19**
See also CA 117; 209; DLB 19; RGEL 2

Johnson, Marguerite Annie
See Angelou, Maya

Johnson, Mel
See Malzberg, Barry N(athaniel)

Johnson, Pamela Hansford
1912-1981 .... **CLC 1, 7, 27**
See also CA 1-4R; 104; CANR 2, 28; CN
1, 2, 3; DLB 15; MTCW 1, 2; MTFW
2005; RGEL 2

Johnson, Paul (Bede) 1928- .... **CLC 147**
See also BEST 89:4; CA 17-20R; CANR
34, 62, 100

Johnson, Robert .... **CLC 70**

Johnson, Robert 1911(?)-1938 .... **TCLC 69**
See also BW 3; CA 174

Johnson, Samuel 1709-1784 . **LC 15, 52, 128;**
WLC 3
See also BRW 3; BRWR 1; CDBLB 1660-
1789; DA; DAB; DAC; DAM MST; DLB
39, 95, 104, 142, 213; LMFS 1; RGEL 2;
TEA

Johnson, Uwe 1934-1984 .. **CLC 5, 10, 15, 40**
See also CA 1-4R; 112; CANR 1, 39; CD-
WLB 2; DLB 75; EWL 3; MTCW 1;
RGWL 2, 3

Johnston, Basil H. 1929- .... **NNAL**
See also CA 69-72; CANR 11, 28, 66;
DAC; DAM MULT; DLB 60

Johnston, George (Benson) 1913- .... **CLC 51**
See also CA 1-4R; CANR 5, 20; CP 1, 2, 3,
4, 5, 6, 7; DLB 88

Johnston, Jennifer (Prudence)
1930- .... **CLC 7, 150**
See also CA 85-88; CANR 92; CN 4, 5, 6,
7; DLB 14

Joinville, Jean de 1224(?)-1317 ..... **CMLC 38**

Jolley, (Monica) Elizabeth 1923- ..... **CLC 46;**
SSC 19
See also CA 127; CAAS 13; CANR 59; CN
4, 5, 6, 7; DLB 325; EWL 3; RGSF 2

Jones, Arthur Llewellyn 1863-1947
See Machen, Arthur
See also CA 104; 179; HGG

Jones, D(ouglas) G(ordon) 1929- ..... **CLC 10**
See also CA 29-32R; CANR 13, 90; CP 1,
2, 3, 4, 5, 6, 7; DLB 53

Jones, David (Michael) 1895-1974 .... **CLC 2,**
4, 7, 13, 42
See also BRW 6; BRWS 7; CA 9-12R; 53-
56; CANR 28; CDBLB 1945-1960; CP 1,
2; DLB 20, 100; EWL 3; MTCW 1; PAB;
RGEL 2

Jones, David Robert 1947-
See Bowie, David
See also CA 103; CANR 104

Jones, Diana Wynne 1934- .... **CLC 26**
See also AAYA 12; BYA 6, 7, 9, 11, 13, 16;
CA 49-52; CANR 4, 26, 56, 120; CLR
23; DLB 161; FANT; JRDA; MAICYA 1,
2; MTFW 2005; SAAS 7; SATA 9, 70,
108, 160; SFW 4; SUFW 2; YAW

Jones, Edward P. 1950- .... **CLC 76, 223**
See also AAYA 71; BW 2, 3; CA 142;
CANR 79, 134; CSW; MTFW 2005

Jones, Gayl 1949- ...... **BLC 2; CLC 6, 9, 131**
See also AFAW 1, 2; BW 2, 3; CA 77-80;
CANR 27, 66, 122; CN 4, 5, 6, 7; CSW;
DA3; DAM MULT; DLB 33, 278; MAL
5; MTCW 1, 2; MTFW 2005; RGAL 4

Jones, James 1921-1977 ...... **CLC 1, 3, 10, 39**
See also AITN 1, 2; AMWS 11; BPFB 2;
CA 1-4R; 69-72; CANR 6; CN 1, 2; DLB
2, 143; DLBD 17; DLBY 1998; EWL 3;
MAL 5; MTCW 1; RGAL 4

Jones, John J.
See Lovecraft, H. P.

Jones, LeRoi .... **CLC 1, 2, 3, 5, 10, 14**
See Baraka, Amiri
See also CN 1, 2; CP 1, 2, 3; MTCW 2

Jones, Louis B. 1953- .... **CLC 65**
See also CA 141; CANR 73

Jones, Madison (Percy, Jr.) 1925- ...... **CLC 4**
See also CA 13-16R; CAAS 11; CANR 7,
54, 83; CN 1, 2, 3, 4, 5, 6, 7; CSW; DLB
152

Jones, Mervyn 1922- .... **CLC 10, 52**
See also CA 45-48; CAAS 5; CANR 1, 91;
CN 1, 2, 3, 4, 5, 6, 7; MTCW 1

Jones, Mick 1956(?)- .... **CLC 30**

Jones, Nettie (Pearl) 1941- .... **CLC 34**
See also BW 2; CA 137; CAAS 20; CANR
88

Jones, Peter 1802-1856 .... **NNAL**

Jones, Preston 1936-1979 .... **CLC 10**
See also CA 73-76; 89-92; DLB 7

Jones, Robert F(rancis) 1934-2003 .... **CLC 7**
See also CA 49-52; CANR 2, 61, 118

Jones, Rod 1953- .... **CLC 50**
See also CA 128

Jones, Terence Graham Parry
1942- .... **CLC 21**
See Jones, Terry; Monty Python
See also CA 112; 116; CANR 35, 93; INT
CA-116; SATA 127

Jones, Terry
See Jones, Terence Graham Parry
See also SATA 67; SATA-Brief 51

Jones, Thom (Douglas) 1945(?)- ..... **CLC 81;**
SSC 56
See also CA 157; CANR 88; DLB 244;
SSFS 23

Jong, Erica 1942- .... **CLC 4, 6, 8, 18, 83**
See also AITN 1; AMWS 5; BEST 90:2;
BPFB 2; CA 73-76; CANR 26, 52, 75,
132; CN 3, 4, 5, 6, 7; CP 2, 3, 4, 5, 6, 7;
CPW; DA3; DAM NOV, POP; DLB 2, 5,
28, 152; FW; INT CANR-26; MAL 5;
MTCW 1, 2; MTFW 2005

Jonson, Ben(jamin) 1572(?)-1637 . **DC 4; LC**
6, 33, 110; PC 17; WLC 3
See also BRW 1; BRWC 1; BRWR 1; CD-
BLB Before 1660; DA; DAB; DAC;
DAM DRAM, MST, POET; DFS 4, 10;
DLB 62, 121; LMFS 1; PFS 23; RGEL 2;
TEA; WLIT 3

Jordan, June 1936-2002 .. **BLCS; CLC 5, 11,**
23, 114; PC 38
See also AAYA 2, 66; AFAW 1, 2; BW 2,
3; CA 33-36R; 206; CANR 25, 70, 114,
154; CLR 10; CP 3, 4, 5, 6, 7; CWP;
DAM MULT, POET; DLB 38; GLL 2;
LAIT 5; MAICYA 1, 2; MTCW 1; SATA
4, 136; YAW

Jordan, June Meyer
See Jordan, June

Jordan, Neil 1950- .... **CLC 110**
See also CA 124; 130; CANR 54, 154; CN
4, 5, 6, 7; GLL 2; INT CA-130

Jordan, Neil Patrick
See Jordan, Neil

Knebel, Fletcher 1911-1993 .... **CLC 14**
See also AITN 1; CA 1-4R; 140; CAAS 3; CANR 1, 36; CN 1, 2, 3, 4, 5; SATA 36; SATA-Obit 75

Knickerbocker, Diedrich
See Irving, Washington

Knight, Etheridge 1931-1991 ... **BLC 2; CLC 40; PC 14**
See also BW 1, 3; CA 21-24R; 133; CANR 23, 82; CP 1, 2, 3, 4, 5; DAM POET; DLB 41; MTCW 2; MTFW 2005; RGAL 4; TCLE 1:1

Knight, Sarah Kemble 1666-1727 .... **LC 7**
See also DLB 24, 200

Knister, Raymond 1899-1932 .... **TCLC 56**
See also CA 186; DLB 68; RGEL 2

Knowles, John 1926-2001 ... **CLC 1, 4, 10, 26**
See also AAYA 10; AMWS 12; BPFB 2; BYA 3; CA 17-20R; 203; CANR 40, 74, 76, 132; CDALB 1968-1988; CLR 98; CN 1, 2, 3, 4, 5, 6, 7; DA; DAC; DAM MST, NOV; DLB 6; EXPN; MTCW 1, 2; MTFW 2005; NFS 2; RGAL 4; SATA 8, 89; SATA-Obit 134; YAW

Knox, Calvin M.
See Silverberg, Robert

Knox, John c. 1505-1572 .... **LC 37**
See also DLB 132

Knye, Cassandra
See Disch, Thomas M(ichael)

Koch, C(hristopher) J(ohn) 1932- .... **CLC 42**
See also CA 127; CANR 84; CN 3, 4, 5, 6, 7; DLB 289

Koch, Christopher
See Koch, C(hristopher) J(ohn)

Koch, Kenneth (Jay) 1925-2002 .... **CLC 5, 8, 44**
See also AMWS 15; CA 1-4R; 207; CAD; CANR 6, 36, 57, 97, 131; CD 5, 6; CP 1, 2, 3, 4, 5, 6, 7; DAM POET; DLB 5; INT CANR-36; MAL 5; MTCW 2; MTFW 2005; PFS 20; SATA 65; WP

Kochanowski, Jan 1530-1584 .... **LC 10**
See also RGWL 2, 3

Kock, Charles Paul de 1794-1871 . **NCLC 16**

Koda Rohan
See Koda Shigeyuki

Koda Rohan
See Koda Shigeyuki
See also DLB 180

Koda Shigeyuki 1867-1947 .... **TCLC 22**
See Koda Rohan
See also CA 121; 183

Koestler, Arthur 1905-1983 ... **CLC 1, 3, 6, 8, 15, 33**
See also BRWS 1; CA 1-4R; 109; CANR 1, 33; CDBLB 1945-1960; CN 1, 2, 3; DLBY 1983; EWL 3; MTCW 1, 2; MTFW 2005; NFS 19; RGEL 2

Kogawa, Joy Nozomi 1935- ...... **CLC 78, 129**
See also AAYA 47; CA 101; CANR 19, 62, 126; CN 6, 7; CP 1; CWP; DAC; DAM MST, MULT; FW; MTCW 2; MTFW 2005; NFS 3; SATA 99

Kohout, Pavel 1928- .... **CLC 13**
See also CA 45-48; CANR 3

Koizumi, Yakumo
See Hearn, (Patricio) Lafcadio (Tessima Carlos)

Kolmar, Gertrud 1894-1943 .... **TCLC 40**
See also CA 167; EWL 3; RGHL

Komunyakaa, Yusef 1947- .. **BLCS; CLC 86, 94, 207; PC 51**
See also AFAW 2; AMWS 13; CA 147; CANR 83; CP 6, 7; CSW; DLB 120; EWL 3; PFS 5, 20; RGAL 4

Konrad, George
See Konrad, Gyorgy

Konrad, Gyorgy 1933- .... **CLC 4, 10, 73**
See also CA 85-88; CANR 97; CDWLB 4; CWW 2; DLB 232; EWL 3

Konwicki, Tadeusz 1926- .... **CLC 8, 28, 54, 117**
See also CA 101; CAAS 9; CANR 39, 59; CWW 2; DLB 232; EWL 3; IDFW 3; MTCW 1

Koontz, Dean R. 1945- .... **CLC 78, 206**
See also AAYA 9, 31; BEST 89:3, 90:2; CA 108; CANR 19, 36, 52, 95, 138; CMW 4; CPW; DA3; DAM NOV, POP; DLB 292; HGG; MTCW 1; MTFW 2005; SATA 92, 165; SFW 4; SUFW 2; YAW

Koontz, Dean Ray
See Koontz, Dean R.

Koontz, Dean Ray
See Koontz, Dean R.

Kopernik, Mikolaj
See Copernicus, Nicolaus

Kopit, Arthur (Lee) 1937- ...... **CLC 1, 18, 33**
See also AITN 1; CA 81-84; CABS 3; CAD; CD 5, 6; DAM DRAM; DFS 7, 14; DLB 7; MAL 5; MTCW 1; RGAL 4

Kopitar, Jernej (Bartholomaus) 1780-1844 .... **NCLC 117**

Kops, Bernard 1926- .... **CLC 4**
See also CA 5-8R; CANR 84; CBD; CN 1, 2, 3, 4, 5, 6, 7; CP 1, 2, 3, 4, 5, 6, 7; DLB 13; RGHL

Kornbluth, C(yril) M. 1923-1958 .... **TCLC 8**
See also CA 105; 160; DLB 8; SCFW 1, 2; SFW 4

Korolenko, V. G.
See Korolenko, Vladimir Galaktionovich

Korolenko, Vladimir
See Korolenko, Vladimir Galaktionovich

Korolenko, Vladimir G.
See Korolenko, Vladimir Galaktionovich

Korolenko, Vladimir Galaktionovich 1853-1921 .... **TCLC 22**
See also CA 121; DLB 277

Korzybski, Alfred (Habdank Skarbek) 1879-1950 .... **TCLC 61**
See also CA 123; 160

Kosinski, Jerzy (Nikodem) 1933-1991 .... **CLC 1, 2, 3, 6, 10, 15, 53, 70**
See also AMWS 7; BPFB 2; CA 17-20R; 134; CANR 9, 46; CN 1, 2, 3, 4; DA3; DAM NOV; DLB 2, 299; DLBY 1982; EWL 3; HGG; MAL 5; MTCW 1, 2; MTFW 2005; NFS 12; RGAL 4; RGHL; TUS

Kostelanetz, Richard (Cory) 1940- .. **CLC 28**
See also CA 13-16R; CAAS 8; CANR 38, 77; CN 4, 5, 6; CP 2, 3, 4, 5, 6, 7

Kostrowitzki, Wilhelm Apollinaris de 1880-1918
See Apollinaire, Guillaume
See also CA 104

Kotlowitz, Robert 1924- .... **CLC 4**
See also CA 33-36R; CANR 36

Kotzebue, August (Friedrich Ferdinand) von 1761-1819 .... **NCLC 25**
See also DLB 94

Kotzwinkle, William 1938- ..... **CLC 5, 14, 35**
See also BPFB 2; CA 45-48; CANR 3, 44, 84, 129; CLR 6; CN 7; DLB 173; FANT; MAICYA 1, 2; SATA 24, 70, 146; SFW 4; SUFW 2; YAW

Kowna, Stancy
See Szymborska, Wislawa

Kozol, Jonathan 1936- .... **CLC 17**
See also AAYA 46; CA 61-64; CANR 16, 45, 96; MTFW 2005

Kozoll, Michael 1940(?)- .... **CLC 35**

Kramer, Kathryn 19(?)- .... **CLC 34**

Kramer, Larry 1935- .... **CLC 42; DC 8**
See also CA 124; 126; CANR 60, 132; DAM POP; DLB 249; GLL 1

Krasicki, Ignacy 1735-1801 .... **NCLC 8**

Krasinski, Zygmunt 1812-1859 .... **NCLC 4**
See also RGWL 2, 3

Kraus, Karl 1874-1936 .... **TCLC 5**
See also CA 104; 216; DLB 118; EWL 3

Kreve (Mickevicius), Vincas 1882-1954 .... **TCLC 27**
See also CA 170; DLB 220; EWL 3

Kristeva, Julia 1941- .... **CLC 77, 140**
See also CA 154; CANR 99; DLB 242; EWL 3; FW; LMFS 2

Kristofferson, Kris 1936- .... **CLC 26**
See also CA 104

Krizanc, John 1956- .... **CLC 57**
See also CA 187

Krleza, Miroslav 1893-1981 .... **CLC 8, 114**
See also CA 97-100; 105; CANR 50; CDWLB 4; DLB 147; EW 11; RGWL 2, 3

Kroetsch, Robert (Paul) 1927- .... **CLC 5, 23, 57, 132**
See also CA 17-20R; CANR 8, 38; CCA 1; CN 2, 3, 4, 5, 6, 7; CP 6, 7; DAC; DAM POET; DLB 53; MTCW 1

Kroetz, Franz
See Kroetz, Franz Xaver

Kroetz, Franz Xaver 1946- .... **CLC 41**
See also CA 130; CANR 142; CWW 2; EWL 3

Kroker, Arthur (W.) 1945- .... **CLC 77**
See also CA 161

Kroniuk, Lisa
See Berton, Pierre (Francis de Marigny)

Kropotkin, Peter (Aleksieevich) 1842-1921 .... **TCLC 36**
See Kropotkin, Petr Alekseevich
See also CA 119; 219

Kropotkin, Petr Alekseevich
See Kropotkin, Peter (Aleksieevich)
See also DLB 277

Krotkov, Yuri 1917-1981 .... **CLC 19**
See also CA 102

Krumb
See Crumb, R.

Krumgold, Joseph (Quincy) 1908-1980 .... **CLC 12**
See also BYA 1, 2; CA 9-12R; 101; CANR 7; MAICYA 1, 2; SATA 1, 48; SATA-Obit 23; YAW

Krumwitz
See Crumb, R.

Krutch, Joseph Wood 1893-1970 ..... **CLC 24**
See also ANW; CA 1-4R; 25-28R; CANR 4; DLB 63, 206, 275

Krutzch, Gus
See Eliot, T(homas) S(tearns)

Krylov, Ivan Andreevich 1768(?)-1844 .... **NCLC 1**
See also DLB 150

Kubin, Alfred (Leopold Isidor) 1877-1959 .... **TCLC 23**
See also CA 112; 149; CANR 104; DLB 81

Kubrick, Stanley 1928-1999 .... **CLC 16; TCLC 112**
See also AAYA 30; CA 81-84; 177; CANR 33; DLB 26

Kumin, Maxine (Winokur) 1925- ..... **CLC 5, 13, 28, 164; PC 15**
See also AITN 2; AMWS 4; ANW; CA 1-4R; CAAS 8; CANR 1, 21, 69, 115, 140; CP 2, 3, 4, 5, 6, 7; CWP; DA3; DAM POET; DLB 5; EWL 3; EXPP; MTCW 1, 2; MTFW 2005; PAB; PFS 18; SATA 12

CPW; DA3; DAM POP; DLB 173, 226; INT CANR-28; MSW; MTCW 1, 2; MTFW 2005; RGAL 4; SATA 163; TCWW 1, 2

Leonard, Hugh .... **CLC 19**
See Byrne, John Keyes
See also CBD; CD 5, 6; DFS 13; DLB 13

Leonov, Leonid (Maximovich)
1899-1994 .... **CLC 92**
See Leonov, Leonid Maksimovich
See also CA 129; CANR 76; DAM NOV; EWL 3; MTCW 1, 2; MTFW 2005

Leonov, Leonid Maksimovich
See Leonov, Leonid (Maximovich)
See also DLB 272

Leopardi, (Conte) Giacomo
1798-1837 .... **NCLC 22, 129; PC 37**
See also EW 5; RGWL 2, 3; WLIT 7; WP

Le Reveler
See Artaud, Antonin (Marie Joseph)

Lerman, Eleanor 1952- .... **CLC 9**
See also CA 85-88; CANR 69, 124

Lerman, Rhoda 1936- .... **CLC 56**
See also CA 49-52; CANR 70

Lermontov, Mikhail Iur'evich
See Lermontov, Mikhail Yuryevich
See also DLB 205

Lermontov, Mikhail Yuryevich
1814-1841 .... **NCLC 5, 47, 126; PC 18**
See Lermontov, Mikhail Iur'evich
See also EW 6; RGWL 2, 3; TWA

Leroux, Gaston 1868-1927 .... **TCLC 25**
See also CA 108; 136; CANR 69; CMW 4; MTFW 2005; NFS 20; SATA 65

Lesage, Alain-Rene 1668-1747 .... **LC 2, 28**
See also DLB 313; EW 3; GFL Beginnings to 1789; RGWL 2, 3

Leskov, N(ikolai) S(emenovich) 1831-1895
See Leskov, Nikolai (Semyonovich)

Leskov, Nikolai (Semyonovich)
1831-1895 .... **NCLC 25; SSC 34**
See Leskov, Nikolai Semenovich

Leskov, Nikolai Semenovich
See Leskov, Nikolai (Semyonovich)
See also DLB 238

Lesser, Milton
See Marlowe, Stephen

Lessing, Doris (May) 1919- ... **CLC 1, 2, 3, 6,
10, 15, 22, 40, 94, 170; SSC 6, 61;
WLCS**
See also AAYA 57; AFW; BRWS 1; CA 9-12R; CAAS 14; CANR 33, 54, 76, 122; CBD; CD 5, 6; CDBLB 1960 to Present; CN 1, 2, 3, 4, 5, 6, 7; CWD; DA; DA3; DAB; DAC; DAM MST, NOV; DFS 20; DLB 15, 139; DLBY 1985; EWL 3; EXPS; FL 1:6; FW; LAIT 4; MTCW 1, 2; MTFW 2005; RGEL 2; RGSF 2; SFW 4; SSFS 1, 12, 20; TEA; WLIT 2, 4

Lessing, Gotthold Ephraim
1729-1781 .... **DC 26; LC 8, 124**
See also CDWLB 2; DLB 97; EW 4; RGWL 2, 3

Lester, Richard 1932- .... **CLC 20**

Levenson, Jay .... **CLC 70**

Lever, Charles (James)
1806-1872 .... **NCLC 23**
See also DLB 21; RGEL 2

Leverson, Ada Esther
1862(?)-1933(?) .... **TCLC 18**
See Elaine
See also CA 117; 202; DLB 153; RGEL 2

Levertov, Denise 1923-1997 .. **CLC 1, 2, 3, 5,
8, 15, 28, 66; PC 11**
See also AMWS 3; CA 1-4R, 178; 163; CAAE 178; CAAS 19; CANR 3, 29, 50, 108; CDALBS; CP 1, 2, 3, 4, 5, 6; CWP;

DAM POET; DLB 5, 165; EWL 3; EXPP; FW; INT CANR-29; MAL 5; MTCW 1, 2; PAB; PFS 7, 17; RGAL 4; RGHL; TUS; WP

Levi, Carlo 1902-1975 .... **TCLC 125**
See also CA 65-68; 53-56; CANR 10; EWL 3; RGWL 2, 3

Levi, Jonathan .... **CLC 76**
See also CA 197

Levi, Peter (Chad Tigar)
1931-2000 .... **CLC 41**
See also CA 5-8R; 187; CANR 34, 80; CP 1, 2, 3, 4, 5, 6, 7; DLB 40

Levi, Primo 1919-1987 ...... **CLC 37, 50; SSC
12; TCLC 109**
See also CA 13-16R; 122; CANR 12, 33, 61, 70, 132; DLB 177, 299; EWL 3; MTCW 1, 2; MTFW 2005; RGHL; RGWL 2, 3; WLIT 7

Levin, Ira 1929- .... **CLC 3, 6**
See also CA 21-24R; CANR 17, 44, 74, 139; CMW 4; CN 1, 2, 3, 4, 5, 6, 7; CPW; DA3; DAM POP; HGG; MTCW 1, 2; MTFW 2005; SATA 66; SFW 4

Levin, Meyer 1905-1981 .... **CLC 7**
See also AITN 1; CA 9-12R; 104; CANR 15; CN 1, 2, 3; DAM POP; DLB 9, 28; DLBY 1981; MAL 5; RGHL; SATA 21; SATA-Obit 27

Levine, Albert Norman 1923-2005
See Levine, Norman
See also CN 7

Levine, Norman 1923-2005 .... **CLC 54**
See also CA 73-76; 240; CAAS 23; CANR 14, 70; CN 1, 2, 3, 4, 5, 6; CP 1; DLB 88

Levine, Norman Albert
See Levine, Norman

Levine, Philip 1928- .. **CLC 2, 4, 5, 9, 14, 33,
118; PC 22**
See also AMWS 5; CA 9-12R; CANR 9, 37, 52, 116; CP 1, 2, 3, 4, 5, 6, 7; DAM POET; DLB 5; EWL 3; MAL 5; PFS 8

Levinson, Deirdre 1931- .... **CLC 49**
See also CA 73-76; CANR 70

Levi-Strauss, Claude 1908- .... **CLC 38**
See also CA 1-4R; CANR 6, 32, 57; DLB 242; EWL 3; GFL 1789 to the Present; MTCW 1, 2; TWA

Levitin, Sonia (Wolff) 1934- .... **CLC 17**
See also AAYA 13, 48; CA 29-32R; CANR 14, 32, 79; CLR 53; JRDA; MAICYA 1, 2; SAAS 2; SATA 4, 68, 119, 131; SATA-Essay 131; YAW

Levon, O. U.
See Kesey, Ken (Elton)

Levy, Amy 1861-1889 .... **NCLC 59**
See also DLB 156, 240

Lewes, George Henry 1817-1878 ... **NCLC 25**
See also DLB 55, 144

Lewis, Alun 1915-1944 .... **SSC 40; TCLC 3**
See also BRW 7; CA 104; 188; DLB 20, 162; PAB; RGEL 2

Lewis, C. Day
See Day Lewis, C(ecil)
See also CN 1

Lewis, Cecil Day
See Day Lewis, C(ecil)

Lewis, Clive Staples
See Lewis, C.S.

Lewis, C.S. 1898-1963 ... **CLC 1, 3, 6, 14, 27,
124; WLC 4**
See also AAYA 3, 39; BPFB 2; BRWS 3; BYA 15, 16; CA 81-84; CANR 33, 71, 132; CDBLB 1945-1960; CLR 3, 27, 109; CWRI 5; DA; DA3; DAB; DAC; DAM MST, NOV, POP; DLB 15, 100, 160, 255; EWL 3; FANT; JRDA; LMFS 2; MAI-

CYA 1, 2; MTCW 1, 2; MTFW 2005; RGEL 2; SATA 13, 100; SCFW 1, 2; SFW 4; SUFW 1; TEA; WCH; WYA; YAW

Lewis, Janet 1899-1998 .... **CLC 41**
See Winters, Janet Lewis
See also CA 9-12R; 172; CANR 29, 63; CAP 1; CN 1, 2, 3, 4, 5, 6; DLBY 1987; RHW; TCWW 2

Lewis, Matthew Gregory
1775-1818 .... **NCLC 11, 62**
See also DLB 39, 158, 178; GL 3; HGG; LMFS 1; RGEL 2; SUFW

Lewis, (Harry) Sinclair 1885-1951 . **TCLC 4,
13, 23, 39; WLC 4**
See also AMW; AMWC 1; BPFB 2; CA 104; 133; CANR 132; CDALB 1917-1929; DA; DA3; DAB; DAC; DAM MST, NOV; DLB 9, 102, 284; DLBD 1; EWL 3; LAIT 3; MAL 5; MTCW 1, 2; MTFW 2005; NFS 15, 19, 22; RGAL 4; TUS

Lewis, (Percy) Wyndham
1884(?)-1957 .. **SSC 34; TCLC 2, 9, 104**
See also BRW 7; CA 104; 157; DLB 15; EWL 3; FANT; MTCW 2; MTFW 2005; RGEL 2

Lewisohn, Ludwig 1883-1955 .... **TCLC 19**
See also CA 107; 203; DLB 4, 9, 28, 102; MAL 5

Lewton, Val 1904-1951 .... **TCLC 76**
See also CA 199; IDFW 3, 4

Leyner, Mark 1956- .... **CLC 92**
See also CA 110; CANR 28, 53; DA3; DLB 292; MTCW 2; MTFW 2005

Lezama Lima, Jose 1910-1976 .... **CLC 4, 10,
101; HLCS 2**
See also CA 77-80; CANR 71; DAM MULT; DLB 113, 283; EWL 3; HW 1, 2; LAW; RGWL 2, 3

L'Heureux, John (Clarke) 1934- ...... **CLC 52**
See also CA 13-16R; CANR 23, 45, 88; CP 1, 2, 3, 4; DLB 244

Li Ch'ing-chao 1081(?)-1141(?) ... **CMLC 71**

Liddell, C. H.
See Kuttner, Henry

Lie, Jonas (Lauritz Idemil)
1833-1908(?) .... **TCLC 5**
See also CA 115

Lieber, Joel 1937-1971 .... **CLC 6**
See also CA 73-76; 29-32R

Lieber, Stanley Martin
See Lee, Stan

Lieberman, Laurence (James)
1935- .... **CLC 4, 36**
See also CA 17-20R; CANR 8, 36, 89; CP 1, 2, 3, 4, 5, 6, 7

Lieh Tzu fl. 7th cent. B.C.-5th cent.
B.C. .... **CMLC 27**

Lieksman, Anders
See Haavikko, Paavo Juhani

Lifton, Robert Jay 1926- .... **CLC 67**
See also CA 17-20R; CANR 27, 78; INT CANR-27; SATA 66

Lightfoot, Gordon 1938- .... **CLC 26**
See also CA 109; 242

Lightfoot, Gordon Meredith
See Lightfoot, Gordon

Lightman, Alan P(aige) 1948- .... **CLC 81**
See also CA 141; CANR 63, 105, 138; MTFW 2005

Ligotti, Thomas (Robert) 1953- ...... **CLC 44;
SSC 16**
See also CA 123; CANR 49, 135; HGG; SUFW 2

Li Ho 791-817 .... **PC 13**

Li Ju-chen c. 1763-c. 1830 .... **NCLC 137**

Lilar, Francoise
See Mallet-Joris, Francoise

Macaulay, (Emilie) Rose
  1881(?)-1958 .... **TCLC 7, 44**
  See also CA 104; DLB 36; EWL 3; RGEL
  2; RHW

Macaulay, Thomas Babington
  1800-1859 .... **NCLC 42**
  See also BRW 4; CDBLB 1832-1890; DLB
  32, 55; RGEL 2

MacBeth, George (Mann)
  1932-1992 .... **CLC 2, 5, 9**
  See also CA 25-28R; 136; CANR 61, 66;
  CP 1, 2, 3, 4, 5; DLB 40; MTCW 1; PFS
  8; SATA 4; SATA-Obit 70

MacCaig, Norman (Alexander)
  1910-1996 .... **CLC 36**
  See also BRWS 6; CA 9-12R; CANR 3, 34;
  CP 1, 2, 3, 4, 5, 6; DAB; DAM POET;
  DLB 27; EWL 3; RGEL 2

MacCarthy, Sir (Charles Otto) Desmond
  1877-1952 .... **TCLC 36**
  See also CA 167

MacDiarmid, Hugh .... **CLC 2, 4, 11, 19, 63;**
    PC 9
  See Grieve, C(hristopher) M(urray)
  See also CDBLB 1945-1960; CP 1, 2; DLB
  20; EWL 3; RGEL 2

MacDonald, Anson
  See Heinlein, Robert A(nson)

Macdonald, Cynthia 1928- .... **CLC 13, 19**
  See also CA 49-52; CANR 4, 44, 146; DLB
  105

MacDonald, George 1824-1905 .... **TCLC 9,**
    113
  See also AAYA 57; BYA 5; CA 106; 137;
  CANR 80; CLR 67; DLB 18, 163, 178;
  FANT; MAICYA 1, 2; RGEL 2; SATA 33,
  100; SFW 4; SUFW; WCH

Macdonald, John
  See Millar, Kenneth

MacDonald, John D(ann)
  1916-1986 .... **CLC 3, 27, 44**
  See also BPFB 2; CA 1-4R; CANR 1,
  19, 60; CMW 4; CPW; DAM NOV, POP;
  DLB 8, 306; DLBY 1986; MSW; MTCW
  1, 2; MTFW 2005; SFW 4

Macdonald, John Ross
  See Millar, Kenneth

Macdonald, Ross ..... **CLC 1, 2, 3, 14, 34, 41**
  See Millar, Kenneth
  See also AMWS 4; BPFB 2; CN 1, 2, 3;
  DLBD 6; MAL 5; MSW; RGAL 4

MacDougal, John
  See Blish, James (Benjamin)

MacDougal, John
  See Blish, James (Benjamin)

MacDowell, John
  See Parks, Tim(othy Harold)

MacEwen, Gwendolyn (Margaret)
  1941-1987 .... **CLC 13, 55**
  See also CA 9-12R; 124; CANR 7, 22; CP
  1, 2, 3, 4; DLB 53, 251; SATA 50; SATA-
  Obit 55

Macha, Karel Hynek 1810-1846 .... **NCLC 46**

Machado (y Ruiz), Antonio
  1875-1939 .... **TCLC 3**
  See also CA 104; 174; DLB 108; EW 9;
  EWL 3; HW 2; PFS 23; RGWL 2, 3

Machado de Assis, Joaquim Maria
  1839-1908 .... **BLC 2; HLCS 2; SSC 24;**
    TCLC 10
  See also CA 107; 153; CANR 91; DLB 307;
  LAW; RGSF 2; RGWL 2, 3; TWA;
  WLIT 1

Machaut, Guillaume de c.
  1300-1377 .... **CMLC 64**
  See also DLB 208

Machen, Arthur .... **SSC 20; TCLC 4**
  See Jones, Arthur Llewellyn
  See also CA 179; DLB 156, 178; RGEL 2;
  SUFW 1

Machiavelli, Niccolo 1469-1527 ... **DC 16; LC**
    8, 36; WLCS
  See also AAYA 58; DA; DAB; DAC; DAM
  MST; EW 2; LAIT 1; LMFS 1; NFS 9;
  RGWL 2, 3; TWA; WLIT 7

MacInnes, Colin 1914-1976 .... **CLC 4, 23**
  See also CA 69-72; 65-68; CANR 21; CN
  1, 2; DLB 14; MTCW 1, 2; RGEL 2;
  RHW

MacInnes, Helen (Clark)
  1907-1985 .... **CLC 27, 39**
  See also BPFB 2; CA 1-4R; 117; CANR 1,
  28, 58; CMW 4; CN 1, 2; CPW; DAM
  POP; DLB 87; MSW; MTCW 1, 2;
  MTFW 2005; SATA 22; SATA-Obit 44

Mackay, Mary 1855-1924
  See Corelli, Marie
  See also CA 118; 177; FANT; RHW

Mackay, Shena 1944- .... **CLC 195**
  See also CA 104; CANR 88, 139; DLB 231,
  319; MTFW 2005

Mackenzie, Compton (Edward Montague)
  1883-1972 .... **CLC 18; TCLC 116**
  See also CA 21-22; 37-40R; CAP 2; CN 1;
  DLB 34, 100; RGEL 2

Mackenzie, Henry 1745-1831 .... **NCLC 41**
  See also DLB 39; RGEL 2

Mackey, Nathaniel (Ernest) 1947- .... **PC 49**
  See also CA 153; CANR 114; CP 6, 7; DLB
  169

MacKinnon, Catharine A. 1946- .... **CLC 181**
  See also CA 128; 132; CANR 73, 140; FW;
  MTCW 2; MTFW 2005

Mackintosh, Elizabeth 1896(?)-1952
  See Tey, Josephine
  See also CA 110; CMW 4

MacLaren, James
  See Grieve, C(hristopher) M(urray)

MacLaverty, Bernard 1942- .... **CLC 31**
  See also CA 116; 118; CANR 43, 88; CN
  5, 6, 7; DLB 267; INT CA-118; RGSF 2

MacLean, Alistair (Stuart)
  1922(?)-1987 .... **CLC 3, 13, 50, 63**
  See also CA 57-60; 121; CANR 28, 61;
  CMW 4; CP 2, 3, 4, 5, 6, 7; CPW; DAM
  POP; DLB 276; MTCW 1; SATA 23;
  SATA-Obit 50; TCWW 2

Maclean, Norman (Fitzroy)
  1902-1990 .... **CLC 78; SSC 13**
  See also AMWS 14; CA 102; 132; CANR
  49; CPW; DAM POP; DLB 206;
  TCWW 2

MacLeish, Archibald 1892-1982 ... **CLC 3, 8,**
    14, 68; PC 47
  See also AMW; CA 9-12R; 106; CAD;
  CANR 33, 63; CDALBS; CP 1, 2; DAM
  POET; DFS 15; DLB 4, 7, 45; DLBY
  1982; EWL 3; EXPP; MAL 5; MTCW 1,
  2; MTFW 2005; PAB; PFS 5; RGAL 4;
  TUS

MacLennan, (John) Hugh
  1907-1990 .... **CLC 2, 14, 92**
  See also CA 5-8R; 142; CANR 33; CN 1,
  2, 3, 4; DAC; DAM MST; DLB 68; EWL
  3; MTCW 1, 2; MTFW 2005; RGEL 2;
  TWA

MacLeod, Alistair 1936- .. **CLC 56, 165; SSC**
    90
  See also CA 123; CCA 1; DAC; DAM
  MST; DLB 60; MTCW 2; MTFW 2005;
  RGSF 2; TCLE 1:2

Macleod, Fiona
  See Sharp, William
  See also RGEL 2; SUFW

MacNeice, (Frederick) Louis
  1907-1963 .... **CLC 1, 4, 10, 53; PC 61**
  See also BRW 7; CA 85-88; CANR 61;
  DAB; DAM POET; DLB 10, 20; EWL 3;
  MTCW 1, 2; MTFW 2005; RGEL 2

MacNeill, Dand
  See Fraser, George MacDonald

Macpherson, James 1736-1796 .... **LC 29**
  See Ossian
  See also BRWS 8; DLB 109; RGEL 2

Macpherson, (Jean) Jay 1931- .... **CLC 14**
  See also CA 5-8R; CANR 90; CP 1, 2, 3, 4,
  6, 7; CWP; DLB 53

Macrobius fl. 430- .... **CMLC 48**

MacShane, Frank 1927-1999 .... **CLC 39**
  See also CA 9-12R; 186; CANR 3, 33; DLB
  111

Macumber, Mari
  See Sandoz, Mari(e Susette)

Madach, Imre 1823-1864 .... **NCLC 19**

Madden, (Jerry) David 1933- .... **CLC 5, 15**
  See also CA 1-4R; CAAS 3; CANR 4, 45;
  CN 3, 4, 5, 6, 7; CSW; DLB 6; MTCW 1

Maddern, Al(an)
  See Ellison, Harlan (Jay)

Madhubuti, Haki R. 1942- ... **BLC 2; CLC 6,**
    73; PC 5
  See Lee, Don L.
  See also BW 2, 3; CA 73-76; CANR 24,
  51, 73, 139; CP 6, 7; CSW; DAM MULT,
  POET; DLB 5, 41; DLBD 8; EWL 3;
  MAL 5; MTCW 2; MTFW 2005; RGAL 4

Madison, James 1751-1836 .... **NCLC 126**
  See also DLB 37

Maepenn, Hugh
  See Kuttner, Henry

Maepenn, K. H.
  See Kuttner, Henry

Maeterlinck, Maurice 1862-1949 ..... **TCLC 3**
  See also CA 104; 136; CANR 80; DAM
  DRAM; DLB 192; EW 8; EWL 3; GFL
  1789 to the Present; LMFS 2; RGWL 2,
  3; SATA 66; TWA

Maginn, William 1794-1842 .... **NCLC 8**
  See also DLB 110, 159

Mahapatra, Jayanta 1928- .... **CLC 33**
  See also CA 73-76; CAAS 9; CANR 15,
  33, 66, 87; CP 4, 5, 6, 7; DAM MULT;
  DLB 323

Mahfouz, Naguib (Abdel Aziz Al-Sabilgi)
  1911(?)- .... **CLC 153; SSC 66**
  See Mahfuz, Najib (Abdel Aziz al-Sabilgi)
  See also AAYA 49; BEST 89:2; CA 128;
  CANR 55, 101; DA3; DAM NOV;
  MTCW 1, 2; MTFW 2005; RGWL 2, 3;
  SSFS 9

Mahfuz, Najib (Abdel Aziz al-Sabilgi)
  .... **CLC 52, 55**
  See Mahfouz, Naguib (Abdel Aziz Al-
  Sabilgi)
  See also AFW; CWW 2; DLBY 1988; EWL
  3; RGSF 2; WLIT 6

Mahon, Derek 1941- .... **CLC 27; PC 60**
  See also BRWS 6; CA 113; 128; CANR 88;
  CP 1, 2, 3, 4, 5, 6, 7; DLB 40; EWL 3

Maiakovskii, Vladimir
  See Mayakovski, Vladimir (Vladimirovich)
  See also IDTP; RGWL 2, 3

Mailer, Norman 1923- ... **CLC 1, 2, 3, 4, 5, 8,**
    11, 14, 28, 39, 74, 111
  See also AAYA 31; AITN 2; AMW; AMWC
  2; AMWR 2; BPFB 2; CA 9-12R; CABS
  1; CANR 28, 74, 77, 130; CDALB 1968-
  1988; CN 1, 2, 3, 4, 5, 6, 7; CPW; DA;
  DA3; DAB; DAC; DAM MST, NOV,

POP; DLB 2, 16, 28, 185, 278; DLBD 3; DLBY 1980, 1983; EWL 3; MAL 5; MTCW 1, 2; MTFW 2005; NFS 10; RGAL 4; TUS

Mailer, Norman Kingsley
See Mailer, Norman

Maillet, Antonine 1929- .... **CLC 54, 118**
See also CA 115; 120; CANR 46, 74, 77, 134; CCA 1; CWW 2; DAC; DLB 60; INT CA-120; MTCW 2; MTFW 2005

Maimonides, Moses 1135-1204 ..... **CMLC 76**
See also DLB 115

Mais, Roger 1905-1955 .... **TCLC 8**
See also BW 1, 3; CA 105; 124; CANR 82; CDWLB 3; DLB 125; EWL 3; MTCW 1; RGEL 2

Maistre, Joseph 1753-1821 .... **NCLC 37**
See also GFL 1789 to the Present

Maitland, Frederic William
1850-1906 .... **TCLC 65**

Maitland, Sara (Louise) 1950- .... **CLC 49**
See also BRWS 11; CA 69-72; CANR 13, 59; DLB 271; FW

Major, Clarence 1936- ... **BLC 2; CLC 3, 19, 48**
See also AFAW 2; BW 2, 3; CA 21-24R; CAAS 6; CANR 13, 25, 53, 82; CN 3, 4, 5, 6, 7; CP 2, 3, 4, 5, 6, 7; CSW; DAM MULT; DLB 33; EWL 3; MAL 5; MSW

Major, Kevin (Gerald) 1949- .... **CLC 26**
See also AAYA 16; CA 97-100; CANR 21, 38, 112; CLR 11; DAC; DLB 60; INT CANR-21; JRDA; MAICYA 1, 2; MAIC-YAS 1; SATA 32, 82, 134; WYA; YAW

Maki, James
See Ozu, Yasujiro

Makine, Andrei 1957- .... **CLC 198**
See also CA 176; CANR 103; MTFW 2005

Malabaila, Damiano
See Levi, Primo

Malamud, Bernard 1914-1986 .. **CLC 1, 2, 3, 5, 8, 9, 11, 18, 27, 44, 78, 85; SSC 15; TCLC 129; WLC 4**
See also AAYA 16; AMWS 1; BPFB 2; BYA 15; CA 5-8R; 118; CABS 1; CANR 28, 62, 114; CDALB 1941-1968; CN 1, 2, 3, 4; CPW; DA; DA3; DAB; DAC; DAM MST, NOV, POP; DLB 2, 28, 152; DLBY 1980, 1986; EWL 3; EXPS; LAIT 4; LATS 1:1; MAL 5; MTCW 1, 2; MTFW 2005; NFS 4, 9; RGAL 4; RGHL; RGSF 2; SSFS 8, 13, 16; TUS

Malan, Herman
See Bosman, Herman Charles; Bosman, Herman Charles

Malaparte, Curzio 1898-1957 .... **TCLC 52**
See also DLB 264

Malcolm, Dan
See Silverberg, Robert

Malcolm, Janet 1934- .... **CLC 201**
See also CA 123; CANR 89; NCFS 1

Malcolm X .... **BLC 2; CLC 82, 117; WLCS**
See Little, Malcolm
See also LAIT 5; NCFS 3

Malherbe, Francois de 1555-1628 .... **LC 5**
See also GFL Beginnings to 1789

Mallarme, Stephane 1842-1898 ...... **NCLC 4, 41; PC 4**
See also DAM POET; DLB 217; EW 7; GFL 1789 to the Present; LMFS 2; RGWL 2, 3; TWA

Mallet-Joris, Francoise 1930- .... **CLC 11**
See also CA 65-68; CANR 17; CWW 2; DLB 83; EWL 3; GFL 1789 to the Present

Malley, Ern
See McAuley, James Phillip

Mallon, Thomas 1951- .... **CLC 172**
See also CA 110; CANR 29, 57, 92

Mallowan, Agatha Christie
See Christie, Agatha (Mary Clarissa)

Maloff, Saul 1922- .... **CLC 5**
See also CA 33-36R

Malone, Louis
See MacNeice, (Frederick) Louis

Malone, Michael (Christopher)
1942- .... **CLC 43**
See also CA 77-80; CANR 14, 32, 57, 114

Malory, Sir Thomas 1410(?)-1471(?) . **LC 11, 88; WLCS**
See also BRW 1; BRWR 2; CDBLB Before 1660; DA; DAB; DAC; DAM MST; DLB 146; EFS 2; RGEL 2; SATA 59; SATA-Brief 33; TEA; WLIT 3

Malouf, (George Joseph) David
1934- .... **CLC 28, 86**
See also CA 124; CANR 50, 76; CN 3, 4, 5, 6, 7; CP 1, 3, 4, 5, 6, 7; DLB 289; EWL 3; MTCW 2; MTFW 2005

Malraux, (Georges-)Andre
1901-1976 .... **CLC 1, 4, 9, 13, 15, 57**
See also BPFB 2; CA 21-22; 69-72; CANR 34, 58; CAP 2; DA3; DAM NOV; DLB 72; EW 12; EWL 3; GFL 1789 to the Present; MTCW 1, 2; MTFW 2005; RGWL 2, 3; TWA

Malthus, Thomas Robert
1766-1834 .... **NCLC 145**
See also DLB 107, 158; RGEL 2

Malzberg, Barry N(athaniel) 1939- ... **CLC 7**
See also CA 61-64; CAAS 4; CANR 16; CMW 4; DLB 8; SFW 4

Mamet, David 1947- .. **CLC 9, 15, 34, 46, 91, 166; DC 4, 24**
See also AAYA 3, 60; AMWS 14; CA 81-84; CABS 3; CAD; CANR 15, 41, 67, 72, 129; CD 5, 6; DA3; DAM DRAM; DFS 2, 3, 6, 12, 15; DLB 7; EWL 3; IDFW 4; MAL 5; MTCW 1, 2; MTFW 2005; RGAL 4

Mamet, David Alan
See Mamet, David

Mamoulian, Rouben (Zachary)
1897-1987 .... **CLC 16**
See also CA 25-28R; 124; CANR 85

Mandelshtam, Osip
See Mandelstam, Osip (Emilievich)
See also EW 10; EWL 3; RGWL 2, 3

Mandelstam, Osip (Emilievich)
1891(?)-1943(?) .... **PC 14; TCLC 2, 6**
See Mandelshtam, Osip
See also CA 104; 150; MTCW 2; TWA

Mander, (Mary) Jane 1877-1949 ... **TCLC 31**
See also CA 162; RGEL 2

Mandeville, Bernard 1670-1733 .... **LC 82**
See also DLB 101

Mandeville, Sir John fl. 1350- ...... **CMLC 19**
See also DLB 146

Mandiargues, Andre Pieyre de .... **CLC 41**
See Pieyre de Mandiargues, Andre
See also DLB 83

Mandrake, Ethel Belle
See Thurman, Wallace (Henry)

Mangan, James Clarence
1803-1849 .... **NCLC 27**
See also RGEL 2

Maniere, J.-E.
See Giraudoux, Jean(-Hippolyte)

Mankiewicz, Herman (Jacob)
1897-1953 .... **TCLC 85**
See also CA 120; 169; DLB 26; IDFW 3, 4

Manley, (Mary) Delariviere
1672(?)-1724 .... **LC 1, 42**
See also DLB 39, 80; RGEL 2

Mann, Abel
See Creasey, John

Mann, Emily 1952- .... **DC 7**
See also CA 130; CAD; CANR 55; CD 5, 6; CWD; DLB 266

Mann, (Luiz) Heinrich 1871-1950 ... **TCLC 9**
See also CA 106; 164, 181; DLB 66, 118; EW 8; EWL 3; RGWL 2, 3

Mann, (Paul) Thomas 1875-1955 . **SSC 5, 80, 82; TCLC 2, 8, 14, 21, 35, 44, 60, 168; WLC 4**
See also BPFB 2; CA 104; 128; CANR 133; CDWLB 2; DA; DA3; DAB; DAC; DAM MST, NOV; DLB 66; EW 9; EWL 3; GLL 1; LATS 1:1; LMFS 1; MTCW 1, 2; MTFW 2005; NFS 17; RGSF 2; RGWL 2, 3; SSFS 4, 9; TWA

Mannheim, Karl 1893-1947 .... **TCLC 65**
See also CA 204

Manning, David
See Faust, Frederick (Schiller)

Manning, Frederic 1882-1935 .... **TCLC 25**
See also CA 124; 216; DLB 260

Manning, Olivia 1915-1980 .... **CLC 5, 19**
See also CA 5-8R; 101; CANR 29; CN 1, 2; EWL 3; FW; MTCW 1; RGEL 2

Mannyng, Robert c. 1264-c.
1340 .... **CMLC 83**
See also DLB 146

Mano, D. Keith 1942- .... **CLC 2, 10**
See also CA 25-28R; CAAS 6; CANR 26, 57; DLB 6

Mansfield, Katherine .... **SSC 9, 23, 38, 81; TCLC 2, 8, 39, 164; WLC 4**
See Beauchamp, Kathleen Mansfield
See also BPFB 2; BRW 7; DAB; DLB 162; EWL 3; EXPS; FW; GLL 1; RGEL 2; RGSF 2; SSFS 2, 8, 10, 11; WWE 1

Manso, Peter 1940- .... **CLC 39**
See also CA 29-32R; CANR 44

Mantecon, Juan Jimenez
See Jimenez (Mantecon), Juan Ramon

Mantel, Hilary (Mary) 1952- .... **CLC 144**
See also CA 125; CANR 54, 101; CN 5, 6, 7; DLB 271; RHW

Manton, Peter
See Creasey, John

Man Without a Spleen, A
See Chekhov, Anton (Pavlovich)

Manzano, Juan Franciso
1797(?)-1854 .... **NCLC 155**

Manzoni, Alessandro 1785-1873 ... **NCLC 29, 98**
See also EW 5; RGWL 2, 3; TWA; WLIT 7

Map, Walter 1140-1209 .... **CMLC 32**

Mapu, Abraham (ben Jekutiel)
1808-1867 .... **NCLC 18**

Mara, Sally
See Queneau, Raymond

Maracle, Lee 1950- .... **NNAL**
See also CA 149

Marat, Jean Paul 1743-1793 .... **LC 10**

Marcel, Gabriel Honore 1889-1973 . **CLC 15**
See also CA 102; 45-48; EWL 3; MTCW 1, 2

March, William .... **TCLC 96**
See Campbell, William Edward March
See also CA 216; DLB 9, 86, 316; MAL 5

Marchbanks, Samuel
See Davies, (William) Robertson
See also CCA 1

Marchi, Giacomo
See Bassani, Giorgio

Marcus Aurelius
See Aurelius, Marcus
See also AW 2

Marguerite
See de Navarre, Marguerite

Marguerite d'Angouleme
See de Navarre, Marguerite
See also GFL Beginnings to 1789

Mass, Anna .... **CLC 59**
Mass, William
    See Gibson, William
Massinger, Philip 1583-1640 .... **LC 70**
    See also BRWS 11; DLB 58; RGEL 2
Master Lao
    See Lao Tzu
Masters, Edgar Lee 1868-1950 ...... **PC 1, 36;
    TCLC 2, 25; WLCS**
    See also AMWS 1; CA 104; 133; CDALB
    1865-1917; DA; DAC; DAM MST,
    POET; DLB 54; EWL 3; EXPP; MAL 5;
    MTCW 1, 2; MTFW 2005; RGAL 4;
    TUS; WP
Masters, Hilary 1928- .... **CLC 48**
    See also CA 25-28R, 217; CAAE 217;
    CANR 13, 47, 97; CN 6, 7; DLB 244
Mastrosimone, William 1947- .... **CLC 36**
    See also CA 186; CAD; CD 5, 6
Mathe, Albert
    See Camus, Albert
Mather, Cotton 1663-1728 .... **LC 38**
    See also AMWS 2; CDALB 1640-1865;
    DLB 24, 30, 140; RGAL 4; TUS
Mather, Increase 1639-1723 .... **LC 38**
    See also DLB 24
Matheson, Richard (Burton) 1926- .. **CLC 37**
    See also AAYA 31; CA 97-100; CANR 88,
    99; DLB 8, 44; HGG; INT CA-97-100;
    SCFW 1, 2; SFW 4; SUFW 2
Mathews, Harry (Burchell) 1930- ..... **CLC 6,
    52**
    See also CA 21-24R; CAAS 6; CANR 18,
    40, 98; CN 5, 6, 7
Mathews, John Joseph 1894-1979 .. **CLC 84;
    NNAL**
    See also CA 19-20; 142; CANR 45; CAP 2;
    DAM MULT; DLB 175; TCWW 1, 2
Mathias, Roland (Glyn) 1915- .... **CLC 45**
    See also CA 97-100; CANR 19, 41; CP 1,
    2, 3, 4, 5, 6, 7; DLB 27
Matsuo Basho 1644(?)-1694 ...... **LC 62; PC 3**
    See Basho, Matsuo
    See also DAM POET; PFS 2, 7, 18
Mattheson, Rodney
    See Creasey, John
Matthews, (James) Brander
    1852-1929 .... **TCLC 95**
    See also CA 181; DLB 71, 78; DLBD 13
Matthews, Greg 1949- .... **CLC 45**
    See also CA 135
Matthews, William (Procter III)
    1942-1997 .... **CLC 40**
    See also AMWS 9; CA 29-32R; 162; CAAS
    18; CANR 12, 57; CP 2, 3, 4, 5, 6; DLB 5
Matthias, John (Edward) 1941- .... **CLC 9**
    See also CA 33-36R; CANR 56; CP 4, 5,
    6, 7
Matthiessen, F(rancis) O(tto)
    1902-1950 .... **TCLC 100**
    See also CA 185; DLB 63; MAL 5
Matthiessen, Peter 1927- ... **CLC 5, 7, 11, 32,
    64**
    See also AAYA 6, 40; AMWS 5; ANW;
    BEST 90:4; BPFB 2; CA 9-12R; CANR
    21, 50, 73, 100, 138; CN 1, 2, 3, 4, 5, 6,
    7; DA3; DAM NOV; DLB 6, 173, 275;
    MAL 5; MTCW 1, 2; MTFW 2005; SATA
    27
Maturin, Charles Robert
    1780(?)-1824 .... **NCLC 6, 169**
    See also BRWS 8; DLB 178; GL 3; HGG;
    LMFS 1; RGEL 2; SUFW
Matute (Ausejo), Ana Maria 1925- .. **CLC 11**
    See also CA 89-92; CANR 129; CWW 2;
    DLB 322; EWL 3; MTCW 1; RGSF 2
Maugham, W. S.
    See Maugham, W(illiam) Somerset

Maugham, W(illiam) Somerset
    1874-1965 .. **CLC 1, 11, 15, 67, 93; SSC
    8; WLC 4**
    See also AAYA 55; BPFB 2; BRW 6; CA
    5-8R; 25-28R; CANR 40, 127; CDBLB
    1914-1945; CMW 4; DA; DA3; DAB;
    DAC; DAM DRAM, MST, NOV; DFS
    22; DLB 10, 36, 77, 100, 162, 195; EWL
    3; LAIT 3; MTCW 1, 2; MTFW 2005;
    NFS 23; RGEL 2; RGSF 2; SATA 54;
    SSFS 17
Maugham, William Somerset
    See Maugham, W(illiam) Somerset
Maupassant, (Henri Rene Albert) Guy de
    1850-1893 . **NCLC 1, 42, 83; SSC 1, 64;
    WLC 4**
    See also BYA 14; DA; DA3; DAB; DAC;
    DAM MST; DLB 123; EW 7; EXPS; GFL
    1789 to the Present; LAIT 2; LMFS 1;
    RGSF 2; RGWL 2, 3; SSFS 4, 21; SUFW;
    TWA
Maupin, Armistead (Jones, Jr.)
    1944- .... **CLC 95**
    See also CA 125; 130; CANR 58, 101;
    CPW; DA3; DAM POP; DLB 278; GLL
    1; INT CA-130; MTCW 2; MTFW 2005
Maurhut, Richard
    See Traven, B.
Mauriac, Claude 1914-1996 .... **CLC 9**
    See also CA 89-92; 152; CWW 2; DLB 83;
    EWL 3; GFL 1789 to the Present
Mauriac, Francois (Charles)
    1885-1970 .... **CLC 4, 9, 56; SSC 24**
    See also CA 25-28; CAP 2; DLB 65; EW
    10; EWL 3; GFL 1789 to the Present;
    MTCW 1, 2; MTFW 2005; RGWL 2, 3;
    TWA
Mavor, Osborne Henry 1888-1951
    See Bridie, James
    See also CA 104
Maxwell, William (Keepers, Jr.)
    1908-2000 .... **CLC 19**
    See also AMWS 8; CA 93-96; 189; CANR
    54, 95; CN 1, 2, 3, 4, 5, 6, 7; DLB 218,
    278; DLBY 1980; INT CA-93-96; MAL
    5; SATA-Obit 128
May, Elaine 1932- .... **CLC 16**
    See also CA 124; 142; CAD; CWD; DLB
    44
Mayakovski, Vladimir (Vladimirovich)
    1893-1930 .... **TCLC 4, 18**
    See Maiakovskii, Vladimir; Mayakovsky,
    Vladimir
    See also CA 104; 158; EWL 3; MTCW 2;
    MTFW 2005; SFW 4; TWA
Mayakovsky, Vladimir
    See Mayakovski, Vladimir (Vladimirovich)
    See also EW 11; WP
Mayhew, Henry 1812-1887 .... **NCLC 31**
    See also DLB 18, 55, 190
Mayle, Peter 1939(?)- .... **CLC 89**
    See also CA 139; CANR 64, 109
Maynard, Joyce 1953- .... **CLC 23**
    See also CA 111; 129; CANR 64
Mayne, William (James Carter)
    1928- .... **CLC 12**
    See also AAYA 20; CA 9-12R; CANR 37,
    80, 100; CLR 25; FANT; JRDA; MAI-
    CYA 1, 2; MAICYAS 1; SAAS 11; SATA
    6, 68, 122; SUFW 2; YAW
Mayo, Jim
    See L'Amour, Louis (Dearborn)
Maysles, Albert 1926- .... **CLC 16**
    See also CA 29-32R
Maysles, David 1932-1987 .... **CLC 16**
    See also CA 191

Mazer, Norma Fox 1931- .... **CLC 26**
    See also AAYA 5, 36; BYA 1, 8; CA 69-72;
    CANR 12, 32, 66, 129; CLR 23; JRDA;
    MAICYA 1, 2; SAAS 1; SATA 24, 67,
    105, 168; WYA; YAW
Mazzini, Guiseppe 1805-1872 .... **NCLC 34**
McAlmon, Robert (Menzies)
    1895-1956 .... **TCLC 97**
    See also CA 107; 168; DLB 4, 45; DLBD
    15; GLL 1
McAuley, James Phillip 1917-1976 .. **CLC 45**
    See also CA 97-100; CP 1, 2; DLB 260;
    RGEL 2
McBain, Ed
    See Hunter, Evan
    See also MSW
McBrien, William (Augustine)
    1930- .... **CLC 44**
    See also CA 107; CANR 90
McCabe, Patrick 1955- .... **CLC 133**
    See also BRWS 9; CA 130; CANR 50, 90;
    CN 6, 7; DLB 194
McCaffrey, Anne 1926- .... **CLC 17**
    See also AAYA 6, 34; AITN 2; BEST 89:2;
    BPFB 2; BYA 5; CA 25-28R; 227; CAAE
    227; CANR 15, 35, 55, 96; CLR 49;
    CPW; DA3; DAM NOV, POP; DLB 8;
    JRDA; MAICYA 1, 2; MTCW 1, 2;
    MTFW 2005; SAAS 11; SATA 8, 70, 116,
    152; SATA-Essay 152; SFW 4; SUFW 2;
    WYA; YAW
McCaffrey, Anne Inez
    See McCaffrey, Anne
McCall, Nathan 1955(?)- .... **CLC 86**
    See also AAYA 59; BW 3; CA 146; CANR
    88
McCann, Arthur
    See Campbell, John W(ood, Jr.)
McCann, Edson
    See Pohl, Frederik
McCarthy, Charles, Jr. 1933-
    See McCarthy, Cormac
    See also CANR 42, 69, 101; CPW; CSW;
    DA3; DAM POP; MTCW 2; MTFW 2005
McCarthy, Cormac ...... **CLC 4, 57, 101, 204**
    See McCarthy, Charles, Jr.
    See also AAYA 41; AMWS 8; BPFB 2; CA
    13-16R; CANR 10; CN 6, 7; DLB 6, 143,
    256; EWL 3; LATS 1:2; MAL 5; TCLE
    1:2; TCWW 2
McCarthy, Mary (Therese)
    1912-1989 .. **CLC 1, 3, 5, 14, 24, 39, 59;
    SSC 24**
    See also AMW; BPFB 2; CA 5-8R; 129;
    CANR 16, 50, 64; CN 1, 2, 3, 4; DA3;
    DLB 2; DLBY 1981; EWL 3; FW; INT
    CANR-16; MAL 5; MAWW; MTCW 1,
    2; MTFW 2005; RGAL 4; TUS
McCartney, James Paul
    See McCartney, Paul
McCartney, Paul 1942- .... **CLC 12, 35**
    See also CA 146; CANR 111
McCauley, Stephen (D.) 1955- .... **CLC 50**
    See also CA 141
McClaren, Peter .... **CLC 70**
McClure, Michael (Thomas) 1932- ... **CLC 6,
    10**
    See also BG 1:3; CA 21-24R; CAD; CANR
    17, 46, 77, 131; CD 5, 6; CP 1, 2, 3, 4, 5,
    6, 7; DLB 16; WP
McCorkle, Jill (Collins) 1958- .... **CLC 51**
    See also CA 121; CANR 113; CSW; DLB
    234; DLBY 1987
McCourt, Frank 1930- .... **CLC 109**
    See also AAYA 61; AMWS 12; CA 157;
    CANR 97, 138; MTFW 2005; NCFS 1
McCourt, James 1941- .... **CLC 5**
    See also CA 57-60; CANR 98, 152

Muske-Dukes, Carol (Anne) 1945-
See Muske, Carol
See also CA 65-68, 203; CAAE 203; CANR 32, 70; CWP; PFS 24

Musset, Alfred de 1810-1857 . **DC 27; NCLC 7, 150**
See also DLB 192, 217; EW 6; GFL 1789 to the Present; RGWL 2, 3; TWA

Musset, Louis Charles Alfred de
See Musset, Alfred de

Mussolini, Benito (Amilcare Andrea) 1883-1945 .... **TCLC 96**
See also CA 116

Mutanabbi, Al-
See al-Mutanabbi, Ahmad ibn al-Husayn Abu al-Tayyib al-Jufi al-Kindi
See also WLIT 6

My Brother's Brother
See Chekhov, Anton (Pavlovich)

Myers, L(eopold) H(amilton) 1881-1944 .... **TCLC 59**
See also CA 157; DLB 15; EWL 3; RGEL 2

Myers, Walter Dean 1937- .. **BLC 3; CLC 35**
See also AAYA 4, 23; BW 2; BYA 6, 8, 11; CA 33-36R; CANR 20, 42, 67, 108; CLR 4, 16, 35, 110; DAM MULT, NOV; DLB 33; INT CANR-20; JRDA; LAIT 5; MAICYA 1, 2; MAICYAS 1; MTCW 2; MTFW 2005; SAAS 2; SATA 41, 71, 109, 157; SATA-Brief 27; WYA; YAW

Myers, Walter M.
See Myers, Walter Dean

Myles, Symon
See Follett, Ken(neth Martin)

Nabokov, Vladimir (Vladimirovich) 1899-1977 .... **CLC 1, 2, 3, 6, 8, 11, 15, 23, 44, 46, 64; SSC 11, 86; TCLC 108; WLC 4**
See also AAYA 45; AMW; AMWC 1; AMWR 1; BPFB 2; CA 5-8R; 69-72; CANR 20, 102; CDALB 1941-1968; CN 1, 2; CP 2; DA; DA3; DAB; DAC; DAM MST, NOV; DLB 2, 244, 278, 317; DLBD 3; DLBY 1980, 1991; EWL 3; EXPS; LATS 1:2; MAL 5; MTCW 1, 2; MTFW 2005; NCFS 4; NFS 9; RGAL 4; RGSF 2; SSFS 6, 15; TUS

Naevius c. 265B.C.-201B.C. .... **CMLC 37**
See also DLB 211

Nagai, Kafu .... **TCLC 51**
See Nagai, Sokichi
See also DLB 180

Nagai, Sokichi 1879-1959
See Nagai, Kafu
See also CA 117

Nagy, Laszlo 1925-1978 .... **CLC 7**
See also CA 129; 112

Naidu, Sarojini 1879-1949 .... **TCLC 80**
See also EWL 3; RGEL 2

Naipaul, Shiva(dhar Srinivasa) 1945-1985 .... **CLC 32, 39; TCLC 153**
See also CA 110; 112; 116; CANR 33; CN 2, 3; DA3; DAM NOV; DLB 157; DLBY 1985; EWL 3; MTCW 1, 2; MTFW 2005

Naipaul, V(idiadhar) S(urajprasad) 1932- .... **CLC 4, 7, 9, 13, 18, 37, 105, 199; SSC 38**
See also BPFB 2; BRWS 1; CA 1-4R; CANR 1, 33, 51, 91, 126; CDBLB 1960 to Present; CDWLB 3; CN 1, 2, 3, 4, 5, 6, 7; DA3; DAB; DAC; DAM MST, NOV; DLB 125, 204, 207, 326; DLBY 1985, 2001; EWL 3; LATS 1:2; MTCW 1, 2; MTFW 2005; RGEL 2; RGSF 2; TWA; WLIT 4; WWE 1

Nakos, Lilika 1903(?)-1989 .... **CLC 29**

Napoleon
See Yamamoto, Hisaye

Narayan, R(asipuram) K(rishnaswami) 1906-2001 .... **CLC 7, 28, 47, 121, 211; SSC 25**
See also BPFB 2; CA 81-84; 196; CANR 33, 61, 112; CN 1, 2, 3, 4, 5, 6, 7; DA3; DAM NOV; DLB 323; DNFS 1; EWL 3; MTCW 1, 2; MTFW 2005; RGEL 2; RGSF 2; SATA 62; SSFS 5; WWE 1

Nash, (Fredric) Ogden 1902-1971 . **CLC 23; PC 21; TCLC 109**
See also CA 13-14; 29-32R; CANR 34, 61; CAP 1; CP 1; DAM POET; DLB 11; MAICYA 1, 2; MAL 5; MTCW 1, 2; RGAL 4; SATA 2, 46; WP

Nashe, Thomas 1567-1601(?) .... **LC 41, 89**
See also DLB 167; RGEL 2

Nathan, Daniel
See Dannay, Frederic

Nathan, George Jean 1882-1958 .... **TCLC 18**
See Hatteras, Owen
See also CA 114; 169; DLB 137; MAL 5

Natsume, Kinnosuke
See Natsume, Soseki

Natsume, Soseki 1867-1916 .... **TCLC 2, 10**
See Natsume Soseki; Soseki
See also CA 104; 195; RGWL 2, 3; TWA

Natsume Soseki
See Natsume, Soseki
See also DLB 180; EWL 3

Natti, (Mary) Lee 1919-
See Kingman, Lee
See also CA 5-8R; CANR 2

Navarre, Marguerite de
See de Navarre, Marguerite

Naylor, Gloria 1950- ..... **BLC 3; CLC 28, 52, 156; WLCS**
See also AAYA 6, 39; AFAW 1, 2; AMWS 8; BW 2, 3; CA 107; CANR 27, 51, 74, 130; CN 4, 5, 6, 7; CPW; DA; DA3; DAC; DAM MST, MULT, NOV, POP; DLB 173; EWL 3; FW; MAL 5; MTCW 1, 2; MTFW 2005; NFS 4, 7; RGAL 4; TCLE 1:2; TUS

Neal, John 1793-1876 .... **NCLC 161**
See also DLB 1, 59, 243; FW; RGAL 4

Neff, Debra .... **CLC 59**

Neihardt, John Gneisenau 1881-1973 .... **CLC 32**
See also CA 13-14; CANR 65; CAP 1; DLB 9, 54, 256; LAIT 2; TCWW 1, 2

Nekrasov, Nikolai Alekseevich 1821-1878 .... **NCLC 11**
See also DLB 277

Nelligan, Emile 1879-1941 .... **TCLC 14**
See also CA 114; 204; DLB 92; EWL 3

Nelson, Willie 1933- .... **CLC 17**
See also CA 107; CANR 114

Nemerov, Howard (Stanley) 1920-1991 .... **CLC 2, 6, 9, 36; PC 24; TCLC 124**
See also AMW; CA 1-4R; 134; CABS 2; CANR 1, 27, 53; CN 1, 2, 3; CP 1, 2, 3, 4, 5; DAM POET; DLB 5, 6; DLBY 1983; EWL 3; INT CANR-27; MAL 5; MTCW 1, 2; MTFW 2005; PFS 10, 14; RGAL 4

Neruda, Pablo 1904-1973 .. **CLC 1, 2, 5, 7, 9, 28, 62; HLC 2; PC 4, 64; WLC 4**
See also CA 19-20; 45-48; CANR 131; CAP 2; DA; DA3; DAB; DAC; DAM MST, MULT, POET; DLB 283; DNFS 2; EWL 3; HW 1; LAW; MTCW 1, 2; MTFW 2005; PFS 11; RGWL 2, 3; TWA; WLIT 1; WP

Nerval, Gerard de 1808-1855 ... **NCLC 1, 67; PC 13; SSC 18**
See also DLB 217; EW 6; GFL 1789 to the Present; RGSF 2; RGWL 2, 3

Nervo, (Jose) Amado (Ruiz de) 1870-1919 .... **HLCS 2; TCLC 11**
See also CA 109; 131; DLB 290; EWL 3; HW 1; LAW

Nesbit, Malcolm
See Chester, Alfred

Nessi, Pio Baroja y
See Baroja, Pio

Nestroy, Johann 1801-1862 .... **NCLC 42**
See also DLB 133; RGWL 2, 3

Netterville, Luke
See O'Grady, Standish (James)

Neufeld, John (Arthur) 1938- .... **CLC 17**
See also AAYA 11; CA 25-28R; CANR 11, 37, 56; CLR 52; MAICYA 1, 2; SAAS 3; SATA 6, 81, 131; SATA-Essay 131; YAW

Neumann, Alfred 1895-1952 .... **TCLC 100**
See also CA 183; DLB 56

Neumann, Ferenc
See Molnar, Ferenc

Neville, Emily Cheney 1919- .... **CLC 12**
See also BYA 2; CA 5-8R; CANR 3, 37, 85; JRDA; MAICYA 1, 2; SAAS 2; SATA 1; YAW

Newbound, Bernard Slade 1930-
See Slade, Bernard
See also CA 81-84; CANR 49; CD 5; DAM DRAM

Newby, P(ercy) H(oward) 1918-1997 .... **CLC 2, 13**
See also CA 5-8R; 161; CANR 32, 67; CN 1, 2, 3, 4, 5, 6; DAM NOV; DLB 15, 326; MTCW 1; RGEL 2

Newcastle
See Cavendish, Margaret Lucas

Newlove, Donald 1928- .... **CLC 6**
See also CA 29-32R; CANR 25

Newlove, John (Herbert) 1938- .... **CLC 14**
See also CA 21-24R; CANR 9, 25; CP 1, 2, 3, 4, 5, 6, 7

Newman, Charles 1938-2006 .... **CLC 2, 8**
See also CA 21-24R; CANR 84; CN 3, 4, 5, 6

Newman, Charles Hamilton
See Newman, Charles

Newman, Edwin (Harold) 1919- ...... **CLC 14**
See also AITN 1; CA 69-72; CANR 5

Newman, John Henry 1801-1890 . **NCLC 38, 99**
See also BRWS 7; DLB 18, 32, 55; RGEL 2

Newton, (Sir) Isaac 1642-1727 ...... **LC 35, 53**
See also DLB 252

Newton, Suzanne 1936- .... **CLC 35**
See also BYA 7; CA 41-44R; CANR 14; JRDA; SATA 5, 77

New York Dept. of Ed. .... **CLC 70**

Nexo, Martin Andersen 1869-1954 .... **TCLC 43**
See also CA 202; DLB 214; EWL 3

Nezval, Vitezslav 1900-1958 .... **TCLC 44**
See also CA 123; CDWLB 4; DLB 215; EWL 3

Ng, Fae Myenne 1957(?)- .... **CLC 81**
See also BYA 11; CA 146

Ngema, Mbongeni 1955- .... **CLC 57**
See also BW 2; CA 143; CANR 84; CD 5, 6

Ngugi, James T(hiong'o) . **CLC 3, 7, 13, 182**
See Ngugi wa Thiong'o
See also CN 1, 2

Ngugi wa Thiong'o
See Ngugi wa Thiong'o
See also CD 3, 4, 5, 6, 7; DLB 125; EWL 3

O'Brien, Flann .... **CLC 1, 4, 5, 7, 10, 47**
See O Nuallain, Brian
See also BRWS 2; DLB 231; EWL 3;
RGEL 2

O'Brien, Richard 1942- .... **CLC 17**
See also CA 124

O'Brien, (William) Tim(othy) 1946- . **CLC 7,**
19, 40, 103, 211; SSC 74
See also AAYA 16; AMWS 5; CA 85-88;
CANR 40, 58, 133; CDALBS; CN 5, 6,
7; CPW; DA3; DAM POP; DLB 152;
DLBD 9; DLBY 1980; LATS 1:2; MAL
5; MTCW 2; MTFW 2005; RGAL 4;
SSFS 5, 15; TCLE 1:2

Obstfelder, Sigbjoern 1866-1900 .... **TCLC 23**
See also CA 123

O'Casey, Sean 1880-1964 .... **CLC 1, 5, 9, 11,**
15, 88; DC 12; WLCS
See also BRW 7; CA 89-92; CANR 62;
CBD; CDBLB 1914-1945; DA3; DAB;
DAC; DAM DRAM, MST; DFS 19; DLB
10; EWL 3; MTCW 1, 2; MTFW 2005;
RGEL 2; TEA; WLIT 4

O'Cathasaigh, Sean
See O'Casey, Sean

Occom, Samson 1723-1792 .... **LC 60; NNAL**
See also DLB 175

Occomy, Marita (Odette) Bonner
1899(?)-1971
See Bonner, Marita
See also BW 2; CA 142; DFS 13; DLB 51,
228

Ochs, Phil(ip David) 1940-1976 .... **CLC 17**
See also CA 185; 65-68

O'Connor, Edwin (Greene)
1918-1968 .... **CLC 14**
See also CA 93-96; 25-28R; MAL 5

O'Connor, (Mary) Flannery
1925-1964 ... **CLC 1, 2, 3, 6, 10, 13, 15,**
21, 66, 104; SSC 1, 23, 61, 82; TCLC
132; WLC 4
See also AAYA 7; AMW; AMWR 2; BPFB
3; BYA 16; CA 1-4R; CANR 3, 41;
CDALB 1941-1968; DA; DA3; DAB;
DAC; DAM MST, NOV; DLB 2, 152;
DLBD 12; DLBY 1980; EWL 3; EXPS;
LAIT 5; MAL 5; MAWW; MTCW 1, 2;
MTFW 2005; NFS 3, 21; RGAL 4; RGSF
2; SSFS 2, 7, 10, 19; TUS

O'Connor, Frank .... **CLC 23; SSC 5**
See O'Donovan, Michael Francis
See also DLB 162; EWL 3; RGSF 2; SSFS 5

O'Dell, Scott 1898-1989 .... **CLC 30**
See also AAYA 3, 44; BPFB 3; BYA 1, 2,
3, 5; CA 61-64; 129; CANR 12, 30, 112;
CLR 1, 16; DLB 52; JRDA; MAICYA 1,
2; SATA 12, 60, 134; WYA; YAW

Odets, Clifford 1906-1963 ..... **CLC 2, 28, 98;**
DC 6
See also AMWS 2; CA 85-88; CAD; CANR
62; DAM DRAM; DFS 3, 17, 20; DLB 7,
26; EWL 3; MAL 5; MTCW 1, 2; MTFW
2005; RGAL 4; TUS

O'Doherty, Brian 1928- .... **CLC 76**
See also CA 105; CANR 108

O'Donnell, K. M.
See Malzberg, Barry N(athaniel)

O'Donnell, Lawrence
See Kuttner, Henry

O'Donovan, Michael Francis
1903-1966 .... **CLC 14**
See O'Connor, Frank
See also CA 93-96; CANR 84

Oe, Kenzaburo 1935- .. **CLC 10, 36, 86, 187;**
SSC 20
See Oe Kenzaburo
See also CA 97-100; CANR 36, 50, 74, 126;
DA3; DAM NOV; DLB 182; DLBY 1994;
LATS 1:2; MJW; MTCW 1, 2; MTFW
2005; RGSF 2; RGWL 2, 3

Oe Kenzaburo
See Oe, Kenzaburo
See also CWW 2; EWL 3

O'Faolain, Julia 1932- .... **CLC 6, 19, 47, 108**
See also CA 81-84; CAAS 2; CANR 12,
61; CN 2, 3, 4, 5, 6, 7; DLB 14, 231, 319;
FW; MTCW 1; RHW

O'Faolain, Sean 1900-1991 ...... **CLC 1, 7, 14,**
32, 70; SSC 13; TCLC 143
See also CA 61-64; 134; CANR 12, 66; CN
1, 2, 3, 4; DLB 15, 162; MTCW 1, 2;
MTFW 2005; RGEL 2; RGSF 2

O'Flaherty, Liam 1896-1984 .... **CLC 5, 34;**
SSC 6
See also CA 101; 113; CANR 35; CN 1, 2,
3; DLB 36, 162; DLBY 1984; MTCW 1,
2; MTFW 2005; RGEL 2; RGSF 2; SSFS
5, 20

Ogai
See Mori Ogai
See also MJW

Ogilvy, Gavin
See Barrie, J(ames) M(atthew)

O'Grady, Standish (James)
1846-1928 .... **TCLC 5**
See also CA 104; 157

O'Grady, Timothy 1951- .... **CLC 59**
See also CA 138

O'Hara, Frank 1926-1966 .... **CLC 2, 5, 13,**
78; PC 45
See also CA 9-12R; 25-28R; CANR 33;
DA3; DAM POET; DLB 5, 16, 193; EWL
3; MAL 5; MTCW 1, 2; MTFW 2005;
PFS 8, 12; RGAL 4; WP

O'Hara, John (Henry) 1905-1970 . **CLC 1, 2,**
3, 6, 11, 42; SSC 15
See also AMW; BPFB 3; CA 5-8R; 25-28R;
CANR 31, 60; CDALB 1929-1941; DAM
NOV; DLB 9, 86, 324; DLBD 2; EWL 3;
MAL 5; MTCW 1, 2; MTFW 2005; NFS
11; RGAL 4; RGSF 2

O'Hehir, Diana 1929- .... **CLC 41**
See also CA 245

Ohiyesa
See Eastman, Charles A(lexander)

Okada, John 1923-1971 .... **AAL**
See also BYA 14; CA 212; DLB 312

Okigbo, Christopher 1930-1967 .... **BLC 3;**
CLC 25, 84; PC 7; TCLC 171
See also AFW; BW 1, 3; CA 77-80; CANR
74; CDWLB 3; DAM MULT, POET; DLB
125; EWL 3; MTCW 1, 2; MTFW 2005;
RGEL 2

Okigbo, Christopher Ifenayichukwu
See Okigbo, Christopher

Okri, Ben 1959- .... **CLC 87, 223**
See also AFW; BRWS 5; BW 2, 3; CA 130;
138; CANR 65, 128; CN 5, 6, 7; DLB
157, 231, 319, 326; EWL 3; INT CA-138;
MTCW 2; MTFW 2005; RGSF 2; SSFS
20; WLIT 2; WWE 1

Olds, Sharon 1942- .. **CLC 32, 39, 85; PC 22**
See also AMWS 10; CA 101; CANR 18,
41, 66, 98, 135; CP 5, 6, 7; CPW; CWP;
DAM POET; DLB 120; MAL 5; MTCW
2; MTFW 2005; PFS 17

Oldstyle, Jonathan
See Irving, Washington

Olesha, Iurii
See Olesha, Yuri (Karlovich)
See also RGWL 2

Olesha, Iurii Karlovich
See Olesha, Yuri (Karlovich)
See also DLB 272

Olesha, Yuri (Karlovich) 1899-1960 . **CLC 8;**
SSC 69; TCLC 136
See Olesha, Iurii; Olesha, Iurii Karlovich;
Olesha, Yury Karlovich
See also CA 85-88; EW 11; RGWL 3

Olesha, Yury Karlovich
See Olesha, Yuri (Karlovich)
See also EWL 3

Oliphant, Mrs.
See Oliphant, Margaret (Oliphant Wilson)
See also SUFW

Oliphant, Laurence 1829(?)-1888 .. **NCLC 47**
See also DLB 18, 166

Oliphant, Margaret (Oliphant Wilson)
1828-1897 .... **NCLC 11, 61; SSC 25**
See Oliphant, Mrs.
See also BRWS 10; DLB 18, 159, 190;
HGG; RGEL 2; RGSF 2

Oliver, Mary 1935- .... **CLC 19, 34, 98**
See also AMWS 7; CA 21-24R; CANR 9,
43, 84, 92, 138; CP 4, 5, 6, 7; CWP; DLB
5, 193; EWL 3; MTFW 2005; PFS 15

Olivier, Laurence (Kerr) 1907-1989 . **CLC 20**
See also CA 111; 150; 129

Olsen, Tillie 1912- ... **CLC 4, 13, 114; SSC 11**
See also AAYA 51; AMWS 13; BYA 11;
CA 1-4R; CANR 1, 43, 74, 132;
CDALBS; CN 2, 3, 4, 5, 6, 7; DA; DA3;
DAB; DAC; DAM MST; DLB 28, 206;
DLBY 1980; EWL 3; EXPS; FW; MAL
5; MTCW 1, 2; MTFW 2005; RGAL 4;
RGSF 2; SSFS 1; TCLE 1:2; TCWW 2;
TUS

Olson, Charles (John) 1910-1970 .. **CLC 1, 2,**
5, 6, 9, 11, 29; PC 19
See also AMWS 2; CA 13-16; 25-28R;
CABS 2; CANR 35, 61; CAP 1; CP 1;
DAM POET; DLB 5, 16, 193; EWL 3;
MAL 5; MTCW 1, 2; RGAL 4; WP

Olson, Toby 1937- .... **CLC 28**
See also CA 65-68; CANR 9, 31, 84; CP 3,
4, 5, 6, 7

Olyesha, Yuri
See Olesha, Yuri (Karlovich)

Olympiodorus of Thebes c. 375-c.
430 .... **CMLC 59**

Omar Khayyam
See Khayyam, Omar
See also RGWL 2, 3

Ondaatje, Michael 1943- ..... **CLC 14, 29, 51,**
76, 180; PC 28
See also AAYA 66; CA 77-80; CANR 42,
74, 109, 133; CN 5, 6, 7; CP 1, 2, 3, 4, 5,
6, 7; DA3; DAB; DAC; DAM MST; DLB
60, 323, 326; EWL 3; LATS 1:2; LMFS
2; MTCW 2; MTFW 2005; NFS 23; PFS
8, 19; TCLE 1:2; TWA; WWE 1

Ondaatje, Philip Michael
See Ondaatje, Michael

Oneal, Elizabeth 1934-
See Oneal, Zibby
See also CA 106; CANR 28, 84; MAICYA
1, 2; SATA 30, 82; YAW

Oneal, Zibby .... **CLC 30**
See Oneal, Elizabeth
See also AAYA 5, 41; BYA 13; CLR 13;
JRDA; WYA

O'Neill, Eugene (Gladstone)
1888-1953 ... **DC 20; TCLC 1, 6, 27, 49;**
WLC 4
See also AAYA 54; AITN 1; AMW; AMWC
1; CA 110; 132; CAD; CANR 131;
CDALB 1929-1941; DA; DA3; DAB;
DAC; DAM DRAM, MST; DFS 2, 4, 5,
6, 9, 11, 12, 16, 20; DLB 7; EWL 3; LAIT
3; LMFS 2; MAL 5; MTCW 1, 2; MTFW
2005; RGAL 4; TUS

Onetti, Juan Carlos 1909-1994 ... **CLC 7, 10;**
HLCS 2; SSC 23; TCLC 131
See also CA 85-88; 145; CANR 32, 63; CD-
WLB 3; CWW 2; DAM MULT, NOV;
DLB 113; EWL 3; HW 1, 2; LAW;
MTCW 1, 2; MTFW 2005; RGSF 2

Paley, Grace 1922- .... **CLC 4, 6, 37, 140; SSC 8**
See also AMWS 6; CA 25-28R; CANR 13, 46, 74, 118; CN 2, 3, 4, 5, 6, 7; CPW; DA3; DAM POP; DLB 28, 218; EWL 3; EXPS; FW; INT CANR-13; MAL 5; MAWW; MTCW 1, 2; MTFW 2005; RGAL 4; RGSF 2; SSFS 3, 20

Palin, Michael (Edward) 1943- .... **CLC 21**
See Monty Python
See also CA 107; CANR 35, 109; SATA 67

Palliser, Charles 1947- .... **CLC 65**
See also CA 136; CANR 76; CN 5, 6, 7

Palma, Ricardo 1833-1919 .... **TCLC 29**
See also CA 168; LAW

Pamuk, Orhan 1952- .... **CLC 185**
See also CA 142; CANR 75, 127; CWW 2; WLIT 6

Pancake, Breece Dexter 1952-1979
See Pancake, Breece D'J
See also CA 123; 109

Pancake, Breece D'J .... **CLC 29; SSC 61**
See Pancake, Breece Dexter
See also DLB 130

Panchenko, Nikolai .... **CLC 59**

Pankhurst, Emmeline (Goulden)
1858-1928 .... **TCLC 100**
See also CA 116; FW

Panko, Rudy
See Gogol, Nikolai (Vasilyevich)

Papadiamantis, Alexandros
1851-1911 .... **TCLC 29**
See also CA 168; EWL 3

Papadiamantopoulos, Johannes 1856-1910
See Moreas, Jean
See also CA 117; 242

Papini, Giovanni 1881-1956 .... **TCLC 22**
See also CA 121; 180; DLB 264

Paracelsus 1493-1541 .... **LC 14**
See also DLB 179

Parasol, Peter
See Stevens, Wallace

Pardo Bazan, Emilia 1851-1921 .... **SSC 30**
See also EWL 3; FW; RGSF 2; RGWL 2, 3

Pareto, Vilfredo 1848-1923 .... **TCLC 69**
See also CA 175

Paretsky, Sara 1947- .... **CLC 135**
See also AAYA 30; BEST 90:3; CA 125; 129; CANR 59, 95; CMW 4; CPW; DA3; DAM POP; DLB 306; INT CA-129; MSW; RGAL 4

Parfenie, Maria
See Codrescu, Andrei

Parini, Jay (Lee) 1948- .... **CLC 54, 133**
See also CA 97-100, 229; CAAE 229; CAAS 16; CANR 32, 87

Park, Jordan
See Kornbluth, C(yril) M.; Pohl, Frederik

Park, Robert E(zra) 1864-1944 ..... **TCLC 73**
See also CA 122; 165

Parker, Bert
See Ellison, Harlan (Jay)

Parker, Dorothy (Rothschild)
1893-1967 . **CLC 15, 68; PC 28; SSC 2; TCLC 143**
See also AMWS 9; CA 19-20; 25-28R; CAP 2; DA3; DAM POET; DLB 11, 45, 86; EXPP; FW; MAL 5; MAWW; MTCW 1, 2; MTFW 2005; PFS 18; RGAL 4; RGSF 2; TUS

Parker, Robert B. 1932- .... **CLC 27**
See also AAYA 28; BEST 89:4; BPFB 3; CA 49-52; CANR 1, 26, 52, 89, 128; CMW 4; CPW; DAM NOV, POP; DLB 306; INT CANR-26; MSW; MTCW 1; MTFW 2005

Parker, Robert Brown
See Parker, Robert B.

Parkin, Frank 1940- .... **CLC 43**
See also CA 147

Parkman, Francis, Jr. 1823-1893 .. **NCLC 12**
See also AMWS 2; DLB 1, 30, 183, 186, 235; RGAL 4

Parks, Gordon 1912-2006 .... **BLC 3; CLC 1, 16**
See also AAYA 36; AITN 2; BW 2, 3; CA 41-44R; CANR 26, 66, 145; DA3; DAM MULT; DLB 33; MTCW 2; MTFW 2005; SATA 8, 108

Parks, Gordon Alexander Buchanan
See Parks, Gordon

Parks, Suzan-Lori 1964(?)- .... **DC 23**
See also AAYA 55; CA 201; CAD; CD 5, 6; CWD; DFS 22; RGAL 4

Parks, Tim(othy Harold) 1954- ...... **CLC 147**
See also CA 126; 131; CANR 77, 144; CN 7; DLB 231; INT CA-131

Parmenides c. 515B.C.-c.
450B.C. .... **CMLC 22**
See also DLB 176

Parnell, Thomas 1679-1718 .... **LC 3**
See also DLB 95; RGEL 2

Parr, Catherine c. 1513(?)-1548 .... **LC 86**
See also DLB 136

Parra, Nicanor 1914- ... **CLC 2, 102; HLC 2; PC 39**
See also CA 85-88; CANR 32; CWW 2; DAM MULT; DLB 283; EWL 3; HW 1; LAW; MTCW 1

Parra Sanojo, Ana Teresa de la
1890-1936 .... **HLCS 2**
See de la Parra, (Ana) Teresa (Sonojo)
See also LAW

Parrish, Mary Frances
See Fisher, M(ary) F(rances) K(ennedy)

Parshchikov, Aleksei 1954- .... **CLC 59**
See Parshchikov, Aleksei Maksimovich

Parshchikov, Aleksei Maksimovich
See Parshchikov, Aleksei
See also DLB 285

Parson, Professor
See Coleridge, Samuel Taylor

Parson Lot
See Kingsley, Charles

Parton, Sara Payson Willis
1811-1872 .... **NCLC 86**
See also DLB 43, 74, 239

Partridge, Anthony
See Oppenheim, E(dward) Phillips

Pascal, Blaise 1623-1662 .... **LC 35**
See also DLB 268; EW 3; GFL Beginnings to 1789; RGWL 2, 3; TWA

Pascoli, Giovanni 1855-1912 .... **TCLC 45**
See also CA 170; EW 7; EWL 3

Pasolini, Pier Paolo 1922-1975 .. **CLC 20, 37, 106; PC 17**
See also CA 93-96; 61-64; CANR 63; DLB 128, 177; EWL 3; MTCW 1; RGWL 2, 3

Pasquini
See Silone, Ignazio

Pastan, Linda (Olenik) 1932- .... **CLC 27**
See also CA 61-64; CANR 18, 40, 61, 113; CP 3, 4, 5, 6, 7; CSW; CWP; DAM POET; DLB 5; PFS 8

Pasternak, Boris (Leonidovich)
1890-1960 ...... **CLC 7, 10, 18, 63; PC 6; SSC 31; WLC 4**
See also BPFB 3; CA 127; 116; DA; DA3; DAB; DAC; DAM MST, NOV, POET; DLB 302; EW 10; MTCW 1, 2; MTFW 2005; RGSF 2; RGWL 2, 3; TWA; WP

Patchen, Kenneth 1911-1972 .... **CLC 1, 2, 18**
See also BG 1:3; CA 1-4R; 33-36R; CANR 3, 35; CN 1; CP 1; DAM POET; DLB 16, 48; EWL 3; MAL 5; MTCW 1; RGAL 4

Pater, Walter (Horatio) 1839-1894 . **NCLC 7, 90, 159**
See also BRW 5; CDBLB 1832-1890; DLB 57, 156; RGEL 2; TEA

Paterson, A(ndrew) B(arton)
1864-1941 .... **TCLC 32**
See also CA 155; DLB 230; RGEL 2; SATA 97

Paterson, Banjo
See Paterson, A(ndrew) B(arton)

Paterson, Katherine 1932- .... **CLC 12, 30**
See also AAYA 1, 31; BYA 1, 2, 7; CA 21-24R; CANR 28, 59, 111; CLR 7, 50; CWRI 5; DLB 52; JRDA; LAIT 4; MAI-CYA 1, 2; MAICYAS 1; MTCW 1; SATA 13, 53, 92, 133; WYA; YAW

Paterson, Katherine Womeldorf
See Paterson, Katherine

Patmore, Coventry Kersey Dighton
1823-1896 .... **NCLC 9; PC 59**
See also DLB 35, 98; RGEL 2; TEA

Paton, Alan (Stewart) 1903-1988 ...... **CLC 4, 10, 25, 55, 106; TCLC 165; WLC 4**
See also AAYA 26; AFW; BPFB 3; BRWS 2; BYA 1; CA 13-16; 125; CANR 22; CAP 1; CN 1, 2, 3, 4; DA; DA3; DAB; DAC; DAM MST, NOV; DLB 225; DLBD 17; EWL 3; EXPN; LAIT 4; MTCW 1, 2; MTFW 2005; NFS 3, 12; RGEL 2; SATA 11; SATA-Obit 56; TWA; WLIT 2; WWE 1

Paton Walsh, Gillian 1937- .... **CLC 35**
See Paton Walsh, Jill; Walsh, Jill Paton
See also AAYA 11; CANR 38, 83; CLR 2, 65; DLB 161; JRDA; MAICYA 1, 2; SAAS 3; SATA 4, 72, 109; YAW

Paton Walsh, Jill
See Paton Walsh, Gillian
See also AAYA 47; BYA 1, 8

Patsauq, Markoosie 1942- .... **NNAL**
See also CA 101; CLR 23; CWRI 5; DAM MULT

Patterson, (Horace) Orlando (Lloyd)
1940- .... **BLCS**
See also BW 1; CA 65-68; CANR 27, 84; CN 1, 2, 3, 4, 5, 6

Patton, George S(mith), Jr.
1885-1945 .... **TCLC 79**
See also CA 189

Paulding, James Kirke 1778-1860 ... **NCLC 2**
See also DLB 3, 59, 74, 250; RGAL 4

Paulin, Thomas Neilson 1949-
See Paulin, Tom
See also CA 123; 128; CANR 98

Paulin, Tom .... **CLC 37, 177**
See Paulin, Thomas Neilson
See also CP 3, 4, 5, 6, 7; DLB 40

Pausanias c. 1st cent. - .... **CMLC 36**

Paustovsky, Konstantin (Georgievich)
1892-1968 .... **CLC 40**
See also CA 93-96; 25-28R; DLB 272; EWL 3

Pavese, Cesare 1908-1950 .... **PC 13; SSC 19; TCLC 3**
See also CA 104; 169; DLB 128, 177; EW 12; EWL 3; PFS 20; RGSF 2; RGWL 2, 3; TWA; WLIT 7

Pavic, Milorad 1929- .... **CLC 60**
See also CA 136; CDWLB 4; CWW 2; DLB 181; EWL 3; RGWL 3

Pavlov, Ivan Petrovich 1849-1936 . **TCLC 91**
See also CA 118; 180

Pavlova, Karolina Karlovna
1807-1893 .... **NCLC 138**
See also DLB 205

Payne, Alan
See Jakes, John (William)

Payne, Rachel Ann
See Jakes, John (William)

Phillips, Caryl 1958- ..... **BLCS; CLC 96, 224**
See also BRWS 5; BW 2; CA 141; CANR
63, 104, 140; CBD; CD 5, 6; CN 5, 6, 7;
DA3; DAM MULT; DLB 157; EWL 3;
MTCW 2; MTFW 2005; WLIT 4; WWE
1

Phillips, David Graham
1867-1911 .... **TCLC 44**
See also CA 108; 176; DLB 9, 12, 303;
RGAL 4

Phillips, Jack
See Sandburg, Carl (August)

Phillips, Jayne Anne 1952- .... **CLC 15, 33,**
139; SSC 16
See also AAYA 57; BPFB 3; CA 101;
CANR 24, 50, 96; CN 4, 5, 6, 7; CSW;
DLBY 1980; INT CANR-24; MTCW 1,
2; MTFW 2005; RGAL 4; RGSF 2; SSFS
4

Phillips, Richard
See Dick, Philip K.

Phillips, Robert (Schaeffer) 1938- .... **CLC 28**
See also CA 17-20R; CAAS 13; CANR 8;
DLB 105

Phillips, Ward
See Lovecraft, H. P.

Philostratus, Flavius c. 179-c.
244 .... **CMLC 62**

Piccolo, Lucio 1901-1969 .... **CLC 13**
See also CA 97-100; DLB 114; EWL 3

Pickthall, Marjorie L(owry) C(hristie)
1883-1922 .... **TCLC 21**
See also CA 107; DLB 92

Pico della Mirandola, Giovanni
1463-1494 .... **LC 15**
See also LMFS 1

Piercy, Marge 1936- .... **CLC 3, 6, 14, 18, 27,**
62, 128; PC 29
See also BPFB 3; CA 21-24R, 187; CAAE
187; CAAS 1; CANR 13, 43, 66, 111; CN
3, 4, 5, 6, 7; CP 1, 2, 3, 4, 5, 6, 7; CWP;
DLB 120, 227; EXPP; FW; MAL 5;
MTCW 1, 2; MTFW 2005; PFS 9, 22;
SFW 4

Piers, Robert
See Anthony, Piers

Pieyre de Mandiargues, Andre 1909-1991
See Mandiargues, Andre Pieyre de
See also CA 103; 136; CANR 22, 82; EWL
3; GFL 1789 to the Present

Pilnyak, Boris 1894-1938 . **SSC 48; TCLC 23**
See Vogau, Boris Andreyevich
See also EWL 3

Pinchback, Eugene
See Toomer, Jean

Pincherle, Alberto 1907-1990 ...... **CLC 11, 18**
See Moravia, Alberto
See also CA 25-28R; 132; CANR 33, 63,
142; DAM NOV; MTCW 1; MTFW 2005

Pinckney, Darryl 1953- .... **CLC 76**
See also BW 2, 3; CA 143; CANR 79

Pindar 518(?)B.C.-438(?)B.C. .... **CMLC 12;**
PC 19
See also AW 1; CDWLB 1; DLB 176;
RGWL 2

Pineda, Cecile 1942- .... **CLC 39**
See also CA 118; DLB 209

Pinero, Arthur Wing 1855-1934 .... **TCLC 32**
See also CA 110; 153; DAM DRAM; DLB
10; RGEL 2

Pinero, Miguel (Antonio Gomez)
1946-1988 .... **CLC 4, 55**
See also CA 61-64; 125; CAD; CANR 29,
90; DLB 266; HW 1; LLW

Pinget, Robert 1919-1997 .... **CLC 7, 13, 37**
See also CA 85-88; 160; CWW 2; DLB 83;
EWL 3; GFL 1789 to the Present

Pink Floyd
See Barrett, (Roger) Syd; Gilmour, David;
Mason, Nick; Waters, Roger; Wright, Rick

Pinkney, Edward 1802-1828 .... **NCLC 31**
See also DLB 248

Pinkwater, D. Manus
See Pinkwater, Daniel Manus

Pinkwater, Daniel
See Pinkwater, Daniel Manus

Pinkwater, Daniel M.
See Pinkwater, Daniel Manus

Pinkwater, Daniel Manus 1941- .... **CLC 35**
See also AAYA 1, 46; BYA 9; CA 29-32R;
CANR 12, 38, 89, 143; CLR 4; CSW;
FANT; JRDA; MAICYA 1, 2; SAAS 3;
SATA 8, 46, 76, 114, 158; SFW 4; YAW

Pinkwater, Manus
See Pinkwater, Daniel Manus

Pinsky, Robert 1940- .... **CLC 9, 19, 38, 94,**
121, 216; PC 27
See also AMWS 6; CA 29-32R; CAAS 4;
CANR 58, 97, 138; CP 3, 4, 5, 6, 7; DA3;
DAM POET; DLBY 1982, 1998; MAL 5;
MTCW 2; MTFW 2005; PFS 18; RGAL
4; TCLE 1:2

Pinta, Harold
See Pinter, Harold

Pinter, Harold 1930- .. **CLC 1, 3, 6, 9, 11, 15,**
27, 58, 73, 199; DC 15; WLC 4
See also BRWR 1; BRWS 1; CA 5-8R;
CANR 33, 65, 112, 145; CBD; CD 5, 6;
CDBLB 1960 to Present; CP 1; DA; DA3;
DAB; DAC; DAM DRAM, MST; DFS 3,
5, 7, 14; DLB 13, 310; EWL 3; IDFW 3,
4; LMFS 2; MTCW 1, 2; MTFW 2005;
RGEL 2; RGHL; TEA

Piozzi, Hester Lynch (Thrale)
1741-1821 .... **NCLC 57**
See also DLB 104, 142

Pirandello, Luigi 1867-1936 .. **DC 5; SSC 22;**
TCLC 4, 29, 172; WLC 4
See also CA 104; 153; CANR 103; DA;
DA3; DAB; DAC; DAM DRAM, MST;
DFS 4, 9; DLB 264; EW 8; EWL 3;
MTCW 2; MTFW 2005; RGSF 2; RGWL
2, 3; WLIT 7

Pirsig, Robert M(aynard) 1928- ... **CLC 4, 6,**
73
See also CA 53-56; CANR 42, 74; CPW 1;
DA3; DAM POP; MTCW 1, 2; MTFW
2005; SATA 39

Pisarev, Dmitrii Ivanovich
See Pisarev, Dmitry Ivanovich
See also DLB 277

Pisarev, Dmitry Ivanovich
1840-1868 .... **NCLC 25**
See Pisarev, Dmitrii Ivanovich

Pix, Mary (Griffith) 1666-1709 .... **LC 8**
See also DLB 80

Pixerecourt, (Rene Charles) Guilbert de
1773-1844 .... **NCLC 39**
See also DLB 192; GFL 1789 to the Present

Plaatje, Sol(omon) T(shekisho)
1878-1932 .... **BLCS; TCLC 73**
See also BW 2, 3; CA 141; CANR 79; DLB
125, 225

Plaidy, Jean
See Hibbert, Eleanor Alice Burford

Planche, James Robinson
1796-1880 .... **NCLC 42**
See also RGEL 2

Plant, Robert 1948- .... **CLC 12**

Plante, David 1940- .... **CLC 7, 23, 38**
See also CA 37-40R; CANR 12, 36, 58, 82,
152; CN 2, 3, 4, 5, 6, 7; DAM NOV;
DLBY 1983; INT CANR-12; MTCW 1

Plante, David Robert
See Plante, David

Plath, Sylvia 1932-1963 ..... **CLC 1, 2, 3, 5, 9,**
11, 14, 17, 50, 51, 62, 111; PC 1, 37;
WLC 4
See also AAYA 13; AMWR 2; AMWS 1;
BPFB 3; CA 19-20; CANR 34, 101; CAP
2; CDALB 1941-1968; DA; DA3; DAB;
DAC; DAM MST, POET; DLB 5, 6, 152;
EWL 3; EXPN; EXPP; FL 1:6; FW; LAIT
4; MAL 5; MAWW; MTCW 1, 2; MTFW
2005; NFS 1; PAB; PFS 1, 15; RGAL 4;
SATA 96; TUS; WP; YAW

Plato c. 428B.C.-347B.C. .... **CMLC 8, 75;**
WLCS
See also AW 1; CDWLB 1; DA; DA3;
DAB; DAC; DAM MST; DLB 176; LAIT
1; LATS 1:1; RGWL 2, 3; WLIT 8

Platonov, Andrei
See Klimentov, Andrei Platonovich

Platonov, Andrei Platonovich
See Klimentov, Andrei Platonovich
See also DLB 272

Platonov, Andrey Platonovich
See Klimentov, Andrei Platonovich
See also EWL 3

Platt, Kin 1911- .... **CLC 26**
See also AAYA 11; CA 17-20R; CANR 11;
JRDA; SAAS 17; SATA 21, 86; WYA

Plautus c. 254B.C.-c. 184B.C. ...... **CMLC 24;**
DC 6
See also AW 1; CDWLB 1; DLB 211;
RGWL 2, 3; WLIT 8

Plick et Plock
See Simenon, Georges (Jacques Christian)

Plieksans, Janis
See Rainis, Janis

Plimpton, George (Ames)
1927-2003 .... **CLC 36**
See also AITN 1; CA 21-24R; 224; CANR
32, 70, 103, 133; DLB 185, 241; MTCW
1, 2; MTFW 2005; SATA 10; SATA-Obit
150

Pliny the Elder c. 23-79 .... **CMLC 23**
See also DLB 211

Pliny the Younger c. 61-c. 112 ...... **CMLC 62**
See also AW 2; DLB 211

Plomer, William Charles Franklin
1903-1973 .... **CLC 4, 8**
See also AFW; BRWS 11; CA 21-22; CANR
34; CAP 2; CN 1; CP 1, 2; DLB 20, 162,
191, 225; EWL 3; MTCW 1; RGEL 2;
RGSF 2; SATA 24

Plotinus 204-270 .... **CMLC 46**
See also CDWLB 1; DLB 176

Plowman, Piers
See Kavanagh, Patrick (Joseph)

Plum, J.
See Wodehouse, P(elham) G(renville)

Plumly, Stanley (Ross) 1939- .... **CLC 33**
See also CA 108; 110; CANR 97; CP 3, 4,
5, 6, 7; DLB 5, 193; INT CA-110

Plumpe, Friedrich Wilhelm
1888-1931 .... **TCLC 53**
See also CA 112

Plutarch c. 46-c. 120 .... **CMLC 60**
See also AW 2; CDWLB 1; DLB 176;
RGWL 2, 3; TWA; WLIT 8

Po Chu-i 772-846 .... **CMLC 24**

Podhoretz, Norman 1930- .... **CLC 189**
See also AMWS 8; CA 9-12R; CANR 7,
78, 135

Poe, Edgar Allan 1809-1849 ..... **NCLC 1, 16,**
55, 78, 94, 97, 117; PC 1, 54; SSC 1,
22, 34, 35, 54, 88; WLC 4
See also AAYA 14; AMW; AMWC 1;
AMWR 2; BPFB 3; BYA 5, 11; CDALB
1640-1865; CMW 4; DA; DA3; DAB;
DAC; DAM MST, POET; DLB 3, 59, 73,
74, 248, 254; EXPP; EXPS; GL 3; HGG;
LAIT 2; LATS 1:1; LMFS 1; MSW; PAB;

Prevert, Jacques (Henri Marie)
1900-1977 .... **CLC 15**
See also CA 77-80; 69-72; CANR 29, 61;
DLB 258; EWL 3; GFL 1789 to the
Present; IDFW 3, 4; MTCW 1; RGWL 2,
3; SATA-Obit 30

Prevost, (Antoine Francois)
1697-1763 .... **LC 1**
See also DLB 314; EW 4; GFL Beginnings
to 1789; RGWL 2, 3

Price, (Edward) Reynolds 1933- ... **CLC 3, 6,**
13, 43, 50, 63, 212; SSC 22
See also AMWS 6; CA 1-4R; CANR 1, 37,
57, 87, 128; CN 1, 2, 3, 4, 5, 6, 7; CSW;
DAM NOV; DLB 2, 218, 278; EWL 3;
INT CANR-37; MAL 5; MTFW 2005;
NFS 18

Price, Richard 1949- .... **CLC 6, 12**
See also CA 49-52; CANR 3, 147; CN 7;
DLBY 1981

Prichard, Katharine Susannah
1883-1969 .... **CLC 46**
See also CA 11-12; CANR 33; CAP 1; DLB
260; MTCW 1; RGEL 2; RGSF 2; SATA
66

Priestley, J(ohn) B(oynton)
1894-1984 .... **CLC 2, 5, 9, 34**
See also BRW 7; CA 9-12R; 113; CANR
33; CDBLB 1914-1945; CN 1, 2, 3; DA3;
DAM DRAM, NOV; DLB 10, 34, 77,
100, 139; DLBY 1984; EWL 3; MTCW
1, 2; MTFW 2005; RGEL 2; SFW 4

Prince 1958- .... **CLC 35**
See also CA 213

Prince, F(rank) T(empleton)
1912-2003 .... **CLC 22**
See also CA 101; 219; CANR 43, 79; CP 1,
2, 3, 4, 5, 6, 7; DLB 20

Prince Kropotkin
See Kropotkin, Peter (Aleksieevich)

Prior, Matthew 1664-1721 .... **LC 4**
See also DLB 95; RGEL 2

Prishvin, Mikhail 1873-1954 .... **TCLC 75**
See Prishvin, Mikhail Mikhailovich

Prishvin, Mikhail Mikhailovich
See Prishvin, Mikhail
See also DLB 272; EWL 3

Pritchard, William H(arrison)
1932- .... **CLC 34**
See also CA 65-68; CANR 23, 95; DLB
111

Pritchett, V(ictor) S(awdon)
1900-1997 ... **CLC 5, 13, 15, 41; SSC 14**
See also BPFB 3; BRWS 3; CA 61-64; 157;
CANR 31, 63; CN 1, 2, 3, 4, 5, 6; DA3;
DAM NOV; DLB 15, 139; EWL 3;
MTCW 1, 2; MTFW 2005; RGEL 2;
RGSF 2; TEA

Private 19022
See Manning, Frederic

Probst, Mark 1925- .... **CLC 59**
See also CA 130

Procaccino, Michael
See Cristofer, Michael

Proclus c. 412-c. 485 .... **CMLC 81**

Prokosch, Frederic 1908-1989 ...... **CLC 4, 48**
See also CA 73-76; 128; CANR 82; CN 1,
2, 3, 4; CP 1, 2, 3, 4; DLB 48; MTCW 2

Propertius, Sextus c. 50B.C.-c.
16B.C. .... **CMLC 32**
See also AW 2; CDWLB 1; DLB 211;
RGWL 2, 3; WLIT 8

Prophet, The
See Dreiser, Theodore

Prose, Francine 1947- .... **CLC 45**
See also CA 109; 112; CANR 46, 95, 132;
DLB 234; MTFW 2005; SATA 101, 149

Protagoras c. 490B.C.-420B.C. ...... **CMLC 85**
See also DLB 176

Proudhon
See Cunha, Euclides (Rodrigues Pimenta)
da

Proulx, Annie
See Proulx, E. Annie

Proulx, E. Annie 1935- .... **CLC 81, 158**
See also AMWS 7; BPFB 3; CA 145;
CANR 65, 110; CN 6, 7; CPW 1; DA3;
DAM POP; MAL 5; MTCW 2; MTFW
2005; SSFS 18, 23

Proulx, Edna Annie
See Proulx, E. Annie

Proust, (Valentin-Louis-George-Eugene)
Marcel 1871-1922 ..... **SSC 75; TCLC 7,**
13, 33; WLC 5
See also AAYA 58; BPFB 3; CA 104; 120;
CANR 110; DA; DA3; DAB; DAC; DAM
MST, NOV; DLB 65; EW 8; EWL 3; GFL
1789 to the Present; MTCW 1, 2; MTFW
2005; RGWL 2, 3; TWA

Prowler, Harley
See Masters, Edgar Lee

Prudentius, Aurelius Clemens 348-c.
405 .... **CMLC 78**
See also EW 1; RGWL 2, 3

Prus, Boleslaw 1845-1912 .... **TCLC 48**
See also RGWL 2, 3

Pryor, Aaron Richard
See Pryor, Richard

Pryor, Richard 1940-2005 .... **CLC 26**
See also CA 122; 152; 246

Pryor, Richard Franklin Lenox Thomas
See Pryor, Richard

Przybyszewski, Stanislaw
1868-1927 .... **TCLC 36**
See also CA 160; DLB 66; EWL 3

Pteleon
See Grieve, C(hristopher) M(urray)
See also DAM POET

Puckett, Lute
See Masters, Edgar Lee

Puig, Manuel 1932-1990 .... **CLC 3, 5, 10, 28,**
65, 133; HLC 2
See also BPFB 3; CA 45-48; CANR 2, 32,
63; CDWLB 3; DA3; DAM MULT; DLB
113; DNFS 1; EWL 3; GLL 1; HW 1, 2;
LAW; MTCW 1, 2; MTFW 2005; RGWL
2, 3; TWA; WLIT 1

Pulitzer, Joseph 1847-1911 .... **TCLC 76**
See also CA 114; DLB 23

Purchas, Samuel 1577(?)-1626 .... **LC 70**
See also DLB 151

Purdy, A(lfred) W(ellington)
1918-2000 .... **CLC 3, 6, 14, 50**
See also CA 81-84; 189; CAAS 17; CANR
42, 66; CP 1, 2, 3, 4, 5, 6, 7; DAC; DAM
MST, POET; DLB 88; PFS 5; RGEL 2

Purdy, James (Amos) 1923- .... **CLC 2, 4, 10,**
28, 52
See also AMWS 7; CA 33-36R; CAAS 1;
CANR 19, 51, 132; CN 1, 2, 3, 4, 5, 6, 7;
DLB 2, 218; EWL 3; INT CANR-19;
MAL 5; MTCW 1; RGAL 4

Pure, Simon
See Swinnerton, Frank Arthur

Pushkin, Aleksandr Sergeevich
See Pushkin, Alexander (Sergeyevich)
See also DLB 205

Pushkin, Alexander (Sergeyevich)
1799-1837 .... **NCLC 3, 27, 83; PC 10;**
SSC 27, 55; WLC 5
See Pushkin, Aleksandr Sergeevich
See also DA; DA3; DAB; DAC; DAM
DRAM, MST, POET; EW 5; EXPS; RGSF
2; RGWL 2, 3; SATA 61; SSFS 9; TWA

P'u Sung-ling 1640-1715 .... **LC 49; SSC 31**

Putnam, Arthur Lee
See Alger, Horatio, Jr.

Puttenham, George 1529(?)-1590 ...... **LC 116**
See also DLB 281

Puzo, Mario 1920-1999 .... **CLC 1, 2, 6, 36,**
107
See also BPFB 3; CA 65-68; 185; CANR 4,
42, 65, 99, 131; CN 1, 2, 3, 4, 5, 6; CPW;
DA3; DAM NOV, POP; DLB 6; MTCW
1, 2; MTFW 2005; NFS 16; RGAL 4

Pygge, Edward
See Barnes, Julian

Pyle, Ernest Taylor 1900-1945
See Pyle, Ernie
See also CA 115; 160

Pyle, Ernie .... **TCLC 75**
See Pyle, Ernest Taylor
See also DLB 29; MTCW 2

Pyle, Howard 1853-1911 .... **TCLC 81**
See also AAYA 57; BYA 2, 4; CA 109; 137;
CLR 22; DLB 42, 188; DLBD 13; LAIT
1; MAICYA 1, 2; SATA 16, 100; WCH;
YAW

Pym, Barbara (Mary Crampton)
1913-1980 .... **CLC 13, 19, 37, 111**
See also BPFB 3; BRWS 2; CA 13-14; 97-
100; CANR 13, 34; CAP 1; DLB 14, 207;
DLBY 1987; EWL 3; MTCW 1, 2; MTFW
2005; RGEL 2; TEA

Pynchon, Thomas (Ruggles, Jr.)
1937- ...... **CLC 2, 3, 6, 9, 11, 18, 33, 62,**
72, 123, 192, 213; SSC 14, 84; WLC 5
See also AMWS 2; BEST 90:2; BPFB 3;
CA 17-20R; CANR 22, 46, 73, 142; CN
1, 2, 3, 4, 5, 6, 7; CPW 1; DA; DA3;
DAB; DAC; DAM MST, NOV, POP;
DLB 2, 173; EWL 3; MAL 5; MTCW 1,
2; MTFW 2005; NFS 23; RGAL 4; SFW
4; TCLE 1:2; TUS

Pythagoras c. 582B.C.-c. 507B.C. . **CMLC 22**
See also DLB 176

Q
See Quiller-Couch, Sir Arthur (Thomas)

Qian, Chongzhu
See Ch'ien, Chung-shu

Qian, Sima 145B.C.-c. 89B.C. .... **CMLC 72**

Qian Zhongshu
See Ch'ien, Chung-shu
See also CWW 2

Qroll
See Dagerman, Stig (Halvard)

Quarles, Francis 1592-1644 .... **LC 117**
See also DLB 126; RGEL 2

Quarrington, Paul (Lewis) 1953- ..... **CLC 65**
See also CA 129; CANR 62, 95

Quasimodo, Salvatore 1901-1968 .... **CLC 10;**
PC 47
See also CA 13-16; 25-28R; CAP 1; DLB
114; EW 12; EWL 3; MTCW 1; RGWL
2, 3

Quatermass, Martin
See Carpenter, John (Howard)

Quay, Stephen 1947- .... **CLC 95**
See also CA 189

Quay, Timothy 1947- .... **CLC 95**
See also CA 189

Queen, Ellery .... **CLC 3, 11**
See Dannay, Frederic; Davidson, Avram
(James); Deming, Richard; Fairman, Paul
W.; Flora, Fletcher; Hoch, Edward
D(entinger); Kane, Henry; Lee, Manfred
B.; Marlowe, Stephen; Powell, (Oval) Tal-
mage; Sheldon, Walter J(ames); Sturgeon,
Theodore (Hamilton); Tracy, Don(ald
Fiske); Vance, Jack
See also BPFB 3; CMW 4; MSW; RGAL 4

Queen, Ellery, Jr.
See Dannay, Frederic; Lee, Manfred B.

Rechy, John 1934- ..... **CLC 1, 7, 14, 18, 107; HLC 2**
See also CA 5-8R; 195; CAAE 195; CAAS 4; CANR 6, 32, 64, 152; CN 1, 2, 3, 4, 5, 6, 7; DAM MULT; DLB 122, 278; DLBY 1982; HW 1, 2; INT CANR-6; LLW; MAL 5; RGAL 4

Rechy, John Francisco
See Rechy, John

Redcam, Tom 1870-1933 .... **TCLC 25**

Reddin, Keith 1956- .... **CLC 67**
See also CAD; CD 6

Redgrove, Peter (William)
1932-2003 .... **CLC 6, 41**
See also BRWS 6; CA 1-4R; 217; CANR 3, 39, 77; CP 1, 2, 3, 4, 5, 6, 7; DLB 40; TCLE 1:2

Redmon, Anne .... **CLC 22**
See Nightingale, Anne Redmon
See also DLBY 1986

Reed, Eliot
See Ambler, Eric

Reed, Ishmael (Scott) 1938- . **BLC 3; CLC 2, 3, 5, 6, 13, 32, 60, 174; PC 68**
See also AFAW 1, 2; AMWS 10; BPFB 3; BW 2, 3; CA 21-24R; CANR 25, 48, 74, 128; CN 1, 2, 3, 4, 5, 6, 7; CP 1, 2, 3, 4, 5, 6, 7; CSW; DA3; DAM MULT; DLB 2, 5, 33, 169, 227; DLBD 8; EWL 3; LMFS 2; MAL 5; MSW; MTCW 1, 2; MTFW 2005; PFS 6; RGAL 4; TCWW 2

Reed, John (Silas) 1887-1920 .... **TCLC 9**
See also CA 106; 195; MAL 5; TUS

Reed, Lou .... **CLC 21**
See Firbank, Louis

Reese, Lizette Woodworth 1856-1935 . **PC 29**
See also CA 180; DLB 54

Reeve, Clara 1729-1807 .... **NCLC 19**
See also DLB 39; RGEL 2

Reich, Wilhelm 1897-1957 .... **TCLC 57**
See also CA 199

Reid, Christopher (John) 1949- .... **CLC 33**
See also CA 140; CANR 89; CP 4, 5, 6, 7; DLB 40; EWL 3

Reid, Desmond
See Moorcock, Michael

Reid Banks, Lynne 1929-
See Banks, Lynne Reid
See also AAYA 49; CA 1-4R; CANR 6, 22, 38, 87; CLR 24; CN 1, 2, 3, 7; JRDA; MAICYA 1, 2; SATA 22, 75, 111, 165; YAW

Reilly, William K.
See Creasey, John

Reiner, Max
See Caldwell, (Janet Miriam) Taylor (Holland)

Reis, Ricardo
See Pessoa, Fernando (Antonio Nogueira)

Reizenstein, Elmer Leopold
See Rice, Elmer (Leopold)
See also EWL 3

Remarque, Erich Maria 1898-1970 . **CLC 21**
See also AAYA 27; BPFB 3; CA 77-80; 29-32R; CDWLB 2; DA; DA3; DAB; DAC; DAM MST, NOV; DLB 56; EWL 3; EXPN; LAIT 3; MTCW 1, 2; MTFW 2005; NFS 4; RGHL; RGWL 2, 3

Remington, Frederic S(ackrider)
1861-1909 .... **TCLC 89**
See also CA 108; 169; DLB 12, 186, 188; SATA 41; TCWW 2

Remizov, A.
See Remizov, Aleksei (Mikhailovich)

Remizov, A. M.
See Remizov, Aleksei (Mikhailovich)

Remizov, Aleksei (Mikhailovich)
1877-1957 .... **TCLC 27**
See Remizov, Alexey Mikhaylovich
See also CA 125; 133; DLB 295

Remizov, Alexey Mikhaylovich
See Remizov, Aleksei (Mikhailovich)
See also EWL 3

Renan, Joseph Ernest 1823-1892 . **NCLC 26, 145**
See also GFL 1789 to the Present

Renard, Jules(-Pierre) 1864-1910 .. **TCLC 17**
See also CA 117; 202; GFL 1789 to the Present

Renart, Jean fl. 13th cent. - .... **CMLC 83**

Renault, Mary .... **CLC 3, 11, 17**
See Challans, Mary
See also BPFB 3; BYA 2; CN 1, 2, 3; DLBY 1983; EWL 3; GLL 1; LAIT 1; RGEL 2; RHW

Rendell, Ruth (Barbara) 1930- .. **CLC 28, 48**
See Vine, Barbara
See also BPFB 3; BRWS 9; CA 109; CANR 32, 52, 74, 127; CN 5, 6, 7; CPW; DAM POP; DLB 87, 276; INT CANR-32; MSW; MTCW 1, 2; MTFW 2005

Renoir, Jean 1894-1979 .... **CLC 20**
See also CA 129; 85-88

Resnais, Alain 1922- .... **CLC 16**

Revard, Carter 1931- .... **NNAL**
See also CA 144; CANR 81, 153; PFS 5

Reverdy, Pierre 1889-1960 .... **CLC 53**
See also CA 97-100; 89-92; DLB 258; EWL 3; GFL 1789 to the Present

Rexroth, Kenneth 1905-1982 .... **CLC 1, 2, 6, 11, 22, 49, 112; PC 20**
See also BG 1:3; CA 5-8R; 107; CANR 14, 34, 63; CDALB 1941-1968; CP 1, 2, 3; DAM POET; DLB 16, 48, 165, 212; DLBY 1982; EWL 3; INT CANR-14; MAL 5; MTCW 1, 2; MTFW 2005; RGAL 4

Reyes, Alfonso 1889-1959 .... **HLCS 2; TCLC 33**
See also CA 131; EWL 3; HW 1; LAW

Reyes y Basoalto, Ricardo Eliecer Neftali
See Neruda, Pablo

Reymont, Wladyslaw (Stanislaw)
1868(?)-1925 .... **TCLC 5**
See also CA 104; EWL 3

Reynolds, John Hamilton
1794-1852 .... **NCLC 146**
See also DLB 96

Reynolds, Jonathan 1942- .... **CLC 6, 38**
See also CA 65-68; CANR 28

Reynolds, Joshua 1723-1792 .... **LC 15**
See also DLB 104

Reynolds, Michael S(hane)
1937-2000 .... **CLC 44**
See also CA 65-68; 189; CANR 9, 89, 97

Reznikoff, Charles 1894-1976 .... **CLC 9**
See also AMWS 14; CA 33-36; 61-64; CAP 2; CP 1, 2; DLB 28, 45; RGHL; WP

Rezzori, Gregor von
See Rezzori d'Arezzo, Gregor von

Rezzori d'Arezzo, Gregor von
1914-1998 .... **CLC 25**
See also CA 122; 136; 167

Rhine, Richard
See Silverstein, Alvin; Silverstein, Virginia B(arbara Opshelor)

Rhodes, Eugene Manlove
1869-1934 .... **TCLC 53**
See also CA 198; DLB 256; TCWW 1, 2

R'hoone, Lord
See Balzac, Honore de

Rhys, Jean 1890-1979 .... **CLC 2, 4, 6, 14, 19, 51, 124; SSC 21, 76**
See also BRWS 2; CA 25-28R; 85-88; CANR 35, 62; CDBLB 1945-1960; CD-WLB 3; CN 1, 2; DA3; DAM NOV; DLB 36, 117, 162; DNFS 2; EWL 3; LATS 1:1; MTCW 1, 2; MTFW 2005; NFS 19; RGEL 2; RGSF 2; RHW; TEA; WWE 1

Ribeiro, Darcy 1922-1997 .... **CLC 34**
See also CA 33-36R; 156; EWL 3

Ribeiro, Joao Ubaldo (Osorio Pimentel)
1941- .... **CLC 10, 67**
See also CA 81-84; CWW 2; EWL 3

Ribman, Ronald (Burt) 1932- .... **CLC 7**
See also CA 21-24R; CAD; CANR 46, 80; CD 5, 6

Ricci, Nino (Pio) 1959- .... **CLC 70**
See also CA 137; CANR 130; CCA 1

Rice, Anne 1941- .... **CLC 41, 128**
See Rampling, Anne
See also AAYA 9, 53; AMWS 7; BEST 89:2; BPFB 3; CA 65-68; CANR 12, 36, 53, 74, 100, 133; CN 6, 7; CPW; CSW; DA3; DAM POP; DLB 292; GL 3; GLL 2; HGG; MTCW 2; MTFW 2005; SUFW 2; YAW

Rice, Elmer (Leopold) 1892-1967 ...... **CLC 7, 49**
See Reizenstein, Elmer Leopold
See also CA 21-22; 25-28R; CAP 2; DAM DRAM; DFS 12; DLB 4, 7; IDTP; MAL 5; MTCW 1, 2; RGAL 4

Rice, Tim(othy Miles Bindon)
1944- .... **CLC 21**
See also CA 103; CANR 46; DFS 7

Rich, Adrienne (Cecile) 1929- ... **CLC 3, 6, 7, 11, 18, 36, 73, 76, 125; PC 5**
See also AAYA 69; AMWR 2; AMWS 1; CA 9-12R; CANR 20, 53, 74, 128; CDALBS; CP 1, 2, 3, 4, 5, 6, 7; CSW; CWP; DA3; DAM POET; DLB 5, 67; EWL 3; EXPP; FL 1:6; FW; MAL 5; MAWW; MTCW 1, 2; MTFW 2005; PAB; PFS 15; RGAL 4; RGHL; WP

Rich, Barbara
See Graves, Robert (von Ranke)

Rich, Robert
See Trumbo, Dalton

Richard, Keith .... **CLC 17**
See Richards, Keith

Richards, David Adams 1950- .... **CLC 59**
See also CA 93-96; CANR 60, 110; CN 7; DAC; DLB 53; TCLE 1:2

Richards, I(vor) A(rmstrong)
1893-1979 .... **CLC 14, 24**
See also BRWS 2; CA 41-44R; 89-92; CANR 34, 74; CP 1, 2; DLB 27; EWL 3; MTCW 2; RGEL 2

Richards, Keith 1943-
See Richard, Keith
See also CA 107; CANR 77

Richardson, Anne
See Roiphe, Anne

Richardson, Dorothy Miller
1873-1957 .... **TCLC 3**
See also CA 104; 192; DLB 36; EWL 3; FW; RGEL 2

Richardson (Robertson), Ethel Florence Lindesay 1870-1946
See Richardson, Henry Handel
See also CA 105; 190; DLB 230; RHW

Richardson, Henry Handel .... **TCLC 4**
See Richardson (Robertson), Ethel Florence Lindesay
See also DLB 197; EWL 3; RGEL 2; RGSF 2

Richardson, John 1796-1852 .... **NCLC 55**
See also CCA 1; DAC; DLB 99

Richardson, Samuel 1689-1761 ...... **LC 1, 44;**
WLC 5
See also BRW 3; CDBLB 1660-1789; DA;
DAB; DAC; DAM MST, NOV; DLB 39;
RGEL 2; TEA; WLIT 3
Richardson, Willis 1889-1977 .... **HR 1:3**
See also BW 1; CA 124; DLB 51; SATA 60
Richler, Mordecai 1931-2001 .... **CLC 3, 5, 9,**
13, 18, 46, 70, 185
See also AITN 1; CA 65-68; 201; CANR
31, 62, 111; CCA 1; CLR 17; CN 1, 2, 3,
4, 5, 7; CWRI 5; DAC; DAM MST, NOV;
DLB 53; EWL 3; MAICYA 1, 2; MTCW
1, 2; MTFW 2005; RGEL 2; RGHL;
SATA 44, 98; SATA-Brief 27; TWA
Richter, Conrad (Michael)
1890-1968 .... **CLC 30**
See also AAYA 21; BYA 2; CA 5-8R; 25-
28R; CANR 23; DLB 9, 212; LAIT 1;
MAL 5; MTCW 1, 2; MTFW 2005;
RGAL 4; SATA 3; TCWW 1, 2; TUS;
YAW
Ricostranza, Tom
See Ellis, Trey
Riddell, Charlotte 1832-1906 .... **TCLC 40**
See Riddell, Mrs. J. H.
See also CA 165; DLB 156
Riddell, Mrs. J. H.
See Riddell, Charlotte
See also HGG; SUFW
Ridge, John Rollin 1827-1867 ...... **NCLC 82;**
NNAL
See also CA 144; DAM MULT; DLB 175
Ridgeway, Jason
See Marlowe, Stephen
Ridgway, Keith 1965- .... **CLC 119**
See also CA 172; CANR 144
Riding, Laura .... **CLC 3, 7**
See Jackson, Laura (Riding)
See also CP 1, 2, 3, 4, 5; RGAL 4
Riefenstahl, Berta Helene Amalia 1902-2003
See Riefenstahl, Leni
See also CA 108; 220
Riefenstahl, Leni .... **CLC 16, 190**
See Riefenstahl, Berta Helene Amalia
Riffe, Ernest
See Bergman, (Ernst) Ingmar
Riggs, (Rolla) Lynn
1899-1954 .... **NNAL; TCLC 56**
See also CA 144; DAM MULT; DLB 175
Riis, Jacob A(ugust) 1849-1914 ..... **TCLC 80**
See also CA 113; 168; DLB 23
Riley, James Whitcomb 1849-1916 .... **PC 48;**
TCLC 51
See also CA 118; 137; DAM POET; MAI-
CYA 1, 2; RGAL 4; SATA 17
Riley, Tex
See Creasey, John
Rilke, Rainer Maria 1875-1926 .... **PC 2;**
TCLC 1, 6, 19
See also CA 104; 132; CANR 62, 99; CD-
WLB 2; DA3; DAM POET; DLB 81; EW
9; EWL 3; MTCW 1, 2; MTFW 2005;
PFS 19; RGWL 2, 3; TWA; WP
Rimbaud, (Jean Nicolas) Arthur
1854-1891 ... **NCLC 4, 35, 82; PC 3, 57;**
WLC 5
See also DA; DA3; DAB; DAC; DAM
MST, POET; DLB 217; EW 7; GFL 1789
to the Present; LMFS 2; RGWL 2, 3;
TWA; WP
Rinehart, Mary Roberts
1876-1958 .... **TCLC 52**
See also BPFB 3; CA 108; 166; RGAL 4;
RHW
Ringmaster, The
See Mencken, H(enry) L(ouis)

Ringwood, Gwen(dolyn Margaret) Pharis
1910-1984 .... **CLC 48**
See also CA 148; 112; DLB 88
Rio, Michel 1945(?)- .... **CLC 43**
See also CA 201
Rios, Alberto (Alvaro) 1952- .... **PC 57**
See also AAYA 66; AMWS 4; CA 113;
CANR 34, 79, 137; CP 6, 7; DLB 122;
HW 2; MTFW 2005; PFS 11
Ritsos, Giannes
See Ritsos, Yannis
Ritsos, Yannis 1909-1990 .... **CLC 6, 13, 31**
See also CA 77-80; 133; CANR 39, 61; EW
12; EWL 3; MTCW 1; RGWL 2, 3
Ritter, Erika 1948(?)- .... **CLC 52**
See also CD 5, 6; CWD
Rivera, Jose Eustasio 1889-1928 ... **TCLC 35**
See also CA 162; EWL 3; HW 1, 2; LAW
Rivera, Tomas 1935-1984 .... **HLCS 2**
See also CA 49-52; CANR 32; DLB 82;
HW 1; LLW; RGAL 4; SSFS 15; TCWW
2; WLIT 1
Rivers, Conrad Kent 1933-1968 .... **CLC 1**
See also BW 1; CA 85-88; DLB 41
Rivers, Elfrida
See Bradley, Marion Zimmer
See also GLL 1
Riverside, John
See Heinlein, Robert A(nson)
Rizal, Jose 1861-1896 .... **NCLC 27**
Roa Bastos, Augusto 1917-2005 ...... **CLC 45;**
HLC 2
See also CA 131; 238; CWW 2; DAM
MULT; DLB 113; EWL 3; HW 1; LAW;
RGSF 2; WLIT 1
Roa Bastos, Augusto Jose Antonio
See Roa Bastos, Augusto
Robbe-Grillet, Alain 1922- .... **CLC 1, 2, 4, 6,**
8, 10, 14, 43, 128
See also BPFB 3; CA 9-12R; CANR 33,
65, 115; CWW 2; DLB 83; EW 13; EWL
3; GFL 1789 to the Present; IDFW 3, 4;
MTCW 1, 2; MTFW 2005; RGWL 2, 3;
SSFS 15
Robbins, Harold 1916-1997 .... **CLC 5**
See also BPFB 3; CA 73-76; 162; CANR
26, 54, 112; DA3; DAM NOV; MTCW
1, 2
Robbins, Thomas Eugene 1936-
See Robbins, Tom
See also CA 81-84; CANR 29, 59, 95, 139;
CN 7; CPW; CSW; DA3; DAM NOV,
POP; MTCW 1, 2; MTFW 2005
Robbins, Tom .... **CLC 9, 32, 64**
See Robbins, Thomas Eugene
See also AAYA 32; AMWS 10; BEST 90:3;
BPFB 3; CN 3, 4, 5, 6, 7; DLBY 1980
Robbins, Trina 1938- .... **CLC 21**
See also AAYA 61; CA 128; CANR 152
Roberts, Charles G(eorge) D(ouglas)
1860-1943 .... **SSC 91; TCLC 8**
See also CA 105; 188; CLR 33; CWRI 5;
DLB 92; RGEL 2; RGSF 2; SATA 88;
SATA-Brief 29
Roberts, Elizabeth Madox
1886-1941 .... **TCLC 68**
See also CA 111; 166; CLR 100; CWRI 5;
DLB 9, 54, 102; RGAL 4; RHW; SATA
33; SATA-Brief 27; TCWW 2; WCH
Roberts, Kate 1891-1985 .... **CLC 15**
See also CA 107; 116; DLB 319
Roberts, Keith (John Kingston)
1935-2000 .... **CLC 14**
See also BRWS 10; CA 25-28R; CANR 46;
DLB 261; SFW 4
Roberts, Kenneth (Lewis)
1885-1957 .... **TCLC 23**
See also CA 109; 199; DLB 9; MAL 5;
RGAL 4; RHW

Roberts, Michele (Brigitte) 1949- .... **CLC 48,**
178
See also CA 115; CANR 58, 120; CN 6, 7;
DLB 231; FW
Robertson, Ellis
See Ellison, Harlan (Jay); Silverberg, Rob-
ert
Robertson, Thomas William
1829-1871 .... **NCLC 35**
See Robertson, Tom
See also DAM DRAM
Robertson, Tom
See Robertson, Thomas William
See also RGEL 2
Robeson, Kenneth
See Dent, Lester
Robinson, Edwin Arlington
1869-1935 .... **PC 1, 35; TCLC 5, 101**
See also AMW; CA 104; 133; CDALB
1865-1917; DA; DAC; DAM MST,
POET; DLB 54; EWL 3; EXPP; MAL 5;
MTCW 1, 2; MTFW 2005; PAB; PFS 4;
RGAL 4; WP
Robinson, Henry Crabb
1775-1867 .... **NCLC 15**
See also DLB 107
Robinson, Jill 1936- .... **CLC 10**
See also CA 102; CANR 120; INT CA-102
Robinson, Kim Stanley 1952- .... **CLC 34**
See also AAYA 26; CA 126; CANR 113,
139; CN 6, 7; MTFW 2005; SATA 109;
SCFW 2; SFW 4
Robinson, Lloyd
See Silverberg, Robert
Robinson, Marilynne 1944- ...... **CLC 25, 180**
See also AAYA 69; CA 116; CANR 80, 140;
CN 4, 5, 6, 7; DLB 206; MTFW 2005
Robinson, Mary 1758-1800 .... **NCLC 142**
See also DLB 158; FW
Robinson, Smokey .... **CLC 21**
See Robinson, William, Jr.
Robinson, William, Jr. 1940-
See Robinson, Smokey
See also CA 116
Robison, Mary 1949- .... **CLC 42, 98**
See also CA 113; 116; CANR 87; CN 4, 5,
6, 7; DLB 130; INT CA-116; RGSF 2
Roches, Catherine des 1542-1587 ...... **LC 117**
Rochester
See Wilmot, John
See also RGEL 2
Rod, Edouard 1857-1910 .... **TCLC 52**
Roddenberry, Eugene Wesley 1921-1991
See Roddenberry, Gene
See also CA 110; 135; CANR 37; SATA 45;
SATA-Obit 69
Roddenberry, Gene .... **CLC 17**
See Roddenberry, Eugene Wesley
See also AAYA 5; SATA-Obit 69
Rodgers, Mary 1931- .... **CLC 12**
See also BYA 5; CA 49-52; CANR 8, 55,
90; CLR 20; CWRI 5; INT CANR-8;
JRDA; MAICYA 1, 2; SATA 8, 130
Rodgers, W(illiam) R(obert)
1909-1969 .... **CLC 7**
See also CA 85-88; DLB 20; RGEL 2
Rodman, Eric
See Silverberg, Robert
Rodman, Howard 1920(?)-1985 .... **CLC 65**
See also CA 118
Rodman, Maia
See Wojciechowska, Maia (Teresa)
Rodo, Jose Enrique 1871(?)-1917 .... **HLCS 2**
See also CA 178; EWL 3; HW 2; LAW
Rodolph, Utto
See Ouologuem, Yambo
Rodriguez, Claudio 1934-1999 .... **CLC 10**
See also CA 188; DLB 134

Rodriguez, Richard 1944- .... **CLC 155;**
HLC 2
　See also AMWS 14; CA 110; CANR 66,
　116; DAM MULT; DLB 82, 256; HW 1,
　2; LAIT 5; LLW; MTFW 2005; NCFS 3;
　WLIT 1

Roelvaag, O(le) E(dvart) 1876-1931
　See Rolvaag, O(le) E(dvart)
　See also CA 117; 171

Roethke, Theodore (Huebner)
　1908-1963 .... **CLC 1, 3, 8, 11, 19, 46,**
　101; PC 15
　See also AMW; CA 81-84; CABS 2;
　CDALB 1941-1968; DA3; DAM POET;
　DLB 5, 206; EWL 3; EXPP; MAL 5;
　MTCW 1, 2; PAB; PFS 3; RGAL 4; WP

Rogers, Carl R(ansom)
　1902-1987 .... **TCLC 125**
　See also CA 1-4R; 121; CANR 1, 18;
　MTCW 1

Rogers, Samuel 1763-1855 .... **NCLC 69**
　See also DLB 93; RGEL 2

Rogers, Thomas Hunton 1927- .... **CLC 57**
　See also CA 89-92; INT CA-89-92

Rogers, Will(iam Penn Adair)
　1879-1935 .... **NNAL; TCLC 8, 71**
　See also CA 105; 144; DA3; DAM MULT;
　DLB 11; MTCW 2

Rogin, Gilbert 1929- .... **CLC 18**
　See also CA 65-68; CANR 15

Rohan, Koda
　See Koda Shigeyuki

Rohlfs, Anna Katharine Green
　See Green, Anna Katharine

Rohmer, Eric .... **CLC 16**
　See Scherer, Jean-Marie Maurice

Rohmer, Sax .... **TCLC 28**
　See Ward, Arthur Henry Sarsfield
　See also DLB 70; MSW; SUFW

Roiphe, Anne 1935- .... **CLC 3, 9**
　See also CA 89-92; CANR 45, 73, 138;
　DLBY 1980; INT CA-89-92

Roiphe, Anne Richardson
　See Roiphe, Anne

Rojas, Fernando de 1475-1541 ... **HLCS 1, 2;**
　LC 23
　See also DLB 286; RGWL 2, 3

Rojas, Gonzalo 1917- .... **HLCS 2**
　See also CA 178; HW 2; LAWS 1

Roland (de la Platiere), Marie-Jeanne
　1754-1793 .... **LC 98**
　See also DLB 314

Rolfe, Frederick (William Serafino Austin
　Lewis Mary) 1860-1913 .... **TCLC 12**
　See Al Siddik
　See also CA 107; 210; DLB 34, 156;
　RGEL 2

Rolland, Romain 1866-1944 .... **TCLC 23**
　See also CA 118; 197; DLB 65, 284; EWL
　3; GFL 1789 to the Present; RGWL 2, 3

Rolle, Richard c. 1300-c. 1349 ...... **CMLC 21**
　See also DLB 146; LMFS 1; RGEL 2

Rolvaag, O(le) E(dvart) .... **TCLC 17**
　See Roelvaag, O(le) E(dvart)
　See also DLB 9, 212; MAL 5; NFS 5;
　RGAL 4

Romain Arnaud, Saint
　See Aragon, Louis

Romains, Jules 1885-1972 .... **CLC 7**
　See also CA 85-88; CANR 34; DLB 65,
　321; EWL 3; GFL 1789 to the Present;
　MTCW 1

Romero, Jose Ruben 1890-1952 .... **TCLC 14**
　See also CA 114; 131; EWL 3; HW 1; LAW

Ronsard, Pierre de 1524-1585 . **LC 6, 54; PC**
　11
　See also EW 2; GFL Beginnings to 1789;
　RGWL 2, 3; TWA

Rooke, Leon 1934- .... **CLC 25, 34**
　See also CA 25-28R; CANR 23, 53; CCA
　1; CPW; DAM POP

Roosevelt, Franklin Delano
　1882-1945 .... **TCLC 93**
　See also CA 116; 173; LAIT 3

Roosevelt, Theodore 1858-1919 ..... **TCLC 69**
　See also CA 115; 170; DLB 47, 186, 275

Roper, William 1498-1578 .... **LC 10**

Roquelaure, A. N.
　See Rice, Anne

Rosa, Joao Guimaraes 1908-1967 ... **CLC 23;**
　HLCS 1
　See Guimaraes Rosa, Joao
　See also CA 89-92; DLB 113, 307; EWL 3;
　WLIT 1

Rose, Wendy 1948- . **CLC 85; NNAL; PC 13**
　See also CA 53-56; CANR 5, 51; CWP;
　DAM MULT; DLB 175; PFS 13; RGAL
　4; SATA 12

Rosen, R. D.
　See Rosen, Richard (Dean)

Rosen, Richard (Dean) 1949- .... **CLC 39**
　See also CA 77-80; CANR 62, 120; CMW
　4; INT CANR-30

Rosenberg, Isaac 1890-1918 .... **TCLC 12**
　See also BRW 6; CA 107; 188; DLB 20,
　216; EWL 3; PAB; RGEL 2

Rosenblatt, Joe .... **CLC 15**
　See Rosenblatt, Joseph
　See also CP 3, 4, 5, 6, 7

Rosenblatt, Joseph 1933-
　See Rosenblatt, Joe
　See also CA 89-92; CP 1, 2; INT CA-89-92

Rosenfeld, Samuel
　See Tzara, Tristan

Rosenstock, Sami
　See Tzara, Tristan

Rosenstock, Samuel
　See Tzara, Tristan

Rosenthal, M(acha) L(ouis)
　1917-1996 .... **CLC 28**
　See also CA 1-4R; 152; CAAS 6; CANR 4,
　51; CP 1, 2, 3, 4, 5, 6; DLB 5; SATA 59

Ross, Barnaby
　See Dannay, Frederic; Lee, Manfred B.

Ross, Bernard L.
　See Follett, Ken(neth Martin)

Ross, J. H.
　See Lawrence, T(homas) E(dward)

Ross, John Hume
　See Lawrence, T(homas) E(dward)

Ross, Martin 1862-1915
　See Martin, Violet Florence
　See also DLB 135; GLL 2; RGEL 2;
　RGSF 2

Ross, (James) Sinclair 1908-1996 ... **CLC 13;**
　SSC 24
　See also CA 73-76; CANR 81; CN 1, 2, 3,
　4, 5, 6; DAC; DAM MST; DLB 88;
　RGEL 2; RGSF 2; TCWW 1, 2

Rossetti, Christina 1830-1894 ... **NCLC 2, 50,**
　66; PC 7; WLC 5
　See also AAYA 51; BRW 5; BYA 4; DA;
　DA3; DAB; DAC; DAM MST, POET;
　DLB 35, 163, 240; EXPP; FL 1:3; LATS
　1:1; MAICYA 1; PFS 10, 14; RGEL 2;
　SATA 20; TEA; WCH

Rossetti, Christina Georgina
　See Rossetti, Christina

Rossetti, Dante Gabriel 1828-1882 . **NCLC 4,**
　77; PC 44; WLC 5
　See also AAYA 51; BRW 5; CDBLB 1832-
　1890; DA; DAB; DAC; DAM MST,
　POET; DLB 35; EXPP; RGEL 2; TEA

Rossi, Cristina Peri
　See Peri Rossi, Cristina

Rossi, Jean-Baptiste 1931-2003
　See Japrisot, Sebastien
　See also CA 201; 215

Rossner, Judith 1935-2005 .... **CLC 6, 9, 29**
　See also AITN 2; BEST 90:3; BPFB 3; CA
　17-20R; 242; CANR 18, 51, 73; CN 4, 5,
　6, 7; DLB 6; INT CANR-18; MAL 5;
　MTCW 1, 2; MTFW 2005

Rossner, Judith Perelman
　See Rossner, Judith

Rostand, Edmond (Eugene Alexis)
　1868-1918 .... **DC 10; TCLC 6, 37**
　See also CA 104; 126; DA; DA3; DAB;
　DAC; DAM DRAM, MST; DFS 1; DLB
　192; LAIT 1; MTCW 1; RGWL 2, 3;
　TWA

Roth, Henry 1906-1995 ..... **CLC 2, 6, 11, 104**
　See also AMWS 9; CA 11-12; 149; CANR
　38, 63; CAP 1; CN 1, 2, 3, 4, 5, 6; DA3;
　DLB 28; EWL 3; MAL 5; MTCW 1, 2;
　MTFW 2005; RGAL 4

Roth, (Moses) Joseph 1894-1939 ... **TCLC 33**
　See also CA 160; DLB 85; EWL 3; RGWL
　2, 3

Roth, Philip 1933- ... **CLC 1, 2, 3, 4, 6, 9, 15,**
　22, 31, 47, 66, 86, 119, 201; SSC 26;
　WLC 5
　See also AAYA 67; AMWR 2; AMWS 3;
　BEST 90:3; BPFB 3; CA 1-4R; CANR 1,
　22, 36, 55, 89, 132; CDALB 1968-1988;
　CN 3, 4, 5, 6, 7; CPW 1; DA; DA3; DAB;
　DAC; DAM MST, NOV, POP; DLB 2,
　28, 173; DLBY 1982; EWL 3; MAL 5;
　MTCW 1, 2; MTFW 2005; RGAL 4;
　RGHL; RGSF 2; SSFS 12, 18; TUS

Roth, Philip Milton
　See Roth, Philip

Rothenberg, Jerome 1931- .... **CLC 6, 57**
　See also CA 45-48; CANR 1, 106; CP 1, 2,
　3, 4, 5, 6, 7; DLB 5, 193

Rotter, Pat ed. .... **CLC 65**

Roumain, Jacques (Jean Baptiste)
　1907-1944 .... **BLC 3; TCLC 19**
　See also BW 1; CA 117; 125; DAM MULT;
　EWL 3

Rourke, Constance Mayfield
　1885-1941 .... **TCLC 12**
　See also CA 107; 200; MAL 5; YABC 1

Rousseau, Jean-Baptiste 1671-1741 ...... **LC 9**

Rousseau, Jean-Jacques 1712-1778 .... **LC 14,**
　36, 122; WLC 5
　See also DA; DA3; DAB; DAC; DAM
　MST; DLB 314; EW 4; GFL Beginnings
　to 1789; LMFS 1; RGWL 2, 3; TWA

Roussel, Raymond 1877-1933 .... **TCLC 20**
　See also CA 117; 201; EWL 3; GFL 1789
　to the Present

Rovit, Earl (Herbert) 1927- .... **CLC 7**
　See also CA 5-8R; CANR 12

Rowe, Elizabeth Singer 1674-1737 ..... **LC 44**
　See also DLB 39, 95

Rowe, Nicholas 1674-1718 .... **LC 8**
　See also DLB 84; RGEL 2

Rowlandson, Mary 1637(?)-1678 .... **LC 66**
　See also DLB 24, 200; RGAL 4

Rowley, Ames Dorrance
　See Lovecraft, H. P.

Rowley, William 1585(?)-1626 ... **LC 100, 123**
　See also DFS 22; DLB 58; RGEL 2

Rowling, J. K. 1966- .... **CLC 137, 217**
　See also AAYA 34; BYA 11, 13, 14; CA
　173; CANR 128; CLR 66, 80, 112; MAI-
　CYA 2; MTFW 2005; SATA 109; SUFW 2

Rowling, Joanne Kathleen
　See Rowling, J. K.

Rowson, Susanna Haswell
　1762(?)-1824 .... **NCLC 5, 69**
　See also AMWS 15; DLB 37, 200; RGAL 4

Scorsese, Martin 1942- .... **CLC 20, 89, 207**
See also AAYA 38; CA 110; 114; CANR 46, 85
Scotland, Jay
See Jakes, John (William)
Scott, Duncan Campbell
1862-1947 .... **TCLC 6**
See also CA 104; 153; DAC; DLB 92; RGEL 2
Scott, Evelyn 1893-1963 .... **CLC 43**
See also CA 104; 112; CANR 64; DLB 9, 48; RHW
Scott, F(rancis) R(eginald)
1899-1985 .... **CLC 22**
See also CA 101; 114; CANR 87; CP 1, 2, 3, 4; DLB 88; INT CA-101; RGEL 2
Scott, Frank
See Scott, F(rancis) R(eginald)
Scott, Joan .... **CLC 65**
Scott, Joanna 1960- .... **CLC 50**
See also CA 126; CANR 53, 92
Scott, Paul (Mark) 1920-1978 ...... **CLC 9, 60**
See also BRWS 1; CA 81-84; 77-80; CANR 33; CN 1, 2; DLB 14, 207, 326; EWL 3; MTCW 1; RGEL 2; RHW; WWE 1
Scott, Ridley 1937- .... **CLC 183**
See also AAYA 13, 43
Scott, Sarah 1723-1795 .... **LC 44**
See also DLB 39
Scott, Sir Walter 1771-1832 .... **NCLC 15, 69, 110; PC 13; SSC 32; WLC 5**
See also AAYA 22; BRW 4; BYA 2; CD-BLB 1789-1832; DA; DAB; DAC; DAM MST, NOV, POET; DLB 93, 107, 116, 144, 159; GL 3; HGG; LAIT 1; RGEL 2; RGSF 2; SSFS 10; SUFW 1; TEA; WLIT 3; YABC 2
Scribe, (Augustin) Eugene 1791-1861 . **DC 5; NCLC 16**
See also DAM DRAM; DLB 192; GFL 1789 to the Present; RGWL 2, 3
Scrum, R.
See Crumb, R.
Scudery, Georges de 1601-1667 .... **LC 75**
See also GFL Beginnings to 1789
Scudery, Madeleine de 1607-1701 .. **LC 2, 58**
See also DLB 268; GFL Beginnings to 1789
Scum
See Crumb, R.
Scumbag, Little Bobby
See Crumb, R.
Seabrook, John
See Hubbard, L. Ron
Seacole, Mary Jane Grant
1805-1881 .... **NCLC 147**
See also DLB 166
Sealy, I(rwin) Allan 1951- .... **CLC 55**
See also CA 136; CN 6, 7
Search, Alexander
See Pessoa, Fernando (Antonio Nogueira)
Sebald, W(infried) G(eorg)
1944-2001 .... **CLC 194**
See also BRWS 8; CA 159; 202; CANR 98; MTFW 2005; RGHL
Sebastian, Lee
See Silverberg, Robert
Sebastian Owl
See Thompson, Hunter S(tockton)
Sebestyen, Igen
See Sebestyen, Ouida
Sebestyen, Ouida 1924- .... **CLC 30**
See also AAYA 8; BYA 7; CA 107; CANR 40, 114; CLR 17; JRDA; MAICYA 1, 2; SAAS 10; SATA 39, 140; WYA; YAW
Sebold, Alice 1963(?)- .... **CLC 193**
See also AAYA 56; CA 203; MTFW 2005
Second Duke of Buckingham
See Villiers, George

Secundus, H. Scriblerus
See Fielding, Henry
Sedges, John
See Buck, Pearl S(ydenstricker)
Sedgwick, Catharine Maria
1789-1867 .... **NCLC 19, 98**
See also DLB 1, 74, 183, 239, 243, 254; FL 1:3; RGAL 4
Seelye, John (Douglas) 1931- .... **CLC 7**
See also CA 97-100; CANR 70; INT CA-97-100; TCWW 1, 2
Seferiades, Giorgos Stylianou 1900-1971
See Seferis, George
See also CA 5-8R; 33-36R; CANR 5, 36; MTCW 1
Seferis, George .... **CLC 5, 11; PC 66**
See Seferiades, Giorgos Stylianou
See also EW 12; EWL 3; RGWL 2, 3
Segal, Erich (Wolf) 1937- .... **CLC 3, 10**
See also BEST 89:1; BPFB 3; CA 25-28R; CANR 20, 36, 65, 113; CPW; DAM POP; DLBY 1986; INT CANR-20; MTCW 1
Seger, Bob 1945- .... **CLC 35**
Seghers, Anna .... **CLC 7**
See Radvanyi, Netty
See also CDWLB 2; DLB 69; EWL 3
Seidel, Frederick (Lewis) 1936- .... **CLC 18**
See also CA 13-16R; CANR 8, 99; CP 1, 2, 3, 4, 5, 6, 7; DLBY 1984
Seifert, Jaroslav 1901-1986 . **CLC 34, 44, 93; PC 47**
See also CA 127; CDWLB 4; DLB 215; EWL 3; MTCW 1, 2
Sei Shonagon c. 966-1017(?) .... **CMLC 6**
Sejour, Victor 1817-1874 .... **DC 10**
See also DLB 50
Sejour Marcou et Ferrand, Juan Victor
See Sejour, Victor
Selby, Hubert, Jr. 1928-2004 ..... **CLC 1, 2, 4, 8; SSC 20**
See also CA 13-16R; 226; CANR 33, 85; CN 1, 2, 3, 4, 5, 6, 7; DLB 2, 227; MAL 5
Selzer, Richard 1928- .... **CLC 74**
See also CA 65-68; CANR 14, 106
Sembene, Ousmane
See Ousmane, Sembene
See also AFW; EWL 3; WLIT 2
Senancour, Etienne Pivert de
1770-1846 .... **NCLC 16**
See also DLB 119; GFL 1789 to the Present
Sender, Ramon (Jose) 1902-1982 ...... **CLC 8; HLC 2; TCLC 136**
See also CA 5-8R; 105; CANR 8; DAM MULT; DLB 322; EWL 3; HW 1; MTCW 1; RGWL 2, 3
Seneca, Lucius Annaeus c. 4B.C.-c. 65 .... **CMLC 6; DC 5**
See also AW 2; CDWLB 1; DAM DRAM; DLB 211; RGWL 2, 3; TWA; WLIT 8
Senghor, Leopold Sedar 1906-2001 ... **BLC 3; CLC 54, 130; PC 25**
See also AFW; BW 2; CA 116; 125; 203; CANR 47, 74, 134; CWW 2; DAM MULT, POET; DNFS 2; EWL 3; GFL 1789 to the Present; MTCW 1, 2; MTFW 2005; TWA
Senior, Olive (Marjorie) 1941- .... **SSC 78**
See also BW 3; CA 154; CANR 86, 126; CN 6; CP 6, 7; CWP; DLB 157; EWL 3; RGSF 2
Senna, Danzy 1970- .... **CLC 119**
See also CA 169; CANR 130
Serling, (Edward) Rod(man)
1924-1975 .... **CLC 30**
See also AAYA 14; AITN 1; CA 162; 57-60; DLB 26; SFW 4
Serna, Ramon Gomez de la
See Gomez de la Serna, Ramon

Serpieres
See Guillevic, (Eugene)
Service, Robert
See Service, Robert W(illiam)
See also BYA 4; DAB; DLB 92
Service, Robert W(illiam)
1874(?)-1958 ... **PC 70; TCLC 15; WLC 5**
See Service, Robert
See also CA 115; 140; CANR 84; DA; DAC; DAM MST, POET; PFS 10; RGEL 2; SATA 20
Seth, Vikram 1952- .... **CLC 43, 90**
See also BRWS 10; CA 121; 127; CANR 50, 74, 131; CN 6, 7; CP 5, 6, 7; DA3; DAM MULT; DLB 120, 271, 282, 323; EWL 3; INT CA-127; MTCW 2; MTFW 2005; WWE 1
Seton, Cynthia Propper 1926-1982 .. **CLC 27**
See also CA 5-8R; 108; CANR 7
Seton, Ernest (Evan) Thompson
1860-1946 .... **TCLC 31**
See also ANW; BYA 3; CA 109; 204; CLR 59; DLB 92; DLBD 13; JRDA; SATA 18
Seton-Thompson, Ernest
See Seton, Ernest (Evan) Thompson
Settle, Mary Lee 1918-2005 .... **CLC 19, 61**
See also BPFB 3; CA 89-92; 243; CAAS 1; CANR 44, 87, 126; CN 6, 7; CSW; DLB 6; INT CA-89-92
Seuphor, Michel
See Arp, Jean
Sevigne, Marie (de Rabutin-Chantal)
1626-1696 .... **LC 11**
See Sevigne, Marie de Rabutin Chantal
See also GFL Beginnings to 1789; TWA
Sevigne, Marie de Rabutin Chantal
See Sevigne, Marie (de Rabutin-Chantal)
See also DLB 268
Sewall, Samuel 1652-1730 .... **LC 38**
See also DLB 24; RGAL 4
Sexton, Anne (Harvey) 1928-1974 ..... **CLC 2, 4, 6, 8, 10, 15, 53, 123; PC 2; WLC 5**
See also AMWS 2; CA 1-4R; 53-56; CABS 2; CANR 3, 36; CDALB 1941-1968; CP 1, 2; DA; DA3; DAB; DAC; DAM MST, POET; DLB 5, 169; EWL 3; EXPP; FL 1:6; FW; MAL 5; MAWW; MTCW 1, 2; MTFW 2005; PAB; PFS 4, 14; RGAL 4; RGHL; SATA 10; TUS
Shaara, Jeff 1952- .... **CLC 119**
See also AAYA 70; CA 163; CANR 109; CN 7; MTFW 2005
Shaara, Michael (Joseph, Jr.)
1929-1988 .... **CLC 15**
See also AAYA 71; AITN 1; BPFB 3; CA 102; 125; CANR 52, 85; DAM POP; DLBY 1983; MTFW 2005
Shackleton, C. C.
See Aldiss, Brian W(ilson)
Shacochis, Bob .... **CLC 39**
See Shacochis, Robert G.
Shacochis, Robert G. 1951-
See Shacochis, Bob
See also CA 119; 124; CANR 100; INT CA-124
Shadwell, Thomas 1641(?)-1692 .... **LC 114**
See also DLB 80; IDTP; RGEL 2
Shaffer, Anthony (Joshua)
1926-2001 .... **CLC 19**
See also CA 110; 116; 200; CBD; CD 5, 6; DAM DRAM; DFS 13; DLB 13
Shaffer, Peter (Levin) 1926- .. **CLC 5, 14, 18, 37, 60; DC 7**
See also BRWS 1; CA 25-28R; CANR 25, 47, 74, 118; CBD; CD 5, 6; CDBLB 1960 to Present; DA3; DAB; DAM DRAM, MST; DFS 5, 13; DLB 13, 233; EWL 3; MTCW 1, 2; MTFW 2005; RGEL 2; TEA

Shulman, Alix Kates 1932- .... **CLC 2, 10**
See also CA 29-32R; CANR 43; FW; SATA 7

Shuster, Joe 1914-1992 .... **CLC 21**
See also AAYA 50

Shute, Nevil .... **CLC 30**
See Norway, Nevil Shute
See also BPFB 3; DLB 255; NFS 9; RHW; SFW 4

Shuttle, Penelope (Diane) 1947- .... **CLC 7**
See also CA 93-96; CANR 39, 84, 92, 108; CP 3, 4, 5, 6, 7; CWP; DLB 14, 40

Shvarts, Elena 1948- .... **PC 50**
See also CA 147

Sidhwa, Bapsi 1939-
See Sidhwa, Bapsy (N.)
See also CN 6, 7; DLB 323

Sidhwa, Bapsy (N.) 1938- .... **CLC 168**
See Sidhwa, Bapsi
See also CA 108; CANR 25, 57; FW

Sidney, Mary 1561-1621 .... **LC 19, 39**
See Sidney Herbert, Mary

Sidney, Sir Philip 1554-1586 . **LC 19, 39; PC 32**
See also BRW 1; BRWR 2; CDBLB Before 1660; DA; DA3; DAB; DAC; DAM MST, POET; DLB 167; EXPP; PAB; RGEL 2; TEA; WP

Sidney Herbert, Mary
See Sidney, Mary
See also DLB 167

Siegel, Jerome 1914-1996 .... **CLC 21**
See Siegel, Jerry
See also CA 116; 169; 151

Siegel, Jerry
See Siegel, Jerome
See also AAYA 50

Sienkiewicz, Henryk (Adam Alexander Pius) 1846-1916 .... **TCLC 3**
See also CA 104; 134; CANR 84; EWL 3; RGSF 2; RGWL 2, 3

Sierra, Gregorio Martinez
See Martinez Sierra, Gregorio

Sierra, Maria (de la O'LeJarraga) Martinez
See Martinez Sierra, Maria (de la O'LeJarraga)

Sigal, Clancy 1926- .... **CLC 7**
See also CA 1-4R; CANR 85; CN 1, 2, 3, 4, 5, 6, 7

Siger of Brabant 1240(?)-1284(?) . **CMLC 69**
See also DLB 115

Sigourney, Lydia H.
See Sigourney, Lydia Howard (Huntley)
See also DLB 73, 183

Sigourney, Lydia Howard (Huntley) 1791-1865 .... **NCLC 21, 87**
See Sigourney, Lydia H.; Sigourney, Lydia Huntley
See also DLB 1

Sigourney, Lydia Huntley
See Sigourney, Lydia Howard (Huntley)
See also DLB 42, 239, 243

Siguenza y Gongora, Carlos de 1645-1700 .... **HLCS 2; LC 8**
See also LAW

Sigurjonsson, Johann
See Sigurjonsson, Johann

Sigurjonsson, Johann 1880-1919 ... **TCLC 27**
See also CA 170; DLB 293; EWL 3

Sikelianos, Angelos 1884-1951 .... **PC 29; TCLC 39**
See also EWL 3; RGWL 2, 3

Silkin, Jon 1930-1997 .... **CLC 2, 6, 43**
See also CA 5-8R; CAAS 5; CANR 89; CP 1, 2, 3, 4, 5, 6; DLB 27

Silko, Leslie (Marmon) 1948- .... **CLC 23, 74, 114, 211; NNAL; SSC 37, 66; WLCS**
See also AAYA 14; AMWS 4; ANW; BYA 12; CA 115; 122; CANR 45, 65, 118; CN 4, 5, 6, 7; CP 4, 5, 6, 7; CPW 1; CWP; DA; DA3; DAC; DAM MST, MULT, POP; DLB 143, 175, 256, 275; EWL 3; EXPP; EXPS; LAIT 4; MAL 5; MTCW 2; MTFW 2005; NFS 4; PFS 9, 16; RGAL 4; RGSF 2; SSFS 4, 8, 10, 11; TCWW 1, 2

Sillanpaa, Frans Eemil 1888-1964 ... **CLC 19**
See also CA 129; 93-96; EWL 3; MTCW 1

Sillitoe, Alan 1928- .. **CLC 1, 3, 6, 10, 19, 57, 148**
See also AITN 1; BRWS 5; CA 9-12R, 191; CAAE 191; CAAS 2; CANR 8, 26, 55, 139; CDBLB 1960 to Present; CN 1, 2, 3, 4, 5, 6; CP 1, 2, 3, 4, 5; DLB 14, 139; EWL 3; MTCW 1, 2; MTFW 2005; RGEL 2; RGSF 2; SATA 61

Silone, Ignazio 1900-1978 .... **CLC 4**
See also CA 25-28; 81-84; CANR 34; CAP 2; DLB 264; EW 12; EWL 3; MTCW 1; RGSF 2; RGWL 2, 3

Silone, Ignazione
See Silone, Ignazio

Silver, Joan Micklin 1935- .... **CLC 20**
See also CA 114; 121; INT CA-121

Silver, Nicholas
See Faust, Frederick (Schiller)

Silverberg, Robert 1935- .... **CLC 7, 140**
See also AAYA 24; BPFB 3; BYA 7, 9; CA 1-4R; CAAE 186; CAAS 3; CANR 1, 20, 36, 85, 140; CLR 59; CN 6, 7; CPW; DAM POP; DLB 8; INT CANR-20; MAICYA 1, 2; MTCW 1, 2; MTFW 2005; SATA 13, 91; SATA-Essay 104; SCFW 1, 2; SFW 4; SUFW 2

Silverstein, Alvin 1933- .... **CLC 17**
See also CA 49-52; CANR 2; CLR 25; JRDA; MAICYA 1, 2; SATA 8, 69, 124

Silverstein, Shel(don Allan) 1932-1999 .... **PC 49**
See also AAYA 40; BW 3; CA 107; 179; CANR 47, 74, 81; CLR 5, 96; CWRI 5; JRDA; MAICYA 1, 2; MTCW 2; MTFW 2005; SATA 33, 92; SATA-Brief 27; SATA-Obit 116

Silverstein, Virginia B(arbara Opshelor) 1937- .... **CLC 17**
See also CA 49-52; CANR 2; CLR 25; JRDA; MAICYA 1, 2; SATA 8, 69, 124

Sim, Georges
See Simenon, Georges (Jacques Christian)

Simak, Clifford D(onald) 1904-1988 . **CLC 1, 55**
See also CA 1-4R; 125; CANR 1, 35; DLB 8; MTCW 1; SATA-Obit 56; SCFW 1, 2; SFW 4

Simenon, Georges (Jacques Christian) 1903-1989 .... **CLC 1, 2, 3, 8, 18, 47**
See also BPFB 3; CA 85-88; 129; CANR 35; CMW 4; DA3; DAM POP; DLB 72; DLBY 1989; EW 12; EWL 3; GFL 1789 to the Present; MSW; MTCW 1, 2; MTFW 2005; RGWL 2, 3

Simic, Charles 1938- .... **CLC 6, 9, 22, 49, 68, 130; PC 69**
See also AMWS 8; CA 29-32R; CAAS 4; CANR 12, 33, 52, 61, 96, 140; CP 2, 3, 4, 5, 6, 7; DA3; DAM POET; DLB 105; MAL 5; MTCW 2; MTFW 2005; PFS 7; RGAL 4; WP

Simmel, Georg 1858-1918 .... **TCLC 64**
See also CA 157; DLB 296

Simmons, Charles (Paul) 1924- .... **CLC 57**
See also CA 89-92; INT CA-89-92

Simmons, Dan 1948- .... **CLC 44**
See also AAYA 16, 54; CA 138; CANR 53, 81, 126; CPW; DAM POP; HGG; SUFW 2

Simmons, James (Stewart Alexander) 1933- .... **CLC 43**
See also CA 105; CAAS 21; CP 1, 2, 3, 4, 5, 6, 7; DLB 40

Simms, William Gilmore 1806-1870 .... **NCLC 3**
See also DLB 3, 30, 59, 73, 248, 254; RGAL 4

Simon, Carly 1945- .... **CLC 26**
See also CA 105

Simon, Claude 1913-2005 ... **CLC 4, 9, 15, 39**
See also CA 89-92; 241; CANR 33, 117; CWW 2; DAM NOV; DLB 83; EW 13; EWL 3; GFL 1789 to the Present; MTCW 1

Simon, Claude Eugene Henri
See Simon, Claude

Simon, Claude Henri Eugene
See Simon, Claude

Simon, Marvin Neil
See Simon, Neil

Simon, Myles
See Follett, Ken(neth Martin)

Simon, Neil 1927- .... **CLC 6, 11, 31, 39, 70; DC 14**
See also AAYA 32; AITN 1; AMWS 4; CA 21-24R; CAD; CANR 26, 54, 87, 126; CD 5, 6; DA3; DAM DRAM; DFS 2, 6, 12, 18; DLB 7, 266; LAIT 4; MAL 5; MTCW 1, 2; MTFW 2005; RGAL 4; TUS

Simon, Paul 1941(?)- .... **CLC 17**
See also CA 116; 153; CANR 152

Simon, Paul Frederick
See Simon, Paul

Simonon, Paul 1956(?)- .... **CLC 30**

Simonson, Rick ed. .... **CLC 70**

Simpson, Harriette
See Arnow, Harriette (Louisa) Simpson

Simpson, Louis (Aston Marantz) 1923- .... **CLC 4, 7, 9, 32, 149**
See also AMWS 9; CA 1-4R; CAAS 4; CANR 1, 61, 140; CP 1, 2, 3, 4, 5, 6, 7; DAM POET; DLB 5; MAL 5; MTCW 1, 2; MTFW 2005; PFS 7, 11, 14; RGAL 4

Simpson, Mona 1957- .... **CLC 44, 146**
See also CA 122; 135; CANR 68, 103; CN 6, 7; EWL 3

Simpson, Mona Elizabeth
See Simpson, Mona

Simpson, N(orman) F(rederick) 1919- .... **CLC 29**
See also CA 13-16R; CBD; DLB 13; RGEL 2

Sinclair, Andrew (Annandale) 1935- . **CLC 2, 14**
See also CA 9-12R; CAAS 5; CANR 14, 38, 91; CN 1, 2, 3, 4, 5, 6, 7; DLB 14; FANT; MTCW 1

Sinclair, Emil
See Hesse, Hermann

Sinclair, Iain 1943- .... **CLC 76**
See also CA 132; CANR 81; CP 5, 6, 7; HGG

Sinclair, Iain MacGregor
See Sinclair, Iain

Sinclair, Irene
See Griffith, D(avid Lewelyn) W(ark)

Sinclair, Mary Amelia St. Clair 1865(?)-1946
See Sinclair, May
See also CA 104; HGG; RHW

Sinclair, May .... **TCLC 3, 11**
See Sinclair, Mary Amelia St. Clair
See also CA 166; DLB 36, 135; EWL 3; RGEL 2; SUFW

Snyder, Zilpha Keatley 1927- .... **CLC 17**
    See also AAYA 15; BYA 1; CA 9-12R;
    CANR 38; CLR 31; JRDA; MAICYA 1,
    2; SAAS 2; SATA 1, 28, 75, 110, 163;
    SATA-Essay 112, 163; YAW
Soares, Bernardo
    See Pessoa, Fernando (Antonio Nogueira)
Sobh, A.
    See Shamlu, Ahmad
Sobh, Alef
    See Shamlu, Ahmad
Sobol, Joshua 1939- .... **CLC 60**
    See Sobol, Yehoshua
    See also CA 200; RGHL
Sobol, Yehoshua 1939-
    See Sobol, Joshua
    See also CWW 2
Socrates 470B.C.-399B.C. .... **CMLC 27**
Soderberg, Hjalmar 1869-1941 ...... **TCLC 39**
    See also DLB 259; EWL 3; RGSF 2
Soderbergh, Steven 1963- .... **CLC 154**
    See also AAYA 43; CA 243
Soderbergh, Steven Andrew
    See Soderbergh, Steven
Sodergran, Edith (Irene) 1892-1923
    See Soedergran, Edith (Irene)
    See also CA 202; DLB 259; EW 11; EWL
    3; RGWL 2, 3
Soedergran, Edith (Irene)
    1892-1923 .... **TCLC 31**
    See Sodergran, Edith (Irene)
Softly, Edgar
    See Lovecraft, H. P.
Softly, Edward
    See Lovecraft, H. P.
Sokolov, Alexander V(sevolodovich) 1943-
    See Sokolov, Sasha
    See also CA 73-76
Sokolov, Raymond 1941- .... **CLC 7**
    See also CA 85-88
Sokolov, Sasha .... **CLC 59**
    See Sokolov, Alexander V(sevolodovich)
    See also CWW 2; DLB 285; EWL 3; RGWL
    2, 3
Solo, Jay
    See Ellison, Harlan (Jay)
Sologub, Fyodor .... **TCLC 9**
    See Teternikov, Fyodor Kuzmich
    See also EWL 3
Solomons, Ikey Esquir
    See Thackeray, William Makepeace
Solomos, Dionysios 1798-1857 .... **NCLC 15**
Solwoska, Mara
    See French, Marilyn
Solzhenitsyn, Aleksandr I. 1918- .. **CLC 1, 2,
    4, 7, 9, 10, 18, 26, 34, 78, 134; SSC 32;
    WLC 5**
    See Solzhenitsyn, Aleksandr Isayevich
    See also AAYA 49; AITN 1; BPFB 3; CA
    69-72; CANR 40, 65, 116; DA; DA3;
    DAB; DAC; DAM MST, NOV; DLB 302;
    EW 13; EXPS; LAIT 4; MTCW 1, 2;
    MTFW 2005; NFS 6; RGSF 2; RGWL 2,
    3; SSFS 9; TWA
Solzhenitsyn, Aleksandr Isayevich
    See Solzhenitsyn, Aleksandr I.
    See also CWW 2; EWL 3
Somers, Jane
    See Lessing, Doris (May)
Somerville, Edith Oenone
    1858-1949 .... **SSC 56; TCLC 51**
    See also CA 196; DLB 135; RGEL 2; RGSF
    2
Somerville & Ross
    See Martin, Violet Florence; Somerville,
    Edith Oenone
Sommer, Scott 1951- .... **CLC 25**
    See also CA 106

Sommers, Christina Hoff 1950- ...... **CLC 197**
    See also CA 153; CANR 95
Sondheim, Stephen (Joshua) 1930- . **CLC 30,
    39, 147; DC 22**
    See also AAYA 11, 66; CA 103; CANR 47,
    67, 125; DAM DRAM; LAIT 4
Sone, Monica 1919- .... **AAL**
    See also DLB 312
Song, Cathy 1955- .... **AAL; PC 21**
    See also CA 154; CANR 118; CWP; DLB
    169, 312; EXPP; FW; PFS 5
Sontag, Susan 1933-2004 ... **CLC 1, 2, 10, 13,
    31, 105, 195**
    See also AMWS 3; CA 17-20R; 234; CANR
    25, 51, 74, 97; CN 1, 2, 3, 4, 5, 6, 7;
    CPW; DA3; DAM POP; DLB 2, 67; EWL
    3; MAL 5; MAWW; MTCW 1, 2; MTFW
    2005; RGAL 4; RHW; SSFS 10
Sophocles 496(?)B.C.-406(?)B.C. .... **CMLC 2,
    47, 51; DC 1; WLCS**
    See also AW 1; CDWLB 1; DA; DA3;
    DAB; DAC; DAM DRAM, MST; DFS 1,
    4, 8; DLB 176; LAIT 1; LATS 1:1; LMFS
    1; RGWL 2, 3; TWA; WLIT 8
Sordello 1189-1269 .... **CMLC 15**
Sorel, Georges 1847-1922 .... **TCLC 91**
    See also CA 118; 188
Sorel, Julia
    See Drexler, Rosalyn
Sorokin, Vladimir .... **CLC 59**
    See Sorokin, Vladimir Georgievich
Sorokin, Vladimir Georgievich
    See Sorokin, Vladimir
    See also DLB 285
Sorrentino, Gilbert 1929-2006 .... **CLC 3, 7,
    14, 22, 40**
    See also CA 77-80; CANR 14, 33, 115; CN
    3, 4, 5, 6, 7; CP 1, 2, 3, 4, 5, 6, 7; DLB 5,
    173; DLBY 1980; INT CANR-14
Soseki
    See Natsume, Soseki
    See also MJW
Soto, Gary 1952- ... **CLC 32, 80; HLC 2; PC
    28**
    See also AAYA 10, 37; BYA 11; CA 119;
    125; CANR 50, 74, 107; CLR 38; CP 4,
    5, 6, 7; DAM MULT; DLB 82; EWL 3;
    EXPP; HW 1, 2; INT CA-125; JRDA;
    LLW; MAICYA 2; MAICYAS 1; MAL 5;
    MTCW 2; MTFW 2005; PFS 7; RGAL 4;
    SATA 80, 120; WYA; YAW
Soupault, Philippe 1897-1990 .... **CLC 68**
    See also CA 116; 147; 131; EWL 3; GFL
    1789 to the Present; LMFS 2
Souster, (Holmes) Raymond 1921- .... **CLC 5,
    14**
    See also CA 13-16R; CAAS 14; CANR 13,
    29, 53; CP 1, 2, 3, 4, 5, 6, 7; DA3; DAC;
    DAM POET; DLB 88; RGEL 2; SATA 63
Southern, Terry 1924(?)-1995 .... **CLC 7**
    See also AMWS 11; BPFB 3; CA 1-4R;
    150; CANR 1, 55, 107; CN 1, 2, 3, 4, 5,
    6; DLB 2; IDFW 3, 4
Southerne, Thomas 1660-1746 .... **LC 99**
    See also DLB 80; RGEL 2
Southey, Robert 1774-1843 .... **NCLC 8, 97**
    See also BRW 4; DLB 93, 107, 142; RGEL
    2; SATA 54
Southwell, Robert 1561(?)-1595 .... **LC 108**
    See also DLB 167; RGEL 2; TEA
Southworth, Emma Dorothy Eliza Nevitte
    1819-1899 .... **NCLC 26**
    See also DLB 239
Souza, Ernest
    See Scott, Evelyn

Soyinka, Wole 1934- .. **BLC 3; CLC 3, 5, 14,
    36, 44, 179; DC 2; WLC 5**
    See also AFW; BW 2, 3; CA 13-16R;
    CANR 27, 39, 82, 136; CD 5, 6; CDWLB
    3; CN 6, 7; CP 1, 2, 3, 4, 5, 6 ,7; DA;
    DA3; DAB; DAC; DAM DRAM, MST,
    MULT; DFS 10; DLB 125; EWL 3;
    MTCW 1, 2; MTFW 2005; RGEL 2;
    TWA; WLIT 2; WWE 1
Spackman, W(illiam) M(ode)
    1905-1990 .... **CLC 46**
    See also CA 81-84; 132
Spacks, Barry (Bernard) 1931- .... **CLC 14**
    See also CA 154; CANR 33, 109; CP 3, 4,
    5, 6, 7; DLB 105
Spanidou, Irini 1946- .... **CLC 44**
    See also CA 185
Spark, Muriel (Sarah) 1918-2006 . **CLC 2, 3,
    5, 8, 13, 18, 40, 94; PC 72; SSC 10**
    See also BRWS 1; CA 5-8R; CANR 12, 36,
    76, 89, 131; CDBLB 1945-1960; CN 1, 2,
    3, 4, 5, 6, 7; CP 1, 2, 3, 4, 5, 6, 7; DA3;
    DAB; DAC; DAM MST, NOV; DLB 15,
    139; EWL 3; FW; INT CANR-12; LAIT
    4; MTCW 1, 2; MTFW 2005; NFS 22;
    RGEL 2; TEA; WLIT 4; YAW
Spaulding, Douglas
    See Bradbury, Ray (Douglas)
Spaulding, Leonard
    See Bradbury, Ray (Douglas)
Speght, Rachel 1597-c. 1630 .... **LC 97**
    See also DLB 126
Spence, J. A. D.
    See Eliot, T(homas) S(tearns)
Spencer, Anne 1882-1975 .... **HR 1:3**
    See also BW 2; CA 161; DLB 51, 54
Spencer, Elizabeth 1921- .... **CLC 22; SSC 57**
    See also CA 13-16R; CANR 32, 65, 87; CN
    1, 2, 3, 4, 5, 6, 7; CSW; DLB 6, 218;
    EWL 3; MTCW 1; RGAL 4; SATA 14
Spencer, Leonard G.
    See Silverberg, Robert
Spencer, Scott 1945- .... **CLC 30**
    See also CA 113; CANR 51, 148; DLBY
    1986
Spender, Stephen (Harold)
    1909-1995 .. **CLC 1, 2, 5, 10, 41, 91; PC
    71**
    See also BRWS 2; CA 9-12R; 149; CANR
    31, 54; CDBLB 1945-1960; CP 1, 2, 3, 4,
    5, 6; DA3; DAM POET; DLB 20; EWL
    3; MTCW 1, 2; MTFW 2005; PAB; PFS
    23; RGEL 2; TEA
Spengler, Oswald (Arnold Gottfried)
    1880-1936 .... **TCLC 25**
    See also CA 118; 189
Spenser, Edmund 1552(?)-1599 ...... **LC 5, 39,
    117; PC 8, 42; WLC 5**
    See also AAYA 60; BRW 1; CDBLB Be-
    fore 1660; DA; DA3; DAB; DAC; DAM
    MST, POET; DLB 167; EFS 2; EXPP;
    PAB; RGEL 2; TEA; WLIT 3; WP
Spicer, Jack 1925-1965 .... **CLC 8, 18, 72**
    See also BG 1:3; CA 85-88; DAM POET;
    DLB 5, 16, 193; GLL 1; WP
Spiegelman, Art 1948- .... **CLC 76, 178**
    See also AAYA 10, 46; CA 125; CANR 41,
    55, 74, 124; DLB 299; MTCW 2; MTFW
    2005; RGHL; SATA 109, 158; YAW
Spielberg, Peter 1929- .... **CLC 6**
    See also CA 5-8R; CANR 4, 48; DLBY
    1981
Spielberg, Steven 1947- .... **CLC 20, 188**
    See also AAYA 8, 24; CA 77-80; CANR
    32; SATA 32
Spillane, Frank Morrison .... **CLC 3, 13**
    See Spillane, Mickey
    See also BPFB 3; CMW 4; DLB 226; MSW

Stevenson, Robert Louis (Balfour)
1850-1894 ...... **NCLC 5, 14, 63; SSC 11, 51; WLC 5**
See also AAYA 24; BPFB 3; BRW 5; BRWC 1; BRWR 1; BYA 1, 2, 4, 13; CDBLB 1890-1914; CLR 10, 11, 107; DA; DA3; DAB; DAC; DAM MST, NOV; DLB 18, 57, 141, 156, 174; DLBD 13; GL 3; HGG; JRDA; LAIT 1, 3; MAICYA 1, 2; NFS 11, 20; RGEL 2; RGSF 2; SATA 100; SUFW; TEA; WCH; WLIT 4; WYA; YABC 2; YAW

Stewart, J(ohn) I(nnes) M(ackintosh)
1906-1994 .... **CLC 7, 14, 32**
See Innes, Michael
See also CA 85-88; 147; CAAS 3; CANR 47; CMW 4; CN 1, 2, 3, 4, 5; MTCW 1, 2

Stewart, Mary (Florence Elinor)
1916- .... **CLC 7, 35, 117**
See also AAYA 29; BPFB 3; CA 1-4R; CANR 1, 59, 130; CMW 4; CPW; DAB; FANT; RHW; SATA 12; YAW

Stewart, Mary Rainbow
See Stewart, Mary (Florence Elinor)

Stifle, June
See Campbell, Maria

Stifter, Adalbert 1805-1868 .. **NCLC 41; SSC 28**
See also CDWLB 2; DLB 133; RGSF 2; RGWL 2, 3

Still, James 1906-2001 .... **CLC 49**
See also CA 65-68; 195; CAAS 17; CANR 10, 26; CSW; DLB 9; DLBY 01; SATA 29; SATA-Obit 127

Sting 1951-
See Sumner, Gordon Matthew
See also CA 167

Stirling, Arthur
See Sinclair, Upton

Stitt, Milan 1941- .... **CLC 29**
See also CA 69-72

Stockton, Francis Richard 1834-1902
See Stockton, Frank R.
See also AAYA 68; CA 108; 137; MAICYA 1, 2; SATA 44; SFW 4

Stockton, Frank R. .... **TCLC 47**
See Stockton, Francis Richard
See also BYA 4, 13; DLB 42, 74; DLBD 13; EXPS; SATA-Brief 32; SSFS 3; SUFW; WCH

Stoddard, Charles
See Kuttner, Henry

Stoker, Abraham 1847-1912
See Stoker, Bram
See also CA 105; 150; DA; DA3; DAC; DAM MST, NOV; HGG; MTFW 2005; SATA 29

Stoker, Bram .... **SSC 62; TCLC 8, 144; WLC 6**
See Stoker, Abraham
See also AAYA 23; BPFB 3; BRWS 3; BYA 5; CDBLB 1890-1914; DAB; DLB 304; GL 3; LATS 1:1; NFS 18; RGEL 2; SUFW; TEA; WLIT 4

Stolz, Mary (Slattery) 1920- .... **CLC 12**
See also AAYA 8; AITN 1; CA 5-8R; CANR 13, 41, 112; JRDA; MAICYA 1, 2; SAAS 3; SATA 10, 71, 133; YAW

Stone, Irving 1903-1989 .... **CLC 7**
See also AITN 1; BPFB 3; CA 1-4R; 129; CAAS 3; CANR 1, 23; CN 1, 2, 3, 4; CPW; DA3; DAM POP; INT CANR-23; MTCW 1, 2; MTFW 2005; RHW; SATA 3; SATA-Obit 64

Stone, Oliver (William) 1946- .... **CLC 73**
See also AAYA 15, 64; CA 110; CANR 55, 125

Stone, Robert (Anthony) 1937- ... **CLC 5, 23, 42, 175**
See also AMWS 5; BPFB 3; CA 85-88; CANR 23, 66, 95; CN 4, 5, 6, 7; DLB 152; EWL 3; INT CANR-23; MAL 5; MTCW 1; MTFW 2005

Stone, Ruth 1915- .... **PC 53**
See also CA 45-48; CANR 2, 91; CP 5, 6, 7; CSW; DLB 105; PFS 19

Stone, Zachary
See Follett, Ken(neth Martin)

Stoppard, Tom 1937- ... **CLC 1, 3, 4, 5, 8, 15, 29, 34, 63, 91; DC 6; WLC 6**
See also AAYA 63; BRWC 1; BRWR 2; BRWS 1; CA 81-84; CANR 39, 67, 125; CBD; CD 5, 6; CDBLB 1960 to Present; DA; DA3; DAB; DAC; DAM DRAM, MST; DFS 2, 5, 8, 11, 13, 16; DLB 13, 233; DLBY 1985; EWL 3; LATS 1:2; MTCW 1, 2; MTFW 2005; RGEL 2; TEA; WLIT 4

Storey, David (Malcolm) 1933- ..... **CLC 2, 4, 5, 8**
See also BRWS 1; CA 81-84; CANR 36; CBD; CD 5, 6; CN 1, 2, 3, 4, 5, 6; DAM DRAM; DLB 13, 14, 207, 245, 326; EWL 3; MTCW 1; RGEL 2

Storm, Hyemeyohsts 1935- ... **CLC 3; NNAL**
See also CA 81-84; CANR 45; DAM MULT

Storm, (Hans) Theodor (Woldsen)
1817-1888 .... **NCLC 1; SSC 27**
See also CDWLB 2; DLB 129; EW; RGSF 2; RGWL 2, 3

Storni, Alfonsina 1892-1938 . **HLC 2; PC 33; TCLC 5**
See also CA 104; 131; DAM MULT; DLB 283; HW 1; LAW

Stoughton, William 1631-1701 .... **LC 38**
See also DLB 24

Stout, Rex (Todhunter) 1886-1975 ..... **CLC 3**
See also AITN 2; BPFB 3; CA 61-64; CANR 71; CMW 4; CN 2; DLB 306; MSW; RGAL 4

Stow, (Julian) Randolph 1935- ... **CLC 23, 48**
See also CA 13-16R; CANR 33; CN 1, 2, 3, 4, 5, 6, 7; CP 1, 2, 3, 4; DLB 260; MTCW 1; RGEL 2

Stowe, Harriet (Elizabeth) Beecher
1811-1896 ..... **NCLC 3, 50, 133; WLC 6**
See also AAYA 53; AMWS 1; CDALB 1865-1917; DA; DA3; DAB; DAC; DAM MST, NOV; DLB 1, 12, 42, 74, 189, 239, 243; EXPN; FL 1:3; JRDA; LAIT 2; MAICYA 1, 2; NFS 6; RGAL 4; TUS; YABC 1

Strabo c. 64B.C.-c. 25 .... **CMLC 37**
See also DLB 176

Strachey, (Giles) Lytton
1880-1932 .... **TCLC 12**
See also BRWS 2; CA 110; 178; DLB 149; DLBD 10; EWL 3; MTCW 2; NCFS 4

Stramm, August 1874-1915 .... **PC 50**
See also CA 195; EWL 3

Strand, Mark 1934- .. **CLC 6, 18, 41, 71; PC 63**
See also AMWS 4; CA 21-24R; CANR 40, 65, 100; CP 1, 2, 3, 4, 5, 6, 7; DAM POET; DLB 5; EWL 3; MAL 5; PAB; PFS 9, 18; RGAL 4; SATA 41; TCLE 1:2

Stratton-Porter, Gene(va Grace) 1863-1924
See Porter, Gene(va Grace) Stratton
See also ANW; CA 137; CLR 87; DLB 221; DLBD 14; MAICYA 1, 2; SATA 15

Straub, Peter 1943- .... **CLC 28, 107**
See also BEST 89:1; BPFB 3; CA 85-88; CANR 28, 65, 109; CPW; DAM POP; DLBY 1985; HGG; MTCW 1, 2; MTFW 2005; SUFW 2

Straub, Peter Francis
See Straub, Peter

Strauss, Botho 1944- .... **CLC 22**
See also CA 157; CWW 2; DLB 124

Strauss, Leo 1899-1973 .... **TCLC 141**
See also CA 101; 45-48; CANR 122

Streatfeild, (Mary) Noel
1897(?)-1986 .... **CLC 21**
See also CA 81-84; 120; CANR 31; CLR 17, 83; CWRI 5; DLB 160; MAICYA 1, 2; SATA 20; SATA-Obit 48

Stribling, T(homas) S(igismund)
1881-1965 .... **CLC 23**
See also CA 189; 107; CMW 4; DLB 9; RGAL 4

Strindberg, (Johan) August
1849-1912 ... **DC 18; TCLC 1, 8, 21, 47; WLC 6**
See also CA 104; 135; DA; DA3; DAB; DAC; DAM DRAM, MST; DFS 4, 9; DLB 259; EW 7; EWL 3; IDTP; LMFS 2; MTCW 2; MTFW 2005; RGWL 2, 3; TWA

Stringer, Arthur 1874-1950 .... **TCLC 37**
See also CA 161; DLB 92

Stringer, David
See Roberts, Keith (John Kingston)

Stroheim, Erich von 1885-1957 ..... **TCLC 71**

Strugatskii, Arkadii (Natanovich)
1925-1991 .... **CLC 27**
See Strugatsky, Arkadii Natanovich
See also CA 106; 135; SFW 4

Strugatskii, Boris (Natanovich)
1933- .... **CLC 27**
See Strugatsky, Boris (Natanovich)
See also CA 106; SFW 4

Strugatsky, Arkadii Natanovich
See Strugatskii, Arkadii (Natanovich)
See also DLB 302

Strugatsky, Boris (Natanovich)
See Strugatskii, Boris (Natanovich)
See also DLB 302

Strummer, Joe 1952-2002 .... **CLC 30**

Strunk, William, Jr. 1869-1946 ...... **TCLC 92**
See also CA 118; 164; NCFS 5

Stryk, Lucien 1924- .... **PC 27**
See also CA 13-16R; CANR 10, 28, 55, 110; CP 1, 2, 3, 4, 5, 6, 7

Stuart, Don A.
See Campbell, John W(ood, Jr.)

Stuart, Ian
See MacLean, Alistair (Stuart)

Stuart, Jesse (Hilton) 1906-1984 ... **CLC 1, 8, 11, 14, 34; SSC 31**
See also CA 5-8R; 112; CANR 31; CN 1, 2, 3; DLB 9, 48, 102; DLBY 1984; SATA 2; SATA-Obit 36

Stubblefield, Sally
See Trumbo, Dalton

Sturgeon, Theodore (Hamilton)
1918-1985 .... **CLC 22, 39**
See Queen, Ellery
See also AAYA 51; BPFB 3; BYA 9, 10; CA 81-84; 116; CANR 32, 103; DLB 8; DLBY 1985; HGG; MTCW 1, 2; MTFW 2005; SCFW; SFW 4; SUFW

Sturges, Preston 1898-1959 .... **TCLC 48**
See also CA 114; 149; DLB 26

Styron, William 1925- .... **CLC 1, 3, 5, 11, 15, 60; SSC 25**
See also AMW; AMWC 2; BEST 90:4; BPFB 3; CA 5-8R; CANR 6, 33, 74, 126; CDALB 1968-1988; CN 1, 2, 3, 4, 5, 6, 7; CPW; CSW; DA3; DAM NOV, POP; DLB 2, 143, 299; DLBY 1980; EWL 3; INT CANR-6; LAIT 2; MAL 5; MTCW 1, 2; MTFW 2005; NCFS 1; NFS 22; RGAL 4; RGHL; RHW; TUS

Su, Chien 1884-1918
See Su Man-shu
See also CA 123

Tanizaki, Jun'ichiro 1886-1965 ... **CLC 8, 14, 28; SSC 21**
　　See Tanizaki Jun'ichiro
　　See also CA 93-96; 25-28R; MJW; MTCW 2; MTFW 2005; RGSF 2; RGWL 2

Tanizaki Jun'ichiro
　　See Tanizaki, Jun'ichiro
　　See also DLB 180; EWL 3

Tannen, Deborah 1945- .... **CLC 206**
　　See also CA 118; CANR 95

Tannen, Deborah Frances
　　See Tannen, Deborah

Tanner, William
　　See Amis, Kingsley (William)

Tao Lao
　　See Storni, Alfonsina

Tapahonso, Luci 1953- .... **NNAL; PC 65**
　　See also CA 145; CANR 72, 127; DLB 175

Tarantino, Quentin (Jerome)
　　1963- .... **CLC 125**
　　See also AAYA 58; CA 171; CANR 125

Tarassoff, Lev
　　See Troyat, Henri

Tarbell, Ida M(inerva) 1857-1944 . **TCLC 40**
　　See also CA 122; 181; DLB 47

Tarkington, (Newton) Booth
　　1869-1946 .... **TCLC 9**
　　See also BPFB 3; BYA 3; CA 110; 143; CWRI 5; DLB 9, 102; MAL 5; MTCW 2; RGAL 4; SATA 17

Tarkovskii, Andrei Arsen'evich
　　See Tarkovsky, Andrei (Arsenyevich)

Tarkovsky, Andrei (Arsenyevich)
　　1932-1986 .... **CLC 75**
　　See also CA 127

Tartt, Donna 1964(?)- .... **CLC 76**
　　See also AAYA 56; CA 142; CANR 135; MTFW 2005

Tasso, Torquato 1544-1595 .... **LC 5, 94**
　　See also EFS 2; EW 2; RGWL 2, 3; WLIT 7

Tate, (John Orley) Allen 1899-1979 .. **CLC 2, 4, 6, 9, 11, 14, 24; PC 50**
　　See also AMW; CA 5-8R; 85-88; CANR 32, 108; CN 1, 2; CP 1, 2; DLB 4, 45, 63; DLBD 17; EWL 3; MAL 5; MTCW 1, 2; MTFW 2005; RGAL 4; RHW

Tate, Ellalice
　　See Hibbert, Eleanor Alice Burford

Tate, James (Vincent) 1943- ..... **CLC 2, 6, 25**
　　See also CA 21-24R; CANR 29, 57, 114; CP 1, 2, 3, 4, 5, 6, 7; DLB 5, 169; EWL 3; PFS 10, 15; RGAL 4; WP

Tate, Nahum 1652(?)-1715 .... **LC 109**
　　See also DLB 80; RGEL 2

Tauler, Johannes c. 1300-1361 ...... **CMLC 37**
　　See also DLB 179; LMFS 1

Tavel, Ronald 1940- .... **CLC 6**
　　See also CA 21-24R; CAD; CANR 33; CD 5, 6

Taviani, Paolo 1931- .... **CLC 70**
　　See also CA 153

Taylor, Bayard 1825-1878 .... **NCLC 89**
　　See also DLB 3, 189, 250, 254; RGAL 4

Taylor, C(ecil) P(hilip) 1929-1981 .... **CLC 27**
　　See also CA 25-28R; 105; CANR 47; CBD

Taylor, Edward 1642(?)-1729 . **LC 11; PC 63**
　　See also AMW; DA; DAB; DAC; DAM MST, POET; DLB 24; EXPP; RGAL 4; TUS

Taylor, Eleanor Ross 1920- .... **CLC 5**
　　See also CA 81-84; CANR 70

Taylor, Elizabeth 1912-1975 ..... **CLC 2, 4, 29**
　　See also CA 13-16R; CANR 9, 70; CN 1, 2; DLB 139; MTCW 1; RGEL 2; SATA 13

Taylor, Frederick Winslow
　　1856-1915 .... **TCLC 76**
　　See also CA 188

Taylor, Henry (Splawn) 1942- .... **CLC 44**
　　See also CA 33-36R; CAAS 7; CANR 31; CP 6, 7; DLB 5; PFS 10

Taylor, Kamala (Purnaiya) 1924-2004
　　See Markandaya, Kamala
　　See also CA 77-80; 227; MTFW 2005; NFS 13

Taylor, Mildred D(elois) 1943- .... **CLC 21**
　　See also AAYA 10, 47; BW 1; BYA 3, 8; CA 85-88; CANR 25, 115, 136; CLR 9, 59, 90; CSW; DLB 52; JRDA; LAIT 3; MAICYA 1, 2; MTFW 2005; SAAS 5; SATA 135; WYA; YAW

Taylor, Peter (Hillsman) 1917-1994 .. **CLC 1, 4, 18, 37, 44, 50, 71; SSC 10, 84**
　　See also AMWS 5; BPFB 3; CA 13-16R; 147; CANR 9, 50; CN 1, 2, 3, 4, 5; CSW; DLB 218, 278; DLBY 1981, 1994; EWL 3; EXPS; INT CANR-9; MAL 5; MTCW 1, 2; MTFW 2005; RGSF 2; SSFS 9; TUS

Taylor, Robert Lewis 1912-1998 .... **CLC 14**
　　See also CA 1-4R; 170; CANR 3, 64; CN 1, 2; SATA 10; TCWW 1, 2

Tchekhov, Anton
　　See Chekhov, Anton (Pavlovich)

Tchicaya, Gerald Felix 1931-1988 .. **CLC 101**
　　See Tchicaya U Tam'si
　　See also CA 129; 125; CANR 81

Tchicaya U Tam'si
　　See Tchicaya, Gerald Felix
　　See also EWL 3

Teasdale, Sara 1884-1933 .... **PC 31; TCLC 4**
　　See also CA 104; 163; DLB 45; GLL 1; PFS 14; RGAL 4; SATA 32; TUS

Tecumseh 1768-1813 .... **NNAL**
　　See also DAM MULT

Tegner, Esaias 1782-1846 .... **NCLC 2**

Teilhard de Chardin, (Marie Joseph) Pierre 1881-1955 .... **TCLC 9**
　　See also CA 105; 210; GFL 1789 to the Present

Temple, Ann
　　See Mortimer, Penelope (Ruth)

Tennant, Emma (Christina) 1937- .. **CLC 13, 52**
　　See also BRWS 9; CA 65-68; CAAS 9; CANR 10, 38, 59, 88; CN 3, 4, 5, 6, 7; DLB 14; EWL 3; SFW 4

Tenneshaw, S. M.
　　See Silverberg, Robert

Tenney, Tabitha Gilman
　　1762-1837 .... **NCLC 122**
　　See also DLB 37, 200

Tennyson, Alfred 1809-1892 ... **NCLC 30, 65, 115; PC 6; WLC 6**
　　See also AAYA 50; BRW 4; CDBLB 1832-1890; DA; DA3; DAB; DAC; DAM MST, POET; DLB 32; EXPP; PAB; PFS 1, 2, 4, 11, 15, 19; RGEL 2; TEA; WLIT 4; WP

Teran, Lisa St. Aubin de .... **CLC 36**
　　See St. Aubin de Teran, Lisa

Terence c. 184B.C.-c. 159B.C. ...... **CMLC 14; DC 7**
　　See also AW 1; CDWLB 1; DLB 211; RGWL 2, 3; TWA; WLIT 8

Teresa de Jesus, St. 1515-1582 .... **LC 18**

Teresa of Avila, St.
　　See Teresa de Jesus, St.

Terkel, Louis .... **CLC 38**
　　See Terkel, Studs
　　See also AAYA 32; AITN 1; MTCW 2; TUS

Terkel, Studs 1912-
　　See Terkel, Louis
　　See also CA 57-60; CANR 18, 45, 67, 132; DA3; MTCW 1, 2; MTFW 2005

Terry, C. V.
　　See Slaughter, Frank G(ill)

Terry, Megan 1932- .... **CLC 19; DC 13**
　　See also CA 77-80; CABS 3; CAD; CANR 43; CD 5, 6; CWD; DFS 18; DLB 7, 249; GLL 2

Tertullian c. 155-c. 245 .... **CMLC 29**

Tertz, Abram
　　See Sinyavsky, Andrei (Donatevich)
　　See also RGSF 2

Tesich, Steve 1943(?)-1996 .... **CLC 40, 69**
　　See also CA 105; 152; CAD; DLBY 1983

Tesla, Nikola 1856-1943 .... **TCLC 88**

Teternikov, Fyodor Kuzmich 1863-1927
　　See Sologub, Fyodor
　　See also CA 104

Tevis, Walter 1928-1984 .... **CLC 42**
　　See also CA 113; SFW 4

Tey, Josephine .... **TCLC 14**
　　See Mackintosh, Elizabeth
　　See also DLB 77; MSW

Thackeray, William Makepeace
　　1811-1863 ...... **NCLC 5, 14, 22, 43, 169; WLC 6**
　　See also BRW 5; BRWC 2; CDBLB 1832-1890; DA; DA3; DAB; DAC; DAM MST, NOV; DLB 21, 55, 159, 163; NFS 13; RGEL 2; SATA 23; TEA; WLIT 3

Thakura, Ravindranatha
　　See Tagore, Rabindranath

Thames, C. H.
　　See Marlowe, Stephen

Tharoor, Shashi 1956- .... **CLC 70**
　　See also CA 141; CANR 91; CN 6, 7

Thelwall, John 1764-1834 .... **NCLC 162**
　　See also DLB 93, 158

Thelwell, Michael Miles 1939- .... **CLC 22**
　　See also BW 2; CA 101

Theobald, Lewis, Jr.
　　See Lovecraft, H. P.

Theocritus c. 310B.C.- .... **CMLC 45**
　　See also AW 1; DLB 176; RGWL 2, 3

Theodorescu, Ion N. 1880-1967
　　See Arghezi, Tudor
　　See also CA 116

Theriault, Yves 1915-1983 .... **CLC 79**
　　See also CA 102; CANR 150; CCA 1; DAC; DAM MST; DLB 88; EWL 3

Theroux, Alexander (Louis) 1939- .... **CLC 2, 25**
　　See also CA 85-88; CANR 20, 63; CN 4, 5, 6, 7

Theroux, Paul (Edward) 1941- ..... **CLC 5, 8, 11, 15, 28, 46**
　　See also AAYA 28; AMWS 8; BEST 89:4; BPFB 3; CA 33-36R; CANR 20, 45, 74, 133; CDALBS; CN 1, 2, 3, 4, 5, 6, 7; CP 1; CPW 1; DA3; DAM POP; DLB 2, 218; EWL 3; HGG; MAL 5; MTCW 1, 2; MTFW 2005; RGAL 4; SATA 44, 109; TUS

Thesen, Sharon 1946- .... **CLC 56**
　　See also CA 163; CANR 125; CP 5, 6, 7; CWP

Thespis fl. 6th cent. B.C.- .... **CMLC 51**
　　See also LMFS 1

Thevenin, Denis
　　See Duhamel, Georges

Thibault, Jacques Anatole Francois
　　1844-1924
　　See France, Anatole
　　See also CA 106; 127; DA3; DAM NOV; MTCW 1, 2; TWA

Thiele, Colin (Milton) 1920- .... **CLC 17**
　　See also CA 29-32R; CANR 12, 28, 53, 105; CLR 27; CP 1, 2; DLB 289; MAICYA 1, 2; SAAS 2; SATA 14, 72, 125; YAW

Thistlethwaite, Bel
　　See Wetherald, Agnes Ethelwyn

Thomas, Audrey (Callahan) 1935- .... **CLC 7, 13, 37, 107; SSC 20**
See also AITN 2; CA 21-24R, 237; CAAE 237; CAAS 19; CANR 36, 58; CN 2, 3, 4, 5, 6, 7; DLB 60; MTCW 1; RGSF 2

Thomas, Augustus 1857-1934 .... **TCLC 97**
See also MAL 5

Thomas, D(onald) M(ichael) 1935- . **CLC 13, 22, 31, 132**
See also BPFB 3; BRWS 4; CA 61-64; CAAS 11; CANR 17, 45, 75; CDBLB 1960 to Present; CN 4, 5, 6, 7; CP 1, 2, 3, 4, 5, 6, 7; DA3; DLB 40, 207, 299; HGG; INT CANR-17; MTCW 1, 2; MTFW 2005; RGHL; SFW 4

Thomas, Dylan (Marlais) 1914-1953 .... **PC 2, 52; SSC 3, 44; TCLC 1, 8, 45, 105; WLC 6**
See also AAYA 45; BRWS 1; CA 104; 120; CANR 65; CDBLB 1945-1960; DA; DA3; DAB; DAC; DAM DRAM, MST, POET; DLB 13, 20, 139; EWL 3; EXPP; LAIT 3; MTCW 1, 2; MTFW 2005; PAB; PFS 1, 3, 8; RGEL 2; RGSF 2; SATA 60; TEA; WLIT 4; WP

Thomas, (Philip) Edward 1878-1917 . **PC 53; TCLC 10**
See also BRW 6; BRWS 3; CA 106; 153; DAM POET; DLB 19, 98, 156, 216; EWL 3; PAB; RGEL 2

Thomas, Joyce Carol 1938- .... **CLC 35**
See also AAYA 12, 54; BW 2, 3; CA 113; 116; CANR 48, 114, 135; CLR 19; DLB 33; INT CA-116; JRDA; MAICYA 1, 2; MTCW 1, 2; MTFW 2005; SAAS 7; SATA 40, 78, 123, 137; SATA-Essay 137; WYA; YAW

Thomas, Lewis 1913-1993 .... **CLC 35**
See also ANW; CA 85-88; 143; CANR 38, 60; DLB 275; MTCW 1, 2

Thomas, M. Carey 1857-1935 .... **TCLC 89**
See also FW

Thomas, Paul
See Mann, (Paul) Thomas

Thomas, Piri 1928- .... **CLC 17; HLCS 2**
See also CA 73-76; HW 1; LLW

Thomas, R(onald) S(tuart) 1913-2000 .... **CLC 6, 13, 48**
See also CA 89-92; 189; CAAS 4; CANR 30; CDBLB 1960 to Present; CP 1, 2, 3, 4, 5, 6, 7; DAB; DAM POET; DLB 27; EWL 3; MTCW 1; RGEL 2

Thomas, Ross (Elmore) 1926-1995 .. **CLC 39**
See also CA 33-36R; 150; CANR 22, 63; CMW 4

Thompson, Francis (Joseph) 1859-1907 .... **TCLC 4**
See also BRW 5; CA 104; 189; CDBLB 1890-1914; DLB 19; RGEL 2; TEA

Thompson, Francis Clegg
See Mencken, H(enry) L(ouis)

Thompson, Hunter S(tockton) 1937(?)-2005 .... **CLC 9, 17, 40, 104**
See also AAYA 45; BEST 89:1; BPFB 3; CA 17-20R; 236; CANR 23, 46, 74, 77, 111, 133; CPW; CSW; DA3; DAM POP; DLB 185; MTCW 1, 2; MTFW 2005; TUS

Thompson, James Myers
See Thompson, Jim (Myers)

Thompson, Jim (Myers) 1906-1977(?) .... **CLC 69**
See also BPFB 3; CA 140; CMW 4; CPW; DLB 226; MSW

Thompson, Judith (Clare Francesca) 1954- .... **CLC 39**
See also CA 143; CD 5, 6; CWD; DFS 22

Thomson, James 1700-1748 .... **LC 16, 29, 40**
See also BRWS 3; DAM POET; DLB 95; RGEL 2

Thomson, James 1834-1882 .... **NCLC 18**
See also DAM POET; DLB 35; RGEL 2

Thoreau, Henry David 1817-1862 .. **NCLC 7, 21, 61, 138; PC 30; WLC 6**
See also AAYA 42; AMW; ANW; BYA 3; CDALB 1640-1865; DA; DA3; DAB; DAC; DAM MST; DLB 1, 183, 223, 270, 298; LAIT 2; LMFS 1; NCFS 3; RGAL 4; TUS

Thorndike, E. L.
See Thorndike, Edward L(ee)

Thorndike, Edward L(ee) 1874-1949 .... **TCLC 107**
See also CA 121

Thornton, Hall
See Silverberg, Robert

Thorpe, Adam 1956- .... **CLC 176**
See also CA 129; CANR 92; DLB 231

Thubron, Colin (Gerald Dryden) 1939- .... **CLC 163**
See also CA 25-28R; CANR 12, 29, 59, 95; CN 5, 6, 7; DLB 204, 231

Thucydides c. 455B.C.-c. 395B.C. . **CMLC 17**
See also AW 1; DLB 176; RGWL 2, 3; WLIT 8

Thumboo, Edwin Nadason 1933- .... **PC 30**
See also CA 194; CP 1

Thurber, James (Grover) 1894-1961 .. **CLC 5, 11, 25, 125; SSC 1, 47**
See also AAYA 56; AMWS 1; BPFB 3; BYA 5; CA 73-76; CANR 17, 39; CDALB 1929-1941; CWRI 5; DA; DA3; DAB; DAC; DAM DRAM, MST, NOV; DLB 4, 11, 22, 102; EWL 3; EXPS; FANT; LAIT 3; MAICYA 1, 2; MAL 5; MTCW 1, 2; MTFW 2005; RGAL 4; RGSF 2; SATA 13; SSFS 1, 10, 19; SUFW; TUS

Thurman, Wallace (Henry) 1902-1934 ..... **BLC 3; HR 1:3; TCLC 6**
See also BW 1, 3; CA 104; 124; CANR 81; DAM MULT; DLB 51

Tibullus c. 54B.C.-c. 18B.C. .... **CMLC 36**
See also AW 2; DLB 211; RGWL 2, 3; WLIT 8

Ticheburn, Cheviot
See Ainsworth, William Harrison

Tieck, (Johann) Ludwig 1773-1853 .... **NCLC 5, 46; SSC 31**
See also CDWLB 2; DLB 90; EW 5; IDTP; RGSF 2; RGWL 2, 3; SUFW

Tiger, Derry
See Ellison, Harlan (Jay)

Tilghman, Christopher 1946- .... **CLC 65**
See also CA 159; CANR 135, 151; CSW; DLB 244

Tillich, Paul (Johannes) 1886-1965 .... **CLC 131**
See also CA 5-8R; 25-28R; CANR 33; MTCW 1, 2

Tillinghast, Richard (Williford) 1940- .... **CLC 29**
See also CA 29-32R; CAAS 23; CANR 26, 51, 96; CP 2, 3, 4, 5, 6; CSW

Timrod, Henry 1828-1867 .... **NCLC 25**
See also DLB 3, 248; RGAL 4

Tindall, Gillian (Elizabeth) 1938- ...... **CLC 7**
See also CA 21-24R; CANR 11, 65, 107; CN 1, 2, 3, 4, 5, 6, 7

Tiptree, James, Jr. .... **CLC 48, 50**
See Sheldon, Alice Hastings Bradley
See also DLB 8; SCFW 1, 2; SFW 4

Tirone Smith, Mary-Ann 1944- .... **CLC 39**
See also CA 118; 136; CANR 113; SATA 143

Tirso de Molina 1580(?)-1648 .... **DC 13; HLCS 2; LC 73**
See also RGWL 2, 3

Titmarsh, Michael Angelo
See Thackeray, William Makepeace

Tocqueville, Alexis (Charles Henri Maurice Clerel Comte) de 1805-1859 .. **NCLC 7, 63**
See also EW 6; GFL 1789 to the Present; TWA

Toer, Pramoedya Ananta 1925-2006 .... **CLC 186**
See also CA 197; RGWL 3

Toffler, Alvin 1928- .... **CLC 168**
See also CA 13-16R; CANR 15, 46, 67; CPW; DAM POP; MTCW 1, 2

Toibin, Colm 1955- .... **CLC 162**
See also CA 142; CANR 81, 149; CN 7; DLB 271

Tolkien, J(ohn) R(onald) R(euel) 1892-1973 .... **CLC 1, 2, 3, 8, 12, 38; TCLC 137; WLC 6**
See also AAYA 10; AITN 1; BPFB 3; BRWC 2; BRWS 2; CA 17-18; 45-48; CANR 36, 134; CAP 2; CDBLB 1914-1945; CLR 56; CN 1; CPW 1; CWRI 5; DA; DA3; DAB; DAC; DAM MST, NOV, POP; DLB 15, 160, 255; EFS 2; EWL 3; FANT; JRDA; LAIT 1; LATS 1:2; LMFS 2; MAICYA 1, 2; MTCW 1, 2; MTFW 2005; NFS 8; RGEL 2; SATA 2, 32, 100; SATA-Obit 24; SFW 4; SUFW; TEA; WCH; WYA; YAW

Toller, Ernst 1893-1939 .... **TCLC 10**
See also CA 107; 186; DLB 124; EWL 3; RGWL 2, 3

Tolson, M. B.
See Tolson, Melvin B(eaunorus)

Tolson, Melvin B(eaunorus) 1898(?)-1966 .... **BLC 3; CLC 36, 105**
See also AFAW 1, 2; BW 1, 3; CA 124; 89-92; CANR 80; DAM MULT, POET; DLB 48, 76; MAL 5; RGAL 4

Tolstoi, Aleksei Nikolaevich
See Tolstoy, Alexey Nikolaevich

Tolstoi, Lev
See Tolstoy, Leo (Nikolaevich)
See also RGSF 2; RGWL 2, 3

Tolstoy, Aleksei Nikolaevich
See Tolstoy, Alexey Nikolaevich
See also DLB 272

Tolstoy, Alexey Nikolaevich 1882-1945 .... **TCLC 18**
See Tolstoy, Aleksei Nikolaevich
See also CA 107; 158; EWL 3; SFW 4

Tolstoy, Leo (Nikolaevich) 1828-1910 . **SSC 9, 30, 45, 54; TCLC 4, 11, 17, 28, 44, 79, 173; WLC 6**
See Tolstoi, Lev
See also AAYA 56; CA 104; 123; DA; DA3; DAB; DAC; DAM MST, NOV; DLB 238; EFS 2; EW 7; EXPS; IDTP; LAIT 2; LATS 1:1; LMFS 1; NFS 10; SATA 26; SSFS 5; TWA

Tolstoy, Count Leo
See Tolstoy, Leo (Nikolaevich)

Tomalin, Claire 1933- .... **CLC 166**
See also CA 89-92; CANR 52, 88; DLB 155

Tomasi di Lampedusa, Giuseppe 1896-1957
See Lampedusa, Giuseppe (Tomasi) di
See also CA 111; DLB 177; EWL 3; WLIT 7

Tomlin, Lily .... **CLC 17**
See Tomlin, Mary Jean

Tomlin, Mary Jean 1939(?)-
See Tomlin, Lily
See also CA 117

Tomline, F. Latour
See Gilbert, W(illiam) S(chwenck)

Tuck, Lily 1938- .... **CLC 70**
See also CA 139; CANR 90

Tu Fu 712-770 .... **PC 9**
See Du Fu
See also DAM MULT; TWA; WP

Tunis, John R(oberts) 1889-1975 ..... **CLC 12**
See also BYA 1; CA 61-64; CANR 62; DLB 22, 171; JRDA; MAICYA 1, 2; SATA 37; SATA-Brief 30; YAW

Tuohy, Frank .... **CLC 37**
See Tuohy, John Francis
See also CN 1, 2, 3, 4, 5, 6, 7; DLB 14, 139

Tuohy, John Francis 1925-
See Tuohy, Frank
See also CA 5-8R; 178; CANR 3, 47

Turco, Lewis (Putnam) 1934- ..... **CLC 11, 63**
See also CA 13-16R; CAAS 22; CANR 24, 51; CP 1, 2, 3, 4, 5, 6, 7; DLBY 1984; TCLE 1:2

Turgenev, Ivan (Sergeevich)
1818-1883 ..... **DC 7; NCLC 21, 37, 122; SSC 7, 57; WLC 6**
See also AAYA 58; DA; DAB; DAC; DAM MST; NOV; DFS 6; DLB 238, 284; EW 6; LATS 1:1; NFS 16; RGSF 2; RGWL 2, 3; TWA

Turgot, Anne-Robert-Jacques
1727-1781 .... **LC 26**
See also DLB 314

Turner, Frederick 1943- .... **CLC 48**
See also CA 73-76, 227; CAAE 227; CAAS 10; CANR 12, 30, 56; DLB 40, 282

Turton, James
See Crace, Jim

Tutu, Desmond M(pilo) 1931- .. **BLC 3; CLC 80**
See also BW 1, 3; CA 125; CANR 67, 81; DAM MULT

Tutuola, Amos 1920-1997 ..... **BLC 3; CLC 5, 14, 29**
See also AFW; BW 2, 3; CA 9-12R; 159; CANR 27, 66; CDWLB 3; CN 1, 2, 3, 4, 5, 6; DA3; DAM MULT; DLB 125; DNFS 2; EWL 3; MTCW 1, 2; MTFW 2005; RGEL 2; WLIT 2

Twain, Mark .... **SSC 6, 26, 34, 87; TCLC 6, 12, 19, 36, 48, 59, 161; WLC 6**
See Clemens, Samuel Langhorne
See also AAYA 20; AMW; AMWC 1; BPFB 3; BYA 2, 3, 11, 14; CLR 58, 60, 66; DLB 11; EXPN; EXPS; FANT; LAIT; MAL 5; NCFS 4; NFS 1, 6; RGAL 4; RGSF 2; SFW 4; SSFS 1, 7, 16, 21; SUFW; TUS; WCH; WYA; YAW

Tyler, Anne 1941- . **CLC 7, 11, 18, 28, 44, 59, 103, 205**
See also AAYA 18, 60; AMWS 4; BEST 89:1; BPFB 3; BYA 12; CA 9-12R; CANR 11, 33, 53, 109, 132; CDALBS; CN 1, 2, 3, 4, 5, 6, 7; CPW; CSW; DAM NOV, POP; DLB 6, 143; DLBY 1982; EWL 3; EXPN; LATS 1:2; MAL 5; MAWW; MTCW 1, 2; MTFW 2005; NFS 2, 7, 10; RGAL 4; SATA 7, 90; SSFS 17; TCLE 1:2; TUS; YAW

Tyler, Royall 1757-1826 .... **NCLC 3**
See also DLB 37; RGAL 4

Tynan, Katharine 1861-1931 .... **TCLC 3**
See also CA 104; 167; DLB 153, 240; FW

Tyndale, William c. 1484-1536 .... **LC 103**
See also DLB 132

Tyutchev, Fyodor 1803-1873 .... **NCLC 34**

Tzara, Tristan 1896-1963 .... **CLC 47; PC 27; TCLC 168**
See also CA 153; 89-92; DAM POET; EWL 3; MTCW 2

Uchida, Yoshiko 1921-1992 .... **AAL**
See also AAYA 16; BYA 2, 3; CA 13-16R; 139; CANR 6, 22, 47, 61; CDALBS; CLR 6, 56; CWRI 5; DLB 312; JRDA; MAICYA 1, 2; MTCW 1, 2; MTFW 2005; SAAS 1; SATA 1, 53; SATA-Obit 72

Udall, Nicholas 1504-1556 .... **LC 84**
See also DLB 62; RGEL 2

Ueda Akinari 1734-1809 .... **NCLC 131**

Uhry, Alfred 1936- .... **CLC 55**
See also CA 127; 133; CAD; CANR 112; CD 5, 6; CSW; DA3; DAM DRAM, POP; DFS 11, 15; INT CA-133; MTFW 2005

Ulf, Haerved
See Strindberg, (Johan) August

Ulf, Harved
See Strindberg, (Johan) August

Ulibarri, Sabine R(eyes)
1919-2003 .... **CLC 83; HLCS 2**
See also CA 131; 214; CANR 81; DAM MULT; DLB 82; HW 1, 2; RGSF 2

Unamuno (y Jugo), Miguel de
1864-1936 .. **HLC 2; SSC 11, 69; TCLC 2, 9, 148**
See also CA 104; 131; CANR 81; DAM MULT, NOV; DLB 108, 322; EW 8; EWL 3; HW 1, 2; MTCW 1, 2; MTFW 2005; RGSF 2; RGWL 2, 3; SSFS 20; TWA

Uncle Shelby
See Silverstein, Shel(don Allan)

Undercliffe, Errol
See Campbell, (John) Ramsey

Underwood, Miles
See Glassco, John

Undset, Sigrid 1882-1949 .. **TCLC 3; WLC 6**
See also CA 104; 129; DA; DA3; DAB; DAC; DAM MST, NOV; DLB 293; EW 9; EWL 3; FW; MTCW 1, 2; MTFW 2005; RGWL 2, 3

Ungaretti, Giuseppe 1888-1970 ... **CLC 7, 11, 15; PC 57**
See also CA 19-20; 25-28R; CAP 2; DLB 114; EW 10; EWL 3; PFS 20; RGWL 2, 3; WLIT 7

Unger, Douglas 1952- .... **CLC 34**
See also CA 130; CANR 94

Unsworth, Barry (Forster) 1930- .... **CLC 76, 127**
See also BRWS 7; CA 25-28R; CANR 30, 54, 125; CN 6, 7; DLB 194, 326

Updike, John 1932- . **CLC 1, 2, 3, 5, 7, 9, 13, 15, 23, 34, 43, 70, 139, 214; SSC 13, 27; WLC 6**
See also AAYA 36; AMW; AMWC 1; AMWR 1; BPFB 3; BYA 12; CA 1-4R; CABS 1; CANR 4, 33, 51, 94, 133; CDALB 1968-1988; CN 1, 2, 3, 4, 5, 6, 7; CP 1, 2, 3, 4, 5, 6, 7; CPW 1; DA; DA3; DAB; DAC; DAM MST, NOV, POET, POP; DLB 2, 5, 143, 218, 227; DLBD 3; DLBY 1980, 1982, 1997; EWL 3; EXPP; HGG; MAL 5; MTCW 1, 2; MTFW 2005; NFS 12; RGAL 4; RGSF 2; SSFS 3, 19; TUS

Updike, John Hoyer
See Updike, John

Upshaw, Margaret Mitchell
See Mitchell, Margaret (Munnerlyn)

Upton, Mark
See Sanders, Lawrence

Upward, Allen 1863-1926 .... **TCLC 85**
See also CA 117; 187; DLB 36

Urdang, Constance (Henriette)
1922-1996 .... **CLC 47**
See also CA 21-24R; CANR 9, 24; CP 1, 2, 3, 4, 5, 6; CWP

Uriel, Henry
See Faust, Frederick (Schiller)

Uris, Leon (Marcus) 1924-2003 ... **CLC 7, 32**
See also AITN 1, 2; BEST 89:2; BPFB 3; CA 1-4R; 217; CANR 1, 40, 65, 123; CN 1, 2, 3, 4, 5, 6; CPW 1; DA3; DAM NOV, POP; MTCW 1, 2; MTFW 2005; RGHL; SATA 49; SATA-Obit 146

Urista (Heredia), Alberto (Baltazar)
1947- .... **HLCS 1**
See Alurista
See also CA 182; CANR 2, 32; HW 1

Urmuz
See Codrescu, Andrei

Urquhart, Guy
See McAlmon, Robert (Menzies)

Urquhart, Jane 1949- .... **CLC 90**
See also CA 113; CANR 32, 68, 116; CCA 1; DAC

Usigli, Rodolfo 1905-1979 .... **HLCS 1**
See also CA 131; DLB 305; EWL 3; HW 1; LAW

Usk, Thomas (?)-1388 .... **CMLC 76**
See also DLB 146

Ustinov, Peter (Alexander)
1921-2004 .... **CLC 1**
See also AITN 1; CA 13-16R; 225; CANR 25, 51; CBD; CD 5, 6; DLB 13; MTCW 2

U Tam'si, Gerald Felix Tchicaya
See Tchicaya, Gerald Felix

U Tam'si, Tchicaya
See Tchicaya, Gerald Felix

Vachss, Andrew 1942- .... **CLC 106**
See also CA 118; 214; CAAE 214; CANR 44, 95, 153; CMW 4

Vachss, Andrew H.
See Vachss, Andrew

Vachss, Andrew Henry
See Vachss, Andrew

Vaculik, Ludvik 1926- .... **CLC 7**
See also CA 53-56; CANR 72; CWW 2; DLB 232; EWL 3

Vaihinger, Hans 1852-1933 .... **TCLC 71**
See also CA 116; 166

Valdez, Luis (Miguel) 1940- ..... **CLC 84; DC 10; HLC 2**
See also CA 101; CAD; CANR 32, 81; CD 5, 6; DAM MULT; DFS 5; DLB 122; EWL 3; HW 1; LAIT 4; LLW

Valenzuela, Luisa 1938- .... **CLC 31, 104; HLCS 2; SSC 14, 82**
See also CA 101; CANR 32, 65, 123; CDWLB 3; CWW 2; DAM MULT; DLB 113; EWL 3; FW; HW 1, 2; LAW; RGSF 2; RGWL 3

Valera y Alcala-Galiano, Juan
1824-1905 .... **TCLC 10**
See also CA 106

Valerius Maximus fl. 20- .... **CMLC 64**
See also DLB 211

Valery, (Ambroise) Paul (Toussaint Jules)
1871-1945 .... **PC 9; TCLC 4, 15**
See also CA 104; 122; DA3; DAM POET; DLB 258; EW 8; EWL 3; GFL 1789 to the Present; MTCW 1, 2; MTFW 2005; RGWL 2, 3; TWA

Valle-Inclan, Ramon (Maria) del
1866-1936 .... **HLC 2; TCLC 5**
See del Valle-Inclan, Ramon (Maria)
See also CA 106; 153; CANR 80; DAM MULT; DLB 134; EW 8; EWL 3; HW 2; RGSF 2; RGWL 2, 3

Vallejo, Antonio Buero
See Buero Vallejo, Antonio

Vallejo, Cesar (Abraham)
1892-1938 .... **HLC 2; TCLC 3, 56**
See also CA 105; 153; DAM MULT; DLB 290; EWL 3; HW 1; LAW; RGWL 2, 3

Valles, Jules 1832-1885 .... **NCLC 71**
See also DLB 123; GFL 1789 to the Present

Winters, Yvor 1900-1968 .... **CLC 4, 8, 32**
See also AMWS 2; CA 11-12; 25-28R; CAP 1; DLB 48; EWL 3; MAL 5; MTCW 1; RGAL 4

Winterson, Jeanette 1959- .... **CLC 64, 158**
See also BRWS 4; CA 136; CANR 58, 116; CN 5, 6, 7; CPW; DA3; DAM POP; DLB 207, 261; FANT; FW; GLL 1; MTCW 2; MTFW 2005; RHW

Winthrop, John 1588-1649 .... **LC 31, 107**
See also DLB 24, 30

Wirth, Louis 1897-1952 .... **TCLC 92**
See also CA 210

Wiseman, Frederick 1930- .... **CLC 20**
See also CA 159

Wister, Owen 1860-1938 .... **TCLC 21**
See also BPFB 3; CA 108; 162; DLB 9, 78, 186; RGAL 4; SATA 62; TCWW 1, 2

Wither, George 1588-1667 .... **LC 96**
See also DLB 121; RGEL 2

Witkacy
See Witkiewicz, Stanislaw Ignacy

Witkiewicz, Stanislaw Ignacy
1885-1939 .... **TCLC 8**
See also CA 105; 162; CDWLB 4; DLB 215; EW 10; EWL 3; RGWL 2, 3; SFW 4

Wittgenstein, Ludwig (Josef Johann)
1889-1951 .... **TCLC 59**
See also CA 113; 164; DLB 262; MTCW 2

Wittig, Monique 1935-2003 .... **CLC 22**
See also CA 116; 135; 212; CANR 143; CWW 2; DLB 83; EWL 3; FW; GLL 1

Wittlin, Jozef 1896-1976 .... **CLC 25**
See also CA 49-52; 65-68; CANR 3; EWL 3

Wodehouse, P(elham) G(renville)
1881-1975 . **CLC 1, 2, 5, 10, 22; SSC 2; TCLC 108**
See also AAYA 65; AITN 2; BRWS 3; CA 45-48; 57-60; CANR 3, 33; CDBLB 1914-1945; CN 1, 2; CPW 1; DA3; DAB; DAC; DAM NOV; DLB 34, 162; EWL 3; MTCW 1, 2; MTFW 2005; RGEL 2; RGSF 2; SATA 22; SSFS 10

Woiwode, L.
See Woiwode, Larry (Alfred)

Woiwode, Larry (Alfred) 1941- ... **CLC 6, 10**
See also CA 73-76; CANR 16, 94; CN 3, 4, 5, 6, 7; DLB 6; INT CANR-16

Wojciechowska, Maia (Teresa)
1927-2002 .... **CLC 26**
See also AAYA 8, 46; BYA 3; CA 9-12R; 183; 209; CAAE 183; CANR 4, 41; CLR 1; JRDA; MAICYA 1, 2; SAAS 1; SATA 1, 28, 83; SATA-Essay 104; SATA-Obit 134; YAW

Wojtyla, Karol (Josef)
See John Paul II, Pope

Wojtyla, Karol (Jozef)
See John Paul II, Pope

Wolf, Christa 1929- .... **CLC 14, 29, 58, 150**
See also CA 85-88; CANR 45, 123; CD-WLB 2; CWW 2; DLB 75; EWL 3; FW; MTCW 1; RGWL 2, 3; SSFS 14

Wolf, Naomi 1962- .... **CLC 157**
See also CA 141; CANR 110; FW; MTFW 2005

Wolfe, Gene 1931- .... **CLC 25**
See also AAYA 35; CA 57-60; CAAS 9; CANR 6, 32, 60, 152; CPW; DAM POP; DLB 8; FANT; MTCW 2; MTFW 2005; SATA 118, 165; SCFW 2; SFW 4; SUFW 2

Wolfe, Gene Rodman
See Wolfe, Gene

Wolfe, George C. 1954- .... **BLCS; CLC 49**
See also CA 149; CAD; CD 5, 6

Wolfe, Thomas (Clayton)
1900-1938 ...... **SSC 33; TCLC 4, 13, 29, 61; WLC 6**
See also AMW; BPFB 3; CA 104; 132; CANR 102; CDALB 1929-1941; DA; DA3; DAB; DAC; DAM MST, NOV; DLB 9, 102, 229; DLBD 2, 16; DLBY 1985, 1997; EWL 3; MAL 5; MTCW 1, 2; NFS 18; RGAL 4; SSFS 18; TUS

Wolfe, Thomas Kennerly, Jr.
1931- .... **CLC 147**
See Wolfe, Tom
See also CA 13-16R; CANR 9, 33, 70, 104; DA3; DAM POP; DLB 185; EWL 3; INT CANR-9; MTCW 1, 2; MTFW 2005; TUS

Wolfe, Tom .... **CLC 1, 2, 9, 15, 35, 51**
See Wolfe, Thomas Kennerly, Jr.
See also AAYA 8, 67; AITN 2; AMWS 3; BEST 89:1; BPFB 3; CN 5, 6, 7; CPW; CSW; DLB 152; LAIT 5; RGAL 4

Wolff, Geoffrey 1937- .... **CLC 41**
See also CA 29-32R; CANR 29, 43, 78, 154

Wolff, Geoffrey Ansell
See Wolff, Geoffrey

Wolff, Sonia
See Levitin, Sonia (Wolff)

Wolff, Tobias (Jonathan Ansell)
1945- .... **CLC 39, 64, 172; SSC 63**
See also AAYA 16; AMWS 7; BEST 90:2; BYA 12; CA 114; 117; CAAS 22; CANR 54, 76, 96; CN 5, 6, 7; CSW; DA3; DLB 130; EWL 3; INT CA-117; MTCW 2; MTFW 2005; RGAL 4; RGSF 2; SSFS 4, 11

Wolfram von Eschenbach c. 1170-c.
1220 .... **CMLC 5**
See Eschenbach, Wolfram von
See also CDWLB 2; DLB 138; EW 1; RGWL 2

Wolitzer, Hilma 1930- .... **CLC 17**
See also CA 65-68; CANR 18, 40; INT CANR-18; SATA 31; YAW

Wollstonecraft, Mary 1759-1797 .... **LC 5, 50, 90**
See also BRWS 3; CDBLB 1789-1832; DLB 39, 104, 158, 252; FL 1:1; FW; LAIT 1; RGEL 2; TEA; WLIT 3

Wonder, Stevie 1950- .... **CLC 12**
See also CA 111

Wong, Jade Snow 1922-2006 .... **CLC 17**
See also CA 109; CANR 91; SATA 112

Woodberry, George Edward
1855-1930 .... **TCLC 73**
See also CA 165; DLB 71, 103

Woodcott, Keith
See Brunner, John (Kilian Houston)

Woodruff, Robert W.
See Mencken, H(enry) L(ouis)

Woolf, (Adeline) Virginia 1882-1941 .. **SSC 7, 79; TCLC 1, 5, 20, 43, 56, 101, 123, 128; WLC 6**
See also AAYA 44; BPFB 3; BRW 7; BRWC 2; BRWR 1; CA 104; 130; CANR 64, 132; CDBLB 1914-1945; DA; DA3; DAB; DAC; DAM MST, NOV; DLB 36, 100, 162; DLBD 10; EWL 3; EXPS; FL 1:6; FW; LAIT 3; LATS 1:1; LMFS 2; MTCW 1, 2; MTFW 2005; NCFS 2; NFS 8, 12; RGEL 2; RGSF 2; SSFS 4, 12; TEA; WLIT 4

Woollcott, Alexander (Humphreys)
1887-1943 .... **TCLC 5**
See also CA 105; 161; DLB 29

Woolrich, Cornell .... **CLC 77**
See Hopley-Woolrich, Cornell George
See also MSW

Woolson, Constance Fenimore
1840-1894 .... **NCLC 82; SSC 90**
See also DLB 12, 74, 189, 221; RGAL 4

Wordsworth, Dorothy 1771-1855 . **NCLC 25, 138**
See also DLB 107

Wordsworth, William 1770-1850 .. **NCLC 12, 38, 111, 166; PC 4, 67; WLC 6**
See also AAYA 70; BRW 4; BRWC 1; CD-BLB 1789-1832; DA; DA3; DAB; DAC; DAM MST, POET; DLB 93, 107; EXPP; LATS 1:1; LMFS 1; PAB; PFS 2; RGEL 2; TEA; WLIT 3; WP

Wotton, Sir Henry 1568-1639 .... **LC 68**
See also DLB 121; RGEL 2

Wouk, Herman 1915- .... **CLC 1, 9, 38**
See also BPFB 2, 3; CA 5-8R; CANR 6, 33, 67, 146; CDALBS; CN 1, 2, 3, 4, 5, 6; CPW; DA3; DAM NOV, POP; DLBY 1982; INT CANR-6; LAIT 4; MAL 5; MTCW 1, 2; MTFW 2005; NFS 7; TUS

Wright, Charles (Penzel, Jr.) 1935- .. **CLC 6, 13, 28, 119, 146**
See also AMWS 5; CA 29-32R; CAAS 7; CANR 23, 36, 62, 88, 135; CP 3, 4, 5, 6, 7; DLB 165; DLBY 1982; EWL 3; MTCW 1, 2; MTFW 2005; PFS 10

Wright, Charles Stevenson 1932- ..... **BLC 3; CLC 49**
See also BW 1; CA 9-12R; CANR 26; CN 1, 2, 3, 4, 5, 6, 7; DAM MULT, POET; DLB 33

Wright, Frances 1795-1852 .... **NCLC 74**
See also DLB 73

Wright, Frank Lloyd 1867-1959 .... **TCLC 95**
See also AAYA 33; CA 174

Wright, Jack R.
See Harris, Mark

Wright, James (Arlington)
1927-1980 .... **CLC 3, 5, 10, 28; PC 36**
See also AITN 2; AMWS 3; CA 49-52; 97-100; CANR 4, 34, 64; CDALBS; CP 1, 2; DAM POET; DLB 5, 169; EWL 3; EXPP; MAL 5; MTCW 1, 2; MTFW 2005; PFS 7, 8; RGAL 4; TUS; WP

Wright, Judith (Arundell)
1915-2000 .... **CLC 11, 53; PC 14**
See also CA 13-16R; 188; CANR 31, 76, 93; CP 1, 2, 3, 4, 5, 6, 7; CWP; DLB 260; EWL 3; MTCW 1, 2; MTFW 2005; PFS 8; RGEL 2; SATA 14; SATA-Obit 121

Wright, L(aurali) R. 1939- .... **CLC 44**
See also CA 138; CMW 4

Wright, Richard (Nathaniel)
1908-1960 ... **BLC 3; CLC 1, 3, 4, 9, 14, 21, 48, 74; SSC 2; TCLC 136, 180; WLC 6**
See also AAYA 5, 42; AFAW 1, 2; AMW; BPFB 3; BW 1; BYA 2; CA 108; CANR 64; CDALB 1929-1941; DA; DA3; DAB; DAC; DAM MST, MULT, NOV; DLB 76, 102; DLBD 2; EWL 3; EXPN; LAIT 3, 4; MAL 5; MTCW 1, 2; MTFW 2005; NCFS 1; NFS 1, 7; RGAL 4; RGSF 2; SSFS 3, 9, 15, 20; TUS; YAW

Wright, Richard B(ruce) 1937- .... **CLC 6**
See also CA 85-88; CANR 120; DLB 53

Wright, Rick 1945- .... **CLC 35**

Wright, Rowland
See Wells, Carolyn

Wright, Stephen 1946- .... **CLC 33**
See also CA 237

Wright, Willard Huntington 1888-1939
See Van Dine, S. S.
See also CA 115; 189; CMW 4; DLBD 16

Wright, William 1930- .... **CLC 44**
See also CA 53-56; CANR 7, 23, 154

Wroth, Lady Mary 1587-1653(?) .... **LC 30; PC 38**
See also DLB 121

Zimmerman, Robert
See Dylan, Bob
Zindel, Paul 1936-2003 ...... **CLC 6, 26; DC 5**
See also AAYA 2, 37; BYA 2, 3, 8, 11, 14;
CA 73-76; 213; CAD; CANR 31, 65, 108;
CD 5, 6; CDALBS; CLR 3, 45, 85; DA;
DA3; DAB; DAC; DAM DRAM, MST,
NOV; DFS 12; DLB 7, 52; JRDA; LAIT
5; MAICYA 1, 2; MTCW 1, 2; MTFW
2005; NFS 14; SATA 16, 58, 102; SATA-
Obit 142; WYA; YAW
Zinn, Howard 1922- .... **CLC 199**
See also CA 1-4R; CANR 2, 33, 90
Zinov'Ev, A.A.
See Zinoviev, Alexander
Zinov'ev, Aleksandr
See Zinoviev, Alexander
See also DLB 302
Zinoviev, Alexander 1922-2006 .... **CLC 19**
See Zinov'ev, Aleksandr
See also CA 116; 133; CAAS 10

Zinoviev, Alexander Aleksandrovich
See Zinoviev, Alexander
Zizek, Slavoj 1949- .... **CLC 188**
See also CA 201; MTFW 2005
Zoilus
See Lovecraft, H. P.
Zola, Emile (Edouard Charles Antoine)
1840-1902 .. **TCLC 1, 6, 21, 41; WLC 6**
See also CA 104; 138; DA; DA3; DAB;
DAC; DAM MST, NOV; DLB 123; EW
7; GFL 1789 to the Present; IDTP; LMFS
1, 2; RGWL 2; TWA
Zoline, Pamela 1941- .... **CLC 62**
See also CA 161; SFW 4
Zoroaster 628(?)B.C.-551(?)B.C. ... **CMLC 40**
Zorrilla y Moral, Jose 1817-1893 .... **NCLC 6**
Zoshchenko, Mikhail (Mikhailovich)
1895-1958 .... **SSC 15; TCLC 15**
See also CA 115; 160; EWL 3; RGSF 2;
RGWL 3

Zuckmayer, Carl 1896-1977 .... **CLC 18**
See also CA 69-72; DLB 56, 124; EWL 3;
RGWL 2, 3
Zuk, Georges
See Skelton, Robin
See also CCA 1
Zukofsky, Louis 1904-1978 ... **CLC 1, 2, 4, 7,**
11, 18; PC 11
See also AMWS 3; CA 9-12R; 77-80;
CANR 39; CP 1, 2; DAM POET; DLB 5,
165; EWL 3; MAL 5; MTCW 1; RGAL 4
Zweig, Paul 1935-1984 .... **CLC 34, 42**
See also CA 85-88; 113
Zweig, Stefan 1881-1942 .... **TCLC 17**
See also CA 112; 170; DLB 81, 118; EWL
3; RGHL
Zwingli, Huldreich 1484-1531 .... **LC 37**
See also DLB 179

Literary Criticism Series
Cumulative Topic Index

This index lists all topic entries in Thompson Gale's *Children's Literature Review* (CLR), *Classical and Medieval Literature Criticism* (CMLC), *Contemporary Literary Criticism* (CLC), *Drama Criticism* (DC), *Literature Criticism from 1400 to 1800* (LC), *Nineteenth-Century Literature Criticism* (NCLC), *Short Story Criticism* (SSC), and *Twentieth-Century Literary Criticism* (TCLC). The index also lists topic entries in the Gale Critical Companion Collection, which includes the following publications: *The Beat Generation* (BG), *Feminism in Literature* (FL), *Gothic Literature* (GL), and *Harlem Renaissance* (HR).

Topic Index

Topic Index

SSC Cumulative Nationality Index

Nationality Index

SSC-93 Title Index